dedication

To Marsha, Joel, Casey, Dan, Molly, Michael, Colin, and Quinn—you have been our strength in the past, our joy in the present, and our hope for the future.

and

To the team that made this edition possible, especially the instructors and students who gave us such valuable guidance as we developed the text and package.

ABOUT THE authors

Bill Nickels is emeritus professor of business at the University of Maryland, College Park. He has over 30 years' experience teaching graduate and undergraduate business courses including introduction to business, marketing, and promotion. He won the Outstanding Teacher on Campus award four times and was nominated for the award dozens of other times. He received his M.B.A. degree from Western Reserve University and his Ph.D. from The Ohio State University. He has written a marketing communications text and two marketing principles texts in addition to many articles in business publications. He has taught many seminars to businesspeople on subjects like power communications, marketing, non-business marketing, and stress and life management. His son, Joel, is a Professor of English at the University of Miami (Florida).

Jim McHugh holds an M.B.A. degree from Lindenwood University and has had broad experience in education, business, and government. As chairman of the Business and Economics Department of St. Louis Community College/Forest Park, Jim coordinated and directed the development of the business curriculum. In addition to teaching several sections of introduction to business each semester for nearly 30 years, Jim taught in the marketing and management areas at both the undergraduate and graduate levels. Jim enjoys conducting business seminars and consulting with small and large businesses. He is actively involved in the public service sector and served as chief of staff to the St. Louis County Executive.

Susan McHugh is a learning specialist with extensive training and experience in adult learning and curriculum development. She holds a M.Ed. degree from the University of Missouri and completed her course work for a Ph.D. in education administration with a specialty in adult learning theory. As a professional curriculum developer, she has directed numerous curriculum projects and educator training programs. She has worked in the public and private sector as a consultant in training and employee development. While Jim and Susan treasure their participation in writing projects, their greatest accomplishment is their collaboration on their three children. Casey is carrying on the family teaching tradition as an adjunct professor at Washington University. Molly and Michael are carrying on the family writing tradition by contributing to the development of several supplementary materials for this text.

walkthrough

A New Approach to Proven Content

McGraw-Hill *Connect Introduction to Business*

Connect Introduction to Business' online features can easily be used for online courses as well as traditional classes. The *Connect* materials include:

1. Interactive Presentations
2. *LearnSmart*—intelligent flashcards that offer feedback and direct students back to the text based on individual performance.
3. Auto-grading Interactive Applications

PREP—STUDY—APPLY

USING CONNECT Every chapter opener in the text features a *Connect* box that offers students a learning path through the course. In addition to reading the chapter, students are encouraged to go to *Connect* to view the Interactive Presentation. These presentations serve as a preparation for understanding the topics covered throughout the chapter. Students can then practice what they have learned by answering the LearnSmart questions and apply their knowledge by using the Interactive Applications.

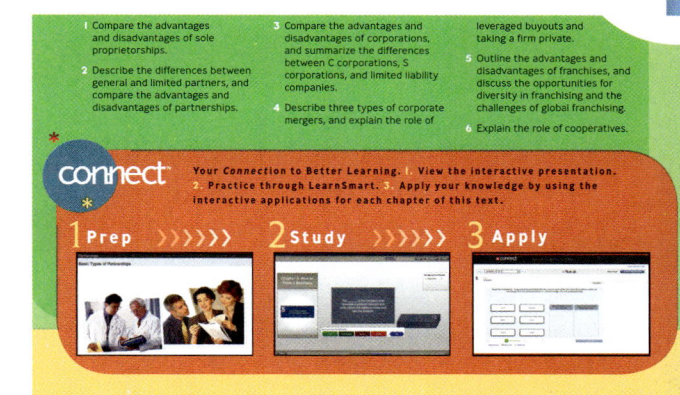

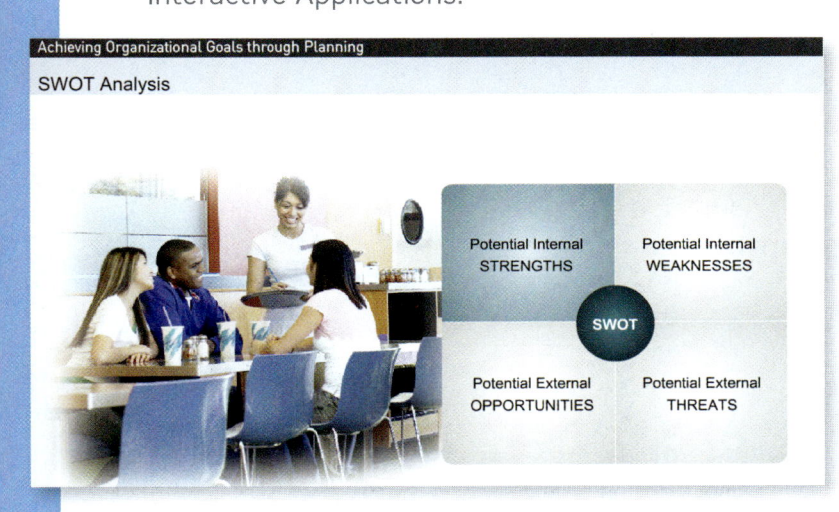

Prep—Interactive Presentations

Specific to the text, the interactive presentations in *Connect* are engaging, with online professional presentations (fully Section 508-compliant) covering the same learning objectives and concepts directly from the chapter. Interactive presentations teach students the core learning objectives in a multimedia format, bringing the course to life. Interactive presentations are a great prep tool for students—when students are better prepared, they are more engaged and better equipped to participate in class.

Study—LearnSmart

Students want to make the best use of their study time. The *LearnSmart* adaptive self-study technology within *Connect Introduction to Business* provides students with a seamless combination of practice, assessment, and remediation for every concept in the textbook. This learning aid is designed to meet the individual needs of each student. *LearnSmart* monitors students' progress as it quizzes them on concepts. It adapts instantly to each student's performance, pinpoints concepts the student doesn't understand and provides a personalized study plan designed to efficiently guide students toward mastery.

Using *LearnSmart*, students spend less time on the topics they understand and practice more of those they have yet to master. Not only do the students get feedback on their responses, they are also guided to the area in the text where more study is needed, and are offered an opportunity to make learning fun by competing against other students for the highest scores. *LearnSmart* provides continual reinforcement and remediation, but gives only as much guidance as students need. *LearnSmart* integrates diagnostics as part of the learning experience. This enables instructors to assess which concepts students have efficiently learned on their own, thus freeing class time for more application and discussion.

Apply—Auto-Grading Interactive Applications

Interactive Applications within *Connect Introduction to Business* engage students beyond simple reading and recall. Students practice key concepts by *applying* them with these textbook-specific interactive applications in every chapter.

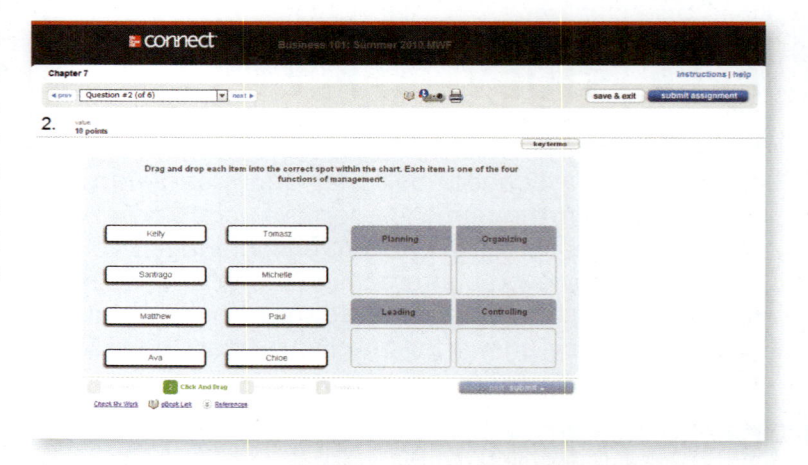

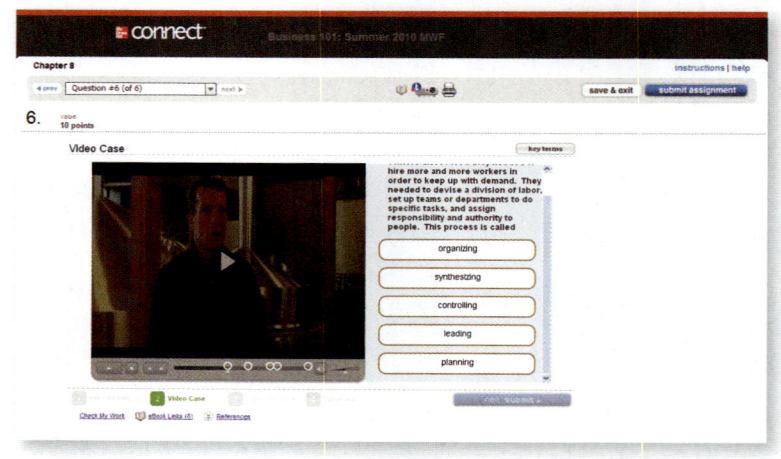

Critical thinking makes for a higher level of learning. Each interactive application is followed by a series of *concept checks* to reinforce key topics and further increase student understanding. Students walk away from an interactive application with more practice and better understanding than simply reading the chapter. All Interactive Applications are automatically scored and entered into the instructor gradebook.

At the close of each text chapter, students are encouraged to use the Interactive Applications within *Connect* for that chapter to apply what they have learned. A brief description of sample interactive applications is offered, along with visuals of the applications. This is just a sampling of the available materials. Additional applications are offered in *Connect* as assigned by each instructor.

More traditional end-of-chapter materials are also available on the text's Online Learning Center (OLC). These include Developing Workplace Skills activities, Critical Thinking Questions, Taking It to the Net exercises, and Cases.

Comprehension Case Interactive: Ethical problems and issues of social responsibility are not unique to the United States. Stakeholders are demanding socially responsible behavior from their U.S. businesses operating abroad. This poses an ethical dilemma for many companies like Motorola. United States' companies have created corporate policy that is guided by ethical business standards and social responsibility. However, the companies are realizing that the policies they adopt do not always align with the cultural values of the host country. Foreign employees are confronted with the dilemma of following corporate policy or adhering to their cultural and family values. In this exercise, you will read the case and answer the questions.

Comprehension Case Interactive: Choices are not always easy, and the obvious ethical solution may have personal or professional drawbacks. Every college student has been warned about plagiarizing material from the Internet, books, periodicals, or other peoples' work. As the text states, plagiarizing is the most common form of cheating. YouTube has become a popular Web site for individuals as well as businesses. However, using material that is protected by copyright is not only unethical, but illegal as well. The "To Tube or Not To Tube" case discusses the issue of video piracy. This case presents a legal and ethical dilemma regarding the use of copyright-protected material. Read the case and answer the questions.

Click and Drag Interactive: There are six steps that businesses can take to improve business ethics in the United States. Review the various steps involved in establishing a corporate code of ethics and assemble the steps on the timeline as instructed.

Video Case Interactive: Corporate social responsibility (CSR) is the concern businesses have for the welfare of society, not just for their owners. CSR goes well beyond being ethical. It is based on a commitment to integrity, fairness, and respect to all the stakeholders of the organization. Organizations have far more responsibility than just pursuing a profit. Corporations have responsibility to their customers, their investors, their employees, and their communities and environment. Through social audits, today's society is demanding that corporations implement socially responsible and responsive programs. View the video case and answer questions when prompted.

Click and Drag Interactive: Corporate social responsibility (CSR) is the concern businesses have for the welfare of society, not just for their owners. Review the various responsibilities listed and place them under the appropriate stakeholder. Next, review the example and place each under the appropriate stakeholder.

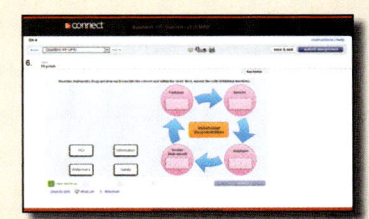

STUDENT RESOURCES

Connect

McGraw-Hill's *Connect Introduction to Business* is an online assignment and assessment solution that connects students with the tools and resources they need to achieve success. Interactive applications help prepare students for their future by prompting them to complete homework in preparation for class, master concepts, and review for exams.

Connect Interactive Presentations and Applications allow students to review chapter content and apply knowledge. Students are presented with a variety of different interactive tools to help them assess their understanding and review chapter sections when needed.

Some of the different applications offered include: video cases, decision generators, comprehension cases, and self-assessments (concept checks).

Video cases give students the opportunity to watch case videos and answer questions as they go.

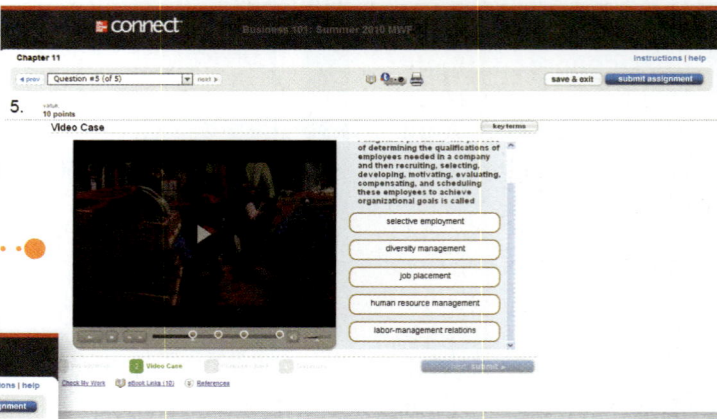

Decision generators require students to make real business decisions based on specific real-world scenarios and cases.

Comprehension cases encourage students to read a case and answer open-ended discussion questions to demonstrate writing and critical-thinking skills.

Concept Checks allow students to evaluate skills and assess personal progress.

Online Learning Center (www.mhhe.com/p2p)

The Online Learning Center will help students use *Business: Connecting Principles to Practice* effectively. Some features on the Web site are:

- Student Assessment and Learning Guide—questions, key-term review, practice tests with answer key, and Internet exercises to help students succeed in their course.

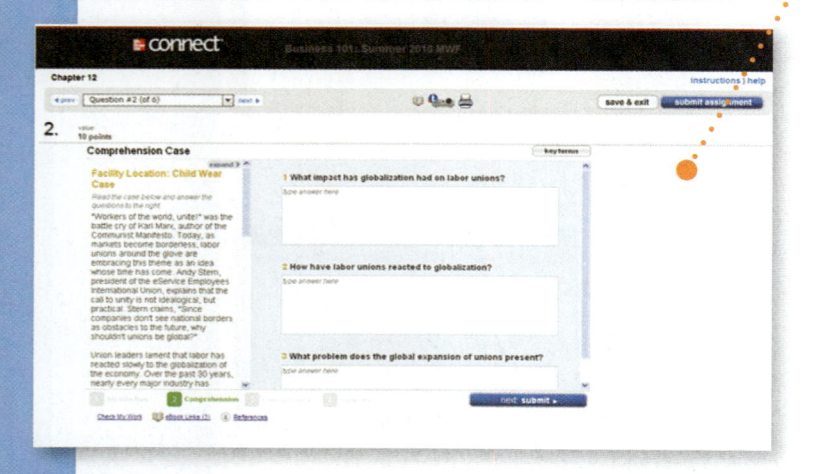

- Casing the Web—short cases that allow students to practice managerial decision making. These discussion starters are provided for every chapter and are intended to replace comprehension cases that can consume class time.
- Multiple choice questions—quizzes focusing on key concepts and providing immediate feedback offer students the opportunity to determine their level of understanding.
- Manager's Hotseat (premium content)—short video cases that show 15 real managers applying their years of experience in confronting certain management and organizational behavior issues. Students assume the role of the manager as they watch the video and answer multiple-choice questions that pop up during the segment, forcing them to make decisions on the spot. Students learn from the managers' mistakes and successes, and then do a report critiquing the managers' approach by defending their reasoning.
- iPod® (premium content)—downloads such as narrated PowerPoint Presentations, audio files, and chapter quizzes.

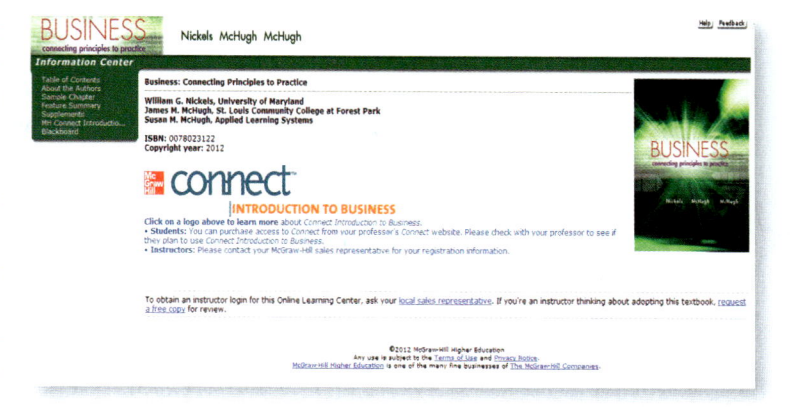

STUDENT-FRIENDLY FEATURES

Getting to Know Business Professionals Every chapter in the text opens with the profile of a business professional whose career relates closely to the material in the chapter. These business professionals work for a variety of businesses from small businesses and nonprofit organizations to large corporations. These career profiles are an engaging way to open the chapter and to introduce students to a variety of business career paths.

Name That Company Every text chapter opens with a Name That Company challenge. The answer for the challenge can be found somewhere in the chapter.

- **Learning Goals** Everything in the text and supplements package ties back to the chapter learning goals. The learning goals listed throughout the chapter help students preview what they should know after reading the chapter. Chapter summaries test students' knowledge by asking questions related to the learning goals. The Test Bank, Instructor's Manual, PowerPoints, Online Course, and Student Assessment and Learning Guide are all organized according to the learning goals.

Progress Assessments help students understand and retain the material in the chapters. Progress Assessment questions stop them at important points in the chapter to assess what they've learned before they continue reading.

progress assessment

- What is human resource management?
- What does it mean to turn an organization chart upside down? What are the five steps in human resource planning?
- What's an internal customer?
- What are contingent workers? Why do companies hire such workers?

Legal Briefcase boxes give students the opportunity to learn about legal issues involving real companies.

Thinking Green boxes highlight corporate responsibility and help students understand the various ways business activities affect the environment.

Spotlight on Small Business boxes feature the ways the concepts in the chapter relate to small business.

Reaching Beyond Our Borders boxes focus on global issues surrounding business.

Making Ethical Decisions boxes offer students ethical dilemmas to consider.

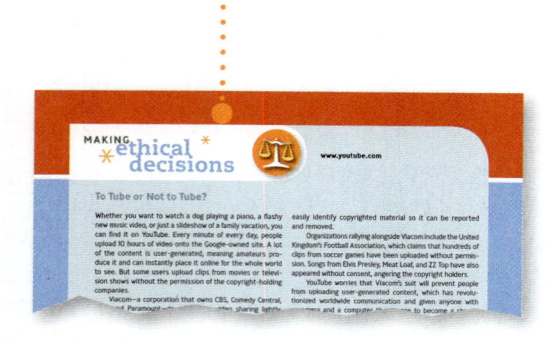

INSTRUCTOR RESOURCES

Student Progress Tracking

Connect Introduction to Business keeps instructors informed about how each student, section, and class is performing, allowing for more productive use of lecture and office hours. The progress-tracking function enables instructors to:

- View scored work immediately and track individual or group performance with assignment and grade reports.
- Access an instant view of student or class performance relative to learning objectives.
- Collect data and generate reports required by many accreditation organizations, such as AACSB.

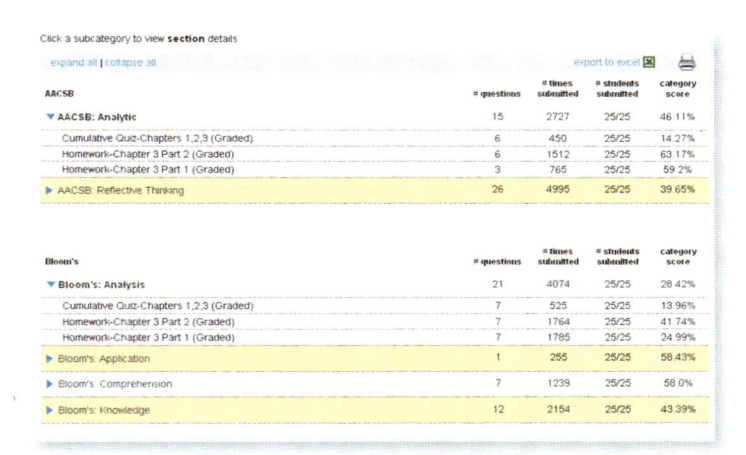

Online Learning Center for Instructors www.mhhe.com/p2p

The Online Learning Center offers instructors a one-stop, secure site for essential course materials, allowing instructors to save prep time before class. The instructor site offers:

- Instructor's Manual
- PowerPoint Presentations
- Testbank/EZ Test
- Monthly Newsletters
- Videos
- Media Resource Guide

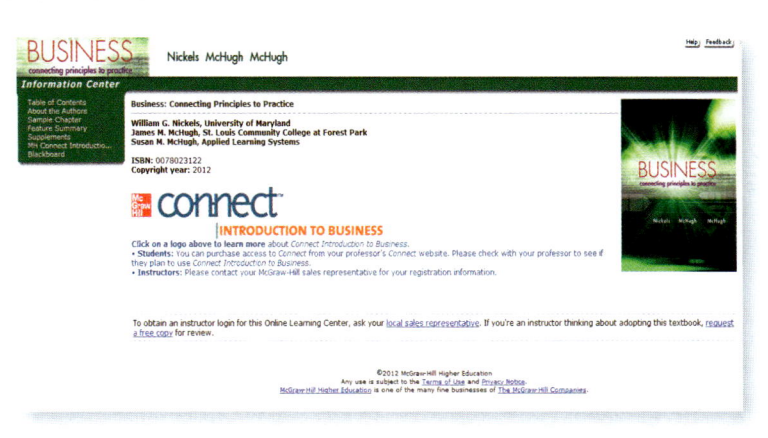

Instructor's Resource CD (IRCD): This CD contains the Instructor's Manual containing everything an instructor needs to prepare a lecture, including lecture outlines, discussion questions, and teaching notes. More than 900 PowerPoint slides offer material from the text, as well as expanded coverage to supplement discussion. The Test Bank and Computerized Test Bank offer over 6000+ multiple-choice, true/false, short answer, essay, and application questions. The Online Learning Center contains a basic version of the media-enhanced PowerPoint Presentations that are found

on the IRCD. The media-enhanced version has video and commercials embedded into the presentations and makes for an engaging and interesting classroom lecture. There is also a lite version of the PowerPoint slides for easier online delivery and customization, as well as auto-narrated slides.
ISBN: 0077482121

Video/DVD
DVD: Case videos, along with video cases included on the OLC discuss the key concepts of each video. Some of the companies featured include: iContact, Netflix, Leo Burnett, and Ball Corporation.
ISBN: 0077482220

Monthly Newsletter
Each month, instructors using *Business: Connecting Principles to Practice* will receive a newsletter that includes many of the hottest topics in business today. Each newsletter contains 10 or more articles and videos on the latest business happenings, with abstracts, discussion questions, and a guide that explains where the information can be implemented in an instructor's course.

Media Resource Guide
This guide includes teaching notes for all of the media materials available with the book. Detailed teaching notes to accompany the chapter videos are available, as well as the Investments Trader. Investments Trader allows students to create a free account at Stock-Trak's new real-time, streaming stock simulation at WallStreetSurvivor.com.

TEACHING OPTIONS AND SOLUTIONS

McGraw-Hill Higher Education and Blackboard have teamed up. What does this mean for you?

1. **Your life, simplified.** Now, you and your students can access McGraw-Hill's *Connect* and Create right from within your Blackboard course—all with one single sign-on. Say goodbye to the days of logging in to multiple applications.

2. **Deep integration of content and tools.** Not only do you get a single sign-on with *Connect* and Create, you also get deep integration of McGraw-Hill content and content engines right in Blackboard. Whether you're choosing a book for your course or building Connect assignments, all the tools you need are right where you want them—inside of Blackboard.

3. **Seamless Gradebooks.** Are you tired of keeping multiple gradebooks and manually synchronizing grades into Blackboard? We thought so. When a student completes an integrated *Connect* assignment, the grade for that assignment automatically (and instantly) feeds your Blackboard grade center.

4. **A solution for everyone.** Whether your institution is already using Blackboard or you just want to try Blackboard on your own, we have a solution for you. McGraw-Hill and Blackboard can now offer you easy access to industry leading technology and content, whether your campus hosts it, or we do. Be sure to ask your local McGraw-Hill representative for details.

McGraw-Hill *Connect Plus Introduction to Business*
McGraw-Hill reinvents the textbook-learning experience for the modern student with *Connect Plus Introduction to Business*. A seamless integration

of an eBook and *Connect Introduction to Business, Connect Plus Introduction to Business* provides all of the *Connect Introduction to Business* features plus the following:

- An integrated eBook, allowing for anytime, anywhere online access to the textbook.
- Dynamic links between the problems or questions assigned to students and the location in the eBook where that problem or question is covered.
- Powerful search function to pinpoint and connect key concepts in a snap.

For more information about *Connect,* go to **connect.mcgraw-hill.com,** or contact your local McGraw-Hill sales representative.

Annotated Instructor's Edition
The AIE is the same as the student edition with the addition of marginal notes that suggest where to use various instructional tools such as PowerPoint, supplementary cases, lecture links, and critical-thinking exercises.
ISBN: 0077482060

CourseSmart
LearnSmart. Choose Smart.
CourseSmart is a new way for faculty to find and review eTextbooks. It's also a great option for students who are interested in accessing their course materials digitally and saving money.

CourseSmart offers thousands of the most commonly adopted textbooks across hundreds of courses from a wide variety of higher education publishers. It is the only place for faculty to review and compare the full text of a textbook online, providing immediate access without the environmental impact of requesting a print exam copy.

With the CourseSmart eTextbook, students can save up to 45 percent off the cost of a print book, reduce their impact on the environment, and access powerful Web tools for learning. CourseSmart is an online eTextbook, which means users access and view their textbook online when connected to the Internet. Students can also print sections of the book for maximum portability. CourseSmart eTextbooks are available in one standard online reader with full text search, notes, and highlighting, and e-mail tools for sharing notes between classmates. For more information on CourseSmart, go to **http://www.coursesmart.com.**

CREATE
Instructors can now tailor their teaching resources to match the way they teach! With McGraw-Hill Create, www.mcgrawhillcreate.com, instructors can easily rearrange chapters, combine material from other content sources, and quickly upload and integrate their own content like course syllabi or teaching notes. Find the right content in Create by searching through thousands of leading McGraw-Hill textbooks. Arrange the material to fit your teaching style. Order a Create book and receive a complimentary print review copy in 3–5 business days or a complimentary electronic review copy (eComp) via email within an hour. Go to **www.mcgrawhillcreate.com** today and register.

Tegrity Campus: Lectures 24/7
Tegrity Campus is a service that makes class time available 24/7 by automatically capturing every lecture in a searchable format for

students to review when they study and complete assignments. With a simple one-click start-and-stop process, you capture all computer screens and corresponding audio. Students can replay any part of any class with easy-to-use browser-based viewing on a PC or Mac.

Educators know that the more students can see, hear, and experience class resources, the better they learn. In fact, studies prove it. With patented Tegrity "search anything" technology, students instantly recall key class moments for replay online, or on iPods® and mobile devices. Instructors can help turn all their students' study time into learning moments immediately supported by their lecture.

To learn more about Tegrity watch a 2-minute Flash demo at **http://tegritycampus.mhhe.com.**

Assurance of Learning Ready

Many educational institutions today are focused on the notion of *assurance of learning,* an important element of some accreditation standards. *Business: Connecting Principles to Practice* is designed specifically to support instructors' assurance of learning initiatives with a simple, yet powerful solution.

Each test bank question for *Business: Connecting Principles to Practice* maps to a specific chapter learning outcome/objective listed in the text. Instructors can use our test bank software, EZ Test and EZ Test Online, to easily query for learning outcomes/objectives that directly relate to the learning objectives for their course. Instructors can then use the reporting features of EZ Test to aggregate student results in similar fashion, making the collection and presentation of assurance of learning data simple and easy.

AACSB Statement

The McGraw-Hill Companies is a proud corporate member of AACSB International. Understanding the importance and value of AACSB accreditation, *Business: Connecting Principles to Practice*, recognizes the curricula guidelines detailed in the AACSB standards for business accreditation by connecting selected questions in the text and the test bank to the six general knowledge and skill guidelines in the AACSB standards.

The statements contained in *Business: Connecting Principles to Practice* are provided only as a guide for the users of this textbook. The AACSB leaves content coverage and assessment within the purview of individual schools, the mission of the school, and the faculty. While *Business: Connecting Principles to Practice* and the teaching package make no claim of any specific AACSB qualification or evaluation, we have within *Business: Connecting Principles to Practice* labeled selected questions according to the six general knowledge and skills areas.

McGraw-Hill Customer Care Contact Information

At McGraw-Hill, we understand that getting the most from new technology can be challenging. That's why our services don't stop after you purchase our products. You can e-mail our Product Specialists 24 hours a day to get product training online. Or you can search our knowledge bank of Frequently Asked Questions on our support Web site. For Customer Support, call **800-331-5094,** e-mail **hmsupport@mcgraw-hill.com,** or visit **www.mhhe.com/support.** One of our Technical Support Analysts will be able to assist you in a timely fashion.

acknowledgements

Our editorial director, Paul Ducham, and executive editor, Doug Hughes, led the talented team at Irwin/McGraw-Hill. We appreciate their dedication to the success of the project and their responsiveness to the demands of the market. Kelly Delso served as our developmental editor and kept everyone on task and on schedule. Michael Hannon provided much appreciated research assistance. Molly and Michael McHugh contributed several of the new boxes and profiles. Matt Baldwin created the new, fresh, open interior design and extraordinary cover. Jeremy Cheshareck carried out the extensive research for photos that was necessary to effectively reflect the concepts presented in the text. Bruce Gin did a splendid job of keeping the production of the text on schedule. Brian Nacik expertly supervised the supplements and media assets.

Many dedicated educators made extraordinary contributions to the quality and utility of this text and package. For this edition, Molly McHugh did an exceptional job in preparing the Test Bank and creating the quizzes for the Online Learning Center and *Connect*, and contributed to and managed the various resources that eventually came together to form the Instructor's Manual and AIE. Molly also did a superb job of creating the PowerPoint slides.

Our outstanding marketing manager, Sarah Reed Schuessler, was up to the challenge of guiding the text to market with the assistance of the market's finest sales professionals. We appreciate her commitment and the renowned product knowledge, service, and dedication of the McGraw-Hill/Irwin sales reps.

We want to thank the many instructors who contributed to the development of *Business: Connecting Principles to Practice*.

REVIEWERS

We would like to thank the following instructors and students who generously provided the input and advice on which the refinements and enhancements contributed to the development of this text.

Nikolas Adamou, *Borough of Manhattan Community College*

Cathy Adamson, *Southern Union State Community College*

Gary Amundson, *Montana State University–Billings*

Kenneth Anderson, *Borough of Manhattan Community College*

Kenneth Anderson, *Mott Community College*

Lydia Anderson, *Fresno City College*

Narita Anderson, *University of Central Oklahoma*

Roanne Angiello, *Bergen Community College*

Chi Anyansi-Archibong, *North Carolina A&T University*

Michael Atchison, *University of Virginia–Charlottesville*

Andrea Bailey, *Moraine Valley Community College*

Sandra Bailey, *Ivy Tech Community College of Indiana*

Scott Bailey, *Troy University*

Wayne Ballantine, *Prairie View A&M University*

Ruby Barker, *Tarleton State University*

Rosalia (Lia) Barone, *Norwalk Community College*

Barbara Barrett, *St. Louis Community College–Meramec*

Barry Barrett, *University of Wisconsin–Milwaukee*

Lorraine Bassette, *Prince George's Community College*

Robb Bay, *College of Southern Nevada–West Charle*

Charles Beavin, *Miami Dade College North*

Charles Beem, *Bucks County Community College*

Cathleen Behan, *Northern Virginia Community College*

Lori Bennett, *Moorpark College*

ACKNOWLEDGEMENTS

Ellen Benowitz, *Mercer Community College*

Patricia Bernson, *County College of Morris*

William Bettencourt, *Edmonds Community College*

Robert Blanchard, *Salem State College*

Mary Jo Boehms, *Jackson State Community College*

James Borden, *Villanova University*

Michael Bravo, *Bentley College*

Dennis Brode, *Sinclair Community College*

Harvey Bronstein, *Oakland Community College–Farmington Hills*

Deborah Brown, *North Carolina State University–Raleigh*

Aaron A. Buchko, *Bradley University*

Laura Bulas, *Central Community College–Hastings*

Judy Bulin, *Monroe Community College*

Barry Bunn, *Valencia Community College–West Camp*

Bill Burton, *Indiana Wesleyan University*

Paul Callahan, *Cincinnati State Technical and Community College*

William Candley, *Lemoyne Owen College*

Nancy Carr, *Community College of Philadelphia*

Ron Cereola, *James Madison University*

Bonnie Chavez, *Santa Barbara City College*

Susan Cisco, *Oakton Community College*

Margaret (Meg) Clark, *Cincinnati State Technical and Community College*

David Clifton, *Ivy Tech Community College of Indiana*

C. Cloud, *Phoenix College*

Doug Cobbs, *JS Reynolds Community College*

Brooks Colin, *University of New Orleans*

Debbie Collins, *Anne Arundel Community College*

Andrew Cook, *Limestone College*

Bob Cox, *Salt Lake Community College*

Susan Cremins, *Westchester Community College*

Julie Cross, *Chippewa Valley Tech College*

Geoffrey Crosslin, *Kalamazoo Valley Community College*

Douglas Crowe, *Bradley University*

John David, *Stark State College of Tech*

Peter Dawson, *Collin County Community College*

Joseph Defilippe, *Suffolk County Community College–Brentwood*

Tim DeGroot, *Midwestern State University*

Len Denault, *Bentley College*

Frances Depaul, *Westmoreland County Community College*

Donna Devault, *Fayetteville Tech Community College*

Sharon Dexter, *Southeast Community College-Beatrice*

John Dilyard, *St. Francis College*

Barbara Dinardo, *Owens Community College*

George Dollar, *St. Petersburg College*

Glenn Doolittle, *Santa Ana College*

Ron Dougherty, *Ivy Tech Community College of Indiana*

Michael Drafke, *College of DuPage*

Karen Eboch, *Bowling Green State University*

Brenda Eichelberger, *Portland State University*

Kelvin Elston, *Nashville State Tech Community College*

Robert Ettl, *Stony Brook University*

Nancy Evans, *Heartland Community College*

Michael Ewens, *Ventura College*

Hyacinth Ezeka, *Coppin State University*

Bob Farris, *Mt. San Antonio College*

Karen Faulkner, *Long Beach City College*

Gil Feiertag, *Columbus State Community College*

Joseph Flack, *Washtenaw Community College*

Lucinda Fleming, *Orange County Community College*

Jackie Flom, *University of Toledo*

Andrea Foster, *John Tyler Community College*

Michael Foster, *Bentley College*

Leatrice Freer, *Pitt Community College*

Alan Friedenthal, *Kingsborough Community College*

Charles Gaiser, *Brunswick Community College*

Ashley Geisewite, *Southwest Tennessee Community College*

Katie Ghahramani, *Johnson County Community College*

Debora Gilliard, *Metropolitan State College–Denver*

James Glover, *Community College of Baltimore County Essex Constance Golden, Lakeland Community College*

Toby Grodner, *Union County College*

Clark Hallpike, *Elgin Community College*

Geri Harper, *Western Illinois University*

Frank Hatstat, *Bellevue Community College*

Spedden Hause, *University of Maryland–University College*

Karen Hawkins, *Miami-Dade College–Kendall*

Travis Hayes, *Chattanooga State Tech*

Jack Heinsius, *Modesto Junior College*

Charlane Held, *Onondaga Community College*

James Hess, *Ivy Tech Community College of Indiana*

Steve Hester, *Southwest Tennessee Community College-Macon Campus*

William Hill, *Mississippi State University*

Nathan Himelstein, *Essex County College*

Paula Hladik, *Waubonsee Community College*

David Ho, *Metropolitan Community College*

Douglas Hobbs, *Sussex County Community College*

Maryanne Holcomb, *Antelope Valley College*

Mary Carole Hollingsworth, *Georgia Perimeter College*

Russell Holmes, *Des Moines Area Community College*

Scott Homan, *Purdue University-West Lafayette*

Stacy Horner, *Southwestern Michigan College*

Dennis Hudson, *University of Tulsa*

Jo Ann Hunter, *Community College Allegheny County in Pittsburgh*

Kimberly Hurns, *Washtenaw Community College*

Victor Isbell, *University of Nevada-Las Vegas*

Deloris James, *University of Maryland-University College*

Pam Janson, *Stark State College of Tech*

William Jedlicka, *William Rainey Harper College*

Carol Johnson, *University of Denver*

Gwendolyn Jones, *University of Akron*

Kenneth Jones, *Ivy Tech Community College of Indiana*

Marilyn Jones, *Friends University*

Michael Jones, *Delgado Community College*

Dmitriy Kalyagin, *Chabot College*

Jack Kant, *San Juan College*

Jimmy Kelsey, *Seattle Central Community College*

Robert Kemp, *University of Virginia-Charlottesville*

David Kendall, *Fashion Institute Technology*

Kristine Kinard, *Shelton State Community College*

Sandra King, *Minnesota State University-Mankato*

John Kurnik, *Saint Petersburg College*

Jeff LaVake, *University of Wisconsin-Oshkosh*

Robert Lewis, *Davenport University*

Byron Lilly, *Deanza College*

Beverly Loach, *Central Piedmont Community College*

Boone Londrigan, *Mott Community College*

Ladonna Love, *Fashion Institute Technology*

Ivan Lowe, *York Technical College*

Yvonne Lucas, *Southwestern College*

Robert Lupton, *Central Washington University*

Megan Luttenton, *Grand Valley State University*

Elaine Madden, *Anne Arundel Community College*

Lawrence Maes, *Davenport University*

Niki Maglaris, *Northwestern College*

James Maniki, *Northwestern College*

Martin Markowitz, *College of Charleston*

Fred Mayerson, *Kingsborough Community College*

Stacy McCaskill, *Rock Valley College*

Vershun L. McClain, *Jackson State University*

Gina McConoughey, *Illinois Central College*

Patricia McDaniel, *Central Piedmont Community College*

Pam McElligott, *St. Louis Community College-Meramec*

Tom McFarland, *Mt. San Antonio College*

Bill McPherson, *Indiana University of Pennsylvania*

Ginger Moore, *York Technical College*

Sandy Moore, *Ivy Tech Community College of Indiana*

Jennifer Morton, *Ivy Tech Community College of Indiana*

Peter Moutsatson, *Central Michigan University*

Rachna Nagi-Condos, *American River College*

Darrell Neron, *Pierce College*

Mihia Nica, *University of Central Oklahoma*

Charles Nichols, *Sullivan University*

Frank Novakowski, *Davenport University*

Mark Nygren, *Brigham Young University-Idaho*

Paul Okello, *Tarrant County College*

Faviana Olivier, *Bentley College*

John Olivo, *Bloomsburg University of Pennsylvania*

Teresa O'Neill, *International Institute of the Americas*

Cathy Onion, *Western Illinois University*

Susan Ontko, *Schoolcraft College*

Glenda Orosco, *Oklahoma State University Institute of Technology*

ACKNOWLEDGEMENTS

Christopher O'Suanah, *J. S. Reynolds Community College*
Daniel Pacheco, *Kansas City Kansas Community College*
Esther Page-Wood, *Western Michigan University*
Lauren Paisley, *Genesee Community College*
John Pappalardo, *Keene State College*
Ron Pardee, *Riverside Community College*
Jack Partlow, *Northern Virginia Community College*
Jeff Pepper, *Chippewa Valley Tech College*
Sheila Petcavage, *Cuyahoga Community College Western-Parma*
Roy Pipitone, *Erie Community College*
Lana Powell, *Valencia Community College-West Campus*
Dan Powroznik, *Chesapeake College*
Litsa Press, *College of Lake County*
Sally Proffitt, *Tarrant County College Northeast*
Michael Quinn, *James Madison University*
Anthony Racka, *Oakland Community College*
Larry Ramos, *Miami-Dade Community College*
Greg Rapp, *Portland Community College-Sylvania*
Robert Reese, *Illinois Valley Community College*
David Reiman, *Monroe County Community College*
Gloria Rembert, *Mitchell Community College*
Levi Richard, *Citrus College*
Clinton Richards, *University of Nevada-Las Vegas*
Patricia Richards, *Westchester Community College*
Susan Roach, *Georgia Southern University*
Sandra Robertson, *Thomas Nelson Community College*
Catherine Roche, *Rockland Community College*
Tim Rogers, *Ozarks Technical College*
Sam Rohr, *University of Northwestern Ohio*
Pamela Rouse, *Butler University*
Carol Rowey, *Community College of Rhode Island*
Jeri Rubin, *University of Alaska-Anchorage*
Storm Russo, *Valencia Community College*
Mark Ryan, *Hawkeye Community College*
Richard Sarkisian, *Camden County College*
Andy Saucedo, *Dona Ana Community College-Las Cruces*
James Scott, *Central Michigan University*
Janet Seggern, *Lehigh Carbon Community College*
Sashi Sekhar, *Purdue University-Calumet-Hammond*
Pat Setlik, *William Rainey Harper College*
Swannee Sexton, *University of Tennessee-Knoxville*
Phyllis Shafer, *Brookdale Community College*
Richard Shortridge, *Glendale Community College*
Louise Stephens, *Volunteer State Community College*
Desiree Stephens, *Norwalk Community College*
Clifford Stalter, *Chattanooga State Technical Community College*
Kurt Stanberry, *University of Houston Downtown*
Martin St. John, *Westmoreland County Community College*
John Striebich, *Monroe Community College*
David Stringer, *Deanza College*
Ron Surmacz, *Duquesne University*
William Syvertsen, *Fresno City College*
Scott Taylor, *Moberly Area Community College*
Jim Thomas, *Indiana University Northwest*
Deborah Thompson, *Bentley College*
Evelyn Thrasher, *University of Massachusetts-Dartmouth*
Jon Tomlinson, *University of Northwestern Ohio*
Bob Trewartha, *Minnesota School of Business*
Bob Urell, *Irvine Valley College*
Dan Vetter, *Central Michigan University*
Andrea Vidrine, *Baton Rouge Community College*
Daniel Viveiros, *Johnson & Wales University*
Joann Warren, *Community College of Rhode Island-Warwick*
R. Patrick Wehner, *Everest University*
Sally Wells, *Columbia College*
Mildred Wilson, *Georgia Southern University*
Karen Wisniewski, *County College of Morris*
Greg Witkowski, *Northwestern College*
Colette Wolfson, *Ivy Tech Community College of Indiana*
Deborah Yancey, *Virginia Western Community College*
Mark Zarycki, *Hillsborough Community College*
Lisa Zingaro, *Oakton Community College*
Mark Zorn, *Butler County Community College*

This edition offers the market's gold standard due to involvement of these committed instructors and students. We thank them all for their help, support, and friendship.

Bill Nickels Jim McHugh Susan McHugh

Preface v

brief CONTENTS

part 1
Business Trends: Cultivating a Business in Diverse, Global Environments
1. Taking Risks and Making Profits within the Dynamic Business Environment 2
2. Understanding How Economics Affects Business 28
3. Doing Business in Global Markets 58
4. Demanding Ethical and Socially Responsible Behavior 88

part 2
Business Ownership: Starting a Small Business
5. How to Form a Business 112
6. Entrepreneurship and Starting a Small Business 144

part 3
Business Management: Empowering Employees to Satisfy Customers
7. Management and Leadership 176
8. Adapting Organizations to Today's Markets 200
9. Production and Operations Management 228

part 4
Management of Human Resources: Motivating Employees to Produce Quality Goods and Services
10. Motivating Employees 254
11. Human Resource Management: Finding and Keeping the Best Employees 282
12. Dealing with Employee–Management Issues and Relationships 316

part 5
Marketing: Developing and Implementing Customer-Oriented Marketing Plans
13. Marketing: Helping Buyers Buy 344
14. Developing and Pricing Goods and Services 372
15. Distributing Products 400
16. Using Effective Promotions 428

part 6
Managing Financial Resources
17. Understanding Accounting and Financial Information 454
18. Financial Management 484
19. Using Securities Markets for Financing and Investing Opportunities 512
20. Money, Financial Institutions, and the Federal Reserve 544

Appendix Working within the Legal Environment

Bonus Chapters (available online only)
A. Using Technology to Manage Information BA
B. Managing Risk BB
C. Managing Your Personal Finances BC

Chapter Notes N
Glossary G
Photo Credits PC-1
Name Index I
Organization Index I-8
Subject Index I-13

contents

Preface v

part I
Business Trends: Cultivating a Business in Diverse, Global Environments

Chapter One

2 Taking Risks and Making Profits within the Dynamic Business Environment

Profile: Getting to Know Nick Graham, Owner of the Main Street Market 2

Entrepreneurship and Wealth Building 4
- Revenues, Profits, and Losses 5
- Matching Risk with Profit 5
- Standard of Living and Quality of Life 5
- Responding to the Various Business Stakeholders 6
- Using Business Principles in Nonprofit Organizations 7

Entrepreneurship versus Working for Others 8
- Opportunities for Entrepreneurs 9
- The Importance of Entrepreneurs to the Creation of Wealth 9
- *Spotlight on Small Business: Hiring People with Special Needs* 10

The Business Environment 11
- The Economic and Legal Environment 12
- The Technological Environment 14
- *Making Ethical Decisions: Ethics Begins with You* 15
- The Competitive Environment 16
- The Social Environment 17
- The Global Environment 18
- *Thinking Green: Getting Involved Personally* 20

The Evolution of U.S. Business 20
- Progress in the Agricultural and Manufacturing Industries 20
- Progress in Service Industries 21
- Your Future in Business 21

***Connect* Interactive Applications** 25

Chapter Two

28 Understanding How Economics Affects Business

Profile: Getting to Know Muhammad Yunus, Founder of the Grameen Bank 28

How Economic Conditions Affect Businesses 30
- What Is Economics? 30
- The Secret to Creating a Wealthy Economy 31
- *Thinking Green: More Profits from the Green Revolution* 32
- Adam Smith and the Creation of Wealth 33
- How Businesses Benefit the Community 33
- *Making Ethical Decisions: Corruption Destroys Economies* 34

Understanding Free-Market Capitalism 34
- The Foundations of Capitalism 35
- *Spotlight on Small Business: The Key to Capitalism Is Capital* 36
- How Free Markets Work 36
- How Prices Are Determined 36
- The Economic Concept of Supply 37
- The Economic Concept of Demand 37
- The Equilibrium Point, or Market Price 37
- Competition within Free Markets 39
- Benefits and Limitations of Free Markets 39

Understanding Socialism 40
- The Benefits of Socialism 41
- The Negative Consequences of Socialism 41

Understanding Communism 41

The Trend toward Mixed Economies 42
- *Reaching Beyond Our Borders: Prospering in Foreign Lands* 43

Understanding the U.S. Economic System 45
- Key Economic Indicators 45
- Productivity in the United States 48
- Productivity in the Service Sector 48
- The Business Cycle 48
- Stabilizing the Economy through Fiscal Policy 49
- Fiscal Policy in Action during the Economic Crisis of 2008–2010 50
- Using Monetary Policy to Keep the Economy Growing 51

***Connect* Interactive Applications** 54

Chapter Three

58 Doing Business in Global Markets

Profile: Getting to Know Sheikha Lubna al-Qasimi, Foreign Trade Minister of the United Arab Emirates 58

The Dynamic Global Market 60

Why Trade with Other Nations? 61

- The Theories of Comparative and Absolute Advantage 61

Getting Involved in Global Trade 62

- Importing Goods and Services 63
- Exporting Goods and Services 63
- *Spotlight on Small Business: Finding Cracks in the Great Wall 64*
- Measuring Global Trade 64

Strategies for Reaching Global Markets 66

- Licensing 66
- Exporting 67
- *Reaching Beyond Our Borders: The Sun Never Sets on Mickey D's 68*
- Franchising 68
- Contract Manufacturing 69
- International Joint Ventures and Strategic Alliances 70
- Foreign Direct Investment 70

Forces Affecting Trading in Global Markets 72

- Sociocultural Forces 72
- Economic and Financial Forces 73
- Legal and Regulatory Forces 74
- Physical and Environmental Forces 75

Trade Protectionism 75

- The World Trade Organization 76
- Common Markets 77
- The North American and Central American Free Trade Agreements 78
- *Legal Briefcase: NAFTA or SHAFTA? 79*

The Future of Global Trade 80

- The Challenge of Offshore Outsourcing 81
- *Making Ethical Decisions: Take Two Aspirins and Go to Thailand 82*
- Globalization and Your Future 83

Connect Interactive Applications 85

Chapter Four

88 Demanding Ethical and Socially Responsible Behavior

Profile: Getting to Know Steve Ells, Founder and CEO of Chipotle Mexican Grill 88

Ethics Is More Than Legality 90

- *Legal Briefcase: Paying the Price 91*
- Ethical Standards Are Fundamental 92
- Ethics Begins with Each of Us 92
- *Making Ethical Decisions: To Tube or Not to Tube? 93*

Managing Businesses Ethically and Responsibly 94

- Setting Corporate Ethical Standards 96

Corporate Social Responsibility 98

- Responsibility to Customers 100
- Responsibility to Investors 101
- Responsibility to Employees 102
- Responsibility to Society and the Environment 102
- *Thinking Green: Green Greed 104*
- Social Auditing 104

International Ethics and Social Responsibility 105

- *Reaching Beyond Our Borders: Ethical Culture Clash 107*

Connect Interactive Applications 109

part 2

Business Ownership: Starting a Small Business

Chapter Five

112 How to Form a Business

Profile: Getting to Know Brian Scudamore, Founder of 1-800-GOT-JUNK? 112

Basic Forms of Business Ownership 114

Sole Proprietorships 115

- Advantages of Sole Proprietorships 115
- Disadvantages of Sole Proprietorships 116

Partnerships 117

- Advantages of Partnerships 118
- *Spotlight on Small Business: Pick Your Partner Wisely 119*
- Disadvantages of Partnerships 119

Corporations 121

- Advantages of Corporations 121
- Disadvantages of Corporations 123
- Individuals Can Incorporate 124
- S Corporations 125
- Limited Liability Companies 126
- *Legal Briefcase: Vermont Wants to Be the Home of Your New Virtual Company 127*

Corporate Expansion: Mergers and Acquisitions 129

- *Thinking Green: Root, Root, Root for the Green Team 131*

Franchises 131

- Advantages of Franchises 132
- Disadvantages of Franchises 133

xxi

Diversity in Franchising   134
Home-Based Franchises   135
E-Commerce in Franchising   136
Using Technology in Franchising   136
Franchising in International Markets   136

Cooperatives   137

Which Form of Ownership Is for You?   138

Connect Interactive Applications   140

Chapter Six

144 Entrepreneurship and Starting a Small Business

Profile: Getting to Know Sheila C. Johnson, Cofounder of Black Entertainment Television (BET)   144

The Age of the Entrepreneur   146

The Job-Creating Power of Entrepreneurs in the United States   146

Spotlight on Small Business: You're Never Too Young to Be an Entrepreneur   147

Why People Take the Entrepreneurial Challenge   147

What Does It Take to Be an Entrepreneur?   148

Thinking Green: Socially Responsible Entrepreneurship   149

Turning Your Passions and Problems into Opportunities   149

Entrepreneurial Teams   150

Micropreneurs and Home-Based Businesses   150

Reaching Beyond Our Borders: Outsourcing Your Small Business   153

Web-Based Businesses   154

Entrepreneurship within Firms   155

Encouraging Entrepreneurship: What Government Can Do   156

Getting Started in Small Business   157

Small versus Big Business   157

Importance of Small Businesses   158

Small-Business Success and Failure   158

Learning about Small-Business Operations   160

Learn from Others   160

Get Some Experience   160

Take Over a Successful Firm   160

Making Ethical Decisions: Going Down with the Ship   161

Managing a Small Business   161

Begin with Planning   162

Writing a Business Plan   162

Getting Money to Fund a Small Business   164

The Small Business Administration (SBA)   165

Knowing Your Customers   166

Managing Employees   167

Keeping Records   167

Looking for Help   167

Going International: Small-Business Prospects   169

Connect Interactive Applications   172

part 3
Business Management: Empowering Employees to Satisfy Customers

Chapter Seven

176 Management and Leadership

Profile: Getting to Know Indra Krishnamurthy Nooyi, CEO of PepsiCo   176

Managers' Roles Are Evolving   178

The Four Functions of Management   179

Reaching Beyond Our Borders: We Need Managers Over Here   180

Planning and Decision Making   181

Spotlight on Small Business: I'd Rather Be Blue   185

Decision Making: Finding the Best Alternative   185

Organizing: Creating a Unified System   186

Tasks and Skills at Different Levels of Management   188

Staffing: Getting and Keeping the Right People   189

Leading: Providing Continuous Vision and Values   189

Making Ethical Decisions: To Share or Not to Share   190

Leadership Styles   190

Empowering Workers   192

Managing Knowledge   192

Controlling: Making Sure It Works   193

A Key Criterion for Measurement: Customer Satisfaction   194

Connect Interactive Applications   197

Chapter Eight

200 Adapting Organizations to Today's Markets

Profile: Getting to Know Anne Mulcahy, Former CEO of Xerox   200

Everyone's Organizing   202

Building an Organization from the Bottom Up   202

Reaching Beyond Our Borders: General Electric Looks for More Profits   203

Making Ethical Decisions: Safety versus Profit   204

The Changing Organization 204
   The Development of Organization Design 205
   Turning Principles into Organization Design 207

Decisions to Make in Structuring Organizations 208
   Choosing Centralized or Decentralized Authority 208
   Choosing the Appropriate Span of Control 208
   Choosing between Tall and Flat Organization Structures 209
   Weighing the Advantages and Disadvantages of Departmentalization 210

Organization Models 213
   Line Organizations 213
   Line-and-Staff Organizations 213
   Matrix-Style Organizations 214
   Cross-Functional Self-Managed Teams 216
   Going Beyond Organizational Boundaries 216

Managing the Interactions among Firms 217
   Transparency and Virtual Organizations 217
   Benchmarking and Core Competencies 218

Adapting to Change 219
   Restructuring for Empowerment 219
   Creating a Change-Oriented Organizational Culture 220
   Managing the Informal Organization 221
   Spotlight on Small Business: Keeping That Small-Company Feeling 222

***Connect* Interactive Applications 225**

Chapter Nine

228 Production and Operations Management

Profile: Getting to Know Samuel J. Palmisano, CEO and President of IBM 228

Manufacturing and Services in Perspective 230
   Thinking Green: The Green Movement Improves the Economy 231
   Manufacturers and Service Organizations Become More Competitive 231

From Production to Operations Management 232
   Operations Management in the Service Sector 233

Production Processes 234
   The Need to Improve Production Techniques and Cut Costs 236
   Computer-Aided Design and Manufacturing 236
   Flexible Manufacturing 237
   Lean Manufacturing 237
   Mass Customization 237

Operations Management Planning 238
   Facility Location 238
   Facility Location for Manufacturers 239

   Making Ethical Decisions: Stay or Leave? 240
   Taking Operations Management to the Internet 240
   Facility Location in the Future 240
   Reaching Beyond Our Borders: Partnering Beyond Country Borders 241
   Facility Layout 241
   Materials Requirement Planning 242
   Purchasing 244
   Just-in-Time Inventory Control 244
   Quality Control 244
   The Baldrige Awards 245
   ISO 9000 and ISO 14000 Standards 245

Control Procedures: PERT and Gantt Charts 246

Preparing for the Future 248

***Connect* Interactive Applications 251**

part 4

Management of Human Resources: Motivating Employees to Produce Quality Goods and Services

Chapter Ten

254 Motivating Employees

Profile: Getting to Know Sergey Brin and Larry Page, Founders of Google 254

The Value of Motivation 256
   Frederick Taylor: The Father of Scientific Management 257
   Legal Briefcase: Upset at UPS 258
   Elton Mayo and the Hawthorne Studies 259

Motivation and Maslow's Hierarchy of Needs 260

Herzberg's Motivating Factors 261

McGregor's Theory X and Theory Y 263
   Theory X 264
   Theory Y 264

Ouchi's Theory Z 265

Goal-Setting Theory and Management by Objectives 267

Meeting Employee Expectations: Expectancy Theory 267

Reinforcing Employee Performance: Reinforcement Theory 268

Treating Employees Fairly: Equity Theory 268

Putting Theory into Action 269
   Motivation through Job Enrichment 270
   Motivating through Open Communication 270
   Thinking Green: Green Team, Go! 271

Applying Open Communication in Self-Managed Teams 272

Recognizing a Job Well Done 272

Spotlight on Small Business: Big Motivators for Small Businesses 273

Personalizing Motivation 274

Motivating Employees across the Globe 274

Motivating Employees across Generations 275

***Connect* Interactive Applications** 279

Chapter Eleven

282 Human Resource Management: Finding and Keeping the Best Employees

Profile: Getting to Know Sally Mainquist, President and CEO of Certes Financial Pros 282

Working with People Is Just the Beginning 284

Developing the Ultimate Resource 284

The Human Resource Challenge 286

Thinking Green: Green Eggs and Green Ham 287

Laws Affecting Human Resource Management 287

Legal Briefcase: Government Legislation 288

Laws Protecting Employees with Disabilities and Older Employees 289

Effects of Legislation 290

Determining a Firm's Human Resource Needs 290

Recruiting Employees from a Diverse Population 292

Selecting Employees Who Will Be Productive 293

Spotlight on Small Business: It's Not Easy Being Small 294

Hiring Contingent Workers 296

Making Ethical Decisions: Motivating Temporary Employees 297

Training and Developing Employees for Optimum Performance 297

Management Development 300

Networking 300

Diversity in Management Development 301

Appraising Employee Performance to Get Optimum Results 301

Compensating Employees: Attracting and Keeping the Best 303

Pay Systems 303

Compensating Teams 304

Fringe Benefits 305

Scheduling Employees to Meet Organizational and Employee Needs 306

Flextime Plans 306

Reaching Beyond Our Borders: Working Worldwide 307

Home-Based Work 308

Job-Sharing Plans 308

Moving Employees Up, Over, and Out 309

Promoting and Reassigning Employees 309

Terminating Employees 310

Retiring Employees 310

Losing Valued Employees 311

***Connect* Interactive Applications** 313

Chapter Twelve

316 Dealing with Employee–Management Issues and Relationships

Profile: Getting to Know Roger Goodell, Commissioner of the National Football League 316

Employee–Management Issues 318

Labor Unions from Different Perspectives 319

The Early History of Organized Labor 319

Labor Legislation and Collective Bargaining 320

Objectives of Organized Labor 323

Reaching Beyond Our Borders: Workers of the World, Unite 325

Resolving Labor–Management Disagreements 325

Mediation and Arbitration 326

Tactics Used in Labor–Management Conflicts 327

Union Tactics 327

Management Tactics 328

Making Ethical Decisions: When Do You Cross the Line? 329

The Future of Unions and Labor–Management Relations 329

Spotlight on Small Business: Nursing the Unions Back to Health 331

Controversial Employee–Management Issues 332

Executive Compensation 332

Legal Briefcase: Paying for Incompetence 333

Pay Equity 334

Sexual Harassment 335

Child Care 336

Elder Care 337

Drug Testing 338

Violence in the Workplace 338

***Connect* Interactive Applications** 341

part 5

Marketing: Developing and Implementing Customer-Oriented Marketing Plans

Chapter Thirteen

344 Marketing: Helping Buyers Buy

Profile: Getting to Know Cricket Lee, Creator of Fitlogic 344

What Is Marketing? 346
- The Evolution of Marketing 347
- *Spotlight on Small Business: Find a Need and Fill It* 348
- Nonprofit Organizations and Marketing 349

The Marketing Mix 350
- Applying the Marketing Process 350
- *Thinking Green: Four Ps Drive Marketing* 351
- Designing a Product to Meet Consumer Needs 352
- Setting an Appropriate Price 353
- Getting the Product to the Right Place 353
- Developing an Effective Promotional Strategy 354

Providing Marketers with Information 354
- The Marketing Research Process 354

The Marketing Environment 357
- *Reaching Beyond Our Borders: Social Marketing Goes Global* 358
- Global Factors 358
- Technological Factors 358
- Sociocultural Factors 359
- Competitive Factors 359
- Economic Factors 359

Two Different Markets: Consumer and Business-to-Business (B2B) 359

The Consumer Market 360
- Segmenting the Consumer Market 361
- Reaching Smaller Market Segments 362
- Moving toward Relationship Marketing 363
- The Consumer Decision-Making Process 363

The Business-to-Business Market 365

Your Prospects in Marketing 366

***Connect* Interactive Applications** 368

Chapter Fourteen

372 Developing and Pricing Goods and Services

Profile: Getting to Know Ratan Tata from the Tata Group 372

Product Development and the Total Product Offer 374
- Developing a Total Product Offer 375
- *Spotlight on Small Business: Home Cooking in Half the Time* 376
- Product Lines and the Product Mix 377

Product Differentiation 378
- Marketing Different Classes of Consumer Goods and Services 378
- Marketing Industrial Goods and Services 379

Packaging Changes the Product 381
- The Growing Importance of Packaging 382

Branding and Brand Equity 382
- Brand Categories 383
- *Thinking Green: Couldn't You Make a Smaller Footprint?* 384
- Generating Brand Equity and Loyalty 384
- Creating Brand Associations 385
- Brand Management 385

The New-Product Development Process 385
- Generating New-Product Ideas 386
- Product Screening 386
- Product Analysis 387
- Product Development and Testing 387
- Commercialization 387

The Product Life Cycle 388
- Example of the Product Life Cycle 388
- Using the Product Life Cycle 389

Competitive Pricing 390
- Pricing Objectives 390
- Cost-Based Pricing 391
- Demand-Based Pricing 391
- *Reaching Beyond Our Borders: When Selling Sweets Goes Sour* 392
- Competition-Based Pricing 392
- Break-Even Analysis 392
- Other Pricing Strategies 393
- How Market Forces Affect Pricing 394

Nonprice Competition 394

***Connect* Interactive Applications** 397

Chapter Fifteen

400 Distributing Products

Profile: Getting to Know Mark Stern of Doggypads.com 400

The Emergence of Marketing Intermediaries 402
- *Spotlight on Small Business: Recycling Is Part of the Whole Supply-Chain Process* 403
- Why Marketing Needs Intermediaries 403
- How Intermediaries Create Exchange Efficiencies 404
- The Value versus the Cost of Intermediaries 405

The Utilities Created by Intermediaries 407
- Form Utility 407
- Time Utility 407
- Place Utility 407
- Possession Utility 408

xxv

Information Utility 408
Service Utility 408
Wholesale Intermediaries 409
Merchant Wholesalers 409
Agents and Brokers 410
Retail Intermediaries 411
Retail Distribution Strategy 411
Nonstore Retailing 412
Electronic Retailing 412
Telemarketing 413
Vending Machines, Kiosks, and Carts 413
Direct Selling 414
Multilevel Marketing 414
Direct Marketing 414
Building Cooperation in Channel Systems 415
Corporate Distribution Systems 415
Contractual Distribution Systems 415
Administered Distribution Systems 416
Supply Chains 416
Reaching Beyond Our Borders: How to Reach the Little Guy 417
Logistics: Getting Goods to Consumers Efficiently 418
Trains Are Great for Large Shipments 419
Trucks Are Good for Small Shipments to Remote Locations 420
Water Transportation Is Inexpensive but Slow 420
Thinking Green: Keeping Your Carbon Footprint Low 421
Pipelines Are Fast and Efficient 421
Air Transportation Is Fast but Expensive 421
Intermodal Shipping 421
The Storage Function 422
Tracking Goods 422
What All This Means to You 422
Connect Interactive Applications 425

Chapter Sixteen

428 Using Effective Promotions

Profile: Getting to Know Laurel Richie, Chief Marketing Officer of the Girl Scouts 428
Promotion and the Promotion Mix 430
Advertising: Informing, Persuading, and Reminding 431
Television Advertising 433
Thinking Green: Finding a Competitive Advantage in Sustainability 434
Product Placement 434
Infomercials 435
Online Advertising 435
Global Advertising 436
Personal Selling: Providing Personal Attention 437
Steps in the Selling Process 438
The Business-to-Consumer Sales Process 440
Public Relations: Building Relationships 441
Publicity: The Talking Arm of PR 441
Sales Promotion: Giving Buyers Incentives 442
Word of Mouth and Other Promotional Tools 444
Viral Marketing 445
Blogging 445
Podcasting 445
E-Mail Promotions 445
Spotlight on Small Business: Fresh-Baked Promotion 446
Mobile Media 446
Managing the Promotion Mix: Putting It All Together 446
Reaching Beyond Our Borders: Going Digital 447
Promotional Strategies 447
Connect Interactive Applications 450

part 6

Managing Financial Resources

Chapter Seventeen

454 Understanding Accounting and Financial Information

Profile: Getting to Know Sean Perich of Bakery Barn 454
The Role of Accounting Information 456
What Is Accounting? 456
Accounting Disciplines 457
Managerial Accounting 457
Financial Accounting 458
Legal Briefcase: Balance Sheet Sherlocks 460
Auditing 460
Tax Accounting 461
Government and Not-for-Profit Accounting 461
The Accounting Cycle 462
Accounting Technology 463
Understanding Key Financial Statements 463
The Fundamental Accounting Equation 464
The Balance Sheet 465
Classifying Assets 466
Liabilities and Owners' Equity Accounts 466
The Income Statement 468
Revenue 469
Cost of Goods Sold 469
Operating Expenses 469
Spotlight on Small Business: Accounting for What's Coming and Going in a Small Business 470

Net Profit or Loss   470
The Statement of Cash Flows   471
The Need for Cash Flow Analysis   472
Making Ethical Decisions: On the Accounting Hot Seat   473

Analyzing Financial Performance Using Ratios   473
Liquidity Ratios   473
Leverage (Debt) Ratios   474
Profitability (Performance) Ratios   475
Activity Ratios   475
Reaching Beyond Our Borders: The Accounting Shot Heard around the World   477

Connect Interactive Applications   480

Chapter Eighteen

484 Financial Management

Profile: Getting to Know Tonya Antonucci, Commissioner of the Women's Professional Soccer League   484

The Role of Finance and Financial Managers   486
The Value of Understanding Finance   487
What Is Financial Management?   488

Financial Planning   489
Forecasting Financial Needs   489
Working with the Budget Process   490
Establishing Financial Controls   491

The Need for Operating Funds   492
Making Ethical Decisions: Sail Smoothly or Rock the Boat?   493
Managing Day-by-Day Needs of the Business   493
Spotlight on Small Business: Keeping the Cash Flowing in Hard Times   494
Controlling Credit Operations   494
Acquiring Needed Inventory   495
Making Capital Expenditures   495
Alternative Sources of Funds   495

Obtaining Short-Term Financing   496
Trade Credit   496
Family and Friends   497
Commercial Banks   497
Different Forms of Short-Term Loans   498
Factoring Accounts Receivable   499
Legal Briefcase: Making Sure It's a Done Deal   500
Commercial Paper   500
Credit Cards   501

Obtaining Long-Term Financing   501
Reaching Beyond Our Borders: Sharing the Wealth?   502
Debt Financing   502
Equity Financing   503
Comparing Debt and Equity Financing   505
Financial Management in Trying Times   506

Connect Interactive Applications   509

Chapter Nineteen

512 Using Securities Markets for Financing and Investing Opportunities

Profile: Getting to Know Warren Buffett, CEO of Berkshire Hathaway   512

The Function of Securities Markets   514
The Role of Investment Bankers   515

Stock Exchanges   515
Securities Regulations and the Securities and Exchange Commission   516
Making Ethical Decisions: Wagging the Dog   518
Foreign Stock Exchanges   518
Reaching Beyond Our Borders: The Wide, Wide World of Investing   519

How Businesses Raise Capital by Selling Stock   519
Advantages and Disadvantages of Issuing Stock   520
Issuing Shares of Common Stock   520
Issuing Shares of Preferred Stock   520

How Businesses Raise Capital by issuing Bonds   521
Learning the Language of Bonds   521
Advantages and Disadvantages of Issuing Bonds   522
Different Classes of Bonds   523
Special Bond Features   523

How Investors Buy Securities   524
Investing through Online Brokers   524
Choosing the Right Investment Strategy   525
Reducing Risk by Diversifying Investments   525

Investing in Stocks   526
Stock Splits   527
Buying Stock on Margin   527
Understanding Stock Quotations   528

Investing in Bonds   529
Investing in High-Risk (Junk) Bonds   529
Understanding Bond Quotations   530

Investing in Mutual Funds and Exchange-Traded Funds   530
Thinking Green: Investing with Integrity   531
Understanding Mutual Fund Quotations   532

Understanding Stock Market Indicators   533
Riding the Market's Roller Coaster   534
Legal Briefcase: Gambling with Investors' Security   536
Investing Challenges in the 21st-Century Market   536

Connect Interactive Applications   540

xxvii

Chapter Twenty

544 Money, Financial Institutions, and the Federal Reserve

Profile: Getting to Know Ben S. Bernanke, Chairman of the Federal Reserve 544

Why Money Is Important 546

    What Is Money? 547

    What Is the Money Supply? 548

    Managing Inflation and the Money Supply 548

    The Global Exchange of Money 549

Control of the Money Supply 549

    Basics about the Federal Reserve 549

    The Reserve Requirement 550

    Open-Market Operations 551

    The Discount Rate 551

    The Federal Reserve's Check-Clearing Role 551

The History of Banking and the Need for the Fed 553

    Banking and the Great Depression 553

The U.S. Banking System 554

    Commercial Banks 554

    Making Ethical Decisions: What to Tell the Teller 555

    Services Provided by Commercial Banks 555

    Services to Borrowers 556

    Savings and Loan Associations (S&Ls) 556

    Credit Unions 556

    Spotlight on Small Business: How the Banking Crisis Affected Small Businesses 557

    Other Financial Institutions (Nonbanks) 557

The Current Banking Crisis and How the Government Protects Your Money 558

    Protecting Your Funds 559

    The Federal Deposit Insurance Corporation (FDIC) 559

    Reaching Beyond Our Borders: The Banking Crisis Goes Global 560

    The Savings Association Insurance Fund (SAIF) 560

    The National Credit Union Administration (NCUA) 560

Using Technology to Make Banking More Efficient 561

    Online Banking 562

International Banking and Banking Services 563

    Leaders in International Banking 563

    The World Bank and the International Monetary Fund (IMF) 563

***Connect* Interactive Applications 567**

Appendix

Working within the Legal Environment

Profile: Getting to Know David Boies, Corporate Attorney A

The Case for Laws A-2

    Statutory and Common Law A-3

    Administrative Agencies A-3

Tort Law A-4

    Product Liability A-4

Legally Protecting Ideas: Patents, Copyrights, and Trademarks A-6

Sales Law: The Uniform Commercial Code A-8

    Warranties A-8

    Negotiable Instruments A-8

Contract Law A-9

    Breach of Contract A-10

Promoting Fair and Competitive Business Practices A-10

    The History of Antitrust Legislation A-11

Laws to Protect Consumers A-12

Tax Laws A-13

Bankruptcy Laws A-14

Deregulation versus Regulation A-17

Bonus Chapters (available online only)

A   Using Technology to Manage Information **BA**

B   Managing Risk **BB**

C   Managing Your Personal Finances **BC**

Chapter Notes N

Glossary G

Photo Credits PC-1

Name Index I

Organization Index I-8

Subject Index I-13

Business

connecting principles
to practice

Taking Risks and Making Profits within the DYNAMIC BUSINESS Environment

profile

Getting to Know
Nick Graham
Owner of the Main Street Market

The business environment in the downtown area of many small U.S. cities does not seem to favor the small businesses that once thrived there. Often big companies come to the outskirts of a town and draw business away from the town center. It is not unusual, therefore, that the Main Street Market, the only grocery store in Truman, Minnesota, went out of business. What is unusual is what happened next.

Nick Graham was a high school senior in Truman. He thought he could provide a community service and create a profitable enterprise by reopening the grocery store. That meant taking some risk, of course, but Nick was ready for the challenge. The community was thrilled, and people came to the Main Street Market to volunteer to do everything from stock the shelves to mop the floor. They were happy to have the store back because the nearest supermarket was 14 miles away—a distance that proved a hardship for older folks.

But where does a 17-year-old boy get the money to buy a grocery store? The Truman Development Corporation, a community investment group, approved Graham's $22,000 loan to buy the store building and fixtures. Since the teen wasn't legally old enough to buy property, the group let him lease the building until he turned 18. Graham got the additional $10,000 he needed to stock the store by shingling roofs and by working on his uncle's turkey farm.

When Graham was only 4, his dad died; he and his mom moved to Iowa when he was 7, and at 15 Graham returned to Truman to live with his grandmother. He works in the Main Street Market every day and has one clerk to help. He carries bags out to the car for his customers, and on Wednesdays he delivers orders to residents at the local retirement home, putting the groceries away if necessary. Everyone appreciates his good service, and customers flow through the door each day.

Graham did so well with his first store that by the end of the first year he was able to pay off his loan and buy another store, Armstrong Foods, in Armstrong, Iowa. He's looking for a pharmacy for his town and has thought of putting a fitness center in the old post office. He bought a refrigerated truck and delivers food to his Truman store and other stores in the

LEARNING goals

After you have read and studied this chapter, you should be able to

1. Describe the relationship between profit and risk, and show how businesses and nonprofit organizations can raise the standard of living for all.
2. Compare and contrast being an entrepreneur and working for others.
3. Analyze the effect of the economic environment and taxes on businesses.
4. Describe the effects of technology on businesses.
5. Demonstrate how businesses can meet and beat competition.
6. Analyze the social changes affecting businesses.
7. Identify what businesses must do to meet global challenges, including war and terrorism.
8. Review how past trends are being repeated in the present and what those trends mean for tomorrow's college graduates.

connect

Your *Connection* to Better Learning. 1. View the interactive presentation. 2. Practice through LearnSmart. 3. Apply your knowledge by using the interactive applications for each chapter of this text.

1 Prep »»»»» **2 Practice**  »»»»» **3 Apply**

---

area. On delivery days, Graham hits the road by 5:30 a.m. A normal workweek for him is 90 to 100 hours, but he thrives on long days and hard work. "I enjoy what I do," Graham says. "Rural America is an underserved market. The challenges are harder, but you're overlooked by the competition, too."

The business environment is constantly changing, as evidenced by the recent economic decline, but along with those changes come opportunities for new entrepreneurs like Graham. The purpose of this chapter, and this text, is to introduce you to the dynamic world of business and to some of the people who run those businesses. You'll learn about all phases of business from planning to management, production, marketing, finance, accounting, and more. You'll also learn about all kinds of businesses: small, large, nonprofit, local, national, and international. Through your studies, you should be able to find attractive career possibilities.

We begin by looking at some key terms you will need to know, terms like *profit* and *loss* and *risk*. Entrepreneurs like Nick Graham contribute much to the communities they serve, and they also make a good living doing so. That's what business is all about.

Sources: Marti Attoun, "Stocking Shelves, Restoring Hope," *American Profile*, January 6–12, 2008; YouTube, accessed June, 2010; and Max Chafkin, "And the Money Comes Rolling In," *Inc.*, January–February 2009.

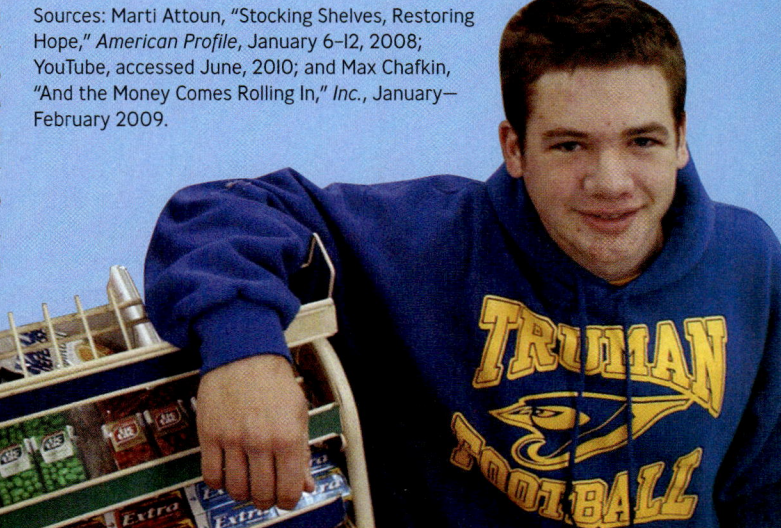

www.youtube.com

NAME THAT company

We are a major competitor in the global automobile industry. Although our company is based in Korea, we do a great deal of our work in the United States. We perform design and engineering work in Detroit, Michigan, and produce cars in our state-of-the-art manufacturing facility in Montgomery, Alabama. Who are we? (Find the answer in the chapter.)

> PPT I-1:
Taking Risks and Making Profits within the Dynamic Business Environment
> PPT I-2:
Nick Graham

LEARNING goal 1 *

Describe the relationship between profit and risk, and show how businesses and nonprofit organizations can raise the standard of living for all.

> PPT I-3:
Goods and Services

goods
Tangible products such as computers, food, clothing, cars, and appliances.

services
Intangible products (i.e., products that can't be held in your hand) such as education, health care, insurance, recreation, and travel and tourism.

business
Any activity that seeks to provide goods and services to others while operating at a profit.

entrepreneur
A person who risks time and money to start and manage a business.

> PPT I-4:
Business and Entrepreneurship

ENTREPRENEURSHIP AND WEALTH BUILDING

One thing you can learn from the chapter-opening Profile is that success in business is often based on the strategy of finding a need and filling it. Nick Graham saw the need for a grocery store in town and he filled it. This strategy lets you help the community in several ways. You provide needed goods, jobs, and services to people in the area. **Goods** are *tangible* products such as computers, food, clothing, cars, and appliances. **Services** are *intangible* products (i.e., products that can't be held in your hand) such as education, health care, insurance, recreation, and travel and tourism.

Although you don't need to have wealth as a primary goal, one result of successfully filling a market need is that you can make money for yourself, sometimes a great deal, by giving customers what they want. Nick Graham may well prosper as a result of his ventures, although his original goal was to save his town's sole grocery store. Sam Walton of Wal-Mart began by opening one store in Arkansas and, over time, became one of the richest people in the United States.[1] The United States is home to more than 11 million millionaires.[2] Maybe you will be one of them some day if you start your own business. A **business** is any activity that seeks to provide goods and services to others while operating at a profit.

An **entrepreneur** is a person who risks time and money to start and manage a business. Entrepreneurs like Nick Graham know there is more to business than just getting started. As Graham opens more and more stores, he will need to have a reliable accountant, a good lawyer, and strong managers and other employees.

To expand in business and to provide even more goods and services and jobs, Graham may have to go to a bank or to venture capital firms to borrow more money. In today's economy, borrowing from a bank is harder than usual.[3] Therefore, later in the text we will talk about ways to get closer to local banks so that they will be more inclined to give you a loan. Graham will also need to learn a lot more about business, including how to deal with unions, what kind of insurance to buy, and how to find the right people to hire.

Usually that means studying business at a community college or university.[4] That is much easier today now that so many courses are available online.[5] Taking this course and reading this text are good ways to start building a foundation for understanding business. In this chapter, we'll give you an overview to help you organize what you'll be learning.

Revenues, Profits, and Losses

Revenue is the total amount of money a business takes in during a given period by selling goods and services. **Profit** is the amount of money a business earns above and beyond what it spends for salaries and other expenses needed to run the operation. A **loss** occurs when a business's expenses are more than its revenues. If a business loses money over time, it will likely have to close, putting its employees out of work. About 80,000 businesses in the United States close each year; even more close during a slowdown like the United States experienced in 2008–2010.[6]

The business environment is constantly changing. What seems like a great opportunity one day—for example, online grocery shopping or SUVs—may become a huge failure when the economy changes. Starting a business may thus come with huge risks. But huge risks often result in huge profits. We'll explore that concept next.

Matching Risk with Profit

Risk is the chance an entrepreneur takes of losing time and money on a business that may not prove profitable. Profit, remember, is the amount of money a business earns *above and beyond* what it pays out for salaries and other expenses. For example, if you were to start a business selling hot dogs from a cart in the summer, you would have to pay for the cart rental. You would also have to pay for the hot dogs and other materials, and for someone to run the cart while you were away. After you paid your employee and yourself, paid for the food and materials you used, paid the rent on the cart, and paid your taxes, any money left over would be profit.

Keep in mind that profit is over and above the money you pay yourself in salary. You could use any profit to rent or buy a second cart and hire other employees. After a few summers, you might have a dozen carts employing dozens of workers. Remember, after he revived the Main Street Market, Nick Graham opened another store in a nearby town and hired other people to work there. By taking more risk, he is likely to make more profit.

Not all enterprises make the same amount of profit. Those that take the most risk may make the most profit. There is high risk, for example, in making a new kind of automobile.[7] It's also risky to open a business in an inner city, because insurance and rent are usually higher than in suburban areas, but reduced competition makes substantial profit possible. Irish entrepreneur Denis O'Brien, of Digicel, makes billions of dollars selling cell phones in the poorest, most violent countries in the world.[8] Big risk, big profits.

Standard of Living and Quality of Life

Entrepreneurs such as Sam Walton (Wal-Mart) and Bill Gates (Microsoft) not only became wealthy themselves; they also provided employment for many other people. Wal-Mart is currently the nation's largest private employer.

◄ PPT I-5:
Revenue, Profit, and Loss
◄ LECTURE LINK I-1:
The World's Richest People
◄ CRITICAL THINKING EXERCISE I-1:
How Much Profit?

revenue
The total amount of money a business takes in during a given period by selling goods and services.

profit
The amount of money a business earns above and beyond what it spends for salaries and other expenses.

loss
When a business's expenses are more than its revenues.

risk
The chance an entrepreneur takes of losing time and money on a business that may not prove profitable.

◄ PPT I-6:
Risks

David Bowie has responded to what he sees as a fundamentally changed music business and struck out on his own as an entrepreneur, with his own recording company called Iso and a short-term distribution deal with Sony. What potential risks and rewards is David Bowie likely anticipating for his new venture?

PPT I-7: How Is Tax Money Used?
PPT I-8: Quality of Life

standard of living
The amount of goods and services people can buy with the money they have.

quality of life
The general well-being of a society in terms of its political freedom, natural environment, education, health care, safety, amount of leisure, and rewards that add to the satisfaction and joy that other goods and services provide.

PPT I-9: Stakeholders

stakeholders
All the people who stand to gain or lose by the policies and activities of a business and whose concerns the business needs to address.

outsourcing
Contracting with other companies (often in other countries) to do some or all of the functions of a firm, like its production or accounting tasks.

Having a high quality of life means having the freedom, safety, health, and leisure to enjoy the satisfaction that goods and services can provide. How does a country's standard of living contribute to its citizens' quality of life?

Businesses and their employees pay taxes that the federal government and local communities use to build hospitals, schools, libraries, playgrounds, roads, and other public facilities. Taxes also help to keep the environment clean, support people in need, and provide police and fire protection. Thus, the wealth businesses generate and the taxes they pay help everyone in their communities. A nation's businesses are part of an economic system that contributes to the standard of living and quality of life for everyone in the country (and, potentially, the world). How has the recent economic slowdown affected the standard of living and quality of life in your part of the world?

The term **standard of living** refers to the amount of goods and services people can buy with the money they have. For example, the United States has one of the highest standards of living in the world, even though workers in some other countries, such as Germany and Japan, may on average make more money per hour. How can that be? Prices for goods and services in Germany and Japan are higher than in the United States, so a person in those countries can buy less than what a person in the United States can buy with the same amount of money. For example, a bottle of beer may cost $7 in Japan and $3 in the United States.

Often, goods cost more in one country than another because of higher taxes and stricter government regulations. Finding the right level of taxes and regulation is important in making a country or city prosperous. We'll explore that issue more deeply in Chapter 2. At this point, it is enough to understand that the United States enjoys a high standard of living largely because of the wealth created by its businesses.

The term **quality of life** refers to the general well-being of a society in terms of its political freedom, natural environment, education, health care, safety, amount of leisure, and rewards that add to the satisfaction and joy that other goods and services provide. Maintaining a high quality of life requires the combined efforts of businesses, nonprofit organizations, and government agencies. The more money businesses create, the more is potentially available to improve the quality of life for everyone. It's important to be careful, however. Working to build a higher standard of living may lower the quality of life if it means less time with family or more stress.[9]

Responding to the Various Business Stakeholders

Stakeholders are all the people who stand to gain or lose by the policies and activities of a business and whose concerns the business needs to address. They include customers, employees, stockholders, suppliers, dealers (retailers), bankers, people in the surrounding community, the media, environmentalists, and elected government leaders (see Figure 1.1).

A primary challenge for organizations of the 21st century will be to recognize and respond to the needs of their stakeholders. For example, the need for the business to make profits may be balanced against the needs of employees to earn sufficient income or the need to protect the environment. Ignore the media, and they might attack your business with articles that hurt sales. Oppose the local community, and it may stop you from expanding.

Staying competitive may call for outsourcing. **Outsourcing** means contracting with other companies (often in other countries) to do some or all the functions of a firm, like its production or accounting tasks.[10] Outsourcing has had serious

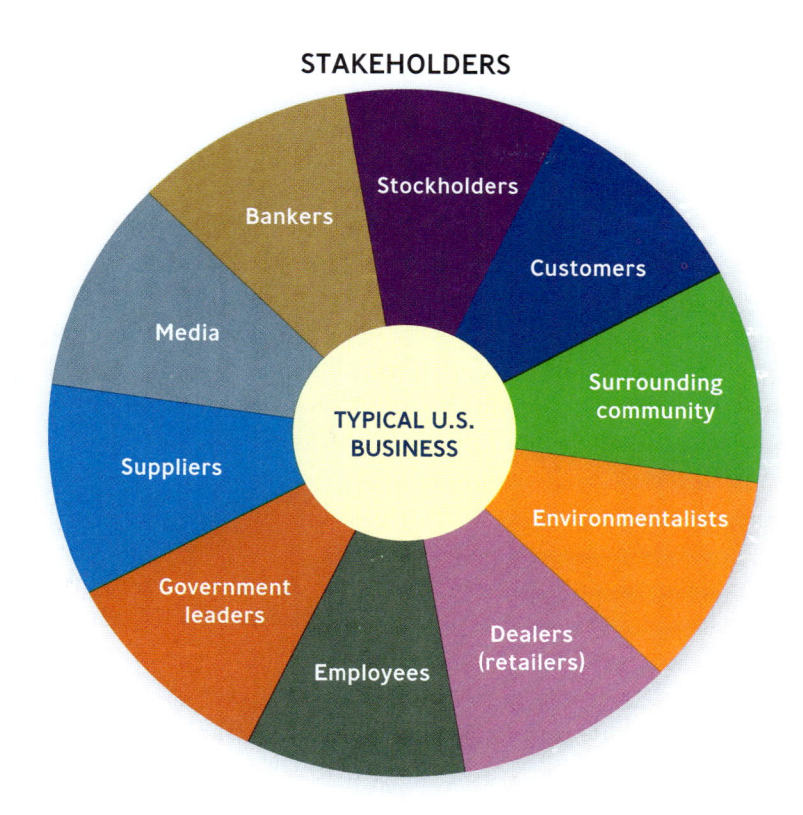

STAKEHOLDERS

Typical U.S. Business stakeholders: Stockholders, Customers, Surrounding community, Environmentalists, Dealers (retailers), Employees, Government leaders, Suppliers, Media, Bankers.

figure 1.1
A BUSINESS AND ITS STAKEHOLDERS
Often the needs of a firm's various stakeholders will conflict. For example, paying employees more may cut into stockholders' profits. Balancing such demands is a major role of business managers.

consequences in some states where jobs have been lost to overseas competitors. We discuss outsourcing in more detail in Chapter 3.

The other side of the outsourcing coin is *insourcing*. Many foreign companies are setting up design and production facilities here in the United States. For example, Korea-based Hyundai operates design and engineering headquarters in Detroit, Michigan, and produces cars in Montgomery, Alabama. Japanese automakers Honda and Toyota have been producing cars in the United States for years. Insourcing creates many new U.S. jobs and helps offset those being outsourced.[11]

It may be legal and profitable to outsource, but is it best for all the stakeholders? Business leaders must make outsourcing decisions based on all factors. Pleasing stakeholders is not easy and often calls for trade-offs.

Using Business Principles in Nonprofit Organizations

Despite their efforts to satisfy their stakeholders, businesses cannot do everything needed to make a community all it can be. Nonprofit organizations—such as public schools, civic associations, charities like United Way and Salvation Army, and groups devoted to social causes—also make a major contribution to the welfare of society. A **nonprofit organization** is an organization whose goals do not include making a personal profit for its owners or organizers. Nonprofit organizations often do strive for financial gains, but they use them to meet their social or educational goals rather than for personal profit.

Social entrepreneurs are people who use business principles to start and manage not-for-profits and help address social issues. Muhammad Yunus won the Nobel Prize for starting the Grameen Bank, a microlending organization (discussed in Chapter 2), that provides small loans to entrepreneurs too poor to qualify for traditional loans. Yunus has started 30 of what he calls

◄ **PPT 1-10:**
Outsourcing and Insourcing

◄ **PPT 1-11:**
Nonprofit Organizations

◄ **BONUS CASE 1-1:**
The World's Largest Charity

◄ **PPT 1-12:**
Well-Known Nonprofit Organizations in the United States

nonprofit organization
An organization whose goals do not include making a personal profit for its owners or organizers.

◄ **LECTURE LINK 1-2:**
Social Entrepreneurship: Village Phones and Yogurt

The goals of nonprofit organizations are social and educational, not profit-oriented. The Red Cross, for instance, responds to more than 70,000 natural and human-made disasters each year, including fires, floods, hurricanes, earthquakes, and accidents. Why do good management principles apply equally to businesses and nonprofits?

➤ **LECTURE LINK I-3:**
Social Entrepreneurship: Mercy Corps

➤ **LECTURE LINK I-4:**
Social Entrepreneurship: Improving World Health without Profits

➤ **PPT I-13:**
Progress Assessment

social businesses that do not have profit as their goal. One, for example, provides cataract operations for a fraction of the usual cost.[12]

Your interests may lead you to work for a nonprofit organization such as those started by Yunus.[13] That doesn't mean, however, that you shouldn't study business in college. You'll still need to learn business skills such as information management, leadership, marketing, and financial management. The knowledge and skills you acquire in this and other business courses are useful for careers in any organization, including nonprofits. We'll explore entrepreneurship in more detail right after the Progress Assessment.

progress assessment

- What is the difference between *revenue* and *profit*?
- What is the difference between *standard of living* and *quality of life*?
- What is risk, and how is it related to profit?
- What do the terms *stakeholders*, *outsourcing*, and *insourcing* mean?

LEARNING goal 2 ✳

Compare and contrast being an entrepreneur and working for others.

ENTREPRENEURSHIP VERSUS WORKING FOR OTHERS

There are two ways to succeed in business. One is to rise through the ranks of large companies. The advantage of working for others is that somebody else assumes the company's entrepreneurial risk and provides you with benefits like paid vacation time and health insurance.[14] It's a good option, and many people choose it.

The other, riskier path is to become an entrepreneur. The national anthem, "The Star Spangled Banner," says that the United States is the "land of the free and the home of the brave." Part of being free is being able to own your own business and reap the profits from it.[15] But freedom to succeed also means freedom to fail, and many small businesses fail each year. It takes a brave person, like Nick Graham in this chapter's opening Profile, to start one. As an entrepreneur, you don't receive any benefits such as paid vacation time, day care, a company car, or health insurance. You have to provide them for yourself! But what you gain—freedom to make your own decisions, opportunity, and possible wealth—is often worth the effort. Before you take on the challenge, you should study successful entrepreneurs to learn the process. You can talk to them personally and read about them in Chapter 6, as well as in other books and magazines.[16]

◄ PPT 1-14:
The Ups and Downs of Entrepreneurship

◄ CRITICAL THINKING EXERCISE 1-2:
Job and Career Versus Owning a Business

Opportunities for Entrepreneurs

Millions of people from all over the world have taken the entrepreneurial challenge and succeeded. For example, the number of Hispanic-owned businesses in the United States has grown dramatically (Hispanics are now the largest ethnic group in the United States).[17] Both Hispanic men and women are doing particularly well.[18] Similar successes are true of businesses owned by Asians, Pacific Islanders, Native Americans, and Alaskan Natives.

Women now own over a third of all businesses. Names you may know include Oprah Winfrey, Donna Karan, and Lillian Vernon. Andrea Jung is the CEO of Avon Products.[19] The world's most powerful women include Ho Ching, the chief executive of Temasek Holdings in Singapore; Indra Nooyi, chief executive of Pepsico, U.S.; and Cynthia Carroll, chief executive of Anglo American in the United Kingdom.[20] The Spotlight on Small Business box on p. 10 discusses a successful woman who employs a very unusual workforce.

The Importance of Entrepreneurs to the Creation of Wealth

Have you ever wondered why some countries are relatively wealthy and others poor? Economists have been studying the issue of wealth creation for many years. They began by identifying five **factors of production** that seemed to contribute to wealth (see Figure 1.2 on p. 10):

1. Land (or natural resources).
2. Labor (workers).
3. Capital. (This includes machines, tools, buildings, or whatever else is used in the production of goods. It may not include money; money is used to buy factors of production but is not always considered a factor by itself.)
4. Entrepreneurship.
5. Knowledge.

factors of production
The resources used to create wealth: land, labor, capital, entrepreneurship, and knowledge.

Traditionally, business and economics textbooks emphasized only four factors of production: land, labor, capital, and entrepreneurship. But management expert and business consultant Peter Drucker said the most important factor of production in our economy is and always will be *knowledge*.

SPOTLIGHT ON SMALL *business

www.artforacause.com

Hiring People with Special Needs

Lisa Knoppe Reed's company, Art for a Cause, creates and sells hand-painted tools and furniture. When she left the corporate world, Reed started the company in her kitchen and donated a percentage of the profits to charities. One day she gave a presentation in a class of students with special needs at a local school. She was so impressed with the students that she came up with an idea to help them and her company at the same time. She showed them how to sand and prime the tools, and was very impressed with the results.

Today, special needs children and adults throughout Michigan help Reed build her tools, which are sold at stores like Ace Hardware and Hallmark. Sales are in the $2.5 million range, and Reed plans to start similar companies in California and Maine.

Sources: J. J. Ramberg, "Doing Good: Cause and Effect," *Entrepreneur*, February 2008; and Andrea Cooper, "Serial Starter," *Entrepreneur*, April 2008; Art For a Cause, www.artforacause.com, accessed July 28, 2010.

▶ PPT I-15:
Hiring People with Special Needs

▶ PPT I-16:
Five Factors of Production

What do we find when we compare the factors of production in rich and poor countries? Some poor countries have plenty of land and natural resources. Russia, for example, has vast areas of land with many resources such as timber and oil, but it is not considered a rich country (yet). Although it ranks second in the world in number of billionaires—with 32, behind America's 359—Russia's per capita gross domestic product (per capita GDP)—the value of all goods and services produced in the country, divided by the population—is only $14,700.[21] In contrast, Japan is a relatively rich country with a per capita GDP of $33,600, but it is poor in land and other natural resources. Therefore, land isn't the critical element for wealth creation.

figure I.2
THE FIVE FACTORS OF PRODUCTION

Land
Land and other natural resources are used to make homes, cars, and other products.

Labor
People have always been an important resource in producing goods and services, but many people are now being replaced by technology.

Capital
Capital includes machines, tools, buildings, and other means of manufacturing.

Entrepreneurship
All the resources in the world have little value unless entrepreneurs are willing to take the risk of starting businesses to use those resources.

Knowledge
Information technology has revolutionized business, making it possible to quickly determine wants and needs and to respond with desired goods and services.

Most poor countries such as Mexico have many laborers, so it's not labor that's the primary source of wealth today. Laborers need to find work to make a contribution; that is, they need entrepreneurs to create jobs for them. Furthermore, capital—machinery and tools—is now fairly easy for firms to find in world markets, so capital isn't the missing ingredient either. Capital is not productive without entrepreneurs to put it to use.

What makes rich countries rich today is a combination of *entrepreneurship* and the effective use of *knowledge*. Entrepreneurs use what they've learned (knowledge) to grow their businesses and increase wealth. Economic and political freedom also matter.

The business environment either encourages or discourages entrepreneurship. That helps explain why some states and cities in the United States grow rich while others remain relatively poor. In the following section, we'll explore what makes up the business environment and how to build an environment that encourages growth and job creation.

To create wealth for its citizens, a country requires more than natural resources like timber. No matter how vast its forests or other inputs like labor, fuel, and waterways, a country needs the efforts of entrepreneurs and the skill and knowledge to produce goods and services. How can the government support entrepreneurship and the spread of knowledge?

progress assessment

- What are some of the advantages of working for others?
- What benefits do you lose by being an entrepreneur, and what do you gain?
- What are the five factors of production? Which ones seem to be the most important for creating wealth?

THE BUSINESS ENVIRONMENT

The **business environment** consists of the surrounding factors that either help or hinder the development of businesses. Figure 1.3 shows the five elements in the business environment:

1. The economic and legal environment.
2. The technological environment.
3. The competitive environment.
4. The social environment.
5. The global business environment.

business environment The surrounding factors that either help or hinder the development of businesses.

◄ PPT 1-17:
Progress Assessment

◄ PPT 1-18:
Today's Dynamic Business Environment

Businesses that create wealth and jobs grow and prosper in a healthy environment. Thus, creating the right business environment is the foundation for social benefits of all kinds, including good schools, clean air and water, good health care, and low rates of crime. Businesses normally can't control their environment, but they need to monitor it carefully and do what they can to adapt as it changes.

figure I.3
TODAY'S DYNAMIC BUSINESS ENVIRONMENT

GLOBAL BUSINESS ENVIRONMENT

The Economic and Legal Environment
1. Freedom of ownership
2. Contract laws
3. Elimination of corruption
4. Tradable currency
5. Taxes and regulation

The Technological Environment
1. Information technology
2. Databases
3. Bar codes
4. The Internet

BUSINESS MANAGEMENT AND JOB CREATION

The Competitive Environment
1. Customer service
2. Stakeholder recognition
3. Employee service
4. Concern for the environment

The Social Environment
1. Diversity
2. Demographic changes
3. Family changes

GLOBAL COMPETITION • FREE TRADE • THE QUALITY IMPERATIVE

LEARNING goal 3 *

Analyze the effect of the economic environment and taxes on businesses.

> PPT I-19:
> Government's Role in Business

The Economic and Legal Environment

People are willing to start new businesses if they believe the risk of losing their money isn't too great. The economic system and the way government works with or against businesses can have a strong impact on that level of risk. For example, a government can *minimize spending* and *keep taxes and regulations to a minimum*, policies that tend to favor business. Much of the debate in recent presidential elections has focused on whether or not to raise taxes and how to lower government spending.[22] President Obama is increasing government spending with the idea of getting the economy moving faster. Some economists agree with such a stimulus, but some do not.[23]

One way for government to actively promote entrepreneurship is to *allow private ownership of businesses.* In some countries, the government owns most businesses, and there's little incentive for people to work hard or create profit. Around the world today, however, some governments are selling those businesses to private individuals to create more wealth. One of the best things the governments of developing countries can do is to *minimize interference with the free exchange of goods and services.*

The government can further lessen the risks of entrepreneurship by *passing laws that enable businesspeople to write enforceable contracts*. In the United States, the Uniform Commercial Code, for example, regulates business agreements like contracts and warranties so that firms know they can rely on one another. In countries that don't yet have such laws, the risks of starting a business are that much greater. You can read more about business laws in the Appendix at the end of this book.

The government can also *establish a currency that's tradable in world markets.* That is, the currency lets you buy and sell goods and services anywhere in the world when it is easily exchanged for that of the other countries where you do business. If the Chinese did not want to trade their yuan for the U.S. dollar, for instance, it's hard to imagine how Coca-Cola or Disney would have been able to sell their products and services there.

Finally, the government can help *minimize corruption* in business and in its own ranks. Where governments are corrupt, it's difficult to build a factory or open a store without a government permit, which is obtained largely through bribery of public officials. Among businesses themselves, unscrupulous leaders can threaten their competitors and unlawfully minimize competition.

◀ PPT I-20:
Corruption Worldwide

Many laws in the United States attempt to minimize corruption. Nonetheless, corrupt and illegal activities at some companies do negatively affect the business community and the economy as a whole. The news media widely reports these scandals.[24] Ethics is so important to the success of businesses and the economy as a whole that we feature stories about ethics in most chapters and devote Chapter 4 to the subject.

The capitalist system relies heavily on honesty, integrity, and high ethical standards. Failure of those fundamentals can weaken the whole system.[25] The faltering economy of 2008–2010 was due in large part to such failure. Some mortgage lenders, for instance, failed to do the research necessary to ensure their borrowers' creditworthiness. Many subprime borrowers forfeited their loans. The ripple effects of these unpaid debts not only cost many people their homes but also reduced the value of housing across the world and made it

Starting a business is much harder in some countries than in others. In India, for example, it requires a time-consuming and bureaucratic process to obtain government permission. Nonetheless, new businesses can become a major source of wealth and employment; this jewelry business is one small example. What do you think would be the effect of a little more freedom to create business opportunities in this country of over a billion people?

difficult even for business borrowers to get new loans. Part of the blame for this economic disaster can be placed on the borrowers who didn't tell the truth about their income or who otherwise deceived the lenders.

It is easy to see the damage caused by the poor moral and ethical behavior of some businesspeople. What is not so obvious is the damage caused by the moral and ethical lapses of the everyday consumer—that is, you and me. The Making Ethical Decisions box discusses that issue in more depth.

LEARNING goal 4 *

Describe the effects of technology on businesses.

The Technological Environment

Since prehistoric times, humans have felt the need to create tools that make work easier. Few technological changes have had a more comprehensive and lasting impact on businesses, however, than the emergence of information technology (IT): computers, networks, cell phones, and especially the Internet.

The iPod, the iPhone, the BlackBerry and other personal digital assistants, and even social networks like MySpace and Facebook have completely changed the way people communicate with one another. Advertisers and other businesspeople have created ways of using these tools to reach their suppliers and customers.[26] Even politicians have harnessed the power of the Internet to advance their causes. Barack Obama has 27 million friends on Facebook.[27] The number is growing every day.

IT is such a major force in business today that we discuss its impact on businesses throughout the entire text.

▶ PPT I-22:
Benefits of Technology

technology
Everything from phones and copiers to computers, medical imaging devices, personal digital assistants, and the various software programs that make business processes more effective, efficient, and productive.

productivity
The amount of output you generate given the amount of input (e.g., hours worked).

▶ LECTURE LINK I-5:
Education's New Whiteboard

▶ PPT I-23:
E-Commerce

e-commerce
The buying and selling of goods over the Internet.

How Technology Benefits Workers and You One of the advantages of working for others is that the company often provides the tools and technology to make your job more productive. **Technology** means everything from phones and copiers to computers, medical imaging devices, personal digital assistants, and the various software programs that make business processes more effective, efficient, and productive. *Effectiveness* means producing the desired result. *Efficiency* means producing goods and services using the least amount of resources.

Productivity is the amount of output you generate given the amount of input, such as the number of hours you work. The more you can produce in any given period, the more money you are worth to companies. The average worker in the United States contributes $63,885 to GDP, making U.S. workers some of the world's most productive employees.[28]

Technology affects people in all industries. For example, Don Glenn, a farmer in Decatur, Alabama, uses his personal computer to compare data from the previous year's harvest with infrared satellite photos of his farm that show which crops are flourishing. He has a desktop terminal called a DTN that allows him to check the latest grain prices, and he uses AgTalk, a Web-based bulletin board, to converse with other farmers from all over the world. He also bids for bulk fertilizer on XSAg.com, an online agricultural exchange. High-tech equipment tells Glenn how and where to spread fertilizer and seed, tracks yields yard by yard, and allows him to maintain high profit margins.

The Growth of E-Commerce **E-commerce** is the buying and selling of goods over the Internet. There are two major types of e-commerce transactions: business-to-consumer (B2C) and business-to-business (B2B). As important as the Internet

MAKING ethical decisions

Ethics Begins with You

It is easy to criticize the ethics of people whose names appear in the headlines. It is more difficult to see the moral and ethical misbehavior of your own social group. Do you find some of the behaviors of your friends morally or ethically questionable?

A survey found that the number of employees calling in sick had reached a five-year high, and three-fifths were not sick at all. Other employees have been caught conducting personal business at work, such as doing their taxes. And others play video games on their work computers. We're sure you can add many more examples.

Many companies today are creating ethics codes to guide their employees' behavior. We believe the trend toward improving ethical behavior is so important that we've made it a major theme of this book. Throughout the text you'll see boxes like this one, called Making Ethical Decisions, that pose ethical dilemmas and ask what you would do to resolve them. The idea is for you to think about the moral and ethical dimensions of every decision you make.

Here is your first one: You're doing a project at home that requires paper, pens, and other materials available at work. You've noticed other employees taking home such materials, and you're thinking about doing the same. What is the problem in this situation? What are your alternatives? What are the consequences of each alternative? Which alternative will you choose? Is your choice ethical?

---

has been to retailers like Amazon.com in the consumer market, it has become even more important in the B2B market, where businesses sell goods and services to one another, such as IBM selling consulting services to a local bank.[29] Web sites have become the new stores.[30]

Traditional businesses must deal with the competition from B2B and B2C firms, and vice versa. Many new parents would just as soon buy used items posted on Craigslist than shop in a baby-goods store.[31] Starting a business on eBay has never been easier.[32] Almost 220 million Chinese citizens were using the Internet in 2008.[33] And what did people do before they could Google? E-commerce has become so important that we will discuss it throughout the text.

Using Technology to Be Responsive to Customers A major theme of this text is that those businesses most responsive to customer wants and needs will succeed.[34] That realization points to one way in which even traditional retailers can use Internet technology. For example, businesses use bar codes to identify products you buy and their size, quantity, and color. The scanner at the checkout counter identifies the price but can also put all your purchase information into a **database**, an electronic storage file for information.

Databases enable stores to carry only the merchandise their local population wants. But because companies routinely trade database information, many retailers know what you buy and from whom you buy it. Thus they can send you catalogs and other direct mail advertising offering the kind of products you might want, as indicated by your past purchases. We discuss other ways businesses use technology to be responsive to consumers throughout the text.

Unfortunately, the legitimate collection of personal customer information also opens the door to identity theft. **Identity theft** is the obtaining of individuals' personal information, such as Social Security and credit card numbers, for illegal purposes. The Federal Trade Commission says millions of U.S. consumers are victims of identity theft each year. What you should learn

◄ PPT I-21:
Ethics Begins with You

◄ CRITICAL THINKING EXERCISE I-3:
Making Ethical Decisions

◄ PPT I-24:
Databases and Identity Theft

◄ PPT I-25:
Protect Yourself from Identity Theft

database
An electronic storage file for information.

◄ LECTURE LINK I-6:
Preventing Identity Theft

identity theft
The obtaining of individuals' personal information, such as Social Security and credit card numbers, for illegal purposes.

Technology makes workers more productive. Instead of spending hours traveling to meet, for instance, these employees use teleconferencing to share information and make decisions. Are some workers likely to be more comfortable with new technology than others?

from these examples is to limit those to whom you give personal information. You also need antivirus software on your computer as well as a firewall and antispyware software. You may also want to monitor your credit report. It is important for you to understand identity theft, security, privacy, stability, and other important IT issues.

LEARNING goal 5 *

Demonstrate how businesses can meet and beat competition.

The Competitive Environment

Competition among businesses has never been greater. Some have found a competitive edge by focusing on quality. The goal for many companies is zero defects—no mistakes in making the product. However, even achieving a rate of zero defects isn't enough to stay competitive in world markets. Companies now have to offer both high-quality products and good value—that is, outstanding service at competitive prices. Figure 1.4 shows how competition has evolved to a new, world-class model.

Competing by Exceeding Customer Expectations Today's customers want not only good quality at low prices but great service as well. Every manufacturing and service organization in the world should have a sign over its door telling its workers that the customer is king. Business is becoming customer-driven, not management-driven as often occurred in the past. Successful organizations must now listen more closely to customers to determine their wants and needs, and then adjust the firm's products, policies, and practices accordingly.[35] We will explore these ideas in more depth in Chapter 13.

Competing by Restructuring and Empowerment To meet the needs of customers, firms must give their frontline workers—for example, office clerks, front-desk people at hotels, and salespeople—the responsibility, authority, freedom, training, and equipment they need to respond quickly to customer requests. They also must allow workers to make other decisions essential to

▶ PPT I-26:
Using Empowerment to Compete in Today's Market

figure 1.4
HOW COMPETITION HAS CHANGED BUSINESS

TRADITIONAL BUSINESSES	MODERN BUSINESSES
Customer satisfaction	Delighting the customer[1]
Customer orientation	Customer and stakeholder orientation[2]
Profit orientation	Profit and social orientation[3]
Reactive ethics	Proactive ethics[4]
Product orientation	Quality and service orientation
Managerial focus	Customer focus

[1] *Delight* is a term from total quality management. *Bewitch* and *fascinate* are alternative terms.
[2] Stakeholders include employees, stockholders, suppliers, dealers (retailers), and the community; the goal is to please *all* stakeholders.
[3] A social orientation goes beyond profit to do what is right and good for others.
[4] *Proactive* means doing the right thing before anyone tells you to do it. *Reactive* means responding to criticism after it happens.

producing high-quality goods and services. The process is called **empowerment**, and we'll be talking about it throughout this book.

As many companies have discovered, it sometimes takes years to restructure an organization so that managers can and will give up some of their authority, and employees will assume more responsibility. We'll discuss such organizational changes in Chapter 8.

LEARNING goal 6 *

Analyze the social changes affecting businesses.

The Social Environment

Demography is the statistical study of the human population with regard to its size, density, and other characteristics such as age, race, gender, and income. In this text, we're particularly interested in the demographic trends that most affect businesses and career choices. The U.S. population is going through major changes that are dramatically affecting how people live, where they live, what they buy, and how they spend their time. Furthermore, tremendous population shifts are leading to new opportunities for some firms and to declining opportunities for others. For example, there are many more retired workers than in the past, creating new markets for all kinds of goods and services.

Managing Diversity *Diversity* has come to mean much more than recruiting and keeping minority and female employees. Diversity efforts now include seniors, disabled people, homosexuals, atheists, extroverts, introverts, married people, singles, and the devout. It also means dealing sensitively with workers and cultures around the world.

Legal and illegal immigrants have had a dramatic effect on many cities. Schools and hospitals have been especially affected. Some local governments are making every effort to adapt, including changing signs, brochures, Web sites, and forms to include other languages. Has your city experienced such changes? What are some of the impacts you've noticed?

The Increase in the Number of Older Citizens People ages 65 to 74 are currently the richest demographic group in the United States.[36] They thus

---

empowerment
Giving frontline workers the responsibility, authority, freedom, training, and equipment they need to respond quickly to customer requests.

demography
The statistical study of the human population with regard to its size, density, and other characteristics such as age, race, gender, and income.

◄ PPT I-27:
U.S. Population Changes

◄ PPT I-28:
Who Will Support Social Security?

◄ PPT I-29:
Demography

represent a lucrative market for companies involved with food service, transportation, entertainment, education, lodging, and so on. By 2020, the percentage of the population over 60 will be 22.8 percent (versus 16 percent in 2000).[37] What do these changes mean for you and for businesses in the future? Think of the products and services that middle-aged and elderly people will need—medicine, nursing homes, assisted-living facilities, adult day care, home health care, recreation, and the like—and you'll see opportunities for successful businesses of the 21st century. Don't rule out computer games and Internet services, even Wii. Businesses that cater to older consumers will have the opportunity for exceptional growth in the near future. The market is huge.

On the other hand, retired people will be draining the economy of wealth. Social Security has become a major issue. The pay-as-you-go system (in which workers today pay the retirement benefits for today's retirees) operated just fine in 1940, when 42 workers supported each retiree in 1940; but by 1960, there were only 5 workers per retiree, and today, as the baby-boom generation (born between 1946 and 1964) begins to retire, that number is under 3 and dropping. In addition, the government has been spending the accumulated Social Security money instead of leaving it in a Social Security account.

Soon, less money will be coming into Social Security than will be going out. The government will have to do something to make up for the shortfall: raise taxes, reduce Social Security benefits (e.g., raise the retirement age at which people qualify for payments), reduce spending elsewhere (e.g., in other social programs like welfare or Medicaid), or borrow on the world market.

In short, paying Social Security to senior citizens in the future will draw huge amounts of money from the working population. That is why there is so much discussion about what to do with Social Security in the media today.

The Increase in the Number of Single-Parent Families It is a tremendous task to work full-time and raise a family. Thus, the rapid growth of single-parent households has also had a major effect on businesses. Single parents, including those forced by welfare rules to return to work after a certain benefit period, have encouraged businesses to implement programs such as family leave (giving workers time off to attend to a sick child or elder relative) and flextime (allowing workers to arrive or leave at selected times). You will read about such programs in more detail in Chapter 11.

LEARNING goal 7   *

Identify what businesses must do to meet global challenges, including war and terrorism.

The Global Environment

The global environment of business is so important that we show it as surrounding all other environmental influences (see again Figure 1.3 on p. 12). Two important changes here are the growth of global competition and the increase of free trade among nations.

World trade, or *globalization*, has grown thanks to the development of efficient distribution systems (we'll talk about these in Chapter 15) and communication advances such as the Internet. Globalization has greatly improved living standards around the world. China and India have become major U.S. competitors. Lenovo, a Chinese firm, bought IBM's PC unit. Shop at Wal-Mart and most other U.S. retail stores, and you can't help but notice the number of "Made in China" stickers you see. Call for computer help, and you are as likely to be talking with someone in India as someone in the United States.

World trade has its benefits and costs. You'll read much more about its importance in Chapter 3 and in the Reaching Beyond Our Borders boxes throughout the text.

War and Terrorism The wars in Iraq and Afghanistan have drawn billions of dollars from the U.S. economy. Some companies—like those that make bullets, tanks, and uniforms—have benefited greatly. Others, however, have lost workers to the armed forces, and still others (e.g., tourism) have grown more slowly as money has been diverted to the war effort. The threat of other wars and terrorism lead the government to spend even more money on the military. Such expenditures are subject to much debate, especially as the United States responds to an economic recession.

The threat of terrorism also adds greatly to organizational costs, including the cost of insurance. In fact, some firms are finding it difficult to get insurance against terrorist attacks. Security, too, is costly. Airlines, for example, have had to install stronger cockpit doors and add more passenger screening devices.

Like all citizens, businesspeople benefit from a peaceful and prosperous world. One way to lessen international tensions is to foster global economic growth among both profit-making and nonprofit organizations.

How Global Changes Affect You As businesses expand to serve global markets, new jobs will be created in both manufacturing and service industries. Global trade also means global competition. The students who will prosper will be those prepared for the markets of tomorrow. Rapid changes create a need for continuous learning, so be prepared to continue your education throughout your career. You'll have every reason to be optimistic about job opportunities in the future if you prepare yourself well.

The Ecological Environment Few issues have captured the attention of the international business community more than climate change.[38] **Climate change** is the movement of the temperature of the planet up or down over time. The issue now is global warming, but the issue may become global cooling. Some of the world's largest firms—including General Electric, Coca-Cola, Shell, Nestlé, DuPont, Johnson & Johnson, British Airways, and Shanghai Electric—say the evidence for climate change is overwhelming. Saving energy and producing products that cause less harm to the environment is a trend called **greening**. Greening has become such a pervasive issue that we devote boxes to that subject throughout the text. (See the Thinking Green box for things you can do to contribute to the cause.)

More and more working families consist of single parents who must juggle the demands of a job and the responsibilities of raising children. What can managers do to try to retain valued employees who face such challenges?

climate change
The movement of the temperature of the planet up or down over time.

greening
The trend toward saving energy and producing products that cause less harm to the environment.

progress assessment

- What are four ways the government can foster entrepreneurship?
- What's the difference between effectiveness, efficiency, and productivity?
- What is *empowerment*?
- What are some of the major issues affecting the economy today?

THINKING green

Getting Involved Personally

There is little doubt humans can take action to protect the environment. What can we do now to start?

It's not necessary to change your lifestyle radically in order to make a difference. Simply heating or cooling your apartment or house more efficiently is a good start. Why not buy a reusable grocery bag? It is also a good idea to change your lightbulbs. A 25-watt compact fluorescent bulb produces about as much light as a 100-watt conventional bulb but uses one-quarter of the energy. You can recycle paper and containers. You can walk or ride a bike instead of driving. You can reduce your use of electrical equipment and of water (pumping water takes a lot of electricity). Buy produce that is grown locally to save the energy used in shipping food from faraway places. If you're in the market for a car, you could "go green" by buying a hybrid or a small, fuel-efficient car.

The idea is to become more ecologically aware and join others throughout the world in using less energy and emitting less carbon into the atmosphere. Everyone benefits when the air is cleaner. That's part of what the green movement is all about.

Sources: Mya Frazier, "Who's in Charge of Green?" *Advertising Age*, June 9, 2008; Anne Underwood, "10 Fixes for the Planet," *Newsweek*, April 14, 2008; Rebecca Smith, "A Little Knowledge . . . ," *The Wall Street Journal*, June 30, 2008; and Arden Dale, "Green Products Gain from New Price Equation," *The Wall Street Journal*, June 24, 2008.

LEARNING goal 8 *

Review how past trends are being repeated in the present and what those trends mean for tomorrow's college graduates.

THE EVOLUTION OF U.S. BUSINESS

Businesses in the United States have become so productive that they need fewer workers than ever before to produce goods. If global competition and improved technology are putting skilled people out of work, should we be concerned about the prospect of high unemployment rates and low incomes? Where will the jobs be when you graduate? These important questions force us all to look briefly at the U.S. economy and its future.

Progress in the Agricultural and Manufacturing Industries

The United States has experienced strong economic development since the 1800s. The agricultural industry led the way, providing food for the United States and much of the world. Cyrus McCormick's invention of the harvester in 1834, other inventions such as Eli Whitney's cotton gin, and modern improvements on such equipment did much to make large-scale farming successful. Technology has made modern farming so efficient that the number of farmers has dropped from about 33 percent of the population to about 1 percent today. However, average farm size is now about 450 acres versus 160 acres in the past.[39]

Agriculture is still a major industry in the United States. What has changed is that the millions of small farms that existed previously have been replaced by some huge farms, some merely large farms, and some small but highly specialized farms. The loss of farm workers over the past century is not a negative sign. It is instead an indication that U.S. agricultural workers are the most productive in the world.

Most farmers who lost their jobs during the 19th and 20th centuries went to work in factories springing up around the country. Manufacturers, like farms, began using technology like tools and machines to become more productive. Eventually the consequence in manufacturing, as in farming, was the elimination of many jobs.

Again, the loss to society is minimized if the wealth created by increased productivity and efficiency creates new jobs elsewhere—and that's exactly what has happened over the past 50 years. Many workers in the industrial sector found jobs in the growing service sector. Most of those who can't find work today are people who need retraining and education to become qualified for jobs that now exist or will exist in the near future, like building wind farms or making electric automobiles. We'll discuss the manufacturing sector and production in more detail in Chapter 9.

Agriculture is one of the largest and most important industries in the United States. Technology has increased productivity and made farmers more efficient, allowing for larger farms. This trend has reduced the price of food for consumers but has also reduced the number of small, family-run farms. Does the new technology also help smaller farms compete?

Progress in Service Industries

In the past, the fastest-growing industries in the United States produced goods like steel, automobiles, and machine tools. Today, the fastest-growing firms provide services in areas like law, health, telecommunications, entertainment, and finance.

Together, services make up about 70 percent of the value of the U.S. economy.[40] Since the mid-1980s, the service industry has generated almost all the increases in employment. Although service-sector growth has slowed, it remains the largest area of growth. Chances are very high that you'll work in a service job at some point in your career. Figure 1.5 on p. 22 lists many service-sector jobs; look it over to see where the careers of the future are likely to be. Retailers like American Eagle are part of the service sector. Each new retail store creates many managerial jobs for college graduates.

Another bit of good news is that there are *more* high-paying jobs in the service sector than in the goods-producing sector. High-paying service-sector jobs abound in health care, accounting, finance, entertainment, telecommunications, architecture, law, software engineering, and more. Projections are that some areas of the service sector will grow rapidly, while others may have much slower growth. The strategy for college graduates is to remain flexible, find out where jobs are being created, and move when appropriate.

◄ PPT I-41:
The Service Era

◄ PPT I-42:
The Information Technology Era

Your Future in Business

Despite the growth in the service sector we've described above, the service era now seems to be coming to a close as a new era is beginning. We're in the midst of an information-based global revolution that will alter all sectors of the economy: agricultural, industrial, and service. It's exciting to think about the role you'll play in that revolution. You may be a leader who will implement the changes and accept the challenges of world competition based on world quality standards. This book will introduce you to some of the concepts that make such leadership possible, not just in business but also in government agencies and nonprofit organizations. Business can't prosper in the future without the cooperation of government and social leaders throughout the world.

There's much talk about the service sector, but few discussions actually list what it includes. Here's a representative list of services as classified by the government:

Lodging Services

Hotels, rooming houses, and other lodging places
Sporting and recreation camps
Trailer parks and camp sites for transients

Personal Services

Laundries
Linen supply
Diaper service
Carpet cleaning
Photographic studios
Health clubs
Child care
Shoe repair
Funeral homes
Tax preparation
Beauty shops

Business Services

Accounting
Ad agencies
Collection agencies
Commercial photography
Commercial art
Stenographic services
Window cleaning
Consulting
Equipment rental
Tax preparation
Exterminating
Employment agencies
Computer programming
Research and development labs
Management services
Public relations
Detective agencies
Interior design
Web design
Trash collection

Automotive Repair Services and Garages

Auto rental
Truck rental
Parking lots
Paint shops
Tire retreading
Exhaust system shops
Car washes
Transmission repair

Miscellaneous Repair Services

Radio and television
Watch
Reupholstery
Welding
Sharpening
Septic tank cleaning

Motion Picture Industry

Production
Distribution
Theaters
Drive-ins

Amusement and Recreation Services

Restaurants
Symphony orchestras
Pool halls
Bowling alleys
Fairs
Botanical gardens
Video rentals
Racetracks
Golf courses
Amusement parks
Carnivals
Ice skating rinks
Circuses
Infotainment

Health Services

Physicians
Dentists
Chiropractors
Nursery care
Medical labs
Dental labs

Legal Services

Educational Services

Libraries
Schools
Computer schools
Online schools

Social Services

Child care
Job training
Family services
Elder care

Noncommercial Museums, Art Galleries, and Botanical and Zoological Gardens

Selected Membership Organizations

Business associations
Civic associations

Financial Services

Banking
Insurance
Real estate agencies
Investment firms (brokers)

Miscellaneous Services

Architectural
Engineering
Telecommunications
Vending
Surveying
Utilities
Lawn care
Delivery

figure I.5

WHAT IS THE SERVICE SECTOR?

progress assessment

- What major factor caused people to move from farming to manufacturing and from manufacturing to the service sector?
- What does the future look like for tomorrow's college graduates?

summary

Learning Goal 1. Describe the relationship between profit and risk, and show how businesses and nonprofit organizations can raise the standard of living for all.

- **What is the relationship of businesses' profit to risk assumption?**

Profit is money a business earns above and beyond the money that it spends for salaries and other expenses. Businesspeople make profits by taking risks. *Risk* is the chance an entrepreneur takes of losing time and money on a business that may not prove profitable. A loss occurs when a business's costs and expenses are higher than its revenues.

- **Who are stakeholders, and which stakeholders are most important to a business?**

Stakeholders include customers, employees, stockholders, suppliers, dealers, bankers, the media, people in the local community, environmentalists, and elected government leaders. The goal of business leaders is to try to recognize and respond to the needs of these stakeholders and still make a profit.

Learning Goal 2. Compare and contrast being an entrepreneur and working for others.

- **What are the advantages and disadvantages of entrepreneurship?**

Working for others means getting benefits like paid vacations and health insurance. Entrepreneurs take more risks and lose those benefits. They gain the freedom to make their own decisions, more opportunity, and possible wealth.

- **What are the five factors of production?**

The five factors of production are land, labor, capital, entrepreneurship, and knowledge. Of these, the most important are entrepreneurship and knowledge. Entrepreneurs are people who risk time and money to start and manage a business. What makes rich countries rich today is a combination of *entrepreneurship* and the effective use of *knowledge*.

Learning Goal 3. Analyze the effect of the economic environment and taxes on businesses.

- **What can governments in developing countries do to reduce the risk of starting businesses and thus help entrepreneurs?**

The government may allow private ownership of businesses, pass laws that enable businesspeople to write contracts that are enforceable in court, establish a currency that's tradable in world markets, help to lessen corruption in business and government, and keep taxes and regulations to a minimum. From a business perspective, lower taxes mean lower risks, more growth, and thus more money for workers and the government.

Learning Goal 4. Describe the effects of technology on businesses.

- **How has technology benefited workers, businesses, and consumers?**

Technology enables workers to be more effective, efficient, and productive. *Effectiveness* means doing the right thing in the right way. *Efficiency* means producing items using the least amount of resources. *Productivity* is the amount of output you generate given the amount of input (e.g., hours worked).

Learning Goal 5. Demonstrate how businesses can meet and beat competition.
- **What are some ways in which businesses meet and beat competition?**

Some companies have found a competitive edge by focusing on making high-quality products, all the way to zero defects. Companies also aim to exceed customer expectations. Often that means *empowering* front-line workers by giving them more training and more responsibility and authority.

Learning Goal 6. Analyze the social changes affecting businesses.
- **How have social changes affected businesses?**

Diversity has come to mean much more than recruiting and keeping minority and female employees. Diversity efforts now include seniors, disabled people, homosexuals, atheists, extroverts, introverts, married people, singles, and the devout. It also means dealing sensitively with workers and cultures around the world. Providing Social Security benefits to senior citizens in the future will draw huge amounts of money from the working population. That is why there is so much discussion about Social Security in the media today.

Learning Goal 7. Identify what businesses must do to meet global challenges, including war and terrorism.
- **Which countries are creating the greatest challenges?**

China and India are two major competitors.
- **What will be the impacts of future wars and terrorism?**

Some businesses, such as those in the defense industry, may prosper. Others, such as tourism, may suffer. One way to minimize world tensions is to help less developed countries to become more prosperous.

Learning Goal 8. Review how past trends are being repeated in the present and what those trends mean for tomorrow's college graduates.
- **What is the history of our economic development in the United States, and what does it tell us about the future?**

Agricultural workers displaced by improved farm technology went to work in factories. Improved manufacturing productivity and increased competition from foreign firms contributed to the development of a service economy in the United States. The service era is now giving way to an information-based global revolution that will affect all sectors of the economy. The secret to long-term success in such an economy is flexibility and continuing education to be prepared for the opportunities that are sure to arise.
- **What job opportunities for college graduates exist in the service sector?**

Check over Figure 1.5, which outlines the service sector. That is where you are most likely to find the fast-growing firms of the future.

key terms

business 4
business environment 11
climate change 19
database 15
demography 17
e-commerce 14
empowerment 17
entrepreneur 4
factors of production 9
goods 4
greening 19
identity theft 15

Taking Risks and Making Profits within the Dynamic Business Environment * CHAPTER 1   25

loss 5
nonprofit organization 7
outsourcing 6
productivity 14
profit 5
quality of life 6
revenue 5
risk 5
services 4
stakeholders 6
standard of living 6
technology 14

connect interactive applications

Reinforcing Your *Connect*ion to Concepts in Business

This chapter offers 12 interactive applications designed to help you apply what you've learned (examples of these exercises appear below). Your instructor has determined which interactive applications will benefit you throughout this course. Please refer to your instructor's assignment list in *Connect* to determine which applications you should complete.

Comprehension Case Interactive: A business started by an entrepreneur faces many challenges, from the characteristics of the entrepreneur to challenges on a global scale. In this comprehension case, you will analyze the case according to your understanding of entrepreneurship and business.

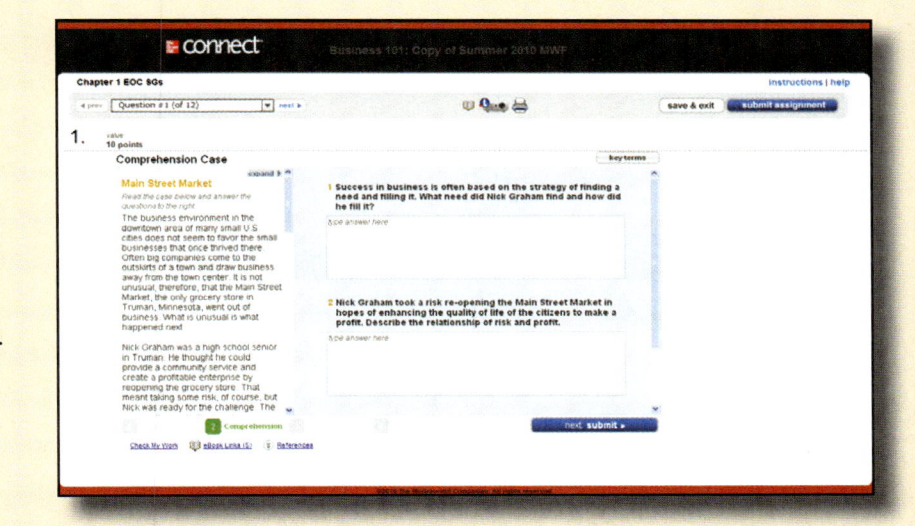

Drag and Drop Interactive: Factors of production differ from country to country. In this drag-and-drop activity, you will need to categorize each country by its factor of production.

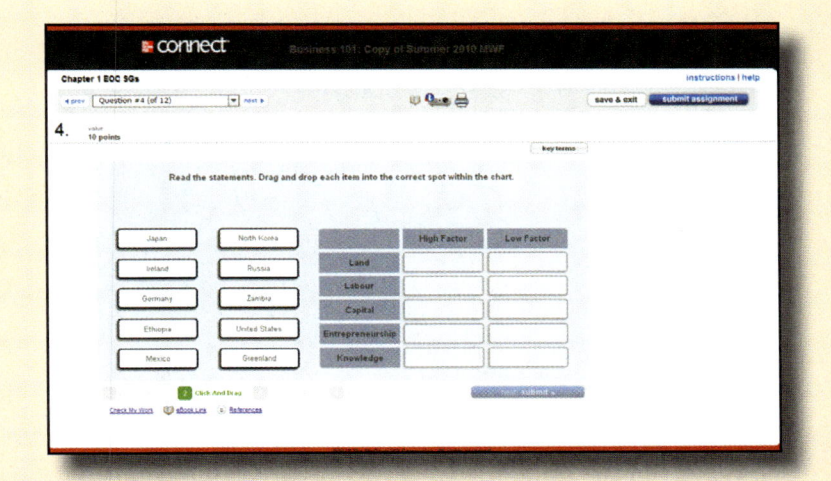

Video Case Interactive: Businesses must deal with various elements in the business environment, including technology and competition. The founders of the company iContact decided to take the associated risk in starting a business and have addressed many of the issues facing a business. As the video plays, you will need to apply concepts from this chapter to answer the questions about iContact's experience.

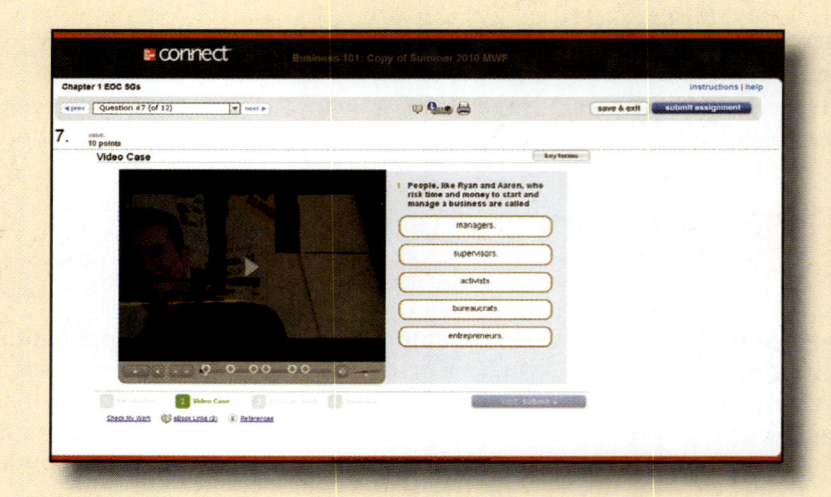

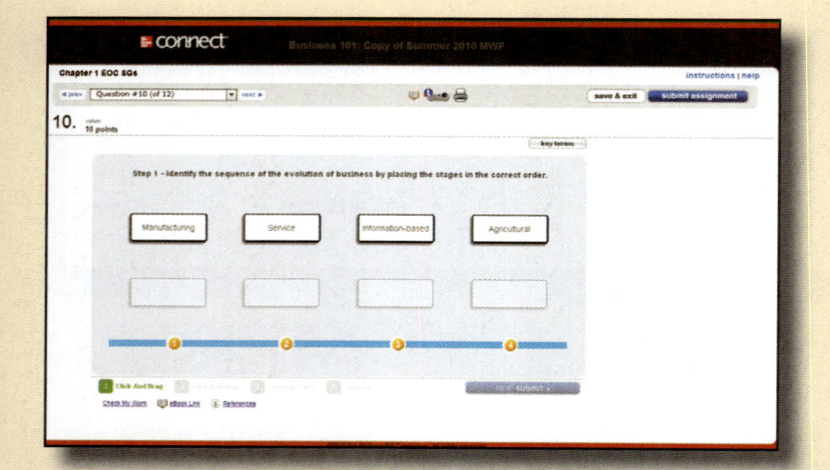

Drag and Drop Interactive: In this drag-and-drop activity, you will apply what you learned about the evolution of business in the United States by placing example businesses on a timeline, beginning with the earliest industry.

2 Understanding HOW Economics Affects Business

profile

In the traditional banking world, credit was given where credit was due. To most banks, that meant credit was due only to people with dependable collateral. That changed somewhat when, before the recent banking crisis, banks began making loans to people with very little or no collateral. (We'll talk more about this later in the text.)

Collateral refers to anything of significant value that a borrower puts up as security for a loan and is forfeited if the loan is not repaid. Historically, if the collateral was sufficient and the person had a good credit history, the bank would grant the loan. But what about people who have no credit history and no collateral, yet still have an entrepreneurial desire to succeed? Bangladeshi economist Muhammad Yunus asked himself this question in 1974, when he loaned $27 out of his own pocket to a group of 42 women in a less developed country to expand their bamboo furniture business.

With no collateral, the women could not get a loan from a bank. Their only other option was to borrow money from the village loan sharks, who charged sky-high interest rates. Yunus's loans not only saved the women from the danger of dealing with the local moneylenders but also allowed them to turn a profit and quickly pay him back.

After the success of his first loan, Yunus began the Grameen Bank in 1976. (*Grameen* means "village" in the Bangla language.) As he developed the bank's policies and procedures, Yunus observed what other banks did and then did the opposite. "Conventional banks go to the rich; we go to the poor," Yunus said. "Their rule is, 'The more you have, the more you get.' So our rule became, 'The less you have, the higher attention you get. If you have nothing, you get the highest priority.'" The bank centered on granting what we would consider very small loans, which he called microcredits, to underprivileged clients. The bank operates on Yunus's firm belief that everyone can be an entrepreneur, even those who are born into societies in which they are unable to access the capital needed to make the most of their innate talents.

Getting to Know

x *Muhammad Yunus*

Founder of the Grameen Bank

LEARNING goals

After you have read and studied this chapter, you should be able to

1. Explain basic economics.
2. Explain what capitalism is and how free markets work.
3. Compare socialism and communism.
4. Analyze the trend toward mixed economies.
5. Describe the economic system of the United States, including the significance of key economic indicators (especially GDP), productivity, and the business cycle.
6. Contrast fiscal policy and monetary policy, and explain how each affects the economy.

connect™

Your *Connection* to Better Learning. 1. View the interactive presentation. 2. Practice through LearnSmart. 3. Apply your knowledge by using the interactive applications for each chapter of this text.

1 Prep >>>>>> 2 Study >>>>>> 3 Apply

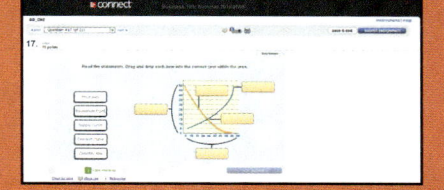

Grameen Bank has lent over $7 billion in microcredits to impoverished people of Bangladesh. Of the 7.5 million borrowers, 97 percent are women. In February 2008, Grameen Bank opened a branch in New York City, its first location in a developed country. Yunus hoped to provide $176 million in loans over five years to some of the 28 million U.S. adults who had no bank accounts, and the 44.7 million who had limited access to financial institutions. The recent banking crisis has made it even more difficult to borrow from some banks, creating even more need for Yunus's services.

Yunus's actions have not gone unnoticed by the international community. At the top of his long list of awards is the 2006 Nobel Peace Prize. But no matter how many accolades he receives, Yunus remains steadfast in his quest to eradicate poverty by changing the economic environment of the entire world through microcredits. As he said in his Nobel Prize acceptance speech, "I firmly believe that we can create a poverty-free world if we collectively believe in it. In a poverty-free world, the only place you would be able to see poverty is in the poverty museums."

Many people don't realize the importance of the economic environment to the success of business. That is what this chapter is all about. You will learn to compare different economic systems to see the benefits and the drawbacks of each. You will learn how the free-market system of the United States works. And you will learn more about what makes some countries rich and other countries poor. By the end of the chapter, you should understand the direct effect economic systems have on the wealth and happiness of communities throughout the world.

Sources: Muhammad Yunus, "Yunus Speaks about Capitalism, Poverty, and the Future of 'Social Business,'" *The Tech,* June 13, 2008; Emily Parker, "Subprime Lender," *The Wall Street Journal,* March 1–2, 2008; www.nobelprize.org; www.grameen-info.org; www.muhammadyunus.org, accessed February 11, 2009; and Yunus Centre, www.muhammadyunus.org, accessed July 28, 2010.

www.muhammadyunus.org

NAME THAT company

▶ **PPT 2-1:**
Understanding How Economics Affects Business

▶ **PPT 2-2:**
Muhammad Yunus

Like the Grameen Bank, this organization lends small amounts of money to people in poor countries. It loaned a woman in Uganda enough to buy a refrigerator. She was able to sell fresh food from the refrigerator and make enough money for her family to succeed. What is the name of this organization? (The answer is in the chapter.)

LEARNING goal 1 *

Explain basic economics.

HOW ECONOMIC CONDITIONS AFFECT BUSINESSES

Compared to, say, Mexico, the United States is a relatively wealthy country. Why? Why is South Korea comparatively wealthy and North Korea suffering economically, with many of its people starving?[1] Why is China's income per person lower than Taiwan's? Such questions are part of the subject of economics. In this chapter, we explore the various economic systems of the world and how they either promote or hinder business growth, the creation of wealth, and a higher quality of life for all.[2]

A major part of the United States' business success in the past was due to an economic and social climate that allowed most businesses to operate freely. People were free to start a business anywhere, and just as free to fail and start again. That freedom motivated people to try until they succeeded because the rewards were often so great.

Any change in the U.S. economic or political system has a major influence on the success of the business system. For example, the recent increase in government involvement in business will have an economic effect (see the discussion of Keynesian economics at the end of this chapter); what that effect will be in the long run, however, remains to be seen.

Global economics and global politics also have a major influence on businesses in the United States. Therefore, to understand business, you must also understand basic economics and politics.

▶ **PPT 2-3:**
The Major Branches of Economics

> **economics**
> The study of how society chooses to employ resources to produce goods and services and distribute them for consumption among various competing groups and individuals.

> **macroeconomics**
> The part of economics study that looks at the operation of a nation's economy as a whole.

> **microeconomics**
> The part of economics study that looks at the behavior of people and organizations in particular markets.

What Is Economics?

Economics is the study of how society chooses to employ resources to produce goods and services and distribute them for consumption among various competing groups and individuals. There are two major branches of economics: **macroeconomics** looks at the operation of a nation's economy as a whole (the whole United States), and **microeconomics** looks at the behavior of people and organizations in markets for particular products or services. A question in microeconomics might be: Why do people buy smaller cars when gas prices go up? Macroeconomic topics in this chapter include gross domestic product (GDP), the unemployment rate, and price indexes. Microeconomic issues include pricing and supply/demand interactions.

Some economists define economics as the study of the allocation of *scarce* resources. They believe resources need to be carefully divided among people, usually by the government. However, there's no way to maintain peace and prosperity in the world by merely dividing the resources we have today among the existing nations. There aren't enough known resources to do that. **Resource development** is the study of how to increase resources (say by getting oil from shale and tar sands) and create conditions that will make better use of them (like recycling and conservation).

Businesses can contribute to an economic system by inventing products that greatly increase available resources. For example, they can discover new energy sources (hydrogen fuel for autos), new ways of growing food (hydroponics), and new ways of creating needed goods and services (nanotechnology). Mariculture, or raising fish in pens out in the ocean, could lead to more food for everyone and more employment.[3] The Thinking Green box on p. 32 explores some new ventures that have been created to help lessen climate change.

The Secret to Creating a Wealthy Economy

Imagine the world when kings and other rich landowners had most of the wealth, and the majority of the people were peasants. The peasants had many children, and it may have seemed a natural conclusion that if things went on as usual there would soon be too many people and not enough food and other resources. Economist Thomas Malthus made this argument in the late 1700s and early 1800s, leading the writer Thomas Carlyle to call economics "the dismal science."

The economic contrast is remarkable. Business is booming in Seoul, South Korea (pictured on left). But North Korea, a communist country, is not doing well, as the picture on the right of thousands of workers using old-fashioned tools in a work-for-food program shows. What do you think accounts for the dramatic differences in the economies of these two neighboring countries?

resource development
The study of how to increase resources and to create the conditions that will make better use of those resources.

◄ PPT 2-4:
Resource Development
◄ PPT 2-5:
Examples of Ways to Increase Resources
◄ CRITICAL THINKING EXERCISE 2-1:
Know Your History of Economics

THINKING green

More Profits from the Green Revolution

Adjusting to climate changes creates as many opportunities as it does challenges. Companies that help lower carbon emissions can prosper as people become more concerned about climate change. Toyota has had success selling its hybrid Prius, and most automakers now offer similar hybrids, which get better mileage with less pollution than gas-only vehicles. Some all-electric cars will soon be available. And several firms are offering cars half the size of regular cars—to get better fuel economy.

Farmers are growing more corn and other crops for use as biofuels. That creates more demand for tractors and other farm equipment, and helps the economy grow. It also causes food prices to skyrocket. Given these outcomes, would you recommend an increase in the use of biofuels?

It's amazing what you find when you begin looking for greener businesses. Have you ever seen hot-dog wrappers blowing around the ballpark? In the future, they'll be recycled. *Reduce. Reuse. Recycle.* These have become the tenets of a greener, more environmentally responsive lifestyle.

Business schools are teaching entrepreneurs how to get rich helping to save the environment. You and I can't solve the problem by ourselves, but together all of us may make a difference. Are you part of the solution or part of the problem? What is your college or university doing to lower its carbon output? Have you volunteered to help clean up the Gulf oil spill?

Sources: Martha Brant and Miyoko Ohtake, "A Growth Industry," *Newsweek*, April 14, 2008; Environmental Protection Agency, "Ready, Set, Green," public service advertisement, 2008; Warren Brown, "Checking the Extremes at the New York Show," *The Washington Post*, March 23, 2008; and Paul H. Rubin, "Why is the Gulf Cleanup So Slow?," *The Wall Street Journal*, July 2, 2010.

▶ **LECTURE LINK 2-I:**
Europe Is Shrinking
▶ **PPT 2-6:**
More Profits From the Green Revolution

New ways of producing goods and services add resources to the economy and create more employment. Fish farms, for instance, create both food and jobs through the new process of mariculture, or the cultivation of marine life in open or closed areas of the ocean. What other new industries might the world's oceans sustain?

Followers of Malthus today (who are called neo-Malthusians) still believe there are too many people in the world and that the solution to poverty is radical birth control, including forced abortions and sterilization.[4] The latest world statistics, however, show population growing more slowly than expected. In some industrial countries—like Japan, Germany, Italy, Russia, and the United States—population growth may be so slow that eventually there will be too many old people and too few young people to care for them. In the developing world, on the other hand, population will climb relatively quickly and may lead to greater poverty and more unrest. Studies about the effects of population growth on the economy are part of macroeconomics.

Some macroeconomists believe that a large population, especially an educated one, can be a valuable resource. You've probably heard the saying "Give a man a fish and you feed him for a day, but teach a man to fish and you feed him for a lifetime." You can add to that: "Teach a person to start a fish farm, and he or she will be able to feed a village for a lifetime." *The secret to economic development is contained in this last statement.* Business owners provide jobs and economic growth for their employees and communities as well as for themselves.

The challenge for macroeconomists is to determine what makes some countries relatively wealthy and other countries relatively poor, and then to implement policies and programs that lead to increased prosperity for everyone in all countries.[5] One way to begin understanding this challenge is to consider the theories of Adam Smith.

Adam Smith and the Creation of Wealth

Rather than believing fixed resources had to be divided among competing groups and individuals, Scottish economist Adam Smith envisioned creating more resources so that everyone could become wealthier. Smith's book *An Inquiry into the Nature and Causes of the Wealth of Nations* (often called simply *The Wealth of Nations*) was published in 1776.

Smith believed *freedom* was vital to the survival of any economy, especially the freedom to own land or property and to keep the profits from working the land or running a business.[6] He believed people will work long and hard if they have incentives for doing so—that is, if they know they'll be rewarded. As a result of those efforts, the economy would prosper, with plenty of food and all kinds of products available to everyone. Smith's ideas were later challenged by Malthus and others who believed economic conditions would only get worse, but Smith, not Malthus, is considered the *father of modern economics.*

How Businesses Benefit the Community

In Adam Smith's view, businesspeople don't necessarily deliberately set out to help others. They work primarily for their own prosperity and growth. Yet as people try to improve their own situation in life, Smith said, their efforts serve as an "invisible hand" that helps the economy grow and prosper through the production of needed goods, services, and ideas. Thus, the phrase **invisible hand** is used to describe the process that turns self-directed gain into social and economic benefits for all.

How do people working in their own self-interest produce goods, services, and wealth for others? The only way farmers can become wealthy is to sell some of their crops to others. To become even wealthier, they have to hire workers to produce more food. So the farmers' self-centered efforts to become wealthy lead to jobs for some and food for almost all. Think about that process for a minute, because it is critical to understanding economic growth in the United States and other free countries.[7] The same principles apply to everything from clothing to houses to iPhones.

◄ PPT 2-7:
Thomas Malthus and the Dismal Science
◄ PPT 2-8:
Population as a Resource
◄ PPT 2-9:
Adam Smith and the Father of Economics
◄ PPT 2-10:
The Invisible Hand Theory

invisible hand
A phrase coined by Adam Smith to describe the process that turns self-directed gain into social and economic benefits for all.

◄ CRITICAL THINKING EXERCISE 2-2:
Applying Economic Principles to Education
◄ PPT 2-11:
Understanding the Invisible Hand Theory

According to Adam Smith's theory, business owners in a market economy are motivated to work hard because they know they will earn, and keep, the rewards of their labor. When they prosper, as the owner of this store has, they are able to add employees and grow, indirectly helping the community and the larger economy grow in the process. What might motivate you to start your own business?

MAKING ethical decisions

Corruption Destroys Economies

You may wonder how men like Mexico's Carlos Slim, the world's second-richest man, can become billionaires in countries that are so poor. Clearly, numerous forces in such countries hinder economic growth and development. One of those forces is corruption. In many countries, a businessperson must bribe government officials to get permission to own land, build on it, and conduct normal business operations.

The United States has seen much corruption among businesspeople, such as use of prostitutes, illegal drug use, alcohol addiction, and gambling. Imagine you need a permit to add liquor to your restaurant menu to increase your profit. You have tried for years to get one, with no results. You have a friend in the government who offers to help you if you make a large contribution to his or her reelection campaign. Would you be tempted to make a campaign contribution? What are your alternatives? What are the consequences of each?

▶ **PPT 2-12:**
Corruption Destroys Economies

Smith assumed that as people became wealthier, they would naturally reach out to help the less fortunate in the community.[8] That has not always happened. Today, however, many businesspeople are becoming more concerned about social issues and their obligation to return to society some of what they've earned.[9] As we mentioned in Chapter 1, it is important for businesses to be ethical as well as generous.[10] Unethical practices undermine the whole economic system. The Making Ethical Decisions box explores a key ethical question.

▶ **PPT 2-13:**
Progress Assessment

progress assessment

- What is the difference between macroeconomics and microeconomics?
- What is better for an economy than teaching a man to fish?
- What does Adam Smith's term *invisible hand* mean? How does the invisible hand create wealth for a country?

LEARNING goal 2 *

Explain what capitalism is and how free markets work.

UNDERSTANDING FREE-MARKET CAPITALISM

Basing their ideas on free-market principles such as those of Adam Smith, businesspeople in the United States, Europe, Japan, Canada, and other countries began to create more wealth than ever before. They hired others to work on their farms and in their factories, and their nations began to prosper as a result. Businesspeople soon became the wealthiest people in society.

However, great disparities in wealth remained or even increased. Many businesspeople owned large homes and fancy carriages, while most workers

▶ **BONUS CASE 2-1:**
Foundations of the Capitalist System

lived in humble surroundings. Nonetheless, there was always the promise of better times. One way to be really wealthy was to start a successful business of your own. Of course, it wasn't that easy—it never has been. Then and now, you have to accumulate some money to buy or start a business, and you have to work long hours to make it grow. But the opportunities are there.

The economic system that has led to wealth creation in much of the world is known as capitalism. Under **capitalism** all or most of the factors of production and distribution—such as land, factories, railroads, and stores—are owned by individuals. They are operated for profit, and businesspeople, not government officials, decide what to produce and how much, what to charge, and how much to pay workers. They also decide whether to produce goods in their own countries or have them made in other countries. No country is purely capitalist, however. Often the government gets involved in issues such as determining minimum wages, setting farm prices, and lending money to some failing businesses—as it does in the United States. But capitalism is the *foundation* of the U.S. economic system, and of the economies of England, Australia, Canada, and most other developed nations. The root word of *capitalism* is "capital." The Spotlight on Small Business box on p. 36 shows how a little capital can help small businesses grow in the poorest countries in the world.

The Foundations of Capitalism

Under free-market capitalism people have four basic rights:

1. *The right to own private property.* This is the most fundamental of all rights under capitalism. Private ownership means that individuals can buy, sell, and use land, buildings, machinery, inventions, and other forms of property. They can also pass property on to their children. Would farmers work as hard if they didn't own the land and couldn't keep the profits from what they earned?

2. *The right to own a business and keep all that business's profits.* Recall from Chapter 1 that profits equal revenues minus expenses (salaries, materials, taxes). Profits act as important incentives for business owners.

3. *The right to freedom of competition.* Within certain guidelines established by the government, individuals are free to compete with other individuals or businesses in selling and promoting goods and services.

4. *The right to freedom of choice.* People are free to choose where they want to work and what career they want to follow. Other choices people are free to make include where to live and what to buy or sell.

One benefit of the four basic rights of capitalism is that people are willing to take more risks than they might otherwise. President Franklin Roosevelt believed four additional freedoms were essential to economic success: freedom of speech and expression, the freedom to worship in your own way, freedom from want, and freedom from fear. Do you see the benefits of these additional freedoms?

Now let's explore how the free market works. What role do consumers play in the process? How do businesses learn what consumers need and want? These questions and more are answered next.

◀ PPT 2-14:
Capitalism

capitalism
An economic system in which all or most of the factors of production and distribution are privately owned and operated for profit.

◀ PPT 2-15:
The Key to Capitalism is Capital

◀ PPT 2-16:
Capitalism's Four Basic Rights

◀ PPT 2-17:
Roosevelt's Four Additional Rights

The right to own private property, including the means of production, and the right to own a business and keep its profits are two of the fundamental rights that exist in the economic system called free-market capitalism. Would either of these rights be viable without the other?

SPOTLIGHT ON SMALL *business

www.villagebanking.org

The Key to Capitalism Is Capital

As you read in the chapter's opening Profile, about Muhammad Yunus of Grameen Bank, one way people in developed countries can help people in less developed countries is to create a local "bank" that lends money to budding entrepreneurs so they can begin or expand their business. The entrepreneurs must pay the money back, with interest, and often must keep some money in the bank. Such banks don't necessarily have to be in a bank building. Village women often assume the role of banker and decide which women will get the loans. The "bankers" meet in a community building of some sort.

A nonprofit similar to Grameen Bank is the Foundation for International Community Assistance (FINCA). In its 10-year history, FINCA has loaned more than $447 million to over 600,000 small-scale entrepreneurs in some of the world's poorest countries. Its borrowers have a 97.6 percent loan repayment rate.

The story of one small entrepreneur will help you understand the process. Pros Magaga lives in Kampala, Uganda. She had a tiny shop in town, but it carried very little inventory. She did not make enough to send her four children to school or to feed them more than once a day. FINCA lent her $50; she used it to buy a refrigerator, which allowed her to carry fresh foods and cold snacks. Later she added a freezer. Now her children are all in school, and the family enjoys two meals a day. Magaga has built a small home with two rooms and plans to add another room soon. She can borrow more money from FINCA because she has already paid back her $50 loan.

Sources: Sheridan Prasso, "Saving the World One Cup of Yogurt at a Time," *Fortune*, February 19, 2007; Opportunity International's quarterly newsletter, Summer 2008; and Ruth David, "In a Microfinance Boom, Echoes of Subprime," Bloomberg Businessweek, June 21–June 27, 2010.

How Free Markets Work

A free market is one in which decisions about what and how much to produce are made by the market—by buyers and sellers negotiating prices for goods and services. You and I and other consumers send signals to tell producers what to make, how many, in what color, and so on. We do that by choosing to buy (or not to buy) certain products and services.

For example, if all of us decided we wanted T-shirts supporting our favorite baseball team, the clothing industry would respond in certain ways. Manufacturers and retailers would increase the price of those T-shirts, because they know people are willing to pay more for the shirts they want. They would also realize they could make more money by making more of those T-shirts. Thus, they have an incentive to pay workers to start earlier and end later. Further, the number of companies making T-shirts would increase. How many T-shirts they make depends on how many we request or buy in the stores. Prices and quantities will continue to change as the number of T-shirts we buy changes.

The same process occurs with most other products. The *price* tells producers how much to produce. If something is wanted but isn't available, the price tends to go up until someone begins making more of that product, sells the ones already on hand, or makes a substitute. As a consequence, there's rarely a long-term shortage of goods in the United States.

How Prices Are Determined

In a free market, prices are not determined by sellers; they are determined by buyers and sellers negotiating in the marketplace. A seller may want to

▶ PPT 2-18:
Free Markets

▶ LECTURE LINK 2-2:
The Circular Flow Model

▶ PPT 2-19:
Circular Flow Model

▶ PPT 2-20:
Pricing

receive $50 for a T-shirt, but the quantity buyers demand at that high price may be quite low. If the seller lowers the price, the quantity demanded is likely to increase. How is a price determined that is acceptable to both buyers and sellers? The answer is found in the microeconomic concepts of supply and demand. We shall explore both next.

The Economic Concept of Supply

Supply refers to the quantities of products manufacturers or owners are willing to sell at different prices at a specific time. Generally speaking, the amount supplied will increase as the price increases, because sellers can make more money with a higher price.

Economists show this relationship between quantity supplied and price on a graph. Figure 2.1 on p. 38 shows a simple supply curve for T-shirts. The price of the shirts in dollars is shown vertically on the left of the graph. The quantity of shirts sellers are willing to supply is shown horizontally at the bottom of the graph. The various points on the curve indicate how many T-shirts sellers would provide at different prices. For example, at a price of $5 a shirt, a T-shirt vendor would provide only 5 shirts, but at $50 a shirt the vendor would supply 50 shirts. The supply curve indicates the relationship between the price and the quantity supplied. All things being equal, the higher the price, the more the vendor will be willing to supply.

The Economic Concept of Demand

Demand refers to the quantity of products that people are willing to buy at different prices at a specific time. Generally speaking, the quantity demanded will increase as the price decreases. Again, we can show the relationship between price and quantity demanded in a graph. Figure 2.2 on p. 38 shows a simple demand curve for T-shirts. The various points on the graph indicate the quantity demanded at various prices. For example, at $45, buyers demand just 5 shirts, but at $5, the quantity demanded would increase to 35 shirts. All things being equal, the lower the price, the more buyers are willing to buy.

The Equilibrium Point, or Market Price

You might realize from Figures 2.1 and 2.2 that the key factor in determining the quantities supplied and demanded is *price*. If you were to lay the two graphs one on top of the other, the supply curve and the demand curve would cross where quantity demanded and quantity supplied are equal. Figure 2.3 illustrates that point. At a price of $15, the quantity of T-shirts demanded and the quantity supplied are equal (25 shirts). That crossing point is known as the *equilibrium point* or equilibrium price. In the long run, that price will become the

supply
The quantity of products that manufacturers or owners are willing to sell at different prices at a specific time.

demand
The quantity of products that people are willing to buy at different prices at a specific time.

The economic concept of demand measures the quantities of goods and services that people are willing to buy. Judging from this photo of people waiting to buy the iPhone on the first day it was available for sale, how would you describe the demand for this product?

figure 2.1

THE SUPPLY CURVE AT VARIOUS PRICES

The supply curve rises from left to right. Think it through. The higher the price of T-shirts goes (the vertical axis), the more sellers will be willing to supply.

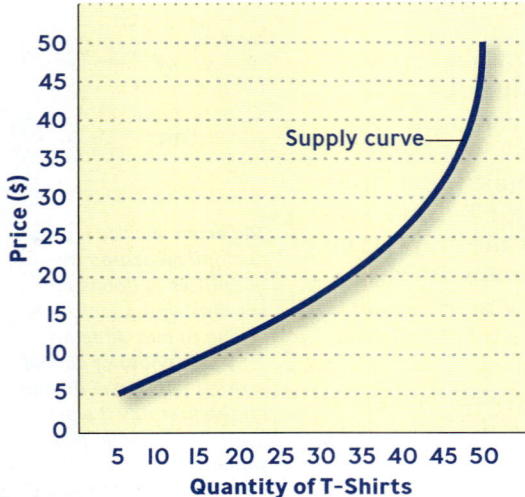

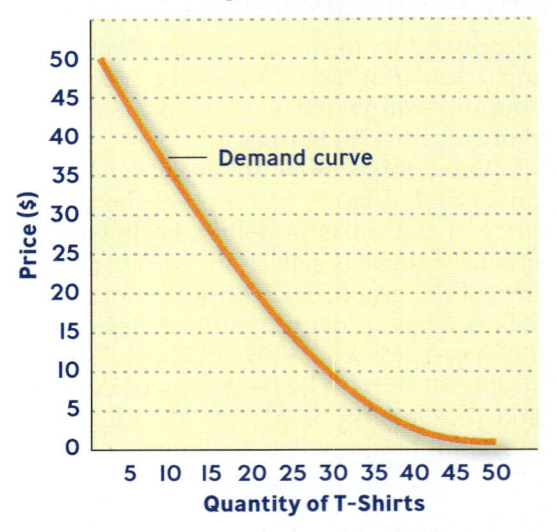

▶ PPT 2-21:
Supply Curves
▶ PPT 2-22:
Demand Curves
▶ PPT 2-23:
Equilibrium
▶ CRITICAL THINKING EXERCISE 2-3:
Finding the Equilibrium Point

figure 2.2

THE DEMAND CURVE AT VARIOUS PRICES

This is a simple demand curve showing the quantity of T-shirts demanded at different prices. The demand curve falls from left to right. It is easy to understand why. The lower the price of T-shirts, the higher the quantity demanded.

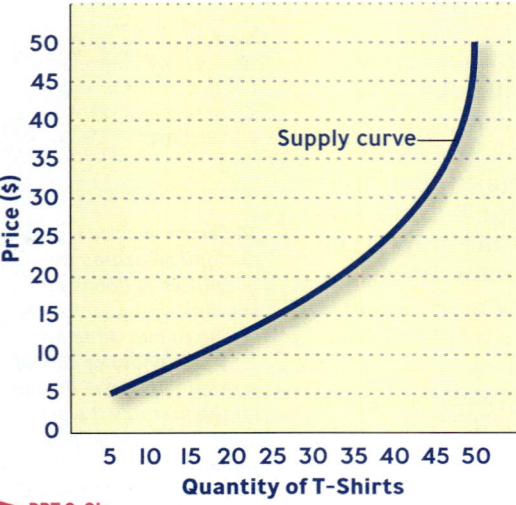

figure 2.3

THE EQUILIBRIUM POINT

The place where quantity demanded and supplied meet is called the equilibrium point. When we put both the supply and demand curves on the same graph, we find that they intersect at a price where the quantity supplied and the quantity demanded are equal. In the long run, the market price will tend toward the equilibrium point.

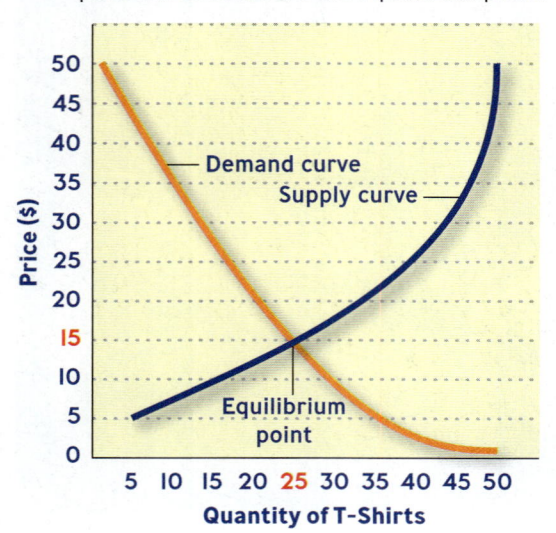

market price. **Market price**, then, is determined by supply and demand.[11] It is the price toward which the market will trend.

Proponents of a free market argue that, because supply and demand interactions determine prices, there is no need for government to set prices. If quantity supplied exceeds quantity demanded, the resulting surplus signals sellers to lower the price. If shortages develop because quantity supplied is less than quantity demanded, it signals sellers to increase the price. Eventually, supply will again equal demand if nothing interferes with market forces.

When supplies of oil were lower because of the Gulf oil spill, for instance, the price of gasoline went up. When supplies were again plentiful, the price of gas fell a little. It may rise if demand increases globally, especially in China and India. Food prices went up when more corn was being used for ethanol fuel and less for food.[12] Note, too, how many alternative fuel sources (wind, solar, tar sands, etc.) were tried when the price of gas went to about $4 a gallon.

In countries without a free market, there is no mechanism to reveal to businesses (via price) what to produce and in what amounts, so there are often shortages (not enough products) or surpluses (too many products). In such countries, the government decides what to produce and in what quantity, but without price signals it has no way of knowing what the proper quantities are. Furthermore, when the government interferes in otherwise free markets, such as when it subsidizes farm goods, surpluses and shortages may develop. Competition differs in free markets, too. We shall explore that concept next.

Competition within Free Markets

Economists generally agree there are four different degrees of competition: (1) perfect competition, (2) monopolistic competition, (3) oligopoly, and (4) monopoly.

Perfect competition exists when there are many sellers in a market and none is large enough to dictate the price of a product. Sellers' products appear to be identical, such as agricultural products like apples, corn, and potatoes. There are no true examples of perfect competition. Today, government price supports and drastic reductions in the number of farms make it hard to argue that even farming represents perfect competition.

Under **monopolistic competition** a large number of sellers produce very similar products that buyers nevertheless perceive as different, such as hot dogs, sodas, personal computers, and T-shirts. Product differentiation—the attempt to make buyers think similar products are different in some way—is a key to success. Think about what that means. Through advertising, branding, and packaging, sellers try to convince buyers that their products are different from competitors', though they may be very similar or even interchangeable. The fast-food industry, with its pricing battles between hamburger places, offers a good example of monopolistic competition.

An **oligopoly** is a degree of competition in which just a few sellers dominate a market, as we see in tobacco, gasoline, automobiles, aluminum, and aircraft. One reason some industries remain in the hands of a few sellers is that the initial investment required to enter the business often is tremendous. Think, for example, of how much it would cost to start a new airplane manufacturing facility.

In an oligopoly, products from different companies tend to be priced about the same. The reason is simple: Intense price competition would lower profits for everyone, since a price cut by one producer would most likely be matched by the others. As in monopolistic competition, product differentiation, rather than price, is usually the major factor in market success in an oligopoly. Note, for example, that most cereals are priced about the same, as are soft drinks. Thus, advertising is a major factor in which of the few available brands consumers buy, because often it is advertising that creates the perceived differences.

A **monopoly** occurs when one seller controls the total supply of a product or service, and sets the price. In the United States, laws prohibit the creation of monopolies. Nonetheless, the U.S. legal system has permitted monopolies in the markets for public utilities that sell natural gas, water, and electric power. These companies' prices and profits are usually controlled by public service commissions to protect the interest of buyers. For example, the Florida Public Service Commission is the administering agency over the Florida Power and Light utility company. New legislation has ended the monopoly status of utilities in some areas, letting consumers choose among providers. The intention of such *deregulation* is to increase competition among utility companies and, ultimately, lower prices for consumers.

Benefits and Limitations of Free Markets

One benefit of the free market is that it allows open competition among companies. Businesses must provide customers with high-quality products at fair prices with good service. If they don't, they lose customers to businesses that do. Do government services have the same incentives?

---

market price
The price determined by supply and demand.

◀ PPT 2-24:
Four Degrees of Competition

perfect competition
The degree of competition in which there are many sellers in a market and none is large enough to dictate the price of a product.

monopolistic competition
The degree of competition in which a large number of sellers produce very similar products that buyers nevertheless perceive as different.

oligopoly
A degree of competition in which just a few sellers dominate the market.

monopoly
A degree of competition in which only one seller controls the total supply of a product or service, and sets the price.

> **CRITICAL THINKING EXERCISE 2-4:**
> Standard of Living Comparison

The free market—with its competition and incentives—was a major factor in creating the wealth that industrialized countries now enjoy. Some people even talk of the free market as an economic miracle. Free-market capitalism, more than any other economic system, provides opportunities for poor people to work their way out of poverty. Capitalism also encourages businesses to be more efficient so they can successfully compete on price and quality.

Yet even as free-market capitalism has brought prosperity to the United States and to much of the rest of the world, it has brought inequality as well.[13] Business owners and managers usually make more money and have more wealth than lower-level workers. Yet people who are old, disabled, or sick may not be able to start and manage a business, and others may not have the talent or the drive. What should society do about such inequality? Not everyone in the United States is as generous as Bill Gates, founder of Microsoft, who with his wife has established the Bill and Melinda Gates Foundation to support world health and education. In fact, the desire to create as much wealth as possible has led some businesspeople throughout history, and still today, to use such practices as slavery and child labor.

> **PPT 2-25:**
> Free Market Benefits and Limitations

One of the dangers of free markets is that some people let greed dictate how they act.[14] Criminal charges brought against some big businesses in banking, oil, accounting, telecommunications, insurance, and pharmaceuticals indicate the scope of the potential problem. Some businesspeople have deceived the public about their products; others have deceived stockholders about the value of their stock, all in order to increase executives' personal assets.

> **PPT 2-26:**
> The Government Needs

Clearly, some government laws and regulations may be necessary to protect businesses' stakeholders and make sure people who cannot work get the basic care they need. To overcome some of capitalism's limitations, some countries have adopted an economic system called socialism. It, too, has its good and bad points. We explore these after the Progress Assessment questions.

> **PPT 2-27:**
> Progress Assessment

progress assessment

- What are the four basic rights that people have under free-market capitalism?
- How do businesspeople know what to produce and in what quantity?
- How are prices determined?
- What are the four degrees of competition, and what are some examples of each?

LEARNING goal 3 *

Compare socialism and communism.

> **PPT 2-28:**
> Socialism

UNDERSTANDING SOCIALISM

socialism
An economic system based on the premise that some, if not most, basic businesses should be owned by the government so that profits can be more evenly distributed among the people.

Socialism is an economic system based on the premise that some, if not most, basic businesses (e.g., steel mills, coal mines, and utilities) should be owned by the government so that profits can be more evenly distributed among the people. Entrepreneurs often own and run smaller businesses, and individuals are often taxed relatively steeply to pay for social programs. The top federal personal income tax rate in the United States, for example, was 35 percent in 2009, but in some socialist countries the top rate can be as much as 60 percent. While U.S. shoppers pay sales taxes ranging from 10.25 percent in Chicago to zero in Delaware,[15] socialist countries charge a similar value-added tax of 15 to 20 percent or more. Socialists acknowledge the major benefit of capitalism—wealth creation—but believe that wealth should be more evenly distributed than occurs in free-market capitalism. They believe the government should carry out the distribution and be much more involved in protecting the environment and providing for the poor. Do you see such a movement occurring in the United States?[16]

Socialism has been more successful in some countries than in others. This photo shows Denmark's clean and modern public transportation system. In France, on the other hand, street riots erupted when young people protested legislation that would have allowed businesses to fire younger workers, and the legislation was withdrawn. What other factors might lead to slower growth in socialist countries?

The Benefits of Socialism

The major benefit of socialism is supposed to be social equality. Ideally it comes about because the government takes income from wealthier people, in the form of taxes, and redistributes it to poorer people through various government programs. Free education through college, free health care, and free child care are some of the benefits socialist governments, using the money from taxes, may provide to their people. Workers in socialist countries usually get longer vacations, work fewer hours per week, and have more employee benefits (e.g., generous sick leave) than those in countries where free-market capitalism prevails.

The Negative Consequences of Socialism

Socialism may create more equality than capitalism, but it takes away some of businesspeople's incentives. For example, tax rates in some nations once reached 83 percent.[17] Today, doctors, lawyers, business owners, and others who earn a lot of money pay very high tax rates. As a consequence, many of them leave socialist countries for capitalistic countries with lower taxes, such as the United States. This loss of the best and brightest people to other countries is called a **brain drain**. What countries are raising taxes now?

Imagine an experiment in socialism in your own class. Imagine that after the first exam, those with grades of 90 and above have to give some of their points to those who make 70 and below so that everyone ends up with grades in the 80s. Would those who got 90s study as hard for the second exam? What about those who got 70s? Can you see why workers may not work as hard or as well if they all get the same benefits regardless of how hard they work?

Socialism also results in fewer inventions and less innovation, because those who come up with new ideas usually don't receive as much reward as they would in a capitalist system. Over the past decade or so, most socialist countries have simply not kept up with the United States in new inventions, job creation, or wealth creation. Communism may be considered a more intensive version of socialism. We shall explore that system next.

brain drain
The loss of the best and brightest people to other countries.

◀ PPT 2-29:
Socialism Benefits

◀ PPT 2-30:
The Negatives of Socialism

◀ PPT 2-31:
Communism

UNDERSTANDING COMMUNISM

Communism is an economic and political system in which the government makes almost all economic decisions and owns almost all the major factors of production. It intrudes further into the lives of people than socialism does. For example, some communist countries have not allowed their citizens to practice certain religions, change jobs, or move to the town of their choice.

communism
An economic and political system in which the government makes almost all economic decisions and owns almost all the major factors of production.

One problem with communism is that the government has no way of knowing what to produce, because prices don't reflect supply and demand as they do in free markets. The government must guess what the people need. As a result, shortages of many items, including food and clothing, may develop. Another problem is that communism doesn't inspire businesspeople to work hard because the incentives are not there. Therefore, communism is slowly disappearing as an economic form.

Most communist countries today are suffering severe economic depression. In North Korea, many people are starving. In Cuba, people suffer a lack of goods and services readily available in most other countries, and some fear the government. Even so, there seems to be a movement toward communist principles in Venezuela, following the Cuban model.[18]

While some parts of the former Soviet Union remain under communist ideals, Russia itself now has a flat tax of only 13 percent. Yet this low rate increased the government's tax revenues by nearly 30 percent, because more people were willing to pay. The trend toward free markets is growing in Vietnam and parts of China as well. The regions of China that are most free have prospered rapidly, while the rest of the country has grown relatively slowly. Remnants of China's communist system, such as political and religious oppression, still exist, however.

> **PPT 2-32:**
> Two Major Economic Systems

free-market economies
Economic systems in which the market largely determines what goods and services get produced, who gets them, and how the economy grows.

command economies
Economic systems in which the government largely decides what goods and services will be produced, who will get them, and how the economy will grow.

Since the communist system in Russia has largely collapsed, the country has been struggling to find its way toward a viable market economy. Poverty has begun to decline and a middle class is emerging, but many of the country's vast natural resources are difficult to tap. Laws that help promote business are few, and there is an active black market for many goods, but many observers are optimistic that Russia can prosper. What do you think?

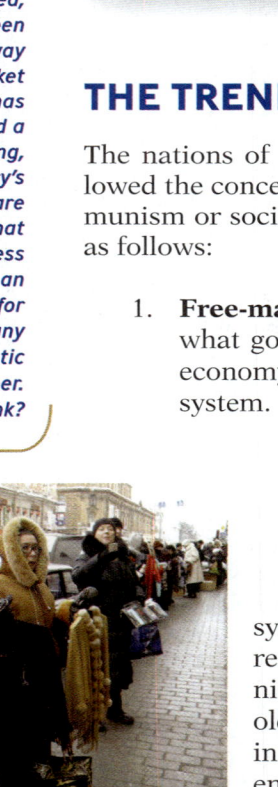

LEARNING goal 4 *

Analyze the trend toward mixed economies.

THE TREND TOWARD MIXED ECONOMIES

The nations of the world have largely been divided between those that followed the concepts of capitalism and those that adopted the concepts of communism or socialism. We can now contrast the two major economic systems as follows:

1. **Free-market economies** exist when the market largely determines what goods and services get produced, who gets them, and how the economy grows. *Capitalism* is the popular term for this economic system.

2. **Command economies** exist when the government largely decides what goods and services will be produced, who gets them, and how the economy will grow. *Socialism* and *communism* are variations on this economic system.

Although all countries actually have some mix of the two systems, neither free-market nor command economies have resulted in optimal economic conditions. Free-market mechanisms don't seem to respond enough to the needs of the poor, the old, or the disabled. Some people also believe that businesses in free-market economies have not done enough to protect the environment. (We shall discuss that issue throughout the text.) Over time, voters in mostly free-market countries, such as the United States, have elected officials who have adopted many social and environmental programs such as Social Security, welfare, unemployment compensation, and various clean air and

REACHING BEYOND our borders

www.yum.com

Prospering in Foreign Lands

China's government controls many of the country's businesses. Is it possible for a U.S. company to prosper there? Yum! Brands, which owns Taco Bell, KFC, and Pizza Hut, is so big in China that it has been reporting its Chinese earnings separately since 2005. A new KFC opened nearly every day in China in 2007, and KFCs and Pizza Huts now number more than 2,300 units. Yum! Brands expects to open 20,000 more units in China.

Selling chicken and pizza in China is one thing, but can Yum! Brands sell Taco Bell fare in Mexico? The company is trying its best. There are now 10 Taco Bells in Mexico, and the goal is 300 more. Taco Bell doesn't pretend to be Mexican. It describes itself as "Mexican inspired." The advertising slogan is "Es otra cosa" (It's something else). Surprisingly, Taco Bell has had a difficult time buying taco shells in Mexico. It now imports them from the United States.

You can find Yum! Brands just about everywhere in the world. What kinds of issues might the company encounter when trying to sell food in other countries?

Source: Lisa Takeuchi Cullen, "When Eat Meets West," *Time,* January 28, 2008; Daniel J. Isenberg, "The Global Entrepreneur," *Harvard Business Review,* December 2008; and Michael Elliott, "The New Global Opportunity," *Fortune,* July 5, 2010.

---

water acts. What new or enhanced social policies do you know of that are being considered today?

Socialism and communism haven't always created enough jobs or wealth to keep economies growing fast enough. Thus, communist governments are disappearing, and some socialist governments have been cutting back on social programs and lowering taxes on businesses and workers to generate more business growth and more revenue.[19] The Reaching Beyond Our Borders box discusses how U.S. companies are expanding overseas regardless of the economic system.

The trend, then, has been for mostly capitalist countries (like the United States) to move toward socialism (government takeover of banks, more involvement of the government in health care), and for mostly socialist countries, such as France and China, to move toward capitalism (more private businesses, lower taxes). All countries have some mix of the two systems. Thus, the long-term global trend is toward a blend of capitalism and socialism. This trend likely will increase with the opening of global markets made easier by the Internet. The net effect is the emergence throughout the world of mixed economies.

Mixed economies exist where some allocation of resources is made by the market and some by the government. Most countries don't have a name for such a system. If free-market mechanisms allocate most resources, the leaders call their system capitalism. If the government allocates most resources, the leaders call it socialism. Figure 2.4 compares the various economic systems.

Like most other nations of the world, the United States has a mixed economy. The U.S. government has now become the largest employer in the country,

◀ PPT 2-35:
Prospering in Foreign Lands

◀ PPT 2-33:
Mixed Economies

◀ PPT 2-34:
Trending Toward Mixed Economies

mixed economies
Economic systems in which some allocation of resources is made by the market and some by the government.

43

	CAPITALISM (United States)*	**SOCIALISM** (Sweden)	**COMMUNISM** (North Korea)	**MIXED ECONOMY** (Germany)
Social and Economic Goals	Private ownership of land and business. Liberty and the pursuit of happiness. Free trade. Emphasis on freedom and the profit motive for economic growth.	Public ownership of major businesses. Some private ownership of smaller businesses and shops. Government control of education, health care, utilities, mining, transportation, and media. Very high taxation. Emphasis on equality.	Public ownership of all businesses. Government-run education and health care. Emphasis on equality. Many limitations on freedom, including freedom to own businesses and to assemble to protest government actions.	Private ownership of land and business with government regulation. Government control of some institutions (e.g., mail). High taxation for defense and the common welfare. Emphasis on a balance between freedom and equality.
Motivation of Workers	Much incentive to work efficiently and hard because profits are retained by owners. Workers are rewarded for high productivity.	Capitalist incentives exist in private businesses. Government control of wages in public institutions limits incentives.	Very little incentive to work hard or to produce quality goods or services.	Incentives are similar to capitalism except in government-owned enterprises, which may have fewer incentives.
Control over Markets	Complete freedom of trade within and among nations. Some government control of markets.	Some markets are controlled by the government and some are free. Trade restrictions among nations vary and include some free-trade agreements.	Total government control over markets except for illegal transactions.	Some government control of trade within and among nations (trade protectionism).
Choices in the Market	A wide variety of goods and services is available. Almost no scarcity or oversupply exists for long because supply and demand control the market.	Variety in the marketplace varies considerably from country to country. Choice is directly related to government involvement in markets.	Very little choice among competing goods.	Similar to capitalism, but scarcity and oversupply may be caused by government involvement in the market (e.g., subsidies for farms).
Social Freedoms	Freedom of speech, press, assembly, religion, job choice, movement, and elections.	Similar to mixed economy. Governments may restrict job choice, movement among countries, and who may attend upper-level schools (i.e., college).	Very limited freedom to protest the government, practice religion, or change houses or jobs.	Some restrictions on freedoms of assembly and speech. Separation of church and state may limit religious practices in schools.

*The United States is a mixed economy based on a foundation of capitalism.

figure 2.4

COMPARISONS OF KEY ECONOMIC SYSTEMS

which means there are more workers in the public sector (government) than in any of the major businesses in the United States. Do you see the government growing or declining in the coming years?

progress assessment

- What led to the emergence of socialism?
- What are the benefits and drawbacks of socialism?
- What countries still practice communism?
- What are the characteristics of a mixed economy?

LEARNING goal 5 *

Describe the economic system of the United States, including the significance of key economic indicators (especially GDP), productivity, and the business cycle.

UNDERSTANDING THE U.S. ECONOMIC SYSTEM

The following sections will introduce the terms and concepts that you, as an informed citizen, will need to understand the issues facing government and business leaders in the United States.

Key Economic Indicators

Three major indicators of economic conditions are (1) the gross domestic product (GDP), (2) the unemployment rate, and (3) price indexes. Another important statistic is the increase or decrease in productivity. When you read business literature, you'll see these terms used again and again. Let's explore what they mean.

Gross Domestic Product **Gross domestic product (GDP)**, which we mentioned briefly in Chapter 1, is the total value of final goods and services produced in a country in a given year. Both domestic and foreign-owned companies can produce the goods and services included in GDP, as long as the companies are located within the country's boundaries. For example, production values from Japanese automaker Honda's factory in Ohio are included in U.S. GDP. Revenue generated by Ford's factory in Mexico is included in Mexico's GDP, even though Ford is a U.S. company.

Almost every discussion about a nation's economy is based on GDP. If growth in GDP slows or declines, businesses may feel many negative effects, such as the slowdown in retail sales experienced in 2008–2010. A major influence on the growth of GDP is the productivity of the workforce—that is,

gross domestic product (GDP)
The total value of final goods and services produced in a country in a given year.

The overall unemployment rate in the United States has been less than 5 percent but has risen to over 9 percent recently. Unemployment insurance goes only so far to relieve such unemployment. How high is the unemployment rate in your area?

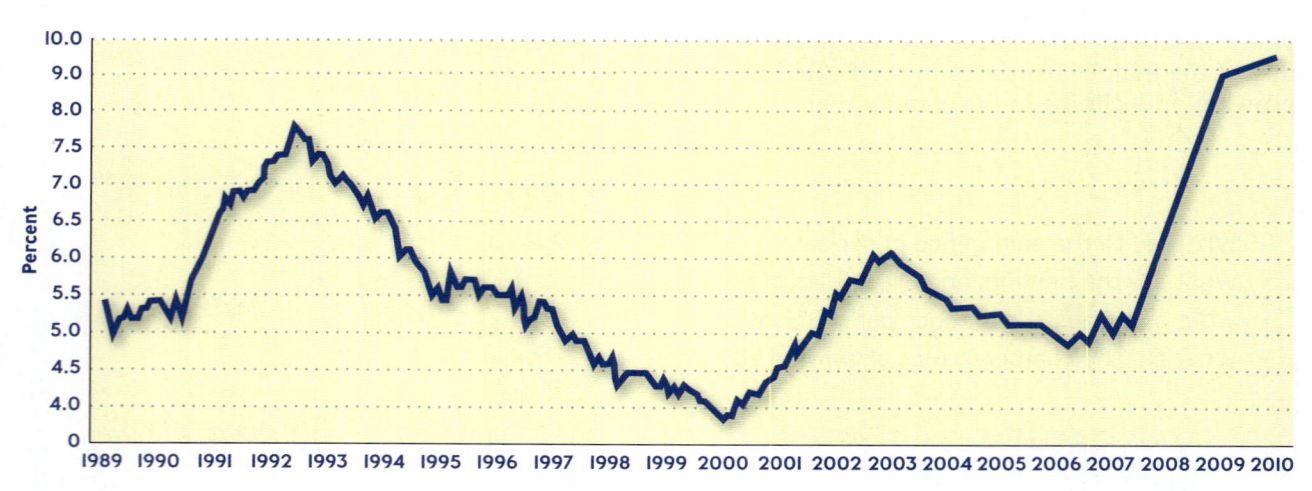

figure 2.5
U.S. UNEMPLOYMENT RATE 1989–2009

▶ PPT 2-38:
Who's Running the World?
▶ PPT 2-39:
The United States GDP

unemployment rate
The number of civilians at least 16 years old who are unemployed and tried to find a job within the prior four weeks.

▶ PPT 2-40:
Playing Catch Up
▶ PPT 2-41:
Unemployment
▶ PPT 2-42:
Unemployment Rate of the U.S.

how much output workers create with a given amount of input. The total U.S. GDP is about $14 trillion.[20] The level of U.S. economic activity is actually larger than the GDP figures show, because those figures don't take into account illicit activities such as sales of illegal drugs. The high GDP in the United States is what enables its citizens to enjoy a high standard of living.

The Unemployment Rate The **unemployment rate** refers to the percentage of civilians at least 16 years old who are unemployed *and tried to find a job within the prior four weeks.* In 2000, the U.S. unemployment rate reached its lowest point in over 30 years, falling as low as 3.9 percent, but by 2010 the rate had risen to over 9.5 percent and was estimated to be climbing higher (see Figure 2.5).

Figure 2.6 describes the four types of unemployment: frictional, structural, cyclical, and seasonal. The United States tries to protect those who are unemployed because of recessions (defined later in the chapter), industry shifts, and other cyclical factors.[21] Nonetheless, the underemployment figure in 2010 was about 17 percent.[22]

figure 2.6
TYPES OF UNEMPLOYMENT

FOUR KINDS OF UNEMPLOYMENT

- *Frictional unemployment* refers to those people who have quit work because they didn't like the job, the boss, or the working conditions and who haven't yet found a new job. It also refers to those people who are entering the labor force for the first time (e.g., new graduates) or are returning to the labor force after significant time away (e.g., parents who reared children). There will always be some frictional unemployment because it takes some time to find a first job or a new job.

- *Structural unemployment* refers to unemployment caused by the restructuring of firms or by a mismatch between the skills (or location) of job seekers and the requirements (or location) of available jobs (e.g., coal miners in an area where mines have been closed).

- *Cyclical unemployment* occurs because of a recession or a similar downturn in the business cycle (the ups and downs of business growth and decline over time). This type of unemployment is the most serious.

- *Seasonal unemployment* occurs where demand for labor varies over the year, as with the harvesting of crops.

If you worry about the U.S. unemployment rate, consider this: the unemployment rate in Zimbabwe is way over 80 percent, and the inflation rate is spectacular.[23] You would enjoy cashing in your dollars in Zimbabwe; one dollar will get you billions of Zimbabwean dollars.[24] Actually, the situation is getting much worse. Do you suppose Zimbabwe is a capitalist economy?

Inflation and Price Indexes Price indexes help gauge the health of the economy by measuring the levels of inflation, disinflation, deflation, and stagflation.[25] **Inflation** is a general rise in the prices of goods and services over time.[26] The official definition is "a persistent increase in the level of consumer prices or a persistent decline in the purchasing power of money, caused by an increase in available currency and credit beyond the proportion of goods and services."[27] Thus, it is also described as "too many dollars chasing too few goods."[28] Go back and review the laws of supply and demand to see how that works. Rapid inflation is scary. If the prices of goods and services go up by just 7 percent a year, they will double in about 10 years. Think of how much fear was generated by the rapid increase in the price of gasoline in 2008–2009.

Disinflation occurs when price increases are slowing (the inflation rate is declining). That was the situation in the United States throughout the 1990s. **Deflation** means that prices are declining. It occurs when countries produce so many goods that people cannot afford to buy them all (too few dollars are chasing too many goods). Several articles indicated that deflation would occur in 2010.[29] **Stagflation** occurs when the economy is slowing but prices are going up anyhow.[30] Some economists fear the United States may face stagflation in the near future.[31]

The **consumer price index (CPI)** consists of monthly statistics that measure the pace of inflation or deflation. The government computes costs of goods and services—including housing, food, apparel, and medical care—to see whether they are going up or down (see Figure 2.7). The CPI is an important figure because some wages and salaries, rents and leases, tax brackets, government benefits, and interest rates are based on it. You may see the term *core inflation*. That means the CPI minus food and energy costs. Since food and energy have been going up rapidly, the core inflation figure is lower than the CPI.[32]

The government created a new index called the chained consumer price index (C-CPI). The CPI failed to take into account that consumers would shift their purchases as prices go up or down. For example, if the price of beef goes up, consumers may switch to chicken, which is less expensive. The C-CPI factors in such decisions; thus, it is usually a lower figure. There is still much debate about government figures on inflation.[33] One only has to look at

◀ **LECTURE LINK 2-3:**
Other Economic Indicators

◀ **LECTURE LINK 2-4:**
New Economic Measures

◀ **PPT 2-43:**
Inflation

inflation
A general rise in the prices of goods and services over time.

disinflation
A situation in which price increases are slowing (the inflation rate is declining).

deflation
A situation in which prices are declining.

stagflation
A situation when the economy is slowing but prices are going up anyhow.

consumer price index (CPI)
Monthly statistics that measure the pace of inflation or deflation.

◀ **PPT 2-44:**
Price Index
◀ **PPT 2-45:**
Productivity
◀ **PPT 2-46:**
Productivity in the Service Sector

figure 2.7

HOW THE CONSUMER PRICE INDEX IS PUT TOGETHER

1. 400 data collectors visit stores and gather 80,000 retail price quotes and 5,000 housing rent quotes, transmitting data daily to Washington.
2. 40 commodity analysts at the Bureau of Labor Statistics review about a quarter of this avalanche of price data.
3. About nine days before the release of the CPI, the office is locked down—with bright red RESTRICTED AREA signs posted on all the doors.
4. 90 people—a mix of commodity analysts and other economists who specialize in assembling the CPI—compute basic indexes for 211 item categories, which are divided into 38 index areas.
5. Final results are released at 8:30 a.m., Eastern time, about two weeks after the end of the month in question.

producer price index (PPI)
An index that measures prices at the wholesale level.

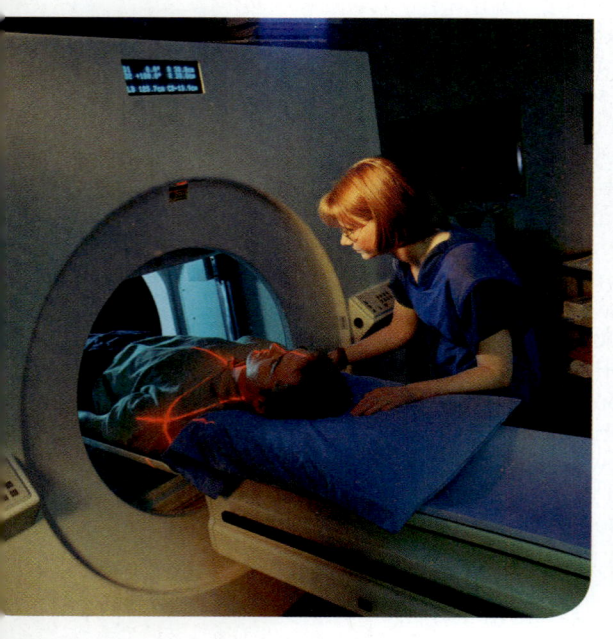

the rising price of milk and other consumer products to see that government-reported inflation may be less than we are actually experiencing.[34]

The **producer price index (PPI)** measures prices at the wholesale level. Other indicators of the economy's condition include housing starts, retail sales, and changes in personal income. You can learn more about such indicators by reading business periodicals, listening to business broadcasts on radio and television, and exploring business sites on the Internet.

Productivity in the United States

An increase in productivity means a worker can produce more goods and services than before in the same time period, usually thanks to machinery or other equipment. Productivity in the United States has risen because computers and other technology have made production faster and easier. The higher productivity, the lower the costs of producing goods and services, and the lower prices can be. Therefore, businesspeople are eager to increase productivity. Remember, however, that high productivity can lead to high unemployment.

Now that the U.S. economy is a service economy, productivity is an issue because service firms are so labor-intensive. Spurred by foreign competition, productivity in the manufacturing sector is rising rapidly. In the service sector, productivity is growing more slowly because service workers—like teachers, clerks, lawyers, and barbers—have fewer new technologies available than there are for factory workers.

It can be difficult to accurately measure productivity in service industries because new technologies, like high-tech medical scanning, can greatly improve the quality of services provided without necessarily increasing the number of people served. A doctor can make much more accurate diagnoses with scans, for instance, but can still see only so many patients in a day. How can productivity measures try to capture improvements in the quality of service?

Productivity in the Service Sector

One problem with the service industry is that an influx of machinery may add to the *quality* of the service provided but not to the *output per worker*. For example, you've probably noticed how many computers there are on college campuses. They add to the quality of education but don't necessarily boost professors' productivity. The same is true of some equipment in hospitals, such as CAT scanners, PET scanners, and MRI scanners. They improve patient care but don't necessarily increase the number of patients doctors can see. In other words, today's productivity measures in the service industry fail to capture the increase in quality caused by new technology.

Clearly, the United States and other countries need to develop new measures of productivity for the service economy that include quality as well as quantity of output. Despite productivity improvement, the economy is likely to go through a series of ups and downs, much as it has over the past few years. We'll explore that process next.

The Business Cycle

Business cycles are the periodic rises and falls that occur in economies over time. Economists look at a number of business cycles, from seasonal cycles that occur within a year to cycles that occur every 48–60 years.[35]

Economist Joseph Schumpeter identified the four phases of long-term business cycles as boom–recession–depression–recovery:

1. An *economic boom* is just what it sounds like—business is booming.
2. **Recession** is two or more consecutive quarters of decline in the GDP.[36] In a recession prices fall, people purchase fewer products, and

business cycles
The periodic rises and falls that occur in economies over time.

▶ PPT 2-47:
Business Cycles

recession
Two or more consecutive quarters of decline in the GDP.

businesses fail.[37] A recession brings high unemployment, increased business failures, and an overall drop in living standards. The 2008–2010 recession is an example.

3. A **depression** is a severe recession, usually accompanied by deflation. Business cycles rarely go through a depression phase. In fact, while there were many business cycles during the 20th century, there was only one severe depression (1930s).[38] Nonetheless some economists are predicting a depression in the coming years.[39]

4. A *recovery* occurs when the economy stabilizes and starts to grow. This eventually leads to an economic boom, starting the cycle all over again.

depression
A severe recession, usually accompanied by deflation.

◄ LECTURE LINK 2-5:
What Is a Depression?

One goal of some economists is to predict such ups and downs. That is very difficult to do. Business cycles are identified according to facts, but we can explain those facts only by using theories. Therefore, we cannot predict with certainty. But one thing is certain: over time, the economy *will* rise and fall as it has done lately.

Since dramatic swings up and down in the economy cause all kinds of disruptions to businesses, the government tries to minimize such changes. It uses fiscal policy and monetary policy to try to keep the economy from slowing too much or growing too rapidly.

LEARNING goal 6 *

Contrast fiscal policy and monetary policy, and explain how each affects the economy.

Stabilizing the Economy through Fiscal Policy

Fiscal policy refers to the federal government's efforts to keep the economy stable by increasing or decreasing taxes or government spending. The first fiscal policy tool is taxation. Theoretically, high tax rates tend to slow the economy because they draw money away from the private sector and put it into the government. High tax rates may discourage small-business ownership because they decrease the profits businesses can earn and make the effort less rewarding. It follows, then, that low tax rates will theoretically give the economy a boost.[40]

In the United States, the percentage of GDP the government takes through taxes at all levels (federal, state, and local) is about 28.2 percent.[41] When you count all fees, sales taxes, and more, taxes on the highest-earning citizens could exceed 50 percent. Is that figure too high or not high enough in your opinion? Why?

The second fiscal policy tool is government spending on highways, social programs, education, infrastructure (e.g., roads and utilities), defense, and so on. The *national deficit* is the amount of money the federal government spends beyond what it gathers in taxes for a given fiscal year. The 2008 federal budget, for example, had a projected deficit of $407 billion.[42] The deficit is expected to rise to over $1 trillion for several years. Such deficits increase the national debt. The **national debt** is the sum of government deficits over time. Recently, the national debt was over $13 trillion (see Figure 2.8 on p. 50) and was growing at a rate of $3.5 billion a day.[43] That is a rather misleading number,

fiscal policy
The federal government's efforts to keep the economy stable by increasing or decreasing taxes or government spending.

◄ PPT 2-48:
Fiscal Policy

◄ CRITICAL THINKING
EXERCISE 2-5:
Balancing the Federal Budget

national debt
The sum of government deficits over time.

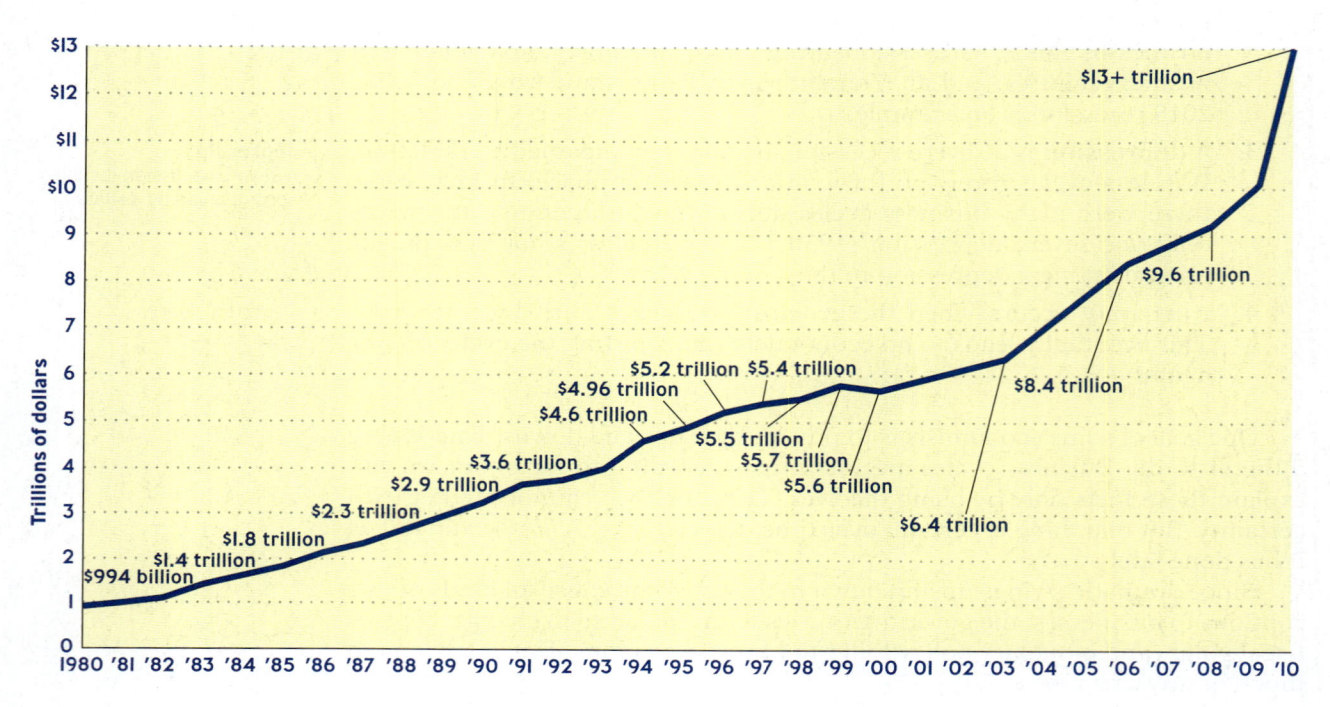

figure 2.8

THE NATIONAL DEBT
Source: Government data.

A line graph titled "Trillions of dollars" shows the national debt from 1980 to 2010:
- 1980: $994 billion
- $1.4 trillion
- $1.8 trillion
- $2.3 trillion
- $2.9 trillion
- $3.6 trillion
- $4.6 trillion
- $4.96 trillion
- $5.2 trillion
- $5.4 trillion
- $5.5 trillion
- $5.7 trillion
- $5.6 trillion
- $6.4 trillion
- $8.4 trillion
- $9.6 trillion
- $13+ trillion

▶ **PPT 2-49:**
National Deficits, Debt, and Surplus

▶ **PPT 2-50:**
What's Our National Debt?

▶ **PPT 2-51:**
What Can a _____ Dollars Buy

▶ **LECTURE LINK 2-6:**
Capitalism in Crisis

Keynesian economic theory
The theory that a government policy of increasing spending and cutting taxes could stimulate the economy in a recession.

however, since the unfunded obligation for Medicare alone is about $34 trillion.[44] The unfunded debt to Social Security is on top of that. If the government takes in more revenue than it spends (i.e., tax revenues exceed expenditures), there is a *national surplus*. That is not likely to happen soon.

One way to lessen deficits is to cut government spending. Many presidents have promised to make the government "smaller," that is, to reduce government spending—but that doesn't happen very often. There seems to be a need for more social programs or more defense spending (such as for the wars in Iraq and Afghanistan) each year, and thus the deficits continue and add to the national debt. Some people believe that government spending helps the economy grow. Others believe that the money the government spends comes out of the pockets of consumers and businesspeople, and thus slows growth. What do you think?

Fiscal Policy in Action during the Economic Crisis of 2008–2010

For most of his presidency, George W. Bush followed the basic economic principles of free markets. By the end of his term, however, the economy was facing a dire economic crisis and President Bush approved the spending of almost $1 trillion of government money in an effort to revive the failing economy (including helping out banks, the auto industry, and others). President Barack Obama promised to spend additional trillions. A trillion dollars is about $3,272 per person in the United States. Both presidents were following a basic economic theory (fiscal policy).

John Maynard Keynes (pronounced *Canes*) wrote a book called *The General Theory of Employment, Interest and Money* in 1936. **Keynesian economic theory** and later adaptations suggest a government policy of increasing spending (e.g., on infrastructure—roads, bridges, schools, and utilities) and cutting taxes could stimulate the economy in a recession. Policy related to taxes and spending is called *fiscal policy*. The goal of cutting taxes would be to increase consumer spending to revive businesses. Conversely, when the economy seems to be growing too fast, Keynesian theory suggests cutting back on government spending and increasing taxes. Such government intervention is supposed to be a short-term solution to wide swings in the business cycle. Once the economy was stabilized, Keynes believed, then free economic principles could be restored. Presidents George W. Bush and Barack Obama adopted Keynesian principles to stem the economic crisis.[45] You will see the results over the coming years.[46]

Using Monetary Policy to Keep the Economy Growing

Have you ever wondered what organization adds or subtracts money from the economy? The answer is the Federal Reserve Bank (the Fed). The Fed is a semiprivate organization that is not under the direct control of the government but does have members appointed by the president. We will discuss the Fed in detail when we look at banking in Chapter 20. Now we simply introduce monetary policy and the role of the Fed in controlling the economy.

Monetary policy is the management of the money supply and interest rates by the Federal Reserve Bank. The Fed's most visible role is the raising and lowering of interest rates. When the economy is booming, the Fed tends to raise interest rates. This makes money more expensive to borrow. Businesses thus borrow less, and the economy slows as businesspeople spend less money on everything they need to grow, including labor and machinery. The opposite is true when the Fed lowers interest rates. Businesses tend to borrow more, and the economy is expected to grow. Raising and lowering interest rates should therefore help control the rapid ups and downs of the economy. In 2010, the Fed kept interest rates near zero, but the economy remained sluggish.[47]

> **monetary policy**
> The management of the money supply and interest rates by the Federal Reserve Bank.

The Fed also controls the money supply. A simple explanation of this function is that the more money the Fed makes available to businesspeople and others, the faster the economy is supposed to grow. To slow the economy (and prevent inflation), the Fed lowers the money supply. The Fed poured money into the economy in 2008–2010. What would you expect the result to be? Is that what happened?

To sum up, there are two major tools for managing the economy of the United States: fiscal policy (government taxes and spending) and monetary policy (the Fed's control over interest rates and the money supply). The goal is to keep the economy growing so that more people can rise up the economic ladder and enjoy a higher standard of living and quality of life.

The economic crisis of 2008–2010 caused much anguish among Wall Street workers and people in general. How effective was the government's response?

progress assessment

- Name the three economic indicators and describe how well the United States is doing based on each indicator.
- What's the difference between a recession and a depression?
- How does the government manage the economy using fiscal policy?
- What does the term *monetary policy* mean? What organization is responsible for monetary policy?

summary

Learning Goal 1. Explain basic economics.
- **What is economics?**

Economics is the study of how society chooses to employ resources to produce goods and services and distribute them for consumption among various competing groups and individuals.
- **What are the two branches of economics?**

There are two major branches of economics: macroeconomics studies the operation of a nation's economy as a whole, and microeconomics studies the behavior of people and organizations in particular markets (e.g., why people buy smaller cars when gas prices go up).
- **How can we be assured of having enough resources?**

Resource development is the study of how to increase resources and create the conditions that will make better use of them.
- **How does capitalism create a climate for economic growth?**

Under capitalism, businesspeople don't often deliberately set out to help others; they work mostly for their own prosperity and growth. Yet people's efforts to improve their own situation in life act like an *invisible hand* to help the economy grow and prosper through the production of needed goods, services, and ideas.

Learning Goal 2. Explain what capitalism is and how free markets work.
- **What is capitalism?**

Capitalism is an economic system in which all or most of the means of production and distribution are privately owned and operated for profit.
- **Who decides what to produce under capitalism?**

In capitalist countries, businesspeople decide what to produce, how much to pay workers, and how much to charge for goods and services. They also decide whether to produce certain goods in their own countries, import those goods, or have them made in other countries.
- **What are the basic rights people have under capitalism?**

The four basic rights under capitalism are (1) the right to private property, (2) the right to own a business and to keep all of that business's profits after taxes, (3) the right to freedom of competition, and (4) the right to freedom of choice. President Franklin D. Roosevelt felt that other economic freedoms were also important: the right to freedom of speech and expression, the right to worship in your own way, and freedom from want and fear.
- **How does the free market work?**

The free market is one in which buyers and sellers negotiating prices for goods and services influence the decisions about what gets produced and in what quantities. Buyers' decisions in the marketplace tell sellers what to produce and in what quantity. When buyers demand more goods, the price goes up, signaling suppliers to produce more. The higher the price, the more goods and services suppliers are willing to produce. Price is the mechanism that allows free markets to work.

Learning Goal 3. Compare socialism and communism.
- **What is socialism?**

Socialism is an economic system based on the premise that some businesses should be owned by the government.
- **What are the advantages and disadvantages of socialism?**

Socialism intends to create more social equity. Workers in socialist countries usually receive more education, health care, and other benefits and also work fewer hours, with longer vacations. The major disadvantage of socialism is that it lowers the incentive to start a business or to work hard. Socialist economies tend to have a higher unemployment rate and a slower growth rate than capitalist economies.

- **How does socialism differ from communism?**

Under communism, the government owns almost all major production facilities and dictates what gets produced and by whom. Communism is also more restrictive when it comes to personal freedoms, such as religious freedom.

Learning Goal 4. Analyze the trend toward mixed economies.

- **What is a mixed economy?**

A mixed economy is part capitalist and part socialist. Some businesses are privately owned, but taxes tend to be high to distribute income more evenly among the population.

- **What countries have mixed economies?**

The United States has a mixed economy, as do most other developed countries.

- **What are the benefits of mixed economies?**

A mixed economy has most of the benefits of wealth creation that free markets bring plus the benefits of greater social equality and concern for the environment that socialism promises.

Learning Goal 5. Describe the economic system of the United States, including the significance of key economic indicators (especially GDP), productivity, and the business cycle.

- **What are the key economic indicators in the United States?**

Gross domestic product (GDP) is the total value of final goods and services produced in a country in a given year. The *unemployment rate* refers to the percentage of civilians at least 16 years old who are unemployed and tried to find a job within the most recent four weeks. The *consumer price index (CPI)* measures changes in the prices of about 400 goods and services that consumers buy.

- **What are the four phases of business cycles?**

In an *economic boom,* businesses do well. A *recession* occurs when two or more quarters show declines in the GDP, prices fall, people purchase fewer products, and businesses fail. A *depression* is a severe recession. *Recovery* occurs when the economy stabilizes and starts to grow.

Learning Goal 6. Contrast fiscal policy and monetary policy, and explain how each affects the economy.

- **What is Keynesian economics?**

The idea is to increase government spending and cut taxes in order to stimulate the economy when the economy is in a recession. When the economy seems to be growing too fast, the idea is to cut back on government spending or increase taxes.

- **What is fiscal policy?**

Fiscal policy consists of government efforts to keep the economy stable by increasing or decreasing taxes or government spending.

- **What is the importance of monetary policy to the economy?**

Monetary policy is the management of the money supply and interest rates. When unemployment gets too high, the Federal Reserve Bank (the Fed) may put more money into the economy and lower interest rates. That is supposed to provide a boost to the economy as businesses borrow and spend more money and hire more people.

key terms

brain drain 41	gross domestic product (GDP) 45	oligopoly 39
business cycles 48	inflation 47	perfect competition 39
capitalism 35	invisible hand 33	producer price index (PPI) 48
command economies 42	Keynesian economic theory 50	recession 48
communism 41	macroeconomics 30	resource development 31
consumer price index (CPI) 47	market price 39	socialism 40
deflation 47	microeconomics 30	stagflation 47
demand 37	mixed economies 43	supply 37
depression 49	monetary policy 51	unemployment rate 46
disinflation 47	monopolistic competition 39	
economics 30	monopoly 39	
fiscal policy 49	national debt 49	
free-market economies 42		

connect interactive applications

Reinforcing Your *Connection* to Concepts in Business

This chapter offers 15 interactive applications designed to help you apply what you've learned (examples of these exercises appear below). Your instructor has determined which interactive applications will benefit you throughout this course. Please refer to your instructor's assignment list in *Connect* to determine which applications you should complete.

Click and Drag Interactive: Businesses must provide customers with high-quality products at fair prices with good service. If they don't, they lose customers to businesses that do. For each industry, identify the appropriate type of competition and drag it to the appropriate spot on the chart.

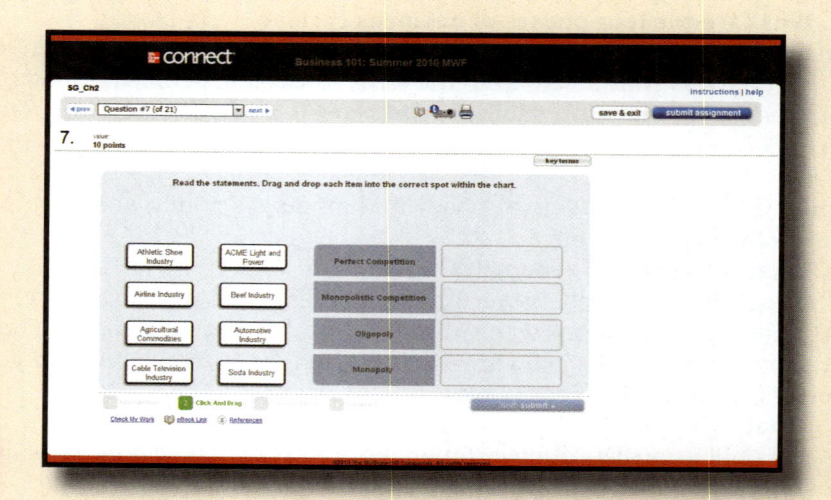

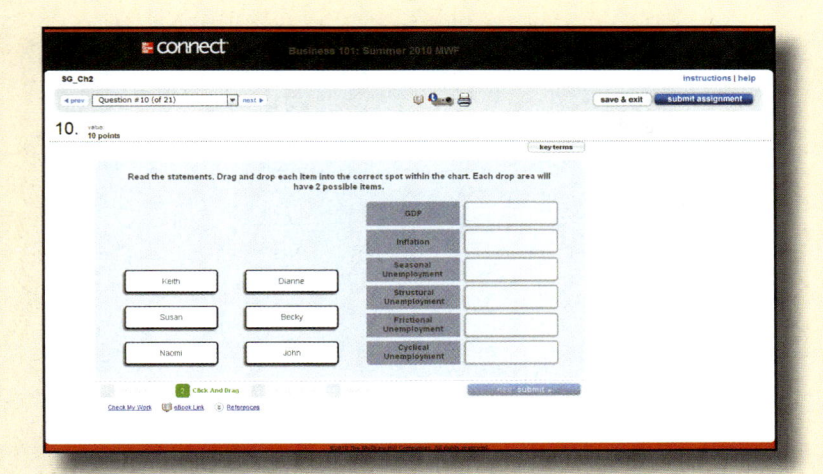

Click and Drag Interactive: The health of the economy of the United States is measured by three major indicators, which include the gross domestic product, the unemployment rate, and price indices. The gross domestic product is the total value of goods and services produced in a country in a year. The unemployment rate measures how many people age 16 or older are out of work. Finally, price indices, which include the consumer price index (CPI) and the producer price index (PPI), measure the pace of inflation and prices at the wholesale level. All of these indicators help us determine the health of the economy in the United States. For this click-and-drag activity, read the statements and drop each item into the correct spot within the chart. Each drop area has two possible items.

Click and Drag Interactive: The different economic systems include capitalism, socialism, communism, and mixed-economies. Each of these economic systems has distinct advantages and disadvantages that can span social and economic goals, worker motivation, market control, market choices, and social freedoms. In this click-and-drag activity, you will read each statement when it appears and place the activity in the correct box in the chart on the right.

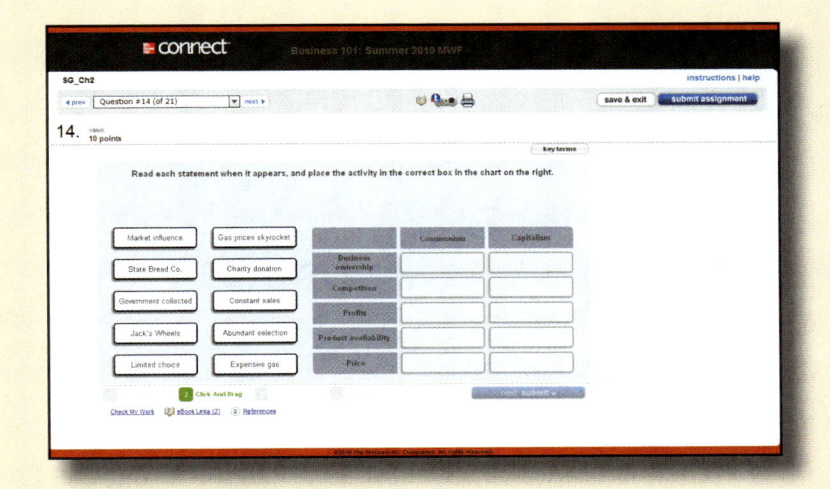

Click and Drag Interactive: Prices are set by buyers and sellers in free market capitalism. The microeconomic concepts of supply and demand establish prices based on buyers and sellers negotiating. Identify the component of the supply and demand chart using the appropriate terminology.

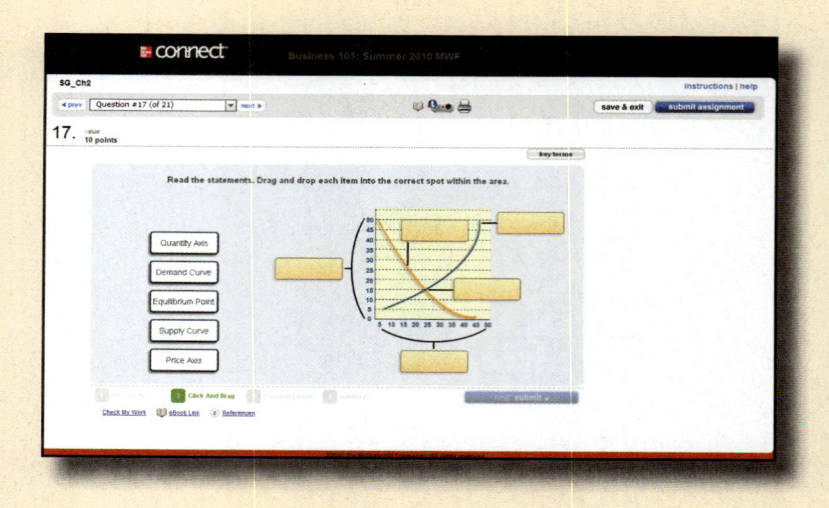

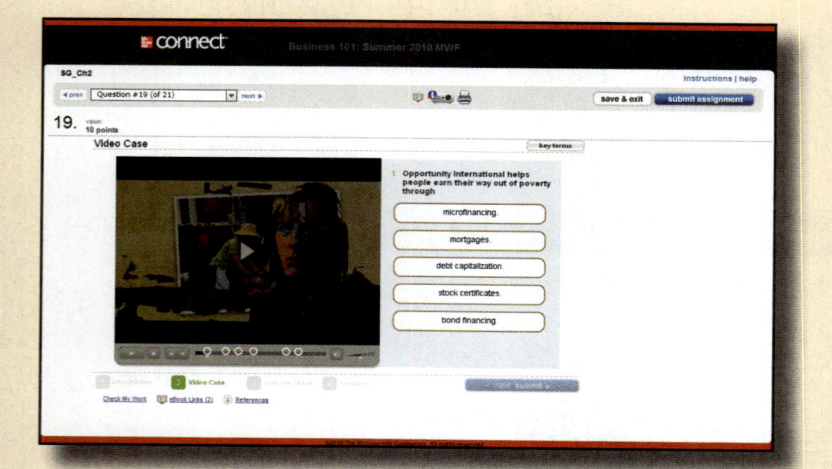

Video Case Interactive: Based on his economic theories, Adam Smith is considered to be the father of modern economics. While others have challenged Smith's theory, it remains one of the basic foundations of the study of economics. Watch the video, *Opportunity International,* and answer the questions as they appear.

3 DOING Business in Global MARKETS

> PPT 3-1:
> Doing Business in Global Markets

> PPT 3-2:
> Sheikha Lubna Al-Quasimi

profile

Getting to Know Sheikha Lubna al-Qasimi
Foreign Trade Minister of the United Arab Emirates

Sheikha Lubna al-Qasimi, the first female foreign trade minister of the United Arab Emirates (UAE), is not like any other trade minister. She's a princess (*sheikha*) who has her own perfume line and who has been described affectionately as a mix of Carly Fiorina (former CEO of Hewlett-Packard), Condoleezza Rice (former secretary of state), and Oprah Winfrey.

One of the most influential women in the Middle East, Sheikha Lubna is comfortable with political and business leaders throughout the world, including former presidents Bill Clinton and George W. Bush and Microsoft founder Bill Gates. Sheikha Lubna is an atypical Arab woman. For example, she firmly shakes hands with men when greeting them, something most Arab women would never consider. Effective leaders in global business acknowledge the practices of other cultures, and Sheikha Lubna very much understands the importance of doing so. As she travels the world, Sheikha Lubna adapts her personal communication processes to match the culture of the person with whom she is interacting.

Though born into the extended royal family of Sharjah, Sheikha Lubna has embraced ambitions and desires beyond what is generally expected of Arab royalty. She learned English in Britain and, at the urging of her two brothers, moved to California for college. After completing her degree in technology at California State University at 22 years old, she returned to the UAE and took a job with an Indian software firm. As her notoriety for her work in the software industry grew, she became the first woman to earn a post on the management team of the Dubai Ports Authority. Though frequently dismissed as a secretary by her male counterparts at the authority, Sheikha Lubna developed a computerized cargo manifest system that won her a $5 million grant to develop her own e-commerce company, Tejari.com. Success at Tejari.com earned her a post in the UAE cabinet as minister of economy and planning. She launched her own perfume line in 2007, and she was named the UAE's first minister of foreign trade in 2008.

LEARNING goals

After you have read and studied this chapter, you should be able to

1. Discuss the importance of the global market and the roles of comparative advantage and absolute advantage in global trade.
2. Explain the importance of importing and exporting, and understand key terms used in global business.
3. Illustrate the strategies used in reaching global markets and explain the role of multinational corporations.
4. Evaluate the forces that affect trading in global markets.
5. Debate the advantages and disadvantages of trade protectionism.
6. Discuss the changing landscape of the global market and the issue of offshore outsourcing.

connect

Your *Connection* to Better Learning. 1. View the interactive presentation. 2. Practice through LearnSmart. 3. Apply your knowledge by using the interactive applications for each chapter of this text.

1 Prep »»»»» 2 Study »»»»» 3 Apply

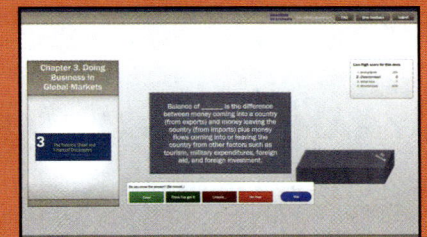

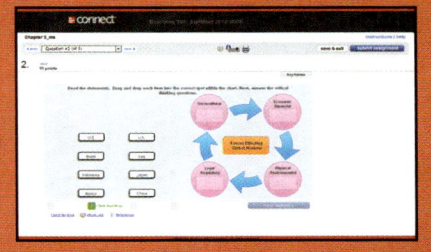

The UAE is less than 40 years old, young by country standards, but is already booming economically. Major businesses have offices in Dubai, a tourist hot spot sometimes called the Las Vegas of the Middle East. Much of this success is due to Sheikha Lubna's efforts. "I think we've achieved a great deal in a generation," she says. Sheikha Lubna is proud of her personal triumphs as well as her country's progress. "My proudest achievement is that I am a bridge," she says. "Women are following my example. I am changing the mindset of young girls, saying, 'It's okay. Look, I'm here. I'm on the other side, and you can breeze through.' . . . Not bad for a geek with a perfume."

Sheikha Lubna al-Qasimi is an example of an emerging global businessperson. She has learned to speak languages, understands cultural and economic differences, and is well schooled in technology. This chapter explains the opportunities and challenges businesspeople like Sheikha Lubna face every day in dealing with the dynamic environment of global business.

Sources: John Arlidge, "Mover *and* Sheikha," *Conde Nast Portfolio*, June 2008; www.tejari.com accessed August 16, 2010; Hassan M. Fattah, "Chipping at Glass Ceiling from Peak of Power," *International Herald Tribune*, November 11, 2006; and "UAE is Boosting Its Economic Achievements Through Economic Diversification," Emirates News Agency, June 22, 2010.

www.tejari.com

NAME THAT company

As I traveled through Italy, I fell in love with the unique coffee shops scattered throughout the towns. Each café was its own little community where people would meet, do work, or simply enjoy the coffee. When I returned to the United States, I knew I had to create this same atmosphere for my countrymen. My name is Howard Shultz. Name my company. (Find the answer in the chapter.)

LEARNING goal 1 *

Discuss the importance of the global market and the roles of comparative advantage and absolute advantage in global trade.

> PPT 3-3:
> Business in the Global Market

THE DYNAMIC GLOBAL MARKET

Have you dreamed of traveling to cities like Paris, Tokyo, Rio de Janeiro, or Cairo? Today, over 90 percent of the companies doing business globally believe it's important for their employees to have experience working in other countries.[1] The reason is not surprising—although the United States is a market of over 300 *million* people, there are over 6.8 *billion* potential customers in the 194 countries that make up the global market.[2] That's too many people to ignore. (See Figure 3.1 for a map of the world and important statistics about world population.)

Today U.S. consumers buy billions of dollars' worth of goods from China.[3] United Parcel Service (UPS) experienced double-digit market growth in its global operations and continues to expand abroad, most recently into Vietnam.[4] Major League Baseball opened its 2008 season in Japan.[5] The National Basketball Association (NBA) and the National Football League (NFL) play games in Mexico, Italy, England, and elsewhere. Chinese-born Yao Ming of the NBA's Houston Rockets is one of the most recognized athletes in the world.[6] U.S. film stars Johnny Depp, Will Smith, and Julia Roberts draw crowds to movie theaters around the globe.

Because the global market is so large, it is important to understand the language of international trade. For example, **importing** is buying products

> The New York Giants were the "away" team to the "host" Miami Dolphins at London's Wembley Stadium for the NFL's first regular-season game to be played outside North America. Major League Baseball opened its 2008 season in Japan, and the NBA now plays games in several countries around the world. What cultural factors must U.S. sports franchises overcome to increase their popularity abroad?

importing
Buying products from another country.

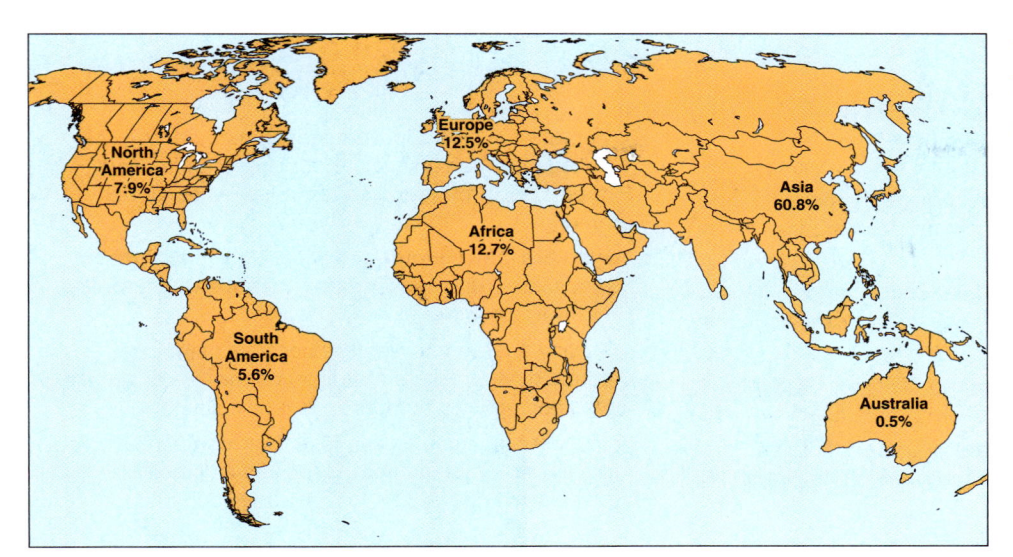

figure 3.1

WORLD POPULATION BY CONTINENT

from another country. **Exporting** is selling products to another country. The United States is the largest importing nation in the world.[7] It is the third largest exporting nation, behind China and Germany.[8] As you might suspect, competition among exporting nations is intense.

This chapter will familiarize you with global business and its many challenges. As competition in global markets increases, the demand for students with training in global business is almost certain to grow. If you choose such a career, prepare yourself to work hard and always be ready for new challenges.

WHY TRADE WITH OTHER NATIONS?

No nation, not even a technologically advanced one, can produce all the products its people want and need. Even if a country did become self-sufficient, other nations would seek to trade with it to meet the needs of their own people. Some nations like Venezuela and Russia have an abundance of natural resources but limited technological know-how. Other countries, such as Japan and Switzerland, have sophisticated technology but few natural resources. Global trade enables a nation to produce what it is most capable of producing and buy what it needs from others in a mutually beneficial exchange relationship. This happens through the process called free trade.[9]

Free trade is the movement of goods and services among nations without political or economic barriers. It has become a hotly debated concept.[10] In fact, many in the United States take the position "fair trade, not free trade."[11] Figure 3.2 on p. 62 offers some of the pros and cons of free trade.

The Theories of Comparative and Absolute Advantage

Countries exchange more than goods and services, however. They also exchange art, sports, cultural events, medical advances, space exploration, and labor. Comparative advantage theory, suggested in the early 19th century by English economist David Ricardo, was the guiding principle that supported the idea of free economic exchange.[12]

Comparative advantage theory states that a country should sell to other countries those products it produces most effectively and efficiently, and buy from other countries those products it cannot produce as effectively or efficiently. The United States has a comparative advantage in producing goods and

exporting
Selling products to another country.

◀ PPT 3-4:
World Population by Continent

◀ PPT 3-5:
Importing and Exporting

◀ PPT 3-6:
Where Are They From?

◀ PPT 3-7:
Can You Spare a Dime?

◀ PPT 3-8:
Trading with Other Nations

◀ PPT 3-9:
How Free Trade Benefits the World

free trade
The movement of goods and services among nations without political or economic barriers.

◀ PPT 3-10:
Comparative and Absolute Advantage

comparative advantage theory
Theory that states that a country should sell to other countries those products that it produces most effectively and efficiently, and buy from other countries those products that it cannot produce as effectively or efficiently.

PROS	CONS
• The global market contains over 6.8 billion potential customers for goods and services.
• Productivity grows when countries produce goods and services in which they have a comparative advantage.
• Global competition and less-costly imports keep prices down, so inflation does not curtail economic growth.
• Free trade inspires innovation for new products and keeps firms competitively challenged.
• Uninterrupted flow of capital gives countries access to foreign investments, which help keep interest rates low.	• Domestic workers (particularly in manufacturing-based jobs) can lose their jobs due to increased imports or production shifts to low-wage global markets.
• Workers may be forced to accept pay cuts from employers, who can threaten to move their jobs to lower-cost global markets.
• Moving operations overseas because of intense competitive pressure often means the loss of service jobs and growing numbers of white-collar jobs.
• Domestic companies can lose their comparative advantage when competitors build advanced production operations in low-wage countries.

figure 3.2

THE PROS AND CONS OF FREE TRADE

services, such as software and engineering services. In contrast, it lacks a comparative advantage in growing coffee or making shoes; thus, we import most of the shoes and coffee we consume. By specializing and trading, the United States and its trading partners can realize mutually beneficial exchanges.[13]

absolute advantage
The advantage that exists when a country has a monopoly on producing a specific product or is able to produce it more efficiently than all other countries.

A country has an **absolute advantage** if it has a monopoly on producing a specific product or is able to produce it more efficiently than all other countries. However, absolute advantage in natural resources does not last forever: for instance, South Africa once had an absolute advantage in diamond production, but that is no longer the case. Global competition also causes other absolute advantages to fade. Today there are very few instances of absolute advantage in global markets.

LEARNING goal 2 *

Explain the importance of importing and exporting, and understand key terms used in global business.

GETTING INVOLVED IN GLOBAL TRADE

People interested in a job in global business often think they are limited to firms like Boeing, Ford, or IBM, which have large multinational accounts.[14] However, the real global job potential may be with small businesses. In the United States, small businesses now account for almost half of private sector commerce, but only about 30 percent of small businesses export. With the help and encouragement of the U.S. Department of Commerce, however, by 2018 half these businesses are expected to be engaged in global trade.[15]

▶ PPT 3-11:
Going Global with a Small Business

▶ PPT 3-12:
Where Do They Invest?

Getting started globally is often a matter of observing, being determined, and taking risks. For example, years ago a U.S. traveler in an African country noticed there was no ice available for drinks or for keeping foods fresh. Further research showed there was no ice factory for hundreds of miles, yet the market seemed huge. The man returned to the United States, found some investors, and returned to Africa to build an ice-making plant. The job was tough; much negotiation was necessary with local authorities (and was often best done by local citizens and businesspeople who know the system). But the plant was built, and this forward-thinking entrepreneur gained a considerable return on his idea, while the people gained a needed product.

Importing Goods and Services

Students attending colleges and universities abroad often notice that some products widely available in their countries are unavailable or more expensive elsewhere. By working with producers in their native country, finding some start-up financing, and putting in long hours of hard work, many have become major importers while still in school.

Howard Schultz, CEO of Starbucks, found his opportunity while traveling in Italy. Schultz was enthralled with the ambience, the aroma, and especially the sense of community in Italian neighborhood coffee and espresso bars. He felt such gathering places would be great in the United States. Schultz bought the original Starbucks coffee shop in Seattle and transformed it according to his vision.[16] Because the Italian coffee bars caught his attention, U.S. coffee lovers now know what a grande latte is.

Exporting Goods and Services

Who would think U.S. firms could sell beer in Germany, home of so many good beers? Well, around the corner from a famous beer hall in Munich you can buy Samuel Adams Boston Lager. If this surprises you, imagine selling sand in the Middle East. Meridan Group exports a special kind of sand used in swimming pool filters that sells well there.

The fact is, you can sell just about any good or service used in the United States to other countries—and sometimes the competition is not nearly so intense as it is at home. You can sell snowplows to Saudi Arabians, who use them to clear sand off their driveways. Tropical Blossom Honey Company in Edgewater, Florida, found that Saudis are significant consumers of honey because the Koran suggests it has healing properties.[17] Transware Corporation, a global consulting company in San Francisco, California, develops client Web sites and software specific to the cultural and linguistic needs of a particular country or region.[18]

Exporting provides a terrific boost to the U.S. economy.[19] C. Fred Bergsten, director of the Peterson Institute for International Economics, estimates that every $1 billion in U.S. exports generates over 20,000 jobs at home. But selling in global markets and adapting products to global customers are by no means easy tasks. The Spotlight on Small Business box on p. 64 explains firsthand the challenges small U.S. businesses face in China. We discuss key forces that affect global trading later in this chapter.

If you are interested in exporting, send for "The Basic Guide to Exporting," a brochure from the U.S. Government Printing Office; Superintendent of Documents; Washington, D.C. 20402. More advice is available at Web sites such as those sponsored by the U.S Department of Commerce (www.doc.gov), the Bureau of Export Administration (www.bea.gov), the Small Business Administration (www.sba.gov), and the Small Business Exporters Association (www.sbea.org).

Things may not have started off "pretty" for Ugly Dolls, a venture founded almost by accident, but the two-person company has grown into a global business selling its products in over 1,000 stores around the world. The original dolls have been joined by books, calendars, action figures, and T-shirts. Does a career in exporting or importing sound appealing to you?

SPOTLIGHT ON SMALL business

www.mfg.com

Finding Cracks in the Great Wall

When Mitch Free launched his new business, MFG.com, in 2000, he never considered China as part of his plans. MFG.com is an online exchange where manufacturers and suppliers can initiate a dialogue to help one another's businesses. Manufacturers needing a part for a computer hard drive or a transmission for a speedboat can load design specifics onto MFG.com. Suppliers view the specs, determine whether they can fill the request, and bid on the job.

The rapid growth of his business pleased Free, but he noticed something he did not expect. Chinese manufacturers had found their way to his site and were eager to pay MFG.com's average $5,000-a-year fee for the right to bid on projects posted there. By mid-2005, he could see that expansion to China was inevitable.

Like other entrepreneurs who venture into the global market, Free had to overcome certain challenges. What surprised him most was that dealing with the Chinese legal system, accounting rules, and banking regulations was easy. The business culture, including the way workers related to their employers, was the tough part. This led him to search for young Chinese managers with good English-speaking skills who could set him on the right cultural path. Free was fortunate to find James Jin, a Beijing native who had graduated from the Thunderbird School of Global Management in Phoenix, Arizona, whom he hired as general manager. Today, China accounts for 11 percent of MFG.com's revenue, and sales are approaching $6 million.

Mitch Free is hard at work trying to expand his *guanxi* (a Chinese concept of doing business based on networks and relationships). When he first came to China, he had no idea how to find possible suppliers, much less sell his concept to them. By 2008, his team had identified 58,000 business possibilities, with a goal of 100,000 by the year's end. Why all the effort? Mitch Free knows MFG.com could lose everything he has built if he gets China wrong; competition is that intense.

Sources: Stephanie Clifford, "How to Get Ahead in China," *Inc.*, May 2008; and "Online Manufacturing Marketplace MFG.com Receives $26 Million Investment Led by Fidelity Ventures and Fidelity Asia Ventures," *Business Wire*, January 9, 2008.

▶ **PPT 3-16:**
Finding Cracks in the Great Wall

balance of trade
The total value of a nation's exports compared to its imports measured over a particular period.

▶ **PPT 3-17:**
How to Measure Global Trade

trade surplus
A favorable balance of trade; occurs when the value of a country's exports exceeds that of its imports.

trade deficit
An unfavorable balance of trade; occurs when the value of a country's imports exceeds that of its exports.

▶ **PPT 3-18:**
Balance of Payments

Measuring Global Trade

In measuring global trade, nations rely on two key indicators: balance of trade and balance of payments. The **balance of trade** is the total value of a nation's exports compared to its imports measured over a particular period. A *favorable* balance of trade, or **trade surplus**, occurs when the value of a country's exports exceeds that of its imports.[20] An *unfavorable* balance of trade, or **trade deficit**, occurs when the value of a country's exports is less than its imports. It's easy to understand why countries prefer to export more than they import. If I sell you $200 worth of goods and buy only $100 worth, I have an extra $100 available to buy other things. However, I'm in an unfavorable position if I buy $200 worth of goods from you and sell you only $100.

The **balance of payments** is the difference between money coming into a country (from exports) and money leaving the country (for imports) plus money flows coming into or leaving a country from other factors such as tourism, foreign aid, military expenditures, and foreign investment. The goal is to have more money flowing into the country than out—a *favorable* balance of payments. Conversely, an *unfavorable* balance of payments exists when more money is flowing out of a country than coming in.

For many years, the United States exported more goods and services than it imported. However, since 1975 it has bought more goods from other nations than it has sold and thus has a trade deficit.[21] Recently, it ran its highest trade deficits with China.[22] How, then, is the United States one of the world's largest *exporting* nations? Even though the United States exports a vast amount of

The United States imports most of its toys from China—and so does the rest of the world. China now produces and exports 80 percent of the toys manufactured in the world. The highest U.S. trade deficit is with China. What products do you use that are imported from China?

goods globally, it exports a much lower *percentage* of its products than other countries, such as Japan and Germany. (Figure 3.3 lists the major trading countries in the world and the leading U.S trading partners.)

In supporting free trade, the United States, like other nations, wants to make certain global trade is conducted fairly. To ensure a level playing field, countries prohibit unfair practices such as dumping.[23] **Dumping** is selling products in a foreign country at lower prices than those charged in the producing country. This tactic is sometimes used to reduce surplus products in foreign markets or to gain a foothold in a new market. Some governments may offer financial incentives to certain industries to sell goods in global markets for less than they sell them at home. China, Brazil, and Russia, for example, have been penalized for dumping steel in the United States.[24] U.S. laws against dumping are specific and require foreign firms to price their products to include 10 percent overhead costs plus an 8 percent profit margin.

Now that you understand some of the basic terms used in global business, we can look at different strategies for entering global markets. First, let's assess your progress so far.

balance of payments
The difference between money coming into a country (from exports) and money leaving the country (for imports) plus money flows from other factors such as tourism, foreign aid, military expenditures, and foreign investment.

dumping
Selling products in a foreign country at lower prices than those charged in the producing country.

◄ PPT 3-19:
Unfair Trade Practices

figure 3.3

THE LARGEST TRADING NATIONS IN THE WORLD AND LARGEST U.S TRADE PARTNERS

World's Largest Trading Nations

- United States
- Germany
- China (includes Hong Kong)
- Japan
- France
- Great Britain
- Canada
- Italy
- Netherlands

Top U.S. Trading Partners

COUNTRY	2007 U.S. EXPORTS (IN BILLIONS)
1. Canada	$248.4
2. Mexico	$136.5
3. China	$65.2
4. Japan	$62.7
5. United Kingdom	$50.3
6. Germany	$49.7
7. South Korea	$34.7
8. Netherlands	$33
9. France	$27.4
10. Taiwan	$26.4

progress assessment

- What are two of the main arguments favoring the expansion of U.S. businesses into global markets?
- What is comparative advantage, and what are some examples of this concept at work in global markets?
- How are a nation's balance of trade and balance of payments determined?
- What is meant by the term *dumping* in global trade?

LEARNING goal 3 *

Illustrate the strategies used in reaching global markets and explain the role of multinational corporations.

STRATEGIES FOR REACHING GLOBAL MARKETS

Businesses use different strategies to compete in global markets. The key strategies include licensing, exporting, franchising, contract manufacturing, international joint ventures and strategic alliances, foreign subsidiaries, and foreign direct investment. Each provides different economic opportunities, along with specific commitments and risks. Figure 3.4 places the strategies on a continuum showing the amount of commitment, control, risk, and profit potential associated with each. Take a few minutes to look it over before you continue.

Licensing

A firm (the licensor) may decide to compete in a global market by **licensing** the right to manufacture its product or use its trademark to a foreign company (the licensee) for a fee (a royalty). A company with an interest in licensing generally sends company representatives to the foreign producer to help set up operations. The licensor may also assist or work with a licensee in such areas as distribution, promotion, and consulting.

licensing
A global strategy in which a firm (the licensor) allows a foreign company (the licensee) to produce its product in exchange for a fee (a royalty).

figure 3.4
STRATEGIES FOR REACHING GLOBAL MARKETS

Licensing → Exporting → Franchising → Contract manufacturing → International joint ventures and strategic alliances → Foreign direct investment

LEAST ← Amount of commitment, control, risk, and profit potential → MOST

Warner Bros. has licensed hundreds of companies to make products related to its series of hit films based on the best-selling Harry Potter books, which have been translated into dozens of languages. Do you think Potter-licensed products will maintain their global popularity with new generations of young readers and viewers?

A licensing agreement can benefit a firm in several ways. First, the firm can gain revenues it would not otherwise have generated in its home market. Also, foreign licensees often must purchase start-up supplies, materials, and consulting services from the licensing firm. Disney and Coca-Cola entered global licensing agreements that have extended into long-term service contracts. For example, Oriental Land Company owns and operates Tokyo Disneyland and Tokyo Disney Sea Park under a licensing agreement that pays Disney management and consulting fees. Disney and competitors like Universal Studios and Marvel Entertainment are seeking to sign licensing agreements for theme parks in the oil-rich Middle East.[25]

A final advantage of licensing is that licensors spend little or no money to produce and market their products. These costs come from the licensee's pocket. Therefore, licensees generally work hard to succeed. However, licensors may also experience problems. Often a firm must grant licensing rights to its product for an extended period, 20 years or longer. If a product experiences remarkable growth in the foreign market, the bulk of the revenues belong to the licensee. Perhaps even more threatening is that the licensing firm is actually selling its expertise. If a foreign licensee learns the company's technology or product secrets, it may break the agreement and begin to produce a similar product on its own. If legal remedies are not available, the licensing firm may lose its trade secrets, not to mention promised royalties.

Exporting

To meet increasing global competition, the U.S. Department of Commerce created Export Assistance Centers (EACs).[26] EACs provide hands-on exporting assistance and trade-finance support for small and medium-sized businesses that wish to directly export goods and services. An EAC network exists in more than 126 U.S. cities and 80 countries, with further expansion planned.[27]

U.S. firms that are still hesitant can engage in indirect exporting through specialists called export-trading companies (or export-management companies) that assist in negotiating and establishing trading relationships. An export-trading company not only matches buyers and sellers from different countries but also deals with foreign customs offices, documentation, and even weights and measures conversions to ease the process of entering global

◀ PPT 3-23:
Export Assistance Centers and Export Trading Centers

REACHING BEYOND our borders

www.mcdonalds.com

The Sun Never Sets on Mickey D's

Go to any city in the United States and you're guaranteed to find some familiar places. Restaurants like KFC, Burger King, and Domino's Pizza have thousands of franchises from coast to coast, making a bucket of extra crispy or a large pepperoni easy to find no matter where you are in the country or, for that matter, in the world. The United States pioneered the expansion of franchising across the planet, and now familiar U.S. brands, large and small, cover the globe. Yum! Brands has more than 2,200 KFCs and 450 Pizza Huts in China, and Burger King reigns over thousands of locations in more than 69 countries.

But the undisputed king of franchising isn't BK; it's Mickey D's. In Mexico and Malaysia, Peru and Portugal, Canada and Qatar, no other company adapts to local culture better than McDonald's. Today, it's the largest food-service company in the world, operating more than 32,000 restaurants in over 117 countries.

In all the markets in which it operates, McDonald's listens to customers and adapts to their culture and preferences. For example, having set up its first franchises in Hong Kong in 1975, McDonald's altered the breakfast menu after realizing customers there liked burgers for breakfast, and chicken or fish for the rest of the day. The company also offers unique products such as curry potato pie and red bean sundaes for its Hong Kong customers. In Israel, all meat served in McDonald's restaurants is 100 percent kosher beef. The company closes many of its restaurants on the Sabbath and on religious holidays. However, it also operates nonkosher restaurants for those Israelis who are not observant Jews. In India, to respect religious sentiments, McDonald's does not include any beef or pork on its menu. Go to www.mcdonalds.com and click on the "I'm Going to McDonald's" link to explore the various Web sites of McDonald's international franchises. Notice how each site blends the culture of the country into the restaurant's image.

The company has also had to respond to challenges like the outbreak of mad cow disease in Europe and Asia, or lawsuits claiming its food has caused customers to be overweight. McDonald's has helped fund research to test for the presence of *E. coli* and mad cow disease in its beef. It has added healthier alternatives to its menus like salads and yogurt, and recently it announced a switch to transfat-free cooking oil for its fries.

Despite such challenges, McDonald's remains the world's top restaurant chain, serving more than 47 million global customers a day. It derives more than half its sales globally, a figure that has continued to increase as rising food prices in the United States have hurt domestic profits. By successfully mixing its image with many cultures, McDonald's has woven itself into the world fabric, and the world is "lovin' it."

Sources: "McDonald's Holds Down Dollar Menu, Making Menu Healthier," *International Business Times,* May 22, 2008; and Mike Harris, "Higher Food Costs in U.S. Eat into Yum Brands' Net," *Wall Street Journal,* February 5, 2008. Yum! Brands, www.yum.com, accessed August 5, 2010; McDonalds, www.mcdonalds.com, accessed August 5, 2010.

---

markets. It also helps exporters get paid. If you are considering a career in global business, export-trading companies often provide internships or part-time opportunities for students.

Franchising

▶ PPT 3-24: Franchising

Franchising is a contractual agreement whereby someone with a good idea for a business sells others the rights to use the business name and sell a product or service in a given territory in a specified manner. Franchising is popular domestically and internationally. (We discuss it in depth in Chapter 5.) Major U.S. franchisors such as Subway, Holiday Inn, and Dunkin' Donuts have many

Tired of studying and want a quick snack? How about a piping hot Domino's pizza with squid and sweet mayonnaise to satisfy your craving? Domino's serves pizzas around the globe that appeal to different tastes. Franchises like Domino's and McDonald's know the world is a big place with wide differences in food preferences. How can franchises ensure their products are appropriate for global markets?

global units operated by foreign franchisees, but global franchising isn't limited to large franchisors. For example, Rocky Mountain Chocolate Factory, a Colorado-based producer of premium chocolate candies, has franchising agreements with the Al Muhairy Group of the United Arab Emirates, where chocolate is considered a gourmet luxury much like caviar in the United States.[28] Mr. Rooter, a full-service plumbing and drain cleaning company, has more than 300 franchise locations globally.[29]

Franchisors have to be careful to adapt their product or service to the countries they serve. KFC's first 11 Hong Kong outlets failed within two years. Apparently the chicken was too greasy, and eating with fingers was too messy for the fastidious people of Hong Kong. Pizza Hut and Domino's Pizza learned that preferences in pizza toppings differ globally. Japanese customers enjoy squid and sweet mayonnaise pizza. Read the Reaching Beyond Our Borders box that highlights McDonald's, the champion of franchisors.

Contract Manufacturing

In **contract manufacturing** a foreign company produces private-label goods to which a domestic company then attaches its own brand name or trademark. For example, Dell contracts with Quanta Computer of Taiwan to make notebook PCs on which it puts the Dell brand name. Flextronics of Singapore manufactures cell phones, printers, and telecom equipment for many U.S. firms. Nike has more than 700 contract factories around the world that manufacture its footwear and apparel.

Contract manufacturing enables a company to experiment in a new market without incurring heavy start-up costs such as building a manufacturing plant. If the brand name becomes a success, the company has penetrated a new market with relatively low risk. A firm can also use contract manufacturing temporarily to meet an unexpected increase in orders, and, of course, labor costs are often very low. Contract manufacturing falls under the broad

◄ PPT 3-25:
Time to Make the Donuts

◄ PPT 3-26:
The Sun Never Sets on Mickey D's

◄ PPT 3-27:
That's at McDonald's?

contract manufacturing
A foreign country's production of private-label goods to which a domestic company then attaches its brand name or trademark; part of the broad category of outsourcing.

◄ PPT 3-28:
Contract Manufacturing

Margin notes

▶ PPT 3-29: Joint Ventures

joint venture
A partnership in which two or more companies (often from different countries) join to undertake a major project.

▶ PPT 3-30: Strategic Alliances

strategic alliance
A long-term partnership between two or more companies established to help each company build competitive market advantages.

foreign direct investment (FDI)
The buying of permanent property and businesses in foreign nations.

foreign subsidiary
A company owned in a foreign country by another company, called the *parent company*.

The United States has been and remains a popular global spot for foreign direct investment. Global automobile manufacturers like Toyota, Honda, and Mercedes have spent millions of dollars building facilities in the United States, like the Mercedes plant in Tuscaloosa, Alabama, pictured here. Do you consider a Mercedes produced in Tuscaloosa to be a U.S. car or a German car?

---

category of *outsourcing*, which we defined in Chapter 1 and will discuss in more depth later in this chapter.

International Joint Ventures and Strategic Alliances

A **joint venture** is a partnership in which two or more companies (often from different countries) join to undertake a major project. Joint ventures are often mandated by governments such as China as a condition of doing business in their country. For example, Colgate-Palmolive entered a joint venture with one of China's largest toothpaste producers. Since then it has doubled its oral hygiene revenues in China and now exports its Chinese products to 70 countries.[30] General Motors and Volkswagen have a joint venture with Shanghai Automotive Industrial Corporation, China's largest domestic car company, to build cars in China.[31] General Motors now sells more Buicks in China than in the United States.[32]

Joint ventures are developed for many different reasons. Campbell Soup Company's joint venture with Japan's Nakano Vinegar, called Campbell Nakano Inc., was designed to expand Campbell's rather low share of the soup market in Japan. Elite Foods is a joint venture between PepsiCo and Elite Industries to market Frito-Lay snacks in Israel. Joint ventures can also be truly unique, such as the University of Pittsburgh and the Italian government's joint venture that brought a new medical transplant center to Sicily.

The benefits of international joint ventures are clear:

1. Shared technology and risk.
2. Shared marketing and management expertise.
3. Entry into markets where foreign companies are often not allowed unless goods are produced locally.

The drawbacks of joint ventures are not so obvious but are important. One partner can learn the other's technology and practices, then use what it learned to its own advantage. Also, a shared technology may become obsolete, or the joint venture may become too large to be as flexible as needed.

The global market is also fueling the growth of strategic alliances. A **strategic alliance** is a long-term partnership between two or more companies established to help each company build competitive market advantages. Unlike joint ventures, strategic alliances don't share costs, risks, management, or even profits. Such alliances provide broad access to markets, capital, and technical expertise. Thanks to their flexibility, strategic alliances can effectively link firms from different countries and firms of vastly different sizes. Hewlett-Packard has strategic alliances with Hitachi and Samsung, and Chevron has alliances with the Western Australia Energy Research Alliance.

Foreign Direct Investment

Foreign direct investment (FDI) is the buying of permanent property and businesses in foreign nations. The most common form of FDI is a **foreign subsidiary**, a company owned in a foreign country by another company, called the *parent company*. The subsidiary operates like a domestic firm, with production, distribution, promotion, pricing, and other business functions under the control of the subsidiary's management. The subsidiary also must observe the legal requirements of both the country where the parent firm is located (called the *home country*) and the foreign country where the subsidiary is located (called the *host country*).

figure 3.5

THE LARGEST MULTINATIONAL CORPORATIONS IN THE WORLD

COMPANY	COUNTRY	MARKET CAPITALIZATION (IN BILLIONS)
1. ExxonMobil	United States	$406
2. Wal-Mart	United States	214
3. China Mobil	China	209
4. Industrial and Commercial Bank of China	China	183
5. General Electric	United States	178
6. Procter & Gamble	United States	177
7. Microsoft	United States	169
8. Volkswagen	Germany	168
9. Royal Dutch Shell	Netherlands	166
10. Petrochina	China	161

Source: *BusinessWeek,* January 12, 2009.

The primary advantage of a subsidiary is that the company maintains complete control over any technology or expertise it may possess. The major shortcoming is the need to commit funds and technology within foreign boundaries. Should relationships with a host country falter, the firm's assets could be *expropriated* (taken over by the foreign government). Swiss-based Nestlé has many foreign subsidiaries. The consumer-products giant spent billions of dollars acquiring foreign subsidiaries such as Ralston Purina, Chef America (maker of Hot Pockets), and Dreyer's Ice Cream in the United States as well as Perrier in France. It employs over 280,000 people in factories and operations in almost every country in the world.[33]

Nestlé is a **multinational corporation**, one that manufactures and markets products in many different countries and has multinational stock ownership and management. Multinational corporations are typically extremely large corporations like Nestlé, but not all large global businesses are multinationals.[34] A business could export everything it produces, deriving 100 percent of its sales and profits globally, and still not be a multinational corporation. Only firms that have *manufacturing capacity* or some other physical presence in different nations can truly be called multinational.[35] Figure 3.5 lists the 10 largest multinational corporations in the world.

One of the fastest-growing forms of foreign direct investment is the use of **sovereign wealth funds (SWFs)**, investment funds controlled by governments holding large stakes in foreign companies. SWFs from Kuwait, Singapore, and China have purchased significant portions of U.S companies such as Citigroup. Analysts estimate SWFs controlled $3 trillion in U.S. firms as of 2008. SWF investments are expected to grow in the next five years even though the financial crisis in 2008 slowed the activity of some funds.[36]

SWFs' size and government ownership make some fear they might be used for achieving geopolitical objectives, gaining control of strategic natural resources, or obtaining sensitive technologies. SWFs could also undermine the management of the companies in which they invest. In contrast, some experts see foreign investment as a vote of confidence in the U.S. economy and a way to create thousands of U.S. jobs.[37] You can read more about SWFs in Chapter 18.

Entering global business requires selecting an entry strategy that best fits your business goals. The different strategies we've discussed reflect different levels of ownership, financial commitment, and risk. However, this is just the

◀ **CRITICAL THINKING EXERCISE 3-2:**
Evaluating Global Expansion

◀ **PPT 3-31:**
Foreign Direct Investment

◀ **PPT 3-32:**
Multinational Corporations

◀ **BONUS CASE 3-1:**
Gap's Evolving View of Ethics

multinational corporation
An organization that manufactures and markets products in many different countries and has multinational stock ownership and multinational management.

sovereign wealth funds (SWFs)
Investment funds controlled by governments holding large stakes in foreign companies.

◀ **PPT 3-33:**
Sovereign Wealth Funds

beginning. You should also be aware of market forces that affect a business's ability to thrive in global markets. After the Progress Assessment, we'll discuss them.

progress assessment

- What are the advantages to a firm of using licensing as a method of entry in global markets? What are the disadvantages?
- What services are usually provided by an export-trading company?
- What is the key difference between a joint venture and a strategic alliance?
- What makes a company a multinational corporation?

LEARNING goal 4 *

Evaluate the forces that affect trading in global markets.

FORCES AFFECTING TRADING IN GLOBAL MARKETS

The hurdles to success are higher and more complex in global markets than in domestic markets. Such hurdles include dealing with differences in sociocultural forces, economic and financial forces, legal and regulatory forces, and physical and environmental forces. Let's analyze each of these market forces to see how they challenge even the most established and experienced global businesses.

Sociocultural Forces

The word *culture* refers to the set of values, beliefs, rules, and institutions held by a specific group of people. Culture can include social structures, religion, manners and customs, values and attitudes, language, and personal communication. If you hope to get involved in global trade, it's critical to be aware of the cultural differences among nations. Unfortunately, while the United States is a multicultural nation, U.S. businesspeople are often accused of *ethnocentricity*, an attitude that your own culture is superior to other cultures.

In contrast, many foreign businesspeople are very good at adapting to U.S. culture. Think how effectively German and Japanese carmakers adapted to U.S. drivers' wants and needs in the auto industry. Asian manufacturers outsell the U.S. Big Three (General Motors, Ford, Chrysler) in the United States, and Toyota replaced General Motors as the global leader in auto sales in 2008.[38] In contrast, for many years U.S. auto producers didn't adapt automobiles to drive on the left side of the road and printed owner's manuals only in English. Liberia, Myanmar, and the United States are the only nations in the world that have not conformed to the metric system of measurement.[39] Let's look at other experiences U.S. businesses face in adapting to social and cultural differences in global markets.

Religion is an important part of any society's culture and can have a significant impact on business operations. Consider the violent clashes between religious communities in India, Pakistan, Northern Ireland, and the Middle East—clashes that have wounded these areas' economies. Companies sometimes ignore religious implications in business decisions. Both McDonald's and Coca-Cola offended Muslims in Saudi Arabia by putting the Saudi Arabian flag on their packaging. The flag's design contains a passage from the Koran, and Muslims believe their holy writ should never be wadded up and thrown away.

In a classic story, a U.S. manager in Islamic Pakistan toured a new plant under his control. While the plant was in full operation, he went to his office to make some preliminary production forecasts. Suddenly all the machinery in the plant stopped. The manager rushed out, suspecting a power failure, only to find his production workers on their prayer rugs. Upon learning that Muslims are required to pray five times a day, he returned to his office and lowered his production estimates.

Understanding sociocultural differences is important in managing employees. In Latin American countries, workers believe that managers are in positions of authority to make decisions about the well-being of the workers under their control. Consider the U.S. manager in Peru who was unaware of this cultural characteristic and believed workers should participate in managerial functions. He was convinced he could motivate his workers to higher levels of productivity by instituting a more democratic decision-making style. Soon workers began quitting in droves. When asked why, they said the new manager did not know his job and was asking the workers what to do. All stated they wanted to find new jobs, since this company was doomed due to its incompetent management.

Many U.S. companies still fail to think globally. A sound philosophy is: *Never assume what works in one country will work in another.* Intel, Nike, IBM, Apple, Honda, Dell, and Wal-Mart have developed brand names with widespread global appeal and recognition. However, even they often face difficulties. To get an idea of the problems companies have faced with translations of advertising, take a look at Figure 3.6.

Economic and Financial Forces

Economic differences muddy the water in global markets. It's hard for us to imagine buying chewing gum by the stick. Yet this behavior is commonplace in economically depressed nations like Haiti, where customers can afford only small quantities. You might suspect with over 1 billion people, India would be a dream market for companies like Pepsi-Cola and Hershey's. However, Indians consume an average of only three soft drinks per person a year, and most cannot afford chocolate due to India's low per-capita income.

Mexicans shop with pesos, South Koreans with won, Japanese with yen, and U.S. consumers with dollars. Globally, the U.S. dollar is considered a

◄ **LECTURE LINK 3-4:**
Blood Type Matters in Japan

◄ **PPT 3-38:**
Ready to Travel Abroad?

◄ **CRITICAL THINKING EXERCISE 3-3:**
Currency Shifts

figure 3.6

OOPS, DID WE SAY THAT?
A global marketing strategy can be very difficult to implement. Look at the problems these well-known companies encountered in global markets.

- PepsiCo attempted a Chinese translation of "Come Alive, You're in the Pepsi Generation" that read to Chinese customers as "Pepsi Brings Your Ancestors Back from the Dead."
- Coors Brewing Company put its slogan "Turn It Loose" into Spanish and found it translated as "Suffer from Diarrhea."
- Perdue Chicken used the slogan "It Takes a Strong Man to Make a Chicken Tender," which was interpreted in Spanish as "It Takes an Aroused Man to Make a Chicken Affectionate."
- KFC's patented slogan "Finger-Lickin' Good" was understood in Japanese as "Bite Your Fingers Off."
- On the other side of the translation glitch, Electrolux, a Scandinavian vacuum manufacturer, tried to sell its products in the U.S. market with the slogan "Nothing Sucks Like an Electrolux."

▶ PPT 3-39:
Exchange Rates

exchange rate
The value of one nation's currency relative to the currencies of other countries.

dominant and stable currency. However, it doesn't always retain the same market value.[40] In a global transaction today, a dollar may be exchanged for eight pesos; tomorrow you may get seven. The **exchange rate** is the value of one nation's currency relative to the currencies of other countries.

Changes in a nation's exchange rates have effects in global markets.[41] A *high value of the dollar* means a dollar is trading for more foreign currency than previously. Therefore, foreign products become cheaper because it takes fewer dollars to buy them. However, U.S.-produced goods become more expensive because of the dollar's high value. Conversely, a *low value of the dollar* means a dollar is traded for less foreign currency—foreign goods become more expensive because it takes more dollars to buy them, but U.S. goods become cheaper to foreign buyers because it takes less foreign currency to buy them.[42]

Global financial markets operate under a system called *floating exchange rates*, which means that currencies "float" in value according to the supply and demand for them in the global market for currency. This supply and demand is created by global currency traders, who develop a market for a nation's currency based on the country's perceived trade and investment potential.

When the dollar is "up," foreign goods and travel are a bargain for U.S. consumers. When the dollar trades for less foreign currency, however, foreign tourists like these often flock to U.S. cities to enjoy relatively cheaper vacations and shopping trips. Do U.S. exporters profit more when the dollar is up or when it is down?

Changes in currency values cause many problems globally. For instance, labor costs for multinational corporations like Nestlé, General Electric, and Sony can vary considerably as currency values shift, causing them to juggle production from one country to another. Medium-sized companies like H. B. Fuller of St. Paul, Minnesota, and smaller businesses like Superior Products of Cleveland, Ohio, are also affected. Fuller has 3,200 employees in 32 countries, and Superior operates in 6 countries.[43] Both have learned to use currency fluctuations to their advantage in dealing with their global markets.

Currency valuation problems can be especially harsh on developing economies.[44] At times a nation's government will intervene and readjust the value of its currency, often to increase the export potential of its products. **Devaluation** lowers the value of a nation's currency relative to others. Sometimes, due to a nation's weak currency, the only way to trade is *bartering*, the exchange of merchandise for merchandise or service for service with no money traded.

devaluation
Lowering the value of a nation's currency relative to other currencies.

countertrading
A complex form of bartering in which several countries may be involved, each trading goods for goods or services for services.

Countertrading is a complex form of bartering in which several countries each trade goods or services for other goods or services. Estimates are that countertrading accounts for over 20 percent of all global exchanges, especially with developing countries. Let's say a developing country such as Jamaica wants to buy vehicles from Ford Motor Company in exchange for bauxite, a mineral compound that is a source of aluminum ore. Ford does not need Jamaican bauxite, but it does need compressors. In a countertrade, Ford may trade vehicles to Jamaica, which trades bauxite to another country, say India, which exchanges compressors with Ford. All three parties benefit and avoid some of the financial problems and currency constraints in global markets.

▶ PPT 3-40:
Devaluation and Countertrading

Legal and Regulatory Forces

In any economy, the conduct and the direction of business are firmly tied to the legal and regulatory environment. In global markets, no central system of law exists, so different systems of laws and regulations may apply in different places. This makes conducting global business difficult as businesspeople navigate a sea of laws and regulations that are often inconsistent. Antitrust rules, labor relations, patents, copyrights, trade practices, taxes, product liability, child labor, prison labor, and other issues are governed differently country by country.[45]

U.S. businesses must follow U.S. laws and regulations in conducting business globally, although legislation such as the Foreign Corrupt Practices Act of 1978 can create competitive disadvantages. This law prohibits "questionable" or "dubious" payments to foreign officials to secure business contracts.[46] That runs contrary to practices in many countries, where corporate or government bribery is not merely acceptable but perhaps the only way to secure a lucrative contract. The Organization for Economic Cooperation and Development (OECD) and Transparency International have led a global effort to fight corruption and bribery in foreign markets, with limited success. Figure 3.7 shows a partial list of countries where bribery or other unethical business practices are most common.

The cooperation and sponsorship of local businesspeople can help a company penetrate the market and deal with laws, regulations, and bureaucratic barriers in their country.

figure 3.7

COUNTRIES RATED HIGHEST ON CORRUPT BUSINESS

1. Somalia
2. Afghanistan
3. Myanmar
4. Sudan
5. Iraq
6. Chad
7. Uzbekistan
8. Turkmenistan
9. Iran
10. Haiti

Source: Transparency International, 2010.

Physical and Environmental Forces

Physical and environmental forces certainly affect a company's ability to conduct global business. Some developing countries have such primitive transportation and storage systems that international distribution is ineffective, if not impossible, especially for perishable food. Add unclean water and lack of effective sewer systems, and you can see the intensity of the problem.

Technological differences also influence the features of exportable products. For example, residential electrical systems in most developing countries do not match those of U.S. homes, in kind or capacity. Computer and Internet use in many developing countries is thin or nonexistent. These facts make for a tough business environment in general and for e-commerce in particular. After the Progress Assessment, we'll explore how another force, trade protectionism, affects global business.

LECTURE LINK 3-5: Bribery Pitfalls

PPT 3-41: Legal Concerns Overseas

BONUS CASE 3-2: Cooling Off the Sweatshops

LECTURE LINK 3-6: E-Mail by Snail-Mail

PPT 3-42: Environmental Forces

progress assessment

- What are four major hurdles to successful global trade?
- What does *ethnocentricity* mean, and how can it affect global success?
- How would a low value of the dollar affect U.S. exports?
- What does the Foreign Corrupt Practices Act prohibit?

PPT 3-43: Progress Assessment

LEARNING goal 5 *

Debate the advantages and disadvantages of trade protectionism.

PPT 3-44: Trade Protectionism

LECTURE LINK 3-7: Does Trade Protection Protect or Risk Your Future?

TRADE PROTECTIONISM

As we discussed in the previous section, sociocultural, economic and financial, legal and regulatory, and physical and environmental forces are all challenges to global trade. What is often a much greater barrier to global trade, however,

PPT 3-45: Tariffs

PPT 3-46: Import Quotas and Embargoes

trade protectionism
The use of government regulations to limit the import of goods and services.

tariff
A tax imposed on imports.

import quota
A limit on the number of products in certain categories that a nation can import.

embargo
A complete ban on the import or export of a certain product, or the stopping of all trade with a particular country.

The United Steelworkers Union claims it lost 70 percent of its members over the past 20 years because of the growth of imported steel. Should governments protect their industries by placing tariffs on imported products? Why or why not?

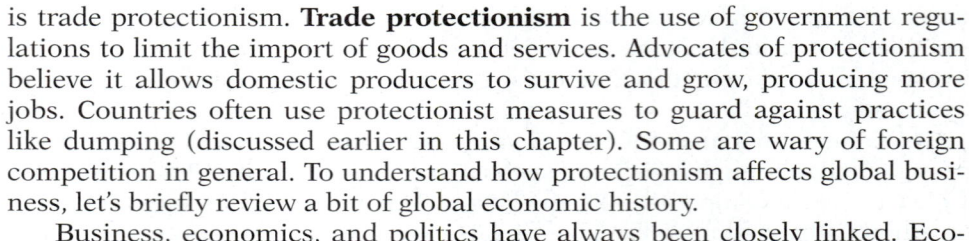

is trade protectionism. **Trade protectionism** is the use of government regulations to limit the import of goods and services. Advocates of protectionism believe it allows domestic producers to survive and grow, producing more jobs. Countries often use protectionist measures to guard against practices like dumping (discussed earlier in this chapter). Some are wary of foreign competition in general. To understand how protectionism affects global business, let's briefly review a bit of global economic history.

Business, economics, and politics have always been closely linked. Economics was once referred to as *political economy*, indicating the close ties between politics (government) and economics. In the 17th and 18th centuries, businesspeople and government leaders endorsed an economic policy called *mercantilism*.[47] The idea was for a nation to sell more goods to other nations than it bought from them, that is, to have a favorable balance of trade. According to mercantilists, this resulted in a flow of money to the country that sold the most globally. The philosophy led governments to implement **tariffs**, taxes on imports, making imported goods more expensive to buy.

There are two kinds of tariffs: protective and revenue. *Protective tariffs* (import taxes) raise the retail price of imported products so that domestic goods are more competitively priced. These tariffs are meant to save jobs for domestic workers and keep industries—especially infant industries that have companies in the early stages of growth—from closing down because of foreign competition. *Revenue tariffs* are designed to raise money for the government.

An **import quota** limits the number of products in certain categories a nation can import. The United States has import quotas on a number of products, including sugar and shrimp, to protect U.S. companies and preserve jobs. An **embargo** is a complete ban on the import or export of a certain product, or the stopping of all trade with a particular country. Political disagreements have caused many countries to establish embargoes, such as the U.S. embargo against Cuba, in effect since 1962.[48]

Nations also prohibit the export of specific products. Antiterrorism laws and the U.S. Export Administration Act of 1979 prohibit exporting goods like high-tech weapons that could endanger national security.

Nontariff barriers are not as specific or formal as tariffs, import quotas, and embargoes but can be as detrimental to free trade. For example, restrictive standards often detail exactly how a product must be sold in a country. Denmark requires companies to sell butter in cubes, not tubs. South Korea sends 700,000 cars to the United States each year but imports only 5,000 due to nontariff barriers such as the size of the engine.[49] Japan argued it had low tariffs and welcomed foreign exports, yet a Japanese tradition called *keiretsu* (pronounced "kay-RET-soo") built "corporate families" (like Mitsui and Mitsubishi) that forged semipermanent ties with suppliers, customers, and distributors. Today, Japan's economy is a much friendlier place for imports.

Would-be exporters might view trade barriers as good reasons to avoid global trade, but overcoming constraints creates business opportunities. Next, we'll look at organizations and agreements that attempt to eliminate barriers.

The World Trade Organization

In 1948, government leaders from 23 nations formed the **General Agreement on Tariffs and Trade (GATT)**, a global forum for reducing trade restrictions on goods, services, ideas, and cultural programs. In 1986, the Uruguay Round of the GATT convened to renegotiate trade agreements. After eight years of meetings, 124 nations voted to lower tariffs an average of 38 percent worldwide and expand new trade rules to areas such as agriculture, services, and the protection of patents.

The Uruguay Round also established the **World Trade Organization (WTO)** to mediate trade disputes among nations. The WTO, headquartered in Geneva, is an independent entity of 153 member nations whose purpose is to oversee cross-border trade issues and global business practices.[50] Trade disputes are presented by member nations with decisions made within a year, rather than languishing for years as in the past.

The WTO has not solved all global trade problems.[51] Legal and regulatory differences (discussed above) often impede trade expansion. And a wide gap separates developing nations (80 percent of the WTO membership) and industrialized nations like the United States.[52] The WTO meetings in Doha, Qatar, began in 2001 to address dismantling protection of manufactured goods, eliminating subsidies on agricultural products, and overturning temporary protectionist measures. Unfortunately, the Doha Round ended in 2008 with no significant agreements.[53]

Common Markets

An issue not resolved by the GATT or the WTO is whether common markets create regional alliances at the expense of global expansion. A **common market** (also called a *trading bloc*) is a regional group of countries with a common external tariff, no internal tariffs, and coordinated laws to facilitate exchange among members. The European Union (EU), Mercosur, and the Association of Southeast Asian Nations (ASEAN) Economic Community are common markets.

The EU began in the late 1950s as an alliance of six trading partners (then known as the Common Market and later the European Economic Community). Today it is a group of 27 nations (see Figure 3.8 on p. 78) with a population of almost 500 million and a GDP of $16.8 trillion.[54] The EU sees continued economic integration as the major way to compete for global business, particularly with the United States, China, and Japan.

The path to European unification was not easy, but the EU took a significant step in 1999 by adopting the euro as a common currency. EU businesses have saved billions by eliminating currency conversions. The euro has proven a worthy challenger to the U.S. dollar's dominance in global markets due to its economic strength.

Mercosur unites Brazil, Argentina, Paraguay, Uruguay, and associate members Chile and Bolivia into a trading bloc.[55] Its economic goals also include a single currency among member nations. Recently a proposal was revived to combine Mercosur and the Andean Pact (Venezuela, Colombia, Peru, and Ecuador) into a Union of South American Nations that would pave the way for an economic free-trade zone spanning South America.[56]

The ASEAN Economic Community was established in 1967 in Thailand to create economic cooperation among its five original members (Indonesia, Malaysia, Philippines, Singapore, and Thailand). ASEAN has expanded to include Brunei, Cambodia, the Lao People's Democratic Republic, Myanmar, and Vietnam, creating a trade association with a population of approximately 560 million and a GDP of $1.2 trillion.[57]

Failure to reach agreement on whether to allow tariff protection for farmers in developing nations marked the end of the recent Doha Round of trade talks among World Trade Organization members. Some disappointed observers feared the failure could also endanger global agreements on other issues like global warming. Do you agree? Why or why not?

General Agreement on Tariffs and Trade (GATT)
A 1948 agreement that established an international forum for negotiating mutual reductions in trade restrictions.

◀ PPT 3-47:
World Trade Organization

World Trade Organization (WTO)
The international organization that replaced the General Agreement on Tariffs and Trade, and was assigned the duty to mediate trade disputes among nations.

common market
A regional group of countries that have a common external tariff, no internal tariffs, and a coordination of laws to facilitate exchange; also called a *trading bloc*. An example is the European Union.

figure 3.8

MEMBERS OF THE EUROPEAN UNION
Current EU members are highlighted in dark blue. Countries that have applied for membership are in light blue.

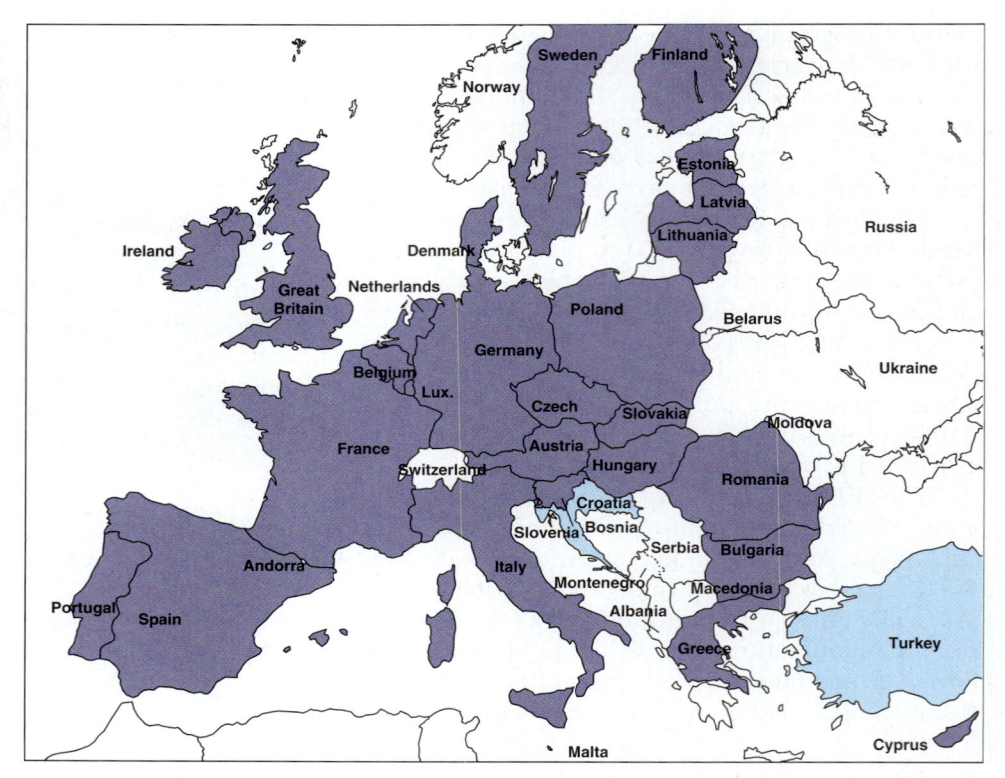

The North American and Central American Free Trade Agreements

A widely debated issue of the early 1990s was the ratification in 1994 of the **North American Free Trade Agreement (NAFTA)**, which created a free-trade area among the United States, Canada, and Mexico. Opponents warned of the loss of U.S. jobs and capital. Supporters predicted that NAFTA would open a vast new market for U.S. exports and create jobs and market opportunities in the long term.[58]

NAFTA's objectives were to (1) eliminate trade barriers and facilitate cross-border movement of goods and services, (2) promote conditions of fair competition, (3) increase investment opportunities, (4) provide effective protection and enforcement of intellectual property rights (patents and copyrights), (5) establish a framework for further regional trade cooperation, and (6) improve working conditions in North America. Today, the three NAFTA countries have a combined population over 450 million and a gross domestic product (GDP) of $16 trillion.

NAFTA remains hotly debated.[59] On the positive side, the value of U.S. exports to NAFTA partners has increased since its signing. Trade volume among the three partners has expanded from $289 billion in 1994 to $930 billion today.[60] On the downside, the U.S. Department of Labor estimates the United States has lost 500,000 jobs to Mexico since enacting NAFTA; some labor economists believe the number is much higher. Annual per capita income in Mexico still lags considerably behind that of the United States, causing illegal immigration to remain a major problem. Critics also argue that working conditions in Mexico are less safe than before NAFTA, especially in southern Mexico. The Legal Briefcase box delves deeper into this emotional topic. See which side you support.

NAFTA controversies have not changed the U.S. commitment to free-trade agreements. In 2005, Congress passed the Central American Free Trade

---

North American Free Trade Agreement (NAFTA)
Agreement that created a free-trade area among the United States, Canada, and Mexico.

▶ CRITICAL THINKING EXERCISE 3-4:
Trade Agreements

▶ PPT 3-48:
Common Markets

▶ PPT 3-49:
NAFTA

▶ PPT 3-50:
CAFTA

LEGAL briefcase

www.nafta.com

NAFTA or SHAFTA?

The North American Free Trade Agreement (NAFTA) was passed in 1994 with promises it would create thousands of U.S. jobs, turn the U.S. trade deficit with Mexico into a surplus, and halt illegal immigration. Unfortunately, the opposite occurred. Thousands of manufacturing jobs have been relocated to other countries, the U.S. trade deficit with Mexico has increased to $47 billion, and illegal immigration has risen. NAFTA even surfaced as an issue during the 2008 presidential primary campaign. Presidential candidate Barack Obama spoke of renegotiating NAFTA in states like Ohio, where the agreement was blamed for many job losses. Shortly after securing the Democratic nomination, President Obama retracted his previous remarks about NAFTA. As president, however, he has indicated that he would like to address labor and environmental protection aspects of the pact. Still, resentment against the trade agreement remains strong in many states and among organized labor.

Despite its criticisms, NAFTA has had its share of positives. Trade with Canada and Mexico has nearly tripled since 1994, bringing $930 billion to the United States. Food exports to Mexico have increased 8 percent annually, and, though manufacturing jobs have decreased in the United States, manufacturing output has increased 54 percent. Many argue that the loss of manufacturing jobs is a result of vast strides in automation and information technology, which has caused reductions in manufacturing jobs across the world, including China.

Though NAFTA has not delivered on all its initial promises, the agreement is not the major cause of our nation's current economic predicament. Blaming NAFTA for the United States' economic difficulties helps little in solving the problem.

Sources: Pete Engardio, Geri Smith, and Jane Sasseen, "Refighting NAFTA," *BusinessWeek,* March 31, 2008; Jack Welch and Suzy Welch, "A Punching Bag Named NAFTA," *BusinessWeek,* April 28, 2008; Darlene Superville, "Obama and Mexican President Meet in Washington," AP Online, January 13, 2009; and U.S. Census Bureau, www.census.gov, accessed August 5, 2010.

Agreement (CAFTA), creating a free-trade zone with Costa Rica, the Dominican Republic, El Salvador, Guatemala, Honduras, and Nicaragua.[61] Again, supporters claimed CAFTA would open new markets, lower tariffs, and ease regulations between the member nations. Critics countered the measure would cost U.S. jobs, especially in the sugar and textile industries. Free traders hope CAFTA is a stepping-stone to the creation of a Free Trade Area of the Americas (FTAA), encompassing 800 million people from Patagonia to Alaska. The FTAA agreement remains stalled, however, due to political and trade differences among potential partners.

Common markets and free-trade areas will be debated far into the 21st century. Some economists resoundingly praise such unions, while others express concern that the world is dividing into major trading blocs (EU, NAFTA, etc.) that will exclude poor and developing nations. After the Progress Assessment, we'll look at the future of global trade and the controversial issue of outsourcing.

progress assessment

- What are the advantages and disadvantages of trade protectionism and of tariffs?
- What is the primary purpose of the WTO?
- What is the key objective of a common market like the EU?
- Which three nations comprise NAFTA? Which nations comprise CAFTA?

LEARNING goal 6 *

Discuss the changing landscape of the global market and the issue of offshore outsourcing.

THE FUTURE OF GLOBAL TRADE

Global trade opportunities grow more interesting and more challenging each day. After all, 6.7 billion customers are hard to pass up. Take, for example, two small companies: New England Pottery Company and Build-A-Bear Workshops. Using the Internet, both companies were able to find new customers online and enjoy an expanded global presence.[62] However, terrorism, nuclear proliferation, rogue states, and other issues cast a dark shadow on global markets. Let's conclude by looking at issues certain to influence global markets, and perhaps your business career, in the 21st century.

With more than 1.3 billion people and incredible exporting prowess, China has transformed the world economic map in the 2000s. As mentioned earlier, China is the world's third-largest exporter behind Germany and the United States.[63] Not long ago, foreign direct investment in China was considered risky and not worth the effort. How things change! Since 2003, China has attracted more global foreign direct investment than the United States. China is the largest global consumer of steel, copper, coal, and cement, and is second only to the United States in the consumption of oil. Manufacturers now use the term *China price* to mean the lowest price possible.

Multinationals like General Motors have invested heavily in China. In eight years auto production and sales in China have quadrupled to 8.8 million.[64] China is already the second largest vehicle market in the world after the United States.[65] If automobile ownership in China rose to current U.S. levels, there would be over 600 million cars on China's roads—more than all the cars in the world today. Wal-Mart began operations in China in 1996 and now has 284 stores with plans to open more.[66]

Many view China as a free trader's dream, where global investment and entrepreneurship are leading to wealth and interdependence with the rest of the world. However, concerns remain about China's one-party political system, human rights abuses, and increasing urban population growth.[67] China's underground economy also generates significant product piracy and counterfeiting, since counterfeit Rolex watches, Callaway golf clubs, and Louis Vuitton bags are readily available.[68] Although China has been more responsive to these latter problems since its 2001 admission to the WTO, few expect the pirating problems to disappear anytime soon. The economic problems of 2008 slowed China down, but it has unquestionably joined the United States, the EU, and Japan as a key driver of the world economy.[69]

While China attracts most of the attention in Asia, India's population of 1.1 billion (600 million under age 25) and Russia's 150 million present enormous business opportunities. India has seen huge growth in information technology, pharmaceuticals, and biotechnology. Still, it remains a nation with difficult trade laws.[70] For example, foreign retailers like Wal-Mart cannot sell directly to consumers. They can, however, direct wholesale operations and give support to Indian retailers.[71]

Russia is an industrialized nation with large reserves of oil, gas, and gold. Multinationals like Chevron, ExxonMobil, and BP are intent on developing Russia's oil reserves, estimated to be the seventh largest in the world. Other multinationals, including Toyota, Ford, and Procter & Gamble, have Russian

> PPT 3-53:
> Future of Global Trade

China's economy is booming, and a highly educated middle class with money to spend is emerging, especially in the cities. Many observers believe China will continue its rapid growth and play a major role in the global economy. Are U.S. firms prepared to compete?

manufacturing facilities.[72] Unfortunately, political, currency, and social problems persist.[73]

The developing nations of Asia, including Indonesia, Thailand, Singapore, the Philippines, Korea, Malaysia, and Vietnam, also offer great potential for U.S. businesses—and possibly for you.

The Challenge of Offshore Outsourcing

Outsourcing, as noted in Chapter 1, is the process whereby one firm contracts with other companies, often in other countries, to do some or all of its functions. In the United States, companies have outsourced payroll functions, accounting, and some manufacturing operations for many years. However, the shift to primarily low-wage global markets, called *offshore outsourcing*, has become a major issue. To take a look at the pros and cons of offshore outsourcing, see Figure 3.9.

◀ **LECTURE LINK 3-8:**
Internet Tutoring

◀ **PPT 3-54:**
Outsourcing

figure 3.9

THE PROS AND CONS OF OFFSHORE OUTSOURCING

PROS

1. Less-strategic tasks can be outsourced globally so that companies can focus on areas in which they can excel and grow.
2. Outsourced work allows companies to create efficiencies that in fact let them hire more workers.
3. Consumers benefit from lower prices generated by effective use of global resources and developing nations grow, thus fueling global economic growth.

CONS

1. Jobs are lost permanently and wages fall due to low-cost competition offshore.
2. Offshore outsourcing reduces product quality and can therefore cause permanent damage to a company's reputation.
3. Communication among company members, with suppliers, and with customers becomes much more difficult.

MAKING ethical decisions

www.medicaltravelsite.com

Take Two Aspirins and Go to Thailand

While many U.S. consumers enjoy standard vacation hot spots like Disneyworld or the beaches of Hawaii, others participate in medical tourism. With U.S. health costs rising to astronomical heights, insurance companies are encouraging patients to seek medical care in foreign countries like Thailand, Singapore, and India. For example, a heart bypass operation costs $130,000 in the United States, while in Thailand it costs only $11,000.

"That's the difference between putting it on your credit card or going into bankruptcy," said Ruben Toral, the former marketing director of Bumrungrand International Hospital in Bangkok, Thailand. Not only do hospitals like Bumrungrand provide medical care at a fraction of the cost; they include top-flight teams of doctors and state-of-the-art facilities better than those in most U.S. hospitals. Bumrungrand even has an adjoining hotel for recovering patients, as well as several restaurants. "This doesn't look like a hospital. It feels more like a hotel or an upscale mall," said Toral.

International hospitals are forging strong partnerships with large U.S. insurance companies, like Blue Cross and Blue Shield and United Healthcare. Private businesses such as Companion Global Healthcare have started up solely to act as travel agents for patients interested in getting medical care overseas.

If medical costs continue their meteoric rise in the United States, outsourcing operations overseas could become so commonplace that insurance companies might require it. Would it be ethical to force patients to travel thousands of miles and be separated from friends and family in a time of crisis, in order to save money?

Sources: Bruce Einhorn, "Outsourcing the Patients," *BusinessWeek*, March 24, 2008; Greg Lindsay, "Medical Leave," *Fast Company*, May 2008; and Emma Wall, "Medical Tourism Costs Under the Microscope," *The Telegraph*, August 13, 2010.

▶ **PPT 3-55:**
Electronics Manufacturing Around the World

▶ **PPT 3-56:**
Take Two Aspirin and Go to Thailand

As lower-level manufacturing became more simplified, U.S. companies like Levi Strauss and Nike outsourced manufacturing offshore. Today, economists suggest, we are moving into the "second wave" of offshore outsourcing, shifting from product assembly to design and architecture. This process is proving more disruptive to the U.S. job market than the first, which primarily affected manufacturing jobs. Today, increasing numbers of skilled, educated, middle-income workers in service-sector jobs such as accounting, law, finance, risk management, health care, and information technology are seeing their jobs outsourced offshore. Forrester Research estimates that more than 3 million U.S. jobs could be moved to global markets in the next 10 years.

Loss of jobs is not the only worry. China has a spotty safety record in manufacturing toys, food, and drugs.[74] Today, concerns are mounting about companies like Medtronic and Siemens shifting production of sensitive medical devices such as MRI and CT machines to China. In an effort to cut costs, U.S. airlines are outsourcing airline maintenance to countries such as El Salvador.[75] India at one time focused on providing call centers, telemarketing, data entry, billing, and low-end software development. Today—with its deep pool of scientists, software engineers, chemists, accountants, lawyers, and physicians—India is providing more sophisticated services. For example, radiologists from Wipro Health Science read CAT scans and MRIs for many U.S. hospitals. Some medical providers are shifting surgical procedures to India and other nations. The Making Ethical Decisions box offers an interesting ethical question.

As technical talent grows around the globe, offshore outsourcing will increase. China and India graduate more engineers each year than the United States. Education and training will be critical for U.S. workers to preserve the skill premium they possess today and stay ahead in the future.

Globalization and Your Future

Whether you aspire to be an entrepreneur, a manager, or some other type of business leader, think globally in planning your career. By studying foreign languages, learning about foreign cultures, and taking business courses (including a global business course), you can develop a global perspective on your future. As you progress through this text, keep two things in mind: globalization is real, and economic competition promises to intensify.

Also keep in mind that global market potential does not belong only to large, multinational corporations. Small and medium-sized businesses have a world of opportunity in front of them. In fact, these firms are often better prepared to leap into global markets and react quickly to opportunities than are large businesses. Finally, don't forget the potential of franchising, which we examine in more detail in Chapter 5.

◄ **PPT 3-57:**
Plan for Your Global Career

progress assessment

- How has the Internet affected doing business in global markets?
- What are the economic risks of doing business in countries like China?
- What might be some important factors that will have an impact on global trading?
- What are the two primary concerns of offshore outsourcing?

◄ **PPT 3-58:**
Progress Assessment

summary

Learning Goal 1. Discuss the importance of the global market and the roles of comparative advantage and absolute advantage in global trade.
- **Why should nations trade with other nations?**

(1) No country is self-sufficient, (2) other countries need products that prosperous countries produce, and (3) natural resources and technological skills are not distributed evenly around the world.
- **What is the theory of comparative advantage?**

The theory of comparative advantage contends that a country should make and then sell those products it produces most efficiently but buy those it cannot produce as efficiently.
- **What is absolute advantage?**

Absolute advantage means that a country has a monopoly on a certain product or can produce the product more efficiently than any other country. There are few examples of absolute advantage.

Learning Goal 2. Explain the importance of importing and exporting, and understand key terms used in global business.
- **What kinds of products can be imported and exported?**

Though it is not necessarily easy, just about any kind of product can be imported or exported.
- **What terms are important in understanding world trade?**

Exporting is selling products to other countries. *Importing* is buying products from other countries. The *balance of trade* is the relationship of exports to imports. The *balance of payments* is the balance of trade plus other money flows such as tourism and foreign aid. *Dumping* is selling products for less in a foreign country than in your own country. See the Key Terms list at the end of this chapter to be sure you know the other important terms.

Learning Goal 3. Illustrate the strategies used in reaching global markets and explain the role of multinational corporations.
- **What are some ways in which a company can engage in global business?**
Ways of entering world trade include licensing, exporting, franchising, contract manufacturing, joint ventures and strategic alliances, and direct foreign investment.
- **How do multinational corporations differ from other companies that participate in global business?**
Unlike companies that only export or import, multinational corporations also have manufacturing facilities or other physical presence abroad.

Learning Goal 4. Evaluate the forces that affect trading in global markets.
- **What are some of the forces that can discourage participation in global business?**
Potential stumbling blocks to world trade include sociocultural forces, economic and financial forces, legal and regulatory forces, and physical and environmental forces.

Learning Goal 5. Debate the advantages and disadvantages of trade protectionism.
- **What is trade protectionism?**
Trade protectionism is the use of government regulations to limit the import of goods and services. Advocates believe it allows domestic producers to grow, producing more jobs. The key tools of protectionism are tariffs, import quotas, and embargoes.
- **What are tariffs?**
Tariffs are taxes on foreign products. Protective tariffs raise the price of foreign products and protect domestic industries; revenue tariffs raise money for the government.
- **What is an embargo?**
An embargo prohibits the importing or exporting of certain products.
- **Is trade protectionism good for domestic producers?**
That is debatable. Trade protectionism offers pluses and minuses.
- **Why do governments continue such practices?**
The theory of mercantilism started the practice of trade protectionism and it has persisted, though in a weaker form, ever since.

Learning Goal 6. Discuss the changing landscape of the global market and the issue of offshore outsourcing.
- **What is offshore outsourcing? Why is it a major concern for the future?**
Outsourcing is the purchase of goods and services from outside a firm rather than providing them inside the company. Today, more businesses are outsourcing manufacturing and services offshore. Many fear that growing numbers of jobs in the United States will be lost due to offshore outsourcing and that the quality of products produced could be inferior.

key terms

- absolute advantage 62
- balance of payments 65
- balance of trade 64
- common market 77
- comparative advantage theory 61
- contract manufacturing 69
- countertrading 74
- devaluation 74
- dumping 65
- embargo 76
- exchange rate 74
- exporting 61
- foreign direct investment (FDI) 70
- foreign subsidiary 70
- free trade 61
- General Agreement on Tariffs and Trade (GATT) 77
- importing 60
- import quota 76
- joint venture 70
- licensing 66
- multinational corporation 71
- North American Free Trade Agreement (NAFTA) 78
- sovereign wealth funds (SWFs) 71
- strategic alliance 70
- tariff 76
- trade deficit 64
- trade protectionism 76
- trade surplus 64
- World Trade Organization (WTO) 77

connect interactive applications

Reinforcing Your *Connection* to Concepts in Business

This chapter offers 12 interactive applications designed to help you apply what you've learned (examples of these exercises appear below). Your instructor has determined which interactive applications will benefit you throughout this course. Please refer to your instructor's assignment list in *Connect* to determine which applications you should complete.

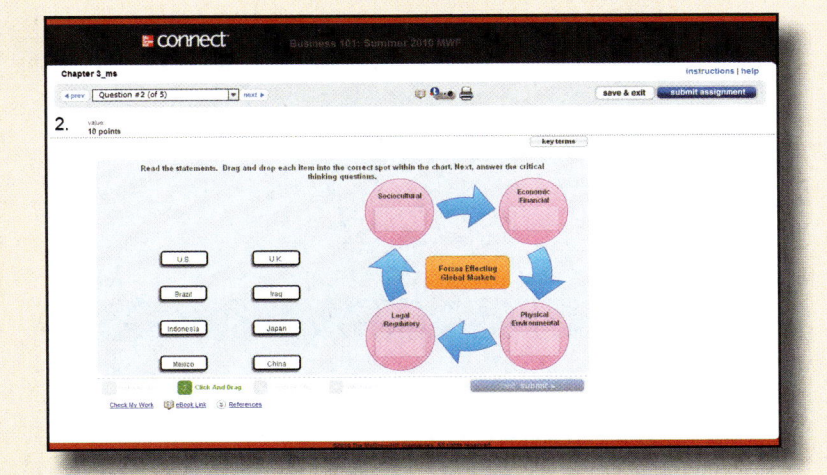

Click and Drag Interactive: Companies expanding into global markets can expect several more obstacles and challenges than those solely competing in domestic markets. Such hurdles include dealing with various global market forces. In this click-and-drag activity, you are asked to read the statements, drag and drop each item into the correct spot within the chart, and answer the critical thinking questions.

Click and Drag Interactive: Businesses use different strategies to compete in global markets. Each provides different economic opportunities, along with specific commitments, control, risk, and profit potential. Review the various strategies and assemble the strategies on the continuum as instructed.

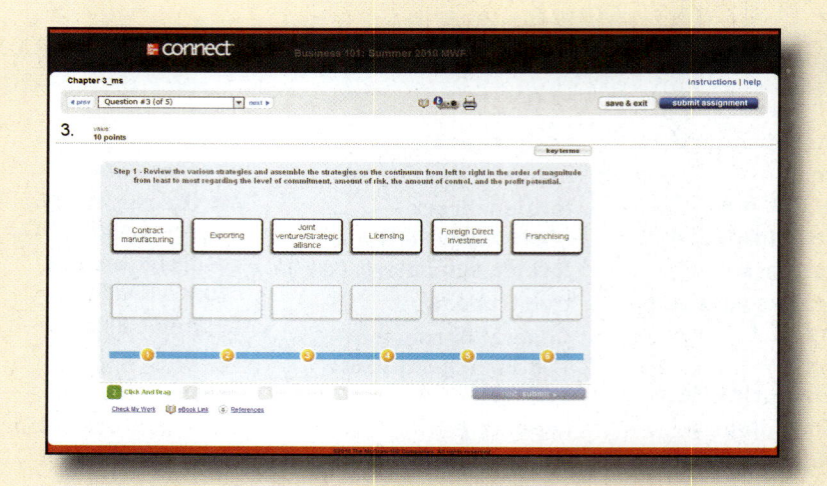

Click and Drag Interactive: When companies outsource, the idea is to save money to keep the prices of their product lower than the competition. This activity will help you identify the pros and cons of offshore outsourcing.

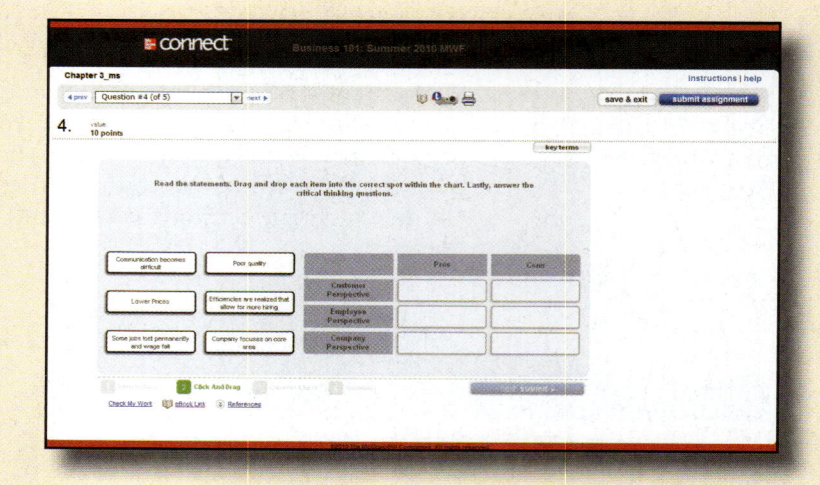

Video Case Interactive: Walt Disney Imagineering, the creative arm of the Walt Disney Company, has realized that people all over the world have similar likes, fears, and imaginations. The product that the Disney theme parks offer taps into these likes, fears, and imaginations. As the video plays, you will be prompted to answer the questions.

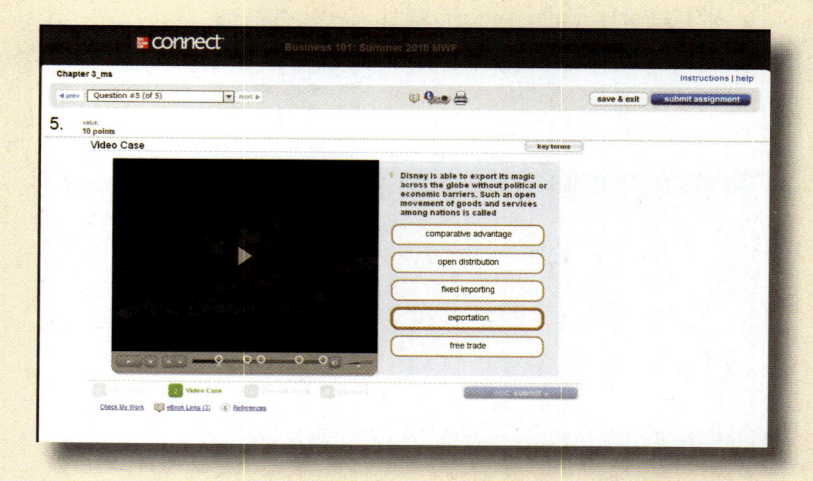

4 Demanding Ethical and Socially Responsible Behavior

profile

Getting to Know Steve Ells, Founder and CEO of Chipotle Mexican Grill

In the mind of burrito baron Steve Ells, founder and CEO of Chipotle Mexican Grill, a fast-food restaurant shouldn't have to sacrifice quality or ethical responsibility in order to be inexpensive and, well, *fast*. Customers agree as they line up for Chipotle's gourmet burritos, made with fresh ingredients right before their eyes. Dedication to quality has made Chipotle a national hit, with current annual sales over $1 billion.

But it's not just big burritos or towering sales that make Chipotle an exceptional restaurant chain. In 2000, Ells visited one of his meat suppliers and could not believe the horrible conditions of the supplier's factory farm. As a result of this eye-opening visit, Ells launched Chipotle's "Food With Integrity" campaign, with "a philosophy that we can always do better in terms of the food we buy," said Ells.

"If people know that the food is based on abusing animals, how satisfying can that dining experience be?" said Ells. All Chipotle's pork now comes from family farms with open pastures, bedded pens, and vegetarian meals for the pigs, with no antibiotics or growth hormones. Although there are not yet enough producers of naturally raised chicken and beef to supply all of Chipotle's meat, the supply is growing: 100 percent of Chipotle's chicken and 60 percent of its beef is humanely raised, and in 2008 Chipotle committed to serving 52 million pounds of humanely raised meat to its customers. Its support of family farms has made Chipotle the leading restaurant buyer of humanely raised meats.

Thanks to its high-quality food and humane treatment of animals, U.S. diners are going hog wild for Chipotle. The average annual revenue for a Chipotle restaurant that has been open more than a year is $1.7 million, and analysts predict Chipotle could expand from 950 locations to more than 3,000 restaurants across the United States. Its environmentally friendly attitude has even rubbed off on fast-food giants Wendy's and Burger King, which have begun to incorporate humanely raised pork in their food. But despite such strides, Ells's mission to serve "Food With Integrity" is far from complete.

LEARNING goals

After you have read and studied this chapter, you should be able to

1. Explain why obeying the law is only the first step in behaving ethically.
2. Ask the three questions to answer when faced with a potentially unethical action.
3. Describe management's role in setting ethical standards.
4. Distinguish between compliance-based and integrity-based ethics codes, and list the six steps in setting up a corporate ethics code.
5. Define *corporate social responsibility* and compare corporations' responsibilities to various stakeholders.
6. Analyze the role of U.S. businesses in influencing ethical behavior and social responsibility in global markets.

connect

Your *Connect*ion to Better Learning. 1. View the interactive presentation. 2. Practice through LearnSmart. 3. Apply your knowledge by using the interactive applications for each chapter of this text.

1 Prep >>>>>> 2 Study >>>>>> 3 Apply

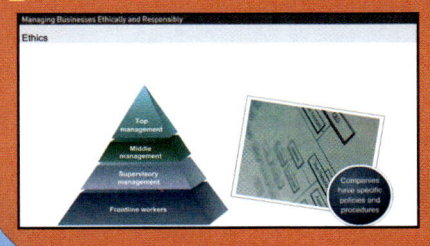

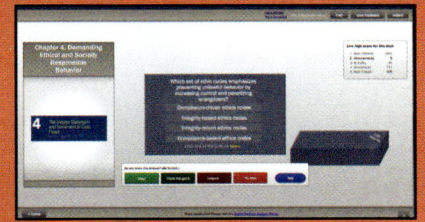

"Have we achieved our mission? No. Will we ever accomplish it? Never, because 'Food With Integrity' is a constant process of searching and improving. But the changes will be noticeable, positive and significant," said Ells.

Though they may not receive as much press as their corrupt colleagues, ethical entrepreneurs are the backbone of the business world. In this chapter, we explore the responsibility of businesses to their stakeholders: customers, investors, employees, and society. We look at the responsibilities of individuals as well. After all, responsible business behavior depends on responsible behavior of each individual in the business.

Sources: Chipotle Mexican Grill, www.chipotle.com/#flash/fwi_story; Humane Farming Association, www.hfa.org/factory/index.html; "Chipotle Commits to Serving More Than 50 Million Pounds of Naturally Raised Meat in 2008," Business Wire, January 7, 2008; Adrianne Cohen, "Ode to a Burrito," *Fast Company*, April 2008; Anna Kuchment, "A Chain That Pigs Would Die For," *Newsweek*, May 12, 2008; and www.chipotle.com, accessed July 2, 2010.

www.chipotle.com

NAME THAT company

Founded in 1985 and based in Texas, this successful energy company was Fortune magazine's "Most Innovative Company" six years in a row. However, things went downhill fast. In 2001, an accounting scandal implicating its chief executive officer and board chairman, chief operating officer, and chief accounting officer led to the company's bankruptcy and the loss of thousands of employees' pensions. Name that company. (Find the answer in the chapter.)

LEARNING goal 1 *

Explain why obeying the law is only the first step in behaving ethically.

> PPT 4-3:
> Life After Scandal

A recent investigation into the activities of the Minerals Management Service, an agency of the U.S. Department of the Interior, alleged that employees and managers accepted gifts from energy companies, abused drugs on the job, and engaged in illicit sexual activities. How can managers ensure ethical conduct if rules are ignored?

ETHICS IS MORE THAN LEGALITY

In the early 2000s, the U.S. public was shocked to learn that Enron, the giant energy trading company, had created off-the-books partnerships to unlawfully hide its debts and losses. The Enron disgrace soon was followed by more scandals at major companies like WorldCom, Tyco International, ImClone, HealthSouth, and Boeing. (See the Legal Briefcase box for a brief summary of a few of these cases.) In recent years, greedy borrowers and lenders alike were among those who brought the real estate, mortgage, and banking industries to the edge of a financial crisis that threatened the entire U.S. and world economies.[1]

Given the ethical lapses prevalent today, how can we restore trust in the free-market system and in leaders in general? First, those who have broken the law should be punished accordingly. New laws making accounting records more transparent (easy to read and understand) and businesspeople and others more accountable for their actions may also help.[2] But laws alone don't make people honest, reliable, or truthful. If they did, crime would disappear.

One danger in writing new laws to correct behavior is that people may begin to think that any behavior that is within the law is also acceptable. The measure of behavior then becomes "Is it legal?" A society gets into trouble when people consider only what is illegal and not also what is unethical. Ethics and legality are two very different things. Although following the law is an important first step, behaving ethically requires more than that. Ethics reflects people's proper relationships with one another: How should we treat others? What responsibility should we feel for others? Legality is narrower. It refers to laws we have written to protect ourselves from fraud, theft, and violence. Many immoral and unethical acts fall well within our laws.

LEGAL briefcase

Paying the Price

The following is a brief summary of some high-profile corporate scandals:

- Enron: Former Enron chairman and chief executive officer (CEO) Kenneth Lay, former CEO Jeffery Skilling, and chief accounting officer Richard Causey were convicted in 2006 of committing accounting fraud by setting up partnerships that the energy company used to improperly enhance profits while removing billions of dollars of debt off its balance sheet. That made the company's financial picture look better than it was and artificially inflated the company's stock and bond prices.

    The company's pension regulations prohibited regular employees from selling their stock, but the executives sold millions of dollars' worth of shares just before the fraud became public. They bankrupted the company yet made fortunes while the employees and other small investors lost millions.

    Skilling is serving a 24-year prison sentence in Minnesota and must pay a $45 million fine. His lawyers are still working to have his conviction overturned. Causey entered a guilty plea and received a shorter sentence than Skilling; he is scheduled to be released from prison in October 2011. Lay suffered a heart attack and passed away before his sentencing; all his convictions were thrown out.

- Arthur Andersen: In 2002, Arthur Andersen, one of the country's largest accounting firms at the time, was convicted of tampering with witnesses when it told its employees to shred two tons of Enron documents. The government claimed that the firm tried to obstruct a Securities and Exchange Commission investigation that company executives knew was coming. At the trial, Andersen executives said they were merely reminding employees to follow the company's established document retention and destruction policy and had not yet been notified of any investigation or asked for any documents. In 2005, the U.S. Supreme Court agreed with Andersen and overturned the conviction. However, there was no one left at Andersen to celebrate—the company's 28,000 employees had already lost their jobs when the earlier conviction forced the company out of business. Currently, Arthur Andersen holds a small staff of under 200 people who are working to dissolve the company.

- Tyco International: In a 2005 retrial, former Tyco CEO Dennis Kozlowski and former chief financial officer Mark Swartz were convicted of stealing $600 million from the global manufacturing company. Both were sentenced to $8\frac{1}{3}$ to 25 years in New York state prison. A state judge had declared the 2004 trial a mistrial because, he said, there had been undue pressure on one juror. Kozlowski and Swartz are expected to leave prison in September 2030.

- Adelphia Communication: In 2004, Adelphia founder John Rigas and his son Timothy were convicted of conspiracy, bank fraud, and securities fraud. John was sentenced to 15 years in prison and Timothy to 20 years. Another Rigas son, Michael, pleaded guilty in 2005 to making a false entry in a financial record, eliminating a need for retrial after his first trial ended in a mistrial. A fourth executive, Michael Mulcahey, was found not guilty of conspiracy and securities fraud. As of this writing, John Rigas's health is failing and he may be allowed to leave prison if a doctor claims he has less than three months to live.

- WorldCom: In June 2002, communications giant WorldCom admitted that intentional accounting irregularities made the company look almost $4 billion more profitable than it was. Further scrutiny of the company's books revealed WorldCom's practice of counting revenue twice dated as far back as 1999, that additional debt continued to be undisclosed, and that revenue not received was entered in the books—pushing the irregularities to more than $11 billion.

    In 2005, former CEO Bernie Ebbers was convicted of fraud, conspiracy, and making false regulatory filings. He was sentenced to 25 years in federal prison. The company has emerged from bankruptcy and now operates under the name of MCI Inc. Ebbers is in Oakdale Federal Correctional Institution in Louisiana and is expected to be released in July 2028.

Sources: Matthew Boyle with Chris Tkaczyk, "Corporate Convicts: Where Are They Now?" *Fortune*, June 9, 2008; and Andrew Clark, "Jailed Boss Seeks to Reverse Enron Verdict," *Guardian*, April 3, 2008.

Ethical Standards Are Fundamental

ethics
Standards of moral behavior, that is, behavior accepted by society as right versus wrong.

> PPT 4-4:
> What Are Ethics?

> PPT 4-5:
> Basic Moral Values

> PPT 4-6:
> Paying the Price

> CRITICAL THINKING EXERCISE 4-1:
> Exploring Community Service

> PPT 4-7:
> Ethics and You

> CRITICAL THINKING EXERCISE 4-2:
> Ethical Dilemmas

We define **ethics** as society's accepted standards of moral behavior, that is, behaviors accepted by society as right rather than wrong. Many Americans today have few moral absolutes. Many decide situationally whether it's OK to steal, lie, or drink and drive. They seem to think that what is right is whatever works best for the individual—that each person has to work out for himself or herself the difference between right and wrong. Such thinking may be part of the behavior that has led to the recent scandals in government and business.

This isn't the way it always was. When Thomas Jefferson wrote that all men have the right to life, liberty, and the pursuit of happiness, he declared it to be a self-evident truth. Going back even further in time, the Ten Commandments were not called the "Ten Highly Tentative Suggestions."

In the United States, with so many diverse cultures, you might think it is impossible to identify common standards of ethical behavior. However, among sources from many different times and places—such as the Bible, Aristotle's *Ethics*, the Koran, and the *Analects* of Confucius—you'll find the following common statements of basic moral values: Integrity, respect for human life, self-control, honesty, courage, and self-sacrifice are right. Cheating, cowardice, and cruelty are wrong. Furthermore, all the world's major religions support a version of what some call the Golden Rule: Do unto others as you would have them do unto you.[3]

> In 2008, the U.S. Justice Department indicted more than 400 developers, mortgage lenders and brokers, lawyers, real estate agents, and appraisers on charges of lending fraud, foreclosure rescue scams, and mortgage-related bankruptcy schemes in almost 150 cases. What motivates people to risk everything by committing fraud?

LEARNING goal 2 *

Ask three questions to answer when faced with a potentially unethical action.

Ethics Begins with Each of Us

It is easy to criticize business and political leaders for moral and ethical shortcomings, and in a recent study both managers and workers cite low managerial ethics as a major cause of U.S. businesses' competitive woes.[4] But employees also reported frequently violating safety standards and goofing off as much as seven hours a week. U.S. adults in general are not always as honest or honorable as they should be. Even though volunteerism is at an all-time high according to the U.S. Census Bureau, three of every four citizens do not give any time to the community in which they live.[5]

Plagiarizing material from the Internet, including cutting and pasting information from Web sites without giving credit, is the most common form of cheating in schools today. To fight this problem, many instructors now use services like TurnItIn.com, which scans students' papers against more than 12 billion online sources to provide evidence of copying in seconds.[6]

In a recent study, most teens said they were prepared to make ethical decisions in the workforce, but an alarming 38 percent felt that lying, cheating, plagiarizing, or behaving violently is sometimes necessary.[7] Two recent studies found a strong relationship between academic dishonesty among undergraduates and dishonesty at work.[8]

MAKING ethical decisions

www.youtube.com

To Tube or Not to Tube?

Whether you want to watch a dog playing a piano, a flashy new music video, or just a slideshow of a family vacation, you can find it on YouTube. Every minute of every day, people upload 10 hours of video onto the Google-owned site. A lot of the content is user-generated, meaning amateurs produce it and can instantly place it online for the whole world to see. But some users upload clips from movies or television shows without the permission of the copyright-holding companies.

Viacom—a corporation that owns CBS, Comedy Central, MTV, and Paramount—does not take video sharing lightly. When Viacom noticed that entire episodes of popular shows like *South Park* and *The Daily Show* appeared on YouTube, it filed a $1 billion lawsuit for copyright infringement. Viacom argues that featuring its content on YouTube violates the Digital Millennium Copyright Act, which requires that Web sites remove copyrighted material uploaded without the owner's permission. Viacom claims it identified 150,000 unauthorized clips viewed a total of 1.5 billion times, supporting its argument that the exposure robbed it of valuable revenue it would have received from television advertisers. Viacom holds YouTube, rather than the individuals who uploaded the video clips, responsible for carrying the illegal content.

YouTube says it diligently tries to delete any videos that generate complaints from copyright owners, but with millions of different users of the site, it is impossible to catch everything. To discourage people from posting copyrighted material, YouTube not only removes the offending videos but also bans any user who uploads copyrighted content without permission. It also provides companies with software to easily identify copyrighted material so it can be reported and removed.

Organizations rallying alongside Viacom include the United Kingdom's Football Association, which claims that hundreds of clips from soccer games have been uploaded without permission. Songs from Elvis Presley, Meat Loaf, and ZZ Top have also appeared without consent, angering the copyright holders.

YouTube worries that Viacom's suit will prevent people from uploading user-generated content, which has revolutionized worldwide communication and given anyone with a camera and a computer the chance to become a star. In their defensive statement YouTube's lawyers said, "Viacom's complaint threatens the way hundreds of millions of people legitimately exchange information, news, entertainment, and political and artistic expression."

In June 2010, a federal judge ruled in YouTube's favor saying that it was not guilty of copyright infringement as long as it promptly removed illegal content when notified of an infringement. Viacom called the judge's decision "fundamentally flawed" and vowed to appeal. What do you think? Who should be held accountable for copyright violations—the people who upload the material or the Web sites that carry it? If Web sites are not held legally responsible, do they still have an ethical responsibility to find and remove such material? What should they do?

Sources: Stephen Foley, "Defender of the Net, or an Infringement Factory?" *The Independent,* June 1, 2008; Larry Neumesiter, "YouTube Suit Called Threat to Online Communication," Associated Press, May 27, 2008; and Michael Liedtke, "Viacom Loses to YouTube in Landmark Copyright Case," www.huffingtonpost.com, accessed July 23, 2010.

In response, many schools are establishing heavier consequences for cheating and requiring students to perform a certain number of hours of community service to graduate. Do you think such policies make a difference in student behavior?

The Making Ethical Decisions boxes throughout the text—like the accompanying one on video piracy—remind you to keep ethics in mind whenever you are making a business decision. Choices are not always easy, and the obvious ethical solution may have personal or professional drawbacks. Imagine that your supervisor has asked you to do something you feel is unethical. You've just taken out a mortgage on a new house to make room for your first baby, due in two months. Not carrying out your supervisor's request may get you fired. What should you do? Sometimes there is no easy alternative in such *ethical dilemmas* because you must choose between equally unsatisfactory alternatives.

◀ PPT 4-9:
To Tube or Not to Tube

It can be difficult to balance ethics and other goals such as pleasing stakeholders or advancing in your career. According to management writer Ken Blanchard and religious leader Norman Vincent Peale, it helps to ask yourself the following questions when facing an ethical dilemma.[9]

1. *Is my proposed action legal?* Am I violating any law or company policy? Whether you're thinking about having a drink and driving home, gathering marketing intelligence, designing a product, hiring or firing employees, getting rid of industrial waste, or using a questionable nickname for an employee, think about the legal implications. This is the most basic question in business ethics, but it is only the first.

2. *Is it balanced?* Am I acting fairly? Would I want to be treated this way? Will I win everything at the expense of another? Win–lose situations often become lose–lose situations and generate retaliation from the loser. Not every situation can be completely balanced, but the health of our relationships requires us to avoid major imbalances over time. An ethical businessperson has a win–win attitude and tries to make decisions that benefit all.

3. *How will it make me feel about myself?* Would I feel proud if my family learned of my decision? My friends? Could I discuss the proposed situation or action with my supervisor? The company's clients? Will I have to hide my actions? Has someone warned me not to disclose them? What if my decision were announced on the evening news? Am I feeling unusually nervous? Decisions that go against our sense of right and wrong make us feel bad—they erode our self-esteem. That is why an ethical businessperson does what is proper as well as what is profitable.

Individuals and companies that develop a strong ethics code and use the three questions above have a better chance than most of behaving ethically. If you would like to know which style of recognizing and resolving ethical dilemmas you favor, fill out the ethical orientation questionnaire in Figure 4.1.

progress assessment

- What are ethics?
- How do ethics differ from legality?
- When faced with ethical dilemmas, what questions can you ask yourself that might help you make ethical decisions?

LEARNING goal 3 *

Describe management's role in setting ethical standards.

MANAGING BUSINESSES ETHICALLY AND RESPONSIBLY

Ethics is caught more than it is taught. That is, people learn their standards and values from observing what others do, not from hearing what they say. This is as true in business as it is at home. Organizational ethics begins at the top, and the leadership and example of strong managers can help instill

Please answer the following questions.

1. Which is worse?
   A. Hurting someone's feelings by telling the truth.
   B. Telling a lie and protecting someone's feelings.
2. Which is the worse mistake?
   A. To make exceptions too freely.
   B. To apply rules too rigidly.
3. Which is it worse to be?
   A. Unmerciful.
   B. Unfair.
4. Which is worse?
   A. Stealing something valuable from someone for no good reason.
   B. Breaking a promise to a friend for no good reason.
5. Which is it better to be?
   A. Just and fair.
   B. Sympathetic and feeling.
6. Which is worse?
   A. Not helping someone in trouble.
   B. Being unfair to someone by playing favorites.
7. In making a decision you rely more on
   A. Hard facts.
   B. Personal feelings and intuition.
8. Your boss orders you to do something that will hurt someone. If you carry out the order, have you actually done anything wrong?
   A. Yes.
   B. No.
9. Which is more important in determining whether an action is right or wrong?
   A. Whether anyone actually gets hurt.
   B. Whether a rule, law, commandment, or moral principle is broken.

To score: The answers fall in one of two categories, J or C. Count your number of J and C answers using this key: 1. A = C; B = J; 2. A = J; B = C; 3. A = C; B = J; 4. A = J; B = C; 5. A = J; B = C; 6. A = C; B = J; 7. A = J; B = C; 8. A = C; B = J; 9. A = C; B = J

What your score means: The higher your J score, the more you rely on an ethic of *justice.* The higher your C score, the more you prefer an ethic of *care.* Neither style is better than the other, but they are different. Because they appear so different, they may seem opposed to one another, but they're actually complementary. In fact, your score probably shows you rely on each style to a greater or lesser degree. (Few people end up with a score of 9 to 0.) The more you can appreciate both approaches, the better you'll be able to resolve ethical dilemmas and to understand and communicate with people who prefer the other style.

An ethic of justice is based on principles like justice, fairness, equality, or authority. People who prefer this style see ethical dilemmas as conflicts of rights that can be solved by the impartial application of some general principle. The advantage of this approach is that it looks at a problem logically and impartially. People with this style try to be objective and fair, hoping to make a decision according to some standard that's higher than any specific individual's interests. The disadvantage of this approach is that people who rely on it might lose sight of the immediate interests of particular individuals. They may unintentionally ride roughshod over the people around them in favor of some abstract ideal or policy. This style is more common for men than women.

An ethic of care is based on a sense of responsibility to reduce actual harm or suffering. People who prefer this style see moral dilemmas as conflicts of duties or responsibilities. They believe that solutions must be tailored to the special details of individual circumstances. They tend to feel constrained by policies that are supposed to be enforced without exception. The advantage of this approach is that it is responsive to immediate suffering and harm. The disadvantage is that, when carried to an extreme, this style can produce decisions that seem not simply subjective, but arbitrary. This style is more common for women than men.

To learn more about these styles and how they might relate to gender, go to www.ethicsandbusiness.org/kgl.htm.

Source: Thomas I. White, *Discovering Philosophy—Brief Edition,* 1e, © Copyright 1996. Adapted by permission of Pearson Education, Inc., Upper Saddle River, NJ.

figure 4.1

ETHICAL ORIENTATION QUESTIONNAIRE

corporate values in employees. The majority of CEOs surveyed recently attributed unethical employee conduct to leadership's failure to establish ethical standards and culture.[10]

Trust and cooperation between workers and managers must be based on fairness, honesty, openness, and moral integrity. The same applies to relationships among businesses and between nations. A business should be managed ethically for many reasons: to maintain a good reputation; to keep existing customers and attract new ones; to avoid lawsuits; to reduce employee turnover; to avoid government intervention in the form of new laws and regulations controlling business activities; to please customers, employees, and society; and simply to do the right thing.[11]

Some managers think ethics is a personal matter—either individuals have ethical principles or they don't. These managers feel that they are not responsible for an individual's misdeeds and that ethics has nothing to do with management. But a growing number of people think ethics has everything to do with management. Individuals do not usually act alone; they need the implied, if not the direct, cooperation of others to behave unethically in a corporation.

For example, there have been reports of cell phone service sales representatives who actually lie to get customers to extend their contracts—or even extend their contracts without the customers' knowledge. Some phone reps intentionally hang up on callers to prevent them from canceling their contracts. Why do these sales reps sometimes resort to overly aggressive tactics? Because poorly designed incentive programs reward them for meeting certain goals, sometimes doubling or tripling their salaries with incentives. Do their managers say directly, "Deceive the customers"? No, but the message is clear. Overly ambitious goals and incentives can create an environment in which unethical actions like this can occur.[12]

LEARNING goal 4 *

Distinguish between compliance-based and integrity-based ethics codes, and list the six steps in setting up a corporate ethics code.

Setting Corporate Ethical Standards

More and more companies have adopted written codes of ethics. Figure 4.2 offers Johnson & Johnson's as a sample. Although these codes vary greatly, we can put them into two categories: compliance-based and integrity-based (see Figure 4.3). **Compliance-based ethics codes** emphasize preventing unlawful behavior by increasing control and penalizing wrongdoers. **Integrity-based ethics codes** define the organization's guiding values, create an environment that supports ethically sound behavior, and stress shared accountability.

Here are six steps many believe can improve U.S. business ethics:[13]

1. Top management must adopt and unconditionally support an explicit corporate code of conduct.
2. Employees must understand that expectations for ethical behavior begin at the top and that senior management expects all employees to act accordingly.
3. Managers and others must be trained to consider the ethical implications of all business decisions.

---

compliance-based ethics codes
Ethical standards that emphasize preventing unlawful behavior by increasing control and by penalizing wrongdoers.

integrity-based ethics codes
Ethical standards that define the organization's guiding values, create an environment that supports ethically sound behavior, and stress a shared accountability among employees.

> Written in 1943 by long-time Chairman General Robert Wood Johnson, the Johnson & Johnson Credo serves as a conscious plan that represents and encourages a unique set of values. Our Credo sums up the responsibilities we have to the four important groups we serve:
>
> - <u>Our customers</u>—We have a responsibility to provide high-quality products they can trust, offered at a fair price.
> - <u>Our employees</u>—We have a responsibility to treat them with respect and dignity, pay them fairly and help them develop and thrive personally and professionally.
> - <u>Our communities</u>—We have a responsibility to be good corporate citizens, support good works, encourage better health and protect the environment.
> - <u>Our stockholders</u>—We have a responsibility to provide a fair return on their investment.
>
> The deliberate ordering of these groups—customers first, stockholders last—proclaims a bold business philosophy: If we meet our first three responsibilities, the fourth will take care of itself . . . To ensure our adherence to Credo values, we periodically ask every employee to evaluate the company's performance in living up to them. We believe that by monitoring our actions against the ethical framework of Our Credo, we will best ensure that we make responsible decisions as a company.

figure 4.2

OVERVIEW OF JOHNSON & JOHNSON'S CODE OF ETHICS
This is an overview of Johnson & Johnson's code of ethics, what it calls its Credo. To see the company's complete Credo, go to www.jnj.com/connect/about=jnj/jnj=credo and click on "Our Credo Values."

FEATURES OF COMPLIANCE-BASED ETHICS CODES		**FEATURES OF INTEGRITY-BASED ETHICS CODES**	
Ideal:	Conform to outside standards (laws and regulations)	Ideal:	Conform to outside standards (laws and regulations) and chosen internal standards
Objective:	Avoid criminal misconduct	Objective:	Enable responsible employee conduct
Leaders:	Lawyers	Leaders:	Managers with aid of lawyers and others
Methods:	Education, reduced employee discretion, controls, penalties	Methods:	Education, leadership, accountability, decision processes, controls, and penalties

figure 4.3

STRATEGIES FOR ETHICS MANAGEMENT
Integrity-based ethics codes move beyond legal compliance to create a "do-it-right" climate that emphasizes core values such as honesty, fair play, good service to customers, a commitment to diversity, and involvement in the community. These values are ethically desirable, but not necessarily legally mandatory.

4. An ethics office must be set up with which employees can communicate anonymously. **Whistleblowers** (insiders who report illegal or unethical behavior) must feel protected from retaliation. In 2002, President George W. Bush signed the Corporate and Criminal Fraud Accountability Act, also called the Sarbanes-Oxley Act. It protects whistleblowers by requiring all public corporations to allow employee concerns about accounting and auditing to be submitted confidentially and anonymously. The act also requires reinstatement and back pay to people who were punished by their employers for passing information about frauds on to authorities. (We cover Sarbanes-Oxley in more detail in Chapter 17.)

5. Outsiders such as suppliers, subcontractors, distributors, and customers must be told about the ethics program. Pressure to put

whistleblowers
Insiders who report illegal or unethical behavior.

◄ PPT 4-14:
How to Improve America's Business Ethics

◄ PPT 4-15:
How to Improve America's Business Ethics

◄ PPT 4-16:
How to Prevent Unethical Behaviors

aside ethical considerations often comes from the outside, and it helps employees resist such pressure when everyone knows what the ethical standards are.

6. The ethics code must be enforced with timely action if any rules are broken. That is the most forceful way to communicate to all employees that the code is serious.

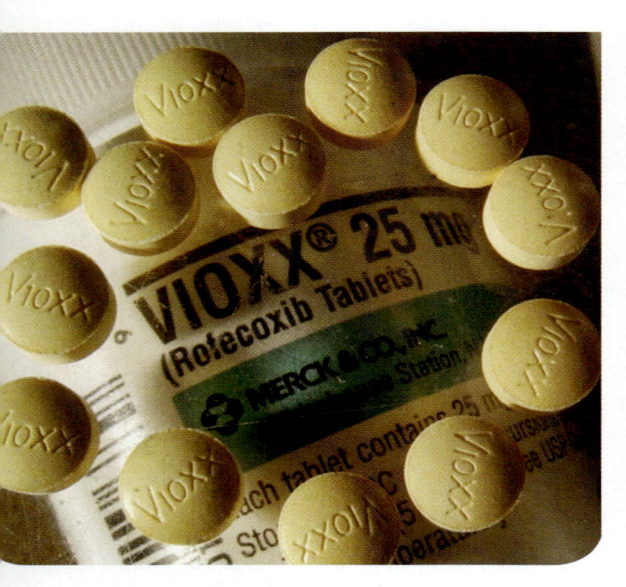

This last step is perhaps the most critical. No matter how well intended a company's ethics code, it is worthless if not enforced. Enron had a written code of ethics. By ignoring it, Enron's board and management sent employees the message that rules could be shelved when inconvenient. In contrast, Johnson & Johnson's response to a cyanide poisoning crisis in the 1980s shows that enforcing ethics codes can enhance the bottom line. Although not legally required to do so, the company recalled its Tylenol products and won great praise and a reputation of corporate integrity.[14]

An important factor in enforcing an ethics code is selecting an ethics officer. The most effective ethics officers set a positive tone, communicate effectively, and relate well to employees at every level. They are equally comfortable as counselors and investigators and can be trusted to maintain confidentiality, conduct objective investigations, and ensure fairness. They can demonstrate to stakeholders that ethics are important in everything the company does.

> *H. Dean Steinke blew the whistle on his former employer, drug company Merck, maker of Vioxx and Zocor, charging that it gave doctors excessive financial incentives to prescribe the drugs and discounts unavailable to government health programs. The case ended with a $671 million settlement and a $68 million reward to Steinke. What motivates whistleblowers?*

progress assessment

- What are compliance-based and integrity-based ethics codes?
- What are the six steps to follow in establishing an effective ethics program in a business?

LEARNING goal 5 *

Define *corporate social responsibility* and compare corporations' responsibilities to various stakeholders.

CORPORATE SOCIAL RESPONSIBILITY

Just as you and I need to be good citizens, contributing what we can to society, corporations need to be good citizens as well. **Corporate social responsibility (CSR)** is the concern businesses have for the welfare of society, not just for their owners. CSR goes well beyond being ethical. It is based on a commitment to integrity, fairness, and respect.

You may be surprised to know that not everyone thinks that CSR is a good thing. Some critics of CSR believe that a manager's sole role is to compete and win in the marketplace. U.S. economist Milton Friedman made the famous statement that the only social responsibility of business is to make money for stockholders. He thought doing anything else was moving dangerously toward socialism. Other CSR critics believe that managers who pursue CSR are doing

corporate social responsibility (CSR)
A business's concern for the welfare of society.

so with other people's money—which they invested to make more money, not to improve society. In this view spending money on CSR activities is stealing from investors.[15]

CSR defenders, in contrast, believe that businesses owe their existence to the societies they serve and cannot succeed in societies that fail. Firms have access to society's labor pool and its natural resources, in which every member of society has a stake. Even Adam Smith, the father of capitalism, believed that self-interested pursuit of profit was wrong and that benevolence was the highest virtue. CSR defenders acknowledge that businesses have deep obligations to investors and should not attempt government-type social responsibility projects. However, they also argue that CSR makes more money for investors in the long run. Studies show that companies with good ethical reputations attract and retain better employees, draw more customers, and enjoy greater employee loyalty.[16]

The social performance of a company has several dimensions:

- **Corporate philanthropy** includes charitable donations to nonprofit groups of all kinds. Eighty percent of the business leaders surveyed in a recent study said that their companies participate in philanthropic activities. Some make long-term commitments to one cause, such as McDonald's Ronald McDonald Houses for families whose critically ill children require treatment away from home. The Bill & Melinda Gates Foundation is by far the nation's largest philanthropic foundation, with assets of more than $35 billion.[17]

- **Corporate social initiatives** include enhanced forms of corporate philanthropy. Corporate social initiatives differ from traditional philanthropy in that they are more directly related to the company's competencies. For example, logistics giant TNT keeps a 50-person emergency-response team on standby to go anywhere in the world at 48 hours' notice. The team has helped in more than two dozen emergencies, including the 2004 Asian tsunami. "We're just faster," says Ludo Oelrich, the director of TNT's Moving the World program.[18]

corporate philanthropy
The dimension of social responsibility that includes charitable donations.

◀ PPT 4-20:
Corporate Philanthropy and Social Initiatives

corporate social initiatives
Enhanced forms of corporate philanthropy directly related to the company's competencies.

◀ PPT 4-21:
Corporate Responsibility and Policy

Timberland is a company with a long-standing commitment to community service. The company's "Path of Service" program offers employees 40 hours of paid time off each year to serve their communities. Here at a sales meeting in Jacksonville, Florida, employees gather for a day of community service. Do companies have responsibilities to the environment beyond obeying environmental laws?

corporate responsibility
The dimension of social responsibility that includes everything from hiring minority workers to making safe products.

corporate policy
The dimension of social responsibility that refers to the position a firm takes on social and political issues.

- **Corporate responsibility** includes everything from hiring minority workers to making safe products, minimizing pollution, using energy wisely, and providing a safe work environment—essentially everything that has to do with acting responsibly within society.

- **Corporate policy** refers to the position a firm takes on social and political issues. For example, Patagonia's corporate policy includes this statement: "A love of wild and beautiful places demands participation in the fight to save them, and to help reverse the steep decline in the overall environmental health of our planet. We donate our time, services and at least 1% of our sales to hundreds of grassroots environmental groups all over the world who work to help reverse the tide."[19]

The problems corporations cause get so much news coverage that people tend to get a negative view of their impact on society. But businesses make positive contributions too. Few people know, for example, that a Xerox program called Social Service Leave allows employees to take up to a year to work for a nonprofit organization while earning their full Xerox salary and benefits, including job security.[20] IBM and Wells-Fargo Bank have similar programs. In fact, many companies allow employees to give part-time help to social agencies of all kinds.

President George W. Bush signed an executive order establishing the USA Freedom Corps to oversee Citizen Corps, a program designed to strengthen homeland security efforts through the help of volunteers. Volunteers handle administrative work at local police departments and spread antiterrorism information as part of expanded Neighborhood Watch programs. Some donate their professional health care skills to support emergency medical efforts, and some train others in disaster response and emergency preparedness.[21]

NetworkforGood.org, 1-800-Volunteer.org, and VolunteerMatch.org are Web-based services that link volunteers with nonprofit and public sector organizations around the country. Volunteers enter a zip code or indicate the geographic area in which they'd like to work, and the programs list organizations that could use their help.

Two-thirds of the MBA students surveyed by a group called Students for Responsible Business said they would take a reduced salary to work for a socially responsible company.[22] But when the same students were asked to define *socially responsible*, things got complicated. Even those who support the idea of social responsibility can't agree on what it is. Instead, let's look at the concept through the eyes of the stakeholders to whom businesses are responsible: customers, investors, employees, and society in general.

Responsibility to Customers

President John F. Kennedy proposed four basic rights of consumers: (1) the right to safety, (2) the right to be informed, (3) the right to choose, and (4) the right to be heard. These rights will be achieved only if business and consumers recognize them and take action in the marketplace.

A recurring theme of this book is the importance of pleasing customers by offering them real value. Since three of five new businesses fail, we know this responsibility is not as easy to meet as it seems. One sure way of failing to please customers is to be less than honest with them. The payoff for socially conscious behavior, however, can be new customers who admire the company's social efforts—a powerful competitive edge. Consumer behavior studies show that, all else being equal, a socially conscious company is likely to be viewed more favorably than others.

It's not enough for companies to brag about their social responsibility efforts; they must live up to the expectations they raise or face the consequences.

▶ **CRITICAL THINKING EXERCISE 4-4:**
Ethics Minicases

▶ **PPT 4-22:**
Positive Impacts of Companies

▶ **PPT 4-23:**
To Whom Much Has Been Given...

▶ **LECTURE LINK 4-3:**
The Pyramid of Corporate Social Responsibility

▶ **LECTURE LINK 4-4:**
Merck and Ethics (Part I)

▶ **PPT 4-24:**
Helping Hands

▶ **PPT 4-25:**
Who Gives?

▶ **PPT 4-26:**
Generous Americans

▶ **PPT 4-27:**
President Kennedy's Basic Rights of Consumers

▶ **BONUS CASE 4-2:**
Merck and Ethics (Part II)

When herbal tea maker Celestial Seasonings ignored its advertised image of environmental stewardship by poisoning prairie dogs on its property, it incurred customers' wrath.[23] Customers prefer to do business with companies they trust and, even more important, don't want to do business with those they don't trust. Companies earn customers' trust by demonstrating credibility over time; they can lose it at any point.

Responsibility to Investors

Ethical behavior doesn't subtract from the bottom line; it adds to it. In contrast, unethical behavior, even if it seems to work in the short term, does financial damage. Those cheated are the shareholders themselves. For example, in just 11 business days in June 2002, 44 CEOs left U.S. corporations amid accusations of wrongdoing, and the stock prices of their companies plummeted.

Some people believe that you must make money before you can do good; others believe that by doing good, you can also do well. Bagel Works, a New England–based chain of bagel stores, has a dual-bottom-line approach that focuses on the well-being of the planet in addition to profits. Each store not only employs environmentally protective practices such as in-store recycling, composting, and using organically grown ingredients and nontoxic cleaners; it also includes donations for community causes in its budget. The company donates 10 percent of its pretax profits to charities each year and has earned national recognition for social responsibility.

Many investors believe that it makes financial as well as moral sense to invest in companies that plan ahead to create a better environment. By choosing to put their money into companies whose goods and services benefit the community and the environment, investors can improve their own financial health while improving society's.[24]

A few investors, however, have chosen unethical means to improve their financial health. For example, **insider trading** uses private company information to further insiders' own fortunes or those of their family and friends. A high-profile case implicated home-style diva Martha Stewart. While Stewart was never convicted of insider trading, she was found guilty of lying to authorities investigating the possibility of such trading.[25]

Insider trading isn't limited to company executives and their friends. Before it was publicly known that IBM was going to take over Lotus Development, an IBM secretary told her husband, who told two co-workers, who told friends, relatives, business associates, and even a pizza delivery man. A total of 25 people traded illegally on the insider tip within a six-hour period. When the deal was announced publicly, Lotus stock soared 89 percent. One of the inside traders, a stockbroker who passed the information to a few customers, made $468,000 in profits. The U.S. Securities and Exchange Commission (SEC) filed charges against the secretary, her husband, and 23 others. Four defendants settled out of court by paying penalties of twice their profits. Prosecutors are increasingly pursuing insider trading cases to ensure that the securities market remains fair and equally accessible to all.

After the deluge of insider trader cases made public in the early 2000s, the SEC adopted a new rule called Regulation FD (for "fair disclosure"). The rule doesn't specify what information can and cannot be disclosed. It simply requires companies that release any information to share it with everybody, not just a few select people. In other words, if companies tell anyone, they must tell everyone—at the same time.[26]

Some companies have misused information for their own benefit at investors' expense. When WorldCom admitted to accounting irregularities

New York's attorney general led an investigation into seven student-loan companies, charging they had misled student borrowers with questionable marketing tactics. The companies agreed to place $1.4 million into a fund to educate students and their families about loans and to follow a code of ethical conduct.

◄ PPT 4-28:
Insider Trading

◄ CRITICAL THINKING EXERCISE 4-5:
Social Responsibility Successes and Failures

insider trading
An unethical activity in which insiders use private company information to further their own fortunes or those of their family and friends.

BREWING a better world
GMCR

Green Mountain Coffee Roasters calls itself "a force for good in the world," and claims: "We celebrate and support the power of businesses and individuals to bring about positive changes, locally and globally." The company sets aside 5 percent of pretax earnings each year for good causes and produces an annual corporate social responsibility report. Do companies owe their investors a responsibility to be profitable, or to do good? Can they do both?

▶ PPT 4-29:
Responsibility to Employees

▶ BONUS CASE 4-3:
A Glance Into the Future: Your Computer Knows

▶ PPT 4-30:
America's Most Admired Companies

▶ LECTURE LINK 4-5:
E-Cycling

▶ LECTURE LINK 4-6:
Saving Lives with LifeStraw

▶ PPT 4-31:
Society and the Environment

misrepresenting its profitability, investors who had purchased its stock on the basis of the false financial reports saw share prices free-fall from the midteens in January 2002 to less than a dime the following July. The pain was even greater for long-term investors, who had bought the stock at around $60 in 1999.

Responsibility to Employees

It's been said that the best social program in the world is a job. Businesses have a responsibility to create jobs if they want to grow. Once they've done so, they must see to it that hard work and talent are fairly rewarded. Employees need realistic hope of a better future, which comes only through a chance for upward mobility. Studies have shown that what most influences a company's effectiveness and financial performance is responsible human resource management.[27] We'll discuss this in Chapter 11.

If a company treats employees with respect, those employees usually will respect the company as well. Mutual respect can make a huge difference in a company's bottom line. In their book *Contented Cows Give Better Milk*, Bill Catlette and Richard Hadden compared "contented cow" companies with "common cow" companies. The companies with contented employees outgrew their counterparts by four to one for more than 10 years. They also out-earned the "common cow" companies by nearly $40 billion and generated 800,000 more jobs. Catlette and Hadden attribute this difference in performance to the commitment and caring the outstanding companies demonstrated for their employees.[28]

One way a company can demonstrate commitment and caring is to give employees salaries and benefits that help them reach their personal goals. The wage and benefit packages offered by warehouse retailer Costco are among the best in hourly retail. Even part-time workers are covered by Costco's health plan, and the workers pay less for their coverage than at other retailers such as Wal-Mart.[29] Increased benefits reduce employee turnover, which at Costco is less than a third of industry average. The U.S. Department of Labor estimates that replacing employees costs between 150 and 250 percent of their annual salaries, so retaining workers is good for business as well as morale.

Getting even is one of the most powerful incentives for good people to do bad things. Few disgruntled workers are desperate enough to commit violence in the workplace, but a great number relieve their frustrations in subtle ways: blaming mistakes on others, not accepting responsibility, manipulating budgets and expenses, making commitments they intend to ignore, hoarding resources, doing the minimum needed to get by, and making results look better than they are.

The loss of employee commitment, confidence, and trust in the company and its management can be costly indeed. Employee fraud costs U.S. businesses approximately 5 percent of annual revenue and causes 30 percent of all business failures, according to the Association of Certified Fraud Examiners.[30] You'll read more about employee–management issues like pay equity, sexual harassment, child and elder care, drug testing, and violence in the workplace in Chapter 12.

Responsibility to Society and the Environment

More than a third of U.S. workers receive salaries from nonprofit organizations that receive funding from others, that in turn receive their money from businesses. Foundations, universities, and other nonprofit organizations own billions of shares in publicly held companies. As stock prices of those firms increase, businesses create more wealth to benefit society.

Businesses are also partly responsible for promoting social justice. Many companies believe they have a role in building communities that goes well beyond simply "giving back." To them, charity is not enough. Their social contributions include cleaning up the environment, building community toilets, providing computer lessons, caring for the elderly, and supporting children from low-income families.

As concern about global warming increased, the green movement emerged in nearly every aspect of daily life. What makes a product green? Some believe that a product's carbon footprint (the amount of carbon released during production, distribution, consumption, and disposal) defines how green it is. Many variables contribute to a product's carbon footprint. The carbon footprint of a package of, say, frozen corn includes not only the carbon released by the fertilizer to grow the corn but also the carbon in the fertilizer itself, the gas used to run the farm equipment and transport the corn to market, the electricity to make the plastic packages and power the freezers, and so on.

No specific guidelines define the carbon footprints of products, businesses, or individuals or outline how to communicate them to consumers. PepsiCo presents carbon information with a label on bags of cheese-and-onion potato chips, for example, that says "75 grams of CO_2." Simple enough, but what does it mean? (We don't know either.)[31]

The green movement has provided consumers with lots of product choices. However, making those choices means sorting through the many and confusing claims made by manufacturers. (See the Thinking Green box on p. 104 for a discussion of misusing the green label.) The noise in the marketplace challenges even the most dedicated green activists, but taking the easy route of buying what's most readily available violates the principles of the green movement.[32]

Environmental efforts may increase a company's costs, but they also allow the company to charge higher prices, increase market share, or both. Ciba Specialty Chemicals, a Swiss textile-dye manufacturer, developed dyes that require less salt than traditional dyes. Since used dye solutions must be treated before being released into rivers or streams, less salt means lower water-treatment costs. Patents protect Ciba's low-salt dyes, so the company can charge more for its dyes than other companies can charge for theirs. Ciba's experience illustrates that, just as a new machine enhances labor productivity, lowering environmental costs can add value to a business.

Not all environmental strategies are as financially beneficial as Ciba's, however. In the early 1990s, tuna producer StarKist responded to consumer concerns about dolphins in the eastern Pacific dying in nets set out for yellowfin tuna. The company announced it would sell only skipjack tuna from the western Pacific, which do not swim near dolphins. Unfortunately, customers were unwilling to pay a premium for dolphin-safe tuna and considered the taste of skipjack inferior. Nor was there a clear environmental gain: for every dolphin saved in the eastern Pacific, thousands of immature tuna and dozens of sharks, turtles, and other marine animals died in the western Pacific fishing process.

The green movement has had a positive impact on the U.S. labor force. Emerging renewable-energy and energy-efficiency industries currently account for 9 million jobs and by 2030 will create as many as 40 million more in engineering, manufacturing, construction, accounting, and management, according to a green-collar job report by the American Solar Energy Society.[33]

Environmental quality is a public good; that is, everyone gets to enjoy it regardless of who pays for it. The challenge for companies is to find the public goods that will appeal to their customers. Many corporations are publishing reports that document their net social contribution. To do that, a company must measure its positive social contributions and subtract its negative social impacts. We discuss that process next.

◄ PPT 4-32:
Responsibility to the Environment

THINKING green

www.greenwashingindex.com

Green Greed

With public concern over the environment at an all-time high, companies are constantly looking for more eco-friendly ways of doing business. Some, however, only want to appear green while still maintaining the same business practices. These corner-cutting companies have been accused of "greenwashing," that is, using deceptive marketing and advertising that portrays their business as environmentally responsible. For example, many paint brands claim to be low in eco-unfriendly volatile organic compounds (VOCs), but when colorant is added to the paint at stores, VOCs are added too and the count in the final product jumps to dangerous levels. Other products simply offer irrelevant information to appear green, such as aerosol cans with green dots to show the product has no ozone-depleting chlorofluorocarbons (CFC). In fact, no aerosol spray sold in the United States today contains CFC, because the chemical was banned in 1978. Since most greenwashed ads are subtle, they fall short of being illegal and fly under the radar of most consumers. To combat this marketing strategy, independent organizations screen hundreds of ads and determine which are genuinely green and which are greenwashing. For more information, visit, for example, *Consumer Reports'* Greener Choices (www.greenerchoices.org) and the University of Oregon's Greenwashing Index (www.greenwashingindex.com) and keep in mind that not everything's as green as it seems.

Sources: Kenneth Stier, "Companies' 'Green' Claims Often Misleading: Experts," *CNBC*, April 22, 2008; Andrea Billups, "Texas Duo Patrols Ads for Abuse of Eco-Claims," *Washington Times*, June 11, 2008.

Social Auditing

Can we measure whether organizations are making social responsibility an integral part of top management's decision making? The answer is yes, and the term that represents that measurement is *social auditing*.

A **social audit** is a systematic evaluation of an organization's progress toward implementing socially responsible and responsive programs. One of the major problems of conducting a social audit is establishing procedures for measuring a firm's activities and their effects on society. What should a social audit measure? Many consider workplace issues, the environment, product safety, community relations, military weapons contracting, international operations and human rights, and respect for the rights of local people.

It remains a question whether we should add up positive actions like charitable donations and pollution control efforts, and then subtract negative effects like layoffs and overall pollution created, to get a net social contribution. Or should we just record positive actions? What do you think? However they are conducted, social audits force organizations to consider their social responsibility beyond the level of just feeling good or managing public relations.

In addition to social audits conducted by companies themselves, four types of groups serve as watchdogs to monitor how well companies enforce their ethical and social responsibility policies:

1. *Socially conscious investors* insist that a company extend its own high standards to its suppliers. Social responsibility investing (SRI) is on the rise, with nearly $3 trillion invested in SRI funds in the United States already.[34]

▶ **PPT 4-33:** Green Greed

▶ **PPT 4-34:** Social Auditing

social audit
A systematic evaluation of an organization's progress toward implementing socially responsible and responsive programs.

2. *Environmentalists* apply pressure by naming companies that don't abide by environmentalists' standards. After months of protests coordinated by the San Francisco–based Rainforest Action Network (RAN), JPMorgan Chase & Co. adopted guidelines that restrict its lending and underwriting practices for industrial projects likely to have a negative impact on the environment. RAN activists first go after an industry leader, like JPMorgan, then tackle smaller companies. "We call it, 'Rank 'em and spank 'em,'" says RAN's executive director.[35]
3. *Union officials* hunt down violations and force companies to comply to avoid negative publicity.
4. *Customers* make buying decisions based on their social conscience. Fifty-five percent of respondents to a recent survey said they make special efforts to patronize retailers with a green reputation, 74 percent said they buy environmentally friendly products, and 60 percent said they are willing to pay more for them.[36]

What these groups look for constantly changes as the worldview changes. Until September 11, 2001, no group formally screened publicly traded companies to determine potential links to terrorism or the spread of weapons of mass destruction. Now some groups have targeted companies that may be peripherally linked. Three-quarters of businesses surveyed in 2008 reported that the number of advocacy groups collecting and reporting information about them increased in the last three years.[37] It isn't enough for a company to be right when it comes to ethics and social responsibility—it also has to convince its customers and society that it's right.

> Green jobs "cannot be easily outsourced, say, to Asia," says the president of Green for All, an organization that promotes renewable energy. "If we are going to weatherize buildings, they have to be weatherized here. If you put up solar panels, you can't ship a building to Asia and have them put the solar panels on and ship it back. These jobs have to be done in the United States." What employee skills will "green" firms look for?

progress assessment

- What is corporate social responsibility, and how does it relate to each of a business's major stakeholders?
- What is a social audit, and what kinds of activities does it monitor?

◄ PPT 4-35:
Progress Assessment

LEARNING goal 6 *

Analyze the role of U.S businesses in influencing ethical behavior and social responsibility in global markets.

INTERNATIONAL ETHICS AND SOCIAL RESPONSIBILITY

◄ PPT 4-36:
International Ethics

Ethical problems and issues of social responsibility are not unique to the United States. Influence-peddling or bribery charges have been brought against top officials in Japan, South Korea, China, Italy, Brazil, Pakistan, and Zaire. What is new about the moral and ethical standards by which government leaders are being judged? They are much stricter than in the past. Top leaders are now being held to higher standards.

◄ PPT 4-37:
Givers Around the World

Many U.S. businesses also demand socially responsible behavior from their international suppliers, making sure they don't violate U.S. human rights and environmental standards. Sears will not import products made by Chinese prison labor. Clothing manufacturer Phillips–Van Heusen will cancel orders from suppliers that violate its ethical, environmental, and human rights code. Dow Chemical expects suppliers to conform to tough U.S. pollution and safety laws rather than just to local laws of their respective countries. McDonald's denied rumors that one of its suppliers grazes cattle on cleared rain-forest land but wrote a ban on the practice anyway.

In contrast are companies criticized for exploiting workers in less developed countries. Nike, the world's largest athletic shoe company, has been accused by human rights and labor groups of treating its workers poorly while lavishing millions of dollars on star athletes to endorse its products. Cartoonist Garry Trudeau featured an anti-Nike campaign in his popular syndicated series *Doonesbury*. An Ernst & Young report on Nike's operations in Asia indicated that thousands of young women labored over 10 hours a day, six days a week, in excessive heat, noise, and foul air, for slightly more than $10 a week.[38]

Nike is working to improve its reputation, in part by joining forces with Patagonia, Gap, five other companies, and six leading anti-sweatshop groups to create a single set of labor standards with a common factory inspection system. The goal of the Joint Initiative on Corporate Accountability and Workers' Rights is to replace current approaches with a single inexpensive and easy-to-use standard that more companies can adopt.[39] If the 30-month experiment works, one outcome is to keep companies from undercutting one another on labor standards. One sticking point is the local living wage, which must be subjectively determined and will likely exceed the local legal minimum wage. Success of the Joint Initiative should benefit all the companies' stakeholders— employees, investors, community, and customers. While customers still favor brand, price, and quality over their perception of a company's humane actions and social responsibility, surveys show that the vast majority would pay a few extra dollars for a garment made in a worker-friendly environment.

The fairness of requiring international suppliers to adhere to U.S. ethical standards is not as clear-cut as you might think. For example, a gift in one

Nike has outsourced the manufacture of its products to plants in other countries and has weathered much criticism for operating in low-wage countries where child labor is common. The company has taken many corrective measures, including working with other companies and advocacy groups on a set of common labor standards and factory guidelines. Can a successful firm overcome past ethical errors?

REACHING BEYOND our borders

www.motorola.com

Ethical Culture Clash

Now that corporations have shattered the world's borders to expand into communities all over the globe, it raises the question: Which communities are they responsible for?

Take communications and electronics giant Motorola. Almost half its employees live outside the United States, and more than half its revenues come from non-U.S. markets. Is it difficult for Motorola employees to adhere to the company's ethical values while at the same time respecting the values of the host countries in which Motorola manufactures and markets its products?

Here's an example of how corporate ethics can clash with cultural ethics. Joe, the oldest son of a poor South American cloth peddler, managed to move to the United States, earn an engineering degree, and get a job with Motorola. After five years, Joe seemed to have bought into the Motorola culture and was happy to be granted a transfer back to his home country. He was told that the company expected him to live there in a safe and presentable home of his choice. To help him afford such a residence, Motorola agreed to reimburse him a maximum of $2,000 a month for the cost of his rent and servants. Each month Joe submitted rental receipts for exactly $2,000. The company later found out that Joe was living in what was, by Western standards, a shack in a dangerous area of town. Such a humble home could not have cost more than $200 a month. The company was concerned for Joe's safety as well as for the effect his residence would have on Motorola's image. The human resource manager was also worried about Joe's lack of integrity, given he had submitted false receipts for reimbursement.

Joe was upset with what he considered the company's invasion of his privacy. He argued he should receive the full $2,000 monthly reimbursement all employees received. He explained his choice of housing by saying he was making sacrifices so he could send the extra money to his family and put his younger siblings through school. This was especially important since his father had died and his family had no one else to depend on. "Look, my family is poor," Joe said, "so poor that most Westerners wouldn't believe our poverty even if they saw it. This money means the difference between hope and despair for all of us. For me to do anything less for my family would be to defile the honor of my late father. Can't you understand?"

Often it is difficult to understand what others perceive as ethical. Different situations often turn the clear waters of "rightness" downright muddy. Joe was trying to do the honorable thing for his family. Yet Motorola's wish to have its higher-level people live in safe housing is not unreasonable, given the dangerous conditions of the city in which Joe lived. The policy of housing reimbursement supports Motorola's intent to make its employees' stay in the country reasonably comfortable and safe, not to increase their salaries. If Joe worked in the United States, where he would not receive a housing supplement, it would be unethical for him to falsify expense reports in order to receive more money to send to his family. In South America, though, the issue is not so clear.

Sources: R. S. Moorthy, Robert C. Solomon, William J. Ellos, and Richard T. De George, "Friendship or Bribery?" *Across the Board,* January 1999, pp. 43–47; and Marina V. Whitman, Mayer N. Zald, Gerald F. Davis, "The Responsibility Paradox," *Stanford Social Innovation Review,* January 2008.

culture can be a bribe in another. Is it always ethical for companies to demand compliance with the standards of their own countries? What about countries where child labor is accepted and families depend on children's salaries for survival? Should foreign companies doing business in the United States expect U.S. companies to comply with their ethical standards? Since multinational corporations span different societies, should they conform to any society's standards? Why is Sears applauded for not importing goods made in Chinese prisons when there are many prison-based enterprises in the United States? None of these questions are easy to answer, but they suggest the complexity of social responsibility in international markets. (See the Reaching Beyond Our Borders box for an example of an ethical culture clash.)

In the 1970s, the Foreign Corrupt Practices Act (discussed in Chapter 3) sent a chill throughout the U.S. business community by criminalizing the act of paying foreign business or government leaders to get business. Many U.S. executives complained this law put their businesses at a competitive disadvantage when bidding against non-U.S. companies, since foreign companies don't have to abide by it.[40]

To identify some form of common global ethic and fight corruption in global markets, partners in the Organization of American States signed the Inter-American Convention Against Corruption. The United Nations adopted a formal condemnation of corporate bribery, as did the European Union and the Organization for Economic Cooperation and Development. The International Organization for Standardization (ISO) plans to publish a standard on social responsibility called ISO 26000, with guidelines on product manufacturing, fair pay rates, appropriate employee treatment, and hiring practices.[41] These standards are advisory only and will not be used for certification purposes. The formation of a single set of international rules governing multinational corporations is unlikely in the near future. In many places "Fight corruption" remains just a slogan, but even a slogan is a start.

progress assessment

- How are U.S. businesses demanding socially responsible behavior from their international suppliers?
- Why is it unlikely that there will be a single set of international rules governing multinational companies soon?

summary

Learning Goal 1. Explain why obeying the law is only the first step in behaving ethically.

- **How is legality different from ethics?**

Ethics goes beyond obeying laws to include abiding by the moral standards accepted by society. Ethics reflects people's proper relationships with one another. Legality is more limiting; it refers only to laws written to protect people from fraud, theft, and violence.

Learning Goal 2. Ask the three questions to answer when faced with a potentially unethical action.

- **How can we tell if our business decisions are ethical?**

We can put our business decisions through an ethics check by asking three questions: (1) Is it legal? (2) Is it balanced? and (3) How will it make me feel?

Learning Goal 3. Describe management's role in setting ethical standards.

- **What is management's role in setting ethical standards?**

Managers often set formal ethical standards, but more important are the messages they send through their actions. Management's tolerance or intolerance of ethical misconduct influences employees more than any written ethics codes.

Learning Goal 4. Distinguish between compliance-based and integrity-based ethics codes, and list the six steps in setting up a corporate ethics code.

- **What's the difference between compliance-based and integrity-based ethics codes?**

Whereas compliance-based ethics codes are concerned with avoiding legal punishment, integrity-based ethics codes define the organization's guiding values, create an environment that supports ethically sound behavior, and stress a shared accountability among employees.

Learning Goal 5. Define *corporate social responsibility* and compare corporations' responsibilities to various stakeholders.

- **What is corporate social responsibility?**

Corporate social responsibility is the concern businesses have for society.

- **How do businesses demonstrate corporate responsibility toward stakeholders?**

Business is responsible to four types of stakeholders: (1) it must *satisfy customers* with goods and services of real value; (2) it must make money for its *investors;* (3) it must create jobs for *employees,* maintain job security, and see that hard work and talent are fairly rewarded; and (4) it must create new wealth for *society,* promote social justice, and contribute to making its own environment a better place.

- **How are a company's social responsibility efforts measured?**

A corporate social audit measures an organization's progress toward social responsibility. Some people believe the audit should add together the organization's positive actions and then subtract the negative effects to get a net social benefit.

Learning Goal 6. Analyze the role of U.S. businesses in influencing ethical behavior and social responsibility in global markets.

- **How can U.S. companies influence ethical behavior and social responsibility in global markets?**

Many U.S. businesses are demanding socially responsible behavior from their international suppliers by making sure their suppliers do not violate U.S. human rights and environmental standards. Companies like Sears, Phillips–Van Heusen, and Dow Chemical will not import products from companies that do not meet their ethical and social responsibility standards.

key terms

compliance-based ethics codes 96
corporate philanthropy 99
corporate policy 100
corporate responsibility 100
corporate social initiatives 99
corporate social responsibility (CSR) 98
ethics 92
insider trading 101
integrity-based ethics codes 96
social audit 104
whistleblowers 97

connect interactive applications

Reinforcing Your *Connect*ion to Concepts in Business

This chapter offers 15 interactive applications designed to help you apply what you've learned (examples of these exercises appear on the following pages). Your instructor has determined which interactive applications will benefit you throughout this course. Please refer to your instructor's assignment list in *Connect* to determine which applications you should complete.

Comprehension Case Interactive: Ethical problems and issues of social responsibility are not unique to the United States. Stakeholders are demanding socially responsible behavior from their U.S. businesses operating abroad. This poses an ethical dilemma for many companies like Motorola. United States' companies have created corporate policy that is guided by ethical business standards and social responsibility. However, the companies are realizing that the policies they adopt do not always align with the cultural values of the host country. Foreign employees are confronted with the dilemma of following corporate policy or adhering to their cultural and family values. In this exercise, you will read the case and answer the questions.

Comprehension Case Interactive: Choices are not always easy, and the obvious ethical solution may have personal or professional drawbacks. Every college student has been warned about plagiarizing material from the Internet, books, periodicals, or other peoples' work. As the text states, plagiarizing is the most common form of cheating. YouTube has become a popular Web site for individuals as well as businesses. However, using material that is protected by copyright is not only unethical, but illegal as well. The "To Tube or Not To Tube" case discusses the issue of video piracy. This case presents a legal and ethical dilemma regarding the use of copyright-protected material. Read the case and answer the questions.

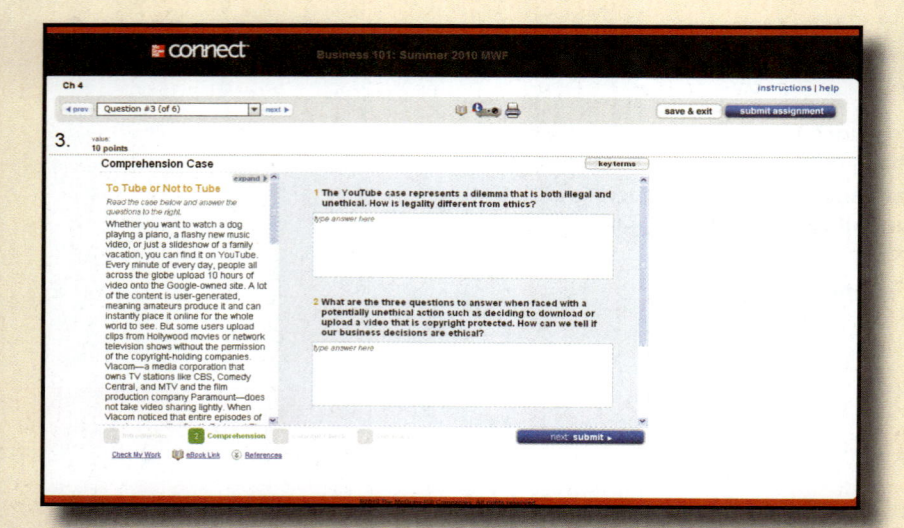

Click and Drag Interactive: There are six steps that businesses can take to improve business ethics in the United States. Review the various steps involved in establishing a corporate code of ethics and assemble the steps on the timeline as instructed.

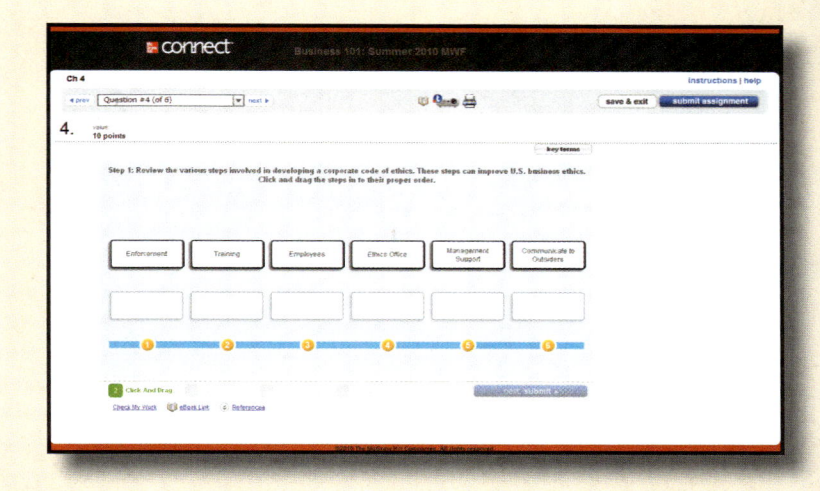

Video Case Interactive: Corporate social responsibility (CSR) is the concern businesses have for the welfare of society, not just for their owners. CSR goes well beyond being ethical. It is based on a commitment to integrity, fairness, and respect to all the stakeholders of the organization. Organizations have far more responsibility than just pursuing a profit. Corporations have responsibility to their customers, their investors, their employees, and their communities and environment. Through social audits, today's society is demanding that corporations implement socially responsible and responsive programs. View the video case and answer the questions when prompted.

Click and Drag Interactive: Corporate social responsibility (CSR) is the concern businesses have for the welfare of society, not just for their owners. Review the various responsibilities listed and place them under the appropriate stakeholder. Next, review the example and place each under the appropriate stakeholder.

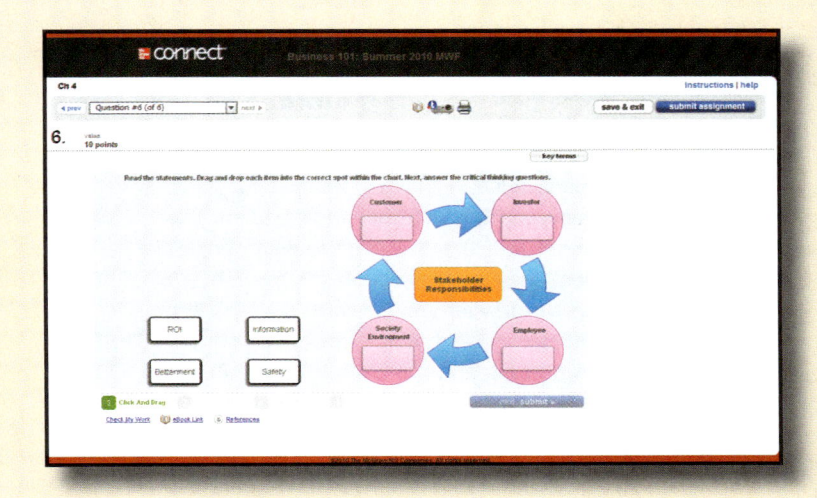

5
HOW to Form a Business

> PPT 5-1:
> How to Form a Business

> PPT 5-2:
> Brian Scudamore

profile

Getting to Know
x Brian Scudamore
Founder of I-800-GOT-JUNK?

In 1989, 18-year-old college student Brian Scudamore couldn't find a summer job, so he decided to start his own business. Inspired by a junk-hauling truck he saw at a McDonald's, Scudamore bought a used truck for $700 and began a junk removal company called the Rubbish Boys (he chose the plural name even though he was the owner and sole employee). His slogan was "We'll Stash Your Trash in a Flash!" Over the following summers Scudamore's business grew, and in 1998 he changed the name to I-800-GOT-JUNK? and expanded his business through franchising.

With uniformed employees and clean, shiny trucks proudly advertising the company's name and telephone number, Scudamore set his company apart from other independent junk haulers, creating an unlikely brand out of hauling people's trash or, as Scudamore sees it, treasure. Most trash removal services require you to drag your junk down to the curb, but I-800-GOT-JUNK? doesn't. Leave your stuff in the garage, basement, attic, or wherever, and the crew will come in and pick it up from there. They will even sort your trash into three categories: recycling, donating, and dumping, so you can rest assured that your reusable castoffs will not end up in a landfill unnecessarily. Now 40, Scudamore is the world's richest garbage man, with $130 million in annual earnings from servicing around 200 million people across North America and Australia. While many companies expand their businesses by transforming into corporations and selling shares on the open market, I-800-GOT-JUNK? expanded solely through entrepreneurs opening licensed franchises in their own towns. By franchising his business and not depending on outside investors, Scudamore has been able to retain 100 percent control of the company. He has, though, handed over the day-to-day operations of the company to Launi Skinner, a former president of Starbucks U.S. Skinner became the new president and chief operating officer of I-800-GOT-JUNK? in August 2008.

Scudamore's achievements have not gone unnoticed. I-800-GOT-JUNK? was listed 97th on the Franchise 500 list and 10th on *Franchise Business Reviews*' Top 50 list for franchisee satisfaction. The company often tops Canadian surveys of the best companies to work for, and Scudamore was named the

LEARNING goals

After you have read and studied this chapter, you should be able to

1. Compare the advantages and disadvantages of sole proprietorships.
2. Describe the differences between general and limited partners, and compare the advantages and disadvantages of partnerships.
3. Compare the advantages and disadvantages of corporations, and summarize the differences between C corporations, S corporations, and limited liability companies.
4. Describe three types of corporate mergers, and explain the role of leveraged buyouts and taking a firm private.
5. Outline the advantages and disadvantages of franchises, and discuss the opportunities for diversity in franchising and the challenges of global franchising.
6. Explain the role of cooperatives.

connect

Your *Connect*ion to Better Learning. 1. View the interactive presentation. 2. Practice through LearnSmart. 3. Apply your knowledge by using the interactive applications for each chapter of this text.

1 Prep >>>>> **2 Study** 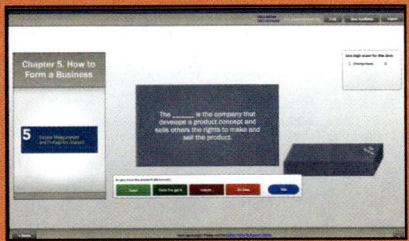 >>>>> **3 Apply**

2007 International Franchise Association's Entrepreneur of the Year. He realized a personal dream by appearing on *The Oprah Winfrey Show.*

Scudamore continues to look to the future. He constantly reminds employees, franchisees, and the media about his clear vision for the company's future, which he calls his "painted picture." His current goal is to earn $1 billion in annual sales with locations in 10 countries by 2012. Perhaps more than anything, though, Scudamore wants 1-800-GOT-JUNK? to be admired across the globe. "Admired not for what we've built, but how we've built it," said Scudamore.

Just like Scudamore, all business owners must decide for themselves which form of business is best for them. Whether you dream of starting a business for yourself, going into business with a partner, forming a corporation, or someday being a leading franchisor, it's important to know that each form of ownership has its advantages and disadvantages. You will learn about them all in this chapter.

Sources: Eric Stites, "Franchise Relations: Different Ideas, Great Solutions," *Franchising World,* May 1, 2008; "Junk Removal Founder Awarded Entrepreneur of the Year by International Franchise Association," PR Newswire, February 11, 2008; 1-800-GOT-JUNK? www.1800gotjunk.com, accessed July 2, 2010.

www.1800gotjunk.com

NAME THAT Company

My name is Mary Ellen Sheets, and I started my company when my sons were in college. They were looking for ways to make some money, so I bought a truck for $350 and placed an advertisement under "Movers" in the classified section of the newspaper. When my sons went back to school, I found more men to fill my trucks. Now we are a large company with 1,300 trucks in 200 franchise locations across North America. What company did I start? (Find the answer in the chapter.)

▶ **LECTURE LINK 5-1:**
The Fortune List of Most Admired Corporations

▶ **PPT 5-3:**
Major Forms of Ownership

▶ **PPT 5-4:**
Forms of Business Ownership

sole proprietorship
A business that is owned, and usually managed, by one person.

partnership
A legal form of business with two or more owners.

BASIC FORMS OF BUSINESS OWNERSHIP

Like Brian Scudamore, hundreds of thousands of people have started new businesses in the United States. In fact, more than 600,000 are started each year.[1] Chances are, you've thought of owning your own business or know someone who has.

How you form your business can make a tremendous difference in your long-term success. The three major forms of business ownership are (1) sole proprietorships, (2) partnerships, and (3) corporations. Each has advantages and disadvantages that we'll discuss.

It can be easy to get started in your own business. You can begin a lawn mowing service, develop a Web site, or go about meeting other wants and needs of your community. A business owned, and usually managed, by one person is called a **sole proprietorship**. That is the most common form of business ownership.

Many people do not have the money, time, or desire to run a business on their own. When two or more people legally agree to become co-owners of a business, the organization is called a **partnership**.

Sole proprietorships and partnerships are relatively easy to form, but there are advantages to creating a business that is separate and distinct from the

figure 5.1
FORMS OF BUSINESS OWNERSHIP

Although corporations make up only 20 percent of the total number of businesses, they make 81 percent of the total receipts. Sole proprietorships are the most common form (72 percent), but they earn only 6 percent of the receipts.
Source: U.S. Internal Revenue Service.

Percentage of Businesses
- Sole proprietorships 72%
- Corporations 20%
- Partnerships 8%

Percentage of Total Receipts
- Corporations 81%
- Partnerships 13%
- Sole proprietorships 6%

owners. This is a **corporation**, a legal entity with authority to act and have liability apart from its owners. The almost 5 million corporations in the United States make up only 20 percent of all businesses, but they earn 81 percent of total U.S. business receipts (see Figure 5.1).

Keep in mind that just because a business starts in one form of ownership, it doesn't have to stay in that form. Many companies start out in one form, then add (or drop) a partner or two, and eventually become corporations, limited liability companies, or franchisors.[2] Let's begin our discussion by looking at the most basic form of ownership—the sole proprietorship.

> **corporation**
> A legal entity with authority to act and have liability apart from its owners.

LEARNING goal 1 *

Compare the advantages and disadvantages of sole proprietorships.

◄ PPT 5-5:
Major Benefits of Sole Proprietorship

SOLE PROPRIETORSHIPS

Advantages of Sole Proprietorships

Sole proprietorships are the easiest kind of businesses to explore in your quest for an interesting career. Every town has sole proprietors you can visit. Talk with some of these businesspeople about the joys and frustrations of being on their own. Most will mention the benefits of being their own boss and setting their own hours. Other advantages include:

1. *Ease of starting and ending the business.* All you have to do to start a sole proprietorship is buy or lease the needed equipment (a saw, a laptop, a tractor, a lawn mower) and put up some announcements saying you are in business. You may have to get a permit or license from the local government, but often that is no problem. It is just as easy to get out of business; you simply stop. There is no one to consult or disagree with about such decisions.

2. *Being your own boss.* Working for others simply does not have the same excitement as working for yourself—at least, that's the way sole proprietors feel. You may make mistakes, but they are your mistakes—and so are the many small victories each day.

3. *Pride of ownership.* People who own and manage their own businesses are rightfully proud of their work. They deserve all the credit for taking the risks and providing needed goods or services.

4. *Leaving a legacy.* Owners can leave an ongoing business for future generations.

5. *Retention of company profit.* Owners not only keep the profits earned but also benefit from the increasing value as the business grows.[3]

6. *No special taxes.* All the profits of a sole proprietorship are taxed as the personal income of the owner, and the owner pays the normal income tax on that money.

> Warren Brown's career is finally "rising." Brown left a promising law career to create Cakelove, a bustling bakery that specializes in making pastries from scratch using natural ingredients. Brown has appeared on The Oprah Winfrey Show and is regularly seen on the Food Network. Do you have a passion you would like to pursue as a business?

However, owners do have to pay the self-employment tax (for Social Security and Medicare). They also have to estimate their taxes and make quarterly payments to the government or suffer penalties for nonpayment.

Disadvantages of Sole Proprietorships

Not everyone is equipped to own and manage a business. Often it is difficult to save enough money to start a business and keep it going. The costs of inventory, supplies, insurance, advertising, rent, computers, utilities, and so on may be too much to cover alone. There are other disadvantages:

1. *Unlimited liability—the risk of personal losses.* When you work for others, it is their problem if the business is not profitable. When you own your own business, you and the business are considered one. You have **unlimited liability**; that is, any debts or damages incurred by the business are your debts and you must pay them, even if it means selling your home, your car, or whatever else you own. This is a serious risk, and undertaking it requires not only thought but also discussion with a lawyer, an insurance agent, an accountant, and others.

2. *Limited financial resources.* Funds available to the business are limited to what the one owner can gather. Since there are serious limits to how much money one person can raise, partnerships and corporations have a greater probability of obtaining the financial backing needed to start and equip a business and keep it going.

3. *Management difficulties.* All businesses need management; someone must keep inventory, accounting, and tax records. Many people skilled at selling things or providing a service are not so skilled at keeping records. Sole proprietors often find it difficult to attract qualified employees to help run the business because often they cannot compete with the salary and benefits offered by larger companies.

4. *Overwhelming time commitment.* Though sole proprietors say they set their own hours, it's hard to own a business, manage it, train people, and have time for anything else in life when there is no one with whom to share the burden. The owner of a store, for example, may put in 12 hours a day at least six days a week—almost twice the hours worked by a nonsupervisory employee in a large company. Imagine how this time commitment affects the sole proprietor's family life. Many sole proprietors will tell you, "It's not a job, it's not a career, it's a way of life."

5. *Few fringe benefits.* If you are your own boss, you lose the fringe benefits that often come with working for others. You have no paid health insurance, no paid disability insurance, no pension plan, no sick leave, and no vacation pay. These and other benefits may add up to 30 percent or more of a worker's income.

Being the sole proprietor of a company, like a dog-walking service, means making a major time commitment to run the business, including constantly seeking out new customers and looking for reliable employees when the time comes to grow. If you were a sole proprietor, how would you need to prepare things at the office if you wanted to take a week's vacation?

unlimited liability
The responsibility of business owners for all of the debts of the business.

▶ PPT 5-6:
Disadvantages of Sole Proprietorship

6. *Limited growth.* Expansion is often slow since a sole proprietorship relies on its owner for most of its creativity, business know-how, and funding.
7. *Limited life span.* If the sole proprietor dies, is incapacitated, or retires, the business no longer exists (unless it is sold or taken over by the sole proprietor's heirs).

Talk with a few local sole proprietors about the problems they've faced in being on their own. They are likely to have many interesting stories about problems getting loans from the bank, problems with theft, and problems simply keeping up with the business. These are reasons why many sole proprietors choose to find partners to share the load.

progress assessment

- Most people who start businesses in the United States are sole proprietors. What are the advantages and disadvantages of sole proprietorships?
- Why would unlimited liability be considered a major drawback to sole proprietorships?

LEARNING goal 2 *

Describe the differences between general and limited partners, and compare the advantages and disadvantages of partnerships.

PARTNERSHIPS

A partnership is a legal form of business with two or more owners. There are several types: (1) general partnerships, (2) limited partnerships, and (3) master limited partnerships. In a **general partnership** all owners share in operating the business and in assuming liability for the business's debts. A **limited partnership** has one or more general partners and one or more limited partners. A **general partner** is an owner (partner) who has unlimited liability and is active in managing the firm. Every partnership must have at least one general partner. A **limited partner** is an owner who invests money in the business but does not have any management responsibility or liability for losses beyond his or her investment. **Limited liability** means that the limited partners' liability for the debts of the business is *limited* to the amount they put into the company; their personal assets are not at risk.

One form of partnership, the **master limited partnership (MLP)**, looks much like a corporation (which we discuss next) in that it acts like a corporation and is traded on the stock exchanges like a corporation, but it is taxed like a partnership and thus avoids the corporate income tax. For example, Sunoco Inc. formed the MLP Sunoco Logistics (SXL) to acquire, own, and operate a group of crude oil and refined-product pipelines and storage facilities. Income received by SXL is not taxed before it is passed on to investors in the form of dividends as it would be if SXL were a corporation.[4]

general partnership
A partnership in which all owners share in operating the business and in assuming liability for the business's debts.

limited partnership
A partnership with one or more general partners and one or more limited partners.

general partner
An owner (partner) who has unlimited liability and is active in managing the firm.

limited partner
An owner who invests money in the business but does not have any management responsibility or liability for losses beyond the investment.

limited liability
The responsibility of a business's owners for losses only up to the amount they invest; limited partners and shareholders have limited liability.

master limited partnership (MLP)
A partnership that looks much like a corporation (in that it acts like a corporation and is traded on a stock exchange) but is taxed like a partnership and thus avoids the corporate income tax.

limited liability partnership (LLP)
A partnership that limits partners' risk of losing their personal assets to only their own acts and omissions and to the acts and omissions of people under their supervision.

▶ PPT 5-8:
Major Types of Partnerships

▶ PPT 5-9:
Other Forms of Partnerships

▶ PPT 5-10:
Types of Partners

▶ PPT 5-11:
Advantages of Partnerships

▶ CRITICAL THINKING EXERCISE 5-1:
Picking Partners

Husband-and-wife teams can make highly successful business partnerships. A case in point: art director and marketer Caterina Fake and her husband, Web designer Stewart Butterfield, founded the free photo-sharing Web site Flickr and sold it to Yahoo a year later for $30 million. What are some of the advantages and disadvantages of being married to your business partner?

Another type of partnership was created to limit the disadvantage of unlimited liability. A **limited liability partnership (LLP)** limits partners' risk of losing their personal assets to the outcomes of only their own acts and omissions and those of people under their supervision. If you are a limited partner in an LLP, you can operate without the fear that one of your partners might commit an act of malpractice resulting in a judgment that takes away your house, car, retirement plan, and collection of vintage Star Wars action figures, as would be the case in a general partnership. However, in many states this personal protection does not extend to contract liabilities such as bank loans, leases, and business debt the partnership takes on; loss of personal assets is still a risk if these are not paid.[5] In states without additional contract liability protections for LLPs, the LLP is in many ways similar to an LLC (discussed later in the chapter).

All states except Louisiana have adopted the Uniform Partnership Act (UPA) to replace earlier laws governing partnerships. The UPA defines the three key elements of any general partnership as (1) common ownership, (2) shared profits and losses, and (3) the right to participate in managing the operations of the business.

Advantages of Partnerships

Often, it is much easier to own and manage a business with one or more partners. Your partner may be skilled at inventory control and accounting, while you do the selling or servicing. A partner can also provide additional money, support, and expertise as well as cover for you when you are sick or on vacation. The Spotlight on Small Business box offers a few tips about choosing a partner.

Partnerships usually have the following advantages:

1. *More financial resources.* When two or more people pool their money and credit, it is easier to pay the rent, utilities, and other bills incurred by a business. A limited partnership is specially designed to help raise money. As mentioned earlier, a limited partner invests money in the business but cannot legally have any management responsibility and has limited liability.

2. *Shared management and pooled/complementary skills and knowledge.* It is simply much easier to manage the day-to-day activities of a business with carefully chosen partners. Partners give each other free time from the business and provide different skills and perspectives. Some people find that the best partner is a spouse. Many husband-and-wife teams manage restaurants, service shops, and other businesses.[6]

3. *Longer survival.* One study that examined 2,000 businesses started since 1960 found that partnerships were four times as likely to succeed as sole proprietorships. Being watched by a partner can help a businessperson become more disciplined.

4. *No special taxes.* As with sole proprietorships, all profits of partnerships are taxed as the personal income of the owners, who pay the normal income tax on that money. Similarly, partners must estimate their taxes and make quarterly payments or suffer penalties for nonpayment.

SPOTLIGHT ON SMALL business

www.entrepreneur.com

Pick Your Partner Wisely

Before you plunge into a partnership, ask yourself these questions regarding your potential partner: Do you share the same goals? Do you share the same vision for the company's future? What skills does the person have? Are those skills the same as yours, or do they complement your skills? What contacts, resources, or special attributes will the person bring to the business? What type of decision maker is the person? Is this someone with whom you could happily share authority for all major business decisions? Do you trust each other? How does the person respond to adversity? Does he or she try to solve the problem or try to defend his or her ego? Can the person accept constructive criticism without getting defensive? To what extent can you build fun into the partnership?

If the answers to many of these questions are negative, this person is not the partner for you. But remember, there's no such thing as a perfect partner, so allow for some imperfection (after all, you aren't going to be the perfect partner either). As in a good marriage, the best way to avoid major conflicts in a business partnership is to begin with an honest communication of what each partner expects to give to and get from the endeavor.

Disadvantages of Partnerships

Anytime two people must agree, conflict and tension are possible. Partnerships have caused splits between relatives, friends, and spouses. Let's explore the disadvantages of partnerships:

1. *Unlimited liability.* Each *general* partner is liable for the debts of the firm, no matter who was responsible for causing them. You are liable for your partners' mistakes as well as your own. Like sole proprietors, general partners can lose their homes, cars, and everything else they own if the business loses a lawsuit or goes bankrupt.

2. *Division of profits.* Sharing risk means sharing profits, and that can cause conflicts. There is no set system for dividing profits in a partnership, and they are not always divided evenly. For example, if one partner puts in more money and the other puts in more hours, each may feel justified in asking for a bigger share of the profits.

3. *Disagreements among partners.* Disagreements over money are just one example of potential conflict in a partnership. Who has final authority over employees? Who hires and fires employees? Who works what hours? What if one partner wants to buy expensive equipment for the firm and the other partner disagrees? All terms of the partnership should be spelled out in writing to protect all parties and minimize misunderstandings.[7]

4. *Difficulty of termination.* Once you have committed yourself to a partnership, it is not easy to get out of it. Sure, you can just quit. However, questions about who gets what and what happens next are often difficult to resolve when the partnership ends. Surprisingly, law firms often have faulty partnership agreements and find that breaking up is hard to do. How do you get rid of a partner you don't like? It is best to decide such questions up front in the partnership agreement. Figure 5.2 on p. 120 gives you more ideas about what to include in partnership agreements.

◀ PPT 5-12:
Disadvantages of Partnerships

◀ PPT 5-13:
Pick Your Partner Wisely

figure 5.2
HOW TO FORM A PARTNERSHIP

It's not hard to form a partnership, but it's wise for each prospective partner to get the counsel of a lawyer experienced with such agreements. Lawyers' services are usually expensive, so would-be partners should read all about partnerships and reach some basic agreements before calling a lawyer.

For your protection, be sure to put your partnership agreement in writing. The Model Business Corporation Act recommends including the following in a written partnership agreement:

1. The name of the business. Many states require the firm's name to be registered with state and/or county officials if the firm's name is different from the name of any of the partners.
2. The names and addresses of all partners.
3. The purpose and nature of the business, the location of the principal offices, and any other locations where business will be conducted.
4. The date the partnership will start and how long it will last. Will it exist for a specific length of time, or will it stop when one of the partners dies or when the partners agree to discontinue?
5. The contributions made by each partner. Will some partners contribute money, while others provide real estate, personal property, expertise, or labor? When are the contributions due?
6. The management responsibilities. Will all partners have equal voices in management, or will there be senior and junior partners?
7. The duties of each partner.
8. The salaries and drawing accounts of each partner.
9. Provision for sharing of profits or losses.
10. Provision for accounting procedures. Who'll keep the accounts? What bookkeeping and accounting methods will be used? Where will the books be kept?
11. The requirements for taking in new partners.
12. Any special restrictions, rights, or duties of any partner.
13. Provision for a retiring partner.
14. Provision for the purchase of a deceased or retiring partner's share of the business.
15. Provision for how grievances will be handled.
16. Provision for how to dissolve the partnership and distribute the assets to the partners.

The best way to learn about the advantages and disadvantages of partnerships is to interview several people who have experience with them. They will give you insights and hints on how to avoid problems.

One fear of owning your own business or having a partner is the fear of losing everything you own if someone sues the business or it loses a lot of money. Many businesspeople try to avoid this and the other disadvantages of sole proprietorships and partnerships by forming corporations. We discuss this basic form of business ownership in the following section.

▶ **LECTURE LINK 5-2:**
The Development of Sears Roebuck, and Company

▶ **PPT 5-14:**
Progress Assessment

progress assessment

- What is the difference between a limited partner and a general partner?
- What are some of the advantages and disadvantages of partnerships?

LEARNING goal 3 *

Compare the advantages and disadvantages of corporations, and summarize the differences between C corporations, S corporations, and limited liability companies.

> **conventional (C) corporation**
> A state-chartered legal entity with authority to act and have liability separate from its owners.

CORPORATIONS

Many corporations—like General Electric, Microsoft, and Wal-Mart—are big and contribute substantially to the U.S. economy. However, it's not necessary to be big to incorporate. Incorporating may be beneficial for small businesses as well.

A **conventional (C) corporation** is a state-chartered legal entity with authority to act and have liability separate from its owners—its *stockholders*. Stockholders are not liable for the debts or other problems of the corporation beyond the money they invest in it by buying ownership shares, or stock, in the company. Corporate owners don't have to worry about losing their house, car, or other property because of some business problem—a significant benefit. A corporation not only limits the liability of owners but often enables many people to share in the ownership (and profits) of a business without working there or having other commitments to it. Corporations can choose whether to offer ownership to outside investors or remain privately held. (We discuss stock ownership in Chapter 19.) Figure 5.3 on p. 122 describes various types of corporations.

Advantages of Corporations

Most people are not willing to risk everything to go into business. Yet for a business to grow, prosper, and create economic opportunity, many people have to be willing to invest money in it. One way to solve this problem is to create an artificial being, an entity that exists only in the eyes of the law—a corporation. Let's explore some of the advantages of corporations:

1. *Limited liability.* A major advantage of corporations is the limited liability of their owners. Remember, limited liability means that the owners of a business are responsible for its losses only up to the amount they invest in it.
2. *Ability to raise more money for investment.* To raise money, a corporation can sell shares of its stock to anyone who is interested. This means that millions of people can own part of major companies like IBM, Xerox, and Cisco, and smaller companies as well. If a company sells 10 million shares for $50 each, it will have $500 million available to build plants, buy materials, hire people, manufacture products, and so on. Such a large amount of money would be difficult to raise any other way.

    Corporations can also borrow money. They borrow from individual investors by issuing bonds, which are promises to repay the loan in the future with interest. Firms can also obtain loans from financial institutions. You can read about how corporations raise funds through the sale of stocks and bonds in Chapter 19.

◄ PPT 5-15:
Conventional Corporations

◄ PPT 5-16:
Advantages of Corporations

◄ LECTURE LINK 5-3:
The Fortune 500 Largest Companies for 2008

> *Burton Baskin and Irvine Robbins ran their ice cream businesses separately for two years. Once they had succeeded apart, Baskin and Robbins became partners and were able to avoid many of the pitfalls of starting a new business from scratch. They flipped a coin to see whose name would come first. What factors besides the partners' individual success do you think contributed to their long-lasting partnership?*

figure 5.3

CORPORATE TYPES

Corporations can fit in more than one category.

> You may find some confusing types of corporations when reading about them. Here are a few of the more widely used terms:
>
> An *alien corporation* does business in the United States but is chartered (incorporated) in another country.
>
> A *domestic corporation* does business in the state in which it's chartered (incorporated).
>
> A *foreign corporation* does business in one state but is chartered in another. About one-third of all corporations are chartered in Delaware because of its relatively attractive rules for incorporation. A foreign corporation must register in states where it operates.
>
> A *closed (private) corporation* is one whose stock is held by a few people and isn't available to the general public.
>
> An *open (public) corporation* sells stock to the general public. General Motors and ExxonMobil are examples of public corporations.
>
> A *quasi-public corporation* is a corporation chartered by the government as an approved monopoly to perform services to the general public. Public utilities are examples of quasi-public corporations.
>
> A *professional corporation* is one whose owners offer professional services (doctors, lawyers, etc.). Shares in professional corporations aren't publicly traded.
>
> A *nonprofit* (or *not-for-profit*) *corporation* is one that doesn't seek personal profit for its owners.
>
> A *multinational corporation* is a firm that operates in several countries.

▶ **LECTURE LINK 5-4:**
Really Big! Business

3. *Size.* "Size" summarizes many of the advantages of some corporations. Because they can raise large amounts of money to work with, big corporations can build modern factories or software development facilities with the latest equipment. They can hire experts or specialists in all areas of operation. They can buy other corporations in different fields to diversify their business risks. In short, a large corporation with numerous resources can take advantage of opportunities anywhere in the world.

But corporations do not have to be large to enjoy the benefits of incorporating. Many doctors, lawyers, and individuals, as well

You can be part owner of a corporation by buying shares of the company's stock. What are the advantages and disadvantages of corporations?

as partners in a variety of businesses, have incorporated. The vast majority of corporations in the United States are small businesses.

4. *Perpetual life.* Because corporations are separate from those who own them, the death of one or more owners does not terminate the corporation.
5. *Ease of ownership change.* It is easy to change the owners of a corporation. All that is necessary is to sell the stock to someone else.
6. *Ease of attracting talented employees.* Corporations can attract skilled employees by offering such benefits as stock options (the right to purchase shares of the corporation for a fixed price).
7. *Separation of ownership from management.* Corporations are able to raise money from many different owners/stockholders without getting them involved in management. The corporate hierarchy in Figure 5.4 shows how the owners/stockholders are separate from the managers and employees. The owners/stockholders elect a board of directors, who hire the officers of the corporation and oversee major policy issues. The owners/stockholders thus have some say in who runs the corporation but have no control over the daily operations.

PPT 5-17: How Owners Affect Management

PPT 5-18: The Big Boys of Business

BONUS CASE 5-1: Building Compudyne

Disadvantages of Corporations

There are so many sole proprietorships and partnerships in the United States that there must be some disadvantages to incorporating. Otherwise, everyone would do it. The following are a few of the disadvantages:

1. *Initial cost.* Incorporation may cost thousands of dollars and require expensive lawyers and accountants. There are less expensive ways

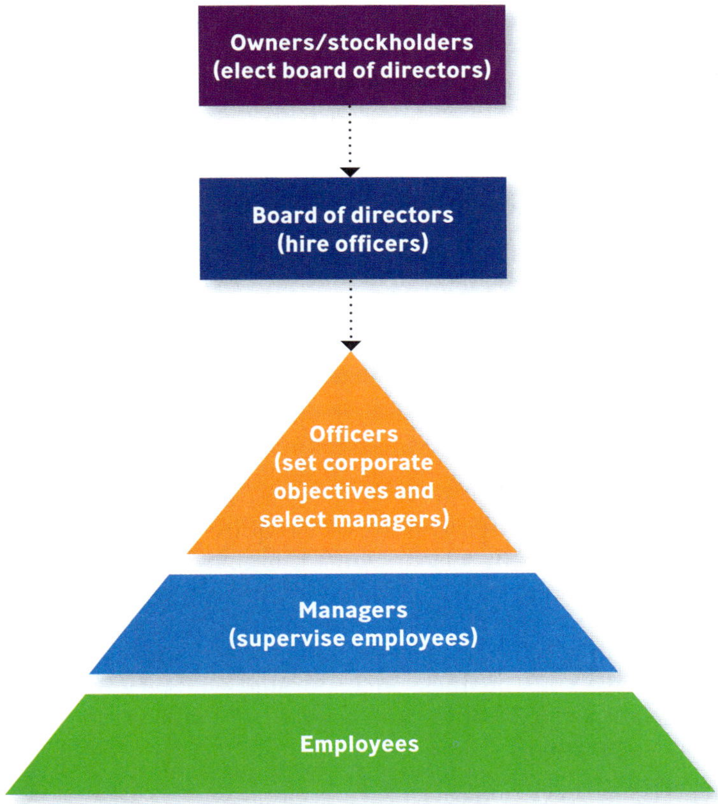
Owners/stockholders (elect board of directors)
Board of directors (hire officers)
Officers (set corporate objectives and select managers)
Managers (supervise employees)
Employees

figure 5.4

HOW OWNERS AFFECT MANAGEMENT

Owners have an influence on how business is managed by electing a board of directors. The board hires the top officers (and fires them if necessary). It also sets the pay for those officers. The officers then select managers and employees with the help of the human resources department.

of incorporating in certain states (see the following subsection), but many people do not have the time or confidence to go through this procedure without the help of a potentially expensive lawyer.

2. *Extensive paperwork.* The paperwork needed to start a corporation is just the beginning. A sole proprietor or partnership may keep rather broad accounting records. A corporation, in contrast, must keep detailed financial records, the minutes of meetings, and more. As noted in Figure 5.3 on p. 122, many firms incorporate in Delaware because the state's laws make the process easier than it is in other states.[8]

3. *Double taxation.* Corporate income is taxed twice. First the corporation pays tax on its income before it can distribute any, as *dividends*, to stockholders. Then the stockholders pay income tax on the dividends they receive. States often tax corporations more heavily than other enterprises, and some special taxes apply only to corporations.

4. *Two tax returns.* An individual who incorporates must file both a corporate tax return and an individual tax return. Depending on the size of the corporation, a corporate return can be quite complex and require the assistance of a certified public accountant (CPA).

5. *Size.* Size may be one advantage of corporations, but it can be a disadvantage as well. Large corporations sometimes become too inflexible and tied down in red tape to respond quickly to market changes, and their profitability can suffer.

6. *Difficulty of termination.* Once a corporation has started, it's relatively hard to end.

7. *Possible conflict with stockholders and board of directors.* Conflict may brew if the stockholders elect a board of directors who disagree with management. Since the board of directors chooses the company's officers, entrepreneurs serving as managers can find themselves forced out of the very company they founded. This happened to Tom Freston, one of the founders of MTV, and Steve Jobs, a founder of Apple Computer (Jobs later returned to the company).

Many businesspeople are discouraged by the costs, paperwork, and special taxes corporations must pay. However, many others believe the advantages of incorporation outweigh the hassles.

Individuals Can Incorporate

Not all corporations are large organizations with hundreds of employees and thousands of stockholders. Truckers, doctors, lawyers, plumbers, athletes, and small-business owners of all kinds can also incorporate. Normally, individuals who incorporate do not issue stock to outsiders; therefore, they do not share all the advantages and disadvantages of large corporations (such as size and more money for investment). Their major advantages are limited liability and possible tax benefits. Although you are not required to file for incorporation through a lawyer, it is usually wise to consult one. In addition to lawyers' fees, the secretary of state's office charges a fee for incorporating a business, varying by state from a low of $50 (in Colorado, Iowa, Kentucky, Mississippi, and Oklahoma) to a high of $300 (in Texas).[9] Like the fee, the length of time it will take to actually have your business incorporated will vary by state. The average time is approximately 30 days from the date of application. Figure 5.5 outlines how to incorporate.

figure 5.5
HOW TO INCORPORATE

The process of forming a corporation varies somewhat from state to state. The articles of incorporation are usually filed with the secretary of state's office in the state in which the company incorporates. The articles contain:

- The corporation's name.
- The names of the people who incorporated it.
- Its purposes.
- Its duration (usually perpetual).
- The number of shares that can be issued, their voting rights, and any other rights the shareholders have.
- The corporation's minimum capital.
- The address of the corporation's office.
- The name and address of the person responsible for the corporation's legal service.
- The names and addresses of the first directors.
- Any other public information the incorporators wish to include.

Before a business can so much as open a bank account or hire employees, it needs a federal tax identification number. To apply for one, get an SS-4 form from the IRS.

In addition to the articles of incorporation listed, a corporation has bylaws. These describe how the firm is to be operated from both legal and managerial points of view. The bylaws include

- How, when, and where shareholders' and directors' meetings are held, and how long directors are to serve.
- Directors' authority.
- Duties and responsibilities of officers, and the length of their service.
- How stock is issued.
- Other matters, including employment contracts.

S Corporations

An **S corporation** is a unique government creation that looks like a corporation but is taxed like sole proprietorships and partnerships. (The name comes from the fact that the rules governing them are in Subchapter S of Chapter 1 of the Internal Revenue Code.) The paperwork and details of S corporations are similar to those of conventional (C) corporations. S corporations have shareholders, directors, and employees, and the benefit of limited liability, but their profits are taxed only as the personal income of the shareholders—thus avoiding the double taxation of C corporations.

Avoiding double taxation is reason enough for approximately 3 million U.S. companies to operate as S corporations. Yet not all businesses can become S corporations. In order to qualify, a company must:

1. Have no more than 100 shareholders. (All members of a family count as one shareholder.)
2. Have shareholders that are individuals or estates, and who (as individuals) are citizens or permanent residents of the United States.
3. Have only one class of stock. (You can read more about the various classes of stock in Chapter 19.)
4. Derive no more than 25 percent of income from passive sources (rents, royalties, interest).

An S corporation that loses its S status may not operate under it again for at least five years. The tax structure of S corporations isn't attractive to all

S corporation
A unique government creation that looks like a corporation but is taxed like sole proprietorships and partnerships.

◄ PPT 5-23:
S Corporations

◄ PPT 5-24:
Who Can Form S Corporations?

businesses. For one thing, the benefits change every time the tax rules change. The best way to learn all the benefits or shortcomings for a specific business is to go over the tax advantages and liability differences with a lawyer, an accountant, or both.

Limited Liability Companies

A **limited liability company (LLC)** is similar to an S corporation but without the special eligibility requirements. LLCs were introduced in Wyoming in 1977 and were recognized by the Internal Revenue Service as a partnership for federal income tax purposes in 1988. By 1996, all 50 states and the District of Columbia recognized LLCs.

The number of LLCs has risen dramatically since 1988, when there were fewer than 100 filings to operate them. Today more than half of new business registrations in some states are LLCs. The Legal Briefcase box features a new type of LLC, a virtual company.

Why the drive toward forming LLCs? Advantages include:[10]

> **PPT 5-25:**
> Limited Liability Companies

> **limited liability company (LLC)**
> A company similar to an S corporation but without the special eligibility requirements.

1. *Limited liability.* Personal assets are protected. Limited liability was previously available only to limited partners and shareholders of C corporations.
2. *Choice of taxation.* LLCs can choose to be taxed as partnerships or as corporations. Partnership-level taxation was previously a benefit normally reserved for partners or S corporation owners.
3. *Flexible ownership rules.* LLCs do not have to comply with ownership restrictions as S corporations do. Owners can be a person, partnership, or corporation.
4. *Flexible distribution of profits and losses.* Profits and losses don't have to be distributed in proportion to the money each person invests, as in corporations. LLC members agree on the percentage to be distributed to each member.
5. *Operating flexibility.* LLCs do have to submit articles of organization, which are similar to articles of incorporation, but they are not required to keep minutes, file written resolutions, or hold annual meetings. An LLC also submits a written operating agreement, similar to a partnership agreement, describing how the company is to be operated.

A secret room uncovered during renovations at the Craftwood Inn contained historic engravings and photos that enhance the inn's turn-of-the-century frontier ambience. The fabled restaurant and banquet hall overlooking Pike's Peak is privately owned. Would you be surprised to learn that the Craftwood Inn is a limited liability corporation?

Of course, LLCs have their disadvantages as well. These include:

1. *No stock.* LLC ownership is nontransferable. LLC members need the approval of the other members in order to sell their interests in the company. In contrast, regular and S corporation stockholders can sell their shares as they wish.
2. *Limited life span.* LLCs are required to identify dissolution dates in the articles of organization (no more than 30 years in some states). The death of a member can cause LLCs to dissolve automatically. Members may choose to reconstitute the LLC after it dissolves.

> **PPT 5-26:**
> Disadvantages of LLCs

LEGAL briefcase

http://vermontvirtual.org

Vermont Wants to Be the Home of Your New Virtual Company

Most companies are required by law to have a physical office and a management team, and to keep a physical paper trail of all transactions. This may soon change. In June 2008, Vermont passed a law that its supporters believe will make Vermont so attractive for LLCs that it will become the "Delaware of the Net." (Delaware collects around $700 million a year in incorporation taxes and fees because of its attractive rules of incorporation.)

The Vermont law creates a new form of LLC called a virtual company, that is, a company that can exist only online. Any documents required to register a company can be filed electronically, company meetings can be held using any type of online communication, and relationships among company members can be established electronically. They can make decisions together using voting structures managed by social networking software.

Traditional companies spend large amounts of money recruiting, hiring, and training employees to serve various roles. In contrast, virtual companies can allow online contributors with different skills, availability, and interests to identify themselves and contribute as they choose. Members of the virtual company decide the value of each member's contribution and the percentage of the LLC's profits that should be passed to each. New York Law School professor David Johnson and his students were instrumental in writing the Vermont law. Johnson concedes that many details remained to be resolved. It will be interesting to see whether Vermont does indeed become the Delaware of the Net.

Sources: David R. Johnson, "Virtual Companies," Do Tank, http://dotank.nyls.edu/june18virtualcorp.html, June 15, 2008; and Max Chafkin, "A Haven for Virtual Companies," *Inc.*, July 2008.

3. *Fewer incentives.* Unlike corporations, LLCs can't deduct the cost of fringe benefits for members owning 2 percent or more of the company. And since there's no stock, they can't use stock options as incentives to employees.
4. *Taxes.* LLC members must pay self-employment taxes—the Medicare/Social Security taxes paid by sole proprietors and partnerships—on their profits. In contrast, S corporations pay self-employment tax on owners' salaries but not on the entire profits.
5. *Paperwork.* While the paperwork required of LLCs is not as great as that required of corporations, it is more than required of sole proprietors.

The start-up cost for an LLC varies. Online legal services such as Legal Zoom (www.legalzoom.com) can file the necessary paperwork for as little as $150.[11] Figure 5.6 on p. 128 summarizes the advantages and disadvantages of the major forms of business ownership.

progress assessment

- What are the major advantages and disadvantages of incorporating a business?
- What is the role of owners (stockholders) in the corporate hierarchy?
- If you buy stock in a corporation and someone gets injured by one of the corporation's products, can you be sued? Why or why not?
- Why are so many new businesses choosing a limited liability company (LLC) form of ownership?

	SOLE PROPRIETORSHIP	GENERAL PARTNERSHIP	LIMITED PARTNERSHIP	CONVENTIONAL CORPORATION	S CORPORATION	LIMITED LIABILITY COMPANY
Documents Needed to Start Business	None; may need permit or license	Partnership agreement (oral or written)	Written agreement; must file certificate of limited partnership	Articles of incorporation, bylaws	Articles of incorporation, bylaws, must meet criteria	Articles of organization and operating agreement; no eligibility requirements
Ease of Termination	Easy to terminate: just pay debts and quit	May be hard to terminate, depending on the partnership agreement	Same as general partnership	Hard and expensive to terminate	Same as conventional corporation	May be difficult, depending upon operating agreement
Length of Life	Terminates on the death of owner	Terminates on the death or withdrawal of partner	Same as general partnership	Perpetual life	Same as conventional corporation	Varies according to dissolution dates in articles of organization
Transfer of Ownership	Business can be sold to qualified buyer	Must have other partner(s)' agreement	Same as general partnership	Easy to change owners; just sell stock	Can sell stock, but with restrictions	Can't sell stock
Financial Resources	Limited to owner's capital and loans	Limited to partners' capital and loans	Same as general partnership	More money to start and operate; may sell stocks and bonds	Same as conventional corporation	Same as partnership
Risk of Losses	Unlimited liability	Unlimited liability	Limited liability	Limited liability	Limited liability	Limited liability
Taxes	Taxed as personal income	Taxed as personal income	Same as general partnership	Corporate, double taxation	Taxed as personal income	Varies
Management Responsibilities	Owner manages *all* areas of the business	Partners share management	Can't participate in management	Separate management from ownership	Same as conventional corporation	Varies
Employee Benefits	Usually fewer benefits and lower wages	Often fewer benefits and lower wages; promising employee could become a partner	Same as general partnership	Usually better benefits and wages, advancement opportunities	Same as conventional corporation	Varies, but are not tax deductible

figure 5.6

COMPARISON OF FORMS OF BUSINESS OWNERSHIP

LEARNING goal 4 *

Define and give examples of three types of corporate mergers, and explain the role of leveraged buyouts and taking a firm private.

◄ **LECTURE LINK 5-6:**
Merck: Finding the Next Big One

merger
The result of two firms forming one company.

acquisition
One company's purchase of the property and obligations of another company.

vertical merger
The joining of two companies involved in different stages of related businesses.

horizontal merger
The joining of two firms in the same industry.

conglomerate merger
The joining of firms in completely unrelated industries.

CORPORATE EXPANSION: MERGERS AND ACQUISITIONS

The merger mania of the late 1990s reached its peak in 2000, when the total spent on mergers and acquisitions hit a stunning $3.4 trillion and a new deal was being struck every 17 minutes. It seemed as though each deal made was intended to top the one before. Most of the new deals involved companies trying to expand within their own fields to save costs, enter new markets, position for international competition, or adapt to changing technologies or regulations. Those proved to be unattainable goals for many of the merged giants; two-thirds of mergers of the late 1990s failed to meet their goals. In 2009, the U.S. economic landscape was so bleak that the volume of mergers and acquisitions plummeted 86 percent.[12]

What's the difference between mergers and acquisitions? A **merger** is the result of two firms joining to form one company. It is similar to a marriage, joining two individuals as one family. An **acquisition** is one company's purchase of the property and obligations of another company. It is more like buying a house than entering a marriage.

There are three major types of corporate mergers: vertical, horizontal, and conglomerate. A **vertical merger** joins two firms operating in different stages of related businesses. A merger between a soft drink company and an artificial sweetener maker would ensure the merged firm a constant supply of an ingredient the soft drink manufacturer needs. It could also help ensure quality control of the soft drink company's products.

A **horizontal merger** joins two firms in the same industry and allows them to diversify or expand their products. A soft drink company and a mineral water company that merge can now supply a variety of drinking products.

A **conglomerate merger** unites firms in completely unrelated industries in order to diversify business operations and investments. A soft drink company and a snack food company would form a conglomerate merger. Figure 5.7 on p. 130 illustrates the differences among the three types of mergers.

Rather than merge or sell to another company, some corporations decide to maintain, or in some cases regain, control of a firm internally. By *taking a firm private*, management or a group of stockholders obtain all the firm's stock for themselves by buying it back from the other stockholders. Suppose employees believe they may lose their jobs, or managers believe they could improve corporate performance if they owned the company. Does either group

Mars, the maker of M&M's, acquired the Wm. Wrigley Jr. Company for $23 billion. Both have long histories as family-owned businesses. Mars president said, "The strong cultural heritage of two legendary American companies with a shared commitment to innovation, quality, and best-in-class global brands provides a great basis for this combination." What other factors might make an acquisition or merger like this a successful one?

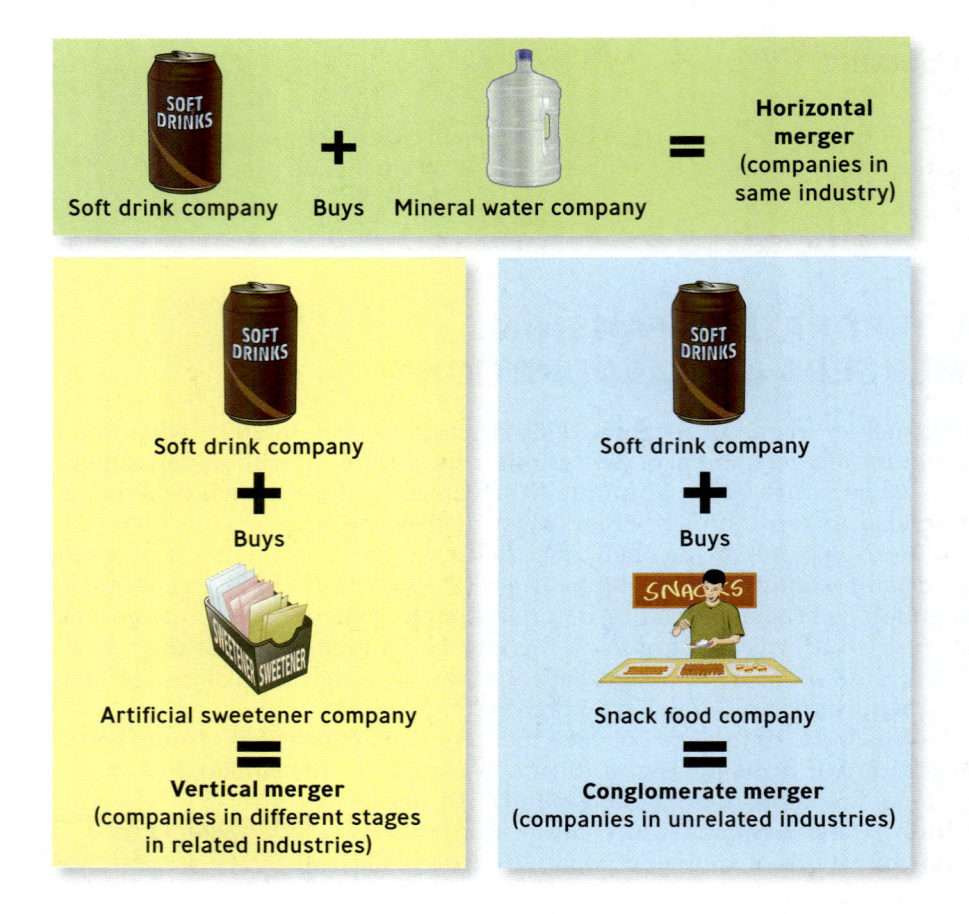

figure 5.7
TYPES OF MERGERS

Soft drink company + Mineral water company = **Horizontal merger** (companies in same industry)

Soft drink company + Artificial sweetener company = **Vertical merger** (companies in different stages in related industries)

Soft drink company + Snack food company = **Conglomerate merger** (companies in unrelated industries)

▶ PPT 5-29:
Mergers and Acquisitions

▶ LECTURE LINK 5-7:
Jam and Coffee

▶ PPT 5-30:
Types of Mergers

▶ PPT 5-31:
Leveraged Buyouts

▶ LECTURE LINK 5-8:
Employee Stock Ownership Plans (ESOPs)

leveraged buyout (LBO)
An attempt by employees, management, or a group of investors to purchase an organization primarily through borrowing.

have an opportunity of taking ownership of the company? Yes—they might attempt a leveraged buyout.

A **leveraged buyout (LBO)** is an attempt by employees, management, or a group of investors to buy out the stockholders in a company, primarily by borrowing the necessary funds. The employees, managers, or investors now become the owners of the firm. LBOs have ranged in size from $50 million to $31 billion and have involved everything from small family businesses to giant corporations like Toys "R" Us, Northwest Airlines, and the former RJR Nabisco.

Today, business acquisitions are not limited to U.S. buyers. In 2007 alone, foreign investors poured a record $414 billion into U.S. companies. That was up 90 percent from the previous year and more than double the average for the last decade. For example, a Saudi Arabian conglomerate bought a Massachusetts plastics maker; a French company set up a new factory in Michigan; a British company bought a New Jersey cough syrup maker.[13] In 2008, Belgium's beverage giant InBev paid $52 billion for one of the United States' largest breweries, Anheuser-Busch.[14]

Foreign companies have found the quickest way to grow is often to buy an established operation and bring the brands and technology back to their home countries. However, such deals are not always welcomed. In 2005, U.S. lawmakers feared the proposed purchase of U.S. oil company Unocal by a Chinese oil company might threaten American economic and national security interests. CNOOC, the Chinese company, eventually withdrew its bid.[15]

THINKING green

www.washington.nationals.mlb.com

Root, Root, Root for the Green Team

Many people think the only thing you can buy at a franchise is fast food. After all, restaurants make up over 80 percent of U.S. franchises. Franchising, however, goes beyond a local Domino's or KFC. Hotels, schools, even professional sports teams are part of the franchise system. For example, Washington, D.C., got its Major League Baseball franchise, the Nationals, when investors lured the Montreal Expos franchise to the nation's capital.

One of the major inducements for the Expos' move was the promise of a new stadium. The D.C. city council went further and insisted that the structure be the first sports stadium to earn a Leadership in Energy and Environmental Design (LEED) rating from the U.S. Green Building Council. The $611 million stadium opened to a national TV audience and the president of the United States in 2008.

As the Nationals took the field on opening day, fans may not have noticed that 95 percent of the stadium's steel was recycled or that its low-flow toilets would save millions of gallons of water each season. They also may not have known that the wastewater system screens out organic debris such as peanut shells and hot-dog bits, or that the park's recycling center is large enough to handle glass, metal, and plastic recyclables amassed during a three-game home stand. They came to see baseball.

But lots of other folks, like other major league franchises, were taking notice and making their own efforts to improve the environment. The San Francisco Giants, Colorado Rockies, and Cleveland Indians have all installed solar panels in their ballparks. The Seattle Mariners started a composting project at their park. The New York Mets and Minnesota Twins have promised LEED certification at their new parks. Play ball! But play green!

Sources: Matthew Phillips, "Not Just Greener Grass," *Newsweek,* April 14, 2008, pp. 66–67; and Jeff Chu, "Take Me Out to the Ballpark," *Fast Company,* April 2008, pp. 72–73.

LEARNING goal 5 *

Outline the advantages and disadvantages of franchises, and discuss the opportunities for diversity in franchising and the challenges of global franchising.

FRANCHISES

In addition to the three basic forms of business ownership, there are two special forms: franchises and cooperatives. Let's look at franchises first. A **franchise agreement** is an arrangement whereby someone with a good idea for a business (the **franchisor**) sells the rights to use the business name and sell a product or service (the **franchise**) to others (the **franchisees**) in a given territory.

Some people, uncomfortable with the idea of starting their own business from scratch, would rather join a business with a proven track record through a franchise agreement. A franchise can be formed as a sole proprietorship, a partnership, or a corporation. Some of the best-known franchises are McDonald's, Jiffy Lube, 7-Eleven, Weight Watchers, and Holiday Inn.

franchise agreement
An arrangement whereby someone with a good idea for a business sells the rights to use the business name and sell a product or service to others in a given territory.

franchisor
A company that develops a product concept and sells others the rights to make and sell the products.

franchise
The right to use a specific business's name and sell its products or services in a given territory.

franchisee
A person who buys a franchise.

More than 900,000 franchised businesses have operated in the United States, employing approximately 10 million people—and those numbers grew as franchises added more than 140,000 new businesses and 1.2 million new jobs between 2001 and 2005.[16] The most popular businesses for franchising are restaurants (more than 80 percent of all franchises), retail stores, hotels and motels, and automotive parts and service centers. McDonald's, the largest restaurant chain in the United States, is often considered the gold standard of franchising. One of the fastest-growing franchise sectors is senior care. In fact, Home Instead Senior Care was the franchise with the highest average net-income growth on *The Wall Street Journal*'s 2008 list of 25 franchise high performers.[17] The Thinking Green box on p. 131 discusses a franchise in the sport known as America's favorite pastime.

Advantages of Franchises

Franchising has penetrated every aspect of U.S. and global business life by offering products and services that are reliable, convenient, and competitively priced. Franchising clearly has some advantages:

1. *Management and marketing assistance.* Compared with someone who starts a business from scratch, a franchisee usually has a much greater chance of succeeding because he or she has an established product to sell, help choosing a location, and assistance in all phases of promotion and operation. It's like having your own store but with full-time consultants when you need them. Franchisors usually provide intensive training. For example, McDonald's sends all new franchisees and managers to Hamburger University in Oak Brook, Illinois.

Some franchisors help their franchisees with local marketing efforts rather than having them depend solely on national advertising. Franchisees also have a network of fellow franchisees facing similar problems who can share their experiences. The UPS Store provides its 4,445 franchisees with a software program that helps them build customer databases along with quick and personal one-on-one phone and e-mail support.[18]

2. *Personal ownership.* A franchise operation is still your business, and you enjoy as much of the incentives and profit as any sole proprietor would. You are still your own boss, although you must follow more rules, regulations, and procedures than with your own privately owned business.

3. *Nationally recognized name.* It is one thing to open a gift shop or an ice cream store. It is quite another to open a new Hallmark store or a Baskin-Robbins. With an established franchise, you get instant recognition and support from a product group with established customers around the world.

4. *Financial advice and assistance.* Two major problems for small-business owners are arranging financing and learning to keep good records. Franchisees get valuable assistance and periodic advice from people with expertise in these areas. In fact, some franchisors provide financing to potential franchisees they feel will be valuable parts of the franchise system. For example, SRA International Inc., an executive-recruiting franchise, eases entry for selected new franchisees by

Door-to-Door Dry Cleaning franchises are the brain child of John Dame and his wife Joey. All franchisees need to get started is a truck to make pickups and deliveries, and a contract with a local dry cleaner. Start-up costs can be as low as $40,000 and profits as high as 26 percent. The Dames provide two weeks of training and plenty of online support. What type of service franchise might appeal to you as a business owner?

▶ **PPT 5-32:**
Franchising

▶ **BONUS CASE 5-2:**
Franchise or Independent? What Fits Your Mold?

▶ **PPT 5-33:**
Advantages of Franchising

allowing $20,000 of the $35,000 initiation fee to be paid from revenue over a period of two years or more.

5. *Lower failure rate.* Historically, the failure rate for franchises has been lower than that of other business ventures. However, franchising has grown so rapidly that many weak franchises have entered the field, so you need to be careful and invest wisely.[19]

Disadvantages of Franchises

There are, however, some potential pitfalls to franchising. Check out any franchise arrangement with present franchisees and discuss the idea with an attorney and an accountant. Disadvantages of franchises include the following:

1. *Large start-up costs.* Most franchises demand a fee for the rights to the franchise. Start-up costs for a Jazzercise franchise range from $2,000 to $3,000, but if it's Krispy Kreme you're after, you'd better have a lot more dough—approximately $2 million.[20]

2. *Shared profit.* The franchisor often demands either a large share of the profits in addition to the start-up fees or a percentage commission based on sales, not profit. This share is called a *royalty*. For example, if a franchisor demands a 10 percent royalty on a franchise's net sales, 10 cents of every dollar the franchisee collects (before taxes and other expenses) must be paid to the franchisor.

3. *Management regulation.* Management "assistance" has a way of becoming managerial orders, directives, and limitations. Franchisees feeling burdened by the company's rules and regulations may lose the drive to run their own business. Often franchisees will band together to resolve their grievances with franchisors rather than each fighting their battles alone. For example, in 2008 Dairy Queen franchisees in 10 states joined together to file a lawsuit that claimed DQ was forcing them to increase the size of restaurants or add table service or risk losing their franchises. The lawsuit contended that such changes would force franchise owners to spend between $275,000 and $450,000 to remodel their stores.[21]

4. *Coattail effects.* What happens to your franchise if fellow franchisees fail? The actions of other franchises have an impact on your future growth and profitability. Due to this *coattail effect*, you could be forced out of business even if your particular franchise has been profitable. Franchisees must also look out for competition from fellow franchisees. For example, TCBY franchisees' love for frozen yogurt melted as the market became flooded with new TCBY stores. McDonald's franchisees complain that due to the company's relentless growth, some new stores have taken business away from existing locations, squeezing franchisees' profits per outlet.

5. *Restrictions on selling.* Unlike owners of private businesses, who can sell their companies to whomever they choose on their own terms, many franchisees face restrictions on the resale of their franchises. To control quality, franchisors often insist on approving the new owner, who must meet their standards.

6. *Fraudulent franchisors.* Most franchisors are not large systems like McDonald's and Subway. Many are small, rather obscure companies that prospective franchisees may know little about. Most are honest, but complaints to the Federal Trade Commission have increased about franchisors that delivered little or nothing of what they promised. Before you buy a franchise, make certain you check out the facts fully.[22] The saying "You get what you pay for" may be old, but it's not old-fashioned. See Figure 5.8 on p. 134 for some tips on evaluating a franchisee.

◄ **PPT 5-34:**
Disadvantages of Franchising

◄ **CRITICAL THINKING EXERCISE 5-3:**
Opportunities in Entrepreneurship

Since buying a franchise is a major investment, be sure to check out a company's financial strength before you get involved. Watch out for scams too. Scams called *bust-outs* usually involve people coming to town, renting nice offices, taking out ads, and persuading people to invest. Then they disappear with the investors' money. For example, in San Francisco a company called T.B.S. Inc. sold distributorships for in-home AIDS tests. It promised an enormous market and potential profits of $3,000 for an investment of less than $200. The "test" turned out to be nothing more than a mail-order questionnaire about lifestyle.

A good source of information about evaluating a franchise deal is the handbook *Investigate before Investing,* available from International Franchise Association Publications.

Checklist for Evaluating a Franchise

The Franchise

Did your lawyer approve the franchise contract you're considering after he or she studied it paragraph by paragraph?

Does the franchise give you an exclusive territory for the length of the franchise?

Under what circumstances can you terminate the franchise contract and at what cost to you?

If you sell your franchise, will you be compensated for your goodwill (the value of your business's reputation and other intangibles)?

If the franchisor sells the company, will your investment be protected?

The Franchisor

How many years has the firm offering you a franchise been in operation?

Does it have a reputation for honesty and fair dealing among the local firms holding its franchise?

Has the franchisor shown you any certified figures indicating exact net profits of one or more going firms that you personally checked yourself with the franchisee? Ask for the company's disclosure statement.

Will the firm assist you with
  A management training program?
  An employee training program?
  A public relations program?
  Capital?
  Credit?
  Merchandising ideas?

Will the firm help you find a good location for your new business?

Has the franchisor investigated you carefully enough to assure itself that you can successfully operate one of its franchises at a profit both to itself and to you?

You, the Franchisee

How much equity capital will you need to purchase the franchise and operate it until your income equals your expenses?

Does the franchisor offer financing for a portion of the franchising fees? On what terms?

Are you prepared to give up some independence of action to secure the advantages offered by the franchise? Do you have your family's support?

Does the industry appeal to you? Are you ready to spend much or all of the remainder of your business life with this franchisor, offering its product or service to the public?

Your Market

Have you made any study to determine whether the product or service that you propose to sell under the franchise has a market in your territory at the prices you'll have to charge?

Will the population in the territory given to you increase, remain static, or decrease over the next five years?

Will demand for the product or service you're considering be greater, about the same, or less five years from now than it is today?

What competition already exists in your territory for the product or service you contemplate selling?

Sources: U.S. Department of Commerce, *Franchise Opportunities Handbook;* and Steve Adams, "Buying a Brand," *Patriot Ledger* (Quincy, MA), March 1, 2008.

figure 5.8
BUYING A FRANCHISE

▶ PPT 5-35:
Women in Franchising

Diversity in Franchising

One issue in franchising is the number of women who own franchises. As franchise cost increases, female franchise ownership decreases. Some think there is not so much a glass ceiling as a green ceiling—lack of money. While women own about half of all U.S. companies, they receive less than 4 percent of venture capital.[23] Many experts believe more needs to be done to educate women business owners about the appropriate forms of financing for each stage of business growth.

Women are getting the message. Firms owned by women have grown at twice the rate of all companies for the past two decades, according to the Center for Women's Business Research.[24] In fact, women aren't just franchisees

Judi Sheppard Missett started a dance-fitness program called Jazzercise in 1969. The worldwide franchise company now takes fitness-minded adults and kids in 32 countries through weekly classes blending jazz dance, resistance training, Pilates, yoga, and kickboxing moves choreographed to the latest popular music. Jazzercise is consistently listed among Entrepreneur *magazine's top 20 franchises. What accounts for its appeal?*

anymore; they're becoming franchisors as well. When they have difficulty obtaining financing for expansion, they often find franchisees to help carry expansion costs. For example, top-rated franchise companies Auntie Anne's, Decorating Den, and Jazzercise are owned by women.

Entrepreneur Mary Ellen Sheets moved into the male-dominated trucking industry when she started Two Men and a Truck as a way to help her college-age sons earn money part-time. Sheets bought an old pickup truck for $350 and managed her sons' moving-job schedules. When the boys went back to school, she kept the business going by hiring two men to do the heavy lifting. Business grew, and Sheets decided to expand through franchising. Today, Two Men and a Truck has 200 locations in North America and a fleet of over 1,300 trucks. Sheets's sons have returned—one as a franchise owner and the other as director of franchise licensing. Her daughter is president and chief operating officer.[25]

Minority-owned businesses are growing at more than six times the national rate. About 20 percent of the franchises in this country are owned by African Americans, Latinos, Asians, and Native Americans, according to the International Franchise Association Education Foundation.[26] Franchisors are becoming more focused on recruiting minority franchisees. For example, Domino's Pizza launched an internal minority franchisee recruitment program called Delivering the Dream. The program is designed to provide financial support to current minority employees to build new stores. "Some of the most successful Domino's stores are those that are owned and operated by franchisees living in the communities we serve," said Mike Mettler, Domino's director of franchise recruitment and sales. "Now, through the Delivering the Dream program, we're helping to eliminate the financial roadblock that may exist for motivated future minority franchisees."[27] Franchising opportunities seem perfectly attuned to the needs of aspiring minority businesspeople. The U.S. Commerce Department's Federal Minority Business Development Agency provides minorities with training in how to run franchises.

Home-Based Franchises

Home-based businesses offer many obvious advantages, including relief from the stress of commuting, extra time for family activities, and low overhead expenses. One disadvantage is the feeling of isolation. Compared to home-based entrepreneurs, home-based franchisees feel less isolated. Experienced franchisors often share their knowledge of building a profitable enterprise with other franchisees. For example, when Henry and Paula Feldman decided to quit sales jobs that kept them on the road for weeks, they wanted to find a business to run at home together.

The Feldmans started their home-based franchise, Money Mailer Inc. (a direct mail advertiser), with a table and a telephone. Five years later, they owned 15 territories, which they ran from an office full of state-of-the-art equipment. They grossed more than $600,000 during their fifth year. Henry says the real value of being in a franchise is that the systems are in place: "You don't have to develop them yourself. Just be willing to work hard, listen, and learn. There's no greater magic than that."[28]

E-Commerce in Franchising

Many brick-and-mortar franchisees are expanding their businesses online. For example, the Web site of Carole Shutts, a Rocky Mountain Chocolate Factory franchisee in Galena, Illinois, generates 15 percent of her sales. Although other Rocky Mountain franchisees have competing Web sites, Shutts isn't concerned because she thinks multiple sites will build brand awareness.

Many franchisors prohibit franchisee-sponsored Web sites because conflicts can erupt if the franchisor creates its own site. Sometimes franchisors send "reverse royalties" to outlet owners who believe their sales were hurt by the franchisor's Internet sales, but that doesn't always bring about peace. Before buying a franchise, read the small print regarding online sales.

Using Technology in Franchising

Franchisors often use technology to meet the needs of both their customers and their franchisees. For example, U.S. Web Corporation set up its Web site to streamline communication for its employees, customers, and vendors. It built a computer network to allow communication among its 50 franchisees, almost eliminating paperwork. Every franchisee has immediate online access to every subject concerning the franchise operation, even the forms to fill out. All franchisees are kept up-to-date on company news via e-mail, and they use a chat room to discuss issues with each other. The company has found the Internet a great way of disseminating information that is revolutionizing franchisor support and franchisee communications.

Holiday Inn's InterContinental Amstel hotel in Amsterdam has been celebrated as the Netherlands' most beautiful and luxurious hotel. Holiday Inn franchises try to complement the environment of the area they serve. This hotel is on the crossroads of Amsterdam's financial and exclusive shopping districts. What do you think would have been the reaction if Holiday Inn had built the typical U.S.-style hotel in this area?

Franchising in International Markets

Today, U.S. franchisors are counting their profits in pesos, won, euros, krona, baht, yen, and many other currencies.[29] McDonald's has more than 32,000 restaurants in 117 countries serving 50 million customers.[30]

Because of proximity and shared language, Canada is by far the most popular target for U.S.-based franchises. Many other franchisors are finding it surprisingly easy to move into South Africa and the Philippines. Even though franchisors find the costs of franchising high in these markets, the costs are usually counterbalanced by less competition and a rapidly expanding consumer base.

Newer, smaller franchises are going international as well. SpeeDee Oil Change & Tune-Up, Rug Doctor Pro, and Merry Maids have all ventured into the international market. Long Island–based Nathan's Famous Inc. sells hot dogs in the Caribbean and the Middle East. Auntie Anne sells hand-rolled pretzels in Indonesia, Malaysia, the Philippines, Singapore, Japan, Venezuela, and Thailand.

What makes franchising successful in international markets is what makes it successful in the United States: convenience and a predictable level of service and quality. Franchisors, though, must be careful to adapt to the region. In France, people thought a furniture-stripping place called Dip 'N' Strip was a bar that featured strippers. In Latin America, one U.S. company was surprised to discover the brand name of the cooking oil it was marketing translated into Spanish as "Jackass Oil."[31] In general, however, U.S. franchises are doing well all over the world and are adapting to the local customs and desires of consumers.

International franchising travels both ways. Just as McDonald's and Subway have exported golden arches and sub sandwiches worldwide, foreign franchises are changing tastes here. For example, Maria's Bakery customers in the United States enjoy sweet pastries made from the recipes perfected by franchisor Maria Lee, considered the Martha Stewart of Hong Kong. Asian franchisors have added stores throughout the United States, while businesses from Latin America more often focus on California, Texas, and Florida. Just as U.S. franchisors must adapt to their foreign markets, foreign franchisors must tinker with menus and store layouts to better fit the U.S. market. For example, Maria's Bakery franchises in the United States carry milk tea drinks and ice cream, products the Hong Kong stores never sold because there was so much competition from other food vendors there.

LEARNING goal 6 *

Explain the role of cooperatives.

COOPERATIVES

Some people dislike the notion of owners, managers, workers, and buyers being separate individuals with separate goals. So they have formed cooperatives, a different kind of organization to meet their needs for electricity, child care, housing, health care, food, and financial services. A **cooperative**, or co-op, is owned and controlled by the people who use it—producers, consumers, or workers with similar needs who pool their resources for mutual gain. In many rural parts of the country, for example, the government sells wholesale power to electric cooperatives at rates 40 to 50 percent below the rates nonfederal utilities charge. Electric cooperatives serve 42 million U.S. consumer-members in 47 states—or 12 percent of the population.[32]

Worldwide, some 750,000 cooperatives serve 730 million members—120 million of them in the United States.[33] Members democratically control these businesses by electing a board of directors that hires professional management. Some co-ops ask members/customers to work for a number of hours a month as part of their membership duties. You may have one of the country's 4,000 food co-ops near you. If so, stop by and chat to learn more about this growing aspect of the U.S. economy. If you are interested in knowing more about cooperatives, contact the National Cooperative Business Association at 202-638-6222 or visit its Web site at www.ncba.coop.

cooperative
A business owned and controlled by the people who use it—producers, consumers, or workers with similar needs who pool their resources for mutual gain.

> **CRITICAL THINKING EXERCISE 5-4:**
> Choosing a Form of Business Ownership

Another kind of cooperative in the United States is formed to give members more economic power as a group than they have as individuals. The best example is a farm cooperative. The goal at first was for farmers to join together to get better prices for their food products. Eventually the idea expanded, and farm cooperatives now buy and sell fertilizer, farm equipment, seed, and other products in a multibillion-dollar industry. Cooperatives have an advantage in the marketplace because they don't pay the same kind of taxes corporations do.[34]

In spite of debt and mergers, cooperatives are still a major force in agriculture and other industries today. Some top co-ops have familiar names such as Land O Lakes, Sunkist, Ocean Spray, Blue Diamond, Associated Press, Ace Hardware, True Value Hardware, Riceland Foods, and Welch's.

WHICH FORM OF OWNERSHIP IS FOR YOU?

You can build your own business in a variety of ways. You can start your own sole proprietorship, partnership, corporation, LLC, or cooperative—or you can buy a franchise and be part of a larger corporation. There are advantages and disadvantages to each. Before you decide which form is for you, evaluate all the alternatives carefully.

The miracle of free enterprise is that the freedom and incentives of capitalism make risks acceptable to many people who go on to create the great corporations of America. You know many of their names: James Cash (J. C.) Penney, Malcolm Forbes, Richard Warren Sears and Alvah C. Roebuck, Levi Strauss, Henry Ford, Thomas Edison, Bill Gates, and so on. They started small, accumulated capital, grew, and became industrial leaders. Could you do the same?

> **PPT 5-42:**
> Progress Assessment

progress assessment

- What are some of the factors to consider before buying a franchise?
- What opportunities are available for starting a global franchise?
- What is a cooperative?

summary

Learning Goal 1. Compare the advantages and disadvantages of sole proprietorships.
- **What are the advantages and disadvantages of sole proprietorships?**
The advantages of sole proprietorships include ease of starting and ending, ability to be your own boss, pride of ownership, retention of profit, and no special taxes. The disadvantages include unlimited liability, limited financial resources, difficulty in management, overwhelming time commitment, few fringe benefits, limited growth, and limited life span.

Learning Goal 2. Describe the differences between general and limited partners, and compare the advantages and disadvantages of partnerships.
- **What are the three key elements of a general partnership?**
The three key elements of a general partnership are common ownership, shared profits and losses, and the right to participate in managing the operations of the business.

- **What are the main differences between general and limited partners?**

General partners are owners (partners) who have unlimited liability and are active in managing the company. Limited partners are owners (partners) who have limited liability and are not active in the company.

- **What does *unlimited liability* mean?**

Unlimited liability means that sole proprietors and general partners must pay all debts and damages caused by their business. They may have to sell their houses, cars, or other personal possessions to pay business debts.

- **What does *limited liability* mean?**

Limited liability means that corporate owners (stockholders) and limited partners are responsible for losses only up to the amount they invest. Their other personal property is not at risk.

- **What is a master limited partnership?**

A master limited partnership is a partnership that acts like a corporation but is taxed like a partnership.

- **What are the advantages and disadvantages of partnerships?**

The advantages include more financial resources, shared management and pooled knowledge, and longer survival. The disadvantages include unlimited liability, division of profits, disagreements among partners, and difficulty of termination.

Learning Goal 3. Compare the advantages and disadvantages of corporations, and summarize the differences between C corporations, S corporations, and limited liability companies.

- **What is the definition of a corporation?**

A corporation is a state-chartered legal entity with authority to act and have liability separate from its owners.

- **What are the advantages and disadvantages of corporations?**

The advantages include more money for investment, limited liability, size, perpetual life, ease of ownership change, ease of drawing talented employees, and separation of ownership from management. The disadvantages include initial cost, paperwork, size, difficulty of termination, double taxation, and possible conflict with a board of directors.

- **Why do people incorporate?**

Two important reasons for incorporating are special tax advantages and limited liability.

- **What are the advantages of S corporations?**

S corporations have the advantages of limited liability (like a corporation) and simpler taxes (like a partnership). To qualify for S corporation status, a company must have fewer than 100 stockholders (members of a family count as one shareholder), its stockholders must be individuals or estates and U.S. citizens or permanent residents, and the company cannot derive more than 25 percent of its income from passive sources.

- **What are the advantages of limited liability companies?**

Limited liability companies have the advantage of limited liability without the hassles of forming a corporation or the limitations imposed by S corporations. LLCs may choose whether to be taxed as partnerships or corporations.

Learning Goal 4. Describe three types of corporate mergers, and explain the role of leveraged buyouts and taking a firm private.

- **What is a merger?**

A merger is the result of two firms forming one company. The three major types are vertical mergers, horizontal mergers, and conglomerate mergers.

- **What are leveraged buyouts, and what does it mean to take a company private?**

Leveraged buyouts are attempts by managers and employees to borrow money and purchase the company. Individuals who, together or alone, buy all the stock for themselves are said to take the company private.

Learning Goal 5. Outline the advantages and disadvantages of franchises, and discuss the opportunities for diversity in franchising and the challenges of global franchising.

- **What is a franchise?**

An arrangement to buy the rights to use the business name and sell its products or services in a given territory is called a franchise.

- **What is a franchisee?**

A franchisee is a person who buys a franchise.

- **What are the benefits and drawbacks of being a franchisee?**

The benefits include getting a nationally recognized name and reputation, a proven management system, promotional assistance, and pride of ownership. Drawbacks include high franchise fees, managerial regulation, shared profits, and transfer of adverse effects if other franchisees fail.

- **What is the major challenge to global franchises?**

It is often difficult to transfer an idea or product that worked well in the United States to another culture. It is essential to adapt to the region.

Learning Goal 6. Explain the role of cooperatives.

- **What is the role of a cooperative?**

Cooperatives are organizations owned by members/customers. Some people form cooperatives to acquire more economic power than they would have as individuals. Small businesses often form cooperatives to gain more purchasing, marketing, or product development strength.

key terms

acquisition 129
conglomerate merger 129
conventional (C) corporation 121
cooperative 137
corporation 115
franchise 131
franchise agreement 131
franchisee 131
franchisor 131
general partner 117
general partnership 117
horizontal merger 129
leveraged buyout (LBO) 130
limited liability 117
limited liability company (LLC) 126
limited liability partnership (LLP) 118
limited partner 117
limited partnership 117
master limited partnership (MLP) 117
merger 129
partnership 114
S corporation 125
sole proprietorship 114
unlimited liability 116
vertical merger 129

connect interactive applications

Reinforcing Your *Connect*ion to Concepts in Business

This chapter offers 15 interactive applications designed to help you apply what you've learned (examples of these exercises appear on the following pages). Your instructor has determined which interactive applications will benefit you throughout this course. Please refer to your instructor's assignment list in *Connect* to determine which applications you should complete.

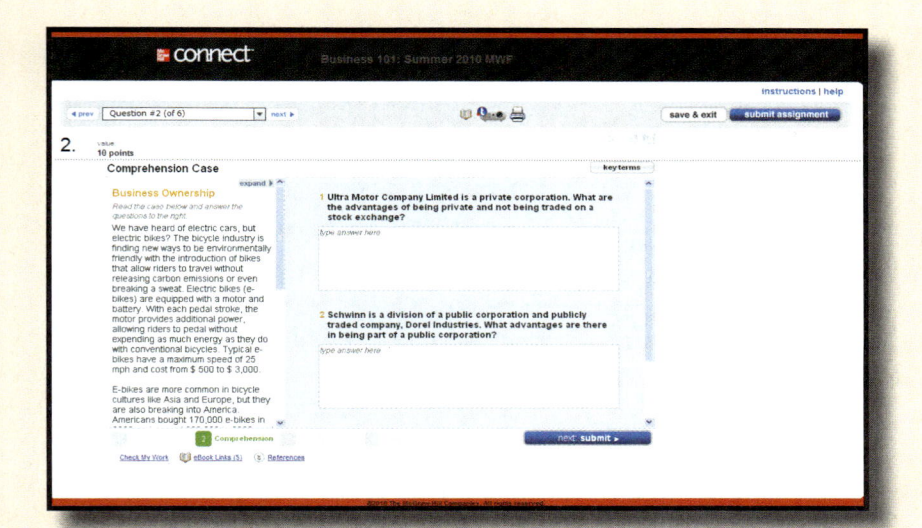

Comprehension Case Interactive: The owners of two companies have chosen different forms of business ownership to best meet their needs as far as liability and taxation are concerned. Read the mini-case that describes the E-Bike industry and answer the questions.

Click and Drag Interactive:
Three primary forms of business ownership—sole proprietorship, partnership, and corporation—are the most often used whether the business is a traditional "bricks and mortar" company, an online-only company, or a combination of both. A business's legal form of ownership affects how it operates, how much tax it pays, and how much control its owners have. In this activity, you will read each statement and drag each item to the appropriate box on the chart.

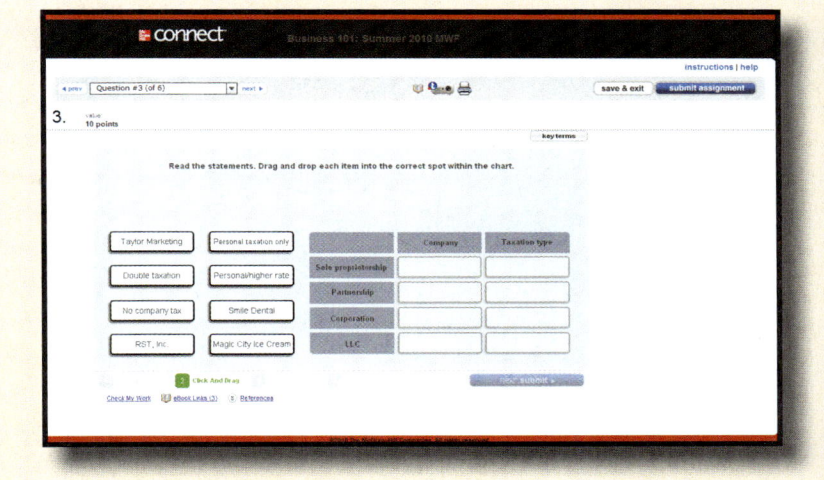

Click and Drag Interactive: A franchise can be formed as a sole proprietorship, a partnership, or a corporation. Franchises provide distinct advantages of starting and managing a small business, but there are potential drawbacks as well. In this activity, you will read each statement and drop it in the appropriate box on the chart. Each item is either an advantage of franchising or a disadvantage of franchising.

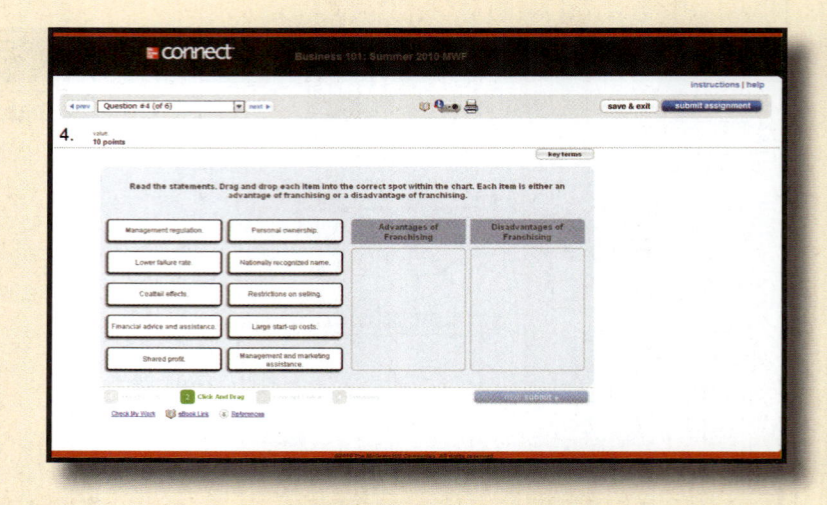

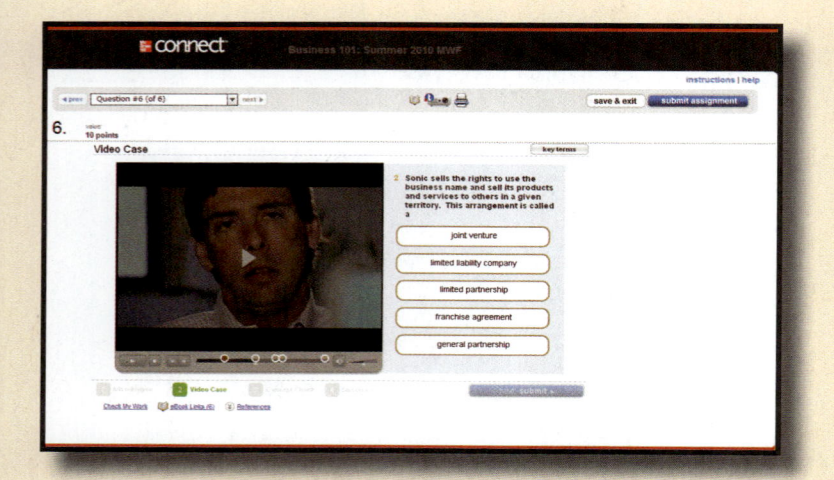

Video Case Interactive: As a business grows, it may change business forms to better meet the needs of its customers and owners. Each business form has advantages and disadvantages. The decision to select one business form over another must be considered carefully. Watch the video and respond to the questions when prompted.

6 Entrepreneurship and STARTING A Small Business

profile

Getting to Know Sheila C. Johnson
Cofounder of Black Entertainment Television (BET)

Entrepreneurs are risk takers who start their own businesses, and their names often appear on the list of firsts in many fields. Sheila Johnson, cofounder of Black Entertainment Television (BET), is no different. Johnson is the first African American woman to become a billionaire and the first African American woman to own three professional sports teams: the Washington Wizards (NBA), the Washington Mystics (WNBA), and the Washington Capitals (NHL). Now Johnson is being compared to domestic and hospitality queen Martha Stewart as she enters a number of new markets.

Before founding BET with her husband, Robert, Sheila Johnson led a simpler life. Married at 20, the University of Illinois cheerleader made her own wedding dress from an "idiot-proof pattern" and was able to use the school's chapel for free. The whole wedding cost less than $50. How did Sheila Johnson get from being a bride on a budget to being a billionaire? In 1979, Robert and Sheila Johnson began to create the first television network targeted to an African American audience. BET debuted in January 1980 with only two hours of programming a week. As BET grew, Sheila Johnson took the post of vice president of corporate affairs and developed many of the network's original shows, most notably the successful and award-winning talk show *Teen Summit*.

In 2000, the Johnsons sold BET to Viacom for a whopping $3 billion. After the sale of the network, Robert stayed on as CEO and Sheila took up new endeavors. She said she is thankful for the sale of BET because it allowed her to spread her entrepreneurial wings and create the kinds of businesses she had always dreamed of owning. She is now part owner in a bath and body products company, Mistral, and CEO of Salamander Hospitality, a company that manages Market Salamander (a gourmet food market) and is developing several luxury hotels in Virginia.

Getting Salamander off the ground has been challenging. In addition to growing the new company, Johnson has had to gain the support of the towns she plans to build in—easier said than done. Some towns are excited that Johnson will put them on the map, while others fear losing their seclusion. However, Johnson is not the type of person who gives

LEARNING goals

After you have read and studied this chapter, you should be able to

1. Explain why people take the risks of entrepreneurship; list the attributes of successful entrepreneurs; and describe entrepreneurial teams, intrapreneurs, and home- and Web-based businesses.

2. Discuss the importance of small business to the American economy and summarize the major causes of small-business failure.

3. Summarize ways to learn about how small businesses operate.

4. Analyze what it takes to start and run a small business.

5. Outline the advantages and disadvantages small businesses have in entering global markets.

connect

Your *Connect*ion to Better Learning. 1. View the interactive presentation. 2. Practice through LearnSmart. 3. Apply your knowledge by using the interactive applications for each chapter of this text.

1 Prep »»»»» **2 Study**  »»»»» **3 Apply**

---

up. She bought and opened her first resort and golf club in the summer of 2007. Her newest establishments were scheduled to debut in Virginia and Florida in 2012.

In addition to her passion for creating new businesses, Johnson is also a proud mother and prominent philanthropist. She donated $7 million to the Parsons School of Design in New York and $2 million to Bennett College. Her $5 million donation to the Curry School of Education at the University of Virginia enabled it to establish a human services center that helps over 7,500 children and their families a year. Johnson is ensuring that her wealth benefits not only her own family but also many other families in the United States.

Stories about people who take risks, like Sheila Johnson, are commonplace in this age of the entrepreneur. As you read about such risk takers in this chapter, maybe you'll be inspired to become an entrepreneur yourself.

Sources: Donna M. Owens, "On The Green: Sheila Johnson Adds $35 Million Golf Resort to Her Expanding Portfolio," *Black Enterprise,* January 1, 2008; "Philanthropy Profile: Sheila C. Johnson," *Black Gives Back,* January 8, 2008; "Sheila C. Johnson: Guided by Love for Entertaining," *Tampa Bay Business Journal,* July 18, 2008; and www.salamanderresort.com, accessed July 2, 2010.

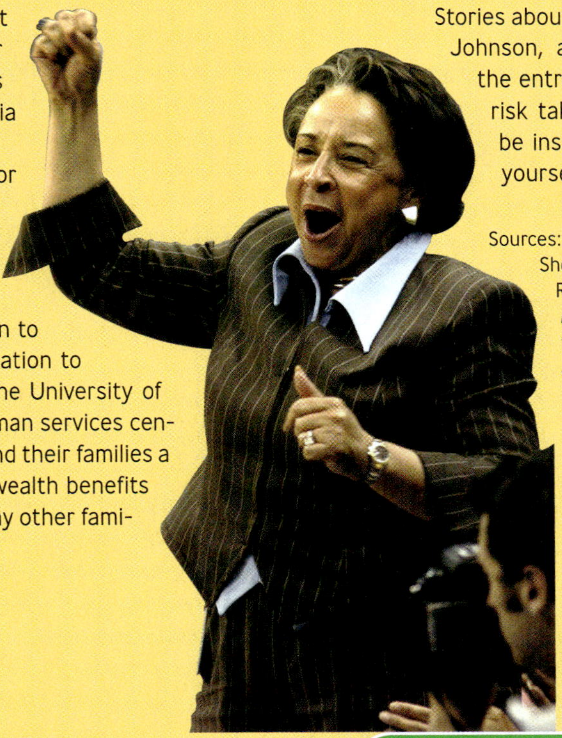

www.bet.com

NAME THAT company

▶ **PPT 6-1:**
Entrepreneurship and Starting a Small Business

▶ **PPT 6-2:**
Sheila C. Johnson

▶ **PPT 6-3:**
What Is Entrepreneurship?

While I was an employee at 3M, I developed a product that has become a staple on most office supply lists. I needed something to mark the pages of a hymnal without falling out or damaging the book. What started as a simple piece of yellow paper with a new adhesive evolved into many different versions—now there are dozens of versions of my invention. Who am I and what did I invent? (Find the answer in the chapter.)

entrepreneurship
Accepting the risk of starting and running a business.

Wacky grocer Jim Bonaminio may put on his wizard suit and roller-skate through his Jungle Jim's International Market, but he's serious when it comes to his business. Instead of competing on price against mega-giants like Wal-Mart, Jungle Jim's competes on product variety. A case holding 1,200 kinds of hot sauce rests beneath an antique fire engine. Why do you think customers might remain loyal to Jungle Jim's?

THE AGE OF THE ENTREPRENEUR

Most young people know it's unlikely they will get a job in a large corporation and stay 30 years. For those who want more control over their destiny, working in or starting a small business makes sense. **Entrepreneurship** is accepting the risk of starting and running a business. Explore this chapter and think about the possibility of entrepreneurship in your future.

THE JOB-CREATING POWER OF ENTREPRENEURS IN THE UNITED STATES

One of the major issues in the United States today is the need to create more jobs. You can begin to understand the job-creating power of entrepreneurs when you look at some of the great U.S. entrepreneurs from the past and the present. The history of the United States is the history of its entrepreneurs. Consider just a few of the many who have helped shape the U.S. economy:[1]

- DuPont, which manufactures thousands of products under such brand names as Teflon and Lycra, was started in 1802 by French immigrant Éleuthère Irénée du Pont de Nemours. Some 18 shareholders provided $36,000 in start-up money.
- Avon, the familiar beauty products retailer, started in 1886 with $500 David McConnell borrowed from a friend.
- George Eastman launched photographic giant Kodak in 1880 with a $3,000 investment.
- Procter & Gamble, now a multinational marketer of household products, was formed in 1837 by William Procter, James Gamble, and a total of $7,000 in capital.
- Ford Motor Company began with an investment of $28,000 by Henry Ford and 11 associates.
  - Amazon.com began with investments by founder Jeff Bezos's family and friends. Bezos's parents invested $300,000, a huge portion of their retirement account. Today they are billionaires.

These stories have much in common. One or a couple of entrepreneurs had a good idea, borrowed some money from friends and family, and started a business. That business now employs thousands of people and helps the country prosper.

SPOTLIGHT ON SMALL business

You're Never Too Young to Be an Entrepreneur

Think you're too young to be making big bucks as a successful entrepreneur? Think again. Age is just a number.

- Leanna Archer, an Islip, New York, 12-year-old, began her business ventures at just 8 years old. Archer's mom made natural hair care products, and the young visionary wanted to do the same. Now she is the owner of Leanna's Inc., a hair care products company. All her products are sold online and in select stores, earning Archer a stellar $5,000 a month!

- Alexis Holmes is a 16-year-old bakery owner. Started as a fund-raising project to support the Oasis Center, a Nashville-based agency that helps kids in crisis, Holmes's Famous Pies bakery now makes pies, cakes, and wedding cakes. Holmes even employs Oasis Center youth to help out. She is currently in the process of building a restaurant/bakery in the Nashville area.

- Jack Short and Daniel Lyons, two Missouri medical students, are the owners of Factory Green, a green apparel company they started as undergrads. Inspired by the knowledge that typical T-shirt production emits 7,600 grams of carbon dioxide per shirt, the two decided there had to be a better way. Factory Green shirts are funny, provocative, and carbon-neutral—the only carbon emissions caused by these shirts are from transport. As these two green businessmen now focus on medical school, their employees continue to try to save the world in a different way.

- Mark Zuckerberg is no stranger to college students. The founder and CEO of Facebook, a social networking Web site that is home to over 400 million users, Zuckerberg started the site in his Harvard dorm room. It grew from a campuswide application to include other colleges nationwide. Now people of all ages around the world connect through Facebook. Zuckerberg has received offers from Yahoo and Viacom, but has no plans to sell just yet. The only thing on his mind is improving the Web site and growing it to over 500 million users.

Sources: Olga Orda, "Factory Green: Young Entrepreneurs Roll Out Shirts with Spunk," Ecopreneurist.com, July 11, 2008; Craig Newmark, "The 2008 Time 100," *Time*, May 12, 2008; Abby Ellin, "3 Kid CEOs Making Big Bucks," *MSN Money*, April 3, 2008.

The United States has plenty of entrepreneurial talent. Names such as Steve Jobs (Apple Computer), Mark Zuckerberg (Facebook), Michael Dell (Dell Inc.), Bill Gates (Microsoft), Howard Schultz (Starbucks), Jack Dorsey (Twitter), Chris DeWolfe and Tom Anderson (MySpace), and Chad Hurley and Steve Chen (YouTube) have become as familiar as those of the great entrepreneurs of the past. The Spotlight on Small Business box highlights several young entrepreneurs who started businesses while still in school.

LEARNING goal 1 *

Explain why people take the risks of entrepreneurship; list the attributes of successful entrepreneurs; and describe entrepreneurial teams, intrapreneurs, and home- and Web-based businesses.

◀ PPT 6-4:
Notable Entrepreneurs

◀ LECTURE LINK 6-1:
History's Greatest Entrepreneurs

◀ PPT 6-5:
You're Never Too Young to Be an Entrepreneur

◀ PPT 6-6:
You're Never Too Old to Be an Entrepreneur Either

WHY PEOPLE TAKE THE ENTREPRENEURIAL CHALLENGE

Taking the risks of starting a business can be scary and thrilling at the same time. One entrepreneur described it as almost like bungee jumping. You might be scared, but if you watch six other people do it and they survive, then you're

> **PPT 6-7:**
> Why Take the Risks?
>
> **LECTURE LINK 6-2:**
> Lucky Office Space
>
> **CRITICAL THINKING EXERCISE 6-1:**
> What Does It Take to Be an Entrepreneur?
>
> **LECTURE LINK 6-3:**
> Success of Women-Owned firms
>
> **PPT 6-8:**
> What Does It Take to Be an Entrepreneur?

more likely to do it yourself. Here are some reasons people are willing to take the entrepreneurial risk:

- *Opportunity.* The opportunity to share in the American dream is a tremendous lure. Many people, including those new to this country, may not have the skills for today's complex organizations, but they do have the initiative and drive to work the long hours demanded by entrepreneurship. The same is true of many corporate managers who leave corporate life (by choice or after downsizing) to run businesses of their own. Other people, including an increasing number with disabilities, find that starting their own businesses offers them more opportunities than working for others.[2]

- *Profit.* Profit is another important reason to become an entrepreneur. Bill Gates, who cofounded Microsoft, is one of the richest men in the world.

- *Independence.* Many entrepreneurs simply do not enjoy working for someone else. Melissa Harvey, whose company Will n' Roses LLC produces all-natural nut and whole-grain Kizo bars, says one of the best things about being an entrepreneur is the freedom to pursue your passion: "It's about independence. You can take something that motivates you, that inspires you and act on it without roadblocks."[3]

- *Challenge.* Some people believe that entrepreneurs are excitement junkies who thrive on risk. Nancy Flexman and Thomas Scanlan, in their book *Running Your Own Business*, point out that entrepreneurs take moderate, calculated risks; they don't just gamble. In general, though, entrepreneurs seek achievement more than power.[4]

What Does It Take to Be an Entrepreneur?

Would you succeed as an entrepreneur? You can learn about the managerial and leadership skills needed to run a firm. However, you may not have the personality to assume the risks, take the initiative, create the vision, and rally others to follow your lead. Such personality traits are harder to learn or acquire than academic skills are. A list of entrepreneurial attributes to look for in yourself includes:[5]

Julie Clark, framed by puppets used in Baby Einstein videos, launched the child video empire in 1996 by making videos in her basement for her own children. In 2000 Clark was named Ernst & Young's Entrepreneur of the Year, and in 2001 she sold the business to Disney. Today there is a Baby Einstein television show as well as books, diaper bag collections, and bath and skin care lines.

- *Self-directed.* You should be self-disciplined and thoroughly comfortable being your own boss. You alone will be responsible for your success or failure.

- *Self-nurturing.* You must believe in your idea even when no one else does, and be able to replenish your own enthusiasm. When Walt Disney suggested the possibility of a full-length animated feature film, *Snow White*, the industry laughed. His personal commitment and enthusiasm caused the Bank of America to back his venture. The rest is history.

- *Action-oriented.* Great business ideas are not enough. Most important is a burning desire to realize, actualize, and build your dream into reality.

- *Highly energetic.* It's your business, and you must be emotionally, mentally, and physically able to work long and hard. Employees have weekends and vacations; entrepreneurs often work seven days a week and don't take vacations for years. Working 18-hour days in your own business can be exhausting, but most entrepreneurs think it is better than working long hours for someone else.

THINKING green

www.stonyfield.com

Socially Responsible Entrepreneurship

Until recently, environmentalism and business did not mix; at least that's what Gary Hirshberg thought. After college, the antibusiness Hirshberg went to work at a small ecological research center, only to have an epiphany at an exposition funded by Kraft Foods. The expo championed the use of fossil fuels, chemicals, and everything else Hirshberg hated about big-business food production. But he realized that more people had attended the exposition in one day than had ever been to his ecological institute, so he went by the old saying "If you can't beat them, join them."

Two years later, Hirshberg started Stonyfield Farm with one question in mind: "Is it possible to run a commercial enterprise that doesn't hurt the planet—and still be highly profitable?" The answer is yes. By entirely offsetting all its carbon dioxide emissions, installing the largest solar photovoltaic array in New Hampshire, and generating all yogurt waste into biogas, Stonyfield runs a 100 percent organic operation. Its manufacturing process is not only environmentally sound but also profitable. Stonyfield's green attitude saves the company millions of dollars a year, and after just 15 years in business, Hirshberg surpassed his old nemesis Kraft Foods in yogurt sales.

Hirshberg is just one of many social entrepreneurs—businesspeople who aim to turn a profit while still being environmentally and socially responsible. Others include Lucas Weingarten, an MBA student at DePaul University who developed a plan for a green business park. "People wonder, 'How can you say you are serving society and you are getting rich off it?' That might be a little myopic. Not that I want to get rich off it, but you absolutely have to be profitable," says Weingarten.

Sources: Gary Hirshberg, "Seven Cows and a Dream," *Newsweek*, February 25, 2008, p. E6; Kris Berggren, "Compassionate Capitalists: Young Social Entrepreneurs Merge Values and Business Savvy to Change the World," *National Catholic Reporter*, May 30, 2008.

- *Tolerant of uncertainty.* Successful entrepreneurs take only calculated risks (if they can help it). Still, they must be able to take *some* risks. Remember, entrepreneurship is not for the squeamish or those bent on security. You can't be afraid to fail. Many well-known entrepreneurs failed several times before achieving success. The late football coach Vince Lombardi summarized the entrepreneurial philosophy when he said, "We didn't lose any games this season, we just ran out of time twice." New entrepreneurs must be prepared to run out of time a few times before they succeed.

Turning Your Passions and Problems into Opportunities

As a young man in Queens, a borough of New York City, Russell Simmons channeled his passion for hip-hop culture into Def Jam Records. Today, his multimillion-dollar empire also includes Phat Farm clothing and Rush Management. Simmons used his time, money, and energy to turn his passion into a sustainable business.[6]

While many entrepreneurs' business ideas are inspired by their passions (see the Thinking Green box for another example), many see business

◀ **LECTURE LINK 6-4:**
Charles Babbage: 19th Century Entrepreneur

◀ **PPT 6-9:**
An Idea Is a Good Opportunity If...

◀ **PPT 6-10:**
Social Entrepreneurship: Responsible and Profitable

◀ **LECTURE LINK 6-5:**
Building A Company With Humanity

opportunities in their problems. For example, Georgette Klinger started her famous skin care company because she had acne. Anita Roddick started The Body Shop, which recycles its bottles and jars, because she hated paying for expensive packaging when she bought makeup.[7]

Most entrepreneurs don't get ideas for products and services from some flash of inspiration. The source of innovation is more like a *flashlight*. Imagine a search party walking in the dark, shining lights, looking around, asking questions, and looking some more. "That's how most creativity happens," says business author Dale Dauten. "Calling around, asking questions, saying 'What if?' till you get blisters on your tongue."

To look at problems and/or passions and see opportunities in them, ask yourself these questions: What do I want, but can never find? What product or service would improve my life? What really irritates me and what product or service would help?

Keep in mind, however, that not all ideas are opportunities. If your idea doesn't meet anyone else's needs, the business won't succeed. You may have a business idea that is a good opportunity if:[8]

- It fills customers' needs.
- You have the skills and resources to start a business.
- You can sell the product or service at a price customers are willing and able to pay—and still make a profit.
- You can get your product or service to customers before your window of opportunity closes (before competitors with similar solutions beat you to the marketplace).
- You can keep the business going.

If you think you may have the entrepreneurial spirit in your blood, complete the Entrepreneurial Readiness Questionnaire on pages 151–152.

Entrepreneurial Teams

An **entrepreneurial team** is a group of experienced people from different areas of business who join to form a managerial team with the skills to develop, make, and market a new product. A team may be better than an individual entrepreneur because team members can combine creative skills with production and marketing skills right from the start. Having a team also can ensure more cooperation and coordination later among functions in the business.

While Steve Jobs was the charismatic folk hero and visionary of Apple Computers, it was Steve Wozniak who invented the first personal computer model and Mike Markkula who offered business expertise and access to venture capital. The key to Apple's early success was that it was built around this "smart team" of entrepreneurs. The team wanted to combine the discipline of a big company with an environment in which people could feel they were participating in a successful venture. The trio of entrepreneurs recruited seasoned managers with similar desires. Everyone worked together to conceive, develop, and market products.[9]

Micropreneurs and Home-Based Businesses

Not everyone who starts a business wants to grow a mammoth corporation. Some are interested in maintaining a balanced lifestyle while doing the kind of work they want to do. Such business owners are called **micropreneurs**. While other entrepreneurs are committed to the quest for growth, micropreneurs know they can be happy even if their companies never appear on a list of top-ranked businesses.

> **LECTURE LINK 6-6:**
> The Myth about Myths

> **entrepreneurial team**
> A group of experienced people from different areas of business who join together to form a managerial team with the skills needed to develop, make, and market a new product.

> **PPT 6-11:**
> Entrepreneurial Teams

> **PPT 6-12:**
> Micropreneurs

> **micropreneurs**
> Entrepreneurs willing to accept the risk of starting and managing the type of business that remains small, lets them do the kind of work they want to do, and offers them a balanced lifestyle.

ENTREPRENEUR READINESS QUESTIONNAIRE

Each of the following items describes something that you may or may not feel represents your personality or other characteristics about you. Read each item and then circle the response (1, 2, 3, 4, or 5) that most nearly reflects the extent to which you agree or disagree that the item seems to fit you.

Looking at My Overall Philosophy of Life and Typical Behavior, I Would Say That . . .	AGREE COMPLETELY (1)	MOSTLY AGREE (2)	PARTIALLY AGREE (3)	MOSTLY DISAGREE (4)	DISAGREE COMPLETELY (5)
1. I am generally optimistic.	1	2	3	4	5
2. I enjoy competing and doing things better than someone else.	1	2	3	4	5
3. When solving a problem, I try to arrive at the best solution first without worrying about other possibilities.	1	2	3	4	5
4. I enjoy associating with co-workers after working hours.	1	2	3	4	5
5. If betting on a horse race I would prefer to take a chance on a high-payoff "long shot."	1	2	3	4	5
6. I like setting my own goals and working hard to achieve them.	1	2	3	4	5
7. I am generally casual and easy-going with others.	1	2	3	4	5
8. I like to know what is going on and take action to find out.	1	2	3	4	5
9. I work best when someone else is guiding me along the way.	1	2	3	4	5
10. When I am right I can convince others.					
11. I find that other people frequently waste my valuable time.	1	2	3	4	5
12. I enjoy watching football, baseball, and similar sports events.	1	2	3	4	5
13. I tend to communicate about myself very openly with other people.	1	2	3	4	5
14. I don't mind following orders from superiors who have legitimate authority.	1	2	3	4	5
15. I enjoy planning things more than actually carrying out the plans.	1	2	3	4	5
16. I don't think it's much fun to bet on a "sure thing."	1	2	3	4	5
17. If faced with failure, I would shift quickly to something else rather than sticking to my guns.	1	2	3	4	5
18. Part of being successful in business is reserving adequate time for family.	1	2	3	4	5
19. Once I have earned something, I feel that keeping it secure is important.	1	2	3	4	5
20. Making a lot of money is largely a matter of getting the right breaks.	1	2	3	4	5
21. Problem solving is usually more effective when a number of alternatives are considered.	1	2	3	4	5
22. I enjoy impressing others with the things I can do.	1	2	3	4	5
23. I enjoy playing games like tennis and handball with someone who is slightly better than I am.	1	2	3	4	5
24. Sometimes moral ethics must be bent a little in business dealings.	1	2	3	4	5
25. I think that good friends would make the best subordinates in an organization.	1	2	3	4	5

(continued)

Scoring:

Give yourself one point for each 1 or 2 response you circled for questions 1, 2, 6, 8, 10, 11, 16, 17, 21, 22, 23.

Give yourself one point for each 4 or 5 response you circled for questions 3, 4, 5, 7, 9, 12, 13, 14, 15, 18, 19, 20, 24, 25.

Add your points and see how you rate in the following categories:

21–25   Your entrepreneurial potential looks great if you have a suitable opportunity to use it. What are you waiting for?
16–20   This is close to the high entrepreneurial range. You could be quite successful if your other talents and resources are right.
11–15   Your score is in the transitional range. With some serious work you can probably develop the outlook you need for running your own business.
6–10   Things look pretty doubtful for you as an entrepreneur. It would take considerable rearranging of your life philosophy and behavior to make it.
0–5   Let's face it. Entrepreneurship isn't really for you. Still, learning what it's all about won't hurt anything.

Source: Kenneth R. Van Voorhis, *Entrepreneurship and Small Business Management* (New York: Allyn & Bacon, 1980).

Many micropreneurs are home-based business owners. More than 66 percent of the self-employed in the United States run businesses from their homes, according to the Bureau of Labor Statistics.[10] Micropreneurs include consultants, video producers, architects, and bookkeepers. Many with professional skills such as graphic design, writing, and translating have found that one way of starting a freelance business is through Web sites such as Elance (www.elance.com) and oDesk (www.odesk.com) that link clients and freelancers. The sites post job openings and client feedback and serve as secure intermediaries for clients' payments.[11] The Reaching Beyond Our Borders box discusses how these Web sites help small-business owners around the world.

Many home-based businesses are owned by people combining career and family. Don't picture just moms with young children; nearly 60 percent are men.[12] Here are more reasons for the growth of home-based businesses:[13]

- Computer technology has leveled the competitive playing field, allowing home-based businesses to look and act as big as their corporate competitors. Broadband Internet connections, personal digital assistants (PDAs) such as the BlackBerry and the iPhone, and other technologies are so affordable that setting up a business takes a much smaller initial investment than it once did.
- Corporate downsizing has led many to venture out on their own. Meanwhile, the work of the downsized employees still needs to be done, and corporations are outsourcing much of it to smaller companies.
- Social attitudes have changed. Whereas home-based entrepreneurs used to be asked when they were going to get a "real" job, they are now likely to be asked for how-to-do-it advice.
- New tax laws have loosened restrictions on deducting expenses for home offices.

Working at home has its challenges, of course. Here are a few:[14]

- *Getting new customers.* Getting the word out can be difficult because you don't have a retail storefront.
- *Managing time.* You save time by not commuting, but it takes self-discipline to use that time wisely.
- *Keeping work and family tasks separate.* It's great to be able to throw a load of laundry in the washer in the middle of the workday if you need to, but you have to keep such distractions to a minimum. It also takes self-discipline to leave your work at the office if the office is at home.

At the age of 26, Chris Lyman sold Hosting.com, the company he had founded, for $30 million. He then bought a big house and an expensive car and traveled. But a life of leisure was not his destiny. "I felt more lost running around the world doing all these fantastic things than being in business." Since 2003 he has been at the helm of another start-up, Fonality, which provides Internet-based phone service, and has taken exactly one week off. What characteristics of an entrepreneur does Lyman seem to have?

▶ PPT 6-13:
Home-Based Business Growth

▶ PPT 6-14:
Benefits of Home-Based Businesses

▶ PPT 6-15:
Downsides of Home-Based Businesses

REACHING BEYOND our borders

www.elance.com

Outsourcing Your Small Business

The term *outsourcing* brings to mind images of manufacturers sending jobs to foreign countries like China. But in the latest outsourcing trend, U.S. small-business owners are harnessing the Internet to find affordable labor all over the globe.

Online-service marketplaces, such as the California-based company Elance, provide small businesses with a central hub to find low-cost software development, accounting, and design work anywhere in the world. Randy and Nicola Wilburn of Dorchester, Massachusetts, own real estate, consulting, design, and, oddly enough, baby food businesses. Using Elance, they hired an Indian artist to design a logo for the baby food; a writer in London to make promotional materials; and virtual assistants in Jerusalem to transcribe voice mail, update their Web site, and design PowerPoint graphics. All this multinational networking is done from the comfort of the Wilburns' Victorian home.

Begun in 1999, Elance now boasts 48,500 small-business clients, an increase of 70 percent from 2007. Like competitors Guru.com and Brickwork India, it owes its rapid growth to the legions of inexpensive freelancers in its databases. It would cost the Wilburns $45,000 for a full-time secretary, while virtual assistants perform the same tasks for under $10,000. With savings like that, it won't be long before online outsourcing gains mass appeal.

Sources: Pete Engardio, "Mom-and-Pop Multinationals," *BusinessWeek,* July 14 and 21, 2008; Erin Conroy, "Busy People Turn to Web Sites for Virtual Errands," Associated Press, June 29, 2008; and Karen Goldberg Goff, "Home-Based Virtual Staffs," *Washington Times,* January 28, 2008.

- *Abiding by city ordinances.* Government ordinances restrict the types of businesses allowed in certain parts of the community and how much traffic a home-based business can attract to the neighborhood.
- *Managing risk.* Home-based entrepreneurs should review their homeowner's insurance policy, since not all policies cover business-related claims. Some even void the coverage if there is a business in the home.

◄ PPT 6-16:
Outsourcing Your Small Business

Home-based entrepreneurs should focus on finding opportunity instead of accepting security, getting results instead of following routines, earning a profit instead of earning a paycheck, trying new ideas instead of avoiding mistakes, and creating a long-term vision instead of seeking a short-term payoff. Figure 6.1 lists 10 ideas for potentially successful home-based businesses, and

figure 6.1

POTENTIAL HOME-BASED BUSINESSES

Many businesses can be started at home. Listed below are 10 businesses that have low start-up costs, don't require an abundance of administrative tasks, and are in relatively high demand:

1. Cleaning service.
2. Gift-basket business.
3. Web merchant.
4. Mailing list service.
5. Microfarming (small plots of land for such high-value crops as mushrooms, edible flowers, or sprouts).
6. Tutoring.
7. Résumé service.
8. Web design.
9. Medical claims assistance.
10. Personal coaching.

Look for a business that meets these important criteria: (1) The job is something you truly enjoy doing; (2) you know enough to do the job well or you are willing to spend time learning it while you have another job; and (3) you can identify a market for your product or service.

figure 6.2
WATCH OUT FOR SCAMS

> PPT 6-17:
> Online Business

You've probably read many newspaper and magazine ads selling home-based businesses. You may have even received unsolicited e-mail messages touting the glory of particular work-at-home opportunities. Beware of work-at-home scams! Here are a few clues that tell you a home business opportunity is a scam:

1. The ad promises that you can earn hundreds or even thousands of dollars a week working at home.
2. No experience is needed.
3. You only need to work a few hours a week.
4. There are loads of CAPITAL LETTERS and exclamation points!!!!!
5. You need to call a 900 number for more information.
6. You're asked to send in some money to receive a list of home-based business opportunities.
7. You're pressured to make a decision NOW!!!!

Do your homework before investing in a business opportunity. Call and ask for references. Contact the Better Business Bureau (www.bbb.org), county and state departments of consumer affairs, and the state attorney general's office. Conduct an Internet search and ask people in forums or on social networking sites if they've dealt with the company. Visit Web sites such as Friends In Business (www.friendsinbusiness.com) to find advice on specific online scams. Most important, don't pay a great deal of money for a business opportunity until you've talked to an attorney.

There are more than 63,000 diamonds for sale on BlueNile.com, a Seattle-based company that recently took in $12.8 million in net income. Customers buy directly from the Web site or through a toll-free number staffed by helpful reps (who don't work on commission). Says CEO Diane Irvine, "This business is all about taking market share." What does Blue Nile offer that other jewelry retailers don't?

Figure 6.2 highlights clues for avoiding home-based business scams. You can find a wealth of online information about starting a home-based business at *Entrepreneur* magazine's Web site (www.entrepreneur.com).

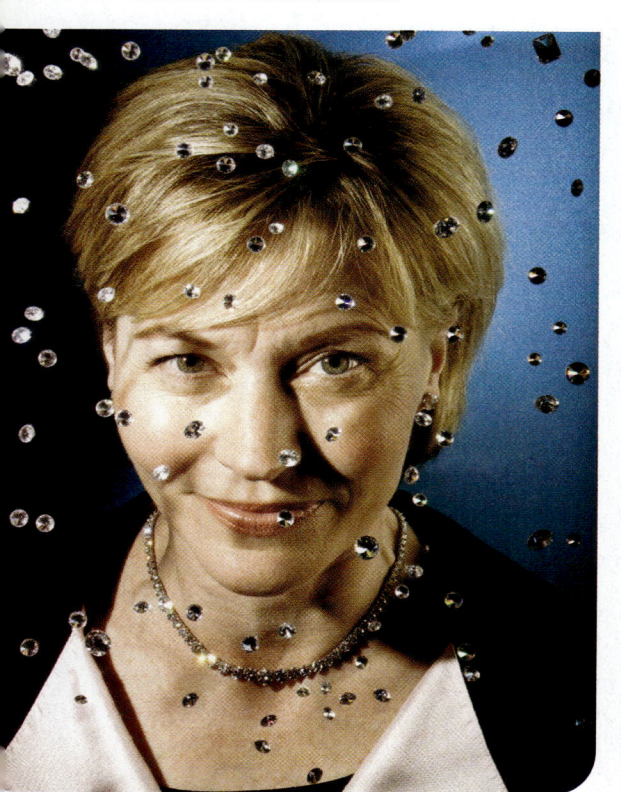

Web-Based Businesses

The Internet has sprouted a world of small Web-based businesses selling everything from staplers to refrigerator magnets to wedding dresses. In 2007, online retail sales reached $165.9 billion, or approximately 8 percent of all retail sales. Online sales grew nearly six times faster than total retail sales, increasing 21.8 percent from a year earlier, while total retail sales grew just 3.9 percent, according to the National Retail Federation.[15]

Web-based businesses have to offer more than the same merchandise customers can buy at stores—they must offer unique products or services. For example, Marc Resnik started his Web-based distribution company after waking up one morning laughing about his business idea. Now ThrowThings.com makes money for him—more than $1 million in revenue in 2008. Although the company's offerings seem like a random collection of unrelated items, everything it sells can be thrown. You can buy promotional products in the "Throw Your Name Around!" section, ventriloquist dummies in the "Throw Your Voice!" section, and sporting equipment in the "Things to Throw!" section. Stranger products include fake vomit ("Throw Up!") and a $3.50 certificate that says you wasted your money ("Throw Your Money Away!"). Resnik doesn't sell very many of those certificates, but he does sell more dummies than anyone else in the United States. About two-thirds of the company's revenue comes from the promotional products section, which allows customers to add a logo to thousands of products. Why is Resnik's business so successful? As one frequent customer said, it's because of Resnik's exceptional service and quick turnaround time.[16]

One of the easiest ways to start a Web-based business is through affiliate marketing. **Affiliate marketing** is an Internet-based marketing strategy in which a business rewards individuals or other businesses (affiliates) for each visitor or customer the affiliate sends to its Web site. For example, imagine you discovered a backpack online made of an extremely lightweight, amazingly strong fabric that holds everything you need for the day, is easy to carry, and looks great. You want to tell all your friends about it, so you register as an affiliate on the seller's Web site and download to your MySpace page a *widget*, a tiny application that links your page to the seller's site. Whenever anyone clicks on the widget (an image of the product) and buys a backpack, the seller pays you a commission.

If you can make a little money in commissions from sales of a single backpack, imagine setting up an online store with many products you love. Building such a store has become easier with the advent of shopping widget operators such as Lemonade Inc.'s Lemonade Stand (www.lemonade.com). Once partnered, an online retailer typically provides Lemonade Stand access to product information and images. Lemonade Stand then funnels that information through its Web site so that users can select which products they would like to appear in their widget product galleries on their Web sites, social network pages, or blogs. Widget users get commissions on sales generated through the widgets. Using a widget operator saves users from the time-consuming task of registering as an affiliate with multiple sellers. "Shopping widgets like Lemonade are allowing Internet users to become what amounts to peer-to-peer affiliates for e-retailers where the users can make money," says Laura Evans, executive director of the retail practice at Resource Interactive, an interactive marketing firm that follows emerging technologies. "Individuals setting up shopping widgets are keying in on a product mix personal to themselves and what their interests are and what they stand behind."[17]

A Web-based business isn't always a fast road to success. It can sometimes be a shortcut to failure. Hundreds of high-flying dot-coms crashed after promising to revolutionize the way we shop. That's the bad news. The good news is that you can learn from someone else's failure and spare yourself some pain.

Entrepreneurship within Firms

Entrepreneurship in a large organization is often reflected in the efforts and achievements of **intrapreneurs**, creative people who work as entrepreneurs within corporations. The idea is to use a company's existing resources—human, financial, and physical—to launch new products and generate new profits.[18] At 3M, which produces a wide array of products from adhesives like Scotch tape to nonwoven materials for industrial use, managers are expected to devote 15 percent of their work time to thinking up new products or services.[19] You know those bright-colored Post-it Notes people use to write messages on just about everything? That product was developed by Art Fry, a 3M employee.

affiliate marketing
An Internet-based marketing strategy in which a business rewards individuals or other businesses (affiliates) for each visitor or customer the affiliate sends to its Web site.

intrapreneurs
Creative people who work as entrepreneurs within corporations.

When you come up with a winning idea, stick with it. That's certainly been the motto of 3M, the maker of Post-it Notes. The company encourages intrapreneurship among its employees by requiring them to devote at least 15 percent of their time to thinking about new products. How has this commitment to innovation paid off for 3M and its employees?

> **PPT 6-18:** Intrapreneurs
>
> **BONUS CASE 6-1:** 3M Company, Intrapreneurial Leader

He needed to mark the pages of his hymnal with something that wouldn't damage the book or fall out. He came up with the idea of the self-stick, repositionable paper slips. The labs at 3M produced a sample, but distributors were unimpressed and market surveys inconclusive. Nonetheless, 3M kept sending samples to secretaries of top executives. Eventually, after a major sales and marketing program, the orders began pouring in, and Post-it Notes became a big winner. The company continues to update the product; making it from recycled paper is one of many innovations. Post-it Notes have gone international as well—the notepads sent to Japan are long and narrow to accommodate vertical writing. You can even use Post-it Notes electronically—the Post-it Software Notes program allows you to type messages onto brightly colored notes and store them on memo boards, embed them in documents, or send them through e-mail.

A classic intrapreneurial venture is Lockheed Martin Corporation's Skunkworks, a research and development center that turned out such monumental products as the United States' first fighter jet in 1943 and the Stealth fighter in 1991.[20]

Encouraging Entrepreneurship: What Government Can Do

> **enterprise zones**
> Specific geographic areas to which governments try to attract private business investment by offering lower taxes and other government support.

> **PPT 6-19:** Government and Entrepreneurship

Part of the Immigration Act passed by Congress in 1990 was intended to encourage more entrepreneurs to come to the United States. The act created a category of "investor visas" that allows 10,000 people to come to the United States each year if they invest $1 million in an enterprise that creates or preserves 10 jobs.[21] Some people are promoting the idea of increasing the allowed number of such immigrants. They believe the more entrepreneurs that can be drawn to the United States, the more jobs will be created and the more the economy will grow.

Another way to encourage entrepreneurship is **enterprise zones**, specific geographic areas to which governments attract private business investment by offering lower taxes and other government support. (These are also sometimes called *empowerment zones* or *enterprise communities*.) The government could have a significant effect on entrepreneurship by offering tax breaks to businesses that make investments to create jobs.[22] President Obama has promoted the idea of offering more tax breaks to businesses to stimulate economic growth. To learn more about the benefits of enterprise zones and to see a list of their locations throughout the United States, go to the USDA Rural Development Web page on the Rural Community Empowerment Program (www.rurdev.usda.gov/rbs/ezec).

States are becoming stronger supporters of entrepreneurs and creating programs that invest directly in new businesses. Often, state commerce departments serve as clearinghouses for such programs. States are also creating incubators and technology centers to reduce start-up capital needs. **Incubators** offer new businesses in the critical stage of early development low-cost offices with basic services such as accounting, legal advice, and secretarial help. According to a recent study conducted by the National Business Incubator Association (NBIA), 87 percent of incubator graduates remain in business.[23] To learn more about what incubators offer and to find links to incubators in your area, visit the NBIA's Web site (www.nbia.org).

> *Incubators, such as this one in Wausau, WI, offer new businesses low-cost offices with basic business services such as accounting, legal advice, and secretarial help. Do you have such incubators in your area?*

> **incubators**
> Centers that offer new businesses low-cost offices with basic business services.

progress assessment

- Why are people willing to take the risks of entrepreneurship?
- What are the advantages of entrepreneurial teams?
- How do micropreneurs differ from other entrepreneurs?
- What are some opportunities and risks of Web-based businesses?

LEARNING goal 2 *

Discuss the importance of small business to the American economy and summarize the major causes of small-business failure.

GETTING STARTED IN SMALL BUSINESS

Let's suppose you have a great idea for a new business, you have the attributes of an entrepreneur, and you're ready to take the leap into business for yourself. How do you start? That's what the rest of this chapter is about.

It may be easier to identify with a small neighborhood business than with a giant global firm, yet the principles of management are similar for each. The management of charities, government agencies, churches, schools, and unions is much the same as the management of small and large businesses. So, as you learn about small-business management, you will take a giant step toward understanding management in general. All organizations demand capital, good ideas, planning, information management, budgets (and financial management in general), accounting, marketing, good employee relations, and good overall managerial know-how. We shall explore these areas as they relate to small businesses and then, later in the book, apply the concepts to large firms and even global organizations.

Small versus Big Business

The Small Business Administration (SBA) defines a **small business** as one that is independently owned and operated, is not dominant in its field of operation, and meets certain standards of size in terms of employees or annual receipts (such as under $2 million a year for service businesses). A small business is considered "small" only in relationship to other businesses in its industry. A wholesaler may sell up to $22 million and still be considered a small business by the SBA. In manufacturing, a plant can have 1,500 employees and still be considered small. Let's look at some interesting statistics about small businesses:[24]

- There are 25.4 million small businesses in the United States.
- Of all nonfarm businesses in the United States, almost 97 percent are considered small by SBA standards.
- Small businesses account for more than 50 percent of the gross domestic product (GDP).

small business
A business that is independently owned and operated, is not dominant in its field of operation, and meets certain standards of size (set by the Small Business Administration) in terms of employees or annual receipts.

- Nearly 600,000 tax-paying, employee-hiring businesses are started every year.
- Small businesses generate 60–80 percent of the new jobs each year.
- Small businesses employ about half of all private-sector employees.
- About 80 percent of U.S. workers find their first jobs in small businesses.

As you can see, small business is really a big part of the U.S. economy. How big? Let's find out.

Importance of Small Businesses

Since 60–80 percent of the nation's new jobs are in small businesses, there's a very good chance you'll either work in a small business someday or start one. In addition to providing employment opportunities, small firms believe they offer other advantages over larger companies—more personal customer service and the ability to respond quickly to opportunities.[25]

Bigger is not always better. Picture a hole in the ground. If you fill it with boulders, there are many empty spaces between them. If you fill it with sand, there is no space between the grains. That's how it is in business. Big businesses don't serve all the needs of the market. There is plenty of room for small companies to make a profit filling those niches.

Small-Business Success and Failure

You can't be naive about business practices, or you'll go broke. According to a study reported in the *Monthly Labor Review*, 44 percent of new businesses don't last four years.[26] Yet a study by economist Bruce Kirchhoff showed that the failure rate is only 18 percent over the first eight years. Kirchhoff contends that other reported failure rates are misinterpretations of Dun & Bradstreet statistics. When small-business owners closed down one business to start another, for instance, they were included in the "failure" category—even though they hadn't failed at all. Similarly, when a business changed its form of ownership or a sole proprietor retired, it was counted as a failure. The good news for entrepreneurs is that business failures are much lower than traditionally reported.

Keep in mind, though, that even the most optimistic interpretation shows that nearly one of five businesses that cease operations is left owing money to creditors.[27] Figure 6.3 lists reasons for small-business failures, among them managerial incompetence and inadequate financial planning.

Choosing the right type of business is critical. Many businesses with low failure rates require advanced training to start—veterinary services, dental practices, medical practices, and so on. While training and degrees may buy security, they do not tend to produce much growth—one dentist can fill only so many cavities. If you want to

Danny Kass, professional snowboarder and Olympic silver medalist, founded Grenade Gloves with his brother Matt and several friends. The company designs snowboarding gear and apparel. Danny's idea was to be "hands-on" rather than just a corporate spokesperson. He and Matt started out by stenciling their new logo around the Winter Olympics Village before they even had anything ready to sell.

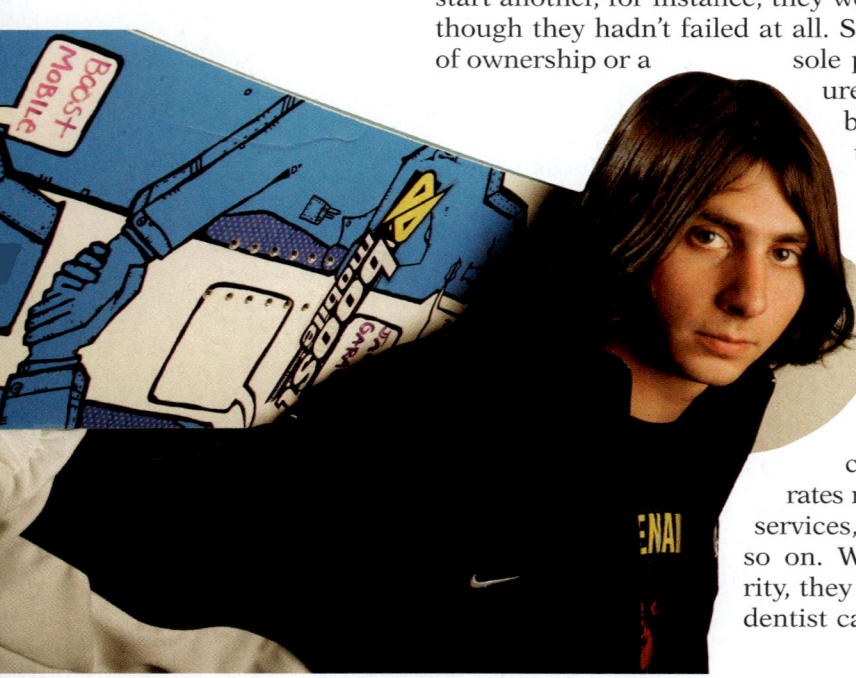

figure 6.3
CAUSES OF SMALL-BUSINESS FAILURE

The following are some of the causes of small-business failure:

- Plunging in without first testing the waters on a small scale.
- Underpricing or overpricing goods or services.
- Underestimating how much time it will take to build a market.
- Starting with too little capital.
- Starting with too much capital and being careless in its use.
- Going into business with little or no experience and without first learning something about the industry or market.
- Borrowing money without planning just how and when to pay it back.
- Attempting to do too much business with too little capital.
- Not allowing for setbacks and unexpected expenses.
- Buying too much on credit.
- Extending credit too freely.
- Expanding credit too rapidly.
- Failing to keep complete, accurate records, so that the owners drift into trouble without realizing it.
- Carrying habits of personal extravagance into the business.
- Not understanding business cycles.
- Forgetting about taxes, insurance, and other costs of doing business.
- Mistaking the freedom of being in business for oneself for the liberty to work or not, according to whim.

be both independent and rich, you need to go after growth. Often high-growth businesses, such as technology firms, are not easy to start and are even more difficult to keep going.[28]

The easiest businesses to start have the least growth and greatest failure rate (like restaurants). The easiest to keep alive are difficult to get started (like manufacturing). And the ones that can make you rich are both hard to start and hard to keep going (like automobile assembly).[29] See Figure 6.4 to get an idea of the business situations most likely to lead to success.

When you decide to start your own business, think carefully. You're unlikely to find everything you want—easy entry, security, and reward—in one business. Choose those characteristics that matter most to you; accept the absence of the others; plan, plan, plan; and then go for it!

◄ **PPT 6-23:**
Advantages of Small Over Big Business

◄ **LECTURE LINK 6-8:**
Failure Is the Best Medicine

◄ **PPT 6-24:**
Business Failures Are Lower Than the Reports Because...

◄ **LECTURE LINK 6-9:**
The Man Who Was Almost Bill Gates

figure 6.4
SITUATIONS FOR SMALL-BUSINESS SUCCESS

The following factors increase the chances of small-business success:

- The customer requires a lot of personal attention, as in a beauty parlor.
- The product is not easily made by mass-production techniques (e.g., custom-tailored clothes or custom auto-body work).
- Sales are not large enough to appeal to a large firm (e.g., a novelty shop).
- The neighborhood is not attractive because of crime or poverty. This provides a unique opportunity for small grocery stores and laundries.
- A large business sells a franchise operation to local buyers. (Don't forget franchising as an excellent way to enter the world of small business.)
- The owner pays attention to new competitors.
- The business is in a growth industry (e.g., computer services or Web design).

LEARNING goal 3 *

Summarize ways to learn about how small businesses operate.

> PPT 6-25:
> They Did What?
>
> PPT 6-26:
> Learning About Small Business

LEARNING ABOUT SMALL-BUSINESS OPERATIONS

Hundreds of would-be entrepreneurs ask the same question: "How can I learn to run my own business?" Here are some hints.

Learn from Others

Investigate your local community college for classes on small business and entrepreneurship; there are thousands of such programs throughout the United States. Many bring together entrepreneurs from diverse backgrounds who form helpful support networks. Talk to others who have already done it. They'll tell you that location is critical and caution you not to be undercapitalized, that is, not to start without enough money. They'll warn you about the problems of finding and retaining good workers. And, most of all, they'll tell you to keep good records and hire a good accountant and lawyer before you start. Free advice like this is invaluable.

Get Some Experience

There is no better way to learn small-business management than by becoming an apprentice or working for a successful entrepreneur. Many small-business owners got the idea for their businesses from their prior jobs. The rule of thumb is: Have three years' experience in a comparable business first.[30]

Lorena Garcia attended law school in Venezuela. Closer to her heart than law, however, was the lure of fine cooking. She eventually entered a culinary school. Today she owns Elements Tierra, a Latin-Asian fusion restaurant in Miami, as well as a deli where she sells her own homemade sauces, and has a net worth of about $2 million. What experiences do you have that could help you start and run a successful business?

Back in 1818, Cornelius Vanderbilt sold his own sailing vessels and went to work for a steamboat company so that he could learn the rules of the new game of steam. After learning what he needed to know, he quit, started his own steamship company, and became the first U.S. business owner to accumulate $100 million.

Running a small business part-time, during your off hours or on weekends, can bring the rewards of working for yourself while still enjoying a regular paycheck at another job. It may save you money too, because you're then less likely to make "rookie mistakes" when you start your own business. The Making Ethical Decisions box presents ethical questions about using the knowledge you've gained as an employee to start your own business.

Take Over a Successful Firm

Small-business owners work long hours and rarely take vacations. After many years, they may feel stuck and think they can't get out because they have too much time and effort invested. Thus millions of small-business owners are eager to get away, at least for a long vacation.

MAKING ethical decisions

Going Down with the Ship

Suppose you've worked for two years in a company and you see signs that it is beginning to falter. You and a co-worker have ideas about how to make a company like your boss's succeed. Rather than share your ideas with your boss, you and your friend are considering quitting your jobs and starting your own company together. Should you approach other co-workers about working for your new venture? Will you try to lure your old boss's customers to your own business? What are your alternatives? What are the consequences of each alternative? What's the most ethical choice?

This is where you come in. Find a successful businessperson who owns a small business. Tell him or her you are eager to learn the business and would like to serve an apprenticeship, that is, a training period. Say that at the end of the training period (one year or so), you would like to help the owner or manager by becoming assistant manager. Thus you can free the owner to take off weekends and holidays and have a long vacation—a good deal for him or her. For another year or so, work very hard to learn all about the business—suppliers, inventory, bookkeeping, customers, promotion. At the end of two years, make this offer: The owner can retire or work only part-time, and you will take over management of the business. You can establish a profit-sharing plan with the owner plus pay yourself a salary. Be generous with yourself; you'll earn it if you manage the business. You can even ask for 40 percent or more of the profits.

The owner benefits by keeping ownership in the business and making 60 percent of what he or she earned before—without having to work. You benefit by making 40 percent of the profits of a successful firm. This is an excellent deal for an owner about to retire—he or she is able to keep the firm and a healthy profit flow. It is also a clever and successful way to share in the profits of a successful small business without making any personal monetary investment.[31]

If profit sharing doesn't appeal to the owner, you may want to buy the business outright. How do you determine a fair price for a business? Value is based on (1) what the business owns, (2) what it earns, and (3) what makes it unique. Naturally, an accountant will need to help you determine the business's value.

If you fail at your efforts to take over the business through either profit sharing or buying, you can quit and start your own business fully trained.

LEARNING goal 4 *

Analyze what it takes to start and run a small business.

MANAGING A SMALL BUSINESS

According to the Small Business Administration, one of the major causes of small business failures is poor management.[32] Keep in mind, though, that *poor management* covers a number of faults. It could mean poor planning, record keeping, inventory control, promotion, or employee relations. Most likely it includes poor capitalization. To help you succeed as a business owner, in the following sections we explore the functions of business in a small-business setting:

- Planning your business.
- Financing your business.
- Knowing your customers (marketing).
- Managing your employees (human resource development).
- Keeping records (accounting).

Although all the functions are important in both the start-up and management phases of the business, the first two—planning and financing—are the primary concerns when you start your business. The others are the heart of your operations once the business is under way.

His love for tinkering with toys led inventor Lonnie Johnson to develop the Super Soaker, at one time the number one toy in the country. After spending $15,000 trying to sell his idea to toy companies, he finally made a deal and today his quarterly royalties have made him a millionaire.

business plan
A detailed written statement that describes the nature of the business, the target market, the advantages the business will have in relation to competition, and the resources and qualifications of the owner(s).

Begin with Planning

Many people eager to start a small business come up with an idea and begin discussing it with professors, friends, and other businesspeople. At this stage the entrepreneur needs a business plan. A **business plan** is a detailed written statement that describes the nature of the business, the target market, the advantages the business will have over competition, and the resources and qualifications of the owner(s). A business plan forces potential small-business owners to be quite specific about the products or services they intend to offer. They must analyze the competition, calculate how much money they need to start, and cover other details of operation. A business plan is also mandatory for talking with bankers or other investors.

Jim Hammersley, director of the Loan Programs Division of the Small Business Administration, says lenders want to know everything about an aspiring business. He offers several tips to entrepreneurs, including picking a bank that serves businesses the size of yours, having a good accountant prepare a complete set of financial statements and a personal balance sheet, making an appointment before going to the bank, going to the bank with an accountant and all the necessary financial information, and demonstrating to the banker that you're a person of good character: civic minded and respected in business and community circles. Finally, ask for *all* the money you need, be specific, and be prepared to personally guarantee the loan.[33]

▶ CRITICAL THINKING EXERCISE 6-3:
Writing a Business Plan

▶ PPT 6-29:
Business Plans

▶ PPT 6-30:
Writing a Business Plan

▶ PPT 6-31:
A Family Affair

Writing a Business Plan

A good business plan takes a long time to write, but you've got only five minutes, in the *executive summary*, to convince readers not to throw it away. Since bankers receive many business plans every day, the summary has to catch their interest quickly.[34] There's no such thing as a perfect business plan, but prospective entrepreneurs do think out the smallest details. The box on pages 163–164 gives an outline of a comprehensive business plan.

Many computer software programs can help you get organized. One highly rated business-plan program is Business Plan Pro by Palo Alto Software. You can find online help with the MiniPlan (www.miniplan.com), a free interactive Web tool that guides you through the process of writing a business plan.

OUTLINE OF A COMPREHENSIVE BUSINESS PLAN

A good business plan is between 25 and 50 pages long and takes at least six months to write.

Cover Letter
Only one thing is certain when you go hunting for money to start a business: You won't be the only hunter out there. You need to make potential funders want to read *your* business plan instead of the hundreds of others on their desks. Your cover letter should summarize the most attractive points of your project in as few words as possible. Be sure to address the letter to the potential investor by name. "To whom it may concern" or "Dear Sir" is not the best way to win an investor's support.

Section 1—Executive Summary
Begin with a two-page or three-page management summary of the proposed venture. Include a short description of the business, and discuss major goals and objectives.

Section 2—Company Background
Describe company operations to date (if any), potential legal considerations, and areas of risk and opportunity. Summarize the firm's financial condition, and include past and current balance sheets, income and cash flow statements, and other relevant financial records (you will read about these financial statements in Chapter 17). It is also wise to include a description of insurance coverage. Investors want to be assured that death or other mishaps do not pose major threats to the company.

Section 3—Management Team
Include an organization chart, job descriptions of listed positions, and detailed résumés of the current and proposed executives. A mediocre idea with a proven management team is funded more often than a great idea with an inexperienced team. Managers should have expertise in all disciplines necessary to start and run a business. If not, mention outside consultants who will serve in these roles and describe their qualifications.

Section 4—Financial Plan
Provide five-year projections for income, expenses, and funding sources. Don't assume the business will grow in a straight line. Adjust your planning to allow for funding at various stages of the company's growth. Explain the rationale and assumptions used to determine the estimates. Assumptions should be reasonable and based on industry/historical trends. Make sure all totals add up and are consistent throughout the plan. If necessary, hire a professional accountant or financial analyst to prepare these statements.

Stay clear of excessively ambitious sales projections; rather, offer best-case, expected, and worst-case scenarios. These not only reveal how sensitive the bottom line is to sales fluctuations but also serve as good management guides.

Section 5—Capital Required
Indicate the amount of capital needed to commence or continue operations, and describe how these funds are to be used. Make sure the totals are the same as the ones on the cash-flow statement. This area will receive a great deal of review from potential investors, so it must be clear and concise.

Section 6—Marketing Plan
Don't underestimate the competition. Review industry size, trends, and the target market segment. Sources like *American Demographics* magazine and the *Rand McNally Commercial Atlas and Marketing Guide* can help you put a plan together. Discuss strengths and weaknesses of the product or service. The most important things investors want to know are what makes the product more desirable than what's already available and whether the product can be patented. Compare pricing to the competition's. Forecast sales in dollars and units. Outline sales, advertising, promotion, and public relations programs. Make sure the costs agree with those projected in the financial statements.

Section 7—Location Analysis
In retailing and certain other industries, the location of the business is one of the most important factors. Provide a comprehensive demographic analysis of consumers in the area of the proposed business as well as a traffic-pattern analysis and vehicular and pedestrian counts.

(continued)

> **Section 8—Manufacturing Plan**
> Describe minimum plant size, machinery required, production capacity, inventory and inventory-control methods, quality control, plant personnel requirements, and so on. Estimates of product costs should be based on primary research.
>
> **Section 9—Appendix**
> Include all marketing research on the product or service (off-the-shelf reports, article reprints, etc.) and other information about the product concept or market size. Provide a bibliography of all the reference materials you consulted. This section should demonstrate that the proposed company won't be entering a declining industry or market segment.
>
> If you would like to see sample business plans that successfully secured funding, go to Bplans.com (www.bplans.com). You can also learn more about writing business plans on the Small Business Administration Web site at www.sba.gov/starting.

Some people may think aging baby boomers are getting ready to retire to their rocking chairs to watch Seinfeld reruns. No way, according to Franny Martin and 5.6 million other U.S. small-business owners aged 50 and over. Martin started her business, Cookies on Call, when she was nearly 56. She sells 52 kinds of chocolate-chunk and fruit-studded cookies through her Web site. Do you think it's ever too late to start a business?

Getting the completed business plan into the right hands is almost as important as getting the right information into the plan. Finding funding requires research. Next we discuss sources of money available to new business ventures. All require a comprehensive business plan. The time and effort you invest before starting a business will pay off many times later. The big payoff is survival.

Getting Money to Fund a Small Business

An entrepreneur has several potential sources of capital: personal savings; relatives; former employers; banks; finance companies; venture capitalists; and government agencies such as the Small Business Administration (SBA), the Farmers Home Administration, the Economic Development Authority, and the Minority Business Development Agency. The most common source of funding after personal savings is friends and family.[35] You may even want to consider borrowing from a potential supplier to your future business. Helping you get started may be in the supplier's interest if there is a chance you will be a big customer later. It's usually not a good idea to ask such an investor for money at the outset. Begin by asking for advice; if the supplier likes your plan, he or she may be willing to help you with funding too.

Individual investors are also a frequent source of capital for most entrepreneurs. *Angel investors* are private individuals who invest their own money in potentially hot new companies before they go public.[36] A number of Web sites match people who want money with those willing to lend it; they include Prosper, Zopa, Lending Club, Virgin Money, CircleLending, and GlobeFunder.[37] This form of individual investing is called peer-to-peer lending (P2P). A creditworthy borrower often gets such money faster and easier than going to the bank. And the cost is often less than a bank loan.[38]

The credit crunch spurred by the subprime mortgage crisis in 2008–2010 made it necessary for small-business owners to do a little extra shopping to find a friendly lender. Many found that smaller community banks were more likely to grant loans than larger regional banks. Since small banks do business in a single town or cluster of towns, they know their customers better. They have more flexibility to make lending decisions based on everything they know about their customers, rather than on a more automated basis as larger banks must.[39]

Venture capitalists may finance your project—for a price. Venture capitalists may ask for a hefty stake in your company (as much as 60 percent) in exchange for the cash to start your business. If the venture capitalist takes too large a stake, you could lose control of the business. Since the widespread failure of early Web start-ups, venture capitalists have been willing to invest less and expect more return on their investment if the new company is sold.[40] Therefore, if you're a very small company, you don't have a very good chance of getting venture capital. You'd have a better chance finding an angel investor.

If your proposed venture does require millions of dollars to start, experts recommend that you talk with at least five investment firms and their clients in order to find the right venture capitalist. To learn more about how to find venture capitalists, visit the National Venture Capital Association's Web site (www.nvca.org).

The Small Business Administration (SBA)

The **Small Business Administration (SBA)** is a U.S. government agency that advises and assists small businesses by providing management training and financial advice and loans (see Figure 6.5 on p. 166). The SBA started a microloan demonstration program in 1991. The program provides very small loans (up to $35,000) and technical assistance to small-business owners. It is administered through a nationwide network of nonprofit organizations chosen by the SBA. Rather than award loans based on collateral, credit history, or previous business success, the program judges worthiness on belief in the borrowers' integrity and the soundness of their business ideas.[41]

The SBA microloan program helps people like Natalie Hughes, who started a mobile auto maintenance business. Hughes didn't even try to get a loan from a bank because she didn't have a great credit history. She was able to get a $4,500 SBA microloan, which allowed her to buy business insurance, oil, and other supplies she need to start her business.[42]

You may also want to consider requesting funds from the **Small Business Investment Company (SBIC) Program**. SBICs are private investment companies licensed by the SBA to lend money to small businesses. An SBIC must have a minimum of $5 million in capital and can borrow up to $2 from the SBA for each $1 of capital it has. It lends to or invests in small businesses that meet its criteria. Often SBICs are able to keep defaults to a minimum by identifying a business's trouble spots early, giving entrepreneurs advice, and in some cases rescheduling loan payments.[43]

Perhaps the best place for young entrepreneurs to start shopping for an SBA loan is a Small Business Development Center (SBDC). SBDCs are funded jointly by the federal government and individual states, and are usually associated with state and community colleges and universities. SBDCs can help you evaluate the feasibility of your idea, develop your business plan, and complete your funding application—all for no charge. The SBA reduced the size of its application from 150 pages to 1 page for loans under $50,000. You

figure 6.5
TYPES OF SBA FINANCIAL ASSISTANCE

The SBA may provide the following types of financial assistance:

- *Guaranteed loans*—loans made by a financial institution that the government will repay if the borrower stops making payments. The maximum individual loan guarantee is capped at $1 million.
- *Microloans*—amounts ranging from $100 to $35,000 (average $10,500) to people such as single mothers and public housing tenants.
- *Export Express*—loans made to small businesses wishing to export. The maximum guaranteed loan amount is $250,000.
- *Community Adjustment and Investment Program (CAIP)*—loans to businesses to create new, sustainable jobs or to preserve existing jobs in eligible communities that have lost jobs due to changing trade patterns with Mexico and Canada following the adoption of NAFTA.
- *Pollution control loans*—loans to eligible small businesses for the financing of the planning, design, or installation of a pollution control facility. This facility must prevent, reduce, abate, or control any form of pollution, including recycling. The maximum guaranteed loan amount is $1 million.
- *504 certified development company (CDC) loans*—loans for purchasing major fixed assets, such as land and buildings for businesses in eligible communities, typically rural communities or urban areas needing revitalization. The program's goal is to expand business ownership by minorities, women, and veterans. The maximum guaranteed loan amount is $1.3 million.

may want to go to the SBA's Web site (www.sba.gov) for the latest information about SBA programs and other business services.

Obtaining money from banks, venture capitalists, and government sources is very difficult for most small businesses. (You will learn more about financing in Chapter 18.) Those who do survive the planning and financing of their new ventures are eager to get their businesses up and running. Your success in running a business depends on many factors, especially knowing your customers, managing your employees, and keeping good records.

Knowing Your Customers

One of the most important elements of small-business success is knowing the **market**, which consists of consumers with unsatisfied wants and needs who have both resources and willingness to buy. Most of our students have the willingness to own a brand-new Maserati sports car. However, few have the resources necessary to satisfy this want. Would they be a good market for a luxury car dealer?

Once you have identified your market and its needs, you must set out to fill those needs. How? Offer top quality at a fair price with great service. Remember, it isn't enough to get customers—you have to *keep* them. As Victoria Jackson, founder of the $50 million company Victoria Jackson Cosmetics, says of the stars who push her products on television infomercials, "All the glamorous faces in the world wouldn't mean a thing if my customers weren't happy with the product and didn't come back for more." Everything must be geared to bring customers the satisfaction they deserve.

One of the greatest advantages small businesses have is the ability to know their customers better and adapt quickly to their ever-changing needs. You will gain more insights about markets in Chapters 13–16. Now let's consider effectively managing the employees who help you serve your market.

---

market
People with unsatisfied wants and needs who have both the resources and the willingness to buy.

Managing Employees

As a business grows, it becomes impossible for an entrepreneur to oversee every detail, even by putting in 60 hours per week.[44] This means hiring, training, and motivating employees is critical.

It is not easy to find good help when you offer less money, skimpier benefits, and less room for advancement than larger firms do. That's one reason employee relations is important for small-business management. Employees of small companies are often more satisfied with their jobs than are their counterparts in big business. Why? Quite often they find their jobs more challenging, their ideas more accepted, and their bosses more respectful.[45]

Often entrepreneurs are reluctant to recognize that to keep growing, they must delegate authority to others. Who should have this delegated authority, and how much?

This can be a particularly touchy issue in small businesses with long-term employees, and in family businesses. As you might expect, entrepreneurs who have built their companies from scratch often feel compelled to promote employees who have been with them from the start—even when they aren't qualified to serve as managers. Common sense tells you this could hurt the business.[46] The idea that you must promote or can't fire people because "they're family" can also hinder growth. Entrepreneurs best serve themselves and the business if they gradually recruit and groom employees for management positions, enhancing trust and support between them. You'll learn more about managing employees in Chapters 7–12.

Keeping Records

Small-business owners often say the most important assistance they received in starting and managing their business was in accounting. A businessperson who sets up an effective accounting system early will save much grief later. Computers simplify record keeping and enable a small-business owner to daily follow sales, expenses, and profits. An inexpensive computer system can also help owners with inventory control, customer records, and payroll.

Many business failures are caused by poor accounting practices that lead to costly mistakes. A good accountant can help you decide whether to buy or lease equipment and whether to own or rent a building. He or she may also help you with tax planning, financial forecasting, choosing sources of financing, and writing requests for funds.

Other small-business owners may tell you where to find an accountant experienced in small business. It pays to shop around for advice. You'll learn more about accounting in Chapter 17.

Looking for Help

Small-business owners have learned, sometimes the hard way, that they need outside consulting advice early in the process. This is especially true of legal, tax, and accounting advice but also of marketing, finance, and other areas. Most small and medium-sized firms cannot afford to hire such experts as employees, so they must turn to outside assistance.

A necessary and invaluable aide is a competent, experienced lawyer who knows and understands small businesses. Lawyers can help with

Not all small businesses stay small; some become business superstars. Take Staples, for example. The world's largest office products company started with an SBA loan in 1986 and is now a $27 billion retailer operating in 25 countries around the world. The government, acting through the Small Business Administration, is a great supporter of entrepreneurship. Have you contacted the SBA for information about starting a small business?

Their love of bacon inspired Dave Lefkow and Justin Esch to create J&D Bacon Salt, a seasoning that adds the flavor of bacon to anything and everything. With a start-up budget of just $5,000, they promoted their product with strategies like MySpace and Facebook pages, a blog, and free samples. Without food-industry connections, Lefkow and Esch created their own network of support the hard way—by picking up the phone and asking for it. Check out their story at www.baconsalt.com.

Service Corps of Retired Executives (SCORE)
An SBA office with volunteers from industry, trade associations, and education who counsel small businesses at no cost (except for expenses).

▶ **PPT 6-41:**
Marketing Research

▶ **LECTURE LINK 6-II:**
Making Entrepreneurship a Major

▶ **PPT 6-42:**
Other Forms of Help

leases, contracts, partnership agreements, and protection against liabilities. They don't have to be expensive. In fact, several prepaid legal plans offer services such as drafting legal documents for a low annual rate. Of course, you can find plenty of legal services online. The SBA offers plain-English guides and mini-tutorials that will help you gain a basic understanding of the laws that affect each phase of the life of a small business. FindForms.com offers a search tool that helps you find free legal forms from all over the Web as well as advice, links, books, and more. Remember, "free" isn't a bargain if the information isn't correct, so check the sources carefully and double-check any legal actions with an attorney.

Make your marketing decisions long before you introduce a product or open a store. An inexpensive marketing research study may help you determine where to locate, whom to select as your target market, and what is an effective strategy for reaching it. Thus a marketing consultant with small-business experience can be of great help to you, especially one who has had experience with the Internet and social media.[47]

Your business will benefit from a presence on the Internet even if you do not directly sell products or services online. Brandt's Cafe, a small restaurant in St. Louis, has a Web site (www.brandtscafe.com) that features the day's menu and specials, highlights the head chef's credentials, and displays photos of the restaurant. It also includes an interactive calendar that lists the scheduled live entertainment and even audio samples of performers' work for you to preview. Web sites such as Workz.com give you access to tools to build your own site, including sources for Web graphic design and search engine submission tactics.

Two other invaluable experts are a commercial loan officer and an insurance agent. The commercial loan officer can help you design an acceptable business plan and give you valuable financial advice as well as lend you money when you need it. An insurance agent will explain all the risks associated with a small business and how to cover them most efficiently with insurance and other means like safety devices and sprinkler systems.

An important source of information for small businesses is the **Service Corps of Retired Executives (SCORE)**. This SBA office has more than 10,500 volunteers from industry, trade associations, and education who counsel small businesses at no cost (except for expenses).[48] You can find a SCORE counselor by logging on to www.score.org. The SBA also offers a free, comprehensive online entrepreneurship course for aspiring entrepreneurs.

Often business professors from local colleges will advise small-business owners free or for a small fee. Some universities have clubs or programs that provide consulting services by master of business administration (MBA) candidates for a nominal fee. The University of Maryland and Virginia Tech have internship programs that pair MBA students with budding companies in local incubator programs. The incubator companies pay half the intern's salary, which is around $20 an hour.

It also is wise to seek the counsel of other small-business owners. The Web site YoungEntrepreneur.com offers experienced entrepreneurs and young start-ups an open forum to exchange advice and ideas. Visitors have access to articles on marketing, business planning, incorporation, and financial management.

Other sources of counsel include local chambers of commerce, the Better Business Bureau, national and local trade associations, the business reference section of your library, and many small-business-related sites on the Internet. Some can match your consulting needs with the proper consultant, like Company Expert (www.4consulting-services.com).

> **progress assessment**
>
> - A business plan is probably the most important document a small business owner will ever create. There are nine sections in the business plan outline on pages 163–164. Can you describe at least five of those sections now?

◀ PPT 6-43:
Progress Assessment

LEARNING goal 5 *

Outline the advantages and disadvantages small businesses have in entering global markets.

GOING INTERNATIONAL: SMALL-BUSINESS PROSPECTS

As we noted in Chapter 3, there are over 310 million people in the United States but more than 6.8 billion people in the world. Obviously, the world market is a much larger, more lucrative market for small businesses than the United States alone. In spite of that potential, many small businesses still do not think internationally. According to the U.S. Department of Commerce, only about a third of small businesses now export, but half are expected to engage in global trade by 2018.[49] Small businesses are well on their way to meeting those expectations; small and medium-sized business accounted for 99 percent of the growth in exporting firms in recent years.[50]

Technological advances have helped increase small business exporting; PayPal makes it possible for small businesses to get paid automatically when they conduct global business online. The Internet also helps small businesses find customers without the expense of international travel. As people acquire more wealth, they often demand specialized products that are not mass-produced and are willing to pay more for niche goods that small businesses offer. Dave Hammond, inventor and founder of Wizard Vending, began to push his gum-ball machines into the international market via a Web site. In the site's first year, he sold machines in Austria, Belgium, and Germany.

◀ PPT 6-44:
Small Business Prospects Abroad

Still, many small businesses have difficulty getting started in global business. Why are so many missing the boat to the huge global markets? Primarily because the voyage includes a few major hurdles: (1) Financing is often difficult to find, (2) would-be exporters don't know how to get started and do not understand the cultural differences between markets, and (3) the bureaucratic paperwork can threaten to bury a small business.

Besides the fact that most of the world's market lies outside the United States, there are other good reasons for going global. Exporting can absorb excess inventory, soften downturns in the domestic market, and extend product lives. It can also spice up dull routines.

Small businesses have several advantages over large businesses in international trade:

- Overseas buyers often enjoy dealing with individuals rather than with large corporate bureaucracies.
- Small companies can usually begin shipping much faster.
- Small companies can provide a wide variety of suppliers.
- Small companies can give customers personal service and undivided attention, because each overseas account is a major source of business to them.

A good place to start finding information about exporting is the Department of Commerce's Bureau of Industry and Security (www.bis.doc.gov). Other sources include the SBA's list of international business resources (www.sba.gov/hotlist/internat.html). The SBA's Export Express loan program provides export financing opportunities for small businesses. The program is designed to finance a variety of needs of small-business exporters, including participation in foreign trade shows, catalog translations for use in foreign markets, lines of credit for export purposes, and real estate and equipment for the production of goods or services to be exported.[51]

progress assessment

- Why do many small businesses avoid doing business overseas?
- What are some of the advantages small businesses have over large businesses in selling in global markets?

summary

Learning Goal 1. Explain why people take the risks of entrepreneurship; list the attributes of successful entrepreneurs; and describe entrepreneurial teams, intrapreneurs, and home- and Web-based businesses.

- **What are a few of the reasons people start their own businesses?**

Reasons include profit, independence, opportunity, and challenge.

- **What are the attributes of successful entrepreneurs?**

Successful entrepreneurs are self-directed, self-nurturing, action-oriented, highly energetic, and tolerant of uncertainty.

- **What have modern entrepreneurs done to ensure longer terms of management?**

They have formed entrepreneurial teams with expertise in the many skills needed to start and manage a business.

- **What is a micropreneur?**

Micropreneurs are people willing to accept the risk of starting and managing the type of business that remains small, lets them do the kind of work they want to do, and offers them a balanced lifestyle.

- **What is intrapreneuring?**

Intrapreneuring is the establishment of entrepreneurial centers within a larger firm where people can innovate and develop new product ideas internally.

- **Why has there been such an increase in the number of home-based and Web-based businesses in the last few years?**

  The increase in power and decrease in price of computer technology has leveled the field and made it possible for small businesses to compete against larger companies—regardless of location.

Learning Goal 2. Discuss the importance of small business to the American economy and summarize the major causes of small business failure.

- **Why are *small* businesses important to the U.S. economy?**

  Small business accounts for almost 50 percent of gross domestic product (GDP). Perhaps more important to tomorrow's graduates, 80 percent of U.S. workers' first jobs are in small businesses.

- **What does the *small* in small business mean?**

  The Small Business Administration defines a small business as one that is independently owned and operated and not dominant in its field of operation, and that meets certain standards of size in terms of employees or sales (depending on the size of others in the industry).

- **Why do many small businesses fail?**

  Many small businesses fail because of managerial incompetence and inadequate financial planning. See Figure 6.3 (page 159) for a list of causes of business failure.

Learning Goal 3. Summarize ways to learn about how small businesses operate.

- **What hints would you give someone who wants to learn about starting a small business?**

  First, learn from others. Take courses and talk with some small-business owners. Second, get some experience working for others. Third, take over a successful firm. Finally, study the latest in small-business management techniques, including the use of computers for functions like payroll, inventory control, and mailing lists.

Learning Goal 4. Analyze what it takes to start and run a small business.

- **What goes into a business plan?**

  See the box on pages 163–164.

- **What sources of funds should someone wanting to start a new business consider investigating?**

  A new entrepreneur has several potential sources of capital: personal savings, relatives, former employers, banks, finance companies, venture capital organizations, government agencies, and more.

- **What are some of the special problems that small-business owners have in dealing with employees?**

  Small-business owners often have difficulty finding competent employees and grooming employees for management responsibilities.

- **Where can budding entrepreneurs find help in starting their businesses?**

  Help can come from many sources: accountants, lawyers, marketing researchers, loan officers, insurance agents, the SBA, SBDCs, SBICs, and even college professors.

Learning Goal 5. Outline the advantages and disadvantages small businesses have in entering global markets.

- **What are some advantages small businesses have over large businesses in global markets?**

  Foreign buyers enjoy dealing with individuals rather than large corporations because (1) small companies provide a wider variety of suppliers and can ship products more quickly and (2) small companies give more personal service.

- **Why don't more small businesses start trading internationally?**
There are several reasons: (1) financing is often difficult to find, (2) many people don't know how to get started and do not understand the cultural differences in foreign markets, and (3) the bureaucratic red tape is often overwhelming.

key terms

affiliate marketing 155
business plan 162
enterprise zones 156
entrepreneurial team 150
entrepreneurship 146
incubators 156
intrapreneurs 155
market 166
micropreneurs 150
Service Corps of Retired Executives (SCORE) 168
small business 157
Small Business Administration (SBA) 165
Small Business Investment Company (SBIC) Program 165
venture capitalists 165

connect interactive applications

Reinforcing Your *Connect*ion to Concepts in Business

This chapter offers 15 interactive applications designed to help you apply what you've learned (examples of these exercises appear below). Your instructor has determined which interactive applications will benefit you throughout this course. Please refer to your instructor's assignment list in *Connect* to determine which applications you should complete.

Comprehension Case Interactive: Entrepreneurs may encounter obstacles that may threaten the success of their business. However, there are strategies that entrepreneurs may employ that can help a small business owner be successful. There are certain attributes and characteristics that make a business more likely to succeed or fail. Read the case regarding pizza and entrepreneurship and answer the questions.

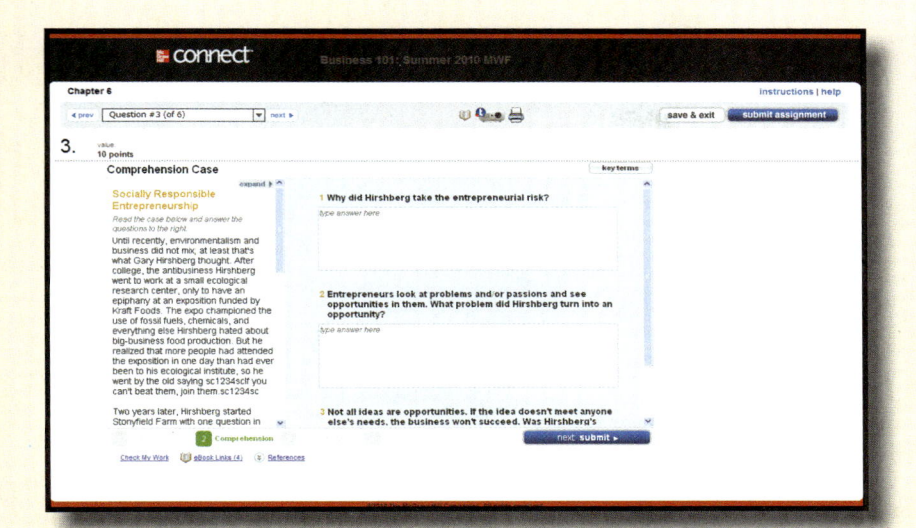

Comprehension Case Interactive: Taking risks is part of becoming an entrepreneur. Starting a business can be scary and thrilling all at the same time. Many entrepreneurs are lured by the opportunity to live the American dream and many are enticed by the potential profit. In general, entrepreneurs seek to achieve rather than seek power. Read the case about socially responsible entrepreneurship and answer the questions.

Comprehension Case Interactive: Small business owners find it easier to focus on a specific group of consumers. Read the case about Burt's Bees and answer the questions.

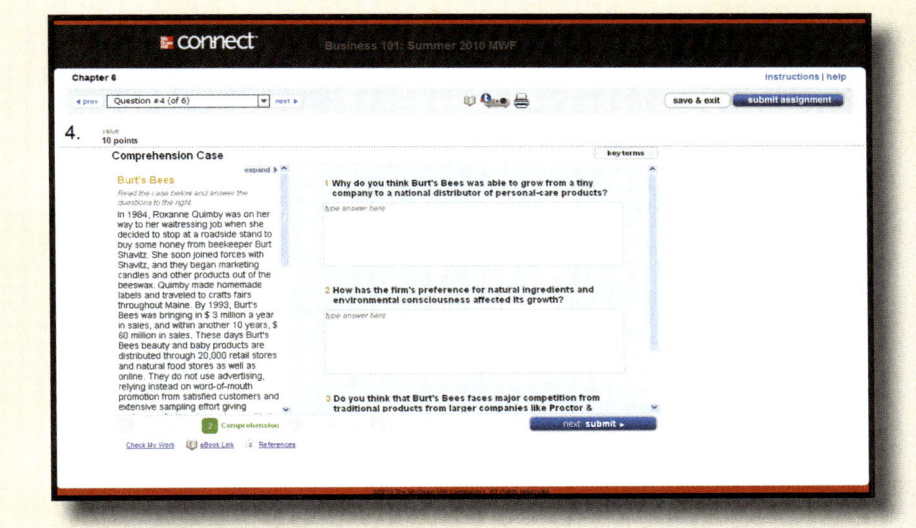

Click and Drag Interactive: A business plan forces potential small-business owners to be specific about the products or services they intend to offer. They must analyze the competition, calculate how much money they need to start, and cover other details of operation. A business plan is also mandatory for talking with bankers and other investors. Read the statements and drag and drop them into the correct spot on the comprehensive business plan.

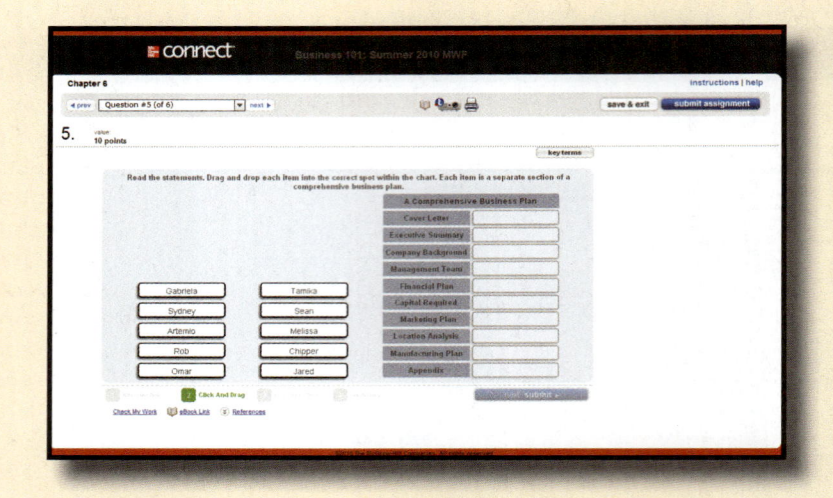

Video Case Interactive: Small businesses are a critical factor to the U.S. economy as they create the majority of new jobs. Watch the video case featuring Broad Reach Sails and answer the questions when prompted.

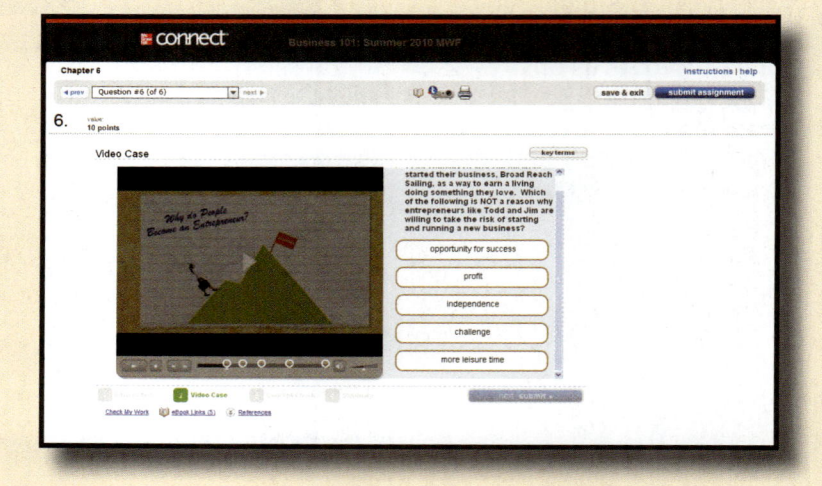

7

MANAGEMENT and Leadership

profile

Getting to Know Indra Krishnamurthy Nooyi, CEO of PepsiCo

Indra Nooyi grew up on the southeast coast of India, the daughter of an accountant and a stay-at-home mom. Every night at dinner, Nooyi's mom would present a world problem to Nooyi and her sister, and they would compete to solve it as if they were a prime minister or a president. In school, Nooyi debated, played cricket, and formed an all-girl rock band in which she played guitar (an instrument she still enjoys).

Eventually, Nooyi earned master's degrees in business from both the Indian School of Management in Calcutta and the Yale School of Management. She worked for the Boston Consulting Group and then moved on to a strategic-planning position at Motorola. She was about to go to work for General Electric when PepsiCo lured her away by saying they needed her more. That was in 1994.

By 1996, Pepsi's sales had slowed. Competitor Coca-Cola was earning 71 percent of its revenues from international sales, and PepsiCo only 29 percent. At that time, Nooyi was strategy chief and the head of mergers and acquisitions. Her long-range planning led Pepsi to buy both Tropicana and Quaker and sell its subsidiaries Pizza Hut, Taco Bell, and KFC. Her goal was to increase sales overseas, introduce more good-for-you products, and put more emphasis on food rather than drinks.

Pepsi had some success by introducing bottled water to its offerings. PepsiCo still produces "fun for you" foods (about 70 percent), but it has "better for you" and "good for you" products too—like Stacy's Simply Naked pita chips and Flat Earth fruit and veggie chips.

When Nooyi became CEO of PepsiCo, she was eager to work closely with other managers, but she also had clear ideas for a company vision she called "Performance with Purpose." She also had a strong commitment to healthier products. She wants the percentage of "better for you" and "good for you" products to reach 50 percent of output, with more fruit, grains, and nuts.

As a top manager, Nooyi excels at the art of persuasion. She is effective at introducing change. And she has a real talent for reaching overseas markets. She tends to use a boss-centered leadership style, but she also is a team

LEARNING goals

After you have read and studied this chapter, you should be able to

1 Describe the changes occurring today in the management function.

2 Describe the four functions of management.

3 Relate the planning process and decision making to the accomplishment of company goals.

4 Describe the organizing function of management.

5 Explain the differences between leaders and managers, and describe the various leadership styles.

6 Summarize the five steps of the control function of management.

connect

Your *Connect*ion to Better Learning. 1. View the interactive presentation. 2. Practice through LearnSmart. 3. Apply your knowledge by using the interactive applications for each chapter of this text.

1 Prep >>>>>>   **2 Study** >>>>>>   **3 Apply**

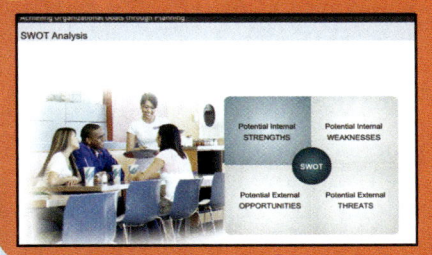

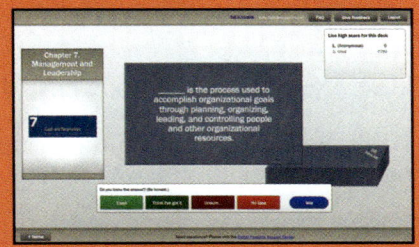

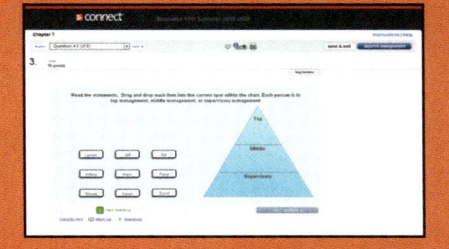

---

www.pepsico.com

player who seeks the input of others (participative leadership). *BusinessWeek* called her one of its "Top 50" managers. Howard Schultz of Starbucks calls her a "world class leader." Her long-term goal is to "go to Washington [to] give back—to work for no money for a while." So look for Nooyi on the world stage in the future. Meanwhile, she has a challenging managerial role because prices of raw materials like corn are skyrocketing, and competition in the snack business is fierce.

Sources: Betsy Morris, "The Pepsi Challenge," *Fortune*, March 3, 2008; Dean Foust, "The BW 50," *BusinessWeek*, April 7, 2008; Howard Schultz, "Indra Nooyi," *Time*, May 12, 2008; and "Pepsi's Plan to Make Litter Green," *Bloomberg BusinessWeek*, April 26 – May 2, 2010, p.28.

NAME THAT company

▶ **PPT 7-1:** Management and Leadership

▶ **PPT 7-2:** Indra Krishnamurthy Nooyi

The father of the "fourth meal," this familiar fast-food chain has actively sought out the late-night crowd with value menu items priced as low as 79 cents. It also tries to appeal to health-conscious customers with its *Fresco* menu. Name that company. (Find the answer in the chapter.)

▶ **PPT 7-3:** America's Most Powerful Female Managers

▶ **LECTURE LINK 7-1:** Beware of Bad Bosses

▶ **LECTURE LINK 7-2:** Best Business Leaders of the 20th Century

LEARNING goal 1 *

Describe the changes occurring today in the management function.

MANAGERS' ROLES ARE EVOLVING

Managers like PepsiCo's Indra Nooyi must practice the art of getting things done through organizational resources, which include workers, financial resources, information, and equipment. At one time, managers were called bosses and their job consisted of telling people what to do, watching over them to be sure they did it, and reprimanding those who didn't. Many managers still behave that way. Perhaps you've witnessed such behavior; many basketball coaches have adopted this style.

Today, however, some managers tend to be more progressive. For example, they emphasize teams and team building; they create drop-in centers, team spaces, and open work areas. They may change the definition of *work* from "a task you do for a specified period in a specific place" to "something you do anywhere, anytime."[1] They tend to guide, train, support, motivate, and coach employees rather than tell them what to do.[2] Managers of high-tech firms, for instance, realize that many workers often know more about technology than they do.[3] Thus most modern managers emphasize teamwork and cooperation rather than discipline and order giving.

Rather than telling employees exactly what to do, managers today tend to give their employees enough independence to make their own informed decisions about how best to please customers. How do you think most employees respond to this new empowerment on the job?

The years 2008–2010 were particularly hard on managers and workers.[4] The financial crisis forced many leading firms—like Boeing, IBM, and Caterpillar—to fire managers and lower-level workers. PepsiCo's Nooyi won praise for rallying employees amid the gloom. But she too announced plans to cut some 3,000 employees.[5] In one day in January 2009, top companies in the United States cut 70,000 jobs![6] Some Dutch, Japanese, and Indian firms made similar cuts.[7] Furthermore, it became more difficult to get financing for new ventures or to modernize existing plants. Managers tended to be cautious in starting new ventures as they waited to see what the economy would do.

The people entering management today are different from those who entered in the past. Leaders of Fortune 100 companies tend to be younger, more of them are female, and fewer of them were educated at elite universities.[8] Managers in the future are more likely to be working in teams and assuming completely new roles in the firm. For one thing, they will be taking a leadership role in adapting to climate change. Further, they'll be doing more expansion overseas[9]—see the Reaching Beyond Our Borders box on p. 180.

What these changes mean for you is that management will demand a new kind of person: a skilled communicator and team player as well as a planner, organizer, motivator, and leader. We'll address these trends in the next few chapters to help you decide whether management is the kind of career you would like.

LEARNING goal 2 *

Describe the four functions of management.

THE FOUR FUNCTIONS OF MANAGEMENT

The following definition of management provides the outline of this chapter: **Management** is the process used to accomplish organizational goals through planning, organizing, leading, and controlling people and other organizational resources (see Figure 7.1).

Planning includes anticipating trends and determining the best strategies and tactics to achieve organizational goals and objectives. One of the major objectives of organizations is to please customers.[10] The trend today is to have *planning teams* to help monitor the environment, find business opportunities, and watch for challenges.[11] *Planning* is a key management function because accomplishing the other functions depends heavily on having a good plan.

◄ **LECTURE LINK 7-3:**
Three Types Of Great Leaders

◄ **PPT 7-4:**
What Is Management?

◄ **PPT 7-5:**
Today's Managers

◄ **PPT 7-6:**
Respect and How to Get It

◄ **PPT 7-7:**
The Best Managers

◄ **PPT 7-8:**
The Worst Managers

◄ **PPT 7-9:**
Four Functions of Management

management
The process used to accomplish organizational goals through planning, organizing, leading, and controlling people and other organizational resources.

planning
A management function that includes anticipating trends and determining the best strategies and tactics to achieve organizational goals and objectives.

◄ **CRITICAL THINKING EXERCISE 7-1:**
Management Functions

figure 7.1
WHAT MANAGERS DO
Some modern managers perform all of these tasks with the full cooperation and participation of workers. Empowering employees means allowing them to participate more fully in decision making.

Planning
- Setting organizational goals.
- Developing strategies to reach those goals.
- Determining resources needed.
- Setting precise standards.

Organizing
- Allocating resources, assigning tasks, and establishing procedures for accomplishing goals.
- Preparing a structure (organization chart) showing lines of authority and responsibility.
- Recruiting, selecting, training, and developing employees.
- Placing employees where they'll be most effective.

Leading
- Guiding and motivating employees to work effectively to accomplish organizational goals and objectives.
- Giving assignments.
- Explaining routines.
- Clarifying policies.
- Providing feedback on performance.

Controlling
- Measuring results against corporate objectives.
- Monitoring performance relative to standards.
- Rewarding outstanding performance.
- Taking corrective action when necessary.

REACHING BEYOND our borders

We Need Managers Over Here

OK, so there are many opportunities for growing a business overseas. What is keeping U.S. companies from expanding rapidly in global markets? Jack Welch, former CEO of General Electric, says the problem is not a lack of engineers or scientists; the problem is a lack of professional managers. Top managers from many companies are complaining that they can't find people to run their operations. That includes managers in all areas, from human resource management to finance. That means lots of opportunity for today's college graduates. If they can broaden their perspective to think of global markets, the potential is awesome.

The challenges are pretty daunting, however. Here is what the *Sloan Management Review* said in 2008: "Village roads can be impassable, home cooking is still a way of life, product prices can be below the cost of production . . . and local products often have generations of loyal customers."

Flexibility is a key to conquering such challenges. For example, companies are using motorcycles to get through on those supposedly impassable roads. Developing products that appeal to local markets is another strategy. That may mean selling cigarettes one by one instead of in packs. It may mean selling crank-up radios that run without electricity. The challenges can be fun as well as daunting. Sure, you'll have to learn how to negotiate with the government. Sure, you'll face all the issues discussed in this chapter. But the payoff is a rewarding managerial position in a growing country. Often the rewards far outstrip the costs.

Sources: Jack Welch and Suzy Welch, "Red Flags for the Decade Ahead," *BusinessWeek*, May 19, 2008; Satish Shankar, Charles Ormiston, Nicolas Bloch, Robert Schaus, and Vijay Vishwanath, "How to Win in Emerging Markets," *Sloan Management Review*, Spring 2008; and Mac Margolis, "Executives Wanted," *Newsweek*, June 14, 2010, pp. 40–41.

---

organizing
A management function that includes designing the structure of the organization and creating conditions and systems in which everyone and everything works together to achieve the organization's goals and objectives.

leading
Creating a vision for the organization and guiding, training, coaching, and motivating others to work effectively to achieve the organization's goals and objectives.

Planning is what helps managers understand the environment in which their business must operate. When people's tastes and preferences for restaurant meals change, food service managers need to be ready to respond with menu alternatives. What changes have occurred in your own preferences?

Organizing includes designing the structure of the organization and creating conditions and systems in which everyone and everything works together to achieve the organization's goals and objectives. Many of today's organizations are being designed around pleasing the customer at a profit.[12] Thus they must remain flexible and adaptable, because when customer needs change, firms must change with them. Whole Foods Market, for example, is known for its high-quality, high-priced food items. But it has introduced many lower-cost items to adjust to the financial losses of its customer base. General Motors lost much of its customer base to manufacturers of more fuel-efficient cars. It hopes to win back market share by offering hydrogen-powered or electric vehicles that cost less to run.[13] Have GM's efforts been successful?

Leading means creating a vision for the organization and communicating, guiding, training, coaching, and motivating others to achieve goals and objectives in a timely manner. The trend is to empower employees, giving them as much freedom as possible to become self-directed and self-motivated. This function was once known as *directing*; that is, telling employees exactly what to do. In many smaller firms, that is still the manager's role. In most large firms, however, managers no longer tell people exactly what to do because knowledge workers and others often know how to do their jobs better than the manager does. Nonetheless, leadership is still necessary to keep employees focused on the right tasks at the right time.

Controlling establishes clear standards to determine whether an organization is progressing toward its goals and objectives, rewarding people for doing a good job, and taking corrective action if they are not. Basically, it means measuring whether what actually occurs meets the organization's goals.

Planning, organizing, leading, and controlling are the heart of management, so let's explore them in more detail. The process begins with planning; we'll look at that right after the Progress Assessment.

controlling
A management function that involves establishing clear standards to determine whether or not an organization is progressing toward its goals and objectives, rewarding people for doing a good job, and taking corrective action if they are not.

progress assessment

- What are some of the changes happening in management today?
- What's the definition of *management* used in this chapter?
- What are the four functions of management?

LEARNING goal 3 *

Relate the planning process and decision making to the accomplishment of company goals.

◄ PPT 7-10:
We Need Managers Here

◄ PPT 7-11:
Sharing the Vision

◄ LECTURE LINK 7-4:
Revisiting Mission at Victoria's Secret

PLANNING AND DECISION MAKING

Planning, the first managerial function, is setting the organization's vision (including its mission statement), goals, and objectives. Executives find planning to be their most valuable tool. A **vision** is more than a goal; it's a broad explanation of why the organization exists and where it's trying to go. It gives the organization a sense of purpose and a set of values that unite workers in a common destiny.[14] Managing an organization without first establishing a vision is like getting everyone in a rowboat excited about going somewhere, but not telling them exactly where. The boat will just keep changing directions rather than speeding toward an agreed-on goal.

Top management usually sets the vision for the organization and then often works with others in the firm to establish a mission statement. A **mission statement** outlines the organization's fundamental purposes. It should address:

- The organization's self-concept.
- Its philosophy.
- Long-term survival needs.
- Customer needs.
- Social responsibility.
- Nature of the product or service.

Starbucks' mission statement appears in Figure 7.2 on p. 182. How well does it address the aspects listed above?

The mission statement becomes the foundation for setting specific goals and objectives. **Goals** are the broad, long-term accomplishments an organization wishes to attain. Because workers and management need to agree on them, setting goals is often a team process. **Objectives** are specific, short-term

vision
An encompassing explanation of why the organization exists and where it's trying to head.

◄ PPT 7-12:
Defining the Mission

◄ PPT 7-13:
Setting Goals and Objectives

mission statement
An outline of the fundamental purposes of an organization.

goals
The broad, long-term accomplishments an organization wishes to attain.

objectives
Specific, short-term statements detailing how to achieve the organization's goals.

figure 7.2
STARBUCKS' MISSION STATEMENT

TO INSPIRE AND NURTURE THE HUMAN SPIRIT—ONE PERSON, ONE CUP, AND ONE NEIGHBORHOOD AT A TIME.

Here are the principles of how we live that every day:

Our Coffee
It has always been, and will always be, about quality. We're passionate about ethically sourcing the finest coffee beans, roasting them with great care, and improving the lives of people who grow them. We care deeply about all of this; our work is never done.

Our Partners
We're called partners, because it's not just a job, it's our passion. Together, we embrace diversity to create a place where each of us can be ourselves. We always treat each other with respect and dignity. And we hold each other to that standard.

Our Customers
When we are fully engaged, we connect with, laugh with, and uplift the lives of our customers—even if just for a few moments. Sure, it starts with the promise of a perfectly made beverage, but our work goes far beyond that. It's really about human connection.

Our Stores
When our customers feel this sense of belonging, our stores become a haven, a break from the worries outside, a place where you can meet with friends. It's about enjoyment at the speed of life—sometimes slow and savored, sometimes faster. Always full of humanity.

Our Neighborhood
Every store is part of a community, and we take our responsibility to be good neighbors seriously. We want to be invited in wherever we do business. We can be a force for positive action—bringing together our partners, customers, and the community to contribute every day. Now we see that our responsibility—and our potential for good—is even larger. The world is looking to Starbucks to set the new standard, yet again. We will lead.

Our Shareholders
We know that as we deliver in each of these areas, we enjoy the kind of success that rewards our shareholders. We are fully accountable to get each of these elements right so that Starbucks—and everyone it touches—can endure and thrive.

▶ **PPT 7-14:** Planning Answers Fundamental Questions

▶ **CRITICAL THINKING EXERCISE 7-2:** Career SWOT Analysis

▶ **PPT 7-15:** SWOT Matrix

SWOT analysis
A planning tool used to analyze an organization's strengths, weaknesses, opportunities, and threats.

statements detailing *how to achieve* the organization's goals. One of your goals for reading this chapter, for example, may be to learn basic concepts of management. An objective you could use to achieve this goal is to answer the chapter's Progress Assessment questions.

Planning is a continuous process. A plan that worked yesterday may not be successful in today's market. Most planning also follows a pattern. The procedure you'll follow in planning your life and career is basically the same as the one businesses use. It answers several fundamental questions:

1. *What is the situation now?* What are the success factors affecting the industry participants and how do we compare? What is the state of the economy and other environments? What opportunities exist for meeting people's needs? What products and customers are most profitable? Who are our major competitors? What threats are they to our business? These questions are part of **SWOT analysis**, which analyses the organization's **s**trengths and **w**eaknesses, and the **o**pportunities and **t**hreats it faces, usually in that order.

figure 7.3

SWOT MATRIX
This matrix identifies potential strengths, weaknesses, opportunities, and threats organizations may consider in a SWOT analysis.

Potential Internal STRENGTHS
- Core competencies in key areas
- An acknowledged market leader
- Well-conceived functional area strategies
- Proven management
- Cost advantages
- Better advertising campaigns

Potential Internal WEAKNESSES
- No clear strategic direction
- Obsolete facilities
- Subpar profitability
- Lack of managerial depth and talent
- Weak market image
- Too narrow a product line

Potential External OPPORTUNITIES
- Ability to serve additional customer groups
- Expand product lines
- Ability to transfer skills/technology to new products
- Falling trade barriers in attractive foreign markets
- Complacency among rival firms
- Ability to grow due to increases in market demand

Potential External THREATS
- Entry of lower-cost foreign competitors
- Rising sales of substitute products
- Slower market growth
- Costly regulatory requirements
- Vulnerability to recession and business cycles
- Changing buyer needs and tastes

Opportunities and threats are often external to the firm and cannot always be anticipated. Weaknesses and strengths are more often internal and therefore more within reach of being measured and fixed. Figure 7.3 lists some of the general issues companies consider when conducting a SWOT analysis: What external success factors affect the industry? How does our firm measure up to other firms? What are our social objectives? What are our personal development objectives? What can we do to survive and prosper during a recession? For more on SWOT analysis, see the Taking It to the Net exercise at the end of this chapter.

2. *How can we get to our goal from here?* Answering this question is often the most important part of planning. It takes four forms: strategic, tactical, operational, and contingency (see Figure 7.4).

Strategic planning is done by top management and determines the major goals of the organization and the policies, procedures, strategies, and resources it will need to achieve them. *Policies* are broad guidelines for action, and *strategies* determine the best way to use resources. At the strategic planning stage,

strategic planning
The process of determining the major goals of the organization and the policies and strategies for obtaining and using resources to achieve those goals.

FORMS OF PLANNING

- **STRATEGIC PLANNING**: The setting of broad, long-range goals by top managers
- **TACTICAL PLANNING**: The identification of specific, short-range objectives by lower-level managers
- **OPERATIONAL PLANNING**: The setting of work standards and schedules
- **CONTINGENCY PLANNING**: Backup plans in case primary plans fail

figure 7.4

PLANNING FUNCTIONS
Very few firms bother to make contingency plans. If something changes the market, such companies may be slow to respond. Most organizations do strategic, tactical, and operational planning.

◂ PPT 7-18:
Planning Functions

Organizations of all kinds need contingency plans for unexpected events. Amtrak and the Transportation Security Administration recently conducted drills at 150 train stations to help officers prepare to work together in case of an emergency. What contingency plans are you aware of on your campus or at work?

> PPT 7-16:
> Strategic and Tactical Planning

tactical planning
The process of developing detailed, short-term statements about what is to be done, who is to do it, and how it is to be done.

operational planning
The process of setting work standards and schedules necessary to implement the company's tactical objectives.

> PPT 7-17:
> Operational and Contingency Planning

> BONUS CASE 7-1:
> DefenseWeb Evaluates a STRATEGIC Expansion

> CRITICAL THINKING EXERCISE 7-3:
> Crisis Management

top managers of the company decide which customers to serve, when to serve them, what products or services to sell, and the geographic areas in which to compete. Take Taco Bell, for example. Recognizing the economic slump, the company introduced a "value menu" of items like cheese roll-ups and bean burritos with prices starting at 79 cents. It also went after the "fourth-meal" (late-night) crowd and introduced several low-calorie, low-fat Fresco items. This strategy resulted in an 8 percent increase in sales.[15]

In today's rapidly changing environment, strategic planning is becoming more difficult because changes are occurring so fast that plans—even those set for just months into the future—may soon be obsolete. Think of how the amusement park company Six Flags had to change its plans when gas went from a couple of dollars per gallon to over four dollars and then dropped back to the three-dollar range again. Clearly, some companies are making shorter-term plans that allow for quick responses to customer needs and requests. The goal is to be flexible and responsive to the market.

Tactical planning is the process of developing detailed, short-term statements about what is to be done, who is to do it, and how. Managers or teams of managers at lower levels of the organization normally make tactical plans. Such plans can include setting annual budgets and deciding on other activities necessary to meet strategic objectives. If the strategic plan of a truck manufacturer, for example, is to sell more trucks in the South, the tactical plan might be to fund more research of southern truck drivers' wants and needs, and to plan advertising to reach them.

Operational planning is the process of setting work standards and schedules necessary to implement the company's tactical objectives. Whereas strategic planning looks at the organization as a whole, operational planning focuses on specific supervisors, department managers, and individual employees. The operational plan is the department manager's tool for daily and weekly operations. An operational plan may include, for example, the specific dates for certain truck parts to be completed and the quality specifications they must meet.

Contingency planning is the process of preparing alternative courses of action the firm can use if its primary plans don't work out. The economic and competitive environments change so rapidly that it's wise to have alternative

SPOTLIGHT ON SMALL business

www.blueman.com

I'd Rather Be Blue

Some of the best-managed organizations can be found in the most unusual situations. Consider, for example, three entrepreneurs whose product involved shaving their heads, slathering themselves with blue paint, and drumming on homemade instruments such as PVC pipe. Enter the Blue Man Group.

Today the original Blue Men—Matt Goldman, Phil Stanton, and Chris Wink—manage an organization of over 500 employees, 70 of whom appear nightly as Blue Men in 12 cities around the world. More than 17 million people have seen their shows.

Like the founders of any other company, the Blue Man Group creators knew they had to tinker with their product if they wanted to expand and be successful. Planning and organization were critical. The partners locked themselves away for several days to write a detailed 132-page Blue Man operating manual. Writing the manual made the partners realize the vast market potential for their concept, but it also taught them the importance of managing the product's growth and everyday operations. They decided that company decisions would not be made on a majority vote but rather by consensus among the three of them. That policy continues today.

Sources: Liz Welch, "How We Did It: The Blue Man Group," *Inc.*, August 2008; and Blue Man Group, www.blueman.com, accessed January 29, 2009.

---

plans of action ready in anticipation of such changes. For example, if an organization doesn't meet its sales goals by a certain date, the contingency plan may call for more advertising or a cut in prices at that time. Crisis planning is a part of contingency planning that anticipates sudden changes in the environment. For example, many cities and businesses have developed plans to respond to terrorist attacks. You can imagine how important such plans would be to hospitals, airlines, the police, and public transportation authorities.

Instead of creating detailed strategic plans, the leaders of market-based companies (companies that respond quickly to changes in competition or to other environmental changes) often simply set direction. They want to stay flexible, listen to customers, and seize opportunities—expected or not. Think of how stores selling to teenagers must adapt to style changes.

The opportunities, however, must fit into the company's overall goals and objectives; if not, the company could lose its focus. Clearly, then, much of management and planning requires decision making. The Spotlight on Small Business box illustrates how one unique small business handles planning and decision making.

◄ PPT 7-19:
I'd Rather Be Blue

contingency planning
The process of preparing alternative courses of action that may be used if the primary plans don't achieve the organization's objectives.

◄ BONUS CASE 7-2:
When Employees Make The Decisions

◄ PPT 7-20:
Decision Making

◄ LECTURE LINK 7-5:
Decision-Making Tips

Decision Making: Finding the Best Alternative

Planning and all the other management functions require decision making. **Decision making** is choosing among two or more alternatives, which sounds easier than it is. In fact, decision making is the heart of all the management functions.

decision making
Choosing among two or more alternatives.

The *rational decision-making model* is a series of steps managers often follow to make logical, intelligent, and well-founded decisions. Think of the steps as the seven Ds of decision making:

1. Define the situation.
2. Describe and collect needed information.
3. Develop alternatives.
4. Develop agreement among those involved.
5. Decide which alternative is best.
6. Do what is indicated (begin implementation).
7. Determine whether the decision was a good one, and follow up.

Managers don't always go through this seven-step process. Sometimes they have to make decisions *on the spot*—with little information available. They still must make good decisions in all such circumstances. **Problem solving** is less formal than decision making and usually calls for quicker action to resolve everyday issues. Both decision making and problem solving call for a lot of judgment.[16]

Problem-solving teams are two or more workers assigned to solve a specific problem (e.g., why aren't customers buying our service contracts?). Problem-solving techniques include **brainstorming**, that is, coming up with as many solutions as possible in a short period of time with no censoring of ideas. Another technique is called **PMI**, or listing all the **p**luses for a solution in one column, all the **m**inuses in another, and the **i**mplications in a third. The idea is to make sure the pluses exceed the minuses.

You can try using the PMI system on some of your personal decisions to get some practice. For example, should you stay home and study tonight? List all the pluses in one column: better grades, more self-esteem, more responsible behavior, and so on. In the other column, put the minuses: boredom, less fun, and so on. We hope the pluses outweigh the minuses most of the time and that you study often. But sometimes it's best to go out and have some fun, as long as doing so won't hurt your grades or job prospects.

problem solving
The process of solving the everyday problems that occur. Problem solving is less formal than decision making and usually calls for quicker action.

brainstorming
Coming up with as many solutions to a problem as possible in a short period of time with no censoring of ideas.

PMI
Listing all the pluses for a solution in one column, all the minuses in another, and the implications in a third column.

progress assessment

- What's the difference between goals and objectives?
- What does a company analyze when it does a SWOT analysis?
- What are the differences between strategic, tactical, and operational planning?
- What are the seven Ds in decision making?

LEARNING goal 4 *

Describe the organizing function of management.

ORGANIZING: CREATING A UNIFIED SYSTEM

After managers have planned a course of action, they must organize the firm to accomplish their goals. That means allocating resources (such as funds for various departments), assigning tasks, and establishing procedures.

An **organization chart** is a visual device that shows relationships among people and divides the organization's work; it shows who reports to whom (see Figure 7.5).

Top management, the highest level, consists of the president and other key company executives who develop strategic plans. Job titles and abbreviations you're likely to see often are chief executive officer (CEO), chief operating officer (COO), chief financial officer (CFO), and chief information officer (CIO) or in some companies chief knowledge officer (CKO). The CEO is often also the president of the firm and is responsible for all top-level decisions. The CEO and president are the same person in 65 percent of the S&P 500 companies, including big companies like United Parcel Service, John Deere, and General Electric.[17]

CEOs are responsible for introducing change into an organization. The COO is responsible for putting those changes into effect. His or her tasks include structuring work, controlling operations, and rewarding people to ensure that everyone strives to carry out the leader's vision. Many companies today are eliminating the COO function as a cost-cutting measure and assigning that role to the CEO. Often, the CFO participates in the decision to cut the COO position. The CFO is responsible for obtaining funds, planning budgets, collecting funds, and so on. The CIO or CKO is responsible for getting the right information to other managers so they can make correct decisions.[18]

Middle management includes general managers, division managers, and branch and plant managers (in colleges, deans and department heads) who are responsible for tactical planning and controlling. Many firms, as a result of the 2008–2010 recession, have eliminated some middle managers through downsizing and have given their remaining managers more employees to supervise.

> **organization chart**
> A visual device that shows relationships among people and divides the organization's work; it shows who reports to whom.
>
> **top management**
> Highest level of management, consisting of the president and other key company executives who develop strategic plans.
>
> ◀ PPT 7-24:
> Organizational Charts
> ◀ PPT 7-25:
> Levels of Management
> ◀ PPT 7-26:
> Management Levels
> ◀ PPT 7-27:
> Top Management
>
> **middle management**
> The level of management that includes general managers, division managers, and branch and plant managers who are responsible for tactical planning and controlling.

TOP MANAGEMENT
President
Vice presidents

MIDDLE MANAGEMENT
Plant managers
Division heads
Branch managers

SUPERVISORY (FIRST-LINE) MANAGEMENT
Supervisors, Foremen
Department heads
Section leaders

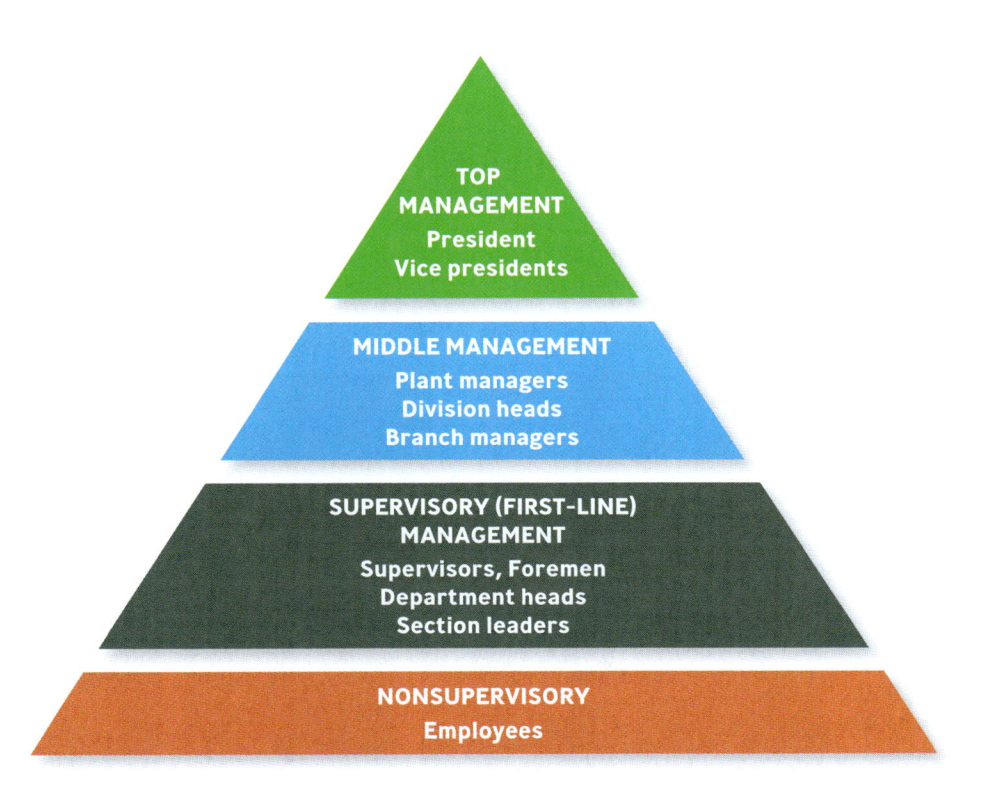

NONSUPERVISORY
Employees

figure 7.5

LEVELS OF MANAGEMENT

This figure shows the three levels of management. In many firms, there are several levels of middle management. Recently, however, firms have been eliminating middle-level managers because fewer are needed to oversee self-managed teams of employees.

supervisory management Managers who are directly responsible for supervising workers and evaluating their daily performance.

Supervisory management includes those directly responsible for supervising workers and evaluating their daily performance; they're often known as first-line managers (or supervisors) because they're the first level above workers. This is the first management position you are most likely to acquire after college.

Tasks and Skills at Different Levels of Management

▶ PPT 7-28:
Managerial Skills

▶ LECTURE LINK 7-6:
Learning Management Skills

▶ CRITICAL THINKING EXERCISE 7-5:
Rate Your Management Skills

Few people are trained to be good managers. Usually a person learns how to be a skilled accountant or sales representative or production-line worker, and then—because of her or his skill—is selected to be a manager. Such managers tend to become deeply involved in showing others how to do things, helping them, supervising them, and generally being active in the operating task.

The further up the managerial ladder a person moves, the less important his or her original job skills become. At the top of the ladder, the need is for people who are visionaries, planners, organizers, coordinators, communicators, morale builders, and motivators. Figure 7.6 shows that a manager must have three categories of skills:

technical skills Skills that involve the ability to perform tasks in a specific discipline or department.

1. **Technical skills** are the ability to perform tasks in a specific discipline (such as selling a product or developing software) or department (such as marketing or information systems).

2. **Human relations skills** include communication and motivation; they enable managers to work through and with people. Skills associated with leadership—coaching, morale building, delegating, training and development, and supportiveness—are also human relations skills.

human relations skills Skills that involve communication and motivation; they enable managers to work through and with people.

3. **Conceptual skills** let the manager picture the organization as a whole and see the relationships among its various parts. They are needed in planning, organizing, controlling, systems development, problem analysis, decision making, coordinating, and delegating.

conceptual skills Skills that involve the ability to picture the organization as a whole and the relationship among its various parts.

Looking at Figure 7.6, you'll notice that first-line managers need to be skilled in all three areas. However, they spend most of their time on technical and human relations tasks, like assisting operating personnel and giving directions, and less time on conceptual tasks. Top managers, in contrast, need to use few technical skills. Instead, they spend almost all their time on human relations and conceptual tasks. A person who is competent at a low level of management may not be competent at higher levels, and vice versa. Different skills are needed at different levels.

▶ PPT 7-29:
Skills Needed at Various Levels of Management

figure 7.6

SKILLS NEEDED AT VARIOUS LEVELS OF MANAGEMENT

All managers need human relations skills. At the top, managers need strong conceptual skills and rely less on technical skills. First-line managers need strong technical skills and rely less on conceptual skills. Middle managers need to have a balance between technical and conceptual skills.

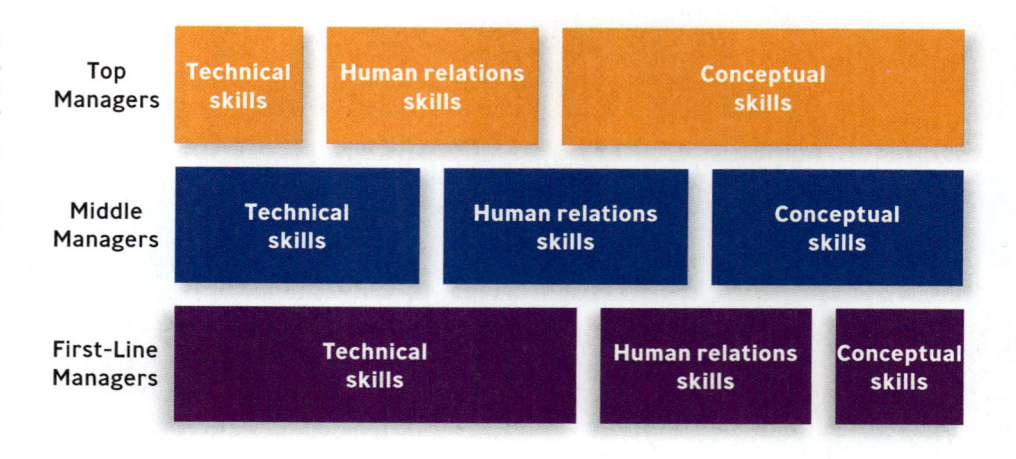

Top Managers	Technical skills	Human relations skills	Conceptual skills
Middle Managers	Technical skills	Human relations skills	Conceptual skills
First-Line Managers	Technical skills	Human relations skills	Conceptual skills

Staffing: Getting and Keeping the Right People

To get the right kind of people to staff an organization, the firm has to offer the right kind of incentives. For example, Google's gourmet chefs cook up free lunches, dinners, and snacks for employees. Would such an incentive appeal to you? How important to you is pay relative to other incentives?

Staffing is recruiting, hiring, motivating, and retaining the best people available to accomplish the company's objectives. Today, staffing is critical, especially in the Internet and high-tech areas. At most high-tech companies, like Google, Sony, and Microsoft, the primary capital equipment is brainpower. A firm with innovative and creative workers can go from start-up to major competitor in just a few years.

Many people are not willing to work at companies unless they are treated well and get fair pay. They may leave to find a better balance between work and home. Staffing is becoming a greater part of each manager's assignment, and all managers need to cooperate with human resource management to win and keep good workers. Chapter 11 is devoted to human resource issues, including staffing.

> **staffing**
> A management function that includes hiring, motivating, and retaining the best people available to accomplish the company's objectives.

LEARNING goal 5 *

Explain the differences between leaders and managers, and describe the various leadership styles.

LEADING: PROVIDING CONTINUOUS VISION AND VALUES

One person might be a good manager but not a good leader. Another might be a good leader without being a good manager. Managers strive to produce order and stability, whereas leaders embrace and manage change. Leadership is creating a vision for others to follow, establishing corporate values and ethics, and transforming the way the organization does business in order to improve its effectiveness and efficiency. Good leaders motivate workers and create the environment for them to motivate themselves. Management is carrying out the leader's vision.

Leaders must therefore:

- *Communicate a vision and rally others around that vision.* The leader should be openly sensitive to the concerns of followers, give them responsibility, and win their trust. A successful leader must influence the actions of others.
- *Establish corporate values.* These include concern for employees, for customers, for the environment, and for the quality of the company's products. When companies set their business goals, they're defining the company's values as well. The number one trait that others look for in a leader is honesty. The second requirement is that the leader be forward looking.[19]

> Although most firms use standard job titles like president, general manager, and chief executive officer, at Matrix Group, an Internet consulting company for nonprofit organizations, founder Joanna Pineda is known as the Chief Troublemaker, and the position of assistant to the CEO was recently advertised under the heading The Enforcer. What do job titles like these tell you about an organization?

MAKING ethical decisions

To Share or Not to Share

First-line managers assist in the decisions made by their department heads. The department heads retain full responsibility for the decisions—if a plan succeeds, it's their success; if a plan fails, it's their failure. Now picture this: As a first-line manager, you have new information that your department head hasn't seen yet. The findings in this report indicate that your manager's recent plans are sure to fail. If the plans do fail, the manager will probably be demoted and you're the most likely candidate to fill the vacancy. Will you give your department head the report? What is the ethical thing to do? What might be the consequences of your decision?

- *Promote corporate ethics.* Ethical behavior includes an unfailing demand for honesty and an insistence that everyone in the company gets treated fairly (see the Making Ethical Decisions box). That's why we stress ethical decision making throughout this text. Many businesspeople have made the news by giving away huge amounts to charity, thus setting a model of social concern for their employees and others.[20]

- *Embrace change.* A leader's most important job may be to transform the way the company does business so that it's more effective (does things better) and more efficient (uses fewer resources to accomplish the same objectives).

- *Stress accountability and responsibility.* If there is anything we have learned from the failures of banking managers and other industry and government managers during the recession of 2008–2010, it is that leaders need to be held accountable and need to feel responsible for their actions. A key word that has emerged from the crisis is transparency. **Transparency** is the presentation of a company's facts and figures in a way that is clear and apparent to all stakeholders. Clearly it is time to make businessess and the government more transparent so that everyone is more aware of what is happening to the economy and to specific businesses and government agencies.

All organizations need leaders, and all employees can help lead. You don't have to be a manager to perform a leadership function. That is, any employee can motivate others to work well, add to a company's ethical environment, and report ethical lapses when they occur.

Leadership Styles

Nothing has challenged management researchers more than the search for the best leadership traits, behaviors, or styles. Thousands of studies have tried to identify characteristics that make leaders different from other people. Intuitively, you might conclude the same thing they did: leadership traits are hard to pin down. Some leaders are well groomed and tactful, while others are unkempt and abrasive—yet both may be just as effective.

Just as no one set of traits describes a leader, no one style of leadership works best in all situations. Even so, we can look at a few of the

transparency
The presentation of a company's facts and figures in a way that is clear and apparent to all stakeholders.

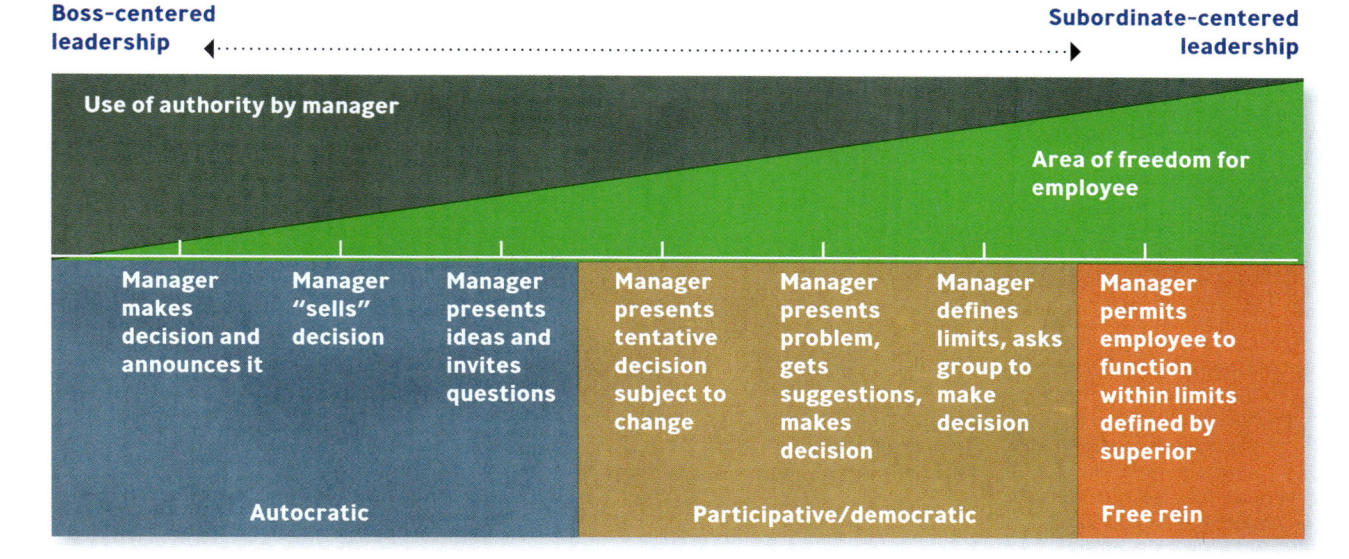

Management and Leadership * CHAPTER 7   191

Boss-centered leadership ◄·······································► **Subordinate-centered leadership**

Use of authority by manager

Area of freedom for employee

| Manager makes decision and announces it | Manager "sells" decision | Manager presents ideas and invites questions | Manager presents tentative decision subject to change | Manager presents problem, gets suggestions, makes decision | Manager defines limits, asks group to make decision | Manager permits employee to function within limits defined by superior |

Autocratic | **Participative/democratic** | **Free rein**

figure 7.7

VARIOUS LEADERSHIP STYLES

Source: Reprinted by permission of the *Harvard Business Review*. An exhibit from "How to Choose a Leadership Pattern" by Robert Tannenbaum and Warren Schmidt (May/June 1973). Copyright © 1973 by the Harvard Business School Publishing Corporation, all rights reserved.

most commonly recognized leadership styles and see how they may be effective (see Figure 7.7):

1. **Autocratic leadership** means making managerial decisions without consulting others. This style is effective in emergencies and when absolute followership is needed—for example, when fighting fires. Autocratic leadership is also effective sometimes with new, relatively unskilled workers who need clear direction and guidance. Coach Phil Jackson used an autocratic leadership style to take the Los Angeles Lakers to three consecutive National Basketball Association championships in his first three seasons. By following his leadership, a group of highly skilled individuals became a winning team. How is the team doing now? What kind of leadership do you see being used most successfully in baseball, football, and other areas?

2. **Participative (democratic) leadership** involves managers and employees working together to make decisions. Research has found that employee participation in decisions may not always increase effectiveness, but it usually does increase job satisfaction. Many large organizations like Wal-Mart, FedEx, IBM, Cisco, and AT&T and most smaller firms have been highly successful using a democratic style of leadership that values traits such as flexibility, good listening skills, and empathy. Employees meet to discuss and resolve management issues by giving everyone some opportunity to contribute to decisions.

3. In **free-rein leadership** managers set objectives and employees are free to do whatever is appropriate to accomplish those objectives. Free-rein leadership is often the

autocratic leadership
Leadership style that involves making managerial decisions without consulting others.

◄ **PPT 7-36:**
Various Leadership Styles

participative (democratic) leadership
Leadership style that consists of managers and employees working together to make decisions.

Coach of the Los Angeles Lakers basketball team, Phil Jackson has been successful as an autocratic leader. That makes sense, since you don't want basketball players deciding whether or not to play as a team. On the other hand, can you see why it is not so good to use autocratic leadership with a team of doctors? What kind of leadership would you expect to succeed in a nonprofit agency full of volunteers?

> **free-rein leadership**
> Leadership style that involves managers setting objectives and employees being relatively free to do whatever it takes to accomplish those objectives.
>
> ▶ **PPT 7-37:**
> Natural Born Leaders?
> ▶ **PPT 7-38:**
> Empowerment

> *Fast-food restaurant employees usually don't have the skill and experience to make empowerment work very well. Instead, their managers generally have to supervise and direct them fairly closely. What do you think are some of the consequences for managers of not being able to empower their staff with decision-making authority?*

most successful leadership style in certain organizations, such as those in which managers supervise doctors, professors, engineers, or other professionals. The traits managers need in such organizations include warmth, friendliness, and understanding. More and more firms are adopting this style of leadership with at least some of their employees.

Individual leaders rarely fit neatly into just one of these categories. We can think of leadership as a continuum along which employee participation varies, from purely boss-centered leadership to subordinate-centered leadership.

Which leadership style is best? Research tells us that it depends largely on what the goals and values of the firm are, who's being led, and in what situations. A manager may be autocratic but friendly with a new trainee, democratic with an experienced employee, and free-rein with a trusted long-term supervisor.

There's no such thing as a leadership trait that is effective in all situations, or a leadership style that always works best. A truly successful leader has the ability to adopt the leadership style most appropriate to the situation and the employees.[21]

Empowering Workers

Many leaders in the past gave explicit instructions to workers, telling them what to do to meet the goals and objectives of the organization. The term for this process is *directing*. In traditional organizations, directing includes giving assignments, explaining routines, clarifying policies, and providing feedback on performance. Many organizations still follow this model, especially fast-food restaurants and small retail establishments where the employees don't have the skill and experience needed to work on their own, at least at first.

Progressive leaders, such as those in some high-tech firms and Internet companies, empower employees to make decisions on their own. *Empowerment* means giving employees the authority to make a decision without consulting the manager, and the responsibility to respond quickly to customer requests. Managers are often reluctant to give up their decision-making power and often resist empowerment. In firms that implement the concept, however, the manager's role is less that of a boss and director and more that of a coach, assistant, counselor, or team member.

Enabling means giving workers the education and tools they need to make decisions. Clearly, it's the key to the success of empowerment. Without the right education, training, coaching, and tools, workers cannot assume the responsibilities and decision-making roles that make empowerment work.

> **enabling**
> Giving workers the education and tools they need to make decisions.
>
> ▶ **PPT 7-39:**
> Work Smarter
> ▶ **PPT 7-40:**
> Managing Knowledge
>
> **knowledge management**
> Finding the right information, keeping the information in a readily accessible place, and making the information known to everyone in the firm.

Managing Knowledge

"Knowledge is power." Empowering employees means giving them knowledge—that is, the information they need to do the best job they can. Finding the right information, keeping it in a readily accessible place, and making it known to everyone in the firm together constitute the tasks of **knowledge management**.

The first step to developing a knowledge management system is determining what knowledge is most important. Do you want to know more about your customers? Do you want to know more about competitors? What kind of information would make your company more effective or more efficient or more responsive to the marketplace? Once you've decided what you need to know, you set out to find answers to those questions.

Knowledge management tries to keep people from reinventing the wheel—that is, duplicating the work of gathering information—every time a decision must be made. A company really progresses when each person continually asks, "What do I still not know?" and "Whom should I be asking?" It's as important to know what's not working as it is to know what *is* working. Employees and managers now have e-mail, text messaging, and other means of keeping in touch with one another, with customers, and with other stakeholders. The key to success is learning how to process information effectively and turn it into knowledge that everyone can use to improve processes and procedures.[22] The benefits are obvious.

LEARNING goal 6 *

Summarize the five steps of the control function of management.

CONTROLLING: MAKING SURE IT WORKS

The control function measures performance relative to the planned objectives and standards, rewards people for work well done, and takes corrective action when necessary.[23] Thus the control process (see Figure 7.8) provides the feedback that lets managers and workers adjust to deviations from plans and to changes in the environment that have affected performance. Controlling consists of five steps:

1. Establishing clear performance standards. This ties the planning function to the control function. Without clear standards, control is impossible.
2. Monitoring and recording actual performance or results.
3. Comparing results against plans and standards.

◀ PPT 7-41:
Five Steps of Controlling

figure 7.8

THE CONTROL PROCESS
The whole control process is based on clear standards. Without such standards, the other steps are difficult, if not impossible. With clear standards, performance measurement is relatively easy and the proper action can be taken.

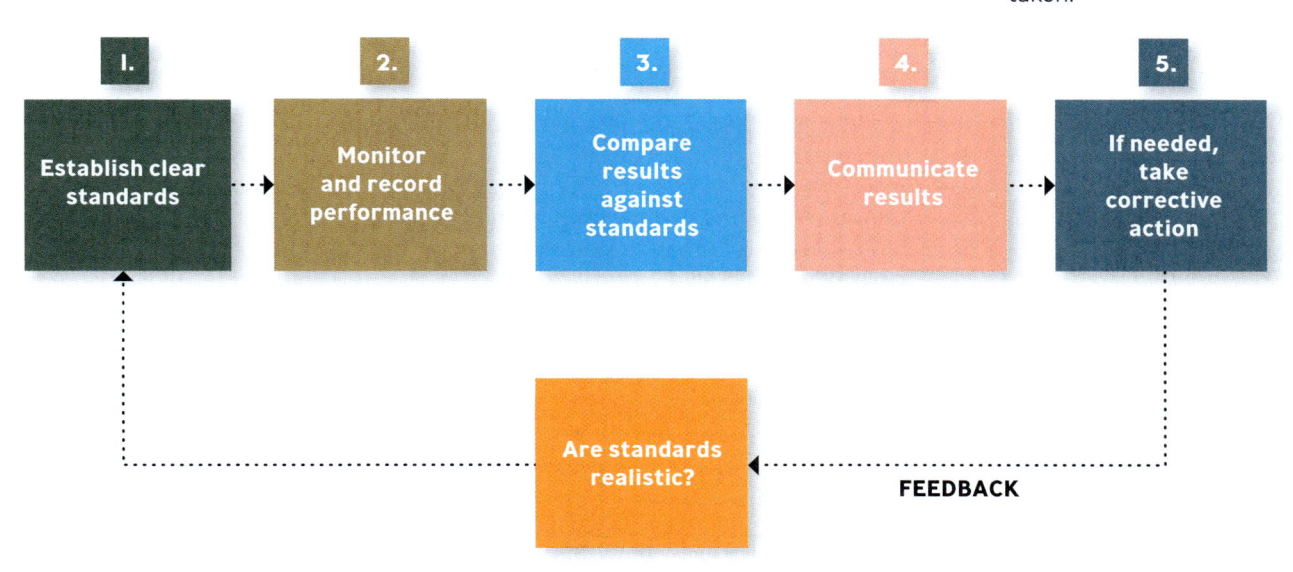

1. Establish clear standards
2. Monitor and record performance
3. Compare results against standards
4. Communicate results
5. If needed, take corrective action

Are standards realistic?

FEEDBACK

4. Communicating results and deviations to the appropriate employees.
5. Taking corrective action when needed and providing positive feedback for work well done.

For managers to measure results, the standards must be specific, attainable, and measurable. Setting such clear standards is part of the planning function. Vague goals and standards such as "better quality," "more efficiency," and "improved performance" aren't sufficient because they don't describe in enough detail what you're trying to achieve. For example, let's say you're a runner and you have made the following statement: "My goal is to improve my distance." When you started your improvement plan last year, you ran 2.0 miles a day; now you run 2.1 miles a day. Did you meet your goal? Well, you did increase your distance, but certainly not by very much.

A more appropriate statement would be "My goal is to increase my running distance from two miles a day to four miles a day by January 1." It's important to establish a time period for reaching goals. The following examples of goals and standards meet these criteria:

- Cutting the number of finished product rejects from 10 per 1,000 to 5 per 1,000 by March 31.
- Increasing the number of times managers praise employees from 3 per week to 12 per week by the end of the quarter.
- Increasing sales of product X from 10,000 per month to 12,000 per month by July.

One way to make control systems work is to establish clear procedures for monitoring performance. Accounting and finance are often the foundations for control systems because they provide the numbers management needs to evaluate progress.

One way colleges and universities measure their performance is to track the number of students who complete their degrees, or who graduate within a certain number of years. What are some of the factors that could affect the achievement of this performance standard, and how do college administrators take corrective action when necessary?

▶ PPT 7-42:
Are You a Micromanager?

▶ PPT 7-43:
Measuring Success

A Key Criterion for Measurement: Customer Satisfaction

Traditional measures of success are usually financial; that is, they define success in terms of profits or return on investment. Certainly these measures are still important, but they're not the whole purpose of the firm. Other purposes may include pleasing employees, stakeholders, and customers—including both external and internal customers.

External customers include dealers, who buy products to sell to others, and ultimate customers (also known as end users) such as you and me, who buy products for their own personal use. **Internal customers** are individuals and units within the firm that receive services from other individuals or units. For example, the field salespeople are the internal customers of the marketing research people who prepare market reports for them. One goal today is to go beyond simply satisfying customers to "delighting" them with unexpectedly good products and services.

We'll discuss management in more detail in the next few chapters. Let's pause now, review, and do some exercises. Management is doing, not just reading.

external customers
Dealers, who buy products to sell to others, and ultimate customers (or end users), who buy products for their own personal use.

internal customers
Individuals and units within the firm that receive services from other individuals or units.

Management and Leadership * CHAPTER 7   195

progress assessment

- How does enabling help achieve empowerment?
- What are the five steps in the control process?
- What's the difference between internal and external customers?

◄ PPT 7-44:
Progress Assessment

summary

Learning Goal 1. Describe the changes occurring today in the management function.

- **What does management look like today?**

At one time, managers were called bosses, and their job consisted of telling people what to do, watching over them to be sure they did it, and reprimanding those who didn't. Many, if not most, managers still behave that way. Today, however, some managers tend to be more progressive. For example, they emphasize teams and team building; they create drop-in centers, team spaces, and open work areas. They tend to guide, train, support, motivate, and coach employees rather than tell them what to do.

- **What reasons can you give to account for changes in management?**

Leaders of Fortune 100 companies today tend to be younger, more of them are female, and fewer of them were educated at elite universities. They know that many of their employees know more about technology and other practices than they do. Therefore, they tend to put more emphasis on motivation, teamwork, and cooperation. Managers in the future are likely to be assuming completely new roles in the firm. For one thing, they will be taking a leadership role in adapting to climate change. Further, they'll be doing more expansion overseas.

Learning Goal 2. Describe the four functions of management.

- **What are the primary functions of management?**

The four primary functions are (1) planning, (2) organizing, (3) leading, and (4) controlling.

- **How do you define each of these functions?**

Planning includes anticipating trends and determining the best strategies and tactics to achieve organizational goals and objectives. Organizing includes designing the structure of the organization and creating conditions and systems in which everyone and everything works together to achieve the organization's goals and objectives. Leading means creating a vision for the organization, and communicating, guiding, training, coaching, and motivating others to achieve goals and objectives. Controlling means measuring whether what actually occurs meets the organization's goals.

Learning Goal 3. Relate the planning process and decision making to the accomplishment of company goals.

- **What's the difference between goals and objectives?**

Goals are broad, long-term achievements that organizations aim to accomplish, whereas objectives are specific, short-term plans made to help reach the goals.

- **What is a SWOT analysis?**

Managers look at the **S**trengths and **W**eaknesses of the firm and the **O**pportunities and **T**hreats facing it.

- **What are the four types of planning, and how are they related to the organization's goals and objectives?**

Strategic planning is broad, long-range planning that outlines the goals of the organization. *Tactical planning* is specific, short-term planning that lists organizational objectives. *Operational planning* is part of tactical planning and sets specific timetables and standards. *Contingency planning* is developing an alternative set of plans in case the first set doesn't work out.

- **What are the steps involved in decision making?**

The seven Ds of decision making are (1) define the situation; (2) describe and collect needed information; (3) develop alternatives; (4) develop agreement among those involved; (5) decide which alternative is best; (6) do what is indicated (begin implementation); and (7) determine whether the decision was a good one, and follow up.

Learning Goal 4. Describe the organizing function of management.

- **What is an organization chart?**

An organization chart is a visual device that shows relationships among people and divides the organization's work; it shows who is accountable for the completion of specific work and who reports to whom.

- **What are the three levels of management in the corporate hierarchy?**

The three levels of management are (1) top management (highest level consisting of the president and other key company executives who develop strategic plans); (2) middle management (general managers, division managers, and plant managers who are responsible for tactical planning and controlling); and (3) supervisory management (first-line managers/supervisors who evaluate workers' daily performance).

- **What skills do managers need?**

Managers must have three categories of skills: (1) technical skills (ability to perform specific tasks such as selling products or developing software), (2) human relations skills (ability to communicate and motivate), and (3) conceptual skills (ability to see organizations as a whole and how all the parts fit together).

- **Are these skills equally important at all management levels?**

Managers at different levels need different skills. Top managers rely heavily on human relations and conceptual skills and rarely use technical skills, while first-line supervisors need strong technical and human relations skills but use conceptual skills less often. Middle managers need to have a balance of all three skills (see Figure 7.6 on p. 188).

Learning Goal 5. Explain the differences between leaders and managers, and describe the various leadership styles.

- **What's the difference between a manager and a leader?**

A manager plans, organizes, and controls functions within an organization. A leader has vision and inspires others to grasp that vision, establishes corporate values, emphasizes corporate ethics, and doesn't fear change.

- **Describe the various leadership styles.**

Figure 7.7 on p. 191 shows a continuum of leadership styles ranging from boss-centered to subordinate-centered leadership.

- **Which leadership style is best?**

The most effective leadership style depends on the people being led and the situation. The challenge of the future will be to empower self-managed teams.

- **What does empowerment mean?**

Empowerment means giving employees the authority and responsibility to respond quickly to customer requests. Enabling is giving workers the education and tools they need to assume their new decision-making powers.

- **What is knowledge management?**

Knowledge management is finding the right information, keeping the information in a readily accessible place, and making the information known to everyone in the firm.

Learning Goal 6. Summarize the five steps of the control function of management.

- **What are the five steps of the control function?**

Controlling incorporates (1) setting clear standards, (2) monitoring and recording performance, (3) comparing performance with plans and standards, (4) communicating results and deviations to employees, and (5) providing positive feedback for a job well done and taking corrective action if necessary.

- **What qualities must standards possess to measure performance results?**

Standards must be specific, attainable, and measurable.

key terms

autocratic leadership 191
brainstorming 186
conceptual skills 188
contingency planning 184
controlling 181
decision making 185
enabling 192
external customers 194
free-rein leadership 192
goals 181
human relations skills 188
internal customers 194
knowledge management 192
leading 180
management 179
middle management 187
mission statement 181
objectives 181
operational planning 184
organization chart 187
organizing 180
participative (democratic) leadership 191
planning 179
PMI 186
problem solving 186
staffing 189
strategic planning 183
supervisory management 188
SWOT analysis 182
tactical planning 184
technical skills 188
top management 187
transparency 190
vision 181

connect interactive applications

Reinforcing Your *Connect*ion to Concepts in Business

This chapter offers 15 interactive applications designed to help you apply what you've learned (examples of these exercises appear on the following pages). Your instructor has determined which interactive applications will benefit you throughout this course. Please refer to your instructor's assignment list in *Connect* to determine which applications you should complete.

Click and Drag Interactive: The four functions of management include: planning, organizing, leading, and controlling. Each of these functions is an important aspect of the management process and must be implemented to achieve organizational goals. Drag and drop each item into the correct spot. Each item is one of the four functions of management.

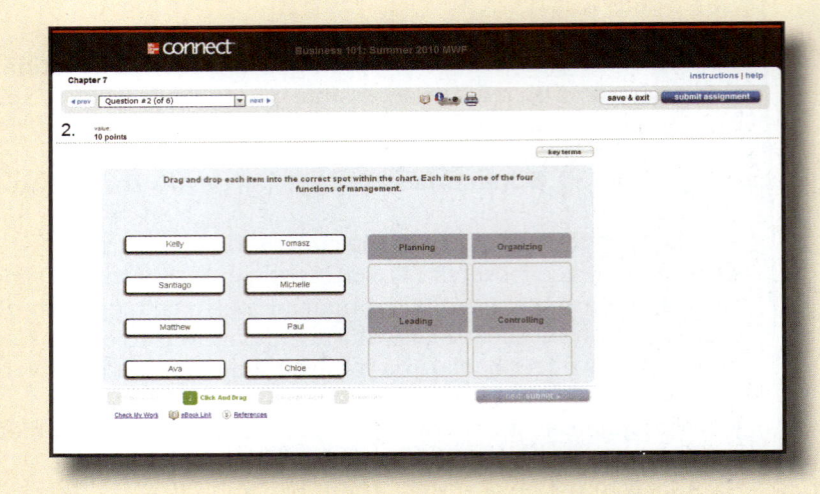

Click and Drag Interactive: An organization chart is a visual device that shows relationships among people and divides the organization's work; it shows who reports to whom. Within the organizational chart, the three levels of management, which include top, middle, and supervisory management, are defined. Read the statements and drop each item into the correct spot within the chart. Each person is in top, middle, or supervisory management.

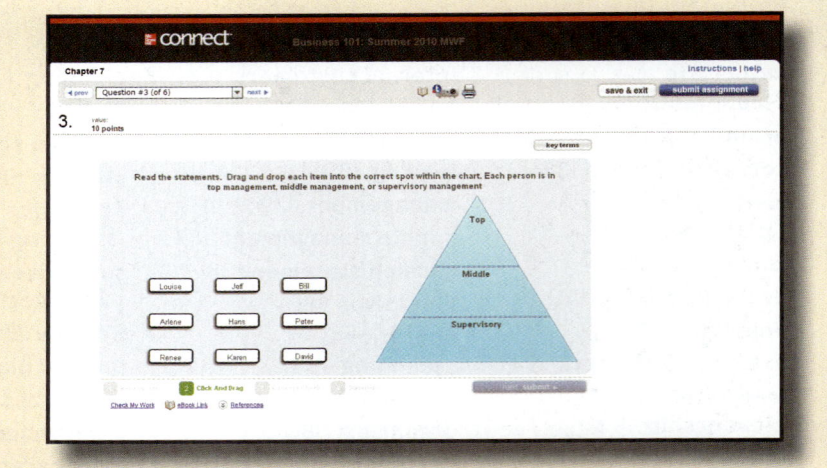

Click and Drag Interactive: Decision making is important in all management functions and levels, whether the decisions are on a strategic, tactical, or operational level. A systematic approach using these seven steps usually leads to more effective decision making. Drag and drop the steps in decision making in the proper order.

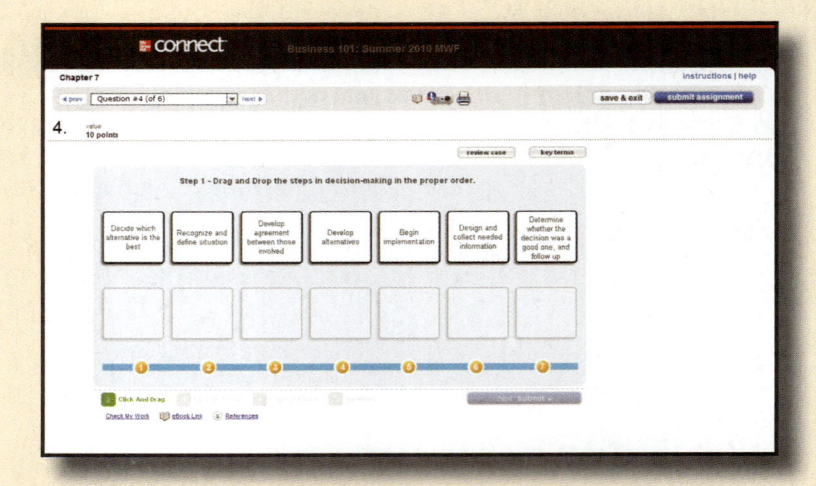

Management and Leadership * CHAPTER 7 199

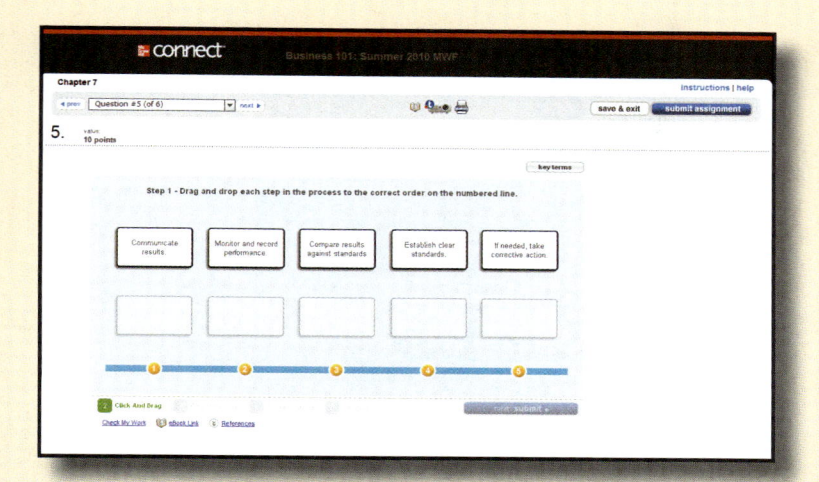

Click and Drag Interactive: The management process includes four functions: planning, organizing, leading, and controlling. All four functions are critical for a manager to be effective. However, in this exercise you are asked to focus on the controlling function of management. The controlling function of management determines if the organization is on target to reach its goals. Drag and drop each step in the process in the correct order.

Video Case Interactive: During the decision-making process, managers may utilize various tools to aid in these decisions. One of the most popular tools is the SWOT analysis. Top management at Best Buy understands that their organization needs to adapt in order to retain their top talent. Watch the video and answer the questions.

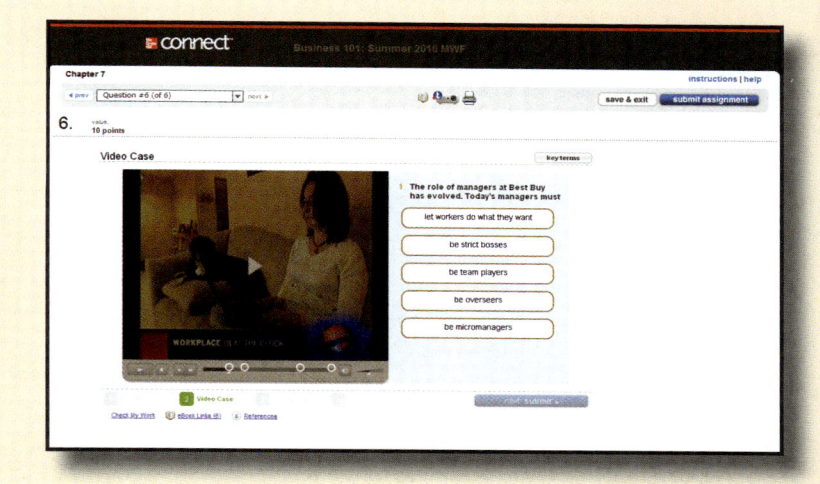

8 Adapting Organizations TO Today's MARKETS

profile

Getting to Know Anne Mulcahy, Former CEO of Xerox

Anne Mulcahy didn't anticipate becoming chief executive officer of Xerox when she majored in English and journalism at Marymount College in New York. But because she had grown up in Connecticut, the company's home state, and her husband and brother worked for the company, it was no surprise that she began her Xerox career as a field sales representative. What was surprising was how quickly she moved up through the organization. She became the vice president for human resources and served from 1992 to 1995. She became chief staff officer in 1997 and corporate senior vice president in 1998. She also gained some experience overseas as vice president and staff officer for customer operations in places like Europe, Asia, and Africa.

Clearly, Mulcahy was not afraid of change or new challenges. But the challenge of being CEO was the biggest of all. When Mulcahy was chosen for the job, Xerox was in bad shape. It had been called before the U.S. Securities and Exchange Commission to explain questionable accounting practices. It was $14 billion in debt. Bankruptcy was on the horizon, but Mulcahy began the work of restructuring the organization. She cut the debt and built up cash reserves. She let 38,000 workers go, brought in a new financial officer, and began meeting with customers to learn how to restore the image of the firm. "Turnaround or growth, it's getting your people focused on the goal that is still the job of leadership," she said. From losses of over $300 million in 2000, Mulcahy created more than $1 billion in profit by 2007.

One of the few women to run a top public company and the first woman to be chosen CEO of the Year by *Chief Executive* magazine, Mulcahy took Xerox back to the foundations of its corporate culture—innovation and customer care. "You need to change and adapt," she said. And changing and adapting is what she did. Her focus was on winning the printing, copying, and services businesses of leading companies like Dell and Kodak.

LEARNING goals

After you have read and studied this chapter, you should be able to

1. Outline the basic principles of organization management.
2. Compare the organizational theories of Fayol and Weber.
3. Evaluate the choices managers make in structuring organizations.
4. Contrast the various organizational models.
5. Identify the benefits of interfirm cooperation and coordination.
6. Explain how organizational culture can help businesses adapt to change.

connect

Your *Connect*ion to Better Learning. **1. View the interactive presentation. 2. Practice through LearnSmart. 3. Apply your knowledge by using the interactive applications for each chapter of this text.**

1 Prep ▶▶▶▶▶▶ 2 Study ▶▶▶▶▶▶ 3 Apply

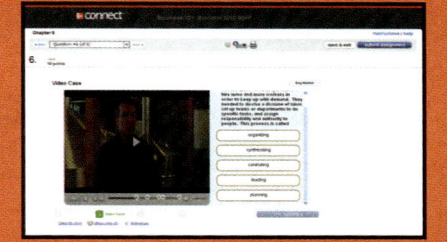

What does Mulcahy say about being a successful manager? "Work hard. Measure the results. Tell the truth." What does she say about reorganizing a business? "First, change is the most difficult thing." She outsourced most of Xerox's manufacturing operations. She also invested in research and development and global services when her company was deep in debt. What most people would consider problems, Mulcahy saw as challenges. She says, "In a crisis, you have the opportunity to move quickly and change a lot. [Then again,] change doesn't happen if you don't work at it."

This chapter is about changing and adapting organizations to today's markets, as Anne Mulcahy did in order to carry Xerox from the brink of disaster to the front ranks among global firms. Most managers never face challenges that big, but there are plenty of opportunities in every firm to use the principles of organizing to manage—and benefit from—change, especially today as firms adapt to the recent economic crisis.

Sources: Xerox, "Executive Biographies," 2008; *University of Rochester News*, April 15, 2008; Xerox Newsroom: Award Announcement, 2008; Marsha Lindsay, "Build Your Own Brand by Thinking Like a Fighter," *Advertising Age*, June 9, 2008; "Fortune 500 Women CEOs," *Fortune*, April 24, 2008; and Diane Brady, "Hard Choices," *Bloomberg Businessweek*, April 26 – May 2, 2010, p. 136.

www.xerox.com

NAME THAT company

Our company is one of the best delivery firms in the business. Whereas most companies are trying to get away from bureaucracy, ours thrives on the rules and regulations that guide our employees. As a result, our workers know what to do and how quickly to do it. It works for us. What is the name of this highly successful company? (Find the answer in the chapter.)

▶ PPT 8-1:
Adapting Organizations to Today's Markets

▶ PPT 8-2:
Anne Mulcahy

▶ PPT 8-3:
Reorganization Is for Everyone

LEARNING goal 1 *

Outline the basic principles of organization management.

The principles of organization apply to businesses of all sizes. Structuring the business, making an appropriate division of labor using job specialization and departmentalization, establishing procedures, and assigning authority are tasks found in most firms. How do these principles operate at your current or most recent job?

EVERYONE'S ORGANIZING

You don't have to look far to find examples of companies reorganizing. Xerox is just one of many—and sometimes the process is quite painful. A. G. Lafley, CEO of legendary company Procter & Gamble, has transformed it into one of the most innovative firms in the United States.[1] Some entrepreneurial companies are organizing globally from the start and succeeding (see the Reaching Beyond Our Borders box). Other organizations have been declining, including automobile makers, homebuilders, and banks.[2] You have been hearing about such failures in the news. Clearly the challenge to reorganize is strong.

You may be wondering what has happened to U.S. producers—so many seem to be failing. But adjusting to changing markets is a normal function in a capitalist economy. There will be big winners, like Google and Facebook, and big losers as well.[3] The key to success is remaining flexible enough to adapt to the changing times. Often that means going back to basic organizational principles and building the firm on a sound foundation.[4] This chapter will discuss such basic principles.

Building an Organization from the Bottom Up

No matter the size of the business, the principles of organization are much the same. Let's say you and two friends plan to start a lawn-mowing business. One of the first steps is to organize your business. *Organizing*, or structuring, begins with determining what work needs to be done (mowing, edging, trimming) and then dividing up the tasks among the three of you; this is called a *division of labor*. One of you might have a special talent for trimming bushes, while another is better at mowing. The success of a firm often depends on management's ability to identify each worker's strengths and assign the right tasks to the right person. Many jobs can be done quickly and well when each person specializes. Dividing tasks into smaller jobs is called *job*

REACHING BEYOND our borders

General Electric Looks for More Profits

When a company is not making as much money as the stock market expects it to make, it has to change perceptions or the market price of its stock may drop. That's what happened to General Electric (GE). Appliance sales dropped as a result of the housing crisis, and GE could not expect to raise profits in that division by 10 percent a year—its overall goal. It therefore planned to sell its appliance business.

Sometimes international units may also have to be sold in a restructuring. For example, GE has been trying to shed its underperforming GE Money unit, which handles consumer finance. That also meant selling its Japanese consumer-lending business.

When all is said and done, GE will have reduced the number of its infrastructure units from six to two, leaving the company with four operational segments: Technology Infrastructure, Energy Infrastructure, GE Capital, and NBC Universal. Further, some people are calling for the sale of NBC Universal. GE must compete on the global market, and that means maintaining growth that can match the growth of companies in other nations, including emerging markets.

Sources: Lauren Pollock, "GE Reorganizes Operations into Four Segments," *The Wall Street Journal*, July 26–27, 2008; and Satish Shankar, Nicolas Bloch, Robert Shaus, and Vijay Vishwanath, "How to Win in Emerging Markets," *Sloan Management Review*, Spring 2008.

---

specialization. For example, you might divide the mowing task into mowing, trimming, and raking.

If your business is successful, you'll probably hire more workers to help. You might organize them into teams or departments to do the various tasks.[5] One team might mow while another uses blowers to clean up leaves and debris. If you're really successful over time, you might hire an accountant to keep records, various people to handle advertising, and a crew to maintain the equipment.

You can see how your business might evolve into a company with several departments: production (mowing and everything related to that), marketing, accounting, and maintenance. The process of setting up individual departments to do specialized tasks is called *departmentalization*. Finally, you'll assign authority and responsibility to people so that you can control the whole process. If something went wrong in the accounting department, for example, you would know who was responsible.

Structuring an organization, then, consists of devising a division of labor (sometimes resulting in specialization); setting up teams or departments to do specific tasks (like production and accounting); and assigning responsibility and authority to people. It also includes allocating resources (such as funds for various departments), assigning specific tasks, and establishing procedures for accomplishing the organizational objectives. From the start, you have to make ethical decisions about how you'll treat your workers (see the Making Ethical Decisions box on p. 204).[6]

You may develop an *organization chart* that shows relationships among people: who is accountable for the completion of specific work, and who reports to whom. Finally, you'll monitor the environment to see what competitors are doing and what customers are demanding. Then you must adjust to the new realities. For example, a major lawn care company may begin promoting itself in your area. You might have to make some organizational changes to offer even better service at competitive prices. What would you do first if you began losing business to competitors?

◄ **LECTURE LINK 8-1:**
Smith's Folly

◄ **PPT 8-4:**
GE Looks for More Profits

◄ **BONUS CASE 8-1:**
Structural Collapse: Responsibility and Accountability

◄ **CRITICAL THINKING EXERCISE 8-1:**
Building an Organization Chart

◄ **PPT 8-5:**
Structuring an Organization

203

MAKING ethical decisions

Safety versus Profit

Imagine you have begun a successful lawn-mowing service in your neighborhood. Other lawn-mowing services in the area seem to hire untrained workers, many from other countries. They pay only the minimum wage or slightly more. Most obviously, however, they often provide no safety equipment. Workers don't have ear protection against the loud mowers and blowers. Most don't wear goggles when operating the shredder. Very few wear masks when spraying potentially harmful fertilizers.

You are aware there are many hazards connected with yard work, but safety gear can be expensive and workers often prefer to work without it. You are interested in making as much money as possible, but you also are concerned about the safety and welfare of your workers. You know yard maintenance equipment creates noise pollution, but quiet equipment is expensive.

The corporate culture you create as you begin your service will last a long time. If you emphasize safety and environmental concern from the start, your workers will adopt your values. On the other hand, you can see the potential for making faster profits by ignoring safety rules and paying little attention to the environment as your competitors seem to do. What are the consequences of each choice? Which will you make?

LEARNING goal 2 *

Compare the organizational theories of Fayol and Weber.

THE CHANGING ORGANIZATION

Never before in the history of business has so much change been introduced so quickly—sometimes too quickly. As we noted in earlier chapters, much of that change is due to the evolving business environment—more global competition, a declining economy, faster technological change, and pressure to preserve the natural environment.[7] Equally important to many businesses is the change in customer expectations. Consumers today expect high-quality products and fast, friendly service—at a reasonable cost.[8]

Managing change, then, has become a critical managerial function. That sometimes includes changing the whole organization structure.[9] Many organizations in the past were designed more to facilitate management than to please the customer. Companies designed many rules and regulations to give managers control over employees. As you'll learn later in this chapter, this reliance on rules is called *bureaucracy*. When Hurricane Katrina hit New Orleans in August 2005, the government seemed paralyzed and didn't know how to respond. The victims placed blame on federal, state, and local bureaucracy. Meanwhile, more flexible businesses in the area and in other states adjusted to the new conditions, reopened, and waited for the government to catch up. The local, state, and federal responses to the oil spill in 2010 were not much better.[10]

To understand where we are in organizational design, it helps to know where we've been. We'll look at that subject next.

The Development of Organization Design

Until the 20th century, most businesses were rather small, the processes for producing goods were relatively simple, and organizing workers was fairly easy. Organizing workers is still not too hard in most small firms, such as a lawn-mowing service or a small shop that produces custom-made boats. Not until the 1900s and the introduction of *mass production* (methods for efficiently producing large quantities of goods) did production processes and business organization become so complex. Usually, the bigger the plant, the more efficient production became.

Business growth led to **economies of scale**. This term refers to the fact that companies can reduce their production costs by purchasing raw materials in bulk. The average cost of goods decreases as production levels rise. The cost of building a car, for example, declined sharply when automobile companies adopted mass production and GM and Ford introduced their huge factories. Over time, such innovations became less meaningful as other companies copied the processes. You may have noticed the benefits of mass production in housing and computers.

During the era of mass production, organization theorists emerged. Two influential thinkers were Henri Fayol and Max Weber. Many of their principles are still being used in businesses throughout the world. Let's explore what they are.

Fayol's Principles of Organization   In France, economic theoretician Henri Fayol published his book *Administration industrielle et générale* in 1919. It was popularized in the United States in 1949 under the title *General and Industrial Management*. Fayol introduced such principles as the following:

- *Unity of command.* Each worker is to report to one, and only one, boss. The benefits of this principle are obvious. What happens if two different bosses give you two different assignments? Which one should you follow? To prevent such confusion, each person should report to only one manager. (Later we'll discuss an organizational plan that seems to violate this principle.)
- *Hierarchy of authority.* All workers should know to whom they report. Managers should have the right to give orders and expect others to follow. (As we discussed in Chapter 7, this concept has changed over time, and empowerment is often more important now.)
- *Division of labor.* Functions are to be divided into areas of specialization such as production, marketing, and finance. (This principle too is being modified, as you'll read later, and cross-functional teamwork is getting more emphasis.)
- *Subordination of individual interests to the general interest.* Workers are to think of themselves as a coordinated team. The goals of the team are more important than the goals of individual workers. (This concept is still very much in use.) Have you heard this concept being applied to football and basketball teams?
- *Authority.* Managers have the right to give orders and the power to enforce obedience. Authority and responsibility are related: whenever authority is exercised, responsibility arises. (This principle is also being modified as managers are beginning to empower employees.)
- *Degree of centralization.* The amount of decision-making power vested in top management should vary by circumstances. In a small organization, it's possible to

◀ **LECTURE LINK 8-2:**
CellularSouth's Katrina Teams

◀ **PPT 8-8:**
Production Changed Organization Design

economies of scale
The situation in which companies can reduce their production costs if they can purchase raw materials in bulk; the average cost of goods goes down as production levels increase.

◀ **PPT 8-9:**
Fayol's Principles

Henri Fayol introduced several management principles still followed today, including the idea that each worker should report to only one manager and that managers, in turn, should have the right to give orders for others to follow and the power to enforce them. Which of Fayol's principles have you observed?

centralize all decision-making power in the top manager. In a larger organization, however, some decision-making power, for both major and minor issues, should be delegated to lower-level managers and employees.

- *Clear communication channels.* All workers should be able to reach others in the firm quickly and easily.
- *Order.* Materials and people should be placed and maintained in the proper location.
- *Equity.* A manager should treat employees and peers with respect and justice.
- *Esprit de corps.* A spirit of pride and loyalty should be created among people in the firm.

Management courses in colleges throughout the world taught Fayol's principles for years, and they became synonymous with the concept of management. Organizations were designed so that no person had more than one boss, lines of authority were clear, and everyone knew to whom to report. Naturally, these principles tended to be written down as rules, policies, and regulations as organizations grew larger.

That process of rule making has often led to rather rigid organizations that haven't always responded quickly to consumer requests. For example, in various cities, the Department of Motor Vehicles (DMV) and auto repair facilities have been slow to adapt to the needs of their customers. So where did the idea of bureaucracy come from? We talk about that next.

Max Weber and Organizational Theory Max Weber's book *The Theory of Social and Economic Organizations*, like Fayol's, appeared in the United States in the late 1940s. Weber, a German sociologist and economist, promoted the pyramid-shaped organization structure that became popular in large firms. Weber put great trust in managers and felt the firm would do well if employees simply did what they were told. The less decision making they had to do, the better. Clearly, this is a reasonable way to operate if you're dealing with relatively uneducated and untrained workers. Such was generally the case at the time Weber was writing. Most employees today, however, have considerably more education and technical skills.[11]

Weber's principles of organization resembled Fayol's. In addition, Weber emphasized:

- Job descriptions.
- Written rules, decision guidelines, and detailed records.
- Consistent procedures, regulations, and policies.
- Staffing and promotion based on qualifications.

Weber believed that large organizations demanded clearly established rules and guidelines to be followed precisely. In other words, he was in favor of *bureaucracy*. Although his principles made sense at the time, rules and procedures became so rigid in some companies that they grew counterproductive. Some organizations today still thrive on Weber's theories. United Parcel Service (UPS), for example, maintains strict written rules and decision guidelines. Those rules enable the firm to deliver packages quickly because employees don't have to pause to make decisions—procedures are clearly spelled out for them.

Some organizations that follow Weber's principles are less effective than UPS because they don't allow employees to respond quickly to new challenges.[12] That has clearly been the case with disaster relief agencies

---

Max Weber promoted an organizational structure composed of middle managers who implement the orders of top managers. He believed less-educated workers were best managed if managers or supervisors gave them strict rules and regulations to follow and monitored their performance. What industries or businesses today would benefit by using such controls?

in many areas. Later, we explore how to make organizations more responsive. First, let's look at some basic terms and concepts.

Turning Principles into Organization Design

Following theories like Fayol's and Weber's, managers in the latter 1900s began designing organizations so that managers could *control* workers. Many companies are still organized that way, with everything set up in a hierarchy. A **hierarchy** is a system in which one person is at the top of the organization and there is a ranked or sequential ordering from the top down of managers and others who are responsible to that person. Since one person can't keep track of thousands of workers, the top manager needs many lower-level managers to help. The **chain of command** is the line of authority that moves from the top of the hierarchy to the lowest level. Figure 8.1 shows a typical hierarchy.

Some organizations have a dozen or more layers of management between the chief executive officer (CEO) and the lowest-level employees. If employees want to introduce work changes, they ask a supervisor (the first level of management), who asks his or her manager, who asks a manager at the next level up, and so on. It can take weeks or months for a decision to be made and passed from manager to manager until it reaches employees.

Max Weber used the word *bureaucrat* to describe a middle manager whose function was to implement top management's orders. Thus, **bureaucracy** came to be the term for an organization with many layers of managers.

When employees in a bureaucracy of any size have to ask managers for permission to make a change, the process may take so long that customers become annoyed. Has this happened to you in a department store or other organization? Since customers want efficient service—and they want it *now*—slow service is simply not acceptable in today's competitive firms.

Some companies are therefore reorganizing to let employees make decisions in order to please customers no matter what. Home Depot has adopted this approach to win more customers from competitors. Nordstrom employees could accept a return from a customer without managerial approval, even if the item was not originally sold at that store. As you read earlier, giving employees such authority is called *empowerment*. Remember that empowerment works only when employees are given the proper training and resources to respond. Can you see how such training would help first responders in crisis conditions?

hierarchy
A system in which one person is at the top of the organization and there is a ranked or sequential ordering from the top down of managers who are responsible to that person.

chain of command
The line of authority that moves from the top of a hierarchy to the lowest level.

bureaucracy
An organization with many layers of managers who set rules and regulations and oversee all decisions.

◀ PPT 8-13:
Typical Organization Chart

figure 8.1

TYPICAL ORGANIZATION CHART
This is a rather standard chart with managers for major functions and supervisors reporting to the managers. Each supervisor manages three employees.

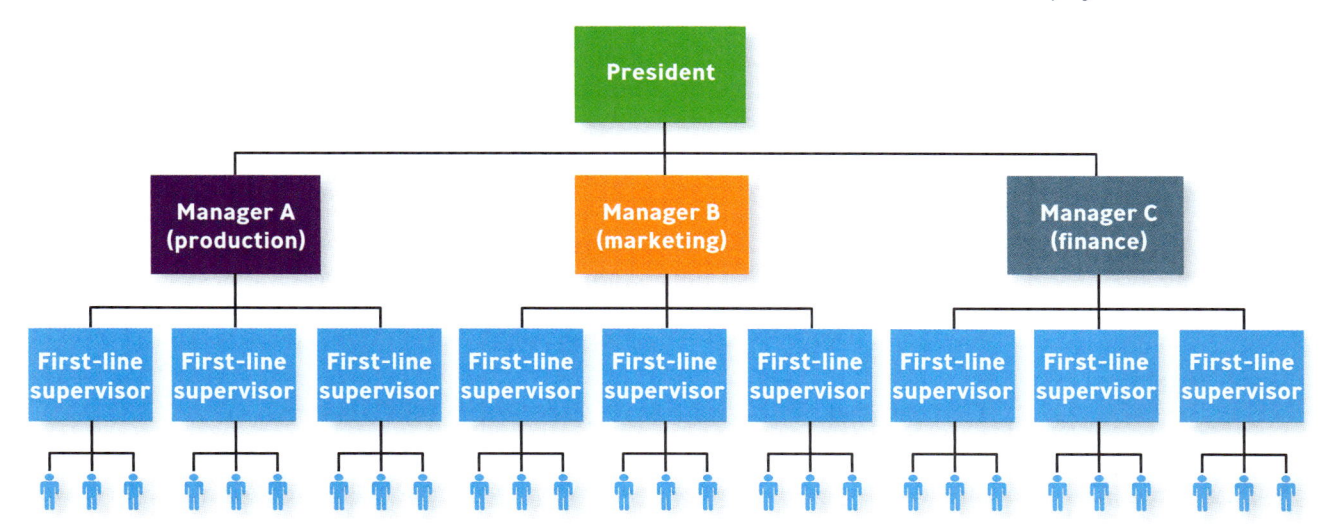

President
├── Manager A (production)
│   ├── First-line supervisor
│   ├── First-line supervisor
│   └── First-line supervisor
├── Manager B (marketing)
│   ├── First-line supervisor
│   ├── First-line supervisor
│   └── First-line supervisor
└── Manager C (finance)
    ├── First-line supervisor
    ├── First-line supervisor
    └── First-line supervisor

progress assessment

- What do the terms *division of labor* and *job specialization* mean?
- What are the principles of management outlined by Fayol?
- What did Weber add to the principles of Fayol?

LEARNING goal 3 *

Evaluate the choices managers make in structuring organizations.

DECISIONS TO MAKE IN STRUCTURING ORGANIZATIONS

▶ PPT 8-14:
Bureaucratic Organizations

When designing responsive organizations, firms have to make decisions about several organizational issues: (1) centralization versus decentralization, (2) span of control, (3) tall versus flat organization structures, and (4) departmentalization.

Choosing Centralized or Decentralized Authority

centralized authority
An organization structure in which decision-making authority is maintained at the top level of management.

Centralized authority occurs when decision making is concentrated at the top level of management. The retailing giant Target, for example, has a very centralized form of management. *Fortune* magazine commented that Target is so top-down that the CEO personally interviews candidates for the top 600 positions.[13] That doesn't mean Target hasn't adapted to different circumstances, however, as you'll see later in this chapter.

McDonald's believes that purchasing, promotion, and other such decisions are best handled centrally. There's usually little need for each McDonald's restaurant in the United States to carry different food products. McDonald's thus leans toward centralized authority. However, today's rapidly changing markets, added to global differences in consumer tastes, tend to favor some decentralization and thus more delegation of authority, even at McDonald's. Its restaurants in England offer tea, those in France offer a Croque McDo (a hot ham-and-cheese sandwich), those in Japan sell rice, and Chinese McDonald's offer taro and red bean desserts.

▶ PPT 8-15:
Centralization or Decentralization?

decentralized authority
An organization structure in which decision-making authority is delegated to lower-level managers more familiar with local conditions than headquarters management could be.

Decentralized authority occurs when decision making is delegated to lower-level managers and employees more familiar with local conditions than headquarters management could be. JCPenney customers in California, for example, demand clothing styles different from what customers in Minnesota or Maine like. It makes sense to delegate to store managers in various cities the authority to buy, price, and promote merchandise appropriate for each area. In response to the economic crisis of 2008–2010, Macy's department store is also shifting to local tastes. The plan, called "My Macy's," proved successful in test markets. Both Home Depot and Lowe's also responded to the crisis with similar moves toward catering to local markets.[14] Figure 8.2 lists some advantages and disadvantages of centralized and decentralized authority.

Choosing the Appropriate Span of Control

span of control
The optimal number of subordinates a manager supervises or should supervise.

Span of control describes the optimal number of subordinates a manager supervises or should supervise. What is the "right" span of control? At lower

ADVANTAGES	DISADVANTAGES
Centralized	
• Greater top-management control	• Less responsiveness to customers
• More efficiency	• Less empowerment
• Simpler distribution system	• Interorganizational conflict
• Stronger brand/corporate image	• Lower morale away from headquarters
Decentralized	
• Better adaptation to customer wants	• Less efficiency
• More empowerment of workers	• Complex distribution system
• Faster decision making	• Less top-management control
• Higher morale	• Weakened corporate image

figure 8.2

ADVANTAGES AND DISADVANTAGES OF CENTRALIZED VERSUS DECENTRALIZED MANAGEMENT

levels, where work is standardized, it's possible to implement a broad span of control (15 to 40 workers). For example, one supervisor can be responsible for 20 or more workers assembling computers or cleaning movie theaters. The appropriate span gradually narrows at higher levels of the organization, because work becomes less standardized and managers need more face-to-face communication.

PPT 8-16: Span of Control

LECTURE LINK 8-4: Choosing the Right Span of Control

The trend today is to expand the span of control as organizations adopt empowerment, reduce the number of middle managers, and hire more talented and better educated lower-level employees. Information technology also allows managers to handle more information, so the span can be broader still.

PPT 8-17: Organizational Structures

At Rowe Furniture in Salem, Virginia, the manufacturing chief dismantled the assembly line and empowered the people who had had limited functions—like sewing, gluing, and stapling—with the freedom to make sofas as they saw fit. Productivity and quality soared.

Choosing between Tall and Flat Organization Structures

In the early 20th century, organizations grew even bigger, adding layer after layer of management to create **tall organization structures**. Some had as many as 14 levels, and the span of control was small (few people reported to each manager).

tall organization structure
An organizational structure in which the pyramidal organization chart would be quite tall because of the various levels of management.

Imagine how a message might be distorted as it moved up the organization and back down through managers, management assistants, secretaries, assistant secretaries, supervisors, trainers, and so on. The cost of all these managers and support people was high, the paperwork they generated was enormous, and the inefficiencies in communication and decision making were often intolerable.

More recently, organizations have adopted **flat organization structures** with fewer layers of management (see Figure 8.3 on p. 210) and a broad span of control (many people report to each manager). Flat structures can respond readily to customer demands because lower-level employees have authority and responsibility for making decisions, and managers can be spared some day-to-day tasks. In a bookstore with a flat organization structure, employees may have authority to arrange shelves by category, process special orders for customers, and so on.

flat organization structure
An organization structure that has few layers of management and a broad span of control.

figure 8.3
A FLAT ORGANIZATION STRUCTURE

Owner/Manager

▶ **PPT 8-18:**
Flat Organizational Structure

Large organizations use flat structures to try to match the friendliness of small firms, whose workers often know customers by name. The flatter organizations become, the broader their spans of control, which means some managers lose their jobs. Figure 8.4 lists advantages and disadvantages of narrow and broad spans of control.

Weighing the Advantages and Disadvantages of Departmentalization

Departmentalization divides organizations into separate units. The traditional way to departmentalize is by *function*—such as design, production, marketing, and accounting. Departmentalization groups workers according to their skills, expertise, or resource use so that they can specialize and work together more effectively. It may also save costs and thus improve efficiency. Other advantages include the following:

departmentalization
The dividing of organizational functions into separate units.

▶ **PPT 8-19:**
Departmentalization

▶ **PPT 8-20:**
Advantages of Departmentalization

1. Employees can develop skills in depth and progress within a department as they master more skills.
2. The company can achieve economies of scale by centralizing all the resources it needs and locate various experts in that area.
3. Employees can coordinate work within the function, and top management can easily direct and control various departments' activities.

A broad span of control allows one supervisor to be responsible for many workers whose work tasks are predictable and standardized. In addition to assembly lines, can you think of other management situations that might benefit from a broad span of control? What about in a service industry?

figure 8.4
ADVANTAGES AND DISADVANTAGES OF A NARROW VERSUS A BROAD SPAN OF CONTROL
The flatter the organization, the broader the span of control.

ADVANTAGES	DISADVANTAGES
Narrow	
• More control by top management	• Less empowerment
• More chances for advancement	• Higher costs
• Greater specialization	• Delayed decision making
• Closer supervision	• Less responsiveness to customers
Broad	
• Reduced costs	• Fewer chances for advancement
• More responsiveness to customers	• Overworked managers
• Faster decision making	• Loss of control
• More empowerment	• Less management expertise

Disadvantages of departmentalization by function include the following:

1. Departments may not communicate well. For example, production may be so isolated from marketing that it does not get needed feedback from customers.
2. Employees may identify with their department's goals rather than the organization's. The purchasing department may find a good value somewhere and buy a huge volume of goods. That makes purchasing look good, but the high cost of storing the goods hurts overall profitability.
3. The company's response to external changes may be slow.
4. People may not be trained to take different managerial responsibilities; rather, they tend to become narrow specialists.
5. Department members may engage in groupthink (they think alike) and may need input from outside to become more creative.

◄ **PPT 8-21:**
Disadvantages of Departmentalization

◄ **PPT 8-22:**
Ways to Departmentalize

◄ **LECTURE LINK 8-5:**
Dell Reorganizes Around Customers

Looking at Alternate Ways to Departmentalize Functional separation isn't always the most responsive form of organization. So what are the alternatives? Figure 8.5 on p. 212 shows five ways a firm can departmentalize. One way is by product. A book publisher might have a trade book department (for books sold to the general public), a textbook department, and a technical book department, each with separate development and marketing processes. Such product-focused departmentalization usually results in good customer relations.

Some organizations departmentalize by customer group. A pharmaceutical company might have one department for the consumer market, another that calls on hospitals (the institutional market), and another that targets doctors. You can see how customer groups can benefit from having specialists satisfying their needs.

Some firms group their units by geographic location because customers vary so greatly by region. Japan, Europe, and South America may deserve separate departments, with obvious benefits.

The decision about how to departmentalize depends on the nature of the product and the customers. A few firms find that it's most efficient to separate activities by *process*. For example, a firm that makes leather coats may have one department cut the leather, another dye it, and a third sew the coat together. Such specialization enables employees to do a better job because they can focus on learning a few critical skills.

Some firms use a combination of departmentalization techniques to create *hybrid forms*. For example, a company could departmentalize by function, geographic location, *and* customer groups.

While departmentalization by function allows employees to hone and develop certain skills, one potential disadvantage of this form of organization is that people tend to become specialists who have a difficult time adapting to changes in their responsibilities. When might employee specialization outweigh this disadvantage?

figure 8.5

WAYS TO DEPARTMENTALIZE

A computer company may want to departmentalize by geographic location (countries), a manufacturer by function, a pharmaceutical company by customer group, a leather manufacturer by process, and a publisher by product. In each case the structure must fit the firm's goals.

▶ **PPT 8-23:**
Ways to Departmentalize

▶ **CRITICAL THINKING EXERCISE 8-2:**
How Do Organizations Group Activities?

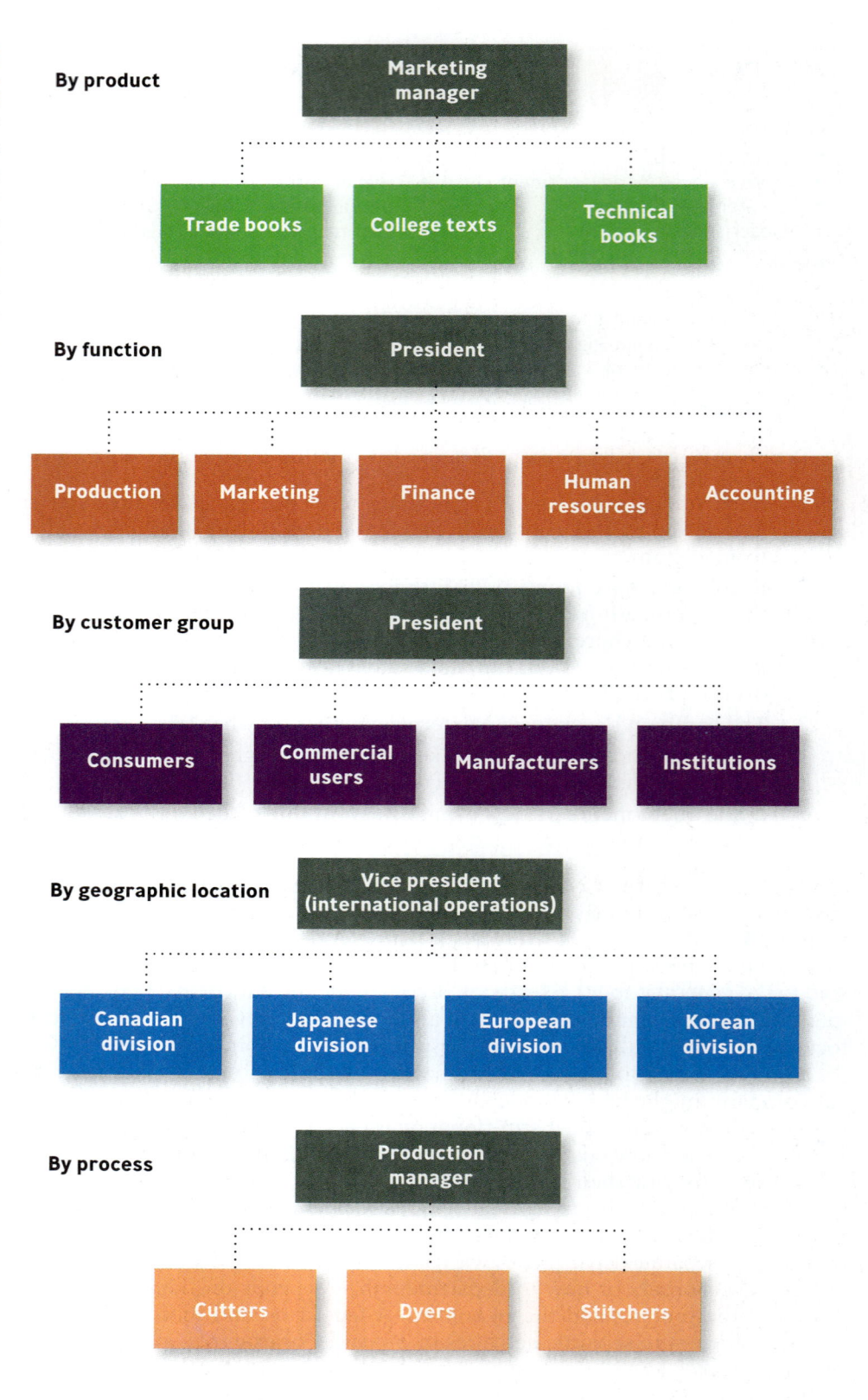

By product
- Marketing manager
  - Trade books
  - College texts
  - Technical books

By function
- President
  - Production
  - Marketing
  - Finance
  - Human resources
  - Accounting

By customer group
- President
  - Consumers
  - Commercial users
  - Manufacturers
  - Institutions

By geographic location
- Vice president (international operations)
  - Canadian division
  - Japanese division
  - European division
  - Korean division

By process
- Production manager
  - Cutters
  - Dyers
  - Stitchers

progress assessment

- Why are organizations becoming flatter?
- What are some reasons for having a narrow span of control in an organization?
- What are the advantages and disadvantages of departmentalization?
- What are the various ways a firm can departmentalize?

LEARNING goal 4 *

Contrast the various organizational models.

ORGANIZATIONAL MODELS

Now that we've explored the basic choices in organization design, let's look in depth at four ways to structure an organization: (1) line organizations, (2) line-and-staff organizations, (3) matrix-style organizations, and (4) cross-functional self-managed teams. You'll see that some of these models violate traditional management principles. The business community is in a period of transition, with some traditional organizational models giving way to new structures. Such transitions can be not only unsettling to employees and managers but also fraught with problems and errors.

Line Organizations

A **line organization** has direct two-way lines of responsibility, authority, and communication running from the top to the bottom of the organization, with everyone reporting to only one supervisor. The military and many small businesses are organized this way. For example, a locally owned pizza parlor might have a general manager and a shift manager. All the general employees report to the shift manager, and he or she reports to the general manager or owner.

A line organization does not have any specialists who provide managerial support. There is no legal department, accounting department, human resources department, or information technology (IT) department. Line organizations follow all of Fayol's traditional management rules. Line managers can issue orders, enforce discipline, and adjust the organization as conditions change.

In large businesses, a line organization may have the disadvantages of being too inflexible, of having few specialists or experts to advise people along the line, and of having lengthy lines of communication. Thus they may be unable to handle complex decisions relating to thousands of products and tons of paperwork. Such organizations usually turn to a line-and-staff form of organization.

Line-and-Staff Organizations

To minimize the disadvantages of simple line organizations, many organizations today have both line and staff personnel. **Line personnel** are responsible for directly achieving organizational goals, and include production workers, distribution people, and marketing personnel. **Staff personnel** advise and assist line personnel in meeting their goals, and include those in marketing research, legal advising, information technology, and human resource management.

---

line organization
An organization that has direct two-way lines of responsibility, authority, and communication running from the top to the bottom of the organization, with all people reporting to only one supervisor.

line personnel
Employees who are part of the chain of command that is responsible for achieving organizational goals.

staff personnel
Employees who advise and assist line personnel in meeting their goals.

See Figure 8.6 for a diagram of a line-and-staff organization. One important difference between line and staff personnel is authority. Line personnel have formal authority to make policy decisions. Staff personnel have authority to advise line personnel and influence their decisions, but they can't make policy changes themselves. The line manager may seek or ignore the advice from staff personnel.

Many organizations benefit from expert staff advice on safety, legal issues, quality control, database management, motivation, and investing. Staff personnel strengthen the line positions and are like well-paid consultants on the organization's payroll.

Matrix-Style Organizations

Both line and line-and-staff organization structures may suffer from inflexibility. Both allow for established lines of authority and communication and work well in organizations with stable environments and slow product development (such as firms selling household appliances). In such firms, clear lines of authority and relatively fixed organization structures are assets that ensure efficient operations.

Today's economy, however, is dominated by high-growth industries like telecommunications, nanotechnology, robotics, biotechnology, and aerospace, where competition is stiff and the life cycle of new ideas is short. Emphasis is on product development, creativity, special projects, rapid communication, and interdepartmental teamwork. From those changes grew the popularity of the

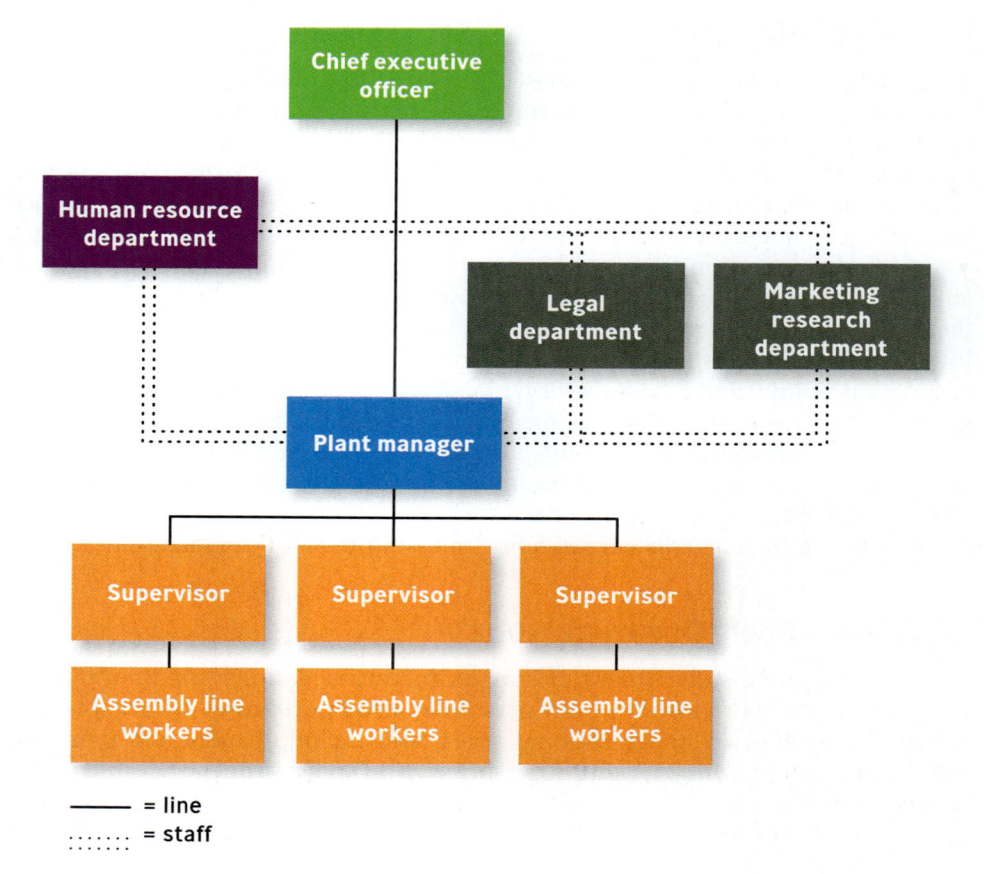

"SEND THIS BACK TO THE LEGAL DEPARTMENT. I THINK THEY COULD MAKE IT MUCH MORE COMPLICATED THAN THIS..."

Members of a legal department are considered staff personnel in a line-and-staff organization. Staff personnel serve in an advisory role and can work with colleagues and departments at every level in the firm's hierarchy. What are some of the advantages of this type of organization model?

▶ PPT 8-30: Matrix Organizations

figure 8.6
A SAMPLE LINE-AND-STAFF ORGANIZATION

—— = line
······ = staff

matrix organization, in which specialists from different parts of the organization work together temporarily on specific projects, but still remain part of a line-and-staff structure (see Figure 8.7). In other words, a project manager can borrow people from different departments to help design and market new product ideas.

The matrix structure was developed in the aerospace industry and is now familiar in areas such as banking, management consulting firms, accounting firms, ad agencies, and school systems. Among its advantages:

- It gives managers flexibility in assigning people to projects.
- It encourages interorganizational cooperation and teamwork.
- It can produce creative solutions to product development problems.
- It makes efficient use of organizational resources.

As for disadvantages:

- It's costly and complex.
- It can confuse employees about where their loyalty belongs—with the project manager or with their functional unit.
- It requires good interpersonal skills as well as cooperative employees and managers to avoid communication problems.
- It may be only a temporary solution to a long-term problem.

If you're thinking that matrix organizations violate some traditional managerial principles, you're right. Normally a person can't work effectively for two bosses. Who has the real authority? Whose directive has first priority?

In reality, however, the system functions more effectively than you might imagine. To develop a new product, a project manager may be given temporary authority to "borrow" line personnel from production, marketing, and other line functions. The employees work together to complete the project and then return to their regular positions. Thus, no one actually reports to more than one manager at a time.

A potential real problem with matrix management, however, is that the project teams are not permanent. They form to solve a problem and then break

> **matrix organization**
> An organization in which specialists from different parts of the organization are brought together to work on specific projects but still remain part of a line-and-staff structure.

◀ PPT 8-31:
Sample Matrix Organization

◀ PPT 8-32:
Advantages of Matrix Style

◀ PPT 8-33:
Disadvantages of Matrix Style

figure 8.7

A MATRIX ORGANIZATION
In a matrix organization, project managers are in charge of teams made up of members of several departments. In this case, project manager 2 supervises employees A, B, C, and D. These employees are accountable not only to project manager 2 but also to the head of their individual departments. For example, employee B, a market researcher, reports to project manager 2 *and* to the vice president of marketing.

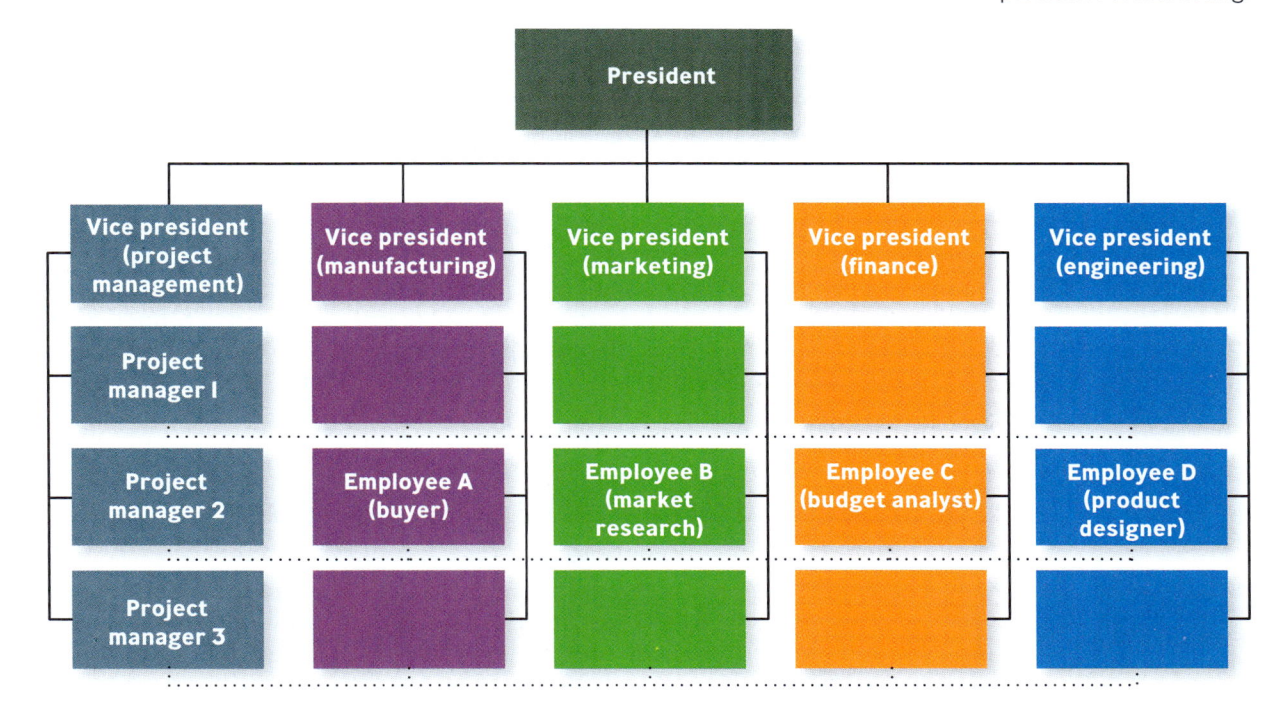

> You can think of a team of medical specialists in an operating room as a cross-functional, self-managed team. Doctors, nurses, technicians, and anesthesiologists from different departments and areas in the hospital work together to complete successful operations. What kinds of tasks do cross-functional, self-managed teams complete in an office or retail environment?

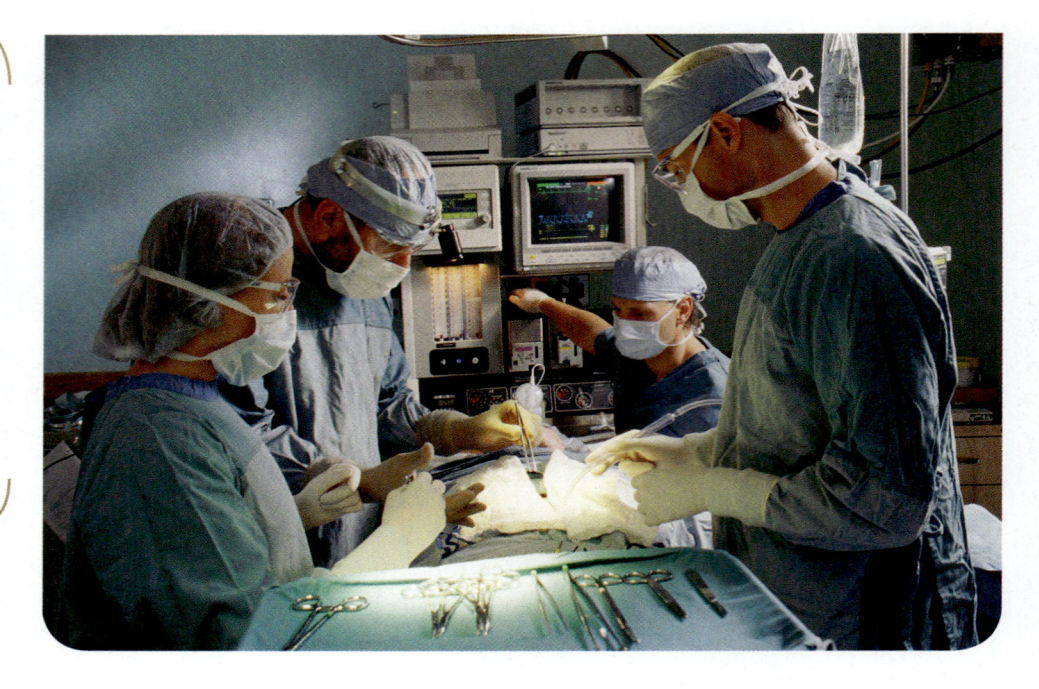

up. There is little chance for cross-functional learning, because teams work together so briefly.

Decision making in the future will be distributed throughout the organization so that people can respond rapidly to change, says the *Harvard Business Review*. Global teams will collaborate on the Internet for a single project and then disband.[15] Young people who play online games will feel quite comfortable working in such groups.

Cross-Functional Self-Managed Teams

One solution to the temporary nature of matrix teams is to establish long-lived teams and empower them to work closely with suppliers, customers, and others to quickly and efficiently bring out new, high-quality products while giving great service. *BusinessWeek* reports that some 82 percent of white-collar workers partner with co-workers. Over 80 percent say they prefer working in groups of three or more. Most work in groups to learn from others, but 30 percent use groups to accomplish a specific task.[16]

Cross-functional self-managed teams are groups of employees from different departments who work together on a long-term basis (as opposed to the temporary teams established in matrix-style organizations). *Self-managed* means that they are empowered to make decisions without management approval. The barriers among design, engineering, marketing, distribution, and other functions fall when interdepartmental teams are created. Sometimes the teams are interfirm; that is, the members come from two or more companies.

Cross-functional teams work best when leadership is shared. An engineer may lead the design of a new product, but a marketing expert may take the leadership position once it's ready for distribution.[17]

Going Beyond Organizational Boundaries

Cross-functional teams work best when the voice of the customer is brought in, especially in product development tasks.[18] Suppliers and distributors should be on the team as well. A cross-functional team that includes customers, suppliers, and distributors goes beyond organizational boundaries. When suppliers and distributors are in other countries, cross-functional teams may share

> **cross-functional self-managed teams**
> Groups of employees from different departments who work together on a long-term basis.

market information across national boundaries. Government coordinators may assist such projects, letting cross-functional teams break the barriers between government and business.

Cross-functional teams are only one way businesses can interact with other companies. Next we look at others.

progress assessment

- What is the difference between line and staff personnel?
- What management principle does a matrix-style organization challenge?
- What is the main difference between a matrix-style organization's structure and the use of cross-functional teams?

LEARNING goal 5 *

Identify the benefits of interfirm cooperation and coordination.

MANAGING THE INTERACTIONS AMONG FIRMS

Whether it involves customers, suppliers, distributors, or the government, **networking** uses communications technology and other means to link organizations and allow them to work together on common objectives.[19] Let's explore this concept further.

Transparency and Virtual Organizations

Networked organizations are so closely linked by the Internet that each can find out what the others are doing in real time. **Real time** simply means the present moment or the actual time in which an event takes place. The Internet has allowed companies to send real-time data to organizational partners as they are developed or collected.[20] The result is transparency (see Chapter 7), which occurs when a company is so open to other companies that electronic information is shared as if the companies were one. With this integration, two companies can work as closely as two departments in traditional firms.

Can you see the implications for organizational design? Most organizations are no longer self-sufficient or self-contained. Rather, they are part of a vast network of global businesses that work closely together. An organization chart showing what people do within any one organization is simply not complete, because the organization is part of a much larger system of firms. A modern chart would show people in different organizations and indicate how they are networked. This is a relatively new concept, however, so few such charts are yet available.

Networked organization structures tend to be flexible. A company may work with a design expert from another company in Italy for a year and then not need that person anymore. It may hire an expert from a company in another country for the next project. Such a temporary network, made of replaceable firms that join and leave as needed, is a **virtual corporation** (see Figure 8.8 on p. 218). This is quite different from a traditional organization structure; in fact, traditional managers sometimes have trouble adapting to the speed of change and the impermanence of relationships in networking. We discuss adaptation to change below; first, we describe how organizations use benchmarking and outsourcing to manage their interactions with other firms.

networking
Using communications technology and other means to link organizations and allow them to work together on common objectives.

real time
The present moment or the actual time in which something takes place.

virtual corporation
A temporary networked organization made up of replaceable firms that join and leave as needed.

figure 8.8

A VIRTUAL CORPORATION
A virtual corporation has no permanent ties to the firms that do its production, distribution, legal, and other work. Such firms are flexible enough to adapt to changes in the market quickly.

[Diagram: CORE Firm in center connected by dotted arrows to Production Firm, Distribution Firm, Advertising Agency, Design Firm, Legal Firm, Accounting Firm]

Benchmarking and Core Competencies

Organizations historically tried to do all functions themselves. Each had its own department for accounting, finance, marketing, production, and so on. As we've noted, today's organizations look to other organizations for help in areas where they do not generate world-class quality.

Benchmarking compares an organization's practices, processes, and products against the world's best. As one example, K2 Skis is a company that makes skis, snowboards, in-line skates, and related products. It studied the compact-disc industry and learned to use ultraviolet inks to print graphics on skis. It went to the aerospace industry to get piezoelectric technology to reduce vibration in its snowboards (the aerospace industry uses the technology for wings on planes). It learned from the cable television industry how to braid layers of fiberglass and carbon, and adapted that knowledge to make skis. As another example, Wyeth, a pharmaceutical company, benchmarked the aerospace industry for project management, the shipping industry for standardization of processes, and computer makers to learn the most efficient way to make prescription drugs.

Benchmarking also has a more directly competitive purpose. In retailing, Target may compare itself to Wal-Mart to see what, if anything, Wal-Mart does better. Target will then try to improve its practices or processes to become even better than Wal-Mart.

If an organization can't do as well as the best in, say, shipping, it will try to outsource the function to an organization like UPS or FedEx that specializes in shipping. Outsourcing, remember, means assigning one or more functions—such as accounting, production, security, maintenance, and legal work—to outside organizations. Even small firms are getting involved in outsourcing.[21] We've already discussed some problems with outsourcing, especially when companies outsource to other countries. Some functions, such as information management and marketing, may be too important to assign to outside firms. In that case, the organization should benchmark the best firms and restructure its departments to try to be equally good.

When a firm has completed its outsourcing process, the remaining functions are its **core competencies**, those functions it can do as well as or better

---

benchmarking
Comparing an organization's practices, processes, and products against the world's best.

▶ **PPT 8-41:**
Benefits and Concerns of Health-Care Outsourcing

▶ **PPT 8-42:**
Which Jobs Will Be Outsourced Next?

▶ **PPT 8-43:**
Benchmarking and Core Competencies

core competencies
Those functions that the organization can do as well as or better than any other organization in the world.

than any other organization in the world. For example, Nike is great at designing and marketing athletic shoes. Those are its core competencies. It outsources manufacturing, however, to other companies that assemble shoes better and less expensively than Nike can. Similarly, Dell is best at marketing computers and outsources most other functions, including manufacturing and distribution.

After you have structured an organization, you must keep monitoring the environment (including customers) to learn what changes are needed. Dell, for example, recently reversed its practice of outsourcing customer support and now offers a premium service that allows U.S. customers to reach tech support in North America. The following section discusses organizational change in more detail.

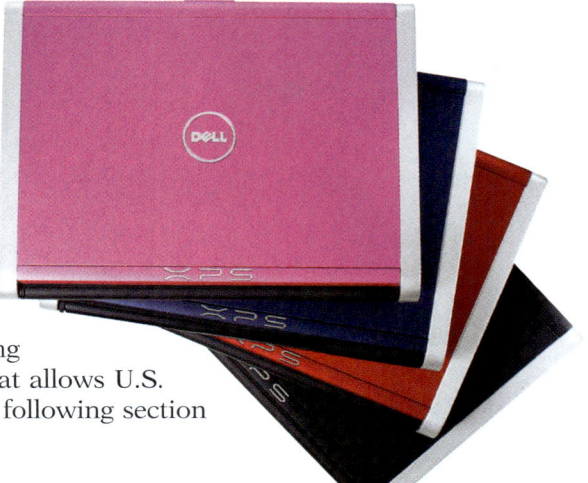

ADAPTING TO CHANGE

Once you have formed an organization, you must be prepared to adapt the structure to changes in the market. That's not always easy to do. Over time, an organization can get stuck in its ways. Employees have a tendency to say, "That's the way we've always done things. If it isn't broken, don't fix it." Managers also get complacent. They may say they have 20 years' experience when in fact they've had 1 year's experience 20 times. Do you think that slow adaptation to change was a factor in the decline of the manufacturing sector in the United States?

Introducing change is thus one of the hardest challenges facing any manager. Nonetheless, change is what's happening at General Motors (GM), Ford, Facebook, and other companies eager to become more competitive.[22] If you have old facilities that are no longer efficient, you have to get rid of them. That's exactly what GM and other companies are doing. In fact, they have asked the government to lend them billions of dollars to help.[23] You may have to cut your labor force to lower costs. From the outset of the recession in December 2007 to the beginning of 2009, U.S. payrolls shrank by 3.6 million jobs.[24] That's a lot of cutting.

The Internet has created whole new opportunities, not only to sell to customers directly but also to ask them questions and provide them with any information they want.[25] To win market share, companies must coordinate the efforts of their traditional departments and their Internet staff to create friendly, easy-to-manage interactions. Young people today are called **digital natives** because they grew up with the Internet. To reach them, companies are retraining older employees to be more tech-savvy.[26] That means becoming familiar with YouTube, Facebook, Wikis, Skype, Twitter, RSS, and more.[27]

We've seen that Target is highly centralized. Nonetheless, the company reacts effectively to changes in consumer preferences throughout the country, in part by keeping in touch with an enormous web of people of all ages, interests, and nationalities—its "creative cabinet"—via the Internet. The members of the "cabinet," who never meet so they cannot influence each other, evaluate various new initiatives and recommend new programs to help Target figure out what belongs on store shelves.

Restructuring for Empowerment

To empower employees, firms often must reorganize dramatically to make frontline workers their most important people. **Restructuring** is redesigning an organization so it can more effectively and efficiently serve its customers.[28]

Delivering reliable and affordable machines built to customers' specifications has long been Dell's core competency. For some time Dell outsourced its customer-support function overseas. Recently, however, the company found it more efficient to base top-quality customer support teams in the United States. Why do you think customer support is so important for a computer maker, even though it may not be a core competency?

◄ PPT 8-44:
Adapting to Market Changes

digital natives
Young people who have grown up using the Internet and social networking.

◄ PPT 8-45:
Keep in Touch

◄ BONUS CASE 8-3:
Restructuring by Eliminating Brands?

restructuring
Redesigning an organization so that it can more effectively and efficiently serve its customers.

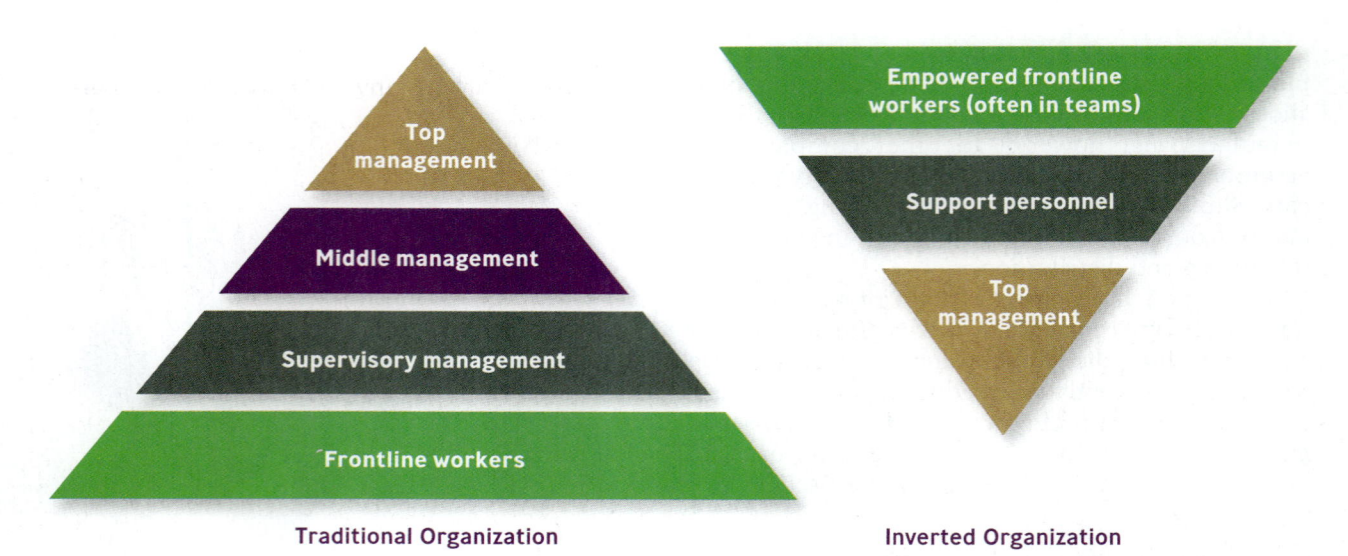

figure 8.9
COMPARISON OF AN INVERTED ORGANIZATION STRUCTURE AND A TRADITIONAL ORGANIZATION STRUCTURE

Traditional Organization: Top management / Middle management / Supervisory management / Frontline workers

Inverted Organization: Empowered frontline workers (often in teams) / Support personnel / Top management

inverted organization
An organization that has contact people at the top and the chief executive officer at the bottom of the organization chart.

➤ PPT 8-46: Restructuring

➤ PPT 8-47: Traditional and Inverted Organizations

Until recently, department store clerks, bank tellers, and front-desk staff in hotels weren't considered key employees. Instead, managers were considered more important, and they were responsible for directing the work of the frontline people. The organization chart in a typical firm looked much like the pyramid in Figure 8.1.

A few service-oriented organizations have turned the traditional organization structure upside down. An **inverted organization** has contact people (like nurses) at the top and the chief executive officer at the bottom. Management layers are few, and the manager's job is to *assist and support* frontline people, not boss them around. Figure 8.9 illustrates the difference between an inverted and a traditional organizational structure.

Companies based on this organization structure support frontline personnel with internal and external databases, advanced communication systems, and professional assistance. Naturally, this means frontline people have to be better educated, better trained, and better paid than in the past. It takes a lot of trust for top managers to implement such a system—but when they do, the payoff in customer satisfaction and profits is often well worth the effort.

In the past, managers controlled information—and that gave them power. In more progressive organizations today, everyone shares information, often through an elaborate database system, and *among* firms as well as *within* them.[29] No matter what organizational model you choose or how much you empower your employees, the secret to successful organization change is to focus on customers and give them what they want.[30]

LEARNING goal 6 *

Explain how organizational culture can help businesses adapt to change.

Creating a Change-Oriented Organizational Culture

organizational (or corporate) culture
Widely shared values within an organization that provide unity and cooperation to achieve common goals.

Any organizational change is bound to cause some stress and resistance among members. Firms adapt best when their culture is already change-oriented. **Organizational (or corporate) culture** is the widely shared values within an organization that foster unity and cooperation to achieve common goals. Usually the culture of an organization is reflected in its stories, traditions, and myths.

Each McDonald's restaurant has the same feel, look, and atmosphere; in short, each has a similar organizational culture. It's obvious from visiting almost any McDonald's that the culture emphasizes quality, service, cleanliness, and value.

An organizational culture can also be negative. Have you ever been in an organization where you feel no one cares about service or quality? The clerks may seem uniformly glum, indifferent, and testy. Their mood pervades the atmosphere, and patrons become unhappy or upset. It may be hard to believe an organization, especially a profit-making one, can be run so badly and still survive. Clearly then, when you search for a job, study the organizational culture to see whether you will thrive in it.

Some of the best organizations have cultures that emphasize service to others, especially customers. The atmosphere reflects friendly, caring people who enjoy working together to provide a good product at a reasonable price. Companies that have such cultures have less need for close supervision of employees. That usually means fewer policy manuals; organization charts; and formal rules, procedures, and controls. The key to a productive culture is mutual trust. You get such trust by giving it. The very best companies stress high moral and ethical values such as honesty, reliability, fairness, environmental protection, and social involvement.[31]

We've been talking as if organizational matters were mostly controllable by management. In fact, the formal structure is just one element of the total organizational system, including its culture. The informal organization is of equal or even greater importance. Let's explore this notion next.

Empowering employees who deal directly with customers to solve problems without needing a manager's approval makes a higher level of customer service possible and helps employees grow as well. What kind of guest issues do you think a frontline hotel employee should be allowed to solve on his or her own?

Managing the Informal Organization

All organizations have two organizational systems. The **formal organization** details lines of responsibility, authority, and position. It's the structure shown on organization charts. The other system is the **informal organization**, the system that develops spontaneously as employees meet and form cliques, relationships, and lines of authority outside the formal organization. It's the human side of the organization that doesn't show on any organization chart (see the Spotlight on Small Business box on p. 222).

No organization can operate effectively without both types of organization. The formal system is often too slow and bureaucratic to let the organization adapt quickly, although it does provide helpful guides and lines of authority for routine situations.

The informal organization is often too unstructured and emotional to allow careful, reasoned decision making on critical matters. It's extremely effective, however, in generating creative solutions to short-term problems and creating camaraderie and teamwork among employees.

In any organization, it's wise to learn quickly who is important in the informal organization. Following formal rules and procedures can take days. Who in the organization knows how to obtain supplies immediately without the normal procedures? Which administrative assistants should you see if you want your work given first priority? Answers to these questions help people work effectively in many organizations.

The informal organization's nerve center is the *grapevine*, the system through which unofficial information flows between and among managers and employees. Key people in the grapevine usually have considerable influence.

formal organization
The structure that details lines of responsibility, authority, and position; that is, the structure shown on organization charts.

informal organization
The system that develops spontaneously as employees meet and form cliques, relationships, and lines of authority outside the formal organization.

SPOTLIGHT ON SMALL business

Keeping That Small-Company Feeling

The informal network is much easier to maintain in small businesses. Camaraderie is often maintained by having a company sports team, informal parties, or bowling outings. There are as many ways of building links among employees as managers' imaginations can create.

Keeping that small-company feeling among larger corporations is not as easy. Merrill Lynch analyst Jessica Cohen wondered why Time Warner, which owned both Warner Music and AOL, didn't come up with something like iTunes. The answer is that communication between and among corporate units in large firms is not managed as well as in small businesses. In fact, research has shown that informal networks may act to inhibit innovation rather than foster it. Workers may slow the process down to avoid change. Large corporations, like smaller businesses, would be wise to form cross-departmental sports teams and sponsor cross-departmental parties.

Some larger companies have *idea brokers* whose job is to promote meetings among people from different parts of the firm at conferences and training programs, as well as in more informal settings. Hewlett-Packard has introduced WaterCooler, a software tool that indexes what employees say on their internal and external blogs. Other companies are giving employees tools to text-message one another and stay in touch through social networking. The idea is to maintain a small-company feel in larger companies so that employees can learn from one another and become more innovative.

Sources: Jena McGregor, "Mining the Office Chatter," *BusinessWeek*, May 19, 2008; Adam M. Kleinbaum and Michael L. Tushman, "Managing Corporate Social Networks," *Harvard Business Review*, July–August 2008; and Lorri Freifeld, "It's the Network," *Training*, February 2008.

Richard Tait (left) calls himself the grand poo-bah for Cranium, producer of the highly successful board game of that name. White Alexander, who does product development and manufacturing, is called the chief noodler. They strive to create products that are clever, high-quality, innovative, friendly, and fun (CHIFF). What kind of leadership style and company culture might you expect in a company that is so casual?

In the old "us-versus-them" system of organizations, where managers and employees were often at odds, the informal system hindered effective management. In more open organizations, managers and employees work together to set objectives and design procedures. The informal organization is an invaluable managerial asset that can promote harmony among workers and establish the corporate culture.

As effective as the informal organization may be in creating group cooperation, it can still be equally powerful in resisting management directives. Employees may form unions, go on strike together, and generally disrupt operations. Learning to create the right corporate culture and work within the informal organization is thus a key to managerial success.

progress assessment

- What is an inverted organization?
- Why do organizations outsource functions?
- What is organizational culture?

summary

Learning Goal 1. Outline the basic principles of organization management.

- **What is happening today to American businesses?**

They are adjusting to changing markets. That is a normal function in a capitalist economy. There will be big winners, like Google and Facebook, and big losers as well. The key to success is remaining flexible and adapting to the changing times.

- **What are the principles of organization management?**

Structuring an organization means devising a division of labor (sometimes resulting in specialization), setting up teams or departments, and assigning responsibility and authority. It includes allocating resources (such as funds), assigning specific tasks, and establishing procedures for accomplishing the organizational objectives. Managers also have to make ethical decisions about how to treat workers.

Learning Goal 2. Compare the organizational theories of Fayol and Weber.

- **What were Fayol's basic principles?**

Fayol introduced principles such as unity of command, hierarchy of authority, division of labor, subordination of individual interests to the general interest, authority, clear communication channels, order, and equity.

- **What principles did Weber add?**

Weber added principles of bureaucracy such as job descriptions, written rules and decision guidelines, consistent procedures, and staffing and promotions based on qualifications.

Learning Goal 3. Evaluate the choices managers make in structuring organizations.

- **What are the four major choices in structuring organizations?**

Choices to make in structuring and restructuring organizations cover (1) centralization versus decentralization, (2) breadth of span of control, (3) tall versus flat organization structures, and (4) type of departmentalization.

- **What are the latest trends in structuring?**

Departments are often replaced or supplemented by matrix organizations and cross-functional teams that decentralize authority. The span of control becomes larger as employees become self-directed. Another trend is to eliminate managers and flatten organizations.

Learning Goal 4. Contrast the various organizational models.

- **What are the two major organizational models?**

Two traditional forms of organization are (1) line organizations and (2) line-and-staff organizations. A line organization has clearly defined responsibility and authority, is easy to understand, and provides each worker with only one supervisor. The expert advice of staff assistants in a line-and-staff organization helps in areas such as safety, quality control, computer technology, human resource management, and investing.

- **What are the key alternatives to the major organizational models?**
Matrix organizations assign people to projects temporarily and encourage interorganizational cooperation and teamwork. Cross-functional self-managed teams have all the benefits of the matrix style and are long-term.

Learning Goal 5. Identify the benefits of interfirm cooperation and coordination.
- **What are the major concepts involved in interfirm communications?**
Networking uses communications technology and other means to link organizations and allow them to work together on common objectives. A virtual corporation is a networked organization of replaceable firms that join and leave as needed. Benchmarking tells firms how their performance measures up to that of their competitors in specific functions. The company may then *outsource* to companies that perform its weaker functions more effectively and efficiently. The functions that are left are the firm's *core competencies*.
- **What is an inverted organization?**
An inverted organization places employees at the top of the hierarchy; managers are at the bottom to train and assist employees.

Learning Goal 6. Explain how organizational culture can help businesses adapt to change.
- **What is organizational culture?**
Organizational (or corporate) culture consists of the widely shared values within an organization that foster unity and cooperation to achieve common goals.
- **What is the difference between the formal and informal organization of a firm?**
The formal organization details lines of responsibility, authority, and position. It's the structure shown on organization charts. The informal organization is the system that develops spontaneously as employees meet and form cliques, relationships, and lines of authority outside the formal organization. It's the human side of the organization. The informal organization is an invaluable managerial asset that often promotes harmony among workers and establishes the corporate culture. As effective as the informal organization may be in creating group cooperation, it can still be equally powerful in resisting management directives.

key terms

benchmarking 218
bureaucracy 207
centralized authority 208
chain of command 207
core competencies 218
cross-functional self-managed teams 216
decentralized authority 208
departmentalization 210
digital natives 219
economies of scale 205
flat organization structure 209
formal organization 221
hierarchy 207
informal organization 221
inverted organization 220
line organization 213
line personnel 213
matrix organization 215
networking 217
organizational (or corporate) culture 220
real time 217
restructuring 219
span of control 208
staff personnel 213
tall organization structure 209
virtual corporation 217

Adapting Organizations to Today's Markets   *   **CHAPTER 8**   225

connect™ interactive applications

Reinforcing Your *Connection* to Concepts in Business

This chapter offers 15 interactive applications designed to help you apply what you've learned (examples of these exercises appear below). Your instructor has determined which interactive applications will benefit you throughout this course. Please refer to your instructor's assignment list in *Connect* to determine which applications you should complete.

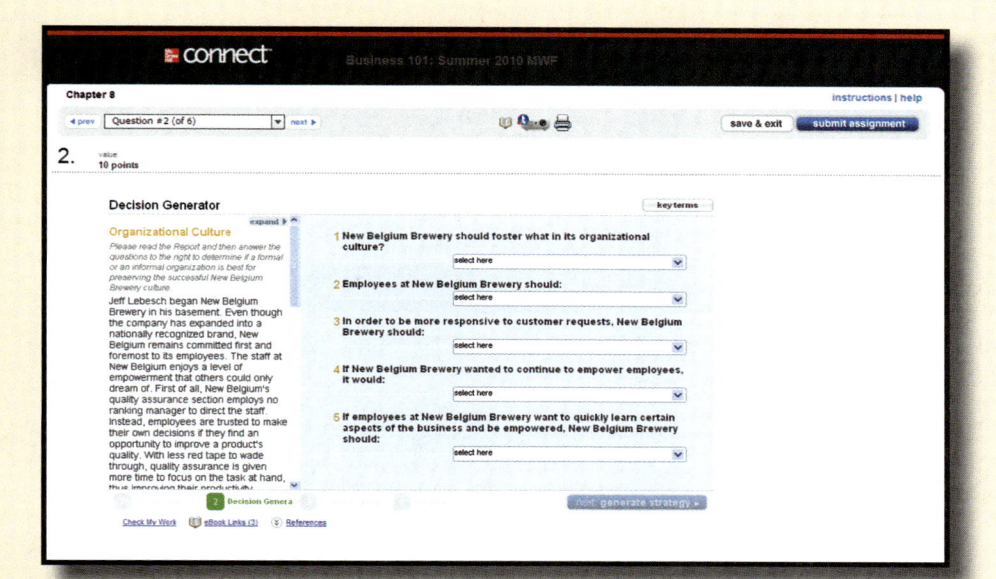

Decision Generator Interactive: An organizational culture contains two systems, the formal organization and the informal organization. The formal organization follows the traditional hierarchy while the informal organization contains the grapevine. The grapevine provides employees with unofficial information. Read the case regarding Belgium Brewery and answer the questions.

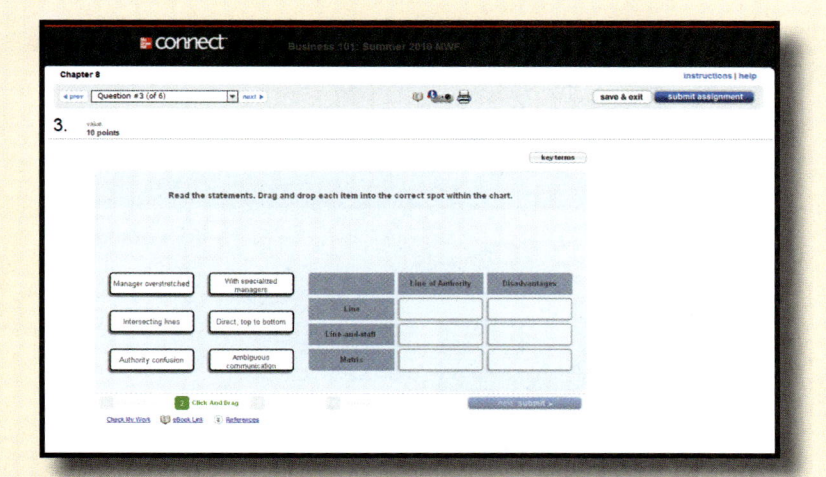

Click and Drag Interactive: Common forms of organization include line organization, line-and-staff organization, and matrix organization. Read the statements and drop each item in the correct box on the chart.

Click and Drag Interactive: Once mass production was introduced, companies had to adapt to new operating principles. As a result, certain organizational theories were introduced by Henri Fayol and Max Weber. Weber emphasized four principles: job descriptions, written rules, consistent procedures, and staffing and promotion based on qualification. Read the statements about each employee and move them to the appropriate place within the chart.

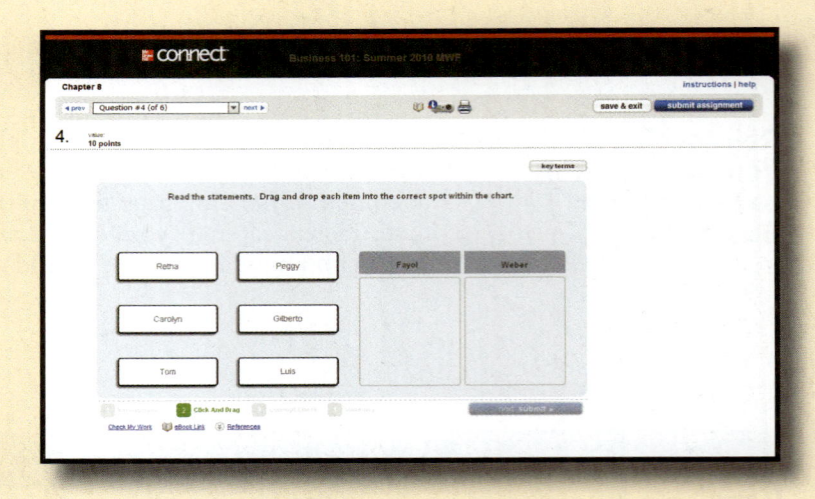

Click and Drag Interactive: Each organization must recognize the advantages and disadvantages of centralization and decentralization and structure their organization accordingly. Read the statements about the different companies and move them to the correct place within the chart.

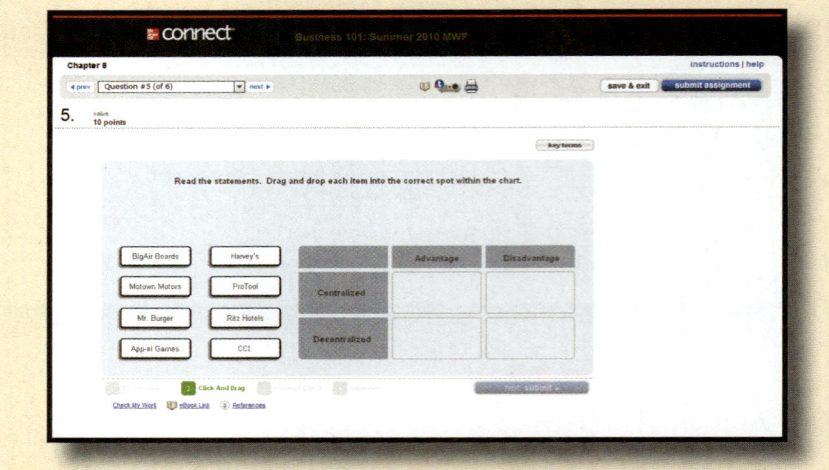

Video Case Interactive: Even though companies may have been founded using one type of organization structure and certain organizational theories, these companies may be changing. These changes are a result of today's business environment, which provides employees with empowerment. View the video regarding New Belgium Brewery and answer questions as prompted.

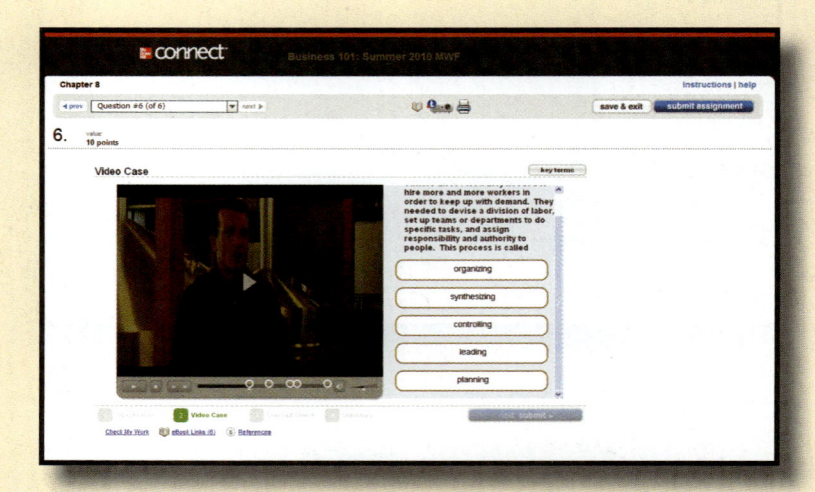

PRODUCTION and Operations Management

profile

Getting to Know x Samuel J. Palmisano
CEO and President of IBM

Few companies in the world are more familiar than IBM. What many people do not know is that although the company still produces servers and storage devices, IBM has shifted its emphasis from products to services. The person in charge of that dramatic change was Sam Palmisano.

Sam Palmisano, current CEO and president of IBM, started working as a salesperson for the company in 1973 after graduating from Johns Hopkins University with a degree in history. He became senior vice president and group executive of global services in 1998, and chairman in 2002.

An international company like IBM must always look toward the future and project what its strengths will be relative to competitors. When IBM looked at the PC market, for example, it decided making and selling PCs was not its strength. It sold its PC business to a Chinese firm and turned to other areas for growth. It turned out IBM had a major advantage in selling software and services. It had also established good relationships with customers in emerging markets like Brazil, Russia, India, and China. By turning toward software and services, IBM began growing much more rapidly. Palmisano believes the company will continue that pace into the future.

IBM also discovered that doing its own new-product development could be a slow and costly process. Thus it invested nearly $16 billion in acquiring more than 60 innovative companies. Now no company offers more information technology (IT) services than IBM. Its employees are able to help customers use less energy for the same or more computing. IBM also helps manage its customers' complex computing systems and integrates the information technologies of merging companies.

By switching IBM's focus from production to services, software, and customer support, Sam Palmisano has led his company into the fastest-growing segment of the global

LEARNING goals

After you have read and studied this chapter, you should be able to

1. Describe the current state of U.S. manufacturing and what manufacturers have done to become more competitive.

2. Describe the evolution from production to operations management.

3. Identify various production processes and describe techniques that improve productivity, including computer-aided design and manufacturing, flexible manufacturing, lean manufacturing, and mass customization.

4. Describe operations management planning issues including facility location, facility layout, materials requirement planning, purchasing, just-in-time inventory control, and quality control.

5. Explain the use of PERT and Gantt charts to control manufacturing processes.

connect

Your *Connect*ion to Better Learning. 1. View the interactive presentation. 2. Practice through LearnSmart. 3. Apply your knowledge by using the interactive applications for each chapter of this text.

1 Prep >>>>> 2 Study >>>>> 3 Apply

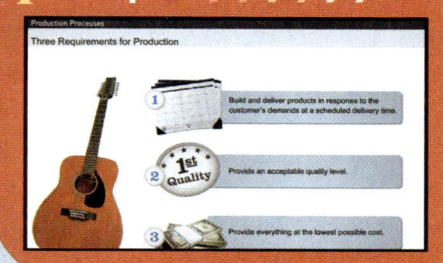

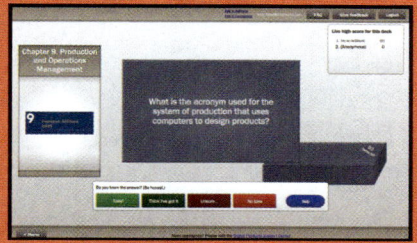

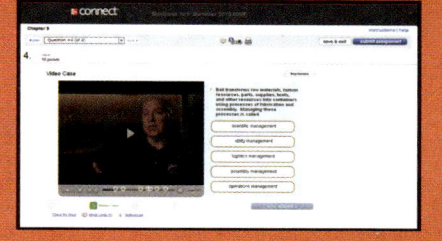

market—emerging markets. This chapter will explore what is occurring in the manufacturing sector now, and how the United States generally is moving from a production-based economy to a service economy.

Sources: Rex Crum, "IBM Earnings Up 22% on Services, Software Deals," *Marketwatch,* July 17, 2008; Mike Daniels, "Why IBM? Global Technology Services," *W3 News* (an IBM publication), March 18, 2008; "Terms of Trade," *The Washington Post,* January 5, 2009; and Samuel J. Palmisano, www.ibm.com, accessed July 28, 2010.

www.ibm.com

NAME THAT company

This hotel company takes its job very seriously, ensuring that all its services are of the highest quality, from the elevators to the restaurants, and staying attuned to what guests may need to make their stay fruitful and comfortable. No wonder this company has set the standard for luxury hotels around the world. Name that company. (Find the answer in the chapter.)

PPT 9-1: Production and Operations Management

PPT 9-2: Samuel J. Palmisano

PPT 9-3: Manufacturing in the U.S.

PPT 9-4: What's Made in the USA?

PPT 9-5: Exporters Extraordinaire

LEARNING goal 1 *

Describe the current state of U.S. manufacturing and what manufacturers have done to become more competitive.

MANUFACTURING AND SERVICES IN PERSPECTIVE

In November 2008, *The Washington Post* reported, "Activity in the nation's manufacturing sector . . . declined last month to the lowest level in more than two decades, offering economists more evidence that the country is entering a deep recession."[1] Soon after that, on January 29, 2009, *The Wall Street Journal* reported, "Joblessness was worst in the West and Midwest, indicating that the industries hit first by the recession—housing and manufacturing—continue to lose jobs."[2] Another *Wall Street Journal* article went on to say that unemployment could reach double-digit levels, home values could plunge a total of 36 percent, and stocks could fall a total of 55 percent.[3] Such events led President Obama and Congress to propose a stimulus package that would spend about a trillion dollars (including interest) to "create or save" millions of jobs and get the economy moving again—including manufacturing.[4] Much of this chapter is devoted to showing you what manufacturers and service providers can do to revive the U.S. economy to become world-class competitors.

From 2001 until the 2008 collapse, manufacturing output rose 4 percent a year.[5] Although some industries had experienced tough times, the United States was still the world's leading manufacturer, accounting for almost 25 percent of all goods produced in the world each year.[6]

Take the steel industry, for example. For the first time in decades, U.S. steel companies had been adding capacity and workers. A German steelmaker built a steel plant in Alabama expected to employ 2,700 workers. A Russian firm purchased a steel plant outside Baltimore, Maryland, and promised to invest half a billion dollars to update it and run it at capacity.[7] In the furniture industry, Ikea opened its first furniture plant in the United States in Danville, Virginia.[8] Wilson Sporting Goods was still making 700,000 footballs a year in Ada, Ohio.[9]

Thus, until recently, some areas of the country were enjoying economic growth from manufacturing while others were experiencing declines. One key to ending such declines was to adapt to the new realities and attract new manufacturers. Boston did that when it attracted many high-tech firms and became another Silicon Valley.

THINKING green

The Green Movement Improves the Economy

While on their honeymoon trip to Hong Kong, Thailand, and Bali, Bianca and Michael Alexander got the idea to start a business that would focus on the environment and promote a green lifestyle. Their new business, Conscious Planet Media Inc., offers a weekly broadband TV program as well as green event planning and consulting.

Overall the green economy is worth more than $209 billion annually and is expected to reach $1 trillion by 2020. Many consumers say that concepts such as "all natural," "locally grown," "company donates to causes I care about," and "energy efficient" all positively affect their purchasing decisions.

Other ideas for green products and services include:

- A green bed-and-breakfast with recycling bins in the bedrooms, a water-wise garden, green light bulbs, organic meals made from locally grown food, and more.
- Low water-use landscaping (xeriscaping) services.
- Green cleaning services that avoid chemicals that irritate the skin.

You get the idea. You don't have to look too far to find companies that promote organic products, companies that sell biodegradable products ranging from golf tees to coffins, companies that sell soy-based insulation, companies that sell worm-fueled composting and composting products in general. The market for new green products and services seems almost endless.

You can use the production and operations management skills discussed in this chapter to become successful in creating green products and services. The green movement is only beginning. Opportunities are everywhere.

Sources: Glenn Croston, "Go Green," *Entrepreneur,* December 2008; "Take a Tour," *Advertising Age,* June 9, 2008; Steve Garmhausen, "Growing a Green Business," *Black Enterprise,* April 2008; Stephanie Simon, "Green Businesses Jump on Opportunity in Denver," *The Wall Street Journal,* August 28, 2008; and Mike Hogan, "An Online Guide to the Green Scene," *Barron's,* March 2, 2009.

American industry is doing what it can to rebuild. The construction industry is ready to build homes that are easier to heat and cool, and U.S. automakers are scrambling to stage a comeback with more competitive vehicles.[10] The Thinking Green box discusses how entrepreneurs are building new green ventures that will lead to more employment and a stronger economy.[11]

Don't expect a comeback to result in the same number of jobs as were available before the recession. Just as U.S. productivity gains in agriculture lowered the number of farmers needed, today's productivity gains in manufacturing have lowered the number of manufacturing workers companies require. *The U.S. economy is no longer manufacturing-based.* About 70 percent of U.S. GDP and 85 percent of U.S. jobs now come from the *service sector.*[12] In fact, the majority of college graduates in the future are likely to be employed in the service sector. Top-paying jobs already exist in legal services; medical services; entertainment; broadcasting; and business services such as accounting, finance, and management consulting.[13] In fact, the service sector in general has suffered along with manufacturing as a result of the economic slowdown, but not nearly as much.[14]

Manufacturers and Service Organizations Become More Competitive

U.S. producers no longer strike fear in the heart of foreign competitors. In fact, they have much to learn from them, although one reason foreign producers have become so competitive is that they are using U.S. technology and

◄ **PPT 9-7:**
The "Green" Movement Improves the Economy

◄ **PPT 9-6:**
Massive Manufacturers

◄ **LECTURE LINK 9-1:**
The Military Learns From NASCAR

◄ **LECTURE LINK 9-2:**
Auto Suppliers Escape the Recession Overseas

concepts to increase effectiveness and efficiency. Overall, that's a good thing because it helps reduce poverty and hunger in developing countries and opens new markets to the developed world. IBM and other major companies are growing by providing needed goods and services to those developing markets.[15]

Foreign producers are also streaming to the United States to take advantage of its labor force and opportunities. The United States is still the leader in nanotechnology, biotechnology, and other areas.[16] Its workforce is creative and dynamic. Nonetheless, U.S. business cannot stand still; it must keep up with the latest production techniques and processes.

As the U.S. service sector becomes a larger part of the overall economy, managers will be more occupied with service productivity, and with blending services and manufacturing through the Internet.[17] How can U.S. manufacturers and service organizations maintain a competitive edge? Most of them can and are:

- Focusing more on customers.
- Maintaining closer relationships with suppliers and other companies to satisfy customer needs.
- Practicing continuous improvement.
- Focusing on quality.
- Saving on costs through site selection.
- Relying on the Internet to unite companies that work together.
- Adopting production techniques such as enterprise resource planning, computer integrated manufacturing, flexible manufacturing, and lean manufacturing.

This chapter explores these and other operations management techniques in both the service and the manufacturing sectors.[18] We'll begin by going over a few key terms.

Honda is just one of many auto manufacturers that have insourced jobs to the United States. Why do you suppose so many news reports emphasize outsourcing when thousands of jobs are created by insourcing?

▶ **PPT 9-8:**
Top Paying Service Jobs

▶ **PPT 9-9:**
Remaining Competitive in Global Markets

▶ **CRITICAL THINKING EXERCISE 9-1:**
Group Project: Organizing Production

production
The creation of finished goods and services using the factors of production: land, labor, capital, entrepreneurship, and knowledge.

production management
The term used to describe all the activities managers do to help their firms create goods.

LEARNING goal 2 *

Describe the evolution from production to operations management.

FROM PRODUCTION TO OPERATIONS MANAGEMENT

Production is the creation of finished goods and services using the factors of production: land, labor, capital, entrepreneurship, and knowledge (see Chapter 1). Production has historically meant *manufacturing*, and the term **production management** has described the management activities that helped firms create goods. But, as noted above, the nature of business has changed significantly over the last 20 years as the service sector, including Internet services, has grown dramatically. *The United States has become a service economy—that is, one dominated by the service sector.*

Operations management is a specialized area in management that converts or transforms resources, including human resources like technical skills and innovation, into goods and services. It includes inventory management, quality control, production scheduling, follow-up services, and more. In an automobile plant, operations management transforms raw materials, human resources, parts, supplies, paints, tools, and other resources into automobiles. It does this through the processes of fabrication and assembly.

In a college or university, operations management takes inputs such as information, professors, supplies, buildings, offices, and computer systems—and creates services that transform students into educated people. It does this through a process called education. For a more extensive discussion, see the Free Management Library's entry on operations management (www.managementhelp.org/ops_mgnt/ops_mgnt.htm).

Some organizations—such as factories, farms, and mines—produce mostly goods. Others—such as hospitals, schools, and government agencies—produce mostly services. Still others produce a combination of goods and services.[19] For example, an automobile manufacturer not only makes cars but also provides services such as repairs, financing, and insurance. At Wendy's you get goods such as hamburgers and fries, but you also get services such as order taking, order filling, food preparation, and cleanup.

Operations Management in the Service Sector

Operations management in the service industry is all about creating a good experience for those who use the service.[20] In a Ritz-Carlton hotel, for example, operations management includes restaurants that offer the finest in service, elevators that run smoothly, and a front desk that processes people quickly. It may include fresh-cut flowers in the lobbies and dishes of fruit in every room. More important, it may mean spending thousands of dollars to provide training in quality management for every new employee.[21]

Ritz-Carlton's commitment to quality is apparent in the many innovations and changes the company has initiated over the years. These innovations included installation of a sophisticated computerized guest-recognition program and a quality management program designed to ensure that all employees are "certified" in their positions.

Hotel customers today want in-room Internet access and a help center with toll-free telephone service. Executives traveling on business may need video equipment and a host of computer hardware and other aids. Foreign visitors would like multilingual customer-support services. Hotel shops need to carry more than souvenirs, newspapers, and some drugstore and food items to serve today's high-tech travelers: the shops may also carry laptop computer supplies, electrical adapters, and the like. Operations management is responsible for locating and providing such amenities to make customers happy. Ritz-Carlton uses an internal measurement system to assess the performance results of its service delivery system.

operations management
A specialized area in management that converts or transforms resources (including human resources) into goods and services.

◀ PPT 9-10:
Production and Production Management

◀ PPT 9-11:
Operations Management

Each year companies discover new ways of automating that eliminate the need for human labor. This photo shows an automated apparatus known as a Flipper. Are McDonald's or any other restaurants in your area using equipment like this?

◀ LECTURE LINK 9-3:
Speeding Up the Drive Through

◀ PPT 9-12:
Progress Assessment

In short, delighting customers by anticipating their needs has become the quality standard for luxury hotels, as it has for most other service businesses. But knowing customer needs and satisfying them are two different things.[22] That's why operations management is so important: it is the implementation phase of management. Can you see the need for better operations management in airports, hospitals, government agencies, schools, and nonprofits like the Red Cross? The opportunities seem almost unlimited. Much of the future of U.S. growth is in these service areas, but growth is also needed in manufacturing. Next we'll explore production processes and what companies are doing to keep the United States competitive in that area.

> Operations management for services is all about enriching the customer experience. Hotels, for instance, have responded to the needs of business travelers with in-room Internet access and other kinds of office-style support, as well as stored information about the preferences of frequent guests. How important do you think guest-recognition programs are to business travelers?

progress assessment

- What have U.S. manufacturers done to regain a competitive edge?
- What must U.S. companies do to continue to strengthen the country's manufacturing base?
- What led companies to focus on operations management rather than production?

LEARNING goal 3 *

Identify various production processes and describe techniques that improve productivity, including computer-aided design and manufacturing, flexible manufacturing, lean manufacturing, and mass customization.

> PPT 9-13:
> The Production Process

form utility
The value producers add to materials in the creation of finished goods and services.

figure 9.1

THE PRODUCTION PROCESS
The production process consists of taking the factors of production (land, etc.) and using those inputs to produce goods, services, and ideas. Planning, routing, scheduling, and the other activities are the means to accomplish the objective—output.

PRODUCTION PROCESSES

Common sense and some experience have already taught you much of what you need to know about production processes. You know what it takes to write a term paper or prepare a dinner. You need money to buy the materials, you need a place to work, and you need to be organized to get the task done. The same is true of the production process in industry. It uses basic inputs to produce outputs (see Figure 9.1). Production adds value, or utility, to materials or processes.

Form utility is the value producers add to materials in the creation of finished goods and services, such as by transforming silicon into computer chips

INPUTS	PRODUCTION CONTROL	OUTPUTS
Land Labor Capital Entrepreneurship Knowledge	Planning Routing Scheduling Dispatching Follow-up	Goods Services Ideas

or putting services together to create a vacation package. Form utility can exist at the retail level as well. For example, a butcher can produce a specific cut of beef from a whole cow, or a baker can make a specific type of cake from basic ingredients. We'll be discussing utility in more detail in Chapter 15.

Manufacturers use several different processes to produce goods. Andrew S. Grove, the former chairman of computer chip manufacturer Intel, uses this analogy to explain production:

> *Imagine that you're a chef . . . and that your task is to serve a breakfast consisting of a three-minute soft-boiled egg, buttered toast, and coffee. Your job is to prepare and deliver the three items simultaneously, each of them fresh and hot.*

Grove says this task encompasses the three basic requirements of production: (1) to build and deliver products in response to the demands of the customer at a scheduled delivery time, (2) to provide an acceptable quality level, and (3) to provide everything at the lowest possible cost.

Let's use the breakfast example to understand process and assembly. **Process manufacturing** physically or chemically changes materials. For example, boiling physically changes the egg. Similarly, process manufacturing turns sand into glass or computer chips. The **assembly process** puts together components (eggs, toast, and coffee) to make a product (breakfast). Cars are made through an assembly process that puts together the frame, engine, and other parts.

Production processes are either continuous or intermittent. A **continuous process** is one in which long production runs turn out finished goods over time. As a chef, you could have a conveyor belt that continuously lowers eggs into boiling water for three minutes and then lifts them out. A three-minute egg would be available whenever you wanted one. A chemical plant, for example, is run on a continuous process.

It usually makes more sense when responding to specific customer orders to use an **intermittent process**. Here the production run is short (one or two eggs) and the producer adjusts machines frequently to make different products (like the oven in a bakery or the toaster in the diner). Manufacturers of custom-designed furniture would use an intermittent process.

Today many manufacturers use intermittent processes. Computers, robots, and flexible manufacturing processes allow firms to turn out custom-made goods almost as fast as mass-produced goods were once produced. We'll discuss how they do that in more detail in the next few sections as we explore advanced production techniques and technology.

◄ **PPT 9-14:**
Form Utility

◄ **PPT 9-15:**
Grove's Basic Production Requirements

◄ **CRITICAL THINKING EXERCISE 9-2:**
Production Processes

◄ **PPT 9-16:**
Process and Assembly in Production

◄ **LECTURE LINK 9-4:**
Innovation: The Totes

◄ **PPT 9-17:**
Key Production Processes

◄ **PPT 9-18:**
Made in a Minute

process manufacturing
That part of the production process that physically or chemically changes materials.

assembly process
That part of the production process that puts together components.

continuous process
A production process in which long production runs turn out finished goods over time.

intermittent process
A production process in which the production run is short and the machines are changed frequently to make different products.

Production lines allow for the efficient and speedy production of goods that are consistent in size, weight, color, and other measures of quality. How many products can you think of that are likely made on a production line?

Margin Notes

▶ PPT 9-19:
Developments Making U.S. Companies More Competitive

computer-aided design (CAD)
The use of computers in the design of products.

computer-aided manufacturing (CAM)
The use of computers in the manufacturing of products.

computer-integrated manufacturing (CIM)
The uniting of computer-aided design with computer-aided manufacturing.

▶ LECTURE LINK 9-5:
Robo-Revolution

3-D CAD tools allow designers to create cloth prototypes without a pattern's traditional stages, seaming, trying on, alterations, etc. What advantages might this technology offer to smaller manufacturing companies?

▶ PPT 9-20:
Computer-Aided Design and Manufacturing

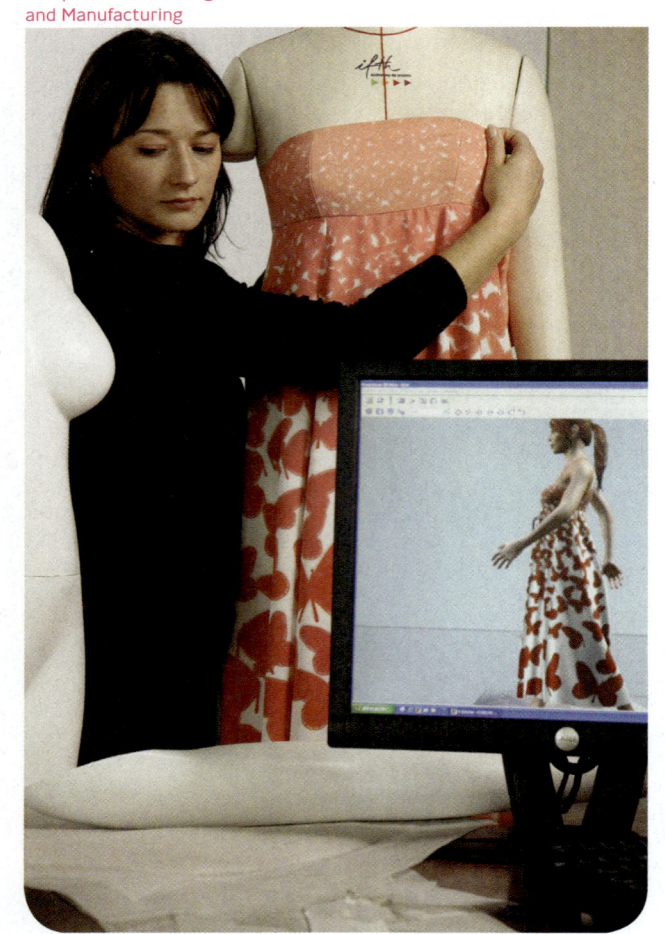

The Need to Improve Production Techniques and Cut Costs

The ultimate goal of operations management is to provide high-quality goods and services instantaneously in response to customer demand. As we stress throughout this book, traditional organizations were simply not designed to be so responsive to the customer. Rather, they were designed to make goods efficiently (inexpensively). The idea behind mass production was to make a large number of a limited variety of products at very low cost.

Over the years, low cost often came at the expense of quality and flexibility. Furthermore, suppliers didn't always deliver when they said they would, so manufacturers had to carry large inventories of raw materials and components to keep producing. Such inefficiencies made U.S. companies vulnerable to foreign competitors who were using more advanced production techniques.

As a result of new global competition, companies have had to make a wide variety of high-quality custom-designed products at very low cost. Clearly, something had to change on the production floor to make that possible. Several major developments have made U.S. companies more competitive: (1) computer-aided design and manufacturing, (2) flexible manufacturing, (3) lean manufacturing, and (4) mass customization.

Computer-Aided Design and Manufacturing

The one development that has changed production techniques more than any other is the integration of computers into the design and manufacturing of products. The first thing computers did was help in the design of products, in a process called **computer-aided design (CAD)**. Today CAD systems allow designers to work in three dimensions.

The next step was to bring computers directly into the production process with **computer-aided manufacturing (CAM)**. CAD/CAM, the use of both computer-aided design and computer-aided manufacturing, makes it possible to custom-design products to meet the needs of small markets with very little increase in cost. A manufacturer programs the computer to make a simple design change, and that change is readily incorporated into production. In the clothing industry, a computer program establishes a pattern and cuts the cloth automatically, even adjusting to a specific person's dimensions to create custom-cut clothing at little additional cost. In food service, CAM supports on-site, small-scale, semiautomated, sensor-controlled baking in fresh-baked cookie shops to make consistent quality easy to achieve.

CAD has doubled productivity in many firms. But in the past CAD machines couldn't talk to CAM machines directly. Today, however, software programs unite CAD and CAM: the result is **computer-integrated manufacturing (CIM)**. The software is expensive, but it cuts as much as 80 percent of the time needed to program machines to make parts. The printing company Johns-Byrne uses CIM in its Niles, Illinois, plant and has noticed decreased overhead, reduced outlay of resources, and fewer errors. Consult the *International Journal of Computer-Integrated Manufacturing* for other examples.

Flexible Manufacturing

Flexible manufacturing means designing machines to do multiple tasks so they can produce a variety of products. Allen-Bradley, part of Rockwell Automation, uses flexible manufacturing to build motor starters. Orders come in daily, and within 24 hours the company's 26 machines and robots manufacture, test, and package the starters—which are untouched by human hands. Allen-Bradley's machines are so flexible that managers can include a special order, even a single item, in the assembly without slowing down the process. Did you notice that these products were made without any labor? One way to compete with cheap overseas labor is to have as few workers as possible.

Lean Manufacturing

Lean manufacturing is the production of goods using less of everything than in mass production: less human effort, less manufacturing space, less investment in tools, and less engineering time to develop a new product. A company becomes lean by continuously increasing its capacity to produce high-quality goods while decreasing its need for resources.[23] Here are some characteristics of lean companies:[24]

- They take half the human effort.[25]
- They have half the defects in the finished product or service.
- They require one-third the engineering effort.
- They use half the floor space for the same output.
- They carry 90 percent less inventory.

Technological improvements are largely responsible for the increase in productivity and efficiency of U.S. plants. That technology made labor more productive and made it possible to pay higher wages. On the other hand, employees can get frustrated by innovations (e.g., they must learn new processes), and companies must constantly train and retrain employees to stay competitive.[26] The need for more productivity and efficiency has never been greater. The solution to the economic crisis depends on such innovations. One step in the process is to make products more individualistic. The next section discusses how that happens.

Mass Customization

To *customize* means to make a unique product or provide a specific service to specific individuals.[27] Although it once may have seemed impossible, **mass customization**, which means tailoring products to meet the needs of a large number of individual customers, is now practiced widely.[28] The National Bicycle Industrial Company in Japan makes 18 bicycle models in more than 2 million combinations, each designed to fit the needs of a specific customer. The customer chooses the model, size, color, and design. The retailer takes various measurements from the buyer and faxes the data to the factory, where robots handle the bulk of the assembly.

More and more manufacturers are learning to customize their products. Some colleges, even, are developing promotions for individual students.[29] Some General Nutrition Center (GNC) stores feature machines that enable shoppers to custom-design their own vitamins, shampoo, and lotions. The Custom Foot stores use infrared scanners to precisely measure each foot so that shoes can be made to fit perfectly. Adidas can make each shoe fit perfectly for each customer. InterActive Custom Clothes

---

flexible manufacturing
Designing machines to do multiple tasks so that they can produce a variety of products.

◀ **LECTURE LINK 9-6:**
Kodak Learns Speed

◀ **PPT 9-21:**
Flexible Manufacturing

◀ **PPT 9-22:**
Lean Manufacturing

lean manufacturing
The production of goods using less of everything compared to mass production.

mass customization
Tailoring products to meet the needs of individual customers.

◀ **PPT 9-23:**
Mass Customization

Dell has refined the process of mass customization by setting up its manufacturing processes so that all its computers can be quickly assembled to individual customer order. What other products could benefit from such an assembly process?

offers a wide variety of options in custom-made jeans, including four different rivet colors. You can even buy custom-made M&M's in colors of your choice.

Mass customization exists in the service sector as well. Capital Protective Insurance (CPI) uses the latest computer software and hardware to sell customized risk-management plans to companies. Health clubs offer unique fitness programs for individuals, travel agencies provide vacation packages that vary according to individual choices, and some colleges allow students to design their own majors. It is much easier to custom-design service programs than to custom-make goods, because there is no fixed tangible good to adapt. Each customer can specify what he or she wants, within the limits of the service organization—limits that seem to be ever-widening.

As you learned in the opening Profile, manufacturing companies may become service companies over time. As you shall see, operations management concepts are applicable in both situations.

progress assessment

- What is form utility?
- Define and differentiate the following: process manufacturing, assembly process, continuous process, and intermittent process.
- What do you call the integration of CAD and CAM?
- What is mass customization?

LEARNING goal 4 *

Describe operations management planning issues including facility location, facility layout, materials requirement planning, purchasing, just-in-time inventory control, and quality control.

OPERATIONS MANAGEMENT PLANNING

Operations management planning helps solve many of the problems in the service and manufacturing sectors. These include facility location, facility layout, materials requirement planning, purchasing, inventory control, and quality control. The resources used may be different, but the management issues are similar.

Facility Location

Facility location is the process of selecting a geographic location for a company's operations. In keeping with the need to focus on customers, one strategy is to find a site that makes it easy for consumers to use the company's services and to communicate about their needs. Flower shops and banks have placed facilities in supermarkets so that their products and services are more accessible than in freestanding facilities. You can find a McDonald's inside some Wal-Mart stores and gas stations. Customers order and pay for their meals at the pumps, and by the time they've filled their tanks, it's time to pick up their food.

The ultimate in convenience is never having to leave home to get services. That's why there is so much interest in Internet banking, Internet shopping, online education, and other services. For brick-and-mortar retailers to beat such competition, they have to choose good locations and offer outstanding

facility location
The process of selecting a geographic location for a company's operations.

service. Study the location of service-sector businesses—such as hotels, banks, athletic clubs, and supermarkets—and you'll see that the most successful are conveniently located. Google is building large data centers in the United States where states give out tax breaks and cheap electricity is readily available in large quantities. They are also located near bodies of water for cooling their servers.[30]

Facility Location for Manufacturers

Volkswagen's factory in Bratislava, Slovakia, turns out 250,000 cars a year, including Audi's Q7 SUV, that used to be made in Western European plants. Geographic shifts in production sometimes result in pockets of unemployment in some geographic areas and tremendous growth in others. We are witnessing such changes in the United States, as automobile production shifted from Detroit to more southern cities.

Why would companies spend millions of dollars to move their facilities from one location to another? In their decisions they consider labor costs; availability of resources, including labor; access to transportation that can reduce time to market; proximity to suppliers; proximity to customers; crime rates; quality of life for employees; cost of living; and the need to train or retrain the local workforce.

Even though labor is becoming a smaller percentage of total cost in highly automated industries, availability of low-cost labor or the right kind of skilled labor remains a key reason many producers move their plants to Malaysia, China, India, Mexico, and other countries. In general, however, U.S. manufacturing firms tend to pay more and offer more benefits than local firms elsewhere in the world. One result of the financial crisis of 2008–2010 is that U.S. workers may be forced to take less pay and receive fewer benefits in order to stay competitive.

Inexpensive resources are another major reason for moving production facilities. Companies usually need water, electricity, wood, coal, and other basic resources. By moving to areas where these are inexpensive and plentiful, firms can significantly lower not only the cost of buying such resources but also the cost of shipping finished products. Often the most important resource is people, so companies tend to cluster where smart and talented people are. Witness Silicon Valley in California and similar areas in Colorado, Massachusetts, Virginia, Texas, Maryland, and other states.

Time-to-market is another decision-making factor. As manufacturers attempt to compete globally, they need sites that allow products to move quickly, at the lowest costs, so they can be delivered to customers fast. Access to highways, rail lines, waterways, and airports is thus critical. Information technology (IT) is also important to quicken response time, so many firms are seeking countries with the most advanced information systems.

Another way to work closely with suppliers to satisfy customers' needs is to locate production facilities near supplier facilities. That cuts the cost of distribution and makes communication easier.

Many businesses are building factories in foreign countries to get closer to their international customers.[31] That's a major reason the Japanese automaker Honda builds cars in Ohio and the German company Mercedes builds them in Alabama. When U.S. firms select foreign sites, they consider whether they are near airports, waterways, and highways so that raw and finished goods can move quickly and easily.

Facility location is a major decision for manufacturing and other companies that must take into account the availability of qualified workers; access to suppliers, customers, and transportation; and local regulations including zoning and taxes. How has the growth of Internet commerce affected company location decisions?

MAKING ethical decisions

www.ethics.ubc.ca/resources/business

Stay or Leave?

Suppose the hypothetical company ChildrenWear Industries has long been the economic foundation for its hometown. Most of the area's small businesses and schools either supply materials the firm needs for production or train its future employees. ChildrenWear has learned that if it were to move its production facilities to Asia, however, it could increase its profits by 25 percent.

Closing operations in the company's hometown would cause many of the town's other businesses, such as restaurants, to fail—leaving a high percentage of the town's adults unemployed, with no options for reemployment there. As a top manager at ChildrenWear, you must help decide whether the plant should be moved and, if so, how soon the firm should tell employees. The law says you must tell them at least 60 days before closing the plant. What alternatives do you have? What are the consequences of each? Which will you choose?

> PPT 9-27:
> Stay or Leave

Businesses also study the quality of life for workers and managers. Are good schools nearby? Is the weather nice? Is the crime rate low? Does the local community welcome new businesses?[32] Do the chief executive and other key managers want to live there? Sometimes a region with a high quality of life is also an expensive one, which complicates the decision. In short, facility location has become a critical issue in operations management. The Making Ethical Decisions box looks at the kinds of decisions companies must make when it comes to locating.

> PPT 9-28:
> Operations Management on the Internet

Taking Operations Management to the Internet

Many rapidly growing companies do very little production themselves. Instead, they outsource engineering, design, manufacturing, and other tasks to companies such as Flextronics and Sanmina-SCI that specialize in those functions. They create new relationships with suppliers over the Internet, making operations management an *interfirm* process in which companies work closely together to design, produce, and ship products to customers.

> CRITICAL THINKING EXERCISE 9-3:
> Site Selection

Manufacturing companies are developing Internet-focused strategies that will enable them and others to compete more effectively in the future. These changes are having a dramatic effect on operations managers as they adjust from a one-firm system to an *interfirm* environment and from a relatively stable environment to one that is constantly changing and evolving.

Facility Location in the Future

> PPT 9-29:
> Future Facility Location

Information technology (IT)—that is computers, modems, e-mail, voice mail, text messaging, and teleconferencing—is giving firms and employees increased flexibility to choose locations while staying in the competitive mainstream.[33] **Telecommuting**, working from home via computer and modem, is a major trend in business. Companies that no longer need to locate near sources of labor will be able to move to areas where land is less expensive and the quality of life may be higher. Furthermore, more salespeople are keeping in touch with the company and its customers through teleconferencing, using computers to talk with and show images to others.[34]

> **telecommuting**
> Working from home via computer and modem.

REACHING BEYOND our borders

www.lockheedmartin.com

Partnering Beyond Country Borders

Can you imagine how hard it is to manage the construction of a combat jet airplane? Now try to imagine how hard it would be if the plane were being built by 80 different suppliers in 187 different locations while the U.S. Air Force, Navy, and Marines; the British Defense Ministry; and eight other U.S. allies (e.g., the United Kingdom, Canada, and Italy) were watching progress, making comments, and changing the plans if necessary. What kind of person could pull all that together?

The man who led this huge project was Dain Hancock of Lockheed Martin. Hancock had the responsibility, with the help of others, of uniting 80 companies into a single production unit. To do that, Lockheed and its partner companies used a system of 90 Web software tools to share designs, track the exchange of documents, and keep an eye on progress.

The Internet enables people from different companies with incompatible computer systems to meet on Web sites, share documents, and speak a common language. They can also use electronic whiteboards on which two or more people can draw pictures or charts as others watch and comment in real time.

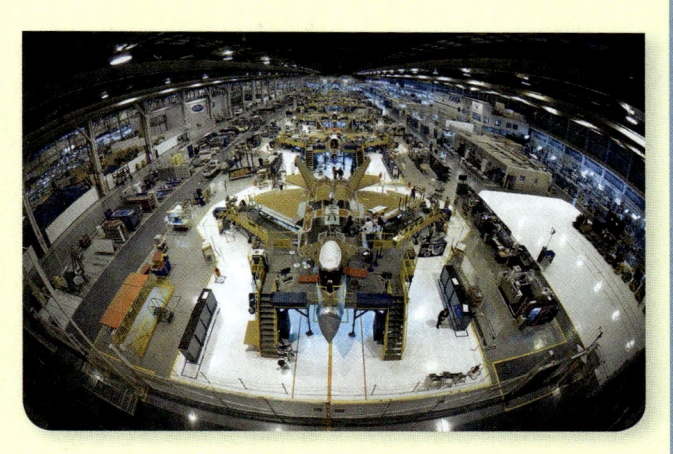

Hancock and other managers are taking operations management beyond the control of one plant to make the best use of multiple plants in multiple locations, often in multiple countries. The Internet has changed business in many ways, but probably none is as dramatic as this.

One big incentive to locate in a particular city or state is the tax situation there and degree of government support. Some states and local governments have higher taxes than others, yet many compete fiercely by offering companies tax reductions and other support, such as zoning changes and financial aid, so they will locate there. The Reaching Beyond Our Borders box explores how one company has handled the complex role of managing production facilities all over the world.

Facility Layout

Facility layout is the physical arrangement of resources, including people, to most efficiently produce goods and provide services for customers. Facility layout depends greatly on the processes that are to be performed. For services, the layout is usually designed to help the consumer find and buy things, including on the Internet. Some stores have kiosks that enable customers to search for goods online and place orders or make returns and credit payments in the store. In short, the facilities and Internet capabilities of service organizations are becoming more customer-oriented.

Some service-oriented organizations, such as hospitals, use layouts that improve efficiency, just as manufacturers do. For manufacturing plants, facilities layout has become critical because cost savings of efficient layouts are enormous.

Many companies are moving from an *assembly-line layout*, in which workers do only a few tasks at a time, to a *modular layout*, in which teams of workers combine to produce more complex units of the final product. There

◀ PPT 9-30:
Partnering Beyond Country Borders

◀ LECTURE LINK 9-7:
Wyeth Biotech

◀ PPT 9-31:
Setting Up the Facility

facility layout
The physical arrangement of resources (including people) in the production process.

> At Cisco Systems, work spaces in some offices are fluid and unassigned, so employees with laptops and mobile phones can choose where to sit when they arrive each day. What do you think are some of the advantages of such nontraditional facility layouts? Are there any disadvantages?

▶ CRITICAL THINKING EXERCISE 9-4:
Designing Plant Layout

▶ PPT 9-32:
Facility Layout Options

▶ LECTURE LINK 9-8:
Spying on the Green Giant

▶ PPT 9-37:
MRP and ERP

materials requirement planning (MRP)
A computer-based operations management system that uses sales forecasts to make sure that needed parts and materials are available at the right time and place.

enterprise resource planning (ERP)
A newer version of materials requirement planning (MRP) that combines the computerized functions of all the divisions and subsidiaries of the firm—such as finance, human resources, and order fulfillment—into a single integrated software program that uses a single database.

may have been a dozen or more workstations on an assembly line to complete an automobile engine in the past, but all that work might be done in one module today.

When working on a major project, such as a bridge or an airplane, companies use a *fixed-position layout* that allows workers to congregate around the product to be completed.

A *process layout* is one in which similar equipment and functions are grouped together. The order in which the product visits a function depends on the design of the item. This allows for flexibility. The Igus manufacturing plant in Cologne, Germany, can shrink or expand in a flash. Its flexible design keeps it competitive in a fast-changing market. Because the layout of the plant changes so often, some employees use scooters in order to more efficiently provide needed skills, supplies, and services to multiple workstations. A fast-changing plant needs a fast-moving employee base to achieve maximum productivity. Figure 9.2 illustrates typical layout designs.

Materials Requirement Planning

Materials requirement planning (MRP) is a computer-based operations management system that uses sales forecasts to make sure needed parts and materials are available at the right time and place. **Enterprise resource planning (ERP)**, a newer version of MRP, combines the computerized functions of all the divisions and subsidiaries of the firm—such as finance, human resources, and order fulfillment—into a single integrated software program that uses a single database. The result is shorter time between orders and payment, less staff needed to do ordering and order processing, reduced inventories, and better customer service. For example, the customer can place an order, either through a customer service representative or online, and immediately see when the order will be filled and how much it will cost. The representative can instantly see the customer's credit rating and order history, the company's inventory, and the shipping schedule. Everyone else in the company can see the new order as well; thus when one department finishes its portion, the order is automatically routed via the ERP system to the next department. The customer can see exactly where the order is at any point by logging into the system.[35]

Production and Operations Management * CHAPTER 9   243

PRODUCT LAYOUT (also called Assembly Line Layout)
Used to produce large quantities of a few types of products.

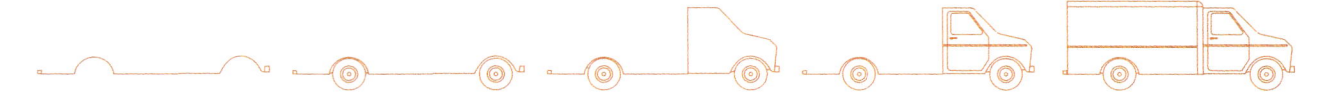

PROCESS LAYOUT
Frequently used in operations that serve different customers' different needs.

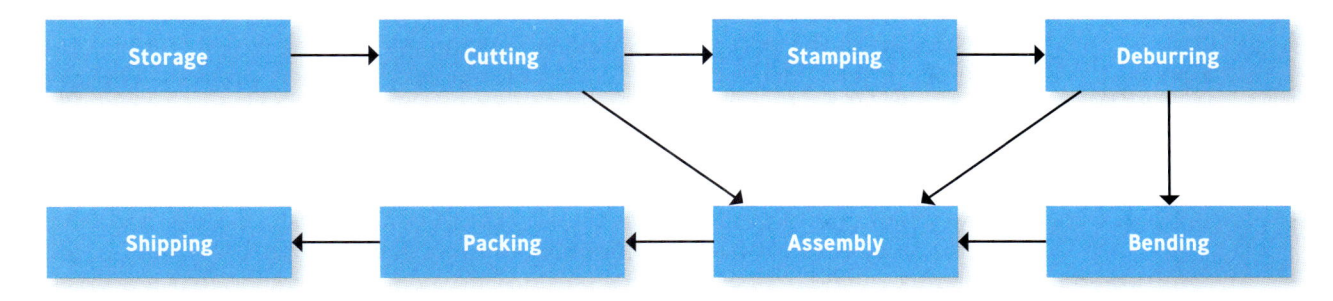

Storage → Cutting → Stamping → Deburring
Shipping ← Packing ← Assembly ← Bending

CELLULAR or MODULE LAYOUT
Can accommodate changes in design or customer demand.

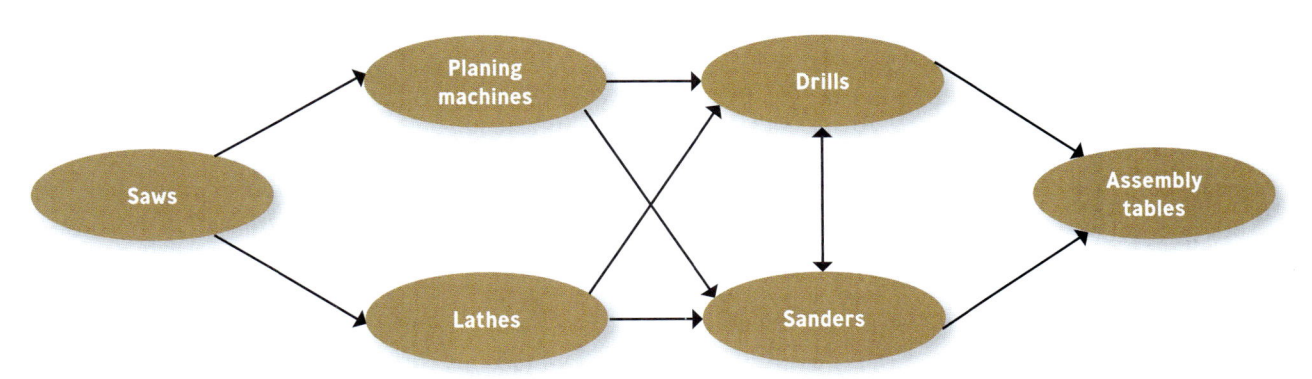

Saws → Planing machines → Drills → Assembly tables
Saws → Lathes → Sanders → Assembly tables

FIXED-POSITION LAYOUT
A major feature of planning is scheduling work operations.

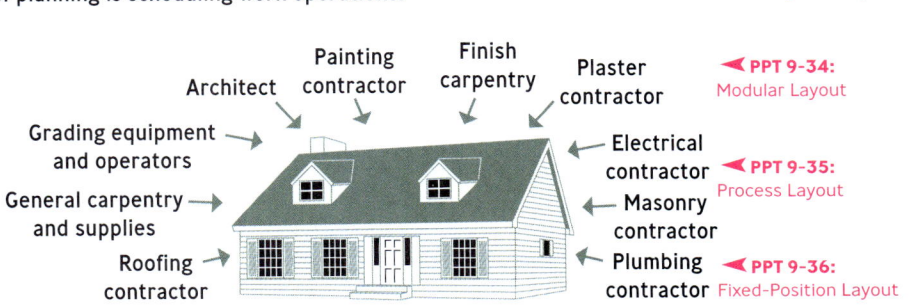

- Architect
- Painting contractor
- Finish carpentry
- Plaster contractor
- Grading equipment and operators
- General carpentry and supplies
- Roofing contractor
- Electrical contractor
- Masonry contractor
- Plumbing contractor

◄ PPT 9-33: Assembly Line Layout
◄ PPT 9-34: Modular Layout
◄ PPT 9-35: Process Layout
◄ PPT 9-36: Fixed-Position Layout

figure 9.2
TYPICAL LAYOUT DESIGNS

Purchasing

Purchasing is the function that searches for high-quality material resources, finds the best suppliers, and negotiates the best price for quality goods and services.[36] In the past, manufacturers dealt with many suppliers so that if one couldn't deliver, the firm could get materials from someone else. Today, however, manufacturers rely more heavily on just one or two suppliers, because the relationship between suppliers and manufacturers is much closer than before. Producers share so much information that they don't want too many suppliers knowing their business.

The Internet has transformed the purchasing function. A business looking for supplies can contact an Internet-based purchasing service and find the best items at the best price. Similarly, a company wishing to sell supplies can use the Internet to find all the companies looking for such supplies. The time and dollar cost of purchasing items has thus been reduced tremendously.

Just-in-Time Inventory Control

One major cost of production is the expense of holding parts, motors, and other items in storage for later use. Storage not only subjects items to obsolescence, pilferage, and damage but also requires construction and maintenance of costly warehouses. To cut such costs, many companies have implemented a concept called **just-in-time (JIT) inventory control**. JIT systems keep a minimum of inventory on the premises—and deliver parts, supplies, and other needs just in time to go on the assembly line. To work effectively, however, the process requires an accurate production schedule (using ERP) and excellent coordination with carefully selected suppliers, who are usually connected electronically so they know what will be needed and when. Sometimes the suppliers build new facilities close to the main producer to minimize distribution time. JIT runs into problems when suppliers are farther away. Weather may delay shipments, for example.

JIT systems make sure the right materials are at the right place at the right time at the cheapest cost to meet both customer and production needs. That's a key step in modern production innovation.

Quality Control

Maintaining **quality** means consistently producing what the customer wants while reducing errors before and after delivery to the customer. In the past, firms often conducted quality control at the end of the production line. Products were completed first and then tested for quality. This resulted in several problems:

1. The need to inspect work required extra people and resources.
2. If an error was found, someone had to correct the mistake or scrap the product. This, of course, was costly.
3. If the customer found the mistake, he or she might be dissatisfied and might even buy from another firm thereafter.

Such problems led to the realization that quality is not an outcome; it is a never-ending process of continually improving what a company produces. Quality control should thus be part of the operations management planning process rather than simply an end-of-the-line inspection.[37]

Companies have turned to the use of modern quality-control standards such as Six Sigma.[38] **Six Sigma quality**, which sets a benchmark of just 3.4 defects per million opportunities, detects potential problems to prevent their occurrence. That's important to a company that makes 4 million transactions a day, like some banks.

Statistical quality control (SQC) is the process some managers use to continually monitor all phases of the production process and assure quality is being built into the product from the beginning. **Statistical process control (SPC)** is the process of testing statistical samples of product components at each stage of production and plotting the test results on a graph. Managers can thus see and correct any deviation from quality standards. Making sure products meet standards all along the production process reduces the need for a quality-control inspection at the end because mistakes are caught much earlier in the process. SQC and SPC thus save companies much time and money.

Some companies use a quality-control approach called the Deming cycle (after the late W. Edwards Deming, the father of the movement toward quality). Its steps are Plan, Do, Check, Act (PDCA). Again, the idea is to find potential errors *before* they happen.

U.S. businesses are getting serious about providing top customer service, and many are already doing it. Service organizations are finding it difficult to provide outstanding service every time because the process is so labor-intensive. Physical goods (e.g., a gold ring) can be designed and manufactured to near perfection. However, it is hard to reach such perfection when designing and providing a service experience such as a dance on a cruise ship or a cab drive through New York City.

The Baldrige Awards

In the United States in 1987, a standard was set for overall company quality with the introduction of the Malcolm Baldrige National Quality Awards, named in honor of the late U.S. secretary of commerce. Companies can apply for these awards in each of the following areas: manufacturing, services, small businesses, education, and health care.

To qualify, an organization has to show quality in seven key areas: leadership, strategic planning, customer and market focus, information and analysis, human resources focus, process management, and business results. Major criteria for earning the award include whether customer wants and needs are being met and whether customer satisfaction ratings are better than those of competitors. As you can see, the focus is shifting away from just making quality goods and services to providing top-quality customer service in all respects.

One Baldrige Award winner was Sunny Fresh Foods, a small company that makes about 200 different egg products. Sunny Fresh was the first food company to win the award, and one of only a few small-company winners. The company used the Baldrige criteria to drive business systems development and business systems redesign.

The Bama Companies of Tulsa, Oklahoma, makes pies, biscuits, and pizza crusts. Using Baldrige criteria, the company increased overall customer satisfaction from 75 percent to almost 100 percent. Richland College, in Dallas, Texas, was the first community college to receive a Baldrige Award. With over 20,000 students, Richland reduced its operational costs while improving services and implemented stakeholder listening services to measure satisfaction.

ISO 9000 and ISO 14000 Standards

The International Organization for Standardization (ISO) is a worldwide federation of national standards bodies from more than 140 countries that set global measures for the quality of individual products. ISO is a nongovernmental organization established in 1947 to promote the development of world standards to facilitate the international exchange of goods and services. (ISO is not an acronym. It

statistical process control (SPC)
The process of testing statistical samples of product components at each stage of the production process and plotting those results on a graph. Any variances from quality standards are recognized and can be corrected if beyond the set standards.

◀ PPT 9-42:
The Baldrige Awards

◀ PPT 9-43:
The Winners Are...

Mercy Health System (MHS), a recent recipient of the prestigious Baldrige National Quality Award, consists of three hospitals and 64 other facilities in Wisconsin and Illinois. The organization has built its "Culture of Excellence" around the four criteria of top quality in patient care, service standards that put patients first, committed partnership with its nearly 4,000 employees and physicians, and cost management for long-term financial success. What other quality criteria do you think a service organization should set for itself?

> **ISO 9000**
> The common name given to quality management and assurance standards.

▶ **PPT 9-44:**
What Is the ISO?

comes from the Greek word *isos,* meaning "oneness.") **ISO 9000** is the common name given to quality management and assurance standards. Some of the latest standards are called ISO 9000: 2008. The 2009–2010 criteria are now available.[39]

The standards require that a company determine what customer needs are, including regulatory and legal requirements, and make communication arrangements to handle issues such as complaints.[40] Other standards cover process control, product testing, storage, and delivery.

What makes ISO 9000 so important is that the European Union (EU) demands that companies that want to do business with the EU be certified by ISO standards. Some major U.S. companies are also demanding suppliers meet these standards. Several accreditation agencies in Europe and the United States will certify that a company meets the standards for all phases of its operations, from product development through production and testing to installation.

> **ISO 14000**
> A collection of the best practices for managing an organization's impact on the environment.

ISO 14000 is a collection of the best practices for managing an organization's impact on the environment. As an environmental management system, it does not prescribe a performance level. Requirements for certification include having an environmental policy, having specific improvement targets, conducting audits of environmental programs, and maintaining top management review of the processes.

Certification in both ISO 9000 and ISO 14000 would show that a firm has a world-class management system in both quality and environmental standards. In the past, firms assigned employees separately to meet each set of standards. Today, ISO 9000 and 14000 standards have been blended so that an organization can work on both at once.[41] ISO is now compiling social responsibility guidelines to go with the other standards.

progress assessment

▶ **PPT 9-45:**
Progress Assessment

- What are the major criteria for facility location?
- What is the difference between MRP and ERP?
- What is just-in-time inventory control?
- What are Six Sigma quality, the Baldrige Award, ISO 9000, and ISO 14000?

LEARNING goal 5 *

Explain the use of PERT and Gantt charts to control manufacturing processes.

▶ **PPT 9-46:**
PERT

▶ **PPT 9-47:**
Steps Involved in PERT

▶ **CRITICAL THINKING EXERCISE 9-5:**
Drawing a PERT Diagram

CONTROL PROCEDURES: PERT AND GANTT CHARTS

▶ **PPT 9-48:**
PERT Chart for a Music Video

Operations managers must ensure products are manufactured and delivered on time, on budget, and to specifications. How can managers be sure all will go smoothly and be completed by the required time? One popular technique for monitoring the progress of production was developed in the 1950s for constructing nuclear submarines: the **program evaluation and review technique (PERT)**. PERT users analyze the tasks to complete a given project, estimate the time needed to complete each, and compute the minimum time needed to complete the whole project.

The steps used in PERT are (1) analyzing and sequencing tasks that need to be done, (2) estimating the time needed to complete each task, (3) drawing a PERT network illustrating the information from steps 1 and 2, and (4) identifying the critical path. The **critical path** is the sequence of tasks that takes the longest time to complete. We use the word *critical* because a delay anywhere along this path will cause the project or production run to be late.

Figure 9.3 illustrates a PERT chart for producing a music video. The squares indicate completed tasks, and the arrows indicate the time needed to complete each. The path from one completed task to another illustrates the relationships among tasks; the arrow from "set designed" to "set materials purchased" indicates we must design the set before we can purchase the materials. The critical path, indicated by the bold black arrows, shows producing the set takes more time than auditioning dancers, choreographing dances, or designing and making costumes. The project manager now knows it's critical that set construction remain on schedule if the project is to be completed on time, but short delays in dance and costume preparation are unlikely to delay it.

A PERT network can be made up of thousands of events over many months. Today, this complex procedure is done by computer. Another, more basic strategy manufacturers use for measuring production progress is a Gantt chart. A **Gantt chart** (named for its developer, Henry L. Gantt) is a bar graph, now also prepared by computer, that clearly shows what projects are being worked on and how much has been completed at any given time. Figure 9.4 on p. 248, a Gantt chart for a doll manufacturer, shows that the dolls' heads and bodies should be completed before the clothing is sewn. It also shows that at the end of week 3, the dolls' bodies are ready, but the heads are about half a week behind. Using a Gantt-like computer program, a manager can trace the production process minute by minute to determine which tasks are on time and which are behind, so that adjustments can be made to allow the company to stay on schedule.

program evaluation and review technique (PERT)
A method for analyzing the tasks involved in completing a given project, estimating the time needed to complete each task, and identifying the minimum time needed to complete the total project.

critical path
In a PERT network, the sequence of tasks that takes the longest time to complete.

Gantt chart
Bar graph showing production managers what projects are being worked on and what stage they are in at any given time.

figure 9.3

PERT CHART FOR A MUSIC VIDEO
The minimum amount of time it will take to produce this video is 15 weeks. To get that number, you add the week it takes to pick a star and a song to the four weeks to design a set, the two weeks to purchase set materials, the six weeks to construct the set, the week before rehearsals, and the final week when the video is made. That's the critical path. Any delay in that process will delay the final video.

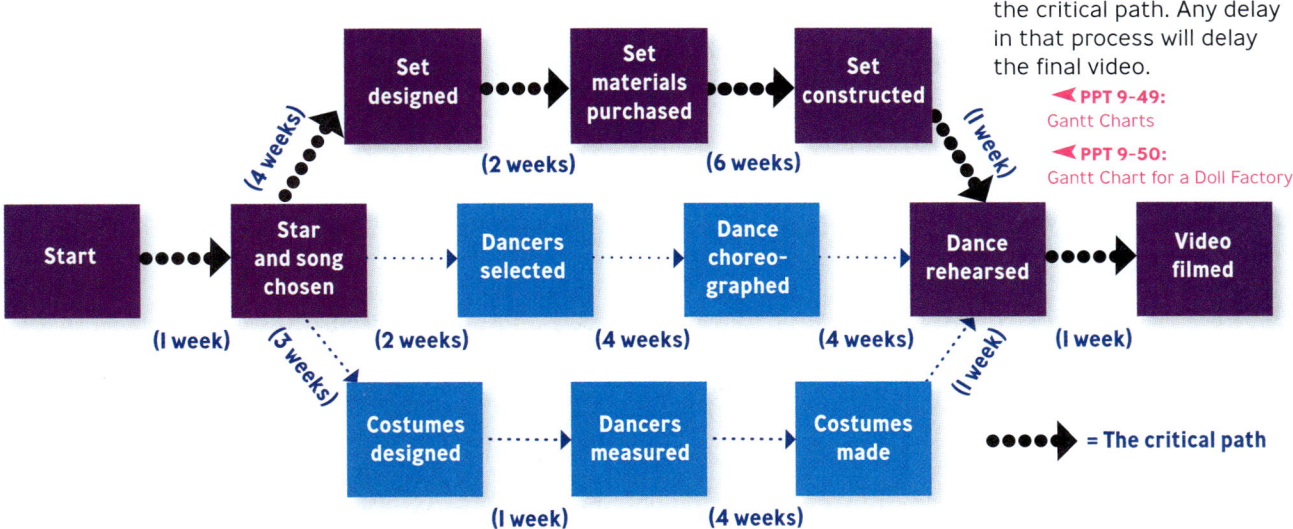

◂ PPT 9-49:
Gantt Charts
◂ PPT 9-50:
Gantt Chart for a Doll Factory

figure 9.4

GANTT CHART FOR A DOLL MANUFACTURER

A Gantt chart enables a production manager to see at a glance when projects are scheduled to be completed and what the status is now. For example, the dolls' heads and bodies should be completed before the clothing is sewn, but they could be a little late as long as everything is ready for assembly in week 6. This chart shows that at the end of week 3, the dolls' bodies are ready, but the heads are about half a week behind.

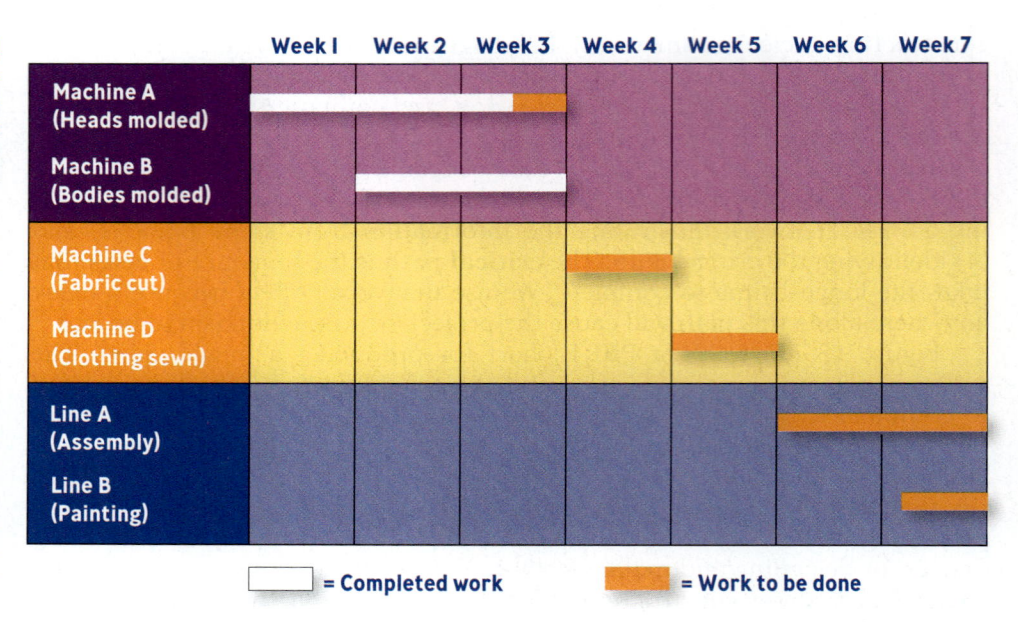

	Week 1	Week 2	Week 3	Week 4	Week 5	Week 6	Week 7
Machine A (Heads molded)							
Machine B (Bodies molded)							
Machine C (Fabric cut)							
Machine D (Clothing sewn)							
Line A (Assembly)							
Line B (Painting)							

☐ = Completed work   ▬ = Work to be done

PREPARING FOR THE FUTURE

The United States remains a major industrial country, but competition grows stronger each year. Tremendous opportunities exist for careers in operations management as both manufacturing and service companies fight to stay competitive. Students who can see future trends and have the skills to own or work in tomorrow's highly automated factories and modern service facilities will benefit.

progress assessment

- Draw a PERT chart for making a breakfast of three-minute eggs, buttered toast, and coffee. Define the critical path.
- How could you use a Gantt chart to keep track of production?

▶ PPT 9-51: Progress Assessment

summary

Learning Goal 1. Describe the current state of U.S. manufacturing and what manufacturers have done to become more competitive.

- **What is the current state of manufacturing in the United States?**

Activity in the nation's manufacturing sector has declined to the lowest level in more than two decades. Joblessness is the worst in the West and Midwest, indicating that the industries hit first by the recession—housing and manufacturing—continue to lose jobs. Unemployment could reach double-digit levels, home values could plunge a total of 36 percent, and stocks could fall a total of 55 percent. Much of this chapter is devoted to showing you what manufacturers and service providers can do to revive the U.S. economy to become world-class competitors.

- **What have U.S. manufacturers done to achieve increased output?**

U.S. manufacturers have increased output by emphasizing close relationships with suppliers and other companies to satisfy customer needs;

continuous improvement; quality; site selection; use of the Internet to unite companies; and production techniques such as enterprise resource planning, computer integrated manufacturing, flexible manufacturing, and lean manufacturing.

Learning Goal 2. Describe the evolution from production to operations management.

- **What is production management?**

Production management consists of all the activities managers do to help their firms create goods. To reflect the change in importance from manufacturing to services, the term *production* is often replaced by the term *operations*.

- **What is operations management?**

Operations management is the specialized area in management that converts or transforms resources, including human resources, into goods and services.

- **What kind of firms use operations managers?**

Firms in both the manufacturing and service sectors use operations managers.

Learning Goal 3. Identify various production processes and describe techniques that improve productivity, including computer-aided design and manufacturing, flexible manufacturing, lean manufacturing, and mass customization.

- **What is process manufacturing, and how does it differ from assembly processes?**

Process manufacturing physically or chemically changes materials. Assembly processes put together components.

- **How do CAD/CAM systems work?**

Design changes made in computer-aided design (CAD) are instantly incorporated into the computer-aided manufacturing (CAM) process. The linking of CAD and CAM is computer-integrated manufacturing (CIM).

- **What is flexible manufacturing?**

Flexible manufacturing means designing machines to produce a variety of products.

- **What is lean manufacturing?**

Lean manufacturing is the production of goods using less of everything than in mass production: less human effort, less manufacturing space, less investment in tools, and less engineering time to develop a new product.

- **What is mass customization?**

Mass customization means making custom-designed goods and services for a large number of individual customers. Flexible manufacturing makes mass customization possible. Given the exact needs of a customer, flexible machines can produce a customized good as fast as mass-produced goods were once made. Mass customization is also important in service industries.

Learning Goal 4. Describe operations management planning issues including facility location, facility layout, materials requirement planning, purchasing, just-in-time inventory control, and quality control.

- **What is facility location and how does it differ from facility layout?**

Facility location is the process of selecting a geographic location for a company's operations. Facility layout is the physical arrangement of resources, including people, to produce goods and services effectively and efficiently.

- **How do managers evaluate different sites?**

Labor costs and land costs are two major criteria for selecting the right sites. Other criteria include whether resources are plentiful and inexpensive, skilled workers are available or are trainable, taxes are low and the local government offers support, energy and water are available, transportation costs are low, and the quality of life and of education are high.

- **What relationship does materials requirement planning (MRP) and enterprise resource planning (ERP) have with the production process?**

MRP is a computer-based operations management system that uses sales forecasts to make sure the needed parts and materials are available at the right time and place. Enterprise resource planning (**ERP**), a newer version of MRP, combines the computerized functions of all the divisions and subsidiaries of the firm—such as finance, material requirements planning, human resources, and order fulfillment—into a single integrated software program that uses a single database. The result is shorter time between orders and payment, less staff to do ordering and order processing, reduced inventories, and better customer service for all the firms involved.

- **What is just-in-time (JIT) inventory control?**

JIT requires suppliers to deliver parts and materials just in time to go on the assembly line so they don't have to be stored in warehouses.

- **What is Six Sigma quality?**

Six Sigma quality sets standards at just 3.4 defects per million opportunities and detects potential problems before they occur. Statistical quality control (**SQC**) is the process some managers use to continually monitor all processes in the production process and ensure quality is being built into the product from the beginning. Statistical process control (**SPC**) tests statistical samples of product components at each stage of the production process and plots the results on a graph so managers can recognize and correct deviations from quality standards.

- **What quality standards do firms use in the United States?**

To qualify for the Malcolm Baldrige National Quality Awards, a company must demonstrate quality in seven key areas: leadership, strategic planning, customer and market focus, information and analysis, human resources focus, process management, and business results. International standards U.S. firms strive to meet include ISO 9000: 2008 (ISO 9001) and ISO 14000. The first is a world standard for quality and the second is a collection of the best practices for managing an organization's impact on the environment.

Learning Goal 5. Explain the use of PERT and Gantt charts to control manufacturing processes.

- **Is there any relationship between a PERT chart and a Gantt chart?**

Figure 9.3 shows a PERT chart. Figure 9.4 shows a Gantt chart. Whereas PERT is a tool used for planning, a Gantt chart is a tool used to measure progress.

key terms

assembly process 235
computer-aided design (CAD) 236
computer-aided manufacturing (CAM) 236
computer-integrated manufacturing (CIM) 236
continuous process 235
critical path 247
enterprise resource planning (ERP) 242
facility layout 241
facility location 238
flexible manufacturing 237
form utility 234
Gantt chart 247
intermittent process 235
ISO 14000 246
ISO 9000 246
just-in-time (JIT) inventory control 244

Production and Operations Management * CHAPTER 9   251

lean manufacturing 237
mass customization 237
materials requirement
  planning (MRP) 242
operations
  management 233
process
  manufacturing 235
production 232
production
  management 232
program evaluation
  and review technique
  (PERT) 247
purchasing 244
quality 244
Six Sigma quality 244
statistical process
  control (SPC) 245
statistical quality
  control (SQC) 244
telecommuting 240

connect interactive applications

Reinforcing Your Connection to Concepts in Business

This chapter offers 9 interactive applications designed to help you apply what you've learned (examples of these exercises appear below). Your instructor has determined which interactive applications will benefit you throughout this course. Please refer to your instructor's assignment list in *Connect* to determine which applications you should complete.

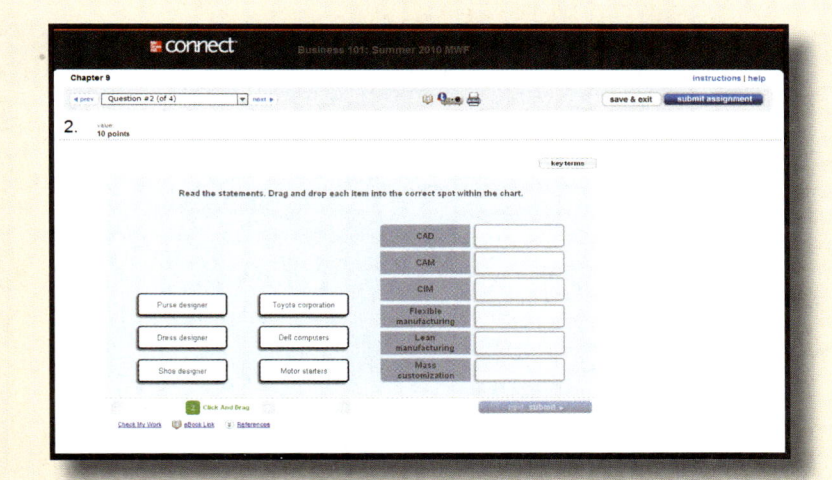

Click and Drag Interactive: Several major developments have made U.S. companies more competitive: (1) computer-aided design and manufacturing, (2) flexible manufacturing, (3) lean manufacturing, and (4) mass customization. Read about the different types of companies to determine where they fit within the chart.

Click and Drag Interactive: The production process uses basic inputs to produce outputs. Manufacturers use several different processes to produce goods. Evaluate the different products and determine where they fit on the chart.

Video Case Interactive: Ball Metal Manufacturing does many things to stay competitive. In this video, you will see how Ball seeks opportunities to improve its manufacturing process and customer and supplier relationships. Watch the video and respond to the questions when prompted.

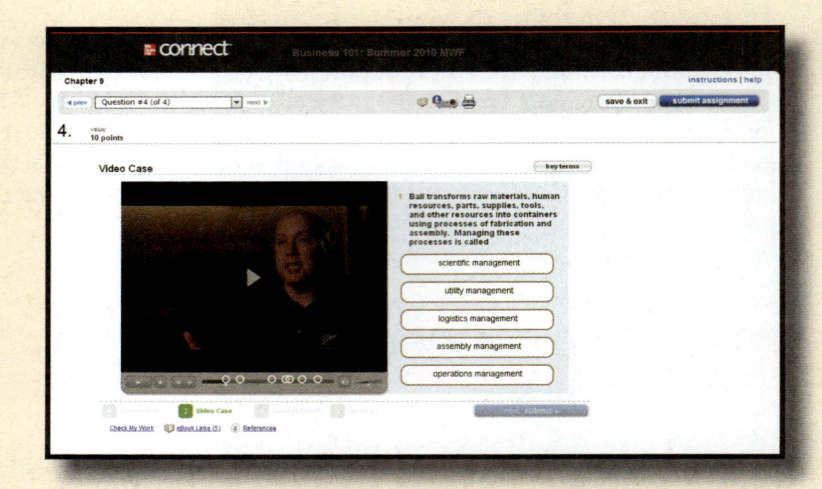

10 Motivating Employees

profile

Getting to Know Sergey Brin and Larry Page, Founders of Google

Few companies serve more of the global marketplace than Google. Founders Sergey Brin and Larry Page began the company in 1998 as a small-time coding operation in a friend's garage. Since then, Google has grown into the Internet's central search hub, becoming so established that the verb *Google* (meaning to do an Internet search) has gone from slang to the dictionary. With its popular e-mail service, G-mail; revolutionary online mapping program, Google Earth; and recent acquisition of the video-sharing site YouTube, what started as a college project has transformed into a multibillion-dollar corporation employing over 10,000 people.

With a business model centered on constantly breaking new technological ground, Brin and Page encourage their employees, or Googlers, to be innovative and to pursue their own interests in the course of their work. To encourage staff to explore their passions, Brin and Page established the "20% Time Initiative," which sets aside one day a week for Googlers to work on projects of their choice. For example, Googler Robyn Beavers began her career as a personal assistant to Brin and Page. In 2004, she approached the two founders and suggested that they create a green strategy group to improve Google's environmental efficiency. Not only did Brin and Page love the idea, but they put Beavers in charge of the operation even though it would take time away from her work assisting them.

Nowhere is Brin and Page's flexibility more apparent than at headquarters. The Googleplex sports a bright, funky facade to match the vibrant environment within. In the lava-lamp-lit hallways, Googlers travel to and from their workspaces, some on scooters and bicycles, some with their dogs. They share offices with up to four other people, working on couches and beanbag chairs, and bouncing ideas off one another. Upper managers work in the same environment as everyone else. Besides the laid-back office environment, the Googleplex provides every kind of convenience, from a gym and massage room to pool tables and a volleyball court. At the Google Café, employees choose from several styles of gourmet cuisine, all prepared by a chef

LEARNING goals

After you have read and studied this chapter, you should be able to

1. Explain Taylor's theory of scientific management.
2. Describe the Hawthorne studies and their significance to management.
3. Identify the levels of Maslow's hierarchy of needs and apply them to employee motivation.
4. Distinguish between the motivators and hygiene factors identified by Herzberg.
5. Differentiate among Theory X, Theory Y, and Theory Z.
6. Explain the key principles of goal-setting, expectancy, reinforcement, and equity theories.
7. Show how managers put motivation theories into action through such strategies as job enrichment, open communication, and job recognition.
8. Show how managers personalize motivation strategies to appeal to employees across the globe and across generations.

connect

Your *Connect*ion to Better Learning. 1. View the interactive presentation. 2. Practice through LearnSmart. 3. Apply your knowledge by using the interactive applications for each chapter of this text.

1 Prep >>>>>> **2 Study** 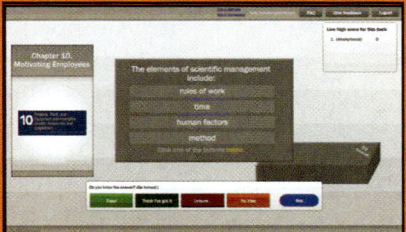 >>>>>> **3 Apply**

who once cooked for the Grateful Dead. But perhaps most impressive is the cost of these amenities to employees—nothing. From food to fun, it's all free for Googlers.

At the core of Brin and Page's generosity is their simple corporate philosophy: "You can make money without doing evil." The duo realized early that too many companies adhere to a restrictive hierarchy in which those low on the totem pole become voiceless drones, leaving the work environment stagnant. Brin and Page took the opposite approach, giving their staff unprecedented resources and influence in the company. It appears to have paid off. Google stock has soared as high as $700 per share, providing another key motivating factor for the 99 percent of Googlers who receive stock options and thus stand to benefit when the company performs well. *Fortune* magazine placed Google at number one on their "100 Best Companies to Work For" list in 2007 and 2008.

In this chapter, you'll learn about the theories and practices managers like Sergey Brin and Larry Page use in motivating their employees to focus on goals common to them and the organization.

Sources: Robert Levering and Milton Moskowitz, "100 Best Companies to Work For," *Fortune*, February 2008; "The New Oases," *The Economist*, April 10, 2008; and Google, www.google.com, accessed July 2, 2010.

www.google.com

NAME THAT company

> PPT 10-1:
> Motivating Employees

> PPT 10-2:
> Sergey Brin & Larry Page

A pioneer in the use of the assembly line, this U.S. automobile company overhauled the development of its signature sports car by granting a 400-person team complete control over the project from engineering to marketing. The highly motivated team delivered the car months ahead of schedule, under budget, to rave reviews and sales. Name that company. (Find the answer in the chapter.)

THE VALUE OF MOTIVATION

"If work is such fun, how come the rich don't do it?" quipped comedian Groucho Marx. Well, the rich do work—Bill Gates didn't make his billions playing computer games. And workers can have fun, if managers make the effort to motivate them.

It's hard to overstate the importance of workers' job satisfaction. Happy workers lead to happy customers, and happy customers lead to successful businesses. On the other hand, unhappy workers are likely to leave. When that happens, the company usually loses more than an experienced employee. It can also lose the equivalent of 6 to 18 months' salary to cover the costs of recruiting and training a replacement.[1] The "soft" costs of losing employees are even greater: loss of intellectual capital, decreased morale of remaining workers, increased employee stress, lower customer service, interrupted product development, and a poor reputation.

While it is costly to recruit and train new workers, it's also expensive to retain those who are disengaged. The word *engagement* is used to describe employees' level of motivation, passion, and commitment.[2] Engaged employees work with passion and feel a connection to their company. Disengaged workers have essentially checked out; they plod through their day putting in time, but not energy. Not only do they act out their unhappiness at work, but disengaged employees undermine the efforts of engaged co-workers. A recent Gallup study showed that 29 percent of U.S. employees are actively engaged in their jobs, 54 percent are not engaged, and 17 percent are actively disengaged. Another Gallup survey estimated that the lower productivity of actively disengaged workers costs the U.S. economy about $300 billion a year.[3]

Motivating the right people to join the organization and stay with it is a key function of managers. Top-performing mangers are usually surrounded by top-performing employees. It is no coincidence that geese fly faster in formation than alone.[4] Although the desire to perform well ultimately comes from within, good managers stimulate people and bring out their natural drive to do a good job. People are willing to work, and work hard, if they feel their work makes a difference and is appreciated.[5]

People are motivated by a variety of things, such as recognition, accomplishment, and status. An **intrinsic reward** is the personal satisfaction you

> *One important type of motivator is intrinsic (inner) rewards, which include the personal satisfaction you feel for a job well done. People who respond to such inner promptings often enjoy their work and share their enthusiasm with others. Are you more strongly motivated by your own desire to do well, or by extrinsic rewards like pay and recognition?*

> CRITICAL THINKING
> EXERCISE 10-1:
> Managing a Family Business

intrinsic reward
The personal satisfaction you feel when you perform well and complete goals.

feel when you perform well and complete goals. The belief that your work makes a significant contribution to the organization or to society is a form of intrinsic reward. An **extrinsic reward** is given to you by someone else as recognition for good work. Pay increases, praise, and promotions are extrinsic rewards.

This chapter will help you understand the concepts, theories, and practice of motivation. We begin with a look at some traditional theories of motivation. Why should you bother to know about these theories? Because sometimes "new" approaches aren't really new; variations of them have been tried in the past. Knowing what has gone before will help you see what has worked and what hasn't. First, we discuss the Hawthorne studies because they created a new interest in worker satisfaction and motivation. Then we look at some assumptions about employees that come from the traditional theorists. You will see the names of these theorists over and over in business literature and future courses: Taylor, Mayo, Maslow, Herzberg, and McGregor. Finally, we'll introduce modern motivation theories and show you how managers apply them.

LEARNING goal 1 *

Explain Taylor's theory of scientific management.

Frederick Taylor: The Father of Scientific Management

Several 19th-century thinkers presented management principles, but not until the early 20th century did any work with lasting implications appear. *The Principles of Scientific Management* was written by U.S. efficiency engineer Frederick Taylor and published in 1911, earning Taylor the title "father of scientific management." Taylor's goal was to increase worker productivity to benefit both the firm and the worker. The solution, he thought, was to scientifically study the most efficient ways to do things, determine the one "best way" to perform each task, and then teach people those methods. This approach became known as **scientific management**. Three elements were basic to Taylor's approach: time, methods, and rules of work. His most important tools were observation and the stopwatch. Taylor's thinking lies behind today's measures of how many burgers McDonald's expects its cooks to flip.

A classic Taylor story describes his study of men shoveling rice, coal, and iron ore with the same type of shovel. Believing different materials called for different shovels, he proceeded to invent a wide variety of sizes and shapes of shovels and, stopwatch in hand, measured output over time in what were called **time-motion studies**. These were studies of the tasks performed in a job and the time needed for each. Sure enough, an average person could shovel 25 to 35 tons more per day using the most efficient motions and the proper shovel. This finding led to time-motion studies of virtually every factory job. As researchers determined the most efficient ways of doing things, efficiency became the standard for setting goals.

Taylor's scientific management became the dominant strategy for improving productivity in the early 1900s. One follower of Taylor was Henry L. Gantt, who developed charts by which managers plotted the work of employees a day in advance down to the smallest detail. (See Chapter 9 for a discussion of Gantt charts.) U.S. engineers Frank and Lillian Gilbreth used Taylor's ideas in a three-year study of bricklaying. They developed the **principle of motion economy**, showing how every job could be broken into a series of elementary motions called a *therblig* (*Gilbreth* spelled backward with the *t* and *h* transposed). They then analyzed each motion to make it more efficient.

◀ PPT 10-3:
Intrinsic Rewards

extrinsic reward
Something given to you by someone else as recognition for good work; extrinsic rewards include pay increases, praise, and promotions.

◀ PPT 10-4:
Extrinsic Rewards

◀ PPT 10-5:
Fringe Benefits

◀ PPT 10-6:
Taylor's Scientific Management

◀ PPT 10-7:
Taylor's Four Key Principles

scientific management
Studying workers to find the most efficient ways of doing things and then teaching people those techniques.

◀ PPT 10-8:
Time-Motion Studies

time-motion studies
Studies, begun by Frederick Taylor, of which tasks must be performed to complete a job and the time needed to do each task.

principle of motion economy
Theory developed by Frank and Lillian Gilbreth that every job can be broken down into a series of elementary motions.

LEGAL briefcase

www.ups.com

Upset at UPS

With over $49 billion in revenue and 408,000 employees in 200 countries and territories, United Parcel Service (UPS) is the world's largest package distribution company. The company grew from a small bicycle messenger service in 1907 to today's mammoth delivery service in part by dictating every task for its employees.

Drivers are required to step out of their trucks with their right foot and carry their keys on their ring finger. If a driver is considered slow, a supervisor rides along, prodding the driver with stopwatches and clipboards. To improve productivity even further to meet increased competition from other delivery services, in 2007 UPS opened a $34 million, 11,500-square-foot training center in Landover, Maryland. It has simulators that teach employees how to properly lift and load boxes, drive their trucks proficiently, and even lessen the risk of slipping and falling when carrying a package.

Drivers have long accepted such work requirements, taking comfort in good wages, generous benefits, and an attractive profit-sharing plan. All the pressure on performance has taken its toll, however. Many UPS drivers have suffered anxiety, phobias, or back strain. At one point the firm had twice the injury rate of other delivery companies. In 1994, UPS settled a $3 million complaint from the Occupational Safety and Health Administration (OSHA) that it did not provide adequate safeguards for workers who handled hazardous wastes. UPS has spent nearly $1.5 billion since 1995 improving health and safety programs. The total of days lost to disability has been on the decline.

UPS is using new technologies and better planning in an effort to achieve greater productivity without overloading employees. Competition from companies such as FedEx (where workers earn 30 to 50 percent less than UPS workers) also requires greater efficiency. The variety of new UPS services requires drivers to remember more things, such as UPS's 340 methods of delivery. Because the jobs require more thinking, the company has begun hiring a new breed of skilled, college-educated workers. Do you think they will be more or less tolerant of the company's rules and demands? Why?

Sources: Nadira A. Hira, "The Making of a UPS Driver," *Fortune*, November 7, 2007; "United Parcel Service Swings to a Loss," *New York Times*, January 31, 2008; UPS, www.ups.com, accessed February 2009; and David Wanetick, "Distinguishing Traits of Elite Performers," *Directors and Boards*, March 22, 2008.

▶ PPT 10-9:
Upset at UPS

▶ PPT 10-10:
Are You Stressed?

Scientific management viewed people largely as machines that needed to be properly programmed. There was little concern for the psychological or human aspects of work. Taylor believed that workers would perform at a high level of effectiveness—that is, be motivated—if they received high enough pay.

Some of Taylor's ideas are still in use. Some companies continue to emphasize conformity to work rules rather than creativity, flexibility, and responsiveness. For example, United Parcel Service (UPS) tells drivers how fast to walk (three feet per second), how many packages to pick up and deliver a day (an average of 400), and how to hold their keys (teeth up, third finger). Drivers wear ring scanners, electronic devices on their index fingers wired to a small computer on their wrists. The devices shoot a pattern of photons at a bar code on a package to let a customer check the Internet and know exactly where a package is at any given moment.⁶ See the Legal Briefcase box for more about scientific management at UPS.

The benefits of relying on workers to come up with solutions to productivity problems have long been recognized, as we shall discover next.

LEARNING goal 2 *

Describe the Hawthorne studies and their significance to management.

◄ PPT 10-11:
Hawthorne Studies:
Purpose and Results

Elton Mayo and the Hawthorne Studies

One study, inspired by Frederick Taylor's research, began at the Western Electric Company's Hawthorne plant in Cicero, Illinois, in 1927 and ended six years later. Let's see why it is one of the major studies in management literature.

Elton Mayo and his colleagues from Harvard University came to the Hawthorne plant to test the degree of lighting associated with optimum productivity. In this respect, their study was a traditional scientific management study. The idea was to keep records of the workers' productivity under different levels of illumination. But the initial experiments revealed what seemed to be a problem. The researchers had expected productivity to fall as the lighting was dimmed. Yet the experimental group's productivity went up regardless of whether the lighting was bright or dim, and even when it was reduced to about the level of moonlight.

In a second series of 13 experiments, a separate test room was set up where researchers could manipulate temperature, humidity, and other environmental factors. Productivity went up each time; in fact, it increased by 50 percent overall. When the experimenters repeated the original condition (expecting productivity to fall to original levels), productivity increased yet again. The experiments were considered a total failure at this point. No matter what the experimenters did, productivity went up. What was causing the increase?

In the end, Mayo guessed that some human or psychological factor was at play. He and his colleagues interviewed the workers, asking about their feelings and attitudes toward the experiment. The answers began a profound change in management thinking that still has repercussions today. Here is what the researchers concluded:

Little did Elton Mayo and his research team from Harvard University know they would forever change managers' beliefs about employee motivation. Their research at the Hawthorne plant of Western Electric in Cicero, Illinois (pictured here), gave birth to the concept of human-based motivation by showing that employees behaved differently simply because they were involved in planning and executing the experiments.

- The workers in the test room thought of themselves as a social group. The atmosphere was informal, they could talk freely, and they interacted regularly with their supervisors and the experimenters. They felt special and worked hard to stay in the group. This motivated them.

- The workers were included in planning the experiments. For example, they rejected one kind of pay schedule and recommended another, which was adopted. They believed their ideas were respected and felt engaged in managerial decision making. This, too, motivated them.

- No matter the physical conditions, the workers enjoyed the atmosphere of their special room and the additional pay for being more productive. Job satisfaction increased dramatically.

Researchers now use the term **Hawthorne effect** to refer to people's tendency to behave differently when they know they're being studied. The Hawthorne study's results encouraged researchers to study human motivation and the managerial styles that lead to higher productivity.[7] Research emphasis shifted from Taylor's scientific management toward Mayo's new human-based management.

Mayo's findings led to completely new assumptions about employees. One was that pay is not the only motivator. In fact, money was found to be a relatively ineffective motivator. New assumptions led to many theories about the human side of motivation. One of the best-known motivation theorists was Abraham Maslow, whose work we discuss next.

> **Hawthorne effect**
> The tendency for people to behave differently when they know they are being studied.

> **LECTURE LINK 10-1:**
> Motivating Without Money

> **CRITICAL THINKING EXERCISE 10-2:**
> Does Money Motivate?

LEARNING goal 3 *

Identify the levels of Maslow's hierarchy of needs and apply them to employee motivation.

> **PPT 10-12:**
> Maslow's Theory of Motivation

MOTIVATION AND MASLOW'S HIERARCHY OF NEEDS

Psychologist Abraham Maslow believed that to understand motivation at work, we must understand human motivation in general. It seemed to him that motivation arises from need. That is, people are motivated to satisfy unmet needs. Needs that have already been satisfied no longer provide motivation.

Figure 10.1 shows **Maslow's hierarchy of needs**, whose levels are:

Physiological needs: Basic survival needs, such as the need for food, water, and shelter.

Safety needs: The need to feel secure at work and at home.

Social needs: The need to feel loved, accepted, and part of the group.

Esteem needs: The need for recognition and acknowledgment from others, as well as self-respect and a sense of status or importance.

Self-actualization needs: The need to develop to one's fullest potential.

> **Maslow's hierarchy of needs**
> Theory of motivation based on unmet human needs from basic physiological needs to safety, social, and esteem needs to self-actualization needs.

When one need is satisfied, another, higher-level need emerges and motivates us to satisfy it. The satisfied need is no longer a motivator. For example, if you just ate a full-course dinner, hunger would not be a motivator (at least for several hours), and your attention may turn to your surroundings (safety needs) or family (social needs). Of course, lower-level needs (perhaps thirst) may reemerge at any time they are not being met and take your attention away from higher-level needs.

Most of the world's workers struggle all day simply to meet the basic physiological and safety needs. In more developed countries, such needs no longer dominate, and workers seek to satisfy growth needs—social, esteem, and self-actualization needs.

To compete successfully, U.S. firms must create a work environment that includes goals such as social contribution, honesty, reliability, service, quality,

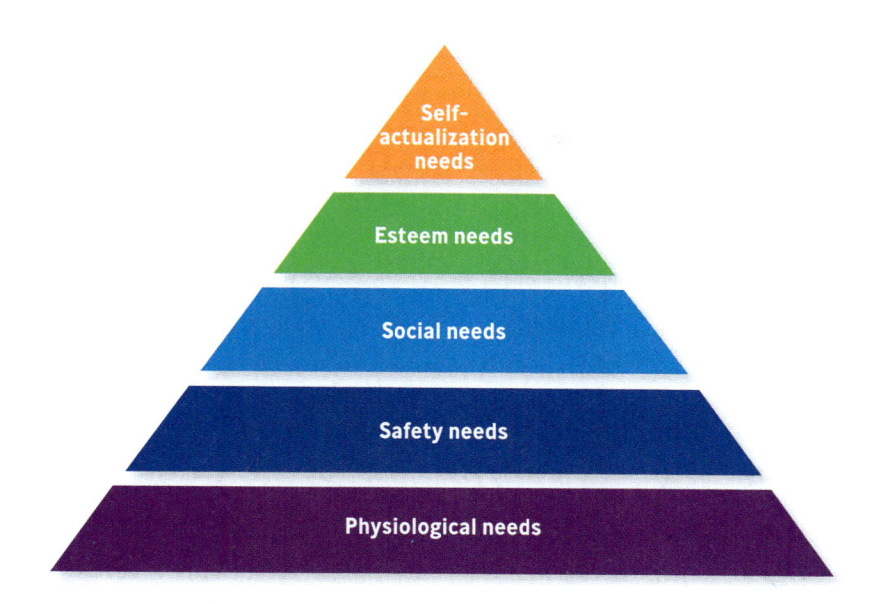

figure 10.1

MASLOW'S HIERARCHY OF NEEDS

Maslow's hierarchy of needs is based on the idea that motivation comes from need. If a need is met, it's no longer a motivator, so a higher-level need becomes the motivator. Higher-level needs demand the support of lower-level needs. This chart shows the various levels of need. Do you know where you are on the chart right now?

(Pyramid from top to bottom: Self-actualization needs; Esteem needs; Social needs; Safety needs; Physiological needs)

dependability, and unity—for all levels of employees. Chip Conley of Joie de Vivre, a chain of 30 boutique hotels, thinks about higher-level needs such as meaning (self-actualization) for all employees, including lower-level workers. Half his employees are housekeepers who clean toilets all day. How does he help them feel they're doing meaningful work? One technique is what he calls the George Bailey exercise, based on the main character in the movie *It's a Wonderful Life*. Conley asks small groups of housekeepers what would happen if they weren't there every day. Trash would pile up, bathrooms would be full of wet towels, and let's not even think about the toilets. Then he asks them to come up with some other name for housekeeping. They offer suggestions like "serenity keepers," "clutter busters," or "the peace-of-mind police." In the end, these employees have a sense of how the customer's experience wouldn't be the same without them. This gives meaning to their work that helps satisfy higher-level needs.[8]

◀ PPT 10-13:
Maslow's Hierarchy of Needs

◀ CRITICAL THINKING EXERCISE 10-3:
Testing Maslow's Hierarchy of Needs

◀ BONUS CASE 10-1:
When Failure Is the Norm

LEARNING goal 4 *

Distinguish between the motivators and hygiene factors identified by Herzberg.

HERZBERG'S MOTIVATING FACTORS

Another direction in managerial theory is to explore what managers can do with the job itself to motivate employees, a modern-day look at Taylor's research. In other words, some theorists ask: Of all the factors controllable by managers, which are most effective in generating an enthusiastic work effort?

In the mid-1960s, psychologist Frederick Herzberg conducted the most-discussed study in this area. Herzberg asked workers to rank various job-related factors in order of importance relative to motivation. The question was: What creates enthusiasm for workers and makes them work to full potential? The most important factors were:

1. Sense of achievement.
2. Earned recognition.

◀ LECTURE LINK 10-2:
The Big Thrill Motivation

◀ PPT 10-14:
Herzberg's Motivating Factors

◀ PPT 10-15:
Job Content

3. Interest in the work itself.
4. Opportunity for growth.
5. Opportunity for advancement.
6. Importance of responsibility.
7. Peer and group relationships.
8. Pay.
9. Supervisor's fairness.
10. Company policies and rules.
11. Status.
12. Job security.
13. Supervisor's friendliness.
14. Working conditions.

> **PPT 10-16:**
> Job Environment

> **LECTURE LINK 10-3:**
> McClelland's Acquired Needs Theory

> **PPT 10-17:**
> Herzberg's Motivators and Hygiene Factors

motivators
In Herzberg's theory of motivating factors, job factors that cause employees to be productive and that give them satisfaction.

hygiene factors
In Herzberg's theory of motivating factors, job factors that can cause dissatisfaction if missing but that do not necessarily motivate employees if increased.

Factors receiving the most votes all clustered around job content. Workers like to feel they contribute to the company (sense of achievement was number 1). They want to earn recognition (number 2) and feel their jobs are important (number 6). They want responsibility (which is why learning is so important) and to earn recognition for that responsibility by having a chance for growth and advancement. Of course, workers also want the job to be interesting. Do you feel the same way about your work?

Workers did not consider factors related to job environment to be motivators. It was interesting to find that one of those factors was pay. Workers felt the *absence* of good pay, job security, and friendly supervisors could cause dissatisfaction, but their presence did not motivate employees to work harder; it just provided satisfaction and contentment. Would you work harder if you were paid more?

Herzberg concluded that certain factors, which he called **motivators**, made employees productive and gave them satisfaction. These factors, as you have seen, mostly related to job content. Herzberg called other elements of the job **hygiene factors** (or maintenance factors). These related to the job environment and could cause dissatisfaction if missing but would not necessarily motivate employees if increased. See Figure 10.2 for a list of motivators and hygiene factors.

Herzberg's motivating factors led to this conclusion: The best way to motivate employees is to make their jobs interesting, help them achieve their objectives, and recognize their achievement through advancement and added responsibility. A review of Figure 10.3 shows the similarity between Maslow's hierarchy of needs and Herzberg's theory.

Look at Herzberg's motivating factors, identify those that motivate you, and rank them in order of importance to you. Keep them in mind as you

figure 10.2

HERZBERG'S MOTIVATORS AND HYGIENE FACTORS

There's some controversy over Herzberg's results. For example, sales managers often use money as a motivator. Recent studies have shown that money can be a motivator if used as part of a recognition program.

MOTIVATORS	HYGIENE (MAINTENANCE) FACTORS
(These factors can be used to motivate workers.)	(These factors can cause dissatisfaction, but changing them will have little motivational effect.)
Work itself	Company policy and administration
Achievement	Supervision
Recognition	Working conditions
Responsibility	Interpersonal relations (co-workers)
Growth and advancement	Salary, status, and job security

figure 10.3

COMPARISON OF MASLOW'S HIERARCHY OF NEEDS AND HERZBERG'S THEORY OF FACTORS

Maslow: Self-actualization, Esteem, Social, Safety, Physiological

Herzberg:
- Motivational: Work itself, Achievement, Possibility of growth; Advancement, Recognition, Status
- Hygiene (Maintenance): Interpersonal relations (Superior, Subordinates, Peers), Supervision; Company policy and administration, Job security, Working conditions; Salary, Personal life

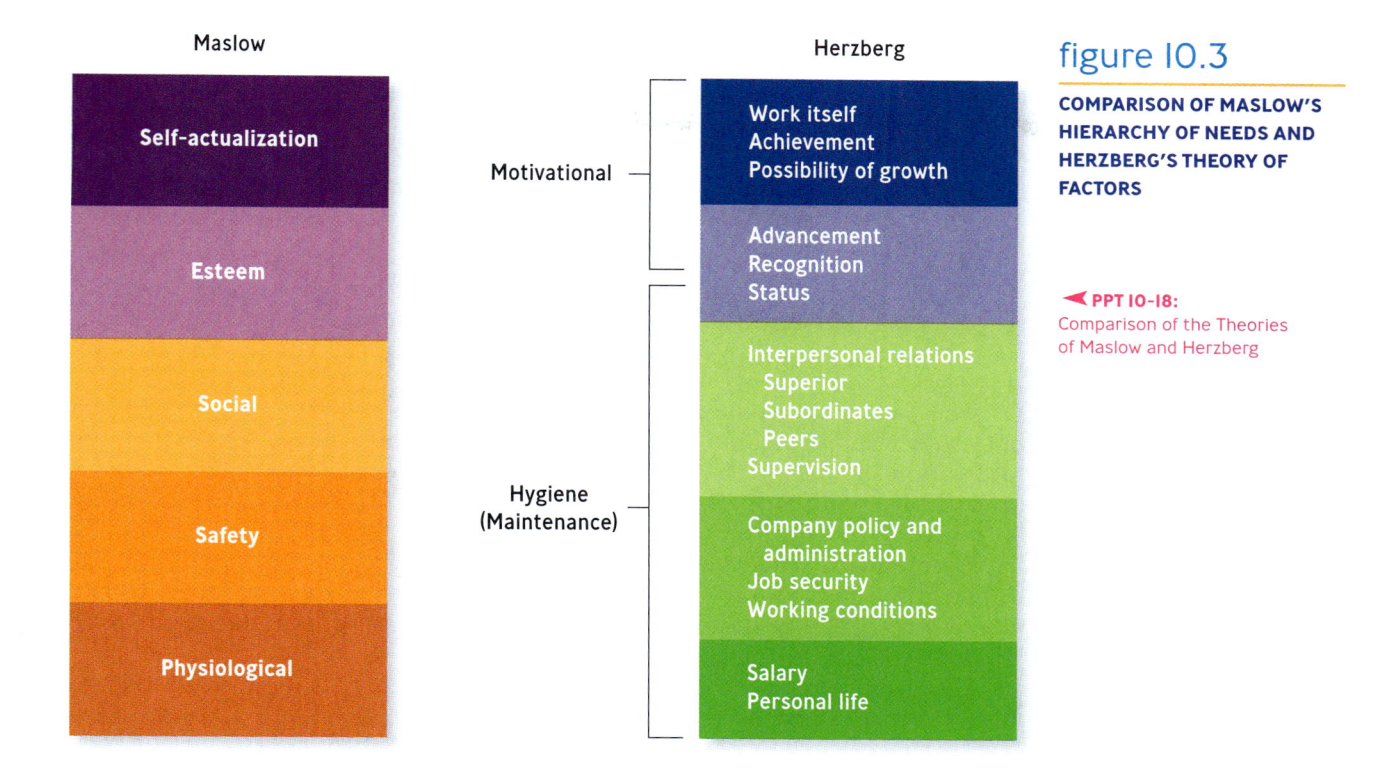

◄ PPT 10-18: Comparison of the Theories of Maslow and Herzberg

consider jobs and careers. What motivators do your job opportunities offer you? Are they the ones you consider important? Evaluating your job offers in terms of what's really important to you will help you make a wise career choice.

progress assessment

- What are the similarities and differences between Taylor's time-motion studies and Mayo's Hawthorne studies?
- How did Mayo's findings influence scientific management?
- Draw a diagram of Maslow's hierarchy of needs. Label and describe the parts.
- Explain the distinction between what Herzberg called motivators and hygiene factors.

◄ PPT 10-19: Progress Assessment

LEARNING goal 5 *

Differentiate among Theory X, Theory Y, and Theory Z.

MCGREGOR'S THEORY X AND THEORY Y

◄ PPT 10-20: Theory X and Theory Y

The way managers go about motivating people at work depends greatly on their attitudes toward workers. Management theorist Douglas McGregor observed that managers' attitudes generally fall into one of two entirely different sets of managerial assumptions, which he called Theory X and Theory Y.

> **PPT 10-21:**
> Assumptions of Theory X Managers

Theory X

The assumptions of Theory X management are:

- The average person dislikes work and will avoid it if possible.
- Because of this dislike, workers must be forced, controlled, directed, or threatened with punishment to make them put forth the effort to achieve the organization's goals.
- The average worker prefers to be directed, wishes to avoid responsibility, has relatively little ambition, and wants security.
- Primary motivators are fear and money.

The natural consequence of these assumptions is a manager who is very busy and watches people closely, telling them what to do and how to do it. Motivation is more likely to take the form of punishment for bad work than reward for good work. Theory X managers give workers little responsibility, authority, or flexibility. Taylor and other theorists who preceded him would have agreed with Theory X. Time-motion studies calculated the one best way to perform a task and the optimal time to devote to it. Researchers assumed workers needed to be trained and carefully watched to see that they conformed to standards.

Many managers and entrepreneurs still suspect that employees cannot be fully trusted and need to be closely supervised. No doubt you have seen such managers in action. How did they make you feel? Were these managers' assumptions accurate regarding workers' attitudes?

Theory Y

Theory Y makes entirely different assumptions about people:

- Most people like work; it is as natural as play or rest.
- Most people naturally work toward goals to which they are committed.
- The depth of a person's commitment to goals depends on the perceived rewards for achieving them.
- Under certain conditions, most people not only accept but also seek responsibility.
- People are capable of using a relatively high degree of imagination, creativity, and cleverness to solve problems.
- In industry, the average person's intellectual potential is only partially realized.
- People are motivated by a variety of rewards. Each worker is stimulated by a reward unique to him or her (time off, money, recognition, and so on).

Rather than authority, direction, and close supervision, Theory Y managers emphasize a relaxed managerial atmosphere in which workers are free to set objectives, be creative, be flexible, and go beyond the goals set by management. A key technique here is *empowerment*, giving employees authority to make decisions and tools to implement the decisions they make. For empowerment to be a real motivator, management should follow these three steps:

1. Find out what people think the problems in the organization are.
2. Let them design the solutions.
3. Get out of the way and let them put those solutions into action.

> *Theory X managers do not come in one-size-fits-all packages. Take Salina Lo of Ruckus Wireless, for example. She doesn't match the typical Theory X stereotype, but on the job this graduate of the University of California at Berkeley is a tough and exacting Theory X manager. Her in-your-face style has earned her a reputation as one of the industry's toughest managers. Would you prefer to work for a Theory X or a Theory Y manager?*

> **LECTURE LINK 10-4:**
> The L Factor

> **BONUS CASE 10-2:**
> The Supermarket Manager

> **PPT 10-22:**
> Assumptions of Theory Y Managers

Often employees complain that although they're asked to engage in company decision-making, their managers fail to actually empower them to make decisions. Have you ever worked in such an atmosphere? How did that make you feel?

OUCHI'S THEORY Z

One reason many U.S. companies choose a more flexible managerial style is to meet competition from firms in Japan, China, and the European Union. In the 1980s, Japanese companies seemed to be outperforming U.S. businesses. William Ouchi, management professor at the University of California–Los Angeles, wondered whether the reason was the way Japanese companies managed their workers. The Japanese approach, which Ouchi called Type J, included lifetime employment, consensual decision-making, collective responsibility for the outcomes of decisions, slow evaluation and promotion, implied control mechanisms, nonspecialized career paths, and holistic concern for employees. In contrast, the U.S. management approach, which Ouchi called Type A, relied on short-term employment, individual decision-making, individual responsibility for the outcomes of decisions, rapid evaluation and promotion, explicit control mechanisms, specialized career paths, and segmented concern for employees.

Type J firms are based on the culture of Japan, which includes a focus on trust and intimacy within the group and family. Conversely, Type A firms are based on American culture, which includes a focus on individual rights and achievements. Ouchi wanted to help U.S. firms adopt successful Japanese strategies, but he realized it wouldn't be practical to expect U.S. managers to accept an approach based on the culture of another country. Judge for yourself. A job for life may sound good until you think of the implications: no chance to change jobs and no opportunity to move quickly through the ranks.

Ouchi recommended a hybrid approach, Theory Z (see Figure 10.4). Theory Z includes long-term employment, collective decision-making, individual responsibility for the outcomes of decisions, slow evaluation and promotion, moderately specialized career paths, and holistic concern for employees

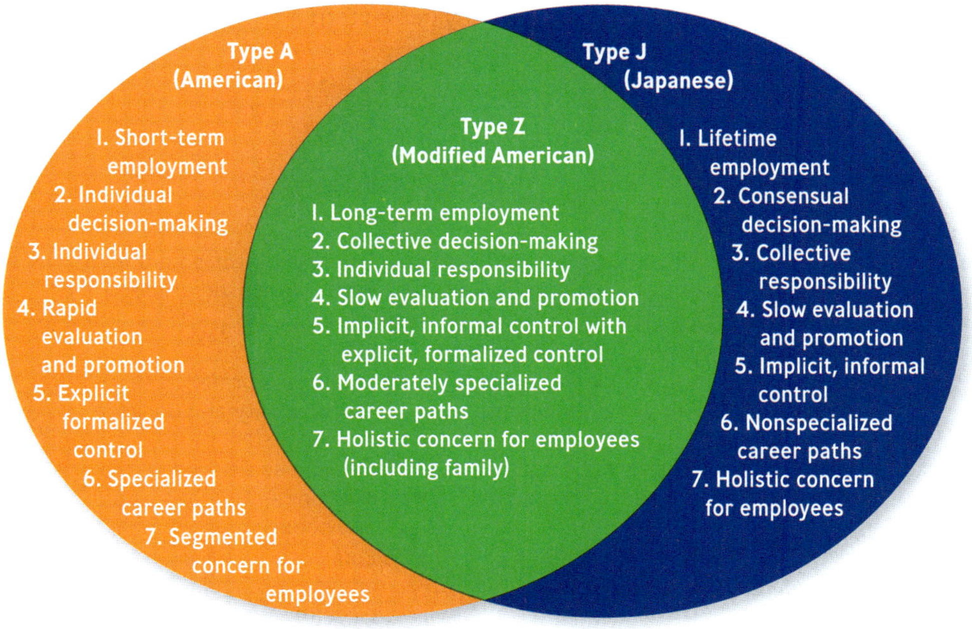

figure 10.4

THEORY Z: A BLEND OF AMERICAN AND JAPANESE MANAGEMENT APPOACHES

Type A (American)
1. Short-term employment
2. Individual decision-making
3. Individual responsibility
4. Rapid evaluation and promotion
5. Explicit formalized control
6. Specialized career paths
7. Segmented concern for employees

Type Z (Modified American)
1. Long-term employment
2. Collective decision-making
3. Individual responsibility
4. Slow evaluation and promotion
5. Implicit, informal control with explicit, formalized control
6. Moderately specialized career paths
7. Holistic concern for employees (including family)

Type J (Japanese)
1. Lifetime employment
2. Consensual decision-making
3. Collective responsibility
4. Slow evaluation and promotion
5. Implicit, informal control
6. Nonspecialized career paths
7. Holistic concern for employees

Great Lakes Industry employee Gary Lykins works out on company fitness equipment during his shift. His employer provides paid health coaches and reduces health insurance premiums and co-payments for employees who participate in its wellness programs. Can you think of any other examples of the kind of holistic concern for employees suggested by William Ouchi's Theory Z style of management?

(including family). Theory Z views the organization as a family that fosters cooperation and organizational values.

Today, demographic and social changes, fierce global competition, and the worst recession in their country's history have forced Japanese managers to reevaluate the way they conduct business. They now need to become both more dynamic and more efficient in order to compete effectively.

Electronics giant Hitachi was the first major Japanese company to quit requiring corporate calisthenics. Having everyone start the day with group exercises had symbolized doing the same thing the same way, and reinforced the cultural belief that employees should not take risks or think for themselves. Many managers think such conformity is what hurt Japanese business. Will Japanese managers move toward the hybrid Theory Z in the future? We'll have to wait and see. An appropriate managerial style matches the culture, situation, and specific needs of the organization and its employees. (See Figure 10.5 for a summary of Theories X, Y, and Z.)

LEARNING goal 6 *

Explain the key principles of goal-setting, expectancy, reinforcement, and equity theories.

figure 10.5
A COMPARISON OF THEORIES X, Y, AND Z

THEORY X	THEORY Y	THEORY Z
1. Employees dislike work and will try to avoid it.	1. Employees view work as a natural part of life.	1. Employee involvement is the key to increased productivity.
2. Employees prefer to be controlled and directed.	2. Employees prefer limited control and direction.	2. Employee control is implied and informal.
3. Employees seek security, not responsibility.	3. Employees will seek responsibility under proper work conditions.	3. Employees prefer to share responsibility and decision making.
4. Employees must be intimidated by managers to perform.	4. Employees perform better in work environments that are nonintimidating.	4. Employees perform better in environments that foster trust and cooperation.
5. Employees are motivated by financial rewards.	5. Employees are motivated by many different needs.	5. Employees need guaranteed employment and will accept slow evaluations and promotions.

GOAL-SETTING THEORY AND MANAGEMENT BY OBJECTIVES

Goal-setting theory says setting ambitious but attainable goals can motivate workers and improve performance if the goals are accepted and accompanied by feedback, and if conditions in the organization pave the way for achievement. All organization members should have some basic agreement about both overall goals and specific objectives for each department and individual. Thus there should be a system to engage everyone in the organization in goal setting and implementation.

Management expert Peter Drucker developed such a system in the 1960s. "Managers cannot motivate people; they can only thwart people's motivation because people motivate themselves," he said. Called **management by objectives (MBO)**, Drucker's system of goal setting and implementation includes a cycle of discussion, review, and evaluation of objectives among top and middle-level managers, supervisors, and employees. It calls on managers to formulate goals in cooperation with everyone in the organization, to commit employees to those goals, and to monitor results and reward accomplishment. Large corporations like Toyota and government agencies like the Department of Defense use MBO.[9]

MBO is most effective in relatively stable situations when managers can make long-range plans and implement them with few changes. Managers must also understand the difference between helping and coaching subordinates. *Helping* means working with the subordinate and doing part of the work if necessary. *Coaching* means acting as a resource—teaching, guiding, and recommending—but not participating actively or doing the task. The central idea of MBO is that employees need to motivate themselves.

Employee input and expectations are important.[10] Problems can arise when management uses MBO as a strategy for forcing managers and workers to commit to goals that are not agreed on together but are instead set by top management.

Victor Vroom identified the importance of employee expectations and developed a process called expectancy theory. Let's examine this concept next.

goal-setting theory
The idea that setting ambitious but attainable goals can motivate workers and improve performance if the goals are accepted, accompanied by feedback, and facilitated by organizational conditions.

management by objectives (MBO)
A system of goal setting and implementation; it involves a cycle of discussion, review, and evaluation of objectives among top and middle-level managers, supervisors, and employees.

MEETING EMPLOYEE EXPECTATIONS: EXPECTANCY THEORY

According to Victor Vroom's **expectancy theory**, employee expectations can affect motivation. That is, the amount of effort employees exert on a specific task depends on their expectations of the outcome. Vroom contends that employees ask three questions before committing their maximum effort to a task: (1) Can I accomplish the task? (2) If I do accomplish it, what's my reward? (3) Is the reward worth the effort? (See Figure 10.6 on p. 268.)

Think of the effort you might exert in class under the following conditions: Suppose your instructor says that to earn an A in the course, you must achieve an average of 90 percent on coursework plus jump eight feet high. Would you exert maximum effort toward earning an A if you knew you could not possibly jump eight feet high? Suppose your instructor said any student can earn an A in the course, but you know this instructor has not awarded an A in 25 years of teaching. If the reward of an A seems unattainable, would you exert significant effort in the course? Better yet, let's say you read online that businesses prefer hiring C-minus students to A-plus students. Does the reward of an A seem worth it? Now think of similar situations that may occur on the job.

expectancy theory
Victor Vroom's theory that the amount of effort employees exert on a specific task depends on their expectations of the outcome.

figure 10.6

EXPECTANCY THEORY
The amount of effort employees exert on a task depends on their expectations of the outcome.

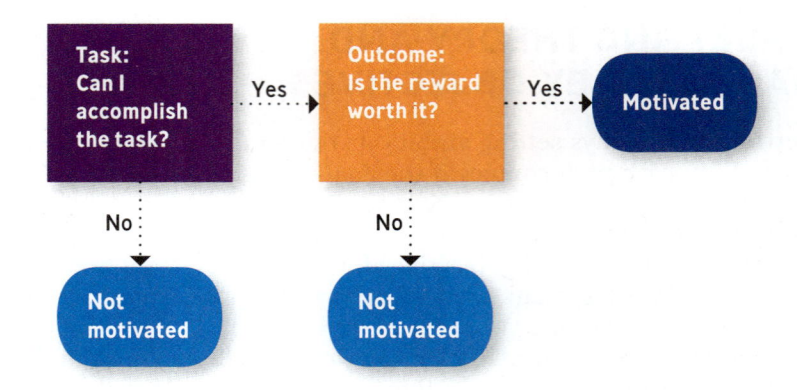

Expectancy theory does note that expectation varies from individual to individual. Employees establish their own views of task difficulty and the value of the reward.[11] Researchers David Nadler and Edward Lawler modified Vroom's theory and suggested that managers follow five steps to improve employee performance:[12]

▶ PPT 10-30:
Nadler & Lawler's Modification

1. Determine what rewards employees value.
2. Determine each employee's desired performance standard.
3. Ensure that performance standards are attainable.
4. Guarantee rewards tied to performance.
5. Be certain that employees consider the rewards adequate.

REINFORCING EMPLOYEE PERFORMANCE: REINFORCEMENT THEORY

reinforcement theory
Theory that positive and negative reinforcers motivate a person to behave in certain ways.

▶ PPT 10-31:
Using Reinforcement Theory

Reinforcement theory says positive and negative reinforcers motivate a person to behave in certain ways. In other words, motivation is the result of the carrot-and-stick approach: individuals act to receive rewards and avoid punishment. Positive reinforcements are rewards such as praise, recognition, and a pay raise. Negative reinforcement includes reprimands, reduced pay, and layoffs or firing. A manager might also try to stop undesirable behavior by not responding to it. This response is called *extinction* because managers hope the unwanted behavior will become extinct. Figure 10.7 illustrates how a manager can use reinforcement theory to motivate workers.

▶ PPT 10-32:
Reinforcement Theory

TREATING EMPLOYEES FAIRLY: EQUITY THEORY

equity theory
The idea that employees try to maintain equity between inputs and outputs compared to others in similar positions.

▶ PPT 10-33:
Equity Theory

Equity theory looks at how employees' perceptions of fairness affect their willingness to perform. It assumes employees ask, "If I do a good job, will it be worth it?" and "What's fair?" Employees try to maintain equity between what they put into the job and what they get out of it, comparing those inputs and outputs to those of others in similar positions. Workers find comparative information through personal relationships, professional organizations, and other sources.

When workers perceive inequity, they will try to reestablish fairness in a number of ways. For example, suppose you compare the grade you earned on a term paper with your classmates' grades. If you think you received a lower grade than someone who put out the same effort as you, you may (1) reduce your effort on future class projects or (2) rationalize the difference by saying, "Grades are overvalued anyway!" If you think your paper received a higher grade than comparable papers, you will probably (1) increase your effort to justify the higher reward in the future or (2) rationalize by saying, "I'm worth it!"

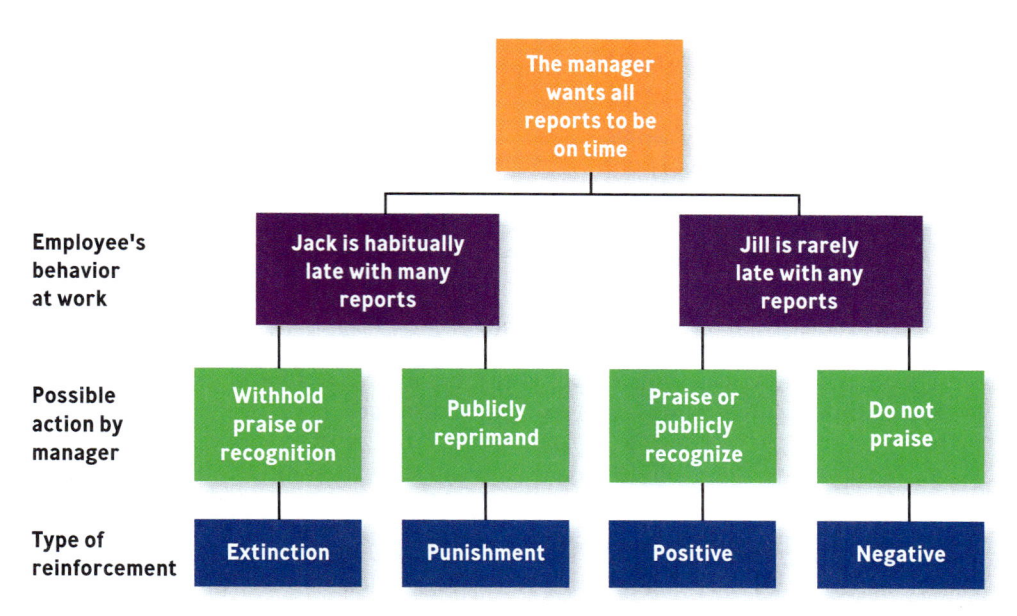

figure 10.7

REINFORCEMENT THEORY
A manager can use both positive and negative reinforcement to motivate employee behavior.

```
                    The manager
                    wants all
                    reports to be
                    on time
                   /              \
Employee's    Jack is habitually    Jill is rarely
behavior      late with many        late with any
at work       reports               reports
              /         \           /          \
Possible   Withhold   Publicly   Praise or    Do not
action by  praise or  reprimand  publicly     praise
manager    recognition           recognize

Type of    Extinction  Punishment  Positive   Negative
reinforcement
```

In the workplace, perceived inequity may lead to lower productivity, reduced quality, increased absenteeism, and voluntary resignation.

Remember that equity judgments are based on perception and are therefore subject to error. When workers overestimate their own contributions—as happens often—they feel *any* rewards given out for performance are inequitable. Sometimes organizations try to deal with this by keeping employee salaries secret, but secrecy may make things worse. Employees are likely to overestimate the salaries of others, in addition to overestimating their own contribution. The best remedy is generally clear and frequent communication. Managers must communicate as clearly as possible both the results they expect and the outcomes that will occur.

progress assessment

- Briefly describe the managerial attitudes behind Theories X, Y, and Z.
- Explain goal-setting theory.
- Evaluate expectancy theory. When could expectancy theory apply to your efforts or lack of effort?
- Explain the principles of equity theory.

◀ PPT 10-34:
Progress Assessment

LEARNING goal 7 *

Show how managers put motivation theories into action through such strategies as job enrichment, open communication, and job recognition.

PUTTING THEORY INTO ACTION

Now that you know what a few theorists have to say about motivation, you might be asking yourself "So what? What do all those theories have to do with what really goes on in the workplace today?" Fair question. Let's look at how companies put the theories into action through job enrichment, open communication, and job recognition.

Motivation through Job Enrichment

Managers have extended both Maslow's and Herzberg's theories through **job enrichment**, a strategy that motivates workers through the job itself. Work is assigned so that individuals can complete an identifiable task from beginning to end and are held responsible for successful achievement. Job enrichment is based on Herzberg's higher motivators, such as responsibility, achievement, and recognition. It stands in contrast to *job simplification*, which produces task efficiency by breaking a job into simple steps and assigning people to each. Review Maslow's and Herzberg's work to see how job enrichment grew from those theories.

Those who advocate job enrichment believe that five characteristics of work are important in motivation and performance:

1. *Skill variety.* The extent to which a job demands different skills.
2. *Task identity.* The degree to which the job requires doing a task with a visible outcome from beginning to end.
3. *Task significance.* The degree to which the job has a substantial impact on the lives or work of others in the company.
4. *Autonomy.* The degree of freedom, independence, and discretion in scheduling work and determining procedures.
5. *Feedback.* The amount of direct and clear information given about job performance.

Variety, identity, and significance contribute to the meaningfulness of the job. Autonomy gives people a feeling of responsibility; feedback contributes to a feeling of achievement and recognition. The Thinking Green box tells the story of how one company uses job enrichment to go green.

One type of job enrichment is **job enlargement**, which combines a series of tasks into one challenging and interesting assignment. Maytag, the home appliance manufacturer, redesigned its washing machine production process so that employees could assemble an entire water pump instead of just adding one part. **Job rotation** also makes work more interesting and motivating by moving employees from one job to another. One problem, of course, is the need to train employees to do several different operations. However, the resulting increase in motivation and the value of having flexible, cross-trained employees usually offsets the costs.

Motivating through Open Communication

Communication and information must flow freely throughout the organization when employees are empowered to make decisions—they can't make them in a vacuum. Procedures for encouraging open communication include the following:

- *Create an organizational culture that rewards listening.* Top managers must create places to talk and show employees that talking with superiors counts—by providing feedback, adopting employee suggestions, and rewarding upward communication—even if the discussion is negative.

---

job enrichment
A motivational strategy that emphasizes motivating the worker through the job itself.

▶ PPT 10-35:
Enriching Jobs

▶ PPT 10-36:
Key Characteristics of Work

One of the hallmarks of job enrichment is the worker's ability to perform a complete task from beginning to end. Why do you think this might be more motivating than simply adding a few parts to an assembly on a production line?

job enlargement
A job enrichment strategy that involves combining a series of tasks into one challenging and interesting assignment.

job rotation
A job enrichment strategy that involves moving employees from one job to another.

▶ BONUS CASE 10-3:
Managing Volunteers

THINKING green

www.paylocity.com

Green Team, Go!

Giving employees room to express and explore their own ideas in the workplace has long been an effective motivation strategy. For Steve Sarowitz, founder of payroll and human resources solutions provider Paylocity, that openness is not only a motivating factor but an environmental one as well. Before the company moved to a different building in 2008, Sarowitz e-mailed the company's 180 employees for advice on how to make the business more eco-friendly. He was flooded with suggestions, and soon he formed a 14-person "green team" to help implement the best ones.

The green team expanded the company's recycling program, increased telecommuting, and switched from paper coffee cups to ceramic ones. Not only was the team successful in greening up the office, but the project got the employees excited about accomplishing something that was not necessarily part of their job. "You just have to say, 'Let's do this,' and your employees will do it for you," Sarowitz said. "Just point your company in the right direction."

Sources: Chris Penttila, "Best Practices: Green Team," *Entrepreneur*, April 2008; and Sonja Sharp, "Torrance Green Team Helps Local Students Find Work, Build Job Skills," *Daily Breeze*, July 25, 2008.

Employees must feel free to say anything they deem appropriate and believe their opinions are valued.[13]

- *Train supervisors and managers to listen.* Most people receive no training in how to listen, in school or anywhere else, so organizations must do such training themselves or hire someone to do it.

- *Use effective questioning techniques.* We get information through questioning. Different kinds of questions yield different kinds of information. Closed questions that generate yes/no answers don't encourage the longer, more thoughtful responses that open questions do. Appropriate personal questions can create a sense of camaraderie between employee and manager.[14]

- *Remove barriers to open communication.* Separate offices, parking areas, bathrooms, and dining rooms for managers only set up barriers. Other barriers are different dress codes and different ways of addressing one another (like calling workers by their first names and managers by their last). Removing such barriers may require imagination and managers' willingness to give up special privileges.

- *Avoid vague and ambiguous communication.* Passive voice appears weak and tentative. Statements such as "Mistakes were made" leave you wondering who made the mistakes. Hedging is another way managers send garbled messages. Terms like *possibly* and *perhaps* sound wishy-washy to employees who need more definitive direction.[15]

- *Make it easy to communicate.* Encouraging organization members to eat together at large lunch tables, allowing employees to gather in conference rooms, having organizational picnics and athletic teams, and so on can help workers at all levels mix with one another.

- *Ask employees what is important to them.* Managers shouldn't wait until the exit interview to ask an employee, "What can I do to keep you?" Then it's too late. Instead they should have frequent *stay interviews* to find out what matters to employees and what they can do to keep them on the job.[16]

◄ PPT 10-37:
Green Team, Go!

◄ LECTURE LINK 10-6:
Recognition: Making Heroes

◄ PPT 10-38:
Types of Job Enrichment

◄ PPT 10-39:
Using Open Communication

Applying Open Communication in Self-Managed Teams

Before the recent economic crisis, the auto companies were often cited for good practices. At Ford Motor Company, for example, a group known as Team Mustang set the guidelines for how production teams should be formed. Given the challenge to create a car that would make people dust off their old "Mustang Sally" records and dance into showrooms, the 400-member team was also given the freedom to make decisions without waiting for approval from headquarters. Everyone worked under one roof in an old warehouse where drafting experts sat next to accountants, engineers next to stylists. Budgetary walls between departments were knocked down too as department managers were persuaded to surrender some control over their subordinates on the team.

When the resulting Mustang convertible displayed shaking problems, engineers were so motivated to finish on time and under budget that they worked late into the night, sleeping on the floor when necessary. Senior Ford executives were tempted to intervene, but they stuck with their promise not to meddle. Working with suppliers, the team solved the shaking problem and still came in under budget and a couple of months early. The new car was a hit with drivers, and sales soared.[17]

To implement such teams, managers at most companies must reinvent work. This means respecting workers, providing interesting work, developing workers' skills, allowing autonomy, decentralizing authority, and rewarding good work. Next we'll take a look at some of the ways companies recognize and reward good work.

In the car business nothing works like the "wow" factor. At Ford, the 400-member Team Mustang group was empowered to create the "wow" response for the company's sleek Mustang convertible. The work team, suppliers, company managers, and even customers worked together to make the Mustang a winner in the very competitive automobile market.

▶ CRITICAL THINKING EXERCISE 10-5:
Which Are the Best Companies to Work For?

▶ LECTURE LINK 10-7:
Positive Feedback

Recognizing a Job Well Done

Letting people know you appreciate their work is usually more powerful than giving a raise or bonus alone. When asked in a recent survey their reason for changing jobs, only 42 percent of the participants listed increased compensation and benefits, while 83 percent said they left for increased responsibilities and/or a more senior role.[18] Clearly, providing advancement opportunity is important in retaining valuable employees.

Promotions aren't the only way to celebrate a job well done. Recognition can be as simple as noticing positive actions out loud, making employees feel their efforts are worthwhile and valued enough to be noticed.[19] For example: "Sarina, you didn't say much in the meeting today. Your ideas are usually so valuable; I missed hearing them." This comment lets Sarina know her ideas are appreciated, and she'll be more apt to participate fully in the next meeting.

Here are just a few examples of ways managers have raised employee spirits without raising paychecks:[20]

- A Los Angeles law firm sent 400 employees and their families to Disneyland for the day. Kinko's did something similar, but it sent

SPOTLIGHT ON SMALL business

Big Motivators for Small Businesses

Often small businesses cannot offer their employees the financial incentives larger businesses can. So how can they motivate their workers to perform their best?

Many strive to create an upbeat, relaxed company culture to encourage employees to bond with one another. For example, at Blurb, a San Francisco–based specialty publishing company, at the end of every Friday the conference room is transformed into a concert venue as employees play the video game Rock Band. The boss provides refreshments along with the game, allowing the staff to relax and let the stress of the workweek pass into memory. Sprout Group, a small marketing firm based in Utah, uses a similarly laid-back strategy with weekly company trips to the movie theater where tickets and popcorn are on the boss.

But employee motivation isn't just about morale-boosting leisure activities like video games and movie nights. Besides providing social interaction, management needs to communicate clearly with the staff in order to give purpose and direction. At the small consulting firm Sonoma Partners, veteran employees mentor new hires to acquaint them with the work environment and show them how to excel. Not only does this method help new employees bond with their colleagues; it also sets them on the path to becoming productive workers.

Small businesses have a greater opportunity to motivate with open communication and broad responsibility. Individual workers can have more say in the company and not feel like just another drone in the great corporate beehive. As long as management encourages innovation from employees (and throws an occasional video game party), small businesses should have no trouble motivating their employees.

Sources: Eileen Gunn, "That's the Spirit! How to Energize Your Team—And Why It Matters," *BusinessWeek SmallBiz,* August/September 2008; and John R. Ingrisano, "Motivation: More Than Money," *Corporate Report Wisconsin,* February 1, 2008.

---

high-achieving employees to Disneyland *and* put the company's top executives in those employees' place while they were gone.

- Accounting firm KPMG gave employees a sundae surprise of gourmet ice cream and toppings.
- Give More Media offers perks like Netflix and XM Satellite Radio memberships. It also encourages participation in its Smile and Give

◀ PPT 10-40:
Big Motivators for Small Business

◀ PPT 10-41:
Recognizing Good Work

◀ PPT 10-42:
Work Well and Others

Gary Kelly (left and right), CEO of Southwest Airlines, has shown up at company Halloween parties dressed as Gene Simmons from the rock group Kiss, and as characters from the films Hairspray *and* Pirates of the Caribbean. *Each year in his blog he asks Southwest employees to suggest his next disguise. How do you think Kelly's Halloween antics help develop happy, productive, and loyal employees?*

> **PPT 10-43:**
> What's Good for You

> **PPT 10-44:**
> What's Bad for You

Travelocity's Gnomie Award, based on the company's mascot, the traveling gnome, is given to employees nominated by their peers for outstanding performance. Winners receive a $750 travel voucher, a paid day off, recognition at the company's quarterly meeting, and a golden gnome. What part do you think these awards play in motivating the winners to continue their outstanding performance?

> **CRITICAL THINKING EXERCISE 10-6:**
> Motivation Survey

> **PPT 10-45:**
> Motivating Employees Across the Globe

program, which gives employees three paid days off to work for a nonprofit of their choice.

- Lotus Public Relations in New York City has an annual "Lotus Day." One year employees sailed the Hudson, ate in an expensive restaurant, and enjoyed a comedy show and drinks. Other everyday perks include a free snack cabinet, free coffee, and free unlimited city commuting.
- Walt Disney World offers more than 200 employee recognition programs. The Spirit of Fred Award is named after an employee named Fred, who makes each award (a certificate mounted and varnished on a plaque) himself. Fred's name became an acronym for Friendly, Resourceful, Enthusiastic, and Dependable.
- Maritz Inc., in Fenton, Missouri, has a Thanks a Bunch program that gives flowers to a selected employee in appreciation of a job well done. That employee passes the bouquet to someone else who helped. The idea is to see how many people are given the flowers throughout the day. The bouquet comes with thank-you cards that are entered into a drawing for awards like binoculars and jackets.
- Hewlett-Packard (HP) bestows its Golden Banana Award for a job well done. The award started when an engineer burst into his manager's office saying he'd found the solution to a long-standing problem. In his haste to find something to give the employee to show his appreciation, the manager grabbed a banana from his lunch and said, "Well done! Congratulations!" The Golden Banana is now one of the most prestigious honors given to an inventive HP employee.

Giving valued employees prime parking spots, more vacation days, or more flexible schedules may help them feel their work is appreciated, but sometimes nothing inspires workers like the prospect of a payout down the road. Companies that offer a small equity stake or stock options often have a good chance of developing loyal employees.[21]

The same things don't motivate all employees. Next we'll explore how employees from different cultures and generations are motivated in different ways.

LEARNING goal 8 *

Show how managers personalize motivation strategies to appeal to employees across the globe and across generations.

PERSONALIZING MOTIVATION

Managers cannot use one motivational formula for all employees. They have to get to know each worker personally and tailor the motivational effort to the individual. This is further complicated by the increase in global business and the fact that managers now work with employees from a variety of cultural backgrounds. Cultural differences also exist between generations raised in the same country. Let's look at how managers personalize their strategies to appeal to employees across the globe and across generations.

Motivating Employees across the Globe

Different cultures experience motivational approaches differently; therefore, managers study and understand these cultural factors in designing a reward system. In a *high-context culture*, workers build personal relationships and develop group trust before focusing on tasks. In a *low-context culture*, workers often view relationship building as a waste of time that diverts attention from the task. Koreans, Thais, and Saudis tend to be high-context workers who often view their U.S. colleagues as insincere due to their need for data and quick decision-making.

Dow Chemical solved a cross-cultural problem with a recognition program for its 52,000 employees in over 37 countries who use a wide variety of languages and currencies. Globoforce Ltd. created a Web-based program for Dow called Recognition@Dow that automatically adjusts for differences created by cultural preferences, tax laws, and even local standards of living. Thus a U.S. employee might receive a gift certificate for Macy's, whereas a Chinese employee receives one for online retailer Dangdang.com. The system even allows employees to nominate colleagues for recognition using an "award wizard" to help determine the appropriate award.[22]

Understanding motivation in global organizations and building effective global teams is still a new task for most companies. Developing group leaders who are culturally astute, flexible, and able to deal with ambiguity is a challenge businesses face in the 21st century.

Motivating Employees across Generations

Baby boomers (born between 1946 and 1964); Generation X members (born between 1965 and 1980); and Generation Y members, also known as Millennials or echo boomers (born between 1980 and 2000), are linked through experiences they shared in their formative years—usually the first 10 years of life. The beliefs you accept as a child affect how you view risk, challenge, authority, technology, relationships, and economics. When you're in a management position, they can even affect whom you hire, fire, or promote.

Boomers were raised in families that experienced unprecedented economic prosperity, secure jobs, and optimism about the future. Gen Xers were raised in dual-career families with parents who focused on work. As children, they attended day care or became latchkey kids. Their parents' layoffs added to their insecurity about a lifelong job. Millennials were raised by indulgent parents, and most don't remember a time without cell phones, computers, and electronic entertainment.[23]

How do generational differences among these groups affect motivation in the workplace? Boomer managers need to be flexible with their Gen X and Millennial employees, or they will lose them. Gen X employees need to use their enthusiasm for change and streamlining to their advantage. Although many are unwilling to pay the same price for success their parents and grandparents did, their concern about undue stress and long hours doesn't mean they lack ambition. They want economic security as much as older workers, but they have a different approach to achieving it. Rather than focusing on job security, Gen Xers tend to focus on career security instead and are willing to change jobs to find it.

Many Gen Xers are now managers themselves, responsible for motivating other employees. What kind of managers are they? In general, they are well equipped to motivate people. They usually understand that there is more to life than work, and they think a big part of motivating is letting people know you recognize that fact. Gen X managers tend to focus more on results than on hours in the workplace. They tend to be flexible and good at collaboration and consensus building. They often think in broader terms than their predecessors because the media have exposed them to problems around the world. They also have a big impact on their team members. They are more likely to

Millennials grew up taking technology for granted. They tend to be skeptical, outspoken, and image-driven as well as adaptable, tech-savvy employees with a sense of fun and tolerance. Many Millennials will work for Gen X managers, who tend to be skilled at collaborating, building consensus, and giving feedback. What are some of the advantages you think Gen Xers as managers might offer Millennial employees?

▶ PPT 10-49:
Millenials in the Workplace

▶ PPT 10-50:
The Best Companies for Workers

give them the goals and outlines of the project and leave them alone to do their work.[24]

Perhaps the best asset of Gen X managers is their ability to give employees feedback, especially positive feedback. One reason might be that they expect more of it themselves. One new employee was frustrated because he hadn't received feedback from his boss since he was hired—two weeks earlier. In short, managers need to realize that young workers demand performance reviews and other forms of feedback more than the traditional one or two times a year.

In every generational shift, the older generation tends to say the same thing about the new: "They break the rules." The generation that lived through the Great Depression and World War II said it of the baby boomers. Boomers look at Gen Xers and say, "Why are they breaking the rules?" And now Gen Xers are looking at Millennials and saying, "What's wrong with these kids?"

In fact, Millennials are entering the job market at 80 million strong, creating a workplace four generations deep.[25] As a group, they tend to share a number of characteristics: they're impatient, skeptical, blunt and expressive, image-driven, and inexperienced. Like any other generation, they can transform their characteristics into unique skills. For example, Millennials tend to be adaptable, tech-savvy, able to grasp new concepts, practiced at multitasking, efficient, and tolerant. Perhaps the most surprising attribute they share is a sense of commitment.[26]

Millennials aren't rushing to find lifetime careers after graduation. They're "job surfing" and aren't opposed to living with their parents while they test out jobs.[27] A recent study found Millennials place a higher value on work-life balance, expect their employers to adapt to them (not the other way around), and are more likely to rank fun and stimulation in their top five ideal-job requirements.[28] What do you think are the most effective strategies managers can use to motivate Millennial workers?

One thing in business is likely to remain constant: much motivation will come from the job itself rather than from external punishments or rewards. Managers need to give workers what they require to do a good job: the right tools, the right information, and the right amount of cooperation. Motivation doesn't have to be difficult. It begins with acknowledging a job well done—and especially doing so in front of others. After all, as we said earlier, the best motivator is frequently a sincere "Thanks, I really appreciate what you're doing."

progress assessment

- What are several steps firms can take to increase internal communications and thus motivation?
- What problems may emerge when firms try to implement participative management?
- Why is it important to adjust motivational styles to individual employees? Are there any general principles of motivation that today's managers should follow?

summary

Learning Goal 1. Explain Taylor's theory of scientific management.
- **What is Frederick Taylor known for?**

Human efficiency engineer Frederick Taylor was one of the first people to study management and has been called the father of scientific management. He conducted time-motion studies to learn the most efficient way of doing a job and then trained workers in those procedures. He published his book The *Principles of Scientific Management* in 1911. Henry L. Gantt and Frank and Lillian Gilbreth were followers of Taylor.

Learning Goal 2. Describe the Hawthorne studies and their significance to management.
- **What led to the more human-based managerial styles?**

The greatest impact on motivation theory was generated by the Hawthorne studies in the late 1920s and early 1930s. In these studies, Elton Mayo found that human factors such as feelings of involvement and participation led to greater productivity gains than did physical changes in the workplace.

Learning Goal 3. Identify the levels of Maslow's hierarchy of needs and apply them to employee motivation.
- **What did Abraham Maslow find human motivation to be based on?**

Maslow studied basic human motivation and found that motivation was based on needs. He said that a person with an unfilled need would be motivated to satisfy it and that a satisfied need no longer served as motivation.
- **What levels of need did Maslow identify?**

Starting at the bottom of Maslow's hierarchy and going to the top, the levels of need are physiological, safety, social, esteem, and self-actualization.
- **Can managers use Maslow's theory?**

Yes, they can recognize what unmet needs a person has and design work so that it satisfies those needs.

Learning Goal 4. Distinguish between the motivators and hygiene factors identified by Herzberg.
- **What is the difference between Frederick Herzberg's motivator and hygiene factors?**

Herzberg found that while some factors motivate workers (motivators), others cause job dissatisfaction if missing but are not motivators if present (hygiene or maintenance factors).
- **What are the factors called motivators?**

The work itself, achievement, recognition, responsibility, growth, and advancement.
- **What are the hygiene (maintenance) factors?**

Company policies, supervision, working conditions, interpersonal relationships, and salary.

Learning Goal 5. Differentiate among Theory X, Theory Y, and Theory Z.
- **Who developed Theory X and Theory Y?**

Douglas McGregor held that managers have one of two opposing attitudes toward employees. He called them Theory X and Theory Y.
- **What is Theory X?**

Theory X assumes the average person dislikes work and will avoid it if possible. Therefore, people must be forced, controlled, and threatened with punishment to accomplish organizational goals.

- **What is Theory Y?**

Theory Y assumes people like working and will accept responsibility for achieving goals if rewarded for doing so.

- **What is Theory Z?**

William Ouchi based Theory Z on Japanese management styles and stresses long-term employment; collective decision-making; individual responsibility; slow evaluation and promotion; implicit, informal control with explicit, formalized control; moderately specialized career paths; and a holistic concern for employees (including family).

Learning Goal 6. Explain the key principles of goal-setting, expectancy, reinforcement, and equity theories.

- **What is goal-setting theory?**

Goal-setting theory is based on the notion that setting ambitious but attainable goals will lead to high levels of motivation and performance if the goals are accepted and accompanied by feedback, and if conditions in the organization make achievement possible.

- **What is management by objectives (MBO)?**

MBO is a system of goal setting and implementation; it includes a cycle of discussion, review, and evaluation of objectives among top and middle-level managers, supervisors, and employees.

- **What is the basis of expectancy theory?**

According to Victor Vroom's expectancy theory, employee expectations can affect an individual's motivation.

- **What are the key elements of expectancy theory?**

Expectancy theory centers on three questions employees often ask about performance on the job: (1) Can I accomplish the task? (2) If I do accomplish it, what's my reward? and (3) Is the reward worth the effort?

- **What are the variables in reinforcement theory?**

Positive reinforcers are rewards like praise, recognition, or raises that a worker might strive to receive after performing well. Negative reinforcers are punishments such as reprimands, pay cuts, or firing that a worker might be expected to try to avoid.

- **According to equity theory, employees try to maintain equity between inputs and outputs compared to other employees in similar positions. What happens when employees perceive that their rewards are not equitable?**

If employees perceive they are under-rewarded, they will either reduce their effort or rationalize that it isn't important. If they perceive that they are over-rewarded, they will either increase their effort to justify the higher reward in the future or rationalize by saying, "I'm worth it!" Inequity leads to lower productivity, reduced quality, increased absenteeism, and voluntary resignation.

Learning Goal 7. Show how managers put motivation theories into action through such strategies as job enrichment, open communication, and job recognition.

- **What characteristics of work affect motivation and performance?**

The job characteristics that influence motivation are skill variety, task identity, task significance, autonomy, and feedback.

- **Name two forms of job enrichment that increase motivation.**

Job enlargement combines a series of tasks into one challenging and interesting assignment. Job rotation makes work more interesting by moving employees from one job to another.

- **How does open communication improve employee motivation?**

Open communication helps both top managers and employees understand the objectives and work together to achieve them.

- **How can managers encourage open communication?**

Managers can create an organizational culture that rewards listening, train supervisors and managers to listen, use effective questioning techniques, remove barriers to open communication, avoid vague and ambiguous communication, and actively make it easier for all to communicate.

Learning Goal 8. Show how managers personalize motivation strategies to appeal to employees across the globe and across generations.

- **What is the difference between high-context and low-context cultures?**

In high-context cultures people build personal relationships and develop group trust before focusing on tasks. In low-context cultures, people often view relationship building as a waste of time that diverts attention from the task.

- **How are Generation X managers likely to be different from their baby boomer predecessors?**

Baby boomers tend to be willing to work long hours to build their careers and often expect their subordinates to do likewise. Gen Xers may strive for a more balanced lifestyle and are likely to focus on results rather than on how many hours their teams work. Gen Xers tend to be better than previous generations at working in teams and providing frequent feedback. They are not bound by traditions that may constrain those who have been with an organization for a long time and are willing to try new approaches to solving problems.

- **What are some common characteristics of Millennials?**

Millennials tend to be adaptable, tech-savvy, able to grasp new concepts, practiced at multitasking, efficient, and tolerant. They often place a higher value on work-life balance, expect their employers to adapt to them, and are more likely to rank fun and stimulation in their top five ideal job requirements.

key terms

equity theory 268
expectancy theory 267
extrinsic reward 257
goal-setting theory 267
Hawthorne effect 260
hygiene factors 262
intrinsic reward 256
job enlargement 270
job enrichment 270
job rotation 270
management by objectives (MBO) 267
Maslow's hierarchy of needs 260
motivators 262
principle of motion economy 257
reinforcement theory 268
scientific management 257
time-motion studies 257

connect interactive applications

Reinforcing Your *Connect*ion to Concepts in Business

This chapter offers 15 interactive applications designed to help you apply what you've learned (examples of these exercises appear on the following pages). Your instructor has determined which interactive applications will benefit you throughout this course. Please refer to your instructor's assignment list in *Connect* to determine which applications you should complete.

Click and Drag Interactive: Assumptions about motivation have led to many theories about the human side of motivation. What do all these theories have to do with what really goes on in the workplace today? Demonstrate your understanding of the concepts, theories, and practice of motivation by categorizing the statements given.

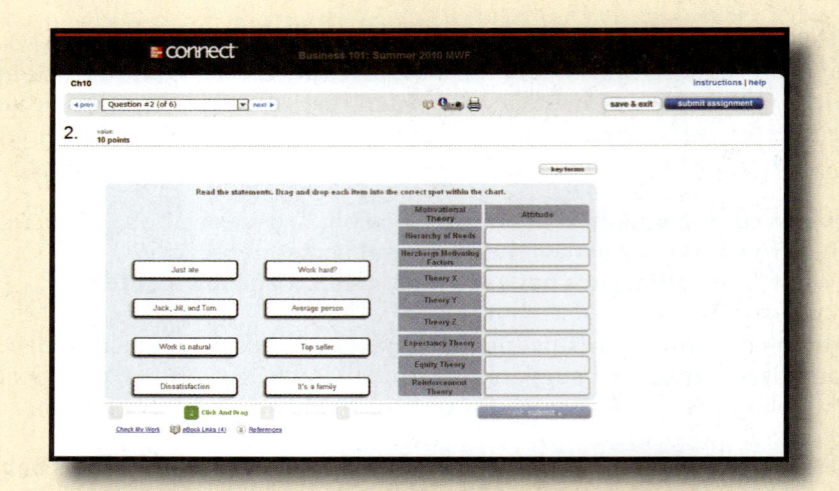

Click and Drag Interactive: Herzberg identified certain factors, which he called motivators, that made employees more productive and gave them satisfaction. Herzberg called other elements of the job hygiene factors (or maintenance factors). These related to the job environment and could cause dissatisfaction if missing but would not necessarily motivate employees if increased. Evaluate the factors listed to determine whether they are motivators or hygiene factors.

Click and Drag Interactive: Some workers struggle all day to simply meet basic physiological and safety needs. For other workers, such needs no longer dominate, and they seek to satisfy growth needs—social, esteem, and self-actualization needs. Evaluate the needs listed and drop them in the correct order on the hierarchy pyramid.

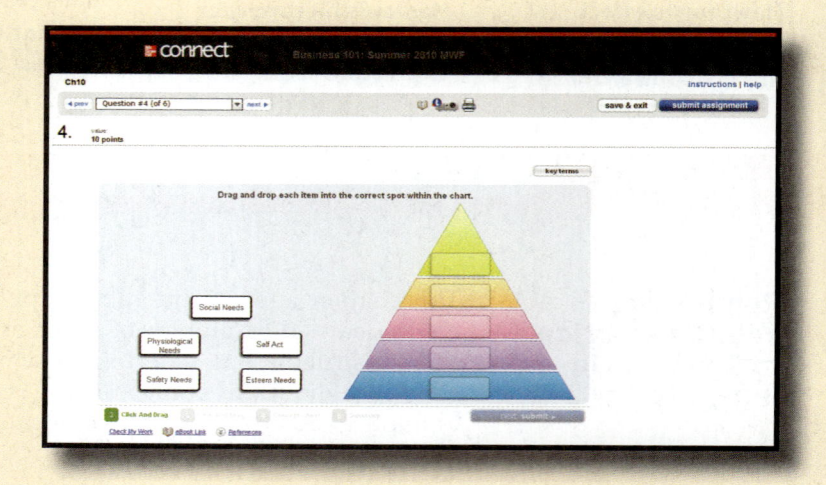

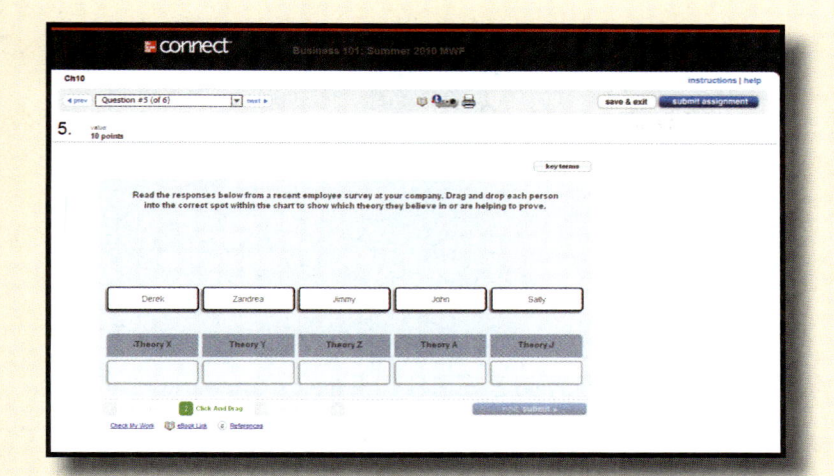

Click and Drag Interactive: William Ouchi investigated the ways in which Japanese companies managed employees and developed a new theory of management called Theory Z. Read the responses and correlate each person into the correct spot within the chart to illustrate which theory they best emulate.

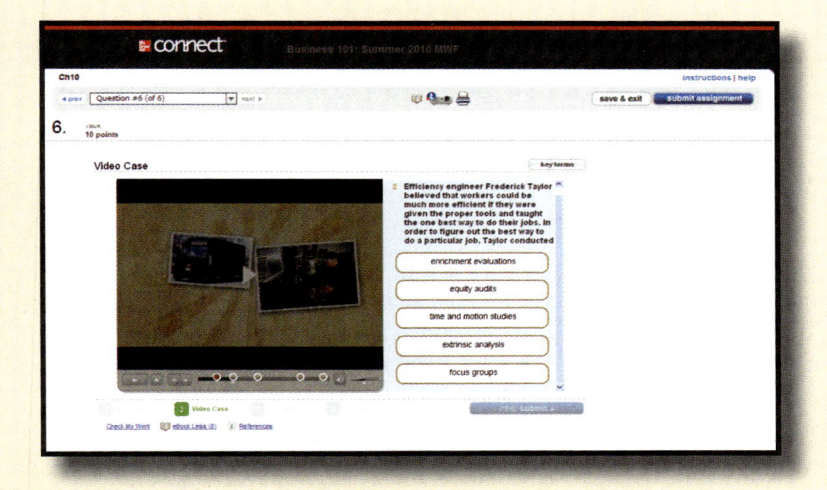

Video Case Interactive: Enterprise managers try to motivate employees by being better listeners, rewarding good work, and creating a climate that fosters enthusiasm for the job and work satisfaction. View the Enterprise Rent-a-Car video to determine how Enterprise goes about training and motivating its employees.

Human Resource Management

FINDING AND KEEPING THE BEST EMPLOYEES

profile

Getting to Know Sally Mainquist, President and CEO of Certes Financial Pros

In today's business world the prospect of lifetime employment at a single company is becoming increasingly unlikely. Thanks to a sluggish economy and never-ending technological innovation, workers no longer have much of a chance to stay in one place until their retirement. As staff sizes rise and fall with the global marketplace, many companies say they require a flexible workforce of people who can come and go as they're needed. Workers in turn demand flexible schedules to help balance work and life, with nontraditional work arrangements such as part-time and temporary jobs.

That's where Sally Mainquist, president and CEO of Minnesota-based Certes Financial Pros, comes in. Her company finds financial professionals to fit flexible work environments on a contingent, or temporary, basis. Certes's 200-plus full- and part-time workers are free to shape their schedules to fit their lifestyles, allowing them to go on vacation, attend a child's sporting event, or even take the entire summer off unimpeded. In fact, Certes employees can take up to six months off and still retain benefits.

"Certes strives to implement programs and practices that create a flexible and supportive workplace, one that allows our employees to express their true needs while providing the highest level of service to our clients," Mainquist said. Besides providing an impressive array of benefits and above-average wages, Certes makes five vacation homes available to workers free of charge. Generous benefits aren't typical of temporary agencies, but they've helped Mainquist attract a loyal workforce. The average tenure of a Certes employee is four years, exceptional in the usually turnover-heavy temporary employment industry. In 2008, the *Minneapolis/St. Paul Business Journal* named Certes the best place to work in the Twin Cities. Recently, an Iowa-based company, Staffing Now, bought Certes with the intention of expanding its business philosophy nationwide.

Besides outstanding perks, Certes workers acquire an unusually broad range of work experience. Today's business environment demands that workers have a diverse set of skills instead of focusing on just one. Contingent workers

LEARNING goals

After you have read and studied this chapter, you should be able to

1. Explain the importance of human resource management, and describe current issues in managing human resources.
2. Illustrate the effects of legislation on human resource management.
3. Summarize the five steps in human resource planning.
4. Describe methods that companies use to recruit new employees, and explain some of the issues that make recruitment challenging.
5. Outline the six steps in selecting employees.
6. Illustrate employee training and development methods.
7. Trace the six steps in appraising employee performance.
8. Summarize the objectives of employee compensation programs, and evaluate pay systems and fringe benefits.
9. Show how managers use scheduling plans to adapt to workers' needs.
10. Describe how employees can move through a company: promotion, reassignment, termination, and retirement.

connect

Your *Connect*ion to Better Learning. 1. View the interactive presentation. 2. Practice through LearnSmart. 3. Apply your knowledge by using the interactive applications for each chapter of this text.

1 Prep »»»»» **2 Study** 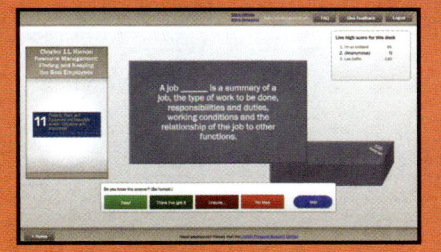 »»»»» **3 Apply**

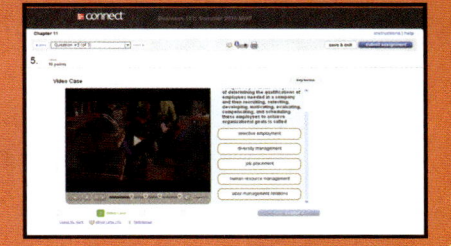

view their temporary positions as opportunities to build their skills and gain necessary experience. Many employers in turn view temporary agencies as excellent training grounds and say hiring people for temporary work is an efficient way to test-drive employees before committing to hire them full-time.

Many contingent workers find the flexibility liberating. It gives them more time with their families, along with opportunities to build new skills or switch careers. For Certes, building morale has been a key to success. Over half the Twin Cities' Fortune 500 companies and 25 percent of all public companies contract workers from Certes, and as the company takes its philosophy to the national stage, it may be destined for even greater success.

In this chapter, you'll learn how successful businesses like Certes recruit, manage, and make the most of their employees.

Sources: Elizabeth Millard, "Benefits Buffet," *Minnesota Business*, July 2008; Dr. John Sullivan, "A Flexible Force," *Workforce Management*, July 14, 2008; Kathryn Tyler, "Treat Contingent Workers with Care," *HRMagazine*, March 1, 2008; and Certes Financial Pros, www.certespros.com, accessed July 2, 2010.

www.certespros.com

NAME THAT company

For this award-winning supermarket chain, friendly customer service is paramount. The shopper-centric company culture sets no limits on the employees' capacity to please the purchaser, even if that means driving to the customer's home to make sure a food order is perfect. The staff is rewarded for their hard work with high wages and unparalleled benefits. Name that company. (Find the answer in the chapter.)

> **PPT 11-1:**
> Human Resource Management: Finding and Keeping the Best Employees

> **PPT 11-2:**
> Sally Mainquist

LEARNING goal 1 *

Explain the importance of human resource management, and describe current issues in managing human resources.

> **PPT 11-3:**
> Human Resource Management

WORKING WITH PEOPLE IS JUST THE BEGINNING

Students often say they want to go into human resource management because they want to "work with people." Human resource managers do work with people, but they are also deeply involved in planning, record keeping, and other administrative duties. To begin a career in human resource management, you need a better reason than "I want to work with people." This chapter will tell you what else human resource management is all about.

> **PPT 11-4:**
> Human Resource Management (HRM)

human resource management (HRM)
The process of determining human resource needs and then recruiting, selecting, developing, motivating, evaluating, compensating, and scheduling employees to achieve organizational goals.

Human resource management (HRM) is the process of determining human resource needs and then recruiting, selecting, developing, motivating, evaluating, compensating, and scheduling employees to achieve organizational goals (see Figure 11.1). For many years, human resource management was called "personnel" and involved clerical functions such as screening applications, keeping records, processing the payroll, and finding new employees when necessary. The roles and responsibilities of HRM have evolved primarily because of two key factors: (1) organizations' recognition of employees as their ultimate resource and (2) changes in the law that rewrote many traditional practices. Let's explore both.

Developing the Ultimate Resource

> **PPT 11-5:**
> Developing the Firm's Ultimate Resource

One reason human resource management is receiving increased attention now is that the U.S. economy has experienced a major shift—from traditional manufacturing industries to service and high-tech manufacturing industries that require highly technical job skills. This shift means that many workers

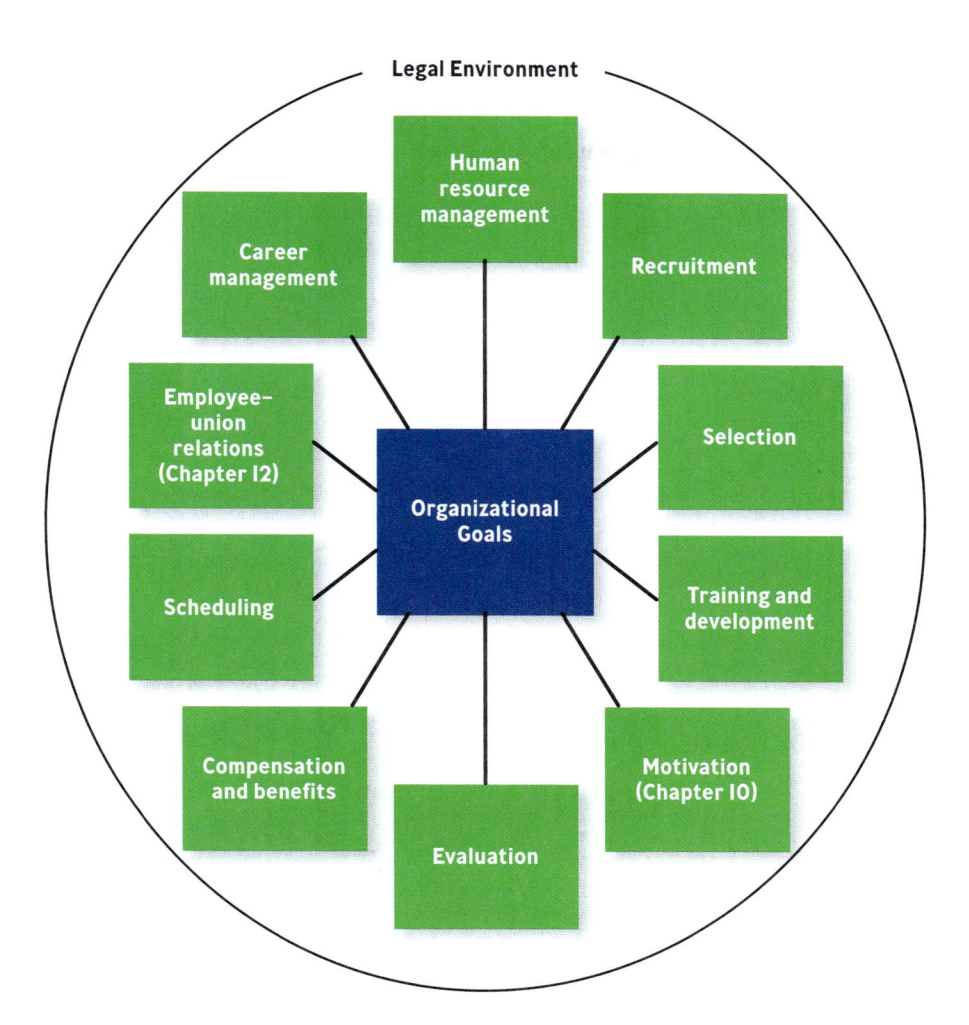

figure 11.1

HUMAN RESOURCE MANAGEMENT

As this figure shows, human resource management is more than hiring and firing personnel. All activities are designed to achieve organizational goals within the laws that affect human resource management. (Note that human resource management includes motivation, as discussed in Chapter 10, and employee–union relations, as discussed in Chapter 12.)

Diagram (Legal Environment encircling): Organizational Goals at center, connected to Human resource management, Recruitment, Selection, Training and development, Motivation (Chapter 10), Evaluation, Compensation and benefits, Scheduling, Employee–union relations (Chapter 12), Career management.

---

must be retrained for new, more challenging jobs. They truly are the ultimate resource. People develop the ideas that eventually become products to satisfy consumers' wants and needs. Take away their creative minds, and leading firms such as Disney, Apple, Procter & Gamble, Google, and General Electric would be nothing.

In the past, human resources were plentiful, so there was little need to nurture and develop them. If you needed qualified people, you simply hired them. If they didn't work out, you fired them and found others. Most firms assigned the job of recruiting, selecting, training, evaluating, compensating, motivating, and, yes, firing people to the functional departments that employed them, like accounting, manufacturing, and marketing. Today the job of human resource management has taken on an increased role in the firm since *qualified* employees are much scarcer, which makes recruiting and retaining people more important and more difficult.[1]

In the future, human resource management may become the firm's most critical function, responsible for dealing with all aspects of a business's most critical resource—people.[2] In fact, the human resource function has become so important that it's no longer the job of just one department; it's a responsibility of *all* managers. What are some human resource challenges all managers face? We'll outline a few next.

▶ **PPT II-6:** Challenges in Finding High-Level Workers

U.S. firms face a shortage of workers skilled in areas like science, green technology, and the development of clean energy sources like these solar panels. What other job markets do you think will grow as companies focus more on environmentally friendly policies? Which ones appeal to you?

The Human Resource Challenge

Many of the changes that have had the most dramatic impact on U.S. business are those in the labor force. The ability to compete in global markets depends on new ideas, new products, and new levels of productivity—in other words, on people with good ideas. These are some of the challenges and opportunities in human resources:

- Shortages of trained workers in growth areas, such as computers, biotechnology, robotics, green technology, and the sciences.[3]
- An increasing number of skilled and unskilled workers from declining industries, such as steel and automobiles, who are unemployed or underemployed and need retraining. *Underemployed workers* are those who have more skills or knowledge than their current jobs require.[4]
- A growing percentage of new workers who are undereducated and unprepared for jobs in the contemporary business environment.[5]
- A shortage of workers in skilled trades due to retirement of aging baby boomers.[6]
- An increasing number of both single-parent and two-income families, resulting in a demand for job sharing, maternity leave, and special career advancement programs for women.[7]
- A shift in employee attitudes toward work. Leisure time has become a much higher priority, as have flextime and a shorter workweek.[8]
- A declining economy that is taking a toll on employee morale as well as increasing the demand for temporary and part-time workers.[9]
- A challenge from overseas labor pools whose members work for lower wages and are subject to fewer laws and regulations than U.S. workers. This results in many jobs being outsourced overseas.[10]
- An increased demand for benefits tailored to the individual yet cost-effective to the company. See the Thinking Green box to see how companies are addressing wellness issues at work.
- A growing concern over health care, elder care, child care, drug testing, workplace violence (all discussed in Chapter 12), and opportunities for people with disabilities.
- A decreased sense of employee loyalty, which raises employee turnover and the cost of replacing lost workers.

Given these issues, you can see why human resource management has taken a central place in management thinking. However, significant changes in laws covering hiring, safety, unionization, equal pay, and affirmative action have also had a major influence. Let's look at their impact on human resource management.

THINKING green

Green Eggs and Green Ham

In many company cafeterias, jelly donuts and sugary sodas are becoming distant memories. Big businesses like Google, Microsoft, and Dow Chemical have begun to supply their company eateries with healthy alternatives like dried fruit, salads, and vegan dishes, while cutting back on fatty burgers and desserts. By helping keep employees healthy, companies will not only have a fitter workforce but also save money on insurance premiums, and may even see an increase in productivity. Dow Chemical aims to reduce health risks to its 43,000 employees by 10 percent by 2014.

Besides conveying health and monetary benefits, eating right in the workplace also helps the environment. Along with eliminating trans fats from cafeteria food, San Diego State University turns 50 tons of leftovers a year into compost for the campus landscape. Cox Enterprises in Atlanta makes all the packaging for its health-oriented food service from sustainable sources. Plates are made of sugar cane and cups from corn; both disintegrate in 60 days. While other organizations may not be as creative, their growing use of organic and renewable sources for food are not only good for the body but also much better for the earth than chemicals and preservatives.

Sources: Stephanie Armour, "Corporate Cafeterias Go the Green, Healthy Route," *USA Today*, February 8, 2008; and Michelle Conlin, "Hide the Doritos! Here Comes HR!" *BusinessWeek*, April 17, 2008.

LEARNING goal 2 *

Illustrate the effects of legislation on human resource management.

LAWS AFFECTING HUMAN RESOURCE MANAGEMENT

Until the 1930s, the U.S. government had little to do with human resource decisions. Since then, legislation and legal decisions have greatly affected all areas of human resource management, from hiring to training to monitoring working conditions (see the Legal Briefcase box on p. 288). These laws were passed because many businesses did not exercise fair labor practices voluntarily.

◄ **PPT 11-7:**
Civil Rights Act of 1964

One of the more important pieces of social legislation passed by Congress was the Civil Rights Act of 1964. This act generated much debate and was amended 97 times before final passage. Title VII of that act brought the government directly into the operations of human resource management. Title VII prohibits discrimination in hiring, firing, compensation, apprenticeships, training, terms, conditions, or privileges of employment based on race, religion, creed, sex, or national origin. Age was later added to the conditions of the act. The Civil Rights Act of 1964 was expected to stamp out discrimination in the workplace, but specific language in it made enforcement quite difficult. Congress took on the task of amending the law.

◄ **PPT 11-8:**
1972 Equal Employment Opportunity Act (EEOA)

In 1972, the Equal Employment Opportunity Act (EEOA) was added as an amendment to Title VII. It strengthened the Equal Employment Opportunity Commission (EEOC), which was created by the Civil Rights Act, by giving it rather broad powers. For example, it permitted the EEOC to issue guidelines for acceptable employer conduct in administering equal employment opportunity. The EEOC also mandated specific record keeping procedures,

LEGAL briefcase

www.eeoc.gov/welcome.html

Government Legislation

National Labor Relations Act of 1935. Established collective bargaining in labor-management relations and limited management interference in the right of employees to have a collective bargaining agent.

Fair Labor Standards Act of 1938. Established a minimum wage and overtime pay for employees working more than 40 hours a week. Amendments expanded the classes of workers covered, raised the minimum wage, redefined regular-time work, raised overtime payments, and equalized pay scales for men and women.

Manpower Development and Training Act of 1962. Provided for the training and retraining of unemployed workers.

Equal Pay Act of 1963. Specified that men and women doing equal jobs must be paid the same wage.

Civil Rights Act of 1964. For firms with 15 or more employees, outlawed discrimination in employment based on sex, race, color, religion, or national origin.

Age Discrimination in Employment Act of 1967. Outlawed employment practices that discriminate against people 40 and above. An amendment outlaws requiring retirement by a specific age.

Occupational Safety and Health Act of 1970. Regulated the degree to which employees can be exposed to hazardous substances and specified the safety equipment the employer must provide.

Equal Employment Opportunity Act of 1972. Strengthened the Equal Employment Opportunity Commission (EEOC) and authorized the EEOC to set guidelines for human resource management.

Comprehensive Employment and Training Act of 1973 (CETA). Provided funds for training unemployed workers.

Employee Retirement Income Security Act of 1974 (ERISA). Regulated and insured company retirement plans.

Immigration Reform and Control Act of 1986. Required employers to verify employment eligibility of all new hires including U.S. citizens.

Supreme Court ruling against set-aside programs (affirmative action), 1989. Declared that setting aside 30 percent of contracting jobs for minority businesses was reverse discrimination and unconstitutional.

Older Workers Benefit Protection Act, 1990. Protects older people from signing away their rights to pensions and protection from illegal age discrimination.

Civil Rights Act of 1991. For firms with over 15 employees, extends the right to a jury trial and punitive damages to victims of intentional job discrimination.

Americans with Disabilities Act of 1990 (1992 implementation). Prohibits employers from discriminating against qualified individuals with disabilities in hiring, advancement, or compensation and requires them to adapt the workplace if necessary.

Family and Medical Leave Act of 1993. Businesses with 50 or more employees must provide up to 12 weeks of unpaid leave per year upon birth or adoption of an employee's child or upon serious illness of a parent, spouse, or child.

Americans with Disabilities Amendments Act of 2008 (ADA). Provides broader protection for disabled workers and reverses Supreme Court decisions deemed too restrictive. Adds disabilities such as epilepsy and cancer to ADA coverage.

---

affirmative action
Employment activities designed to "right past wrongs" by increasing opportunities for minorities and women.

and Congress vested it with the power of enforcement to ensure these mandates were carried out. The EEOC became a formidable regulatory force in the administration of human resource management.

The most controversial policy enforced by the EEOC was **affirmative action**, designed to "right past wrongs" by increasing opportunities for minorities and women. Interpretation of the affirmative action law led employers to actively recruit, and in some cases give preference to, women and minority group members. Questions persist about the legality of affirmative action and the effect it may have in creating a sort of reverse discrimination in the workplace. **Reverse discrimination** has been defined as discrimination against whites or males, as when companies are perceived as unfairly giving preference to women or minority group members in hiring and promoting. The issue has generated much heated debate as well as many lawsuits.[11]

The Civil Rights Act of 1991 expanded the remedies available to victims of discrimination by amending Title VII of the Civil Rights Act of 1964. Now victims of discrimination have the right to a jury trial and punitive damages. Though the number of discrimination lawsuits has dropped considerably, human resource managers must follow court decisions closely to see how the law is enforced.[12] The issue is likely to persist for years to come.

The Office of Federal Contract Compliance Programs (OFCCP) ensures that employers comply with nondiscrimination and affirmative action laws and regulations when doing business with the federal government.[13]

Laws Protecting Employees with Disabilities and Older Employees

As you read above, laws prohibit discrimination related to race, sex, or age in hiring, firing, and training. The Vocational Rehabilitation Act of 1973 extended protection to people with any physical or mental disability.

The Americans with Disabilities Act of 1990 (ADA) requires employers to give applicants with physical or mental disabilities the same consideration for employment as people without disabilities. It also requires making "reasonable accommodations" for employees with disabilities, such as modifying equipment or widening doorways. Accommodations are not always expensive; an inexpensive headset can allow someone with cerebral palsy to talk on the phone. The ADA also protects individuals with disabilities from discrimination in public accommodations, transportation, and telecommunications.[14]

Most companies have no trouble making structural changes to be accommodating. Some, however, find cultural changes difficult. Employers used to think that being fair meant treating everyone the same, but *accommodation* in fact means treating people *according to their specific needs*. That can include putting up barriers to isolate people readily distracted by noise, reassigning workers to new tasks, and making changes in supervisors' management styles.

In 2008, Congress passed the Americans with Disabilities Amendments Act, which overturned Supreme Court decisions that had reduced protections for certain people with disabilities such as diabetes, epilepsy, heart disease, and cancer.[15] Enforcement promises to be a continuing issue for human resource management.[16]

The Age Discrimination in Employment Act of 1967 (ADEA) protects individuals 40 or older from employment and workplace discrimination in hiring, firing, promotion, layoff, compensation, benefits, job assignments, and training. The ADEA is enforced by the EEOC, applies to employers with 20 or more employees, and protects both

◀ PPT II-9:
Controversial Procedures of the EEOC

reverse discrimination
Discrimination against members of a dominant or majority group (e.g. white males) usually as a result of policies designed to correct discrimination against minority or disadvantaged groups.

◀ PPT II-10:
Civil Rights Act of 1991 and OFCCP

◀ PPT II-11:
Laws Protecting Employees with Disabilities

The Americans with Disabilities Act guarantees that all U.S. workers have equal opportunity in employment. This legislation requires businesses to make "reasonable accommodations" on the job for people with disabilities. What required accommodations do you think would be reasonable?

> **PPT 11-12:**
> Age Discrimination in Employment Act (ADEA)

employees and job applicants.[17] It also outlaws mandatory retirement in most organizations. It does, however, allow age restrictions for certain job categories like airline pilot or bus driver if evidence shows that the ability to perform significantly diminishes with age or that age imposes a danger to society.

Effects of Legislation

> **PPT 11-13:**
> Minding the Law in HRM

Clearly, laws ranging from the Social Security Act of 1935 to the 2008 Americans with Disabilities Amendments Act require human resource managers to keep abreast of laws and court decisions to effectively perform their jobs. Choosing a career in human resource management offers a challenge to anyone willing to put forth the effort. Remember:

- Employers must know and act in accordance with the legal rights of their employees or risk costly court cases.
- Legislation affects all areas of human resource management, from hiring and training to compensation.
- Court cases demonstrate that it is sometimes legal to go beyond providing equal rights for minorities and women to provide special employment (affirmative action) and training to correct discrimination in the past.
- New court cases and legislation change human resource management almost daily; the only way to keep current is to read the business literature and stay familiar with emerging issues.

progress assessment

> **PPT 11-14:**
> Progress Assessment

- What is human resource management?
- What did Title VII of the Civil Rights Act of 1964 achieve?
- What is the EEOC, and what was the intention of affirmative action?
- What does *accommodations* mean in the Americans with Disabilities Act of 1990?

LEARNING goal 3 *

Summarize the five steps in human resource planning.

DETERMINING A FIRM'S HUMAN RESOURCE NEEDS

> **PPT 11-15:**
> Human Resource Planning Process

All management, including human resource management, begins with planning. The five steps in the human resource planning process are:

> **CRITICAL THINKING EXERCISE 11-1:**
> Expanding the Work Force

1. *Preparing a human resource inventory of the organization's employees.* This inventory should include ages, names, education, capabilities, training, specialized skills, and other relevant information (such as languages spoken). It reveals whether the labor force is technically up-to-date and thoroughly trained.

> **job analysis**
> A study of what employees do who hold various job titles.

2. *Preparing a job analysis.* A **job analysis** is a study of what employees do who hold various job titles. It's necessary in order to recruit and

figure 11.2

JOB ANALYSIS

A job analysis yields two important statements: job descriptions and job specifications. Here you have a job description and job specifications for a sales representative.

JOB ANALYSIS

Observe current sales representatives doing the job.
Discuss job with sales managers.
Have current sales reps keep a diary of their activities.

JOB DESCRIPTION	JOB SPECIFICATIONS
Primary objective is to sell company's products to stores in Territory Z. Duties include servicing accounts and maintaining positive relationships with clients. Responsibilities include: • Introducing the new products to store managers in the area. • Helping the store managers estimate the volume to order. • Negotiating prime shelf space. • Explaining sales promotion activities to store managers. • Stocking and maintaining shelves in stores that wish such service.	Characteristics of the person qualifying for this job include: • Two years' sales experience. • Positive attitude. • Well-groomed appearance. • Good communication skills. • High school diploma and two years of college credit.

◄ PPT 11-16:
What's a Job Analysis

job description
A summary of the objectives of a job, the type of work to be done, the responsibilities and duties, the working conditions, and the relationship of the job to other functions.

job specifications
A written summary of the minimum qualifications required of workers to do a particular job.

train employees with the necessary skills to do the job.[18] The results of job analysis are two written statements: job descriptions and job specifications. A **job description** specifies the objectives of the job, the type of work, the responsibilities and duties, working conditions, and the job's relationship to other functions. **Job specifications** are a written summary of the minimal education and skills to do a particular job. In short, job descriptions are about the job, and job specifications are about the person who does the job. Visit the Occupational Information Network (O*NET) at www.onetcenter.org for detailed information about job analyses and job descriptions. See Figure 11.2 for a hypothetical job description and job specifications.

3. *Assessing future human resource demand.* Because technology changes rapidly, effective human resource managers are proactive; that is, they forecast the organization's requirements and train people ahead of time or ensure trained people are available when needed.[19]

4. *Assessing future labor supply.* The labor force is constantly shifting: getting older, becoming more technically oriented, attracting more women. Some workers will be scarcer in the future, like computer and robotic repair workers, and others will be oversupplied, like assembly-line workers.

5. *Establishing a strategic plan.* The human resource strategic plan must address recruiting, selecting, training, developing, appraising, compensating, and scheduling the labor force. Because the first four steps lead up to this one, we'll focus on them in the rest of the chapter.

Some companies use advanced technology to perform the human resource planning process more efficiently. IBM manages its global workforce of about 100,000 employees and 100,000 subcontractors with a database that matches employee skills, experiences, schedules, and references with jobs available. If a client in Quebec, Canada, has a month-long project requiring a consultant who speaks English and French, has an advanced degree in engineering, and is experienced with Linux programming, IBM's database can find the best-suited consultant available and put him or her in touch with the client.

LEARNING goal 4 *

Describe methods that companies use to recruit new employees, and explain some of the issues that make recruitment challenging.

> **PPT II-17:**
> Recruiting Employees

> **LECTURE LINK II-1:**
> Where Have All the Want Ads Gone?

> **recruitment**
> The set of activities used to obtain a sufficient number of the right employees at the right time.

> **LECTURE LINK II-2:**
> Finding Google People

> **CRITICAL THINKING EXERCISE II-2:**
> Management Selection

> **CRITICAL THINKING EXERCISE II-3:**
> Job Search Via the Internet

Human resource managers today have the opportunity to recruit people from a wide range of cultural and ethnic backgrounds. What are some of the advantages of a diverse workforce?

RECRUITING EMPLOYEES FROM A DIVERSE POPULATION

Recruitment is the set of activities for obtaining the right number of qualified people at the right time. Its purpose is to select those who best meet the needs of the organization. You might think a continuous flow of new people into the workforce makes recruiting easy. On the contrary, it's become very challenging for several reasons:

- Some organizations have policies that demand promotions from within, operate under union regulations, or offer low wages, which makes recruiting and keeping employees difficult or subject to outside influence and restrictions.
- The emphasis on corporate culture, teamwork, and participative management makes it important to hire people who not only are skilled but also fit in with the culture and leadership style of the organization. Wegmans Food Markets (a perennial member of *Fortune* magazine's list of best companies to work for) encourages employees to do whatever they think is necessary to make a customer happy. For example, they don't have to ask a supervisor if they need to cook a Thanksgiving turkey at the store for a customer whose oven is too small or go to a customer's home to check a food order.
- Sometimes people with the necessary skills are not available; then workers must be hired and trained internally.

Human resource managers can turn to many sources for recruiting assistance (see Figure 11.3). *Internal sources* include current employees who can be transferred or promoted or who can recommend others to hire. Using internal sources is less expensive than recruiting from outside and helps maintain employee morale. However, it isn't always possible to find qualified workers within the company, so human resource managers also use *external sources* such as advertisements, public and private employment agencies, college placement bureaus, management consultants, Internet sites, professional organizations, referrals, and online and walk-in applications.

Recruiting qualified workers may be particularly difficult for small businesses with few staff

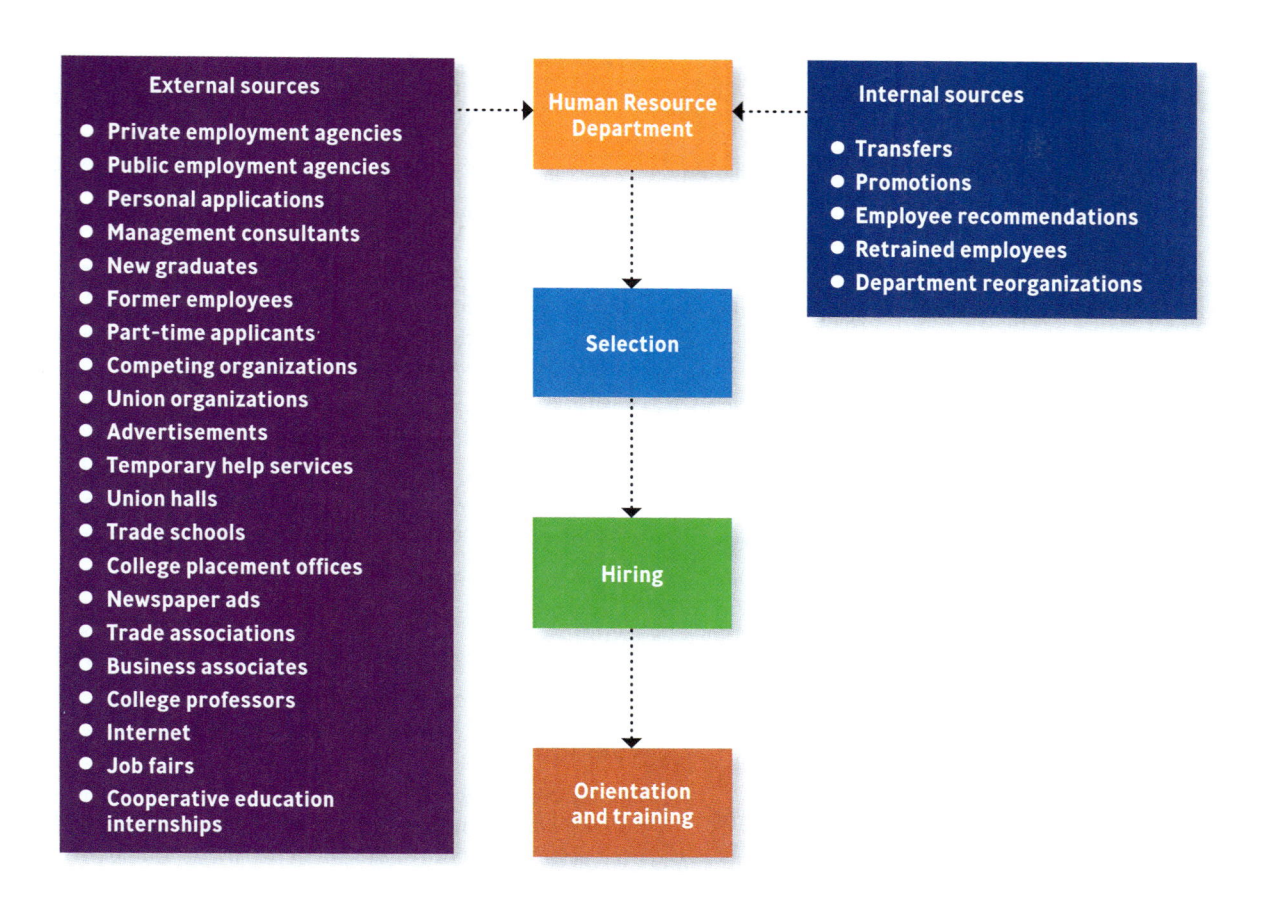

Human Resource Management: Finding and Keeping the Best Employees * CHAPTER 11   293

External sources
- Private employment agencies
- Public employment agencies
- Personal applications
- Management consultants
- New graduates
- Former employees
- Part-time applicants
- Competing organizations
- Union organizations
- Advertisements
- Temporary help services
- Union halls
- Trade schools
- College placement offices
- Newspaper ads
- Trade associations
- Business associates
- College professors
- Internet
- Job fairs
- Cooperative education internships

Internal sources
- Transfers
- Promotions
- Employee recommendations
- Retrained employees
- Department reorganizations

Human Resource Department → Selection → Hiring → Orientation and training

figure 11.3
EMPLOYEE SOURCES
Internal sources are often given first consideration, so it's useful to get a recommendation from a current employee of the firm for which you want to work. College placement offices are also an important source. Be sure to learn about such facilities early so that you can plan a strategy throughout your college career.

◄ PPT 11-19:
Employee Sources

◄ PPT 11-20:
Selection

selection
The process of gathering information and deciding who should be hired, under legal guidelines, to serve the best interests of the individual and the organization.

◄ LECTURE LINK 11-3:
Interview Blunders

members and less-than-competitive compensation to attract external sources. CareerBuilder.com and Monster.com have helped such firms. They attract more than 80 million visitors per month.[20] The Spotlight on Small Business box on p. 294 offers additional ways small businesses can recruit.

LEARNING goal 5 *

Outline the six steps in selecting employees.

SELECTING EMPLOYEES WHO WILL BE PRODUCTIVE

Selection is the process of gathering information and deciding who should be hired, under legal guidelines, to serve the best interests of the individual and the organization. Selecting and training employees are extremely expensive processes in some firms. Just think what's involved: advertising or recruiting agency fees, interview time, medical exams, training costs, unproductive time spent learning the job, possible travel and moving expenses, and more. It can cost one and a half times the employee's annual salary to recruit, process, and train even an entry-level worker, and over six figures for a top manager.

SPOTLIGHT ON SMALL business

www.monster.com

It's Not Easy Being Small

To survive, it's critical for small businesses to recruit and retain qualified workers. However, competing for top talent is difficult when you can't afford corporate-level benefits or expensive recruiters to hunt down the best people. Despite these hurdles, small-business management consultants say there are many ways to lure desirable workers:

- *Transform ads into promotional tools.* Ecoprint, a small print shop in Maryland, touts the benefits of working for this collegial company in its regular advertisements.

- *Post job openings on the Internet.* Running an ad on an online service like CareerBuilder.com or Monster.com for 30 days costs about one-fourth the price of a comparable ad in the *New York Times* that runs for one week.

- *Let your staff help recruit and select hires.* The more staff engaged in the search and interview process, the better chance to find recruits with the personality and skills to fit in.

- *Create a dynamic workplace that attracts local, energetic applicants.* Sometimes word of mouth is the most effective recruiting tool.

- *Test-drive an employee.* Hiring contingent workers allows you to test candidates for a few months before deciding whether to make an offer of permanent employment.

- *Hire customers.* Loyal customers sometimes make the smartest employees. Build-A-Bear Workshop often hires customers who come into its stores and exhibit a real interest in the company and its products.

- *Check community groups and local government agencies.* Don't forget to check state-run employment agencies. Many nonprofit organizations serve immigrants new to a region or people in need of a job who become excellent candidates you can train.

- *Work hard for publicity in local media.* Publicity is more believable than advertising.

- *Lure candidates with a policy of promotions and raises.* Most employees want to know they can move up. Give employees an incentive for learning the business.

- *Outsource fringe benefit management to a professional employer organization (PEO).* It's tough to build a benefits program equivalent to those offered by large companies, but PEOs may offer lower insurance rates due to economies of scale. Face it, any way you can close the gap may help attract qualified workers.

Sources: "Why Are Your Employees Leaving?" *Nonprofit World,* July 1, 2008; Dwayne Orrick, "Making Recruitment and Retention a Priority," *Law and Order,* March 1, 2008; Mila Stahl, "How to Hire (or Fire) an Employee," *Wisconsin State Journal,* March 1, 2008; and "Finding, Hiring and Keeping Next-Generation Talent," Executive Quotes and Information Service, May 26, 2008.

▶ **PPT 11-18:**
It's Not Easy Being Small

▶ **LECTURE LINK 11-4:**
Memorable Job Interviews

▶ **LECTURE LINK 11-5:**
Personality Testing for Job Applicants

A typical selection process has six steps:

1. *Obtaining complete application forms.* Although equal employment laws limit the kinds of questions that can appear, applications help reveal the applicant's educational background, work experience, career objectives, and other qualifications directly related to the job.

    Large retail employers like Winn-Dixie and Finish Line make the application process more efficient by using an automated program called Workforce Acquisition.[21] An applicant sits at a computer and answers questions about job experience, time available to work, and personality. The software e-mails a report to the hiring manager recommending whether to interview the applicant and, if so, suggesting questions to ask. Mike Marchetti, executive vice president of store operations for Finish Line, says his company processed 330,000 applications, eliminating 60,000 interview hours and reducing turnover 24 percent.[22]

2. *Conducting initial and follow-up interviews.* A staff member from the human resource department often screens applicants in a first interview. If the interviewer considers the applicant a potential hire, the manager who will supervise the new employee may interview the applicant as well. It's important that managers prepare adequately for the interview to avoid selection decisions they may regret. No matter how innocent the intention, missteps such as asking about pregnancy or child care could later be evidence if the applicant files discrimination charges.[23]

3. *Giving employment tests.* Organizations often use tests to measure basic competency in specific job skills like welding or fire fighting, and to help evaluate applicants' personalities and interests. The tests should always be directly related to the job. Employment tests have been legally challenged as potential means of discrimination.[24] UPS was sued under the Americans with Disabilities Act for requiring all drivers to pass a hearing test approved by the Department of Transportation (DOT), even though DOT does not require a hearing test for drivers who operate local delivery trucks weighing less than 10,000 pounds. The hearing-impaired drivers who applied to drive these trucks challenged the application of the test as a job requirement.[25] Many companies test potential employees in assessment centers where they perform actual job tasks. Such testing can make the selection process more efficient and will generally satisfy legal requirements.

4. *Conducting background investigations.* Most organizations now investigate a candidate's work record, school record, credit history, and references more carefully than in the past to help identify those most likely to succeed. It is simply too costly to hire, train, and motivate people only to lose them and have to start the process over. Services such as LexisNexis allow prospective employers not only to conduct speedy background checks of criminal records, driving records, and credit histories but also to verify work experience and professional and educational credentials.[26]

5. *Obtaining results from physical exams.* There are obvious benefits to hiring physically and mentally healthy people. However, according to the Americans with Disabilities Act, medical tests cannot be given just to screen out individuals. In some states, physical exams can be given only after an offer of employment has been accepted. In states that allow pre-employment physical exams, they must be given to everyone applying for the same position. Pre-employment testing to detect drug or alcohol abuse has been controversial, as has screening to detect carriers of HIV, the virus that causes AIDS. Over 70 percent of U.S. companies now test both current and potential employees for drug use.

◄ PPT 11-21:
Steps in the Selection Process

◄ PPT 11-22:
Oops!

Choosing qualified employees is a challenge. Psychologist Turhan Canli believes he can tell what makes some people better suited to a job than others by using human physiology mechanisms. Canli uses brain scans to see how people react to certain word-image combinations and believes you can read personalities from them. What do you think are key criteria for evaluating job candidates?

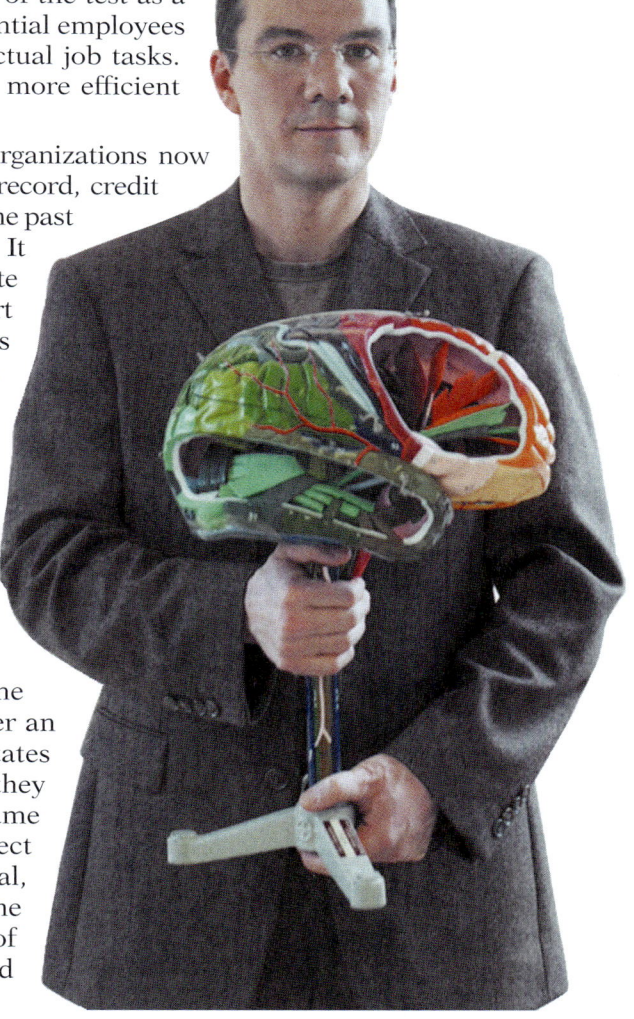

> **LECTURE LINK II-6:**
> Background Checks: Security and Privacy Issues

> **BONUS CASE II-I:**
> Should You Hire Back a Former Employee?

6. *Establishing trial (probationary) periods.* Often an organization will hire an employee conditionally to let the person prove his or her value on the job. After a specified probationary period (perhaps six months or a year), the firm can either permanently hire or discharge that employee on the basis of supervisors' evaluations. Although such systems make it easier to fire inefficient or problem employees, they do not eliminate the high cost of turnover.

The selection process is often long and difficult, but it is worth the effort to select new employees carefully because of the high cost of replacing them.[27] Care helps ensure that new employees meet all requirements, including communication skills, education, technical skills, experience, personality, and health.

Hiring Contingent Workers

A company with employment needs that vary—from hour to hour, day to day, week to week, or season to season—may find it cost-effective to hire contingent workers.[28] **Contingent workers** include part-time workers (anyone who works 1 to 34 hours per week), temporary workers (workers paid by temporary employment agencies), seasonal workers, independent contractors, interns, and co-op students.

> **contingent workers**
> Employees that include part-time workers, temporary workers, seasonal workers, independent contractors, interns, and co-op students.

Companies may also hire contingent workers when full-timers are on some type of leave (such as maternity leave), when there is a peak demand for labor or products (like the holiday shopping season), or when quick service to customers is a priority. Cathy Villhard of Batter-Up Bakery, for example, partnered with the International Institute of St. Louis to hire contingent workers during the holiday season when last-minute cookie orders came from her largest clients.[29]

Companies also tend to hire more contingent workers in an uncertain economy, particularly when they are available and qualified, and when the jobs require minimal training.

> **PPT II-23:**
> Hiring Contingent Workers

Contingent workers receive few benefits; they are rarely offered health insurance, vacation time, or company pensions. They also tend to earn less than permanent workers do. On the positive side, many on temporary assignments are eventually offered full-time positions. Managers see using temporary workers as a way of weeding out poor workers and finding good hires. Temporary workers who are told that they may at some point be hired as permanent staff are often more productive than those on the regular payroll (see the Making Ethical Decisions box).

> **PPT II-24:**
> Why Hire Contingent Workers?

Although exact numbers are difficult to gather, the Bureau of Labor Statistics estimates there are approximately 5.7 million contingent workers in the United States, with the majority under age 25.[30] Experts say temps are filling openings in an increasingly broad range of jobs, from unskilled manufacturing and distribution positions to middle management. Increasing numbers of contingent workers are educated professionals such as accountants, attorneys, and engineers. Certes Financial Pros, described in the chapter opening Profile, provides contingent financial specialists to companies.

Many companies include college students in their contingent workforce plan. Ryan Falvey of Gentle Giant Moving Company in Somerville, Massachusetts, targets students looking for summer work (the firm's peak time) and encourages them to come back year after year.[31] As a student, Daniel Butrym found that the transition to temp worker wasn't difficult. He says, "The first time you walk into [the temporary staffing] office, they meet you, sit you down, and they find out your skills. Once you're in their computer, they have all your stats and know what you can do. You came back in town, didn't

MAKING ethical decisions

www.manpower.com

Motivating Temporary Employees

Contingent workers often perform effectively because they believe that they might be offered a permanent position. Suppose you manage a prestigious department store called Highbrow's. Each winter you must hire temporary workers to handle the large number of holiday shoppers. Store policy and budget constraints mandate that all temporaries must be discharged on January 15.

As you interview prospective employees, however, you give them the impression the store will hire at least two new full-time retail salespeople for the coming year. You hope this will motivate the temporary workers and even foster some competition among them. You also instruct your permanent salespeople to reinforce that good work during the Christmas season is the path to full-time employment. Is this an ethical way to try to motivate your employees? What are the dangers of using this tactic?

---

have to interview or run across town and do a drug test or waste a lot of time looking for a job. If I called from school to say 'I'm going to be home and need some money,' I was put into the system for work assignments." Randstad USA, a global staffing services giant with over 400 branches in the United States, welcomes college students primarily because of their computer skills and familiarity with many of the popular software programs companies use.[32]

In an era of rapid change and economic uncertainty, some contingent workers have even found that temping can be more secure than full-time employment.

◀ PPT II-25:
Motivating Temporary Employees

progress assessment

- What are the five steps in human resource planning?
- What factors make it difficult to recruit qualified employees?
- What are the six steps in the selection process?
- Who is considered a contingent worker, and why do companies hire such workers?

◀ PPT II-26:
Progress Assessment

LEARNING goal 6 *

Illustrate employee training and development methods.

◀ PPT II-27:
Training and Developing Employees

TRAINING AND DEVELOPING EMPLOYEES FOR OPTIMUM PERFORMANCE

As technology and other innovations change the workplace, companies must offer training programs that often are quite sophisticated. The term **training and development** includes all attempts to improve productivity by increasing an employee's ability to perform. A well-designed training program often leads

training and development
All attempts to improve productivity by increasing an employee's ability to perform. Training focuses on short-term skills, development on long-term abilities.

297

At FedEx, time is money. That's why the company spends six times more on employee training than the average firm. Does the added expense pay off? You bet. FedEx enjoys a remarkably low 4 percent employee turnover rate. Should other companies follow FedEx's financial commitment to training? Why?

to higher retention rates, increased productivity, and greater job satisfaction. Employers in the United States generally find that money for training—an estimated $130 billion a year—is well spent.[33] *Training* focuses on short-term skills, whereas *development* focuses on long-term abilities. Both include three steps: (1) assessing organization needs and employee skills to determine training needs; (2) designing training activities to meet identified needs; and (3) evaluating the training's effectiveness. Some common training and development activities are employee orientation, on-the-job training, apprenticeships, off-the-job training, vestibule training, job simulation, and management training.

- **Orientation** is the activity that initiates new employees into the organization; to fellow employees; to their immediate supervisors; and to the policies, practices, and objectives of the firm. Orientation programs range from informal talks to formal activities that last a day or more and often include scheduled visits to various departments and required reading of handbooks. For example, at Aflac, one of the nation's largest insurance companies, new employees are schooled about the company's history, values, and product integrity. They also learn about industry certifications that can be earned through on-site courses offered at the company during business hours. Aflac has been recognized by both *Fortune* and *Training Magazine* as one of the best 100 U.S. companies for which to work.[34]

- **On-the-job training** lets the employee learn by doing, or by watching others for a while and then imitating them, right at the workplace. Salespeople, for example, are often trained by watching experienced salespeople perform (often called *shadowing*). Naturally, this can be either quite effective or disastrous, depending on the skills and habits of the person being observed. On-the-job training is the easiest kind of training to implement when the job is relatively simple (such as clerking in a store) or repetitive (such as collecting refuse, cleaning carpets, or mowing lawns). More demanding or intricate jobs require a more intense training effort. Intranets and other forms of technology make cost-effective on-the-job training programs available 24 hours a day. Computer systems can monitor workers' input and give them instructions if they become confused about what to do next.

- In **apprentice programs** a learner works alongside an experienced employee to master the skills and procedures of a craft. Some apprentice programs include classroom training. Trade unions in skilled crafts, such as bricklaying and plumbing, require a new worker to serve as an apprentice for several years to ensure excellence as well as to limit entry to the union. Workers who successfully complete an apprenticeship earn the classification *journeyman*. As baby boomers retire from skilled trades such as pipefitting, welding, and carpentry, shortages of trained workers will result.[35] Apprentice programs may be shortened to prepare people for skilled jobs in changing industries such as auto repair and aircraft maintenance that require increased knowledge of computer technology.

orientation
The activity that introduces new employees to the organization; to fellow employees; to their immediate supervisors; and to the policies, practices, and objectives of the firm.

on-the-job training
Training at the workplace that lets the employee learn by doing or by watching others for a while and then imitating them.

apprentice programs
Training programs during which a learner works alongside an experienced employee to master the skills and procedures of a craft.

▶ **PPT II-28:**
Three Steps of Training and Development

About 450,000 apprentices are registered with the U.S. Department of Labor.[36]

- **Off-the-job training** occurs away from the workplace and consists of internal or external programs to develop any of a variety of skills or to foster personal development. Training is becoming more sophisticated as jobs become more sophisticated. Furthermore, training is expanding to include education (through the Ph.D.) and personal development. Subjects may include time management, stress management, health and wellness, physical education, nutrition, and even art and languages.

- **Online training** demonstrates how technology is improving the efficiency of many off-the-job training programs. Most colleges and universities now offer a wide variety of Internet classes, sometimes called *distance learning*, including introductory business courses.[37] Both nonprofit and profit-seeking businesses make extensive use of online training. The Red Cross offers an online tutorial called "Be Red Cross Ready" to help citizens prepare for disasters such as floods, tornadoes, or hurricanes.[38] Technology giants like EMC and large manufacturers like Timken use the online training tool GlobeSmart to teach employees how to operate in different cultures.[39] Online training's key advantage is the ability to provide a large number of employees with consistent content tailored to specific training needs at convenient times.[40]

- **Vestibule training** (or near-the-job training) is done in classrooms with equipment similar to that used on the job so that employees learn proper methods and safety procedures before assuming a specific job assignment. Computer and robotics training is often completed in a vestibule classroom.

- **Job simulation** is the use of equipment that duplicates job conditions and tasks so that trainees can learn skills before attempting them on the job. It differs from vestibule training in that it duplicates the *exact* combination of conditions that occur on the job. This is the kind of training given to astronauts, airline pilots, army tank operators, ship captains, and others who must learn difficult procedures off the job.

---

off-the-job training
Internal or external training programs away from the workplace that develop any of a variety of skills or foster personal development.

online training
Training programs in which employees complete classes via the Internet.

◄ PPT II-29:
Most Commonly Used Training and Development Activities

vestibule training
Training done in schools where employees are taught on equipment similar to that used on the job.

job simulation
The use of equipment that duplicates job conditions and tasks so trainees can learn skills before attempting them on the job.

This job simulator at the Federal Aviation Administration Academy in Oklahoma City helps air traffic controllers learn how to manage aircraft departures and arrivals. Experts see a coming shortage of trained controllers, who face mandatory retirement at 56. Do you think simulation training is effective for jobs like this? Why or why not?

Management Development

Managers often need special training. To be good communicators, they need to learn listening skills and empathy. They also need time management, planning, and human relations skills.

Management development, then, is the process of training and educating employees to become good managers, and then monitoring the progress of their managerial skills over time. Management development programs are widespread, especially at colleges, universities, and private management development firms. Managers may participate in role-playing exercises, solve various management cases, and attend films and lectures.

Management development is increasingly being used as a tool to accomplish business objectives. General Electric's and Motorola's management teams were built with significant investment in their development. Most management training programs include several of the following:

- *On-the-job coaching.* A senior manager assists a lower-level manager by teaching needed skills and providing direction, advice, and helpful feedback. E-coaching is being developed to coach managers electronically, though it will take time and experimentation before firms figure out how to make coaches come to life online.[41]

- *Understudy positions.* Job titles such as *undersecretary* and *assistant* are part of a relatively successful way of developing managers. Selected employees work as assistants to higher-level managers and participate in planning and other managerial functions until they are ready to assume such positions themselves.

- *Job rotation.* So that they can learn about different functions of the organization, managers are often given assignments in a variety of departments. Such job rotation gives them the broad picture of the organization they need to succeed.[42]

- *Off-the-job courses and training.* Managers periodically go to classes or seminars for a week or more to hone technical and human relations skills. Major universities like the University of Michigan, MIT, and the University of Chicago offer specialized short courses to assist managers in performing their jobs more efficiently. McDonald's Corporation has its own Hamburger University. Managers and potential franchisees attend six days of classes and complete a course of study equivalent to 36 hours of college business-school credit.[43]

Networking

Networking is the process of establishing and maintaining contacts with key managers in your own and other organizations, and using those contacts to weave strong relationships that serve as informal development systems.[44] Of equal or greater importance may be a **mentor**, a corporate manager who supervises, coaches, and guides selected lower-level employees by introducing them to the right people and generally acting as their organizational sponsor. In most organizations informal mentoring occurs as experienced employees assist less experienced workers.[45] However, many organizations formally assign mentors to employees considered to have strong potential.

It's also important to remember that networking and mentoring go beyond the business environment. For example, college is a perfect place to begin networking. Associations you nurture with professors, with local businesspeople through internships, and especially with your classmates can provide a valuable network to turn to for the rest of your career.

Diversity in Management Development

As more women moved into management, they learned the importance of networking and of having mentors. Unfortunately, women often have more difficulty than men in networking or finding mentors, since most senior managers are male. Women, however, won a major legal victory when the U.S. Supreme Court ruled it illegal to bar women from certain clubs, long open to men only, where business activity flows and contacts are made. This decision allowed more women to enter established networking systems or, in some instances, create their own.

Similarly, African American and Hispanic managers learned the value of networking. Both groups are forming pools of capital and new opportunities helping many individuals overcome traditional barriers to success. *Black Enterprise* magazine sponsors several networking forums each year for African American professionals. The Hispanic Alliance for Career Enhancement (HACE) is committed to building career opportunities and career advancement for Hispanics.[46] Monte Jade is an association that helps Taiwanese and Chinese assimilate in U.S. business. Sulekha is an Indian networking group that unites Indians in the United States and around the world.[47]

Companies that take the initiative to develop female and minority managers understand three crucial principles: (1) grooming women and minorities for management positions isn't about legality, morality, or even morale but rather about bringing more talent in the door, the key to long-term profitability; (2) the best women and minorities will become harder to attract and retain, so companies that commit to development early have an edge; and (3) having more women and minorities at all levels lets businesses serve their increasingly female and minority customers better.[48] If you don't have a diversity of people working in the back room, how are you going to satisfy the diversity of people coming in the front door?

Informal networking gatherings like this one are sponsored by Likemind, an association of creative professionals who meet weekly in 55 cities worldwide. "We just show up over coffee and talk," said one participant in Detroit. Why do you think younger workers prefer such informal gatherings?

LEARNING goal 7 *

Trace the six steps in appraising employee performance.

APPRAISING EMPLOYEE PERFORMANCE TO GET OPTIMUM RESULTS

Managers must be able to determine whether their workers are doing an effective and efficient job, with a minimum of errors and disruptions. They do so by using a **performance appraisal**, an evaluation that measures employee performance against established standards in order to make decisions about promotions, compensation, training, or termination. Performance appraisals have six steps:

1. *Establishing performance standards.* This step is crucial. Standards must be understandable, subject to measurement, and reasonable. Both manager and subordinate must accept them.

◄ CRITICAL THINKING EXERCISE 11-5:
Best Companies for Working Mothers

performance appraisal
An evaluation that measures employee performance against established standards in order to make decisions about promotions, compensation, training, or termination.

> **PPT II-33:**
> Appraising Performance on the Job

> **PPT II-34:**
> Six Steps of Performance Appraisals

2. *Communicating those standards.* It's dangerous to assume that employees know what is expected of them. They must be told clearly and precisely what the standards and expectations are, and how to meet them.
3. *Evaluating performance.* If the first two steps are done correctly, performance evaluation is relatively easy. It is a matter of evaluating the employee's behavior to see whether it matches standards.
4. *Discussing results with employees.* Employees often make mistakes and fail to meet expectations at first. It takes time to learn a job and do it well. Discussing an employee's successes and areas that need improvement can provide managers an opportunity to be understanding and helpful and guide the employee to better performance. The performance appraisal can also allow employees to suggest how a task could be done better.
5. *Taking corrective action.* As part of performance appraisal, a manager can take corrective action or provide feedback to help the employee perform better. The key word is *perform*. The primary purpose of appraisal is to improve employee performance if possible.
6. *Using the results to make decisions.* Decisions about promotions, compensation, additional training, or firing are all based on performance evaluations. An effective performance appraisal system is also a way of satisfying legal requirements about such decisions.

> **PPT II-35:**
> Major Uses of Performance Appraisals

> **LECTURE LINK II-7:**
> Microsoft Revises Performance Appraisals

> **PPT II-36:**
> Performance Appraisal Mistakes

Managing effectively means getting results through top performance. That's what performance appraisals are for at all levels of the organization, including at the top where managers benefit from reviews by their subordinates and peers.

In the *360-degree review*, management gathers opinions from all around the employee, including those under, above, and on the same level, to get an accurate, comprehensive idea of the worker's abilities.[49] Figure 11.4 illustrates how managers can make performance appraisals more meaningful.

figure II.4
CONDUCTING EFFECTIVE APPRAISALS AND REVIEWS

1. **DON'T** attack the employee personally. Critically evaluate his or her work.
2. **DO** allow sufficient time, without distractions, for appraisal. (Take the phone off the hook or close the office door.)
3. **DON'T** make the employee feel uncomfortable or uneasy. *Never* conduct an appraisal where other employees are present (such as on the shop floor).
4. **DO** include the employee in the process as much as possible. (Let the employee prepare a self-improvement program.)
5. **DON'T** wait until the appraisal to address problems with the employee's work that have been developing for some time.
6. **DO** end the appraisal with positive suggestions for employee improvement.

> **PPT II-37:**
> Progress Assessment

progress assessment

- Name and describe four training techniques.
- What is the primary purpose of a performance appraisal?
- What are the six steps in a performance appraisal?

LEARNING goal 8 *

Summarize the objectives of employee compensation programs, and describe various pay systems and fringe benefits.

COMPENSATING EMPLOYEES: ATTRACTING AND KEEPING THE BEST

Companies don't just compete for customers; they also compete for employees. Compensation is one of the main tools companies use to attract qualified employees, and one of their largest operating costs. The long-term success of a firm—perhaps even its survival—may depend on how well it can control employee costs and optimize employee efficiency. Service organizations like hospitals and airlines struggle with high employee costs since these firms are *labor-intensive* (the primary cost of operations is the cost of labor). Manufacturing firms in the auto and steel industries have asked employees to take reductions in wages (called givebacks) to make the firms more competitive. (We discuss this in depth in Chapter 12.) Those are just a few reasons compensation and benefit packages require special attention. In fact, some experts believe determining how best to compensate employees is today's greatest human resources challenge.[50]

A carefully managed and competitive compensation and benefit program can accomplish several objectives:

- Attracting the kinds of people the organization needs, and in sufficient numbers.
- Providing employees with the incentive to work efficiently and productively.
- Keeping valued employees from going to competitors or starting competing firms.
- Maintaining a competitive position in the marketplace by keeping costs low through high productivity from a satisfied workforce.
- Providing employees with some sense of financial security through fringe benefits such as insurance and retirement benefits.

Pay Systems

The way an organization chooses to pay its employees can have a dramatic effect on efficiency and productivity. Managers thus look for a system that compensates employees fairly.

Many companies still use the pay system known as the Hay system, devised by Edward Hay. This plan is based on job tiers, each of which has a strict pay range. The system is set up on a point basis with three key factors considered: know-how, problem solving, and accountability.

Firms like San Francisco–based Skyline Construction let workers pick their own pay system. They can earn a fixed salary or collect a lower salary with potential for a bonus.[51] John Whitney, author of *The Trust Factor*, believes that companies should set pay at the market level or better and then award all employees the same percentage merit raise. Doing so, he says, sends the message that everyone in the company is important. Figure 11.5 on p. 304 outlines some of the most common pay systems. Which do you think is the fairest?

◄ **LECTURE LINK II-8:**
Keeping Talented Employees: It's the Fringe That Counts

◄ **PPT II-38:**
Compensation Programs

◄ **PPT II-39:**
Types of Pay Systems

figure II.5
PAY SYSTEMS

Some of the different pay systems are as follows:

- **Salary:** Fixed compensation computed on weekly, biweekly, or monthly pay periods (e.g., $1,600 per month or $400 per week). Salaried employees do not receive additional pay for any extra hours worked.
- **Hourly wage or daywork:** Wage based on number of hours or days worked, used for most blue-collar and clerical workers. Often employees must punch a time clock when they arrive at work and when they leave. Hourly wages vary greatly. The federal minimum wage is $7.25, and top wages go as high as $40 per hour for skilled craftspeople. This does not include benefits such as retirement systems, which may add 30 percent or more to the total package.
- **Piecework system:** Wage based on the number of items produced rather than by the hour or day. This type of system creates powerful incentives to work efficiently and productively.
- **Commission plans:** Pay based on some percentage of sales. Often used to compensate salespeople, commission plans resemble piecework systems.
- **Bonus plans:** Extra pay for accomplishing or surpassing certain objectives. There are two types of bonuses: monetary and cashless. Money is always a welcome bonus. Cashless rewards include written thank-you notes, appreciation notes sent to the employee's family, movie tickets, flowers, time off, gift certificates, shopping sprees, and other types of recognition.
- **Profit-sharing plans:** Annual bonuses paid to employees based on the company's profits. The amount paid to each employee is based on a predetermined percentage. Profit sharing is one of the most common forms of performance-based pay.
- **Gain-sharing plans:** Annual bonuses paid to employees based on achieving specific goals such as quality measures, customer satisfaction measures, and production targets.
- **Stock options:** Right to purchase stock in the company at a specific price over a specific period. Often this gives employees the right to buy stock cheaply despite huge increases in the price of the stock. For example, if over the course of his employment a worker received options to buy 10,000 shares of the company stock at $10 each and the price of the stock eventually grows to $100, he can use those options to buy the 10,000 shares (now worth $1 million) for $100,000.

▶ **PPT II-40:**
Compensating Teams

Compensating Teams

Thus far, we've talked about compensating individuals. What about teams? Since you want your teams to be more than simply a group of individuals, would you compensate them like individuals? If you can't answer that question immediately, you're not alone. Most managers believe in using teams, but fewer are sure about how to pay them. Team-based pay programs are not as effective or as fully developed as managers would hope. Measuring and rewarding individual performance on teams, while at the same time rewarding team performance, is tricky—but it can be done. Professional football players, for example, are rewarded as a team when they go to the playoffs and to the Super Bowl, but they are paid individually as well. Companies are now experimenting with and developing similar incentive systems.

Jim Fox, founder and senior partner of compensation and human resource specialist firm Fox Lawson & Associates, insists that setting up the team right in the first place is the key element to designing an appropriate team compensation plan. He believes the pay model to enhance performance will be a natural outcome of the team's development process.[52] Jay Schuster, coauthor of a study of team pay, found that when pay is based strictly on individual performance, it erodes team cohesiveness and makes the team less likely meet its goals as a collaborative effort. Workplace studies indicate over 50 percent of team compensation plans are based on team goals. Skill-based pay and gain-sharing systems are the two most common compensation methods for teams.

Skill-based pay rewards the growth of both the individual and the team. Base pay is raised when team members learn and apply new skills. Baldrige Award winner Eastman Chemical Company rewards its teams for proficiency in technical, social, and business knowledge skills. A cross-functional compensation policy team defines the skills. The drawbacks of skill-based pay are twofold: the system is complex, and it is difficult to relate the acquisition of skills directly to profit gains.

Most *gain-sharing systems* base bonuses on improvements over previous performance. Nucor Steel, one of the largest U.S. steel producers, calculates bonuses on quality—tons of steel that go out the door with no defects. There are no limits on bonuses a team can earn; they generally run from 100 to 220 percent of base salary. With bonuses, the typical Nucor steel mill worker can earn over $70,000 per year.[53]

It is important to reward individual team players also. Outstanding team players—who go beyond what is required and make an outstanding individual contribution—should be separately recognized, with cash or noncash rewards. A good way to compensate for uneven team participation is to let the team decide which members get what type of individual award. After all, if you really support the team process, you need to give teams freedom to reward themselves.

Fringe Benefits

Fringe benefits include sick-leave pay, vacation pay, pension plans, and health plans that provide additional compensation to employees beyond base wages. Benefits in recent years grew faster than wages and can't really be considered fringe anymore. In 1929, such benefits accounted for less than 2 percent of payroll; today they account for about 30 percent. Health care costs have soared, forcing employees to pay a larger share of their own health insurance bill. Since 2000, the cost to the employee for employee-only coverage has increased 86 percent; the cost of family coverage premiums has increased 80 percent.[54] Employees often request more fringe benefits instead of salary, in order to avoid higher taxes. This has resulted in increased debate and government investigation.

Fringe benefits can include recreation facilities, company cars, country club memberships, discounted massages, special home-mortgage rates, paid and unpaid sabbaticals, day care services, and executive dining rooms. Employees often want dental care, mental health care, elder care, legal counseling, eye care, and even short workweeks.

Understanding that it takes many incentives to attract and retain the best employees, dozens of firms among *Fortune* magazine's "100 Best Companies to Work For" list offer so-called soft benefits. *Soft benefits* help workers maintain the balance between work and family life that is often as important to hardworking employees as the nature of the job itself.[55] These perks include onsite haircuts and shoe repair, concierge services, and free breakfasts. Freeing employees from errands and chores gives them more time for family—and work. Biotechnology firm Genentech even offers doggie day care and an onsite farmer's market.[56]

At one time, most employees sought benefits that were similar. Today, however, some may seek child-care benefits while others prefer attractive pension plans. To address such growing demands, over half

◀ **PPT II-41:**
Fringe Benefits on the Job

◀ **PPT II-42:**
The Range of Fringe Benefits

fringe benefits
Benefits such as sick-leave pay, vacation pay, pension plans, and health plans that represent additional compensation beyond base wages.

Some companies encourage employees to take short naps during the workday so that they replenish their energy and creativity. These EnergyPods block noise and light and are in use at some firms including Cisco Systems, Google, and Procter & Gamble. Is napping a job benefit that appeals to you?

◀ **LECTURE LINK II-9**
Encouraging Healthy Work-Life Balance

cafeteria-style fringe benefits
Fringe benefits plan that allows employees to choose the benefits they want up to a certain dollar amount.

▶ PPT II-43:
Special Perks at Dreamworks

▶ PPT II-44:
Cafeteria-Style and Soft Benefits

▶ PPT II-45:
Changing Times, Changing Employee Benefits

▶ PPT II-46:
Let's Go to the Beach!

flextime plan
Work schedule that gives employees some freedom to choose when to work, as long as they work the required number of hours.

core time
In a flextime plan, the period when all employees are expected to be at their job stations.

figure II.6

A FLEXTIME CHART
At this company, employees can start work anytime between 6:30 and 9:30 a.m. They take a half hour for lunch anytime between 11:00 a.m. and 1:30 p.m. and can leave between 3:00 and 6:30 p.m. Everyone works an eight-hour day. The blue arrows show a typical employee's flextime day.

of all large firms offer **cafeteria-style fringe benefits**, in which employees can choose the benefits they want up to a certain dollar amount. Such plans let human resource managers equitably and cost-effectively meet employees' individual needs by allowing them choice.

As the cost of administering benefits programs has accelerated, many companies have chosen to outsource this function. Administaff and Workforce Solutions Inc., both of which are members of the Professional Employers Organization (PEO), handle employee benefits administration for firms with up to 2,500 employees. Culpepper Compensation & Benefits Surveys estimates that over 50 percent of all companies outsource some portion of their human resource tasks.[57] Managing benefits can be especially complicated when employees are located in other countries. The Reaching Beyond Our Borders box discusses the human resource challenges faced by global businesses. To put it simply, benefits are often as important to recruiting top talent as salary and may even become more important in the future.

LEARNING goal 9 *

Show how managers use scheduling plans to adapt to workers' needs.

SCHEDULING EMPLOYEES TO MEET ORGANIZATIONAL AND EMPLOYEE NEEDS

Workplace trends and the increasing costs of transportation have led employees to look for scheduling flexibility. Flextime, in-home employment, and job sharing are becoming important benefits employees seek.

Flextime Plans

A **flextime plan** gives employees some freedom to choose which hours to work, as long as they work the required number. The most popular plans allow employees to arrive between 7:00 and 9:00 a.m. and leave between 4:00 and 6:00 p.m. Flextime plans generally incorporate core time. **Core time** is the period when all employees are expected to be at their job stations. An organization may designate core time as 9:00 to 11:00 a.m. and 2:00 to 4:00 p.m. During these hours all employees are required to be at work (see Figure 11.6).

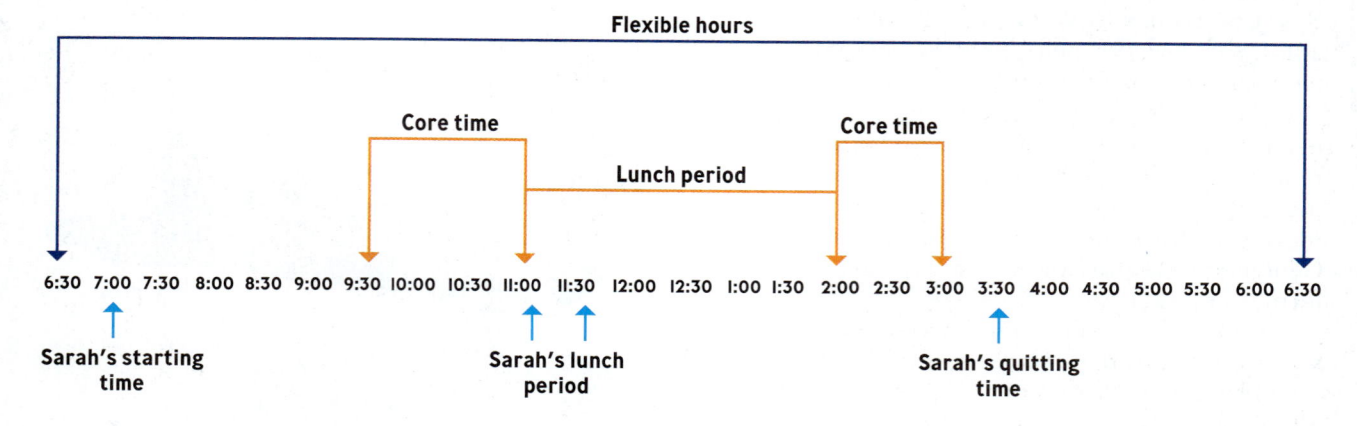

REACHING BEYOND our borders

www.shrm.org

Working Worldwide

Human resource management of a global workforce begins with an understanding of the customs, laws, and local business needs of every country in which the organization operates. Country-specific cultural and legal standards can affect a variety of human resource functions:

- *Compensation.* Salaries must be converted to and from foreign currencies. Often employees with international assignments receive special allowances for relocation, children's education, housing, travel, and other business-related expenses.

- *Health and pension standards.* There are different social contexts for benefits in other countries. In the Netherlands the government provides retirement income and health care.

- *Paid time off.* Four weeks of paid vacation is the standard of many European employers. But many other countries lack the short-term and long-term absence policies offered in the United States, including sick leave, personal leave, and family and medical leave. Global companies need a standard definition of *time off.*

- *Taxation.* Different countries have varying taxation rules, and the payroll department is an important player in managing immigration information.

- *Communication.* When employees leave to work in another country, they often feel disconnected from their home country. Wise companies use their intranet and the Internet to help these faraway employees keep in direct contact.

Human resource policies at home are influenced more and more by conditions and practices in other countries and cultures. Human resource managers need to sensitize themselves and their organizations to overseas cultural and business practices.

Sources: "Mercer Survey Reveals New Challenges and Solutions as HR Takes on Expanded Global Role," Business Wire, September 26, 2008; and Charles E. Carraher, Sarah C. Carraher, Shawn M. Carraher, Gerald R. Ferris, and Ronald M. Buckley, "Human Resource Issues in Global Entrepreneurial High Technology Firms: Do They Differ?" *Journal of Applied Management and Entrepreneurship,* January 1, 2008.

Flextime allows employees to adjust to work/life demands. Two-income families find them especially helpful.[58] Sun Microsystems finds that flextime boosts employee productivity and morale.

Flextime is not for all organizations, however. It doesn't suit shift work like fast-food or assembly processes like manufacturing, where everyone on a given shift must be at work at the same time. Another disadvantage is that managers often have to work longer days to assist and supervise in organizations that may operate from 6:00 a.m. to 6:00 p.m. Flextime also makes communication more difficult since certain employees may not be there when others need to talk to them. Furthermore, if not carefully supervised, some employees could abuse the system, causing resentment among others.

Another option that about 1 in 4 companies use is a **compressed workweek**. An employee works the full number of hours, but in fewer than the

◀ **PPT II-47:** Working Worldwide
◀ **PPT II-48:** Flexible Scheduling Plans
◀ **PPT II-49:** Using Flextime Plans
◀ **PPT II-50:** A Flextime Chart
◀ **PPT II-51:** Compressed Workweeks

compressed workweek
Work schedule that allows an employee to work a full number of hours per week but in fewer days.

307

standard number of days. For example, an employee may work four 10-hour days and then enjoy a long weekend, instead of working five 8-hour days with a traditional weekend.⁵⁹ There are obvious advantages of compressed workweeks, but some employees get tired working such long hours, and productivity can decline. Others find the system a great benefit, however, and are enthusiastic about it. Nurses often work compressed weeks.

Home-Based Work

As we noted in Chapter 1, nearly 10 million U.S. workers now telecommute, working at home at least several days per month. Approximately 12 percent of businesses use some home-based work.⁶⁰ Home-based workers can choose their own hours, interrupt work for child care or other tasks, and take time out for personal reasons. Working at home isn't for everyone. It requires discipline to stay focused on the job and not be easily distracted.

Home-based work can be a cost saver for employers. Conseco Inc., an insurance provider, needed to trim costs after emerging from bankruptcy. It had a surplus of office space, so it cut back on the number of offices it maintained for employees traveling or telecommuting and established a reservations system called hoteling that temporarily assigned employees to a desk when needed.⁶¹ Almost 73 percent of Fortune 500 companies offer "hot-desking," or sharing a desk with other employees who work at different times.⁶²

Many companies are hiring U.S. home-based call agents rather than using either more expensive in-house operators or less-qualified offshore call centers. Office Depot shifted to home-based call agents in 2005 and saved 30 or 40 percent on the cost of each call by not providing workspace (or benefits) for its home-based call-center workers. Figure 11.7 outlines the benefits and challenges of home-based work to organizations, individuals, and society.

Job-Sharing Plans

Job sharing lets two or more part-time employees share one full-time job. Students and parents with small children, for instance, may work only during school hours, and older workers can work part-time before fully retiring or after retiring. Benefits of job sharing include:

- Employment opportunities for those who cannot or prefer not to work full-time.
- An enthusiastic and productive workforce.
- Reduced absenteeism and tardiness.
- Ability to schedule part-time workers into peak demand periods (e.g., banks on payday).
- Retention of experienced employees who might otherwise have retired.

Disadvantages include the need to hire, train, motivate, and supervise at least twice as many people and perhaps prorate some fringe benefits. But firms are finding that the advantages generally outweigh the disadvantages.

All Jet Blue's reservations agents work from home through the company's virtual reservations center. What do you think would be the biggest problem for you of working from home?

▶ **BONUS CASE 11-3:**
Human Resource Planning and Women Workers

job sharing
An arrangement whereby two part-time employees share one full-time job.

▶ **PPT 11-52:**
Job Sharing Benefits

	BENEFITS	CHALLENGES
To Organization	• Increases productivity due to fewer sick days, fewer absences, higher job satisfaction, and higher work performance ratings • Broadens available talent pool • Reduces costs of providing on-site office space	• Makes it more difficult to appraise job performance • Can negatively affect the social network of the workplace and can make it difficult to promote team cohesiveness • Complicates distribution of tasks (should office files, contact lists, and such be allowed to leave the office?)
To Individual	• Makes more time available for work and family by reducing or eliminating commute time • Reduces expenses of buying and maintaining office clothes • Avoids office politics • Helps balance work and family • Expands employment opportunities for disabled individuals	• Can cause feeling of isolation from social network • Can raise concerns regarding promotions and other rewards due to being out of sight, out of mind • May diminish individual's influence within company due to limited opportunity to learn the corporate culture
To Society	• Decreases traffic congestion • Discourages community crime that might otherwise occur in bedroom communities • Increases time available to build community ties	• Increases need to resolve zoning regulations forbidding business deliveries in residential neighborhoods • May reduce ability to interact with other people in a personal, intimate manner

LEARNING goal 10 *

Describe how employees can move through a company: promotion, reassignment, termination, and retirement.

figure 11.7

BENEFITS AND CHALLENGES OF HOME-BASED WORK
Home-based work (also known as telecommuting) offers many benefits and challenges to organizations, individuals, and society as a whole.

◄ PPT 11-53:
Movement of Employees

MOVING EMPLOYEES UP, OVER, AND OUT

Employees don't always stay in the position they were hired to fill. They may excel and move up the corporate ladder or fail and move out the door. Employees can also be reassigned or retire. Of course, some choose to move themselves by going to another company.

Promoting and Reassigning Employees

Many companies find that promotion from within the company improves employee morale. It's also cost-effective in that the promoted employees are already familiar with the corporate culture and procedures and don't need to spend valuable time on basic orientation.

In the new, flatter corporate structures (see Chapter 8), there are fewer levels for employees to reach than in the past. Thus they often move *over* to a new position rather than *up*. Such lateral transfers allow employees to develop and display new skills and learn more about the company overall. Reassignment

As the economic crisis grew, managers had to terminate a growing number of employees. Do you think they will rehire full-time employees when the economy recovers? Why or why not? What alternatives do they have?

▶ **PPT 11-54:**
Terminating Employees

▶ **LECTURE LINK 11-10:**
Why Employees Leave

▶ **BONUS CASE 11-2:**
The Department Store Dilemma

▶ **LECTURE LINK 11-11:**
Using the Exit Interview for Feedback

figure 11.8
HOW TO AVOID WRONGFUL-DISCHARGE LAWSUITS

Sources: "In Economics Old and New, Treatment of Workers Is Paramount," *The Washington Post*, February 11, 2001, p. L1; and U.S. Law, www.uslaw.com.

is one way of motivating experienced employees to remain in a company with few advancement opportunities.

Terminating Employees

We've seen that the relentless pressure of global competition, shifts in technology, increasing customer demands for greater value, and uncertain economic conditions have human resource managers struggling to manage layoffs and firings. Even if the economy is booming, many companies are hesitant to hire or rehire workers full-time. Why is that the case? One reason is that the cost of terminating employees is prohibitively high in terms of lost training costs and possible damages and legal fees for wrongful discharge suits. That's why many companies are either using temporary employees or outsourcing certain functions.

At one time the prevailing employment doctrine in the United States was "employment at will." This meant managers had as much freedom to fire workers as workers had to leave voluntarily. Most states now limit the at-will doctrine to protect employees from wrongful firing. An employer can no longer fire someone for exposing the company's illegal actions or refusing to violate a law. Employees who are members of a minority or other protected group also may have protections under equal employment law. In some cases, workers fired for using illegal drugs have sued on the ground that they have an illness (addiction) and are therefore protected by laws barring discrimination under the Americans with Disabilities Act (ADA). Well-intended legislation has in some ways restricted management's ability to terminate employees as it increased workers' rights to their jobs. See Figure 11.8 for advice about how to minimize the chance of wrongful discharge lawsuits.

Retiring Employees

Companies looking to downsize sometimes offer early retirement benefits to entice older (and more expensive) workers to retire. Such benefits can include one-time cash payments, known in some companies as *golden handshakes*. The

---

Consultants offer this advice to minimize the chance of a lawsuit for wrongful discharge:

- Prepare before hiring by requiring recruits to sign a statement that retains management's freedom to terminate at will.
- Don't make unintentional promises by using such terms as *permanent employment*.
- Document reasons before firing and make sure you have an unquestionable business reason for the firing.
- Fire the worst first and be consistent in discipline.
- Buy out bad risk by offering severance pay in exchange for a signed release from any claims.
- Be sure to give employees the true reasons they are being fired. If you do not, you cannot reveal it to a recruiter asking for a reference without risking a defamation lawsuit.
- Disclose the reasons for an employee's dismissal to that person's potential new employers. For example, if you fired an employee for dangerous behavior and you withhold that information from your references, you can be sued if the employee commits a violent act at his or her next job.

advantage early retirement benefits have over layoffs or firing is the increased morale of surviving employees. Retiring senior workers earlier also increases promotion opportunities for younger employees.

Losing Valued Employees

In spite of a company's efforts to retain them, some talented employees will choose to pursue opportunities elsewhere. Knowing their reasons for leaving can be invaluable in preventing the loss of other good people in the future. One way to learn the reasons is to have an outside expert conduct an *exit interview*. Outsiders can provide confidentiality and anonymity that earns more honest feedback than employees are comfortable giving in face-to-face interviews with their bosses. Web-based systems can capture, track, and statistically analyze employee exit interview data to generate reports that identify trouble areas. Such programs can also coordinate exit interview data with employee satisfaction surveys to predict which departments should expect turnover to occur.

Attracting and retaining the best employees is the key to success in the competitive global business environment. Dealing with controversial issues employees have on the job is challenging and never-ending. Chapter 12 discusses such issues.

progress assessment

- Can you name and describe five alternative compensation techniques?
- What advantages do compensation plans such as profit sharing offer an organization?
- What are the benefits and challenges of flextime? Telecommuting? Job sharing?

◀ PPT 11-55:
Progress Assessment

summary

Learning Goal 1. Explain the importance of human resource management, and describe current issues in managing human resources.

- **What are current challenges and opportunities in the human resource area?**

Many current challenges and opportunities arise from changing demographics: more women, minorities, immigrants, and older workers in the workforce. Others include a shortage of trained workers and an abundance of unskilled workers, skilled workers in declining industries requiring retraining, changing employee work attitudes, and complex laws and regulations.

Learning Goal 2. Illustrate the effects of legislation on human resource management.

- **What are some of the key laws?**

See the Legal Briefcase box on page 288 and review the text section on laws.

Learning Goal 3. Summarize the five steps in human resource planning.

- **What are the steps in human resource planning?**

The five steps are (1) preparing a human resource inventory of the organization's employees; (2) preparing a job analysis; (3) assessing future demand; (4) assessing future supply; and (5) establishing a plan for recruiting, hiring, educating, appraising, compensating, and scheduling employees.

Learning Goal 4. Describe methods that companies use to recruit new employees, and explain some of the issues that make recruitment challenging.
- **What methods do human resource managers use to recruit new employees?**

Recruiting sources are classified as either internal or external. Internal sources include those hired from within (transfers, promotions, reassignments) and employees who recommend others to hire. External recruitment sources include advertisements, public and private employment agencies, college placement bureaus, management consultants, professional organizations, referrals, walk-in applications, and the Internet.
- **Why has recruitment become more difficult?**

Legal restrictions complicate hiring and firing practices. Finding suitable employees can be more difficult if companies are considered unattractive workplaces.

Learning Goal 5. Outline the six steps in selecting employees.
- **What are the six steps in the selection process?**

The steps are (1) obtaining complete application forms, (2) conducting initial and follow-up interviews, (3) giving employment tests, (4) conducting background investigations, (5) obtaining results from physical exams, and (6) establishing a trial period of employment.

Learning Goal 6. Illustrate employee training and development methods.
- **What are some training activities?**

Training activities include employee orientation, on- and off-the-job training, apprentice programs, online training, vestibule training, and job simulation.
- **What methods help develop managerial skills?**

Management development methods include on-the-job coaching, understudy positions, job rotation, and off-the-job courses and training.
- **How does networking fit in this process?**

Networking is the process of establishing contacts with key managers within and outside the organization to get additional development assistance.

Learning Goal 7. Trace the six steps in appraising employee performance.
- **How do managers evaluate performance?**

The steps are (1) establish performance standards; (2) communicate those standards; (3) compare performance to standards; (4) discuss results; (5) take corrective action when needed; and (6) use the results for decisions about promotions, compensation, additional training, or firing.

Learning Goal 8. Summarize the objectives of employee compensation programs, and describe various pay systems and fringe benefits.
- **What are common types of compensation systems?**

They include salary systems, hourly wages, piecework, commission plans, bonus plans, profit-sharing plans, and stock options.
- **What types of compensation are appropriate for teams?**

The most common are gain-sharing and skill-based compensation programs. Managers also reward outstanding individual performance within teams.

- **What are fringe benefits?**
Fringe benefits include sick leave, vacation pay, company cars, pension plans, and health plans that provide additional compensation to employees beyond base wages. Cafeteria-style fringe benefits plans let employees choose the benefits they want, up to a certain dollar amount.

Learning Goal 9. Show how managers use scheduling plans to adapt to workers' needs.
- **What scheduling plans can adjust work to employees' need for flexibility?**
Such plans include job sharing, flextime, compressed workweeks, and working at home.

Learning Goal 10. Describe how employees can move through a company: promotion, reassignment, termination, and retirement.
- **How can employees move within a company?**
Employees can be moved up (promotion), over (reassignment), or out (termination or retirement) of a company. They can also choose to leave a company to pursue opportunities elsewhere.

key terms

affirmative action 288
apprentice programs 298
cafeteria-style fringe benefits 306
compressed workweek 307
contingent workers 296
core time 306
flextime plan 306
fringe benefits 305
human resource management (HRM) 284
job analysis 290
job description 291
job sharing 308
job simulation 299
job specifications 291
management development 300
mentor 300
networking 300
off-the-job training 299
online training 299
on-the-job training 298
orientation 298
performance appraisal 301
recruitment 292
reverse discrimination 289
selection 293
training and development 297
vestibule training 299

connect interactive applications

Reinforcing Your Connection to Concepts in Business

This chapter offers 12 interactive applications designed to help you apply what you've learned (examples of these exercises appear on the following pages). Your instructor has determined which interactive applications will benefit you throughout this course. Please refer to your instructor's assignment list in *Connect* to determine which applications you should complete.

Click and Drag Interactive:
IBM manages its global workforce of about 100,000 employees and 100,000 subcontractors with a database that matches employees' skills, experiences, schedules, and references with jobs available. Place the five steps of the human resource planning process in the correct order.

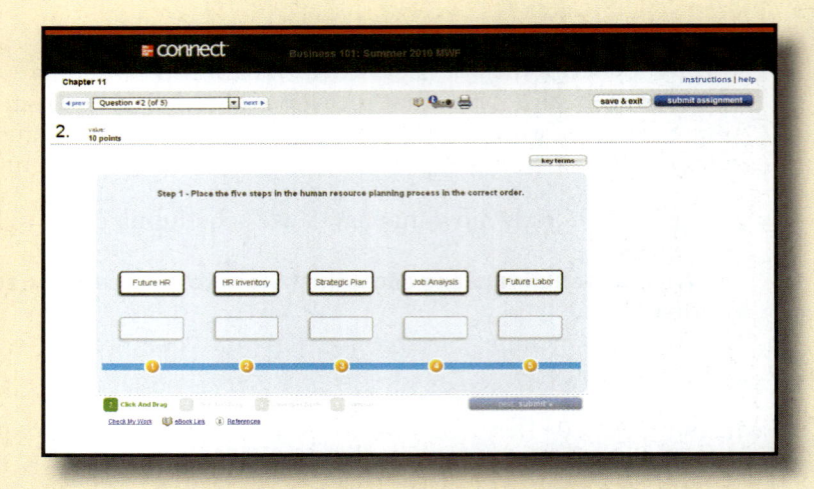

Click and Drag Interactive:
Managers use performance appraisals to measure employee performance against established standards in order to make decisions about promotions, compensation, training, or termination. Review the steps in the performance appraisal process and place them in the correct order.

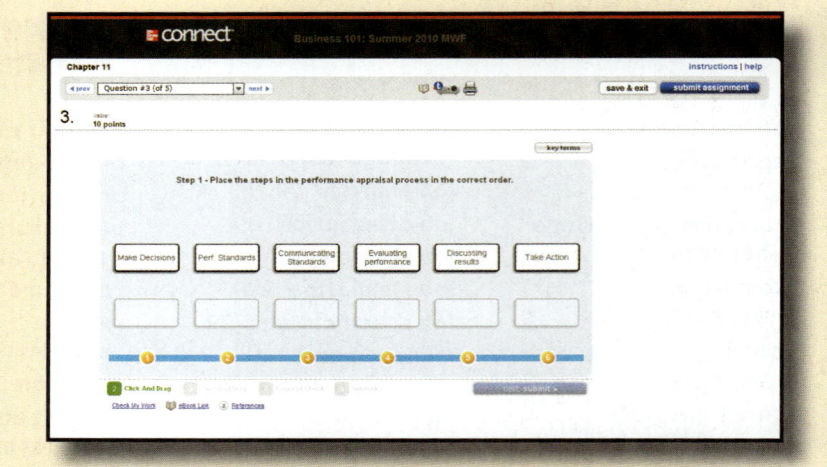

Click and Drag Interactive:
The selection process is often long and difficult, but it is worth the effort to select new employees carefully because of the high cost of replacing them. Review the six steps in the selection process, then review the list of activities and place that activity under the appropriate step on the timeline.

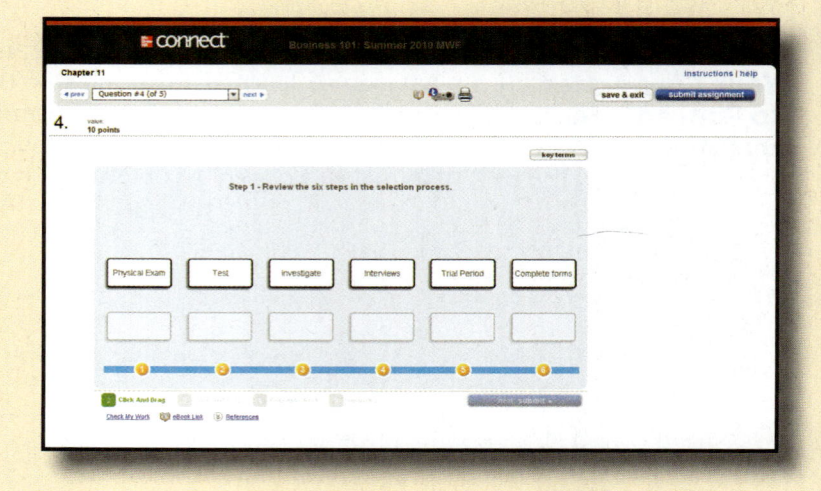

Video Case Interactive:
Patagonia believes in offering long-lasting products backed by a full customer-satisfaction guarantee. Not only do they want to satisfy customers, they also want to produce products that have minimal impact on the environment. Watch the video featuring the CEO of Patagonia and respond to the questions when prompted.

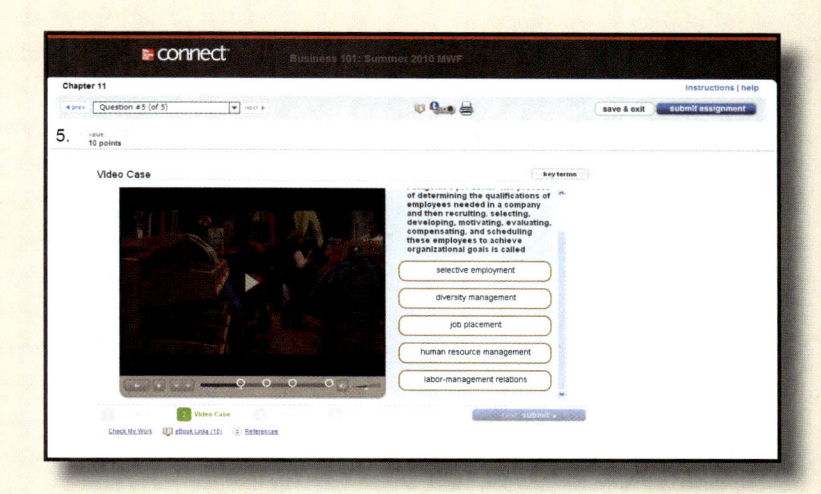

12 Dealing with Employee–Management Issues and Relationships

profile

Getting to Know Roger Goodell, Commissioner of the National Football League

When some people think of employee–management issues, they think of the latest labor problem making the news. However, employee–management relationships are about much more than job issues and strikes. Just ask Roger Goodell, commissioner of the National Football League (NFL). In his short tenure on the job, Goodell has already dealt with issues like drug use, cheating, and dog fighting. In addition, Goodell and the National Football League Players Association (NFLPA) have created a new policy that protects players who have suffered concussions.

Goodell has always had a role in sports. He was a high school athlete, lettering in baseball, basketball, and football. Son of the late New York senator Charles E. Goodell, he attended Washington and Jefferson College and earned a degree in economics. After graduation, Goodell got right back into sports. In 1982, he started at the NFL as a public relations intern, where officials, most notably Commissioner Pete Rozelle, took notice of his knowledge, skill, and drive. Soon Goodell was a key aide to future commissioner Paul Tagliabue. In 2001, after nearly 20 years with the organization, Goodell was named chief operating officer (COO).

Few were surprised when Goodell took the NFL reins on September 1, 2006, over some 185 others mentioned to succeed Tagliabue. Goodell's "rookie season" was memorable to say the least. He revised the current conduct policy and placed stronger penalties on players defaming the league. His policy didn't focus just on the players' behaviors, however; it also held *teams* accountable for bad player conduct.

Goodell's new policy was put to the test when a narcotics search of a house owned by star quarterback Michael Vick led to Vick's conviction and sentencing as part of a dog-fighting ring. Goodell suspended Vick without pay indefinitely. He also suspended all-pro cornerback Pacman Jones for the entire 2007 season after an accumulation of arrests and legal problems. Jones was allowed to return in 2008 pending good behavior. Overall, Goodell's crackdown on player behavior has resulted in 20 percent fewer incidents of player misconduct.

316

LEARNING goals

After you have read and studied this chapter, you should be able to

1. Trace the history of organized labor in the United States.
2. Discuss the major legislation affecting labor unions.
3. Outline the objectives of labor unions.
4. Describe the tactics used by labor and management during conflicts, and discuss the role of unions in the future.
5. Assess some of today's controversial employee–management issues, such as executive compensation, pay equity, child care and elder care, drug testing, and violence in the workplace.

connect

Your *Connection* to Better Learning. 1. View the interactive presentation. 2. Practice through LearnSmart. 3. Apply your knowledge by using the interactive applications for each chapter of this text.

1 Prep >>>>>> **2 Study**  >>>>>> **3 Apply**

As commissioner, Goodell also deals with the other side of the labor spectrum—owner relations. Many team owners are unhappy with the league's collective bargaining agreement (CBA), which directs nearly 60 percent of league revenue straight to the players, allowing some players to earn more than the owners. The CBA expires on November 8, 2010, and owners must vote on whether to renew it. The owners and the players' union are prepared for a serious labor battle. The NFL takes pride in being the only major professional sports organization that has never had a work stoppage, a record Goodell dearly wants to keep intact. In 2009, he encouraged NFL teams to freeze ticket prices during the economic crisis. He voluntarily cut his total compensation in 2008 and froze his pay in 2009. *BusinessWeek* rated him the most powerful man in sports. His skills and influence will surely be tested over the next several years.

Professional sports, of course, is not the only industry that has problems dealing with labor-management relations, employee compensation, and other work-related issues. This chapter discusses such issues and other employee–management concerns, including executive pay, pay equity, child care and elder care, drug testing, and violence in the workplace.

Sources: John Czarnecki, "Labor Crisis Clearly Looming for NFL," *FOX Sports,* April 8, 2008; Geoff Colvin, "Roger Goodell, Now in His Third Year as NFL Commissioner Is Facing His Toughest Challenges Yet—from the Players' Off-Field Behavior to Potential Labor Unrest," *Fortune,* September 29, 2008; and Michael McCarthy, "Goodell to Take Pay Cut amid NFL Drive to Cut Costs," *USA Today,* February 13, 2009.

www.nfl.com

NAME THAT person

> PPT 12-1:
> Dealing with Employee–Management Issues and Relationships

> PPT 12-2:
> Roger Goodell

> LECTURE LINK 12-1:
> The Complicated Legacy of Henry Ford

> PPT 12-3:
> Goals of Organized Labor

> PPT 12-4:
> Organized Labor

Mine may be the most fabled name in labor union history. In 1998, I was elected president of the 1.3-million-member Teamsters Union, 41 years after my father was elected. In 2005, along with six other unions, my union renounced membership in the AFL-CIO and formed a new coalition called Change to Win. Who am I? (Find the answer in the chapter.)

EMPLOYEE–MANAGEMENT ISSUES

The relationship between managers and employees isn't always smooth. Management's responsibility to produce a profit by maximizing productivity sometimes necessitates hard decisions, which limit managers' chances to win popularity contests. Labor (the collective term for nonmanagement workers) is interested in fair and competent management, human dignity, and a reasonable share in the wealth its work generates. Like other managerial challenges, employee–management issues require open discussion, goodwill, and compromise.

A good starting point in discussing employee–management relations in the United States is a discussion of labor unions. A **union** is an employee organization whose main goal is representing its members in employee–management negotiation of job-related issues. Workers originally formed unions to protect themselves from intolerable work conditions and unfair treatment. They also secured some say in the operation of their jobs. As the number of union members grew, workers gained more negotiating power with managers and more political power.

union
An employee organization whose main goal is representing its members in employee–management negotiation of job-related issues.

Labor unions were largely responsible for the establishment of minimum-wage laws, overtime rules, workers' compensation, severance pay, child-labor laws, job safety regulations, and more.[1] Union strength, however, has waned as labor unions have failed to retain the economic and political power they once had, and membership has continued to decline. Economists suggest that increased global competition, shifts from manufacturing to service and high-tech industries that are less heavily unionized, growth in part-time work, and changes in management philosophies are some of the reasons for labor's decline.[2] Others contend the decline is a result of labor's success in seeing the issues it championed become law.

Some labor analysts forecast that unions will regain strength as companies engage in more unpopular practices, such as outsourcing; others insist that unions have seen their brightest days.[3] Few doubt that the role and influence of unions—particularly in selected regions—will continue to arouse emotions and opinions that contrast considerably. Let's briefly look at labor unions and then analyze some other key issues affecting employee–management relations.

LEARNING goal 1 *

Trace the history of organized labor in the United States.

◄ CRITICAL THINKING
EXERCISE 12-1:
Are Unions Good or Bad For Business?

LABOR UNIONS FROM DIFFERENT PERSPECTIVES

Are labor unions necessary in the U.S. economy today? Yes, says an electrician carrying a picket sign in New York City. He or she might even elaborate on the dangers to workers if employers continue to try to bust or break apart unions.[4] A small manufacturer in Illinois would disagree, and complain about being restricted by union wage and benefit obligations in an increasingly competitive global economy.

Historians generally agree that today's unions are an outgrowth of the economic transition caused by the Industrial Revolution of the 19th and early 20th centuries. Workers who once toiled in the fields, dependent on the mercies of nature for survival, found themselves relying on the continuous roll of factory presses and assembly lines for their living. Making the transition from an agricultural economy to an industrial economy was quite difficult.[5] Over time, workers learned that strength through unity (unions) could lead to improved job conditions, better wages, and job security.

Today's critics of organized labor maintain that few of the inhuman conditions once dominant in U.S. industry exist in the modern workplace.[6] Organized labor is an industry in itself, they charge, and protecting workers has become secondary. Some analysts maintain that the current legal system and changing management philosophies minimize odds that sweatshops (workplaces of the late 19th and early 20th centuries with unsatisfactory, unsafe, or oppressive labor conditions) will reappear in the United States. Let's look at some of the history of labor unions.

While the technological achievements of the Industrial Revolution brought countless new products to market and reduced the need for physical labor in many industries, they also put pressure on workers to achieve higher productivity in factory jobs that called for long hours and low pay. Can you see how these conditions made it possible for labor unions to take hold by the turn of the 20th century?

The Early History of Organized Labor

Formal labor organizations in the United States date to the time of the American Revolution. As early as 1792, cordwainers (shoemakers) in Philadelphia met to discuss fundamental work issues of pay, hours, conditions, and job security—pretty much the same issues that dominate labor negotiations today. The cordwainers were a **craft union**, an organization of skilled specialists in a particular craft or trade, typically local or regional.[7] Most craft unions were established to achieve some short-range goal, such as curtailing the use of convict labor as an alternative to available free labor (an issue still present in some states). Often, after attaining that goal, they disbanded. This situation changed dramatically in the late 19th century with the expansion of the Industrial Revolution, which changed the economic structure of the United States. Enormous productivity increases, gained through mass production and job specialization, made the United States an economic world power. This growth, however, brought problems for workers in terms of productivity expectations, hours of work, wages, and unemployment.

Workers were faced with the reality that productivity was vital. Those who failed to produce, or who stayed home because they were ill or had family problems, lost their job. Over time, the increased emphasis on production led firms to expand the hours of work. The length of the average workweek in 1900 was 60 hours, compared to 40 today, but an 80-hour week was not uncommon for some industries. Wages were low, and child labor was widespread.

craft union
An organization of skilled specialists in a particular craft or trade.

◄ PPT 12-5:
History of Organized Labor

◄ PPT 12-6:
Emergency of Labor Organizations

Minimum-wage laws and unemployment benefits were nonexistent, which made periods of unemployment hard on families who earned subsistence wages. As you can sense, these were not short-term issues that would easily go away. The workplace was ripe for the emergence of national labor organizations.

The first truly national labor organization was the **Knights of Labor**, formed by Uriah Smith Stephens in 1869. By 1886, the organization claimed a membership of 700,000. The organization offered membership to all working people, including employers, and promoted social causes as well as labor and economic issues. The Knights' intention was to gain significant *political* power and eventually restructure the entire U.S. economy. The organization fell from prominence after being blamed for a bomb that killed eight policemen during a labor rally at Haymarket Square in Chicago in 1886.[8]

A rival group, the **American Federation of Labor (AFL)**, was formed that same year. By 1890, the AFL, under the dynamic leadership of Samuel Gompers, stood at the forefront of the labor movement.[9] The AFL was an organization of craft unions that championed fundamental labor issues. It intentionally limited membership to skilled workers (craftspeople), assuming they would have better bargaining power than unskilled workers in obtaining concessions from employers. The AFL was never one big union. It still functions as a federation of many individual unions that can become members yet keep their separate union status.

Over time, an unauthorized AFL group called the Committee of Industrial Organizations began to organize **industrial unions**, which consisted of unskilled and semiskilled workers in mass-production industries such as automobile manufacturing and mining. John L. Lewis, president of the United Mine Workers, led this committee. His objective was to organize both craftspeople and unskilled workers.

When the AFL rejected his proposal in 1935, Lewis broke away to form the **Congress of Industrial Organizations (CIO)**. The CIO soon rivaled the AFL in membership, partly because of the passage of the National Labor Relations Act (also called the Wagner Act) that same year (see the next section). For 20 years, the two organizations struggled for power. It wasn't until passage of the Taft-Hartley Act in 1947 (see Figure 12.1) that they saw the benefits of a merger. In 1955, under the leadership of George Meany, 16 million labor members united to form the powerful AFL-CIO. Recently, however, the AFL-CIO's influence has weakened. Seven unions, including the Service Employees International Union (SEIU) and the Teamsters, led by James P. Hoffa, left the AFL-CIO in 2005 and formed a coalition called Change to Win.[10] The SEIU was the AFL-CIO's largest union, with 1.8 million members. The AFL-CIO today maintains affiliations with 56 national and international labor unions and has about 11.5 million members.[11]

LEARNING goal 2 *

Discuss the major legislation affecting labor unions.

LABOR LEGISLATION AND COLLECTIVE BARGAINING

The growth and influence of organized labor in the United States has depended primarily on two major factors: the law and public opinion.[12] Figure 12.1 outlines five major federal laws with a significant impact on the rights and operations of labor unions. Take a few moments to read it before going on.

Knights of Labor
The first national labor union; formed in 1869.

American Federation of Labor (AFL)
An organization of craft unions that championed fundamental labor issues; founded in 1886.

▶ PPT 12-7:
Industrial Unions

industrial unions
Labor organizations of unskilled and semiskilled workers in mass-production industries such as automobiles and mining.

Congress of Industrial Organizations (CIO)
Union organization of unskilled workers; broke away from the American Federation of Labor (AFL) in 1935 and rejoined it in 1955.

yellow-dog contract
A type of contract that required employees to agree as a condition of employment not to join a union; prohibited by the Norris-LaGuardia Act in 1932.

Norris–LaGuardia Act, 1932	Prohibited courts from issuing injunctions against nonviolent union activities; outlawed contracts forbidding union activities; outlawed the use of yellow-dog contracts by employers. (Yellow-dog contracts were contractual agreements forced on workers by employers whereby the employee agreed not to join a union as a condition of employment.)
National Labor Relations Act (Wagner Act), 1935	Gave employees the right to form or join labor organizations (or to refuse to form or join); the right to collectively bargain with employers through elected union representatives; and the right to engage in labor activities such as strikes, picketing, and boycotts. Prohibited certain unfair labor practices by the employer and the union, and established the National Labor Relations Board to oversee union election campaigns and investigate labor practices. This act gave great impetus to the union movement.
Fair Labor Standards Act, 1938	Set a minimum wage and maximum basic hours for workers in interstate commerce industries. The first minimum wage set was 25 cents an hour, except for farm and retail workers.
Labor–Management Relations Act (Taft-Hartley Act), 1947	Amended the Wagner Act; permitted states to pass laws prohibiting compulsory union membership (right-to-work laws); set up methods to deal with strikes that affect national health and safety; prohibited secondary boycotts, closed-shop agreements, and featherbedding (the requiring of wage payments for work not performed) by unions. This act gave more power to management.
Labor–Management Reporting and Disclosure Act (Landrum-Griffin Act), 1959	Amended the Taft-Hartley Act and the Wagner Act; guaranteed individual rights of union members in dealing with their union, such as the right to nominate candidates for union office, vote in union elections, attend and participate in union meetings, vote on union business, and examine union records and accounts; required annual financial reports to be filed with the U.S. Department of Labor. One goal of this act was to clean up union corruption.

figure 12.1

MAJOR LEGISLATION AFFECTING LABOR–MANAGEMENT RELATIONS

◀ PPT 12-8:
Effects of Laws on Labor Unions

collective bargaining
The process whereby union and management representatives form a labor–management agreement, or contract, for workers.

◀ PPT 12-9:
Forming a Union in the Workplace

certification
Formal process whereby a union is recognized by the National Labor Relations Board (NLRB) as the bargaining agent for a group of employees.

decertification
The process by which workers take away a union's right to represent them.

The Norris-LaGuardia Act paved the way for union growth in the United States. This legislation prohibited employers from using contracts that forbid union activities such as yellow dog contracts.[13] A **yellow-dog contract** required employees to agree, as a condition of employment, not to join a union. The National Labor Relations Act (or Wagner Act) provided labor with clear legal justification to pursue key issues that were strongly supported by Samuel Gompers and the AFL. One of these, **collective bargaining**, is the process whereby union and management representatives negotiate a contract for workers. The Wagner Act expanded labor's right to collectively bargain. It obligated employers to meet at reasonable times and bargain in good faith with respect to wages, hours, and other terms and conditions of employment. Gompers believed that collective bargaining was critical to obtaining a fairer share of the economic pie for workers and improving work conditions on the job. The Wagner Act also established an administrative agency, the National Labor Relations Board (NLRB), to oversee labor–management relations.[14]

The NLRB consists of five members appointed by the U.S. president. It provides workplace guidelines and legal protection to workers seeking to vote on organizing a union to represent them. **Certification** is the formal process whereby the NLRB recognizes a labor union as the authorized bargaining agent for a group of employees. Figure 12.2 on p. 322 describes the steps in a union-organizing campaign leading to certification. After the election, both the union and company have five days to contest the results with the NLRB. The Wagner Act also provided workers with a clear process to remove a union as its workplace representative. **Decertification**, described in Figure 12.2, is the process by which workers can take away a union's right to represent them.

figure 12.2

STEPS IN UNION-ORGANIZING AND DECERTIFICATION CAMPAIGNS

Note that the final vote in each case requires that the union receive over 50 percent of the *votes cast.* Note, too, that the election is secret.

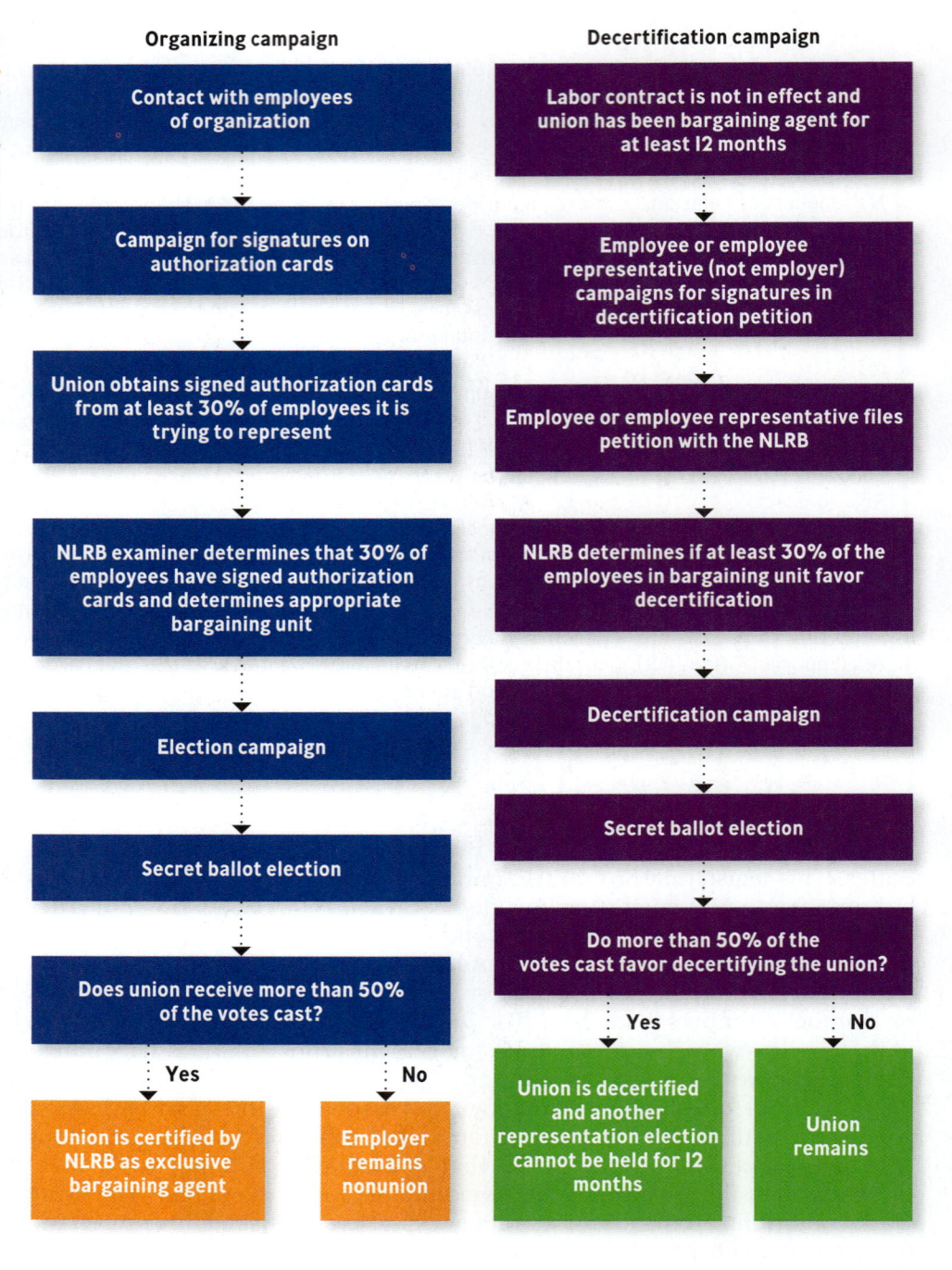

Organizing campaign

- Contact with employees of organization
- ↓
- Campaign for signatures on authorization cards
- ↓
- Union obtains signed authorization cards from at least 30% of employees it is trying to represent
- ↓
- NLRB examiner determines that 30% of employees have signed authorization cards and determines appropriate bargaining unit
- ↓
- Election campaign
- ↓
- Secret ballot election
- ↓
- Does union receive more than 50% of the votes cast?
  - Yes → Union is certified by NLRB as exclusive bargaining agent
  - No → Employer remains nonunion

Decertification campaign

- Labor contract is not in effect and union has been bargaining agent for at least 12 months
- ↓
- Employee or employee representative (not employer) campaigns for signatures in decertification petition
- ↓
- Employee or employee representative files petition with the NLRB
- ↓
- NLRB determines if at least 30% of the employees in bargaining unit favor decertification
- ↓
- Decertification campaign
- ↓
- Secret ballot election
- ↓
- Do more than 50% of the votes cast favor decertifying the union?
  - Yes → Union is decertified and another representation election cannot be held for 12 months
  - No → Union remains

> **CRITICAL THINKING EXERCISE 12-2:** Union Negotiations

As of this writing, unions are hoping that Congress passes the Employee Free Choice Act, which is designed to make it much easier for unions to organize workers.[15] This legislation would replace the secret ballot now used in union certification with a *card check* whereby workers would openly approve union representation simply by signing a card.[16] If a majority of workers sign the cards, the union would be certified. Business leaders promise to fight this legislation because it takes away secret ballots and makes unionization easier.

LEARNING goal 3 *

Outline the objectives of labor unions.

PPT 12-10: Why Join a Union?

PPT 12-11: Labor/Management Agreements

Objectives of Organized Labor

The objectives of labor unions frequently shift with social and economic trends.[17] In the 1970s, the primary objective was additional pay and benefits for members. In the 1980s, job security and union recognition were uppermost. In the 1990s and into the 2000s, unions again focused on job security due to the growth of global competition and outsourcing. The AFL-CIO, for example, was a major opponent of the North American Free Trade Agreement (NAFTA) and the Central American Free Trade Agreement (CAFTA), fearing its members would lose jobs to low-wage workers in other nations.[18] Organized labor has also strongly opposed the increase in offshore outsourcing, claiming this practice will cost U.S. jobs.

The **negotiated labor–management agreement**, more informally referred to as the labor contract, sets the tone and clarifies the terms and conditions under which management and the union will function over a specific period. Negotiations cover a wide range of work topics, and it can take a long time to reach an agreement. Figure 12.3 lists topics commonly negotiated by management and labor.

Labor unions generally insist that a contract contain a **union security clause** stipulating that employees who reap union benefits either officially join or at least pay dues to the union. After passage of the Wagner Act, labor unions sought strict security in the form of the **closed shop agreement**, which specified that workers had to be members of a union before being hired for a job.

negotiated labor–management agreement (labor contract)
Agreement that sets the tone and clarifies the terms under which management and labor agree to function over a period of time.

union security clause
Provision in a negotiated labor–management agreement that stipulates that employees who benefit from a union must either officially join or at least pay dues to the union.

closed shop agreement
Clause in a labor–management agreement that specified workers had to be members of a union before being hired (was outlawed by the Taft-Hartley Act in 1947).

PPT 12-12: Union Security Agreements

1. Management rights
2. Union recognition
3. Union security clause
4. Strikes and lockouts
5. Union activities and responsibilities
   - *a.* Dues checkoff
   - *b.* Union bulletin boards
   - *c.* Work slowdowns
6. Wages
   - *a.* Wage structure
   - *b.* Shift differentials
   - *c.* Wage incentives
   - *d.* Bonuses
   - *e.* Piecework conditions
   - *f.* Tiered wage structures
7. Hours of work and time-off policies
   - *a.* Regular hours of work
   - *b.* Holidays
   - *c.* Vacation policies
   - *d.* Overtime regulations
   - *e.* Leaves of absence
   - *f.* Break periods
   - *g.* Flextime
   - *h.* Mealtime allotments
8. Job rights and seniority principles
   - *a.* Seniority regulations
   - *b.* Transfer policies and bumping
   - *c.* Promotions
   - *d.* Layoffs and recall procedures
   - *e.* Job bidding and posting
9. Discharge and discipline
   - *a.* Suspension
   - *b.* Conditions for discharge
10. Grievance procedures
    - *a.* Arbitration agreement
    - *b.* Mediation procedures
11. Employee benefits, health, and welfare

figure 12.3

ISSUES IN A NEGOTIATED LABOR–MANAGEMENT AGREEMENT

Labor and management often meet to discuss and clarify the terms that specify employees' functions within the company. The topics listed in this figure are typically discussed during these meetings.

figure 12.4

DIFFERENT FORMS OF UNION AGREEMENTS

TYPE OF AGREEMENT	DESCRIPTION
Closed shop	The Taft-Hartley Act made this form of agreement illegal. Under this type of labor agreement, employers could hire only current union members for a job.
Union shop	The majority of labor agreements are of this type. In a union shop, the employer can hire anyone, but as a condition of employment, employees hired must join the union to keep their jobs.
Agency shop	Employers may hire anyone. Employees need not join the union, but are required to pay a union fee. A small percentage of labor agreements are of this type.
Open shop	Union membership is voluntary for new and existing employees. Those who don't join the union don't have to pay union dues. Few union contracts are of this type.

union shop agreement
Clause in a labor–management agreement that says workers do not have to be members of a union to be hired, but must agree to join the union within a prescribed period.

agency shop agreement
Clause in a labor–management agreement that says employers may hire nonunion workers; employees are not required to join the union but must pay a union fee.

right-to-work laws
Legislation that gives workers the right, under an open shop, to join or not join a union if it is present.

open shop agreement
Agreement in right-to-work states that gives workers the option to join or not join a union, if one exists in their workplace.

To labor's dismay, the Labor–Management Relations Act (Taft-Hartley Act) outlawed this practice in 1947 (see Figure 12.4).

Today, unions favor the **union shop agreement**, under which workers do not have to be members of a union to be hired but must agree to join within a prescribed period (usually 30, 60, or 90 days). However, under a contingency called an **agency shop agreement**, employers may hire nonunion workers who are not required to join the union but must pay a special union fee or regular union dues. Labor leaders believe that such fees or dues are justified because the union represents all workers in collective bargaining, not just its members.

The Taft-Hartley Act recognized the legality of the union shop but granted individual states the power to outlaw such agreements through **right-to-work laws**. To date, 22 states have passed such legislation (see Figure 12.5). In a right-to-work state, an **open shop agreement** gives workers the option to join or not join a union if one exists.[19] A worker who does not join cannot be forced to pay a fee or dues.

Future union negotiations will most likely focus on child care and elder care, worker retraining, two-tiered wage plans, offshore outsourcing, employee

figure 12.5

STATES WITH RIGHT-TO-WORK LAWS

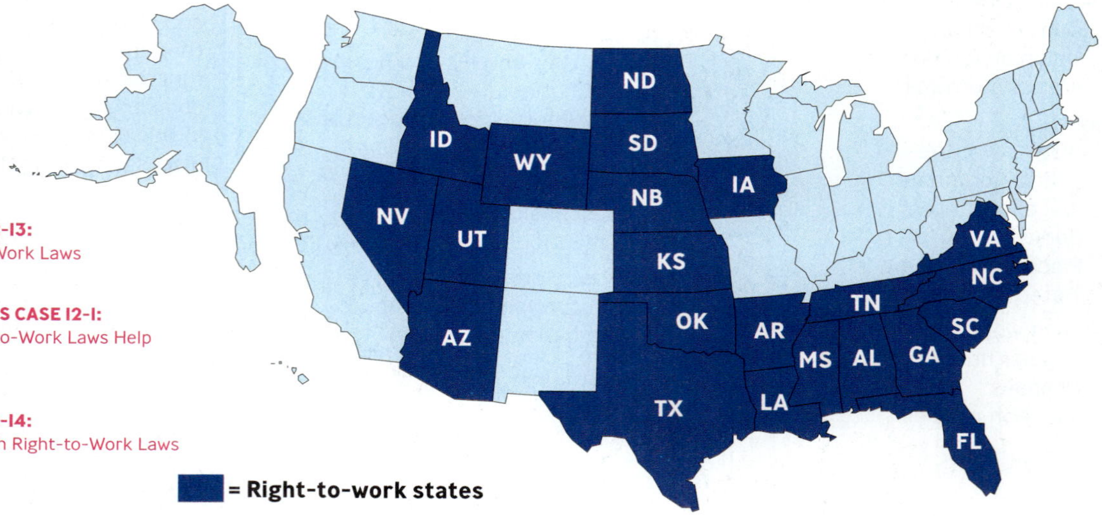

▶ PPT 12-13:
Right-to-Work Laws

▶ BONUS CASE 12-1:
Do Right-to-Work Laws Help States?

▶ PPT 12-14:
States with Right-to-Work Laws

■ = Right-to-work states

REACHING BEYOND our borders

www.unite.com

Workers of the World, Unite

"Workers of the world, unite," was the battle cry of Karl Marx, author of the *Communist Manifesto*. Today, as markets become borderless, labor unions around the globe are embracing this theme as an idea whose time has come. Andy Stern, president of the Service Employees International Union, explains that the call to unity is not ideological, but practical. Stern claims, "Since companies don't see national borders as obstacles to the future, why shouldn't unions be global?"

Union leaders lament that labor has reacted slowly to the globalization of the economy. Over the past 30 years, nearly every major industry has become active in global trade. The global workforce has doubled in size, due primarily to additions from China and India. However, the percentage of the world's workers represented by unions has declined dramatically. In the United States, only about 12 percent of workers belong to a union. In Europe, where unions have long been an integral part of the economic fabric, membership has declined in all but three small nations in the EU. This reduction has significantly limited labor unions' bargaining power in negotiating with global employers.

Labor unions, however, are not about to roll over and give up hope. Union leaders from 64 countries have formed the Council of Global Unions to bring various national union movements into one, powerful global labor movement. Several U.S. unions have already begun to move globally. United Steelworkers (USW) has proposed joining with Britain's largest union, and United Food and Commercial Workers (UFCW) has forged ties with its European counterparts. According to USW president Leo Gerard, "Setting global standards in the 21st century is as critical as setting national standards was in the 20th century."

Obviously, some companies are determined that labor's global ambitions do not succeed and plan a counteroffensive. Kimberly Elliott, of the Peterson Institute for International Economics, warns that attempts to form global unions have not succeeded in the past. Political problems in large nations like China and India also pose large problems for global unionism. Nonetheless, outgoing AFL-CIO president John Sweeney says the goal is to make labor as global as capital has become. As union numbers continue to dwindle, globalization may be labor's best hope.

Sources: Renuka Rayasam, "Labor Unions without Borders," *U.S. News & World Report,* July 8, 2007; Harold Meyerson, "Labor's Global Push," *The Washington Post,* December 12, 2007; AFL-CIO, www.aflcio.com, accessed February 17, 2009; and Change to Win, www.changetowin.com, accessed February 17, 2009.

empowerment, and even integrity and honesty testing. Unions also intend to carefully monitor immigration policies and free trade agreements such as NAFTA and CAFTA to see that U.S. jobs are not lost.

Labor unions play a key role in other countries as well. The Reaching Beyond Our Borders box discusses the possibility of unionizing workers on a global scale, a formidable challenge.

Resolving Labor–Management Disagreements

The negotiated labor–management agreement outlines the rights of both labor and management. Upon acceptance by both sides, it becomes a guide to work relations between them. However, it doesn't necessarily end negotiations. There are sometimes differences concerning interpretations of the agreement. For example, managers may interpret a certain clause in the agreement to mean they are free to select who works overtime. Union members may interpret the same clause to mean that managers must select employees for overtime on the basis of seniority. If the parties can't resolve such controversies, employees may file a grievance.

A **grievance** is a charge by employees that management is not abiding by or fulfilling the terms of the negotiated labor–management agreement as

◀ PPT 12-15:
Workers of the World, Unite

◀ PPT 12-16:
Resolving Disagreements

grievance
A charge by employees that management is not abiding by the terms of the negotiated labor–management agreement.

they perceive it. Overtime rules, promotions, layoffs, transfers, and job assignments are generally sources of employee grievances. Handling them demands a good deal of contact between union officials and managers. Grievances, however, do not imply that a company has broken the law or the labor agreement. In fact, the vast majority of grievances are negotiated and resolved by **shop stewards** (union officials who work permanently in an organization and represent employee interests on a daily basis) and supervisory-level managers. However, if a grievance is not settled at this level, formal grievance procedures will begin. Figure 12.6 illustrates the steps a formal grievance procedure could follow.

Mediation and Arbitration

During the negotiation process, there is generally a **bargaining zone**, which is the range of options between the initial and final offers that each party will consider before negotiations dissolve or reach an impasse. If labor–management negotiators aren't able to agree on alternatives within this bargaining zone, mediation may be necessary.

Mediation is the use of a third party, called a *mediator*, who encourages both sides in a dispute to continue negotiating and often makes suggestions for resolving the matter. Keep in mind that mediators evaluate facts in the dispute and then make suggestions, not decisions.[20] Elected officials (current and past), attorneys, and college professors often serve as mediators in labor disputes. The National Mediation Board provides federal mediators when

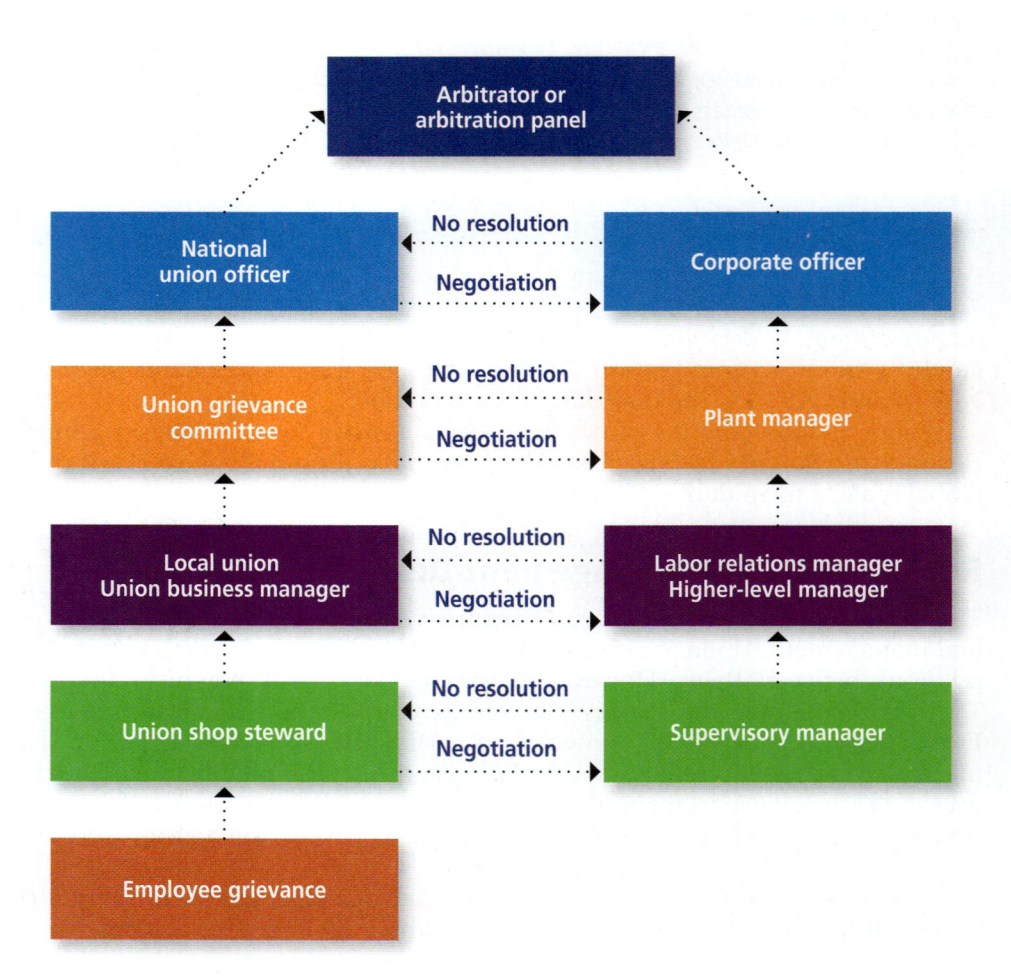

---

shop stewards
Union officials who work permanently in an organization and represent employee interests on a daily basis.

▶ PPT 12-17:
Using Mediation and Arbitration

bargaining zone
The range of options between the initial and final offer that each party will consider before negotiations dissolve or reach an impasse.

mediation
The use of a third party, called a mediator, who encourages both sides in a dispute to continue negotiating and often makes suggestions for resolving the dispute.

▶ PPT 12-18:
The Grievance Resolution Process

figure 12.6
THE GRIEVANCE RESOLUTION PROCESS
The grievance process may move through several steps before the issue is resolved. At each step, the issue is negotiated between union officials and managers. If no resolution comes internally, an outside arbitrator may be mutually agreed on. If so, the decision by the arbitrator is binding (legally enforceable).

requested in a dispute.[21] The Allied Pilots Association that represents 12,000 pilots of American Airlines asked for such assistance in negotiating a new contract with the nation's largest air carrier.[22]

A more extreme option used to resolve conflicts is **arbitration**,[23] an agreement to bring an impartial third party—a single arbitrator or a panel—to render a binding decision in a labor dispute. The arbitrator(s) must be acceptable to both labor and management. You may have heard of professional baseball players filing for arbitration to resolve a contract dispute with their teams. Many negotiated labor–management agreements in the United States call for the use of an arbitrator to end labor disputes. The nonprofit American Arbitration Association is the dominant organization used in dispute resolution.[24]

◀ LECTURE LINK 12-2:
Hollywood Labor Disputes

arbitration
The agreement to bring in an impartial third party (a single arbitrator or a panel of arbitrators) to render a binding decision in a labor dispute.

LEARNING goal 4 *

Describe the tactics used by labor and management during conflicts, and discuss the role of unions in the future.

TACTICS USED IN LABOR–MANAGEMENT CONFLICTS

If labor and management cannot reach an agreement through collective bargaining, and negotiations break down, either side, or both, may use specific tactics to enhance its negotiating position and perhaps sway public opinion. Unions primarily use strikes and boycotts, as well as pickets and work slowdowns. Management, for its part, may implement lockouts, injunctions, and even strikebreakers. The following sections look briefly at each tactic.

◀ PPT 12-19:
Tactics Used in Conflicts

Union Tactics

A **strike** occurs when workers collectively refuse to go to work. Strikes have been the most potent union tactic. They attract public attention to a labor dispute and can cause operations in a company to slow down or totally cease. Besides refusing to work, strikers may also picket the company, walking around the outside of the location carrying signs and talking with the public and the media about the issues in the dispute. Unions also often use picketing as an

strike
A union strategy in which workers refuse to go to work; the purpose is to further workers' objectives after an impasse in collective bargaining.

These members of the International Association of Machinists and Aerospace Workers were among the 27,000 workers who voted to reject a new contract and go on strike against airplane manufacturer Boeing. What other tactics could they have used to bring public attention to their complaints?

▶ **PPT 12-20:**
Strike and Boycotts

▶ **LECTURE LINK 12-3:**
Additional Labor/Management Tactics

cooling-off period
When workers in a critical industry return to their jobs while the union and management continue negotiations.

primary boycott
When a union encourages both its members and the general public not to buy the products of a firm involved in a labor dispute.

Writer/actor Tina Fey joined about 12,000 movie and television writers in a strike against the Alliance of Motion Picture and Television Producers in 2007, delaying the production of dozens of new TV episodes and movies. Can the public impartially evaluate job actions supported by celebrities?

▶ **PPT 12-21:**
Tactics Used in Conflicts

▶ **PPT 12-22:**
Lockouts, Injunctions, and Strikebreakers

informational tool before going on strike. The purpose is to alert the public to an issue stirring labor unrest, even though no strike has been voted.

Strikes sometimes lead to the resolution of a labor dispute; however, they also have generated violence and extended bitterness. Often after a strike is finally settled, labor and management remain openly hostile toward each other and mutual complaints of violations of the negotiated labor–management agreement continue. This occurred after the United Auto Workers strike against Caterpillar and the Teamsters strike against Overnite Transit, the latter of which lasted almost four years.[25]

The public often realizes how important a worker is when he or she goes on strike. Imagine the economic and social disaster if a town's police force or firefighters went on strike. That's why many states prohibit such public safety workers from striking, even though they can be unionized. Employees of the federal government, such as postal workers, can organize unions but are also denied the right to strike. When strikes are prohibited, workers sometimes display their frustrations by engaging in sick-outs (often called the *blue flu*). That is, they arrange in groups to be absent from work and claim illness as the reason.

Under the Taft-Hartley Act, the U.S. president can ask for a **cooling-off period**, during which workers return to their jobs while negotiations continue, to prevent a strike in a critical industry. The cooling-off period can last up to 80 days.

Today, both labor and management seek to avoid strikes. Still, you may recall the 100-day screenwriters' strike in 2007–2008 that shut down your favorite television shows and moved many famous faces to the picket lines.[26] As technological change, offshore outsourcing, and reductions in worker benefits such as health insurance continue, it's unlikely that strikes will disappear. Strikes in entertainment, health care, transportation, professional sports, and other industries demonstrate that the strike is not dead as a labor tactic.

Unions also use boycotts as a means to obtain their objectives in a labor dispute. Boycotts can be classified as primary or secondary. A **primary boycott** occurs when organized labor encourages both its members and the general public not to buy the products or services of a firm engaged in a labor dispute. A **secondary boycott** is an attempt by labor to convince others to stop doing business with a firm that is the subject of a primary boycott. Labor unions can legally authorize primary boycotts, but the Taft-Hartley Act prohibits the use of secondary boycotts.[27] For example, a union could not initiate a secondary boycott against a supermarket chain because that chain carries goods produced by a company that's the target of a primary boycott.

Management Tactics

Like labor, management also uses specific tactics to achieve its workplace goals. A **lockout** is an attempt by managers to put pressure on union workers by temporarily closing the business. When workers don't work, they don't get paid. Today, management rarely uses lockouts to achieve its objectives. However, the high-profile lockout of National Hockey League players that caused the cancellation of the entire 2004–2005 season reminds us this tactic is still viable.[28] Still, management today most often uses injunctions and strikebreakers to counter labor demands it sees as excessive.

An **injunction** is a court order directing someone to do something or to refrain from doing something. Management has sought injunctions to order

MAKING ethical decisions

www.ethics.ubc.ca/resources/business

When Do You Cross the Line?

You just opened your wallet and unfortunately saw only one picture of George Washington staring back at you. Money is obviously tight, and the costs of your education, food, and other expenses keep going up. You read last weekend that Shop-Till-You-Drop, a local grocery chain in your town, is seeking workers to replace members of United Commercial Food Workers (UCFW). The workers are currently on strike against the company due to a reduction in health insurance benefits.

Several classmates at your college are UCFW members employed at Shop-Till-You-Drop stores, and many other students are supporting the strike. The stores also employ many people from your neighborhood. Shop-Till-You-Drop argues that the company has made a fair offer to the union, but the workers' demands are excessive and could ruin the company.

Shop-Till-You-Drop is offering replacement workers an attractive wage rate and flexible schedules to cross the picket line and work during the strike. The company has suggested the possibility of permanent employment. As a struggling student, you could certainly use the job and the extra money for tuition and expenses. Will you cross the picket line and apply? What could be the consequences of your decision? Is your choice ethical?

---

striking workers back to work, limit the number of pickets during a strike, or otherwise deal with actions that could be detrimental to the public welfare. For a court to issue an injunction, management must show a just cause, such as the possibility of violence or destruction of property. The use of strikebreakers has been a particular source of hostility and violence in labor relations.

Strikebreakers (called scabs by unions) are workers hired to do the jobs of striking employees until the labor dispute is resolved. Employers have had the right to replace strikers since a 1938 Supreme Court ruling, but this tactic was infrequently used until the 1980s. Be sure to read the Making Ethical Decisions box, which deals with this issue.

The Future of Unions and Labor–Management Relations

New issues that affect labor–management relations include increased global competition, advancing technology, offshore outsourcing, and the changing nature of work.[29] To save jobs, many unions have granted management concessions, or **givebacks**, of previous gains. Unions at airlines such as United and American agreed to give back previous wage and benefit gains just to keep the airlines flying due to high fuel costs.[30] The United Auto Workers agreed to discuss givebacks to help General Motors and Chrysler obtain financial assistance from the federal government.[31] However, unions have resisted any givebacks of retiree benefits.

Organized labor is at a crossroads. The United Auto Workers (UAW) has lost two-thirds of its membership since 1979.[32] The unionized share of the workforce overall has declined from a peak of 35.5 percent in 1945 to 12.3 percent today. Only 7.4 percent of workers in the private sector are unionized, and union membership by state varies considerably (see Figure 12.7 on p. 330).[33] Organized labor, however, has seen increases in membership over the past two years, and hopes a new trend is emerging.[34] The largest labor organization in the United States today is the National Education Association (NEA), which represents 3.2 million members.[35]

◀ PPT 12-23:
When Do You Cross the Line?

secondary boycott
An attempt by labor to convince others to stop doing business with a firm that is the subject of a primary boycott; prohibited by the Taft-Hartley Act.

◀ PPT 12-24:
Challenges Facing Labor Unions

lockout
An attempt by management to put pressure on unions by temporarily closing the business.

◀ LECTURE LINK 12-4:
Reshaping the Union to Save the Union

injunction
A court order directing someone to do something or to refrain from doing something.

◀ PPT 12-25:
Labor Unions in the Future

strikebreakers
Workers hired to do the jobs of striking workers until the labor dispute is resolved.

givebacks
Concessions made by union members to management; gains from labor negotiations are given back to management to help employers remain competitive and thereby save jobs.

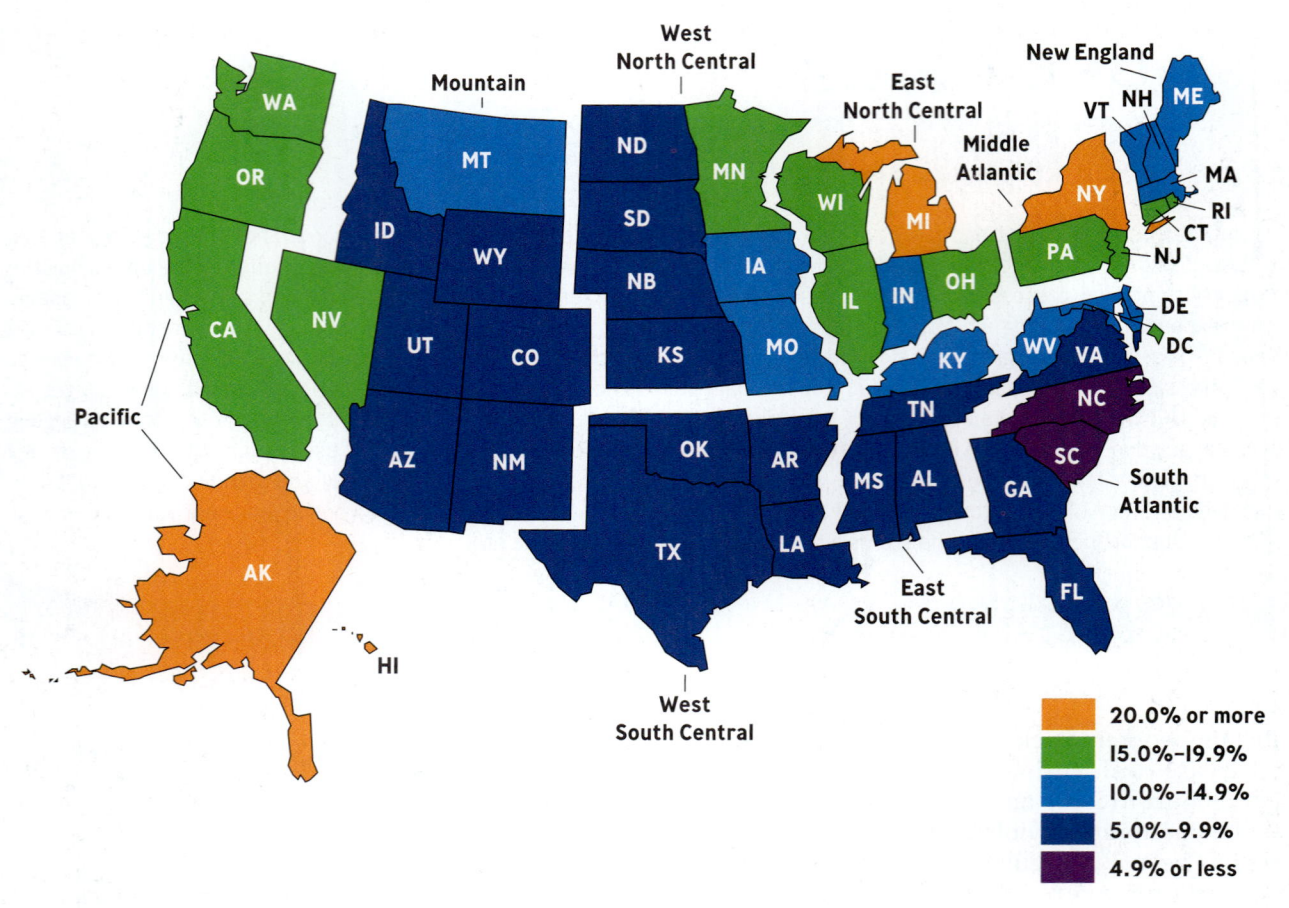

figure 12.7

UNION MEMBERSHIP BY STATE

Source: AFL-CIO, www.aflcio.org, 2009.

Legend:
- 20.0% or more
- 15.0%–19.9%
- 10.0%–14.9%
- 5.0%–9.9%
- 4.9% or less

▶ **PPT 12-26:**
Union Membership by State

▶ **BONUS CASE 12-2:**
Pension Plans Under Attack

▶ **LECTURE LINK 12-5:**
Unions Turn to the Service Industry for Growth

After Petro Canada locked out 260 union members in a labor dispute, the Canadian Labour Congress urged its 3.2 million members to boycott Petro Canada gas stations across the country. What effect do you think such retaliatory actions have on labor–management relations?

To grow, unions will have to include more white-collar, female, and foreign-born workers than they have traditionally included. The Teamsters Union and the Service Employees International Union have begun plans to specifically target workers in health care (14.6 million workers), finance (8.9 million workers), and information technology (3.2 million workers).[36] The Spotlight on Small Business box discusses efforts to organize health care workers.

Unions in the future will be quite different from those in the past. Their members understand that U.S. firms must remain competitive with foreign firms, and labor must do its best to maintain competitiveness. Many unions have taken on a new role in assisting management in training workers, redesigning jobs, and assimilating the changing workforce. They help recruit and train foreign workers, unskilled workers, and others who need special help in

SPOTLIGHT ON SMALL business

www.calnurses.org

Nursing the Unions Back to Health

Globalization has altered many industries, and demographic changes have shifted the composition and characteristics of many jobs. The aging of the baby boomers has driven the need for increased health care services and promises to increase the number of health care professionals needed in the future. Labor unions are well aware of this fact and see health care—particularly its largest area, nursing—as an occupation ripe for growth in union membership.

Nationwide, more than 500,000 registered nurses (RNs) belong to unions. The Service Employees International Union (SEIU) represents approximately 900,000 health care workers, including 110,000 nurses. The SEIU believes that 1 million nurses could be incorporated into organized labor by 2016. However, the task will not be simple, since a good deal of competition exists from labor groups such as the United American Nurses (an affiliate of the AFL-CIO), the American Nurses Association, and the California Nurses Association.

Unions know that to increase membership among nurses they must promise the respect and professionalism nurses deserve. Key issues important to nurses include safe staffing, a voice in hospital policies, professional growth and development (including tuition reimbursement), and increased pay and benefits.

Labor is not forgetting about physicians. Many private-practice physicians have embraced unionization as a means to collectively bargain with managed health care organizations such as health maintenance organizations (HMOs). The possibility of a national health policy is also leading doctors to consider organizing. In 1999, the American Medical Association (AMA) launched a physicians union called Physicians for Responsible Negotiations (PRN). The group became affiliated with the SEIU in 2004 and counts 40,000 doctors as members.

Demographic shifts could cause the number of union members in the health care industry to grow significantly in the years ahead. Naturally, the care and well-being of patients must remain the key focus of the medical profession. Still, it's possible you may someday go to the doctor and ask to see a union card before opening wide and saying "Ahhh." It's not as absurd as you may think.

Sources: "Outliers; Asides and Insides," *Modern Healthcare,* April 14, 2008; "Rival Unions Battle in Ohio over Workers at Hospitals," *New York Times,* March 12, 2008; SEIU, www.seiu.com, accessed February 12, 2009; and California Nurses Association, www.calnurses.org, accessed February 12, 2009.

---

adapting to the job requirements of the new service and knowledge-work economy.

Unions today seek improved job security, profit sharing, and increased wages. Management looks for a productive, dedicated workforce capable of handling the challenges of global competition. How organized labor and management handle these challenges may well define the future for labor unions. After the Progress Assessment, we will look at other issues facing employees and managers in the 21st century.

> PPT 12-28:
> Progress Assessment

progress assessment

- What are the major laws that affected union growth, and what does each one cover?
- How do changes in the economy affect the objectives of unions?
- What are the major tactics used by unions and by management to assert their power in contract negotiations?
- What types of workers do unions hope to organize in the future?

> Because of economic concerns about globalization, free trade, and the relocation of jobs to low-wage countries, organized labor has fiercely opposed trade agreements such as NAFTA and CAFTA. Should the U.S. government protect workers in globalized industries from the loss of their jobs?

LEARNING goal 5 *

Assess some of today's controversial employee–management issues, such as executive compensation, pay equity, child care and elder care, drug testing, and violence in the workplace.

CONTROVERSIAL EMPLOYEE–MANAGEMENT ISSUES

This is an interesting time in the history of employee–management relations. Organizations are active in global expansion, offshore outsourcing, and technology change. The government has eliminated some social benefits to workers and is taking a more active role in mandating what benefits and assurances businesses must provide to workers. Employees are raising questions of fairness and workplace security. Let's look at several rather controversial workplace issues, starting with executive compensation.

Executive Compensation

Tiger Woods putts his way to over $110 million a year, Johnny Depp acts his way to $72 million a year, Oprah Winfrey talks her way to over $275 million a year, and J. K. Rowling rode the Hogwarts train for over $300 million a year.[37] Is it out of line, then, for Lawrence Ellison, CEO of Oracle, to make $84 million a year?[38] Chapter 2 explained that the U.S. free-market system is built on incentives that allow top executives to make such large amounts—or more. Today, however, the government, boards of directors, stockholders, unions, and employees are challenging this principle and arguing that executive compensation has gotten out of line.[39] In fact, way out of line. In 2007, CEOs at the 500 largest U.S. firms actually took a pay cut. Still, the average total CEO compensation (salary, bonuses, and incentives) at a major company was $12.8 million, compared to just a bit over $35,000 for the average worker.[40] Even after adjusting for inflation, this represents an enormous increase from the $160,000 average CEO compensation in 1960.

In the past, CEO compensation and bonuses were determined by the firm's profitability or an increase in its stock price. The logic of this assumption was that as the fortunes of a company and its stockholders grew, so would the rewards of the CEO. Today, however, executives generally receive stock options

> PPT 12-29:
> Compensating Executives

> PPT 12-30:
> Play Ball!

> CRITICAL THINKING
> EXERCISE 12-3:
> Executive Pay Watch

LEGAL briefcase

www.rileyguide.com/execpay.html

Paying for Incompetence

Most workers understand that if they are fired for incompetence, they are lucky to get their last paycheck. The practice of rewarding someone for failure simply goes against common sense. Unfortunately, many companies seem to be missing this point. Some corporate executives who exited their companies under fire wound up better off than if they had stayed—at least financially.

Take former Sprint CEO Gary Forsee. He was fired after he bungled a merger with Nextel, kicking Sprint's stock price from $25 to $7.40 a share. Forsee managed to land on his feet. According to his contract, he was entitled to a $40 million severance check, along with a $1.5 million salary through 2009, $5 million in other bonuses, $23 million in stock options, and an $84,000 pension for life.

Former Home Depot CEO Robert Nardelli had a similar "golden handshake" in his contract, giving him $210 million when he left the company after a lackluster tenure. Along with the enormous severance, Nardelli's contract also stated he would get 90 percent of his salary, regardless of his performance.

Even CEOs who had a heavy hand in causing the subprime mortgage crisis received healthy compensation upon their departure. Stanley O'Neal of Merrill Lynch earned a tidy salary of $87 million during five years of service as he engaged in risky investments in mortgage markets. As $30.5 billion in mortgage write-downs led to losses of billions of dollars, O'Neal resigned, forcing Merrill Lynch to pay him $136 million in deferred compensation and stock options even as the company and the national housing market tanked. Other mortgage lender CEOs, like Angelo Mozilo of Countrywide Financial and Kerry Killinger of Washington Mutual Bank, received performance bonuses worth millions of dollars even as their companies lost billions. Ultimately, Merrill Lynch and Countrywide Financial were taken over by Bank of America; Washington Mutual Bank was purchased by JPMorgan Chase.

Such "corporate benevolence" even extends beyond a CEO's lifetime due to controversial provisions called golden coffins. If Nabors Industries' boss Eugene Isenberg were to die while still CEO, his heirs would be entitled to $288 million of the company's money, more than its 2008 first-quarter earnings.

This type of questionable compensation is causing people like Nell Minow, cofounder of the business watchdog group Corporate Library, to clamor for reform. But the ultimate decision to change the inflated incomes of CEOs lies in the hands of the companies themselves.

Sources: Geoff Colvin, "Rewarding Failure," *Fortune,* April 28, 2008; Neil Weinberg, Michael Maiello, David K. Randall, "Paying for Failure," *Forbes,* May 19, 2008; and Mark Maremont, "Companies Promise CEOs Lavish Posthumous Paydays," *The Wall Street Journal,* June 11, 2008.

(the ability to buy company stock at a set price at a later date) and restricted stock (stock issued directly to the CEO that can't be sold usually for three or four years) as part of their compensation. In fact, stock options now account for over 50 percent of a CEO's compensation, and restricted stock makes up almost 25 percent—even when the company does not meet expectations.[41]

Richard Fuld, CEO of Lehman Brothers, received restricted stock valued at $35 million even though his firm's value plummeted due to the nationwide credit crisis and the company was forced out of business.[42] What's even more frustrating, however, are instances when CEOs are forced to resign because of poor performance but still walk away with lofty compensation.[43] Chuck Prince of Citigroup was shown the door after the company lost $64 billion in market value, yet he left with $68 million and a cash bonus of $12.5 million.[44] Many CEOs are also awarded fat retainers, consulting contracts, and lavish perks when they retire. Make sure to read the Legal Briefcase box for further discussion of this controversial trend.

Management consultant Peter Drucker (1909–2005) long criticized executive pay levels. He suggested CEOs should not earn much more than 20 times the salary of the company's lowest-paid employee. Not many companies,

◀ PPT 12-31:
Take Me Out to the Ball Game

◀ LECTURE LINK 12-6:
Golden Goodbyes

◀ PPT 12-32:
Paying for Incompetence

◀ PPT 12-33:
Compensating Executives in the Future

333

however, have placed such limits on executive compensation.[45] Some numbers can be staggering. For example, a custodian earning minimum wage at Oracle would have to work approximately 5,609 years to make what CEO Larry Ellison earned in 2009 ($84 million).

As global competition intensifies, executive paychecks in Europe have increased, too, but European CEOs typically earn only about 40 percent what U.S. CEOs make.[46] In some European countries, such as Germany, workers account for 50 percent of the seats on the board of directors of major firms according to a process called *co-determination* (cooperation between management and workers in decision making). Since boards set executive pay, this could be a reason why the imbalance in pay is less in Europe.

Today, government and shareholder pressure for full disclosure of executive compensation puts U.S. boards of directors on notice that they are not there simply to enrich CEOs.[47] The financial crisis of 2008–2010 strengthened shareholders intentions to propose an overhaul of executive compensation.[48] President Obama and Congress put limits on executive compensation of firms receiving money under the federal government bailout programs.

Most U.S. executives are responsible for multibillion-dollar corporations, work 70-plus hours a week, and often travel. Many have made decisions that turned potential problems into successes and reaped huge compensation for employees and stockholders as well as themselves. Furthermore, there are few seasoned, skilled professionals who can manage large companies, especially troubled companies looking for the right CEO to accomplish a turnaround. There's no easy answer to the question of what is fair compensation for executives, but it's a safe bet the controversy will not go away.[49]

Pay Equity

The Equal Pay Act of 1963 requires companies to give equal pay to men and women who do the same job. For example, it's against the law to pay a female nurse less than a male nurse unless factors such as seniority, merit pay, or performance incentives are involved. But *pay equity* goes beyond the concept of equal pay for equal work; it says people in jobs that require similar levels of education, training, or skills should receive equal pay. Pay equity compares the value of jobs like bank teller or librarian (traditionally women's jobs) with jobs like truck driver or plumber (traditionally men's jobs). Such a comparison shows that "women's" jobs tend to pay less—sometimes much less.

In the United States today, women earn 80.2 percent of what men earn, though the disparity varies by profession, job experience and tenure, and level of education.[50] In the past, the primary explanation for this disparity was that women worked only 50 to 60 percent of their available years once they left school, whereas men normally worked all those years. This explanation doesn't have much substance today because fewer women leave the workforce for an extended time. Other explanations suggest many women devote more time to their families than men do and thus accept lower-paying jobs with more flexible hours.

In 2008, a 1980s concept called *comparable worth* was reintroduced. This legislative proposal required that people in jobs requiring similar levels of education, training, or skills should receive equal pay. Evidence did not support

Hundreds of workers protested outside the Bank of America before marching toward AIG offices in Chicago. The group protested the actions of major banks and investment businesses whose behavior has weakened the economy—both before and since the government bailout. They argued that CEO and corporate excess benefited executives at the expense of workers.

▶ PPT 12-34:
The Question of Pay Equity

▶ PPT 12-35:
Equal Pay for Equal Work

the idea that comparable worth would lead to better market equilibrium. Many suggested it would create more chaos and inequity.[51]

Today women appear to be competing financially with men in fields such as health care, biotechnology, information technology, and other knowledge-based jobs. Studies at the University of Michigan found earnings of women with baccalaureate degrees were 96 percent of men's. Female engineers and anesthesiology nurses often earn more than their male counterparts, and women today hold 52 percent of well-paid middle management positions.[52] Still, Heather Boushey, an economist at the Economic Policy Institute, believes that the government puts too much faith in the idea that education will automatically close the pay gap. She and other critics claim that women, especially women with children, still earn less, are less likely to go into business, and are more likely to live in poverty than men.[53] In 2009, Congress passed the Paycheck Fairness Act, which strengthens protections against compensation discrimination.[54] There is no question that pay equity promises to remain a challenging employee–management issue.

◀ PPT 12-36:
The Salary Gender Gap

◀ PPT 12-37:
What's Sexual Harassment

sexual harassment
Unwelcome sexual advances, requests for sexual favors, and other conduct (verbal or physical) of a sexual nature that creates a hostile work environment.

Sexual Harassment

Sexual harassment refers to unwelcome sexual advances, requests for sexual favors, and other verbal or physical conduct of a sexual nature that creates a hostile work environment. Conduct on the job can be considered illegal under specific conditions:[55]

- The employee's submission to such conduct is explicitly or implicitly made a term or condition of employment, or an employee's submission to or rejection of such conduct is used as the basis for employment decisions affecting the worker's status. A threat like "Go out with me or you're fired" or "Go out with me or you'll never be promoted here" constitutes *quid pro quo sexual harassment*.

- The conduct unreasonably interferes with a worker's job performance or creates an intimidating, hostile, or offensive work environment. This type of harassment is *hostile work environment sexual harassment*.

The Civil Rights Act of 1991 governs sexual harassment of both men and women.[56] This fact was reinforced in 1997, when the Supreme Court said same-sex harassment also falls within the purview of sexual harassment law. The number of complaints filed to the Equal Employment Opportunity Commission (EEOC) has declined by about 25 percent since 2000. The Supreme Court in 1996 broadened the scope of what can be considered a hostile work environment; the key word seemed to be *unwelcome*, a term for behavior that would offend a reasonable person.

Companies have found that the courts mean business if they violate sexual harassment laws. Madison Square Garden lost a judgment of $11.6 million to a former executive who sued New York Knicks' basketball coach Isiah Thomas for sexual harassment.[57]

Managers and workers are now much more sensitive to sexual comments and behavior than they were in the past. Still, EEOC statistics show sexual harassment remains a persistent employee

Unwelcome sexual advances, requests for sexual favors, and other verbal or physical conduct are prohibited under the Civil Rights Act of 1991. While most employees are aware of sexual harassment policies in the workplace, they are often not certain what sexual harassment actually means. Thus many companies have turned to the Internet to train employees about the dos and don'ts of acceptable sexual conduct on the job.

> **PPT 12-38:**
> Kinds of Sexual Harassment

> **PPT 12-39:**
> You Make the Call

complaint. A key problem is that workers and managers often know a policy concerning sexual harassment exists but have no idea what it says. California is the first state to require all companies with 50 employees or more to provide sexual harassment prevention training to supervisors. Much training can be done at work through information on the Internet.

Foreign companies doing business in the United States are not immune to sexual harassment charges. Hideaki Otaka, CEO of Toyota Motor North America, resigned under pressure after sexual harassment charges were brought against him by a former assistant.[58]

Many companies have set up rapid, effective grievance procedures and reacted promptly to allegations of harassment. Such efforts may save businesses millions of dollars in lawsuits and make the workplace more productive and harmonious. Nonetheless, the workplace has a way to go before sexual harassment as a key employee–management issue disappears.

> **PPT 12-40:**
> Facing Child Care Issues

Child Care

Since 1975, the percentage of women in the workforce with children under 18 has increased from 47 to 72 percent; among mothers with children under the age of 3, workforce participation has increased from 34 to 61 percent.[59] Such statistics concern employers for two reasons: (1) absences related to child care cost U.S. businesses billions of dollars annually, and (2) the issue of who should pay for employee child care raises a question that often divides employees. Many workers oppose child care benefits for parents or single parents, arguing that single workers and single-income families should not subsidize child care. Others contend that employers and the government have the responsibility to create child care systems that allow employees to be the best workers and best parents they can be. Federal child care assistance has not risen significantly since the passage of the Welfare Reform Act in 1996. Thus, child care remains an important issue.

Questions about responsibilities for child care subsidies, child care programs, and parental leave have spurred much debate in the private and public sectors. The number of large companies offering child care as an employee benefit is growing. *Working Mother* magazine highlighted Bristol-Myers Squibb, IBM, and JPMorgan Chase as particularly sympathetic and cooperative with working mothers.[60] Other large firms with extensive child care programs include Johnson & Johnson, American Express, and Campbell Soup. Some firms provide emergency child care services for employees whose children are ill or whose regular child care arrangements are disrupted.

Unfortunately, just 3 percent of businesses with fewer than 100 employees provide child care at work. Some small companies, however, have found that implementing creative child care programs helps them compete with larger organizations in the challenge to hire and keep qualified employees. Guerra DeBerry Coody, a full-service marketing firm in San Antonio, Texas, set up a child care facility right in its office. Between snacks, naps, and lessons, children play on a roof deck playground watched by caregivers while their parents work. Employees can drop off the kids around 8:00 a.m. and pick them up as late as 6:30 p.m. Every May,

On-site day care is still a relatively uncommon employee benefit in the United States today. Although it is often expensive to operate, it can pay big dividends in employee satisfaction and productivity. Who should pay for employee benefits like child care and elder care, the employee or the company?

the youngsters "graduate" with caps and gowns in a procession down an office hall.[61] The company loses only about one employee per year.

Entrepreneurs Roger Brown and Linda Mason recognized the emerging attraction of child care as a benefit in the workplace. The husband-and-wife team started Bright Horizons Family Solutions Inc. to provide child care at worksites for employers. Today, their company is the leading provider in the $1 billion corporate-sponsored child care market and runs nearly 700 child care centers for about 400 companies.[62]

Working parents consider safe, affordable child care an issue of critical importance. Companies have responded by providing

- Discount arrangements with national child care chains.
- Vouchers that offer payments toward child care the employee selects.
- Referral services that help identify high-quality child care facilities to employees.
- On-site child care centers at which parents can visit children at lunch or during lag times throughout the workday.
- Sick-child centers to care for moderately ill children.

Increasing numbers of two-income households and the 13 million single-parent households in the United States ensure that child care will remain a hotly debated employee–management issue, along with elder care.

Elder Care

Since 1990, the number of people 65 and over has jumped 12 percent, to 35 million. It's expected to double by 2040, to 77 million people over 65.[63] In 2012, the overall labor force will grow by 12 percent, while the percentage 55 and older will increase by 52 percent. Most workers will not have to concern themselves with finding child care but will confront another problem: how to care for older parents and other relatives. The number of households with at least one adult providing elder care has tripled since 1992. It's estimated that more than 20 million U.S. workers now provide such care, a number expected to grow over the next decade. Companies are losing $11 billion a year in reduced productivity, absenteeism, and turnover from employees responsible for aging relatives. Sandra Timmerman, director of MetLife's Mature Market Institute, suggests elder care is *the* key workplace issue of the next decade.[64]

The U.S. Office of Personnel Management (OPM) found that employees with elder care responsibilities need information about medical, legal, and insurance issues, as well as the full support of their supervisors and company. The OPM also suggests such caregivers may require flextime, telecommuting, part-time employment, or job sharing. Some firms offer employee assistance programs. JPMorgan Chase provides elder care management services that include a consultant who conducts a full-fledged needs assessment program for the employee. AAA and UPS offer health-spending accounts in which employees can put aside pretax income for elder care expenses. But the numbers are still small, due to the rising cost of employee health insurance. A Towers-Watson survey found only 28.5 percent of companies surveyed offer elder care services.[65] The government does not provide much relief since both Medicare and Medicaid place heavy financial burdens on family caregivers. Average nursing home costs, for example, top $70,000 per year, with around-the-clock care costing even more.[66]

As more experienced and high-ranking employees begin caring for older parents and relatives, the costs to companies will rise even higher, according to AARP. This argument makes sense, since older workers often hold jobs more critical to a company than those held by younger workers (who are most affected by child care problems). Costs to employers could skyrocket to $25 billion annually. Many firms now realize that transfers and promotions are sometimes out of the question for employees whose elderly parents need ongoing care. Unfortunately, as the nation gets older, the elder care situation will grow considerably worse. With an aging workforce, this employee–management issue promises to persist well into the 21st century.

Drug Testing

Not long ago, acquired immunodeficiency syndrome (AIDS) caused great concern in the workplace. Thankfully, the spread of AIDS has declined somewhat in the United States—good news for all citizens and for business. However, alcohol and drug abuse are serious workplace issues that touch far more workers than AIDS does, from factory floors to construction sites to the locker rooms of professional sports teams.

Alcohol is the most widely used drug in the workplace, with an estimated 6.2 percent of full-time U.S. employees believed to be heavy drinkers.[67] Approximately 40 percent of industrial injuries and fatalities can be linked to alcohol consumption. More than 8 percent of full-time workers ages 18–49 use illegal drugs, according to the Department of Health and Human Services' Substance Abuse & Mental Health Services Association.[68] In some industries, such as construction, the rate is over 13 percent.[69]

Individuals who use illegal drugs are three and a half times more likely to be in workplace accidents and five times more likely to file a workers' compensation claim than other employees. According to the National Institute on Drug Abuse, employed drug users cost their employers about twice as much in medical and workers' compensation claims than drug-free co-workers. The U.S. Department of Labor projects that over a one-year period, drug abuse costs the U.S. economy $276 billion in lost work, health care costs, crime, traffic accidents, and other expenses, and over $140 billion in lost productivity. The National Institute of Health estimates each drug abuser can cost an employer approximately $10,000 annually. Drug abusers are typically associated with 50 percent on-the-job accident rates, 10 percent higher absenteeism, 30 percent more turnover, and more frequent workplace violence incidents. Today, over 70 percent of major companies test workers and job applicants for substance abuse.[70]

Violence in the Workplace

Employers are also struggling with a growing trend toward violence in the workplace. The Occupational Safety and Health Administration (OSHA) reports that homicides account for 16 percent of all workplace deaths and are the number one cause of death for women in the workplace.[71] In fact, one in six violent crimes in the United States occurs at work.[72] The nation first faced the shock of large-scale workplace violence in 1986, when a postal service employee in Oklahoma killed 14 fellow workers before taking his own life.

Many companies have taken action to prevent problems before they occur. They have held focus groups that invite employee input, hired managers with strong interpersonal skills, and employed skilled consultants to deal with any growing potential for workplace violence. State Farm Insurance and Verizon Wireless are among companies that have initiated policies to deal with this growing threat.[73] At software firm Mindbridge, based in Worchester,

Pennsylvania, two company officials must be present whenever an employee is disciplined or fired.[74] Nine states have passed laws allowing an employer to seek a temporary restraining order on behalf of workers experiencing threats or harassment.

Some companies believe that reports of workplace violence are overblown by the media. According to the Bureau of Labor Statistics, 70 percent of U.S. workplaces neither provide any formal training for dealing with prevention of violence at work nor have a policy that addresses workplace violence.[75] Unfortunately, organizations such as the U.S. Postal Service, Edgewater Technology, and Xerox can attest that workplace violence is all too real and promises to be a major issue for the foreseeable future.

Firms that have healthy employee–management relations have a better chance to prosper than those that don't. Taking a proactive approach is the best way to ensure positive employee–management environments. The proactive manager anticipates potential problems and works toward resolving them before they get out of hand—a good lesson for any manager.

◄ **LECTURE LINK 12-7:**
Employee Stock Ownership Plans

progress assessment

- How does top-executive pay in the United States compare with top-executive pay in other countries?
- What's the difference between pay equity and equal pay for equal work?
- How is the term *sexual harassment* defined, and when does sexual behavior become illegal?
- What are some of the issues related to child care and elder care, and how are companies addressing those issues?

◄ **PPT 12-46:**
Progress Assessment

summary

Learning Goal 1. Trace the history of organized labor in the United States.
- **What was the first union?**

The cordwainers (shoemakers) organized a craft union of skilled specialists in 1792. The Knights of Labor, formed in 1869, was the first national labor organization.
- **How did the AFL-CIO evolve?**

The American Federation of Labor (AFL), formed in 1886, was an organization of craft unions. The Congress of Industrial Organizations (CIO), a group of unskilled and semiskilled workers, broke off from the AFL in 1935. Over time, the two organizations saw the benefits of joining and became the AFL-CIO in 1955. The AFL-CIO is a federation of labor unions, not a national union.

Learning Goal 2. Discuss the major legislation affecting labor unions.
- **What are the provisions of the major legislation affecting labor unions?**

See Figure 12.1 on page 321.

Learning Goal 3. Outline the objectives of labor unions.
- **What topics typically appear in labor–management agreements?**

See Figure 12.3 on page 323.

Learning Goal 4. Describe the tactics used by labor and management during conflicts, and discuss the role of unions in the future.

- **What are the tactics used by unions and management in conflicts?**

Unions can use strikes and boycotts. Management can use strikebreakers, injunctions, and lockouts.

- **What will unions have to do to cope with declining membership?**

Unions must adapt to an increasingly white-collar, female, and culturally diverse workforce. To help keep U.S. businesses competitive in international markets, many unions have taken on a new role in assisting management in training workers, redesigning jobs, and assimilating the changing workforce.

Learning Goal 5. Assess some of today's controversial employee–management issues, such as executive compensation, pay equity, child care and elder care, drug testing, and violence in the workplace.

- **What is a fair wage for managers?**

The market and the businesses in it set managers' salaries. What is fair is open to debate.

- **How are equal pay and pay equity different?**

The Equal Pay Act of 1963 provides that workers receive equal pay for equal work (with exceptions for seniority, merit, or performance). Pay equity is the demand for equivalent pay for jobs requiring similar levels of education, training, and skills.

- **Isn't pay inequity caused by sexism?**

There is some evidence that supports that statement and counterarguments that refute the charge. It's believed that education and training lead to pay equity, but that is not always the case.

- **How are some companies addressing the child care issue?**

Responsive companies are providing child care on the premises, emergency care when scheduled care is interrupted, discounts with child care chains, vouchers to be used at the employee's chosen care center, and referral services.

- **What is elder care, and what problems do companies face with regard to this growing problem?**

Workers who need to provide elder care for dependent parents or others are generally more experienced and vital to the mission of the organization than younger workers are. The cost to business is very large and growing.

- **Why are more and more companies now testing workers and job applicants for substance abuse?**

More than 8 percent of employed U.S. adults between 18 and 49 are believed to be illicit drug users. Individuals who use drugs are three and a half times more likely to be in workplace accidents and five times more likely to file a workers' compensation claim than those who do not use drugs.

key terms

agency shop agreement 324
American Federation of Labor (AFL) 320
arbitration 327
bargaining zone 326
certification 321
closed shop agreement 323
collective bargaining 321
Congress of Industrial Organizations (CIO) 320

Dealing with Employee–Management Issues and Relationships ✳ **CHAPTER 12** 341

cooling-off period 328
craft union 319
decertification 321
givebacks 329
grievance 325
industrial unions 320
injunction 329
Knights of Labor 320
lockout 329
mediation 326
negotiated labor–management agreement (labor contract) 323
open shop agreement 324
primary boycott 328
right-to-work laws 324
secondary boycott 329
sexual harassment 335
shop stewards 326
strike 327
strikebreakers 329
union 318
union security clause 323
union shop agreement 324
yellow-dog contract 320

connect interactive applications

Reinforcing Your *Connect*ion to Concepts in Business

This chapter offers 15 interactive applications designed to help you apply what you've learned (examples of these exercises appear below). Your instructor has determined which interactive applications will benefit you throughout this course. Please refer to your instructor's assignment list in *Connect* to determine which applications you should complete.

Comprehension Case Interactive: As union numbers dwindle, globalization may be labor's best hope. Read the Child Wear case and respond to the questions.

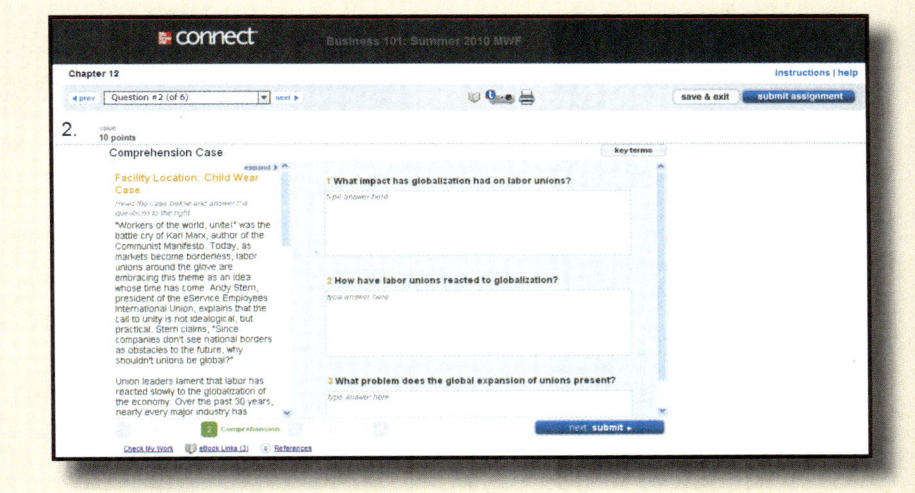

Click and Drag Interactive: After the passage of the Wagner Act, labor unions sought strict security in the form of the closed shop agreement, which specified that workers had to be members of a union before being hired for a job. To labor's dismay, the Labor-Management Relations Act (Taft-Hartley Act) outlawed this practice in 1947. Today, unions favor the union shop. Read about each person and determine, based on their circumstances, where each best fits in terms of type of union agreement.

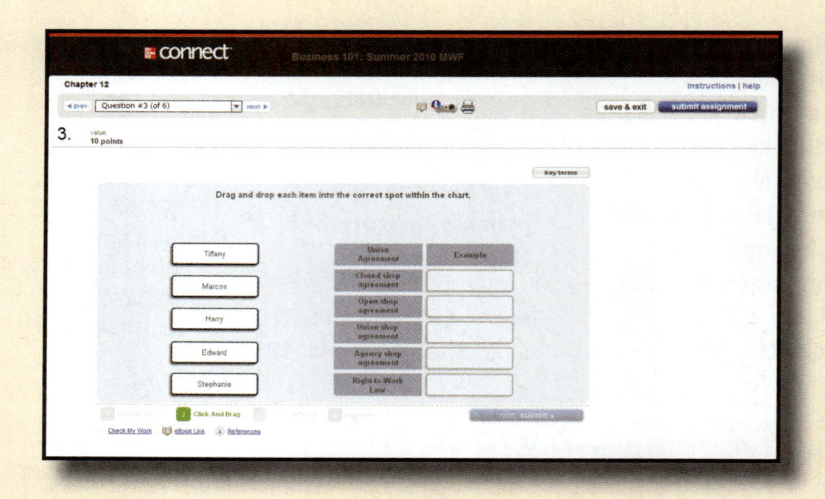

Click and Drag Interactive: If labor-management negotiators are not able to agree on alternative offerings, mediation may be in order. Review each person's statement and determine where each would fall in the listed categories.

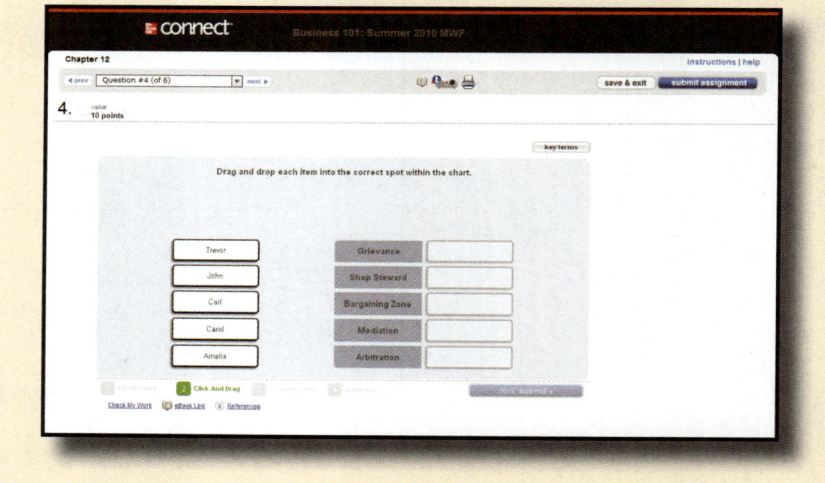

Dealing with Employee–Management Issues and Relationships * **CHAPTER 12** 343

Click and Drag Interactive: The technological achievements of the Industrial Revolution offered new products that, in some instances, reduced the need for physical labor. However, these achievements also put pressure on workers to produce more while enduring longer work days and earning less pay. Consider the labor organizations listed and organize them in the timeline in the order in which they were formed.

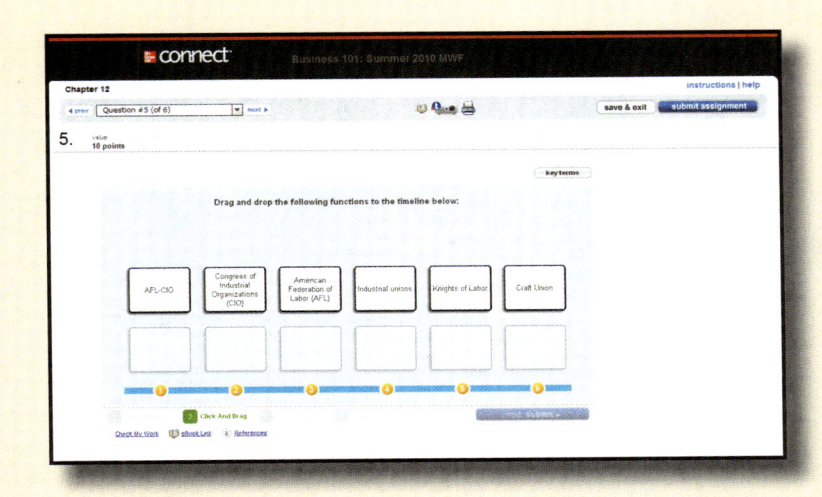

Video Case Interactive: The Writers' Guild of America (WGA) represents writers in the motion picture, broadcast, and news media industries. Like actors, writers have to negotiate pay and benefits relative to the work they do. Watch the video featuring Hollywood labor unions and respond to the questions when prompted.

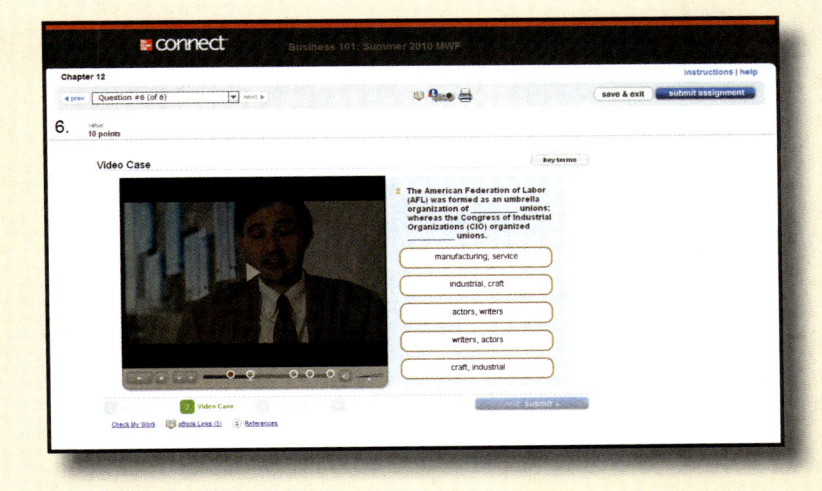

13

Marketing

HELPING BUYERS BUY

profile

Getting to Know

Cricket Lee

Creator of Fitlogic

The traditional motto of marketing is "Find a need and fill it," but for product designer Cricket Lee, "Find a need and *fit* it" may be more appropriate. After a lifetime of frustration trying to find clothes that fit properly, Lee developed her own sizing system, called Fitlogic, in the hope of establishing universal sizing standards for women's clothes based on body types as well as measurements.

The current system is based on limited data collected in the 1940s on a select group of women, mostly Caucasians in good shape in their 20s. Lee discovered this narrow data set accounted for only 20 percent of female body types, leaving plus-sized and minority women with little representation. Many clothing lines interpret the data differently too, leading to inconsistent size standards from one company to the next. Meanwhile, women have grown taller and heavier over the past 60 or so years. The increased use of vanity sizing (putting a smaller number on a larger garment to make the customer feel better about buying it) compounds the difficulty. It's no wonder that women who don't match the industry norm have a tough time finding clothes that fit well, especially pants. A recent study revealed 84 percent have difficulty finding apparel that fits, and 40 percent of purchased apparel is returned due to improper fit.

Lee's system aims to standardize sizes and provide flexibility for many female body types. Lee and a pattern maker used new data to develop the Fitlogic system, based on three common female body types. One of the first challenges was to find names for them. Lee's team came up with *straight, curvy,* and *round*. However, when Lee's 11-year-old daughter balked at being called a "straight," Lee renamed the figures *1, 2,* and *3,* respectively: *1* for a thick waist with small hips, *2* for curvy but proportional, and *3* for thin waist with a round bottom and large thighs. She then paired these body types with the industry's standard sizing numbers, so a size 6 woman with a 1 body type would wear a size 6.1 outfit. Women who have tried the system feel the clothes come as close to custom-made as you can get off the rack. Over 90 percent are happy with the results!

The fashion industry has been hesitant to adopt the system, however. Even though Lee attracted $3.5 million from

LEARNING goals

After you have read and studied this chapter, you should be able to

1. Define *marketing*, and apply the marketing concept to both for-profit and nonprofit organizations.
2. Describe the four Ps of marketing.
3. Summarize the marketing research process.
4. Show how marketers use environmental scanning to learn about the changing marketing environment.
5. Explain how marketers apply the tools of market segmentation, relationship marketing, and the study of consumer behavior.
6. Compare the business-to-business market and the consumer market.

connect

Your *Connect*ion to Better Learning. 1. View the interactive presentation. 2. Practice through LearnSmart. 3. Apply your knowledge by using the interactive applications for each chapter of this text.

1 Prep »»»»» **2 Study** 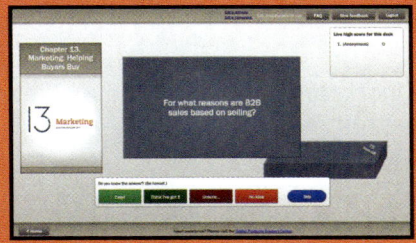 »»»»» **3 Apply**

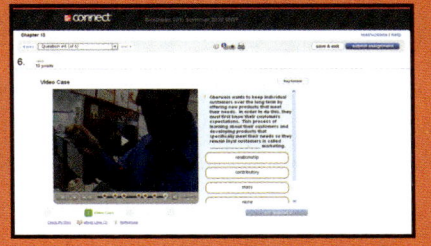

---

investors who had faith in it, she received countless rejections from garment companies concerned about its feasibility. Some stores worry that adopting Fitlogic will require them to carry triple the merchandise to account for the three body types, causing unnecessary overstock. Lee's first break came in 2004 when Jones Apparel Group Inc. used Fitlogic for a line of pants sold on the QVC shopping network. Jones has since supplied Fitlogic in other settings, including 20 Macy's department stores. While Fitlogic clothes sold well at Macy's, most sales came from in-store events held by Lee where she taught customers about the new system. Though stores like Lee's system in theory, she still has more marketing work ahead of her. Clearly, it's easier to find a market need than to fill it.

Marketing research finds needs, and marketing practitioners come up with clever ways of filling them. As Cricket Lee knows, marketing can include personal selling (getting companies to use the new system), distribution (getting stores to carry the products), advertising, publicity (getting the story in the media), and more. That's what this chapter is all about.

Sources: Ann Zimmerman, "Cricket Lee Takes On the Fashion Industry," *The Wall Street Journal*, March 17, 2008; Maria Halkias, "Cricket's Idea Is Ready to Wear," *Dallas Morning News*, November 20, 2005; and Fitlogic, www.fitlogic.com, accessed June 2010.

www.fitlogic.com

NAME THAT company

> PPT 13-1:
> Marketing: Helping Buyers Buy

> PPT 13-2:
> Cricket Lee

> PPT 13-3:
> What's Marketing?

Famous for U.S. soup standards like tomato and chicken noodle, this company studies population growth and regional trends to expand its product line for specific areas of the country. Its research led to the creation of a Creole soup targeted primarily to the South and a spicy nacho cheese soup made especially for Texas and California. Name that company. (Find the answer in the chapter.)

LEARNING goal 1 *

Define *marketing,* and apply the marketing concept to both for-profit and nonprofit organizations.

WHAT IS MARKETING?

The term marketing means different things to different people. Many think of marketing as simply "selling" or "advertising." Yes, selling and advertising are part of marketing, but it's much more. The American Marketing Association defines **marketing** as the activity, set of institutions, and processes for creating, communicating, delivering, and exchanging offerings that have value for customers, clients, partners, and society at large. We can also think of marketing, more simply, as the activities buyers and sellers perform to facilitate mutually satisfying exchanges.[1]

marketing
The activity, set of institutions, and processes for creating, communicating, delivering, and exchanging offerings that have value for customers, clients, partners, and society at large.

> BONUS CASE 13-1:
> Customer-Oriented Marketing Concepts at Thermos

In the past marketing focused almost entirely on helping the seller sell. That's why many people still think of it as mostly selling, advertising, and distribution *from the seller to the buyer.* Today, much of marketing is instead about *helping the buyer buy.* Let's examine a couple of examples.

Today, when people want to buy a new or used car, they often turn to the Internet first.[2] They go to a Web site like Vehix (www.vehix.com) to search for the vehicle they want and even take a virtual ride. At other Web sites they compare prices and features. By the time they go to the dealer, they may know exactly which car they want and the best price available.

The Web sites have *helped the buyer buy.* Not only are customers spared searching one dealership after another to find the best price, but manufacturers and dealers are eager to participate so that they don't lose customers. The future of marketing is doing everything you can to help the buyer buy.[3] Can you see how Fitlogic (see the opening Profile) helps shoppers find satisfying clothes?

Let's look at another case. In the past, one of the few ways students and parents could find the college with the right "fit" was to travel from campus to campus, a grueling and expensive process. Today, colleges use podcasts, virtual tours, live chats, and other interactive technologies to make on-campus visits less necessary.[4] Such virtual tours help students and their parents buy.

Of course, helping the buyer buy also helps the seller sell. Think about that for a minute.

Here's an example from *The Wall Street Journal*: "In the vacation market now, many people hunt out the holiday they want themselves. They use the Internet to find and then make choices, sometimes questioning potential sellers online. In industries like this, the role of marketing is to make sure that a company's products or services are easily found online, and that the company responds effectively to potential customers."[5]

These are only a few examples of the marketing trend toward helping buyers buy. Consumers today spend hours searching the Internet for good deals. Wise marketers provide a wealth of information online and even cultivate customer relationships using blogs and social networking sites such as Facebook and Twitter.[6] Online communities provide an opportunity to observe people (customers and others) interacting with one another, expressing their own opinions, forming relationships, and commenting on various goods and services. It is important for marketers to track what relevant bloggers are writing by doing blog searches using key terms that define their market. Vendors who have text-mining tools can help companies measure conversations about their products and their personnel. Much of the future of marketing lies in mining such online conversations and responding appropriately.[7]

Retailers and other marketers who rely solely on *traditional* advertising and selling are losing out to the new ways of marketing.[8] The Spotlight on Small Business box on p. 348 discusses how one young marketer used the Internet to his advantage.

◀ PPT 13-4:
Focus of Contemporary Marketing

The Evolution of Marketing

What marketers do at any particular time depends on what they need to do to fill customers' needs and wants, which continually change. Let's take a brief look at how those changes have influenced the evolution of marketing. Marketing in the United States has passed through four eras: (1) production, (2) selling, (3) marketing concept, and (4) customer relationship (see Figure 13.1).

The Production Era From the time the first European settlers began their struggle to survive in America until the early 1900s, the general philosophy of business was "Produce as much as you can, because there is a limitless market for it." Given the limited production capability and vast demand for products in those days, a production philosophy was both logical and profitable.

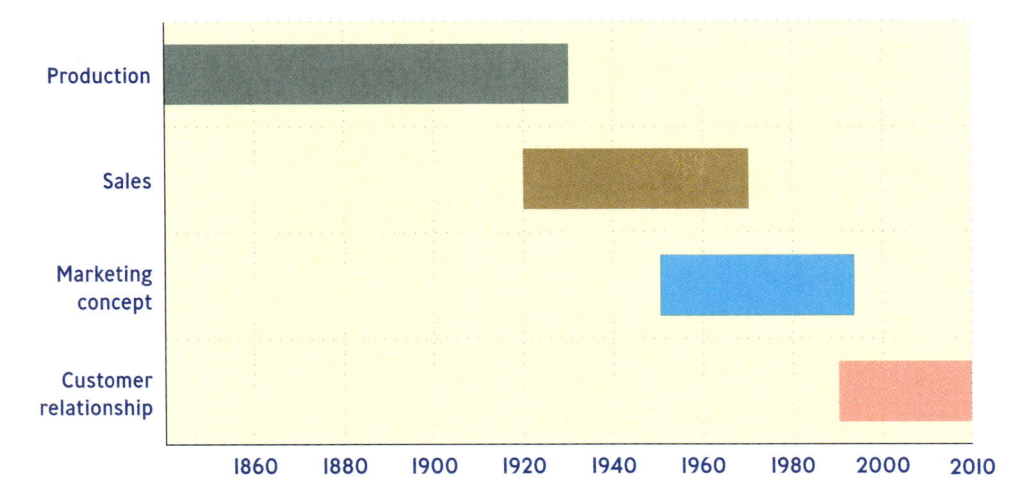

figure 13.1

MARKETING ERAS

The evolution of marketing in the United States involved four eras: (1) production, (2) selling, (3) marketing concept, and (4) customer relationship.

SPOTLIGHT ON SMALL business

www.freestyleaudio.com

Find a Need and Fill It

Lance Fried was an electrical engineer before he became a marketer. One day while watching surfers near his home in Del Mar, California, he thought about how much fun it would be to listen to your favorite music while surfing. That thought merely bounced around in his head for a while until a friend dropped an iPod into a cooler full of water and ice, making it useless. Fried began working on a waterproof MP3 player. After a while, he completed a lightweight prototype. Now what?

The fastest way to market such a product would be to go to large retailers and get wide distribution. But Fried expected that his waterproof MP3 player would not get the personal attention it needed at such large stores. Furthermore, he knew it would be hard to produce enough units to serve large retail outlets. At smaller surfing shops, however, the waterproof player could be of major interest.

Fried took the MP3 player to a trade show and placed it at the bottom of a large fish tank with earphones sticking out so that potential customers could try it. As he hoped, the player was a big hit and several smaller retailers ordered it. *Surfer* magazine put the waterproof MP3 player at the top of its Christmas wish list. In 2007, Fried's company, Freestyle Audio, was honored with National Geographic's *Adventure* magazine's "Best of Adventure" water gear award and selected as an ISPO BrandNew Award product finalist in 2006. You can imagine the interest such exposure created.

Fried sells his MP3 player online and helps the buyer buy with a Web site that's easy to read and use. What might be his next step for reaching a larger customer base? What more can he do to help the buyer buy? Would you recommend that he establish a blog, form a surfer-type community, or otherwise get more deeply involved with the market?

Source: Jonathan Sidener, "Five Questions: Lance Fried," *San Diego Union Tribune*, April 30, 2007; Freestyle Audio, www.freestyleaudio.com, accessed February 2009.

▶ PPT 13-5:
Find a Need and Fill It

▶ PPT 13-6:
Four Eras of U.S. Marketing

▶ PPT 13-7:
The Production and Selling Eras

▶ PPT 13-8:
The Marketing Concept Era

▶ LECTURE LINK 13-1:
Updating the Marketing Concept

▶ PPT 13-9:
Applying the Marketing Concept

marketing concept
A three-part business philosophy: (1) a customer orientation, (2) a service orientation, and (3) a profit orientation.

Business owners were mostly farmers, carpenters, and trade workers. They needed to produce more and more, so their goals centered on *production*. You can see this same process occurring in the oil industry today, where producers can often sell as much oil as they can produce. The greatest marketing need in this industry is for more production and less expensive distribution and storage.

The Selling Era By the 1920s, businesses had developed mass-production techniques (such as automobile assembly lines), and production capacity often exceeded the immediate market demand. Therefore, the business philosophy turned from producing to *selling*. Most companies emphasized selling and advertising in an effort to persuade consumers to buy existing products; few offered extensive service after the sale.

The Marketing Concept Era After World War II ended in 1945, returning soldiers starting new careers and beginning families sparked a tremendous demand for goods and services. The postwar years launched the sudden increase in the birthrate that we now call the baby boom, and also a boom in consumer spending. Competition for the consumer's dollar was fierce. Businesses recognized that they needed to be responsive to consumers if they wanted to get their business, and a philosophy emerged in the 1950s called the marketing concept.

The **marketing concept** had three parts:

1. *A customer orientation*. Find out what consumers want and provide it for them.[9] That's exactly what Cricket Lee did with her new pants sizes.

348

(Note the emphasis on meeting consumer needs rather than on promotion or sales.)

2. *A service orientation.* Make sure everyone in the organization has the same objective: customer satisfaction. This should be a total and integrated organizational effort.[10] That is, everyone from the president of the firm to the delivery people should be customer-oriented. Does that seem to be the norm today?
3. *A profit orientation.* Focus on those goods and services that will earn the most profit and enable the organization to survive and expand to serve more consumer wants and needs.

It took a while for businesses to implement the marketing concept. The process went slowly during the 1960s and 70s. During the 1980s, businesses began to apply the marketing concept more aggressively than they had done over the preceding 30 years. That led to a focus on customer relationship management (CRM) that has become very important today.[11] We explore that concept next.

The Customer Relationship Era   In the 1990s and early 2000s managers extended the marketing concept by adopting the practice of customer relationship management.[12] **Customer relationship management (CRM)** is the process of learning as much as possible about present customers and doing everything you can over time to satisfy them—or even to exceed their expectations—with goods and services. The idea is to enhance customer satisfaction and stimulate long-term customer loyalty.[13] For example, most airlines offer frequent-flier programs that reward loyal customers with free flights. The newest in customer relationship building, as mentioned earlier, involves social networks, online communities, tweets, and blogs.[14]

Clearly, the degree of consumer dissatisfaction that exists, especially with services such as airlines and phone companies, shows that marketers have a long way to go to create customer satisfaction and loyalty. According to a recent study, only 6.8 percent of marketers said they have excellent knowledge of their customers when it comes to demographic, behavioral, and psychographic (how they think) data.[15]

The newest in CRM efforts is customer-managed relationships (CMR). The idea is to give the customer the power to build relationships with suppliers and consumers.[16] Web sites like Expedia, Travelocity, and Priceline allow customers to find the best price or set their own.

Nonprofit Organizations and Marketing

Even though the marketing concept emphasizes a profit orientation, marketing is a critical part of almost all organizations, including nonprofits. Charities use marketing to raise funds for combating world hunger, for instance,

In the selling era, the focus of marketing was on selling, with little service afterward and less customization. What economic and social factors made this approach appropriate for the times?

customer relationship management (CRM)
The process of learning as much as possible about customers and doing everything you can to satisfy them—or even exceed their expectations—with goods and services.

◄ LECTURE LINK 13-2:
Pat Croce's Ten Commandments
◄ PPT 13-10:
The Customer Relationship Era
◄ BONUS CASE 13-2:
Food Marketing in the Inner City
◄ PPT 13-11:
Nonprofit Marketing
◄ PPT 13-12:
Marketing Strategies for Nonprofits

or to obtain other resources. The Red Cross uses promotion to encourage people to donate blood when local or national supplies run low. Greenpeace uses marketing to promote ecologically safe technologies. Environmental groups use marketing to try to cut carbon emissions.[17] Churches use marketing to attract new members and raise funds. Politicians use marketing to get votes. Recall the record-breaking expenditures in the presidential election of 2008.

States use marketing to attract new businesses and tourists. Many states, for example, have competed to get automobile companies from other countries to locate plants in their area.[18] Schools use marketing to attract new students. Other organizations, such as arts groups, unions, and social groups, also use marketing. The Ad Council, for example, uses public service ads to create awareness and change attitudes on such issues as drunk driving and fire prevention.

Organizations use marketing, in fact, to promote everything from environmentalism and crime prevention ("Take A Bite Out Of Crime") to social issues ("Choose Life").

The Ad Council sponsors many public service ads like this one. The idea is to make the public more aware of various needs that only nonprofit organizations are meeting. The ads then encourage the public to get engaged in the issue somehow, if only by donating money. Have you responded to any Ad Council advertisements?

LEARNING goal 2 *

Describe the four Ps of marketing.

THE MARKETING MIX

We can divide much of what marketing people do into four factors, called the four Ps to make them easy to remember. They are:

1. Product
2. Price
3. Place
4. Promotion

Managing the controllable parts of the marketing process means (1) designing a want-satisfying *product,* (2) setting a *price* for the product, (3) putting the product in a *place* where people will buy it, and (4) *promoting* the product. These four factors are called the **marketing mix** because businesses blend them together in a well-designed marketing program (see Figure 13.2). The Thinking Green box explores how "going green" in the automobile industry has affected the application of the four Ps to that market. It may be too late for many U.S. manufacturers, but there are many other auto manufacturers that are providing good-paying jobs while going green.

marketing mix
The ingredients that go into a marketing program: product, price, place, and promotion.

Applying the Marketing Process

The four Ps are a convenient way to remember the basics of marketing, but they don't necessarily include everything that goes into the marketing process for all products. One of the best ways to understand the entire marketing process is to take a product or a group of products and follow the process that led to their development and sale (see Figure 13.3 on p. 352).

THINKING green

Four Ps Drive Marketing

You can see the four Ps of marketing in action in the automobile industry. U.S. auto manufacturers have failed to capture the market and are looking at foreign producers for direction—perhaps too late. Today, the emphasis seems to be on green cars that don't harm the environment as much as traditional cars do. Such cars include really little vehicles like the Naro, the BMW Clever, the Smart ForTwo, and the Toyota IQ. There are hybrid cars, electric cars, diesel-run cars, and flex-fuel cars. Foreign automobile companies truly seem to be listening to customers, especially environmentally concerned customers, and trying to meet their needs. This is the *product* part of the four Ps.

When it comes to *pricing*, Web sites such as Autobytel.com and Autoweb.com provide product and price information and dealer referrals. Customers can determine the best price before going to a dealership. Even with green cars, price is still a major consideration. To eliminate one of the most annoying parts of buying a car, some dealers offer no-haggle pricing, a real benefit when some dealers are asking for more than the sticker price for popular green cars.

Web sites also contribute to helping customers buy at a convenient *place*. Autobytel.com and Autoweb.com help customers find the dealer closest to them that will offer the best price for the green car they choose.

Promotion for new and used cars is also changing. Dealers are trying low-pressure salesmanship because they know customers are armed with much more information than in the past. Newspapers, magazines, TV shows, and more are all discussing the benefits of going green.

Sources: David Kiley, "The Little Engines That Would," *BusinessWeek*, April 7, 2008; Eric Peters, "Sneak Peak at the 2009 Cars," *Bottom Line Personal*, April 1, 2008; Nate Chapnick, "Driving Ambition," *Forbes*, Spring 2008; Jill Amadio, "Put It in Drive," *Entrepreneur*, April 2008; and Michael S. Hopkins, "Sustainability and Competitive Advantage," *MIT Sloan Management Review*, Fall 2009.

Imagine, for example, that you and your friends want to start a money-making business near your college. You've noticed a lot of vegetarians among your acquaintances. You do a quick survey in a few dorms, sororities, and fraternities and find many vegetarians—and other students who like to eat vegetarian meals once in a while.[19] Your preliminary research indicates some demand for a vegetarian restaurant nearby. You check the fast-food stores in

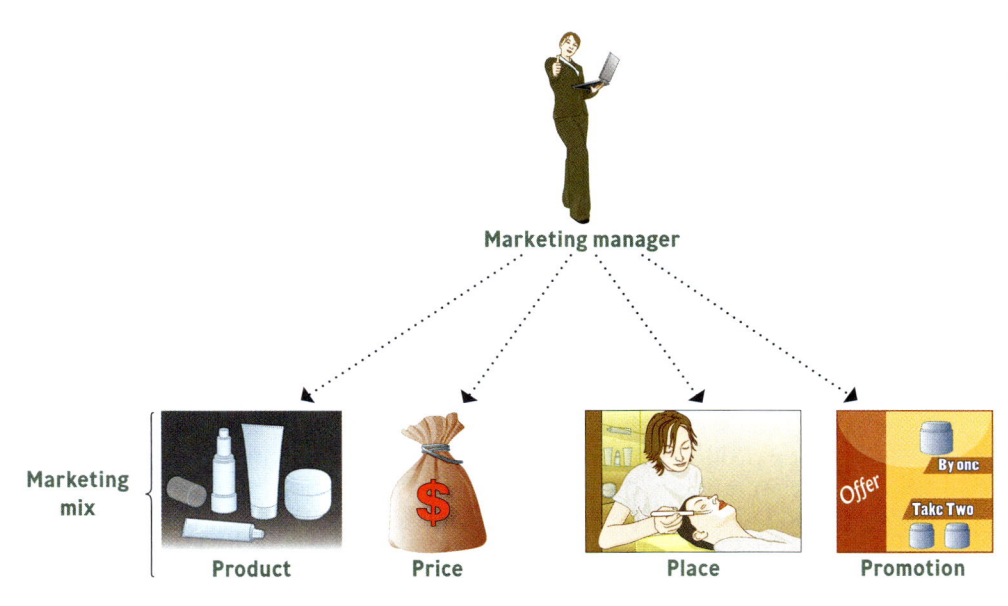

figure 13.2

MARKETING MANAGERS AND THE MARKETING MIX

Marketing managers must choose how to implement the four Ps of the marketing mix: product, price, place, and promotion. The goals are to please customers and make a profit.

Marketing manager

Marketing mix: Product | Price | Place | Promotion

figure 13.3

THE MARKETING PROCESS WITH THE FOUR Ps

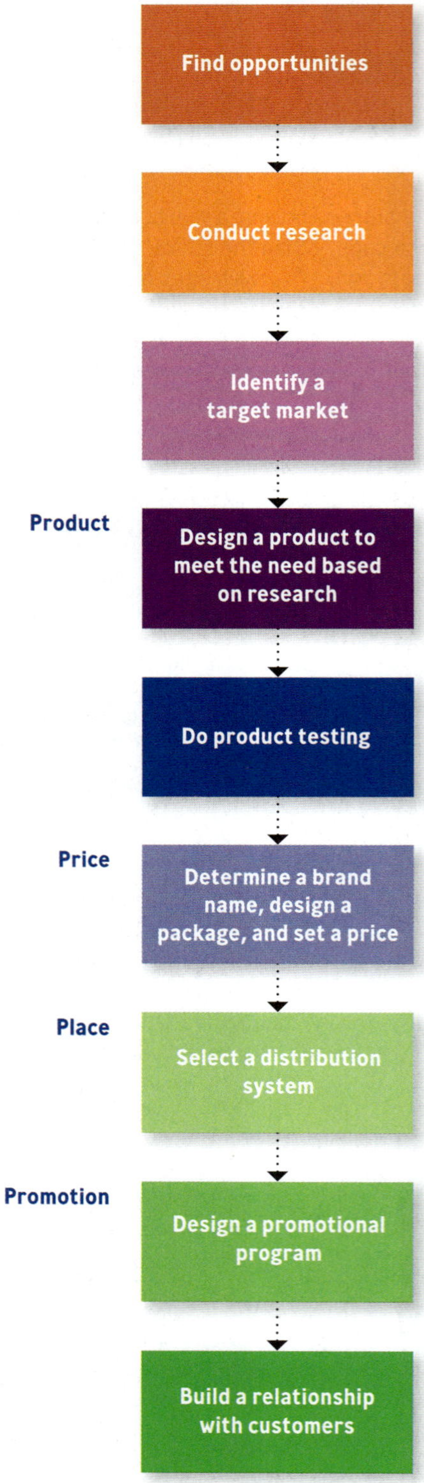

Find opportunities
↓
Conduct research
↓
Identify a target market
↓
Product — Design a product to meet the need based on research
↓
Do product testing
↓
Price — Determine a brand name, design a package, and set a price
↓
Place — Select a distribution system
↓
Promotion — Design a promotional program
↓
Build a relationship with customers

▶ **CRITICAL THINKING EXERCISE 13-1:** Find a Need and Fill It

▶ **PPT 13-13:** Developing a Product

product
Any physical good, service, or idea that satisfies a want or need plus anything that would enhance the product in the eyes of consumers, such as the brand.

test marketing
The process of testing products among potential users.

---

the area and find that none offer more than one or two vegetarian meals. In fact, most don't have any, except salads and some soups.

Further research identifies a number of different kinds of vegetarians. Lacto-ovo vegetarians eat dairy products and eggs. Lacto-vegetarians eat dairy products but no eggs. Fruitarians eat mostly raw fruits, grains, and nuts. Vegans eat neither eggs nor dairy products. Your research identifies vegan farmers who don't use any synthetic chemical fertilizers, pesticides, herbicides, or genetically modified ingredients.[20] You also find that KFC Canada offers a vegan version of its chicken sandwich in 500 of its 750 outlets.[21] Is the Colonel on to something? He may be, since there are successful vegetarian restaurants even in Argentina, where the per-capita consumption of beef is the highest in the world.[22] You conclude that a vegetarian restaurant would have to appeal to all kinds of vegetarians to be a success.

You've just performed the first few steps in the marketing process. You noticed an opportunity (a need for vegetarian food near campus). You conducted some preliminary research to see whether your idea had any merit. And then you identified groups of people who might be interested in your product. They will be your *target market* (the people you will try to persuade to come to your restaurant).

Designing a Product to Meet Consumer Needs

Once you've researched consumer needs and found a target market (which we'll discuss in more detail later) for your product, the four Ps of marketing come into play. You start by developing a product or products. A **product** is any physical good, service, or idea that satisfies a want or need, plus anything that would enhance the product in the eye of consumers, such as the brand name. In this case, your proposed product is a restaurant that would serve different kinds of vegetarian meals.

It's a good idea at this point to do *concept testing*. That is, you develop an accurate description of your restaurant and ask people, in person or online, whether the idea of the restaurant and the kind of meals you intend to offer appeals to them. If it does, you might go to a supplier, like Amy's Kitchen, that makes vegetarian meals, to get samples you can take to consumers to test their reactions. The process of testing products among potential users is called **test marketing**.

If consumers like the products and agree they would buy them, you have the information you need to find investors and look for a convenient location to open a restaurant. You'll have to think of a catchy name. (For practice, stop for a minute and try to think of one.) We'll use Very Vegetarian in this text, although we're sure you can think of a better name. Meanwhile, let's continue with the discussion of product development.

You may want to offer some well-known brand names to attract people right away. A **brand name** is a word, letter, or group of words or letters that differentiates one seller's goods and services from those of competitors.[23] Brand names of vegetarian products include Tofurky, Mori-Nu, and Yves Veggie Cuisine. We'll discuss the product development process in detail in Chapter 14, and follow the Very Vegetarian case to show you how all marketing and other business decisions tie together. For now, we're simply sketching the whole marketing process to give you an overall picture. So far, we've covered the first P of the marketing mix: product. Next comes price.

Carolyn Coquillette keeps the waiting area of her specialty mechanic's shop, called Luscious Garage, immaculate and comfortable as a way of enhancing her relationships with her San Francisco Bay Area customers. How do you think customers respond to this unusual setting?

◀ PPT 13-14:
Pricing and Placing a Product

brand name
A word, letter, or group of words or letters that differentiates one seller's goods and services from those of competitors.

Setting an Appropriate Price

After you've decided what products and services you want to offer consumers, you have to set appropriate prices. Those depend on a number of factors. In the restaurant business, the price could be close to what other restaurants charge to stay competitive. Or you might charge less to attract business, especially at the beginning.[24] Or you may offer high-quality products for which customers are willing to pay a little more (as Starbucks does).[25] You also have to consider the costs of producing, distributing, and promoting the product, which all influence your price. We'll discuss pricing issues in more detail in Chapter 14.

Getting the Product to the Right Place

There are several ways you can serve the market for vegetarian meals. You can have people come in, sit down, and eat at the restaurant, but that's not the only alternative—think of pizza. You could deliver the food to customers' dorms, apartments, and student unions. You may want to sell your products in supermarkets or health-food stores, or through organizations that specialize in distributing food products. Such *intermediaries* are the middle links in a series of organizations that distribute goods from producers to consumers. (The more traditional word for them is *middlemen*.) Getting the product to consumers when and where they want it is critical to market success. Don't forget to consider the Internet as a way to reach consumers.[26] We'll discuss the importance of marketing intermediaries and distribution in detail in Chapter 15.

A vegetarian restaurant might fill a popular need in the neighborhood of many college campuses today. Is there one near your school? What can you tell about its manager's application of the four Ps of marketing—product, price, place, and promotion?

Developing an Effective Promotional Strategy

The last of the four Ps of marketing is promotion. **Promotion** consists of all the techniques sellers use to inform people about and motivate them to buy their products or services. Promotion includes advertising; personal selling; public relations; publicity; word of mouth (viral marketing); and various sales promotion efforts, such as coupons, rebates, samples, and cents-off deals. We'll discuss promotion in detail in Chapter 16.

Promotion often includes relationship building with customers.[27] Among other activities, that means responding to suggestions consumers make to improve the products or their marketing, including price and packaging. For Very Vegetarian, postpurchase, or after-sale, service may include refusing payment for meals that weren't satisfactory and stocking additional vegetarian products customers say they would like. Listening to customers and responding to their needs is the key to the ongoing process that is marketing.[28]

> **promotion**
> All the techniques sellers use to inform people about and motivate them to buy their products or services.

▶ **LECTURE LINK 13-3:**
Marketing Is More Listening Than Persuading

▶ **PPT 13-15:**
Promoting the Product

▶ **PPT 13-16:**
Progress Assessment

> **marketing research**
> The analysis of markets to determine opportunities and challenges, and to find the information needed to make good decisions.

progress assessment

- What does it mean to "help the buyer buy"?
- What are the three parts of the marketing concept?
- What are the four Ps of the marketing mix?

LEARNING goal 3 ✳

Summarize the marketing research process.

> *Personal interviews are one way of collecting primary research data about customers' needs, wants, and buying habits. Perhaps someone has stopped you in a shopping mall recently to ask you some questions about a product or product category you use. What might contribute to the difficulty of collecting information through such interviews, and how can marketers improve the process?*

PROVIDING MARKETERS WITH INFORMATION

Every decision in the marketing process depends on information. When they conduct **marketing research**, marketers analyze markets to determine opportunities and challenges, and to find the information they need to make good decisions.

Marketing research helps identify what products customers have purchased in the past, and what changes have occurred to alter what they want now and what they're likely to want in the future. Marketers also conduct research on business trends, the ecological impact of their decisions, global trends, and more. Businesses need information to compete effectively, and marketing research is the activity that gathers it. Besides listening to customers, marketing researchers also pay attention to what employees, shareholders, dealers, consumer advocates, media representatives, and other stakeholders have to say. As noted earlier, some of that research is now being gathered online through blogs and social networks.[29]

The Marketing Research Process

A simplified marketing research process consists of at least four key steps:

1. Defining the question (the problem or opportunity) and determining the present situation.
2. Collecting research data.

3. Analyzing the research data.
4. Choosing the best solution and implementing it.

The following sections look at each of these steps.

Defining the Question and Determining the Present Situation Marketing researchers need the freedom to discover what the present situation is, what the problems or opportunities are, what the alternatives are, what information they need, and how to go about gathering and analyzing data.

Collecting Data Usable information is vital to the marketing research process. Research can become quite expensive, however, so marketers must often make a trade-off between the need for information and the cost of obtaining it. Normally the least expensive method is to gather information already compiled by others and published in journals and books or made available online.

Such existing data are called **secondary data**, since you aren't the first one to gather them. Figure 13.4 lists the principal sources of secondary marketing research information. Despite its name, *secondary* data is what marketers

◀ PPT 13-17:
Searching for Information

secondary data
Information that has already been compiled by others and published in journals and books or made available online.

figure 13.4

SELECTED SOURCES OF PRIMARY AND SECONDARY INFORMATION
You should spend a day or two at the library becoming familiar with these sources. You can read about primary research in any marketing research text from the library.

PRIMARY SOURCES	SECONDARY SOURCES		
Interviews Surveys Observation Focus groups Online surveys Questionnaires Customer comments Letters from customers	**Government Publications** *Statistical Abstract of the United States* *Survey of Current Business* *Census of Retail Trade*	*Census of Transportation* *Annual Survey of Manufacturers*	
	Commercial Publications ACNielsen Company studies on retailing and media Marketing Research Corporation of America studies on consumer purchases Selling Areas—Marketing Inc. reports on food sales		
	Magazines *Entrepreneur* *BusinessWeek* *Fortune* *Inc.* *Advertising Age* *Forbes* *Harvard Business Review* *Journal of Marketing*	*Journal of Retailing* *Journal of Consumer Research* *Journal of Advertising* *Journal of Marketing Research* *Marketing News*	*Journal of Advertising Research* Trade magazines appropriate to your industry such as *Progressive Grocer* Reports from various chambers of commerce
	Newspapers *The Wall Street Journal, Barron's,* your local newspapers		
	Internal Sources Company records Balance sheets	Income statements Prior research reports	
	General Sources Internet searches Google-type searches	Commercial databases	

> **PPT 13-18:**
> Four Steps in the Marketing Research Process
>
> **PPT 13-19:**
> Defining the Problem or Opportunity
>
> **PPT 13-20:**
> Collecting Secondary Research Data

primary data
Data that you gather yourself (not from secondary sources such as books and magazines).

> **CRITICAL THINKING EXERCISE 13-2:**
> Good to the Last Drop

focus group
A small group of people who meet under the direction of a discussion leader to communicate their opinions about an organization, its products, or other given issues.

> **PPT 13-21:**
> Collecting Primary Research Data
>
> **PPT 13-22:**
> Focus Groups
>
> **PPT 13-23:**
> Analyzing the Data and Implementing the Decision

The authors of this text enjoy the benefits of using focus groups. College faculty and students come to these meetings and tell us how to improve this book. We listen carefully and make as many changes as we can in response. Suggestions have included adding more descriptive captions to the photos in the book and making the text as user-friendly as possible. How are we doing so far?

should gather *first* to avoid incurring unnecessary expense. To find secondary data about vegetarians, go to the Web site for *Vegetarian Times* (www.vegetariantimes.com) or search other Web sites on vegetarianism.

Often, secondary data don't provide all the information managers need for important business decisions. To gather additional in-depth information, marketers must do their own research. The results of such *new studies* are called **primary data**. One way to gather primary data is to conduct a survey.

Telephone surveys, online surveys, mail surveys, and personal interviews are the most common forms of primary data collection. Focus groups (defined below) are another popular method of surveying individuals. What do you think would be the best way to survey students about your potential new restaurant? Would you do a different kind of survey after it had been open a few months? How could you help vegetarians find your restaurant? That is, how could you help your buyers buy? One question researchers pay close attention to is: "Would you recommend this product to a friend?"

A **focus group** is a group of people who meet under the direction of a discussion leader to communicate their opinions about an organization, its products, or other given issues. This textbook is updated periodically using many focus groups made up of faculty and students. They tell us, the authors, what subjects and examples they like and dislike, and the authors follow their suggestions for changes.

Marketers can now gather both secondary and primary data online. The authors of this text, for example, do much research online, but they also gather data from books, articles, interviews, and other sources.

Analyzing the Research Data Marketers must turn the data they collect in the research process into useful information. Careful, honest interpretation of the data can help a company find useful alternatives to specific marketing challenges. For example, by doing primary research, Fresh Italy, a small Italian pizzeria, found that its pizza's taste was rated superior to that of the larger pizza chains. However, the company's sales lagged behind the competition. Secondary research on the industry revealed that free delivery (which Fresh Italy did not offer) was more important to customers than taste. Fresh Italy now delivers—and has increased its market share.

Choosing the Best Solution and Implementing It After collecting and analyzing data, market researchers determine alternative strategies and make recommendations about which may be best and why. This final step in a research effort also includes following up on actions taken to see whether the results were what was expected. If not, the company can take corrective action and conduct new studies in its ongoing attempt to provide consumer satisfaction at the lowest cost. You can see, then, that marketing research is a *continuous process* of responding to changes in the marketplace and in consumer preferences.[30]

LEARNING goal 4 *

Show how marketers use environmental scanning to learn about the changing marketing environment.

THE MARKETING ENVIRONMENT

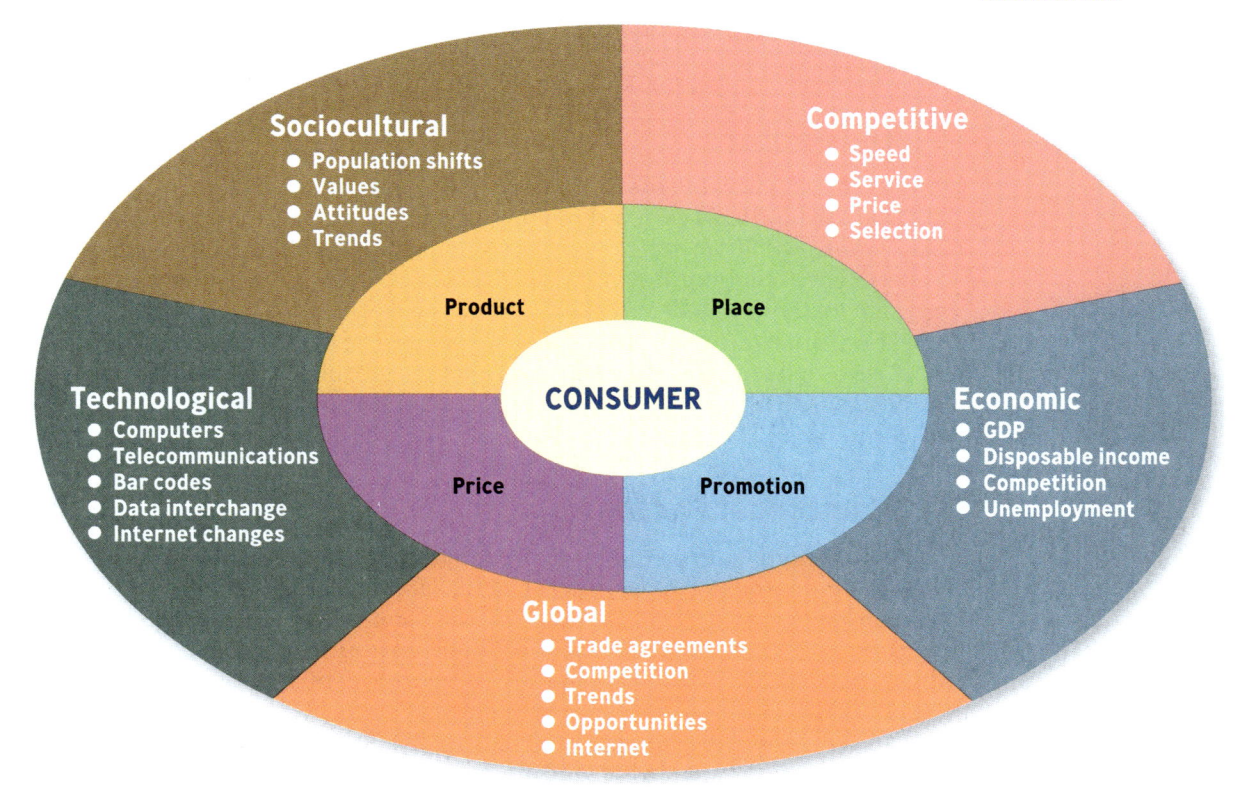

Marketing managers must be aware of the surrounding environment when making marketing mix decisions. **Environmental scanning** is the process of identifying factors that can affect marketing success. As you can see in Figure 13.5, they include global, technological, sociocultural, competitive, and economic influences. We discussed these factors in some detail in Chapter 1, but now let's review them from a strictly marketing perspective.

environmental scanning
The process of identifying the factors that can affect marketing success.

figure 13.5

THE MARKETING ENVIRONMENT

Sociocultural
- Population shifts
- Values
- Attitudes
- Trends

Competitive
- Speed
- Service
- Price
- Selection

Technological
- Computers
- Telecommunications
- Bar codes
- Data interchange
- Internet changes

Economic
- GDP
- Disposable income
- Competition
- Unemployment

Global
- Trade agreements
- Competition
- Trends
- Opportunities
- Internet

CONSUMER: Product, Place, Price, Promotion

REACHING BEYOND our borders

www.whiteflash.com

Social Marketing Goes Global

Debra Wexler is CEO of Whiteflash.com, an online diamond jewelry dealer. She cofounded the business with Brian Gavin, a fifth-generation diamond cutter. Diamonds are a relatively expensive purchase for which customers usually spend face-to-face time with sellers. Wexler and Gavin hope to reach wealthy customers around the world in places like Singapore and Russia. They do this by using live online chat during all hours of the day, and by staying close to bloggers who keep the company name prominent in search engines.

Whiteflash.com gets about 10,000 visitors a month from all over the world. Working with Web.com, Wexler has created a social marketing campaign that leads to a dialogue about fashion, gossip, and, yes, jewelry. She also posts pictures of celebrities wearing Whiteflash designs and publishes 10 to 20 fashion and style articles per month on the Whiteflash Web site. The company has a MySpace page where customers can share stories and photos. Whiteflash's total expenditure on social marketing comes to about $10,000 a month.

The next step in the marketing campaign is to use LivePerson.com (an interactive site) to provide customers all over the world with quick answers to their questions.

Sources: Heather Clancy, "Website Social Marketing," *Entrepreneur,* November 2008; Rebekah Tsadik, "Social Networks Starting to Click," *BtoB,* January 14, 2008; Logan Kugler, "Make Social Networks Work for You," *Advertising Age Career Guide,* September 22, 2008; and Suzanne Kapner, "Facebook Tries to Sell Its Friends Again," *Fortune,* February 16, 2009.

Global Factors

Using the Internet, businesses can reach many of the world's consumers relatively easily and carry on a dialogue with them about the goods and services they want. By 2018, half of all small businesses will be engaged in global trade.[31] The Reaching Beyond Our Borders box discusses the use of the Internet and social marketing to reach global markets.

The globalization process puts more pressure on those whose responsibility it is to deliver products. Many marketers outsource delivery to companies like FedEx, UPS, and DHL, which have a solid reputation for shipping goods quickly.

Technological Factors

The most important technological changes also relate to the Internet. Using consumer databases, blogs, social networking, and the like, companies can develop products and services that closely match consumers' needs.[32] As you read in Chapter 9, firms can now produce customized goods and services for about the same price as mass-produced goods. Thus flexible manufacturing and mass customization are also major influences on marketers. You can imagine, for example, using databases to help you devise custom-made fruit mixes and various salads for your customers at Very Vegetarian.

> PPT 13-28:
Social Marketing Goes Global

Sociocultural Factors

Marketers must monitor social trends to maintain their close relationship with customers, since population growth and changing demographics can have an effect on sales. One of the fastest-growing segments of the U.S. population in the 21st century is people over 65. The increase in the number of older adults creates growing demand for nursing homes, health care, prescription drugs, recreation, continuing education, and more.

Other shifts in the U.S. population are creating new challenges for marketers as they adjust their products to meet the tastes and preferences of Hispanic, Asian, and other growing ethnic groups. To appeal to diverse groups, marketers must listen better and be more responsive to unique ethnic needs. What might you do to appeal to specific ethnic groups with Very Vegetarian?

Competitive Factors

Of course, marketers must pay attention to the dynamic competitive environment. Many brick-and-mortar companies must be aware of new competition from the Internet, including firms that sell automobiles, insurance, music, and clothes. In the book business, Barnes & Noble and Borders Books are still adjusting to the new reality of Amazon.com's huge selection of books at good prices. Now that consumers can literally search the world for the best buys through the Internet, marketers must adjust their pricing, delivery, and services accordingly. Can you see any opportunities for Very Vegetarian to make use of the Internet?

◄ **BONUS CASE 13-3:**
Marketing to the Baby Boom Generation

◄ **PPT 13-29:**
The ABCs of Marketing

Economic Factors

Marketers must pay close attention to the economic environment. As we began the new millennium, the United States was experiencing unparalleled growth, and customers were eager to buy even the most expensive automobiles, watches, and vacations. But as the economy slowed, marketers had to adapt by offering products that were less expensive and more tailored to consumers with modest incomes.

The economic collapse beginning in 2008 really slowed sales and became global in scope.[33] You can see why environmental scanning is critical to a company's success during rapidly changing economic times. What economic changes are occurring around your school that might affect a new restaurant? How have the economic crisis, the wars in Iraq and Afghanistan, or natural disasters affected your area?

◄ **PPT 13-30:**
The Consumer and B2B Market

TWO DIFFERENT MARKETS: CONSUMER AND BUSINESS-TO-BUSINESS (B2B)

Marketers must know as much as possible about the market they wish to serve. As we defined it in Chapter 6, a *market* consists of people with unsatisfied wants and needs who have both the resources and the willingness to buy. There are two major markets in business: the *consumer market* and the *business-to-business market*. The **consumer market** consists of all the individuals or households that want goods and services for personal consumption or use and have the resources to buy them.

The **business-to-business (B2B) market** consists of all the individuals and organizations that want goods and services to use in producing other

consumer market
All the individuals or households that want goods and services for personal consumption or use.

business-to-business (B2B) market
All the individuals and organizations that want goods and services to use in producing other goods and services or to sell, rent, or supply goods to others.

goods and services or to sell, rent, or supply goods to others. Oil-drilling bits, cash registers, display cases, office desks, public accounting audits, and business software are B2B goods and services. Traditionally, they have been known as *industrial* goods and services because they are used in industry.

The important thing to remember is that the buyer's reason for buying—that is, the end use of the product—determines whether a product is a consumer product or a B2B product. A cup of yogurt that a student buys for breakfast is a consumer product. However, when Very Vegetarian purchases the same cup of yogurt to sell to its breakfast customers, it has purchased a B2B product. The following sections outline consumer and B2B markets.

> **The business-to-business (B2B) market** consists of individuals and organizations that sell goods and services to other businesses. A manufacturer, for instance, buys its parts and supplies in the B2B market. How many ways can you think of in which B2B products differ from those you buy, like toothpaste and laundry detergent?

progress assessment

- What are the four steps in the marketing research process?
- What is environmental scanning?
- What factors are included in environmental scanning?

LEARNING goal 5 *

Explain how marketers apply the tools of market segmentation, relationship marketing, and the study of consumer behavior.

THE CONSUMER MARKET

The total potential consumer market consists of the 7 billion or so people in global markets. Because consumer groups differ greatly by age, education level, income, and taste, a business usually can't fill the needs of every group. It must decide which groups to serve, and then develop products and services specially tailored to their needs.

Take the Campbell Soup Company, for example. You know Campbell for its traditional soups such as chicken noodle and tomato. You may also have noticed that Campbell has expanded its U.S. product line to appeal to a number of different tastes. Aware of population growth in the South and in Latino communities in cities across the nation, it introduced a Creole soup for the southern market and a red bean soup for the Latino market. In Texas and California, where people like their food with a bit of kick, Campbell makes its nacho cheese soup spicier than in other parts of the country. It's just one company that has had some success studying the consumer market, breaking it down into categories, and developing products for separate groups.

The process of dividing the total market into groups with similar characteristics is called **market segmentation**. Selecting which groups or segments

> PPT 13-31:
> Progress Assessment

> PPT 13-32:
> Marketing to Consumers

> CRITICAL THINKING EXERCISE 13-3:
> Identifying the Target Market

> LECTURE LINK 13-5:
> Dewalt Identifies Its Target Market

> **market segmentation** The process of dividing the total market into groups whose members have similar characteristics.

figure 13.6

MARKET SEGMENTATION
This table shows some of the methods marketers use to divide the market. The aim of segmentation is to break the market into smaller units.

MAIN DIMENSION	SAMPLE VARIABLES	TYPICAL SEGMENTS
Geographic segmentation	Region	Northeast, Midwest, South, West
	City or county size	Under 5,000; 5,000–10,999; 20,000–49,000; 50,000 and up
	Density	Urban, suburban, rural
Demographic segmentation	Gender	Male, female
	Age	Under 5; 5–10; 11–18; 19–34; 35–49; 50–64; 65 and over
	Education	Some high school or less, high school graduate, some college, college graduate, postgraduate
	Race	Caucasian, African American, Indian, Asian, Hispanic
	Nationality	American, Asian, Eastern European, Japanese
	Life stage	Infant, preschool, child, teenager, collegiate, adult, senior
	Income	Under $15,000; $15,000–$24,999; $25,000–$44,999; $45,000–$74,999; $75,000 and over
	Household size	1; 2; 3–4; 5 or more
	Occupation	Professional, technical, clerical, sales supervisors, farmers, students, home-based business owners, retired, unemployed
Psychographic segmentation	Personality	Gregarious, compulsive, extroverted, aggressive, ambitious
	Values	Actualizers, fulfillers, achievers, experiencers, believers, strivers, makers, strugglers
	Lifestyle	Upscale, moderate
Benefit segmentation	Comfort	(Benefit segmentation divides an already established market into smaller, more homogeneous segments. Those people who desire economy in a car would be an example. The benefit desired varies by product.)
	Convenience	
	Durability	
	Economy	
	Health	
	Luxury	
	Safety	
	Status	
Volume segmentation	Usage	Heavy users, light users, nonusers
	Loyalty status	None, medium, strong

an organization can serve profitably is **target marketing**. For example, a shoe store may choose to sell only women's shoes, only children's shoes, or only athletic shoes. The issue is finding the right *target market*—the most profitable segment—to serve.

Segmenting the Consumer Market

A firm can segment the consumer market several ways (see Figure 13.6). Rather than selling your product throughout the United States, you might focus on just one or two regions where you can be most successful, say southern states

target marketing
Marketing directed toward those groups (market segments) an organization decides it can serve profitably.

◄ PPT 13-33:
Segmenting the Consumer Market

such as Florida, Texas, and South Carolina. Dividing a market by cities, counties, states, or regions is **geographic segmentation**.

Alternatively, you could aim your product's promotions toward people ages 25 to 45 who have some college education and above-average incomes. Automobiles such as Lexus are often targeted to this audience. Age, income, and education level are criteria for **demographic segmentation**. So are religion, race, and occupation. Demographics are the most widely used segmentation variable, but not necessarily the best.

You may want your ads to portray a target group's lifestyle. To do that, you would study the group's values, attitudes, and interests in a strategy called **psychographic segmentation**. If you decide to target Generation Y, you would do an in-depth study of members' values and interests, like which TV shows they watch and which personalities they like best. With that information you would develop advertisements for those TV shows using those stars.

In marketing for Very Vegetarian, what benefits of vegetarianism might you talk about? Should you emphasize freshness, heart-healthiness, taste, or something else? Determining which product benefits your target market prefers and using those benefits to promote a product is **benefit segmentation**.

You can also determine who are the big eaters of vegetarian food. Does your restaurant seem to attract more men or more women? More students or more faculty members? Are your repeat customers from the local community or are they commuters? Separating the market by volume of product use is called **volume (or usage) segmentation**. Once you know who your customer base is, you can design your promotions to better appeal to that specific group or groups.

The best segmentation strategy is to use all the variables to come up with a consumer profile that represents a sizable, reachable, and profitable target market. That may mean not segmenting the market at all and instead going after the total market (everyone). Or it may mean going after ever-smaller segments. We'll discuss that strategy next.

Reaching Smaller Market Segments

Niche marketing is identifying small but profitable market segments and designing or finding products for them. Because it so easily offers an unlimited choice of goods, the Internet is transforming a consumer culture once based on big hits and best-sellers into one that supports more specialized niche products.[34] The *long tail* is a phrase coined by Chris Anderson, editor-in-chief of *Wired* magazine, in an article explaining how companies selling more products with lower demand can easily compete with (or even surpass) those solely dependent on big sellers.[35] Just how small such a segment can be is illustrated by FridgeDoor.com. This company sells refrigerator magnets on the Internet. It keeps some 1,500 different magnets in stock and sells as many as 400 a week.

One-to-one marketing means developing a unique mix of goods and services for *each individual customer*. Travel agencies often develop such packages, including airline reservations, hotel reservations, rental cars, restaurants, and admission to museums and other attractions for individual customers. This is relatively easy to do in B2B markets where each customer may buy in huge volume. But one-to-one marketing is now becoming possible in consumer markets as well. Dell produces a unique computer system for each customer. Can you envision designing special Very Vegetarian menu items for individual customers?

Moving toward Relationship Marketing

In the world of mass production following the Industrial Revolution, marketers responded by practicing mass marketing. **Mass marketing** means developing products and promotions to please large groups of people. That is, there is little market segmentation. The mass marketer tries to sell the same products to as many people as possible. That means using mass media, such as TV, radio, and newspapers to reach them. Although mass marketing led many firms to success, marketing managers often got so caught up with their products and competition that they became less responsive to the market. Airlines, for example, were so intent on meeting competition that they often annoyed their customers.

Relationship marketing tends to lead away from mass production and toward custom-made goods and services. The goal is to keep individual customers over time by offering them new products that exactly meet their requirements. The latest in technology enables sellers to work with individual buyers to determine their wants and needs and to develop goods and services specifically designed for them, like hand-tailored shirts and unique vacations.

Understanding consumers is so important to marketing that a whole area of marketing emerged called consumer behavior. We explore that area next.

◀ **LECTURE LINK 13-6:**
Relationship Marketing: Going Beyond the Expected

relationship marketing
Marketing strategy with the goal of keeping individual customers over time by offering them products that exactly meet their requirements.

The Internet has dramatically increased the ways in which companies can reach out to customers and conduct relationship marketing. It can even assist marketers in customizing products like clothing and travel. Have you formed any relationships with retailers based on your use of their Web sites? What appeals to you about these firms?

The Consumer Decision-Making Process

Figure 13.7 on p. 364 shows the consumer decision-making process and some outside factors that influence it. The five steps in the process are often studied in courses on consumer behavior.

The first step is problem recognition, which may occur when your washing machine breaks down and you realize you need a new one. This leads to an information search—you look for ads and brochures about washing machines. You may consult a secondary data source like *Consumer Reports* or other information, perhaps online. And you'll likely seek advice from other people who have purchased washing machines.

After compiling all this information, you evaluate alternatives and make a purchase decision. But your buying process doesn't end here. After the purchase, you may ask the people you spoke to previously how their machines perform and then do other comparisons to your new washer.

Marketing researchers investigate these consumer thought processes and behavior at each stage in a purchase to determine the best way to help the buyer buy. This area of study is called *consumer behavior*.

Consumer behavior researchers also study the influences that affect consumer behavior. Figure 13.7 shows several: marketing mix variables (the four Ps); psychological influences, such as perception and attitudes; situational influences, such as the type of purchase and the physical

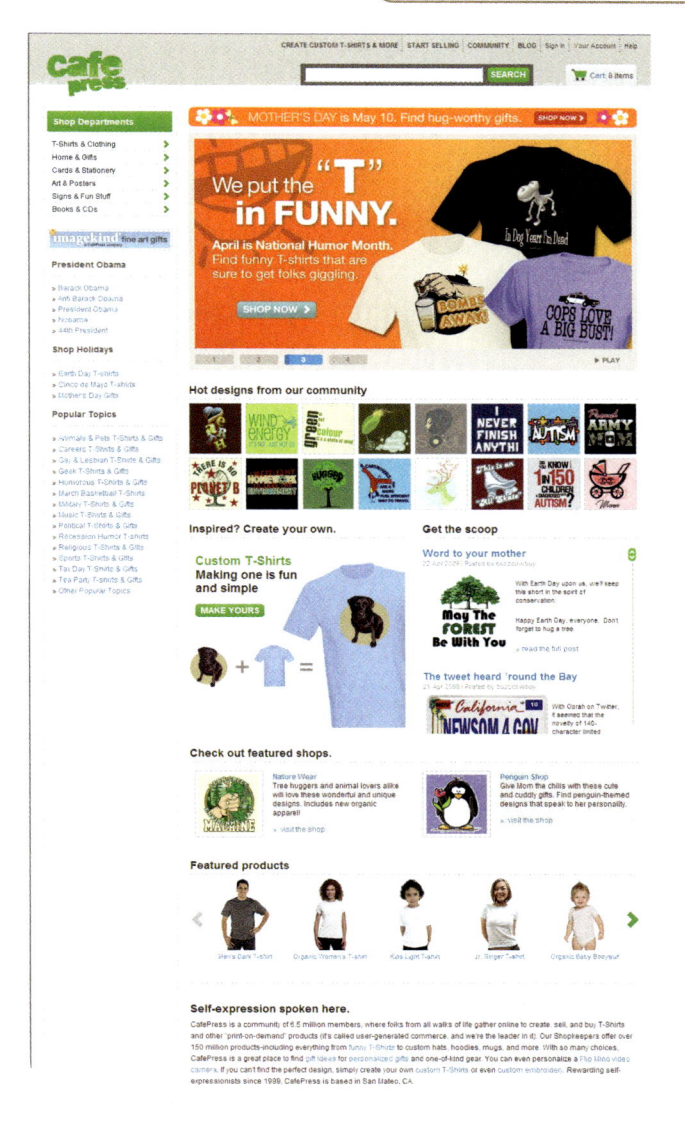

figure 13.7

THE CONSUMER DECISION-MAKING PROCESS AND OUTSIDE INFLUENCES

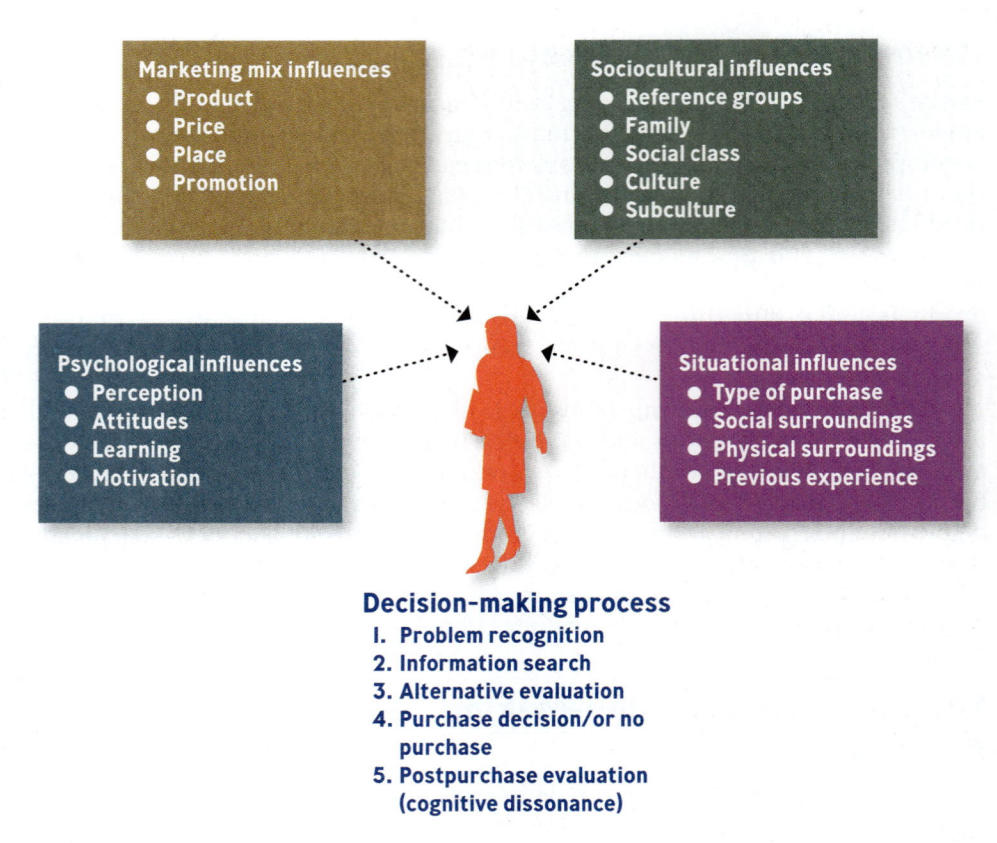

There are many influences on consumers as they decide which goods and services to buy. Marketers have some influence, but it's not usually as strong as sociocultural influences. Helping consumers in their information search and their evaluation of alternatives is a major function of marketing.

Marketing mix influences
- Product
- Price
- Place
- Promotion

Sociocultural influences
- Reference groups
- Family
- Social class
- Culture
- Subculture

Psychological influences
- Perception
- Attitudes
- Learning
- Motivation

Situational influences
- Type of purchase
- Social surroundings
- Physical surroundings
- Previous experience

Decision-making process
1. Problem recognition
2. Information search
3. Alternative evaluation
4. Purchase decision/or no purchase
5. Postpurchase evaluation (cognitive dissonance)

▶ PPT 13-39:
The Consumer Decision-Making Process and Outside Influences

▶ PPT 13-38:
Steps in the Consumer Decision-Making Process

▶ CRITICAL THINKING EXERCISE 13-4:
The Marketing Opportunity

▶ LECTURE LINK 13-7:
Family Life Cycle Theory Updated

▶ PPT 13-40:
Key Factors in Consumer Decision-Making

surroundings; and sociocultural influences, such as reference groups and culture. Other important factors include these:

- *Learning* creates changes in an individual's behavior resulting from previous experiences and information. If you've tried a particular brand of shampoo and don't like it, you've learned not to buy it again.

- *Reference group* is the group an individual uses as a reference point in forming beliefs, attitudes, values, or behavior. A college student who carries a briefcase instead of a backpack may see businesspeople as his or her reference group.

- *Culture* is the set of values, attitudes, and ways of doing things transmitted from one generation to another in a given society. The U.S. culture emphasizes and transmits the values of education, freedom, and diversity.

- *Subculture* is the set of values, attitudes, and ways of doing things that results from belonging to a certain ethnic group, racial group, or other group with which one closely identifies (e.g., teenagers).

- *Cognitive dissonance* is a type of psychological conflict that can occur after a purchase. Consumers who make a major purchase may have doubts about whether they got the best product at the best price. Marketers must reassure such consumers after the sale that they made a good decision. An auto dealer, for example, may send positive press articles about the particular car a consumer purchased, offer product guarantees, and provide certain free services.

Many universities have expanded the marketing curriculum to include courses in business-to-business marketing. As you'll learn below, that market is huge.

LEARNING goal 6 *

Compare the business-to-business market and the consumer market.

Consumer behavior researchers investigate people's buying decisions and the factors that influence their choices. Social, psychological, and marketing-mix factors are important when we decide to buy, and so are the store environment and our previous buying experiences. What influences the choices you make in your local supermarket?

THE BUSINESS-TO-BUSINESS MARKET

Business-to-business (B2B) marketers include manufacturers; intermediaries such as retailers; institutions like hospitals, schools, and charities; and the government. The B2B market is larger than the consumer market because items are often sold and resold several times in the B2B process before they reach the final consumer. B2B marketing strategies also differ from consumer marketing because business buyers have their own decision-making process.[36] Several factors make B2B marketing different, including these:

1. Customers in the B2B market are relatively few; there are just a few construction firms or mining operations compared to the 70 million or so households in the U.S. consumer market.
2. Business customers are relatively large; that is, big organizations account for most of the employment and production of various goods and services. Nonetheless, there are many small to medium-sized firms in the United States that together make an attractive market.
3. B2B markets tend to be geographically concentrated. For example, oilfields are found in the Southwest and Alaska. Thus B2B marketers can concentrate their efforts on a particular area and minimize distribution problems by locating warehouses near industrial centers.
4. Business buyers are generally more rational and less emotional than ultimate consumers; they use product specifications to guide buying choices and often more carefully weigh the total product offer, including quality, price, and service.
5. B2B sales tend to be direct, but not always. Tire manufacturers sell directly to auto manufacturers but use intermediaries, such as wholesalers and retailers, to sell to ultimate consumers.
6. Whereas consumer promotions are based more on *advertising*, B2B sales are based on *selling*. There are fewer customers and they usually demand more personal service.

Figure 13.8 on p. 366 shows some of the differences between buying behavior in the B2B and consumer markets. B2B buyers also use the Internet to make purchases.[37] You'll learn more about the business-to-business market in advanced marketing courses.

◄ **CRITICAL THINKING EXERCISE 13-5:**
Consumer or B2B Good?

◄ **PPT 13-41:**
Business-to-Business Market (B2B)

◄ **PPT 13-42:**
B2B Market Differences

	BUSINESS-TO-BUSINESS MARKET	**CONSUMER MARKET**
Market Structure	Relatively few potential customers Larger purchases Geographically concentrated	Many potential customers Smaller purchases Geographically dispersed
Products	Require technical, complex products Frequently require customization Frequently require technical advice, delivery, and after-sale service	Require less technical products Sometimes require customization Sometimes require technical advice, delivery, and after-sale service
Buying Procedures	Buyers are trained Negotiate details of most purchases Follow objective standards Formal process involving specific employees Closer relationships between marketers and buyers Often buy from multiple sources	No special training Accept standard terms for most purchases Use personal judgment Informal process involving household members Impersonal relationships between marketers and consumers Rarely buy from multiple sources

figure 13.8

COMPARING BUSINESS-TO-BUSINESS AND CONSUMER BUYING BEHAVIOR

YOUR PROSPECTS IN MARKETING

There is a wider variety of careers in marketing than in most business disciplines. If you major in marketing, an array of career options will be available to you. You could become a manager in a retail store like Saks or Target. You could do marketing research or work in product management. You could go into selling, advertising, sales promotion, or public relations. You could work in transportation, storage, or international distribution. You could design interactive Web sites to implement CRM. These are just a few of the possibilities. As you read through the following marketing chapters, consider whether a marketing career would interest you.

▶ PPT 13-43:
Progress Assessment

progress assessment

- Can you define the terms *consumer market* and *business-to-business market*?
- Can you name and describe five ways to segment the consumer market?
- What is niche marketing, and how does it differ from one-to-one marketing?
- What are four key factors that make B2B markets different from consumer markets?

summary

Learning Goal 1. Define *marketing*, and apply the marketing concept to both for-profit and nonprofit organizations.

- **What is marketing?**

Marketing is the activity, set of institutions, and processes for creating, communicating, delivering, and exchanging offerings that have value for customers, clients, partners, and society at large.

- **How has marketing changed over time?**

During the *production era*, marketing was largely a distribution function. Emphasis was on producing as many goods as possible and getting them to markets. By the early 1920s, during the *selling era*, the emphasis turned to selling and advertising to persuade customers to buy the existing goods produced by mass production. After World War II, the tremendous demand for goods and services led to the *marketing concept era*, when businesses recognized the need to be responsive to customers' needs. During the 1990s, marketing entered the *customer relationship era*, focusing on enhancing customer satisfaction and stimulating long-term customer loyalty. The newest in customer relationship building involves social networks, online communities, and blogs.

- **What are the three parts of the marketing concept?**

The three parts of the marketing concept are (1) a customer orientation, (2) a service orientation, and (3) a profit orientation (that is, marketing goods and services that will earn a profit and enable the firm to survive and expand).

- **What kinds of organizations are involved in marketing?**

All kinds of organizations use marketing, including for-profit and nonprofit organizations like states, charities, churches, politicians, and schools.

Learning Goal 2. Describe the four Ps of marketing.

- **How do marketers implement the four Ps?**

The idea behind the four Ps is to design a *product* people want, *price* it competitively, *place* it where consumers can find it easily, and *promote* it so consumers know it exists.

Learning Goal 3. Summarize the marketing research process.

- **What are the steps in conducting marketing research?**

(1) Define the problem and determine the present situation, (2) collect data, (3) analyze the data, and (4) choose the best solution.

Learning Goal 4. Show how marketers use environmental scanning to learn about the changing marketing environment.

- **What is environmental scanning?**

Environmental scanning is the process of identifying factors that can affect marketing success. Marketers pay attention to all the environmental factors that create opportunities and threats.

- **What are some of the more important environmental trends in marketing?**

The most important global and technological change is probably the growth of the Internet. Another is the growth of consumer databases, with which companies can develop products and services that closely match consumers' needs. Marketers must monitor social trends like population growth and shifts to maintain their close relationship with customers. They must also monitor the dynamic competitive and economic environments.

Learning Goal 5. Explain how marketers apply the tools of market segmentation, relationship marketing, and the study of consumer behavior.

- **What are some of the ways marketers segment the consumer market?**

Geographic segmentation means dividing the market into different regions. Segmentation by age, income, and education level are types of *demographic segmentation*. We study a group's values, attitudes, and interests using *psychographic segmentation*. Determining which benefits customers prefer and using them to promote a product is *benefit segmentation*. Separating the market by usage is called *volume segmentation*. The best segmentation strategy is to use all the variables to come up with a consumer profile for a target market that's sizable, reachable, and profitable.

- **What is the difference between mass marketing and relationship marketing?**

Mass marketing means developing products and promotions to please large groups of people. Relationship marketing tends to lead away from mass production and toward custom-made goods and services. Its goal is to keep individual customers over time by offering them products or services that meet their needs.

- **What are some of the factors that influence the consumer decision-making process?**

See Figure 13.7 for some of the major influences on consumer decision-making. Other factors are learning, reference group, culture, subculture, and cognitive dissonance.

Learning Goal 6. Compare the business-to-business market and the consumer market.

- **What makes the business-to-business market different from the consumer market?**

Customers in the B2B market are relatively few and large. B2B markets tend to be geographically concentrated, and industrial buyers generally are more rational than ultimate consumers in their selection of goods and services. B2B sales tend to be direct, and there is much more emphasis on personal selling than in consumer markets.

key terms

benefit segmentation 362
brand name 353
business-to-business (B2B) market 359
consumer market 359
customer relationship management (CRM) 349
demographic segmentation 362
environmental scanning 357
focus group 356
geographic segmentation 362
marketing 346
marketing concept 348
marketing mix 350
marketing research 354
market segmentation 360
mass marketing 362
niche marketing 362
one-to-one marketing 362
primary data 356
product 352
promotion 354
psychographic segmentation 362
relationship marketing 363
secondary data 355
target marketing 361
test marketing 352
volume (or usage) segmentation 362

connect interactive applications

Reinforcing Your Connection to Concepts in Business

This chapter offers 15 interactive applications designed to help you apply what you've learned (examples of these exercises appear on the following pages). Your instructor has determined which interactive applications will benefit you throughout this course. Please refer to your instructor's assignment list in *Connect* to determine which applications you should complete.

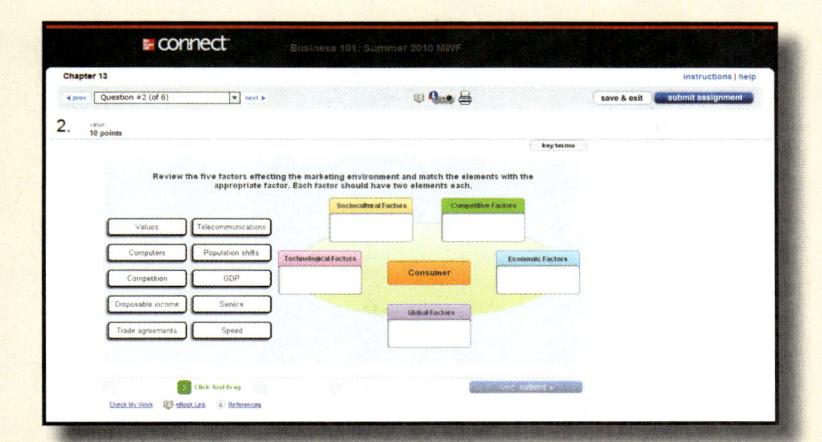

Click and Drag Interactive: Marketing managers must be aware of their environment when making marketing mix decisions. Environmental scanning is the process of identifying global, technological, sociocultural, competitive, and economic factors that can affect marketing success. These factors can impact a company's ability to build and maintain relationships with business and consumer markets. Review the factors affecting the marketing environment and match them with the appropriate element.

Click and Drag Interactive: The emphasis of marketing has shifted from understanding a product to understanding the customer. Each of the four eras in the history of marketing is defined by evolving business philosophies. Review the four eras in the history of marketing and place them in chronological order on the timeline.

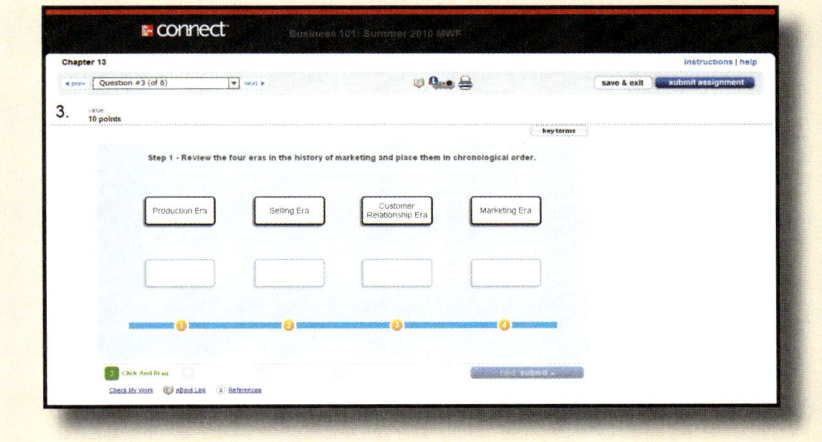

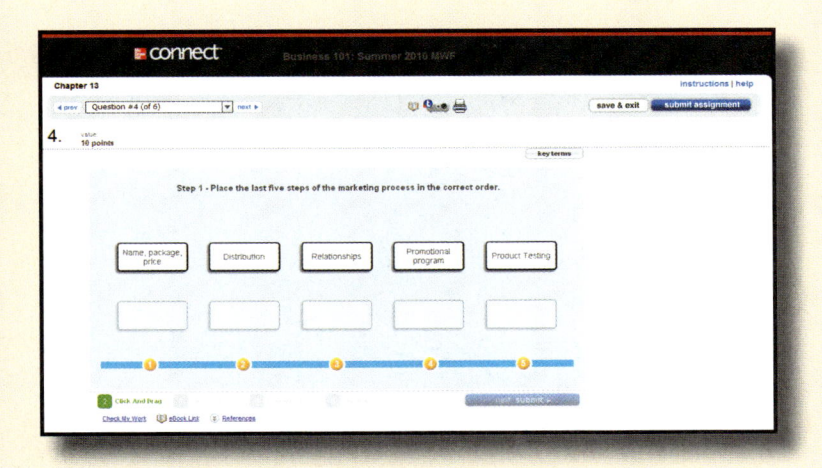

Click and Drag Interactive: There are nine steps in the marketing process. Place the last five steps of the marketing process in the correct order on the timeline.

Click and Drag Interactive: Besides listening to customers, marketing researchers also pay attention to what employees, shareholders, dealers, consumer advocates, media representatives, and other stakeholders have to say. Review the four steps involved in the market research process and place them in the correct sequence on the timeline.

Video Case Interactive: Marketing can be thought of as the activities buyers and sellers perform to facilitate mutually satisfying exchanges. Watch the video featuring Oberweis and respond to the questions when prompted.

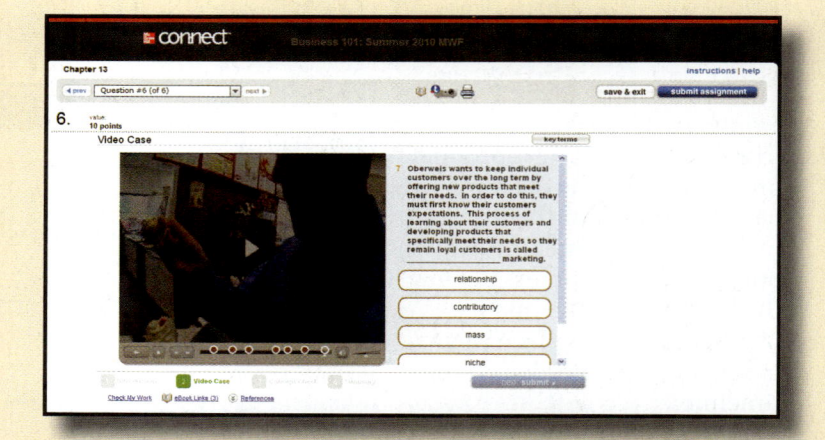

14 Developing and Pricing Goods and Services

profile

Getting to Know Ratan Tata from the Tata Group

Few people caught the business world's attention quite like Ratan Tata did in 2008 with his production of a revolutionary $2,500 "people's car." Tata rose in the span of a few months from a shy, insular executive known to few people outside his own country to a global titan of industry. With command of 98 other manufacturing companies in his family's firm, the Tata Group, Ratan Tata was on *Esquire*'s "75 Most Influential People of the 21st Century" list in October 2008.

Tata was born in Mumbai, India, in 1937 to a wealthy family. After early studies in India, he received a degree in architecture and structural engineering from Cornell University in 1962. Tata then went back to India, rejecting a lucrative offer from IBM. He took a job with the Tata Group, but despite his education and obvious connections with the ownership, he began shoveling limestone and handling the blast furnace for a Tata Steel plant. After paying his dues on the factory floor, Tata was awarded various high-level positions within the family's stable of companies. He eventually became director of Empress Mills, an ailing asset that he turned profitable in 1977. After that success, Ratan was made director of Tata Industries, a corporate division that included the vehicle he would ride to fame.

From the outset, Ratan wanted to revolutionize Indian transportation. For most Indian families, the only affordable motorized transport is a motorcycle—not only impractical but also unsafe on the nation's overcrowded roads. In 2003, Tata began development of the Nano, a small, inexpensive car that answered the dream of four-wheeled transportation for millions of Indian families.

In 2008, the Nano was released to rave reviews across India. People marveled at its diminutive size and surprisingly sturdy structure, but what truly amazed them was its $2,500 price tag. The car is not without faults, however. Despite its affordable sticker price, it still costs many times most Indians' annual income. With India's streets already choked with traffic, the introduction of a new fleet of bargain cars poses pollution hazards. The car isn't available for sale in the United States because it fails to meet U.S. safety standards.

With Tata Motors at the forefront, India's burgeoning auto market is on course to be the largest in the world. Experts

LEARNING goals

After you have read and studied this chapter, you should be able to

1. Describe a total product offer.
2. Identify the various kinds of consumer and industrial goods.
3. Summarize the functions of packaging.
4. Contrast *brand*, *brand name*, and *trademark*, and show the value of brand equity.
5. Explain the steps in the new-product development process.
6. Describe the product life cycle.
7. Identify various pricing objectives and strategies.

connect™

Your *Connect*ion to Better Learning. 1. View the interactive presentation. 2. Practice through LearnSmart. 3. Apply your knowledge by using the interactive applications for each chapter of this text.

1 Prep »»»»» **2 Study** »»»»» **3 Apply**

---

predict India's auto industry will produce 600 million units by 2050. That is more than twice the number of registered cars in the United States today. With foreign auto sales poised to expand on the success of small cars like the Nano, U.S. companies have taken notice. In 2008, Ford Motor Company announced it was selling its luxury brands, Jaguar and Range Rover, to generate capital for a new line of smaller cars. Ratan Tata hit headlines again when he bought the luxury brands for $2.3 billion, less than half what Ford had paid for them.

This chapter is all about developing and pricing new products and services. As shown by the success of Ratan Tata, the companies that command the business world are innovative pioneers.

Sources: Mira Kamdar, "It Costs Just $2,500. It's Cute as a Bug. And It Could Mean Global Disaster," *The Washington Post*, January 13, 2008; Eric Bellman, "Tata's High-Stakes Bet on Low-Cost Car," *The Wall Street Journal*, January 10, 2008; Chris Jones, "Ratan Tata," *Esquire*, October 2008; Eric Bellman and Jackie Range, "Merger, Indian Style: Buy a Brand, Leave It Alone," *The Wall Street Journal*, March 22–23, 2008; Jessica Liebman, "Ratan Tata," *Condé Nast Portfolio,* May 2008; and "Tata Nano Superdrive Concludes," www.forbes.com, accessed June 2010.

www.tatamotors.com

NAME THAT company

You've been using my product for years, yet it took over 15 years for it to be accepted in the market. It finally became popular during World War I, and today you'll find it on your pants, your travel bags, and your hoodie. Who am I and what do I make? (Find the answer in the chapter.)

▶ **PPT 14-1:** Developing and Pricing Goods and Services

▶ **PPT 14-2:** Ratan Tata

▶ **LECTURE LINK 14-1:** There is No Such Thing as a "Better" Product

▶ **PPT 14-3:** Developing Value

▶ **PPT 14-4:** Products "Untouchable" by Spending Cuts

▶ **PPT 14-5:** Products "Expendable" by Spending Cuts

LEARNING goal 1 *

Describe a total product offer.

value
Good quality at a fair price. When consumers calculate the value of a product, they look at the benefits and then subtract the cost to see if the benefits exceed the costs.

PRODUCT DEVELOPMENT AND THE TOTAL PRODUCT OFFER

Clearly, businesspeople like Ratan Tata will be challenging U.S. managers with new products at low prices.[1] The only way to compete is to design and promote better products, meaning products that customers perceive to have the best **value**—good quality at a fair price.[2] You may have noticed that many restaurants were pushing "value meals" when the economy slowed from 2008 to 2010.[3] One of the American Marketing Association's definitions of marketing says it's "a set of processes for creating, communicating, and delivering *value* to customers." When consumers calculate the value of a product, they look at the benefits and then subtract the cost (price) to see whether the benefits exceed the costs, including the cost of driving to the store (or shipping fees if they buy the product online).

Whether consumers perceive a product as the best value depends on many factors, including the benefits they seek and the service they receive. To satisfy consumers, marketers must learn to listen better and constantly adapt to changing market demands.[4] For example, traditional phone companies must now compete with Voice over Internet Protocol (VoIP)—a system that allows people to make very inexpensive phone calls through the Internet. And U.S. automobile companies must adapt to foreign producers by offering more competitive cars, or face extinction.[5]

Marketers have learned that adapting products to new competition and new markets is an ongoing need. We're sure you've noticed menu changes at your local fast-food restaurant over time. An organization can't do a one-time survey of consumer wants and needs, design a group of products to meet those needs, put them in the stores, and then just relax. It must constantly monitor changing consumer wants and needs, and adapt products, policies, and services accordingly. Did you know that McDonald's sells as much chicken as beef these days?[6] Some is being sold as a Chicken Biscuit for breakfast.[7] Those double cheeseburgers fast-food restaurants were serving for $1.00 turned out to be a moneyloser, even though they were popular with consumers.[8] You can't give consumers *too* good a deal or you can go out of business.[9]

McDonald's and other restaurants are constantly trying new ideas. In Kokomo, Indiana, McDonald's tried waiter service and a more varied menu. In New York, it offered McDonuts to compete with Krispy Kreme. In Atlanta and other cities, McDonald's had computer stations linked to the Internet. In Hawaii, it tried a Spam breakfast platter, and in Columbus, Ohio, a mega-McDonald's had a karaoke booth. And watch out, Starbucks—McDonald's has a McCafé in Chicago's Loop that sells premium coffee, pastries, and wrapped sandwiches. It has more than 300 such cafés in other countries. Some McDonald's even have digital-media kiosks that allow customers to burn custom CDs from a catalog of 70,000 songs, print digital photos, and download ringtones for mobile phones. McDonald's plans to add cappuccinos, lattes, and other fancy coffee drinks at all its U.S. locations.[10] That process was delayed a bit when the banking crisis hit and credit was difficult to find.[11] Nonetheless, some McD's now have coffee bars.

What was Starbucks' answer to the new challenge by McDonald's, Dunkin' Donuts, Target, and others? It began offering more food products. Oatmeal has become a huge success at Starbucks.[12] The new menu also includes fruit smoothies and more—like regular coffee at lower prices.[13]

All fast-food organizations must constantly monitor all sources of information for new-product ideas. McDonald's isn't alone in that. Look at those baguettes and cream cheese croissants at 7-Eleven—they're right next to the cappuccino machine. KFC put in a new line of chicken sandwiches. Arby's introduced a new salad. Burger King tried a new X-treme Double Cheeseburger. Wendy's is trying a major new coffee program in Mississippi, including iced coffee, and introducing a whole new lineup of other products.[14]

Offerings may differ in various locations according to the wants of the local community. In Iowa pork tenderloin is big, but in Oklahoma City it's tortilla scramblers. Overseas, companies must adapt to local tastes. At Bob's Big Boy in Thailand, you can get Tropical Shrimp; at Carl's Junior in Mexico, you can order the Machaca Burrito; and at Shakey's Pizza in the Philippines, you can get Cali Shandy, a Filipino beer. McDonald's now has restaurants in over 119 countries offering local menus to 52 million people a day—and is still growing.[15]

Product development, then, is a key activity in any modern business, anywhere in the world. The Spotlight on Small Business on p. 376 box shows how the whole process gets started. There's a lot more to new-product development than merely introducing goods and services, however. What marketers do to create excitement for those products is as important as the products themselves.

How would you like a beer or glass of wine with your Big Mac? You can get both at this McDonald's in Paris. Notice how the restaurant's architecture fits the style of the city. The same is true of the food in McDonald's restaurants outside the United States. In Europe, the menus and interior designs are frequently adapted to fit the tastes and cultural preferences of each country.

◀ BONUS CASE 14-1:
The Value of a Product Offer

Developing a Total Product Offer

From a strategic marketing viewpoint, a product is more than just the physical good or service. A **total product offer** consists of everything consumers evaluate when deciding whether to buy something. Thus, the basic product or service may be a washing machine, an insurance policy, or a beer, but the total

total product offer
Everything that consumers evaluate when deciding whether to buy something; also called a value package.

SPOTLIGHT ON SMALL business

Home Cooking in Half the Time

Men and women today are often very busy with work and don't have much time to make home-cooked meals. Nonetheless, they would like to offer their families good meals. Such meals create more family time and are often more nutritious than restaurant fare. What can marketers do to help working families prepare meals? One answer: a company called Let's Dish. Let's Dish does the planning, shopping, and chopping for you. All you have to do is combine the ingredients, then cook at home whenever you're ready.

The idea behind Let's Dish is popular. A competitor, Dream Dinners, relies on a similar concept. It's like a community kitchen where moms and dads can whip up a couple of weeks' worth of meals in just one or two hours. Here's how it works. Customers go to a Web site to pick a time and date and the meals they would like to prepare, like herb-crusted flank steak. When they arrive at Dream Dinners, the ingredients are ready. Customers mix and package them and bring them home, uncooked. They put the meals in the refrigerator until needed. No shopping for groceries. No looking for recipes. Just meals, ready to go. Sound good?

Dream Dinners now has over 115 stores in 19 states, with many more to come. Of course, a good idea brings in competitors. Besides Let's Dish and Dream Dinners, companies with names like Designed Dinners and Simply Cook It have sprung up. Simply Cook It goes a step further and helps you make a minimum of 24 dinners at the store. You have the assistance of a professional chef and take home what could be a month's worth of dinners.

What does such a company offer as its "product"? First, it provides a place to meet others and have a good time preparing meals. Second, it saves time for people too busy to shop for groceries and prepare meals at home every night. Third, it saves a lot of stress and mess. Finally, the company saves people money, because they don't have to buy big supplies of condiments they'll use only sparingly. Perhaps most important, the company offers a quick and easy way to create healthy and satisfying meals for the whole family. What else might such a company add to its product offer?

Sources: "Get Dishing," an advertising supplement to the *Gaithersburg Gazette*, March 2008; Dream Dinners, www.dreamdinners.com, accessed February 2009; and Simply Cook It, www.simplycookit.net, accessed July 2010.

▶ PPT 14-6:
Home Cooking in Half the Time

▶ PPT 14-7:
Developing a Total Product

▶ PPT 14-8:
Product Innovation During the Great Depression

Apple's iPhone offers a superb range of features and functions, including the ability to take photos, check e-mail, browse Web sites, get directions, tell time, start a shopping list, record appointments in your calendar, download songs, and even make and receive phone calls. What would you like Apple to add to the iPhone's total product offer? The product will likely continue to evolve and improve.

product offer includes some or all the *value* enhancers in Figure 14.1. You may hear some people call the basic product the "core product" and the total product offer the "augmented product."[16]

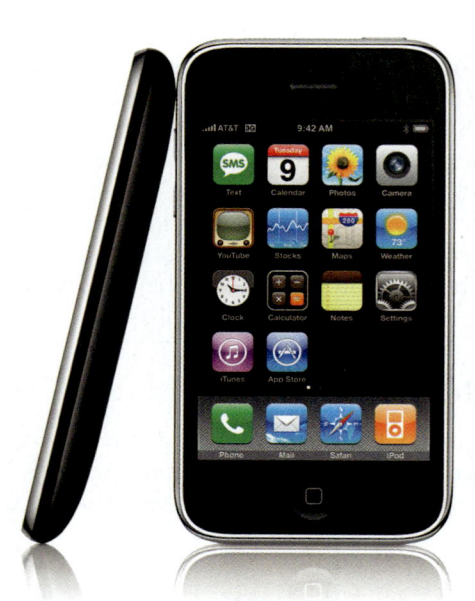

When people buy a product, they may evaluate and compare total product offers on many dimensions.[17] Some are tangible (the product itself and its package); others are intangible (the producer's reputation and the image created by advertising). A successful marketer must begin to think like a consumer and evaluate the total product offer as a collection of impressions created by all the factors listed in Figure 14.1. It is wise to talk with consumers to see which features and benefits are most important to them and which value enhancers they want in the final offerings.[18] What questions might you ask consumers when developing the total product offer for Very Vegetarian? (Recall the business

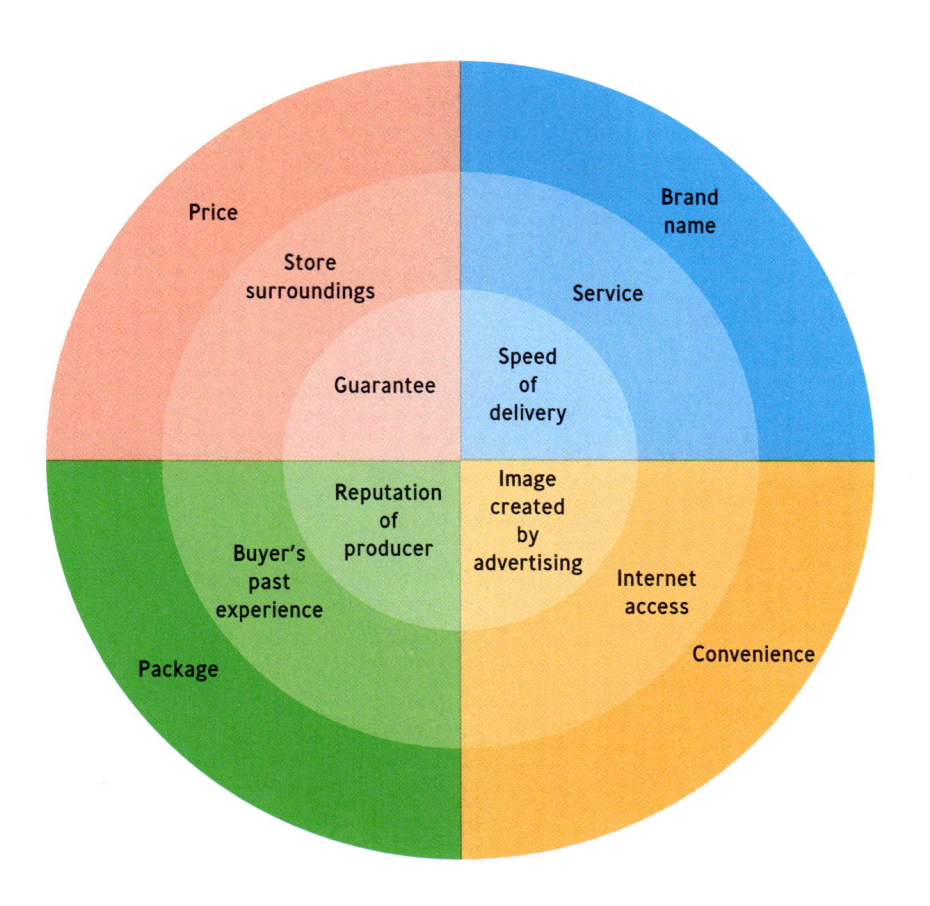

figure 14.1

POTENTIAL COMPONENTS OF A TOTAL PRODUCT OFFER

idea we introduced in Chapter 13.) Remember, store surroundings are important in the restaurant business, as are the parking lot and the condition of bathrooms.

Sometimes an organization can use low prices to create an attractive total product offer. For example, outlet stores offer brand-name goods for less. Shoppers like getting high-quality goods and low prices, but they must be careful. Outlets also carry lower-quality products with similar but not exactly the same features as goods carried in regular stores. Different consumers may want different total product offers, so a company must develop a variety of offerings.

Product Lines and the Product Mix

Companies usually don't sell just one product. A **product line** is a group of products that are physically similar or intended for a similar market. They usually face similar competition. In one product line, there may be several competing brands. Notice, for example, Diet Coke, Diet Coke with Splenda, Coke Zero, Diet Coke with Lemon, Diet Coke with Lime, Diet Vanilla Coke, and Diet Cherry Coke. Makes it kind of hard to choose, doesn't it? Have you seen the new aluminum Coke bottle? It's recyclable, resealable, less costly to make than a plastic or glass bottle, and feels cooler to the touch.[19] Both Coke and Pepsi have added water and sports drinks to their product lines to meet new consumer tastes.

Procter & Gamble (P&G) has many brands in its laundry detergent product line, including Tide, Era, Downy, and Bold. P&G's product lines together make up its **product mix**, the combination of all product lines offered by a manufacturer. Have you tried P&G's Swiffer?

◀ **PPT 14-9:**
Potential Components of a Total Product Offer

◀ **PPT 14-10:**
Understanding Product Lines

◀ **BONUS CASE 14-2:**
Whole Foods Markets Naturally

product line
A group of products that are physically similar or are intended for a similar market.

◀ **PPT 14-11:**
The Product Mix

product mix
The combination of product lines offered by a manufacturer.

PPT 14-12:
Differentiating Products

product differentiation
The creation of real or perceived product differences.

convenience goods and services
Products that the consumer wants to purchase frequently and with a minimum of effort.

shopping goods and services
Those products that the consumer buys only after comparing value, quality, price, and style from a variety of sellers.

Vending machines provide a variety of convenience goods like snacks, gum, candy, soft drinks, bottled water, and newspapers. What convenience goods do you buy, and where do you find them?

Service providers have product lines and product mixes as well. A bank or credit union may offer a variety of services from savings accounts, automated teller machines, and computer banking to money market funds, safety deposit boxes, car loans, mortgages, traveler's checks, online banking, and insurance. AT&T combines services (communications) with goods (phones) in its product mix, with special emphasis on wireless.[20]

LEARNING goal 2 *

Identify the various kinds of consumer and industrial goods.

PRODUCT DIFFERENTIATION

Product differentiation is the creation of real or perceived product differences. Actual product differences are sometimes quite small, so marketers must use a creative mix of pricing, advertising, and packaging (value enhancers) to create a unique, attractive image. Various bottled water companies, for example, have successfully attempted product differentiation. The companies made their bottled waters so attractive through pricing and promotion that now restaurant customers often order water by brand name.

There's no reason why you couldn't create a similar attractive image for Very Vegetarian, your vegetarian restaurant. Small businesses can often win market share with creative product differentiation. Yearbook photographer Charlie Clark competes by offering multiple clothing changes, backgrounds, and poses along with special allowances, discounts, and guarantees. His small business has the advantage of being more flexible in adapting to customer needs and wants, and he's able to offer attractive product options. Clark has been so successful that companies use him as a speaker at photography conventions. How could you respond creatively to the consumer wants of vegetarians?

Marketing Different Classes of Consumer Goods and Services

One popular classification of consumer goods and services has four general categories—convenience, shopping, specialty, and unsought.

1. **Convenience goods and services** are products the consumer wants to purchase frequently and with a minimum of effort, like candy, gum, milk, snacks, gas, and banking services. One store that sells mostly convenience goods is 7-Eleven. Location, brand awareness, and image are important for marketers of convenience goods and services. The Internet has taken convenience to a whole new level, especially for banks and other service companies. Companies that don't offer such services are likely to lose market share to those that do unless they offer outstanding service to customers who visit in person.

2. **Shopping goods and services** are products the consumer buys only after comparing value, quality, price, and style from a variety of sellers. Shopping goods and services are sold largely through *shopping* centers where consumers can make comparisons of products like clothes, shoes, appliances, and auto repair services. Target is one store that sells mostly shopping goods. Because many consumers carefully

compare such products, marketers can emphasize price differences, quality differences, or some combination of the two. Think how the Internet has helped you find the right shopping goods.

3. **Specialty goods and services** are consumer products with unique characteristics and brand identity. Because consumers perceive that specialty goods have no reasonable substitute, they put forth a special effort to purchase them. Examples include fine watches, expensive wine, fur coats, jewelry, imported chocolates, and services provided by medical specialists or business consultants.

    Specialty goods are often marketed through specialty magazines. Specialty skis may be sold through sports magazines and specialty foods through gourmet magazines. Again, the Internet helps buyers find specialty goods. In fact, some specialty goods can be sold exclusively on the Internet.[21]

4. **Unsought goods and services** are products consumers are unaware of, haven't necessarily thought of buying, or suddenly find they need to solve an unexpected problem. They include emergency car-towing services, burial services, and insurance.

The marketing task varies according to the category of product; convenience goods are marketed differently from specialty goods. The best way to promote convenience goods is to make them readily available and create the proper image. Some combination of price, quality, and service is the best appeal for shopping goods. Specialty goods rely on reaching special market segments through advertising. Unsought goods such as life insurance often rely on personal selling. Car towing relies heavily on Yellow Pages advertising.

Whether a good or service falls into a particular class depends on the individual consumer. Coffee can be a shopping good for one consumer, while flavored gourmet roast is a specialty good for another. Some people shop around to compare different dry cleaners, so dry cleaning is a shopping service for them. Others go to the closest store, making it a convenience service. Marketers must carefully monitor their customer base to determine how consumers perceive their products.

Marketing Industrial Goods and Services

Many goods could be classified as consumer goods or industrial goods, based on their uses. A computer kept at home for personal use is clearly a consumer good. But in a commercial setting, such as an accounting firm or manufacturing plant, the same computer is an industrial good.

---

specialty goods and services
Consumer products with unique characteristics and brand identity. Because these products are perceived as having no reasonable substitute, the consumer puts forth a special effort to purchase them.

unsought goods and services
Products that consumers are unaware of, haven't necessarily thought of buying, or find that they need to solve an unexpected problem.

Many goods could be classified as consumer goods or industrial goods, based on their uses. For example, a computer that a person uses at home for personal use would clearly be a consumer good. But that same computer used in a commercial setting, such as an accounting firm or a manufacturing plant, would be classified as an industrial good. What difference does it make how a good is classified?

> **industrial goods**
> Products used in the production of other products. Sometimes called business goods or B2B goods.

Industrial goods (sometimes called business goods or B2B goods) are products used in the production of other products. They are sold in the business-to-business (B2B) market. Some products can be both consumer and industrial goods. We've seen how personal computers fit in both categories. As a consumer good, a computer might be sold through electronics stores like Best Buy or computer magazines. Most of the promotion would be advertising. As an industrial good, personal computers are more likely to be sold through salespeople or on the Internet. Advertising is less of a factor when selling industrial goods. Thus, you can see that classifying goods by user category helps marketers determine the proper marketing-mix strategy.

Figure 14.2 shows some categories of both consumer and industrial goods and services. *Installations* consist of major capital equipment such as new factories and heavy machinery. *Capital items* are expensive products that last a long time. A new factory building is both a capital item and an installation. *Accessory equipment* consists of capital items that are not quite as long-lasting or expensive as installations—like computers, copy machines, and various tools. Other industrial goods and examples are labeled in the chart.

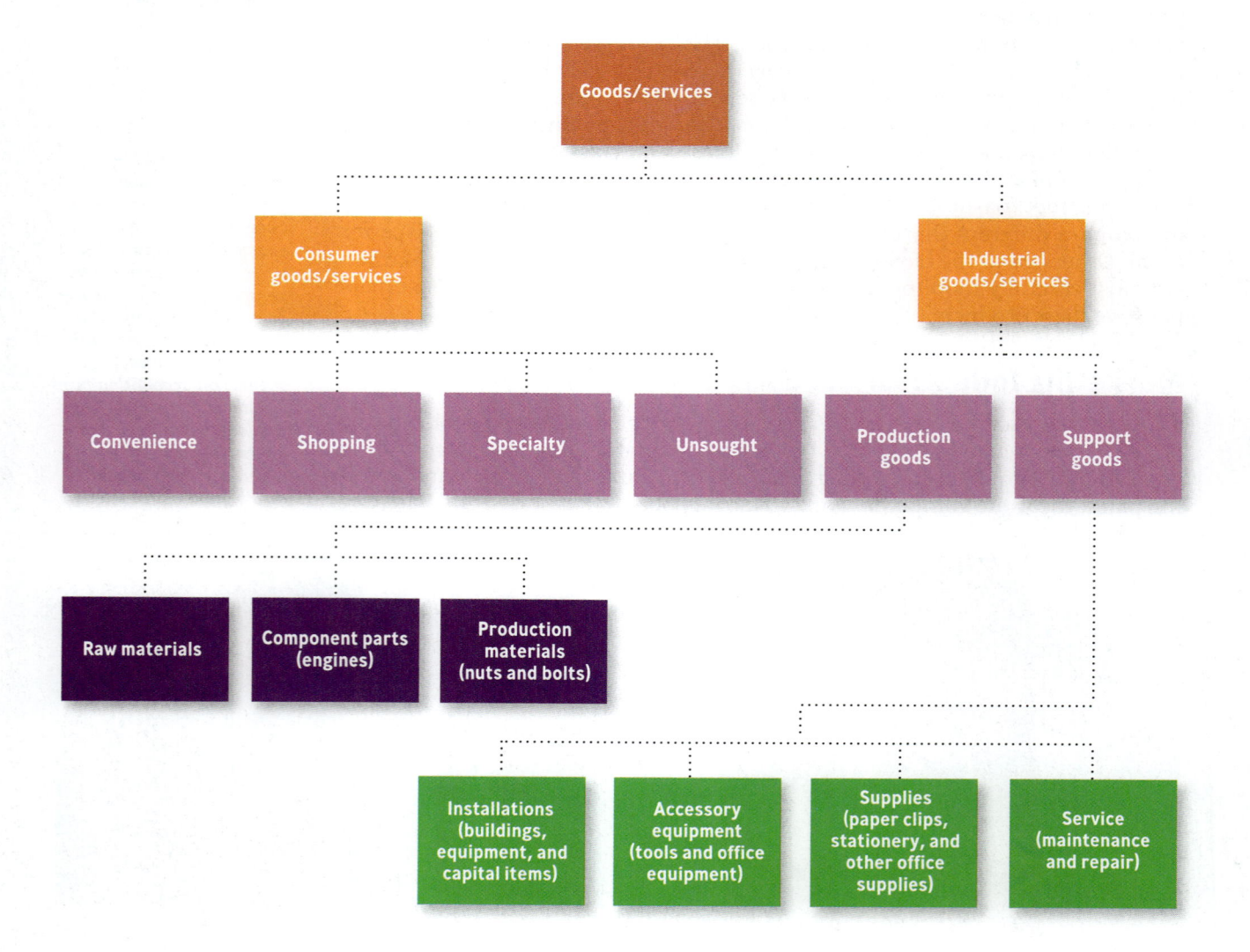

figure 14.2

VARIOUS CATEGORIES OF CONSUMER AND INDUSTRIAL GOODS AND SERVICES

Goods/services
- Consumer goods/services
  - Convenience
  - Shopping
  - Specialty
  - Unsought
- Industrial goods/services
  - Production goods
    - Raw materials
    - Component parts (engines)
    - Production materials (nuts and bolts)
  - Support goods
    - Installations (buildings, equipment, and capital items)
    - Accessory equipment (tools and office equipment)
    - Supplies (paper clips, stationery, and other office supplies)
    - Service (maintenance and repair)

progress assessment

- What value enhancers may be included in a total product offer?
- What's the difference between a product line and a product mix?
- Name the four classes of consumer goods and services, and give examples of each.
- Describe three different types of industrial goods.

LEARNING goal 3 *

Summarize the functions of packaging.

PACKAGING CHANGES THE PRODUCT

We've said that consumers evaluate many aspects of the total product offer, including the brand. It's surprising how important packaging can be in such evaluations. Many companies have used packaging to change and improve their basic product. We have squeezable ketchup bottles that stand upside down; square paint cans with screw tops and integrated handles; plastic bottles for motor oil that eliminate the need for funnels; toothpaste pumps; packaged dinners and other foods, like popcorn, that can be cooked in a microwave oven; single-use packets of spices; and so forth.[22] Another interesting innovation is aromatic packaging. Arizona Beverage Company now has aromatic caps on its flavored iced teas.

In each case, the package changed the product in consumers' minds and opened large new markets. Do you sometimes have difficulty opening plastic packaging? Which packaging innovations do you like best? Can you see some market potential in developing better packaging? Packaging has even become a profession. Check out the Michigan State University School of Packaging, for example. Packages must perform the following functions:

1. Attract the buyer's attention.
2. Protect the goods inside, stand up under handling and storage, be tamperproof, and deter theft.
3. Be easy to open and use.
4. Describe and give information about the contents.
5. Explain the benefits of the good inside.
6. Provide information on warranties, warnings, and other consumer matters.
7. Give some indication of price, value, and uses.

Packaging can also make a product more attractive to retailers. The Universal Product Codes (UPCs) on many packages help stores control inventory. They combine a bar code and a preset number that gives the retailer information about the product's price, size, color, and other attributes. In short, packaging changes the product by changing its visibility, usefulness, or attractiveness.

Marketers have created innovative packages for everyday products that prove it's still possible to improve a good product with a great new idea. For example, Bumble Bee canned some of their cans and now offer tuna packaged in easy-to-open, resealable pouches. Has the new package changed your use of the product?

Even industrial products can benefit from innovative packaging. This foot-tall High-Tech C.F.O. Action Figure is a talking doll created by a design consulting firm in response to a client's request for a written report for business analysts. Long after a written report would have been filed, the Chief Financial Officer doll is still sitting on executives' desks. Can you think of other packaging innovations for office products?

▶ **LECTURE LINK 14-4:**
Frustration-Free Packaging Initiative

bundling
Grouping two or more products together and pricing them as a unit.

▶ **CRITICAL THINKING EXERCISE 14-1:**
Choosing a Brand Name

▶ **LECTURE LINK 14-5:**
The Most Valuable Brands

▶ **PPT 14-23:**
Understanding Branding

▶ **PPT 14-24:**
Key Brand Categories

▶ **CRITICAL THINKING EXERCISE 14-2:**
Most Valuable Global Brands

brand
A name, symbol, or design (or combination thereof) that identifies the goods or services of one seller or group of sellers and distinguishes them from the goods and services of competitors.

trademark
A brand that has exclusive legal protection for both its brand name and its design.

One relatively new packaging technology for tracking products is the radio frequency identification (RFID) chip, especially the ones made with nanoparticle powder.[23] When attached to a product, the chip sends out signals telling a company where the product is at all times. RFID chips carry more information than bar codes, don't have to be read one at a time (whole pallets can be read in an instant), and can be read at a distance. Wal-Mart has been a leader in using RFID technology.

The Growing Importance of Packaging

Packaging has always been an important aspect of the product offer, but today it's carrying more of the promotional burden than in the past. Many products once sold by salespersons are now sold in self-service outlets, and the package has acquired more sales responsibility. The Fair Packaging and Labeling Act was passed to give consumers much more quantity and value information on product packaging.

Packaging may make use of a strategy called **bundling**, which combines goods and/or services for a single price. Virgin Airlines has bundled door-to-door limousine service and in-flight massages in its total product offer. Financial institutions are offering everything from financial advice to help in purchasing insurance, stocks, bonds, mutual funds, and more. When combining goods or services into one package, marketers must not include so much that the price gets too high. It's best to work with customers to develop value enhancers that meet their individual needs.

LEARNING goal 4 ∗

Contrast *brand*, *brand name*, and *trademark*, and show the value of brand equity.

BRANDING AND BRAND EQUITY

A **brand** is a name, symbol, or design (or combination thereof) that identifies the goods or services of one seller or group of sellers and distinguishes them from the goods and services of competitors. The word *brand* includes practically all means of identifying a product. As we noted in Chapter 13, a *brand name* consists of a word, letter, or group of words or letters that differentiates one seller's goods and services from those of competitors.[24] Brand names you may be familiar with include Red Bull, Sony, Del Monte, Campbell, Levi's, Google, Borden, and Michelob. Brand names give products a distinction that tends to make them attractive to consumers. What's the number one brand name today? It's Google.[25]

A **trademark** is a brand that has exclusive legal protection for both its brand name and its design. Trademarks like McDonald's golden arches are widely recognized and help represent the company's reputation and image. McDonald's might sue to prevent a company from selling, say, McDonnel hamburgers. Did you know there are Starsbuck coffee shops in China? (Look closely at that name.)

People are often impressed by certain brand names, even though they say there's no difference between brands in a given product category. For example, even when people say that all aspirin is alike, if you put two aspirin bottles in front of them—one with the Anacin label and one with an unknown name—most choose the one with the well known brand name. Gasoline buyers often choose a brand name (e.g., Exxon) over price.[26]

For the buyer, a brand name ensures quality, reduces search time, and adds prestige to purchases. For the seller, brand names facilitate new-product introductions, help promotional efforts, add to repeat purchases, and differentiate products so that prices can be set higher. What brand names do you prefer?

Brand Categories

Several categories of brands are familiar to you. **Manufacturers' brand names** represent manufacturers that distribute products nationally—Xerox, Kodak, Sony, and Dell, for example.

Dealer (private-label) brands are products that don't carry the manufacturer's name but carry a distributor or retailer's name instead. Kenmore and Diehard are dealer brands sold by Sears. These brands are also known as *house brands* or *distributor brands*.

Many manufacturers fear having their brand names become generic names. A *generic name* is the name for a whole product category. Did you know that aspirin and linoleum were once brand names? So were nylon, escalator, kerosene, and zipper. All those names became so popular, so identified with the product, that they lost their brand status and became generic. (Such issues are decided in the courts.) Their producers then had to come up with new names. The original Aspirin, for example, became Bayer aspirin. Companies working hard to protect their brand names today include Xerox and Rollerblade (in-line skates).

Generic goods are nonbranded products that usually sell at a sizable discount compared to national or private-label brands. They feature basic packaging and are backed with little or no advertising. Some are of poor quality, but many come close to the same quality as the national brand-name goods they copy. There are generic tissues, generic cigarettes, generic drugs, and so on. Consumers today are buying large amounts of generic products because their overall quality has improved so much in recent years. What has been your experience trying generic products?

Knockoff brands are illegal copies of national brand-name goods. If you see an expensive brand-name item such as a Polo shirt or a Rolex watch for sale at a ridiculously low price, you can be pretty sure it's a knockoff.[27] Often the brand name is just a little off, too, like Palo (Polo) or Bolex (Rolex). Look carefully.

Whether it's contained in a name like Tide, a symbol like Nike's swoosh, a design like Coca-Cola's logo, or a combination of those, a brand distinguishes one marketer's goods and services from everyone else's. How do familiar brands influence consumers' choices of products every day?

manufacturers' brand names
The brand names of manufacturers that distribute products nationally.

dealer (private-label) brands
Products that don't carry the manufacturer's name but carry a distributor or retailer's name instead.

◀ **LECTURE LINK 14-6:**
Brand Management Icons

generic goods
Nonbranded products that usually sell at a sizable discount compared to national or private-label brands.

knockoff brands
Illegal copies of national brand-name goods.

THINKING green

Couldn't You Make a Smaller Footprint?

To help consumers make "green" choices, companies are putting carbon labels on products. Timberland shoes, for example, puts a card in each shoebox that provides a carbon rating of 0 to 10. A 0 rating means less than 2.5 kilograms of carbon and other greenhouse gases were emitted when the shoes were produced and shipped. If a shoe gets a 10 rating, its manufacture created as much carbon output as a car driven 240 miles.

The British-based grocery chain Tesco is in the process of putting carbon labels on all its products—from bags of parsley to flat-panel TVs. Boots, Britain's largest pharmaceutical chain, put up signs in the store explaining the carbon output from making its Botanics shampoo. Many other marketers are taking advantage of environmental awareness to help promote their products. Meanwhile, China continues to build coal-powered plants (about one per week), and India is building roads that will eventually allow millions of additional cars to go from city to city. Clearly, the focus on climate change varies greatly from country to country.

Do you pay attention to your carbon footprint? Are you doing anything to lower it? How do you feel about marketers using concern about climate change as a promotional device?

Source: Heather Green and Kerry Capell, "Carbon Confusion," *BusinessWeek*, March 17, 2008; George Anders, "Carbon-Market Concept Moves to Mainstream," *The Wall Street Journal*, May 14, 2008; Edward Taylor, "Start-Ups Race to Produce 'Green' Cars," *The Wall Street Journal*, May 6, 2008; and Kenneth T. Walsh, "Changing America's Energy Ways," *U.S. News & World Report*, April 2009.

▶ PPT 14-28:
Couldn't You Make a Smaller Footprint?

brand equity
The value of the brand name and associated symbols.

▶ LECTURE LINK 14-7:
Is Blackberry a Verb?

▶ PPT 14-25:
Key Brand Categories

brand loyalty
The degree to which customers are satisfied, like the brand, and are committed to further purchases.

brand awareness
How quickly or easily a given brand name comes to mind when a product category is mentioned.

▶ LECTURE LINK 14-8:
The Mystique of Coca-Cola

▶ PPT 14-26:
Establishing Brand Equity and Loyalty

▶ PPT 14-27:
Origins of Automobile Symbols

Generating Brand Equity and Loyalty

A major goal of marketers in the future will be to reestablish the notion of brand equity. **Brand equity** is the value of the brand name and associated symbols. Usually, a company cannot know the value of its brand until it sells it to another company.[28] Brand names with high reported brand equity ratings include Reynolds Wrap aluminum foil and Ziploc food bags. In the past, companies tried to boost their short-term performance by offering coupons and price discounts to move goods quickly. This eroded consumers' commitment to brand names, especially of grocery products. Now companies realize the value of brand equity, and are trying harder to measure the earning power of strong brand names.[29]

The core of brand equity is **brand loyalty**, the degree to which customers are satisfied, like the brand, and are committed to further purchases. A loyal group of customers represents substantial value to a firm, and that value can be calculated. One way manufacturers are trying to create more brand loyalty is by lowering the carbon footprint of their products.[30] The Thinking Green box explains this process.

Brand awareness refers to how quickly or easily a given brand name comes to mind when someone mentions a product category.[31] Advertising helps build strong brand awareness. Established brands, such as Coca-Cola and Pepsi, are usually among the highest in brand awareness. Sponsorship of events, like football's FedEx Orange Bowl and NASCAR's Nextel Cup Series, helps improve brand awareness. Simply being there over and over also increases brand awareness. That's one way Google became such a popular brand.[32]

Perceived quality is an important part of brand equity. A product that's perceived as having better quality than its competitors can be priced accordingly. The key to creating a perception of quality is to identify what consumers look for in a high-quality product, and then to use that information in every message the company sends out. Factors influencing the perception of quality include price, appearance, and reputation.

Consumers often develop *brand preference*—that is, they prefer one brand over another—because of such cues. When consumers reach the point of *brand insistence*, the product becomes a specialty good. For example, a consumer may insist on Goodyear tires for his or her car.

It's now so easy to copy a product's benefits that off-brand products can draw consumers away from brand-name goods. Brand-name manufacturers like Intel Corporation have to develop new products and new markets faster and promote their names better than ever before to hold off challenges from competitors.

Creating Brand Associations

The name, symbol, and slogan a company uses can assist greatly in brand recognition for that company's products. **Brand association** is the linking of a brand to other favorable images, like famous product users, a popular celebrity, or a particular geographic area. Note, for example, how ads for Mercedes-Benz and Buick associate those companies' cars with rich people who may spend their leisure time playing or watching golf or polo. Tiger Woods was once chosen as a spokesperson for Buick because of his popularity among golf fans. The person responsible for building brands is known as a brand manager or product manager. We'll discuss that position next.

brand association
The linking of a brand to other favorable images.

Brand Management

A **brand manager** (known as a *product manager* in some firms) has direct responsibility for one brand or product line, and manages all the elements of its marketing mix: product, price, place, and promotion. Thus, you might think of the brand manager as the president of a one-product firm.

One reason many large consumer-product companies created this position was to have greater control over new-product development and product promotion. Some companies have brand-management *teams* to bolster the overall effort. In B2B companies, brand managers are often known as product managers.

brand manager
A manager who has direct responsibility for one brand or one product line; called a *product manager* in some firms.

progress assessment

- What six functions does packaging now perform?
- What's the difference between a brand name and a trademark?
- Can you explain the difference between a manufacturer's brand, a dealer brand, and a generic brand?
- What are the key components of brand equity?

LEARNING goal 5 *

Explain the steps in the new-product development process.

THE NEW-PRODUCT DEVELOPMENT PROCESS

The odds a new product will fail are high. Over 80 percent of products introduced in any year fail to reach their business objectives. Not delivering what is promised is a leading cause of new-product failure. Other causes include poor

figure 14.3

THE NEW-PRODUCT DEVELOPMENT PROCESS
Product development is a six-stage process. Which stage do you believe to be the most important?

▶ **PPT 14-32:**
The New Product Development Process

▶ **LECTURE LINK 14-9:**
Top Ten New Products in History

▶ **PPT 14-33:**
Bringing New Products to the Market

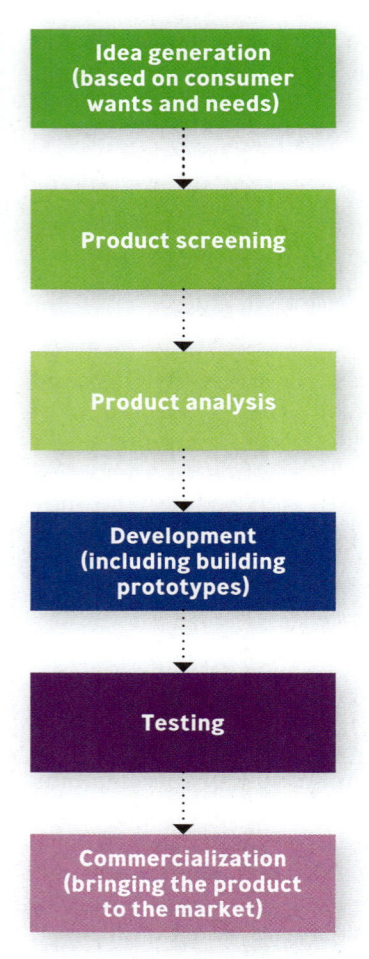

▶ **PPT 14-34:**
Bringing New Products to the Market

```
Idea generation
(based on consumer
wants and needs)
        ↓
Product screening
        ↓
Product analysis
        ↓
Development
(including building
prototypes)
        ↓
Testing
        ↓
Commercialization
(bringing the product
to the market)
```

product screening
A process designed to reduce the number of new-product ideas being worked on at any one time.

Tom Szaky of TerraCycle makes new products such as plant food, planters, pencil cases, and tote bags from discarded products made by other companies. (To see his bags made from drink pouches and Oreo cookie wrappers, go to www.teracycle.net.) Next could be computer bags from recycled billboards and possibly messenger bags from old film reels. What products do you own that are made of recycled material?

positioning, too few differences from competitors, and poor packaging. Small firms especially may experience a low success rate unless they do proper product planning and new product development. As Figure 14.3 shows, new-product development for producers consists of six stages.

New products continue to pour into the market every year, and their profit potential looks tremendous. Think, for example, of the potential of home video conferencing, interactive TV, Wii games and products, Internet-connected phones, iPads, and other innovations. Where do these ideas come from? How are they tested? What's the life span for an innovation? Let's look at these issues.

Generating New-Product Ideas

It now takes about seven ideas to generate one commercial product. Most ideas for new industrial products come from employee suggestions rather than research and development. Research and development, nonetheless, is a major source of new products. Employees are a major source for new consumer-goods ideas. Firms should also listen to their suppliers for new-product ideas because suppliers are often exposed to new ideas.

Product Screening

Product screening reduces the number of new-product ideas a firm is working on at any one time so it can focus on the most promising. *Screening* applies criteria to determine whether the product fits well with present products, has good profit potential, and is marketable. The company may assign each of these factors a weight and compute a total score for each new product so that it can compare their potentials.

Product Analysis

After product screening comes **product analysis**, or making cost estimates and sales forecasts to get a feeling for the profitability of new-product ideas. Products that don't meet the established criteria are withdrawn from consideration.

Product Development and Testing

If a product passes the screening and analysis phase, the firm begins to develop it further, testing many different product concepts or alternatives. A firm that makes packaged meat products may develop the concept of a chicken dog—a hot dog made of chicken that tastes like an all-beef hot dog. It will develop a prototype, or sample, so that consumers can try the taste.

Concept testing takes a product idea to consumers to test their reactions. Do they see the benefits of this new product? How frequently would they buy it? At what price? What features do they like and dislike? What changes in it would they make? The firm tests samples using different packaging, branding, and ingredients until a product emerges that's desirable from both production and marketing perspectives. As you plan for Very Vegetarian, can you see the importance of concept testing for new vegetarian dishes?

Commercialization

Even if a product tests well, it may take quite a while to achieve success in the market. Take the zipper, for example, the result of one of the longest development efforts on record for a consumer product. After Whitcomb Judson received the first patents for his clothing fastener in the early 1890s, it took more than 15 years to perfect the product—and even then consumers weren't interested. Judson's company suffered numerous financial setbacks, name changes, and relocations before settling in Meadville, Pennsylvania. Finally, the U.S. Navy started using zippers during World War I. Today, Talon Inc. is the leading U.S. maker of zippers, producing some 500 million of them a year.

The example of the zipper shows why the marketing effort must include **commercialization**, which includes (1) promoting the product to distributors and retailers to get wide distribution, and (2) developing strong advertising and sales campaigns to generate and maintain interest in the product among distributors and consumers. New products are now getting rapid exposure to global markets through commercialization on the Internet. Interactive Web sites enable consumers to view new products, ask questions, and make purchases easily and quickly.

How do firms test services? JetBlue gave mock air travel tickets to volunteers in order to test its new terminal and facilities at New York's JKF Airport as it prepared to move into the former TWA terminal. What features and benefits was JetBlue probably testing for?

product analysis
Making cost estimates and sales forecasts to get a feeling for profitability of new-product ideas.

concept testing
Taking a product idea to consumers to test their reactions.

commercialization
Promoting a product to distributors and retailers to get wide distribution, and developing strong advertising and sales campaigns to generate and maintain interest in the product among distributors and consumers.

LEARNING goal 6 *

Describe the product life cycle.

▶ PPT 14-35:
The Four Stages of a Product Life Cycle

product life cycle
A theoretical model of what happens to sales and profits for a product class over time; the four stages of the cycle are introduction, growth, maturity, and decline.

THE PRODUCT LIFE CYCLE

Once a product has been developed and tested, it goes to market. There it may pass through a **product life cycle** of four stages: introduction, growth, maturity, and decline (see Figure 14.4). This cycle is a *theoretical* model of what happens to sales and profits for a *product class* over time. However, not all individual products follow the life cycle, and particular brands may act differently. For example, while frozen foods as a generic class may go through the entire cycle, one brand may never get beyond the introduction stage. Some product classes, such as microwave ovens, stay in the introductory stage for years. Some products, like catsup, become classics and never experience decline. Others, such as fad clothing, may go through the entire cycle in a few months. Still others may be withdrawn from the market altogether. Nonetheless, the product life cycle may provide some basis for anticipating future market developments and for planning marketing strategies.

Example of the Product Life Cycle

▶ LECTURE LINK 14-10:
Extending the Life Cycle on a Roller Coaster

▶ LECTURE LINK 14-11:
Extending Sweethearts

▶ PPT 14-36:
Sales and Profits During the Product Life Cycle

The product life cycle can give marketers valuable clues to successfully promoting a product over time. Some products, like crayons and sidewalk chalk, have very long product life cycles, change very little, and never seem to go into decline. Crayola Crayons has been successful for 100 years!

You can see how the theory works by looking at the product life cycle of instant coffee. When it was introduced, most people didn't like it as well as

figure 14.4

SALES AND PROFITS DURING THE PRODUCT LIFE CYCLE

Note that profit levels start to fall *before* sales reach their peak. This is due to increasing price competition. When profits and sales start to decline, it's time to come out with a new product or to remodel the old one to maintain interest and profits.

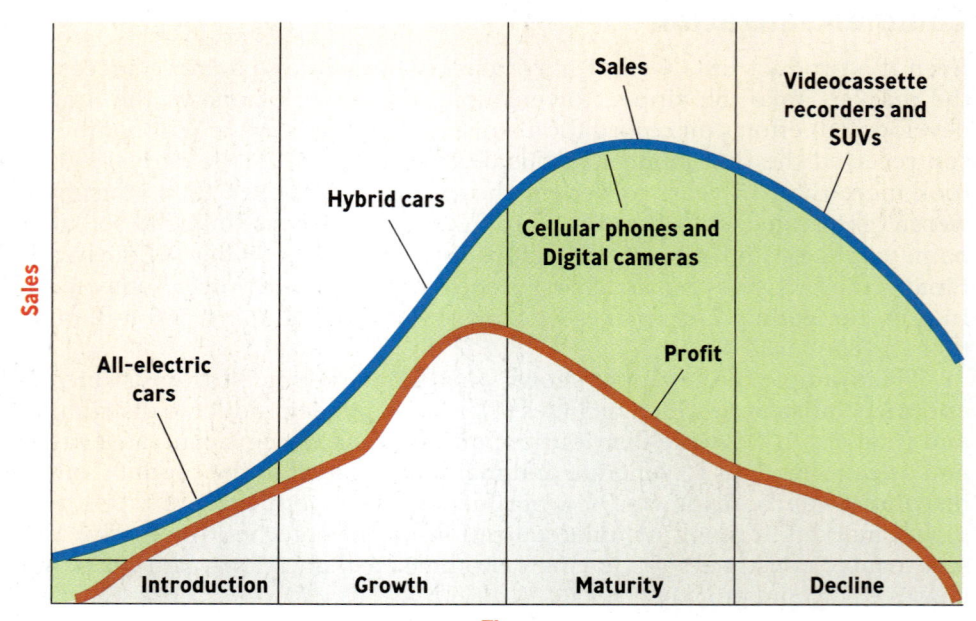

"regular" coffee, and it took several years for instant coffee to gain general acceptance (introduction stage). At one point, though, instant coffee grew rapidly in popularity, and many brands were introduced (growth stage). After a while, people became attached to one brand and sales leveled off (maturity stage). Sales then went into a slight decline when freeze-dried coffees were introduced (decline stage). Now freeze-dried coffee is, in turn, at the decline stage as consumers are buying fresh specialty beans from companies such as Starbucks and grinding them at home. It's extremely important for marketers to recognize what stage a product is in so that they can make intelligent and efficient marketing decisions about it.

Using the Product Life Cycle

Different stages in the product life cycle call for different marketing strategies. Figure 14.5 outlines the marketing mix decisions you might make. As you go through the figure, you'll see that each stage calls for multiple marketing mix changes. Remember, these concepts are largely theoretical and you should use them only as guidelines. We'll discuss the price strategies mentioned in the figure later in this chapter.

Figure 14.6 on p. 390 shows in theory what happens to sales volume, profits, and competition during the product life cycle. Compare it to Figure 14.4. Both figures show that product at the mature stage may reach the top in sales growth while profit is decreasing. At that stage, a marketing manager may decide to create a new image for the product to start a new growth cycle. You may have noticed how Arm & Hammer baking soda gets a new image every few years to generate new sales. One year it's positioned as a deodorant for refrigerators and the next as a substitute for harsh chemicals in swimming pools. Knowing what stage in the cycle a product has reached helps marketing managers decide when such strategic changes are needed.

figure 14.5

SAMPLE STRATEGIES FOLLOWED DURING THE PRODUCT LIFE CYCLE

LIFE CYCLE STAGE	PRODUCT	PRICE	PLACE	PROMOTION
Introduction	Offer market-tested product; keep mix small	Go after innovators with high introductory price (skimming strategy) or use penetration pricing	Use wholesalers, selective distribution	Dealer promotion and heavy investment in primary demand advertising and sales promotion to get stores to carry the product and consumers to try it
Growth	Improve product; keep product mix limited	Adjust price to meet competition	Increase distribution	Heavy competitive advertising
Maturity	Differentiate product to satisfy different market segments	Further reduce price	Take over wholesaling function and intensify distribution	Emphasize brand name as well as product benefits and differences
Decline	Cut product mix; develop new-product ideas	Consider price increase	Consolidate distribution; drop some outlets	Reduce advertising to only loyal customers

figure 14.6

HOW SALES, PROFITS, AND COMPETITION VARY OVER THE PRODUCT LIFE CYCLE
Theoretically, all products go through these stages at various times in their life cycle. What happens to sales as a product matures?

LIFE CYCLE STAGE	SALES	PROFITS	COMPETITORS
Introduction	Low sales	Losses may occur	Few
Growth	Rapidly rising sales	Very high profits	Growing number
Maturity	Peak sales	Declining profits	Stable number, then declining
Decline	Falling sales	Profits may fall to become losses	Declining number

> PPT 14-38:
> Progress Assessment

progress assessment

- What are the six steps in the new-product development process?
- What is the difference between product screening and product analysis?
- What are the two steps in commercialization?
- What is the theory of the product life cycle?

LEARNING goal 7 *

Identify various pricing objectives and strategies.

COMPETITIVE PRICING

> PPT 14-39:
> Pricing Objectives

Pricing is so important to marketing and the development of total product offers that it has been singled out as one of the four Ps in the marketing mix, along with product, place, and promotion. It's one of the most difficult of the four Ps for a manager to control, however, because price is such a critical ingredient in consumer evaluations of the product. In this section, we'll explore price both as an ingredient of the total product offer and as a strategic marketing tool.

Pricing Objectives

A firm may have several objectives in mind when setting a pricing strategy. When pricing a new vegetarian offering, we may want to promote the product's image. If we price it *high* and use the right promotion, maybe we can make it the Evian of vegetarian meals. We also might price it high to achieve a certain profit objective or return on investment. We could also price our product *lower* than its competitors, because we want low-income people to afford this healthy meal. That is, we could have some social or ethical goal in mind. Low pricing may also discourage competition because it reduces the profit potential, but it may help us capture a larger share of the market.

Thus a firm may have several pricing objectives over time, and it must formulate these objectives clearly before developing an overall pricing strategy. Popular objectives include the following:

1. *Achieving a target return on investment or profit.* Ultimately, the goal of marketing is to make a profit by providing goods and services to others. Naturally, one long-run pricing objective of almost all firms is to optimize profit.

2. *Building traffic.* Supermarkets often advertise certain products at or below cost to attract people to the store. These products are called *loss leaders*. The long-run objective is to make profits by following the short-run objective of building a customer base. The Internet portal Yahoo once provided a free auction service to compete with eBay. Why give such a service away? To increase advertising revenue on the Yahoo site and attract more people to Yahoo's other services.

3. *Achieving greater market share.* One way to capture a larger part of the market is to offer lower prices, low finance rates (like 0 percent financing), low lease rates, or rebates.

4. *Creating an image.* Certain watches, perfumes, and other socially visible products are priced high to give them an image of exclusivity and status.

5. *Furthering social objectives.* A firm may want to price a product low so people with little money can afford it. The government often subsidizes the price of farm products to keep basic necessities like milk and bread easily affordable.

A firm may have short-run objectives that differ greatly from its long-run objectives. Managers should understand both types at the beginning and put both into their strategic marketing plan. They should also set pricing objectives in the context of other marketing decisions about product design, packaging, branding, distribution, and promotion. All these marketing decisions are interrelated.

Intuition tells us the price charged for a product must bear some relationship to the cost of producing it. Prices usually *are* set somewhere above cost. But as we'll see, price and cost aren't always related. In fact, there are three major approaches to pricing strategy: cost-based, demand-based (target costing), and competition-based.

Cost-Based Pricing

Producers often use cost as a primary basis for setting price. They develop elaborate cost accounting systems to measure production costs (including materials, labor, and overhead), add in a margin of profit, and come up with a price. Picture the process in terms of producing a car. You add up all the various components—engine parts, body, tires, radio, door locks and windows, paint, and labor—add a profit margin, and come up with a price. The question is whether the price will be satisfactory to the market as well. How has the market responded to the prices of U.S. cars lately? In the long run, the market—not the producer—determines what the price will be (see Chapter 2). Pricing should take into account costs, but it should also include the expected costs of product updates, the marketing objectives for each product, and competitor prices. The Reaching Beyond Our Borders box discusses how difficult it is, at times, to adjust to new higher costs of materials when pricing goods.

Some products are priced high to create a high-status image of exclusivity and desirability. Patek Phillipe watches fall into this category. What is the total product offer for a product like this?

Demand-Based Pricing

Unlike cost-based pricing, **target costing** is demand-based. That means we design a product so it not only satisfies customers but also meets the profit

target costing
Designing a product so that it satisfies customers and meets the profit margins desired by the firm.

REACHING BEYOND our borders

www.chocologo.com

When Selling Sweets Goes Sour

Don Johnson owns Choco-Logo, a producer of gourmet chocolates in Buffalo, New York. He signed on with his global suppliers to a variable-price contract for chocolate. That meant that, as chocolate prices rose, Johnson's costs would rise as well. In fact, the price of chocolate rose 35 percent in one year! The prices of milk and sugar also rose dramatically. What do you do when your profit margin is about 10 percent?

One response to higher prices for supplies is to cut back on expenses. Johnson did that by using less expensive packaging and reducing the size of each box of chocolate. Another option is to lower the quality of the chocolate ingredient, but Johnson did not want to go that route because his firm was known for its quality. Of course, another option is to increase prices, but that is of limited effectiveness in a competitive marketing environment.

Johnson did turn to premium domestic suppliers and found one that was about 25 percent lower than his European source. He also tried different blends to keep the high-quality taste and lower the cost.

The moral of the story is this: Pricing goods and services is a dynamic process of constantly adjusting to fluctuations in the global price of supplies. The answer is never as easy as simply raising prices, because you might lose your customer base. Instead, you have to be creative and make all kinds of adjustments to keep quality high and prices reasonable.

Sources: Alex Salkever, "A Chocolate Maker Is Buffeted by Global Forces Beyond His Control," *Inc.*, April 2008; Rod Norland and Daniel Gross, "Now It's the $6 Loaf of Bread," *Newsweek*, May 5, 2008; and Joseph Weber, "Over a Buck for Dinner? Outrageous," *BusinessWeek*, March 9, 2009.

▶ PPT 14-40:
Pricing Strategies

▶ PPT 14-41:
When Selling Sweets Goes Sour

▶ CRITICAL THINKING EXERCISE 14-3:
Silky Skin Solution

competition-based pricing
A pricing strategy based on what all the other competitors are doing. The price can be set at, above, or below competitors' prices.

price leadership
The strategy by which one or more dominant firms set the pricing practices that all competitors in an industry follow.

margins we've set. Target costing makes the final price an *input* to the product development process, not an outcome of it. You first estimate the selling price people would be willing to pay for a product and then subtract your desired profit margin. The result is your target cost of production, or what you can spend to profitably produce the item. Imagine how you would use this process to make custom-made jewelry.

Competition-Based Pricing

Competition-based pricing is a strategy based on what all the other competitors are doing. The price can be at, above, or below competitors' prices. Pricing depends on customer loyalty, perceived differences, and the competitive climate. **Price leadership** is the strategy by which one or more dominant firms set pricing practices all competitors in an industry follow. You may have noticed that practice among oil companies.

Break-Even Analysis

Before you begin selling a new vegetarian sandwich, it may be wise to determine how many sandwiches you'd have to sell before making a profit. You'd then determine whether you could reach such a sales goal. **Break-even analysis** is the process used to determine profitability at various levels of sales. The break-even point is the point where revenues from sales equal all costs. The formula for calculating the break-even point is as follows:

$$\text{Break-even point (BEP)} = \frac{\text{Total fixed costs (FC)}}{\text{Price of one unit (P)} - \text{Variable costs (VC) of one unit}}$$

Total fixed costs are all the expenses that remain the same no matter how many products are made or sold. Among the expenses that make up fixed costs are the amount paid to own or rent a factory or warehouse and the amount paid for business insurance. **Variable costs** change according to the level of production. Included are the expenses for the materials used in making products and the direct costs of labor used in making those goods. For producing a specific product, let's say you have a fixed cost of $200,000 (for mortgage interest, real estate taxes, equipment, and so on). Your variable cost (e.g., labor and materials) per item is $2. If you sold the products for $4 each, the break-even point would be 100,000 items. In other words, you wouldn't make any money selling this product unless you sold more than 100,000 of them:

$$\text{BEP} = \frac{\text{FC}}{\text{P} - \text{VC}} = \frac{\$200,000}{\$4.00 - \$2.00} = \frac{\$200,000}{\$2.00} = 100,000 \text{ boxes}$$

Other Pricing Strategies

Let's say a firm has just developed a new line of products, such as Blu-ray players. The firm has to decide how to price these sets at the introductory stage of the product life cycle. A **skimming price strategy** prices a new product high, to recover research and development costs and make as much profit as possible while there's little competition. Of course, those large profits will eventually attract new competitors.

A second strategy is to price the new players low. Low prices will attract more buyers and discourage other companies from making sets because profits are slim. This **penetration strategy** enables the firm to penetrate or capture a large share of the market quickly.

Retailers use several pricing strategies. **Everyday low pricing (EDLP)** is the choice of Home Depot and Wal-Mart. They set prices lower than competitors and don't usually have special sales. The idea is to bring consumers to the store whenever they want a bargain rather than having them wait until there is a sale.

Department stores and some other retailers most often use a **high–low pricing strategy**. Regular prices are higher than at stores using EDLP, but during special sales they're lower. The problem with such pricing is that it encourages consumers to wait for sales, thus cutting into profits. As online shopping continues to grow, you may see fewer stores with a high–low strategy because consumers will be able to find better prices on the Internet.

Retailers can use price as a major determinant of the goods they carry. Some promote goods that sell only for 99 cents, or only for $10. Some of those 99-cent stores have raised their prices to over a dollar because of rising costs.[33]

You learned earlier in this chapter that bundling means grouping two or more products together and pricing them as a unit. For example, a store might price washers and dryers as a unit. Jiffy Lube offers an oil change and lube, checks your car's fluid levels and air pressure, and bundles all these services into one price.

Shoppers around the world look for bargains, as these consumers in Seoul, South Korea, are doing. How many different ways can marketers appeal to shoppers' desire to find the lowest price? Do online retailers adopt different pricing strategies?

psychological pricing
Pricing goods and services at price points that make the product appear less expensive than it is.

Psychological pricing means pricing goods and services at price points that make the product appear less expensive than it is. A house might be priced at $299,000 because that sounds like a lot less than $300,000.³⁴ Gas stations almost always use psychological pricing.

How Market Forces Affect Pricing

Recognizing that different consumers may be willing to pay different prices, marketers sometimes price on the basis of consumer demand rather than cost or some other calculation. That's called *demand-oriented pricing*, and you can observe it at movie theaters with low rates for children and drugstores with discounts for senior citizens. The Washington Opera Company in Washington, D.C., raised prices on prime seating and lowered them on less-attractive seats. This strategy raised the company's revenues 9 percent.

Marketers are facing a new pricing problem: Customers can now compare prices of many goods and services on the Internet, at Web sites like DealTime.com and MySimon.com. Priceline.com introduced consumers to a "demand collection system," in which buyers post the prices they are willing to pay and invite sellers to accept or decline the price. Consumers can get great prices on airlines, hotels, and other products by naming their price. They can also buy used goods online. Clearly, price competition is going to heat up as consumers have more access to price information from all around the world. As a result, nonprice competition is likely to increase.

NONPRICE COMPETITION

Marketers often compete on product attributes other than price. You may have noted that price differences are small for products like gasoline, candy bars, and even major products such as compact cars and private colleges.

You won't typically see price as a major promotional appeal on television. Instead, marketers tend to stress product images and consumer benefits such as comfort, style, convenience, and durability.

Many small organizations promote the services that accompany basic products rather than price in order to compete with bigger firms. Good service will enhance a relatively homogeneous product. Danny O'Neill, for example, is a small wholesaler who sells gourmet coffee to upscale restaurants. He has to watch competitors' prices *and* the services they offer so that he can charge the premium prices he wants. To charge high prices, he has to offer and then provide superior service. Larger companies often do the same thing. Some airlines stress friendliness, large "sleeping" seats, promptness, abundant flights, and other such services. Many hotels stress "no surprises," business services, health clubs, and other extras.

◄ CRITICAL THINKING EXERCISE 14-5:
Comparison Shopping Online

progress assessment

- Can you list two short-term and two long-term pricing objectives? Can the two be compatible?
- What are the limitations of a cost-based pricing strategy?
- What is psychological pricing?

◄ PPT 14-45:
Progress Assessment

summary

Learning Goal 1: Describe a total product offer.
- **What's included in a total product offer?**

A total product offer consists of everything consumers evaluate when deciding whether to buy something. It includes price, brand name, and satisfaction in use.
- **What's the difference between a product line and a product mix?**

A product line is a group of physically similar products with similar competitors. A product line of gum may include bubble gum and sugarless gum. A product mix is a company's combination of product lines. A manufacturer may offer lines of gum, candy bars, and breath mints in its product mix.
- **How do marketers create product differentiation for their goods and services?**

Marketers use a combination of pricing, advertising, and packaging to make their products seem unique and attractive.

Learning Goal 2. Identify the various kinds of consumer and industrial goods.
- **What are consumer goods?**

Consumer goods are sold to ultimate consumers like you and me for personal use.
- **What are the four classifications of consumer goods and services, and how are they marketed?**

There are convenience goods and services (requiring minimum shopping effort); shopping goods and services (for which people search and compare price and quality); specialty goods and services (which consumers go out of their way to get, and for which they often demand specific brands); and unsought goods and services (products consumers are unaware of, haven't thought of buying, or need to solve an unexpected problem). Convenience goods and services are best promoted by location, shopping goods and services by some price/quality appeal, and specialty goods and services by specialty magazines and interactive Web sites.
- **What are industrial goods, and how are they marketed differently from consumer goods?**

Industrial goods are products sold in the business-to-business (B2B) market and used in the production of other products. They're sold largely through salespeople and rely less on advertising.

Learning Goal 3. Summarize the functions of packaging.
- **What are the seven functions of packaging?**

Packaging must (1) attract the buyer's attention; (2) protect the goods inside, stand up under handling and storage, be tamperproof, and deter theft; (3) be easy to open and use; (4) describe the contents; (5) explain the benefits of the good inside; (6) provide information about warranties, warnings, and other consumer matters; and (7) indicate price, value, and uses. Bundling means grouping two or more products into a unit, through packaging, and charging one price for them.

Learning Goal 4. Contrast *brand*, *brand name*, and *trademark*, and show the value of brand equity.
- **Can you define brand, brand name, and trademark?**

A *brand* is a name, symbol, or design (or combination thereof) that identifies the goods or services of one seller or group of sellers and distinguishes them from the goods and services of competitors. The word *brand* includes all means of identifying a product. A *brand name* consists of a word, letter, or group of words or letters that differentiates one seller's goods and services from those of competitors. A *trademark* is a brand that has exclusive legal protection for both its brand name and design.
- **What is brand equity, and how do managers create brand associations?**

Brand equity is the value of a brand name and associated symbols. Brand association is the linking of a brand to other favorable images such as product users, a popular celebrity, or a geographic area.
- **What do brand managers do?**

Brand managers coordinate product, price, place, and promotion decisions for a particular product.

Learning Goal 5. Explain the steps in the new-product development process.
- **What are the six steps of the product development process?**

The steps of product development are (1) generation of new-product ideas, (2) product screening, (3) product analysis, (4) development, (5) testing, and (6) commercialization.

Learning Goal 6. Describe the product life cycle.
- **What is the product life cycle?**

The product life cycle is a theoretical model of what happens to sales and profits for a product class over time.
- **What are the four stages in the product life cycle?**

The four product life cycle stages are introduction, growth, maturity, and decline.

Learning Goal 7. Identify various pricing objectives and strategies.
- **What are pricing objectives?**

Pricing objectives include achieving a target profit, building traffic, increasing market share, creating an image, and meeting social goals.
- **What strategies can marketers use to determine a product's price?**

A skimming strategy prices the product high to make big profits while there's little competition. A penetration strategy uses low price to attract more customers and discourage competitors. Demand-oriented pricing starts with consumer demand rather than cost. Competition-oriented pricing is based on all competitors' prices. Price leadership occurs when all competitors follow the pricing practice of one or more dominant companies.

- **What is break-even analysis?**
Break-even analysis is the process used to determine profitability at various levels of sales. The break-even point is the point where revenues from sales equal all costs.
- **Why do companies use nonprice strategies?**
Pricing is one of the easiest marketing strategies to copy. It's often not a good long-run competitive tool.

key terms

brand 382
brand association 385
brand awareness 384
brand equity 384
brand loyalty 384
brand manager 385
break-even analysis 393
bundling 382
commercialization 387
competition-based pricing 392
concept testing 387
convenience goods and services 378
dealer (private-label) brands 383
everyday low pricing (EDLP) 393
generic goods 383
high–low pricing strategy 393
industrial goods 380
knockoff brands 383
manufacturers' brand names 383
penetration strategy 393
price leadership 392
product analysis 387
product differentiation 378
product life cycle 388
product line 377
product mix 377
product screening 386
psychological pricing 394
shopping goods and services 378
skimming price strategy 393
specialty goods and services 379
target costing 391
total fixed costs 393
total product offer 375
trademark 382
unsought goods and services 379
value 374
variable costs 393

connect interactive applications

Reinforcing Your *Connect*ion to Concepts in Business

This chapter offers 15 interactive applications designed to help you apply what you've learned (examples of these exercises appear below). Your instructor has determined which interactive applications will benefit you throughout this course. Please refer to your instructor's assignment list in *Connect* to determine which applications you should complete.

Comprehension Case Interactive:
From a strategic marketing viewpoint, a product is more than just the physical good or service. A total product offer consists of everything consumers evaluate when deciding whether to buy something. The basic product or service may be a cell phone or a hotel room, but the total product offer includes other aspects of the good or service. Review the case regarding Apple's Web site and answer the questions.

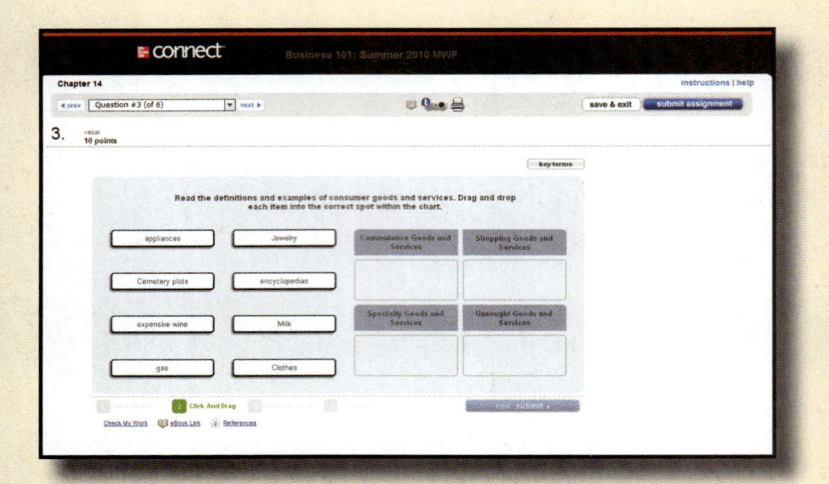

Click and Drag Interactive: The most accepted method of classifying consumer goods and services is based on consumer buying behavior. This method divides consumer goods and services into four general categories: convenience, shopping, specialty, and unsought. Evaluate the definition of each consumer good or service category and match it to the appropriate example of products.

Video Case Interactive: Companies like Clorox have learned that adapting products to new competition and new markets is an ongoing need. With the amount of attention being given to the "green" concept, Clorox has introduced new products to meet the wants and needs of the consumer. An organization must constantly monitor changing consumer wants and needs and adapt to them. Watch the video case featuring Clorox and respond to the questions when prompted.

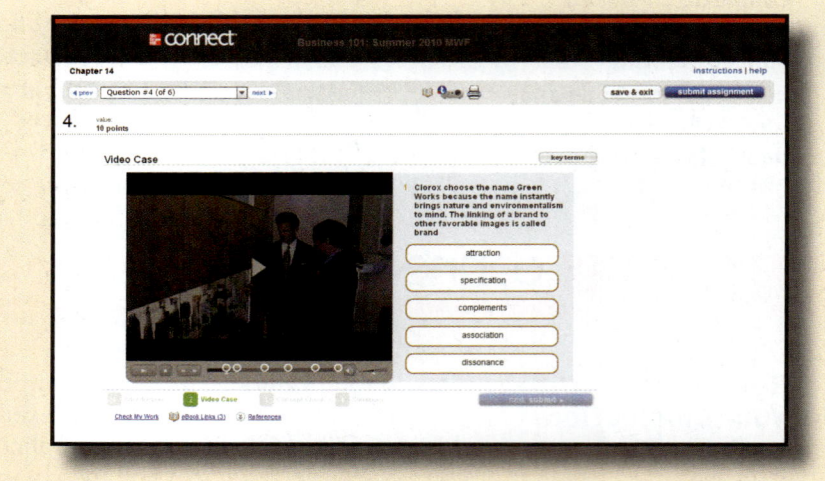

Click and Drag Interactive: For producers, new product development consists of six stages that begin with an idea and end with the commercialization of the idea. Order each step in the product development process.

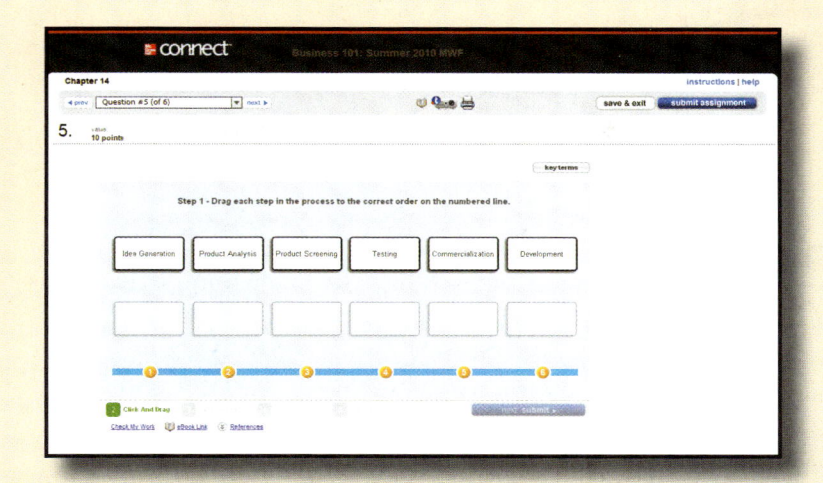

Click and Drag Interactive: The product life cycle may provide some basis for anticipating future market development and for planning marketing strategies. Different stages in the product life cycle call for different marketing strategies. Evaluate each company and determine where they fall within the product development cycle.

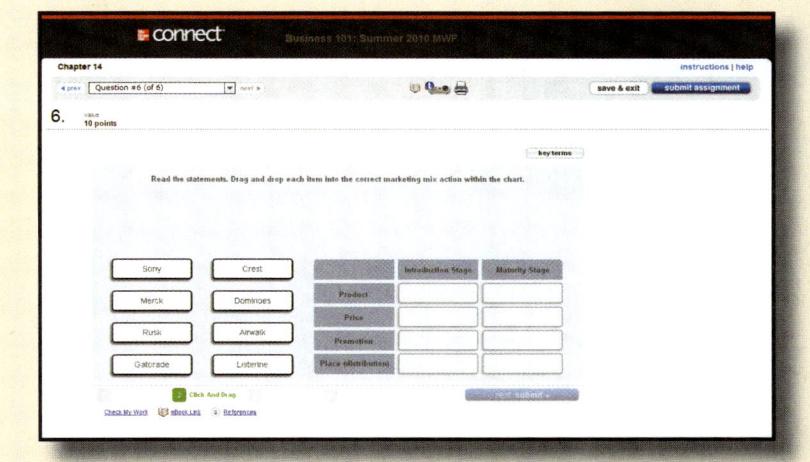

15

DISTRIBUTING Products

profile

Getting to Know
x Mark Stern
of Doggypads.com

Mark Stern knows what it means to find a need and fill it. In his case, the need was for high-quality doggy housebreaking pads at wholesale prices. Where do you go to find such a product? Stern sought out Chinese manufacturers and found what he wanted. The next step was to create a Web site so that customers could place orders online. Orders began pouring in, so Stern rented a 3,000-square-foot warehouse. The only problem was that dealing with storage, inventory, and shipping took all his time. He wanted to spend more time on quality control and marketing.

Stern went to the Internet to find product fulfillment companies that would manage warehousing and shipping functions for him. They turned out to be too expensive. He continued his search until he found a company called Shipwire Inc., a leader in Internet-delivered storage and shipping services.

Stern trusted the company to handle his distribution functions. Now he takes orders, processes the payment, and sends the order to Shipwire. Shipwire does all the rest: inventory keeping, order processing, and delivery. Delivery usually takes just a few days. Stern enjoys the ability to ship from multiple sites in Los Angeles, Chicago, Reno, Toronto, and East Sussex, England. He can handle more orders than before and recover costs related to damaged or undelivered shipments. He still orders from manufacturers, who send the products directly to Shipwire. Thanks to Shipwire, Stern was able to get rid of his warehouse, cut insurance and other inventory-related costs, and reduce his staff.

Shipwire's operations are easy to understand. For a monthly fee, starting at $29.95 for 16 cubic feet of space

LEARNING goals

After you have read and studied this chapter, you should be able to

1. Explain the concept of marketing channels and their value.
2. Demonstrate how intermediaries perform the six marketing utilities.
3. Identify the types of wholesale intermediaries in the distribution system.
4. Compare the distribution strategies retailers use.
5. Explain the various kinds of nonstore retailing.
6. Explain the various ways to build cooperation in channel systems.
7. Describe logistics and outline how intermediaries manage the transportation and storage of goods.

connect™

Your *Connect*ion to Better Learning. 1. View the interactive presentation. 2. Practice through LearnSmart. 3. Apply your knowledge by using the interactive applications for each chapter of this text.

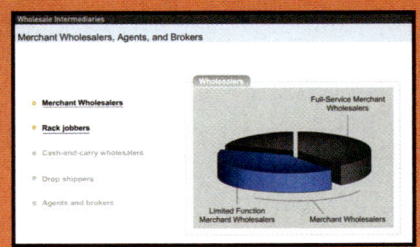

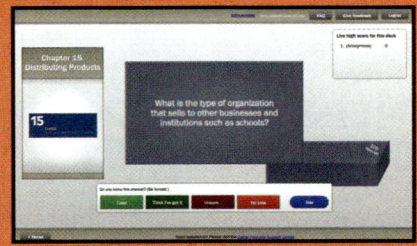

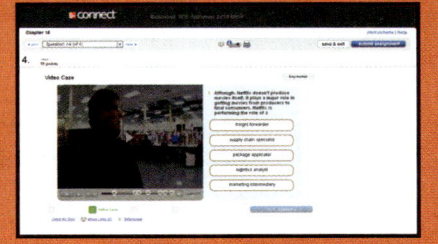

1 Prep »»»»» **2 Study** »»»»» **3 Apply**

---

spread out among its warehouses, companies get storage and delivery services. Some 30,000 online stores have integrated Shipwire's services into their e-commerce sites. You'll learn more about marketing intermediaries such as Shipwire in this chapter.

Marketing's four Ps are product, place, promotion, and price. This chapter is all about *place*. The place function goes by many names, including shipping, warehousing, distribution, logistics, and supply-chain management. We'll explore all these concepts in this chapter so that you can have a much better understanding of the many steps required to get products from the mine to the factory, or from the producer to the consumer.

Sources: "Shipwire Helps Doggypads.com Clean Up Mess That Came with Success," Business Wire, November 27, 2007; Heather Clancy, "Web Site Shipping 2.0," *Entrepreneur*, April 2008; "Shipwire Makes It Easy for E-Tailers to Expand into Europe Using Its New UK Warehouse," Business Wire, June 9, 2008; and www.doggypads.com, accessed May 2010.

www.doggypads.com

NAME THAT company

▶ **PPT 15-1:** Distributing Products
▶ **PPT 15-2:** Mark Stern
▶ **LECTURE LINK 15-1:** Why There are No Indian Wal-Marts

One company in the United States is known for having low prices always. One way it keeps prices low is by eliminating the wholesaler and doing the wholesale function itself. What is the name of the company? (Find the answer in the chapter.)

marketing intermediaries Organizations that assist in moving goods and services from producers to businesses (B2B) and from businesses to consumers (B2C).

▶ **PPT 15-3:** What are Marketing Intermediaries?

channel of distribution A whole set of marketing intermediaries, such as agents, brokers, wholesalers, and retailers, that join together to transport and store goods in their path (or channel) from producers to consumers.

▶ **PPT 15-4:** What are Marketing Intermediaries?

Distribution warehouses store goods until they are needed. Have you ever thought about the benefits of having food, furniture, clothing, and other needed goods close at hand?

LEARNING goal 1 *

Explain the concept of marketing channels and their value.

THE EMERGENCE OF MARKETING INTERMEDIARIES

It's easy to overlook distribution and storage in marketing, where the focus is often on advertising, selling, marketing research, and other functions. But it doesn't take much to realize how important distribution is. Imagine the challenge Timberland faces of getting raw materials together, making 12 million pairs of shoes, and then distributing those shoes to stores throughout the world. That's what thousands of manufacturing firms—making everything from automobiles to toys—have to deal with every day.

Fortunately there are hundreds of thousands of companies and individuals whose job it is to help move goods from the raw-material state to producers and then on to consumers. Then, as is often the case, the products are sent from consumers to recyclers and back to manufacturers or assemblers.[1] Did you know that only 20 percent of plastic water bottles are recycled?[2] See the Spotlight on Small Business box for more on recycling.

Managing the flow of goods has become one of the most important managerial functions for many organizations.[3] Let's look at how this function is carried out.

Marketing intermediaries (once called *middlemen*) are organizations that assist in moving goods and services from producers to businesses (B2B) and from businesses to consumers (B2C). They're called intermediaries because they're in the middle of a series of organizations that join together to help distribute goods from producers to consumers. A **channel of distribution** consists of a whole set of marketing intermediaries, such as agents, brokers, wholesalers, and retailers, that join together to transport and store goods in their path (or channel) from producers

SPOTLIGHT ON SMALL business

www.copart.com

Recycling Is Part of the Whole Supply-Chain Process

What happens to cars that are destroyed in a wreck or a natural disaster? Where do stolen cars go if they are recovered after the insurance settlement? How do buyers learn about the availability of such cars? The answers to these questions involve a company called Copart Inc., in Fairfield, California, that sells damaged cars and used parts.

Copart's customers are mostly rebuilders, licensed dismantlers, and used-car dealers and exporters. Copart offers them an Internet auction for cars and parts. It has over 110 facilities in the United States and Canada, and also provides services such as towing and storage.

Copart processes many of the cars salvaged in the United States. Because of its reputation, it is able to attract major sellers like State Farm. Kemper Auto and Home Group uses Copart exclusively to sell its salvaged vehicles. And over 20 percent of Copart's sales are made overseas, to countries as far away as Cambodia and the United Arab Emirates. Victor Viaden lives in Minsk, Belarus. He spotted a 1995 Ford Probe on the Copart Web site and bought it for $150. He paid $3,500 to transport it to Belarus, fixed it up, and sold it for $4,500.

Companies such as Copart remind us that the supply-chain process doesn't end until the materials used are recycled into other goods.

Sources: Copart, www.copart.com, accessed, June 2010; and Carey Wilson, "Where Does It Go?" *Quality Digest*, March 2008.

---

to consumers. **Agents/brokers** are marketing intermediaries who bring buyers and sellers together and assist in negotiating an exchange but don't take title to the goods—that is, at no point do they own the goods. Think of real estate agents as an example.

A **wholesaler** is a marketing intermediary that sells to other organizations, such as retailers, manufacturers, and hospitals. Wholesalers are part of the B2B system. Because of high distribution costs, Wal-Mart has been trying to eliminate independent wholesalers from its system and do the job itself.[4] That is, Wal-Mart provides its own warehouses and has its own trucks. Finally, a **retailer** is an organization that sells to ultimate consumers (people like you and me).

Channels of distribution help ensure communication flows *and* the flow of money and title to goods. They also help ensure that the right quantity and assortment of goods will be available when and where needed. Figure 15.1 on p. 404 shows selected channels of distribution for both consumer and industrial goods.

You can see the distribution system in the United States at work when you drive down any highway and see the thousands of trucks and trains moving goods from here to there. Less visible, however, are the many distribution warehouses that store goods until they are needed. Have you ever thought about the benefits of having food, furniture, and other needed goods close at hand? Have you seen distribution warehouses along the road as you drive from town to town?

Why Marketing Needs Intermediaries

Figure 15.1 shows that some manufacturers sell directly to consumers. So why have marketing intermediaries at all? The answer is that intermediaries perform certain marketing tasks—such as transporting, storing, selling, advertising, and relationship building—faster and more cheaply than most manufacturers could. Here's a simple analogy: You could personally deliver

---

agents/brokers
Marketing intermediaries who bring buyers and sellers together and assist in negotiating an exchange but don't take title to the goods.

wholesaler
A marketing intermediary that sells to other organizations.

retailer
An organization that sells to ultimate consumers.

403

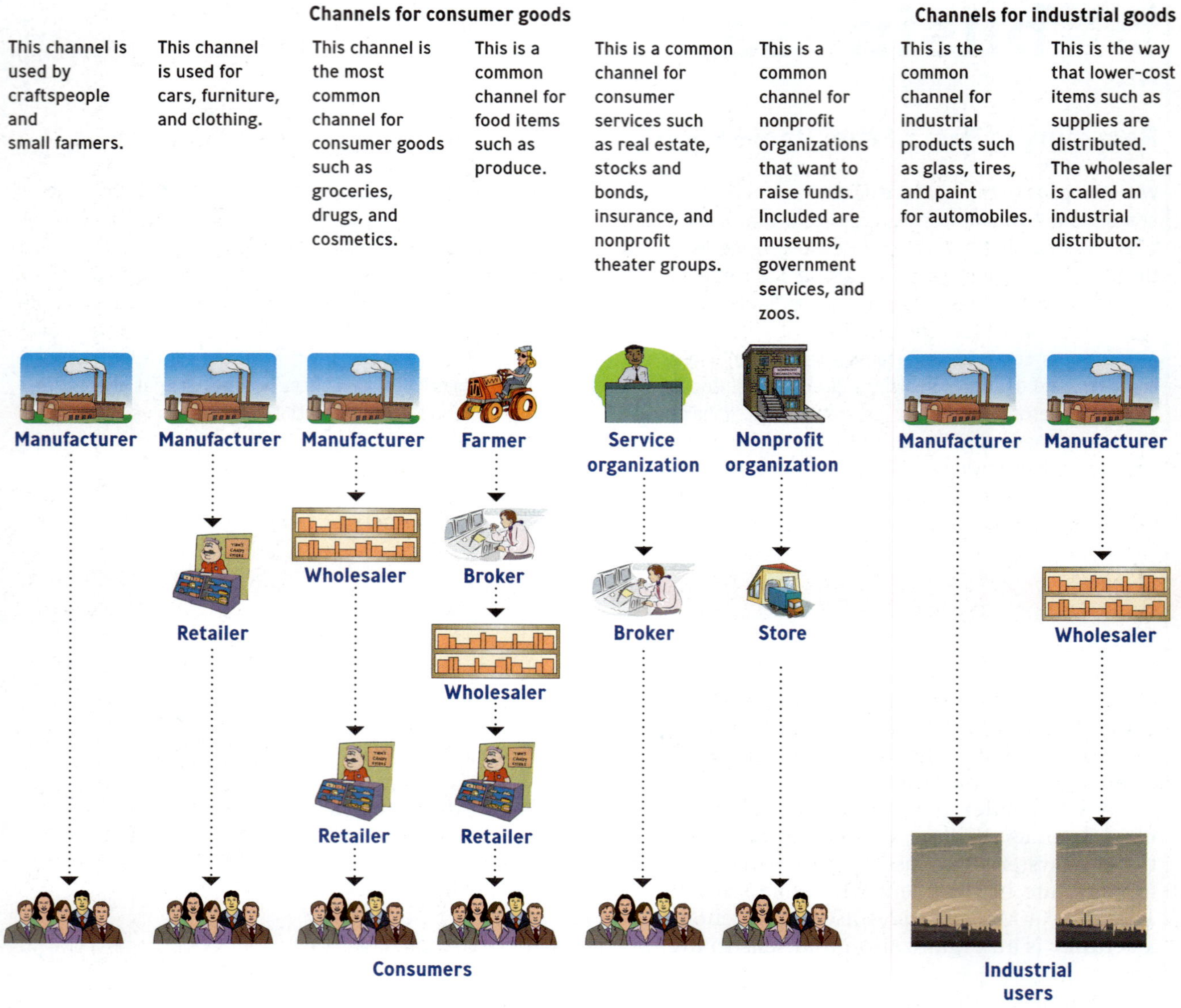
Channels for consumer goods
This channel is used by craftspeople and small farmers.
This channel is used for cars, furniture, and clothing.
This channel is the most common channel for consumer goods such as groceries, drugs, and cosmetics.
This is a common channel for food items such as produce.
This is a common channel for consumer services such as real estate, stocks and bonds, insurance, and nonprofit theater groups.
This is a common channel for nonprofit organizations that want to raise funds. Included are museums, government services, and zoos.
Channels for industrial goods
This is the common channel for industrial products such as glass, tires, and paint for automobiles.
This is the way that lower-cost items such as supplies are distributed. The wholesaler is called an industrial distributor.
Manufacturer
Manufacturer
Manufacturer
Farmer
Service organization
Nonprofit organization
Manufacturer
Manufacturer
Retailer
Wholesaler
Broker
Broker
Store
Wholesaler
Wholesaler
Retailer
Retailer
Consumers
Industrial users

figure 15.1

SELECTED CHANNELS OF DISTRIBUTION FOR CONSUMER AND INDUSTRIAL GOODS AND SERVICES

PPT 15-7: Selected Channels of Distribution for Consumer and Industrial Goods and Services

packages to people anywhere in the world, but usually you don't. Why not? Because it's generally cheaper and faster to have them delivered by the U.S. Postal Service or a private firm such as UPS or FedEx.

Similarly, you could sell your home by yourself or buy stock directly from individual companies, but you probably wouldn't. Why? Again, because agents and brokers are marketing intermediaries who make the exchange process more efficient and easier. In the next section, we'll explore how intermediaries improve the efficiency of various exchanges.

How Intermediaries Create Exchange Efficiency

BONUS CASE 15-1: United Stationers: Office Supply Intermediary

Here is an easy way to see the benefits of using marketing intermediaries. Suppose five manufacturers of various food products each tried to sell directly to five retailers. The number of exchange relationships needed to create this market is 5 times 5, or 25.

But picture what happens when a wholesaler enters the system. The five manufacturers each contact the wholesaler, establishing five exchange

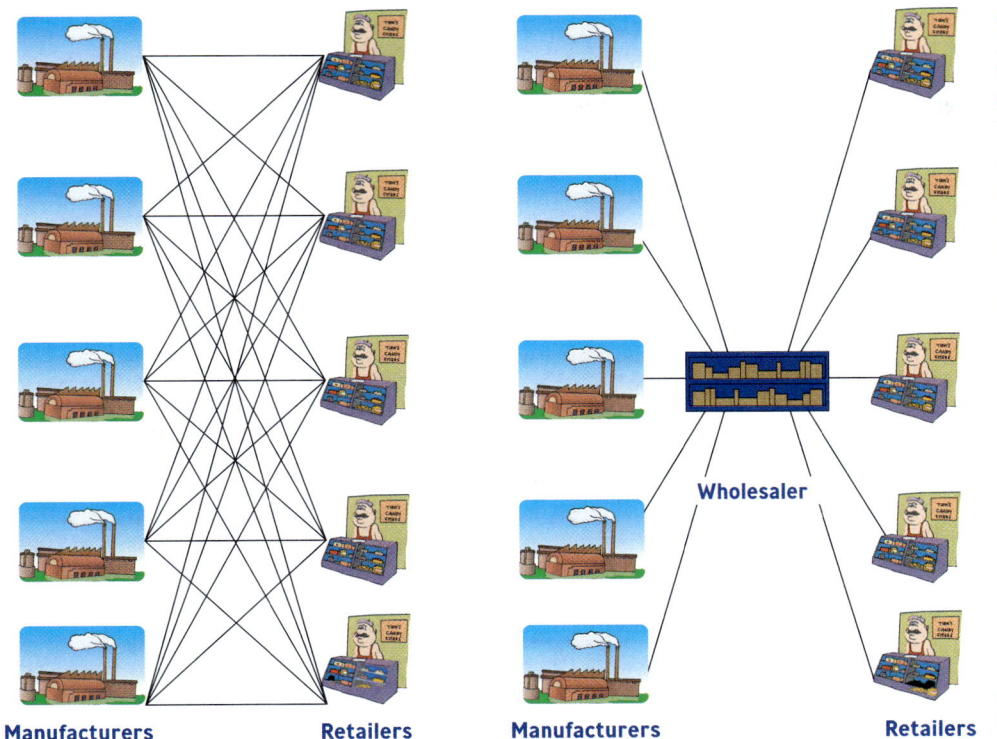

figure 15.2

HOW INTERMEDIARIES CREATE EXCHANGE EFFICIENCY

This figure shows that adding a wholesaler to the channel of distribution cuts the number of contacts from 25 to 10. This improves the efficiency of distribution.

Manufacturers   **Retailers**   **Manufacturers**   **Wholesaler**   **Retailers**

◀ PPT 15-9:
How Intermediaries Create Exchange Efficiency

◀ PPT 15-10:
Three Key Facts About Marketing Intermediaries

relationships. The wholesaler then establishes contact with the five retailers, creating five more exchange relationships. The wholesaler's existence reduces the number of exchanges from 25 to only 10. Figure 15.2 shows this process.

Some economists have said that intermediaries add *costs* and should be eliminated. Marketers say intermediaries add *value*, and that the *value greatly exceeds the cost*. Let's explore this debate and see what value intermediaries provide.

The Value versus the Cost of Intermediaries

The public has often viewed marketing intermediaries with a degree of suspicion. Some surveys show about half the cost of what we buy is marketing costs that go largely to pay for the work of intermediaries. If we could only get rid of intermediaries, people reason, we could greatly reduce the cost of everything we buy. Sounds good, but is the solution really that simple?

Take a box of cereal that sells for $4. How could we, as consumers, get the cereal for less? Well, we could all drive to Michigan, where some cereal is produced, and save shipping costs. But imagine millions of people getting in their cars and driving to Michigan just to buy cereal. No, it doesn't make sense. It's much cheaper to have intermediaries bring the cereal to major cities. That might make transportation and warehousing by wholesalers necessary. These steps add cost, don't they? Yes, but they add value as well—the value of not having to drive to Michigan.

The cereal is now in a warehouse somewhere on the outskirts of the city. We could all drive down to the wholesaler and pick it up. But that still isn't the most economical way to buy cereal. If we figure in the cost of gas and time, the cereal will again be too expensive. Instead, we prefer to have someone move the cereal from the warehouse to a truck, drive it to the corner supermarket, unload it, unpack it, price it, shelve it, and wait for us to come in to buy it. To make it even more convenient, the supermarket may stay open for 24 hours a day, seven days a week. Think of the costs. But think also of the value! For $4, we can get a box of cereal *when* we want it, and with little effort.

If we were to get rid of the retailer, we could buy a box of cereal for slightly less, but we'd have to drive farther and spend time in the warehouse looking through rows of cereals. If we got rid of the wholesaler, we could save a little more money, not counting our drive to Michigan. But a few cents here and there add up—to the point where distribution (marketing) may add up to 75 cents for every 25 cents in manufacturing costs. Figure 15.3 shows where your money goes in the distribution process. The largest percentage goes to people who drive trucks and work in wholesale and retail organizations. Note that only 3.5 cents goes to profit.

Here are three basic points about intermediaries:

1. Marketing intermediaries can be eliminated, but their activities can't; that is, you can eliminate some wholesalers and retailers, but then consumers or someone else would have to perform the intermediaries' tasks, including transporting and storing goods, finding suppliers, and establishing communication with suppliers.
2. Intermediary organizations have survived because they perform marketing functions faster and more cheaply than others can. To maintain their competitive position in the channel, they now must adopt the latest technology.[5] That includes search engine optimization, social networking (on sites like Facebook), and analyzing Web site statistics to understand their customers better.[6]
3. Intermediaries add costs to products, but these costs are usually more than offset by the values they create.

> **PPT 15-11:**
> Distribution's Effect on Your Food Dollar

figure 15.3

DISTRIBUTION'S EFFECT ON YOUR FOOD DOLLAR
Note that the farmer gets only 25 cents of your food dollar. The bulk of your money goes to intermediaries to pay distribution costs. Their biggest cost is labor (truck drivers, clerks), followed by warehouses and storage.

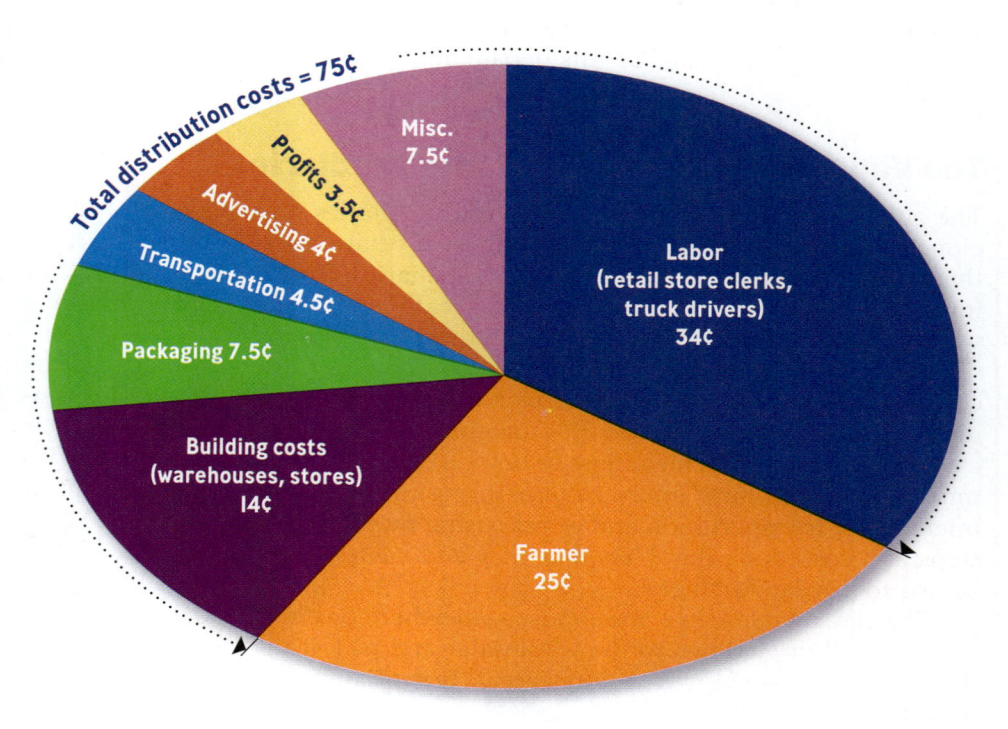

Total distribution costs = 75¢
- Misc. 7.5¢
- Profits 3.5¢
- Advertising 4¢
- Transportation 4.5¢
- Packaging 7.5¢
- Building costs (warehouses, stores) 14¢
- Farmer 25¢
- Labor (retail store clerks, truck drivers) 34¢

LEARNING goal 2 *

Demonstrate how intermediaries perform the six marketing utilities.

THE UTILITIES CREATED BY INTERMEDIARIES

Utility, in economics, is the want-satisfying ability, or value, that organizations add to goods or services by making them more useful or accessible to consumers than they were before. The six kinds of utility are form, time, place, possession, information, and service. Although producers provide some utilities, marketing intermediaries provide most. Let's look at how.

Form Utility

Traditionally, producers rather than intermediaries have provided form utility (see Chapter 9) by changing raw materials into useful products. Thus, a farmer who separates the wheat from the chaff and the processor who turns the wheat into flour are creating form utility. Retailers and other marketers sometimes provide form utility as well. For example, retail butchers cut pork chops from a larger piece of meat and trim off the fat. The servers at Starbucks make coffee just the way you want it. Dell assembles computers according to customers' wishes.

Time Utility

Intermediaries, such as retailers, add **time utility** to products by making them available when consumers need them. Devar Tennent lives in Boston. One winter evening while watching TV with his brother, Tennent suddenly got the urge for a hot dog and a Coke. The problem was, there were no hot dogs or Cokes in the house.

Devar ran down to the corner delicatessen and bought some hot dogs, buns, Cokes, and potato chips. He also bought some frozen strawberries and ice cream. Devar was able to get these groceries at midnight because the local deli was open 24 hours a day. That's time utility. You can buy goods at any time on the Internet, but you can't beat having them available right around the corner *when you want them*. On the other hand, note the value an Internet company provides by staying accessible 24 hours a day.

Place Utility

Intermediaries add **place utility** to products by placing them *where* people want them. While traveling through the badlands of South Dakota, Juanita Ruiz got hungry and thirsty. There are no stores for miles in this part of the country, but Juanita saw signs along the road saying a 7-Eleven was ahead. Following the signs, she stopped at the store for refreshments. She also bought some sunglasses and souvenir items there. The goods and services provided by 7-Eleven are in a convenient place for vacationers. Throughout the United States, 7-Eleven stores remain popular because they are usually in easy-to-reach locations. They provide place utility. As more and more sales become global, place utility will grow in importance.

◀ CRITICAL THINKING EXERCISE 15-2:
Forms of Utility

utility
In economics, the want-satisfying ability, or value, that organizations add to goods or services.

◀ PPT 15-12:
Intermediaries Create Utility

time utility
Adding value to products by making them available when they're needed.

◀ PPT 15-13:
How Marketers Use Utility

place utility
Adding value to products by having them where people want them.

◀ PPT 15-14:
How Marketers Use Utility

Think of how many stores provide time utility by making goods and services available to you 24 hours a day, seven days a week. Have you ever needed to renew a prescription late at night or needed a late night snack? Can you see how time utility offers added value?

> **LECTURE LINK 15-2:**
Whatever Happened to Door-to-Door Delivery?

possession utility
Doing whatever is necessary to transfer ownership from one party to another, including providing credit, delivery, installation, guarantees, and follow-up service.

> **PPT 15-15:**
How Marketers Use Utility

information utility
Adding value to products by opening two-way flows of information between marketing participants.

> **PPT 15-16:**
Progress Assessment

service utility
Adding value by providing fast, friendly service during and after the sale and by teaching customers how to best use products over time.

Possession Utility

Intermediaries add **possession utility** by doing whatever is necessary to transfer ownership from one party to another, including providing credit. Activities associated with possession utility include delivery, installation, guarantees, and follow-up service. Larry Rosenberg wanted to buy a nice home in the suburbs. He found just what he wanted, but he didn't have the money he needed. So he went with the real estate broker to a local savings and loan and borrowed money to buy the home. Both the real estate broker and the savings and loan are marketing intermediaries that provide possession utility. For those who don't want to own goods, possession utility makes it possible for them to use goods through renting or leasing.

Information Utility

Intermediaries add **information utility** by opening two-way flows of information between marketing participants. Jerome Washington couldn't decide what kind of TV set to buy. He looked at various ads in the newspaper, talked to salespeople at several stores, and read material at the library and on the Internet. Newspapers, salespeople, libraries, Web sites, and government publications are all information sources made available by intermediaries. They provide information utility.

Service Utility

Intermediaries add **service utility** by providing fast, friendly service during and after the sale and by teaching customers how to best use products over time. Sze Leung bought a personal computer for his home office. Both the computer manufacturer and the retailer Leung used continue to offer help whenever he needs it. He also gets software updates for a small fee to keep his computer up-to-date. What attracted Leung to the retailer in the first place was the helpful, friendly service he received from the salesperson in the store. Service utility is rapidly becoming the most important utility for many retailers, because without it they would lose business to direct marketing (e.g., marketing by catalog or on the Internet). Can you see how the Internet can provide some forms of service utility?

Service after the sale is one of the contributing factors to Apple's success. Customers can call to make an appointment with an Apple Genius who will help them learn how to use their computers or iPods. How does this service add value to Apple's products?

progress assessment

- What is a channel of distribution, and what intermediaries participate in it?
- Why do we need intermediaries? Illustrate how intermediaries create exchange efficiency. How would you defend intermediaries to someone who said getting rid of them would save consumers millions of dollars?
- Can you give examples of the utilities intermediaries create and how they provide them?

LEARNING goal 3 *

Identify the types of wholesale intermediaries in the distribution system.

WHOLESALE INTERMEDIARIES

Let's distinguish wholesaling from retailing, and clearly define the functions of each. Some producers deal only with wholesalers and won't sell directly to retailers or to end users (consumers). Some producers deal with both wholesalers and retailers but give wholesalers a bigger discount. In turn, some wholesalers sell to both retailers and consumers. The office superstore Staples is a good example. It sells office supplies to small businesses and to consumers as well. Warehouse clubs such as Sam's Club and Costco are other companies with both wholesale and retail functions.

The difference is this: A *retail sale* is the sale of goods and services to consumers *for their own use*. A *wholesale sale* is the sale of goods and services to businesses and institutions like schools or hospitals *for use in the business*, or to wholesalers or retailers *for resale*.

Wholesalers make business-to-business sales. Most people are not as familiar with the various kinds of wholesalers as they are with retailers. Let's explore some of these helpful wholesale intermediaries. Most of them provide a lot of marketing jobs and offer you a good opportunity.

Merchant Wholesalers

Merchant wholesalers are independently owned firms that take title to the goods they handle. About 80 percent of wholesalers fall in this category. There are two types of merchant wholesalers: full-service and limited-function. *Full-service wholesalers* perform all the distribution functions (see Figure 15.4 on p. 410). *Limited-function wholesalers* perform only selected functions, but try to do them especially well. Three common types of limited-function wholesalers are rack jobbers, cash-and-carry wholesalers, and drop shippers.

Rack jobbers furnish racks or shelves full of merchandise like music, toys, hosiery, and health and beauty aids to retailers. They display the products and sell them on consignment, meaning they keep title to the goods until they're sold and then share the profits with the retailer. Have you seen shelves at the supermarket full of CDs and related items? Rack jobbers likely put them there.

Cash-and-carry wholesalers serve mostly smaller retailers with a limited assortment of products. Traditionally, retailers went to such wholesalers, paid cash, and carried the goods back to their stores—thus the term *cash-and-carry*. Today, stores such as Staples allow retailers and others to use credit cards for wholesale purchases. Thus the term *cash-and-carry* is becoming obsolete for wholesalers.

Drop shippers solicit orders from retailers and other wholesalers and have the merchandise shipped directly from a producer to a buyer. They own the merchandise but don't handle, stock, or deliver it. That's done by the producer. Drop shippers tend to handle bulky products such as coal, lumber, and chemicals.

◄ PPT 15-17:
Wholesale Intermediaries

◄ LECTURE LINK 15-3:
What Intermediaries to Use When Going International

◄ PPT 15-18:
Types of Wholesale Intermediaries

◄ CRITICAL THINKING EXERCISE 15-3:
Distribution Channels

merchant wholesalers
Independently owned firms that take title to the goods they handle.

rack jobbers
Wholesalers that furnish racks or shelves full of merchandise to retailers, display products, and sell on consignment.

◄ PPT 15-19:
Types of Limited-Function Wholesalers

cash-and-carry wholesalers
Wholesalers that serve mostly smaller retailers with a limited assortment of products.

drop shippers
Wholesalers that solicit orders from retailers and other wholesalers and have the merchandise shipped directly from a producer to a buyer.

figure 15.4

A FULL-SERVICE WHOLESALER

A FULL-SERVICE WHOLESALER WILL:	THE WHOLESALER MAY PERFORM THE FOLLOWING SERVICES FOR CUSTOMERS:
1. Provide a sales force to sell the goods to retailers and other buyers.	1. Buy goods the end market will desire and make them available to customers.
2. Communicate manufacturers' advertising deals and plans.	2. Maintain inventory, thus reducing customers' costs.
3. Maintain inventory, thus reducing the level of the inventory suppliers have to carry.	3. Transport goods to customers quickly.
4. Arrange or undertake transportation.	4. Provide market information and business consulting services.
5. Provide capital by paying cash or quick payments for goods.	5. Provide financing through granting credit, which is especially critical to small retailers.
6. Provide suppliers with market information they can't afford or can't obtain themselves.	6. Order goods in the types and quantities customers desire.
7. Undertake credit risk by granting credit to customers and absorbing any bad debts, thus relieving the supplier of this burden.	
8. Assume the risk for the product by taking title.	

Source: Thomas C. Kinnear, *Principles of Marketing*, 4th ed., © 1995, p. 394. Reprinted by permission of Pearson Education, Inc., Upper Saddle River, NJ.

Agents and brokers are a familiar type of intermediary. Typically they don't take possession of the goods they sell. A real estate broker, for instance, facilitates the transaction between seller and buyer but never holds title to the house. What functions does a realtor provide in a home sale?

▶ **PPT 15-20:**
Roles of Agents and Brokers

▶ **LECTURE LINK 15-4:**
How Retailers Compete

Agents and Brokers

Agents and brokers bring buyers and sellers together and assist in negotiating an exchange. However, unlike merchant wholesalers, agents and brokers never own the products they distribute. Usually they do not carry inventory, provide credit, or assume risks. While merchant wholesalers earn a profit from the sale of goods, agents and brokers earn commissions or fees based on a percentage of the sales revenues. Agents maintain long-term relationships with the people they represent, whereas brokers are usually hired on a temporary basis.

Agents who represent producers are either *manufacturer's agents* or *sales agents*. As long as they do not carry competing products, manufacturer's agents may represent several manufacturers in a specific territory. They often work in the automotive supply, footwear, and fabricated steel industries. Sales agents represent a single producer in a typically larger territory.

Brokers have no continuous relationship with the buyer or seller. Once they negotiate a contract between the parties, their relationship ends. Producers of seasonal products like fruits and vegetables often use brokers, as does the real estate industry.

LEARNING goal 4 *

Compare the distribution strategies retailers use.

RETAIL INTERMEDIARIES

A retailer, remember, is a marketing intermediary, like a supermarket, that sells to ultimate consumers. The United States boasts approximately 2.3 million retail stores, not including retail Web sites. Retail organizations employ more than 11 million people and are one of the major employers of marketing graduates. The recent recession has affected retailers, forcing many to cut back on employees.[7] Figure 15.5 lists, describes, and gives examples of various kinds of retailers. Have you shopped in each kind of store? What seem to be the advantages of each? Would you enjoy working in a retail store of some kind? Some retailers seem to compete mostly on price, but others, such as specialty stores, use variety as a competitive tool. Marketers use several strategies for retail distribution. We explain them next.

PPT 15-21: Retailing in the U.S.

PPT 15-22: Top Online Retailers

PPT 15-23: Fastest Growing Retail Categories

CRITICAL THINKING EXERCISE 15-4: Retail Distribution Strategy

Retail Distribution Strategy

Because different products call for different retail distribution strategies, a major decision marketers must make is selecting the right retailers to sell their products. There are three categories of retail distribution: intensive, selective, and exclusive.

PPT 15-24: Types of Retail Stores

figure 15.5

TYPES OF RETAIL STORES

TYPE	DESCRIPTION	EXAMPLE
Department store	Sells a wide variety of products (clothes, furniture, housewares) in separate departments	Sears, JCPenney, Nordstrom
Discount store	Sells many different products at prices generally below those of department stores	Wal-Mart, Target
Supermarket	Sells mostly food with other nonfood products such as detergent and paper products	Safeway, Kroger, Albertson's
Warehouse club	Sells food and general merchandise in facilities that are usually larger than supermarkets and offer discount prices; membership may be required	Costco, Sam's Club
Convenience store	Sells food and other often-needed items at convenient locations; may stay open all night	7-Eleven
Category killer	Sells a huge variety of one type of product to dominate that category of goods	Toys "R" Us, Bass Proshops, Office Depot
Outlet store	Sells general merchandise directly from the manufacturer at a discount; items may be discontinued or have flaws ("seconds")	Nordstrom Rack, Liz Claiborne, Nike, TJ Maxx
Specialty store	Sells a wide selection of goods in one category	Jewelry stores, shoe stores, bicycle shops

> **intensive distribution**
> Distribution that puts products into as many retail outlets as possible.

> **selective distribution**
> Distribution that sends products to only a preferred group of retailers in an area.

> **exclusive distribution**
> Distribution that sends products to only one retail outlet in a given geographic area.

▶ **PPT 15-25:**
Retail Distribution Strategies

▶ **PPT 15-26:**
Pick a Strategy

▶ **PPT 15-27:**
Progress Assessment

▶ **CRITICAL THINKING EXERCISE 15-6:**
Internet Auctions: Bypassing the Retailer

▶ **PPT 15-28:**
Forms of Nonstore Retailing

▶ **BONUS CASE 15-2:**
Starting an Online Business

> **electronic retailing**
> Selling goods and services to ultimate customers (e.g., you and me) over the Internet.

Intensive distribution puts products into as many retail outlets as possible, including vending machines. Products that need intensive distribution include convenience goods such as candy, cigarettes, gum, and popular magazines.

Selective distribution uses only a preferred group of the available retailers in an area. Such selection helps ensure producers of quality sales and service. Manufacturers of appliances, furniture, and clothing (shopping goods) use selective distribution.

Exclusive distribution is the use of only one retail outlet in a given geographic area. The retailer has exclusive rights to sell the product and is therefore likely to carry a large inventory, give exceptional service, and pay more attention to this brand than to others. Luxury auto manufacturers often use exclusive distribution, as do producers of specialty goods such as skydiving equipment and fly-fishing products.

progress assessment

- Describe the activities of rack jobbers and drop shippers.
- What kinds of products would call for each of the different distribution strategies: intensive, selective, exclusive?

LEARNING goal 5 *

Explain the various kinds of nonstore retailing.

NONSTORE RETAILING

Nothing else in retailing has received more attention recently than electronic retailing. Internet retailing is just one form of nonstore retailing. Other categories are telemarketing; vending machines, kiosks, and carts; direct selling; multilevel marketing; and direct marketing. Small businesses can use nonstore retailing to open up new channels of distribution for their products.

Electronic Retailing

Electronic retailing consists of selling goods and services to ultimate consumers over the Internet. Thanks to Web site improvements and discounting, online retail sales reached $204 billion in 2008.[8] But getting customers is only half the battle. The other half is delivering the goods, providing helpful service, and keeping your customers. When electronic retailers lack sufficient inventory or fail to deliver goods on time (especially at holidays and other busy periods), customers often give up and go back to brick-and-mortar stores.

Most Internet retailers now offer e-mail order confirmation. But sometimes they are less good at handling complaints, accepting returns, and providing personal help. Some are improving customer service by adding help buttons that lead customers to real-time online assistance from a human employee.

Old brick-and-mortar stores that add online outlets are sometimes called brick-and-click stores. They allow customers to choose which shopping technique suits them best. Most companies that want to compete in the future will probably need both a real store and an online presence to provide consumers with all the options they want.

Traditional retailers like Sears have learned that selling on the Internet calls for a new kind of distribution. Sears's warehouses were accustomed to delivering truckloads of goods to the company's retail outlets. But they were not prepared to deliver to individual consumers, except for large orders like furniture and appliances. It turns out, therefore, that both traditional and Internet retailers have to develop new distribution systems to meet the demands of today's Internet-savvy shoppers. It's often easy to sell goods and services on eBay, but there is always the need to distribute those goods. Most people outsource that function to FedEx or UPS, which have the needed expertise.[9]

Telemarketing

Telemarketing is the sale of goods and services by telephone. Some 80,000 companies use it to supplement or replace in-store selling and complement online selling. Many send a catalog to consumers, who order by calling a toll-free number. Many electronic retailers provide a help feature online that serves the same function.

Vending Machines, Kiosks, and Carts

Vending machines dispense convenience goods when consumers deposit sufficient money. They carry the benefit of location—they're found in airports, office buildings, schools, service stations, and other areas where people want convenience items. In Japan, they sell everything from bandages and face cloths to salads and spiced seafood. Vending by machine will be an interesting area to watch as more innovations are introduced in the United States. U.S. vending machines are already selling iPods, Bose headphones, sneakers, digital cameras, and DVD movies.

Carts and kiosks have lower overhead costs than stores do, so they can offer lower prices on items such as T-shirts, purses, watches, and cell phones.[10] You often see vending carts outside stores or along walkways in malls. Many mall owners love them because they're colorful and create a marketplace atmosphere. Kiosk workers often dispense coupons and helpful product information. You may have noticed airlines are using kiosks to speed the process of getting on the plane. Most provide a boarding pass and allow you to change

> Many brick-and-mortar stores have added Internet services for the added convenience of their customers. Some people shop online and then go to the store to buy the merchandise. Others both shop and buy on the Internet. What motivates you to shop at a store rather than online? What are the advantages and disadvantages of shopping and buying on the Internet?

telemarketing
The sale of goods and services by telephone.

◄ LECTURE LINK 15-5:
The Cost of Violating the "Do Not Call" Registration Law

◄ LECTURE LINK 15-6:
Party On

your seat. Many kiosks serve as gateways to the Internet, so in one place consumers can shop at a store and still have access to all the products available on the Internet. What's your reaction to such kiosks?

Direct Selling

Direct selling reaches consumers in their homes or workplaces. Because so many men and women work outside the home and aren't in during the day, companies that use direct selling are sponsoring parties at workplaces or evenings and weekends. Major users of this sales category include cosmetics producers and vacuum cleaner manufacturers. Trying to copy their success, other businesses are venturing into direct selling with lingerie, artwork, and candles sold at house parties they sponsor. Some companies, however, such as those in encyclopedia sales, have dropped most of their direct selling efforts in favor of Internet selling.

Multilevel Marketing

Over 1,000 U.S. companies have had success using multilevel marketing (MLM) and salespeople who work as independent contractors. One of the most successful MLM firms today is called Team. It sells MonaVie, a fruit juice in a wine bottle for $39. Salespeople earn commissions on their own sales, create commissions for the "upliners" who recruited them, and receive commissions from any "downliners" they recruit to sell. When you have hundreds of downliners—people recruited by the people you recruit—your commissions can be sizable. Some people make tens of thousands of dollars a month this way. That doesn't mean you should get involved with such schemes. More often than not, people at the bottom buy the products themselves and sell a bare minimum to others.[11]

The main attraction of multilevel marketing for employees, other than the potential for making money, is the low cost of entry. For a small investment, the average person can start up a business and begin recruiting others. Many people question MLM because some companies using it have acted unethically.[12] Potential employees must be very careful to examine the practices of such firms.[13] Nonetheless, MLM's sales of $30 billion a year demonstrate the potential for success in this form of marketing.

Direct Marketing

Direct marketing includes any activity that directly links manufacturers or intermediaries with the ultimate consumer. One of the fastest-growing types of retailing, it includes direct mail, catalog sales, and telemarketing as well as online marketing. Popular consumer catalog companies that use direct marketing include Coldwater Creek, L. L. Bean, and Lands' End (now owned by Sears). Direct marketing has created tremendous competition in some high-tech areas as well.

Direct marketing has become popular because shopping from home or work is more convenient for consumers than going to stores. Instead of driving to a mall, people can shop in catalogs and advertising supplements in the newspaper and then buy by phone, mail, or computer. Interactive online selling is expected to provide increasing competition for retail stores.

Vending machines and kiosks are convenient and easy for customers to use. They also have lower overhead than stores do. What do stores provide that kiosks and vending machines don't?

direct selling
Selling to consumers in their homes or where they work.

▶ PPT 15-29:
Forms of Nonstore Retailing

▶ BONUS CASE 15-3:
Multilevel Marketing

▶ PPT 15-30:
What We Need

direct marketing
Any activity that directly links manufacturers or intermediaries with the ultimate consumer.

▶ PPT 15-31:
Come Back Again!

▶ PPT 15-32:
Retail Web Sites with the Lowest Customer Rating

Direct marketing took on a new dimension with *interactive video*. Producers now provide all kinds of information on CD-ROMs or Web sites. Consumers can ask questions, seek the best price, and order goods and services—all online. Companies that use interactive video have become major competitors for those who market through paper catalogs.

To offer consumers the maximum benefit, marketing intermediaries must work together to ensure a smooth flow of goods and services.[14] There hasn't always been total harmony in the channel of distribution. As a result, channel members have created systems to make the flows more efficient. We'll discuss those next.

◄ CRITICAL THINKING EXERCISE 15-5:
Careers in Distribution

LEARNING goal 6 *

Explain the various ways to build cooperation in channel systems.

corporate distribution system
A distribution system in which all of the organizations in the channel of distribution are owned by one firm.

contractual distribution system
A distribution system in which members are bound to cooperate through contractual agreements.

BUILDING COOPERATION IN CHANNEL SYSTEMS

One way traditional retailers can compete with online retailers is to be so efficient that online retailers can't beat them on cost—given the need for customers to pay for delivery. That means manufacturers, wholesalers, and retailers must work closely to form a unified system. How can manufacturers get wholesalers and retailers to cooperate in such a system? One way is to link the firms in a formal relationship. Four systems have emerged to tie firms together: corporate systems, contractual systems, administered systems, and supply chains.

Corporate Distribution Systems

In a **corporate distribution system** one firm owns all the organizations in the channel of distribution. If the manufacturer owns the retail firm, clearly it can maintain a great deal of control over its operations. Sherwin Williams, for example, owns its own retail stores and coordinates everything: display, pricing, promotion, inventory control, and so on.

Franchisors like Chocolate Chocolate Chocolate Company use a contractual distribution system that requires franchisees to follow the franchisors' rules and procedures. How does such a system ensure consistent quality and level of service?

Contractual Distribution Systems

If a manufacturer can't buy retail stores, it can try to get retailers to sign a contract to cooperate with it. In a **contractual distribution system** members are bound to cooperate through contractual agreements. There are three forms of contractual systems:

1. *Franchise systems* such as McDonald's, KFC, Baskin-Robbins, and AAMCO. The franchisee agrees to all the rules, regulations, and procedures established by the franchisor. This results in the consistent quality and level of service you find in most franchised organizations.

2. *Wholesaler-sponsored chains* such as Ace Hardware and IGA food stores. Each store signs an agreement to use the same name, participate in chain promotions, and cooperate as a unified system of stores, even though each is independently owned and managed.

3. *Retail cooperatives* such as Associated Grocers. This arrangement is much like a wholesaler-sponsored chain except it is initiated by the retailers. The same degree of cooperation exists, and the stores remain independent. Normally in such a system, retailers agree to focus their purchases on one wholesaler, but cooperative retailers could also purchase a wholesale organization to ensure better service.

Administered Distribution Systems

If you were a producer, what would you do if you couldn't get retailers to sign an agreement to cooperate? You might manage all the marketing functions yourself, including display, inventory control, pricing, and promotion. A system in which producers manage all the marketing functions at the retail level is called an **administered distribution system**. Kraft does that for its cheeses. Scott does it for its seed and other lawn care products. Retailers cooperate with producers in such systems because they get a great deal of free help. All the retailer has to do is ring up the sale.

Supply Chains

A **supply chain (or value chain)** consists of all the linked activities various organizations must perform to move goods and services from the source of raw materials to ultimate consumers.[15] A supply chain is longer than a channel of distribution because it includes links from suppliers to manufacturers, whereas the channel of distribution begins with manufacturers. Channels of distribution are part of the overall supply chain (see Figure 15.6).

Included in the supply chain are farmers, miners, suppliers of all kinds (parts, equipment, supplies), manufacturers, wholesalers, and retailers. **Supply-chain management** is the process of managing the movement of raw materials, parts, work in progress, finished goods, and related information through all the organizations in the supply chain; managing the return of such goods if necessary; and recycling materials when appropriate.[16]

One complex supply chain is that for the automaker Kia's Sorento model. The Sorento is assembled in South Korea and made of over 30,000 components from all over the world. The shock and front-loading system is from AF Sachs AG, the front-wheel drive is from BorgWarner, and the tires are from Michelin. Airbags are sometimes flown in from Swedish company Autoliv Inc., which makes them in Utah.[17] As you can see, supply-chain management is interfirm and international. To learn about how large companies have learned to distribute their products to very small overseas outlets, see the Reaching Beyond Our Borders box.

figure 15.6
THE SUPPLY CHAIN

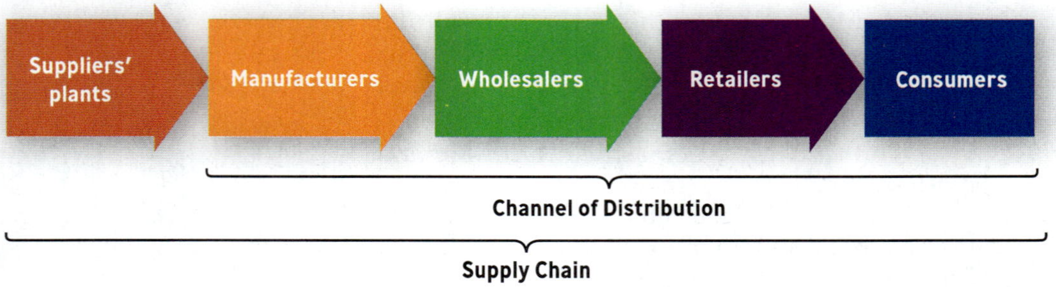

Suppliers' plants → Manufacturers → Wholesalers → Retailers → Consumers

Channel of Distribution: Manufacturers through Consumers
Supply Chain: Suppliers' plants through Consumers

REACHING BEYOND our borders

How to Reach the Little Guy

One of the things some people notice when traveling to a less developed country is how many small entrepreneurs there are. These retailers may set up a small shop on any available plot of land, soon to be joined by many more. They usually charge more than supermarkets and department stores, but they are very convenient, often have close ties with the community, and may sell individual cigarettes and other items not found in larger stores. They also serve more than 80 percent of the developing world's population. How do you reach such stores with products like Coke and Hershey bars?

Coca-Cola used its Peruvian bottler, the Lindley Group, but a local competitor charged lower prices. The Lindley Group eventually outsourced its entire distribution function to local wholesalers that had lower costs and knew the local market better. The Lindley Group then taught those wholesalers how to set up sales routes and use sales management techniques. It also taught them how to use information technology, including cheap cell phones. As a result, distribution costs were cut by a third.

Distributing goods in overseas markets the same way as in the United States has proved foolish and unproductive. Both Coke and Pepsi have done pilot studies to learn how to market to smaller businesses in less developed countries. They've gone on to use the best new practices in other countries.

Sources: Carlos Niezen and Julio Rodriquez, "Distribution Lessons from Mom and Pop," *Harvard Business Review*, April 2008; Jean-Louis Warnholz, "Even the Poorest Can Be a Thriving Market," *Harvard Business Review*, May 2008; Jennifer L. Schenker, "A Solar-Powered Night-Light for the Poor," *BusinessWeek*, July 28, 2008; and Rajiv Shah, "Planting Seeds for Self Sufficiency," World Ark, March/April 2009.

Companies like SAP, PeopleSoft, i2, and Manugistics have developed software to coordinate the movement of goods and information so that producers can translate consumer wants into products with the least amount of materials, inventory, and time. Firms can move parts and information so smoothly, they look like one firm.[18]

Computers make such links possible. Naturally, the systems are quite complex and expensive, but they can pay for themselves in the long run because of inventory savings, customer service improvement, and responsiveness to market changes. Because such systems are so effective and efficient, they are sometimes called *value chains* instead of supply chains.

Not all supply chains are as efficient as they can be.[19] Some companies have struggled with high distribution costs, including the cost of gas, inefficient truck routes, and excess inventory.[20] The complexity of supply-chain management often leads firms to outsource the whole process to experts that know how to integrate it. Richardson Electronics of La Fox, Illinois, does business in 125 countries with 37 different currencies. It relies on PeopleSoft's Supply Chain Management and Financial Management solutions. PeopleSoft also provides financial help, making it easier and less expensive to ship goods anywhere in the world and be sure of payment. Outsourcing is on the rise as more firms realize how complex distribution is.

◀ **PPT 15-39:**
How to Reach the Little Guy

LEARNING goal 7 *

Describe logistics and outline how intermediaries manage the transportation and storage of goods.

LOGISTICS: GETTING GOODS TO CONSUMERS EFFICIENTLY

> **PPT 15-40:**
> Using Logistics

> **logistics**
> The marketing activity that involves planning, implementing, and controlling the physical flow of materials, final goods, and related information from points of origin to points of consumption to meet customer requirements at a profit.

> **inbound logistics**
> The area of logistics that involves bringing raw materials, packaging, other goods and services, and information from suppliers to producers.

> **PPT 15-41:**
> Logistics Applications

> **materials handling**
> The movement of goods within a warehouse, from warehouses to the factory floor, and from the factory floor to various workstations.

> **PPT 15-42:**
> Logistics Applications

Shipping costs have risen dramatically in recent years. When shipping from country to country, it is often impossible to use trucks or trains because the goods have to travel over water. Shipping by air is often prohibitively expensive, which sometimes narrows the choice to moving goods by ship. But how do you get the goods to the ship—and from the ship to the buyer? How do you keep costs low enough to make exchanges beneficial for you and your customers? And how do you handle foreign trade duties and taxes? Distributing goods globally is more complicated than you probably thought. As transportation and distribution have grown more complex, marketers have responded by developing more sophisticated systems.[21]

To better manage customs problems, for instance, many turn to Web-based trade compliance systems. Firms like ClearCross and Xporta determine what paperwork is needed, cross-checking their databases for information about foreign trade duties and taxes, U.S. labor law restrictions, and federal regulations from the Food and Drug Administration or the Bureau of Alcohol, Tobacco, and Firearms. In other words, they manage logistics.

Logistics is the planning, implementing, and controlling of the physical flow of materials, final goods, and related information from points of origin to points of consumption to meet customer requirements at a profit. **Inbound logistics** brings raw materials, packaging, other goods and services, and information from suppliers to producers. **Materials handling** is the movement of goods within a warehouse, from warehouses to the factory floor, and from the factory floor to various workstations. *Factory processes* change raw materials and parts and other inputs into outputs, such as finished goods like shoes, cars, and clothes.

How do you move heavy raw materials like timber from one country to another? This photo shows some of the firms engaged in the logistics process. A trucking firm brings the logs to a dock where huge cranes lift them into the hold of a ship. The ship must be unloaded and the logs put on another truck to travel to a processing plant. Why is managing the logistics process a key to survival in some industries?

Outbound logistics manages the flow of finished products and information to business buyers and ultimately to consumers like you and me. **Reverse logistics** brings goods back to the manufacturer because of defects or for recycling materials.[22]

Logistics is as much about the movement of *information* as it is about the movement of goods. Customer wants and needs must flow through the system all the way to suppliers and must do so in real time. Information must also flow down through the system with no delay. That, of course, demands sophisticated hardware and software. One company in India, Fabindia (a seller of hand-woven garments and home furnishings), ensures close relationships with its suppliers by having its suppliers become shareholders.[23]

Third-party logistics is the use of outside firms to help move goods from here to there. It is part of the trend to outsource functions your firm cannot do more efficiently than outside firms. Texas Instruments (TI) is one of the world's largest makers of silicon chips. About 75 percent of its semiconductor products move through its distribution network. The company uses a regional distribution center in Singapore to serve customers in Asia; one in Dallas to serve North America; one in Utrecht, the Netherlands, to serve Europe; and one in Tsubuka, Japan, to serve markets in that country. TI uses a third-party logistics service to handle the day-to-day operations of those warehouses.[24] Moving goods from one place to another is a major part of logistics.

How do you get products to people around the world after the sale? What are your options? You could send goods by truck, by train, ship, or pipeline. You could use a shipping specialist, such as UPS, FedEx, or the U.S. Postal Service, but often that is expensive, especially for large items. Nonetheless, some of the most sophisticated marketers outsource the distribution process to such specialists. All transportation modes can be evaluated on basic service criteria: cost, speed, dependability, flexibility, frequency, and reach. Figure 15.7 compares the various transportation modes on these criteria.

Trains Are Great for Large Shipments

The largest percentage of goods in the United States (by volume) is shipped by rail. Railroad shipment is best for bulky items such as coal, wheat, automobiles, and heavy equipment. In *piggyback* shipping, a truck trailer is detached from the cab; loaded onto a railroad flatcar; and taken to a destination where it will be offloaded, attached to a truck, and driven to the customer's plant. Railroads should continue to hold their own in competition with other modes of transportation. They offer a relatively energy-efficient way to move goods and could experience significant gains if fuel prices climb.[25]

A company may not ship enough goods to think of using a railroad. Such smaller manufacturers or marketers can get good rates and service by using a **freight forwarder**, which puts many small shipments together to create a

outbound logistics
The area of logistics that involves managing the flow of finished products and information to business buyers and ultimate consumers (people like you and me).

reverse logistics
The area of logistics that involves bringing goods back to the manufacturer because of defects or for recycling materials.

◄ LECTURE LINK 15-8:
Wal-Mart to the Rescue

freight forwarder
An organization that puts many small shipments together to create a single large shipment that can be transported cost-effectively to the final destination.

◄ PPT 15-43:
Comparing Transportation Modes

figure 15.7

COMPARING TRANSPORTATION MODES

Combining trucks with railroads lowers cost and increases the number of locations reached. The same is true when combining trucks with ships. Combining trucks with airlines speeds goods over long distances and gets them to almost any location.

MODE	COST	SPEED	ON-TIME DEPENDABILITY	FLEXIBILITY HANDLING PRODUCTS	FREQUENCY OF SHIPMENTS	REACH
Railroad	Medium	Slow	Medium	High	Low	High
Trucks	High	Fast	High	Medium	High	Highest
Pipeline	Low	Medium	Highest	Lowest	Highest	Lowest
Ships (water)	Lowest	Slowest	Lowest	Highest	Lowest	Low
Airplane	Highest	Fastest	Low	Low	Medium	Medium

Railroads carry over a third of all goods shipped within the United States and are expected to remain a dominant transportation mode. What are some of the advantages of shipping by rail, for both large and small producers?

single large one that can be transported cost-effectively by truck or train. Some freight forwarders also offer warehousing, customs assistance, and other services along with pickup and delivery. You can see the benefits of such a company to a smaller seller. A freight forwarder is just one of many distribution specialists that have emerged to help marketers move goods from one place to another.

Trucks Are Good for Small Shipments to Remote Locations

The second largest surface transportation mode is motor vehicles (trucks and vans). As Figure 15.7 shows, trucks reach more locations than trains and can deliver almost any commodity door-to-door.

You could buy your own truck to make deliveries, but for widespread delivery you can't beat trucking specialists. Like freight forwarders, they have emerged to supply one important marketing function—transporting goods. Railroads have joined with trucking firms to further the process of piggybacking with 20-foot-high railroad cars, called double stacks, that carry two truck trailers, one on top of the other.

When fuel prices rise, trucking companies look for ways to cut costs. The newest measure of transportation from farm to consumer is the *carbon cost*. Some argue that the fewer miles food travels, the better for the environment, but that may not always be true, as the story in the Thinking Green box shows.

Water Transportation Is Inexpensive but Slow

When sending goods overseas, often the least expensive way is by ship. Obviously, ships are slower than ground or air transportation, so water transportation isn't appropriate for goods that need to be delivered quickly. There was a huge dropoff in shipping in 2008 when oil prices skyrocketed, but the situation improved somewhat as oil prices came down.[26] Water transport is local as well as international. If you live near the Mississippi River, you've likely seen towboats hauling as many as 30 barges at a time, with a cargo of up to 35,000 tons. On smaller rivers, towboats can haul about eight barges, carrying up to 20,000 tons—that's the equivalent of four 100-car railroad trains. Add to that Great Lakes shipping, shipping from coast to coast and along the coasts, and international shipments, and water transportation takes on a new dimension as a key transportation mode. When truck trailers are placed on ships to travel

THINKING green

Keeping Your Carbon Footprint Low

Many news stories report the benefits of buying local produce. But buying locally doesn't necessarily reduce your carbon footprint. As Iowa State University's Leopold Center for Sustainable Agriculture reports, "Very few studies support the idea that local-food systems are greener." The reason? The *method of transportation* means as much as the distance from the farm to your table. If you live east of Columbus, Ohio, for example, it may be greener to drink a French wine than a California wine that has been shipped by truck over the Rockies, especially if the French wine came by ship. Sea-freight emissions are less than half those associated with airplanes, and trains are cleaner than trucks.

How food is grown and harvested is also important. Sometimes growing conditions far away can provide more food using less energy and causing less pollution. In short, measuring the effects of carbon output is more complex than you might imagine.

Sources: Tony Dokoupil, "The Carbon Cost from Farm to Fork," *Newsweek*, March 17, 2008; Heather Green and Kerry Capell, "Carbon Confusion," *BusinessWeek*, March 17, 2008; and "Driving a Green Supply Chain," *Quality Digest*, January 2009.

---

long distances at lower rates, it's called *fishyback* (see the explanation of piggyback above). When they are placed in airplanes, by the way, that's *birdyback*.

Pipelines Are Fast and Efficient

One transportation mode we don't often observe is pipeline. Pipelines primarily transport water, petroleum, and petroleum products—but a lot more products than you may imagine. For example, coal can be sent by pipeline by first crushing it and mixing it with water.

Air Transportation Is Fast but Expensive

Today, only a small proportion of shipping goes by air. Nonetheless, air transportation is a critical factor in many industries, carrying everything from small packages to luxury cars and elephants. Its primary benefit is speed. No firms know this better than FedEx and UPS. As just two of several competitors vying for the fast-delivery market, FedEx and UPS have used air transport to expand into global markets.

The air freight industry is starting to focus on global distribution. Emery has been an industry pioneer in establishing specialized sales and operations teams aimed at serving the distribution needs of specific industries. KLM Royal Dutch Airlines has cargo/passenger planes that handle high-profit items such as diplomatic pouches and medical supplies. Specializing in such cargo has enabled KLM to compete with FedEx, TNT, and DHL.

Intermodal Shipping

Intermodal shipping uses multiple modes of transportation—highway, air, water, rail—to complete a single long-distance movement of freight. Services that specialize in intermodal shipping are known as intermodal marketing companies. Today, railroads are merging with each other and with other transportation companies to offer intermodal distribution.

Picture an automobile made in Japan for sale in the United States. It's shipped by truck to a loading dock, and from there moved by ship to a port

◄ PPT 15-47:
Keeping Your Carbon Footprint Low

intermodal shipping
The use of multiple modes of transportation to complete a single long-distance movement of freight.

in the United States. It may be placed on another truck and then taken to a railroad station for loading on a train that will take it across the country, to again be loaded on a truck for delivery to a local dealer. No doubt you've seen automobiles being hauled across the country by train and by truck. Now imagine that one integrated shipping firm handled all that movement. That's what intermodal shipping is all about.

The Storage Function

The preceding sections detailed the various ways of shipping goods once the company has sold them. But that's only the first step in understanding the system that moves goods from one point to another. Another important part of a complex logistics system is storage.

Buyers want goods delivered quickly. That means marketers must have goods available in various parts of the country ready to be shipped locally when ordered.[27] A good percentage of the total cost of logistics is for storage. This includes the cost of the storage warehouse (distribution facility) and its operation, plus movement of goods within the warehouse.

There are two major kinds of warehouses: storage and distribution. A *storage warehouse* holds products for a relatively long time. Seasonal goods such as lawn mowers are kept in such a warehouse. *Distribution warehouses* are facilities used to gather and redistribute products. You can picture a distribution warehouse for FedEx or UPS handling thousands of packages in a very short time. The packages are picked up at places throughout the country and then processed for reshipment at these centers. General Electric's combination storage and distribution facility in San Gabriel Valley, California, gives you a feel for how large such buildings can be. It is nearly half a mile long and 465 feet wide—that's enough to hold almost 27 football fields.

Tracking Goods

How do producers keep track of where their goods are at any given time? As we noted in Chapter 14, companies use Universal Product Codes—the familiar black-and-white bar codes and a preset number—to keep track of inventory.[28] The latest in tracking technology, which we also mentioned earlier, is radio frequency identification (RFID).

RFID technology tags merchandise so that it can be tracked from its arrival on the supplier's docks to its exit through the retailer's door. Wal-Mart, Target, and other organizations all plan to require suppliers to use RFID. Currently, RFID tags cost about 10 cents each, but the goal is to get the cost down to about 1 cent.[29]

Few companies are more interested in tracking items than UPS, which now uses a mix of Bluetooth's short-range radio capability and wireless receivers to track merchandise. It claims the system is even better than RFID. The U.S. State Department is producing an electronic passport card as a substitute for booklet passports to be used by U.S. citizens who travel often to Canada, Mexico, and the Caribbean. It uses an RFID chip to provide data about the user. The card is very controversial, however, because some people believe it can be easily altered.

WHAT ALL THIS MEANS TO YOU

The life or death of a firm often depends on its ability to take orders, process orders, keep customers informed about the progress of their orders, get the goods out to customers quickly, handle returns, and manage any recycling

▶ PPT 15-48:
Storage Warehouses

RFID tags are being used in all kinds of situations, from the movement of goods to the tracking of hurricane evacuees. The Radio Frequency Identification (RFID) wristbands like the one shown here were used to track Hurricane Gustav evacuees as they moved though shelters. Sensors read the wristbands and computers allowed emergency workers to follow and find the evacuees if they moved to different shelters or hospitals.

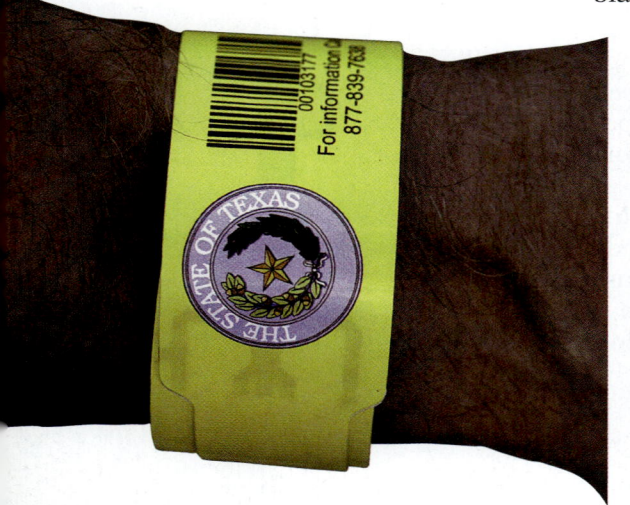

issues. Some of the most exciting firms in the marketplace are those that assist in some aspect of supply-chain management.

What all this means to you is that many new jobs are becoming available in the exciting area of supply-chain management. These include jobs in distribution: trains, airplanes, trucks, ships, and pipelines. It also means jobs handling information flows between and among companies, including Web site development. Other jobs include processing orders, keeping track of inventory, following the path of products as they move from seller to buyer and back, recycling goods, and much more.

progress assessment

- What four systems have evolved to tie together members of the channel of distribution?
- How does logistics differ from distribution?
- What are inbound logistics, outbound logistics, and reverse logistics?

summary

Learning Goal 1. Explain the concept of marketing channels and their value.

- **What is a channel of distribution?**

A channel of distribution consists of a whole set of marketing intermediaries, such as agents, brokers, wholesalers, and retailers, that join together to transport and store goods in their path (or channel) from producers to consumers.

- **How do marketing intermediaries add value?**

Intermediaries perform certain marketing tasks—such as transporting, storing, selling, advertising, and relationship building—faster and more cheaply than most manufacturers could. Channels of distribution ensure communication flows and the flow of money and title to goods. They also help ensure that the right quantity and assortment of goods will be available when and where needed.

- **What are the principles behind the use of such intermediaries?**

Marketing intermediaries can be eliminated, but their activities can't. Without wholesalers and retailers, consumers would have to perform the tasks of transporting and storing goods, finding suppliers, and establishing communication with them. Intermediaries add costs to products, but these costs are usually more than offset by the values they create.

Learning Goal 2. Demonstrate how intermediaries perform the six marketing utilities.

- **How do intermediaries perform the six marketing utilities?**

A retail grocer may cut or trim meat, providing some form utility. But marketers are more often responsible for the five other utilities. They provide time utility by having goods available *when* people want them, and place utility by having goods *where* people want them. Possession utility makes it possible for people to own things and includes credit, delivery, installation, guarantees, and anything else that completes the sale. Marketers also inform consumers of the availability of goods and services with advertising, publicity, and other means. That provides information utility. Finally, marketers provide fast, friendly, and efficient service during and after the sale (service utility).

Learning Goal 3. Identify the types of wholesale intermediaries in the distribution system.
- **What is a wholesaler?**

  A wholesaler is a marketing intermediary that sells to organizations and individuals, but not to final consumers.
- **What are some wholesale organizations that assist in the movement of goods from manufacturers to consumers?**

  Merchant wholesalers are independently owned firms that take title to the goods they handle. *Rack jobbers* furnish racks or shelves full of merchandise to retailers, display products, and sell on consignment. *Cash-and-carry wholesalers* serve mostly small retailers with a limited assortment of products. *Drop shippers* solicit orders from retailers and other wholesalers and have the merchandise shipped directly from a producer to a buyer.

Learning Goal 4. Compare the distribution strategies retailers use.
- **What is a retailer?**

  A retailer is an organization that sells to ultimate consumers. Marketers develop several strategies based on retailing.
- **What are three distribution strategies marketers use?**

  Marketers use three basic distribution strategies: intensive (putting products in as many places as possible), selective (choosing only a few stores in a chosen market), and exclusive (using only one store in each market area).

Learning Goal 5. Explain the various kinds of nonstore retailing.
- **What are some of the forms of nonstore retailing?**

  Nonstore retailing includes online marketing; telemarketing (marketing by phone); vending machines, kiosks, and carts (marketing by putting products in convenient locations, such as in the halls of shopping centers); direct selling (marketing by approaching consumers in their homes or places of work); multilevel marketing (marketing by setting up a system of salespeople who recruit other salespeople and help them to sell directly to customers); and direct marketing (direct mail and catalog sales). Telemarketing and online marketing are also forms of direct marketing.

Learning Goal 6. Explain the various ways to build cooperation in channel systems.
- **What are the four types of distribution systems?**

  The four distribution systems that tie firms together are (1) *corporate systems*, in which all organizations in the channel are owned by one firm; (2) *contractual systems*, in which members are bound to cooperate through contractual agreements; (3) *administered systems*, in which all marketing functions at the retail level are managed by manufacturers; and (4) *supply chains*, in which the various firms in the supply chain are linked electronically to provide the most efficient movement of information and goods possible.

Learning Goal 7. Describe logistics and outline how intermediaries manage the transportation and storage of goods.
- **What is logistics?**

  Logistics includes planning, implementing, and controlling the physical flow of materials, final goods, and related information from points of origin to points of consumption to meet customer requirements at a profit.
- **What is the difference between logistics and distribution?**

  Distribution generally means transportation. Logistics is more complex. *Inbound logistics* brings raw materials, packaging, other goods and services, and information from suppliers to producers. *Materials handling* is the moving of goods from warehouses to the factory floor and to various workstations. *Outbound logistics* manages the flow of finished products and information to business buyers and ultimate consumers (people like you and me). *Reverse logistics* brings goods back to the manufacturer because of defects or for recycling materials.

- **What are the various transportation modes?**

Transportation modes include rail (for heavy shipments within the country or between bordering countries); trucks (for getting goods directly to consumers); ships (for slow, inexpensive movement of goods, often internationally); pipelines (for moving water and oil and other such goods); and airplanes (for shipping goods quickly).

- **What is intermodal shipping?**

Intermodal shipping uses multiple modes of transportation—highway, air, water, rail—to complete a single long-distance movement of freight.

- **What are the different kinds of warehouses?**

A storage warehouse stores products for a relatively long time. Distribution warehouses are used to gather and redistribute products.

key terms

administered distribution system 416
agents/brokers 403
cash-and-carry wholesalers 409
channel of distribution 402
contractual distribution system 415
corporate distribution system 415
direct marketing 414
direct selling 414
drop shippers 409
electronic retailing 412
exclusive distribution 412
freight forwarder 419
inbound logistics 418
information utility 408
intensive distribution 412
intermodal shipping 421
logistics 418
marketing intermediaries 402
materials handling 418
merchant wholesalers 409
outbound logistics 419
place utility 407
possession utility 408
rack jobbers 409
retailer 403
reverse logistics 419
selective distribution 412
service utility 408
supply chain (or value chain) 416
supply-chain management 416
telemarketing 413
time utility 407
utility 407
wholesaler 403

connect interactive applications

Reinforcing Your *Connect*ion to Concepts in Business

This chapter offers 15 interactive applications designed to help you apply what you've learned (examples of these exercises appear on the following pages). Your instructor has determined which interactive applications will benefit you throughout this course. Please refer to your instructor's assignment list in *Connect* to determine which applications you should complete.

Click and Drag Interactive: There are two types of merchant wholesalers. Full-service wholesalers perform all the distribution functions. Limited-function wholesalers perform only selected functions, but try to do them especially well. Three common types of limited-function wholesalers are rack jobbers, case-and-carry wholesalers, and drop shippers. Evaluate the examples of the various merchant intermediaries. Then, match them according to the type of wholesaler they best represent.

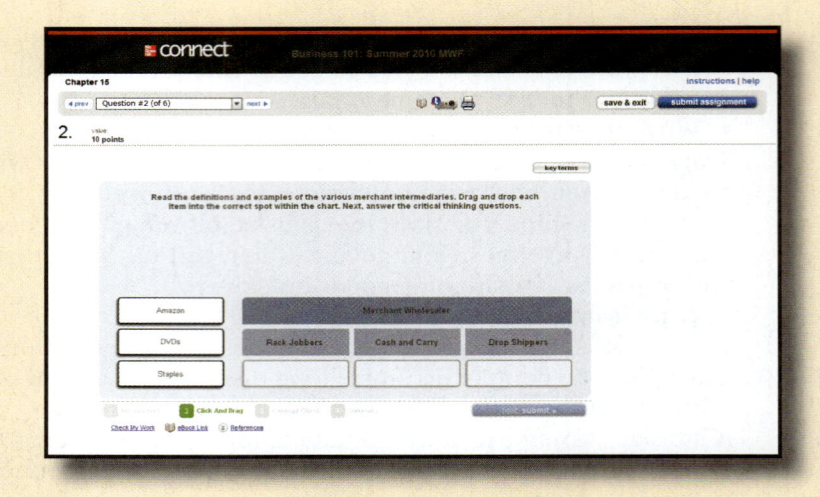

Click and Drag Interactive: The six kinds of utility are form, time, place, possession, information, and service. Review the definitions and examples of the kinds of utility. Then, align them with the correct type in the corresponding chart.

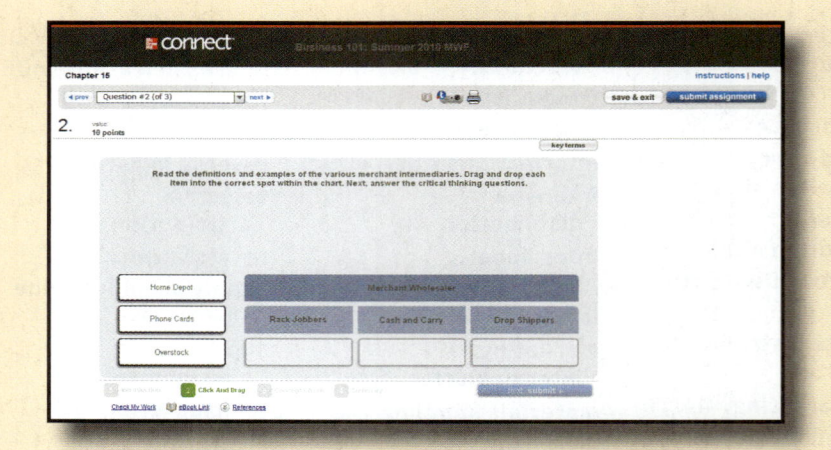

Video Case Interactive: Marketing intermediaries are organizations that assist in moving goods and services from producer to businesses and from businesses to consumers. Intermediaries perform certain marketing tasks, such as transporting, storing, selling, advertising, and relationship building. Utility, in economics, is the want-satisfying ability, or value, that organizations add to goods or services by making them more useful or accessible to consumers than they were before. Watch the video case featuring Netflix and respond to the questions.

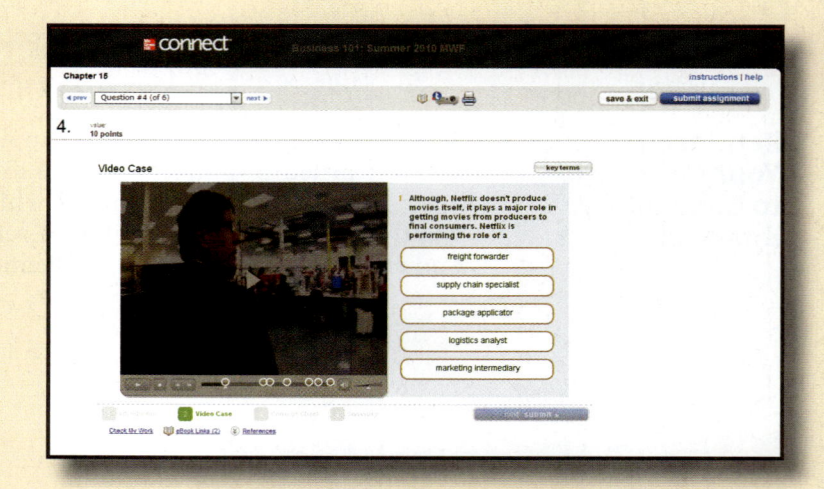

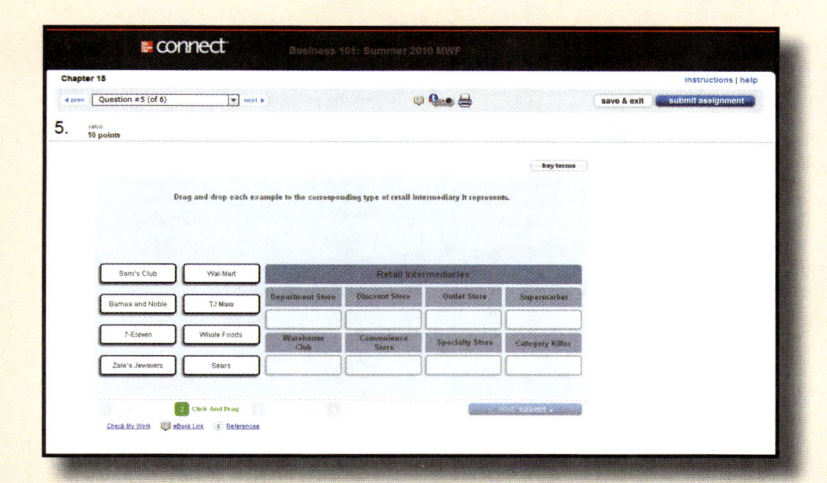

Click and Drag Interactive: Because different products call for different retail distribution strategies, a major decision marketers must make is selecting the right retailers to sell their products. There are three categories of retail distribution: intensive, selective, and exclusive. Review each example and match it to the corresponding type of retail intermediary.

Click and Drag Interactive: A channel of distribution consists of a whole set of marketing intermediaries, such as agents, brokers, wholesalers, and retailers, that join together to transport and store goods in its path (or channel) from producers to consumers. Intermediaries perform certain marketing tasks. These tasks add value to the product, making the intermediaries an important part of the marketing channel. Review the various marketing intermediaries involved in delivering goods and services to the consumer. Then, match each product type or industry to the channel of distribution it best represents.

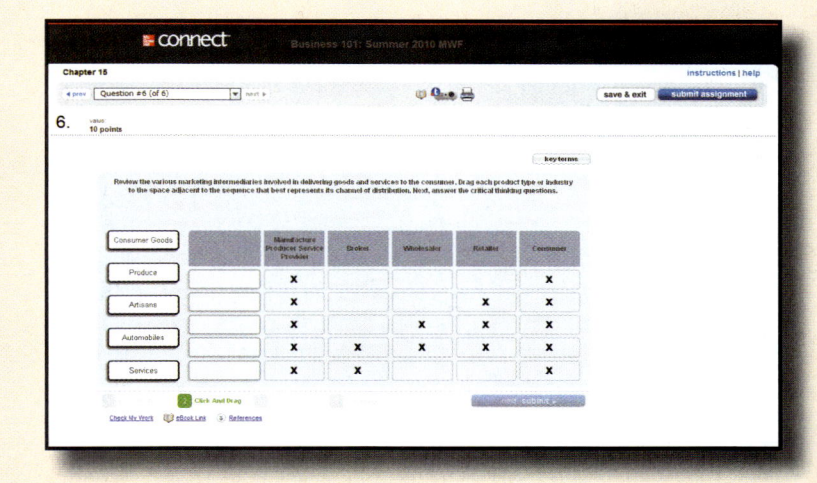

16

USING Effective Promotions

profile

Getting to Know
x Laurel Richie
Chief Marketing Officer of the Girl Scouts

What's the first thing that comes to mind when you think of Girl Scouts? Is it cookies, camping, crafts? You may think such images are old-fashioned and not appealing to young women today. Then how can the Girl Scouts change their image? One answer is to hire someone with great promotional experience, and that's just what the Girl Scouts did when they hired Laurel Richie to be their chief marketing officer (CMO).

Richie worked briefly at the Leo Burnett advertising agency before joining another agency, Ogilvy and Mather, as senior partner, executive group director. There she developed successful promotional campaigns for companies such as American Express, Campbell Soup, Oscar Mayer, and the Partnership for a Drug-Free America. Her challenge now is to change the image of an organization for girls that was started in 1912 by Juliette Gordon Low.

Few people realize that 80 percent of female business leaders were once Girl Scouts. Today, however, only about 2.6 million girls (10 percent) are Scouts, and 1 million adults are Girl Scout volunteers. Membership isn't increasing, as young girls are finding many other ways to grow, achieve, and interact with their peers. Competition for their attention includes sports, clubs, after-school classes, online activities, part-time jobs, volunteering, community and religious groups, and even the occasional trip to the mall.

Richie realizes that part of her mission is to promote Scouting in a whole new way. Today's young women rely on cell phones, text messaging, iPods, Tweets, social networks like MySpace and Facebook, and video sharing on YouTube and other sites. They play video games, blog, and shop online. Part of Richie's challenge is simply to reach them with her message, through communication channels unheard of when Scouting was born. That's why her story is relevant to our chapter on promotion. Richie's idea is to develop a whole new brand image for the Girl Scouts and to develop new communications, publishing, marketing, and Web-based initiatives. It will be interesting to follow Richie's efforts as she begins to implement them,

In this chapter, we explore all the traditional and new elements of promotion. We'll explain how marketers use

LEARNING goals

After you have read and studied this chapter, you should be able to

1. Identify the new and traditional tools that make up the promotion mix.
2. Contrast the advantages and disadvantages of various advertising media, including the Internet.
3. Illustrate the steps of the B2B and B2C selling processes.
4. Describe the role of the public relations department, and show how publicity fits in that role.
5. Assess the effectiveness of various forms of sales promotion, including sampling.
6. Show how word of mouth, e-mail marketing, viral marketing, blogging, podcasting, and mobile marketing work.

connect

Your *Connect*ion to Better Learning. 1. View the interactive presentation. 2. Practice through LearnSmart. 3. Apply your knowledge by using the interactive applications for each chapter of this text.

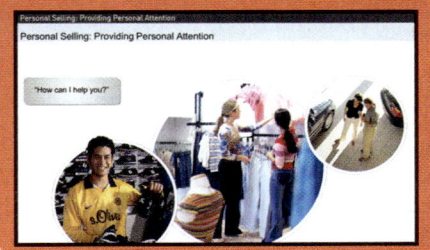

1 Prep   2 Study   3 Apply

different media for promotion and the advantages and disadvantages of each. We'll compare B2C and B2B promotions and look at the role of public relations. Throughout the chapter we'll pay particular attention to promotional uses of electronic media like blogging, social networking, and podcasts.

Sources: Rupal Parekh, "Girl Scouts' New CMO Faces Trial By Campfire," *Advertising Age*, March 31, 2008; a March 2008 release from the Girl Scouts of the USA dated March 24, 2008; Ellen Byron, "Girl Scouts Seek an Image Makeover," *The Wall Street Journal*, March 25, 2008; Megan Greenwell, "Blogs in, Badges Out as Girl Scouts Modernizes," *The Washington Post*, March 2, 2009; and Laurel Richie, www.girlscouts.org, accessed July 2010.

www.girlscouts.org

NAME THAT company

I am an online retailer of garden products and services. We developed an interactive Web site through which customers could chat with each other and ask questions. Such relationship building really helped sales. What is the name of my company? (Find the answer in the chapter.)

▶ PPT 16-1:
Using Effective Promotions

▶ PPT 16-2:
Laurel Richie

▶ LECTURE LINK 16-1:
Murphy's Laws of Marketing

▶ PPT 16-4:
Integrated Marketing Communication

LEARNING goal 1 *

Identify the new and traditional tools that make up the promotion mix.

PROMOTION AND THE PROMOTION MIX

Promotion is one of the four Ps of marketing. As noted in Chapter 13, promotion consists of all the techniques sellers use to motivate people to buy their products or services. Both profit-making and nonprofit organizations use promotional techniques to communicate with people in their target market about goods and services, and to persuade them to participate in a marketing exchange. Marketers use many different tools to promote their products. Traditionally, those tools were advertising, personal selling, public relations, and sales promotion. Today they also include e-mail promotions, mobile promotions (those that use cell phones), social networking, blogging, podcasting, tweets, and more.

The combination of promotional tools an organization uses is called its **promotion mix**; see Figure 16.1. We show the product in the middle of the figure to illustrate that the product itself can also be a promotional tool, such as when marketers give away free samples.

Integrated marketing communication (IMC) combines the promotional tools into one comprehensive, unified promotional strategy.[1] With IMC,

promotion mix
The combination of promotional tools an organization uses.

integrated marketing communication (IMC)
A technique that combines all the promotional tools into one comprehensive, unified promotional strategy.

figure 16.1
THE TRADITIONAL PROMOTION MIX

▶ PPT 16-3:
Promotion in an Organization

1. Identify a target market. (Refer back to Chapter 13 for a discussion of segmentation and target marketing.)
2. Define the objectives for each element of the promotion mix. Goals should be clear and measurable.
3. Determine a promotional budget. The budgeting process will clarify how much can be spent on advertising, personal selling, and other promotional efforts.
4. Develop a unifying message. The goal of an integrated promotional program is to have one clear message communicated by advertising, public relations, sales, and every other promotional effort.
5. Implement the plan. Advertisements, blogs, and other promotional efforts must be scheduled to complement efforts being made by public relations and sales promotion. Salespeople should have access to all materials to optimize the total effort.
6. Evaluate effectiveness. Measuring results depends greatly on clear objectives. Each element of the promotional mix should be evaluated separately, and an overall measure should be taken as well. It is important to learn what is working and what is not.

figure 16.2

STEPS IN A PROMOTIONAL CAMPAIGN

◄ PPT 16-5:
Steps in a Promotional Campaign

◄ PPT 16-6:
Dear Mr. Postman

◄ PPT 16-7:
Advertising in the Firm

◄ PPT 16-8:
Impact of Advertising

◄ PPT 16-9:
I'll Sponsor You

marketers can create a positive brand image, meet the needs of the consumer, and meet the strategic marketing and promotional goals of the firm.[2]

Figure 16.2 shows the six steps in a typical promotional campaign. Let's begin exploring promotional tools by looking at advertising—the most visible tool.

LEARNING goal 2 *

Contrast the advantages and disadvantages of various advertising media, including the Internet.

ADVERTISING: INFORMING, PERSUADING, AND REMINDING

Advertising is paid, nonpersonal communication through various media by organizations and individuals who are in some way *identified in the message*. Identification of the sender separates advertising from *propaganda*, which is nonpersonal communication that *does not have an identified sponsor*. Propaganda is often distributed by the government in various countries. Figure 16.3 on p. 432 lists various categories of advertising. Take a minute to look it over; you'll see there's a lot more to advertising than just television commercials.

It's also easy to appreciate the impact of advertising spending on the U.S. economy; see Figure 16.4 on p. 432. Total ad volume exceeds $294 billion yearly. Note that direct mail is the number one medium, with expenditures over $63 billion. Would you have guessed that direct mail is number one? Television in all its forms (broadcast and cable) is number two, with expenditures of over $48 billion.

How do we, as consumers, benefit from these advertising expenditures? First, ads are informative. Direct mail is full of information about products, prices, features, store policies, and more. So is newspaper advertising. Second, not only does advertising inform us, but the money advertisers spend for commercial time pays the production costs of TV and radio programs. Advertising also covers the major costs of producing newspapers and magazines. Subscriptions and newsstand revenues cover only mailing and promotional

advertising
Paid, nonpersonal communication through various media by organizations and individuals who are in some way identified in the advertising message.

figure 16.3

MAJOR CATEGORIES OF ADVERTISING

Different kinds of advertising are used by various organizations to reach different market targets.

- *Retail advertising*—advertising to consumers by various retail stores such as supermarkets and shoe stores.
- *Trade advertising*—advertising to wholesalers and retailers by manufacturers to encourage them to carry their products.
- *Business-to-business advertising*—advertising from manufacturers to other manufacturers. A firm selling motors to auto companies would use business-to-business advertising.
- *Institutional advertising*—advertising designed to create an attractive image for an organization rather than for a product. "We Care about You" at Giant Food is an example. "Virginia Is for Lovers" and "I ❤ New York" were two institutional campaigns by government agencies.
- *Product advertising*—advertising for a good or service to create interest among consumer, commercial, and industrial buyers.
- *Advocacy advertising*—advertising that supports a particular view of an issue (e.g., an ad in support of gun control or against nuclear power plants). Such advertising is also known as cause advertising.
- *Comparison advertising*—advertising that compares competitive products. For example, an ad that compares two different cold care products' speed and benefits is a comparative ad.
- *Interactive advertising*—customer-oriented communication that enables customers to choose the information they receive, such as interactive video catalogs that let customers select which items to view.
- *Online advertising*—advertising messages that appear on computers as people visit different Web sites.
- *Mobile advertising*—advertising that reaches people on their cell phones.

➤ **PPT 16-10:** Major Categories of Advertising

➤ **PPT 16-11:** Major Categories of Advertising

costs. Figure 16.5 compares the advantages and disadvantages for marketers of various advertising media. Notice that newspapers, radio, and the Yellow Pages are especially attractive to local advertisers.

Marketers must choose which media will best reach the audience they desire. Radio advertising, for example, is less expensive than TV advertising and often reaches people when they have few other distractions, such as while they're driving. Radio is thus especially effective at selling services people don't usually read about in print media—banking, mortgages, continuing education, and brokerage services, to name a few. On the other hand, radio has become so commercial-ridden that many people are paying to switch to commercial-free

➤ **LECTURE LINK 16-2:** Outdoor Advertising: Watch the Phone Booth

➤ **PPT 16-13:** Match Game

➤ **PPT 16-14:** It's a Dog's Life

figure 16.4

ADVERTISING EXPENDITURE BY MEDIA (IN MILLIONS OF DOLLARS)

➤ **PPT 16-12:** Advertising Expenditures by Media in $ Millions

		PROJECTED ADVERTISING SPENDING			
RANK	**MEDIUM**	**2008**	**2007**	**% CHG**	**% TOTAL**
1	Direct mail	$63,732	$60,988	4.5	21.6
2	Broadcast TV (network, spot, synd.)	48,300	45,749	5.6	16.4
3	Newspaper	42,147	42,939	−1.8	14.3
4	Cable TV networks	21,718	20,479	6.1	7.4
5	Radio	18,635	18,592	0.2	6.3
6	Yellow Pages	14,705	14,538	1.1	5.0
7	Consumer magazine	14,106	13,695	3.0	4.8
8	Internet	12,722	10,920	16.5	4.3
	All other	58,311	55,977	4.2	19.8
	Total	294,376	283,877	3.7	100.0

Source: Robert J. Cohen, "U.S. Ad Spending Totals by Medium," *Advertising Age*, December 31, 2007.

MEDIUM	ADVANTAGES	DISADVANTAGES
Newspapers	Good coverage of local markets; ads can be placed quickly; high consumer acceptance; ads can be clipped and saved.	Ads compete with other features in paper; poor color; ads get thrown away with paper (short life span).
Television	Uses sight, sound, and motion; reaches all audiences; high attention with no competition from other material.	High cost; short exposure time; takes time to prepare ads. Digital video recorders skip over ads.
Radio	Low cost; can target specific audiences; very flexible; good for local marketing.	People may not listen to ad; depends on one sense (hearing); short exposure time; audience can't keep ad.
Magazines	Can target specific audiences; good use of color; long life of ad; ads can be clipped and saved.	Inflexible; ads often must be placed weeks before publication; cost is relatively high.
Outdoor	High visibility and repeat exposures; low cost; local market focus.	Limited message; low selectivity of audience.
Direct mail	Best for targeting specific markets; very flexible; ad can be saved.	High cost; consumers may reject ad as junk mail; must conform to post office regulations.
Yellow Pages– type advertising	Great coverage of local markets; widely used by consumers; available at point of purchase.	Competition with other ads; cost may be too high for very small businesses.
Internet	Inexpensive global coverage; available at any time; interactive.	Customers may leave the site before buying.
Mobile advertising	Great reach among younger shoppers.	Easy to ignore, avoid.

satellite radio. Marketers also search for other places to put advertising, such as on video screens mounted in elevators.[3] Have you noticed ads on park benches and grocery carts?[4] You've certainly seen them on Web sites you visit.

Mobile marketing via cell phones started out mostly as text messages, but now Starbucks can send signals to your phone as you approach the store, reminding you to stop in for a latte. Kraft Food developed the iPhone Assistant, an iPhone application that serves up recipes for users—recipes made with Kraft products.[5] Other retailers use e-mail advertisements to build brand awareness and drive people to their stores or Web sites.[6]

Another way to get more impact from advertising is to appeal to the interest in green marketing among consumers and businesses. A brief glance through magazines and the business press reveals all kinds of new appeals to sustainability and carbon-cutting measures (see the Thinking Green box on p. 434). In the next sections, we'll look in more depth at some popular advertising media.

Television Advertising

Television offers many advantages to national advertisers, but it's expensive. Thirty seconds of advertising during the Super Bowl telecast cost about $3 million.[7] How many bottles of beer or bags of dog food must a company sell to pay for such commercials? A lot, but few media besides television allow advertisers to reach so many people with such impact. Denny's spent about $5 million on Super Bowl advertising and the free breakfasts it offered in the ads, but it got 2 million people to visit its restaurants and try its food.[8] Super Bowl XLII was watched by over 98 million viewers, making it the most watched Super Bowl ever.[9]

Despite what you may read about the growth of alternative promotional tools, TV advertising is still a dominant medium.[10] Digital video recorders

figure 16.5

ADVANTAGES AND DISADVANTAGES OF VARIOUS ADVERTISING MEDIA
The most effective media are often very expensive. The inexpensive media may not reach your market. The goal is to use the medium that can reach your desired market most effectively and efficiently.

◄ PPT 16-15:
Popular Advertising Media

◄ CRITICAL THINKING EXERCISE 16-1:
Advertising on Google

◄ CRITICAL THINKING EXERCISE 16-2:
Advertising Appeals

THINKING green

Finding a Competitive Advantage in Sustainability

One way marketers are gaining a competitive advantage is by touting their efforts on behalf of the environment. Mars Drinks North America sells its Flavia brewing machines and hot drinks through distributors. Many of the companies that Mars sells to have sustainability goals, and Mars uses its promotions to sell its efforts to promote sustainability. The overall promotional effort is called "Thirsty for Change." Under that rubric, the company promotes its efforts to use less water, send less waste to landfills, and help customers reduce their own energy use and waste. The company uses several means to get its message across: direct mail, print media, and a new Web site that explains the company's position on sustainability and its activities, such as turning used filters into energy.

How do you compete against such well-known and respected companies as FedEx and United Parcel Service? The answer for First Global Express (FGX) was to use "greening" as a promotional tool. FGX decided to cut the number of miles it flew (thus using much less gas and causing much less pollution) by shipping packages to customers on direct flights. Typically, courier packages go through three or four waypoints before reaching their final destination. FGX used print advertising as well as a completely redesigned Web site, e-mail marketing, thank-you cards, and other sales-related materials to promote its carbon-cutting program. The punch line in the company's ads said, "Ship Greener. Ship Direct." There is also much copy talking about green efforts, including a green thermometer that displays FGX's efforts to make its operations more eco-friendly. FGX also has a ShipGreener blog that talks about environmental and humanitarian topics. The company also helps its customers do a "green audit."

What other companies have you noticed promoting green products and green processes?

Sources: Karen J. Bannan, "Carrier Makes Big Impression with Smaller Carbon Footprint," *BtoB*, December 2008; "Ensuring a Sustainable Future," advertisement, *Fortune*, September 2008; and Kelly Girad, "Entrepreneur Magazine's Emerging Entrepreneur of 2009," *Entrepreneur*, January 2010, p. 25.

▶ **PPT 16-19:**
Finding a Competitive Advantage in Sustainability

▶ **LECTURE LINK 16-3:**
Effective Advertising: Celebrity Voiceovers

▶ **LECTURE LINK 16-4:**
Measuring the Television Audience in the Age of the DVR

product placement
Putting products into TV shows and movies where they will be seen.

▶ **LECTURE LINK 16-5:**
Network Advertising Glut Turns Off Viewers

▶ **CRITICAL THINKING EXERCISE 16-3:**
Identifying Product Placement

(DVRs) enable consumers to skip the ads on TV. This may make TV less attractive to advertisers unless commercials get so much better that people *want* to watch them.[11] New program delivery systems, such as video on demand, make it even more difficult for TV advertisers to catch consumers' eyes. Thus marketers are demanding better and more accurate measures of TV advertising's effectiveness.[12]

Product Placement

TV advertising isn't limited to traditional commercials; sometimes the products appear in the programs themselves. With **product placement**, advertisers pay to put their products into TV shows and movies where the audience will see them. Have you noticed the products that are subtly shown on TV shows and in movies like the James Bond films?[13] Did you ever notice the Coca-Cola cups on the judges' table on *American Idol*?[14] Many placements are more subtle, like the wheeled luggage from Zuca Inc. that appeared on the TV show *CSI*.

The latest wrinkle in product placement puts virtual products into video games. Cadillac, for example, put its V-series Collection luxury vehicles into a high-speed driving game called Project Gotham Racing 3. If you're a gamer, you've also seen in-game ads, like ads around the court in basketball games.[15]

Infomercials

An **infomercial** is a full-length TV program devoted exclusively to promoting a particular good or service. Infomercials have been successful because they show the product and how it works in great detail. They are the equivalent of sending your very best salespeople to a person's home and having them use all of their techniques to make the sale: drama, demonstration, testimonials, graphics, and more.

Products that have earned over $1 billion in sales through infomercials include Proactiv (acne cream), Soloflex, Total Gym, Bowflex (exercise machines), the George Foreman Grill, and Ron Popeil's Rotisserie and Grill. Some products, such as personal development seminars, real estate programs, and workout tapes, are hard to sell without showing people a sample of their contents and using testimonials. Have you purchased any products that you saw in an infomercial?

Online Advertising

When marketers advertise on an online search engine such as Google or Bing, they can reach the people they most want to reach—consumers researching vacations, exploring the car market, or checking stocks.[16] One goal of online advertising is to get potential customers to a Web site where they can learn more about the company and its products—and the company can learn more about them. If users click through an ad to get to the Web site, the company has an opportunity to gather their names, addresses, opinions, and preferences. Online advertising thus brings customers and companies together. Another advantage is that it enables advertisers to see just how many people have clicked on a commercial and how much of it each potential customer has read or watched. It has been one of the fastest-growing parts of advertising.[17] Spending on online advertising is expected to increase greatly in the next three years, although the financial crisis may slow that growth.[18]

E-mail marketing has become a huge component of online advertising.[19] However, advertisers have to be careful not to overuse it because customers don't like to see too many promotional e-mails in their in-boxes. Thus some companies are starting to use e-mail as an alert to send users to other social media such as Facebook, MySpace, and Twitter.[20]

Product placement is often subtle. You can see it in the carefully chosen car an actor drives in a film, or even in the drinks provided to television hosts on the set of their show. In any case, the goal is to influence you to want that product yourself. What product placements have you noticed in your favorite TV shows?

infomercial
A full-length TV program devoted exclusively to promoting goods or services.

◄ CRITICAL THINKING EXERCISE 16-4:
Ethics in Advertising

◄ PPT 16-16:
Infomercials and Online Advertising

◄ PPT 16-17:
Infomercial Hall of Fame

◄ CRITICAL THINKING EXERCISE 16-5:
Developing a Web Site

Interactive promotion allows marketers to go beyond a *monologue*, in which sellers try to persuade buyers to buy things, to a *dialogue*, in which buyers and sellers work together to create mutually beneficial exchange relationships.[21] Garden.com is an online retailer of garden products and services. Dionn Schaffner, the company's vice president of marketing, once said that gardening is an information-intensive activity. Customers obviously want to learn about gardening, but they also seek inspiration by communicating with fellow gardeners and experts. Garden.com's answer to such customers has been to include a forum on its Web site where people can chat with each other and ask gardening questions. (At the Garden.com home page, find the Information Center box and click on the Forum button.)

Technology has greatly improved customer communications. Many companies provide online videos, chat rooms, and other services in a *virtual store* where customers are able to talk to each other, ask questions of salespeople, examine goods and services, and buy products. The Internet is fundamentally changing the way marketers are working with customers. Notice we said *working with* rather than *promoting to*. Marketers now want to *build relationships* with customers over time. That means carefully listening to what consumers want, tracking their purchases, providing them with excellent service, and giving them access to a full range of information.

Here's how online interactive promotion helped one traditional marketer stay competitive. Vita-Mix Corporation makes expensive food blenders. In the beginning, when there was little competition, the company relied mostly on 140 independent contractors to sell the blenders at state fairs, food events, and stores. Eventually Vita-Mix began using infomercials, and sales passed $100 million. Then commercial blender maker K-Tec in Orem, Utah, began going after Vita-Mix's consumer market. K-Tec promoted its new product on a Web site that showed the CEO blending things like golf balls, a rotisserie chicken, and, believe it or not, an Apple iPhone. The video eventually got on YouTube, and sales of this new competitor took off.[22] Vita-Mix successfully responded by creating its own Web site called Vita-Village, showing how to create healthy meals and snacks, and a social network that enables blender fans to share recipes. Online marketers should strive to make sure that their efforts fit into an overall multimedia strategy.[23]

Global Advertising

Global advertising requires the marketer to develop a single product and promotional strategy it can implement worldwide, like MasterCard's "Priceless" campaign.[24] Certainly global advertising that's the same everywhere can save companies money in research and design. In some cases, however, promotions tailored to specific countries or regions may be more successful since each country or region has its own culture, language, and buying habits.

Some problems do arise when marketers use one campaign in all countries. When a Japanese company tried to use English words to name a popular drink, it came up with Pocari Sweat, not a good image for most English-speaking people. In England, the Ford Probe didn't go over too well

---

Online advertising is the fastest-growing type of advertising. Do you think some types of products or services are likely to be promoted more effectively online than others? Which ones and why?

interactive promotion
Promotion process that allows marketers to go beyond a monologue, where sellers try to persuade buyers to buy things, to a dialogue in which buyers and sellers work together to create mutually beneficial exchange relationships.

▶ PPT 16-18:
Global Advertising

because the word *probe* made people think of doctors' waiting rooms and medical examinations. People in the United States may have difficulty with Krapp toilet paper from Sweden. But perhaps worse was the translation of Coors' slogan "Turn it loose," which became "Suffer from diarrhea." Clairol introduced its curling iron, the Mist Stick, to the German market, not realizing *mist* in German can mean "manure." A T-shirt promoting the Pope's visit to Miami read *la papa*, which in Spanish means "the potato." (It should have said *el Papa*.) As you can see, getting the words right in international advertising is tricky and critical. So is understanding the culture, which calls for researching each country, designing appropriate ads, and testing them.

In the United States, some groups are large enough and different enough to call for specially designed promotions. Masterfoods USA, for example, tried to promote dulce de leche (caramel) M&M's to the Hispanic market in cities like Los Angeles, Miami, and San Antonio. The promotion was not successful, however. Knowing the market had potential, Masterfoods changed course and bought a candy company called the Lucas Group, which has had success selling such candies as Felix Sour Fruit and Lucas Hot and Spicy in Mexico. Masterfoods had much more success selling those candies in the United States.

Many marketers today are moving from globalism (one ad for everyone in the world) to regionalism (specific ads for each country or for specific groups within a country). In the future, marketers will prepare more custom-designed promotions to reach even smaller audiences—audiences as small as one person.

This Maybelline ad is designed for the African American woman. There are many ads directed toward the Latina and Asian markets as well. What other groups may prove to be attractive candidates for targeted ads?

LEARNING goal 3 *

Illustrate the steps of the B2B and B2C selling processes.

PERSONAL SELLING: PROVIDING PERSONAL ATTENTION

Personal selling is the face-to-face presentation and promotion of goods and services, including the salesperson's search for new prospects and follow-up service after the sale. Effective selling isn't simply a matter of persuading others to buy. In fact, it's more accurately described today as helping others satisfy their wants and needs (again, helping the buyer buy).[25]

Given that perspective, you can see why salespeople use the Internet, laptop computers, paging devices, fax machines, and other technology to help customers search for information, design custom-made products, look over prices, and generally do everything it takes to complete the order. The benefit of personal selling is having a person help you complete a transaction.

personal selling
The face-to-face presentation and promotion of goods and services.

◀ **LECTURE LINK 16-6:**
Dealing with Changes in Personal Selling

◀ **PPT 16-20:**
Personal Selling

The salesperson should listen to your needs, help you reach a solution, and do everything possible to make accomplishing it smoother and easier.

It's costly for firms to provide customers with personal attention, so those companies that retain salespeople must train them to be especially effective, efficient, and helpful. To attract new salespeople, companies are paying them quite well. The average cost of a single sales call to a potential business-to-business (B2B) buyer is about $400. Surely no firm would pay that much to send anyone but a skillful and highly trained professional salesperson and consultant.

Steps in the Selling Process

The best way to understand personal selling is to go through the selling process. Imagine you are a software salesperson whose job is to show business users the advantages of various programs your firm markets. One product critically important to establishing long-term relationships with customers is customer relationship management (CRM) software. Let's go through the seven steps of the selling process to see what you can do to sell CRM software.

Although this is a business-to-business (B2B) example, the process in consumer selling is similar but less complex. In both cases the salesperson must have deep *product* knowledge—that is, he or she must know the product—and competitors' products—thoroughly.

1. Prospect and Qualify The first step in the selling process is **prospecting**, researching potential buyers and choosing those most likely to buy.[26] The selection process is called **qualifying**. To qualify people means to make sure they have a need for the product, the authority to buy, and the willingness to listen to a sales message. Some people call prospecting and qualifying the process of *lead generation*.[27]

A person who meets the qualifying criteria is called a **prospect**. You often meet prospects at trade shows, where they come to booths sponsored by manufacturers and ask questions. Others may visit your Web site seeking information. But often the best prospects are people recommended to you by others who use or know about your product.[28] Salespeople often e-mail prospects with proposals to see whether there is any interest before making a formal visit.

2. Preapproach The selling process may take a long time, and gathering information before you approach the customer is critical.[29] Before making a sales call, you must do some further research. In the preapproach phase, you learn as much as possible about customers and their wants and needs. Before you try to sell the CRM software, you'll want to know which people in the company are most likely to buy or use it. What kind of customers do they deal with? What kind of relationship strategies are they using now? How is their system set up, and what kind of improvements are they looking for? All that information should be in a database so that, if one representative leaves the firm, the company can carry information about customers to the new salesperson.[30]

You're familiar with all kinds of situations in which people do personal selling. They work in the local department store and sell all kinds of goods and services like automobiles, insurance, and real estate. What could they do to be more helpful to you, the customer? Could you be a successful salesperson? What would you like to sell?

prospecting
Researching potential buyers and choosing those most likely to buy.

qualifying
In the selling process, making sure that people have a need for the product, the authority to buy, and the willingness to listen to a sales message.

prospect
A person with the means to buy a product, the authority to buy, and the willingness to listen to a sales message.

▶ PPT 16-21:
Prospecting and Qualifying in the B2B Selling

3. Approach "You don't have a second chance to make a good first impression." That's why the approach is so important. When you call on a customer for the first time, you want to give an impression of friendly professionalism, create rapport, build credibility, and start a business relationship. Often a company's decision to use a new software package is based on the buyer's perception of reliable service from the salesperson. In selling CRM products, you can make it known from the start that you'll be available to help your customer train its employees and to upgrade the package when necessary.

4. Make a Presentation In your actual presentation of the software, you'll match the benefits of your value package to the client's needs. Companies such as Ventaso Inc. and the Sant Group now provide sales proposal software that includes everything from PowerPoint presentations to competitive analysis. Since you've done your homework and know the prospect's wants and needs, you can tailor your sales presentation accordingly. The presentation is a great time to use testimonials showing potential buyers that they're joining leaders in other firms who are using the product.

5. Answer Objections You should anticipate any objections the prospect may raise and determine the proper responses. Think of questions as opportunities for creating better relationships, not as challenges to what you're saying. Customers may have legitimate doubts, and you are there to resolve them. Successfully and honestly working with others helps you build relationships based on trust. Often you can introduce the customer to others in your firm who can answer their questions and provide them with anything they need. Using a laptop computer, you may set up a virtual meeting in which the customer can chat with your colleagues and begin building a relationship.

6. Close the Sale After you've answered questions and objections, you may present a **trial close**, a question or statement that moves the selling process toward the actual purchase. You might ask, "When would be the best time to train your staff to use the new software?" The final step is to ask for the order and show the client where to sign. Once you've established a relationship, the goal of your sales call may be to get a testimonial from the customer.

7. Follow Up The selling process isn't over until the order is approved and the customer is happy. Salespeople need to be providers of solutions for their customers and to think about what happens after the sale. The follow-up step includes handling customer complaints, making sure the customer's questions are answered, and quickly supplying what the customer wants. Often, customer service is as important to the sale as the product itself. That's why most manufacturers have Web sites where customers can find information and get questions answered. You can see why we describe selling as a process of *establishing relationships*, not just exchanging goods or services. The sales

◄ PPT 16-22:
Steps in the B2B Selling Process

trial close
A step in the selling process that consists of a question or statement that moves the selling process toward the actual close.

Making the sale isn't the end of the salesperson's relationship with the customer. The salesperson should follow up on the sale to make sure the customer is happy and perhaps suggest something to complement what the customer purchased. Have salespeople been able to sell you more because they used effective follow-up procedures? How did they do it?

relationship may continue for years as you respond to new requests for information and provide new services.

The selling process varies somewhat among different goods and services, but the general idea stays the same. Your goals as a salesperson are to help the buyer buy and make sure the buyer is satisfied after the sale. Sales force automation (SFA) includes hundreds of software programs that help salespeople design products, close deals, tap into company intranets, and more. Some salespeople use it to conduct virtual reality tours of the manufacturing plant for the customer. An IBM salesperson may rely on everything from a BlackBerry and sales management software to wikis (collaborative Web sites that users can edit), blogs, podcasts, and IBM's intranet.[31]

The Business-to-Consumer Sales Process

Most sales to consumers take place in retail stores, where the role of the salesperson differs somewhat from that in B2B selling. In both cases, knowing the product comes first. However, in business-to-consumer (B2C) sales, the salesperson does not have to do much prospecting or qualifying. The seller assumes most people who come to the store are qualified to buy the merchandise (except in sales of expensive products such as automobiles and furniture, during which salespeople may have to ask a few questions to qualify prospective customers before spending too much time with them).

Similarly, retail salespeople don't usually have to go through a preapproach step, although they should understand as much as possible about the type of people who shop at a given store. The salesperson does need to focus on the customer and refrain from talking to fellow salespeople, however—or, worse, to friends on the phone. Have you ever experienced such rude behavior from salespeople? What did you think?

The first formal step in the B2C sales process is the approach. Too many salespeople begin with a line like "May I help you?" but the answer too often is "No." A better approach is "How can I help you?" or, simply, "Welcome to our store." The idea is to show the customer you are there to help and are friendly and knowledgeable.

Discover what the customer wants first, and then make a presentation. Show customers how your products meet their needs and answer questions that help them choose the right products for them.

As in B2B selling, it is important to make a trial close, like "Would you like me to put that on hold?" or "Will you be paying for that with your store credit card?" Selling is an art, and a salesperson must learn how to walk the fine line between being helpful and being pushy. Often individual buyers need some time alone to think about the purchase. The salesperson must respect that need but still be clearly available when needed.

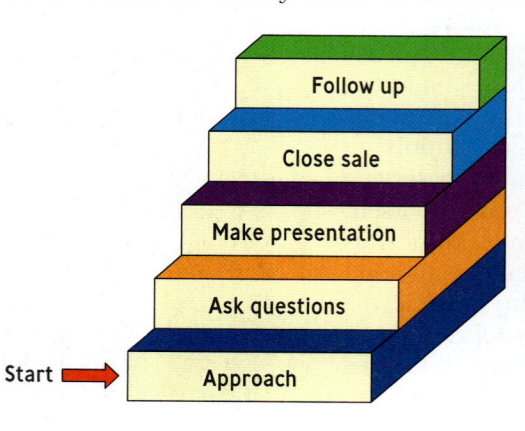

After-sale follow-up is an important but often neglected step in B2C sales. If the product is to be delivered, the salesperson should follow up to be sure it is delivered on time. The same is true if the product has to be installed. There is often a chance to sell more merchandise when a salesperson follows up on a sale. Figure 16.6 shows the whole B2C selling process. Compare it to the seven-step process we outlined earlier for B2B selling.

figure 16.6
STEPS IN THE BUSINESS-TO-CONSUMER (B2C) SELLING PROCESS

Start → Approach → Ask questions → Make presentation → Close sale → Follow up

progress assessment

- What are the four traditional elements of the promotion mix?
- What are the three most important advertising media in order of dollars spent?
- What are the seven steps in the B2B selling process?

◄ PPT 16-26:
Progress Assessment

LEARNING goal 4 *

Describe the role of the public relations department, and show how publicity fits in that role.

PUBLIC RELATIONS: BUILDING RELATIONSHIPS

Public relations (PR) is the management function that evaluates public attitudes, changes policies and procedures in response to the public's requests, and executes a program of action and information to earn public understanding and acceptance. In other words, a good public relations program has three steps:

1. *Listen to the public.* Public relations starts with good marketing research to evaluate public attitudes.
2. *Change policies and procedures.* Businesses earn understanding not by bombarding the public with propaganda but by creating programs and practices in the public interest. The best way to learn what the public wants is to listen to people often—in different forums, including on the Internet. That includes being able to handle a crisis by communicating online.[32]
3. *Inform people you're responsive to their needs.* It's not enough to simply have programs in the public interest. You have to *tell* the public about those programs. Public relations has more power to influence consumers than other corporate communications because the message comes via the media, a source usually perceived as trustworthy.[33]

public relations (PR)
The management function that evaluates public attitudes, changes policies and procedures in response to the public's requests, and executes a program of action and information to earn public understanding and acceptance.

◄ PPT 16-27:
Using Public Relations in Promotion

The PR department maintains close ties with company stakeholders (customers, media, community leaders, government officials, and other corporate stakeholders). Marketers are looking for alternatives to advertising. Public relations is a good alternative. As newspapers cut back on their reporting staff, they are looking for other sources of news information, including publicity releases.[34] Linking up with bloggers has also become an important way to keep company names in the news.[35]

◄ PPT 16-28:
Publicity

Publicity: The Talking Arm of PR

Publicity is the talking arm of public relations and one of the major functions of almost all organizations. Here's how it works: Suppose you want to introduce your store, Very Vegetarian, to consumers, but you have little money to promote it. You need to get some initial sales to generate funds. One effective way to reach the public is through publicity.

Publicity is any information about an individual, product, or organization that's distributed to the public through the media and is not paid for or

publicity
Any information about an individual, product, or organization that's distributed to the public through the media and that's not paid for or controlled by the seller.

A recent New York Times article about electronics recycling company e-Scrap Destruction provided free publicity about the company's efforts to deal responsibly with scrap. Which do you think would attract more attention for a firm, an appealing news story or a paid ad?

▶ PPT 16-29:
Disadvantages of Publicity

controlled by the seller. It takes skill to write interesting or newsworthy press releases that the media will want to publish.[36] You may need to write different stories for different media. One may introduce the new owners. Another may describe the unusual product offerings. If the stories are published, news about your store will reach many potential consumers (and investors, distributors, and dealers), and you may be on your way to becoming a successful marketer. John D. Rockefeller once remarked, "Next to doing the right thing, the most important thing is to *let people know* that you are doing the right thing." What might Very Vegetarian do to help the community and thus create more publicity?

Besides being free, publicity has several further advantages over other promotional tools like advertising. It may reach people who wouldn't read an ad. It may appear on the front page of a newspaper or in some other prominent position, or be given air time on a television news show. Perhaps the greatest advantage of publicity is its believability. When a newspaper or magazine publishes a story as news, the reader treats that story as news—and news is more believable than advertising.

Publicity has several disadvantages as well. For example, marketers have no control over whether, how, and when the media will use the story. The media aren't obligated to use a publicity release, most of which are thrown away. Furthermore, the media may alter the story so that it's not positive. There's good publicity (iPod sales are taking off) and bad publicity (GM is going bankrupt).[37] Also, once a story has run, it's not likely to be repeated. Advertising, in contrast, can be repeated as often as needed. One way to see that the media handle your publicity well is to establish a friendly relationship with media representatives and be open with them when they seek information. Then, when you want their support, they're more likely to cooperate.

LEARNING goal 5 *

Assess the effectiveness of various forms of sales promotion, including sampling.

SALES PROMOTION: GIVING BUYERS INCENTIVES

sales promotion
The promotional tool that stimulates consumer purchasing and dealer interest by means of short-term activities.

▶ PPT 16-30:
Sales Promotion

▶ PPT 16-31:
Some Key Consumer Promotions

Sales promotion is the promotional tool that stimulates consumer purchasing and dealer interest by means of short-term activities. These activities include such things as displays, trade shows and exhibitions, event sponsorships, and contests. Figure 16.7 lists some B2B sales promotion techniques.

For consumer sales promotion activities, think of those free samples you get in the mail, cents-off coupons you clip from newspapers, contests that various retail stores sponsor, and prizes in cereal boxes (see Figure 16.8). You can

figure 16.7
BUSINESS-TO-BUSINESS SALES PROMOTION TECHNIQUES

Trade shows	Catalogs
Portfolios for salespeople	Conventions
Deals (price reductions)	

figure 16.8

CONSUMER SALES PROMOTION TECHNIQUES

Coupons	Bonuses (buy one, get one free)
Cents-off promotions	Catalogs
Sampling	Demonstrations
Premiums	Special events
Sweepstakes	Lotteries
Contests	In-store displays

stimulate sales at Very Vegetarian by putting half-off coupons in the school paper and home mailers.

Sales promotion programs are designed to supplement personal selling, advertising, public relations, and other promotional efforts by creating enthusiasm for the overall promotional program. There was a big increase in such promotions as the 21st century began, especially online. The recent financial crisis has people looking more closely for coupons and other promotional deals.[38]

Sales promotion can take place both within and outside the company. The most important internal sales promotion efforts are directed at salespeople and other customer-contact people, such as customer service representatives and clerks. Internal sales promotion efforts include (1) sales training; (2) the development of sales aids such as flip charts, portable audiovisual displays, and videos; and (3) participation in trade shows where salespeople can get leads. Other employees who deal with the public may also receive special training to improve their awareness of the company's offerings and make them an integral part of the total promotional effort.

After generating enthusiasm internally, marketers want to make distributors and dealers eager to help promote the product. Trade shows allow marketing intermediaries to see products from many different sellers and make comparisons among them. Today, virtual trade shows on the Internet, called Webinars, enable buyers to see many products without leaving the office. Such promotions are usually interactive, so buyers can ask questions, and the information is available 24 hours a day, seven days a week.[39]

After the company's employees and intermediaries have been motivated with sales promotion efforts, the next step is to promote to final consumers using samples, coupons, cents-off deals, displays, store demonstrations, premiums, contests, rebates, and so on. Sales promotion is an ongoing effort to

◀ **PPT 16-32:**
Clip These

◀ **LECTURE LINK 16-7:**
Wrap Your SUV

This International Manufacturing Trade Show in Chicago featured 4,000 booths, giving buyers for other businesses thousands of new products to explore and purchase. Can you see why trade shows in many industries are an efficient and necessary way to stay abreast of the latest developments, competitors, and consumer reactions and needs?

maintain enthusiasm, so sellers use different strategies over time to keep the ideas fresh. You could put food displays in your Very Vegetarian store to show customers how attractive the products look. You could also sponsor in-store cooking demonstrations to attract new vegetarians.

One popular sales promotion tool is **sampling**—letting consumers have a small sample of the product for no charge. Because many consumers won't buy a new product unless they've had a chance to see it or try it, grocery stores often have people standing in the aisles handing out small portions of food and beverage products. Sampling is a quick, effective way of demonstrating a product's superiority when consumers are making a purchase decision. Standing outside Very Vegetarian and giving out samples would surely attract attention.

Pepsi introduced its FruitWorks product line with a combination of sampling, event marketing, and a new Web site. *Event marketing* means sponsoring events such as rock concerts or being at various events to promote your products. In the case of FruitWorks, Pepsi first sent samples to Panama City, Florida, and South Padre Island, Texas, during spring break. Students got free rides on Pepsi trucks and samples of the drinks. Similar sampling and event marketing efforts had been successful for SoBe (herbal fortified drinks) and Snapple (fruit drinks and iced teas).

Everyone likes a free sample. Sampling is a promotional strategy that lets people try a new product, often in a situation when they can buy it right away if they like it. What are some advantages of sampling food products that advertising can't duplicate?

progress assessment

- What are the three steps in setting up a public relations program?
- What are the sales promotion techniques used to reach consumers?
- What sales promotion techniques are used to reach businesses?

sampling
A promotional tool in which a company lets consumers have a small sample of a product for no charge.

word-of-mouth promotion
A promotional tool that involves people telling other people about products they've purchased.

▶ PPT 16-33:
Progress Assessment

▶ PPT 16-34:
Using Word-of-Mouth Promotion

LEARNING goal 6 *

Show how word of mouth, e-mail marketing, viral marketing, blogging, podcasting, and mobile marketing work.

WORD OF MOUTH AND OTHER PROMOTIONAL TOOLS

Although word of mouth was not traditionally listed as one of the major promotional efforts (it was not considered to be manageable), it is now one of the most effective, especially on the Internet. In **word-of-mouth promotion**, people tell other people about products they've purchased.

When James and Ann Scaggs started a company that repairs iPods, customers were hesitant to part with their units without assurance they would be fixed properly. The Scaggs went to RatePoint, a Web 2.0 system for collecting and displaying word of mouth in the form of customer feedback. Sales immediately went up.[40]

Anything that encourages people to talk favorably about an organization can be effective word of mouth. Notice, for example, how stores use clowns, banners, music, fairs, and other attention-getting devices to create word of mouth. Clever commercials can also generate word of mouth. The more that people talk about your products and your brand name, the more easily customers remember them when they shop. You might enjoy brainstorming strategies for creating word of mouth about Very Vegetarian.

Viral Marketing

A number of companies have begun creating word of mouth by rewarding customers for promoting their products to others. One such strategy encourages people to go into Internet chat rooms and hype bands, movies, video games, and sports teams. People who agree to promote products in this way may get what the industry calls *swag*—free tickets, backstage passes, T-shirts, and other such merchandise. What do you think of the ethics of rewarding people to promote goods and services?

Viral marketing describes everything from paying customers to say positive things on the Internet (e.g., using Twitter) to setting up multilevel selling schemes whereby consumers get commissions for directing friends to specific Web sites.

One especially effective strategy for spreading positive word of mouth is to send testimonials to current customers. Most companies use these only in promoting to new customers, but testimonials are also effective in confirming customers' belief that they chose the right company. Therefore, some companies make it a habit to ask customers for referrals.

Word of mouth is so powerful that negative word of mouth can hurt a firm badly. Criticism of a product or company can spread through online forums, chat rooms, bulletin boards, and Web sites. Addressing consumer complaints quickly and effectively is one of the best ways to reduce the effects of negative word of mouth.

Blogging

A **blog**—short for Web log—is an online diary that looks like a Web page but is easier to create and update by posting text, photos, or links to other sites. There are millions of blogs on the Internet, and thousands of new ones are added each day. How do blogs affect marketing? When a book called *Freakonomics* was about to be released, the publisher sent advance copies to 100 bloggers. These bloggers sent reviews to other bloggers (word of mouth), and soon *Freakonomics* was number three on Amazon.com's list of most-ordered books. You can imagine what blogging can do to promote movies, TV shows, and more.[41] See the box called Spotlight on Small Business for more on blogging and entrepreneurs.

Podcasting

Podcasting is a means of distributing audio and video programs via the Internet. It lets users subscribe to a number of files, also known as feeds, and then hear or view the material when they choose. Podcasting allows you to become your own newscaster, since—besides giving broadcast radio and TV a new distribution medium—it enables independent producers to create self-published, syndicated "radio shows." Many companies have also found success in creating video for YouTube.

E-Mail Promotions

Armstrong, the flooring manufacturer, has an e-mail marketing program designed to increase brand awareness among commercial suppliers. At one time it sent out monthly e-mails to announce new products and product updates and to keep people loyal to the brand. Over time, however, those e-mails lost their power. Armstrong then turned to an e-mail service provider that completely

SPOTLIGHT ON SMALL business

www.amysbread.com

Fresh-Baked Promotion

Many entrepreneurs have little time for marketing because they spend nearly all of their time just keeping the business running. One of those entrepreneurs is Amy Scherber. She owns Amy's Bread in New York City. She has more than 100 employees in three retail stores. Baking bread is labor-intensive and doesn't leave much time for traditional marketing. Scherber says that she doesn't use a marketing company or a public relations firm. She does, however, build relationships with people—a major goal of promotion.

Scherber generates media attention by pitching story ideas to the *New York Times* and other publications. She doesn't send them press releases. Instead, she calls the editors who assign articles to see if they would be interested in a particular story. Why would the editors listen to her? Because some of them shop at her stores and she has developed relationships with them. She also attends food industry events where she mingles with reporters. Such contacts enable Scherber to know what editors would be interested in what stories.

Scherber has no advertising budget, but she invests $2,000 to $3,000 a year for printed materials such as T-shirts. Her employees also wear T-shirts, and customers sometimes buy them. Selling T-shirts is one more aspect of marketing. Selected as Alumnus of the Year by her high school, Scherber maintains contact with that community. She also maintains contact with her college alumni to build relationships. As Scherber shows us, building customer relationships doesn't require fancy PR firms or expensive advertising to stay close to your customers.

Sources: Morey Stettner, "Do-It-Yourself Marketing Creates Surprising Results," *Investors Business Daily*, July 7, 2008; Robert Scoble, "Meet the Press," *Fast Company*, April 2008; and Craig Matsuda, "Yes, I Blog at the Office," *Entrepreneur*, March 2010.

> PPT 16-37:
> Fresh-Baked Promotion

revamped the program. The provider divided the market into four separate segments and tracked the success of the e-mails much more closely.

E-mail promotions are gaining in popularity. Most marketers make sure their e-newsletters are also viewable on mobile devices like BlackBerry or Treo. One key to success, therefore, is to keep the message brief, because mobile users don't want to go through much text.

Mobile Media

With mobile media, marketers make use of the cell phone, using text messaging to promote sweepstakes, send customers news or sports alerts, and give them company information.[42] We've seen that companies can now determine where you are and send you messages about restaurants and other services in your vicinity.[43] Despite some technological glitches to work through, mobile marketing is catching on.

Are you getting the idea that traditional promotional methods are slowly but surely being replaced by new technology? If so, you're getting the right idea. By keeping up with the latest trends, you may be able to grab a good job in promotion while traditionalists are still wondering what happened. The Reaching Beyond Our Borders box goes into more detail about the latest media trends.

MANAGING THE PROMOTION MIX: PUTTING IT ALL TOGETHER

Each target group calls for a separate promotion mix. Advertising is most efficient for reaching large groups of consumers whose members share similar traits. Personal selling is best for selling to large organizations. To motivate

> Mobile media allow marketers to reach customers through text messaging. Have you received such promotional messages? For which products are they most effective?

446

REACHING BEYOND our borders

www.publicisgroupe.com

Going Digital

In 2008, David Doty of the Interactive Advertising Bureau (IAB) said, "This is the year when we're seeing more and more marketers understand that digital is the fulcrum for advertising." Rather than blasting a message across media and hoping to get a response, advertisers are recognizing that interactive ads deliver the message in the context where people want to see it and often at the point of decision. So what do you do if you are a very large and traditional advertising agency? You have seen your clients turning to smaller, interactive agencies. The chief marketing officers, who are your clients, are trying hard to show a clear return on their advertising dollars. Digital media are able to do that, and the future is clear. Digital is the way to go.

The situation was this: Publicis Groupe is a French holding company that was fourth in the advertising industry, with about 44,000 employees in 104 countries. It was made up of names like Leo Burnett, Fallon, and Saatchi & Saatchi. It had been creating ads for many very large companies, and their relationships with clients were very strong. Nonetheless, companies wanted more measurement of results, closer relationships with customers, and better promotions. In short, they wanted to use digital media. Publicis's answer was to buy Digitas, an interactive ad agency, for $1.3 billion.

Blending a creative advertising agency with an interactive firm is no easy task. The answer for Publicis is something called the Global Marketing Navigator. The Navigator simplifies masses of data generated by a client's marketing program. Clients can see an ad in the context in which it is running and evaluate key measures of effectiveness. Campaigns can be changed on the fly as consumers react to the messages. Clients can see how an ad is downloading, how long consumers are spending with it, and how consumers are manipulating the information (blowing it up to full screen, etc). The job now is for creative people to use the new media so that the lessons learned in traditional media can be carried over to digital.

Sources: Marcia A. Reed-Woodard, "International Growth," *Black Enterprise*, July 2008; Randy Falco, "AOL CEO: It's Our Fault You're So Confused about Digital," *Advertising Age*, November 3, 2008; "The Digital Issue," *Advertising Age*, March 30, 2009; and Amy Reeves, "Pitch Perfect: Ads Go Digital," *Investor's Business Daily*, May 3, 2010.

---

people to buy now rather than later, marketers use sales promotions like sampling, coupons, discounts, special displays, and premiums. Publicity supports other efforts and can create a good impression among all consumers. Word of mouth is often the most powerful promotional tool. Generate it by listening, being responsive, and creating an impression worth passing on to others that you spread through blogging and podcasting.

Promotional Strategies

How do producers move products to consumers? In a **push strategy**, the producer uses advertising, personal selling, sales promotion, and all other promotional tools to convince wholesalers and retailers to stock and sell merchandise, *pushing* it through the distribution system to the stores. If the push strategy works, consumers will walk into a store, see the product, and buy it.

A **pull strategy** directs heavy advertising and sales promotion efforts toward *consumers*. If the pull strategy works, consumers will go to the store and ask for the products. The store owner will order them from the wholesaler, who in turn will order them from the producer. Products are thus *pulled* through the distribution system.

Dr Pepper has used TV advertising in a pull strategy to increase distribution. Tripledge, a maker of windshield wipers, also tried to capture the interest of retail stores through a pull strategy. Of course, a company could use both

◀ PPT 16-39:
Going Digital
◀ BONUS CASE 16-4:
Wieden & Kennedy: Experimental Promotions

push strategy
Promotional strategy in which the producer uses advertising, personal selling, sales promotion, and all other promotional tools to convince wholesalers and retailers to stock and sell merchandise.

◀ PPT 16-38:
Push, Pull, and Pick Promotional Strategies

pull strategy
Promotional strategy in which heavy advertising and sales promotion efforts are directed toward consumers so that they'll request the products from retailers.

pick economy
Customers who pick out their products from online outlets or who do online comparison shopping.

447

strategies in a major promotional effort. The latest pull and push strategies are being conducted on the Internet, with companies sending messages to both consumers and businesses.

It has been important to make promotion part of a total systems approach to marketing. That is, promotion was part of supply-chain management. In such cases, retailers would work with producers and distributors to make the supply chain as efficient as possible. Then a promotional plan would be developed for the whole system. The idea would be to develop a total product offer that would appeal to everyone: manufacturers, distributors, retailers, and consumers.

Today push and pull strategies have lost some of their effectiveness. Still, customers are interested in searching online outlets like Drugstore.com or Zappos and doing online comparison shopping as they pick the products that appeal to them. Some leading marketers sell directly to consumers with products that really stand out because of their design, packaging, price, or color, like the Dyson vacuum and the Michael Graves teapot. The idea is to help the consumer distinguish your product from the competitors. The term **pick economy** refers to those consumers who pick out their products from online outlets or who do online comparison shopping.

Ads in bus shelters are nothing new, but Kraft recently pumped hot air into 10 Chicago bus stops to promote its Stove Top stuffing mix. The idea was to remind consumers of the warm feeling they get when eating the product. Do you think giving consumers experiences (like warmth on a cold day) is an effective way to remind them of a product?

PPT 16-40:
Progress Assessment

progress assessment

- What is viral marketing?
- What are blogging and podcasting?
- Describe a push strategy, a pull strategy, and the pick economy.

summary

Learning Goal 1. Identify the new and traditional tools that make up the promotion mix.

- **What is promotion?**

Promotion is an effort by marketers to inform and remind people in the target market about products and to persuade them to participate in an exchange.

- **What are the four traditional promotional tools that make up the promotion mix?**

The four traditional promotional tools are advertising, personal selling, public relations, and sales promotion. The product itself can also be a promotional tool—that's why it is shown in the middle of Figure 16.1.

- **What are some of the newer tools used in promotion?**

Today's promotional tools include e-mail promotions, mobile promotions (those that use cell phones), social networking, blogging, podcasting, and YouTubing.

Learning Goal 2. Contrast the advantages and disadvantages of various advertising media, including the Internet.
- **What is advertising?**

Advertising is limited to paid, nonpersonal (not face-to-face) communication through various media by organizations and individuals who are in some way identified in the advertising message.
- **What are the advantages of using the various media?**

Review the advantages and disadvantages of the various advertising media in Figure 16.5.
- **Why the growing use of infomercials?**

Infomercials are growing in importance because they show products in use and present testimonials to help sell goods and services.

Learning Goal 3. Illustrate the steps of the B2B and B2C selling processes.
- **What is personal selling?**

Personal selling is the face-to-face presentation and promotion of products and services. It includes the search for new prospects and follow-up service after the sale.
- **What are the seven steps of the B2B selling process?**

The steps of the selling process are (1) prospect and qualify, (2) preapproach, (3) approach, (4) make presentation, (5) answer objections, (6) close sale, and (7) follow up.
- **What are the steps in the B2C selling process?**

The steps are the approach, which includes asking questions; the presentation, which includes answering questions; the close; and the follow-up.

Learning Goal 4. Describe the role of the public relations department, and show how publicity fits in that role.
- **What is public relations?**

Public relations (PR) is the function that evaluates public attitudes, changes policies and procedures in response to the public's requests, and executes a program of action and information to earn public understanding and acceptance.
- **What are the three major steps in a good public relations program?**

(1) Listen to the public; (2) develop policies and procedures in the public interest; and (3) tell people you're being responsive to their needs.
- **What is publicity?**

Publicity is the talking part of sales promotion; it is information distributed by the media that's not paid for, or controlled by, the seller. Publicity's greatest advantage is its believability.

Learning Goal 5. Assess the effectiveness of various forms of sales promotion, including sampling.
- **How are sales promotion activities used both within and outside the organization?**

Internal sales promotion efforts are directed at salespeople and other customer-contact people to keep them enthusiastic about the company. Internal sales promotion activities include sales training, sales aids, audiovisual displays, and trade shows. External sales promotions to consumers rely on samples, coupons, cents-off deals, displays, store demonstrators, premiums, and other incentives.

Learning Goal 6. Show how word of mouth, e-mail marketing, viral marketing, blogging, podcasting, and mobile marketing work.

- **Is word of mouth a major promotional tool?**

Word of mouth was not considered one of the traditional forms of promotion because it was not considered to be manageable, but it has always been an effective way of promoting goods and services.

- **How is word of mouth used in promotion today?**

Some companies reward people to blog or go into Internet chat rooms and talk enthusiastically about bands, movies, video games, and sports teams. People who agree to hype products in this way get *swag*—free tickets, backstage passes, T-shirts, and other merchandise. *Viral marketing* is everything from paying people to say positive things on the Internet to setting up multilevel selling schemes whereby consumers get commissions for directing friends to specific Web sites. Podcasting is like blogging with an audiovisual focus.

- **What are the major promotional strategies?**

In a *push strategy*, the producer uses advertising, personal selling, sales promotion, and all other promotional tools to convince wholesalers and retailers to stock and sell merchandise. In a *pull strategy*, heavy advertising and sales promotion efforts are directed toward consumers so they'll request the products from retailers. The term *pick economy* refers to those consumers who pick out their products from online outlets such as Drugstore.com or Zappos or who do online comparison shopping.

key terms

advertising 431
blog 445
infomercial 435
integrated marketing communication (IMC) 430
interactive promotion 436
personal selling 437
pick economy 447
podcasting 445
product placement 434
promotion mix 430
prospect 438
prospecting 438
publicity 441
public relations (PR) 441
pull strategy 447
push strategy 447
qualifying 438
sales promotion 442
sampling 444
trial close 439
viral marketing 445
word-of-mouth promotion 444

connect interactive applications

Reinforcing Your *Connect*ion to Concepts in Business

This chapter offers 15 interactive applications designed to help you apply what you've learned (examples of these exercises appear on the following pages). Your instructor has determined which interactive applications will benefit you throughout this course. Please refer to your instructor's assignment list in *Connect* to determine which applications you should complete.

Using Effective Promotions   ✳   CHAPTER 16   451

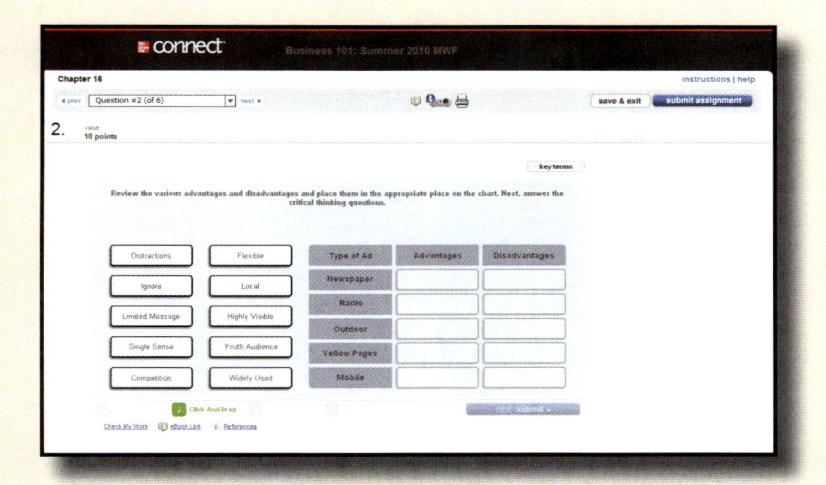

Click and Drag Interactive: Marketers must choose which media will best reach the audience they desire. Radio advertising is less expensive than TV advertising, and it often reaches people when they have few other distractions. Radio is especially effective at selling services people don't usually read about in print media. Evaluate the advantages and disadvantages different types of media face and place them with the form of media they best represent.

Comprehension Case Interactive: Sales promotion programs are designed to supplement personal selling, advertising, public relations, and other efforts by creating enthusiasm for the overall promotional program. Membership in the Girl Scouts is not increasing. The goal of the Girl Scouts organization is to use sales promotion to increase membership. Review the Comprehension Case featuring the Girl Scout's sales promotion campaign and respond to the questions.

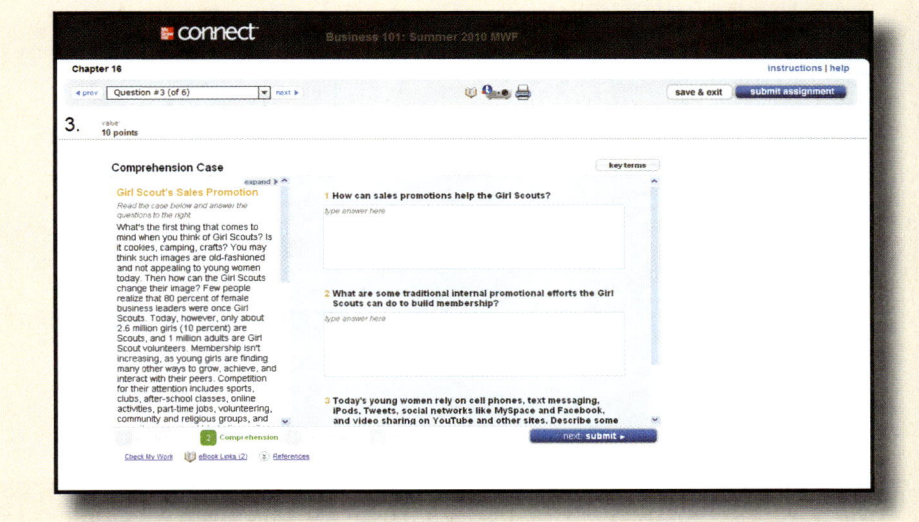

Video Case Interactive: The combination of promotional tools an organization uses is called its promotion mix. Integrated marketing communication (IMC) combines the promotional tools into one comprehensive, unified promotional strategy. With IMC, marketers can create a positive brand image, meet the needs of the consumer, and meet the strategic marketing and promotional goals of the firm. Watch the video featuring Leo Burnett and respond to the questions when prompted.

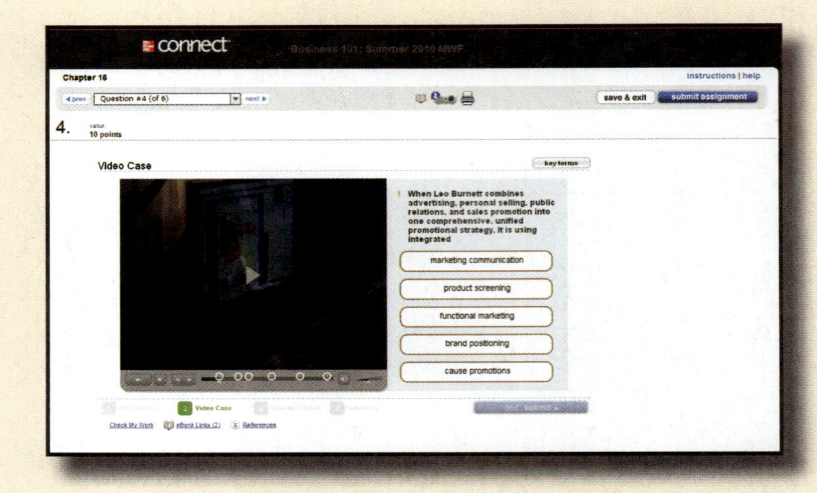

Click and Drag Interactive: The selling process varies somewhat among different goods and services, but the general idea stays the same. The goal of the salesperson is to help the buyer buy and make sure the buyer is satisfied after the sale. Review the seven steps involved in the personal selling process and place them in the correct order on the timeline.

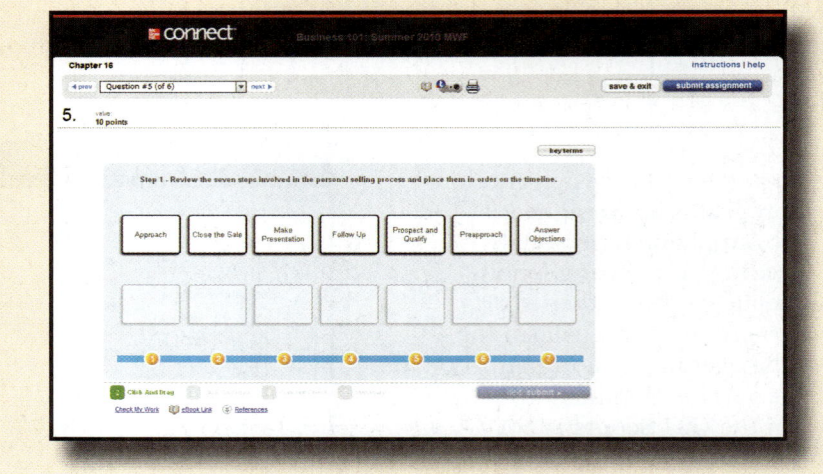

Click and Drag Interactive: Integrated marketing communication (IMC) combines the promotional tools into one comprehensive, unified promotional strategy. With IMC, marketers can create a positive brand image, meet the needs of the consumer, and meet the marketing and promotional goals of the firm. Evaluate the definitions and match them with the type of promotional mix element they best represent.

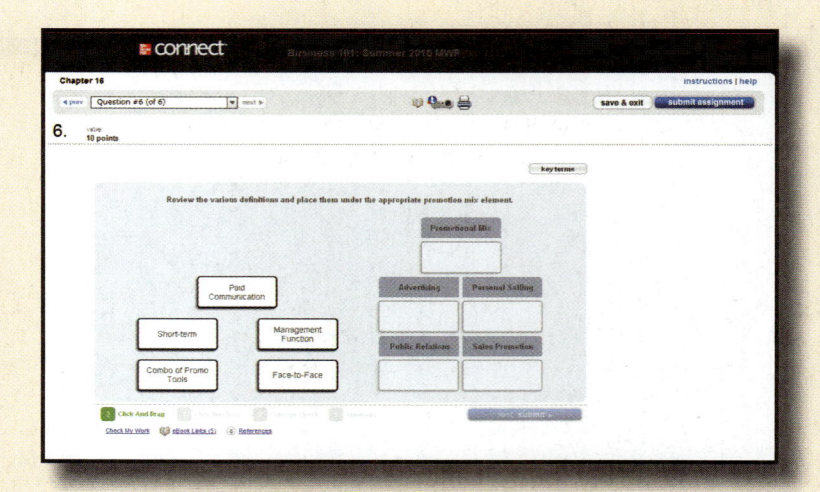

17

UNDERSTANDING Accounting and Financial Information

profile

Getting to Know
x *Sean Perich*
of Bakery Barn

As a lifelong weight lifter, Sean Perich longed for a good-tasting protein-packed cookie he could take with him to the gym. When he couldn't find what he wanted in the stores, he decided to make some himself. Unfortunately, his first attempt at mixing up a batch of protein-fortified chocolate chip cookies blew up his mixer. Perich persisted, however, and using his family and friends from the gym as test subjects, he perfected his recipe. After he finally got a unanimous thumbs-up from his colleagues on the matter of taste, Perich thought about his next step. He decided to change careers from accounting to running his own commercial cookie-baking business.

A Duquesne University graduate and certified public accountant (CPA), Perich worked for KPMG, one of the nation's largest accounting firms. He was familiar with measures of business health like financial analysis, balance sheets, and return on equity and assets. When he decided to open a bakery, his family and friends thought his new business, Bakery Barn, would be in sound financial hands. Perich soon found that baking cookies was the easy part of the transition. Surviving financially was something else.

Perich started Bakery Barn with more than $200,000 from his personal finances, a loan from his father, and a small line of credit. He hired several family members at relatively low wages, which helped keep costs down. However, the financial condition of the company deteriorated quickly. Perich could not get a bank loan, and family and friends were tapped out financially. Bakery Barn was operating on a poor cash-flow basis. Inventory was moving too slowly, costs were too high, and the company was not turning a profit. Even though Perich was a CPA, accounting issues seemed the weakest area of his business.

Perich realized his dream of creating his own line of nutritional cookies would become a nightmare if he didn't swallow his pride and pursue a brighter financial future. He decided to bake cookies for other companies instead, and signed a contract with Apex Fitness Group. Apex began selling Perich's cookies in its 350 health clubs as well as 900 other clubs with which it had associations. The Apex deal became the financial turning point for Bakery Barn, grossing over $1 million the first year.

LEARNING goals

After you have read and studied this chapter, you should be able to

1. Demonstrate the role that accounting and financial information play for a business and for its stakeholders.
2. Identify the different disciplines within the accounting profession.
3. List the steps in the accounting cycle, distinguish between accounting and bookkeeping, and explain how computers are used in accounting.
4. Explain how the major financial statements differ.
5. Demonstrate the application of ratio analysis in reporting financial information.

connect

Your *Connect*ion to Better Learning. 1. View the interactive presentation. 2. Practice through LearnSmart. 3. Apply your knowledge by using the interactive applications for each chapter of this text.

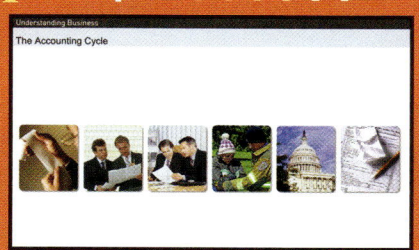

1 Prep ›››››› **2 Study** ›››››› **3 Apply**

As the company grew to 32 employees, Perich knew the high-performance/cheap-labor model he started with wouldn't work. The company sorely needed a business overhaul, and Perich, the accountant, was ready to implement it. He hired a full-time comptroller (chief accountant) to set financial standards, manage cash flow, and measure return on investment. Then he announced a major change; he hired a CEO. Perich felt he had taken the company as far as he could, and a new leader was needed to move the business from its current $6 million a year range to $25 or even $50 million.

Controlling costs, managing cash flows, understanding profit margins and taxes, and reporting finances accurately are keys to survival for both large and small organizations like Bakery Barn. This chapter will introduce you to the accounting fundamentals and financial information critical to business success. It also briefly explores financial ratios that measure business performance in a large or small business.

Sources: Kerry Miller, "Are You the Best Boss for Your Business?" *BusinessWeek,* November 26, 2007; Kerry Miller, "Risky Financing for Cash-Strapped Startups," *BusinessWeek,* November 26, 2007; and Bakery Barn, www.bakery-barn.com, accessed July 2, 2010.

www.bakery-barn.com

NAME THAT company

We were one of the largest accounting firms in the United States until our involvement in the Enron scandal forced us out of business. Our company was convicted of obstruction of justice in the case that led to our downfall. The U.S. Supreme Court later reversed the conviction, but it was too late to save the company. Name our company. (Find the answer in the chapter.)

➤ **PPT 17-1:**
Understanding Accounting and Financial Information

➤ **PPT 17-2:**
Sean Perich

LEARNING goal 1 *

Demonstrate the role that accounting and financial information play for a business and for its stakeholders.

THE ROLE OF ACCOUNTING INFORMATION

Stories like Bakery Barn's are repeated every day throughout the business community. Small and large businesses often survive or fail according to how well they handle financial procedures. Financial management is the heartbeat of competitive businesses, and accounting information helps keep the heartbeat stable.

Accounting reports and financial statements reveal as much about a business's health as pulse and blood pressure readings tell us about a person's health. Thus, you have to know something about accounting if you want to succeed in business. It's almost impossible to understand business operations without being able to read, understand, and analyze accounting reports and financial statements.[1]

By the end of the chapter, you should have a good idea what accounting is, how it works, and the value it offers. You should also know some accounting terms and understand the purpose of accounting statements. Your new understanding will pay off as you become more active in business or simply in understanding what's going on in the world of business and finance.

➤ **PPT 17-3:**
What's Accounting?

➤ **LECTURE LINK 17-1:**
Managerial Accounting and the Budget Process

What Is Accounting?

Accounting is the recording, classifying, summarizing, and interpreting of financial events and transactions in an organization to provide management and other interested parties the financial information they need to make good decisions about its operation. Financial transactions include buying and selling goods and services, acquiring insurance, paying employees, and using supplies. Usually we group all purchases together, and all sales transactions together. The method we use to record and summarize accounting data into reports is an *accounting system* (see Figure 17.1).

A major purpose of accounting is to help managers make well-informed decisions. Another is to report financial information about the firm to interested stakeholders, such as employees, owners, creditors, suppliers, unions,

accounting
The recording, classifying, summarizing, and interpreting of financial events and transactions to provide management and other interested parties the information they need to make good decisions.

figure 17.1

Inputs — Accounting Documents
- Sales documents
- Purchasing documents
- Shipping documents
- Payroll records
- Bank records
- Travel records
- Entertainment records

Processing
1. Entries are made into journals: recording
2. The effects of these journal entries are transferred or posted into ledgers: classifying
3. All accounts are summarized

Outputs — Financial Statements
- Balance sheet
- Income statement
- Statement of cash flows
- Other reports (e.g., annual reports)

THE ACCOUNTING SYSTEM
The inputs to an accounting system include sales documents and other documents. The data are recorded, classified, and summarized. They're then put into summary financial statements such as the income statement and balance sheet and statement of cash flows.

◄ PPT 17-4:
The Accounting System

◄ PPT 17-5:
Accountant's Responsibilities

◄ PPT 17-6:
Managerial Accounting

community activists, investors, and the government (for tax purposes) (see Figure 17.2). Accounting is divided into several major disciplines. Let's look at those next.

LEARNING goal 2 *

Identify the different disciplines within the accounting profession.

ACCOUNTING DISCIPLINES

You may think accounting is only for profit-seeking firms.[2] Nothing could be further from the truth. Accounting, also called the language of business, allows us to report financial information about nonprofit organizations such as churches, schools, hospitals, fraternities, and government agencies. The accounting profession is divided into five key working areas: managerial accounting, financial accounting, auditing, tax accounting, and governmental and not-for-profit accounting. All five are important, and all create career opportunities. Let's explore each.

Managerial Accounting

Managerial accounting provides information and analysis to managers *inside* the organization to assist them in decision making. Managerial accounting is concerned with measuring and reporting costs of production, marketing, and other functions; preparing budgets (planning); checking whether or not

managerial accounting
Accounting used to provide information and analyses to managers inside the organization to assist them in decision making.

figure 17.2

USERS OF ACCOUNTING INFORMATION AND THE REQUIRED REPORTS
Many types of organizations use accounting information to make business decisions. The reports needed vary according to the information each user requires. An accountant must prepare the appropriate forms.

USERS	TYPE OF REPORT
Government taxing authorities (e.g., the Internal Revenue Service)	Tax returns
Government regulatory agencies	Required reports
People interested in the organization's income and financial position (e.g., owners, creditors, financial analysts, suppliers)	Financial statements found in annual reports (e.g., income statement, balance sheet, statement of cash flows)
Managers of the firm	Financial statements and various internally distributed financial reports

Assembling a marine diesel engine requires many tools, parts, raw materials, and other components as well as labor costs. Keeping these costs at a minimum and setting realistic production schedules is critical to a business's survival. What other internal departments must management accountants team with to ensure company competitiveness?

▶ **PPT 17-7:**
Users of Accounting Information

▶ **CRITICAL THINKING EXERCISE 17-1:**
Annual Reports Online

▶ **PPT 17-8**
Financial Accounting

▶ **PPT 17-9**
How to Read an Annual Report

▶ **PPT 17-10**
Public vs. Private Accountants

certified management accountant (CMA)
A professional accountant who has met certain educational and experience requirements, passed a qualifying exam, and been certified by the Institute of Certified Management Accountants.

financial accounting
Accounting information and analyses prepared for people outside the organization.

annual report
A yearly statement of the financial condition, progress, and expectations of an organization.

private accountant
An accountant who works for a single firm, government agency, or nonprofit organization.

units are staying within their budgets (controlling); and designing strategies to minimize taxes.[3]

If you are a business major, you'll probably take a course in managerial accounting.[4] You may even pursue a career as a certified management accountant. A **certified management accountant (CMA)** is a professional accountant who has met certain educational and experience requirements, passed a qualifying exam, and been certified by the Institute of Certified Management Accountants.[5] With growing emphasis on global competition, outsourcing, and organizational cost-cutting, managerial accounting is one of the most important areas you may study in your college career.

Financial Accounting

Financial accounting differs from managerial accounting in that the financial information and analyses it generates are for people primarily *outside* the organization. The information goes not only to company owners, managers, and employees but also to creditors and lenders, employee unions, customers, suppliers, government agencies, and the general public. External users are interested in questions like: Is the organization profitable? Is it able to pay its bills? How much debt does it owe? These questions and others are often answered in the company's **annual report**, a yearly statement of the financial condition, progress, and expectations of an organization. As pressure from stakeholders for detailed financial information has grown, companies have poured more information than ever into their annual reports.

It's critical for firms to keep accurate financial information. Therefore, many organizations employ a **private accountant** who works for a single firm, government agency, or nonprofit organization. However, not all firms or nonprofit organizations want or need a full-time accountant. Fortunately, thousands of accounting firms in the United States provide the accounting services an organization needs through public accountants.

For a fee, a **public accountant** will provide accounting services to individuals or businesses that include designing an accounting system, helping select the correct software to run the system, and analyzing an organization's financial performance. An accountant who passes a series of examinations established by the American Institute of Certified Public Accountants (AICPA) and meets the state's requirement for education and experience is recognized as a **certified public accountant (CPA)**. CPAs find careers as private or public accountants and are often sought to fill other financial positions within organizations. Today, there are over 650,000 CPAs in the United States, 350,000 of whom are members of the AICPA.[6]

Accountants know it's vital for users of a firm's accounting information to be assured the information is accurate.[7] The independent Financial Accounting Standards Board (FASB) defines the *generally accepted accounting principles (GAAP)* that accountants must follow.[8] If accounting reports are prepared in accordance with GAAP, users can expect the information to meet standards accounting professionals have agreed on.

The accounting profession suffered the darkest period in its history in the early 2000s. Accounting scandals engulfed companies including WorldCom, Enron, and Tyco, raising public suspicions of the profession and of corporate integrity in general.[9] Arthur Andersen, one of the nation's leading accounting firms, went out of business after being convicted of obstruction of justice for shredding records in the Enron case (the conviction was later overturned by the U.S. Supreme Court).

Scrutiny of the accounting industry intensified, and it culminated in the U.S. Congress's passage of the Sarbanes-Oxley Act.[10] This legislation created new government reporting standards for publicly traded companies. It also created the Public Company Accounting Oversight Board (PCAOB), which is charged with overseeing the AICPA.[11] In 2008, the PCAOB was challenged in federal court regarding its legal standing. If the ruling goes against the PCAOB, the Sarbanes-Oxley Act's implementation could be in trouble.[12] Figure 17.3 lists a few of the major provisions of Sarbanes-Oxley.

To be effective, accountants must be considered as professional as doctors or lawyers. Besides completing more than 150 hours of intense training and a rigorous exam, CPAs on average take 40 hours of continuing education training a year, are subject to recertification, undergo ethics training requirements, and must pass an ethics exam.[13] The Legal Briefcase box on p. 460 offers an example of how intense accounting scrutiny has become and what some companies are doing about it.

public accountant
An accountant who provides accounting services to individuals or businesses on a fee basis.

certified public accountant (CPA)
An accountant who passes a series of examinations established by the American Institute of Certified Public Accountants (AICPA).

◄ **LECTURE LINK 17-2:**
Coming Soon—The Wide World of Accounting

◄ **PPT 17-12:**
Steps to Control Accounting Practices

◄ **PPT 17-13:**
Auditing Checks Accuracy

- Prohibits accounting firms from providing certain non-auditing work (such as consulting services) to companies they audit.
- Strengthens the protection for whistle-blowers who report wrongful actions of company officers.
- Requires company CEOs and CFOs to certify the accuracy of financial reports and imparts strict penalties for any violation of securities reporting (e.g., earnings misstatements).
- Prohibits corporate loans to directors and executives of the company.
- Establishes the five-member Public Company Accounting Oversight Board (PCAOB) under the Securities and Exchange Commission (SEC) to oversee the accounting industry.
- Stipulates that altering or destroying key audit documents will result in felony charges and significant criminal penalties.

figure 17.3

KEY PROVISIONS OF THE SARBANES-OXLEY ACT

LEGAL briefcase

www.forensisgroup.com

Balance Sheet Sherlocks

Sherlock Holmes might say, "Elementary, my dear Watson, elementary," but forensic accounting is anything but elementary. In the accounting world, forensic accountants are crime-scene investigators. When a company or organization is suspected of fraud, a court will commission a forensic accountant to search for corporate foul play by analyzing computer hard drives, financial papers, bank records, and billing receipts. *Accounting Today* magazine estimates that 78 percent of the nation's top CPA firms use forensic accounting in fraud and litigation.

Forensic accountants are far from simple pencil pushers. They view their job as behavioral, meaning they get out and listen to employees who might have concerns about supervisors encouraging them to cook the books or hide some costs. Though crooked CEOs were once the primary target for forensic accountants, now middle managers are more likely to be scrutinized in their bookkeeping.

Several companies have found out the hard way that even the slightest whiff of accounting irregularities can be detrimental to their health. The financial records of corrupt companies like Enron and WorldCom were exposed as fraudulent once forensic accountants studied their books and noticed many errors and embellishments in their accounting. In 2007, forensic accountants discovered that the government had been losing $146 million annually from employees who used taxpayer money for improper upgrades to first class on airplane flights. Lenders caught in the current subprime mortgage crisis have been plagued by the exposure of their shoddy balance sheets. Unfortunately, it looks like forensic accountants won't have any trouble keeping busy in the future.

Sources: Mara Der Hovanesian, "Lenders Face Still More Misery," *BusinessWeek*, March 13, 2008; Jeffrey Steinhoff, "Forensic Auditing: A Window to Identifying and Combating Fraud, Waste and Abuse," *Journal of Government Financial Management*, July 1, 2008; and Lynn Lofton, "Fraud Examination Growing Part of Forensics," *Mississippi Business Journal*, January 5, 2009.

▶ **PPT 17-11:**
Balance Sheet Sherlocks

auditing
The job of reviewing and evaluating the information used to prepare a company's financial statements.

▶ **LECTURE LINK 17-3:**
The Power of the Internal Auditor

independent audit
An evaluation and unbiased opinion about the accuracy of a company's financial statements.

▶ **LECTURE LINK 17-4:**
Is There a Doctor in the House?

certified internal auditor (CIA)
An accountant who has a bachelor's degree and two years of experience in internal auditing, and who has passed an exam administered by the Institute of Internal Auditors.

Auditing

Reviewing and evaluating the information used to prepare a company's financial statements is referred to as **auditing**. Private accountants within an organization often perform internal audits to guarantee that it is carrying out proper accounting procedures and financial reporting. Public accountants also conduct independent audits of accounting information and related records. An **independent audit** is an evaluation and unbiased opinion about the accuracy of a company's financial statements. Annual reports often include an auditor's unbiased written opinion.

As a result of the accounting scandals mentioned above, many people questioned the ethics of allowing an accounting firm to do both auditing and consulting work for the same company. In response, the Sarbanes-Oxley Act put in place new rules about auditing and consulting to ensure the integrity of the auditing process.[14]

Auditors not only examine the financial health of an organization but also look into operational efficiencies and effectiveness.[15] Accountants who have a bachelor's degree and two years of experience in internal auditing, and who pass an exam administered by the Institute of Internal Auditors, can earn professional accreditation as a **certified internal auditor (CIA)**.[16]

Tax Accounting

Taxes enable governments to supply roads, parks, schools, police protection, the military, and other functions. Federal, state, and local governments require individuals and organizations to file tax returns at specific times and in a precise format. A **tax accountant** is trained in tax law and is responsible for preparing tax returns or developing tax strategies. Since governments often change tax policies according to specific needs or objectives, the job of the tax accountant is always challenging.[17] And as the burden of taxes grows in the economy, the role of the tax accountant becomes increasingly valuable to the organization, individual, or entrepreneur.

Government and Not-for-Profit Accounting

Government and not-for-profit accounting supports organizations whose purpose is not generating a profit but serving ratepayers, taxpayers, and others according to a duly approved budget. Federal, state, and local governments require an accounting system that helps taxpayers, special interest groups, legislative bodies, and creditors ensure that the government is fulfilling its obligations and making proper use of taxpayers' money. Government accounting standards are set by an organization called the Governmental Accounting Standards Board (GASB).[18] The Federal Bureau of Investigation, the Internal Revenue Service, the Missouri Department of Natural Resources, and the Cook County Department of Revenue are just a few of the many government agencies that offer career possibilities to accountants seeking to work in government accounting.

Not-for-profit organizations also require accounting professionals. In fact, their need for trained accountants is growing since donors to nonprofits want to see exactly how and where the funds they contribute are being spent. Charities like the Salvation Army, Red Cross, museums, and hospitals all hire accountants to show contributors where their money goes.[19] Some charities were having a particularly hard time in early 2009 because of losses they suffered from the illegal activities of Bernard Madoff and others like him, as well as from the financial crisis.[20] As a result, some individuals cut back on donations, and accounting for every dollar became even more important.

As you can see, managerial and financial accounting, auditing, tax accounting, and governmental and not-for-profit accounting each require specific training and skill. After the Progress Assessment, we will clarify the difference between accounting and bookkeeping.

The National Park Service, with its workforce of over 26,000 employees, maintains and protects places special to the people of the United States, like the geysers of Yellowstone. Such government organizations employ accountants, auditors, and financial managers.

tax accountant
An accountant trained in tax law and responsible for preparing tax returns or developing tax strategies.

government and not-for-profit accounting
Accounting system for organizations whose purpose is not generating a profit but serving ratepayers, taxpayers, and others according to a duly approved budget.

progress assessment

- What is the key difference between managerial and financial accounting?
- How is the job of a private accountant different from that of a public accountant?
- What is the job of an auditor?

accounting cycle
A six-step procedure that results in the preparation and analysis of the major financial statements.

bookkeeping
The recording of business transactions.

journal
The record book or computer program where accounting data are first entered.

double-entry bookkeeping
The practice of writing every business transaction in two places.

ledger
A specialized accounting book or computer program in which information from accounting journals is accumulated into specific categories and posted so that managers can find all the information about one account in the same place.

trial balance
A summary of all the financial data in the account ledgers that ensures the figures are correct and balanced.

▶ PPT 17-16:
The Accounting Cycle

figure 17.4
STEPS IN THE ACCOUNTING CYCLE

LEARNING goal 3 *

List the steps in the accounting cycle, distinguish between accounting and bookkeeping, and explain how computers are used in accounting.

THE ACCOUNTING CYCLE

The **accounting cycle** is a six-step procedure that results in the preparation and analysis of the major financial statements (see Figure 17.4). It relies on the work of both a bookkeeper and an accountant. **Bookkeeping**, the recording of business transactions, is a basic part of financial reporting. Accounting, however, goes far beyond the mere recording of financial information. Accountants classify and summarize financial data provided by bookkeepers, and then interpret the data and report the information to management. They also suggest strategies for improving the firm's financial condition and prepare financial analyses and income tax returns.

A bookkeeper's first task is to divide all the firm's transactions into meaningful categories such as sales documents, purchasing receipts, and shipping documents, being very careful to keep the information organized and manageable. Bookkeepers then record financial data from the original transaction documents (sales slips and so forth) into a record book or computer program called a **journal**. The word *journal* comes from the French word *jour*, which means "day." Therefore, a journal is where the day's transactions are kept.

It's quite possible to make a mistake when recording financial transactions, like entering $10.98 as $10.89. Bookkeepers record all transactions in two places so that they can check one list of transactions against the other to make sure both add up to the same amount. If the amounts are not equal, the bookkeeper knows there is a mistake. The practice of writing every transaction in two places is called **double-entry bookkeeping**. It requires two entries in the journal and in the ledgers (discussed next) for each transaction.

Suppose a business wanted to determine how much it paid for office supplies in the first quarter of the year. Without a specific bookkeeping tool, that would be difficult—even with accurate accounting journals. Therefore, bookkeepers use a specialized accounting book or computer program called a **ledger**. In the ledger, they transfer (or post) information from accounting journals into specific categories so managers can find all the information about a single account, like office supplies or cash, in one place.

The next step in the accounting cycle is to prepare a **trial balance**, a summary of all the financial data in the account ledgers that ensures the figures

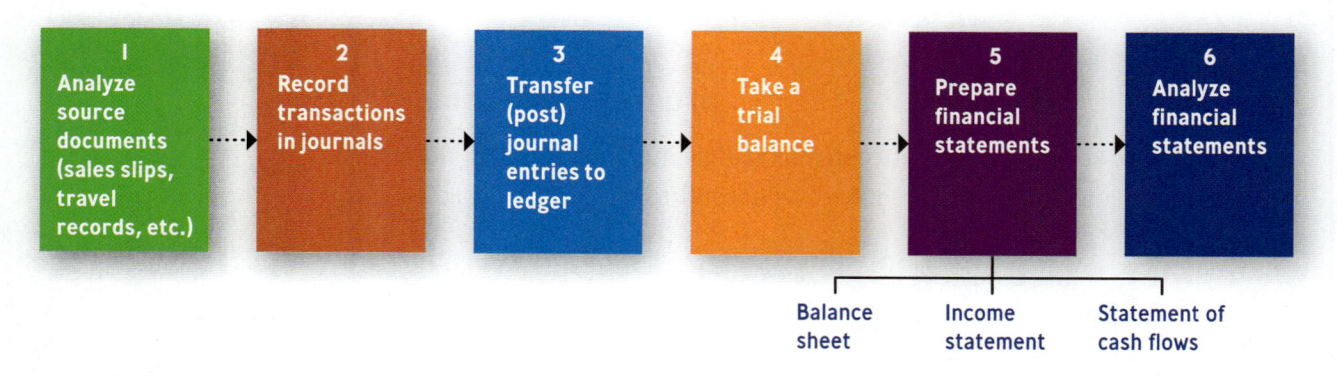

---

1. Analyze source documents (sales slips, travel records, etc.) ┄▶ 2. Record transactions in journals ┄▶ 3. Transfer (post) journal entries to ledger ┄▶ 4. Take a trial balance ┄▶ 5. Prepare financial statements ┄▶ 6. Analyze financial statements

From step 5: Balance sheet | Income statement | Statement of cash flows are correct and balanced. If the information in the account ledgers is not accurate, the accountant must correct it before preparing the firm's financial statements. Then he or she prepares the firm's financial statements—including a balance sheet, an income statement, and a statement of cash flows—according to generally accepted accounting principles.

◀ PPT 17-17:
Bookkeeping's Role

◀ PPT 17-18:
Bookkeeping's Role

Accounting Technology

Computers and accounting software have considerably simplified the accounting process. Computerized accounting programs post information from journals instantaneously, even from remote locations, so that financial information is readily available whenever the organization needs it. That frees accountants for more important tasks such as financial analysis.[21] Computerized accounting programs are particularly helpful to small-business owners who often lack the strong accounting support within their companies that larger firms enjoy. Accounting software—such as Intuit's QuickBooks and Sage's Peachtree—addresses the specific needs of small businesses, often significantly different from the needs of a major corporation. Business owners should, however, understand exactly which computer systems and programs are best suited for their particular needs.[22] That's one reason entrepreneurs planning to start a company should either hire or consult with an accountant to identify the particular needs of their firm. They can then develop a specific computer accounting system that works with the accounting software they've chosen.

A computer is a wonderful tool for businesspeople and helps ease the monotony of bookkeeping and accounting work, but no computer has yet been programmed to make good financial decisions by itself.[23] The work of an accountant requires training and very specific competencies. After the Progress Assessment, we'll explore the balance sheet, income statement, and statement of cash flows. It's from the information in these financial statements that the accountant analyzes and evaluates the financial condition of the firm.

progress assessment

- How is the job of the bookkeeper different from an accountant?
- What's the purpose of accounting journals and a ledger?
- Why is it necessary for a bookkeeper to prepare a trial balance?
- What advantages do computers provide businesses in maintaining and compiling accounting information?

LEARNING goal 4 *

Explain how the major financial statements differ.

UNDERSTANDING KEY FINANCIAL STATEMENTS

A **financial statement** is a summary of all the financial transactions that have occurred over a particular period. Financial statements indicate a firm's financial health and stability, and are key factors in management decision

financial statement
A summary of all the transactions that have occurred over a particular period.

making. That's why stockholders (the owners of the firm), bondholders and banks (people and institutions that lend money to the firm), labor unions, employees, and the Internal Revenue Service are all interested in a firm's financial statements.[24] The key financial statements of a business are:

1. The *balance sheet*, which reports the firm's financial condition *on a specific date*.
2. The *income statement*, which summarizes revenues, cost of goods, and expenses (including taxes), for a specific period and highlights the total profit or loss the firm experienced *during that period*.
3. The *statement of cash flows*, which provides a summary of money coming into and going out of the firm that tracks a company's cash receipts and cash payments.

The differences among the financial statements can best be summarized this way: The balance sheet details what the company owns and owes on a certain day; the income statement shows the revenue a firm earned selling its products compared to its selling costs (profit or loss) over a specific period of time; and the statement of cash flows highlights the difference between cash coming in and cash going out of a business. To fully understand this important financial information, you need to know the purpose of an organization's financial statements. To help with this task, we'll explain each statement in more detail next.

The Fundamental Accounting Equation

Imagine you don't owe anybody money. That is, you have no liabilities (debts). In this case, your assets (cash and so forth) are equal to what you *own* (your equity). However, if you borrow some money from a friend, you have incurred a liability. Your assets are now equal to what you *owe* plus what you own. Translated into business terms, Assets = Liabilities + Owners' equity.

In accounting, this equation must always be balanced. For example, suppose you have $50,000 in cash and decide to use that money to open a small coffee shop. Your business has assets of $50,000 and no debts. The accounting equation would look like this:

Assets   = Liabilities + Owners' equity
$50,000 = $0   + $50,000

You have $50,000 cash and $50,000 owners' equity (the amount of your investment in the business—sometimes referred to as net worth). However, before opening the business, you borrow $30,000 from a local bank; now the equation changes. You have $30,000 of additional cash, but you also have a debt (liability) of $30,000. (Remember, in double-entry bookkeeping we record each business transaction in two places.)

Your financial position within the business has changed. The equation is still balanced but we change it to reflect the borrowing transaction:

Assets   = Liabilities + Owners' equity
$80,000 = $30,000   + $50,000

This **fundamental accounting equation** is the basis for the balance sheet.

PPT 17-19: Financial Statements

Service firms like veterinarian offices rely on the same set of financial statements as manufacturers like Honda and retail sales firms like Macy's. What are some of the assets and liabilities a typical service business like this one would carry on its balance sheet?

PPT 17-20: The Fundamental Accounting Equation

LECTURE LINK 17-5: Finding a Friendly Factor

fundamental accounting equation
Assets = Liabilities + Owners' equity; this is the basis for the balance sheet.

The Balance Sheet

A **balance sheet** is the financial statement that reports a firm's financial condition at a specific time. As highlighted in the sample balance sheet in Figure 17.5 (for our hypothetical vegetarian restaurant Very Vegetarian introduced in Chapter 13), assets are listed in a separate column from liabilities and owners' (or stockholders') equity. The assets are equal to, or *balanced* with, the liabilities and owners' (or stockholders') equity. The balance sheet is that simple.

> **balance sheet**
> Financial statement that reports a firm's financial condition at a specific time and is composed of three major accounts: assets, liabilities, and owners' equity.

VERY VEGETARIAN
Balance Sheet
December 31, 2011

Assets

① Current assets
Cash		$ 15,000
Accounts receivable		200,000
Notes receivable		50,000
Inventory		335,000
Total current assets		**$600,000**

② Fixed assets
Land		$ 40,000	
Building and improvements	$200,000		
Less: Accumulated depreciation	−90,000		
		110,000	
Equipment and vehicles	$ 120,000		
Less: Accumulated depreciation	−80,000		
		40,000	
Furniture and fixtures	$ 26,000		
Less: Accumulated depreciation	−10,000		
		16,000	
Total fixed assets			206,000

③ Intangible assets
Goodwill	$ 20,000	
Total intangible assets		20,000
Total assets		**$ 826,000**

Liabilities and Owners' Equity

④ Current liabilities
Accounts payable	$ 40,000	
Notes payable (due June 2011)	8,000	
Accrued taxes	150,000	
Accrued salaries	90,000	
Total current liabilities		$ 288,000

⑤ Long-term liabilities
Notes payable (due Mar. 2015)	$ 35,000	
Bonds payable (due Dec. 2020)	290,000	
Total long-term liabilities		325,000
Total liabilities		**$ 613,000**

⑥ Owners' equity
Common stock (1,000,000 shares)	$ 100,000	
Retained earnings	113,000	
Total owners' equity		213,000
Total liabilities & owners' equity		**$ 826,000**

figure 17.5
SAMPLE VERY VEGETARIAN BALANCE SHEET

① Current assets: Items that can be converted to cash within one year.
② Fixed assets: Items such as land, buildings, and equipment that are relatively permanent.
③ Intangible assets: Items of value such as patents and copyrights that don't have a physical form.
④ Current liabilities: Payments that are due in one year or less.
⑤ Long-term liabilities: Payments not due for one year or longer.
⑥ Owners' equity: The value of what stockholders own in a firm (also called stockholders' equity).

Since it's critical that businesspeople understand the financial information on the balance sheet, let's take a closer look at what is in the asset account and what is in the liabilities and owners' equity accounts.

Let's say you want to know what your financial condition is at a given time. Maybe you want to buy a house or car and therefore need to calculate your available resources. One of the best measuring sticks is your balance sheet. First, add up everything you own—cash, property, and money owed you. These are your assets. Subtract from that the money you owe others—credit card debt, IOUs, car loan, and student loan. These are your liabilities. The resulting figure is your net worth, or equity. This is fundamentally what companies do in preparing a balance sheet: follow the procedures set in the fundamental accounting equation. In that preparation, it's important to follow generally accepted accounting principles (GAAP).

Classifying Assets

Assets are economic resources (things of value) owned by a firm. Assets include productive, tangible items such as equipment, buildings, land, furniture, and motor vehicles that help generate income, as well as intangible items with value like patents, trademarks, copyrights, and goodwill. Goodwill represents the value attached to factors such as a firm's reputation, location, and superior products. Goodwill is included on a balance sheet when one firm acquires another and pays more for it than the value of its tangible assets. Intangible assets like brand names can be among the firm's most valuable resources. Think of the value of brand names such as Starbucks, Coca-Cola, McDonald's, and Intel.[25] Not all companies, however, list intangible assets on their balance sheets.

We list assets on the firm's balance sheet in order of their **liquidity**, or the ease with which we can convert them to cash. Speedier conversion means higher liquidity. For example, an *account receivable* is an amount of money owed to the firm that it expects to receive within one year. It is considered a liquid asset because it can be quickly converted to cash. Land, however, is not considered a liquid asset because it takes time, effort, and paperwork to sell. It is considered as a fixed or long-term asset. Assets are thus divided into three categories, according to how quickly they can be turned into cash:

1. **Current assets** are items that can or will be converted into cash within one year. They include cash, accounts receivable, and inventory.
2. **Fixed assets** are long-term assets that are relatively permanent such as land, buildings, and equipment. (On the balance sheet we also refer to these as property, plant, and equipment.)
3. **Intangible assets** are long-term assets that have no physical form but do have value. Patents, trademarks, copyrights, and goodwill are intangible assets.

Liabilities and Owners' Equity Accounts

Liabilities are what the business owes to others—its debts. *Current liabilities* are debts due in one year or less. *Long-term liabilities* are debts not due for one year or more. The following are common liability accounts recorded on a balance sheet (see Figure 17.5 again):

1. **Accounts payable** are current liabilities or bills the company owes others for merchandise or services it purchased on credit but has not yet paid for.

---

assets
Economic resources (things of value) owned by a firm.

▶ PPT 17-21:
Assets

▶ PPT 17-22:
Classifying Assets

liquidity
The ease with which an asset can be converted into cash.

current assets
Items that can or will be converted into cash within one year.

fixed assets
Assets that are relatively permanent, such as land, buildings, and equipment.

intangible assets
Long-term assets (e.g., patents, trademarks, copyrights) that have no real physical form but do have value.

liabilities
What the business owes to others (debts).

accounts payable
Current liabilities are bills the company owes to others for merchandise or services purchased on credit but not yet paid for.

2. **Notes payable** can be short-term or long-term liabilities (like loans from banks) that a business promises to repay by a certain date.
3. **Bonds payable** are long-term liabilities; money lent to the firm that it must pay back. (We discuss bonds in depth in Chapters 18 and 19.)

As we saw in the fundamental accounting equation, the value of things you own (assets) minus the amount of money you owe others (liabilities) is called *equity*. The value of what stockholders own in a firm (minus liabilities) is called *stockholders' equity* or *shareholders' equity*. Because stockholders are the owners of a firm, we also call stockholders' equity **owners' equity**, or the amount of the business that belongs to the owners, minus any liabilities the business owes. The formula for owners' equity, then, is assets minus liabilities.

The owners' equity account will differ according to the type of organization. For sole proprietors and partners, owners' equity means the value of everything owned by the business minus any liabilities of the owner(s), such as bank loans. Owners' equity in these firms is called the *capital account*.

For corporations, the owners' equity account records the owners' claims to funds they have invested in the firm (such as stock), as well as retained earnings. **Retained earnings** are accumulated earnings from the firm's profitable operations that are reinvested in the business and not paid out to stockholders in distributions of company profits. (Distributions of profits, called dividends, are discussed in Chapter 19.) Take a few moments to look again at Figure 17.5 and see what facts you can determine about the vegetarian restaurant, Very Vegetarian, from its balance sheet. After the Progress Assessment, have some fun and estimate your own personal net worth, following the directions in Figure 17.6.

notes payable
Short-term or long-term liabilities that a business promises to repay by a certain date.

◀ PPT 17-23:
Classifying Liabilities

bonds payable
Long-term liabilities that represent money lent to the firm that must be paid back.

owners' equity
The amount of the business that belongs to the owners minus any liabilities owed by the business.

◀ PPT 17-24:
Owners' Equity Accounts

retained earnings
The accumulated earnings from a firm's profitable operations that were reinvested in the business and not paid out to stockholders in dividends.

progress assessment

- What do we call the formula for the balance sheet? What three accounts does it include?
- What does it mean to list assets according to liquidity?
- What is included in the liabilities account on the balance sheet?
- What is owners' equity and how do we determine it?

◀ PPT 17-25:
Progress Assessment

◀ LECTURE LINK 17-6:
When is a Sale a Sale?

figure 17.6

YOU INCORPORATED

How do you think You Inc. stacks up financially? Let's take a little time to find out. You may be pleasantly surprised, or you may realize that you need to think hard about planning your financial future. Remember, your net worth is nothing more than the difference between what you own (assets) and what you owe (liabilities). Be honest, and do your best to give a fair evaluation of your private property's value.

ASSETS		LIABILITIES	
Cash	$ _____	Installment loans & interest	$ _____
Savings account	_____	Other loans & interest	_____
Checking account	_____	Credit card accounts	_____
Home	_____	Mortgage	_____
Stocks & bonds	_____	Taxes	_____
Automobile	_____	Cell phone service	_____
IRA or Keogh	_____		
Personal property	_____		
Other assets	_____		
Total assets	$ _____	Total liabilities	$ _____

Determine your net worth:

Total assets	$ _____
Total liabilities	− _____
Net worth	$ _____

> **CRITICAL THINKING EXERCISE 17-2:**
> The Pizza Stand

income statement
The financial statement that shows a firm's profit after costs, expenses, and taxes; it summarizes all of the resources that have come into the firm (revenue), all the resources that have left the firm, and the resulting net income.

> **PPT 17-26:**
> The Income Statement

net income or net loss
Revenue left over after all costs and expenses, including taxes, are paid.

figure 17.7
SAMPLE VERY VEGETARIAN INCOME STATEMENT

① Revenue: Value of what's received from goods sold, services rendered, and other financial sources.
② Cost of goods sold: Cost of merchandise sold or cost of raw materials or parts used for producing items for resale.
③ Gross profit: How much the firm earned by buying or selling merchandise.
④ Operating expenses: Cost incurred in operating a business.
⑤ Net income after taxes: Profit or loss over a specific period after subtracting all costs and expenses, including taxes.

The Income Statement

The financial statement that shows a firm's bottom line—that is, its profit after costs, expenses, and taxes—is the **income statement**. The income statement summarizes all the resources, called *revenue*, that have come into the firm from operating activities, money resources the firm used up, expenses it incurred in doing business, and resources it has left after paying all costs and expenses, including taxes. The resources (revenue) left over or depleted are referred to as **net income or net loss** (see Figure 17.7).

The income statement reports the firm's financial operations over a particular period of time, usually a year, a quarter of a year, or a month. It's the financial statement that reveals whether the business is actually earning a profit or losing money.[26] The income statement includes valuable financial information for stockholders, lenders, potential investors, employees, and of course the government. Because it's so valuable, let's take a quick look at

VERY VEGETARIAN
Income Statement
For the Year Ended December 31, 2011

① **Revenues**			
Gross sales		$720,000	
Less: Sales returns and allowances	$12,000		
Sales discounts	8,000	−20,000	
Net sales			$700,000
② **Cost of goods sold**			
Beginning inventory, Jan. 1		$200,000	
Merchandise purchases	$400,000		
Freight	40,000		
Net purchases		440,000	
Cost of goods available for sale	$640,000		
Less ending inventory, Dec. 31		−230,000	
Cost of goods sold			−410,000
③ **Gross profit**			$290,000
④ **Operating expenses**			
Selling expenses			
Salaries for salespeople	$90,000		
Advertising	18,000		
Supplies	2,000		
Total selling expenses		$110,000	
General expenses			
Office salaries	$67,000		
Depreciation	1,500		
Insurance	1,500		
Rent	28,000		
Light, heat, and power	12,000		
Miscellaneous	2,000		
		112,000	
Total operating expenses			222,000
Net income before taxes			$68,000
Less: Income tax expense			19,000
⑤ **Net income after taxes**			$49,000

how to compile the income statement. Then we will discuss what each element in it means.

> Revenue
> − Cost of goods sold
> = Gross Profit (gross margin)
> − Operating expenses
> = Net income before taxes
> − Taxes
> = Net income or loss

Revenue

Revenue is the monetary value of what a firm received for goods sold, services rendered, and other payments (such as rents received, money paid to the firm for use of its patents, and interest earned). Be sure not to confuse the terms *revenue* and *sales*; they are not the same thing. True, most revenue the firm earns does come from sales, but companies can also have other sources of revenue. Also, a quick glance at the income statement shows you that *gross sales* refers to the total of all sales the firm completed. *Net sales* are gross sales minus returns, discounts, and allowances.

Cost of Goods Sold

The **cost of goods sold (or cost of goods manufactured)** measures the cost of merchandise the firm sells or the cost of raw materials and supplies it used in producing items for resale. It makes sense to compare how much a business earned by selling merchandise and how much it spent to make or buy the merchandise. The cost of goods sold includes the purchase price plus any freight charges paid to transport goods, plus any costs associated with storing the goods.

In financial reporting, it doesn't matter when a firm places a particular item in its inventory, but it does matter how an accountant records the cost of the item when the firm sells it. To find out why, read the Spotlight on Small Business box on p. 470 about two inventory valuation methods.

When we subtract the cost of goods sold from net sales, we get gross profit or gross margin. **Gross profit (or gross margin)** is how much a firm earned by buying (or making) and selling merchandise. In a service firm, there may be no cost of goods sold; therefore, gross profit could *equal* net sales. Gross profit does not tell you everything you need to know about the firm's financial performance. To get that, you must also subtract the business's expenses.

Operating Expenses

In selling goods or services, a business incurs certain **operating expenses** such as rent, salaries, supplies, utilities, and insurance. Other operating expenses, like depreciation, are a bit more complex.

Have you ever heard that a new car depreciates in market value as soon as you drive it off the dealer's lot? The same principle holds true for assets such as equipment and machinery. **Depreciation** is the systematic write-off of the cost of a tangible asset over its estimated useful life. Under accounting rules set by GAAP and the Internal

---

cost of goods sold (or cost of goods manufactured)
A measure of the cost of merchandise sold or cost of raw materials and supplies used for producing items for resale.

◄ PPT 17-27:
The Income Statement

gross profit (or gross margin)
How much a firm earned by buying (or making) and selling merchandise.

operating expenses
Costs involved in operating a business, such as rent, utilities, and salaries.

depreciation
The systematic write-off of the cost of a tangible asset over its estimated useful life.

◄ PPT 17-28:
Accounts of the Income Statement

Jennifer Behar runs a small Miami bakery that sells products like chocolate biscotti and rosemary flatbread to high-end food retailers like Whole Foods Market and Dean & DeLuca. Behar began her business with borrowed funds and doubled revenues in one recent year. What is the difference between revenue and sales?

◄ PPT 17-29:
Accounts of the Income Statement

◄ PPT 17-30:
Accounting for What's Coming and Going in Small Business

SPOTLIGHT ON SMALL *business

www.aicpa.org

Accounting for What's Coming and Going in a Small Business

Generally accepted accounting principles (GAAP) sometimes permit an accountant to use different methods of accounting for a firm's inventory. Let's look at two possible treatments—FIFO and LIFO.

Say a college bookstore buys 100 copies of a particular textbook in July at $70 a copy. When classes begin, the bookstore sells 50 copies of the text to students at $90 each. Since the book will be used again next term, the store places the 50 copies not sold in its inventory until then.

In late December, when the bookstore orders 50 additional copies of the text to sell for the coming term, the publisher's price has increased to $80 a copy due to inflation and other costs. The bookstore now has in its inventory 100 copies of the same textbook from different purchase cycles. If it sells 50 copies to students at $100 each at the beginning of the new term, what's the bookstore's cost of the book for accounting purposes?

It depends.

The books are identical, but the accounting treatment is different. If the bookstore uses a method called first in, first out (FIFO), the cost of goods sold is $70 for each textbook, because the textbook the store bought first—the *first in*—cost $70. The bookstore could use another method, however. Under last in, first out (LIFO), its *last* purchase of the textbooks, at $80 each, determines the cost of each of the 50 textbooks sold.

If the book sells for $100, what is the difference in gross margin between using FIFO and using LIFO?

Most businesses incur operating expenses including rent, salaries, utilities, supplies, and insurance. What are some of the likely operating expenses for this firm?

Revenue Service (which are beyond the scope of this chapter), companies are permitted to recapture the cost of these assets over time by using depreciation as an operating expense.

We can classify operating expenses as either selling or general expenses. *Selling expenses* are related to the marketing and distribution of the firm's goods or services, such as advertising, salespeople's salaries, and supplies. *General expenses* are administrative expenses of the firm such as office salaries, depreciation, insurance, and rent. Accountants are trained to help you record all applicable expenses and find other relevant expenses you need to deduct from your taxable income as a part of doing business.

Net Profit or Loss

After deducting all expenses, we can determine the firm's net income before taxes, also referred to as net earnings or net profit (see Figure 17.7 again). After allocating for taxes, we get to the *bottom line*, which is the net income (or perhaps net loss) the firm incurred from revenue minus sales returns, costs, expenses, and taxes over a period of time. We can now answer the question "Did the business earn or lose money in the specific reporting period?"

The basic principles of the balance sheet and income statement are already familiar to you. You know how to keep track of costs and expenses when you prepare your own budget. If your rent and utilities exceed your earnings, you know you're in trouble. If you need more money, you may need to sell some of the things you own to meet your expenses. The same is true in business. Companies need to keep track of how much money they earn and spend, and how much cash they have on hand. The only difference is that they tend to have more complex problems and a good deal more information to record than you do.

Users of financial statements are interested in how a firm handles the flow of cash coming in and flowing out. Cash flow problems can plague both businesses and individuals. Keep this in mind as we look at the statement of cash flows next.

◀ LECTURE LINK 17-7:
It's the Earnings That Count

◀ CRITICAL THINKING EXERCISE 17-3:
Preparing Financial Statements

The Statement of Cash Flows

The **statement of cash flows** reports cash receipts and cash disbursements related to the three major activities of a firm:

- *Operations* are cash transactions associated with running the business.
- *Investments* are cash used in or provided by the firm's investment activities.
- *Financing* is cash raised by taking on new debt, or equity capital or cash used to pay business expenses, past debts, or company dividends.

statement of cash flows
Financial statement that reports cash receipts and disbursements related to a firm's three major activities: operations, investments, and financing.

◀ PPT 17-31:
The Statement of Cash Flow

Accountants analyze all changes in the firm's cash that have occurred from operating, investing, and financing in order to determine the firm's net cash position. The statement of cash flows also gives the firm some insight into how to handle cash better so that no cash-flow problems occur—such as having no cash on hand.

Figure 17.8 shows a sample statement of cash flows, again using the example of Very Vegetarian. As you can see, this financial statement answers such

VERY VEGETARIAN
Statement of Cash Flows
For the Year Ended December 31, 2011

① Cash flows from operating activities		
Cash received from customers	$700,000	
Cash paid to suppliers and employees	(567,000)	
Interest paid	(64,000)	
Income tax paid	(19,000)	
Interest and dividends received	2,000	
Net cash provided by operating activities		$52,000
② Cash flows from investing activities		
Proceeds from sale of plant assets	$ 4,000	
Payments for purchase of equipment	(23,000)	
Net cash provided by investing activities		(19,000)
③ Cash flows from financing activities		
Proceeds from issuance of short-term debt	$ 2,000	
Payment of long-term debt	(8,000)	
Payment of dividends	(15,000)	
Net cash inflow from financing activities		(21,000)
Net change in cash and equivalents		$ 12,000
Cash balance (beginning of year)		3,000
Cash balance (end of year)		$ 15,000

figure 17.8

SAMPLE VERY VEGETARIAN STATEMENT OF CASH FLOWS

① Cash receipts from sales, commissions, fees, interest, and dividends. Cash payments for salaries, inventories, operating expenses, interest, and taxes.

② Includes cash flows that are generated through a company's purchase or sale of long-term operational assets, investments in other companies, and its lending activities.

③ Cash inflows and outflows associated with the company's own equity transactions or its borrowing activities.

> **LECTURE LINK 17-8:**
> Using the Statement of Cash Flows
>
> **BONUS CASE 17-1:**
> The Best Laid Plans Often Go Awry
>
> **PPT 17-32:**
> Understanding Cash Flow

cash flow
The difference between cash coming in and cash going out of a business.

Cash flow is the difference between money coming into and going out of a business. Careful cash flow management is a must for a business of any size, but it's particularly important for small businesses and for seasonal businesses like ski resorts. Have you read of any firms that were forced into bankruptcy because of cash flow problems?

questions as: How much cash came into the business from current operations such as buying and selling goods and services? Did the firm use cash to buy stocks, bonds, or other investments? Did it sell some investments that brought in cash? How much money did the firm take in from issuing stock?

We analyze these and other financial transactions to see their effect on the firm's cash position. Managing cash flow can mean success or failure of any business, which is why we analyze it in more depth in the next section.

The Need for Cash Flow Analysis

Cash flow, if not properly managed, can cause a business much concern.[27] But cash flow analysis is not difficult to understand.[28] Let's say you borrow $100 from a friend to buy a used bike and agree to pay her back at the end of the week. You then sell the bike for $150 to someone else, who also agrees to pay you by the end of the week. Unfortunately, by the weekend your buyer does not have the money as promised, and says he will have to pay you next month. Meanwhile, your friend wants the $100 you agreed to pay her by the end of the week!

What seemed a great opportunity to make an easy $50 profit is now a cause for concern. You owe $100 and have no cash. What do you do? If you were a business, you might default on the loan and possibly go bankrupt, even though you had the potential for profit.

It's possible for a business to increase sales and profit yet still suffer cash flow problems.[29] **Cash flow** is simply the difference between cash coming in and cash going out of a business. Poor cash flow constitutes a major operating problem for many companies and is particularly difficult for small and seasonal businesses.[30] Accountants sometimes face tough ethical challenges in reporting the flow of funds into a business. Read the Making Ethical Decisions box to see how such an ethical dilemma can arise.

How do cash flow problems start? Often in order to meet the growing demands of customers, a business buys goods on credit (using no cash). If it then sells a large number of goods on credit (getting no cash), the company needs more credit from a lender (usually a bank) to pay its bills. When the firm has reached its credit limit and can borrow no more, it has a severe cash flow problem. That problem could, unfortunately, force the firm into bankruptcy, even though sales may be strong—because no cash was available when it was most needed.

Cash flow analysis shows that a business's relationship with its lenders is critical to preventing cash flow problems.[31] Accountants provide valuable insight and advice to businesses in managing cash flow, suggesting whether they need cash and how much.[32] After the Progress Assessment, we will see how accountants analyze financial statements using ratios.

progress assessment

- What are the key steps in preparing an income statement?
- What's the difference between revenue and income on the income statement?
- Why is the statement of cash flows important in evaluating a firm's operations?

MAKING ethical decisions

www.fasb.gov

On the Accounting Hot Seat

You are the only accountant employed by a small manufacturing firm suffering an economic downturn. You know your employer is going to ask the bank for an additional loan so that the firm can continue to pay its bills. Unfortunately, the financial statements for the year will not show good results, and your best guess is that the bank will not approve a loan on the basis of the financial information you will present.

Your boss approaches you in early January, before you have closed the books for the preceding year, and suggests you might "improve" the company's financial statements by treating the sales made at the beginning of January as if they were made in December. He says you can cover up the trail so that auditors will not discover the discrepancy.

You know this step is against the professional rules of the Financial Accounting Standards Board (FASB), and you argue with your boss about it. He tells you that without the bank loan, the business is likely to close. That means you and everyone else in the firm will be out of a job. You believe he's probably right, and in the current economic downturn it will be tough to find a new job. What are your alternatives? What are the likely consequences of each? What will you do?

LEARNING goal 5 *

Demonstrate the application of ratio analysis in reporting financial information.

ANALYZING FINANCIAL PERFORMANCE USING RATIOS

The firm's financial statements—its balance sheet, income statement, and statement of cash flows—form the basis for financial analyses performed by accountants inside and outside the firm. **Ratio analysis** is the assessment of a firm's financial condition, using calculations and financial ratios developed from the firm's financial statements. Financial ratios are especially useful in comparing the company's performance to its financial objectives and to the performance of other firms in its industry. You probably are already familiar with the use of ratios. For example, in basketball, we express the number of shots made from the foul line with a ratio: shots made to shots attempted. A player who shoots 85 percent from the foul line is considered an outstanding foul shooter; you don't want to foul this player in a close game.

Whether ratios measure an athlete's performance or the financial health of a business, they provide valuable information. Financial ratios provide key insights into how a firm compares to other firms in its industry on liquidity, amount of debt, profitability, and overall business activity. Understanding and interpreting business ratios is a key to sound financial analysis. Let's look briefly at four key types of ratios businesses use to measure financial performance.

Liquidity Ratios

We've seen that *liquidity* refers to how fast an asset can be converted to cash. Liquidity ratios measure a company's ability to turn assets into cash to pay its

ratio analysis
The assessment of a firm's financial condition using calculations and interpretations of financial ratios developed from the firm's financial statements.

◀ PPT 17-33:
On the Accounting Hot Seat

◀ PPT 17-34:
Using Financial Ratios

◀ LECTURE LINK 17-9:
Staying Alive in Tough Economic Times

◀ CRITICAL THINKING EXERCISE 17-4:
Calculating Financial Ratios (Advanced)

◀ PPT 17-35:
Commonly Used Liquidity Ratios

short-term debts (liabilities that must be repaid within one year). These short-term debts are of particular importance to lenders of the firm who expect to be paid on time. Two key liquidity ratios are the current ratio and the acid-test ratio.[33]

The *current ratio* is the ratio of a firm's current assets to its current liabilities. This information appears on the firm's balance sheet. Look back at Figure 17.5, which details Very Vegetarian's balance sheet. The company lists current assets of $600,000 and current liabilities of $288,000, yielding a current ratio of 2.08, which means Very Vegetarian has $2.08 of current assets for every $1 of current liabilities. See the following calculation:

$$\text{Current ratio} = \frac{\text{Current assets}}{\text{Current liabilities}} = \frac{\$600,000}{\$288,000} = \$2.08$$

The question is: Is Very Vegetarian financially secure for the short term (less than one year)? It depends! Usually a company with a current ratio of 2 or better is considered a safe risk for lenders granting short-term credit, since it appears to be performing in line with market expectations. However, lenders will also compare Very Vegetarian's current ratio to that of competing firms in its industry and to its current ratio from the previous year to note any significant changes.

Another key liquidity ratio, called the *acid-test* or *quick ratio*, measures the cash, marketable securities (such as stocks and bonds), and receivables of a firm, compared to its current liabilities:

$$\text{Acid-test ratio} = \frac{\text{Cash} + \text{Accounts receivable} + \text{Marketable securities}}{\text{Current liabilities}}$$

$$= \frac{\$265,000}{\$288,000} = 0.92$$

This ratio is particularly important to firms with difficulty converting inventory into quick cash. It helps answer such questions as: What if sales drop off and we can't sell our inventory? Can we still pay our short-term debt? Though ratios vary among industries, an acid-test ratio between 0.50 and 1.0 is usually considered satisfactory, but bordering on cash-flow problems. Therefore, Very Vegetarian's acid-test ratio of 0.92 could raise concerns that perhaps the firm may not meet its short-term debt and may have to go to a high-cost lender for financial assistance.

Leverage (Debt) Ratios

Leverage (debt) ratios measure the degree to which a firm relies on borrowed funds in its operations. A firm that takes on too much debt could experience problems repaying lenders or meeting promises made to stockholders. The *debt to owners' equity ratio* measures the degree to which the company is financed by borrowed funds that it must repay. Again, let's use Figure 17.5 to measure Very Vegetarian's level of debt:

$$\text{Debt to owners' equity ratio} = \frac{\text{Total liabilities}}{\text{Owners' equity}} = \frac{\$613,000}{\$213,000} = 288\%$$

Anything above 100 percent shows a firm has more debt than equity. With a ratio of 288 percent, Very Vegetarian has a rather high degree of debt compared to its equity, which implies that lenders and investors may perceive the firm to be quite risky. However, again *it's important to compare a firm's debt ratios to those of other firms in its industry,* because debt financing is more acceptable in

Profitability (Performance) Ratios

Profitability (performance) ratios measure how effectively a firm's managers are using its various resources to achieve profits. Three of the more important ratios are earnings per share (EPS), return on sales, and return on equity.

EPS is a revealing ratio because earnings help stimulate the firm's growth and provide for stockholders' dividends.[34] The Financial Accounting Standards Board requires companies to report their quarterly EPS in two ways: basic and diluted. The *basic earnings per share (basic EPS) ratio* helps determine the amount of profit a company earned for each share of outstanding common stock. The *diluted earnings per share (diluted EPS) ratio* measures the amount of profit earned for each share of outstanding common stock, but also considers stock options, warrants, preferred stock, and convertible debt securities the firm can convert into common stock. For simplicity's sake, we will compute only the basic EPS for Very Vegetarian:

$$\text{Basic earnings per share} = \frac{\text{Net income after taxes}}{\text{Number of common stock shares outstanding}}$$

$$= \frac{\$49,000}{\$1,000,000} = \$.049 \text{ per share}$$

Another reliable indicator of performance is *return on sales*, which tells us whether the firm is doing as well as its competitors in generating income from sales. We calculate it by comparing net income to total sales. Very Vegetarian's return on sales is 7 percent, a figure we must measure against similar numbers for competing firms to judge Very Vegetarian's performance:

$$\text{Return on sales} = \frac{\text{Net income}}{\text{Net sales}} = \frac{\$49,000}{\$700,000} = 7\%$$

The higher the risk of failure or loss in an industry, the higher the return investors expect on their investment; they expect to be well compensated for shouldering such odds. *Return on equity* indirectly measures risk by telling us how much a firm earned for each dollar invested by its owners.[35] We calculate it by comparing a company's net income to its total owners' equity. Very Vegetarian's return on equity looks reasonably sound since some believe anything over 15 percent is considered a reasonable return:

$$\text{Return on equity} = \frac{\text{Net income after tax}}{\text{Total owners' equity}} = \frac{\$49,000}{\$213,000} = 23\%$$

Remember that profits help companies like Very Vegetarian grow. That's why profitability ratios are such closely watched measurements of company growth and management performance.

Activity Ratios

Converting the firm's inventory to profits is a key function of management. Activity ratios tell us how effectively management is turning over inventory.

Inventory turnover ratio measures the speed with which inventory moves through the firm and gets converted into sales. Idle inventory sitting in a

---

After being turned down for a bank loan, John Halko found a novel way to finance the growth of his restaurant that keeps his leverage ratio exceptionally low: He sells customers "V.I.P. cards" for $500 to $10,000 that guarantee them discounted meals for years into the future. "I don't have to pay interest and it doesn't cost me as much to recoup," says Halko. What are some potential drawbacks of Halko's unusual approach to financing?

◄ PPT 17-37:
Profitability Ratios

◄ PPT 17-38:
Activity Ratios

Inventory turnover is critical to just about any business, particularly restaurants that serve perishable items and that must turn over tables to keep the flow of food moving and profits up. Can you think of other businesses that need to watch their inventory turnover closely?

warehouse earns nothing and costs money.[36] The more efficiently a firm sells or turns over its inventory, the higher its revenue. We can measure the inventory turnover ratio for Very Vegetarian as follows:

$$\text{Inventory turnover} = \frac{\text{Costs of goods sold}}{\text{Average inventory}} = \frac{\$410,000}{\$215,000} = 1.91 \text{ times}$$

A lower-than-average inventory turnover ratio often indicates obsolete merchandise on hand or poor buying practices. A higher-than-average ratio may signal that the firm has lost sales because of inadequate stock. Rates of inventory turnover vary from industry to industry.

Managers need to be aware of proper inventory control and expected inventory turnover to ensure proper performance. Have you ever worked as a food server in a restaurant like Very Vegetarian? How many times did your employer expect you to *turn over* a table (keep changing customers at the table) in an evening? The more times a table turns, the higher the return to the owner.

Accountants and other finance professionals use several other specific ratios, in addition to the ones we've discussed. To review where the accounting information in ratio analysis comes from, see Figure 17.9 for a quick reference. Remember, financial analysis begins where the accounting financial statements end.

Like other business disciplines, accounting is subject to change. Currently, the accounting profession is feeling the impact of the global market. The Reaching Beyond Our Borders box discusses a movement to globalize accounting procedures. It's worth saying once more that, as the language of business, accounting is a worthwhile language to learn.

▶ **BONUS CASE 17-2:**
Managing by the Numbers

▶ **LECTURE LINK 17-10:**
Knowing the Numbers

▶ **LECTURE LINK 17-11:**
Small Business Accounting

▶ **PPT 17-39:**
Progress Assessment

progress assessment

- What is the primary purpose of performing ratio analysis using the firm's financial statements?
- What are the four main categories of financial ratios?

REACHING BEYOND our borders

www.sec.gov

The Accounting Shot Heard around the World

You have read throughout this text about the tremendous impact of the global market on business. Companies like Coca-Cola and Nestlé earn more than 50 percent of their revenues from global markets, helping them grow but creating a number of accounting headaches. Multinationals must adapt their accounting reporting to the rules of multiple countries, since no global system of accounting exists. However, that situation could soon change.

As a growing number of countries have adopted the International Financial Reporting Standards (IFRS), the International Accounting Standards Board (IASB) has pushed to make them the clear accounting authority worldwide. The U.S. Securities and Exchange Commission (SEC) seems to agree and has suggested the IFRS replace the long-standing generally accepted accounting principles (GAAP) in the near future. Many in the accounting profession believe the move from GAAP to IFRS is a certainty and will probably happen by 2013.

Many others believe, however, that the accounting profession still needs to resolve some questions: Do international standards produce the same quality of reporting as GAAP? Would application and enforcement of international standards in the United States be as rigorous as they have been for GAAP? Professor Sue Haka of Michigan State University also points out that accounting exams and textbooks must be ready for implementation of IFRS. Stay tuned for the possibility of big changes on the accounting front.

Sources: David Katz, "Global Standards: Jilted at the Altar," CFO.com, accessed October 26, 2008; Edward Iwata, "Will Going Global Extend to Accounting?" *USA Today*, January 6, 2009; and Alix Stuart, "Which One When?" *CFO*, February 2009.

Balance Sheet Accounts

ASSETS	LIABILITIES	OWNERS' EQUITY
Cash	Accounts payable	Capital stock
Accounts receivable	Notes payable	Retained earnings
Inventory	Bonds payable	Common stock
Investments	Taxes payable	Treasury stock
Equipment		
Land		
Buildings		
Motor vehicles		
Goodwill		

Income Statement Accounts

REVENUES	COST OF GOODS SOLD	EXPENSES	
Sales revenue	Cost of buying goods	Wages	Interest
Rental revenue	Cost of storing goods	Rent	Donations
Commissions revenue		Repairs	Licenses
Royalty revenue		Travel	Fees
		Insurance	Supplies
		Utilities	Advertising
		Entertainment	Taxes
		Storage	

figure 17.9

ACCOUNTS IN THE BALANCE SHEET AND INCOME STATEMENT

summary

Learning Goal 1. Demonstrate the role that accounting and financial information play for a business and for its stakeholders.

- **What is accounting?**

Accounting is the recording, classifying, summarizing, and interpreting of financial events and transactions that affect an organization. The methods we use to record and summarize accounting data into reports are called an accounting system.

Learning Goal 2. Identify the different disciplines within the accounting profession.

- **How does managerial accounting differ from financial accounting?**

Managerial accounting provides information and analyses to managers within the firm to assist them in decision making. Financial accounting provides information and analyses to external users of data such as creditors and lenders.

- **What is the job of an auditor?**

Auditors review and evaluate the standards used to prepare a company's financial statements. An independent audit is conducted by a public accountant and is an evaluation and unbiased opinion about the accuracy of a company's financial statements.

- **What is the difference between a private accountant and a public accountant?**

A public accountant provides services for a fee to a variety of companies, whereas a private accountant works for a single company. Private and public accountants do essentially the same things with the exception of independent audits. Private accountants do perform internal audits, but only public accountants supply independent audits.

Learning Goal 3. List the steps in the accounting cycle, distinguish between accounting and bookkeeping, and explain how computers are used in accounting.

- **What are the six steps of the accounting cycle?**

The six steps of the accounting cycle are (1) analyzing documents; (2) recording information into journals; (3) posting that information into ledgers; (4) developing a trial balance; (5) preparing financial statements—the balance sheet, income statement, and statement of cash flows—and (6) analyzing financial statements.

- **What is the difference between bookkeeping and accounting?**

Bookkeeping is part of accounting and includes the systematic recording of data. Accounting includes classifying, summarizing, interpreting, and reporting data to management.

- **What are journals and ledgers?**

Journals are the first place bookkeepers record transactions. Bookkeepers them summarize journal entries by posting them to ledgers. Ledgers are specialized accounting books that arrange the transactions by homogeneous groups (accounts).

- **How do computers help accountants?**

Computers can record and analyze data and provide financial reports. Software can continuously analyze and test accounting systems to be sure they are functioning correctly. Computers can help decision making by providing appropriate information, but they cannot themselves make good financial decisions. Accounting applications and creativity are still human functions.

Learning Goal 4. Explain how the major financial statements differ.
- **What is a balance sheet?**

A balance sheet reports the financial position of a firm on a particular day. The fundamental accounting equation used to prepare the balance sheet is Assets = Liabilities + Owners' equity.
- **What are the major accounts of the balance sheet?**

Assets are economic resources owned by the firm, such as buildings and machinery. Liabilities are amounts the firm owes to creditors, bondholders, and others. Owners' equity is the value of everything the firm owns—its assets—minus any liabilities; thus, Owners' equity = Assets − Liabilities.
- **What is an income statement?**

An income statement reports revenues, costs, and expenses for a specific period of time (say, the year ended December 31, 2010). The formulas we use in preparing the income statement are:
  - Revenue − Cost of goods sold = Gross margin
  - Gross margin − Operating expenses = Net income before taxes
  - Net income before taxes − Taxes = Net income (or net loss)

Net income or loss is also called the bottom line.
- **What is a statement of cash flows?**

Cash flow is the difference between cash receipts (money coming in) and cash disbursements (money going out). The statement of cash flows reports cash receipts and disbursements related to the firm's major activities: operations, investments, and financing.

Learning Goal 5. Demonstrate the application of ratio analysis in reporting financial information.
- **What are the four key categories of ratios?**

The four key categories of ratios are liquidity ratios, leverage (debt) ratios, profitability (performance) ratios, and activity ratios.
- **What is the major value of ratio analysis to the firm?**

Ratio analysis provides the firm with information about its financial position in key areas *for comparison to other firms in its industry and its own past performance.*

key terms

accounting 456
accounting cycle 462
accounts payable 466
annual report 458
assets 466
auditing 460
balance sheet 465
bonds payable 467
bookkeeping 462
cash flow 472
certified internal auditor (CIA) 460
certified management accountant (CMA) 458
certified public accountant (CPA) 459
cost of goods sold (or cost of goods manufactured) 469
current assets 466
depreciation 469
double-entry bookkeeping 462
financial accounting 458
financial statement 463
fixed assets 466
fundamental accounting equation 464
government and not-for-profit accounting 461
gross profit (or gross margin) 469
income statement 468
independent audit 460
intangible assets 466
journal 462
ledger 462
liabilities 466
liquidity 466
managerial accounting 457

net income or net loss 468
notes payable 467
operating expenses 469
owners' equity 467
private accountant 458
public accountant 459
ratio analysis 473
retained earnings 467
statement of cash flows 471
tax accountant 461
trial balance 462

connect interactive applications

Reinforcing Your Connection to Concepts in Business

This chapter offers 15 interactive applications designed to help you apply what you've learned (examples of these exercises appear below). Your instructor has determined which interactive applications will benefit you throughout this course. Please refer to your instructor's assignment list in *Connect* to determine which applications you should complete.

Comprehension Case Interactive: One major purpose of accounting is to help managers make well-informed decisions. Another is to report financial information about the firm to interested stakeholders. Review the Comprehension Case featuring Bakery Barn and answer the questions about how financial information leads to important business decisions.

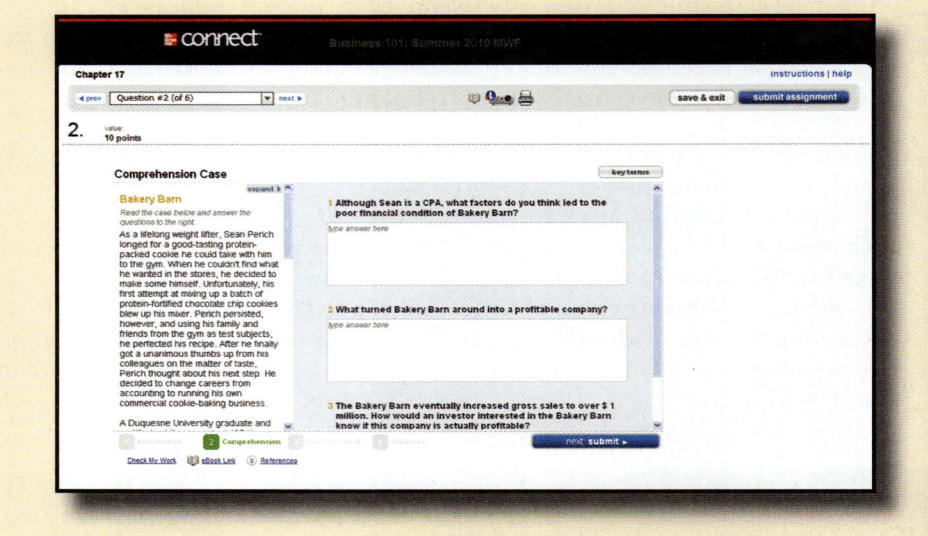

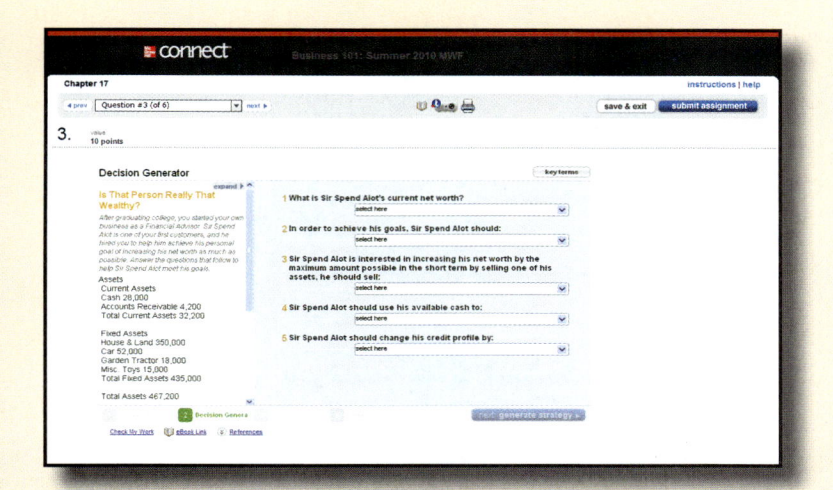

Decision Generator Interactive: You may have friends that seem to have nice cars and expensive possessions. Are these people actually wealthy or are the items actually owned by their creditors? Can a balance sheet be used to determine a person's net worth? Analyze the assets and liabilities in the scenario provided and evaluate the net worth of the individual in question.

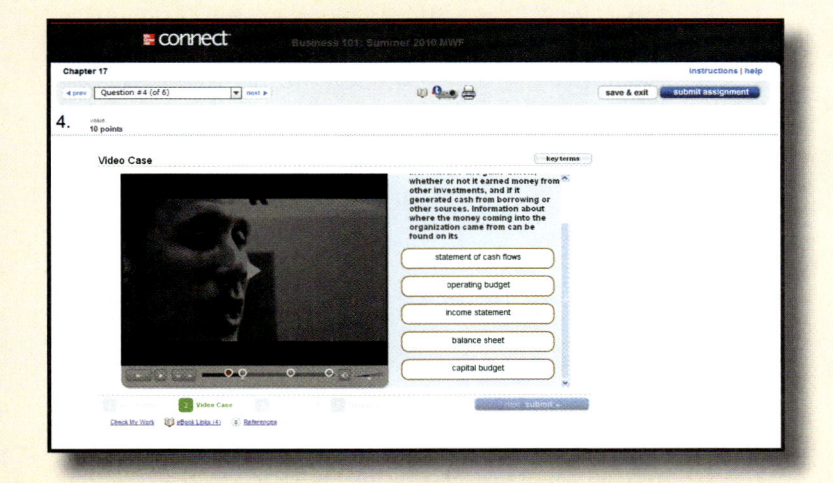

Video Case Interactive: In a start-up industry, it is crucial that firms have good financial management in order to stay in business long enough to see profits generated. Watch the video featuring arena football team, Chicago Rush, and respond to the questions when prompted.

Click and Drag Interactive: The accounting cycle is a six-step procedure that results in the preparation and analysis of major financial statements. These financial statements determine the firm's health and stability and are key factors in management decision making. Place each activity on the timeline in the correct order based on the accounting cycle. Once you have completed this step, you will be provided with a case scenario to evaluate and apply these steps.

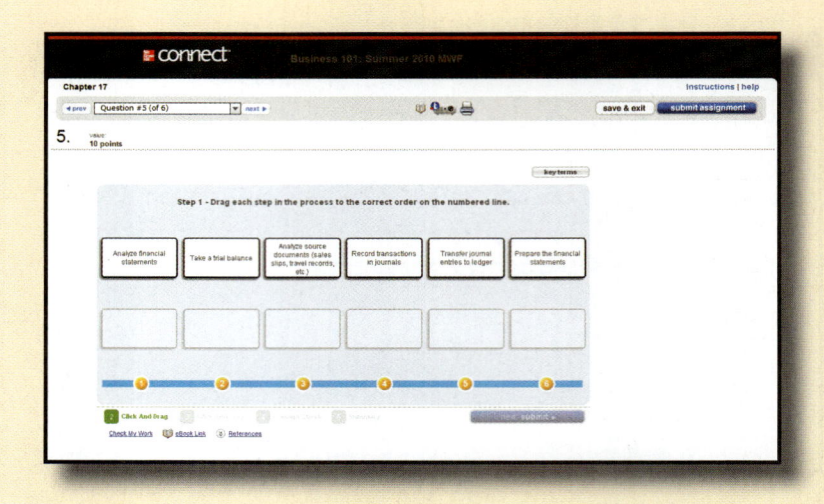

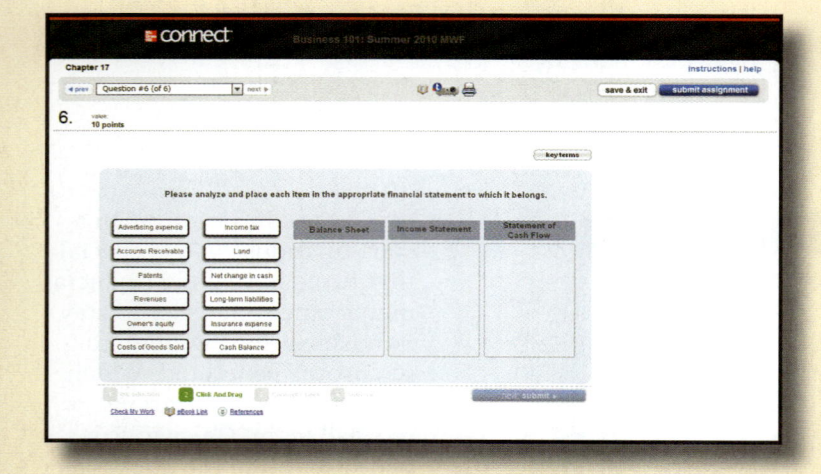

Click and Drag Interactive: The three major financial statements offer information as to the viability of a company. Analyze each item and determine where it would fall on the financial statement.

18 Financial MANAGEMENT

profile

Getting to Know
x Tonya Antonucci
Commissioner of the Women's Professional Soccer League

Lifelong soccer fanatic Tonya Antonucci is realizing a dream she's had since she was nine years old and joined her first soccer team. The former Stanford player and coach is now the commissioner of the new Women's Professional Soccer (WPS) league, launched in 2009.

Antonucci has worked in sports-related jobs since earning her MBA from Santa Clara University. She started as a project manager at Starwave, the Paul Allen–backed Internet-content company, where she worked on the Web site that eventually became ESPN.com. From there she moved to Yahoo, where she helped launch its fantasy sports arena. She eventually became general manager of Yahoo's partnership with soccer's governing global body, the Fédération Internationale de Football Association (FIFA). Antonucci ran the official Web sites for both the men's and women's World Cups.

After leaving Yahoo Sports in 2004, Antonucci attended a Stanford soccer alumni party where she met former teammate and professional star Julie Foudy. Foudy asked Antonucci whether she wanted to help revive professional women's soccer. The original Women's United Soccer Association (WUSA) folded in 2003 due to its failure to meet revenue expectations and low attendance and television ratings. Antonucci knew that to succeed this time the league had to take a different approach. She decided immediately to accept the challenge.

One of the first steps Antonucci took in planning the new league was to examine what went wrong with the WUSA. She knew that in 1999 the U.S. victory in the Women's World Cup sent the nation on a soccer high, and the team became the darling of the sports world. With the U.S. women's soccer team's popularity still soaring when the WUSA began in 2001, league officials predicted great financial rewards for its investors. Unfortunately, they also set unrealistic and unreachable financial goals. For example, operating budgets (money the league needed to operate as a business) exceeded revenue (money the league brought in through ticket sales, television earnings, and other sources). The salaries of top players were too high, the television deal was bad (viewers could not find the games), and corporate sponsorships were not as lucrative as expected. The WUSA had planned to sell at least eight national sponsorships but was able to make only

LEARNING goals

After you have read and studied this chapter, you should be able to

1. Explain the role and responsibilities of financial managers.
2. Outline the financial planning process, and explain the three key budgets in the financial plan.
3. Explain why firms need operating funds.
4. Identify and describe different sources of short-term financing.
5. Identify and describe different sources of long-term financing.

connect

Your *Connect*ion to Better Learning. 1. View the interactive presentation. 2. Practice through LearnSmart. 3. Apply your knowledge by using the interactive applications for each chapter of this text.

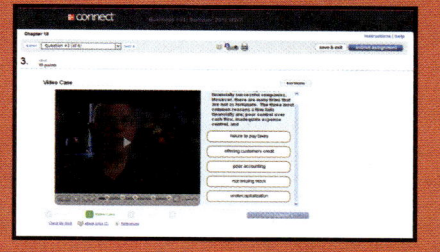

1 Prep »»»»» **2 Study** »»»»» **3 Apply**

---

two deals. The league quickly spent its entire $40 million budget the first season.

Antonucci could see that her task was challenging. She understood that the new WPS needed to limit operating costs and find as many cost-cutting opportunities as possible. WUSA teams had often played in large stadiums that typically hosted National Football League teams. Unfortunately, the stadiums looked empty on television, and renting them was expensive. Antonucci decided the WPS teams would play in smaller, soccer-specific stadiums where rent is lower and gate revenues (money from ticket sales and concessions) higher. Players' salaries also had to be addressed. She realized the $40,000 average salary set by WUSA was too high, so she instituted a team salary cap.

The WPS's seven teams are franchises, and each franchise owner has an equal financial share in the league. WPS shares marketing costs with men's Major League Soccer (MLS), saving the cost of creating a flashy marketing plan of its own. Rather than depending on TV ads to build game attendance, the WPS is community-driven; its players go to local girls' practices and ask them to come watch the teams play, engaging not only the kids but also their families. Antonucci knows that the WPS faces many financial challenges. However, by establishing realistic goals and allocating the league's funds more efficiently, she hopes to make their new league shine as brightly as the gold medals earned by many of its players.

Risk and uncertainty clearly define the role of financial management. In this chapter, you'll explore the role of finance in business. We'll discuss the challenges as well as the tools top managers like Tonya Antonucci use to attain financial stability and growth.

Sources: Liza Porteus Viana, "Women's Soccer's Tonya Antonucci," *Condé Nast Portfolio,* December 28, 2007; Kate O'Sullivan, "Going for the Gold," *CFO,* July–August 2008; Kartik Krishnaiyer, "Tonya Antonucci Interview: Women's Professional Soccer," *Soccer Lens,* July 25, 2008; and R. B. Fallstrom, "Women's Soccer League Confident Despite Recession," AP Online, January 16, 2009.

www.womensprosoccer.com

NAME THAT Company

At one time we were one of the largest companies in the United States and one of the big three in our industry. Due to severe financial problems in the late 1970s, however, our company came very close to extinction. Luckily, a government-backed loan of $1 billion helped us survive and avoid joining other companies that had failed in our industry. Who are we? (Find the answer in the chapter.)

> PPT 18-1:
> Financial Management

> PPT 18-2:
> Tonya Antonucci

> PPT 18-3:
> What's Finance?

LEARNING goal 1 *

Explain the role and responsibilities of financial managers.

THE ROLE OF FINANCE AND FINANCIAL MANAGERS

> PPT 18-4:
> Financial Management

> PPT 18-5:
> Financial Managers

finance
The function in a business that acquires funds for the firm and manages those funds within the firm.

financial management
The job of managing a firm's resources so it can meet its goals and objectives.

financial managers
Managers who examine financial data prepared by accountants and recommend strategies for improving the financial performance of the firm.

> LECTURE LINK 18-1:
> The Expanding Role of the CFO

The goal of this chapter is to answer two major questions: "What is finance?" and "What do financial managers do?" **Finance** is the function in a business that acquires funds for the firm and manages them within the firm. Finance activities include preparing budgets; doing cash flow analysis; and planning for the expenditure of funds on such assets as plant, equipment, and machinery. **Financial management** is the job of managing a firm's resources to meet its goals and objectives. Without a carefully calculated financial plan, a firm has little chance for survival, regardless of its product or marketing effectiveness. Let's briefly review the roles of accountants and financial managers.

We can compare an accountant to a skilled laboratory technician who takes blood samples and other measures of a person's health and writes the findings on a health report (in business, this process is the preparation of financial statements). A financial manager is like the doctor who interprets the report and makes recommendations that will improve the patient's health. In short, **financial managers** examine financial data prepared by accountants and recommend strategies for improving the financial performance of the firm.

Clearly financial managers can make sound financial decisions only if they understand accounting information. That's why we examined accounting in Chapter 17. Similarly, a good accountant needs to understand finance. Accounting and finance go together like peanut butter and jelly. In large and medium-sized organizations, both the accounting and finance functions are generally under the control of a chief financial officer (CFO).[1] However, financial management could also be in the hands of a person who serves as company treasurer or vice president of finance. A comptroller is the chief *accounting* officer.[2]

Figure 18.1 highlights a financial manager's tasks. As you can see, two key responsibilities are to obtain funds and to effectively control the use of those

figure 18.1
WHAT FINANCIAL MANAGERS DO

Planning • Auditing • Managing taxes • Budgeting • Advising top management on financial matters • Obtaining funds • Cash • Collecting funds (credit management) • Controlling funds (funds management)

◄ **PPT 18-6:** What Financial Managers Do

◄ **PPT 18-7:** What Worries Financial Managers

◄ **PPT 18-8:** Why Do Firms Fail Financially?

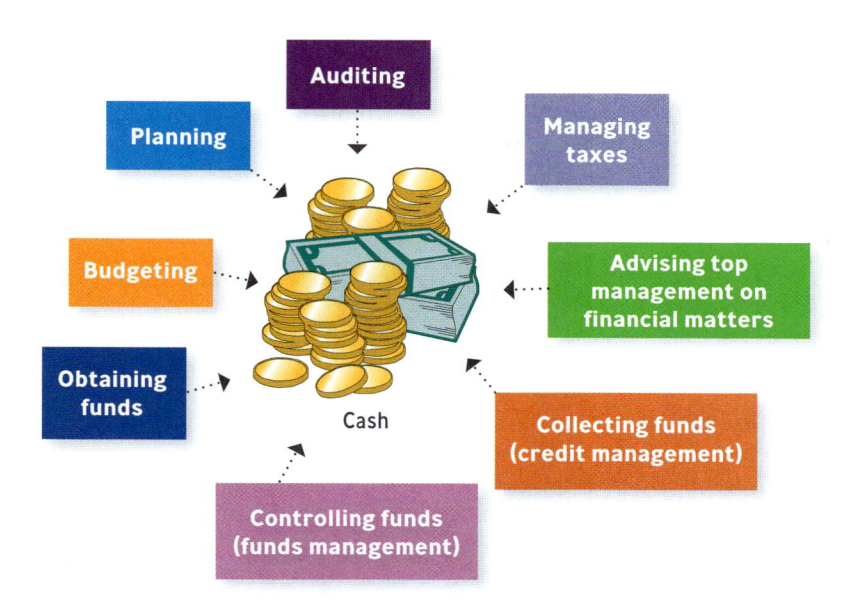

funds.[3] Controlling funds includes managing the firm's cash, credit accounts (accounts receivable), and inventory. Finance is a critical activity in both profit-seeking and nonprofit organizations.

Finance is important, no matter what the firm's size. As you may remember from Chapter 6, financing a small business is essential if the firm expects to survive its important first five years. But the need for careful financial management remains a challenge that a business, large or small, must face throughout its existence. Chrysler Corporation faced extinction in the late 1970s because of severe financial problems and was able to survive due to a government-backed loan of $1 billion. (However, the company, along with the other U.S. automakers, had to come back for a government loan in 2008.)[4] Also in 2008, financial giant Bear Stearns was on the brink of collapse when the government helped JPMorgan purchase it. That same year, the government also backed an $85 billion loan for insurance giant American International Group (AIG) and a $700 billion package to help restore the economy.

Michael Miller overhauled the underperforming Goodwill Industries operations in Portland, Oregon, by treating the nonprofit like a for-profit business. He trimmed operating expenses 30 percent by comparing sales by store, closing weak outlets and opening new ones in better locations, and cutting distribution costs. Sales soared from $4 million to over $50 million.

The Value of Understanding Finance

Three of the most common reasons a firm fails financially are:

1. Undercapitalization (insufficient funds to start the business).
2. Poor control over cash flow.
3. Inadequate expense control.

You can see all three in the following story.

Two friends, Elizabeth Bertani and Pat Sherwood, started a company called Parsley Patch on what can best be described as a shoestring budget. It began when Bertani prepared salt-free seasonings for her husband, who was on a no-salt

> **PPT 18-9:**
> Top Financial Concerns of Company CFOs

diet. Her friend Sherwood thought the seasonings were good enough to sell. Bertani agreed, and Parsley Patch Inc. was born. The business began with an investment of $5,000, rapidly depleted on a logo and label design. Bertani and Sherwood quickly learned about the need for capital in getting a business going. Eventually, they invested more than $100,000 of their own money to keep the business from being undercapitalized.

Everything started well, and hundreds of gourmet shops adopted the product line. But when sales failed to meet expectations, the women decided the health-food market offered more potential because salt-free seasonings were a natural for people with restricted diets. The choice was a good one. Sales soared, approaching $30,000 a month. Still, the company earned no profits.

Bertani and Sherwood weren't trained in monitoring cash flow or in controlling expenses. In fact, they were told not to worry about costs, and they hadn't. They eventually hired a certified public accountant (CPA) and an experienced financial manager, who taught them how to compute the costs of their products, and how to control expenses as well as cash moving in and out of the company (cash flow). Soon Parsley Patch was earning a comfortable margin on operations that ran close to $1 million a year. Luckily, the owners were able to turn things around before it was too late. Eventually, they sold the firm to spice and seasonings giant McCormick.

If Bertani and Sherwood had understood finance before starting their business, they may have been able to avoid the problems they encountered. The key word here is *understood*. You do not have to pursue finance as a career to understand it. Financial understanding is important to anyone who wants to start a small business, invest in stocks and bonds, or plan a retirement fund.[5] In short, finance and accounting are two areas everyone in business should study. Since we discussed accounting in Chapter 17, let's look more closely at what financial management is all about.

What Is Financial Management?

Financial managers are responsible for paying the company's bills at the appropriate time, and for collecting overdue payments to make sure the company does not lose too much money to bad debts (people or firms that don't pay their bills). Therefore, finance functions such as buying merchandise on credit (accounts payable) and collecting payment from customers (accounts receivable) are key components of the financial manager's job. While these functions are vital to all types of businesses, they are particularly critical to small- and medium-sized businesses, which typically have smaller cash or credit cushions than large corporations.[6]

It's essential that financial managers stay abreast of changes or opportunities in finance such as changes in tax law, since taxes represent an outflow of cash from the business.[7] Financial managers must also analyze the tax implications of managerial decisions to minimize the taxes the business must pay. Usually a member of the firm's finance department, the internal auditor, also checks the journals, ledgers, and financial statements the accounting department prepares, to make sure all transactions are in accordance with generally accepted accounting principles (GAAP).[8] Without such audits, accounting statements would be less reliable.[9] Therefore, it is important that internal auditors be objective and

> *Most businesses have predictable day-to-day needs, like the need to buy supplies, pay for fuel and utilities, and pay employees. Financial management is the function that helps ensure firms have the funds they need when they need them. What would happen to the company providing the work in this photo if it couldn't buy gas for its trucks or tools for its employees?*

critical of any improprieties or deficiencies noted in their evaluation. Thorough internal audits assist the firm in financial planning, which we'll look at next.

LEARNING goal 2 *

Outline the financial planning process, and explain the three key budgets in the financial plan.

FINANCIAL PLANNING

Financial planning means analyzing short-term and long-term money flows to and from the firm. Its overall objective is to optimize the firm's profitability and make the best use of its money.[10] It has three steps: (1) forecasting the firm's short-term and long-term financial needs, (2) developing budgets to meet those needs, and (3) establishing financial controls to see whether the company is achieving its goals (see Figure 18.2). Let's look at each step and the role it plays in improving the organization's financial health.

Forecasting Financial Needs

Forecasting is an important part of any firm's financial plan.[11] A **short-term forecast** predicts revenues, costs, and expenses for a period of one year or less. Part of the short-term forecast may be a **cash flow forecast**, which predicts the cash inflows and outflows in future periods, usually months or quarters. The inflows and outflows of cash recorded in the cash flow forecast are based on expected sales revenues and various costs and expenses incurred, as well

◄ PPT 18-10:
Financial Planning

◄ PPT 18-11:
Who's Who in Finance

short-term forecast
Forecast that predicts revenues, costs, and expenses for a period of one year or less.

cash flow forecast
Forecast that predicts the cash inflows and outflows in future periods, usually months or quarters.

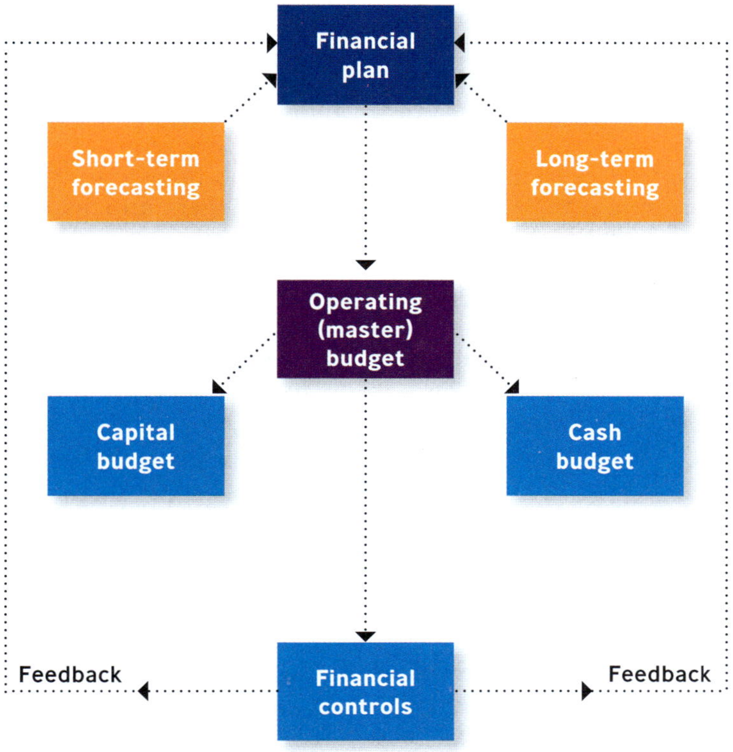

figure 18.2

FINANCIAL PLANNING
Note the close link between financial planning and budgeting.

◄ PPT 18-15:
Financial Planning

> **PPT 18-12:**
> Financial Forecasting

as when they are due for payment.¹² The company's sales forecast estimates projected sales for a particular period.¹³ A business often uses its past financial statements as a basis for projecting expected sales and various costs and expenses.

A **long-term forecast** predicts revenues, costs, and expenses for a period longer than 1 year, sometimes as long as 5 or 10 years. This forecast plays a crucial part in the company's long-term strategic plan, which asks questions such as: What business are we in? Should we be in it five years from now? How much money should we invest in technology and new plant and equipment over the next decade? Will we have cash available to meet long-term obligations? Innovations in Web-based software help financial managers address these long-term forecasting questions.

> **long-term forecast**
> Forecast that predicts revenues, costs, and expenses for a period longer than 1 year, and sometimes as far as 5 or 10 years into the future.

The long-term financial forecast gives top management, as well as operations managers, some sense of the income or profit potential of different strategic plans. It also helps in preparing company budgets.

> **CRITICAL THINKING EXERCISE 18-2:**
> Budgetary Control

Working with the Budget Process

A **budget** sets forth management's expectations for revenues and, on the basis of those expectations, allocates the use of specific resources throughout the firm. As a financial plan, it depends heavily on the accuracy of the firm's balance sheet, income statement, statement of cash flows, and short-term and long-term financial forecasts, which all need to be as accurate as possible. To prepare budgets, financial managers must therefore take their forecasting responsibilities seriously.¹⁴ A budget becomes the primary guide for the firm's financial operations and expected financial needs.

> **budget**
> A financial plan that sets forth management's expectations, and, on the basis of those expectations, allocates the use of specific resources throughout the firm.

There are usually several types of budgets in a firm's financial plan:

> **PPT 18-13:**
> Budgeting in the Firm

- A capital budget.
- A cash budget.
- An operating or master budget.

> **PPT 18-14:**
> Types of Budgets

Let's look at each.

A **capital budget** highlights a firm's spending plans for major asset purchases that often require large sums of money, like property, buildings, and equipment.

> **capital budget**
> A budget that highlights a firm's spending plans for major asset purchases that often require large sums of money.

A **cash budget** estimates cash inflows and outflows during a particular period, like a month or a quarter. It helps managers anticipate borrowing needs, debt repayment, operating expenses, and short-term investments, and is often the last budget prepared. A sample cash budget for our example company, Very Vegetarian, is provided in Figure 18.3.

> **cash budget**
> A budget that estimates cash inflows and outflows during a particular period like a month or a quarter.

The **operating (or master) budget** ties together the firm's other budgets and summarizes its proposed financial activities. More formally, it estimates costs and expenses needed to run a business, given projected revenues. The firm's spending on supplies, travel, rent, advertising, and salaries is determined in the operating budget, generally the most detailed a firm prepares.

> **operating (or master) budget**
> The budget that ties together the firm's other budgets and summarizes its proposed financial activities.

Financial planning obviously plays an important role in the firm's operations and often determines what long-term investments it makes, when it will need specific funds, and how it will generate them. Once a company forecasts its short-term and long-term financial needs and compiles budgets to show how it will allocate funds, the final step in financial planning is to establish financial controls. Before we talk about those, however, Figure 18.4 on p. 492 challenges you to check your personal financial-planning skill by developing a monthly budget for "You Incorporated."

figure 18.3

A SAMPLE CASH BUDGET FOR VERY VEGETARIAN

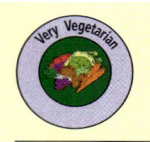

VERY VEGETARIAN
Monthly Cash Budget

	January	February	March
Sales forecast	$50,000	$45,000	$40,000
Collections			
Cash sales (20%)		$ 9,000	$ 8,000
Credit sales (80% of past month)		$40,000	$36,000
Monthly cash collection		$49,000	$44,000
Payments schedule			
Supplies and material		$ 11,000	$ 10,000
Salaries		12,000	12,000
Direct labor		9,000	9,000
Taxes		3,000	3,000
Other expenses		7,000	6,000
Monthly cash payments		$42,000	$39,000
Cash budget			
Cash flow		$ 7,000	$ 5,000
Beginning cash		−1,000	6,000
Total cash		$ 6,000	$ 11,000
Less minimum cash balance		−6,000	−6,000
Excess cash to market securities		$ 0	$ 5,000
Loans needed for minimum balance		0	0

Establishing Financial Controls

Financial control is a process in which a firm periodically compares its actual revenues, costs, and expenses with its budget. Most companies hold at least monthly financial reviews as a way to ensure financial control. Such control procedures help managers identify variances to the financial plan and allow them to take corrective action if necessary. Financial controls also help reveal which specific accounts, departments, and people are varying from the financial plan. Finance managers can judge whether these variances are legitimate and thereby merit adjustments to the plan. The rapid spike and equally rapid fall in oil prices in 2008 caused many companies to adjust their financial plans.[15] The credit crisis that year also forced many companies to alter their long-term financing plans. The Making Ethical Decisions box on p. 493 details a management situation related to financial control. After the Progress Assessment, we'll see why firms need readily available funds.

> **financial control**
> A process in which a firm periodically compares its actual revenues, costs, and expenses with its budget.

◄ PPT 18-16:
Establishing Financial Control

◄ PPT 18-17:
Factors Used in Assessing Financial Control

◄ PPT 18-19:
Progress Assessment

progress assessment

- Name three finance functions important to the firm's overall operations and performance.
- What three primary financial problems cause firms to fail?
- How do short-term and long-term financial forecasts differ?
- What is the purpose of preparing budgets in an organization? Can you identify three different types of budgets?

	EXPECTED	ACTUAL	DIFFERENCE
Monthly income			
Wages (net pay after taxes)	_____	_____	_____
Savings account withdrawal	_____	_____	_____
Family support	_____	_____	_____
Loans	_____	_____	_____
Other sources	_____	_____	_____
Total monthly income	_____	_____	_____
Monthly expenses			
Fixed expenses			
Rent or mortgage	_____	_____	_____
Car payment	_____	_____	_____
Health insurance	_____	_____	_____
Life insurance	_____	_____	_____
Tuition or fees	_____	_____	_____
Other fixed expenses	_____	_____	_____
Subtotal of fixed expenses	_____	_____	_____
Variable expenses			
Food	_____	_____	_____
Clothing	_____	_____	_____
Entertainment	_____	_____	_____
Transportation	_____	_____	_____
Phone	_____	_____	_____
Utilities	_____	_____	_____
Publications	_____	_____	_____
Internet connection	_____	_____	_____
Cable television	_____	_____	_____
Other expenses	_____	_____	_____
Subtotal of variable expenses	_____	_____	_____
Total expenses	_____	_____	_____
Total income − Total expenses = Cash on hand/(Cash deficit)	_____	_____	_____

figure 18.4

YOU INCORPORATED MONTHLY BUDGET

In Chapter 17, you compiled a sample balance sheet for You Inc. (see p. 467). Now, let's develop a monthly budget for You Inc. Be honest and think of everything that needs to be included for an accurate monthly budget for You!

LEARNING goal 3 *

Explain why firms need operating funds.

THE NEED FOR OPERATING FUNDS

In business, the need for operating funds never seems to end. That's why sound financial management is essential to all businesses. And like our personal financial needs, the capital needs of a business change over time. Remember the example of Parsley Patch to see why a small business's financial requirements can shift considerably. The same is true for large corporations such as Intel, Johnson & Johnson, and PepsiCo when they venture into new-product

MAKING ethical decisions

Sail Smoothly or Rock the Boat?

Assume you have recently taken a new job as financial manager at a midsized pharmaceutical company. After working there just a few months, you sense the attitude of most employees at the company is "Who cares?" Salespeople don't turn in detailed expense reports for their travel, nor do they provide receipts to receive reimbursement for meals and other expenses, though the company operations manual says such documentation is required. You also notice employees readily help themselves to office supplies like pens, paper, printer cartridges, and staplers, with no questions asked.

At a meeting of the firm's executive committee you cite the many financial control flaws you have noted and suggest that the company toughen up on lax employee behavior. The CEO says, "My dad started this company twenty-eight years ago, and frankly this is the way it's always been. Probably the best thing we can do is not rock the boat." What will you do? What could result from your decision?

---

areas or new markets. Virtually all organizations have operational needs for which they need funds. Key areas include:

- Managing day-by-day needs of the business.
- Controlling credit operations.
- Acquiring needed inventory.
- Making capital expenditures.

Let's look carefully at these financial needs, which affect both the smallest and the largest of businesses.

Managing Day-by-Day Needs of the Business

If workers expect to be paid on Friday, they don't want to wait until Monday for their paychecks. If tax payments are due on the 15th of the month, the government expects the money on time. If the interest payment on a business loan is due on the 30th of this month, the lender doesn't mean the 1st of next month. As you can see, funds have to be available to meet the daily operational costs of the business.

Financial managers must ensure that funds are available to meet daily cash needs without compromising the firm's opportunities to invest money for its future. Money has *time value*.[16] In other words, if someone offered to give you $200 either today or one year from today, you would benefit by taking the $200 today. Why? It's very simple. You could invest the $200 you receive today and over a year's time it would grow. The same is true in business; the interest a firm gains on its investments is important in maximizing the profit it will gain. That's why financial managers often try to minimize cash expenditures to free up funds for investment in interest-bearing accounts. They suggest the company pay its bills as late as possible (unless a cash discount is available for early payment). They also advise companies to try to collect what's owed them as fast as possible, to maximize the investment potential of the firm's funds. Efficient cash management is particularly important to small firms since their access to capital is much more limited than that of larger businesses.[17] Software from companies like Peachtree assists small firms in handling day-to-day

◀ PPT 18-18:
Sail Smoothly or Rock the Boat?

◀ PPT 18-20:
Key Needs for Operational Funds in a Firm

◀ PPT 18-21:
Ways to Raise Start-Up Capital

493

SPOTLIGHT ON SMALL business

Keeping the Cash Flowing in Hard Times

As the media focuses on the financial problems of the Big Three automakers (Ford, General Motors, and Chrysler) and Wall Street banking giants, small businesses seem to be the forgotten link in the financial dilemma. Saying the recession and continuing financial crisis is hurting small business is an understatement. Small businesses across the nation are in a death struggle to stay afloat as lending institutions continue to hoard cash and customers take longer to pay their bills. Intuit's survey of 751 businesses with fewer than 10 employees found that owners have average overdue customer payments of $1,500 a month. With 22 million businesses falling into this category, the overdue payments add up to a cash flow strain of $33 billion.

A small-business owner in Texas is a good example of small businesses with big cash flow problems. James "Hoss" Boyd owns an electrical contracting and solar energy installation firm. His products and services are in demand, so sales are great, but that doesn't help his cash flow position. A big part of his day is trying to collect his receivables (money owed his company) so that he can pay what he owes to other firms. Boyd knows he isn't alone. "I got a call today from our print shop," he says. "We owe them $400 to $500 for blueprints." It was the company owner on the line making collection calls, Mr. Boyd says, adding, "I would venture to say he's waiting on invoices, too." Boyd sought help from lenders for months but could only get a line of credit through his credit card company. Unfortunately, he is behind on his payments that carry a 29.99 percent interest rate.

Boyd joins the multitude of small-business owners hoping for an economic turnaround and some solution to the short-term lack of credit. Raymond J. Keating, chief economist with the Small Business and Entrepreneurship Council, is quick to remind government policymakers that, for a recovery to occur, small business must be invited to the party. According to Keating, some 60 to 80 percent of new jobs come from small businesses. Fifty percent of private-sector gross domestic product (GDP) is also created by small business. Perhaps Hoss Boyd said it best: "We're on the mend, but we have a long way to go."

Sources: Mickey Meece, "The Fight to Survive, Writ Small," *New York Times*, December 18, 2008; and Anita Huslin, "Businesses Go to Source of Fast Cash," *The Washington Post*, October 27, 2008.

▶ PPT 18-22:
Keeping the Cash Flowing in Hard Times

▶ CRITICAL THINKING EXERCISE 18-3:
Extending Credit

cash management.[18] The Spotlight on Small Business box illustrates the challenge of managing cash flow in small businesses.

Controlling Credit Operations

Financial managers know that making credit available helps keep current customers happy and attracts new ones, especially in today's highly competitive business environment. Credit for customers was especially important during the recent financial crisis since banks were hesitant to make loans.

The problem with selling on credit is that as much as 25 percent of the business's assets could be tied up in its credit accounts (accounts receivable). This forces the firm to use its own funds to pay for goods or services sold to customers who bought on credit. Financial managers in such firms often develop efficient collection procedures, like offering cash or quantity discounts to buyers who pay their accounts by a certain time. They also scrutinize old and new credit customers to see whether they have a history of meeting credit obligations on time.

One convenient way to decrease the time and expense of collecting accounts receivable is to accept bank credit cards such as MasterCard or Visa. The banks that issue these cards have already established the customer's creditworthiness, which reduces the business's risk. Businesses must pay a fee to accept credit cards, but they are usually offset by the benefits.

Acquiring Needed Inventory

As we saw in Chapter 13, effective marketing requires focusing on the customer and providing high-quality service and readily available goods. A carefully constructed inventory policy helps manage the firm's available funds and maximize profitability. Maggie Moo's, a neighborhood ice cream parlor in St. Louis, Missouri, deliberately ties up fewer funds in its inventory of ice cream in winter. It's obvious why: demand for ice cream is lower in winter.

Just-in-time inventory control (see Chapter 9) and other such methods can reduce the funds a firm must tie up in inventory. Carefully evaluating its inventory turnover ratio (see Chapter 17) can also help a firm control outflow of cash for inventory. A business of any size must understand that poorly managed inventory can seriously affect cash flow and drain its finances dry.

Making Capital Expenditures

Capital expenditures are major investments in either tangible long-term assets such as land, buildings, and equipment, or intangible assets such as patents, trademarks, and copyrights. In many organizations the purchase of major assets—such as land for future expansion, manufacturing plants to increase production capabilities, research to develop new-product ideas, and equipment to maintain or exceed current levels of output—is essential. Expanding into new markets can be expensive with no guarantee of success. Therefore, it's critical that companies weigh all possible options before committing a large portion of available resources.

Consider a firm that needs to expand its production capabilities due to increased customer demand. It could buy land and build a new plant, purchase an existing plant, or rent space. Can you think of financial and accounting considerations at play in this decision?

The need for operating funds raises several questions for financial managers: How does the firm obtain funds to finance operations and other business needs? Will it require specific funds in the long or the short term? How much will it cost to obtain these funds? Will they come from internal or external sources? We address these questions next.

Alternative Sources of Funds

We described finance earlier as the function in a business responsible for acquiring and managing funds. Sound financial management determines the amount of money needed and the most appropriate sources from which to obtain it. A firm can raise needed capital by borrowing money (debt), selling ownership (equity), or earning profits (retained earnings). **Debt financing** refers to funds raised through various forms of borrowing that must be repaid. **Equity financing** is money raised from within the firm, from operations or

It's difficult to think of a business that doesn't make credit available to its customers. However, collecting accounts receivables can be time-consuming and expensive. Accepting credit cards such as Visa, MasterCard, and American Express can simplify transactions for sellers and guarantee payment. What types of products do you regularly purchase with a credit card?

capital expenditures
Major investments in either tangible long-term assets such as land, buildings, and equipment or intangible assets such as patents, trademarks, and copyrights.

◄ PPT 18-23:
How Small Businesses Can Improve Cash Flow

◄ PPT 18-24:
Using Alternative Sources of Funds

debt financing
Funds raised through various forms of borrowing that must be repaid.

equity financing
Money raised from within the firm, from operations or through the sale of ownership in the firm (stock).

figure 18.5
WHY FIRMS NEED FUNDS

SHORT-TERM FUNDS	LONG-TERM FUNDS
Monthly expenses	New-product development
Unanticipated emergencies	Replacement of capital equipment
Cash flow problems	Mergers or acquisitions
Expansion of current inventory	Expansion into new markets (domestic or global)
Temporary promotional programs	New facilities

▶ **PPT 18-25:** Short- and Long-Term Financing

short-term financing Funds needed for a year or less.

long-term financing Funds needed for more than a year (usually 2 to 10 years).

through the sale of ownership in the firm (stock). Firms can borrow funds either short-term or long-term. **Short-term financing** refers to funds needed for a year or less. **Long-term financing** covers funds needed for more than a year (usually 2 to 10 years).[19] Figure 18.5 highlights why firms may need short-term and long-term funds.

We'll explore the different sources of short- and long-term financing next. Let's first pause to check your understanding by doing the Progress Assessment.

▶ **PPT 18-26:** Why Firms Need Financing

▶ **PPT 18-27:** Progress Assessment

progress assessment

- Money has time value. What does this mean?
- Why is accounts receivable a financial concern to the firm?
- What's the primary reason an organization spends a good deal of its available funds on inventory and capital expenditures?
- What's the difference between debt and equity financing?

LEARNING goal 4 *

Identify and describe different sources of short-term financing.

▶ **PPT 18-28:** Types of Short-Term Financing

OBTAINING SHORT-TERM FINANCING

The bulk of a finance manager's job does not relate to obtaining *long-term* funds.[20] In small businesses, for example, long-term financing is often out of the question. Instead, day-to-day operations call for the careful management of *short-term* financial needs. Firms may need to borrow short-term funds for purchasing additional inventory or for meeting bills that come due unexpectedly. Like an individual, a business, especially a small business, sometimes needs to secure short-term funds when its cash reserves are low. Let's see how it does so.

▶ **PPT 18-29:** Different Forms of Short-Term Loans

Trade Credit

trade credit The practice of buying goods and services now and paying for them later.

Trade credit is the practice of buying goods or services now and paying for them later. It is the most widely used source of short-term funding, the least expensive, and the most convenient. Small businesses rely heavily on trade credit from firms such as United Parcel Service, as do large firms such as Kmart. When a firm buys merchandise, it receives an invoice (a bill) much like the one you receive when you buy something with a credit card. As you'll see, however, the terms businesses receive are often different from those on your monthly statement.

Business invoices usually contain terms such as *2/10, net 30*. This means the buyer can take a 2 percent discount for paying the invoice within 10 days. Otherwise the total bill (net) is due in 30 days. Finance managers pay close attention to such discounts because they create opportunities to reduce the firm's costs. Think about it for a moment: If the terms are 2/10, net 30, the customer will pay 2 percent more by waiting an extra 20 days to pay the invoice. If the firm *can* pay its bill within 10 days, it is needlessly increasing its costs by not doing so.

Some suppliers hesitate to give trade credit to an organization with a poor credit rating, no credit history, or a history of slow payment. They may insist the customer sign a **promissory note**, a written contract with a promise to pay a supplier a specific sum of money at a definite time. Promissory notes are negotiable. The supplier can sell them to a bank at a discount (the amount of the note less a fee for the bank's services in collecting the amount due).

promissory note
A written contract with a promise to pay a supplier a specific sum of money at a definite time.

Family and Friends

As we discussed in Chapter 17, firms often have several bills coming due at the same time with no sources of funds to pay them. Many small firms obtain short-term funds by borrowing money from family and friends. Such loans can create problems, however, if both lender and borrower do not understand cash flow. It is sometimes better to go to a commercial bank that fully understands the business's risk and can help analyze its future financial needs rather than borrow from friends or relatives.

Entrepreneurs appear to be listening to this advice. According to the National Federation of Independent Business, entrepreneurs today are relying less on family and friends as a source of borrowed funds than they have in the past.[21] If an entrepreneur decides to ask family or friends for financial assistance, it's important that both parties (1) agree to specific loan terms, (2) put the agreement in writing, and (3) arrange for repayment in the same way they would for a bank loan. Such actions help keep family relationships and friendships intact.

Commercial Banks

Banks, being sensitive to risk, generally prefer to lend short-term money to larger, established businesses. Imagine the different types of businesspeople who go to banks for a loan, and you'll get a better idea of the requests bankers evaluate. Picture, for example, a farmer going to the bank in spring to borrow funds for seed, fertilizer, equipment, and other needs that will be repaid after the fall harvest. Or consider a local toy store buying merchandise for Christmas sales. The store borrows the money for such purchases in the summer and plans to pay it back after Christmas. Restaurants often borrow funds at the beginning of the month and pay at the end of the month.

How much a business borrows and for how long depends on the kind of business it is, and how quickly it can resell the merchandise it purchases with a bank loan or use it to generate funds. In a large business, specialists in a company's finance and accounting departments do a cash flow forecast. Small-business owners generally lack such specialists and monitor cash flow themselves.

Nonetheless, a promising and well-organized small business may be able to get a bank loan. In fact, commercial banks provide almost half of small

◄ **CRITICAL THINKING EXERCISE 18-1:**
Finding the Cost of Bank Loans

◄ **LECTURE LINK 18-2:**
The Numbers Speak When Dealing with Your Banker

Did you ever wonder how retail stores get the money to buy all the treasures we splurge on during the holidays? Department stores and other large retailers make extensive use of commercial banks and other lenders to borrow the funds they need to buy merchandise and stock their shelves. How do the stores benefit from using this type of financing?

business financing today. If a small firm gets a bank loan, the owner or person in charge of finance should keep in close touch with the bank and send regular financial statements to keep the bank up-to-date on its operations. The bank may spot cash flow problems early or be willing to lend money in a crisis if the business has established a strong relationship built on trust and sound management.

Different Forms of Short-Term Loans

secured loan
A loan backed by collateral, something valuable such as property.

Commercial banks offer different types of short-term loans. A **secured loan** is backed by *collateral*, something valuable such as property. If the borrower fails to pay the loan, the lender may take possession of the collateral. An automobile loan is a secured loan. If the borrower doesn't repay it, the lender will repossess the car. Inventory of raw materials like coal and steel often serves as collateral for business loans. Collateral removes some of the bank's risk in lending the money.

Accounts receivable are company assets often used as collateral for a loan; this process is called *pledging* and works as follows: A percentage of the value of a firm's accounts receivable pledged (usually about 75 percent) is advanced to the borrowing firm. As customers pay off their accounts, the funds received are forwarded to the lender in repayment of the funds that were advanced.

unsecured loan
A loan that doesn't require any collateral.

An **unsecured loan** is more difficult to obtain because it doesn't require any collateral. Normally, lenders give unsecured loans only to highly regarded customers—long-standing businesses or those considered financially stable.

line of credit
A given amount of unsecured short-term funds a bank will lend to a business, provided the funds are readily available.

revolving credit agreement
A line of credit that's guaranteed but usually comes with a fee.

If a business develops a strong relationship with a bank, the bank may open a **line of credit** for the firm, a given amount of unsecured short-term funds a bank will lend to business, provided the funds are readily available. A line of credit is *not* guaranteed to a business. However, it speeds up the borrowing process since a firm does not have to apply for a new loan every time it needs funds. As businesses mature and become more financially secure, banks will often increase their line of credit. Some even offer a **revolving credit agreement**, a line of credit that's guaranteed but usually comes with a fee. Both lines of credit and revolving credit agreements are particularly good sources of funds for unexpected cash needs.

A secured loan is backed by collateral, a tangible item of value. A car loan, for instance, is a secured loan in which the car itself is the collateral. What is the collateral in a mortgage loan?

If a business is unable to secure a short-term loan from a bank, the financial manager may seek short-term funds from **commercial finance companies**. These non-deposit-type organizations make short-term loans to borrowers who offer tangible assets like property, plant, and equipment as collateral.[22] Commercial finance companies will often make loans to businesses that cannot get short-term funds elsewhere.[23] Since commercial finance companies assume higher degrees of risk than commercial banks, they usually charge higher interest rates. General Electric Capital is the largest commercial finance company in the United States, with $335 billion in assets and operations in 35 countries around the world.[24]

commercial finance companies
Organizations that make short-term loans to borrowers who offer tangible assets as collateral.

Factoring Accounts Receivable

One relatively expensive source of short-term funds for a firm is **factoring**, the process of selling accounts receivable for cash. Factoring dates as far back as 4,000 years, during the days of ancient Babylon. Here's how it works: Let's say a firm sells many of its products on credit to consumers and other businesses, creating a number of accounts receivable. Some buyers may be slow in paying their bills, so a large amount of money is due the firm. A *factor* is a market intermediary (usually a financial institution like CIT Group or a commercial bank) that agrees to buy the firm's accounts receivable, at a discount, for cash.[25] The discount depends on the age of the accounts receivable, the nature of the business, and the condition of the economy. When it collects the accounts receivable that were originally owed to the firm, the factor keeps them. While factors charge more than banks' loan rates, remember many small businesses cannot qualify for a loan.[26] So even though factoring is an expensive way of raising short-term funds, it is popular among small businesses.[27] A company can often reduce its factoring cost if it agrees to reimburse the factor for slow-paying accounts, or to assume the risk for customers who don't pay at all. Remember factoring is not a loan; it is the sale of a firm's asset (accounts receivable).[28]

Large firms can also use factoring as a source of short-term funds. Macy's, the department store giant, employed factoring during its reorganization

factoring
The process of selling accounts receivable for cash.

◄ **LECTURE LINK 18-3:**
Making Payments Overseas

LEGAL briefcase

www.factoring.org

Making Sure It's a Done Deal

With 6.7 billion potential customers on planet Earth, the lure of global markets is just too enticing for businesses to ignore. Unfortunately, the path of would-be exporters is often blocked by financing constraints such as the complications of trading in foreign currencies and difficulty in collecting money from global accounts. Combine these financing challenges with political instability, high loan defaults, threats of terrorism, and unstable currencies, and the prospects of doing business globally look iffy at best. This shaky global environment requires U.S. companies to use creative financing methods, such as international factoring (also called forfeiting), for protection in global markets. International factoring includes negotiating with intermediaries who make sure payment gets from the foreign buyer back to the seller.

There are four parties in an international factoring transaction: the exporter, the U.S. factor (called the export factor), the foreign factor (called the import factor), and the importer. The exporter and the export factor sign a factoring agreement that transfers the exporter's accounts receivable to the U.S. factor in exchange for coverage against any credit losses that could occur. In other words, the export factor guarantees the exporter will receive the money it is owed and selects and supervises an import factor to act on the seller's behalf. The import factor assists in finding local customers in global markets to whom the seller can sell its goods or services.

When an exporter receives an order from a customer, the import factor collects payment, deducts a fee, and gives the remainder to the export factor. The export factor deducts a fee and gives that remainder to the exporter. Complicated? Yes, but by using these agreements U.S. exporters can do business even in risky global markets without risking significant credit losses. Today, international factoring accounts for almost $1 trillion in global trade.

Sources: Myra A. Thomas, "The Global Marketplace: A World of Opportunity and Challenges," *The Secured Lender*, July 1, 2008; Karen Kroll, "Factoring Comes into Fashion," *Business Finance*, September 1, 2007; and "Help for Small Businesses in a Tightening Credit Market," Business Wire, October 14, 2008.

▶ PPT 18-31:
Making Sure It's a Done Deal

▶ PPT 18-30:
Commercial Paper

commercial paper
Unsecured promissory notes of $100,000 and up that mature (come due) in 270 days or less.

several years ago. Factoring is common in the clothing and furniture businesses, and in growing numbers of global trade ventures.[29] The Legal Briefcase box explains the process of factoring in global markets. Today, the Internet can help a firm find factors quickly.

Commercial Paper

Often a corporation needs funds for just a few months and prefers not to have to negotiate with a commercial bank. One strategy available to larger firms is to sell commercial paper. **Commercial paper** consists of *unsecured* promissory notes, in amounts of $100,000 and up, that mature or come due in 270 days or less. Commercial paper states a fixed amount of money the business agrees to repay to the lender (investor) on a specific date at a specified rate of interest.

Because commercial paper is unsecured, only financially stable firms (mainly large corporations with excellent credit reputations) are able to sell it.[30] For these companies it's a quick path to short-term funds for less interest than charged by commercial banks. Since most commercial paper matures in 30 to 90 days, it's an investment opportunity for buyers who can afford to put up cash for short periods to earn some interest on their money. During the financial crisis beginning in 2008, however, the risk of commercial paper increased so much that investors were reluctant to purchase it. The Federal Reserve chose to step in and assist many companies by purchasing their short-term commercial paper.[31]

Credit Cards

According to the National Small Business Association (NSBA), about half of all small businesses now use credit cards to finance their businesses.[32] Credit cards provide a readily available line of credit that can save time and the likely embarrassment of being rejected for a bank loan. Of course, in contrast to the convenience credit cards offer, they are extremely risky and costly. Interest rates can be exorbitant, and there are considerable penalties if users fail to make their payments on time. James and Heather Mills of MHN PR & Internet Marketing in Elgin, Illinois, saw the interest rate on their credit card jump from 11.7 percent to over 30 percent after they were late on a few payments.[33] Credit cards are an expensive way to borrow money and are probably best used as a last resort.

After checking your progress below, we'll look into long-term financing options.

progress assessment

- What does an invoice containing the terms *2/10, net 30* mean?
- What's the difference between trade credit and a line of credit?
- What's the key difference between a secured and an unsecured loan?
- What is factoring? What are some of the considerations factors consider in establishing their discount rate?

LEARNING goal 5 *

Identify and describe different sources of long-term financing.

OBTAINING LONG-TERM FINANCING

In a financial plan, forecasting determines the amount of funding the firm will need over various periods and the most appropriate sources for obtaining those funds. In setting long-term financing objectives, financial managers generally ask three questions:

1. What are our organization's long-term goals and objectives?
2. What funds do we need to achieve the firm's long-term goals and objectives?
3. What sources of long-term funding (capital) are available, and which will best fit our needs?

Firms need long-term capital to purchase expensive assets such as plant and equipment, to develop new products, or perhaps finance their expansion. In major corporations, the board of directors and top management usually make decisions about long-term financing, along with finance and accounting executives. Pfizer, the world's largest research-based biomedical and pharmaceutical company, spends over $8 billion a year researching and developing new products.[34] The development of a single new drug could take 10 years and cost the firm close to $1 billion before it brings in any profit. It's easy to see why high-level managers make the long-term financing decisions at Pfizer.

◄ PPT 18-32:
Setting Long-Term Financing Objectives

◄ PPT 18-33:
The Five C's of Credit

◄ BONUS CASE 18-1:
The Rebuilding Decision

REACHING BEYOND our borders

Sharing the Wealth?

When a nation's government has a budget surplus, it usually has many ways to invest the extra cash back into the country. But sometimes the surplus is too great to distribute immediately, so the country puts the money away in a sovereign wealth fund (SWF), where it can hold the excess assets for future investment.

For years, oil rich nations like United Arab Emirates (UAE) and Kuwait have been blessed with enormous budgetary surpluses, causing their SWFs to swell with capital. Kuwait's SWF boasts an impressive value of $200 billion, while UAE's fund Abu Dhabi Investment Authority (ADIA) is valued at an unbelievable $875 billion. With so much capital at their fingertips, these countries have started to run out of investment opportunities within their own borders, sending them on a search for foreign businesses to support, and their biggest target is the United States.

With the value of the dollar dropping and the subprime mortgage crisis ravaging real estate, SWFs have set their sights on several struggling U.S. businesses. In 2007, a Chinese SWF invested billions of dollars in Morgan Stanley, a giant in the investment community. Similarly, ADIA dropped $7.5 billion in Citigroup, the largest bank in the United States, and bought out high-end retailer Barneys New York for $875 million.

Though SWFs provide these distressed companies with much-needed capital, the presence of foreign governments in the U.S. business world concerns some who think SWFs will try to use their financial footholds to influence or even dictate U.S. governmental policy. Meanwhile the United States will remain an ideal investment target for foreign governments flush with funds.

Sources: Geoff Colvin, "America for Sale," *Fortune*, February 18, 2008; Emily Thornton and Stanley Reed, "A Power Player Emerges in the Gulf," *BusinessWeek*, June 23, 2008; Daniel Gross, "Exec Desperately Seeks SWF," *Newsweek*, January 7, 2008; and Bob Davis, "U.S. Pushes Sovereign Funds to Open to Outside Scrutiny," *The Wall Street Journal*, February 26, 2008.

> **PPT 18-36:**
> Sharing the Wealth?

Owners of small- and medium-sized businesses are almost always actively engaged in analyzing their long-term financing decisions.

As we noted earlier, long-term funding comes from two major sources, debt financing and equity financing. Let's look at these sources next. But first check out the Reaching Beyond Our Borders box to learn why a source of long-term funding is raising eyebrows in the financial community.

Debt Financing

> **PPT 18-34:**
> Using Long-Term Debt Financing

Debt financing is borrowing money the company has a legal obligation to repay. Firms can borrow by either getting a loan from a lending institution or issuing bonds.

> **term-loan agreement**
> A promissory note that requires the borrower to repay the loan in specified installments.

Debt Financing by Borrowing from Lending Institutions Long-term loans are usually due within 3 to 7 years but may extend to 15 or 20 years. A **term-loan agreement** is a promissory note that requires the borrower to repay the loan with interest in specified monthly or annual installments. A major advantage is that the interest is tax deductible.

> **risk/return trade-off**
> The principle that the greater the risk a lender takes in making a loan, the higher the interest rate required.

Long-term loans are both larger and more expensive to the firm than short-term loans. Since the repayment period can be quite long, lenders assume more risk and usually require collateral, which may be real estate, machinery, equipment, company stock, or other items of value. The interest rate is based on the adequacy of collateral, the firm's credit rating, and the general level of market interest rates. The greater the risk a lender takes in making a loan, the higher the rate of interest. This principle is known as the **risk/return trade-off**.

Lenders may also require certain restrictions to force the firm to act responsibly.

Debt Financing by Issuing Bonds If an organization is unable to obtain its long-term financing needs by getting a loan from a lending institution, it may try to issue bonds. To put it simply, a bond is like an IOU with a promise to repay the amount borrowed, with interest, on a certain date. The terms of the agreement in a bond issue are the **indenture terms**. The types of organizations that can issue bonds include federal, state, and local governments; federal government agencies; foreign governments; and corporations.

You may already be familiar with bonds. You may own investments like U.S. government savings bonds, or perhaps you volunteered your time to help a local school district pass a bond issue. If your community is building a new stadium or cultural center, it may sell bonds to finance the project.

Businesses and governments compete when issuing bonds. Potential investors (individuals and institutions) measure the risk of purchasing a bond against the return the bond promises to pay—the interest—and the issuer's ability to repay when promised.

Like other forms of long-term debt, bonds can be secured or unsecured. A **secured bond** is issued with some form of collateral, such as real estate, equipment, or other pledged assets. If the bond's indenture terms are violated (e.g., not paying interest payments), the bondholder can issue a claim on the collateral. An **unsecured bond**, called a debenture bond, is backed only by the reputation of the issuer. Investors in such bonds simply trust that the organization issuing the bond will make good on its financial commitments.

Bonds are a key means of long-term financing for many organizations. They can also be valuable investments for private individuals or institutions. Given this importance, we will discuss bonds in depth in Chapter 19.

Equity Financing

If a firm cannot obtain a long-term loan from a lending institution or is unable to sell bonds to investors, it may seek equity financing. Equity financing makes

---

indenture terms
The terms of agreement in a bond issue.

◀ PPT 18-35:
Using Debt Financing by Issuing Bonds

secured bond
A bond issued with some form of collateral.

unsecured bond
A bond backed only by the reputation of the issuer; also called a debenture bond.

◀ PPT 18-37:
When Government Bailouts Pay Off

Major League Baseball is a big business, and building a new stadium requires big dollars. When the St. Louis Cardinals needed financing to replace their old stadium with a new state-of-the-art facility, St. Louis County issued bonds that helped finance the construction of the Cardinals' new home. What organizations in your community have issued bonds, and for what purpose?

> **PPT 18-38:**
> Securing Equity Financing

> **CRITICAL THINKING EXERCISE 18-4:**
> Financing Options

funds available when the owners of the firm sell shares of ownership to outside investors in the form of stock, when they reinvest company earnings in the business, or obtain funds from venture capitalists.

Equity Financing by Selling Stock The key thing to remember about stock is that stockholders become owners in the organization. Generally, the corporation's board of directors decides the number of shares of stock that will be offered to investors for purchase. The first time a company offers to sell its stock to the general public the event is called an *initial public offering (IPO)*. We discuss IPOs further in Chapter 19.

Selling stock to the public to obtain funds is by no means easy or automatic. U.S. companies can issue stock for public purchase only if they meet requirements set by the Securities and Exchange Commission (SEC) and various state agencies. They can offer different types of stock such as common and preferred; we discuss both in Chapter 19.

Equity Financing from Retained Earnings You probably remember from Chapter 17 that the profits the company keeps and reinvests in the firm are called *retained earnings*. Retained earnings often are a major source of long-term funds, especially for small businesses. They often have fewer financing alternatives, such as selling stock or bonds, than large businesses do. However, large corporations also depend on retained earnings for needed long-term funding. In fact, retained earnings are usually the most favored source of meeting long-term capital needs. A company that uses them saves interest payments, dividends (payments for investing in stock), and any possible underwriting fees for issuing bonds or stock. Retained earnings also create no new ownership in the firm, as stock does.

Suppose you wanted to buy an expensive personal asset such as a new car. Ideally you would go to your personal savings account and take out the necessary cash. No hassle! No interest! Unfortunately, few people have such large amounts of cash available. Most businesses are no different. Even though they

> *When credit grew tight in the recent financial crisis, John Mickey, who makes promotional items with corporate logos, tapped his retirement funds to obtain start-up money for his new venture. Why is this financing strategy considered risky?*

would like to finance long-term needs from operations, few have the resources available to accomplish this.

Equity Financing from Venture Capital The hardest time for a business to raise money is when it is starting up or just beginning to expand. A start-up business typically has few assets and no market track record, so the chances of borrowing significant amounts of money from a bank are slim. **Venture capital** is money invested in new or emerging companies that some investors—venture capitalists—believe have great profit potential. Venture capital helped firms like Intel, Apple, and Cisco Systems get started and let Facebook and Google expand and grow.[35] Venture capitalists invest in a business in return for part ownership of the business. They expect higher-than-average returns and competent management performance for their investment.

The venture capital industry originally began as an alternative investment vehicle for wealthy families. The Rockefeller family, for example (whose vast fortune came from John D. Rockefeller's Standard Oil Company, started in the 19th century), financed Sanford McDonnell when he was operating his company from an airplane hangar. That small venture grew into McDonnell Douglas, a large aerospace and defense contractor that merged with Boeing Corporation in 1997. The venture capital industry grew significantly in the 1990s, especially in high-tech centers like California's Silicon Valley, where venture capitalists concentrated on Internet-related companies. In the 2000s, problems in the technology industry and a slowdown in the overall economy reduced venture capital expenditures. The recent financial crisis has caused venture capitalists to spend cautiously and hold companies to strict standards before investing their capital.[36]

Comparing Debt and Equity Financing

Figure 18.6 compares debt and equity financing options. Raising funds through borrowing to increase the firm's rate of return is referred to as **leverage**. Though debt increases risk because it creates a financial obligation that must be repaid, it also enhances the firm's ability to increase profits. Recall that two key jobs of the financial manager or CFO are forecasting the firm's need for borrowed funds and planning how to manage these funds once they are obtained.

Cost of capital is the rate of return a company must earn in order to meet the demands of its lenders and expectations of its equity holders (stockholders

venture capital
Money that is invested in new or emerging companies that are perceived as having great profit potential.

◀ LECTURE LINK 18-4:
The Myths of Venture Capital

◀ PPT 18-39:
Differences Between Debt and Equity Financing

leverage
Raising needed funds through borrowing to increase a firm's rate of return.

◀ PPT 18-40:
Using Leverage for Funding Needs

cost of capital
The rate of return a company must earn in order to meet the demands of its lenders and expectations of its equity holders.

figure 18.6
DIFFERENCES BETWEEN DEBT AND EQUITY FINANCING

	Type of Financing	
CONDITIONS	**DEBT**	**EQUITY**
Management influence	There's usually none unless special conditions have been agreed on.	Common stockholders have voting rights.
Repayment	Debt has a maturity date. Principal must be repaid.	Stock has no maturity date. The company is never required to repay equity.
Yearly obligations	Payment of interest is a contractual obligation.	The firm isn't legally liable to pay dividends.
Tax benefits	Interest is tax deductible.	Dividends are paid from after-tax income and aren't deductible.

> **CRITICAL THINKING EXERCISE 18-5:**
> Obtaining Financing

> **LECTURE LINK 18-5:**
> Going Overboard on Leverage

or venture capitalists). Firms are obviously concerned with the cost of capital. If the firm's earnings are larger than the interest payments on borrowed funds, business owners can realize a higher rate of return than if they used equity financing. Figure 18.7 describes an example, again involving our vegetarian restaurant, Very Vegetarian (introduced in Chapter 13). If Very Vegetarian needed $200,000 in new financing, it could consider debt by selling bonds or equity through offering stock. Comparing the two options in this situation, you can see that Very Vegetarian would benefit by selling bonds since the company's earnings are greater than the interest paid on borrowed funds (bonds). However, if the firm's earnings were less than the interest paid on borrowed funds (bonds), Very Vegetarian could lose money. It's also important to remember that bonds, like all debt, have to be repaid at a specific time.

Individual firms must determine exactly how to balance debt and equity financing by comparing the costs and benefits of each. Leverage ratios (discussed in Chapter 17) can also give companies an industry standard for this balance, to which they can compare themselves. Sands and Trump Hotels and Casinos carry billions of dollars of debt to finance their hotels, condos, and golf courses. Goldman Sachs relied so heavily on borrowed funds the strategy almost caused its downfall in 2008.[37] In contrast, tech giant Microsoft has no long-term debt and has had almost $50 billion in cash available at times.[38] According to Standard & Poor's and Moody's Investor Services (firms that provide corporate and financial research), the debt of a large industrial corporation typically ranges between 33 and 40 percent of its total assets. The amount of small-business debt varies considerably from firm to firm.

Financial Management in Trying Times

The collapse of financial markets in 2008 put the spotlight directly on the failure of financial managers to do their job effectively. Poor investment decisions and risky financial dealings (especially in areas such as real estate) caused financial markets to suffer their worst fall since the 1920s and 1930s (we discuss this in depth in Chapter 19). As the requirements of financial institutions become more stringent due to the financial crisis and the significant degree of government intervention, the job of the financial manager promises to become more challenging. Investors who watched long-standing financial firms such as Lehman Brothers close their doors not only saw respected businesses

figure 18.7

USING LEVERAGE (DEBT) VERSUS EQUITY FINANCING

Very Vegetarian wants to raise $200,000 in new capital. Compare the firm's debt and equity options.

ADDITIONAL DEBT		ADDITIONAL EQUITY	
Stockholders' equity	$500,000	Stockholders' equity	$500,000
Additional equity	—	Additional equity	$200,000
Total equity	$500,000	Total equity	$700,000
Bond @ 8% interest	200,000	Bond interest	—
Total shareholder equity	$700,000	Total shareholder equity	$700,000

YEAR-END EARNINGS			
Gross profit	$100,000	Gross profit	$100,000
Less bond interest	−16,000	Less interest	—
Operating profit	$84,000	Operating profit	$100,000
Return on equity	16.6%	Return on equity	14.2%
($84,000 ÷ $500,000 = 16.6%)		($100,000 ÷ $700,000 = 14.2%)	

disappear but also saw their invested funds disappear with them. Financial managers have a long road back to earning the trust of the public.

Chapter 19 takes a closer look at bonds and stocks, both as long-term financing tools for businesses and as investment options for private investors. You will learn how securities exchanges work, how firms issue stocks and bonds, how to choose the right investment strategy, how to buy and sell stock, where to find up-to-date information about stocks and bonds, and more. Finance takes on a new dimension when you see how you can participate in financial markets yourself.

progress assessment

- What are the two major forms of debt financing available to a firm?
- How does debt financing differ from equity financing?
- What are the major forms of equity financing available to a firm?
- What is leverage, and why do firms choose to use it?

◄ PPT 18-41: Progress Assessment

summary

Learning Goal 1. Explain the role and responsibilities of financial managers.

- **What are the most common ways firms fail financially?**

The most common financial problems are (1) undercapitalization, (2) poor control over cash flow, and (3) inadequate expense control.

- **What do financial managers do?**

Financial managers plan, budget, control funds, obtain funds, collect funds, conduct audits, manage taxes, and advise top management on financial matters.

Learning Goal 2. Outline the financial planning process, and explain the three key budgets in the financial plan.

- **What are the three budgets in a financial plan?**

The capital budget is the spending plan for expensive assets such as property, plant, and equipment. The cash budget is the projected cash balance at the end of a given period. The operating (master) budget summarizes the information in the other two budgets. It projects dollar allocations to various costs and expenses given various revenues.

Learning Goal 3. Explain why firms need operating funds.

- **What are firms' major financial needs?**

Businesses need financing for four major tasks: (1) managing day-by-day operations, (2) controlling credit operations, (3) acquiring needed inventory, and (4) making capital expenditures.

- **What's the difference between debt financing and equity financing?**

Debt financing raises funds by borrowing. Equity financing raises funds from within the firm through investment of retained earnings, sale of stock to investors, or sale of part ownership to venture capitalists.

- **What's the difference between short-term and long-term financing?**

Short-term financing raises funds to be repaid in less than a year, whereas long-term financing raises funds to be repaid over a longer period.

Learning Goal 4. Identify and describe different sources of short-term financing.

- **Why should businesses use trade credit?**

Trade credit is the least expensive and most convenient form of short-term financing. Businesses can buy goods today and pay for them sometime in the future.

- **What is meant by a line of credit and a revolving credit agreement?**

A line of credit is an agreement by a bank to lend a specified amount of money to the business at any time, if the money is available. A revolving credit agreement is a line of credit that guarantees a loan will be available—for a fee.

- **What's the difference between a secured loan and an unsecured loan?**

An unsecured loan has no collateral backing it. Secured loans have collateral backed by assets such as accounts receivable, inventory, or other property of value.

- **Is factoring a form of secured loan?**

No, factoring means selling accounts receivable at a discounted rate to a factor (an intermediary that pays cash for those accounts and keeps the funds it collects on them).

- **What's commercial paper?**

Commercial paper is a corporation's unsecured promissory note maturing in 270 days or less.

Learning Goal 5. Identify and describe different sources of long-term financing.

- **What are the major sources of long-term financing?**

Debt financing is the sale of bonds to investors and long-term loans from banks and other financial institutions. Equity financing is obtained through the sale of company stock, from the firm's retained earnings, or from venture capital firms.

- **What are the two major forms of debt financing?**

Debt financing comes from two sources: selling bonds and borrowing from individuals, banks, and other financial institutions. Bonds can be secured by some form of collateral or unsecured. The same is true of loans.

- **What's leverage, and how do firms use it?**

Leverage is borrowing funds to invest in expansion, major asset purchases, or research and development. Firms measure the risk of borrowing against the potential for higher profits.

key terms

budget 490
capital budget 490
capital expenditures 495
cash budget 490
cash flow forecast 489
commercial finance companies 499
commercial paper 500
cost of capital 505
debt financing 495
equity financing 495
factoring 499
finance 486
financial control 491
financial management 486
financial managers 486
indenture terms 503
leverage 505
line of credit 498
long-term financing 496
long-term forecast 490
operating (or master) budget 490
promissory note 497
revolving credit agreement 498
risk/return trade-off 502
secured bond 503
secured loan 498

Financial Management * CHAPTER 18   509

short-term financing 496
short-term forecast 489
term-loan agreement 502
trade credit 496
unsecured bond 503
unsecured loan 498
venture capital 505

connect interactive applications

Reinforcing Your *Connect*ion to Concepts in Business

This chapter offers 15 interactive applications designed to help you apply what you've learned (examples of these exercises appear below). Your instructor has determined which interactive applications will benefit you throughout this course. Please refer to your instructor's assignment list in *Connect* to determine which applications you should complete.

Comprehension Case Interactive: In business, the need for operating funds never seems to end. Virtually all organizations have operational needs for which they require funds including: managing daily business costs, controlling credit operations, acquiring inventory, and making capital expenditures. Read the Comprehension Case featuring a business owner with cash flow problems and answer the questions.

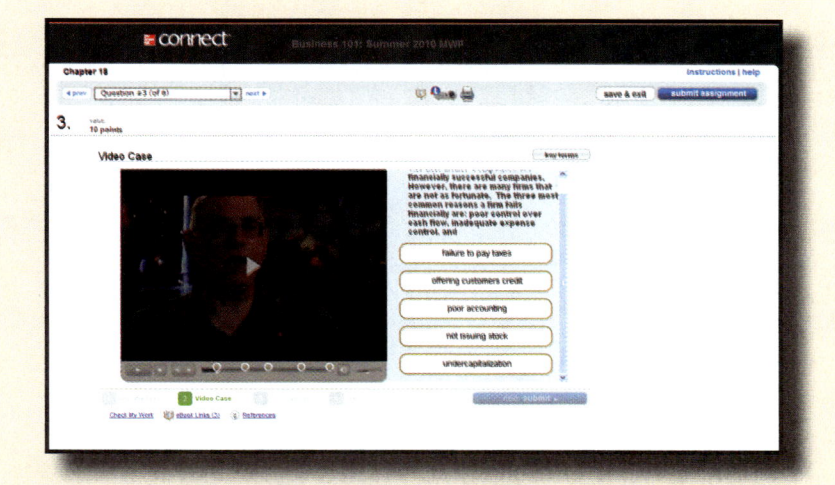

Video Case Interactive: The McFarlane Company uses a unique blend of artistic expertise and financial control to create a company that is successful and financially viable. Watch the video featuring Todd McFarlane and answer the questions when prompted.

Click and Drag Interactive: Forecasting is an important part of any firm's financial plan. Financial managers create forecasts by preparing budgets. These budgets are analyzed in order to determine if or when a firm will need to secure internal or external financing. Evaluate the following actions that would be performed by a financial manager and organize them in the most appropriate order.

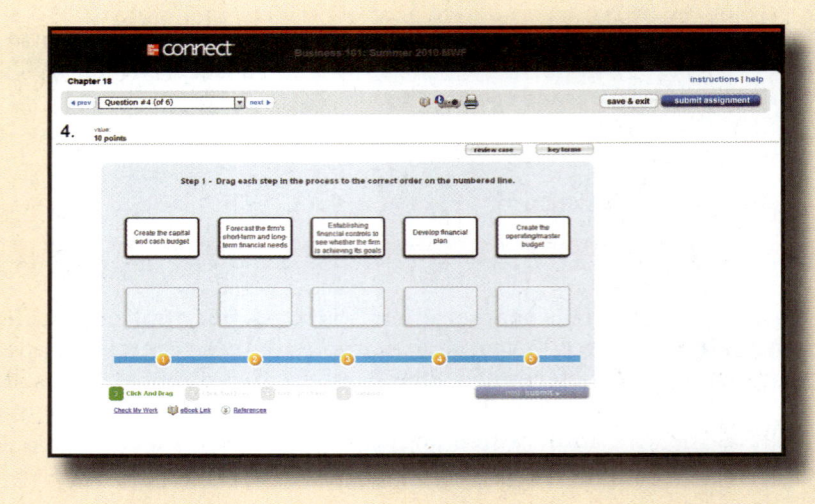

Click and Drag Interactive: A company needs to carefully develop a sound financial plan in order to be successful, regardless of its product or marketing effectiveness. Analyze the activities each person is pursuing and place them in the appropriate category.

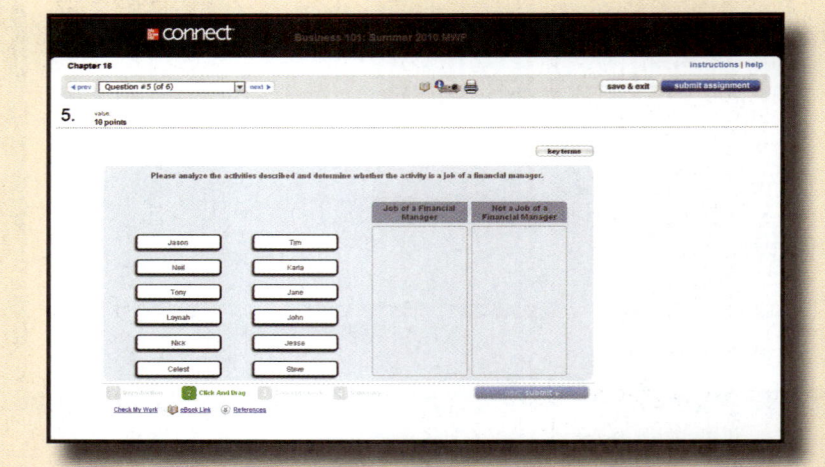

Click and Drag Interactive: Companies secure funding from a variety of sources. Some, in fact, come with a high price attached. These costs could include high interest rates, long payback periods, and increased ownership, which could result in the company losing control of its interests. Analyze the various funding options and determine whether it is a long-term or short-time strategy.

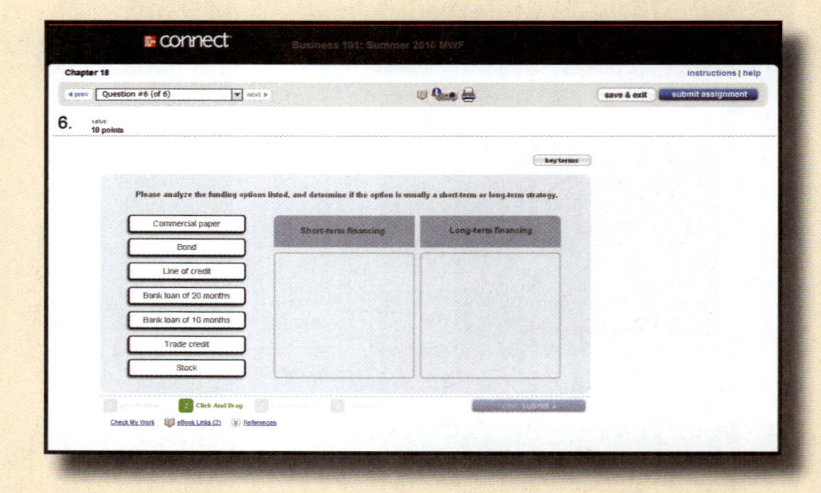

19 USING Securities Markets for Financing AND Investing Opportunities

profile

Getting to Know Warren Buffett, CEO of Berkshire Hathaway

As corporate excesses contributed to sending the U.S. economy tumbling in 2008, they also undermined U.S. investors' already waning trust in executives at business's highest level. Many corporate CEOs seemed more like James Bond villains than stewards of the U.S. economy as reports of enormous, undeserved compensation packages and near-total lack of accountability filled the media. An exception was investment mastermind Warren Buffett.

With a net worth of $47 billion, Buffett was the richest person on earth in 2008 (the downward market spiral knocked him out of the top spot in 2009). But he has been as responsible with his money as when he first began investing in the 1950s. He still lives in the same house in Omaha, Nebraska, that he bought in 1957 for $31,500, and instead of accepting a multimillion-dollar salary like so many other CEOs, he has limited his annual pay to $100,000. He says he is confounded that his secretary pays a greater percentage of salary in taxes than he does. There aren't many billionaire CEOs who ask for a smaller salary and more taxes, but Warren Buffett is not like most billionaire CEOs. Morningstar Inc., a leading provider of independent investment research, named him CEO of the year for 2008.

The son of a stockbroker, Buffett began managing money early in life, filing his first tax return at age 13 and claiming a $35 deduction for his bicycle. He received his undergraduate degree from the University of Pennsylvania and his master's degree in economics from Columbia University's business school, studying under famed economist and investor Benjamin Graham. After working at Graham's investment partnership for a few years, in 1956 Buffett moved back to Omaha and formed his own investment firm, Buffett Partnership Ltd. The turning point in his career came in 1962 when he began investing heavily in a textile firm called Berkshire Hathaway. By 1965, Buffett had taken complete control of the company and begun shifting it away from textiles toward insurance and other investment holdings. Soon he liquidated his old partnership and put the money into his burgeoning investment empire.

Over the following decades, Buffett amassed a considerable fortune from his Berkshire holdings and from continuously investing his revenue in a wide array of new ventures. A large portion of Berkshire's revenue comes from insurance, with automobile insurance company GEICO as its core. Berkshire

LEARNING goals

After you have read and studied this chapter, you should be able to

1. Describe the role of securities markets and of investment bankers.
2. Identify the stock exchanges where securities are traded.
3. Compare the advantages and disadvantages of equity financing by issuing stock, and detail the differences between common and preferred stock.
4. Compare the advantages and disadvantages of obtaining debt financing by issuing bonds, and identify the classes and features of bonds.
5. Explain how to invest in securities markets and set investment objectives such as long-term growth, income, cash, and protection from inflation.
6. Analyze the opportunities stocks offer as investments.
7. Analyze the opportunities bonds offer as investments.
8. Explain the investment opportunities in mutual funds and exchange-traded funds (ETFs).
9. Describe how indicators like the Dow Jones Industrial Average affect the market.

---

connect

Your *Connection* to Better Learning. 1. View the interactive presentation. 2. Practice through LearnSmart. 3. Apply your knowledge by using the interactive applications for each chapter of this text.

1 Prep >>>>>> **2 Study** >>>>>> **3 Apply**

Hathaway also owns large, noncontrolling stakes in Dairy Queen, Coca-Cola, Wells Fargo, Borsheims Fine Jewelry, and more than 70 other large companies. Buffett's investment expertise has earned him the nickname "the Oracle of Omaha," but his investment strategy relies on anything but fortune telling.

Buffett created Berkshire's $200 billion empire by investing in undervalued companies with strong management and raking in sizable profits when the stock rebounded. Buffett used this method with his $5 billion investment in Goldman Sachs, an investment banking company battered by the credit crisis of 2008. Though Buffett won't see a return for many years, his initial stake not only lays the groundwork for an eventual profit but also provides much-needed capital for the struggling firm.

If Buffett's multibillion-dollar investments make a surprising contrast to his modest lifestyle, his massive philanthropic projects are even more impressive. In 2006, Buffett announced he would gradually donate 85 percent of Berkshire's holdings to five foundations, with the largest contribution going to the Bill and Melinda Gates Foundation. Buffett also said he will not leave his fortune to his children because he wants them to find their own success in life instead of falling back on his riches. With his sensible personal philosophies, business genius, and giving spirit, Warren Buffett is truly the "billionaire next door."

Sources: Duncan Greenberg and Tatiana Serafin, "Up in Smoke," *Forbes,* March 30, 2009; Kay Marquadt, "Why Buffett Will Make Out Like a Bandit in This Market Crisis," *U.S. News and World Report,* September 30, 2008; and Shaun Rein, "Warren Buffett is All Wrong About Goldman," *Forbes,* May 17, 2010.

www.berkshirehathaway.com

NAME THAT company

▶ **PPT 19-1:**
Using Securities Markets for Financing and Investing Opportunities

▶ **PPT 19-2:**
Warren Buffett

▶ **PPT 19-3:**
The Basics of Securities Markets

▶ **PPT 19-4:**
Types of Securities Markets

▶ **LECTURE LINK 19-1:**
The IPO from Hell

initial public offering (IPO)
The first public offering of a corporation's stock.

David and Tom Gardner, the Motley Fools, are passionate about spreading the message that securities markets can provide opportunities for all. The brothers have built their careers on providing high-quality financial information to investors regardless of education or income. Visit their Web site at www.fool.com for more information.

For many years we have offered investors assistance by evaluating investment options like bond issues and rating them according to our perception of their risk. Our bond ratings range from the highest quality to midlevel. We even classify some bonds as junk. Who are we? (Find the answer in the chapter.)

LEARNING goal 1 *

Describe the role of securities markets and of investment bankers.

THE FUNCTION OF SECURITIES MARKETS

Securities markets—financial marketplaces for stocks and bonds—serve two major functions. First, they assist businesses in finding long-term funding to finance capital needs, such as expanding operations, developing new products, or buying major goods and services. Second, they provide private investors a place to buy and sell securities (investments) such as stocks and bonds that can help them build their financial future. In this chapter, we look at securities markets from the perspectives of both businesses and private investors.

Securities markets are divided into primary and secondary markets. *Primary markets* handle the sale of *new* securities. This is an important point to understand. Corporations make money on the sale of their securities (stock) only once—when they sell it on the primary market. The first public offering of a corporation's stock is called an **initial public offering (IPO)**. After that, the *secondary market* handles the trading of these securities between investors, with the proceeds of the sale going to the investor selling the stock, not to the corporation whose stock is sold. For example, imagine your vegetarian restaurant, Very Vegetarian, has grown into a chain and your products are available in many retail stores throughout the country. You want to raise additional funds to expand further. If you offer 1 million shares of stock in your company at $10 a share, you can raise $10 million at this initial offering. However, after the initial sale, if Shareholder Jones decides to sell 100 shares of her Very Vegetarian stock to Investor Smith, Very Vegetarian collects nothing from that transaction. Smith buys the stock from Jones, not from Very Vegetarian. It is possible, however, for companies like Very Vegetarian to offer additional shares of stock for sale to raise additional capital.

As Chapter 18 implied, we can't overemphasize the importance to businesses of long-term funding. Given a choice, businesses normally prefer to meet their long-term financial needs by using retained earnings or borrowing from a lending institution (bank, pension fund, insurance company). However, if long-term funds are not available from retained earnings or a lender, a company may be able to raise funds by issuing corporate stock or bonds. (Recall from Chapter 18 that selling stock in the corporation is a form of *equity financing* and issuing corporate bonds is a form of *debt financing*.) Visa, the world's largest processor of debit and credit cards, raised $18 billion from its IPO in 2008.[1] These sources of equity and debt financing are not available to all companies, especially small businesses.

Imagine you need further long-term financing to *expand* operations at Very Vegetarian. Your chief financial officer (CFO) says the company lacks sufficient retained earnings and she doesn't think it can secure the needed funds from a lender. She suggests you offer shares of stock or issue corporate bonds to private investors to secure financing. She warns, however, that issuing shares of stock or corporate bonds is not automatic. To get the necessary approval for stock or bond issues you must make extensive financial disclosures and undergo detailed scrutiny by the U.S. Securities and Exchange Commission (SEC). Because of these requirements, your CFO recommends that the company turn to an investment banker for assistance. Let's see why.

◄ CRITICAL THINKING EXERCISE 19-1:
Financing Growth

The Role of Investment Bankers

Investment bankers are specialists who assist in the issue and sale of new securities. Large financial firms can help companies like Very Vegetarian prepare the extensive financial analyses necessary to gain SEC approval for bond or stock issues.[2] Investment bankers can also *underwrite* new issues of stocks or bonds. That is, the investment banking firm buys the entire stock or bond issue at an agreed-on discount, which can be quite sizable, and then sells the issue to private or institutional investors at full price.[3]

Institutional investors are large organizations—such as pension funds, mutual funds, and insurance companies—that invest their own funds or the funds of others. Because of their vast buying power, institutional investors are a powerful force in securities markets.[4]

Before we look at stocks and bonds as long-term financing and investment opportunities in more depth, it's important to understand stock exchanges—the places where stocks and bonds are traded.

investment bankers
Specialists who assist in the issue and sale of new securities.

◄ PPT 19-5:
Investment Bankers and Institutional Investors

institutional investors
Large organizations—such as pension funds, mutual funds, and insurance companies—that invest their own funds or the funds of others.

LEARNING goal 2 *

Identify the stock exchanges where securities are traded.

STOCK EXCHANGES

As the name implies, a **stock exchange** is an organization whose members can buy and sell (exchange) securities on behalf of companies and individual investors. The New York Stock Exchange (NYSE) was founded in 1792 and was primarily a floor-based exchange, which means trades physically took place on the floor of the stock exchange. In 2005, the NYSE merged with Archipelago, a securities trading company that specialized in electronic trading.[5] In 2007, it merged with Europe's Euronext exchange, and in 2008 the NYSE Euronext acquired the second largest national exchange in the United States, the American Stock Exchange (AMEX).[6] Today the NYSE Euronext is the world's largest securities exchange, boasting a family of stock exchanges in six countries. Its 8,000 listed companies include 78 of the 100 largest companies in the world.

Not all securities are traded on registered stock exchanges. The **over-the-counter (OTC) market** provides companies and investors with a means to trade stocks not listed on the national securities exchanges. The OTC

stock exchange
An organization whose members can buy and sell (exchange) securities for companies and individual investors.

◄ PPT 19-6:
Stock Exchanges

over-the-counter (OTC) market
Exchange that provides a means to trade stocks not listed on the national exchanges.

Stock exchanges, like the NYSE, pictured here, are places—or, increasingly, electronic networks—where stocks and bonds are bought and sold. What are some of the advantages of being "listed" on one of the world's stock exchanges?

▶ **PPT 19-7:**
Top Stock Exchanges

▶ **LECTURE LINK 19-2:**
The Tokyo Exchange Typing Error

NASDAQ
A nationwide electronic system that links dealers across the nation so that they can buy and sell securities electronically.

▶ **PPT 19-8:**
The Securities and Exchange Commission

▶ **BONUS CASE 19-1:**
Is It Time for a NYSE Code of Ethics?

Securities and Exchange Commission (SEC)
Federal agency that has responsibility for regulating the various stock exchanges.

market is a network of several thousand brokers who maintain contact with one another and buy and sell securities through a nationwide electronic system. Trading is conducted between two parties directly, instead of through an exchange like the NYSE Euronext.

The **NASDAQ** (originally known as the National Association of Securities Dealers Automated Quotations) evolved from the OTC market but is no longer part of it. The NASDAQ is a telecommunications network that links dealers across the nation so that they can buy and sell securities electronically rather than in person. It is the largest U.S. electronic stock trading market. Originally it dealt mostly with small firms, but today well-known companies such as Microsoft, Intel, Google, Starbucks, Cisco, and Dell trade their stock on the NASDAQ. The NASDAQ also handles federal, state, and city government bonds and lists approximately 3,200 companies.[7]

Adding a company to an exchange is a highly competitive undertaking, and the battle between the stock exchanges is often fierce.[8] Stocks can be delisted from an exchange if a company fails to meet the exchange's requirements.[9] To find the requirements for registering (listing) stocks on the NYSE Euronext and NASDAQ exchanges, go to www.sec.gov/answers/listings.htm.

Securities Regulations and the Securities and Exchange Commission

The **Securities and Exchange Commission (SEC)** is the federal agency that has responsibility for regulating the various stock exchanges. The Securities Act of 1933 helps protect investors by requiring full disclosure of financial information by firms selling bonds or stock. The U.S. Congress passed this legislation to deal with the free-for-all atmosphere that existed in the securities markets during the 1920s and the early 1930s that helped cause the Great Depression. The Securities and Exchange Act of 1934 created the SEC.

Companies trading on the national exchanges must register with the SEC and provide it with annual updates. The 1934 act also established specific guidelines that companies must follow when issuing financial securities such as stocks or bonds. For example, before issuing either stocks or bonds for sale to the public, a company must file a detailed registration statement with the SEC that includes extensive economic and financial information. The condensed version of that registration document—called a **prospectus**—must be sent to prospective investors.

The 1934 act also established guidelines to prevent insiders within the company from taking advantage of privileged information they may have. *Insider trading* is using knowledge or information that individuals gain through their position that allows them to benefit unfairly from fluctuations in security prices. The key words here are *benefit unfairly.* Insiders within a firm are permitted to buy and sell stock in the company they work for, so long as they do not take unfair advantage of information.

Originally, the SEC defined the term *insider* rather narrowly as covering a company's directors and employees and their relatives. Today the term has been broadened to include just about anyone with securities information not available to the general public. Let's say the CFO of Very Vegetarian tells her next-door neighbor she is finalizing paperwork to sell the company to a large corporation, and the neighbor buys the stock based on this information. A court may well consider the purchase an insider trade. Penalties for insider trading can include fines or imprisonment.[10] Look at Figure 19.1 and test your

prospectus
A condensed version of economic and financial information that a company must file with the SEC before issuing stock; the prospectus must be sent to prospective investors.

figure 19.1

IS IT INSIDER TRADING OR NOT?

Insider trading involves buying or selling a stock on the basis of company information not available to the investing public. It's sometimes difficult to identify insider trading. The following hypothetical examples will give you an idea of what's legal and what's illegal. See how many of the questions you can answer. The answers are at the end of this box.

1. You work in research and development at a large company and have been involved in a major effort that should lead to a blockbuster new product coming to the market. News about the product is not public, and very few other workers even know about it. Can you purchase stock in the company?

2. Pertaining to the above situation, you are in a local coffee bar and mention to a friend about what's going on at the company. Another customer seated at an adjoining table overhears your discussion. Can this person legally buy stock in the company before the public announcement?

3. You work as an executive secretary at a major investment banking firm. You are asked to copy documents that detail a major merger about to happen that will keenly benefit the company being taken over. Can you buy stock in the company before the announcement is made public?

4. Your stockbroker recommends that you buy shares in a little-known company. The broker seems to have some inside information, but you don't ask any questions about his source. Can you buy stock in this company?

5. You work as a cleaning person at a major securities firm. At your job you come across information from the trash cans and computer printers of employees of the firm that provide detailed information about several upcoming deals the firm will be handling. Can you buy stock in the companies involved?

Answers: 1. No; 2. Yes; 3. No; 4. Yes; 5. No.

MAKING ethical decisions

Wagging the Dog

After 35 years of hard work you finally made it to the post of chief executive officer of Laddie Come Home, a large producer of pet foods. As part of your new compensation package, you are entitled to bonuses based on the company's stock performance. If the stock price of Laddie Come Home exceeds $50 a share during the current fiscal year, you could realize close to $3 million in bonuses. The stock is currently selling for $42.

A financial institution specializing in mergers and acquisitions tells you that a major competitor, Barking up the Wrong Tree, wants to acquire your company for upward of $50 a share. Your attorney says the merger is perfectly legal and poses no antitrust problems. You realize your board of directors would probably agree if you suggested selling the company. Unfortunately, at least half your current employees would lose their jobs in the merger. Many of these employees have been with the company over 20 years.

You plan to retire within the next two years, and a $3 million bonus could make life easier. What are the ethical considerations in this situation? What are your alternatives? What are the consequences of each alternative? What will you do?

---

skill in identifying insider trading. Then assess the manager's dilemma in the Making Ethical Decisions box.

Foreign Stock Exchanges

Thanks to expanded communications and the relaxation of many legal barriers, investors can buy securities from companies almost anywhere in the world. If you uncover a foreign company you feel has great potential for growth, you can purchase shares of its stock with little difficulty from U.S. brokers who have access to foreign stock exchanges. Foreign investors can also invest in U.S. securities, and large foreign stock exchanges, like those in London and Tokyo, trade large amounts of U.S. securities daily. The number of U.S. companies listed on foreign stock exchanges is growing. In addition to the London and Tokyo exchanges, other major stock exchanges are located in Shanghai, Paris, Sydney, Buenos Aires, Frankfurt, Zurich, Hong Kong, and Taiwan. There are several stock exchanges in Africa as well. The Reaching Beyond Our Borders box offers advice on how U.S. investors can become active in the global market.

Raising long-term funds using equity financing (stock) is an option many companies pursue. After the Progress Assessment, let's look in more depth at stock and bonds as long-term financing alternatives.

progress assessment

- What is the primary purpose of a stock exchange? Can you name the world's largest stock exchange?
- What does NASDAQ stand for? How does this exchange work?

REACHING BEYOND our borders

www.jpmorgan.com

The Wide, Wide World of Investing

When you consider the unpredictability of the U.S. stock market, it's fair to question whether investing in global markets makes any sense. After all, many countries have unstable currencies and can be politically volatile. Remembering the risk/return trade-off, you might be inclined to just forget about global securities. Many financial analysts, however, argue that investing some money in global markets might be a good idea. From 2003 until 2008, global markets like China and Brazil outperformed the U.S. market. They also fell dramatically when the U.S. market fell.

As an investor, or perhaps a future investor, you may want to explore opportunities in global markets. But do your research. Take a close look at the following suggestions:

- Invest in global companies with a solid track record like Shell Oil, Nestlé, Sony, Unilever, and Siemens.
- Invest in global companies listed on U.S. stock exchanges. They must comply with U.S. accounting procedures and rules of the Securities and Exchange Commission.
- Look into American depository receipts (ADRs), which you can purchase from U.S. brokers. ADRs represent a set number of shares in a foreign company that are held on deposit at a foreign branch of a U.S. bank.
- Consider mutual funds and exchange-traded funds. Both offer global portfolios as well as securities that focus on individual countries such as China or regions such as Europe, Asia, or Latin America.
- Trade with an established broker that has an office abroad. Many U.S. brokers also produce detailed research about foreign companies.
- Be careful of investing in securities from countries that have a history of currency problems or political instability.

Keep the risk/return trade-off, as well as your long-term financial goals, in mind in considering any investments, especially global ones.

Sources: Kunai Kapoor, "The Markets That Roared: When to Invest Globally and When to Avoid It," *On Wall Street,* April 1, 2008; Elizabeth O'Brien, "Going Global Now: Your Clients Still Need International Diversification but Navigating the World's Investment Opportunities Has Become Trickier, to Say the Least," *Financial Planning,* May 1, 2008; and Zachary Karabell, "It's Still a Small World After All," *Newsweek International,* September 22, 2008.

LEARNING goal 3 *

Compare the advantages and disadvantages of equity financing by issuing stock, and detail the differences between common and preferred stock.

◀ PPT 19-12:
Learning the Language of Stocks

◀ PPT 19-11:
The Wide, Wide World of Investing

stocks
Shares of ownership in a company.

stock certificate
Evidence of stock ownership that specifies the name of the company, the number of shares it represents, and the type of stock being issued.

◀ PPT 19-13:
Advantages of Issuing Stocks

dividends
Part of a firm's profits that the firm may distribute to stockholders as either cash payments or additional shares of stock.

HOW BUSINESSES RAISE CAPITAL BY SELLING STOCK

Stocks are shares of ownership in a company. A **stock certificate** represents stock ownership. It specifies the name of the company, the number of shares owned, and the type of stock it represents. Today, stock is generally held electronically; that is, the owners don't get a paper certificate unless they specially want to hold the certificates themselves.

Stock certificates sometimes indicate a stock's *par value*, which is a dollar amount assigned to each share of stock by the corporation's charter. Today, since par values do not reflect the market value of the stock, most companies issue *no-par* stock. **Dividends** are part of a firm's profits that the firm may (but is not required to) distribute to stockholders as either cash payments or additional shares of stock. Dividends are declared by a corporation's board of directors and are generally paid quarterly.

When Country Garden, an obscure real estate company in China, issued its initial public offering (IPO), the company gained more than $1.5 billion from the sale. Here the head of the Hong Kong stock exchange (left) toasts the event with the company's CEO. Can you see why issuing stock can be an appealing option for financing a company's growth?

Advantages and Disadvantages of Issuing Stock

Some advantages to a firm of issuing stock include:

- As owners of the business, stockholders never have to be repaid their investment.
- There's no legal obligation to pay dividends to stockholders; therefore, the firm can reinvest income (retained earnings) to finance future needs.
- Selling stock can improve the condition of a firm's balance sheet since issuing stock creates no debt. (A corporation may also buy back its stock to improve its balance sheet and make the company appear stronger financially.)

Disadvantages of issuing stock include:

- As owners, stockholders (usually only common stockholders) have the right to vote for the company's board of directors. (Typically, one vote is granted for each share of stock.) Issuing new shares of stock can thus alter the control of the firm.
- Dividends are paid from profit after taxes and are not tax-deductible.
- The need to keep stockholders happy can affect managers' decisions.

Companies can issue two classes of stock: common and preferred. Let's see how these two forms of equity financing differ.

Issuing Shares of Common Stock

Common stock is the most basic form of ownership in a firm. In fact, if a company issues only one type of stock, by law it must be common stock. Holders of common stock have the right to (1) elect members of the company's board of directors and vote on important issues affecting the company and (2) share in the firm's profits through dividends, if approved by the firm's board of directors. Having voting rights in a corporation allows common stockholders to influence corporate policy because the board members they elect choose the firm's top management and make major policy decisions. Common stockholders also have a *preemptive right* to purchase new shares of common stock before anyone else. This allows common stockholders to maintain their proportional share of ownership in the company.

common stock
The most basic form of ownership in a firm; it confers voting rights and the right to share in the firm's profits through dividends, if approved by the firm's board of directors.

▶ **PPT 19-14:**
Disadvantages of Issuing Stock

▶ **PPT 19-15:**
Two Classes of Stock

preferred stock
Stock that gives its owners preference in the payment of dividends and an earlier claim on assets than common stockholders if the company is forced out of business and its assets sold.

Issuing Shares of Preferred Stock

Owners of **preferred stock** are given preference in the payment of company dividends and must be paid their dividends in full before any common stock dividends can be distributed (hence the term *preferred*). They also have a prior claim on company assets if the firm is forced out of business and its assets sold. Normally, however, preferred stockholders do not get voting rights in the firm.

Preferred stock is generally issued with a par value that becomes the base for a fixed dividend the firm is willing to pay. For example, if a preferred stock's par value is $50 a share and its dividend rate is 4 percent, the dividend is $2 a share. An owner of 100 preferred shares receives a fixed yearly dividend of $200 if dividends are declared by the board of directors.

Preferred stock can have other special features that common stock doesn't have. For example it can be *callable*, which means preferred stockholders could be required to sell their shares back to the corporation. Preferred stock can also be converted to shares of common stock (but not the other way around), and it can be *cumulative.* That is, if one or more dividends are not paid when promised, they accumulate and the corporation must pay them later before it can distribute any common stock dividends.[11]

progress assessment

- Name at least two advantages and two disadvantages of issuing stock as a form of equity financing.
- What are the major differences between common stock and preferred stock?

LEARNING goal 4 *

Compare the advantages and disadvantages of obtaining debt financing by issuing bonds, and identify the classes and features of bonds.

HOW BUSINESSES RAISE CAPITAL BY ISSUING BONDS

A **bond** is a corporate certificate indicating that an investor has lent money to a firm (or a government). An organization that issues bonds has a legal obligation to make regular interest payments to investors and to repay the entire bond principal amount at a prescribed time. Let's further explore the language of bonds so you understand exactly how they work.

Learning the Language of Bonds

Bonds are usually issued in units of $1,000. The *principal* is the face value of a bond, which the issuing company is legally bound to repay in full to the bondholder on the **maturity date**. **Interest** is the payment the bond issuer makes to the bondholders to compensate them for the use of their money. If Very Vegetarian issues a $1,000 bond with an interest rate of 5 percent and a maturity date of 2020, it is agreeing to pay the bondholder a total of $50 interest each year until a specified date in 2020, when it must repay the full $1,000. Maturity dates can vary. Firms such as Disney and Coca-Cola have issued bonds with 50-year maturity dates.

Bond interest is sometimes called the *coupon rate*, a term that dates back to when bonds were issued as bearer bonds. The holder, or bearer, was considered the owner. Back then, the company issuing the bond kept no record of changes in ownership. Bond interest was paid to whoever clipped coupons attached to the bond and sent them to the issuing company for payment.

---

bond
A corporate certificate indicating that a person has lent money to a firm (or a government).

maturity date
The exact date the issuer of a bond must pay the principal to the bondholder.

interest
The payment the issuer of the bond makes to the bondholders for use of the borrowed money.

Today, bonds are registered to specific owners and changes in ownership are recorded electronically.

The interest rate paid by U.S. government bonds influences the bond interest rate businesses must pay. Government bonds are considered safe investments, so they can pay lower interest. Figure 19.2 describes several types of government bonds that compete with U.S. corporate bonds in securities markets. Bond interest rates also vary according to the state of the economy, the reputation of the issuing company, and the interest rate for bonds of similar companies. Though bond interest is quoted for an entire year, it is usually paid in two installments, and the rate generally cannot be changed.

Independent rating firms such as Standard & Poor's and Moody's Investors Service rate bonds according to their degree of risk.[12] Bonds can range from the highest quality to junk bonds (which we discuss later in this chapter).[13] Figure 19.3 describes the range of ratings.

Advantages and Disadvantages of Issuing Bonds

Bonds offer long-term financing advantages to an organization:

- Bondholders are creditors of the firm, not owners. They seldom vote on corporate matters; thus, management maintains control over the firm's operations.
- Bond interest is tax-deductible to the firm (see Chapter 17).
- Bonds are a temporary source of funding. They're eventually repaid and the debt obligation is eliminated.
- Bonds can be repaid before the maturity date if they contain a *call provision*. They can also be converted to common stock. (We discuss both features below.)

Bonds also have drawbacks:

- Bonds increase debt (long-term liabilities) and may adversely affect the market's perception of the firm.
- Paying interest on bonds is a legal obligation. If interest is not paid, bondholders can take legal action to force payment.
- The face value must be repaid on the maturity date. Without careful planning, this obligation can cause cash flow problems when the repayment comes due.

figure 19.2
TYPES OF GOVERNMENT SECURITIES THAT COMPETE WITH CORPORATE BONDS

BOND	DESCRIPTION
U.S. government bond	Issued by the federal government; considered the safest type of bond investment
Treasury bill (T-bill)	Matures in less than a year; issued with a minimum denomination of $1,000
Treasury note	Matures in 10 years or less; sold in denominations of $1,000 and $5,000
Treasury bond	Matures in 25 years or more; sold in denominations of $1,000 and $5,000
Municipal bond	Issued by states, cities, counties, and other state and local government agencies; usually exempt from federal taxes
Yankee bond	Issued by a foreign government; payable in U.S. dollars

▶ PPT 19-18:
Advantages of Issuing Bonds

▶ PPT 19-19:
Disadvantages of Issuing Bonds

▶ PPT 19-20:
Bond Ratings

figure 19.3
BOND RATINGS: MOODY'S INVESTORS SERVICE AND STANDARD & POOR'S INVESTOR SERVICE

Rating		
MOODY'S	**STANDARD & POOR'S**	**DESCRIPTIONS**
Aaa	AAA	Highest quality (lowest default risk)
Aa	AA	High quality
A	A	Upper medium grade
Baa	BBB	Medium grade
Ba	BB	Lower medium grade
B	B	Speculative
Caa	CCC, CC	Poor (high default risk)
Ca	C	Highly speculative
C	D	Lowest grade

Different Classes of Bonds

Corporations can issue two different classes of corporate bonds. *Unsecured bonds*, usually called **debenture bonds**, are not backed by any specific collateral (such as land or equipment). Only firms with excellent reputations and credit ratings can issue debenture bonds, due to the lack of security they provide investors. *Secured bonds*, sometimes called mortgage bonds, are backed by collateral such as land or buildings that is pledged to bondholders if interest or principal isn't paid when promised.

A bond issuer can choose to include different bond features. Let's look at some.

debenture bonds
Bonds that are unsecured (i.e., not backed by any collateral such as equipment).

Special Bond Features

By now you should understand that bonds are issued with an interest rate, are unsecured or secured by some type of collateral, and must be repaid at their maturity date. This repayment requirement often leads companies to establish a reserve account called a **sinking fund**. Its primary purpose is to ensure that enough money will be available to repay bondholders on the bond's maturity date. Firms issuing sinking-fund bonds periodically *retire* (set aside) some part of the principal prior to maturity so that enough funds will accumulate by the maturity date to pay off the bond. Sinking funds are attractive to both issuing firms and investors for several reasons:

- They provide for an orderly retirement (repayment) of a bond issue.
- They reduce the risk the bond will not be repaid.
- They support the market price of the bond because they reduce the risk the bond will not be repaid.

sinking fund
A reserve account in which the issuer of a bond periodically retires some part of the bond principal prior to maturity so that enough capital will be accumulated by the maturity date to pay off the bond.

A *callable bond* permits the bond issuer to pay off the principal before its maturity date.[14] This gives companies some discretion in their long-term forecasting. Suppose Very Vegetarian issued $10 million in 20-year bonds at 10 percent. Its yearly interest expense is $1 million ($10 million times 10 percent). If market conditions change and bonds of the same quality now pay only 7 percent, Very Vegetarian will be paying 3 percent, or $300,000 ($10 million times 3 percent), in excess interest yearly. The company could benefit by calling in (paying off) the old bonds and issuing new bonds at the lower rate. If a company calls a bond before maturity, it often pays investors a price above the bond's face value.

Investors can convert *convertible bonds* into shares of common stock in the issuing company.[15] This can be an incentive for an investor because common stock value tends to grow faster than a bond. Therefore, if the value of the firm's common stock grows sizably over time, bondholders can compare the value of continued bond interest earned with the potential profit of a specified number of shares of common stock.[16]

Now that you understand the advantages and disadvantages of stocks and bonds from a company's perspective, let's explore the opportunities stocks and bonds provide for *investors*. First, though, let's check your progress.

> **PPT 19-23:**
> Progress Assessment

> **CRITICAL THINKING EXERCISE 19-2:**
> Playing the Stock Market

> **PPT 19-24:**
> Buying Securities

stockbroker
A registered representative who works as a market intermediary to buy and sell securities for clients.

*Online brokers like Ameritrade and E*Trade specialize in providing information for investors. What are some of the features of this Web site (www.etrade.com) that seem designed to provide investment information?*

progress assessment

- Why are bonds considered a form of debt financing?
- What does it mean if a firm issues a 9 percent debenture bond due in 2025?
- Explain the difference between an unsecured and a secured bond.
- Why are convertible bonds attractive to investors?

LEARNING goal 5 *

Explain how to invest in securities markets and various investment objectives such as long-term growth, income, cash, and protection from inflation.

HOW INVESTORS BUY SECURITIES

Investing in stocks and bonds is not difficult. First, you decide what stock or bond you want to buy. After that, you find a registered representative authorized to trade securities to execute your order. A **stockbroker** is a registered representative who works as a market intermediary to buy and sell securities for clients. Stockbrokers place an order where the stock or bond is traded and negotiate a price. After the transaction is completed, the trade is reported to your broker, who notifies you. Large brokerage firms maintain automated order systems that allow brokers to enter your order the instant you make it. The order can be confirmed in seconds.

A broker can also be a source of information about what stocks or bonds would best meet your financial objectives, but it's still important to learn about stocks and bonds on your own.[17] Investment analysts' advice may not always meet your specific expectations and needs.

Investing through Online Brokers

Instead of using traditional brokerage services, investors today can choose from multiple online trading services to buy and sell stocks and bonds. Ameritrade, E*Trade, and Scottrade are among the leaders. Their investors are generally willing to do their own research and make investment decisions without the direct assistance of a broker, so the commissions these services charge are low. The leading services do provide important market information, such as company financial data, price histories of a stock, and analysts' reports. Often the level of information services you can get depends on the size of your account and your level of trading.

Whether you decide to use an online broker or to invest through a traditional stockbroker, remember that investing means committing your money with the hope of making a profit. The dot-com bubble burst in the early 2000s, and the financial crisis beginning in 2008 proved that investing is often a risky business. Therefore, the first step in any investment program is to analyze your level of risk tolerance. Other factors to consider include your desired income, cash requirements, and need to hedge against inflation, along with the investment's growth prospects.

You are never too young or too old to invest, but you should first ask questions and consider alternatives. Let's take a look.

Choosing the Right Investment Strategy

Investment objectives change over the course of a person's life. A young person can better afford to invest in high-risk investment options such as stocks than a person nearing retirement. Younger investors generally look for significant growth in the value of their investments over time. If stocks go into a tailspin and decrease in value, as they did in 2008, a younger person has time to wait for stock values to rise again. Older people, perhaps on a fixed income, lack the luxury of waiting and may be more inclined to invest in bonds that offer a steady return as a protection against inflation.

Consider five key criteria when selecting investment options:

1. *Investment risk.* The chance that an investment will be worth less at some future time than it's worth now.
2. *Yield.* The expected rate of return on an investment, such as interest or dividends, usually over a period of one year.
3. *Duration.* The length of time your money is committed to an investment.
4. *Liquidity.* How quickly you can get back your invested funds if you want or need them.
5. *Tax consequences.* How the investment will affect your tax situation.

What's important in any investment strategy is the risk/return trade-off. Setting investment objectives such as *growth* (choosing stocks you believe will increase in price) or *income* (choosing stocks that pay consistent dividends) should set the tone for your investment strategy.

Reducing Risk by Diversifying Investments

Diversification involves buying several different types of investments to spread the risk of investing. An investor may put 25 percent of his or her money into U.S. stocks that have relatively high risk but strong growth potential, another 25 percent in conservative government bonds, 25 percent in dividend-paying stocks that provide income, 10 percent in an international mutual fund, and the rest in the bank for emergencies and other possible investment opportunities.

◄ BONUS CASE 19-2:
Investing an Inheritance

◄ PPT 19-25:
Primary Investment Services Consumers Need

◄ LECTURE LINK 19-3:
The Dominican Nuns' Stock Portfolio

◄ PPT 19-26:
Five Investment Criteria

◄ PPT 19-27:
Average Annual Return of Asset Classes

diversification
Buying several different investment alternatives to spread the risk of investing.

> *Securities markets are like financial supermarkets—there are lots of investment options to choose from. That's why it's important to determine what investment strategy is right for you. Identifying the risk/return trade-off is a good starting point. A firm like Charles Schwab could help. How do you think your investment objectives will change over your lifetime?*

By diversifying with such a *portfolio strategy* or *allocation model*, investors decrease the chance of losing everything they have invested.[18]

Both stockbrokers and certified financial planners (CFPs) are trained to give advice about the investment portfolio that would best fit each client's financial objectives.[19] However, the more investors themselves read and study the market, the higher their potential for gain. A short course in investments can also be useful. Stocks and bonds provide opportunities for investors to enhance their financial future. Before we look at each, check your understanding with the Progress Assessment.

progress assessment

- What is the key advantage of investing through online brokers? What is the key disadvantage?
- What is the primary purpose of diversifying investments?

LEARNING goal 6 *

Analyze the opportunities stocks offer as investments.

INVESTING IN STOCKS

Buying stock makes investors part owners of a company who participate in its success. Stockholders can also lose money if a company does not do well or the overall stock market declines. The market freefall of 2008–2010 was proof of that.

Stock investors are often called bulls or bears according to their perceptions of the market.[20] *Bulls* believe that stock prices are going to rise; they buy stock in anticipation of the increase. A bull market is when overall stock prices are rising. *Bears* expect stock prices to decline and sell their stocks in anticipation of falling prices.[21] When the prices of stocks decline steadily, the market is called a bear market.

The market price and growth potential of most stock depends heavily on how well the corporation is meeting its business objectives. A company that achieves its objectives offers great potential for **capital gains**, the positive difference between the price at which you bought a stock and what you sell it for.[22] For example, an investment of $2,250 in 100 shares of McDonald's when it first went public in 1965 would have grown to 74,360 shares (after the company's 12 stock splits) worth approximately $4.6 million as of year-end market close on December 31, 2009. Now that's a lot of Big Macs![23]

Investors may select stocks depending on their investment strategy. Stocks issued by higher-quality companies such as Coca-Cola, Johnson & Johnson, and Procter & Gamble are referred to as *blue-chip stocks*; they pay regular dividends and generally experience consistent stock price appreciation.[24]

Stocks of corporations in emerging fields such as technology, biotechnology, or Internet-related firms, whose earnings are expected to grow at a faster rate than other stocks, are referred to as *growth stocks*. While a little riskier, growth stocks offer the potential for higher returns. Stocks of public utilities are considered *income stocks* because they usually offer investors a high dividend yield that generally keeps pace with inflation.[25] There are even *penny stocks*, representing ownership in companies that compete in high-risk industries like oil exploration. Penny stocks sell for less than $2 (some analysts say less than $5) and are considered risky investments.[26]

Stock investors have choices when placing buy orders. A *market order* tells a broker to buy or to sell a stock immediately at the best price available. A *limit order* tells the broker to buy or sell a stock at a specific price, if that price becomes available. Let's say a stock is selling for $40 a share. You believe the price will eventually go higher but could drop to $36 first. You can place a limit order at $36, so your broker will buy the stock at $36 if it drops to that price. If the stock never falls to $36, the broker will not purchase it for you.

Stock Splits

Brokers prefer to make stock purchases in *round lots* of 100 shares at a time. Investors, however, usually cannot afford to buy 100 shares, which may sell for as much as $100 each, and therefore often buy in *odd lots*, or fewer than 100 shares at a time.[27] High per-share prices often induce companies to declare **stock splits**, in which they issue two or more shares for every one that's outstanding. If Very Vegetarian stock were selling for $100 a share, the firm could declare a two-for-one stock split. Investors who owned one share of Very Vegetarian would now own two, each worth only $50 (half as much as before the split).

Stock splits cause no change in the firm's ownership structure and no immediate change in the investment's value. Investors generally approve of stock splits, however, because demand for a stock may be greater at $50 than at $100, and the price may then go up in the near future. A company cannot be forced to split its stock. Warren Buffett's firm, Berkshire Hathaway, has never split its Class A stock even when its per-share price surpassed $150,000.[28]

Buying Stock on Margin

Buying stock on margin means borrowing some of the stocks' purchase cost from the brokerage firm. The margin is the portion of the stocks' purchase price that the investors must pay with their own money. The board of governors of the Federal Reserve System sets *margin rates* in the U.S. market. Briefly, if the margin rate is 50 percent, an investor who qualifies for a margin account may borrow up to 50 percent of the stock's purchase price from the broker.

---

capital gains
The positive difference between the purchase price of a stock and its sale price.

◀ PPT 19-31:
Selecting Stocks

◀ PPT 19-32:
Stock Splits

stock splits
An action by a company that gives stockholders two or more shares of stock for each one they own.

◀ PPT 19-33:
Buying Stock on Margin

buying stock on margin
Purchasing stocks by borrowing some of the purchase cost from the brokerage firm.

Although buying on margin sounds like an easy way to buy more stocks, the downside is that investors must repay the credit extended by the broker, plus interest. If the investor's account goes down in value, the broker may issue *a margin call*, requiring the investor to come up with more money to cover the losses the account has suffered.[29] If the investor is unable to fulfill the margin call, the broker can legally sell off shares of the investor's stock to reduce the broker's chance of loss. Margin calls can force an investor to repay a significant portion of his or her account's loss within days or even hours. Buying on margin is thus a risky way to invest in stocks.

Understanding Stock Quotations

Publications like *The Wall Street Journal*, *Barron's*, and *Investor's Business Daily* carry a wealth of information concerning stocks and other investments. Your local newspaper may carry similar information as well. Financial Web sites like MSN Money and Yahoo! Finance carry up-to-the-minute information about companies that is much more detailed and only a click away. Take a look at Figure 19.4 to see an example of a stock quote from MSN Money for Microsoft. Microsoft trades on the NASDAQ exchange under the symbol MSFT. Preferred stock is identified by the letters *pf* following the company symbol. Remember, corporations can have several different preferred stock issues.

Information provided in the quote includes the highest and lowest price the stock traded for that day, the stock's high and low over the past 52 weeks, the dividend paid (if any), the stock's dividend yield (annual dividend as a percentage of the price per share), important ratios like the price/earnings (P/E) ratio (the price of the stock divided by the firm's per share earnings), and the return on equity. Investors can also see the number of shares outstanding and the total market capitalization of the firm. More technical features, such as the stock's beta (which measures degree of risk), may also appear. Figure 19.4 illustrates the stock's intraday trading (trading throughout the current day), but you can also click to see charts for different time

If you stroll through Times Square in New York City, you never have to wonder how stocks on the NASDAQ exchange are performing. The NASDAQ price wall continuously updates prices and the number of shares being traded. Originally, the NASDAQ dealt primarily with small companies; today it competes with the NYSE for new stock listings.

figure 19.4
UNDERSTANDING STOCK QUOTATIONS

▶ PPT 19-34:
Understanding Stock Quotations

periods. Similar information about bonds, mutual funds, and other investments is available online.

You might want to follow the market behavior of specific stocks that catch your interest, even if you lack the money to invest in them. Many successful investors started by building hypothetical portfolios of stocks and tracking their performance. The more you know about investing before you actually risk your money, the better. (See the Developing Workplace Skills and Taking It to the Net exercises at the end of this chapter for suggested exercises.)

LEARNING goal 7 *

Analyze the opportunities bonds offer as investments.

INVESTING IN BONDS

Investors looking for guaranteed income and limited risk often turn to U.S. government bonds for a secure investment. These bonds have the financial backing and full faith and credit of the federal government. Municipal bonds, also secure, are offered by local governments and often have advantages such as tax-free interest.[30] Some may even be insured. Corporate bonds are a bit more risky and challenging.

First-time corporate bond investors often ask two questions. The first is, "If I purchase a corporate bond, do I have to hold it until the maturity date?" No, you do not. Bonds are bought and sold daily on major securities exchanges (the secondary market we discussed earlier). However, if you decide to sell your bond to another investor before its maturity date, you may not get its face value (usually $1,000). If your bond does not have features that make it attractive to other investors, like a high interest rate or early maturity, you may have to sell at a *discount*, that is, a price less than the bond's face value. But if other investors do highly value it, you may be able to sell your bond at a *premium*, a price above its face value. Bond prices generally fluctuate inversely with current market interest rates. *As interest rates go up, bond prices fall, and vice versa.* Like all investments, bonds have a degree of risk.

The second question is, "How can I assess the investment risk of a particular bond issue?" Standard & Poor's and Moody's Investors Service rate the risk of many corporate and government bonds (look back at Figure 19.3). And recall the risk/return trade-off: The higher the risk of a bond, the higher the interest rate the issuer must offer.[31] Investors will invest in a bond considered risky only if the potential return is high enough. In fact, some will invest in bonds considered junk.

Investing in High-Risk (Junk) Bonds

Although bonds are considered relatively safe investments, some investors look for higher returns through riskier bonds called **junk bonds**. Standard & Poor's Investment Advisory Service and Moody's Investors Service define junk bonds as those with high risk *and* high default rates. Junk bonds pay investors interest as long as the value of the company's assets remains high and its cash flow stays strong.[32] Although the interest rates are attractive and often tempting, if the company can't pay off the bond, the investor is left with an investment that isn't worth more than the paper it's written on—in other words, junk.[33]

junk bonds
High-risk, high-interest bonds.

Understanding Bond Quotations

Bond prices are quoted as a percentage of $1,000, and their interest rate is often followed by an *s* for easier pronunciation. For example, 9 percent bonds due in 2020 are called 9s of 20.

Figure 19.5 is an example of a bond quote for Goldman Sachs from Yahoo! Finance. The quote highlights the bond's interest rate (coupon rate), maturity date, rating, current price, and whether it's callable. The more you know about bonds, the better prepared you will be to talk intelligently with investment counselors and brokers. Always be sure their advice is consistent with your best interests and investment objectives.

LEARNING goal 8 *

Explain the investment opportunities in mutual funds and exchange-traded funds (ETFs).

INVESTING IN MUTUAL FUNDS AND EXCHANGE-TRADED FUNDS

mutual fund
An organization that buys stocks and bonds and then sells shares in those securities to the public.

➤ PPT 19-37:
Investing in Mutual Funds and Exchange-Traded Funds

➤ PPT 19-38:
Percentage of Households Owning Mutual Funds

A **mutual fund** buys stocks and bonds and then sells shares in those securities to the public. A mutual fund is like an investment company that pools investors' money and then buys stocks or bonds in many companies in accordance with the fund's specific purpose. Mutual fund managers are specialists who pick what they consider to be the best stocks and bonds available.

Investors can buy shares of the mutual fund and thus take part in the ownership of many different companies they could not afford to invest in individually. Funds range from very conservative funds that invest only in government securities to others that specialize in emerging high-tech firms, Internet companies, foreign companies, precious metals, and other investments with greater risk. Some mutual funds invest exclusively in socially responsible companies (see the Thinking Green box). Thus, for a fee, mutual funds provide professional investment management and help investors diversify. U.S. investors have invested $12 trillion in mutual funds.[34]

Young or new investors are often advised to buy shares in *index funds* that invest in a certain kind of stocks or bonds or in the market as a whole.[35] An index fund may focus on large companies, small companies, emerging countries, or

figure 19.5
UNDERSTANDING BOND QUOTATIONS

GOLDMAN SACHS GROUP INC

OVERVIEW	
Price:	104.32
Coupon (%):	7.350
Maturity Date:	1-Oct-2009
Yield to Maturity (%):	-3.289
Current Yield (%):	7.045
Fitch Ratings:	A
Coupon Payment Frequency:	Semi-Annual
First Coupon Date:	1-Apr-2000
Type:	Corporate
Callable:	No

THINKING green

www.paxworld.com

Investing with Integrity

As the economy continues to stagger, it may be hard to believe there are still socially responsible high-profile investors. But despite the unfortunate image the credit crisis has bestowed on Wall Street's elite, a number of socially responsible investment funds (SRIs) still manage to prosper.

SRIs invest solely in companies with exceptional environmental, social, and governance (ESG) practices, a method that has netted them a surprisingly tidy profit. While other investment funds have been losing money by pouring capital into traditional, fossil-fuel-focused energy companies, SRIs have been making huge gains by investing in green and alternative energy companies. Their assets have grown more than those of any other type of investment fund, from $629 billion in 1995 to $2.71 trillion in 2005, a 324 percent rise over 10 years. According to Joe Keefe, chief executive of the Pax World Balance Fund, socially responsible investing is beneficial not only for the world at large but also for long-term investing, since companies with high ESG standards are lower risk than other companies.

Sources: Neil Rubin, "The Challenge of Socially Responsible Investments," *CPA Journal,* July 1, 2008; David Bogoslaw, "Socially Responsible Funds Hang Tough," *BusinessWeek,* May 14, 2008; Pax World Mutual Funds, www.paxworld.com, accessed March 4, 2009.

---

real estate (real estate investment trusts, or REITs). One idea is to diversify your investments by investing in a variety of index funds. A stockbroker, certified financial planner (CFP), or banker can help you find the option that best fits your investment objectives. The newsletter *Morningstar Investor* is an excellent resource for evaluating mutual funds, as are business publications such as *BusinessWeek, The Wall Street Journal, Money,* and *Investor's Business Daily.*

With mutual funds it's simple to change your investment objectives if your financial objectives change. Moving your money from a bond fund to a stock fund and back is no more difficult than calling an 800 number or clicking a mouse. Figure 19.6 on p. 532 gives you a list of some mutual fund investment options. Another advantage of mutual funds is that you can buy most directly from the fund and avoid broker fees or commissions.

A *load fund* charges investors a commission to buy or sell its shares; a *no-load fund* charges no commission. Check for fees and charges because they can differ significantly. Also check the long-term performance of the fund's management. Mutual funds called *open-end funds* will accept the investments of any interested investors. *Closed-end funds,* however, limit the number of shares; once the fund reaches its target number, no new investors can buy into the fund.

Exchange-traded funds (ETFs) resemble both stocks and mutual funds. They are collections of stocks and bonds that are traded on securities exchanges but themselves are traded more like individual stocks than like mutual funds.[36] Mutual funds, for example, permit investors to buy and sell shares only at the close of the trading day. ETFs can be purchased or sold at any time during the trading day.

◀ PPT 19-41:
Investing with Integrity

◀ PPT 19-42:
Growth of Socially Responsible Investing

◀ PPT 19-39:
Three Varieties of ETFs

exchange-traded funds (ETFs)
Collections of stocks and bonds that are traded on exchanges but are traded more like individual stocks than like mutual funds.

531

figure 19.6

MUTUAL FUND OBJECTIVES

Mutual funds have a wide array of investment categories. They range from low-risk, conservative funds to others that invest in high-risk industries. Listed here are abbreviations of funds and what these abbreviations stand for.

AB	Investment-grade corporate bonds	MP	Stock and bond fund
AU	Gold oriented	MT	Mortgage securities
BL	Balanced	MV	Mid-cap value
EI	Equity income	NM	Insured municipal bonds
EM	Emerging markets	NR	Natural resources
EU	European region	PR	Pacific region
GL	Global	SB	Short-term corporate bonds
GM	General municipal bond	SC	Small-cap core
GT	General taxable bonds	SE	Sector funds
HB	Health/biotech	SG	Small-cap growth
HC	High-yield bonds	SM	Short-term municipal bonds
HM	High-yield municipal bonds	SP	S&P 500
IB	Intermediate-term corporate bonds	SQ	Specialty
IG	Intermediate-term government bonds	SS	Single-state municipal bonds
IL	International	SU	Short-term government bonds
IM	Intermediate-term municipal bonds	SV	Small-cap value
LC	Large-cap core	TK	Science & technology
LG	Large-cap growth	UN	Unassigned
LT	Latin America	UT	Utility
LU	Long-term U.S. bonds	WB	World bonds
LV	Large-cap value	XC	Multi-cap core
MC	Mid-cap core	XG	Multi-cap growth
MG	Mid-cap growth	XV	Multi-cap value

Sources: *The Wall Street Journal* and *Investor's Business Daily*.

The key points to remember about mutual funds and ETFs is that they offer small investors a way to spread the risk of stock and bond ownership and have their investments managed by a financial specialist for a fee. Financial advisers put mutual funds and ETFs high on the list of recommended investments, particularly for small or beginning investors.

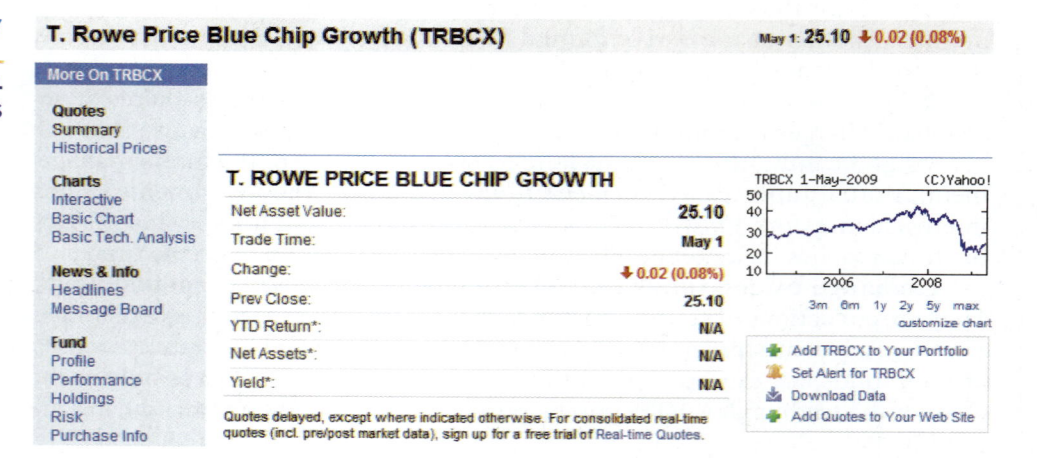

▶ PPT 19-43:
Comparing Investments

▶ PPT 19-40:
Understanding Mutual Fund Quotations

Understanding Mutual Fund Quotations

You can investigate the specifics of various funds by contacting a broker or contacting the fund directly by phone or through its Web site. Business publications and online sources also provide information about mutual funds.

Look at the example of the T. Rowe Price Blue Chip Growth fund from Yahoo! Finance in Figure 19.7. The fund's name is listed in large letters. The

figure 19.7

UNDERSTANDING MUTUAL FUND QUOTATIONS

T. Rowe Price Blue Chip Growth (TRBCX) May 1: 25.10 ↓ 0.02 (0.08%)

More On TRBCX
Quotes
 Summary
 Historical Prices
Charts
 Interactive
 Basic Chart
 Basic Tech. Analysis
News & Info
 Headlines
 Message Board
Fund
 Profile
 Performance
 Holdings
 Risk
 Purchase Info

T. ROWE PRICE BLUE CHIP GROWTH
Net Asset Value: 25.10
Trade Time: May 1
Change: ↓0.02 (0.08%)
Prev Close: 25.10
YTD Return*: N/A
Net Assets*: N/A
Yield*: N/A

Quotes delayed, except where indicated otherwise. For consolidated real-time quotes (incl. pre/post market data), sign up for a free trial of Real-time Quotes.

TRBCX 1-May-2009 (C)Yahoo!

3m 6m 1y 2y 5y max
customize chart

+ Add TRBCX to Your Portfolio
+ Set Alert for TRBCX
+ Download Data
+ Add Quotes to Your Web Site

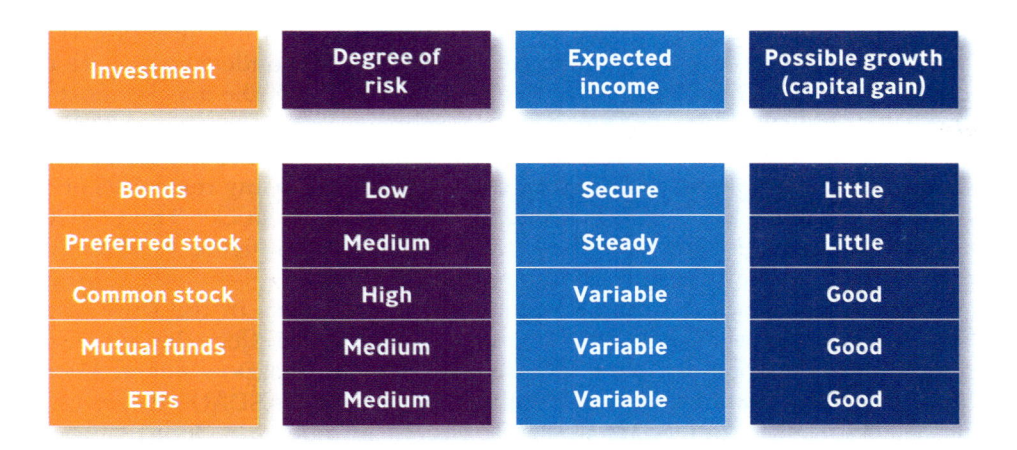

figure 19.8
COMPARING INVESTMENTS

Investment	Degree of risk	Expected income	Possible growth (capital gain)
Bonds	Low	Secure	Little
Preferred stock	Medium	Steady	Little
Common stock	High	Variable	Good
Mutual funds	Medium	Variable	Good
ETFs	Medium	Variable	Good

net asset value (NAV) is the price per share of the mutual fund. The NAV is calculated by dividing the market value of the mutual fund's portfolio by the number of shares it has outstanding. The chart also shows the fund's year-to-date (YTD) return, the change in the NAV from the previous day's trading, and the fund's net assets.

Figure 19.8 evaluates bonds, stocks, mutual funds, and ETFs according to risk, income, and possible investment growth (capital gain).

progress assessment

- What is a stock split? Why do companies sometimes split their stock?
- What does buying stock on margin mean?
- What are mutual funds and ETFs?
- What is the key benefit to investors in investing in a mutual fund or ETF?

LEARNING goal 9 *

Describe how stock market indicators like the Dow Jones Industrial Average affect the market.

UNDERSTANDING STOCK MARKET INDICATORS

Investors today find an enormous wealth of investment information in newspapers and magazines, on television, and on Web sites. Look through *The Wall Street Journal*, *Barron's*, *Investor's Business Daily*, *USA Today*, and your local newspaper's business section. Listen to business reports on radio and TV for investment analysis and different viewpoints. Visit different Web sites that provide information about companies and markets. By doing so, you will begin to better understand investment information. But keep in mind that investing is an inexact science, and rarely are investors as successful as the subject of this chapter's Profile, Warren Buffett. Every time someone sells a stock, believing it will fall, someone else is buying it, believing its price will go higher.

Dow Jones Industrial Average (the Dow)
The average cost of 30 selected industrial stocks, used to give an indication of the direction (up or down) of the stock market over time.

> **CRITICAL THINKING EXERCISE 19-3:**
> Dow Jones Components

News reports often end with the announcer saying something like "The Dow was up 190 points today in active trading." Ever wonder what that's all about? The **Dow Jones Industrial Average (the Dow)** is the average cost of 30 selected industrial stocks. The financial industry uses it to give an indication of the direction (up or down) of the stock market over time. Charles Dow began the practice of measuring stock averages in 1884, using the prices of 12 key stocks. In 1982, the Dow was broadened to include 30 stocks. The 12 original and the 30 current stocks in the Dow are illustrated in Figure 19.9. Do you recognize any of the 12 original companies?

Today, Dow Jones & Company substitutes new stocks in the Dow when it's deemed appropriate. In 1991, Disney was added to reflect the increased economic importance of the service sector. In 1999, the Dow added Home Depot and SBC Communications along with its first NASDAQ stocks, Intel and Microsoft. Chevron, Sears Roebuck, Union Carbide, and Goodyear were eliminated. In 2004, American International Group (AIG), Pfizer, and Verizon replaced AT&T, International Paper, and Eastman Kodak. (In 2005, AT&T rejoined the Dow when it merged with SBC.) In 2008, Chevron, Bank of America, and Kraft Foods replaced Altria Group, Honeywell, and AIG. In 2009, Travelers and Cisco replaced Citigroup and General Motors.

Critics argue that the 30-company Dow sample is too small to get a good statistical representation of the direction of the market over time. Many investors and analysts prefer to follow stock indexes like the Standard & Poor's 500 (S&P 500), which tracks the performance of 400 industrial, 40 financial, 40 public utility, and 20 transportation stocks. Investors also closely follow the NASDAQ average, which is quoted each trading day to show trends in this important exchange.

Staying abreast of the market will help you decide what investments seem most appropriate to your needs and objectives. Remember two key investment realities: Your personal financial objectives and needs change over time, and markets can be volatile. Let's look at market volatility and the challenges that present investors with new risks and opportunities.

Riding the Market's Roller Coaster

Throughout the 1900s, the stock market had its ups and downs, spiced with several major tremors. The first major crash occurred on Tuesday,

> **LECTURE LINK 19-5:**
> The Day They Call "Black Tuesday"

figure 19.9

THE ORIGINAL DOW AND CURRENT DOW

THE ORIGINAL DOW 12	THE 30 CURRENT DOW COMPANIES	
American Cotton Oil	Alcoa	Intel
American Sugar Refining Co.	American Express	Johnson & Johnson
American Tobacco	AT&T	JPMorgan Chase
Chicago Gas	Bank of America	Kraft
Distilling & Cattle Feeding Co.	Boeing	McDonald's
General Electric Co.	Caterpillar	Merck
Laclede Gas Light Co.	Chevron	Microsoft
National Lead	Cisco	Pfizer
North American Co.	Coca-Cola	Procter & Gamble
Tennessee Coal, Iron & Railroad Co.	DuPont	3M
U.S. Leather	ExxonMobil	United Technologies
U.S. Rubber Co.	General Electric	Travelers
	Hewlett-Packard	Verizon
	Home Depot	Wal-Mart Stores
	IBM	Walt Disney

October 29, 1929, when the stock market lost almost 13 percent of its value in a single day. That day, Black Tuesday, brought home to investors the reality of market volatility, especially to those who bought stocks heavily on margin. On October 19, 1987, the stock market suffered the largest one-day drop in its history, losing over 22 percent of its value. On October 27, 1997, investors felt the fury of the market once again. Fears of an impending economic crisis in Asian markets caused panic and widespread losses in the market. Luckily, the market regained its strength after a short downturn.

◀ PPT 19-46:
Market Turmoil

The market was not so fortunate in the early 2000s. All told, investors lost $7 trillion in market value from 2000 through 2002. In 2008, the financial crisis fueled a massive exodus from the stock market, resulting in record losses.

What caused the market turmoils of 1987, 1997, 2000–2002, and 2008? In 1987, analysts agreed it was **program trading**, in which investors give their computers instructions to sell automatically to avoid potential losses if the price of their stock dips to a certain point. On October 19, 1987, computers' sell orders caused many stocks to fall to unbelievable depths. The crash of 1987 prompted the U.S. exchanges to create mechanisms called *curbs* and *circuit breakers* to restrict program trading whenever the market moves up or down by a large number of points in a trading day. A key computer is turned off and program trading is halted. Then you'll see the phrase *curbs in* if you watch programming like CNBC or MSNBC.

program trading
Giving instructions to computers to automatically sell if the price of a stock dips to a certain point to avoid potential losses.

Circuit breakers are more drastic than curbs and are triggered when the Dow falls 10, 20, or 30 percent in a day. That happened on October 27, 1997, when the market suffered an approximate 7 percent decline and the market closed for the day at 3:30 p.m. instead of 4:00. Many believe the 1997 market drop (caused by the financial crisis in Asia) could have been much worse without the trading restrictions. Depending on the rate of decline and the time of day, circuit breakers will halt trading for half an hour to two hours so that traders have time to assess the situation.

The market reached unparalleled heights in the late 1990s only to collapse into a deep decline in 2000–2002. The bursting of the dot-com bubble was the primary cause. A bubble is caused when too many investors drive the price of something unrealistically high.

Before 2000, investors had believed the real value of companies was fairly reflected in their financial statements. This trust was shattered by disclosures of financial fraud at companies such as WorldCom, Enron, Global Crossing, and Tyco. Investment analysts also came under fire as information revealed they often provided clients with wildly optimistic evaluations and recommendations about companies they knew were not worth their current prices.

After the financial downturn caused by the dot-com bubble bursting, the market surged upward again in the mid-2000s. The Dow, in fact, set a record high in October 2007.[37] The market's improvement was dramatic, especially in the real estate sector. From 2000 to 2006 the prices of existing homes rose 50 percent.[38] This real estate bubble was like the tech bubble before it: Investors believed that home prices would increase forever. Financial institutions reduced their lending requirements in order to make more mortgage loans, homebuilders overbuilt, and buyers overspent. The government contributed to the problem by requiring more mortgages be given to low- and moderate-income buyers, many with weak credit scores or no verification of income or assets. These *subprime* loans were pooled together and repackaged as securities that were sold to investors through a process called securitization (described in the Legal Briefcase box on p. 536).

LEGAL briefcase

Gambling with Investors' Security

In the classic 1946 film *It's a Wonderful Life,* friendly savings and loan banker George Bailey made home loans to local residents. He granted loans only to people he expected would repay. He took the risk of being repaid and kept the loans on his books.

George's way of doing things changed in the 1970s when the U.S. government sponsored the creation of large entities like the Federal National Mortgage Association (FNMA), commonly referred to as Fannie Mae. Fannie Mae bought huge numbers of home mortgages from lenders like George, bundled them together in mortgage-backed securities, and then sold these securities to investors.

Since the loan standards at that time were clear, George's risk and return were easy to compute. However, by the 1990s, home loans were riskier and more complex. Borrowers, some of whom would not have qualified for loans in the past, were enticed by lenders offering a wide range of mortgage options with varying repayment plans that many did not understand or would not have qualified for in George's day. Investment banks saw a chance to earn higher fees by combining subprime loans (loans to high-risk borrowers) and other risky securities into asset-backed securities (ABSs) for sale globally. The market for ABSs experienced huge growth in 2003 and by 2007 had grown to $13 trillion.

Rating agencies measured the risk of ABSs with complex computer models. Many were rated AAA and considered risk-free. Raters assumed that these investments would be safe even if subprime borrowers defaulted in large numbers, because such defaults would have no effect on ever-rising real estate prices. What the agencies failed to take into account was that these complex securities were based on millions of mortgages that required someone to make payments every month. The subprime market had tripled in size, and the bulk of these loans were made to borrowers who had no chance of ever repaying them. Raters also did not calculate that, like all investments, real estate prices *can* go down.

Securitization of subprime real estate loans can be blamed for a great part of the recent global market crisis. However, other market weaknesses also helped lead to an economic challenge that could be with us for some time.

Sources: Nomi Prins, "The Risk Fallacy," *Fortune,* October 28, 2008; Elizabeth Spiers, "Putting Lipstick on a Pig," *Fortune,* September 14, 2008; "Securitization 2.0," *Forbes,* April 3, 2008; and Vikas Bajaj, "U.S. Tries a Trillion-Dollar Key for Locked Lending," *New York Times,* February 19, 2009.

▶ **PPT 19-47:**
Turmoil in the 2000s

In 2008, the collapse of the real estate market, as prices peaked and began to fall, drove most financial institutions into a panic and some into default. Financial giants such as Lehman Brothers went out of business. Wall Street icon Merrill Lynch was purchased by Bank of America, and investment banking giant Bear Stearns was taken over by JPMorgan Chase. The federal government took control of mortgage giants Fannie Mae and Freddie Mac. Congress passed a $700 billion financial package called the Troubled Assets Relief Program (TARP) to bolster banks and the automotive industry and to bail out insurer American International Group (AIG). While the troubled banks have repaid some of the money they received through TARP, the financial crisis will affect the economy for a long time.

▶ **PPT 19-48:**
Who's at Fault for the Economic Crisis?

Investing Challenges in the 21st-Century Market

▶ **PPT 19-49:**
Gambling with Investors' Security

In the stock market, what goes up also goes down. Financial markets may experience changes in the future that will only heighten investor risk. The recent financial crisis also reinforced that the world's economies are closely linked. The United States was not the only nation affected by the financial crisis; financial markets in Europe, Asia, and South America felt the pain as well.[39] Persistent challenges and even political and social change promise to make securities markets exciting but not stable places to be in the 21st century.

Diversify your investments, and be mindful of the risks of investing. Taking a long-term perspective is also a wise idea. There's no such thing as easy money or a sure thing. If you carefully research companies and industries, keep up with the news, and make use of investment resources—such as newspapers, magazines, newsletters, the Internet, and TV programs—the payoff can be rewarding over time.

◄ **LECTURE LINK 19-6:**
Investing in Commodities

progress assessment

- What does the Dow Jones Industrial Average measure? Why is it important?
- Why do the 30 companies comprising the Dow change periodically?
- Explain program trading and the problems it can create.

◄ **PPT 19-50:**
Progress Assessment

summary

Learning Goal 1. Describe the role of securities markets and of investment bankers.

- **What opportunities do securities markets provide businesses and individual investors?**

By issuing securities businesses are able to raise much-needed funding to help finance their major expenses. Individual investors can share in the success and growth of emerging firms by investing in them.

- **What role do investment bankers play in securities markets?**

Investment bankers are specialists who assist in the issue and sale of new securities.

Learning Goal 2. Identify the stock exchanges where securities are traded.

- **What are stock exchanges?**

Stock exchanges are securities markets whose members are engaged in buying and selling securities such as stocks and bonds.

- **What are the different exchanges?**

The largest U.S. exchange is the NYSE Euronext. The NASDAQ is a telecommunications network that links dealers across the nation so that they can buy and sell securities electronically rather than in person. It is the largest U.S. electronic stock trading market. There are stock exchanges all over the world.

- **What is the over-the-counter (OTC) market?**

The OTC market is a system for exchanging stocks not listed on the national exchanges.

- **How are securities exchanges regulated?**

The Securities and Exchange Commission (SEC) regulates securities exchanges and requires companies that intend to sell bonds or stock to provide a prospectus to potential investors.

- **What is insider trading?**

Insider trading is the use of information or knowledge individuals gain that allows them to benefit unfairly from fluctuations in security prices.

Learning Goal 3. Compare the advantages and disadvantages of equity financing by issuing stock, and detail the differences between common and preferred stock.

- **What are the advantages and disadvantages to a firm of selling stock?**
  The advantages of selling stock include the following: (1) the stock price never has to be repaid to stockholders, since they become owners in the company; (2) there is no legal obligation to pay stock dividends; and (3) the company incurs no debt, so it may appear financially stronger. Disadvantages of selling stock include the following: (1) stockholders become owners of the firm and can affect its management by voting for the board of directors; (2) it is more costly to pay dividends since they are paid in after-tax profits; and (3) managers may be tempted to make stockholders happy in the short term rather than plan for long-term needs.
- **What are the differences between common and preferred stock?**
  Holders of common stock have voting rights in the company. In exchange for having no voting rights, preferred stockholders receive a fixed dividend that must be paid in full before common stockholders receive a dividend. Preferred stockholders are also paid back their investment before common stockholders if the company is forced out of business.

Learning Goal 4. Compare the advantages and disadvantages of obtaining debt financing by issuing bonds, and identify the classes and features of bonds.
- **What are the advantages and disadvantages of issuing bonds?**
  The advantages of issuing bonds include the following: (1) management retains control since bondholders cannot vote; (2) interest paid on bonds is tax-deductible; (3) bonds are only a temporary source of financing, and after they are paid off the debt is eliminated; (4) bonds can be paid back early if they are issued with a call provision; and (5) sometimes bonds can be converted to common stock. The disadvantages of bonds include the following: (1) because bonds are an increase in debt, they may adversely affect the market's perception of the company; (2) the firm must pay interest on its bonds; and (3) the firm must repay the bond's face value on the maturity date.
- **What are the different types of bonds?**
  Unsecured bonds are not supported by collateral, whereas secured bonds are backed by tangible assets such as mortgages, buildings, and equipment.

Learning Goal 5. Explain how to invest in securities markets and set investment objectives such as long-term growth, income, cash, and protection from inflation.
- **How do investors normally make purchases in securities markets?**
  Investors purchase investments through market intermediaries called stockbrokers, who provide many different services. Online investing is increasingly popular.
- **What are the criteria for selecting investments?**
  Investors should determine their overall financial objectives and evaluate investments according to (1) risk, (2) yield, (3) duration, (4) liquidity, and (5) tax consequences.
- **What is diversification?**
  Diversification means buying several different types of investments (government bonds, corporate bonds, preferred stock, common stock, international stock) with different degrees of risk. The purpose is to reduce the overall risk an investor would assume by investing in just one type of security.

Learning Goal 6. Analyze the opportunities stocks offer as investments.
- **What is a market order?**
  A market order tells a broker to buy or to sell a security immediately at the best price available.

- **A limit order?**

A limit order tells the broker to buy or sell if the stock reaches a specific price.

- **What does it mean when a stock splits?**

When a stock splits, stockholders receive two (or more) shares of stock for each share they own. Each is worth half (or less) of the original share, so while the number of the shares increases, the total value of stockholders' holdings stays the same. The lower per-share price that results may increase demand for the stock.

- **What does buying on margin mean?**

An investor buying on margin borrows up to 50 percent of the cost of a stock from the broker to get shares of stock without immediately paying the full price

- **What information do stock quotations give you?**

Stock quotations provide the highest and lowest price in the last 52 weeks; the dividend yield; the price/earnings ratio; the total shares traded that day; and the closing price and net change in price from the previous day.

Learning Goal 7. Analyze the opportunities bonds offer as investments.

- **What is the difference between a bond selling at a discount and a bond selling at a premium?**

In the secondary market a bond selling at a premium is priced above its face value. A bond selling at a discount sells below its face value.

- **What is a junk bond?**

Junk bonds are high-risk (rated BB or below), high-interest debenture bonds that speculative investors often find attractive.

- **What information does a bond quotation give you?**

A bond quotation gives the bond's interest rate (coupon rate), maturity date, rating, current price, and whether it's callable.

Learning Goal 8. Explain the investment opportunities in mutual funds and exchange-traded funds (ETFs).

- **How can mutual funds help individuals diversify their investments?**

A mutual fund is an organization that buys stocks and bonds and then sells shares in those securities to the public, enabling individuals to invest in many more companies than they could otherwise afford.

- **What are ETFs?**

Like mutual funds ETFs are collections of stocks that are traded on exchanges, but they are traded more like individual stocks.

Learning Goal 9. Describe how stock market indicators like the Dow Jones Industrial Average affect the market.

- **What is the Dow Jones Industrial Average?**

The Dow Jones Industrial Average is the average price of 30 specific stocks that analysts use to track the direction (up or down) of the stock market.

key terms

bond 521
buying stock on margin 527
capital gains 527
common stock 520
debenture bonds 523
diversification 525
dividends 519
Dow Jones Industrial Average (the Dow) 534
exchange-traded funds (ETFs) 531
initial public offering (IPO) 514
institutional investors 515
interest 521
investment bankers 515

PART 6 * Managing Financial Resources

junk bonds 529
maturity date 521
mutual fund 530
NASDAQ 516
over-the-counter (OTC) market 515
preferred stock 520
program trading 535
prospectus 517
Securities and Exchange Commission (SEC) 516
sinking fund 523
stockbroker 524
stock certificate 519
stock exchange 515
stocks 519
stock splits 527

connect interactive applications

Reinforcing Your Connection to Concepts in Business

This chapter offers 12 interactive applications designed to help you apply what you've learned (examples of these exercises appear below). Your instructor has determined which interactive applications will benefit you throughout this course. Please refer to your instructor's assignment list in *Connect* to determine which applications you should complete.

Decision Generator Interactive: Companies are constantly faced with the need to secure more financing from investors and creditors. Each has advantages and disadvantages. For some, stocks provide the best equity financing. For others, bonds are the most attractive option. Analyze the options for the SWB publishing company and respond to the questions. You will be offered the opportunity to revise your response based on the "Your Strategy" box provided.

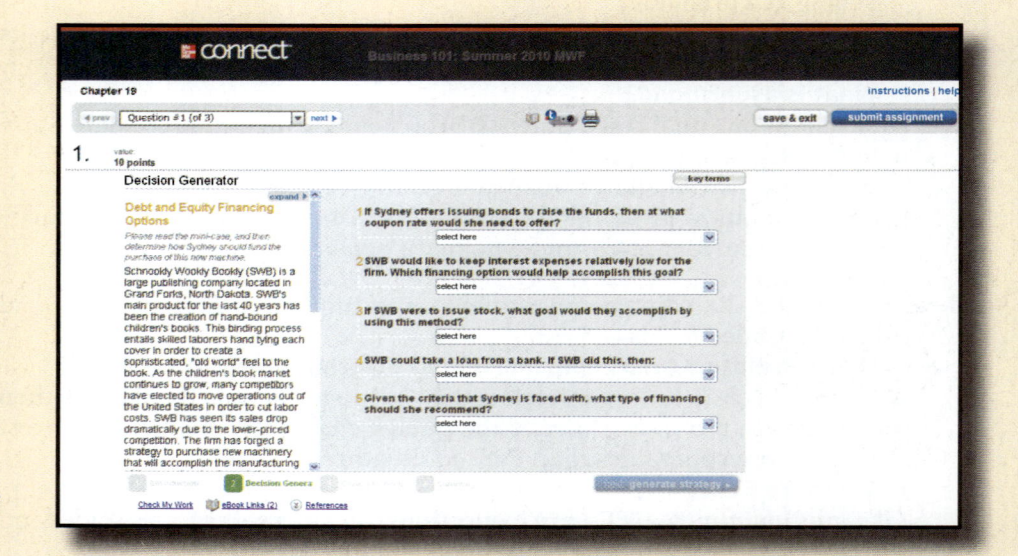

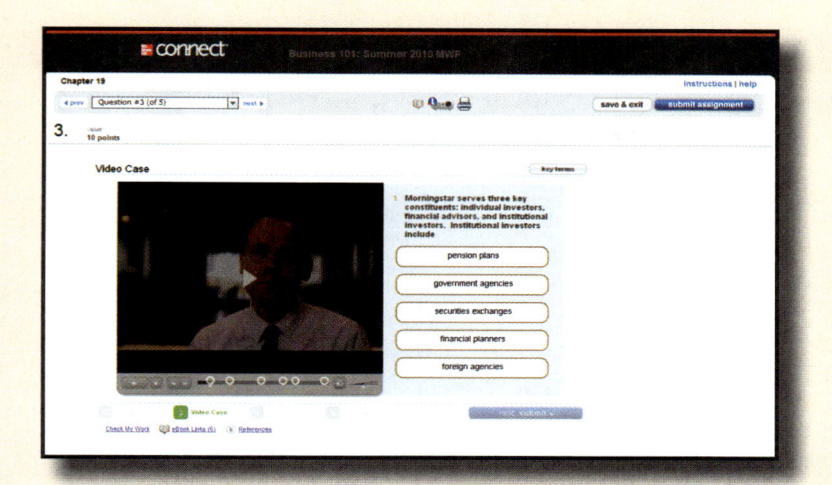

Video Case Interactive: Investors look for clear, unbiased information that can help point them in the right direction. Morningstar provides financial and investment information to investors. Watch the video case featuring Morningstar and respond to the questions when prompted.

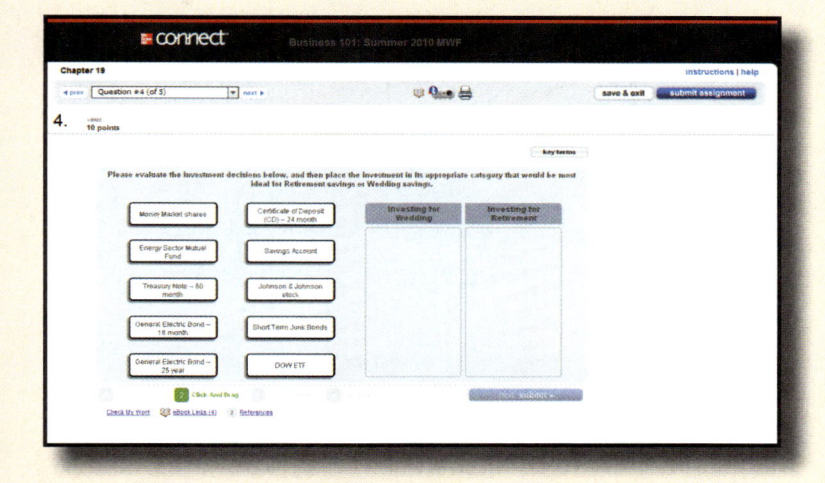

Click and Drag Interactive: There are key factors involved in evaluating investment decisions, including the length of time of the investment, the amount of risk involved, and the potential tax implications. Evaluate the investment opportunity and determine whether it constitutes a long-term or a short-term investment.

Click and Drag Interactive: Stocks are shares of ownership in a company. A stock offers a way of getting large amounts of money into a company relatively easily and this can be very appealing to most companies. However, there are drawbacks. Analyze the statements provided and evaluate the advantages and disadvantages of issuing stock.

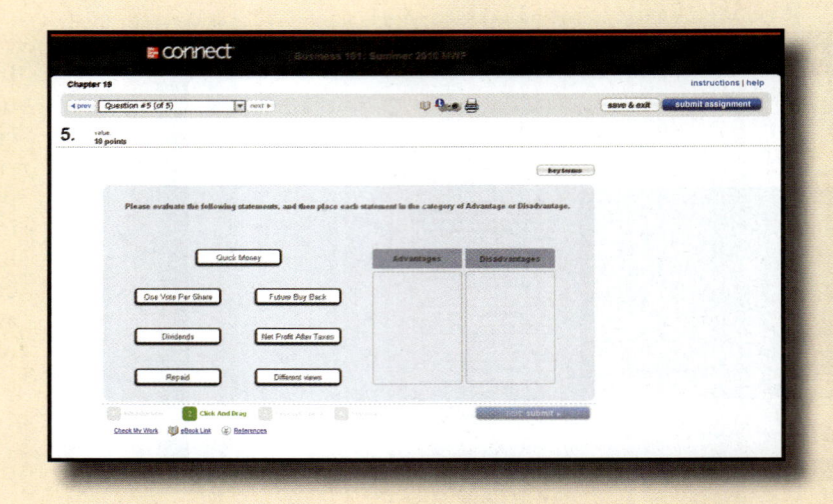

20

Money, Financial INSTITUTIONS, AND the Federal Reserve

profile

Ben Bernanke (pronounced ber-*nan*-kee) was born in Augusta, Georgia. He taught himself calculus in high school, scored 1590 of a possible 1600 on his college entrance exams, and graduated from Harvard summa cum laude with a bachelor's degree in economics. After earning a PhD from MIT, he was an economics professor and department chair at Princeton. He then served as chair of the President's Council of Economic Advisors in 2005 and was a member of the Board of Governors at the Federal Reserve from 2002 to 2005, alongside Alan Greenspan, who was the head of the U.S. Federal Reserve from 1987 to 2006.

Former president George W. Bush appointed Bernanke to succeed Greenspan at the Fed, making him one of the most powerful people in the United States. It was Bernanke, along with former Treasury secretary Henry Paulson, who talked Congress into committing about $700 billion to try to end the banking collapse in 2008. It was Bernanke who mediated between Citicorp and Wells Fargo when both wanted to buy Wachovia bank (Wells Fargo made the purchase). Bernanke lowered interest rates for banks to near zero and was among the group of advisers who made billions available to banks to try to ease the credit crisis.

Bernanke's challenges include keeping inflation in check, increasing the value of the dollar, and getting the economy moving upward again. Part of that plan includes credit easing and buying more than a trillion dollars in debt and mortgage-backed securities. As you can see, almost everything about the economy is affected by the choices Bernanke makes.

> **Getting to Know**
> **x** Ben S. Bernanke
> **Chairman of the Federal Reserve**

LEARNING goals

After you have read and studied this chapter, you should be able to

1. Explain what money is and what makes money useful.
2. Describe how the Federal Reserve controls the money supply.
3. Trace the history of banking and the Federal Reserve System.
4. Classify the various institutions in the U.S. banking system.
5. Briefly trace the causes of the banking crisis of 2008–2010 and explain how the government protects your funds during such crises.
6. Describe how technology helps make banking more efficient.
7. Evaluate the role and importance of international banking, the World Bank, and the International Monetary Fund.

connect

Your *Connect*ion to Better Learning. 1. View the interactive presentation. 2. Practice through LearnSmart. 3. Apply your knowledge by using the interactive applications for each chapter of this text.

1 Prep >>>>>> **2 Study** 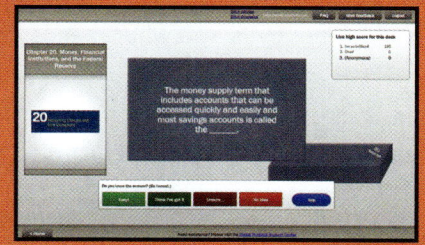 >>>>>> **3 Apply**

You will learn more about the Federal Reserve and the banking system in general in this chapter. Using that information, you can better understand Bernanke's decisions. Keep up with what he is doing by reading the business press and listening to business reports. His successes and failures will be making headlines for a long time.

Sources: Peter Coy, "Quietly, the Fed Seeks More Power," *BusinessWeek,* June 2, 2008; "Bernanke's Busy-Ness," *Washington Times,* March 22, 2008; Allan Sloan, "On the Brink of Disaster," *Fortune,* April 14, 2008; Michael Hirsh, "The Money Man," *Newsweek,* October 27, 2008; Harry Maurer and Cristina Lindblad, "The Whole World Is Watching Washington," *BusinessWeek,* October 6, 2008; James C. Cooper, "Waiting for 'Credit Easing' to Kick In," *BusinessWeek,* February 9, 2009; and Patrick Hill, "Senate OKs 2nd Term for Bernanke as Fed Chief," *The Washington Times*, Janurary 29, 2010, pp. Al and All.

www.federalreserve.gov

NAME THAT company

These are nonprofit, member-owned financial cooperatives that offer the full variety of banking services to their members. Typically they provide interest-bearing checking accounts at relatively high rates, short-term loans at relatively low rates, financial counseling, life insurance policies, and a limited number of home mortgage loans. What are these organizations called? (Find the answer in the chapter.)

> PPT 20-1:
> Money, Financial Institutions, and the Federal Reserve
>
> PPT 20-2:
> Ben Bernanke
>
> LECTURE LINK 20-1:
> Fixed Assets, or Why a Loan in Yap is Hard to Roll Over

LEARNING goal 1 *

Explain what money is and what makes money useful.

WHY MONEY IS IMPORTANT

The Federal Reserve, or the Fed, is the organization in charge of money in the United States. You will be hearing a lot about it and its head, Ben Bernanke, in the coming years. The banking crisis and the moves being made globally by the Fed and other banks to halt a global financial crisis are too complex to discuss in detail here.[1] Our goal in this chapter is simply to introduce you to the world of banking and the role of the Federal Reserve.

Economic growth and the creation of jobs depend on the ready availability of money. Money is so important to the economy that many institutions have evolved to manage it and make it available when you need it. Today you can get cash from an automated teller machine (ATM) almost anywhere in the world, and most organizations will also accept a check, credit card, debit card, or smart card for purchases.[2] Behind the scenes is a complex system of banking that makes the free flow of money possible. Each day, more than $1.9 *trillion* is exchanged in the world's currency markets.[3] Therefore, what happens to any major country's economy has an effect on the U.S. economy and vice versa.[4]

Newly engraved bills make counterfeiting much harder than in the past. The bills look a little different from older ones and are different colors. If you owned a store, would you teach your employees how to recognize a counterfeit bill?

That's why the financial crisis in the United States affected economies throughout the world, including China and the United Kingdom.[5]

There's no way to understand the U.S. economy without understanding global money exchanges and the institutions involved in the creation and management of money. Let's start at the beginning by discussing exactly what the word *money* means and how the supply of money affects the prices you pay for goods and services.

What Is Money?

Money is anything people generally accept as payment for goods and services. In the past, objects as diverse as salt, feathers, fur pelts, stones, rare shells, tea, and horses have served as money.[6] In fact, until the 1880s, cowrie shells were one of the world's most popular currencies.

Barter is the direct trading of goods or services for other goods or services.[7] Though barter may sound like something from the past, many people have discovered the benefits of bartering online.[8] Others barter goods and services the old-fashioned way—face-to-face. In Siberia people have bought movie tickets with two eggs, and in Ukraine people have paid their energy bills with sausages and milk. Today you can go to a *barter exchange* where you can put goods or services into the system and get trade credits for other goods and services that you need. The barter exchange makes it easier to barter because you don't have to find people with whom to barter. The exchange does that for you.

The problem with traditional barter is that eggs and milk are difficult to carry around. Most people need some object that's portable, divisible, durable, and stable so that they can trade goods and services without carrying the actual goods around with them. One solution is coins and paper bills. The five standards for a useful form of money are:

- *Portability*. Coins and paper money are a lot easier to take to market than pigs or other heavy products.
- *Divisibility*. Different-sized coins and bills can represent different values. Prior to 1963, a U.S. quarter had half as much silver content as a half-dollar coin, and a dollar had four times the silver of a quarter. Because silver is now too expensive, today's coins are made of other metals, but the accepted values remain.
- *Stability*. When everybody agrees on the value of coins, the value of money is relatively stable. In fact, U.S. money has become so stable that much of the world has used the U.S. dollar as the measure of value. If the value of the dollar fluctuates too rapidly, the world may turn to some other form of money, such as the euro, for the measure of value.
- *Durability*. Coins last for thousands of years, even when they've sunk to the bottom of the ocean, as you've seen when divers find old coins in sunken ships.
- *Uniqueness*. It's hard to counterfeit, or copy, elaborately designed and minted coins. With the latest color copiers, people are able to duplicate the look of paper money relatively easily. Thus, the government has had to go to extra lengths to make sure *real* dollars are readily identifiable. That's why you have newer paper money with the picture slightly off center and with invisible lines that quickly show up when reviewed by banks and stores. Note the color-changing bell on the new $100 bill.

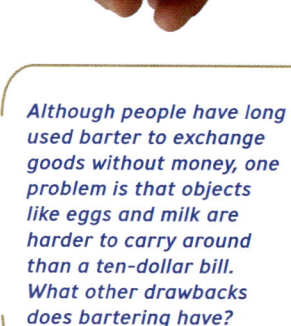

Although people have long used barter to exchange goods without money, one problem is that objects like eggs and milk are harder to carry around than a ten-dollar bill. What other drawbacks does bartering have?

money
Anything that people generally accept as payment for goods and services.

barter
The direct trading of goods or services for other goods or services.

◀ PPT 20-3:
What's Money?

◀ CRITICAL THINKING EXERCISE 20-1:
Bartering: Buying a Pair of Jeans

◀ LECTURE LINK 20-2:
The Fate of the Penny

◀ PPT 20-4:
Standards for a Useful Form of Money

◀ LECTURE LINK 20-3:
Euro Portraits

◀ LECTURE LINK 20-4:
Dirty Money

◀ LECTURE LINK 20-5:
Currency for Visually-Impaired Consumers?

◀ LECTURE LINK 20-6:
Money Facts

◀ CRITICAL THINKING EXERCISE 20-2:
Test Your Knowledge of Money

Coins and paper money simplified exchanges. Most countries have their own currencies, and they're all about equally portable, divisible, and durable. However, they're not always equally stable.

Electronic cash (e-cash) is one of the newest forms of money. You can make online payments using Quicken or Microsoft Money or e-mail e-cash using PayPal. Recipients can choose automatic deposit to their bank, e-dollars for spending online, or a traditional check in the mail.

LEARNING goal 2 *

Describe how the Federal Reserve controls the money supply.

> PPT 20-5:
> The Money Supply

> PPT 20-6:
> How Long Does Paper Money Last?

> PPT 20-7:
> Money Milestones

money supply
The amount of money the Federal Reserve Bank makes available for people to buy goods and services.

M-1
Money that can be accessed quickly and easily (coins and paper money, checks, traveler's checks, etc.).

M-2
Money included in M-1 plus money that may take a little more time to obtain (savings accounts, money market accounts, mutual funds, certificates of deposit, etc.).

M-3
M-2 plus big deposits like institutional money market funds.

What Is the Money Supply?

As Fed chairman, Ben Bernanke is in control of the U.S. money supply. Two questions emerge from that sentence. What is the money supply? Why does it need to be controlled?

The **money supply** is the amount of money the Federal Reserve makes available for people to buy goods and services.[9] And, yes, the Federal Reserve, in tandem with the U.S. Treasury, can print more money if it is needed. For example, some of the trillions of dollars that are being spent over the next few years to get the economy moving again were printed with authorization from the Federal Reserve.[10]

There are several ways of referring to the U.S. money supply. They're called M-1, M-2, and M-3. The *M* stands for money, and the 1, 2, and 3 stand for different definitions of the money supply.

M-1 includes coins and paper bills, money that's available by writing checks (demand deposits and share drafts), and money held in traveler's checks—that is, money that can be accessed quickly and easily. **M-2** includes everything in M-1 plus money in savings accounts, and money in money market accounts, mutual funds, certificates of deposit, and the like—that is, money that may take a little more time to obtain than coins and paper bills. M-2 is the most commonly used definition of money. **M-3** is M-2 plus big deposits like institutional money market funds.

Managing Inflation and the Money Supply

Imagine what would happen if governments (or in the case of the United States, the Federal Reserve, a nongovernmental organization) were to generate twice as much money as exists now. There would be twice as much money available, but still the same amount of goods and services. What would happen to prices? (Hint: Remember the laws of supply and demand from Chapter 2.) Prices would go up, because more people would try to buy goods and services with their money and bid up the price to get what they wanted. This rise in price is called inflation, which some people call "too much money chasing too few goods."[11]

Now think about the opposite: What would happen if the Fed took money out of the economy? Prices would go down because there would be an oversupply of goods and services compared to the money available to buy them; this decrease in prices is called deflation.[12]

Now we come to our second question about the money supply: Why does it need to be controlled? The reason is that doing so allows us to manage, somewhat, the prices of goods and services. The size of the money supply also affects employment and economic growth or decline.[13] That's why the Fed and Ben Bernanke are so important.

The Global Exchange of Money

A *falling dollar value* means that the amount of goods and services you can buy with a dollar decreases. A *rising dollar value* means that the amount of goods and services you can buy with a dollar goes up. Thus, the price in euros you pay for a German car will be lower if the U.S. dollar rises relative to the euro. However, if the euro rises relative to the dollar, the cost of cars from Germany will go up and U.S. consumers may buy fewer German cars.

What makes the dollar weak (falling value) or strong (rising value) is the position of the U.S. economy relative to other economies. When the economy is strong, the demand for dollars is high and the value of the dollar rises. When the economy is perceived as weakening, however, the demand for dollars declines and the value of the dollar falls. The value of the dollar thus depends on a relatively strong economy. (See Chapter 3 for further discussion of effects of changes in currency values or exchange rates.) In the following section, we'll discuss in more detail the money supply and how it's managed. Then we'll explore the U.S. banking system and how it lends money to businesses and individuals, like you and me.

◀ PPT 20-8:
Exchanging Money Globally

◀ CRITICAL THINKING EXERCISE 20-3:
Currency Trading

◀ PPT 20-9:
The Impact of a Falling Dollar

◀ BONUS CASE 20-1:
Keeping Ahead of Counterfeiters

CONTROL OF THE MONEY SUPPLY

Theoretically, with the proper monetary policy in place to control the money supply, one can keep the economy growing without causing inflation. (See Chapter 2 to review monetary policy.) Again, the organization in charge of monetary policy is the Federal Reserve.

Basics about the Federal Reserve

The Federal Reserve System consists of five major parts: (1) the board of governors; (2) the Federal Open Market Committee (FOMC); (3) 12 Federal Reserve banks; (4) three advisory councils; and (5) the member banks of the system. Figure 20.1 shows where the 12 Federal Reserve banks are located.

◀ PPT 20-11:
The 12 Federal Reserve District Banks

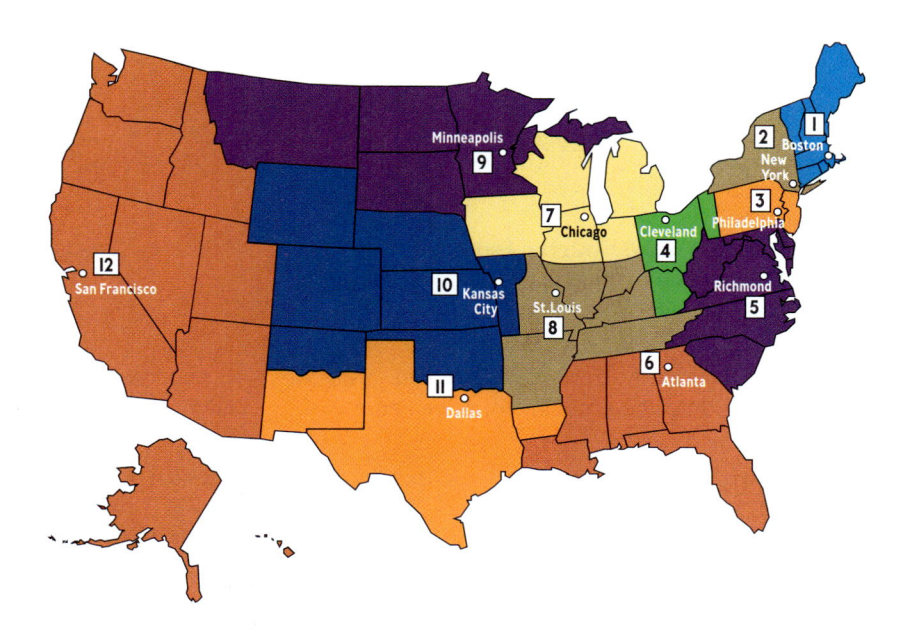

figure 20.1

THE 12 FEDERAL RESERVE DISTRICT BANKS

> **PPT 20-10:**
> Five Major Parts of the Federal Reserve System

The board of governors administers and supervises the 12 Federal Reserve banks. The seven members of the board are appointed by the president and confirmed by the senate. The board's primary function is to set monetary policy. The Federal Open Market Committee (FOMC) has 12 voting members and is the policymaking body. The committee is made up of the seven-member board of governors plus the president of the New York reserve bank and four members who rotate in from the other reserve banks. The advisory councils represent the various banking districts, consumers, and member institutions, including banks, savings and loan institutions, and credit unions. They offer suggestions to the board and to the FOMC.

The Fed buys and sells foreign currencies, regulates various types of credit, supervises banks, and collects data on the money supply and other economic activity. As part of monetary policy, the Fed determines the reserve requirement, that is, the level of reserve funds all financial institutions must keep at one of the 12 Federal Reserve banks. It buys and sells government securities in *open-market operations*. Finally, it lends money to member banks at an interest rate called the *discount rate*.

> **CRITICAL THINKING EXERCISE 20-4:**
> Researching the Federal Reserve's Tools

As noted, the three basic tools the Fed uses to manage the money supply are reserve requirements, open-market operations, and the discount rate (see Figure 20.2). Let's explore how it administers each.

The Reserve Requirement

> **reserve requirement**
> A percentage of commercial banks' checking and savings accounts that must be physically kept in the bank.

The **reserve requirement** is a percentage of commercial banks' checking and savings accounts they must keep in the bank (as cash in the vault) or in a non-interest-bearing deposit at the local Federal Reserve district bank. The reserve requirement is one of the Fed's most powerful tools. When it increases the reserve requirement, money becomes scarcer, which in the long run tends to reduce inflation. For instance, if Omaha Security Bank holds deposits of $100 million and the reserve requirement is, say, 10 percent, then the bank must keep $10 million on reserve. If the Fed were to increase the reserve requirement to 11 percent, then the bank would have to put an additional $1 million on reserve, reducing the amount it could lend out. Since this

figure 20.2
HOW THE FEDERAL RESERVE CONTROLS THE MONEY SUPPLY

CONTROL METHOD	IMMEDIATE RESULT	LONG-TERM EFFECT
Reserve Requirements		
A. Increase.	Banks put more money into the Fed, *reducing* money supply; thus, there is less money available to lend to customers.	Economy slows.
B. Decrease.	Banks put less money into the Fed, *increasing* the money supply; thus, there is more money available to lend to customers.	Economy speeds up.
Open-Market Operations		
A. Fed sells bonds.	Money flows from the economy to the Fed.	Economy slows.
B. Fed buys bonds.	Money flows into the economy from the Fed.	Economy speeds up.
Managing the Discount Rate		
A. Rate increases.	Banks borrow less from the Fed; thus, there is less money to lend.	Economy slows.
B. Rate decreases.	Banks borrow more from the Fed; thus, there is more money to lend.	Economy speeds up.

increase in the reserve requirement would affect all banks, the money supply would be reduced and prices would likely fall.

A decrease of the reserve requirement, in contrast, *increases* the funds available to banks for loans, so they make more loans and money becomes more readily available. An increase in the money supply can *stimulate the economy* to achieve higher growth rates, but it can also create inflationary pressures. That is, the prices of goods and services may go up. Can you see why the Fed may want to decrease the reserve requirement when the economy is in a recession?

Open-Market Operations

Open-market operations consist of the buying and selling of government bonds. To decrease the money supply, the federal government sells U.S. government bonds to the public. The money it gets as payment is no longer in circulation, decreasing the money supply. If the Fed wants to increase the money supply, it buys government bonds back from individuals, corporations, or organizations that are willing to sell. The money the Fed pays for these securities enters circulation, increasing the money supply. That's why the Fed's Bernanke bought bonds during the recent recession. The idea was to get the economy growing again.

The Discount Rate

The Fed has often been called the bankers' bank, because member banks can borrow money from the Fed and pass it on to their customers in the form of loans. The **discount rate** is the interest rate the Fed charges for loans to member banks. An increase in the discount rate discourages banks from borrowing and reduces the number of available loans, decreasing the money supply. In contrast, lowering the discount rate encourages member banks to borrow money and increases the funds they have available for loans, which increases the money supply.[14] Late in 2008, the Fed lowered the discount rate to almost zero, hoping to increase bank lending. Nonetheless, many banks still seemed reluctant to make loans.

The discount rate is one of two interest rates the Fed controls.[15] The other is the rate banks charge each other, called the *federal funds rate*.

The Federal Reserve's Check-Clearing Role

If you write a check to a local retailer that uses the same bank you do, it is a simple matter to reduce your account by the amount of the check and increase the amount in the retailer's account. But what happens if you write a check to a retailer in another state? That's where the Fed's check-clearing function comes into play.

That retailer will take the check to its bank. That bank will deposit the check for credit in the closest Federal Reserve bank. That bank will send the check to your local Federal Reserve bank for collection. The check will then be sent to your bank and the amount of the check will be withdrawn. Your bank will authorize the Federal Reserve bank in your area to deduct the amount of the check. That bank will pay the Federal Reserve bank that began the process in the first place. It will then credit the deposit account in the bank where the retailer has its account. That bank will then credit the account of the retailer. (See Figure 20.3 on p. 552 for a diagram of such an interstate transaction.) This long and involved process is a costly one;

◀ **LECTURE LINK 20-7:**
Wrenching Inflation Out of the Economy

◀ **PPT 20-12:**
Managing the Money Supply

open-market operations
The buying and selling of U.S. government bonds by the Fed with the goal of regulating the money supply.

discount rate
The interest rate that the Fed charges for loans to member banks.

The Federal Reserve system includes 12 member banks (see Figure 20.1). This is the Federal Reserve bank in New York City. What special role in the Fed does the president of this particular bank play?

therefore, banks take many measures to lessen the use of checks. Such efforts include the use of credit cards, debit cards, and other electronic transfers of money.

As you can see, the whole economy is affected by the Federal Reserve System's actions. Next we'll briefly discuss the history of banking to give you some background about why the Fed came into existence. Then we'll explore what's happening in banking today.

> **PPT 20-13:**
> Progress Assessment

> **PPT 20-14:**
> Check-Clearing Process Through the Federal Reserve

progress assessment

- What is money?
- What are the five characteristics of useful money?
- What is the money supply, and why is it important?
- How does the Federal Reserve control the money supply?
- What are the major functions of the Federal Reserve? What other functions does it perform?

figure 20.3
CHECK-CLEARING PROCESS THROUGH THE FEDERAL RESERVE BANK SYSTEM

Suppose Mr. Brown, a farmer from Quince Orchard, Maryland, purchases a tractor from a dealer in Austin, Texas.

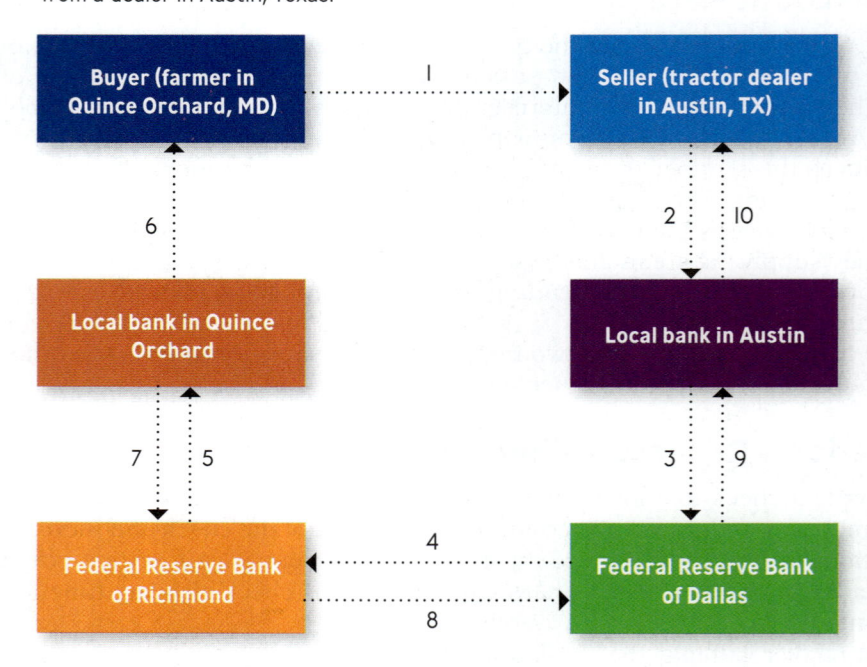

1. Mr. Brown sends his check to the tractor dealer.
2. The dealer deposits the check in his account at a local bank in Austin.
3. The Austin bank deposits the check for credit in its account at the Federal Reserve Bank of Dallas.
4. The Federal Reserve Bank of Dallas sends the check to the Federal Reserve Bank of Richmond for collection.
5. The Federal Reserve Bank of Richmond forwards the check to the local bank in Quince Orchard, where Mr. Brown opens his account.
6. The local bank in Quince Orchard deducts the check amount from Mr. Brown's account.
7. The Quince Orchard bank authorizes the Federal Reserve Bank of Richmond to deduct the check amount from its deposit account with the Federal Reserve Bank.
8. The Federal Reserve Bank of Richmond pays the Federal Reserve Bank of Dallas.
9. The Federal Reserve Bank of Dallas credits the Austin bank's deposit account.
10. The Austin bank credits the tractor dealer's account.

LEARNING goal 3 *

Trace the history of banking and the Federal Reserve System.

THE HISTORY OF BANKING AND THE NEED FOR THE FED

At first, there were no banks in the United States. Strict laws in Europe limited the number of coins people could bring to the colonies in the New World. Thus, colonists were forced to barter for goods; for example, they might trade cotton and tobacco for shoes and lumber.

The demand for money was so great that Massachusetts issued its own paper money in 1690, and other colonies soon followed suit. But continental money, the first paper money printed in the United States, became worthless after a few years because people didn't trust its value.

Land banks were established to lend money to farmers. But Great Britain, still in charge of the colonies at that point, ended land banks by 1741. The colonies rebelled against these and other restrictions on their freedom, and a new bank was formed in Pennsylvania during the American Revolution to finance the war against England.

In 1791, after the United States gained independence, Alexander Hamilton persuaded Congress to form a *central bank* (a bank at which other banks could keep their funds and borrow funds if needed). This first version of a federal bank closed in 1811, only to be replaced in 1816 because state-chartered banks couldn't support the War of 1812. The battle between the Second (Central) Bank of the United States and state banks got hot in the 1830s. Several banks in Tennessee were hurt by pressure from the Central Bank. The fight ended when the Central Bank was closed in 1836. You can see that there was great resistance to a central bank, like the Federal Reserve, through much of U.S. history.

By the time of the Civil War, the U.S. banking system was a mess. Different banks issued different kinds of currencies. People hoarded gold and silver coins because they were worth more as precious metal than as money. The chaos continued long after the war ended, reaching something of a climax in 1907, when many banks failed. People got nervous about the safety of banks and in a run on the banks attempted to withdraw their funds. Soon the cash was depleted and some banks had to refuse money to depositors. This caused people to distrust the banking system in general.

Despite the long history of opposition to a central bank, the cash shortage problems of 1907 led to the formation of an organization that could lend money to banks—the Federal Reserve System. It was to be a "lender of last resort" in such emergencies. Under the Federal Reserve Act of 1913, all federally chartered banks had to join the Federal Reserve. State banks could also join. The Federal Reserve became the bankers' bank.[16] If banks had excess funds, they could deposit them in the Fed; if they needed extra money, they could borrow from the Fed. The Federal Reserve System has been intimately related to banking ever since, but never more than now.

Banking and the Great Depression

The Federal Reserve System was designed to prevent a repeat of the 1907 panic. Nevertheless, the stock market crash of 1929 led to bank failures in the early 1930s.[17] When the stock market began tumbling, people hurried to banks to withdraw cash. In spite of the Federal Reserve System, the banks ran out of

The Federal Reserve System was designed in 1913 to prevent the kind of run on banks that had occurred in 1907. Yet the stock market crash of 1929 caused depositors to make another run on their banks and take big withdrawals. Federal deposit insurance was established in 1933 to protect depositors' money. Do you think these protections are enough?

▶ **BONUS CASE 20-2:**
When Money Loses Its Meaning

▶ **PPT 20-16:**
Largest Bank Failures

money and states were forced to close them. President Franklin D. Roosevelt extended the period of bank closings in 1933, to gain time to come up with a solution to the problem. In 1933 and 1935, Congress passed legislation to strengthen the banking system. The most important move was to establish federal deposit insurance to further protect the public from bank failures. As you can see, bank crises are nothing new; they often occur during a recession. From 1945 to 2007, the United States experienced 10 recessions. The average duration was 10 months.[18]

LEARNING goal 4 *

Classify the various institutions in the U.S. banking system.

▶ **CRITICAL THINKING EXERCISE 20-5:**
Banking as a Business

▶ **PPT 20-17:**
The U.S. Banking System

▶ **PPT 20-18:**
Commercial Banks

THE U.S. BANKING SYSTEM

The U.S. banking system consists of commercial banks, savings and loan associations, and credit unions. In addition, there are various financial organizations, or nonbanks, that accept no deposits but offer many of the services of regular banks. Let's discuss the activities and services of each, starting with commercial banks.

Commercial Banks

commercial bank
A profit-seeking organization that receives deposits from individuals and corporations in the form of checking and savings accounts and then uses some of these funds to make loans.

A **commercial bank** is a profit-seeking organization that receives deposits from individuals and corporations in the form of checking and savings accounts and uses these funds to make loans.[19] It has two types of customers—depositors and borrowers—and is equally responsible to both. A commercial bank makes a profit by efficiently using depositors' funds as inputs (on which

MAKING ethical decisions

What to Tell the Teller

You are at the teller window of your bank making a withdrawal. The teller counts out your money and says: "OK, here's your $300." You count the money and see the teller has given you $320 by mistake. When you point this out, the teller replies indignantly, "I don't think so. I counted the money in front of you."

You are upset by her quick denial of a mistake and her attitude. You have to decide whether or not to give her back the overpayment of $20. What are your alternatives? What would you do? Is that the ethical thing to do?

---

it pays interest) to invest in interest-bearing loans to other customers. If the revenue generated by loans exceeds the interest paid to depositors plus operating expenses, the bank makes a profit. The Making Ethical Decisions box discusses a specific transaction in a commercial bank.

Services Provided by Commercial Banks

Individuals and corporations that deposit money in a checking account can write personal checks to pay for almost any purchase or transaction. The technical name for a checking account is a **demand deposit** because the money is available on demand from the depositor. Typically, banks impose a service charge for check-writing privileges or demand a minimum deposit. They might also charge a small handling fee for each check written. For corporate depositors, the amount of the service charge depends on the average daily balance in the checking account, the number of checks written, and the firm's credit rating and credit history.

In the past, checking accounts paid no interest to depositors, but interest-bearing checking accounts have experienced phenomenal growth in recent years. Commercial banks also offer a variety of savings account options. A savings account is technically a **time deposit** because the bank can require a prior notice before you make a withdrawal. Compare online and neighborhood banks to find where your money can earn the most interest.

A **certificate of deposit (CD)** is a time-deposit (savings) account that earns interest, to be delivered on the certificate's maturity date. The depositor agrees not to withdraw any of the funds until then. CDs are now available for periods of months to years; usually the longer the period, the higher the interest rate. The interest rates also depend on economic conditions.

Commercial banks also offer credit cards to creditworthy customers, life insurance, inexpensive brokerage services, financial counseling, automatic payment of bills, safe-deposit boxes, individual retirement accounts (IRAs), traveler's checks, trust departments, automated teller machines, and overdraft checking account privileges. The latter means preferred customers can automatically get loans when they've written checks exceeding their account balance.

ATMs can dispense maps and directions, phone cards, and postage stamps. They can sell tickets to movies, concerts, and sporting events and show movie trailers, news tickers, and video ads. Some can take orders for flowers and DVDs and download music and games.

◄ PPT 20-19:
Commercial Banks' Services

◄ PPT 20-20:
What to Tell the Teller

◄ LECTURE LINK 20-9:
Toward a Cashless Society

demand deposit
The technical name for a checking account; the money in a demand deposit can be withdrawn anytime on demand from the depositor.

time deposit
The technical name for a savings account; the bank can require prior notice before the owner withdraws money from a time deposit.

certificate of deposit (CD)
A time-deposit (savings) account that earns interest to be delivered at the end of the certificate's maturity date.

Services to Borrowers

Commercial banks offer a variety of services to individuals and corporations in need of a loan. Generally, loans are given on the basis of the recipient's creditworthiness, although the real estate collapse of 2008–2010 was largely due to banks ignoring that rule. Banks want to manage their funds effectively and are supposed to screen loan applicants carefully to ensure that the loan plus interest will be paid back on time. Clearly banks failed to do that in the period leading up to the banking crisis. We will discuss why that happened later in the chapter.

Small businesses and minority businesses often search out banks that cater to their needs. The Spotlight on Small Business box discusses the new relationship between small businesses and banks after the recent banking crisis.

Savings and Loan Associations (S&Ls)

A **savings and loan association (S&L)** is a financial institution that accepts both savings and checking deposits and provides home mortgage loans. S&Ls are often known as thrift institutions because their original purpose (starting in 1831) was to promote consumer thrift and home ownership. To help them encourage home ownership, thrifts were permitted for many years to offer slightly higher interest rates on savings deposits than banks. Those rates attracted a large pool of funds, which S&Ls used to offer long-term fixed-rate mortgages. They no longer offer better rates than banks, however.

Between 1979 and 1983, about 20 percent of the nation's S&Ls failed. Perhaps the biggest reason is that capital gains taxes were raised, making it less attractive to invest in real estate (because the added tax reduced profits). Investors therefore walked away from their real estate loans, leaving S&Ls with lots of properties worth less than the outstanding loans on them. When they sold those properties, the S&Ls lost money. The recent drop in real estate prices has caused similar problems for banks and S&Ls.

In the 1980s, the government stepped in to strengthen S&Ls, permitting them to offer higher interest rates, allocate up to 10 percent of their funds to commercial loans, and offer mortgages with adjustable interest rates based on market conditions. You can learn more about this by looking up the Glass-Steagall Act. In addition, S&Ls were permitted to offer a variety of new banking services, such as financial counseling to small businesses and credit cards. As a result, they became much more similar to commercial banks.

Credit Unions

Credit unions are nonprofit, member-owned financial cooperatives that offer the full variety of banking services to their members—interest-bearing checking accounts at relatively high rates, short-term loans at relatively low rates, financial counseling, life insurance policies, and a limited number of home mortgage loans.[20] They are organized by government agencies, corporations, unions, and professional associations.

As nonprofit institutions, credit unions enjoy an exemption from federal income taxes. You might want to visit a local credit union to see whether you are eligible to belong, and then compare the rates to those at local banks. Credit unions often have

---

PPT 20-21: Savings and Loan Associations

PPT 20-22: Credit Unions

savings and loan association (S&L)
A financial institution that accepts both savings and checking deposits and provides home mortgage loans.

credit unions
Nonprofit, member-owned financial cooperatives that offer the full variety of banking services to their members.

Credit unions are member-owned financial cooperatives that offer their members a wide range of banking services and, because they are nonprofits, are exempt from federal income tax. Do you belong to a credit union?

SPOTLIGHT ON SMALL business

How the Banking Crisis Affected Small Businesses

One of the consequences of the banking crisis of 2008–2010 was that it became more difficult to get a loan from a bank, especially if you ran a small business. It used to be that small businesses could get an "air-ball loan," that is, a loan based more on the borrower's personal relationship with the banker than on his or her assets. Today, however, banks are more reluctant to give out loans. Sometimes the bank will demand that the borrower make a "substantial" deposit—up to half the loan amount—in order to get a loan. Some banks have even cut lending to new customers to conserve available funds for existing customers. Further increasing the pressure on banks, Federal Deposit Insurance Corporation (FDIC) officials say that they may increase the insurance premium banks pay to replenish the insurance fund after the expenses of recent failures.

Because borrowing from a bank has become so difficult, you might have to look to alternative sources of funds. For example, if you are buying equipment, you might ask the vendor for financing.

Despite its name, the Small Business Administration (SBA) is not likely to give small businesses money either. In fact, the SBA has actually reduced its government-guaranteed loan program. Commercial banks' interest rates are often too high for small businesses. What about nonbanks? Small businesses are too small to borrow from pension funds, insurance companies, or brokerage firms.

Some small businesses use credit cards to get started, but the fees can be extremely high if the bills are not paid promptly. Many small businesses turn to friends and family for loans, but that too can be dicey if the business does not do well. What other sources of funds are available?

Angel investors are wealthy individuals who use their own money to fund start-up companies at the early stages of their development. They usually seek out high-growth companies in fields like technology and biotech that might issue stock or get profitably bought out in a few years. Local companies like restaurants, roofers, and deck cleaners usually cannot get a hearing, much less a loan. In short, banks and nonbanks are often reluctant to loan money to small businesses. That opens the door for alternative investors and others to fill the gaps. That includes peer-to-peer (P2P) lending. Web sites like Loanio and Prosper match borrowers with lenders so that borrowers get the money they need and lenders earn more than they can get at the bank.

Sources: Norm Brodsky, "What the Financial Crisis Means to You," *Inc.*, November 2008; Binyamin Appelbaum and David Cho, "Small Banks, Tight Credit," *The Washington Post*, August 27, 2008; C. J. Prince, "Something to Bank On," *Entrepreneur*, August 2008; and Joan Goldwasser, "Little Banks, Better Deals," *Kiplinger's Personal Finance*, May 2010.

---

fewer branches than banks and less access to ATMs. It's best to determine what services you need and then compare *those* services to the same services offered by banks.[21]

Other Financial Institutions (Nonbanks)

Nonbanks are financial organizations that accept no deposits but offer many of the services provided by regular banks. Nonbanks include life insurance companies, pension funds, brokerage firms, commercial finance companies, and corporate financial services (like GE Capital). Nonbanks cut back their lending considerably during the banking crisis of 2008–2010. Such a drop-off in lending contributed to slowing the economy greatly.[22]

As competition between banks and nonbanks has increased, the dividing line between them has become less apparent. This is equally true in Europe, where U.S. companies compete with European banks. The diversity of financial services and investment alternatives nonbanks offer has led banks to expand their own services. In fact, many banks have merged with brokerage firms to offer full-service financial assistance.

nonbanks
Financial organizations that accept no deposits but offer many of the services provided by regular banks (pension funds, insurance companies, commercial finance companies, consumer finance companies, and brokerage houses).

Life insurance companies provide financial protection for policyholders, who periodically pay premiums. In addition, insurers invest the funds they receive from policyholders in corporate and government bonds. In recent years, more insurance companies have begun to provide long-term financing for real estate development projects. Do you think that was a wise decision?

Pension funds are monies put aside by corporations, nonprofit organizations, or unions to help fund their members' financial needs when they retire. Contributions to pension funds are made by employees, employers, or both. To generate additional income, pension funds typically invest in low-return but safe corporate stocks or other conservative investments such as government securities and corporate bonds.

Many financial services organizations that provide retirement and health benefits, such as TIAA-CREF, are becoming a major force in U.S. financial markets. They also lend money directly to corporations.

Brokerage firms have traditionally offered investment services in stock exchanges in the United States and abroad. They have also made serious inroads into regular banks' domain by offering high-yield combination savings and checking accounts. In addition, they offer money market accounts with check-writing privileges and allow investors to borrow, using their securities as collateral.

Commercial and consumer finance companies offer short-term loans to those who cannot meet the credit requirements of regular banks, such as new businesses, or who have exceeded their credit limit and need more funds. College students with no credit history often turn to consumer finance companies for education loans. Be careful when borrowing from such institutions because their interest rates can be quite high.

> **pension funds**
> Amounts of money put aside by corporations, nonprofit organizations, or unions to cover part of the financial needs of members when they retire.

> **PPT 20-25:**
> Progress Assessment

progress assessment

- Why did the United States need a Federal Reserve Bank?
- What's the difference between a bank, a savings and loan association, and a credit union?
- What is a consumer finance company?

LEARNING goal 5 *

Briefly trace the causes of the banking crisis of 2008–2010 and explain how the government protects your funds during such crises.

THE CURRENT BANKING CRISIS AND HOW THE GOVERNMENT PROTECTS YOUR MONEY

What led to the recent banking crisis? There is no simple answer. Some people believe the Federal Reserve is partly responsible because it kept the cost of borrowing so low that people were tempted to borrow more than they could afford to pay back.[23] Congress, very interested in creating more "affordable housing," prodded banks to lend to people with minimal assets.[24] The Community Reinvestment Act further encouraged loans to families with questionable ability to repay.[25]

Other organizations pressured banks, normally quite risk-averse, to make risky loans. Banks learned they could avoid much of the risk by dividing their portfolios of mortgages up and selling the mortgage-backed securities (MBSs) to other banks all over the world. These securities seemed quite safe because they were backed by the homes that were mortgaged. Fannie Mae and Freddie Mac are both quasi-government agencies that seemed to guarantee the value of MBSs. Banks sold more and more of such seemingly safe securities, hoping to make lots of money. Bankers were also accused of pushing loans onto naive consumers.[26]

Meanwhile, the Federal Reserve and the Securities and Exchange Commission failed to issue sufficient warnings. That is, they failed in their regulatory duties.[27] When the value of homes began to decline, people began defaulting on their loans (not paying them) and turned the properties back over to the banks. Since the banks owned the mortgages on those homes, their profits declined dramatically, leading to the recent banking crisis—and the need for the government to help the banks out.[28] Not doing so was considered too risky because the whole economy might fail. The long-term effects of that process are not yet known.

So whom do we blame for the banking crisis? The answer is that we could blame the Fed for suppressing interest rates, the Congress for promoting questionable loans, the banks for making such loans and creating mortgage-backed securities that were not nearly as safe as promoted, government regulatory agencies for not doing their job, and people who took advantage of low interest rates to borrow money they couldn't reasonably hope to repay. No matter who was to blame, the crisis still needed to be solved.

Toward the end of George W. Bush's presidency, the Treasury Department proposed a $700 billion "bailout" package, known as the Troubled Assets Relief Program (TARP). The program was enacted in October 2008 but did not succeed as expected. President Barack Obama, who took office in January 2009, proposed over $800 billion in additional government spending plus a stimulus package. We won't see the results of those proposals for years. The Reaching Beyond Our Borders box on p. 560 discusses what happened to foreign banks, partially as a result of the crisis.

To limit economic effects of the 2009 financial crisis, the Bush administration announced a $700 billion bailout of the financial industry. The Obama administration promised fast action to implement the plan. What are the most recent developments in the bailout?

Protecting Your Funds

The recent banking crisis is nothing new. The government had seen similar problems during the Great Depression of the 1930s. To prevent investors from ever again being completely wiped out during an economic downturn, it created three major organizations to protect your money: the Federal Deposit Insurance Corporation (FDIC); the Savings Association Insurance Fund (SAIF); and the National Credit Union Administration (NCUA). All three insure deposits in individual accounts up to a certain amount. Because these organizations are so important to the safety of your money, let's explore them individually in more depth.

The Federal Deposit Insurance Corporation (FDIC)

The **Federal Deposit Insurance Corporation (FDIC)** is an independent agency of the U.S. government that insures bank deposits. If a bank were to fail, the FDIC would arrange to have that bank's accounts transferred to another

Federal Deposit Insurance Corporation (FDIC)
An independent agency of the U.S. government that insures bank deposits.

REACHING BEYOND our borders

The Banking Crisis Goes Global

The banking crisis has become a global phenomenon, even in countries that appeared to be doing well, such as China. Even though the Chinese government could force banks to make loans, it is reluctant to do so now that capitalism seems to be working. Because banks began holding on to their money, some 67,000 small businesses in China went into bankruptcy in the first half of 2008. Even some larger state-owned businesses felt the effects of the crisis.

Pakistan recently went to China to borrow funds but could not get them and turned to the International Monetary Fund (IMF) for help. Several Eastern and Central European countries and former Soviet republics are also in trouble. The IMF has agreed to lend Ukraine over $16 billion and Hungary over $15 billion. Turkey could need as much as $90 billion. Other countries such as Greece and Spain were in similar straits. Even oil-rich Bahrain suffered from the crisis.

Should the IMF and World Bank continue to give funds to countries suffering financial crises? Where do those funds come from? Should the United States continue to help provide money for such loans as it has pledged to do?

Sources: "Back in Business," *The Wall Street Journal*, October 30, 2008; David Stringer, "Struggling Nations Depleting IMF's Bailout," *Washington Times*, October 29, 2008; Ariana Eunjung Cha and Maureen Fan, "China Unveils $586 Billion Stimulus Plan," *The Washington Post*, November 10, 2008; Chip Cummins, "Bahrain Credit Outlook Is Downgraded," *The Wall Street Journal*, January 7, 2009; and Mark Scott, "The Pain in Spain Falls Mainly on the Cajas," *Bloomberg Businessweek*, March 8, 2010.

▶ **PPT 20-27:** Protecting Depositors' Money

▶ **PPT 20-28:** The Banking Crisis Goes Global

Savings Association Insurance Fund (SAIF)
The part of the FDIC that insures holders of accounts in savings and loan associations.

bank or reimburse depositors up to $100,000. (In 2008, as a result of the banking crisis, the FDIC temporarily raised the amount covered to $250,000 until December 31, 2013.) The FDIC covers about 13,000 institutions, mostly commercial banks.

The Savings Association Insurance Fund (SAIF)

The **Savings Association Insurance Fund (SAIF)** insures holders of accounts in savings and loan associations. A brief history will show why it was created. Some 1,700 bank and thrift institutions had failed during the early 1930s, and people were losing confidence in them. The FDIC and the Federal Savings and Loan Insurance Corporation (FSLIC) were designed (in 1933 and 1934, respectively) to create more confidence in banking institutions by protecting people's savings from loss. In the 1980s, to get more control over the banking system in general, the government placed the FSLIC under the FDIC and gave it a new name: the Savings Association Insurance Fund (SAIF).

The National Credit Union Administration (NCUA)

The National Credit Union Administration (NCUA) provides up to $100,000 coverage per individual depositor per institution. This coverage includes all accounts—checking accounts, savings accounts, money market accounts, and certificates of deposit. Depositors qualify for additional protection by holding accounts jointly or in trust. Individual retirement accounts (IRAs) are also separately insured up to $250,000. Credit unions, like banks, suffered from the banking crisis of 2008–2010 and got money from the federal government to make more loans.[29]

LEARNING goal 6 *

Describe how technology helps make banking more efficient.

USING TECHNOLOGY TO MAKE BANKING MORE EFFICIENT

Imagine the cost to a bank of approving a written check, physically processing it through the banking system, and mailing it back to you. It's expensive. Bankers have long looked for ways to make the system more efficient.

One solution was to issue credit cards to reduce the flow of checks, but they too have their costs: there's still paper to process. Accepting Visa and MasterCard costs retailers about $2 per $100 purchase; Amex costs them about $2.50. In the future we'll see much more electronic rather than physical exchange of money, because it is the most efficient way to transfer funds.

If you must use a credit card, be sure to search for one that offers the best deal for you. Some offer cash back, others offer free travel, and so forth. Don't just sign up for whatever card is offering free T-shirts on campus. Do your research.[30]

In an **electronic funds transfer (EFT) system**, messages about a transaction are sent from one computer to another. Thus, organizations can transfer funds more quickly and economically than with paper checks. EFT tools include electronic check conversion, debit cards, smart cards, direct deposits, and direct payments. The latest technology, developed by information commerce company First Data, is the GO-Tag, a pea-shaped chip with a radio transmitter inside that can stick to a cell phone or ID badge to make payments fast and easy. It takes only a second to complete a transaction with a GO-Tag, much faster than even a credit card.[31]

A **debit card** serves the same function as a check—it withdraws funds from a checking account. It looks like a credit card but withdraws (debits) money that is already in your account. When the sale is recorded, the debit card sends an electronic signal to the bank, automatically transferring funds from your account to the store's. A record of transactions immediately appears online. Although debit cards can work better than credit cards for those who need to control their spending, some banks are now letting customers spend more than is in their accounts and are charging them fees of up to $29 per transaction.[32]

Payroll debit cards are an efficient way for some firms to pay their workers and an alternative to cash for those who don't qualify for a credit or debit card—the so-called unbanked. Employees can access funds in their accounts immediately after they are posted, withdraw them from an ATM, pay bills online, or transfer funds to another

◀ **LECTURE LINK 20-10:**
Send Money Home—Bypass the Bank

◀ **PPT 20-29:**
Technological Advancements in Banking

electronic funds transfer (EFT) system
A computerized system that electronically performs financial transactions such as making purchases, paying bills, and receiving paychecks.

debit card
An electronic funds transfer tool that serves the same function as checks: it withdraws funds from a checking account.

> Short-range technology is already available to allow cell phones to communicate with electronic readers that register purchases. Thus, in Tokyo, you can pay for candy with your phone. One problem with embedding a credit card in a cell phone is determining how to split revenue between the phone carrier and the credit card issuer. What other problems could there be with such capabilities?

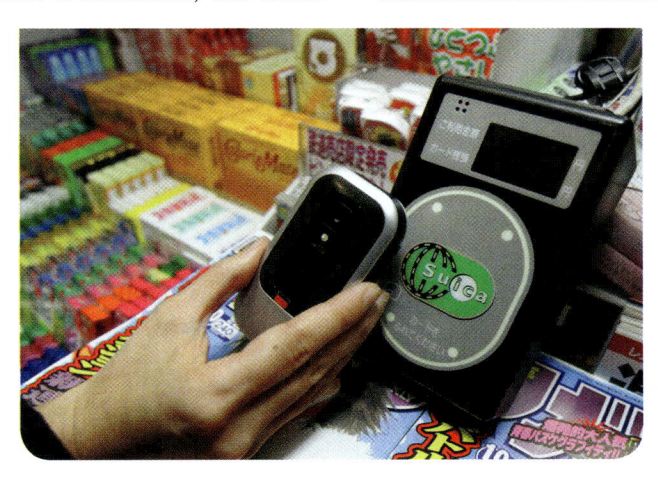

cardholder. The system is much cheaper for companies than issuing checks and more convenient for employees. On the other hand, debit cards don't offer the same protection as credit cards.[33] If someone steals your credit card, you are liable only for a certain amount. You are liable for everything when someone steals your debit card.

A **smart card** is an electronic funds transfer tool that combines a credit card, debit card, phone card, driver's license card, and more. Smart cards replace the typical magnetic strip on a credit or debit card with a microprocessor. The card can then store a variety of information, including the holder's bank balance. Merchants can use this information to check the card's validity and spending limits, and transactions can debit up to the amount on the card.

Some smart cards have embedded radio-frequency identification (RFID) chips that make it possible to enter buildings and secure areas and to buy gas and other items with a swipe of the card. A biometric function lets you use your fingerprint to boot up your computer. Students are using smart cards to open locked doors to dorms and identify themselves to retailers near campus and online. The cards also serve as ATM cards.

For many, the ultimate convenience in banking is automatic transactions such as direct deposit and direct payments. A *direct deposit* is a credit made directly to a checking or savings account in place of a paycheck. The employer contacts the bank and orders it to transfer funds from the employer's account to the worker's account. Individuals can use direct deposits to transfer funds to other accounts, such as from a checking account to a savings or retirement account.

A *direct payment* is a preauthorized electronic payment. Customers sign a separate form for each company whose bill they would like to automatically pay from their checking or savings account on a specified date. The customer's bank completes each transaction and records it on the customer's monthly statement.

Online Banking

All top U.S. retail banks now allow customers to access their accounts online, and most have bill-paying capacity. Thus, you can complete all your financial transactions from home, using your telephone or your computer to transfer funds from one account to another, pay your bills, and check the balance in each of your accounts. You can apply for a car loan or mortgage and get a response while you wait. Buying and selling stocks and bonds is equally easy.

Internet banks such as E*Trade Bank offer online banking only, not physical branches. They can offer customers higher interest rates and lower fees because they do not have the overhead costs traditional banks have. While many consumers are pleased with the savings and convenience, not all are happy with the service. Why? Some are nervous about security. People fear putting their financial information into cyberspace, where others may see it despite all the assurances of privacy. Further, some people want to be able to talk to a knowledgeable person one on one when they have banking problems.

The future thus seems to be with traditional banks that offer both online services and brick-and-mortar facilities. Even small, local banks offer online services now.

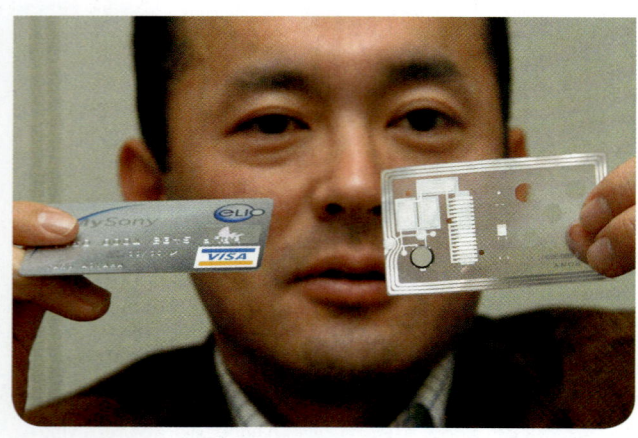

Need to pass the security check in your office building, put gas in your car, and get cash at the ATM? No problem. Smart cards with embedded RFID chips can take care of these tasks and then some. Has cash become a thing of the past?

▶ PPT 20-30:
Smart Cards

smart card
An electronic funds transfer tool that is a combination credit card, debit card, phone card, driver's license card, and more.

LEARNING goal 7 ✴

Evaluate the role and importance of international banking, the World Bank, and the International Monetary Fund.

INTERNATIONAL BANKING AND BANKING SERVICES

Banks help companies conduct business in other countries by providing three services: letters of credit, banker's acceptances, and money exchange. If a U.S. company wants to buy a product from Germany, the company could pay a bank to issue a letter of credit. A **letter of credit** is a promise by the bank to pay the seller a given amount if certain conditions are met. For example, the German company may not be paid until the goods have arrived at the U.S. company's warehouse. A **banker's acceptance** promises that the bank will pay some specified amount at a particular time. No conditions are imposed. Finally, a company can go to a bank and exchange U.S. dollars for euros to use in Germany; that's called *currency* or *money exchange*.

Banks are making it easier than ever for travelers and businesspeople to buy goods and services overseas. Automated teller machines now provide yen, euros, and other foreign currencies through your personal Visa, MasterCard, Cirrus, Plus, or American Express card.

Leaders in International Banking

It would be shortsighted to discuss the U.S. economy apart from the world economy. If the Federal Reserve decides to lower interest rates, within minutes foreign investors can withdraw their money from the United States and put it in countries with higher rates. Of course, the Fed's increasing of interest rates can draw money to the United States equally quickly.

Today's money markets thus form a global market system of which the United States is just a part. International bankers make investments in any country where they can get a maximum return for their money at a reasonable risk. That's how more than $1.9 trillion is traded daily! The net result of international banking and finance has been to link the economies of the world into one interrelated system with no regulatory control. U.S. firms must compete for funds with firms all over the world. An efficient firm in London or Tokyo is more likely to get international financing than a less efficient firm in Detroit or Chicago. Global markets mean that banks do not necessarily keep their money in their own countries. They make investments where they get the maximum return.

What this means for you is that banking is no longer a domestic issue; it's a global one. To understand the U.S. financial system, you must learn about the global financial system. To understand the state of the U.S. economy, you need to learn about the economic condition of countries throughout the world. In the new world economy financed by international banks, the United States is just one player. To be a winner, it must stay financially secure and its businesses must stay competitive in world markets. Is that happening today?

The World Bank and the International Monetary Fund (IMF)

The bank primarily responsible for financing economic development is the International Bank for Reconstruction and Development, or the **World Bank**. After

◀ PPT 20-31:
Making Transactions in Other Countries

letter of credit
A promise by the bank to pay the seller a given amount if certain conditions are met.

banker's acceptance
A promise that the bank will pay some specified amount at a particular time.

◀ PPT 20-32:
Leading Institutions in International Banking

World Bank
The bank primarily responsible for financing economic development; also known as the International Bank for Reconstruction and Development.

564 PART 6 * Managing Financial Resources

World War II, it lent money to countries in Western Europe so they could rebuild. Today, it lends most of its money to less-developed nations to improve their productivity and help raise standards of living and quality of life. That includes working to eliminate diseases that kill millions of people each year.

The World Bank has faced considerable criticism and protests around the world. Environmentalists charge that it finances projects damaging to the ecosystem. Human rights activists and unionists say the bank supports countries that restrict religious freedoms and tolerate sweatshops. AIDS activists complain that it does not do enough to get low-cost AIDS drugs to developing nations.

Despite its efforts to improve, the World Bank still has many critics. Some want it to forgive the debts of less developed countries and others want it to stop making such loans until the countries institute free markets and the right to own property. Some changes in World Bank policy may lie ahead.

In contrast to the World Bank, the **International Monetary Fund (IMF)** was established to foster cooperative monetary policies that stabilize the exchange of one national currency for another. About 185 countries are voluntary members of the IMF and allow their money to be freely exchanged for foreign money, keep the IMF informed about changes in monetary policy, and modify those policies on the advice of the IMF to accommodate the needs of the entire membership.[34]

The IMF is designed to oversee member countries' monetary and exchange rate policies. Its goal is to maintain a global monetary system that works best for all nations and enhances world trade. While it is not primarily a lending institution like the World Bank, its members do contribute funds according to their ability, and those funds are available to countries in financial difficulty. Recently, partly as a consequence of the U.S. banking crisis, Iceland, Ukraine, Hungary, and Pakistan have asked the IMF for loans. The agency was running out of funds while facing pressure to forgive the debts of countries that could not feed their people.[35] As a result, the IMF has looked to the nations of the world to increase its available funds.[36]

The World Bank and the International Monetary Fund (IMF) are intergovernmental organizations that help support the global banking community. Both draw protests from the public for their actions. Why?

International Monetary Fund (IMF)
Organization that assists the smooth flow of money among nations.

▶ PPT 20-33:
Progress Assessment

progress assessment

- What are some of the causes for the banking crisis of 2008–2010?
- What is the role of the FDIC?
- How does a debit card differ from a credit card?
- What is the World Bank and what does it do?
- What is the IMF and what does it do?

summary

Learning Goal 1. Explain what money is and what makes money useful.
- **What is money?**
Money is anything people generally accept as payment for goods and services.
- **What are the five standards for a useful form of money?**
The five standards for a useful form of money are portability, divisibility, stability, durability, and uniqueness.

Learning Goal 2. Describe how the Federal Reserve controls the money supply.
- **How does the Federal Reserve control the money supply?**

The Federal Reserve makes financial institutions keep funds in the Federal Reserve System (reserve requirement), buys and sells government securities (open-market operations), and lends money to banks (the discount rate). To increase the money supply, the Fed can cut the reserve requirement, buy government bonds, and lower the discount rate.

Learning Goal 3. Trace the history of banking and the Federal Reserve System.
- **How did banking evolve in the United States?**

Massachusetts issued its own paper money in 1690; other colonies followed suit. British land banks lent money to farmers but ended such loans by 1741. After the American Revolution, there was much debate about the role of banking, and heated battles between the Central Bank of the United States and state banks. Eventually, a federally chartered and state-chartered system was established, but chaos continued until many banks failed in 1907. The system was revived by the Federal Reserve only to fail again during the Great Depression. There have been 10 recessions since then, including the recession of 2008–2010. The Federal Reserve is doing all it can to solve the banking crisis again.

Learning Goal 4. Classify the various institutions in the U.S. banking system.
- **What institutions make up the banking system?**

Savings and loans, commercial banks, and credit unions are all part of the banking system.
- **How do they differ from one another?**

Before deregulation in 1980, commercial banks were unique in that they handled both deposits and checking accounts. At that time, savings and loans couldn't offer checking services; their main function was to encourage thrift and home ownership by offering high interest rates on savings accounts and providing home mortgages. Deregulation closed the gaps between banks and S&Ls and they now offer similar services.
- **What kinds of services do they offer?**

Banks and thrifts offer such services as savings accounts, checking accounts, certificates of deposit, loans, individual retirement accounts (IRAs), safe-deposit boxes, online banking, life insurance, brokerage services, and traveler's checks.
- **What is a credit union?**

A credit union is a member-owned cooperative that offers everything a bank does—it takes deposits, allows you to write checks, and makes loans. It also may sell life insurance and offer mortgages. Credit union interest rates are sometimes higher than those from banks, and loan rates are often lower.
- **What are some of the other financial institutions that make loans and perform bank-like operations?**

Nonbanks include life insurance companies that lend out their funds, pension funds that invest in stocks and bonds and make loans, brokerage firms that offer investment services, and commercial finance companies.

Learning Goal 5. Briefly trace the causes of the banking crisis of 2008–2010 and explain how the government protects your funds during such crises.
- **What caused the banking crisis of 2008–2010?**

The goal was to have affordable housing, so the government urged banks to make loans to some who could not afford to repay. The banks wanted to minimize the risk of such loans, so they created mortgage-backed securities and sold them to other banks and organizations throughout the world. The government did not regulate these transactions well, and many banks failed because housing values fell and people defaulted on their loans. Many have been blamed for the loss: the Fed, Congress, bank managers, Fannie Mae, and Freddie Mac among them.

- **What agencies insure the money you put into a bank, S&L, or credit union?**

Money deposited in banks is insured by the Federal Deposit Insurance Corporation (FDIC). Money in S&Ls is insured by another agency connected to the FDIC, the Savings Association Insurance Fund (SAIF). Money in credit unions is insured by the National Credit Union Administration (NCUA).

Learning Goal 6. Describe how technology helps make banking more efficient.

- **What are debit cards and smart cards?**

A debit card looks like a credit card but withdraws money that is already in your account. When the sale is recorded, the debit card sends an electronic signal to the bank, automatically transferring funds from your account to the store's. A smart card is an electronic funds transfer tool that combines a credit card, debit card, phone card, driver's license card, and more. Smart cards replace the typical magnetic strip on a credit or debit card with a microprocessor.

- **What is the benefit of automatic transactions and online banking?**

A *direct deposit* is a credit made directly to a checking or savings account in place of a paycheck. A *direct payment* is a preauthorized electronic payment. Customers sign a separate form for each company whose bill they would like to automatically pay from their checking or savings account on a specified date. The customer's bank completes each transaction and records it on the customer's monthly statement. All top U.S. retail banks now allow customers to access their accounts online, and most have bill-paying capacity.

Learning Goal 7. Evaluate the role and importance of international banking, the World Bank, and the International Monetary Fund.

- **What do we mean by global markets?**

Global markets mean that banks do not necessarily keep their money in their own countries. They make investments where they get the maximum return. What this means for you is that banking is no longer a domestic issue; it's a global one.

- **What roles do the World Bank and the IMF play?**

The World Bank (also called the International Bank for Reconstruction and Development) is primarily responsible for financing economic development. The International Monetary Fund (IMF), in contrast, was established to assist the smooth flow of money among nations. It requires members (who join voluntarily) to allow their own money to be exchanged for foreign money freely, to keep the IMF informed about changes in monetary policy, and to modify those policies on the advice of the IMF to accommodate the needs of the entire membership. Lately the IMF has been lending money to countries affected by the U.S. banking crisis, and the U.S. has promised more money to the IMF.

key terms

banker's acceptance 563
barter 547
certificate of deposit (CD) 555
commercial bank 554
credit unions 556
debit card 561
demand deposit 555
discount rate 551
electronic funds transfer (EFT) system 561
Federal Deposit Insurance Corporation (FDIC) 559
International Monetary Fund (IMF) 564
letter of credit 563

Money, Financial Institutions, and the Federal Reserve * CHAPTER 20   567

M-1 548
M-2 548
M-3 548
money 546
money supply 548
nonbanks 557

open-market operations 551
pension funds 558
reserve requirement 550
savings and loan association (S&L) 556

Savings Association Insurance Fund (SAIF) 560
smart card 562
time deposit 555
World Bank 563

connect™ interactive applications

Reinforcing Your Connection to Concepts in Business

This chapter offers 12 interactive applications designed to help you apply what you've learned (examples of these exercises appear below). Your instructor has determined which interactive applications will benefit you throughout this course. Please refer to your instructor's assignment list in *Connect* to determine which applications you should complete.

Comprehension Case Interactive: The valuation of a nation's currency is based on supply and demand. If the demand is high for a currency and there is little of it, the value of that currency becomes quite high compared to other currencies. Analyze the current market conditions and determine the advantages and disadvantages associated with a currency's valuation relative to others.

Decision Generator Interactive: The amount of money in circulation has a tremendous effect on the economy and inflation. The Federal Reserve uses monetary policy in order to try and keep the economy in check. Evaluate the economic condition of a country and make decisions that will keep the economy steady. Upon answering the questions, you will be provided with a strategy based on your responses. You will have the option to change your approach.

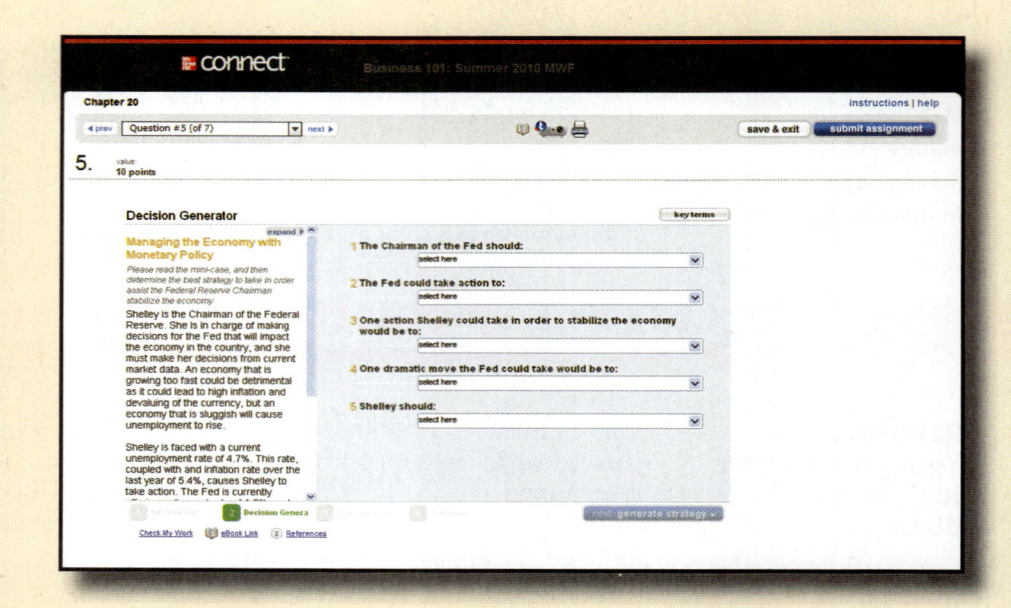

Video Case Interactive: When money is printed and put into circulation, people and government spend it. The amount of money in circulation has a tremendous effect on the economy and inflation. Watch the video case featuring the Federal Reserve. Consider the impact of money in circulation and how this can impact the value of currency, and respond to the questions.

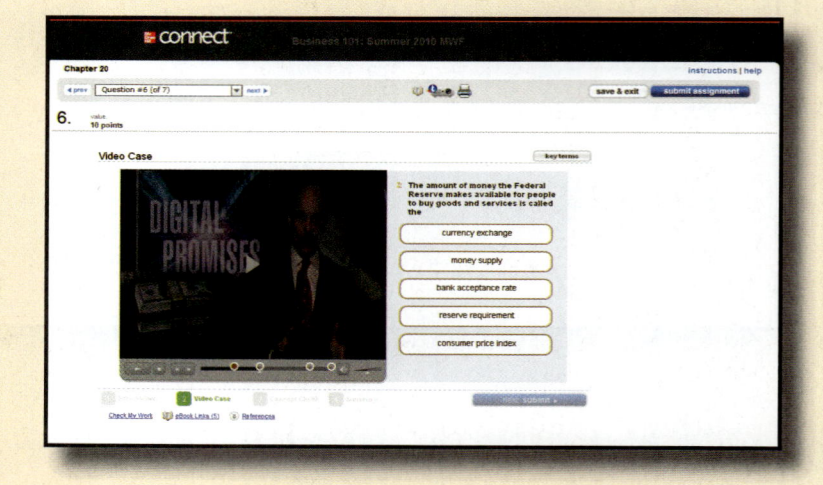

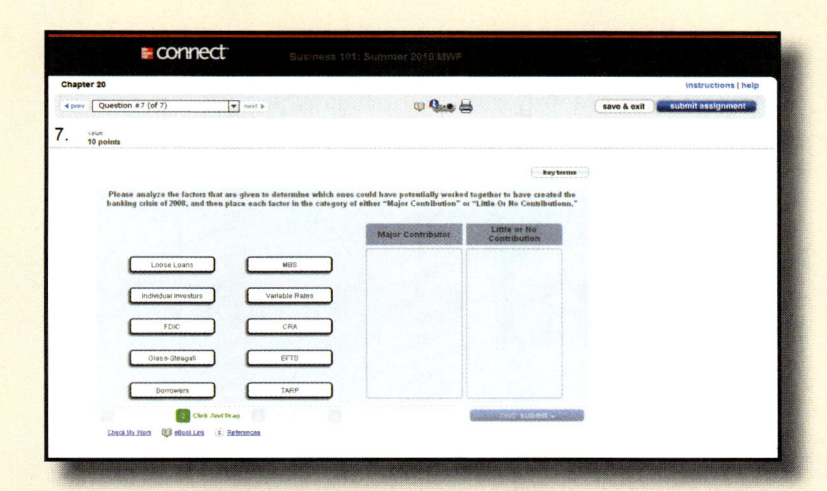

Click and Drag Interactive: There were many factors that contributed to the recent banking crisis. Analyzing and understanding these factors offers an opportunity to prevent a similar situation in the future. Evaluate the factors that led to this crisis and determine which ones could have worked together to create the crisis. Categorize each event as either a major contributor or having little or no effect in contributing to the crisis.

APPENDIX

WORKING within the Legal ENVIRONMENT

profile

Getting to Know David Boies, Corporate Attorney

For most lawyers, a normal day's work is not nearly as exciting as the legal circus acts fictional attorneys perform on television week after week. Most U.S. attorneys will never handle a spectacular case that pulls them into the media spotlight.

But for famed corporate attorney David Boies, big-name clients, major media coverage, and public praise are everyday occurrences. Often called the best trial lawyer in the United States, Boies has represented an impressive list of prominent clients such as IBM, CBS, Calvin Klein, the New York Yankees, and financial services corporation Wachovia. In addition to acquiring a long résumé of A-list clients, Boies has participated in some of the most important trials in recent history. He defended the file-sharing service Napster when it was sued by the Recording Industry Association of American (RIAA) and represented the Justice Department in the government's famous antitrust suit against Microsoft. In perhaps his most famous case, Boies served as chief legal counsel to Al Gore during the disputed presidential election in 2000.

Boies's success did not come easily. Due to a learning disability, dyslexia, Boies did not learn to read until he was in the third grade. Dyslexia slows his reading ability to this day. Still, Boies did not let this challenge overwhelm his inner drive and desire to make a difference. He studied hard and completed his undergraduate degree at Redlands University in three years. He then graduated with honors from Yale Law School. Boies credits the intense concentration his dyslexia requires as the root of his ability to recall key facts and legal citations in the course of his work. In fact, Boies prepares for cases so thoroughly that he said for the two days before the Wachovia case, "The only time I saw daylight was when I walked to court." Dyslexia has also made Boies sensitive to others with disabilities. His law firm has six employees with developmental disabilities who sort and deliver interoffice mail.

Many attribute Boies's success to his ability to take extremely complex subjects and present them simply. He uses his gift for straightforward explanation not only in court but in the classroom. He has taught courses at New York University Law School and Benjamin N. Cardoza School of Law and has also authored many publications, including *Courting Justice* (2004). In recognition of his broad range of talents, Boies has

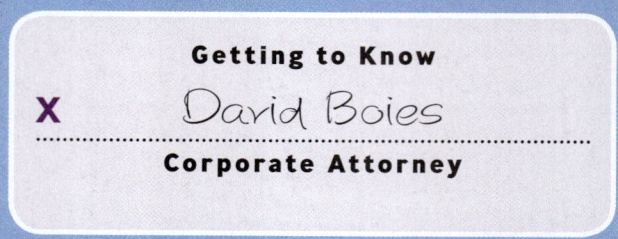

LEARNING goals

After you have read and studied this chapter, you should be able to

1. Define *business law*, distinguish between statutory and common law, and explain the role of administrative agencies.

2. Define *tort law* and explain the role of product liability in tort law.

3. Identify the purposes and conditions of patents, copyrights, and trademarks.

4. Describe warranties and negotiable instruments as covered in the Uniform Commercial Code.

5. List and describe the conditions necessary to make a legally enforceable contract, and describe the possible consequences if such a contract is violated.

6. Summarize several laws that regulate competition and protect consumers in the United States.

7. Explain the role of tax laws in generating income for the government and as a method of discouraging or encouraging certain behaviors among taxpayers.

8. Distinguish among the various types of bankruptcy as outlined by the Bankruptcy Code.

9. Explain the role of deregulation as a tool to encourage competition.

---

been named Lawyer of the Year by the *National Law Journal* and was a runner-up for *Time*'s Person of the Year Award. Today, he heads Boies, Schiller & Flexner, a New York–based law firm with a staff of over 200 lawyers that *The Wall Street Journal* describes as a "litigation powerhouse." What new cases will come across his desk in the future? It's hard to say, but according to Stephen Gillers, a law professor at New York University, "David Boies is on the cusp of becoming one of those lawyers who has achieved legendary status." There doesn't seem to be anyone objecting to that statement.

Legal issues affect almost every area of our lives and of business too. The United States has more lawyers than any other developed nation in the world and is clearly the world's most litigious society. In this chapter, we will look briefly at the history and structure of the U.S. legal system. Then we will discuss key areas of business law such as torts, patents, copyrights and trademarks, sales law, contract law, laws to protect competition and consumers, tax law, and bankruptcy law. We will also discuss the controversial topic of deregulation. You probably won't be able to go head-to-head with David Boies after reading this chapter, but if you use it as a foundation to the study of law, who knows what your future may be?

Sources: Eric Dash and Jonathan Glater, "Citigroup Says Judge Suspends Wachovia Deal," *New York Times*, October 4, 2008; Joe Phalon, "It's Good to Be David Boies," *AM Law Litigation Daily*, October 7, 2008; and Boies, Schiller & Flexner, www.bsfllp.com/index.html, accessed March 2, 2009.

www.boies-schiller.com

NAME THAT company

This fast-food chain has had its share of supersized lawsuits. While one case that blamed the company for causing obesity in its customers was dismissed, another incident with scalding hot coffee cost the restaurant years of unwanted publicity and a large financial judgment against the company. Name that company. (Find the answer in the chapter.)

LEARNING goal 1 *

Define *business law*, distinguish between statutory and common law, and explain the role of administrative agencies.

> PPT A-1: Working within the Legal Environment
>
> PPT A-2: David Boies
>
> PPT A-3: The Need for Laws
>
> PPT A-4: Types of Court

judiciary
The branch of government chosen to oversee the legal system through the court system.

> PPT A-5: Types of Law
>
> PPT A-6: Major Areas of Law

business law
The rules, statutes, codes, and regulations that provide a legal framework for the conduct of business and that are enforceable by court action.

THE CASE FOR LAWS

Imagine a society without laws. Just think: no speed limits, no age restrictions on the consumption of alcohol, no limitations on who can practice law or medicine—a society where people are free to do whatever they choose, with no interference. Obviously, the more we consider this possibility, the more unrealistic we realize it is. Laws are an essential part of a civilized nation. Over time, though, the depth and scope of the body of laws must change to continue reflecting the needs of society. The **judiciary** is the branch of government chosen to oversee the legal system through a system of courts.

The U.S. court system is organized at the federal, state, and local levels. At both the federal and state levels, trial courts hear cases of criminal and civil law. *Criminal law* defines crimes, establishes punishments, and regulates the investigation and prosecution of people accused of committing crimes. *Civil law* proceedings cover noncriminal acts—marriage, personal injury suits, and so on. Both federal and state systems have appellate courts that hear appeals from the losing party about decisions made at the trial-court level. Appellate courts can review and overturn these decisions.

The judiciary also governs the activities and operations of business, including hiring and firing practices, unpaid leave for family emergencies, environmental protection, worker safety, freedom from sexual harassment at work, and more. As you may suspect, businesspeople prefer to set their own standards of behavior and often complain that the government is overstepping its bounds in governing business. Unfortunately, as was evident in the economic crisis of 2008–2010, the U.S. business community did not implement acceptable standards—particularly in financial markets—causing government to expand its control and enforcement procedures.[1] This chapter will look at specific laws and regulations and how they affect businesses.

Business law refers to the rules, statutes, codes, and regulations that provide a legal framework for the conduct of business and that are enforceable by court action. A businessperson must be familiar with laws regarding product liability, sales, contracts, fair competition, consumer protection, taxes, and bankruptcy. Let's start by discussing the foundations of law and what the legal system is all about.

Statutory and Common Law

Two major fields of law are important to businesspeople: statutory law and common law.

Statutory law includes state and federal constitutions, legislative enactments, treaties of the federal government, and ordinances—in short, written law. You can read the statutes that make up this body of law, but they are often written in language whose meaning must be determined in court. That's one reason there are more than 1.1 million lawyers in the United States, including 150,000 in New York State alone.[2]

Common law is the body of law that comes from decisions handed down by courts. We often call it *unwritten law* because it does not appear in any legislative enactment, treaty, or other written document. Under common law principles, what judges have decided in previous cases is very important in deciding today's cases. Such decisions are called **precedent**, and they guide judges in the handling of new cases. Common law evolves through decisions made in trial courts, appellate courts, and special courts (e.g., probate courts or bankruptcy courts). Lower courts (trial courts) must abide by the precedents set by higher courts (e.g., appellate courts) such as the U.S. Supreme Court.

Administrative Agencies

Administrative agencies are federal or state institutions and other government organizations created by Congress or state legislatures with delegated power to create rules and regulations within their given area of authority.

Legislative bodies can create administrative agencies and also terminate them. Some administrative agencies hold quasi-legislative, quasi-executive, and quasi-judicial powers. This means that an agency is allowed to pass rules and regulations within its area of authority, conduct investigations in cases of suspected rules violations, and hold hearings if it feels rules and regulations have been violated.

Administrative agencies issue more rulings affecting business and settle more business disputes than courts do. Such agencies include the Securities and Exchange Commission (SEC), the Federal Reserve Board, and the Equal Employment Opportunity Commission (EEOC). Figure A.1 on p. A-4 lists and describes the powers and functions of several administrative agencies at the federal, state, and local levels of government.

In the U.S. judicial system, judges are guided in their decisions by the precepts of common law, often called unwritten law because it is based on previous decisions handed down by judges. Such decisions become precedent and assist other judges in making legal rulings. What are some practical benefits of this process?

◄ PPT A-7:
Administrative Agencies

statutory law
State and federal constitutions, legislative enactments, treaties of the federal government, and ordinances—in short, written law.

common law
The body of law that comes from decisions handed down by courts; also referred to as unwritten law.

precedent
Decisions judges have made in earlier cases that guide the handling of new cases.

administrative agencies
Federal or state institutions and other government organizations created by Congress or state legislatures with delegated power to create rules and regulations within their mandated area of authority.

progress assessment

- What is business law?
- What's the difference between statutory and common law?
- What is an administrative agency?

figure A.1
EXAMPLES OF FEDERAL, STATE, AND LOCAL ADMINISTRATIVE AGENCIES

EXAMPLES	POWERS AND FUNCTIONS
Federal Agencies	
Federal Trade Commission	Enforces laws and guidelines regarding unfair business practices and acts to stop false and deceptive advertising and labeling.
Food and Drug Administration	Enforces laws and regulations to prevent distribution of adulterated or misbranded foods, drugs, medical devices, cosmetics, and veterinary products, as well as any hazardous consumer products.
State Agencies	
Public utility commissions	Set rates that can be charged by various public utilities to prevent unfair pricing by regulated monopolies (e.g., natural gas, electric power companies).
State licensing boards	License various trades and professions within a state (e.g., state cosmetology board, state real estate commission).
Local Agencies	
Maricopa County Planning Commission	Oversees land-use proposals, long-term development objectives, and other long-range issues in Maricopa County, Arizona.
City of Chesterfield Zoning Board	Sets policy regarding zoning of commercial and residential property in the city of Chesterfield, Missouri.

> PPT A-8: Progress Assessment

LEARNING goal 2 *

Define *tort law* and explain the role of product liability in tort law.

> PPT A-9: What's Tort Law?

TORT LAW

tort
A wrongful act that causes injury to another person's body, property, or reputation.

A **tort** is a wrongful act that causes injury to another person's body, property, or reputation. Although torts often are noncriminal acts, courts can award victims compensation if the conduct that caused the harm is considered intentional. Legally, an *intentional* tort is a willful act that results in injury. The question of intent was a major factor in the lawsuits against the U.S. tobacco industry. Courts had to decide whether tobacco makers intentionally withheld information from the public about the harmful effects of their products.

negligence
In tort law, behavior that causes unintentional harm or injury.

Negligence, in tort law, describes behavior that causes *unintentional* harm or injury. A court's finding of negligence can lead to huge judgments against businesses. In a classic case in 1994, McDonald's lost a lawsuit to an elderly person severely burned by hot coffee bought at a drive-through window. The jury felt that McDonald's failed to provide an adequate warning on the cup. Product liability is a controversial area of tort law, so let's take a closer look at this issue.

product liability
Part of tort law that holds businesses liable for harm that results from the production, design, or use of products they market.

Product Liability

Few issues in business law raise as much debate as product liability.[3] Critics believe product liability laws have gone too far; others feel these laws should be expanded.[4] **Product liability** holds businesses liable for harm that results from the production, design, or inadequate warnings of products they market. The average product liability case costs businesses $5 million, including defense costs, out-of-court settlements, and jury awards.[5]

At one time the legal standard for measuring product liability was whether a producer knowingly placed a hazardous product on the market. Today, many states have extended product liability to the level of **strict product liability**—legally meaning liability without regard to fault. That is, a company that places a defective product on the market can be held liable for damages—a monetary settlement awarded to a person injured by another's actions—even if the company did not know of the defect at the time of sale.[6]

Strict liability is a major concern for businesses. More than 70 companies have been forced into bankruptcy due to asbestos litigation, and a new wave of asbestos lawsuits may be coming related to secondhand asbestos exposure.[7] Lead-based paint producers have faced expensive lawsuits even though lead paint has been banned in the United States for nearly three decades.[8] Mattel was forced to recall 500,000 toy cars produced in China due to lead paint concerns.[9]

Manufacturers of chemicals and drugs are vulnerable to lawsuits under strict product liability if a side effect or other health problem emerges, even if the product has been government-approved and is considered safe. Pharmaceutical giants Merck and Pfizer reached settlements to end thousands of lawsuits filed regarding their painkillers Vioxx and Bextra.[10] Merck agreed to pay $4.85 billion to end lawsuits over Vioxx, and Pfizer paid $894 million to end claims against Bextra.[11]

Some product liability cases have raised intriguing questions about responsibility. Gun manufacturers were unsuccessfully sued by cities including Chicago, Philadelphia, and Miami for the costs of police work and medical care necessitated by gun violence. McDonald's was named in a product liability suit (later dismissed) claiming that its food caused obesity, diabetes,

> **strict product liability**
> Legal responsibility for harm or injury caused by a product regardless of fault.

◄ PPT A-10:
Product Liability Laws

◄ PPT A-11:
Major Product Liability Cases

figure A.2

MAJOR PRODUCT LIABILITY CASES

COMPANY	YEAR	SETTLEMENT
Ford Motor Company	1978	$125 million in punitive damages awarded in the case of a 13-year-old boy severely burned in a rear-end collision involving a Ford Pinto
A. H. Robins	1987	Dalkon Shield intrauterine birth-control devices recalled after eight separate punitive-damage awards
Playtex Company	1988	Considered liable and suffered a $10 million damage award in the case of a toxic shock syndrome fatality in Kansas; removed certain types of tampons from the market
Jack in the Box	1993	Assessed large damages after a two-year-old child who ate at Jack in the Box died of *E. coli* poisoning and others became ill
Sara Lee Corporation	1998	Costly company recall necessitated when tainted hot dogs caused food-poisoning death of 15 people
General Motors	1999	Suffered $4.8 billion punitive award in faulty fuel-tank case
Major Tobacco Firms	2004	$130 billion sought by the federal government for smoking cessation programs (settled for $10 billion)

Sources: U.S. Department of Justice; and American Trial Lawyers Association.

and other health problems in children. Communities have reacted by banning trans fats in food, regulating menu information, and requiring the posting of calorie content at fast-food restaurants.[12] Schools have replaced soft drinks in vending machines with fruit juice and water.

Tort and product liability reform has been a key objective of business for many years. Congress took a step forward with passage of the Class Action Fairness Act in 2005, which expanded federal jurisdiction over many large class-action lawsuits.[13] Businesses and insurance companies argue that much more needs to be done, and few expect the issue to go away. Figure A.2 on p. A-5 highlights several major product liability awards that have cost companies dearly.

LEARNING goal 3 *

Identify the purposes and conditions of patents, copyrights, and trademarks.

LEGALLY PROTECTING IDEAS: PATENTS, COPYRIGHTS, AND TRADEMARKS

Have you ever invented a product you think may have commercial value? Many people have, and to protect their ideas they took the next step and applied for a patent.[14] A **patent** is a document that gives inventors exclusive rights to their inventions for 20 years from the date they file the patent applications.

The 5,500 examiners in the U.S. Patent and Trademark Office (USPTO) review about 362,000 patent requests each year and grant more than 180,000.[15] The agency has a current backlog of 760,000 patents that have been filed. Patent approval may take two to four years.[16] To reduce the backlog, the U.S. Supreme Court imposed stricter standards of "obviousness" on the process, which means that a patent cannot be granted for an invention that is an obvious extension of an existing product.[17] An inventor must make sure a product is truly unique.

Patent applicants should seek the advice of a lawyer; in fact, fewer than 2 percent of product inventors file on their own.[18] How good are your chances of receiving a patent if you file for one? Over 60 percent of patent applications are approved, with fees that vary according to the complexity of the patent. A patent dealing with complex technology can cost anywhere from $10,000 to $30,000.[19] A patent dealing with simpler concepts will cost the inventor about $7,000.

Patent owners have the right to sell or license the use of their patent to others. Foreign companies are also eligible to file for U.S. patents. They account for nearly half the U.S. patents issued. Penalties for violating a patent can be costly. Dr. Gary Michelson received a settlement of $1.35 billion from Medtronic Inc. to end litigation and license patents covering a range of back-surgery products.[20] The USPTO does not take action on behalf of patent holders if patent infringement occurs. The defense of patent rights is solely the job of the patent holder and can be quite expensive.[21]

The American Inventor's Protection Act requires that patent applications be made public after 18 months regardless of whether a patent has been awarded. This law was passed in part to address critics who argued that some inventors intentionally delayed or dragged out a patent application because they expected others to eventually develop similar products or technology. Then when someone (usually a large company) filed for a similar patent, the inventor surfaced to claim the patent—referred to as a *submarine patent*—and demanded large royalties (fees) for its use. The late engineer Jerome Lemelson, for example, reportedly collected more than $1.5 billion in patent royalties for a series of long-delayed patents—including forerunners of the fax machine, the Walkman, and the bar-code scanner—from auto, computer, retailer, and electronics companies.[22]

Technology companies like Verizon, Google, and Cisco have taken additional action to defend themselves against patent infringement suits by joining Allied Security Trust, a not-for-profit firm that acquires intellectual property of interest to its members.[23] The idea is to buy up patents before they fall into the hands of law firms and venture capitalists looking to pursue settlements or legal damages against the tech firms.[24]

Just as a patent protects an inventor's right to a product or process, a **copyright** protects a creator's rights to materials such as books, articles, photos, paintings, and cartoons. Copyrights are filed with the Library of Congress and require a minimum of paperwork. They last for the lifetime of the author or artist plus 70 years and can be passed on to the creator's heirs. The Copyright Act of 1978, however, gives a special term of 75 years from publication to works published before January 1, 1978, whose copyrights had not expired by that date. The holder of a copyright can either prevent anyone from using the copyrighted material or charge a fee for using it. Author J. K. Rowling won a lawsuit against a fan who violated her copyright when he planned to publish a Harry Potter encyclopedia.[25] If a work is created by an employee in the normal course of a job, the copyright belongs to the employer and lasts 95 years from publication or 120 years from creation, whichever comes first.

A *trademark* is a legally protected name, symbol, or design (or combination of these) that identifies the goods or services of one seller and distinguishes them from those of competitors.[26] Trademarks generally belong to the owner forever, as long as they are properly registered and renewed every 10 years.[27] Some well-known trademarks include the Aflac duck, Disney's Mickey Mouse, the Nike swoosh, and the golden arches of McDonald's. Like a patent, a trademark is protected against infringement.[28] Businesses fight hard to protect trademarks, especially in global markets where trademark pirating can be extensive. Chapter 14 discusses trademarks in more detail.

Media companies have sued YouTube for carrying videos of their popular television shows on their Web site. YouTube says that it makes every effort to remove any copyrighted video that users download to the site. Do you think YouTube should be held liable for copyrighted video downloaded by others? Why or why not?

copyright
A document that protects a creator's rights to materials such as books, articles, photos, paintings, and cartoons.

progress assessment

- What is tort law?
- What is product liability?
- For how long is a patent protected?
- What is a copyright?

Sidebar

PPT A-15: What's the Uniform Commercial Code?

PPT A-16: Understanding Warranties

Uniform Commercial Code (UCC)
A comprehensive commercial law, adopted by every state in the United States, that covers sales laws and other commercial laws.

express warranties
Specific representations by the seller that buyers rely on regarding the goods they purchase.

implied warranties
Guarantees legally imposed on the seller.

negotiable instruments
Forms of commercial paper (such as checks) that are transferable among businesses and individuals and represent a promise to pay a specified amount.

Would you buy a new car if the dealer offered no warranty? How about an iPhone or a plasma TV with no guarantee of performance? Warranties are an important part of a product and are generally of major concern to purchasers. It's important to check whether a product's warranty is full or limited. Should colleges offer students warranties with their degree programs?

LEARNING goal 4 *

Describe warranties and negotiable instruments as covered in the Uniform Commercial Code.

SALES LAW: THE UNIFORM COMMERCIAL CODE

At one time, laws governing businesses varied from state to state, making interstate trade extremely complicated. Today, all states have adopted the same commercial law. The **Uniform Commercial Code (UCC)** is a comprehensive commercial law that covers sales laws and other commercial laws. Since all 50 states have adopted the law (although it does not apply in certain sections of Louisiana), the UCC simplifies commercial transactions across state lines.

The UCC has 11 articles, which contain laws covering sales; commercial paper such as promissory notes and checks; bank deposits and collections; letters of credit; bulk transfers; warehouse receipts, bills of lading, and other documents of title; investment securities; and secured transactions. We do not have space in this text to discuss all 11 articles, but we will discuss two: Article 2, which regulates warranties, and Article 3, which covers negotiable instruments.

Warranties

A *warranty* guarantees that the product sold will be acceptable for the purpose for which the buyer intends to use it. There are two types of warranties. **Express warranties** are specific representations by the seller that buyers rely on regarding the goods they purchase. The warranty you receive in the box with an iPhone or a toaster is an express warranty.

Implied warranties are legally imposed on the seller, who implies that a product will conform to the customary standards of the trade or industry in which it competes. An implied warranty entitles you to expect that a toaster will toast your bread to your desired degree (light, medium, dark) or that food you buy for consumption off an establishment's premises is fit to eat.

Warranties can be either full or limited. A full warranty requires a seller to replace or repair a product at no charge if the product is defective, whereas a limited warranty typically limits the defects or mechanical problems the seller covers. Many of the rights of buyers, including the right to accept or reject goods, are spelled out in Article 2 of the UCC.

Negotiable Instruments

Negotiable instruments are forms of commercial paper (such as checks) that are transferable among businesses and individuals; they represent a promise to pay a specified amount. Article 3 of the Uniform Commercial Code requires negotiable instruments to follow four conditions. They must (1) be written and signed by the maker or drawer, (2) be made payable on demand or at a certain time, (3) be made payable to the bearer (the person holding the instrument) or to specific order, and (4) contain an unconditional promise to pay a specified amount of money. Checks or other forms of negotiable instruments are transferred (negotiated for payment) when the payee signs the back. The payee's signature is called an *endorsement*.

LEARNING goal 5 *

List and describe the conditions necessary to make a legally enforceable contract, and describe the possible consequences if such a contract is violated.

CONTRACT LAW

If I offer to sell you my bike for $50 and later change my mind, can you force me to sell the bike by saying we had a contract? If I lose $120 to you in a poker game, can you sue in court to get your money? If I agree to sing at your wedding for free and back out at the last minute, can you claim I violated a contract? These are the kinds of questions contract law answers.

A **contract** is a legally enforceable agreement between two or more parties. **Contract law** specifies what constitutes a legally enforceable agreement. Basically, a contract is legally binding if the following conditions are met:

1. *An offer is made.* An offer to do something or sell something can be oral or written. If I agree to sell you my bike for $50, I have made an offer. That offer is not legally binding, however, until the following other conditions are met.

2. *There is a voluntary acceptance of the offer.* The principle of *mutual acceptance* means that both parties to a contract must agree on the terms. If I use duress—coercion through force or threat of force—in getting you to agree to buy my bike, the contract will not be legal. You couldn't use duress to get me to sell my bike, either. Even if we both agree, though, the contract is still not legally binding without the next four conditions.

3. *Both parties give consideration.* **Consideration** means something of value. If I agree to sell you my bike for $50, the bike and the $50 are consideration, and we have a legally binding contract. If I agree to sing at your wedding and you do not give me anything in return (consideration), we have no contract.

4. *Both parties are competent.* A person under the influence of alcohol or drugs, or a person of unsound mind (one who has been legally declared incompetent), cannot be held to a contract. In many cases, a minor may not be held to a contract either. If a 15-year-old agrees to pay $10,000 for a car, the seller will not be able to enforce the contract due to the buyer's lack of competence.

5. *The contract covers a legal act.* A contract covering the sale of illegal drugs or stolen merchandise is unenforceable since such sales are violations of criminal law. (If gambling is prohibited by state law in your state, you cannot sue to collect the poker debt.)

6. *The contract is in proper form.* An agreement for the sale of goods worth $500 or more must be in writing. Contracts that cannot be fulfilled within one year also must be put in writing. Contracts regarding real property (land and everything attached to it) must be in writing.

◀ **PPT A-17:**
Negotiable Instruments

◀ **LECTURE LINK A-2:**
Negotiable Instrument Forgery and the Uniform Commercial Code

◀ **PPT A-18:**
Contract Law

contract
A legally enforceable agreement between two or more parties.

contract law
Set of laws that specify what constitutes a legally enforceable agreement.

◀ **PPT A-19:**
Contract Requirements

consideration
Something of value; consideration is one of the requirements of a legal contract.

Breach of Contract

breach of contract
When one party fails to follow the terms of a contract.

Both parties in a contract may voluntarily choose to end the agreement. **Breach of contract** occurs when one party fails to follow the terms of a contract. If that happens the following may occur:

1. *Specific performance.* The party who violated the contract may be required to live up to the agreement if money damages would not be adequate. If I legally offered to sell you a rare painting, I would have to sell you that painting.
2. *Payment of damages.* If I fail to live up to a contract, you can sue me for **damages**, usually the amount you would lose from my nonperformance. If we had a legally binding contract for me to sing at your wedding, for example, and I failed to come, you could sue me for the cost of hiring a new singer.
3. *Discharge of obligation.* If I fail to live up to my end of a contract, you can agree to drop the matter. Generally you would not have to live up to your end of the agreement either.

damages
The monetary settlement awarded to a person who is injured by a breach of contract.

Lawyers would not be paid so handsomely if the law were as simple as implied in these rules of contracts.[29] That's why it's always best to put a contract in writing even though oral contracts can be enforceable under contract law. The contract should clearly specify the offer and consideration, and the parties to the contract should sign and date it. A contract does not have to be complicated as long as (1) it is in writing, (2) it specifies mutual consideration, and (3) it contains a clear offer and agreement.

progress assessment

- What is the purpose of the Universal Commercial Code (UCC)?
- Compare express and implied warranties.
- What are the four elements of a negotiable instrument specified in the UCC?
- What are the six conditions for a legally binding contract? What could happen if a contract is breached?

LEARNING goal 6 *

Summarize several laws that regulate competition and protect consumers in the United States.

PROMOTING FAIR AND COMPETITIVE BUSINESS PRACTICES

Competition is a cornerstone of the free-market system (see Chapter 2). A key responsibility of legislators is to pass laws that ensure a competitive atmosphere among businesses and promote fair business practices. The U.S. Justice Department's antitrust division and other government agencies serve as watchdogs to guarantee competition among sellers flows freely, and new competitors have open access to the market. The government's power here is broad.[30] The Justice Department's antitrust division has investigated the competitive practices of market giants such as Microsoft, Visa, and Google.[31] Figure A.3 highlights several high-profile antitrust cases.

Antitrust oversight was not always the rule, however. Big businesses were once able to force smaller competitors out of business with little government resistance. The following brief history details how government responded to past problems. We'll also look at new challenges government regulators face today.

The History of Antitrust Legislation

In the late 19th century, big oil companies, railroads, steel companies, and other industrial firms dominated the U.S. economy. Some feared that such large and powerful companies would be able to crush any competitors and then charge high prices. In that atmosphere, Congress passed the Sherman Antitrust Act in 1890 to prevent large organizations from stifling the competition of smaller or newer firms. The Sherman Act forbids (1) contracts, combinations, or conspiracies in restraint of trade, and (2) the creation of actual monopolies or attempts to monopolize any part of trade or commerce.

Because some of the law's language was vague, there was doubt about just what practices it prohibited. To clarify its intentions Congress enacted the following laws.

- *The Clayton Act of 1914.* The Clayton Act prohibits exclusive dealing, tying contracts, and interlocking directorates. It also prohibits buying large amounts of stock in competing corporations. *Exclusive dealing* is selling goods with the condition that the buyer will not buy from a competitor (when the effect lessens competition). A *tying contract* requires a buyer to purchase unwanted items in order to purchase desired items. Let's say I wanted to purchase 20 cases of Pepsi-Cola per week to sell in my restaurant. Pepsi, however, says it will sell me the 20 cases only if I also agree to buy 10 cases each of its Mountain Dew and Diet Pepsi products. My purchase of Pepsi-Cola would be *tied* to the purchase of the other two products. An *interlocking directorate* occurs when a company's board of directors includes members of the boards of competing corporations.
- *The Federal Trade Commission Act of 1914.* The Federal Trade Commission Act prohibits unfair methods of competition in commerce. This legislation set up the five-member Federal Trade Commission (FTC)

◀ PPT A-22:
The Clayton Act of 1914

◀ PPT A-23:
Antitrust Legislation

figure A.3

HISTORY OF HIGH-PROFILE ANTITRUST CASES

CASE	OUTCOME
United States v. Standard Oil 1911	Standard Oil broken up into 34 companies; Amoco, Chevron, and ExxonMobil are results of the breakup
United States v. American Tobacco 1911	American Tobacco split into 16 companies; British Tobacco and R. J. Reynolds are results of the breakup
United States v. E. I. du Pont de Nemours 1961	DuPont ordered to divest its 23 percent ownership stake in General Motors
United States v. AT&T 1982	Settled after Ma Bell agreed to spin off its local telephone operations into seven regional operating companies
United States v. Microsoft 2000	Microsoft ordered to halt prior anticompetitive practices

Source: U.S. Department of Justice.

to enforce compliance with the act. The FTC deals with a wide range of competitive issues—everything from preventing companies from making misleading "Made in the USA" claims to regulating telemarketers' practices and insisting funeral providers give consumers accurate, itemized price information about funeral goods and services. The activity level of the FTC typically depends on its members at the time.[32] It has the added responsibility for overseeing mergers and acquisitions (Chapter 5) in the health care, energy, computer hardware, automotive, and biotechnology industries. The Wheeler-Lea Amendment of 1938 gave the FTC additional jurisdiction over false or misleading advertising, along with the power to increase fines if its requirements are not met within 60 days.

- *The Robinson-Patman Act of 1936.* The Robinson-Patman Act prohibits price discrimination and applies to both sellers and buyers who knowingly induce or receive price discrimination. Certain types of price-cutting are criminal offenses punishable by fine and imprisonment. That includes price differences that "substantially" weaken competition unless they can be justified by lower selling costs associated with larger purchases. In 2008, four large supermarket chains sued 16 drug makers, charging they were forced to pay more for prescription drugs than institutional pharmacies and health maintenance organizations (HMOs).[33] The law also prohibits advertising and promotional allowances unless they are offered to all retailers, large and small.[34] Remember that this legislation applies to business-to-business transactions and not to business-to-consumer transactions.

The change in U.S. business from manufacturing to knowledge-based technology has created new regulatory challenges for federal agencies. In the early 2000s, Microsoft's competitive practices were the focus of an intense investigation by the Justice Department. The government charged that Microsoft hindered competition by refusing to sell its Windows operating system to computer manufacturers that refused to sell Windows-based computers exclusively. Microsoft settled with the Justice Department, but the case broadened the definition of anticompetitive behavior.[35] The Justice Department's antitrust investigation of the agreement between Google and Yahoo, whereby Google would have provided some search advertising for Yahoo, prompted the companies to drop their proposal.[36] The FTC has opened an antitrust inquiry into anticompetitive activities by Intel, and antitrust issues promise to persist in the future.

LAWS TO PROTECT CONSUMERS

Consumerism is a social movement that seeks to increase and strengthen the rights and powers of buyers in relationship to sellers. It is the people's way of getting a fair share in marketing exchanges. The Public Company Accounting Reform and the Sarbanes/Oxley Act (Chapter 17) were passed to allay concerns about falsified financial statements. The market meltdown of 2008–2010 raised consumer anger, particularly against the Treasury Department, Federal Reserve, and Securities and Exchange Commission (SEC) for their lack of oversight of the securities market.[37] Quasi-governmental agencies such as Fannie Mae and Freddie Mac shouldered much of the blame for the real estate market collapse.[38] Consumers doubted they would see much gain from the $700 billion of taxpayer money needed to bail out financial markets.[39] President Obama's stimulus package faced similar criticism. Figure A.4 lists major consumer protection laws.

> **PPT A-24:**
> History of High Profile Antitrust Cases

> **consumerism**
> A social movement that seeks to increase and strengthen the rights and powers of buyers in relation to sellers.

> **PPT A-25:**
> Consumer Protections

> **PPT A-26:**
> Number of Identity Theft Complaints

Fair Packaging and Labeling Act (1966)	Makes unfair or deceptive packaging or labeling of certain consumer commodities illegal.
Child Protection Act (1966)	Removes from sale potentially harmful toys and allows the FDA to pull dangerous products from the market.
Truth-in-Lending Act (1968)	Requires full disclosure of all finance charges on consumer credit agreements and in advertisements of credit plans.
Child Protection and Toy Safety Act (1969)	Protects children from toys and other products that contain thermal, electrical, or mechanical hazards.
Fair Credit Reporting Act (1970)	Requires that consumer credit reports contain only accurate, relevant, and recent information and are confidential unless a proper party requests them for an appropriate reason.
Consumer Product Safety Act (1972)	Created an independent agency to protect consumers from unreasonable risk of injury arising from consumer products and to set safety standards.
Magnuson-Moss Warranty–Federal Trade Commission Improvement Act (1975)	Provides for minimum disclosure standards for written consumer products warranties and allows the FTC to prescribe interpretive rules and policy statements regarding unfair or deceptive practices.
Alcohol Labeling Legislation (1988)	Provides for warning labels on liquor saying that women shouldn't drink when pregnant and that alcohol impairs a person's abilities.
Nutrition Labeling and Education Act (1990)	Requires truthful and uniform nutritional labeling on every food the FDA regulates.
Consumer Credit Reporting Reform Act (1997)	Increases responsibility of credit issuers for accurate credit data and requires creditors to verify that disputed data are accurate. Consumer notification is necessary before reinstating the data.
Children's Online Privacy Protection Act (2000)	Gives parents control over what information is collected online from their children under age 13; requires Web site operators to maintain the confidentiality, security, and integrity of the personal information collected from children.
Country of Origin Labeling Law (2009)	Requires that the product label on most food products sold in U.S. supermarkets gives the product's country of origin.

figure A.4

CONSUMER PROTECTION LAWS

LEARNING goal 7 *

Explain the role of tax laws in generating income for the government and as a method of discouraging or encouraging certain behaviors among taxpayers.

TAX LAWS

Mention taxes and most people frown. **Taxes** are the way federal, state, and local governments raise money. They affect almost every individual and business in the United States.

Traditionally, governments have used taxes primarily as a source of funding for their operations and programs. Taxes can also help discourage or encourage certain behaviors among taxpayers. If the government wishes to reduce consumer use of certain classes of products like cigarettes or liquor, it can pass *sin taxes* on them to raise their cost.[40] In other situations, the government may

◀ PPT A-27:
Taxes

taxes
How the government (federal, state, and local) raises money.

◀ PPT A-28:
Sin Taxes

figure A.5
TYPES OF TAXES

TYPE	PURPOSE
Income taxes	Taxes paid on the income received by businesses and individuals. Income taxes are the largest source of tax income received by the federal government.
Property taxes	Taxes paid on real and personal property. *Real property* is real estate owned by individuals and businesses. *Personal property* is a broader category that includes any movable property such as tangible items (wedding rings, equipment, etc.) or intangible items (stocks, checks, mortgages, etc.). Taxes are based on their assessed value.
Sales taxes	Taxes paid on merchandise sold at the retail level.
Excise taxes	Taxes paid on selected items such as tobacco, alcoholic beverages, airline travel, gasoline, and firearms. These are often referred to as *sin taxes*. Income generated from the tax goes toward a specifically designated purpose. For example, gasoline taxes often help the federal government and state governments pay for highway construction or improvements.

encourage businesses to hire new employees or purchase new equipment by offering a *tax credit*, an amount firms can deduct from their tax bill.

Taxes are levied from a variety of sources. Income taxes (personal and business), sales taxes, and property taxes are the major bases of tax revenue. The federal government receives its largest share of taxes from income. States and local communities make extensive use of sales taxes. School districts generally depend on property taxes.

The tax policies of states and cities are important considerations when businesses seek to locate operations. They also affect personal decisions such as retirement. As government revenues at all levels dwindle, new tax issues are sure to be debated. States claim they are losing over $15 billion in sales taxes by not collecting from Internet sales transactions. Some states have taken action. New York passed a law that requires out-of-state online companies to collect sales taxes from New York shoppers.[41] Other states are petitioning Congress to pass a law permitting them to collect sales taxes from e-commerce transactions.[42] The European Union levies certain Internet taxes, so expect the U.S. debate to intensify. Figure A.5 highlights the primary types of taxes levied on individuals and businesses.

▶ PPT A-29:
Do the Rich Pay Taxes?

LEARNING goal 8 *

Distinguish among the various types of bankruptcy as outlined by the Bankruptcy Code.

BANKRUPTCY LAWS

Bankruptcy is the legal process by which a person, business, or government entity, unable to meet financial obligations, is relieved of those debts by a court. Courts divide any of the debtor's assets among creditors, allowing them to recover at least part of their money and freeing the debtor to begin anew.

bankruptcy
The legal process by which a person, business, or government entity unable to meet financial obligations is relieved of those obligations by a court that divides any assets among creditors, allowing creditors to get at least part of their money and freeing the debtor to begin anew.

The U.S. Constitution gives Congress the power to establish bankruptcy laws, and legislation has existed since the 1890s. Major amendments to the bankruptcy code include the Bankruptcy Amendments and Federal Judgeships Act of 1984, the Bankruptcy Reform Acts of 1994, and the Bankruptcy Abuse Prevention and Consumer Protection Act of 2005.

The 1984 law allows a person who is bankrupt to keep part of the equity (ownership) in a house and car, and some other personal property. The 1994 Act amended more than 45 sections of the bankruptcy code and created reforms to speed up and simplify the process. The Bankruptcy Reform Act of 2005 was passed to reduce the total number of bankruptcy filings and to eliminate the perceived ease of filing. The legislation increased the cost of filing and made it difficult for people (especially those with high incomes) to escape overwhelming debt from credit cards, medical bills, student loans, or other loans not secured through a home or other asset. It also requires debtors to receive credit counseling.[43]

Bankruptcies increased in the late 1980s and have grown tremendously since. Many attributed the increase to a lessening of the stigma of bankruptcy, an increase in understanding of bankruptcy law and its protections, and increased advertising by bankruptcy attorneys. Some suggest that the ease with which certain consumers could get credit contributed to the number of filings by allowing people to readily overspend.[44] The 2005 reform reduced the number of bankruptcy filings to approximately 600,000 in 2006, compared to an average of 1.5 million between 2001 and 2004.[45] However, with the economic decline in 2008, 1.2 million U.S. households filed for bankruptcy compared to 826,000 in 2007.[46] Though high-profile bankruptcies of businesses—such as Lehman Brothers, Circuit City, GM, and Mrs. Fields Cookies—tend to dominate the news, over 90 percent of bankruptcy filings each year are by individuals.

Bankruptcy can be either voluntary or involuntary. In **voluntary bankruptcy**, the debtor applies for bankruptcy; in **involuntary bankruptcy**, the creditors start legal action against the debtor. Most bankruptcies are voluntary, since creditors usually wait in hopes they will be paid all the money due them rather than settle for only part of it.

Bankruptcy procedures begin when a petition is filed with the court under one of the following sections of the Bankruptcy Code:

Chapter 7—"straight bankruptcy" or liquidation (used by businesses and individuals).

Chapter 11—reorganization (used almost exclusively by businesses).

Chapter 13—repayment (used by individuals).

Chapter 7 is the most popular form of bankruptcy among individuals; it requires the sale of nonexempt assets.[47] Under federal exemption statutes, a debtor may be able to retain (exempt) up to $20,200 of equity in a home; up to $3,225 of equity in an automobile; up to $9,850 in household furnishings, apparel, and musical instruments; and up to $1,225 in jewelry.[48] States can choose different exemption statutes. When the sale of assets is over, creditors, including the government if taxes are owed, divide the remaining cash as stipulated by law. First, creditors with secured claims receive the collateral for their claims or repossess the claimed asset (such as an automobile or home); then unsecured claims (backed by no asset) are paid in this order:

1. Costs of the bankruptcy case.
2. Any business costs incurred after bankruptcy was filed.
3. Wages, salaries, or commissions owed (limited to $2,000 per creditor).

voluntary bankruptcy Legal procedures initiated by a debtor.

involuntary bankruptcy Bankruptcy procedures filed by a debtor's creditors.

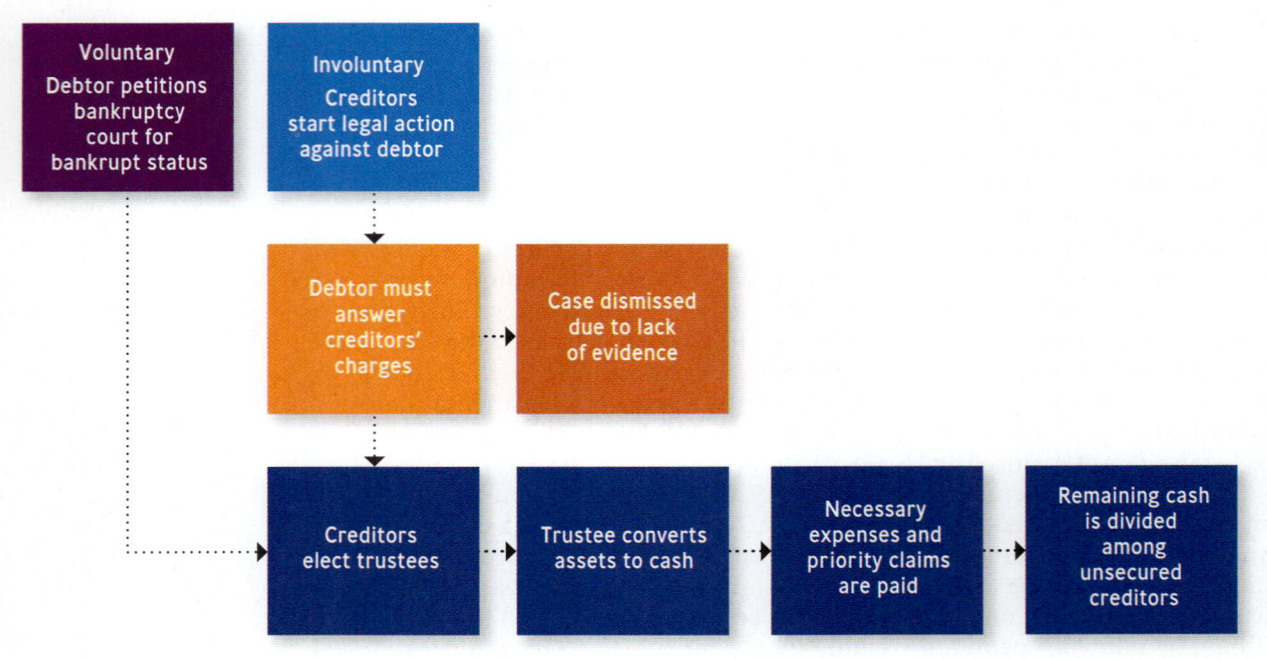

[Flowchart:
Voluntary: Debtor petitions bankruptcy court for bankrupt status
Involuntary: Creditors start legal action against debtor → Debtor must answer creditors' charges → Case dismissed due to lack of evidence
→ Creditors elect trustees → Trustee converts assets to cash → Necessary expenses and priority claims are paid → Remaining cash is divided among unsecured creditors]

figure A.6

HOW ASSETS ARE DIVIDED IN BANKRUPTCY

This figure shows that the creditor (the person owed money) selects the trustee (the person or organization that handles the sale of assets). Note that the process may be started by the debtor or the creditors.

▶ **PPT A-32:**
How Assets are Divided in Bankruptcy

Under Chapter II bankruptcy law, the mighty can fall. Giant electronic retailer Circuit City was forced to declare bankruptcy when it could not pay its suppliers. Do you know other companies forced into bankruptcy due to the recent recession?

4. Contributions to employee benefit plans.
5. Refunds to consumers who paid for products that weren't delivered (limited to $900 per claimant).
6. Federal and state taxes.

Figure A.6 outlines the steps used in liquidating assets under Chapter 7.

In Chapter 11 bankruptcy, a company sued by creditors continues to operate under court protection while it tries to work out a plan for paying off its debts. Under certain conditions it may sell assets, borrow money, and change company officers to strengthen its market position. A court-appointed trustee supervises the proceedings and protects the creditors' interests.

A company does not have to be insolvent to file for relief under Chapter 11. In theory, it is a way for sick companies to recover, designed to help both debtors and creditors find the best solution. In reality, however, less than one-third of Chapter 11 companies survive—usually those with lots of cash available. The Bankruptcy Reform Act of 1994 provides a fast-track procedure for small businesses filing under Chapter 11. Individuals can also file under Chapter 11, but it's uncommon.

Chapter 13 permits individuals, including small-business owners, to pay back creditors over three to five years. Chapter 13 proceedings are less complicated and less expensive than Chapter 7 proceedings. The debtor files a proposed plan with the court for paying off debts. If the plan is approved, the debtor pays a court-appointed trustee in monthly installments as agreed on in the repayment plan. The trustee then pays each creditor.

LEARNING goal 9 *

Explain the role of deregulation as a tool to encourage competition.

DEREGULATION VERSUS REGULATION

At one time, the United States had laws and regulations covering almost every aspect of business. Some felt there were too many laws and regulations, costing the public too much money (see Figure A.7). A movement toward deregulation took hold. **Deregulation** means that the government withdraws certain laws and regulations that seem to hinder competition. The most publicized examples occurred in the airline and telecommunications industries.

Consumers clearly benefited from the Airline Deregulation Act of 1978 that ended federal control of commercial airlines.[49] Before passage of the act, the government restricted where airlines could land and fly. When the restrictions were lifted, airlines began competing for different routes and charging lower prices. The skies were also opened to new competitors, such as Southwest, to take advantage of new opportunities. Today, however, some argue that the industry needs more government intervention, since airlines have lost $40 billion since 2001 and every pre-deregulation carrier except American has filed for bankruptcy protection.[50]

Passage of the Telecommunications Act in 1996 brought similar deregulation to telecommunications and gave consumers a flood of options in local telephone service markets. There was also a significant increase in retail video competition. In the past, most households received only four TV channels (the

deregulation
Government withdrawal of certain laws and regulations that seem to hinder competition.

◄ PPT A-33:
Deregulating Commerce

◄ PPT A-34:
Hamburger Regulations

figure A.7

HAMBURGER REGULATIONS
Does this amount of regulation seem just right, too little, or too much for you?

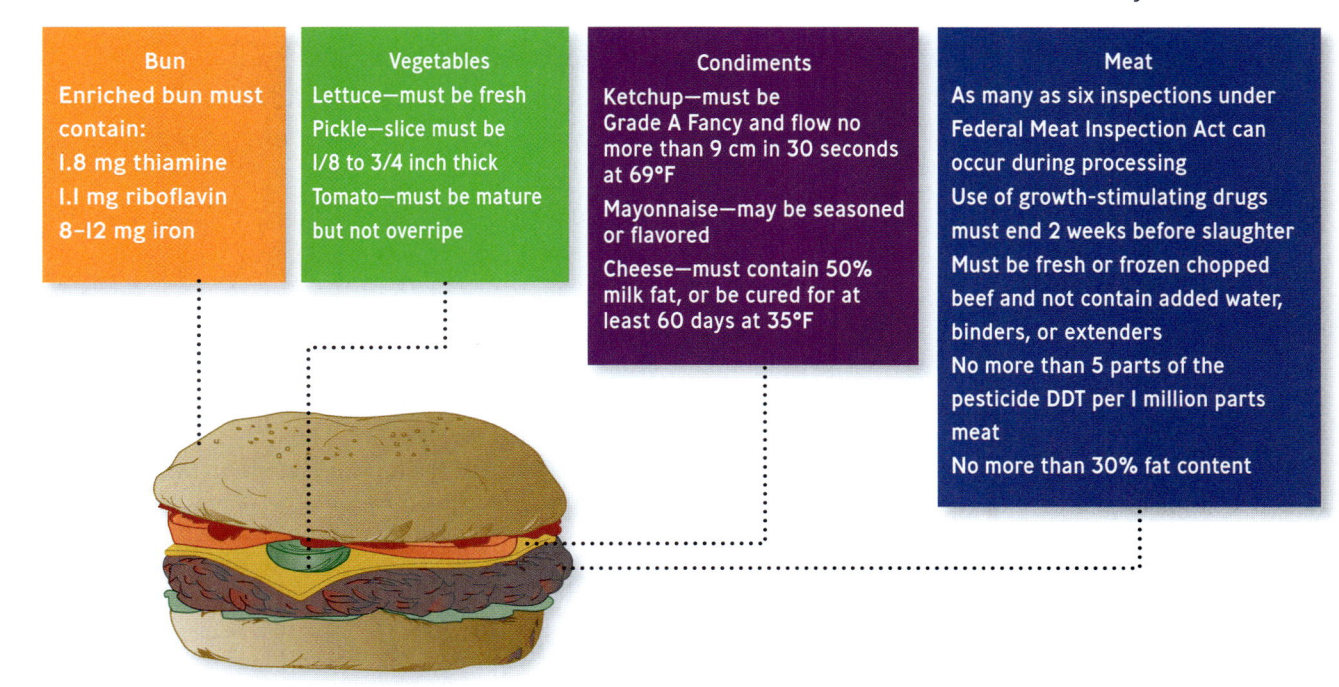

Bun	Vegetables	Condiments	Meat
Enriched bun must contain: 1.8 mg thiamine 1.1 mg riboflavin 8–12 mg iron	Lettuce—must be fresh Pickle—slice must be 1/8 to 3/4 inch thick Tomato—must be mature but not overripe	Ketchup—must be Grade A Fancy and flow no more than 9 cm in 30 seconds at 69°F Mayonnaise—may be seasoned or flavored Cheese—must contain 50% milk fat, or be cured for at least 60 days at 35°F	As many as six inspections under Federal Meat Inspection Act can occur during processing Use of growth-stimulating drugs must end 2 weeks before slaughter Must be fresh or frozen chopped beef and not contain added water, binders, or extenders No more than 5 parts of the pesticide DDT per 1 million parts meat No more than 30% fat content

three major networks—NBC, CBS, and ABC—and public broadcasting). Today most households receive a dozen or more over-the-air stations and hundreds more on cable, satellite, and the Internet.[51]

Unfortunately, deregulation has not always worked as desired. New regulations in the banking and investments industries changed the nature of financial markets and created huge problems. For example, the Federal Reserve System's reluctance to toughen mortgage regulations contributed to the collapse in the real estate market.[52] Events such as the government's takeover of mortgage giants Fannie Mae and Freddie Mac, the Treasury Department's investment in private banks, the bailout of insurance giant AIG, and the infusion of $700 billion into the financial systems caused consumer panic in the stock market. This breakdown of financial markets in 2008–2010 reopened the question of how much deregulation is too much.[53]

More than 20 states have passed utility deregulation laws that were intended to increase competition and provide consumers lower price options.[54] California became the first to deregulate the electric power industry in the late 1990s. State leaders envisioned customers shopping for electricity in a market packed with power suppliers jockeying for their business—with consumers choosing the best option. Instead the state experienced significant problems, causing many to question the deregulation of electric power. Other states have halted deregulation programs to deal with the problems they caused. Still, not everyone is endorsing a move back to government-controlled regulation of utilities. In Texas and New York, deregulation programs have been somewhat successful. Time will tell whether utility deregulation will survive and prosper.

Some regulation of business seems necessary to ensure fair and honest dealings with the public. Corporate scandals in the early 2000s and the financial market collapse of 2008–2010 led to a further demand for better government regulation and oversight of business operations to protect consumers, workers, and investors. With increasing global competition, U.S. business must work with government to create a competitive environment that is fair and open and accept responsibilities to all stakeholders.

progress assessment

- What is the purpose of antitrust law?
- Describe bankruptcy provisions under Chapters 7, 11, and 13.
- What is deregulation? Give examples of successful and unsuccessful deregulation.

summary

Learning Goal 1. Define *business law*, distinguish between statutory and common law, and explain the role of administrative agencies.

- **What is the difference between statutory law and common law?**

Statutory law includes state and federal constitutions, legislative enactments, treaties of the federal government, and ordinances—in short, written law. Common law is the body of unwritten law that comes from decisions handed down by judges.

- **What are administrative agencies?**

    Administrative agencies are federal or state institutions and other government organizations created by Congress or state legislatures with power to create rules and regulations within their area of authority.

Learning Goal 2. Define *tort law* and explain the role of product liability in tort law.

- **What is an intentional tort?**

    An intentional tort is a willful act that results in injury.

- **What is negligence?**

    Negligence, in tort law, is behavior that causes *unintentional* harm or injury. Findings of negligence can lead to huge judgments against businesses.

Learning Goal 3. Identify the purposes and conditions of patents, copyrights, and trademarks.

- **What are patents and copyrights?**

    A patent is a document that gives inventors exclusive rights to their inventions for 20 years from the date they file the patent applications. A copyright protects a creator's rights to materials such as books, articles, photos, paintings, and cartoons.

- **What is a trademark?**

    A trademark is a legally protected name, symbol, or design (or combination of these) that identifies the goods or services of one seller and distinguishes them from those of competitors.

Learning Goal 4. Describe warranties and negotiable instruments as covered in the Uniform Commercial Code.

- **What does Article 2 of the UCC cover?**

    Article 2 contains laws regarding warranties. Express warranties are guarantees made by the seller, whereas implied warranties are guarantees imposed on the seller by law.

- **What does Article 3 of the UCC cover?**

    Article 3 covers negotiable instruments such as checks. A negotiable instrument must (1) be written and signed by the maker or drawer, (2) be made payable on demand or at a certain time, (3) be made payable to the bearer (the person holding the instrument) or to specific order, and (4) contain an unconditional promise to pay a specified amount of money.

Learning Goal 5. List and describe the conditions necessary to make a legally enforceable contract, and describe the possible consequences if such a contract is violated.

- **What makes a contract enforceable under the law?**

    An enforceable contract must meet six conditions: (1) an offer must be made, (2) the offer must be voluntarily accepted, (3) both parties must give consideration, (4) both parties must be competent, (5) the contract must be legal, and (6) the contract must be in proper form.

- **What are the possible consequences if a contract is violated?**

    If a contract is violated, one of the following may be required: (1) specific performance, (2) payment of damages, or (3) discharge of obligation.

Learning Goal 6. Summarize several laws that regulate competition and protect consumers in the United States.

- **What does the Sherman Act cover?**

    The Sherman Act forbids contracts, combinations, or conspiracies in restraint of trade and actual monopolies or attempts to monopolize any part of trade or commerce.

- **What does the Clayton Act add?**

The Clayton Act prohibits exclusive dealing, tying contracts, interlocking directorates, and buying large amounts of stock in competing corporations.

- **Which act regulates false and deceptive advertising?**

The Federal Trade Commission Act prohibits unfair methods of competition in commerce, including deceptive advertising.

- **Which act prohibits price discrimination and demands proportional promotional allowances?**

The Robinson-Patman Act applies to both sellers and buyers who knowingly induce or receive an unlawful discrimination in price.

Learning Goal 7. Explain the role of tax laws in generating income for the government and as a method of discouraging or encouraging certain behaviors among taxpayers.

- **How does the government use taxes to encourage or discourage certain behavior among taxpayers?**

If the government wishes to change citizens' behavior, it can reduce their use of certain classes of products (cigarettes, liquor) by passing *sin taxes* to raise their cost. In other situations, the government may offer tax credits to encourage businesses to hire new employees or purchase new equipment.

Learning Goal 8. Distinguish among the various types of bankruptcy as outlined by the Bankruptcy Code.

- **What are the bankruptcy laws?**

Chapter 7 calls for straight bankruptcy, in which all assets are divided among creditors after exemptions. Chapter 11 allows a firm to reorganize and continue operation after paying only a limited portion of its debts. Chapter 13 allows individuals to pay their creditors over an extended period of time.

Learning Goal 9. Explain the role of deregulation as a tool to encourage competition.

- **What are a few of the most publicized examples of deregulation?**

Perhaps the most publicized examples of deregulation have been those in the airline and telecommunications industries.

key terms

administrative agencies A-3
bankruptcy A-14
breach of contract A-10
business law A-2
common law A-3
consideration A-9
consumerism A-12
contract A-9
contract law A-9
copyright A-7
damages A-10
deregulation A-17
express warranties A-8
implied warranties A-8
involuntary bankruptcy A-15
judiciary A-2
negligence A-4
negotiable instruments A-8
patent A-6
precedent A-3
product liability A-4
statutory law A-3
strict product liability A-5
taxes A-13
tort A-4
Uniform Commercial Code (UCC) A-8
voluntary bankruptcy A-15

chapter notes

CHAPTER 1

1. Patricia Sellers, "Melinda Gates Goes Public," www.fortune.com, accessed July 1, 2010.
2. "The Numbers," *Barron's*, June 14, 2010.
3. Robin White Goode, "Credit Where It's Due," *Black Enterprise*, June 2010.
4. Jim McElhatton, "Community Colleges Seen as Essential," *The Washington Times*, April 14, 2008.
5. Heron Marquez Estrada, "EdCampus Aims to Transform Higher Education," *The Washington Times*, March 31, 2008.
6. Neil Irwin, "Jobless Rate Jumps to 7.2%," *The Washington Post*, January 10, 2009.
7. Mike Spector and Sharon Terlep, "'Old GM' to Sell Plant as 'New GM' Preens," *The Wall Street Journal*, June 29, 2010.
8. Bernard Condon, "Babble Rouser," *Forbes*, August 11, 2008.
9. Marshal Goldsmith and Kelly Goldsmith, "How Happiness Happens," *Bloomberg BusinessWeek*, May 16, 2010.
10. Phanish Puranam and Kannan Srikanth, "Seven Myths about Outsourcing," *The Wall Street Journal*, June 16–17, 2008.
11. Matthew Slaughter, "What Tata Tells Us," *The Wall Street Journal*, March 27, 2008.
12. Steve Hamm, "When the Bottom Line Is Ending Poverty," *BusinessWeek*, March 10, 2008.
13. Bruce Einhorn and Ruth David, "An IPO for India's Top Lender to the Poor," *Bloomberg Businessweek*, May 10–May 16, 2010.
14. John Cuneo, "10 Perks We Love," *Inc.*, June 2010.
15. Andrea Cooper, "Serial Starter," *Entrepreneur*, April 2008.
16. Nichole L. Torres, "First—Stick with It," *Entrepreneur*, March 2008.
17. Jennifer Harper, "Census: Hispanics Largest Ethnic Group," *The Washington Times*, May 2, 2008.
18. Joshua Molina, "Hispanic Executives Continue Their Rise to Prominence amid a Shaky Economy," *Hispanic Business*, January/February, 2009.
19. Bill George, "A New Makeover for an Old Retail Face," *U.S. News and World Report*, November 19, 2007.
20. Elizabeth MacDonald and Chana R. Schoenberger, "The Top 10," *Forbes*, September 17, 2007.
21. Matthew Miller, "Gates No Longer World's Richest Man," *Forbes*, March 5, 2008; and *The World Factbook*, www.cia.gov, July 24, 2008.
22. Richard Rahn, "Running from Success," *The Washington Times*, February 18, 2008.
23. "The Keynesian Dead End," *The Wall Street Journal*, June 26–27, 2010.
24. Alina Dizik, "Social Concerns Gain New Urgency," *The Wall Street Journal*, March 4, 2010.
25. Annys Shin, "Economic Picture Bleak in Fed Report," *The Washington Post*, January 15, 2009.
26. Jason Meyers, "Innovators + The Future," *Entrepreneur*, July 2010.
27. Facebook.com, accessed July 2010.
28. An editorial in *Time*, September 17, 2007.
29. Carol Krol, "Best Buy for Business Builds Data Powerhouse," *BtoB's Lead Generation Guide*, 2008.
30. Mark Wachen, "How to Design a Winning Web Site," *Bottom Line Personal*, March 1, 2008.
31. Craigslist.com, accessed July 2010.
32. Marcia Layton Turner, "Get Sold on eBay," *Entrepreneur*, March 2008.
33. "Numbers," *Time*, May 5, 2008.
34. Jena McGregor, "Customer Service Champs," *BusinessWeek*, March 3, 2008.
35. Patrick Barwise and Sean Meehan, "Is Your Company as Customer-Focused as You Think?" *MIT Sloan Management Review*, Spring 2010.
36. Elderweb.com, accessed July 2010.
37. Bill Novelli, "The Future of Aging," *AARP Bulletin*, June 2008.
38. Andrea Cooper, "The Influencers," *Entrepreneur*, March 2008.
39. Infoplease.com, accessed July 2010.
40. Mark Gongloff, "For Economy, More Widget, Less Services?" *The Wall Street Journal*, January 6, 2009.

CHAPTER 2

1. William W. Beach, "Greater Freedom Is the Answer to Our Economic Woes," *The Washington Times*, January 28, 2010.
2. William H. Peterson, "Indexing Freedom," *The Washington Times*, February 26, 2008.
3. Tamera Nielsen, "An Unlikely Life Aquatic," *Entrepreneur*, March 2010.
4. Justin Lahart, Patrick Barta, and Andrew Batson, "New Limits to Growth Revive Malthusian Fears," *The Wall Street Journal*, March 24, 2008.
5. Daniel Fisher, "The Global Debt Bomb," *Forbes*, February 8, 2010.
6. P. J. O'Rourke, "Adam Smith: Web Junkie," *Forbes*, May 7, 2007.
7. Alex Tokarev, "Three Mighty Men," *World*, April 19/26, 2008.
8. Carol J. Loomis, "The $600 Billion Challenge," *Fortune*, July 5, 2010.
9. Alina Dizik, "Social Concerns Gain New Urgency," *The Wall Street Journal*, March 4, 2010.
10. Jack Welch and Suzy Welch, "Resolutions for the Recession," *BusinessWeek*, January 12, 2009.
11. David Kreutzer, "Supply, Demand and Prices," *The Washington Times*, April 8, 2008.
12. Romano Prodi, "To Avoid a Food Disaster," *The Washington Times*, April 27, 2008.
13. Jim Manzi, "A More Equal Capitalism," *National Review*, February 25, 2008.
14. Peter Burrows, "The SEC's Madoff Misery," *BusinessWeek*, January 12, 2009.
15. "Second City No More," *The Wall Street Journal*, March 5, 2008.
16. Steve Forbes, "Marx Would Be Impressed," *Forbes*, April 12, 2010.
17. Richard Rahn, "Running from Success," *The Washington Times*, February 18, 2008.
18. Peter Coy, "Guess Who Likes the Dollar," *Bloomberg BusinessWeek*, January 25, 2010.
19. Keith Marsden, "New Evidence on Government and Growth," *The Wall Street Journal*, June 16, 2008.
20. www.cia.gov, accessed August 12, 2008.
21. Robert J. Samuelson, "Protecting the Jobless," *Newsweek*, May 12, 2008.
22. George F. Will, "No Rational Exuberance," *Newsweek*, January 25, 2010.
23. "South Africa's Crime," *The Washington Post*, December 21, 2008.

24. Dale McFeatters, "Zimbabwe's Long Descent," *The Washington Times*, March 19, 2008.
25. Daniel Fisher, "Stagpanic," *Forbes*, February 11, 2008.
26. Robert J. Samuelson, "The Specter of Stagflation," *Newsweek*, March 3, 2008.
27. Alan Abelson, "No Place to Hide," *Barron's*, June 23, 2008.
28. Samuelson, "Specter of Stagflation."
29. James C. Cooper, "A Deflation Maelstrom in the Making," *BusinessWeek*, December 29, 2008.
30. Greg Ip, "Fears of Stagflation Return as Price Increases Gain Pace," *The Wall Street Journal*, February 21, 2008.
31. Jeffrey D. Sachs, "Stagflation Is Back. Here's How to Beat It," *Fortune*, June 9, 2008.
32. Rich Karlgaard, "The Crazy Data Decade," *Forbes*, May 10, 2010.
33. David Ranson, "Inflation May Be Worse Than We Think," *The Wall Street Journal*, February 27, 2008.
34. Spiers, "The Great Inflation Cover-Up."
35. Michael Mandel, "A Business Cycle Ends, and Many U.S. Workers Lose Ground," *BusinessWeek*, March 31, 2008.
36. George Will, "Stimulating Talk, Redux," *Newsweek*, January 28, 2008.
37. Phil Izzo, "Economists Raise the Odds of a Recession to 49%," *The Wall Street Journal*, February 7, 2008.
38. Matt Krantz, "Markets' Fall Was Worst in Seven Decades," *USA Today*, January 2, 2009.
39. Matthew Craft, "The 'D' Word," *Forbes*, March 2, 2009.
40. Knight Kiplinger, "Fuzzy Tax Talk," *Kiplinger's Personal Finance*, May 2008.
41. *OECD Factbook 2008: Economic, Environmental and Social Statistics*, www.miranda.sourceoecd.org, accessed August 12, 2008.
42. Robert J. Samuelson, "The $3 Trillion Cop-Out," *Newsweek*, February 18, 2008.
43. Debt Clock, www.brillig.com/debt_clock, accessed July 28, 2010.
44. Geoff Colvin, "The $34 Trillion Problem," *Fortune*, March 17, 2008.
45. "The Keynesian Dead End," *The Wall Street Journal*, June 26-27, 2010.
46. Gerald P. O'Driscoll Jr., " Keynes vs. Hayek: The Great Debate Continues," *The Wall Street Journal*, July 7, 2010.
47. Peter Coy, "Keynes Vs. Alesina: Alesina Who?" *Bloomberg Businessweek*, July 11, 2010.

CHAPTER 3

1. Sattar Bawany, "Transition Coaching Helps Ensure Success for Global Assignments," *Today's Manager*, December 1, 2008.
2. "World Population Clock," U.S. Census Bureau, www.census.gov/ipc/www/popclockworld.html, accessed August 5, 2010.
3. Martin Curtsinger, "Paulson Says U.S. Is Following a Policy of Robust Engagement with China on Trade Issues," AP Worldstream, June 10, 2008; and "U.S. Declines to Say China Manipulates Its Currency," *The New York Times*, May 16, 2008.
4. Reshma Kapadia and Russell Pearlman, "Ready to Roll," *Smart Money*, June 2008; and UPS, www.ups.com, accessed August 5, 2010.
5. "The Old Ball Game," *The Economist*, March 29, 2008; and William Lee Adams, "Major League Baseball's Season Opener in Japan," *Fast Company*, March 2008.
6. Brad Rock, "Jazz-Lakers Playoff Series Is Spiced with International Flavor," *Deseret News (Salt Lake City)*, May 14, 2008; and Xu Guiqi, "Something to Prove: In Modern China Sports Have Always Been Political," *The Washington Post*, May 25, 2008.
7. "A Few Good Machines," *The Economist*, March 15, 2008.
8. World Bank, www.worldbank.org, accessed January 28, 2009; and World Trade Organization, www.wto.org, accessed July 2, 2010.
9. James C. Cooper, "Strong Exports Could Mean a Weak Recession," *BusinessWeek*, April 22, 2008.
10. David Rocks, "In Praise of Not-So-Free Trade," *BusinessWeek*, March 8, 2008; Paul J. Nyden, "Wanna Trade? Markets Free People More Often Than Armies, WVU Professor Argues," *Sunday Gazette-Mail*, February 10, 2008; and Steve Forbes, "Marketing Free Trade," *Forbes*, www.forbes.com, accessed August 3, 2010.
11. Nina Easton, "Make the World Go Away," *Fortune*, February 4, 2008.
12. Thomas Palley, "Institutionalism and New Trade Theory: Rethinking Comparative Advantage and Trade Policy," *Journal of Economic Issues*, March 1, 2008.
13. "The Fragility of Perfection," *The Economist*, May 3, 2008; and Rich Miller and Simon Kennedy, "Next China Currency Shift May Help to Balance Trade," *BusinessWeek*, www.businessweek.com, accessed August 5, 2010.
14. Keith Epstein and Judith Crown, "Globalization Bites Boeing," *BusinessWeek*, March 24, 2008.
15. Matthew Bandyk, "Small Businesses Go Global," *U.S. News & World Report*, February 22, 2008; and Dan Brutto, "It's Time to Go Global," *Forbes*, www.forbes.com, accessed August 5, 2010.
16. Andy Serwer, "Starbucks Fix," *Fortune*, January 18, 2008.
17. Tropical Blossom Honey, www.tropicalblossomhoney.com, accessed January 26, 2009.
18. Transware, www.transware.com, accessed January 13, 2009.
19. Anthony Faiola, "U.S. Downturn Effects May Ease Worldwide," *The Washington Post*, January 30, 2008; and Courtney Rubin, "Obama Encourages Small Firms to Go Global," *Inc.*, Mar 15, 2010.
20. Greg Robb and Kelly Evans, "Slow Spending Helps Narrow Trade Deficit," *The Wall Street Journal*, February 15, 2008.
21. Daniel Cross, "How Pigs Saved Our Bacon," *Newsweek*, March 17, 2008.
22. Martin Crutsinger, "Trade Deficit Eased Last Year," AP Online, February 14, 2008; and Ian Talley and Tom Barkley, "U.S. Presses China Over Trade, Yuan," *The Wall Street Journal*, June 11, 2010.
23. John W. Miller, "EU Opens Probe into Dumping of Chinese Steel," *The Wall Street Journal Asia*, February 4, 2008.
24. Martin Crutsinger, "U.S. Wins Victory over China Imports," AP Online, June 21, 2008; and Pete Engardio, "China: An Early Test for Obama," *BusinessWeek*, January 12, 2009.
25. Ryan Nakashima, "Hollywood Hopes Theme Parks, Superheroes Fly in Middle East," AP Worldstream, April 22, 2008; and Amol Sharma, "Reliance, Universal Entertain Idea of U.S.-Style Theme Park in India," *The Wall Street Journal*, July 29, 2014.
26. "Lending a Hand: SBA, AICPA Partner to Help Small Businesses," *Journal of Accountancy*, May 1, 2008; and "Fiscal 2009 Appropriations: Commerce, Justice, Science," Finance Wire, April 10, 2008.
27. "SBA Chief to Highlight Small Business Trade during Portugal Visit," US Newswire, October 5, 2007; and U.S. Department of Commerce, www.doc.gov, accessed January 26, 2009.
28. Rocky Mountain Chocolate Factory, www.rmcf.com, accessed January 26, 2009.
29. "Top Franchises Named," *Reeves Journal*, March 1, 2008; and Mr. Rooter Plumbing, www.mrrooter.com, accessed January 26, 2009.
30. Orit Gadiesh and Till Vestring, "The Consequences of China's Rising Global Heavyweights," *MIT Sloan Management Review*, Spring 2008.
31. "Collision Ahead," *The Economist*, April 24, 2008.
32. Ibid.
33. Nestlé, www.nestle.com, accessed August 5, 2010.
34. Michael Mandel, "Multinationals: Are They Good for America?" *BusinessWeek*, March 10, 2008.
35. Godwin Maidment, "The Globe's New Stars," *Forbes*, March 24, 2008.

36. Ernesto Zedillo, "Governments as Global Investors," *Forbes*, May 19, 2008; Adam Schreck, "Arab Government Funds Lost Big as Markets Fell," AP Worldstream, January 14, 2009; and Howard Schneider, "U.S. Looks Abroad for Housing Help; Governments Took a Hit When the Boom Went Bust. Will They Return?" *The Washington Post*, February 16, 2010.
37. Geoff Colvin, "America for Sale," *Fortune*, February 18, 2008; and Zedillo, "Governments as Global Investors."
38. Shu-Ching Jean Chen, "Asian Carmakers Reach Primacy in U.S. Market," *Forbes*, June 4, 2008; and Bree Fowler, "Toyota Takes GM's Global Sales Crown," *St. Louis Post Dispatch*, January 23, 2009.
39. Fareed Zakaria, "The Rise of the Rest," *Newsweek*, May 12, 2008.
40. Michelle Higgins, "The Greenback Is Losing Universal Appeal," *The New York Times*, February 10, 2008; and Daryll E. Ray, "Exchange Rates Affect Export Volumes," *Southwest Farm Press*, May 4, 2010.
41. Roger Lowenstein, "If the Dollar Could Speak," *Condé Nast Portfolio*, March 2008.
42. Jack Ewing, "Dollar Daze in Europe," *BusinessWeek*, March 31, 2008.
43. H. B. Fuller, www.hbfuller.com, accessed January 27, 2009; and Superior Products, www.superiorprod.com, accessed January 27, 2009.
44. Katy Marquardt, "Frontier Markets Offer a Wild Ride," *U.S. News & World Report*, January 4, 2008.
45. Nathan Vardi, "Justice, Russian Style," *Forbes*, March 24, 2008; and Peter Burrows, "Why China Is Finally Tackling Video Piracy," *BusinessWeek*, June 9, 2008.
46. Janet Moore, "AGA Medical Fined $2 Million," *Star Tribune (Minneapolis)*, June 4, 2008; and Peter Key, "Executives at Mushriqui of Upper Darby Arrested in Foreign Bribery Sting," *Philadelphia Business Journal*, January 20, 2010.
47. Robert J. Samuelson, "Goodbye, Free Trade: Hello Mercantilism," *Newsweek*, January 7, 2008.
48. Geri Smith, "After the Smoke Clears," *BusinessWeek*, March 10, 2008; "Castro's Legacy," *The Economist*, February 23, 2008; and Paul Haven, "Some U.S. Foes Appear Ready to Give Obama a Chance," *Deseret News (Salt Lake City)*, January 26, 2009.
49. Scot Lehigh, "Smart Trade, the Clinton Way," *Boston Globe*, October 12, 2007; and Choe Sang-Hun, "Washington and Seoul Set Trade Pact," *International Herald Tribune*, July 2, 2007.
50. World Trade Organization, www.wto.org, accessed July 2, 2010.
51. Bradley S. Klapper, "New WTO Drafts Will Show Little Progress toward a Global Trade Pact," AP Worldstream, February 6, 2008.
52. "The Doha Dilemma," *The Economist*, May 31, 2008.
53. Peter Coy, "Free Trade after Doha's Collapse," *BusinessWeek*, July 31, 2008; and "WTO Chief Lamy Only Candidate for Next Term," AP Online, January 5, 2009.
54. "Chicken or Kiev?" *The Economist*, May 31, 2008; European Union, www.eu.com, accessed January 28, 2009; and Abdullah Karatash, "Is the EU's Future Deutschland Über Alles?" *BusinessWeek*, www.businessweek.com, accessed August 6, 2010.
55. Angel Perez, "Latin America/EU: Leaders Agree to Accelerate Trade Talks," International Press Service English News Wire, May 19, 2008; and Natacha Pisarenko, "Mercosur Trade Bloc Agrees to Reduce Customs Fees," www.businessweek.com, accessed, August 6, 2010.
56. Martin Arostegui, "Brazil Proposes Alliance of Latin American Nations: Security Plan Part of Larger Union without U.S.," *The Washington Times*, June 5, 2008; and "Speak Fraternally but Carry a Stick; South American Defence," *The Economist*, May 31, 2008.
57. ASEAN, www.asean.org, accessed January 27, 2009.
58. Pete Engardio, Geri Smith, and Jane Sasseen, "Refighting NAFTA," *BusinessWeek*, March 31, 2008; and Denise Bedell, "Can NAFTA Fill the Gap?" *Global Finance*, March 1, 2010.
59. Jack Welch and Suzy Welch, "A Punching Bag Named NAFTA," *BusinessWeek*, April 28, 2008.
60. Ibid.
61. Stan Modic, "Export More Goods to Produce Balance: Do Free Trade Agreements Really 'Suck' as Critic Says?" *Tooling and Production*, June 1, 2008.
62. New England Pottery, www.newenglandpottery.com, accessed January 28, 2009; and Build-A-Bear, www.buildabear.com, accessed January 28, 2009.
63. World Bank, www.worldbank.com, accessed January 27, 2009.
64. "China's Car Culture," *BusinessWeek*, June 16, 2008.
65. Joe McDonald, "Beijing Auto Show Spotlights Automakers' Hopes for China," AP Online, April 17, 2008.
66. Wal-Mart, www.walmart.com, accessed August 5, 2010.
67. "Beyond the 'Genocide Olympics,'" *The Economist*, April 26, 2008; and Diana Farrell, Janamitra Devan, and Jonathan Woetzel, "Where Big Is Best," *Newsweek International*, May 26, 2008.
68. William Triplett, "China, Russia Still Serious Piracy Threat," *Daily Variety*, April 28, 2008.
69. Tini Tran, "China's Year of the Ox Not So Bullish," AP Worldstream, January 26, 2009.
70. "What's Holding India Back?" *The Economist*, March 8, 2008.
71. Gaurav Baghuvanshi and Eric Bellman, "Wal-Mart Sets India Plans, Aims to Back Local Players," *The Wall Street Journal*, February 21, 2008.
72. Andrew Kramer, "Ford Production Cut by a Strike in Russia Action Underscores Tight Labor Market," *International Herald Tribune*, December 8, 2007; and Luca Ciferri, "Toyota's Russia Plant to Start Slowly," *Automotive News Europe*, April 30, 2008.
73. "Trouble in the Pipeline; Russia's Oil Industry," *The Economist*, May 10, 2008; and Jason Bush, "Russia's Raiders," *BusinessWeek*, June 16, 2008.
74. Bruce Einhorn, "Made in China: MRI Machines," *BusinessWeek*, May 12, 2008.
75. Geri Smith and Justin Bachman, "Flying In for a Tune-Up Overseas," *BusinessWeek*, April 21, 2008.

CHAPTER 4

1. Dan Small, "One Small Step vs. Lending Fraud," *Boston Herald*, May 21, 2008; and Herbert Jack Rotfeld, "Financial Aliteracy," *Journal of Consumer Affairs*, Summer 2008.
2. Michael D. Guttentag, Christine L. Porath, and Samuel N. Fraidin, "Brandeis' Policeman: Results from a Laboratory Experiment on How to Prevent Corporate Fraud," *Journal of Empirical Legal Studies*, June 2008; and "Legal and Ethical Violations Risks Seen Rising, But Not Resources to Control the Risk," U.S. Newswire, January 6, 2009.
3. Religious Tolerance, www.religioustolerance.org/reciproc.htm, accessed August 6, 2008.
4. Pursey P. M. A. R. Heugens, Muel Kaptein, and J. (Hans) van Oosterhout, "Contracts to Communities: A Processual Model of Organizational Virtue," *Journal of Management Studies*, January 2008; and Martha Perego, "Focus on the Fundamentals," *Public Management*, January 1, 2009.
5. U.S. Census Bureau.
6. Turn It In, www.turnitin.com; Sue R. Whittle and Deborah G. Murdoch-Eaton, "Learning about Plagiarism Using TurnItIn Detection Software," *Medical Education*, May 2008.
7. Kathy Gurchiek, "Ethics, Schmethics, U.S. Teens Say," *HR News*, February 1, 2008.
8. Jacqueline A. Burke, Ralph S. Polimeni, and Nathan S. Slavin, "Academic Dishonesty: A Crisis on Campus," *CPA Journal*, May 2007.
9. Kenneth Blanchard and Norman Vincent Peale, *The Power of Ethical Management* (New York: William Morrow, 1996).
10. Richard F. Stolz, "Taking the Lead," *Human Resource Executive*, May 16, 2007; Tom Floyed, "Executive Teams

May Benefit from Coaching on Ethics," *Boston Business Journal*, January 25, 2008; and Jeff Waller, "Creating Ethical Business Standards: Adopt a Modern Ethics Policy and Make It Public," *Alaska Business Monthly*, April 1, 2010.
11. Amy Johnson, "Practicing Good Ethics Gives Competitive Advantage," *St. Louis Business Journal*, February 29, 2008.
12. Bob Sullivan, "Can't Cancel That Service? Blame 'Perverse Incentives,'" www.redtape.msnbc.com, posted May 13, 2008; Gill Corkindale, "What the SocGen Mess Means for Your Company," *Harvard Business Online*, posted January 30, 2008; and Peter R. Kensicki, "Code-Dependent: Creating a Companywide Ethics Policy Will Spur Professionalism and Success," *Best's Review*, January 1, 2010.
13. Frank C. Bucaro, "If Good Ethics Is Good Business, What's the Problem?" *Business First*, January 4, 2008; Dave Blanchard, "How Ethical Is Your Supply Chain?" *Industry Week*, January 1, 2008; Michael Smigocki, "Complying with New Ethics Rules," *Set-Aside Alert*, February 8, 2008; Kurt A. Powell, "More Than the Math: CFOs Should Be 'People People' Too," *HRMagazine*, February 1, 2008; and Eric Krell, "How to Conduct an Ethics Audit: An Ethics Audit Can Reveal Gaps in Your Ethics Policies and Practices," *HRMagazine*, April 1, 2010.
14. Sean M. Connolly and David T. Hickey, "Codes of Conduct Don't Always Protect Reputation," *National Defense*, January 1, 2008.
15. "The Next Question," *The Economist*, January 19, 2008; Allen L. White, "Confessions of a CSR Champion," *Stanford Social Innovation Review*, January 1, 2009; and Pat Galagan, "Not Your Father's MBA," *T + D*, January 1, 2009; and "Does Corporate Social Responsibility Matter?" *Gallup Management Journal*, January 28, 2010.
16. "Just Good Business," *The Economist*, January 19, 2008; Adrienee Fox, "Be an Insider on Social Responsibility," *HRMagazine*, February 1, 2008; "A Stitch in Time," *The Economist*, January 19, 2008; Sheena Harrison, "Philanthropy Good for Business," *Crain's Detroit Business*, February 18, 2008; and Kent Byus, Donald Deis, and Bo Ouyang, "Doing Well by Doing Good: Corporate Social Responsibility and Profitability," *SAM Advanced Management Journal*, January 1, 2010.
17. Gates Foundation, www.gatesfoundation.org, accessed July 2, 2010; and Geoff Kirbyson, "Giving Good for the Soul . . . and Business," *Winnipeg Free Press*, January 14, 2009.
18. "The Feel Good Factor," *The Economist*, January 19, 2008.
19. Patagonia, www.patagonia.com, accessed September 2, 2008.
20. "Xerox Awards Six Employees Social Service Leave for 2008," Business Wire, February 11, 2008.
21. John M. Bridgeland, "Citizen Service," *The Washington Times*, February 1, 2008; and "President Bush Honors America's Armies of Compassion during National Volunteer Week Celebration," U.S. Fed News Service, April 29, 2008.
22. Samantha Marshall, "Incorporating the Cause; Gen Y Entrepreneurs Pair Profits with Philanthropy," *Crain's New York Business*, January 14, 2008.
23. Don Frischmann, "Nothing Is Insignificant When It Comes to Brand Fulfillment," *Advertising Age*, January 21, 2008.
24. Stephen Payne, "Investors Oppose SEC Proposal on Shareholder Rights," *Oil & Gas Investor*, January 1, 2008; and Clay Holtzman, "Venture Capital with a Conscience," *Washington Business Journal*, June 25, 2010.
25. Christine Hurt, "The Undercivilization of Corporate Law," *Journal of Corporation Law*, January 1, 2008; and David Mills and Robert Weisberg, "Corrupting the Harm Requirement in White Collar Crime," *Stanford Law Review*, March 1, 2008.
26. Delbert Goff, Heather Hulburt, Terrill Keasler, and Joe Walsh, "Isolating the Information Content of Equity Analysts' Recommendation Changes, Post Reg FD," *Financial Review*, May 2008; Baljit Sidhu, Tom Smith, Robert E. Whaley, and Richard H. Willis, "Regulation Fair Disclosure and the Cost of Adverse Selection," *Journal of Accounting Research*, June 2008; and Brooks Barnes, "2 Charged with Selling Insider Data from Disney," *The New York Times*, May 26, 2010.
27. David Saxby, "What Makes a Satisfied Employee?" *Rural Telecommunications*, January 1, 2008; and Dennis Huspeni, "Human Resource Personnel Balance Process, Compassion," *Denver Business Journal*, March 19, 2010.
28. Cheryl Winokur Munk, "Winning Workplaces," *Community Banker*, January 1, 2008; Andrew Thomas, "Arizona Businesses Help Employees during Economic Slump," *Arizona Capitol Times*, January 9, 2009; and Melanie Scarborough, "The Rewards of Recognition: Six Strategies for Successful Employee Programs," *Community Banker*, January 1, 2009.
29. Andrea James, "A Compassionate Look at Handling Business; Do Good, Get a 'Positive Result,' Dalai Lama Says," *Seattle Post-Intelligencer*, April 15, 2008; and Steven Greenhouse, "Inequality and Solidarity: Why a Resurgent Labor Movement Is Closer Than You Think," *Washington Monthly*, April 1, 2008.
30. Toni Nuernberg, "Not 'If,' But 'When,'" *Collector*, January 1, 2008; and Vijay R. Chemuturi, "Accounting & Assurance," *Pennsylvania CPA Journal*, January 1, 2008.
31. Heather Green and Kerry Capell, "Carbon Confusion," *BusinessWeek*, March 6, 2008.
32. Wade Vonasek and Matt Warnockm, "Green Building Movement Continues to Grow," *Wood & Wood Products*, February 1, 2008; and Timothy Burn, "Green Guru Shows Firms Way to Help Environment," *Washington Business Journal*, November 6, 2009.
33. Libby Tucker, "Need a Job? Look to Green Economy," *Daily Journal of Commerce (Portland, OR)*, June 4, 2008; "UW School of Business Forums Push 'Green Economy,'" *Capitol Times (Madison, WI)*, January 18, 2009; and American Solar Energy Society, www.ases.org, accessed July 2, 2010.
34. Matt Chandler, "Area Cool to Social Responsibility Investing," *Business First of Buffalo*, April 18, 2008; and "Kellog Company Releases First Corporate Responsibility Report," *Energy Resource*, January 13, 2009; and Social Investment Forum, www.socialinvest.org, accessed July 2, 2010.
35. Rainforest Action Network, www.ran.org, accessed August 1, 2008.
36. "Holiday Shoppers Influenced by 'Social Conscience,'" *Tampa Bay Business Journal*, December 27, 2007; and Cindy F. Crawford, "Environment Top of Mind for Holiday Shoppers," *Nashville Business Journal*, December 31, 2007.
37. "IBM Study Says Businesses Seeking Growth through Social Responsibility," *Wireless News*, February 16, 2008.
38. Min-Dong Paul Lee, "A Review of the Theories of Corporate Social Responsibility," *International Journal of Management Reviews*, March 2008.
39. Joint Initiative on Corporate Accountability and Workers' Rights, www.jo-in.org, accessed August 1, 2008.
40. Bill George, "Ethics Must Be Global, Not Local," *BusinessWeek*, February 12, 2008.
41. Hank Lindborg, "Corporations Tout Social Responsibility," *Quality Progress*, February 1, 2008.

CHAPTER 5

1. Small Business Administration, www.sba.gov.
2. Alan B. Graves, "As Your Small Business Grows, It's Time to Think about Incorporating," *San Diego Business Journal*, March 10, 2008.
3. "Why Be an Entrepreneur?" *The Washington Times*, May 12, 2008; and Trey Cox, "Common Legal Mistakes for Entrepreneurs to Avoid," *Dallas Business Journal*, July 2, 2010.

4. "Sunoco at UBS Global Oil & Gas Conference," *Fair Disclosure Wire*, May 22, 2008; and Peter Key, "Sunoco Logistics to Buy Texon Butane Blending Unit," *Philadelphia Business Journal*, June 28, 2010.
5. Adam Creighton, "Taxing Private Equity," *Policy Review*, April 1, 2008; and Marty Roos and Laura Mason, "How Your Partnership Interest May Be Used as Loan Collateral," *San Antonio Business Journal*, April 16, 2010.
6. Sarah A. Klein, "Focus: Small Business," *Crain's Chicago Business*, June 9, 2008; and Ivy Chang, "Partnerships Grow Construction Businesses," *Construction Bulletin*, January 19, 2009.
7. "Choosing a Business Structure," *Indiana Business Magazine*, March 1, 2008.
8. "California, Delaware or Nevada—Choosing Where to Incorporate," Mondaq Business Briefing, February 25, 2008.
9. Incorporate 101, http://incorporate101.com, accessed January 24, 2009.
10. Melvin Daskal, "Limited Liability Companies," *Agency Sales*, January 1, 2008; Mark E. Battersby, "Unlimited Possibilities with Limited Liability," *Air Conditioning, Heating & Refrigeration News*, January 7, 2008; and Matthew Bandyk, "Turning Your Small Business into a Corporation," *U.S. News & World Report*, March 14, 2008.
11. Legal Zoom, www.legalzoom.com, accessed January 27, 2009; and "Neveda Company Offers Free Incorporation Service to Aid Economic Recovery," U.S. Newswire, January 13, 2009.
12. Andrew Ross Sorkin, "For Merger Success, Best to Drive the Bandwagon," *International Herald Tribune*, February 27, 2008; Danielle Ulman, "Credit Crisis Led to Big Mergers and Acquisitions Decreases in 2008 in Md.," *Daily Record (Baltimore)*, January 23, 2009; and Alexandra Zendrian, "Mergers and Acquisitions Activity at the Start of This Year Was Down Significantly, but Business Is About to Pick Up," *Forbes*, www.forbes.com, accessed July 19, 2009.
13. Peter S. Goodman and Louise Story, "Price Is Right in the U.S. as Foreigners Buy Stakes Tight Credit and Weak Dollar Exploited," *International Herald Tribune*, January 21, 2008.
14. "For Five Generations, St. Louis–Based Anheuser-Busch Has Been Not Only an American Success Story But a Family-Run Business," *National Review*, July 14, 2008; Maureen Ogle, "The Belgians Want Bud? I'll Drink to That," *The Washington Post*, July 6, 2008; and Dean Foust, "Anheuser-Busch's Troubled Brew," *BusinessWeek*, July 16, 2008.
15. Michael Flaherty, "Chinese Deal Makers Get Another Hard Lesson in U.S. Dealtalk," *International Herald Tribune*, March 19, 2008.
16. Lee Conrad, "In Pursuit of the Next Whopper," *US Banker*, January 1, 2008; Terry Hill, "Franchising Outpaces Other Sectors of Economy in Growth, Jobs," *Public Record*, March 18, 2008; Tim Schooley, "More Businesspeople Looking to Franchise in Down Economy," *Pittsburgh Business Times*, May 9, 2008; and "Franchise Business to See Slow Growth in 2010: Industry Forecast Predicts Modest Increases in Jobs, Economic Growth and Number of Establishments," *Franchising World*, February 1, 2010.
17. Raymund Flandez, "A Look at High-Performing Franchises," *The Wall Street Journal*, February 15, 2008; Bethany Clough, "Road Map to Becoming Your Own Boss," *Fresno Bee*, February 28, 2008; and Samantha Maziarz Christmann, "Out of Work? Try Working for Yourself; Owning a Franchise Takes Hard Work, But Can Offer Big Rewards," *Buffalo News*, May 9, 2010.
18. UPS Store, www.theupsstore.com, accessed July 2, 2010.
19. Ian Mount, "New Franchise Rule: More Disclosure, Same High Risks," *Fortune Small Business*, February 29, 2008; Courtney Dentch, "Fewer Franchises Is Chain Reaction to Bad Economy," *Deseret News (Salt Lake City)*, January 8, 2009; and Elizabeth Cooney, "Buying into a Franchise Can Take Uncertainty out of Getting Started," *The Boston Globe* (Boston, MA), October 11, 2009.
20. Jonathan Maze, "Downward Spiral," *Franchise Times*, November/December 2007.
21. Tim Huber, "Franchisees Sue Dairy Queen over Renovation Plan," *Columbus Dispatch*, February 28, 2008; and Stewart Ain, "Want a Franchise? Do Your Homework," *Long Island Business News*, April 13, 2010.
22. Carmen Caruso and Brandi Van Leeuwen, "Communicating a Franchisor's Value without Crossing the Line," *Franchising World*, March 1, 2008; and Mary Beth Brody, "Addressing the Most Common Franchisee Claims," *Franchising World*, May 1, 2008.
23. Carlotta Mast, "Doyennes of the Digital Age," *ColoradoBiz*, February 1, 2008.
24. Tamara Holmes, "Franchising the Family," *Working Mother*, April 1, 2008; and "Woman Starts Own Business after Getting Laid Off," *Idaho State Journal*, June 13, 2010.
25. Lynne Jeter, "On the Move: Two Men and a Truck Franchisee Filling Niche," *Mississippi Business Journal*, May 26, 2008; and Two Men and a Truck, www.twomenandatruck.com, accessed January 24, 2009.
26. Anita Huslin, "Even with a Map, the Road Is Rocky," *The Washington Post*, March 24, 2008; and International Franchise Association, www.franchise.org, accessed July 2, 2010.
27. Miriam L. Brewer, "Attracting Women and Minority Franchisees," *Franchising World*, June 2008; and "The Donut Man," *The Boston Banner*, April 1, 2010.
28. Melanie Turner, "Direct Mail Company Hits Mailboxes with Four Area Franchises," *Sacramento Business Journal*, April 25, 2008.
29. Lawrence Bivins, "U.S. Franchisors Are Making Major Global Inroads," *The Wall Street Journal*, April 10, 2008.
30. McDonald's, www.mcdonalds.com, accessed July 2, 2010.
31. Bachir Mihoubi, "Expanding Your Brand Culturally," *Franchising World*, March 2008.
32. National Cooperative Business Association, www.ncba.coop, accessed January 25, 2009; and National Rural Electric Cooperative Association, www.nreca.org, accessed July 2, 2010.
33. Ibid.
34. "Cooperative to Build Distribution Center in Kenosha," *Business Journal of Milwaukee*, May 14, 2008; and "Co-op Spreads the Word," *Sun-Journal (Lewiston, ME)*, January 2, 2009.

CHAPTER 6

1. Deborah Heisz, Lisa Ocker, and K. Shelby Skrhak, "50 Greatest Entrepreneurs of All Time," *Success*, June/July 2008.
2. Jeremy Quittner, "Starting at the Bottom," *BusinessWeek*, February/March 2008; and Rick Sandella, "Marotti, An Entrepreneur and Business Owner from East Haven, Believes That the Time Has Come for Ordinary," *New Haven Register*, January 19, 2009.
3. Cindy Kibbe, "Stonyfield Institute: A Success Story," *New Hampshire Business Review*, February 29, 2008; and Matthew Bandyk, "How Entrepreneurs Make Money and Lead Happy Lives," *U.S. News & World Report*, May 30, 2008.
4. Keith McFarland, "Myth of the Fearless Entrepreneur," *Time*, June 2, 2008; "Entrepreneur Takes Kastalon to New Heights," *Rubber & Plastics News*, January 12, 2009; and Venkatesan Vembu, "Entrepreneurs Aren't Born, They're Made," *DNA: Daily News & Analysis*, May 29, 2010.
5. Michelle Simms, "Are Entrepreneurial Characteristics Inherited or Learned?" *Bellingham Business Journal*, June 1, 2008; Sarah Pierce, "Spirit of the Entrepreneur," Entrepreneur.com, February 28, 2008; Thomas Duening, "Nature vs. Nurture: Are Entrepreneurs Made, or Are They Born?" *Phoenix Business Journal*, January 18, 2009; and Karen E. Klein, "Starting a Startup," *BusinessWeek*, June 11, 2008.

6. "Living a Life You Will Love," *The Washington Times*, May 13, 2008 ; and Shara Tibken, "Before You Moonlight…," *The Wall Street Journal*, June 21, 2010.
7. "Where Others See Problems, Entrepreneurs Recognize Opportunities," *The Washington Times*, May 13, 2008; and Tennille M. Robinson, "BE Next: Fearless Young Entrepreneurs Reveal Their MVP—Most Valuable Play," *Black Enterprise*, January 1, 2009.
8. "An Idea Is Not Necessarily an Opportunity," *The Washington Times*, May 13, 2008; and Robert Celaschi, "Startup Savvy: A Little Planning Can See the Smallest Businesses through the Rough Times," *Boston Business Journal*, July 2, 2010.
9. Matthew Bandyk, "5 Things Entrepreneurs Should Know about Business Partners," *U.S. News & World Report*, May 6, 2008.
10. Bureau of Labor Statistics, www.bls.gov, accessed January 27, 2009.
11. Sue Shellenbarger, "Nice Work If You Can Get It," *The Wall Street Journal*, July 10, 2008.
12. Bureau of Labor Statistics, www.bls.gov, accessed January 27, 2009.
13. Karen Goldberg Goff, "Home-Based Virtual Staffs," *The Washington Times*, January 28, 2008; Joyce Rosenberg, "Some Small Businesses Forced to Move Back Home," *Telegraph-Herald (Dubuque, IA)*, June 22, 2008; and Spencer E. Ante, "Silicon Valley: Uh-Oh for Web 2.0," *BusinessWeek*, January 5, 2009.
14. Todd Nelson, "Work-From-Home Moms Get Balance," *Star Tribune (Minneapolis, MN)*, February 18, 2008; Lisa Druxman, "Mom's Can Have It All, They Just Can't Do It All," *Entrepreneur*, July 28, 2008; Bethany Clough, "'Mompreneurs' Find Balance in Home-Based Businesses," *Columbia Daily Tribune*, July 9, 2008.
15. Mark Brohan, "Store and Catalog Sales Stalled in 2007, but E-Commerce Roared Along as the Retail Industry's Growth Engine," *Internet Retailer*, June 2008; and 2010 Statistical Abstract, *U.S. Census Bureau*, www.census.gov, accessed July 2, 2010.
16. Chuck Soder, "Got a Good Idea? Throw It Out There," *Crain's Cleveland Business*, January 14, 2008; and Kyle Swenson, "Sales for Dummies," *All Business*, www.allbusiness.com, accessed July 2, 2010.
17. Bill Siwicki, "Selling Widgets," Internet Retailers, www.internetretailers.com, accessed January 27, 2009.
18. Farrah Gray, "Entrepreneurship: Making More Money in 2008," *New Pittsburg Courier*, January 9, 2008; Robert Cassidy, "How Well Are You Treating Your Employees?" *Building Design & Construction*, March 1, 2008; Kingsley Kanu Jr., "Showing Your Business Skills on the Job," *Black Enterprise*, June 1, 2008; and Donald L. Ariail, Gregory R. Quinet, and Robert M. Thacker, "Creating and Fostering Sustainable Intrapreneurship: A Conversation with David Gutierrez," *Journal of Applied Management and Entrepreneurship*, April 1, 2010.
19. 3M, www.3m.com, accessed January 27, 2009.
20. Carol Bidwell, " 'Skunkworks': A Secret Success Clandestine," *Daily News (Los Angeles)*, March 20, 2008.
21. "Immigration through Investment," U.S. Citizenship and Immigration Service, www.uscis.gov, accessed August 17, 2008.
22. Jeff St. John, "Enterprise Zone Pays Off for Business Owners," *Fresno Bee (Fresno, CA)*, July 6, 2008; and Mary Pat Angelini, "Enterprise Zones Are Effective Urban Aid," *The Record (Bergen County, NJ)*, July 9, 2008.
23. National Business Incubator Association, www.nbia.org, accessed July 2, 2010; Martin Cash, "Educating Entrepreneurs a Capital Idea," *Winnipeg Free Press*, January 7, 2009; and Joseph De Avila, "Varick Street Incubator Hatches City Start-Ups," *The Wall Street Journal*, May 20, 2010.
24. Small Business Administration, www.sba.gov, accessed July 2, 2010; and U.S. Census Bureau, www.census.gov, accessed July 2, 2010.
25. Simona Covel and Raymund Flandez, "Three Strategies to Get Customers to Say 'Yes,'" *The Wall Street Journal*, May 29, 2008; and Nina Wu, "Hawaii's Small Businesses Sustain Half of Private Jobs," *Honolulu Star-Bulletin*, January 24, 2009.
26. Rob Hurtt, "Thinking Big for Your Small Business," *St. Louis Business Journal*, May 9, 2008; and National Business Incubator Association, www.nbia.org, accessed July 2, 2010.
27. Small Business Administration, www.sba.gov, accessed January 27, 2009; and Martin Willoughby, "Reality Is That Every Business Will Shut Down or Be Sold," *The Mississippi Business Journal*, March 22, 2010.
28. Thomas Duening, "Many Ingredients Are Essential for Entrepreneurial Success," *Phoenix Business Journal*, May 2, 2008.
29. Chris Birk, "Small Business Owners Unfazed by Slow Economy," *St. Louis Business Journal*, May 9, 2008.
30. Matthew Bandyk, "3 Ways to Make College Pay for Young Entrepreneurs," *U.S. News & World Report*, June 6, 2008; Neal St. Anthony, "Volunteers Help Budding Entrepreneurs through Legal Thickets," *Star Tribune (Minneapolis, MN)*, January 16, 2009; and Hilary Costa, "Antioch Business Workshops Try to Keep Small Employers Afloat," *Oakland Tribune*, January 24, 2009.
31. Brad Sugars, "6 Strategies to Recession-Proof Your Startup," *Entrepreneur*, May 13, 2008.
32. Small Business Administration, www.sba.gov, accessed January 27, 2009.
33. Megan Hupp and Deborah Held Maslia, "Solid Business Plan Crucial in Securing SBA Loan," *Atlanta Business Chronicle*, June 27, 2008; and Jennifer Niemela, "Banking on Entrepreneurs, Firm Offers Flat-Rate Startup Service," *Minneapolis / St. Paul Business Journal*, July 31, 2009.
34. Matt Berkley, "Reviewing Nuts and Bolts of Business Plans," *St. Louis Business Journal*, May 9, 2008.
35. James Montgomery, "Startup Backed by Financing Plan Stands Best Chance of Success," *San Antonio Business Journal*, July 4, 2008.
36. Christopher Farrell, "How Angel Investors Get Their Wings," *Black Enterprise*, August 2008.
37. John Tozzi, "Click Here for Money," *BusinessWeek*, February/March 2008.
38. John Sviokla, "Forget Citibank—Borrow from Bob," *Harvard Business Review*, February 2009.
39. Amy Barrett, "Little Lenders," *BusinessWeek*, February/March 2008; Beth Fitzgerald, "Microloans Fill a Small-Business Cash Need," *NJBIZ*, January 12, 2009; and Joseph De Avila, "Microfinance Groups Think Big," *The Wall Street Journal*, July 6, 2010.
40. Mark Calvey, "Venture Capitalists Say Startup Community Is in Crisis," *Phoenix Business Journal*, July 2, 2008; Michael DeMasi, "The ABCs of Venture Capital," *Business Review (Albany)*, June 7, 2008; Scott Lenet and Oleg Kaganovich, "Venture Fund 101," *Sacramento Business Journal*, June 6, 2008; and John Tozzi, "The Truth about Venture Capital," *BusinessWeek*, February 1, 2008.
41. Small Business Administration, www.sba.gov, accessed August 19, 2008; Jeremy Quittner, "The Squeeze Is On," *BusinessWeek SmallBiz*, June/July 2008; Tamara E. Holmes, "Reel in the Resources," *Black Enterprise*, June 2008; David Doege, "SBA Plays Important Role with State Small Business," *Business Journal of Milwaukee*, June 6, 2008; "SBA Loan Programs," *San Diego Business Journal*, April 21, 2008; and Marshall Eckblad, "The SBA Has a Deal for You," *The Wall Street Journal*, June 21, 2010.
42. Angela Tablac, "When Credit Is Hard to Get, Micro-Loans Lend Mega-Hand," *St. Louis Post-Dispatch*, April 2, 2008.
43. National Association of Small Business Investment Companies, www.nasbic.org, accessed January 27, 2009.
44. Brad Sugars, "Top 7 Hiring Mistakes for Startups," *Entrepreneur*, June 30, 2008.
45. Stephen Baker, "Will Work for Praise," *BusinessWeek*, February 16, 2009; and Jennifer Heldt Powell, "Color Your Employees Happy," *The Boston Herald*, May 16, 2010.

46. Andreas Schwab and John Cater, "Turnaround Strategies in Established Small Family Firms," *Family Business Review*, March 1, 2008; Patricia M. Buhler, "Managing in the New Millennium," *Supervision*, March 1, 2008; and Justin Moresco, "Keeping Families in Business," *Silicon Valley/San Jose Business Journal*, June 6, 2008.
47. Christopher Hosford, "Measuring the Social," *B2B*, December 8, 2008.
48. Patrick O'Grady, "SCORE Combines Phoenix-Area Chapters into One," *Phoenix Business Journal*, July 1, 2008; Dan Reynolds, "Help for Business at a Crossroads," *San Fernando Valley Business Journal*, April 14, 2008; Tonya Layman, "SCORE Atlanta Volunteers Earn Chapter Top Award," *Atlanta Business Chronicle*, May 16, 2008; "SCORE Launches Web Site for Women Entrepreneurs," *Phoenix Business Journal*, July 15, 2008; and "SCORE Helps Create Jobs and Businesses as the Economy Recovers," *U.S. Newswire*, January 27, 2010.
49. Matthem Bandyk, "Small Businesses Go Global," *U.S. News & World Report*, February 22, 2008.
50. "Small Business Firms Fuel Trade Growth," *Manufacturing & Technology News*, June 30, 2008; and "Export Goal is a Tall Order, But Some Minnesota Firms Will Give It a Shot," *Star Tribune* (Minneapolis, MN), May 18, 2010.
51. Small Business Administration, www.sba.gov, January 27, 2009; and "Small Businesses in Kansas, Missouri, Indiana Sell to Latin American Markets, Backed by EX-IM Bank Insurance," US Fed News Service, January 21, 2009.

CHAPTER 7

1. Tamara J. Erickson, "Task, Not Time: Profile of a Gen Y Job," *Harvard Business Review*, February 2008.
2. Gary Hamel, "Moon Shots for Management," *Harvard Business Review*, February 2009.
3. Josh Quittner, "A Tech Pioneer's Newspaper Deathwatch," *Fortune*, March 3, 2008.
4. Daniel Fisher, "The Global Debt Bomb," *Forbes*, February 8, 2010.
5. Erin White and Scott Thurm, "Best CEOs Braved a Brutal Year," *The Wall Street Journal*, December 22, 2008.
6. Patrice Hill, "Top Companies Slash 70,000 Jobs in One Day," *The Washington Times*, January 27, 2009.
7. Ibid.
8. Johanna Neuman, "The Year of the (Business) Woman," *U.S. News and World Report*, Summer 2010.
9. Satish Shankar, Charles Ormiston, Nicolas Bloch, Robert Schaus, and Vijay Vishwanath, "How to Win in Emerging Markets," *MIT Sloan Management Review*, Spring 2008.
10. Beth Snyder Bulik, "Consumers to Providers: Do You Know Who I Am?" *Advertising Age*, March 10, 2008.
11. Keith R. McFarland, "Should You Build Strategy Like You Build Software?" *Sloan Management Review*, Spring 2008.
12. Bulik, "Consumers to Providers."
13. Cait Murphy, "Three Continents, Two Teams, One Goal," *Fortune*, March 3, 2008.
14. Herminia Ibarra and Otila Obodaru, "What Does It mean to Have Vision?" *Harvard Business Review*, January 2009.
15. David Ovens, "Taco Bell," *Advertising Age*, November 17, 2008.
16. Jack Welch and Suzy Welch, "The Loyalty Fallacy," *BusinessWeek*, January 19, 2009.
17. Gary Wilson, "How to Rein In the Imperial CEO," *The Wall Street Journal*, July 9, 2008.
18. Peter S. DeLisi, Dennis Moberg, and Ronald Danielson, "Why CIOs Are Last Among Equals," *The Wall Street Journal*, May 24, 2010
19. James M. Kouzes and Barry Z. Pozner, "To Lead, Create a Shared Vision," *Harvard Business Review*, January 2009.
20. Alina Dizik, "Social Concerns Gain New Urgency," *The Wall Street Journal*, March 4, 2010.
21. Paul Blow, "The Ultimate Business Makeover," *Inc.*, March 2009.
22. Katrina Pugh and Nancy M. Dixon, "Don't Just Capture Knowledge—Put It to Work," *Harvard Business Review*, May 2008.
23. Jack Welch and Suzy Welch, "Emotional Management," *BusinessWeek*, July 28, 2008.

CHAPTER 8

1. Ram Charan, "Making P&G New and Improved," *Time*, April 28, 2008.
2. Michael Mandel, "A Business Cycle Ends, and Many U.S. Workers Lose Ground," *BusinessWeek*, March 31, 2008.
3. Pankaj Ghemawat, "Finding Your Strategy in the New Landscape," *Harvard Business Review*, March 2010.
4. Roger L. Martin, "The Effective Organization," *Harvard Business Review*, July–August 2010.
5. Nadine Heintz, "In Spanish, It's Un Equipo: In English, It's a Team—Either Way, It's Tough to Build," *Inc.*, April 2008.
6. Remi Trudel and June Cotte, "Does Being Ethical Pay?" *The Wall Street Journal*, May 12, 2008.
7. Stephen H. Wildstrom, "A Stroll through the IPhone App Store," *BusinessWeek*, July 28, 2008.
8. Mark Johnson and Joe Sinfield, "Focusing on Consumer Needs Is Not Enough," *Advertising Age*, April 28, 2008.
9. John P. Kotter, "Combating Complacency," *BusinessWeek*, September 15, 2008.
10. William Underhill, "Britain's BP Problem," *Newsweek*, June 21, 2010.
11. Katrina Pugh and Nancy M. Dixon, "Don't Just Capture Knowledge—Put It to Work," *Harvard Business Review*, May 2008.
12. Ram Charan, "Stop Whining, Start Thinking," *BusinessWeek*, September 1, 2008.
13. Jena McGregor, "Customer Service Champs," *BusinessWeek*, March 3, 2008.
14. Jennifer Reingold, "Target's Inner Circle," *Fortune*, March 31, 2008.
15. Byron Reeves, Thomas W. Malone, and Tony O'Driscoll, "Online Labs," *Harvard Business Review*, May 2008.
16. Matt Vella, "White-Collar Workers Shoulder Together—Like It or Not," *BusinessWeek*, April 28, 2008.
17. Craig L. Pearce, "Follow the Leaders," *The Wall Street Journal*, July 7, 2008.
18. Anthony W. Ulwick and Lance A. Bettencourt, "Giving Customers a Fair Hearing," *Sloan Management Review*, Spring 2008.
19. David A. Garvin and Lynne C. Levesque, "The Multinational Enterprise," *Harvard Business Review*, June 2008.
20. Mike Richman, "Moving Forward at the Speed of Video," *Quality Digest*, August 2008.
21. Pete Engardio, "Mom-and-Pop Multinationals," *BusinessWeek*, July 14 and 21, 2008.
22. JoAnn Muller, "Can China Save GM?" *Forbes*, May 10, 2010.
23. Frank Ahrens, "CEO of GM Leads Lobby of Lawmakers for Loans," *The Washington Post*, September 12, 2008.
24. Alan Abelson, "Mission Impossible," *Barron's*, February 9, 2009.
25. Christopher Hosford, "Optimum Results," *BtoB*, May 5, 2008.
26. Leslie Laredo, "How Older Pros Can Transition to Digital," *Advertising Age*, March 24, 2008.
27. Tim Miner, "How Yammer Helps Me Run My Business," *Inc.*, June 2010.
28. Joseph A. De Feo and Matt Barney, "The Future of Manufacturing," *Quality Digest*, February 2008.
29. Martha E. Mangelsdorf, "A New Way to Collaborate," *Sloan Management Review*, Spring 2008.
30. Tony Hsieh, "Zappos' CEO on Going to Extremes for Customers," *Harvard Business Review*, July–August 2010.
31. Chris Meyer and Julia Kirby, "Where Does a Company's Responsibility End?" *Harvard Business Review*, July–August 2010.

CHAPTER 9

1. Michael S. Rosenwald, "Manufacturing Falls to 26-Year Low," *The Washington Post*, November 4, 2008.
2. Conor Dougherty, "Unemployment Rises in Every State," *The Wall Street Journal*, January 28, 2009.
3. Carmen M. Reinhart and Kenneth S. Rogoff, "What Other Financial Crises Tell Us," *The Wall Street Journal*, February 3, 2009.
4. Jonathan Wisman, Greg Hitt, and Nafali Bendavid, "House Passes Stimulus Package," *The Wall Street Journal*, January 29, 2009.
5. Knight Kiplinger, "Our Mighty Factories," *Kiplinger's Personal Finance*, January 2008.
6. Ibid.
7. Michael A. Fletcher, "Steel, Forging a Comeback," *The Washington Post*, May 28, 2008.
8. Ylan Q. Mui, "Ikea Helps a Town Put It Together," *The Washington Post*, May 31, 2008.
9. Matthew Boyle, "Super Bucks," *Fortune*, February 4, 2008.
10. Tom Keene, "EconoChat," *Bloomberg Businessweek*, June 21–June 27, 2010.
11. "Entrepreneur Magazine's Emerging Entrepreneur of 2009: Kelly Giard," *Entrepreneur*, January 2010.
12. Shawn Tully, "Fortune 500: Profits Bounce Back," *Fortune*, May 3, 2010.
13. Arnaud de Borchgrave, "Bandit Capitalism?" *The Washington Times*, September 18, 2008.
14. "Service-Sector Contraction Slows for 2nd Month in a Row," *The Wall Street Journal*, February 5, 2009.
15. Knight Kiplinger, "Plenty to Cheer About in Manufacturing, Too," *The Kiplinger Letter*, May 2010.
16. Joseph A. De Feo and Matt Barney, "The Future of Manufacturing," *Quality Digest*, February 2008.
17. Werner Reinartz and Wolfgang Ulaga, "How to Sell Services More Profitablly," *Harvard Business Review*, May 2008.
18. Frances X. Frei, "The Four Things a Service Business Must Get Right," *Harvard Business Review*, April 2008.
19. Werner Reinartz and Wolfgang Ulaga, "How to Sell Services More Profitably," *Harvard Business Review*, May 2008.
20. Josh Hyatt, "Keen to Be Lean," *CFO*, December 2009.
21. Forrest W. Breyfogle III, "The Future of Quality Management," *Quality Digest*, February 2008.
22. James C. Cooper, "Services: A Heavyweight in a Hard Fight," *BusinessWeek*, May 19, 2008.
23. Robin Cooper and Brian Maskell, "How to Manage through Worse-before-Better," *Sloan Management Review*, Summer 2008.
24. Jerry Feingold, "Lean Roots—A Quick History Lesson," *Quality Digest*, May 2008.
25. Dennis Sowards, "Lean Construction," *Quality Digest*, November 2007.
26. Thomas R. Cutler, "Bored by Lean," *Quality Digest*, May 2008.
27. Anita Elberse, "Should You Invest in the Long Tail?" *Harvard Business Review*, July–August 2008.
28. Jane McGregor, "At Best Buy, Marketing Goes Micro," *BusinessWeek*, May 26, 2008.
29. Michael Rubinkam, "Marketing Matriculation," *The Washington Times*, May 1, 2008.
30. "From Sea to Shining Sea," *Condé Nast Portfolio*, March 2009.
31. William Shugart, "Folly of Incentives," *The Washington Times*, January 25, 2009.
32. Jacquelyn Lynn, "Love Where You Work," *Entrepreneur*, January 2009.
33. Gabe Goldberg, "Tech That Makes Telecommuting Work," *The Washington Post*, June 1, 2008.
34. Michelle Conlin, "The Waning Days of the Road Warrior," *BusinessWeek*, June 2, 2008.
35. Luis R. Gomez-Mejia, David B. Balkin, and Robert L. Cardy, *Management* (New York: McGraw-Hill, 2008).
36. John E. West, "Buyer Beware—and in Control," *Quality Digest*, August 2008.
37. Bretta Kelly, "ISO 9001 Documentation Is Like a Box of Chocolates," *Quality Digest*, January 29, 2009.
38. S. Bala, "A Practical Approach to Lean Six Sigma," *Quality Digest*, July 2008.
39. "Baldrige Criteria—New and Improved," *Quality Digest*, February 2009.
40. John E. West, "Making Products Better," *Quality Digest*, February 2008.
41. John E. West, "Beware the Mechanical IMS," *Quality Digest*, March 2008.

CHAPTER 10

1. Cari Tuna, "In Some Offices, Keeping Workers Earns a Bonus," *The Wall Street Journal*, June 30, 2008; and Rick Brimeyer, "Motivating Employees So That They Give a Rip," *Telegraph-Herald* (Dubuque), March 15, 2010.
2. Paula Ketter, "What's the Big Deal about Employee Engagement?" *Training and Development*, January 1, 2008; "Study Finds 'Spillover Effect' from Positive Employees," *Credit Union Journal*, January 12, 2009; and Jamie Flinchbaugh, "Keys to Employee Engagement," *Assembly*, April 1, 2010.
3. Grace M. Endres, "The Human Resource Craze," *Organization Development Journal*, April 1, 2008.
4. David Wanetick, "Distinguishing Traits of Elite Performers," *Directors & Boards*, March 22, 2008.
5. Bryan Schaffer, "Leadership and Motivation," *Supervision*, February 1, 2008; and Susan Adams, "In Praise of Praise," *Forbes*, www.forbes.com, accessed July 12, 2010.
6. Nadira A. Hira, "The Making of a UPS Driver," *Fortune*, November 7, 2007.
7. Barbara Kiviat, "It's What's on the Outside That Counts," *Time*, September 3, 2007; and Bahaudin G. Mujtaba, "Becoming a Management Legend by Making History through the Hawthorne Studies," *Journal of Applied Management and Entrepreneurship*, January 1, 2008.
8. Mike Hofman, "The Idea That Saved My Company," *Inc.*, October 2007; and Joie de Vivre Hotels, www.jdvhotels.com, accessed July 2, 2010.
9. Ira Jackson, "The Drucker Difference and Toyota's Success," *Inland Valley Daily Bulletin*, July 7, 2008.
10. Leonard Karakowsky and Sara L. Mann, "Setting Goals and Taking Ownership," *Journal of Leadership & Organizational Studies*, February 1, 2008; and Steve Schumacher, "Employee Evaluation," *Rock Products*, May 1, 2010.
11. Brian Horn, "Fast Lane," *Smart Business Detroit*, March 1, 2008.
12. David Nadler and Edward Lawler, "Motivation—a Diagnostic Approach," *Perspectives on Behavior in Organizations* (New York: McGraw-Hill, 1977).
13. Carri Degenhardt-Burke, "Nice Guys Finish Successful," *On Wall Street*, March 1, 2008; Meredyth McKenzie, "Giving Employees a Voice," *Smart Business Broward/Palm Beach*, January 1, 2009; and Cameron Kauffman, "Employee Involvement: A New Blueprint for Success," *Journal of Accountancy*, May 1, 2010.
14. Mila Stahl, "Listen Up!" *Wisconsin State Journal*, April 1, 2008; and Ellen M. Heffes, "Communication with Staff: Morale-Lifter," *Financial Executive*, January 1, 2009.
15. Michael Nowicki and Jim Summers, "When Participative Management Leads to Garbled Communication," *Healthcare Financial Management*, February 1, 2008; and Erik Cassano, "Clear Communication," *Smart Business Indianapolis*, January 1, 2009.
16. Paula Ketter, "What's the Big Deal about Employee Engagement?" *Training and Development*, January 1, 2008;

17. Steven Cole Smith, "Copycat Auto Companies Bank on Pony Cars," *Pittsburgh Tribune-Review*, May 17, 2008.
18. "The Global Star Search," *Fortune*, February 4, 2008.
19. Joan Lloyd, "The Holy Grail of Motivation," *Minneapolis/St. Paul Business Journal*, January 11, 2008; and Melanie Scarborough, "The Rewards of Recognition: Six Strategies for Successful Employee Programs," *Community Banker*, January 1, 2009.
20. Jack Welch and Suzy Welch, "What's Hobbling the IRS," *BusinessWeek*, September 15, 2008; Kelly Spors, "Want to Retain Employees? Think Dogs and Free Lunch," *The Wall Street Journal*, February 15, 2009; Bob Nelson, "Find Simple Ways to Reward Employees to Get That Return on People," *Memphis Business Journal*, January 18, 2008; and Michelle Conlin, "Glum Chums? Call in the Happiness Police," *BusinessWeek*, August 25, 2008.
21. Paul Orfalea, "Ask *Inc.*," *Inc.*, June 2008.
22. "What Really Motivates," *Fortune*, February 4, 2008; and Dow Chemical Company, www.dow.com, accessed July 2, 2010.
23. Michael D. Hais and Morley Winograd, "The Boomers Had Their Day," *The Washington Post*, February 3, 2008; Kathryn Tyler, "Generation Gaps," *HR Magazine*, January 1, 2008; and David Javitch, "Motivating Gen X, Gen Y Workers," *Entrepreneur*, www.entrepreneur.com, accessed July 12, 2010.
24. Tim Shaver, "Make the Workplace Fun to Retain Your Gen X, Y Workers," *Nashville Business Journal*, March 28, 2008; Anne Houlihan, "When Gen-X Is in Charge," *Supervision*, April 1, 2008; and Athima Chansanchai, "To Him, Gen X Still Marks the Spot," *Seattle Post-Intelligencer*, April 9, 2008.
25. Jaclyn C. Stevenson, "Managing the 'Millennials,'" *BusinessWeek*, February 18, 2009; and James Kimberly, "Are You Ready for the Next Generation of Workers?" *New Hampshire Business Review*, January 2, 2009.
26. Rebecca R. Hastings, "Millennials Expect a Lot from Leaders," *HR Magazine*, January 1, 2008; "Generation Y Goes to Work," *The Economist*, January 3, 2009; and Patricia Quinn, "A Multigenerational Perspective on Employee Communications," *Risk Management*, January 1, 2010.
27. Colin Simpson, "A New Work Force Wave," *Bellingham Business Journal*, June 1, 2008; Kinglsey Kanu Jr. "Here's What I'm Looking For!" *Black Enterprise*, April 2008; and Kathryn Yeaton, "Recruiting and Managing the 'Why?' Generation," *CPA Journal*, April 1, 2008.
28. Robert Rodriquez, "Millennials on Board," *Fresno Bee*, April 20, 2008; and Mark Szakonyi, "Different Generations Require Different Feedback, Motivation," *Jacksonville Business Journal*, January 4, 2008.

CHAPTER 11

1. Erin White, "HR Departments Get New Star Power at Some Firms," *The Wall Street Journal*, June 23, 2008; and J. Bret Becton and Mike Schraeder, "Strategic Human Resources Management: Are We There Yet?" *Journal for Quality and Participation*, January 1, 2009.
2. Matthew D. Breitfelder and Daisy Wademan Dowling, "Why Did We Ever Go into HR?" *Harvard Business Review*, July–August 2008; Marcia A. Reed-Woodard, "The People Advantage: An HR Executive Employs a New Company Strategy," *Black Enterprise*, February 1, 2009; and Bill Taylor, "Why We (Shouldn't) Hate HR," *Harvard Business Review*, www.hbr.org, accessed July 14, 2010.
3. Richard Epstein, "Understanding Immigration and Trade: What Will a Shortage of Skilled Labor Do to the U.S.?" *Chief Executive*, April 1, 2008; and "IT Shortage Worries Businesses, Educators," Associated Press, June 24, 2008.
4. Bill Berry, "Memo to Workers: You're on Your Own, Suckers," *Capital Times (Madison, WI)*, June 10, 2008; and "Unionization Bill May Require HR to Hone Skills in Labor Relations," *Workforce Management*, January 19, 2009.
5. Joel E. Anderson, "Help Wanted," *Arkansas Business*, January 28, 2008.
6. Anton Troianovski, "Skilled Trades Seek Workers," *The Wall Street Journal*, August 19, 2008; and Mark Anderson, "Workers Needed: Retiring Baby Boomers Will Leave Shortage of Skilled Trades People," *Wisconsin State Journal*, August 3, 2008.
7. Gina Chen, "Faces of Fatherhood: These Dads Talk about Life as a Parent," *Post-Standard (Syracuse, NY)*, June 15, 2008; and Maryann Tan, "Flexibility at Work on the Rise," *Financial Adviser*, September 25, 2008.
8. Karen Springen, "Cutting Back Your Hours," *Newsweek*, May 12, 2008.
9. Tara Weiss, "Layoff Lessons," *Forbes*, September 9, 2008.
10. Joshua Zumbrun, "Help Wanted," *Forbes*, March 27, 2008.
11. Armstrong Williams, "Should Black People Let Affirmative Action Die? Yes. (Two Sides)," *Ebony*, January 1, 2008; Ellis Cose, "Should Black People Let Affirmative Action Die? No. (Two Sides)," *Ebony*, January 1, 2008; and Judy Greenwald, "More Pro-Employee Laws on the Way?" *Business Insurance*, February 8, 2010.
12. Elizabeth Stull, "Cornell University Law Professors Report; Discrimination Suits Declining in Federal Court," *Daily Record (Rochester, NY)*, September 25, 2008.
13. John Anderson, "When Will They Ever Get It? Employment Law Compliance Is Not an Option," *Business First of Louisville*, February 15, 2008.
14. Leadership Conference on Civil Rights and Leadership Conference on Civil Rights Education Fund, www.civilrights.org, accessed February 17, 2009; and Becky Gillette, "Strong ADA Provisions Go into Effect This Year," *Mississippi Business Journal*, January 5, 2009.
15. Leadership Conference on Civil Rights and Leadership Conference on Civil Rights Education Fund, www.civilrights.org, accessed February 17, 2009; and Anjanette Riley, "Expansion of ADA Law Expected to Cause Windfall of Claims," *Arizona Capitol Times*, January 9, 2009.
16. Suzanne Robitaille, "Support Grows for Disabled Job Seekers," *The Wall Street Journal*, July 22, 2008.
17. Maggie Jackson, "Job Market Wasted on the Young: In an Aging Society, Mature Workers Still Get Passed Over," *Boston Globe*, July 27, 2008.
18. "How to Find and Recruit the Best Hourly Employees," Business Wire, June 24, 2008.
19. Lee Froschheiser, "Business Recruitment Fundamentals: How to Onboard More 'A' Players," *Supervision Magazine*, July 1, 2008.
20. "Leveraging Social Networks within the Current Job Market," Business Wire, September 25, 2008; Steven E.F. Brown, "Survey: Social Networks Top Hiring Tool," *San Francisco Business Times*, June 30, 2010; and Susan Adams, "Expert Tips for Using LinkedIn," *Forbes*, www.forbes.com, accessed July 14, 2010.
21. "Winn-Dixie Extends Use of Kronos Solution," *Food & Beverage Close-Up*, February 12, 2008.
22. Kronos, http://talent.kronos.com, accessed February 17, 2009.
23. Carol A. Dawson, "Serious Warning: Do Not Ask a Pregnant Woman Whether She Is Pregnant," *Business First of Louisville*, May 9, 2008.
24. Allen Smith, "Experts: Tests, Job Steering Raise Flags," *HRMagazine*, June 1, 2008.
25. Chuck Thompson, "Standard Should Not Have Been Applied to Hearing Test," *HR Magazine*, March 1, 2008; and Jim Rendon, "10 Things Human Resources Won't Say," *SmartMoney Magazine*, www.smartmoney.com, accessed July 14, 2010.

26. Lexis Nexis, www.lexisnexis.com/screenapplicants, accessed February 17, 2009; and Judy Stringer, "Background Checks; They're Vital to Finding Dishonest Job Seekers," *Tire Business*, January 5, 2009.
27. Morey Stettner, "Select Top Job Candidates While Screening Out Duds," *Investors Business Daily*, September 15, 2008; and "Avoid Hiring That Bad Apple . . . ," *Credit Management*, February 1, 2009.
28. Dr. John Sullivan, "A Flexible Force," *Workforce Management*, July 14, 2008; and Leslie Rose McDonald, "Maximize Contingent Workers," *Post-Standard (Syracuse, NY)*, February 7, 2009.
29. Angela Tablac, "Temp Workers," *St. Louis Post Dispatch*, January 16, 2008.
30. Kathryn Tyler, "Treat Contingent Workers with Care," *HR Magazine*, March 1, 2008.
31. Ibid.
32. Randstad, www.randstad.com, accessed February 17, 2009.
33. Vicki Swisher, "Using the Company as the Classroom," *BusinessWeek*, June 4, 2008; Marilyn Gardner, "Learn While You Earn," *Christian Science Monitor*, August 11, 2008; and Charley Hannagan, "Raising the Standard of Service: Turning Stone Refocuses Employees on Training, Quality," *Post-Standard (Syracuse, NY)*, February 12, 2009.
34. Mike Neag, "Great Starts: Orientation Ovation," *Training Magazine*, September 16, 2008; Aparna Nancherla, "Money Matters, but Training Doesn't?" *T + D*, February 1, 2009; and "Aflac Named to Computerworld's List of 100 Best Places to Work in IT," *Computer Weekly*, July 8, 2010.
35. Anton Troianovski, "Skilled Trades Seek Workers," *The Wall Street Journal*, August 19, 2008.
36. Harvey Meyer, "Apprenticeships Enable Small Firms to Grow Their Own Skilled Employees," *Costco Connection*, August 2008.
37. "Explanation of Words Used in the E-Learning Guide," *U.S. News & World Report*, October 1, 2008.
38. "Be Ready for Next Disaster," *St. Joseph News Press*, September 8, 2008; and Red Cross, www.redcross.org/flash/brr/English-flash/default.asp, accessed February 17, 2009.
39. Steve Hamm, "Aperian: Helping Companies Bridge Cultures," *BusinessWeek*, September 5, 2008; and Aperian Global, www.aperianglobal.com, accessed February 17, 2009.
40. Becky Gillette, "Companies Turn to Web-Casting to Save Time, Money," *Mississippi Business Journal*, January 21, 2008.
41. Marshall Goldsmith, "E-Tools That Help Teach Leadership," *BusinessWeek*, September 2, 2008; and Diana Middleton, "Want to Know Which Training Works? Take This Course," *The Wall Street Journal*, www.wsj.com, accessed July 15, 2010.
42. Scott Walker, Jerry Davis, and Desai Deepesh, "Postural Assignments & Job Rotation: A Survey of One Company's Assembly Line Supervisors," *Professional Safety*, February 1, 2008.
43. "Big Bite; American History," *The Economist*, April 26, 2008; and McDonald's, www.mcdonald's.com, accessed February 17, 2009.
44. Brad Karsh, "What Does 'Networking' Really Mean?" *Advertising Age*, September 22, 2008.
45. Julie Bird, "Proper Mentor Unlocks Mentee's Potential," *Charlotte Business Journal*, March 14, 2008; and Beth N. Carvin, "The Great Mentor Match," *T + D*, January 1, 2009.
46. Hispanic Alliance for Career Enhancement, www.hace-usa.org, accessed February 17, 2009.
47. Monte Jade, www.montejade.org, accessed February 17, 2009; and Sulekha, www.sulekha.com, accessed February 17, 2009.
48. Laura Weiner, "GM a Leader in Corporate Diversity since 1968," *Crain's Detroit Business*, May 12, 2008.
49. Anthony J. Kubica, "Transitioning Middle Managers," *Healthcare Executive*, March 1, 2008.
50. Bill Boyar, "Compensation Should Be Viewed as a Strategic Asset, Not an Expense," *Houston Business Journal*, November 9, 2007; Stephen D. Kirkland, "Compensation Plans That Pay Back," *Business and Economic Review*, January 1, 2009; and Dave Willmer, "8 Ways to Keep Your Best Workers on Board," *Computerworld,* computerworld.com accessed July 15, 2010.
51. Cari Tuna, "Pay, Your Own Way: Firm Lets Workers Pick Salary," *The Wall Street Journal*, July 7, 2008.
52. Matt Botch, "Rewarding the Team: Make Sure Team-Oriented Compensation Plans Are Designed Carefully," *HR Magazine*, February 1, 2007.
53. Ibid.
54. Paul Fronstin and Stephanie Blakely, "Is the Tipping Point in Health Benefits Near?" *The Wall Street Journal*, April 22, 2008; Josh Heck, "Study: Health Insurance Accounts for 8 Percent of Total Employee Compensation," *Wichita Business Journal,* June 9, 2010; and "Employee Compensation Averages $29.39 an Hour," *Charlotte Business Journal*, June 12, 2010.
55. Colleen Diskin, "Flexible Schedules Can Pay Off for Employers, Too," *The Record (Bergen County, NJ)*, May 28, 2008; and Sarah E. Needleman, "Should a Business Offer Paid Maternity Leave?" *The Wall Street Journal*, www.wsj.com, accessed July 14, 2010.
56. Jeffrey M. O'Brien, Patricia Neering, and Christopher Tkaczyk, "100 Best Companies to Work for in 2008," *Fortune*, February 4, 2008.
57. Taylor Mallory, "May I Handle That for You? Companies That Will Take Payroll—and the Rest of the HR Department—Off Your Plate," *Inc.*, March 2008.
58. Colleen Diskin, "Flexible Schedules Can Pay Off for Employers, Too," *The Record (Bergen County, NJ)*, May 28, 2008.
59. Lori Aratani, "Flextime Has Green Appeal and Lures Younger Workers," *The Washington Post*, August 23, 2008.
60. Lydia Saad, "Telecommuting Still a Rare Perk; No Increase in 2006 in Percentage Punching In from Home," Gallup Poll News Service, August 15, 2008; and Rachel Kenshalo, "Evolving Office Technologies: Telecommuting, Conserving Energy and Resources," *Alaska Business Monthly*, February 1, 2010.
61. Karen Kroll, "Finding a Cure for Your Real Estate Blues," *Business Finance*, August 1, 2008.
62. Tom Albin, "Adjustable Shared Workstations: Savings on the Move," *Buildings Magazine*, May 1, 2008.

CHAPTER 12

1. "Union History Lesson," *Bangor Daily News*, June 16, 2008.
2. Kevin O'Marah, "The Real Threat to U.S. Manufacturing," *Forbes*, April 23, 2008; and Steven Greenhouse, "Union Membership Up Sharply in 2008, Report Says," *New York Times*, January 29, 2009.
3. Nina Easton, "America Sours on Free Trade," CNNMoney.com, accessed April 8, 2009; and Rich Rovito, "End of the Line for Rockwell Union," *The Business Journal of Milwaukee*, www.bizjournals.com, accessed July 16, 2010.
4. Nick Coleman, "Union Busting Thrives in Office of Labor-Backed Attorney General," *Star Tribune (Minneapolis)*, May 29, 2008; and George Pyle, "Value of Labor Unions Depends On Reference Point: New York Leads U.S. in Percentage of Organized Workers," *Buffalo News*, February 28, 2010.
5. Robert J. Samuelson, "Globalization's Achilles' Heel," *Newsweek*, July 21, 2008.
6. Steve Elbow, "State Responds to Report Alleging Sweatshop Contracts," *Capital Times (Madison, WI)*, July 1, 2008; and Alec MacGillis, "Troubles in Service Workers' Union May Dim Hopes for Labor," *The Washington Post*, January 9, 2009.

7. Francine Knowles, "Union Dogfight at United: Teamsters Push to Represent Airline's Mechanics," *Chicago Sun-Times*, December 4, 2007.
8. Mark Lewis, "The History of Labor Day," *Forbes*, August 3, 2007; "Strikes and Brawls," *Current Events*, February 25, 2008; and Murray Weidenbaum, "Unions Rarely Miss Their Payday," *USA Today*, March 1, 2010.
9. AFL-CIO, www.afl-cio.org, accessed February 10, 2009.
10. "Greg Tarpinian to Step Down as Change to Win Executive Director," *U.S. Newswire*, May 27, 2008; and Jeffrey Krasner, "Caritas and SEIU Reach Accord Deal Paves Way for Union Effort," *Boston Globe*, January 27, 2009.
11. AFL-CIO, www.aflcio.org, accessed July 2, 2010.
12. Brian Wingfield, "Supreme Court Favors Business, Again," *Forbes*, June 19, 2008.
13. "Nonunion Coal Companies Offer Individual Contracts to Miners as Coal Prices Double," AP Worldstream, May 1, 2008.
14. Andy Lewis, "Labor Unions Poised for a Resurgence with Change in Tactics," *Register Guard (Eugene, OR)*, July 1, 2008.
15. Jane Sasseen, "Labor Elections: Why Obama May Disappoint the Unions," *BusinessWeek*, February 2, 2009; GovTrack, www.govtrack.us, accessed July 2, 2010; and "Employee Free Choice Act Sounds Too Good to Be True," *The Beacon News* (Aurora, Illinois), May 5, 2010.
16. Matthew Cooper, "Labor Pains," *Condé Nast Portfolio*, February 2009.
17. Brian Wingfield, "Fears of a Union Renaissance," *Forbes*, June 5, 2008.
18. Pete Engardio, Geri Smith, and Jane Sasseen, "What You Don't Know about NAFTA," *BusinessWeek*, March 19, 2008.
19. Jack Markowitz, "Volkswagen Speeds Away from Pa.," *Tribune Review/Pittsburgh Tribune*, July 20, 2008.
20. Sholnn Freeman, "Rail Strike Averted as Amtrak, Unions Reach Tentative Deal," *The Washington Post*, January 19, 2008.
21. National Mediation Board, www.nmb.gov, accessed September 10, 2008; Liz Fedor, "Mediation Board Declares Delta, NWA a Single System," *Star Tribune (Minneapolis, MN)*, January 8, 2009; and "Teamsters Union Requests That NMB Release UPS Aircraft Mechanics from Mediation and Begin Countdown to Potential Strike," *Journal of Transportation*, June 19, 2010.
22. "Allied Pilots Association Calls on National Mediation Board to Expedite Negotiations with American Airlines," US Newswire, May 1, 2008.
23. Al Baker and Steven Greenhouse, "Arbitration Panel Gives Raise to City Police," *The New York Times*, May 20, 2008; and Kimberly Atkins, "U.S. Supreme Court Considers Labor Contract Arbitration," *Lawyers USA*, January 20, 2010.
24. American Arbitration Association, www.adr.org, accessed March 2, 2009.
25. Steven Greenhouse, "Teamsters and U.P.S. Reach Deal on Pensions," *The New York Times*, October 1, 2007.
26. Troy Anderson, "Filming Hits High," *Press-Telegram (Long Beach, CA)*, July 17, 2008.
27. Howard Schweber, "Epic's Power Should Not Be Used to Silence Others," *Capital Times (Madison WI)*, July 9, 2008; and Joseph Lawrence, "As Unions Fall, Lawsuits Rise," *In These Times*, May 1, 2008.
28. Corey Masisak, "NHL's Cup Runneth Over: Final Matchup Is Ideal for Showcasing League," *The Washington Times*, May 21, 2008; John Jackson, "Another Lockout on Horizon?" *Chicago Sun-Times*, February 1, 2009; and Alan Schwarz, "Offering Grim Picture, Union Chief Says Teams Are Preparing for '11 Lockout," *The New York Times*, February 5, 2010.
29. Charley Reese, "Free-Market Economies Are Killing Unions," *Columbia Daily Tribune*, July 18, 2008.
30. Richard Newman, "Air Travails," *The Record (Bergen County, NJ)*, May 4, 2008; and Steve Pearlstein, "A Sacred Cow in the Cockpit," *The Washington Post*, March 21, 2008.
31. Kendra Marr and Peter Whoriskey, "GM, Chrysler Struggling to Strike UAW Deal," *The Washington Post*, February 14, 2009; and Thomas Hartley, "GM Seeks Delphi Givebacks," *Business First of Buffalo*, January 21, 2010.
32. Ken Thomas, "UAW Membership Drops Below 500,000," AP Online, March 29, 2008; and "UAW Membership Falls by 14 Percent," *Columbia Daily Tribune*, March 31, 2008.
33. Steven Greenhouse, "Union Membership Sees Biggest Rise since '83," *The New York Times*, January 26, 2008; and U.S. Bureau of Labor Statistics, www.bls.gov, accessed July 2, 2010.
34. Sam Hananel, "Union Membership Rises for a Second Year," *USA Today*, January 28, 2009.
35. National Education Association, www.nea.org, accessed February 10, 2009.
36. Kevin O'Marah, "The Real Threat to U.S. Manufacturing," *Forbes*, March 4, 2008; and Chris Rauber, "Rival Unions Trade Charges on Election to Represent 45,000 Kaiser Workers," *San Francisco Business Times*, July 14, 2010.
37. Matthew Miller, "Celebrity Star Power," *Forbes*, June 30, 2008.
38. Barry Burr, "CEO Compensation Up by 12.7% in '07: Increase Below Previous Year's Median Hike Although S&P 500 Firms Saw Bigger Gains," *Pensions and Investments*, January 7, 2008; Kurt Badenhausen, "The World's Highest Paid Athletes," *Forbes*, www.forbes.com, accessed July 2, 2010; and Douglas McIntyre, "Larry Ellison's $84 Million Makes Him 2009's Highest Paid CEO," *Daily Finance*, www.dailyfinance.com, accessed July 2, 2010.
39. Joann S. Lublin, "Boards Flex Their Pay Muscles," *The Wall Street Journal*, April 14, 2008.
40. Scott DeCarlo, "Top-Paid CEOs," *Forbes*, April 30, 2008; and Katharine Grayson, "General Mills CEO Powell Received $12.3M in '10," *Minneapolis/St. Paul Business Journal*, July 21, 2010.
41. Rachel Beck, "Wall Street CEOs Should Return Bloated Bonuses," *Telegraph-Herald (Dubuque)*, July 13, 2008.
42. Allan Sloan, "The Lurches of Lehman," *The Washington Post*, June 24, 2008; and Josh Fineman, "Lehman Employees Lost $10 Billion," *The Washington Post*, June 14, 2008.
43. John Cassidy, "The C.E.O.'s New Armor," *Condé Nast Portfolio*, June 2008.
44. John Swartz, "I'm Asking Nicely: Please Show Me the Door," *The New York Times*, January 13, 2008.
45. Carol Hymowitz, "Pay Gap Fuels Worker Woes," *The Wall Street Journal*, April 28, 2008; Chuck Collins, "Put a Cap on Runaway CEO Pay," *The Record (Bergen County, NJ)*, February 4, 2009; and Mark E Aldrich and Michael More Delune, "Navigating Through Executive Compensation Rules Under Tarp," *Orange County Business Journal*, February 22, 2010.
46. "Pay Attention," *The Economist*, June 14, 2008; and "Let the Fight Begin," *The Economist*, June 14, 2008.
47. Phred Dvorak, "Firms Measure a CEO's (Net) Worth," *The Wall Street Journal*, June 23, 2008, p. B-1; and Jack Welch and Suzy Welch, "CEO Pay: No Easy Answer," *BusinessWeek*, July 14, 2008.
48. Cari Tuna, "Shareholders to Focus on Executive Compensation," *The Wall Street Journal*, January 12, 2009.
49. Mark Gongloff and Craig Karmin, "Shareholders Bring the Heat on Executive Pay," *The Wall Street Journal*, April 8, 2008; and Daniel J. Ryterband, "Dodd-Frank: What It Means for Comp and Governance," *BusinessWeek*, www.businessweek.com, accessed July 22, 2010.
50. Harriett Rubin, "Weren't We Supposed to Be Beyond This by Now? After Years of Progress Women's Gains at Work Have Come to a Baffling Halt," *Condé Nast Portfolio*, April 2008; Lyric Wallwork Winik and Meg Massey, "A New Push for Equal Pay," *Parade*, January 18, 2009; Institute for Women's Policy Research, www.iwpr.org, accessed July 2, 2010; and Tara Siegel Bernard, "A Toolkit for Women Seeking a Raise," *The New York Times*, May 14, 2010.
51. Roger Clegg, "Equal Rights Nonsense," *The Wall Street Journal*, February 9, 2008.

52. Rubin, "Weren't We Supposed to Be Beyond This by Now?"; and "Another Shot at Pay Equity," *Boston Globe*, January 8, 2009.
53. Erica Williams, "The Economic Status of Women in Michigan: Wide Disparities by Race and Ethnicity," *Briefing Paper Series*, September 1, 2007.
54. "President Obama Signs Ledbetter Fair Pay Act, Placing New Burdens on Employers," *Mondaq Business Briefing*, February 9, 2009.
55. Shirley Williams and Harsh K. Luthar, "DOTA's Software Re-Engineering Group: What's Going On in Your Department, Jimmy?" *Journal of the International Academy for Case Studies*, November 1, 2008.
56. Equal Employment Opportunity Commission, www.eeoc.gov, accessed September 10, 2008; and Adam Liptak, "Court Expands Ability to Sue in Sexual Harassment Investigations," *The New York Times*, January 27, 2009.
57. "Holding Back Women Can Carry Huge Cost: Companies End Up Paying for Their Bad Behavior," *Chicago-Sun Times*, October 4, 2007.
58. Chris Woodyard, "Toyota to Review Conduct Policies," *USA Today*, May 12, 2006.
59. Dina Bakst, "Equal Pay for Mother's Day," *Forbes*, May 8, 2008.
60. *Working Mother*, www.workingmother.com, accessed September 10, 2008; and Andy Lewis, "Family Leave Law Changes Create New Challenges for Employers," *Register Guard (Eugene, OR)*, January 1, 2009.
61. Nadine Heintz, "Can I Bring the Kids?" *Inc.*, June 2004; and Guerra DeBerry Coody, www.gdc-co.com, accessed February 15, 2009.
62. Bright Horizons, www.brighthorizons.com, accessed July 2, 2010.
63. U.S. Department of Commerce, www.commerce.gov, accessed February 17, 2009.
64. Loren Faulkner, "Keeping the Old, Recruiting the New," *California Builder and Engineer*, November 19, 2007; and Anya Martin, "Geriatric-Care Manager May Be Useful To Families," *Deseret News* (Salt Lake City), February 16, 2010.
65. Amy Joyce, "Caring for Dear Old Dad Gets a Little Easier: More Companies Are Offering Benefits," *The Washington Post*, March 4, 2007; and Towers-Watson, www.towerswatson.com, accessed July 2, 2010.
66. Martin Shannon, "Sandwich Generation Survival Skills," *Forbes*, July 25, 2007; and Jennifer Shaw, "Finding Balance Critical for Caregivers," *Oakland Tribune*, January 6, 2009.
67. Marilyn Blake, "Creating a Drug-Free Workplace: Sobering Facts That May Impact Your Safety Efforts," *Rural Telecommunications*, July 1, 2005.
68. Beth Gorczyca Ryan, "Workplace Dilemma," *State Journal*, August 31, 2007.
69. Nick Bajzek, "Testing, Testing," *Professional Builder*, January 1, 2008.
70. Peter Cholakis and Mari Ryan, "Hurting the Bottom Line," *Occupational Safety and Health*, June 2007.
71. Chuck Mannila, "How to Avoid Becoming a Workplace Violence Statistic," *T + D Magazine*, July 1, 2008.
72. Ibid; and Teresa Long, "Workplace Violence: Can Put Your Company at Risk," *EHS Today*, June 1, 2010.
73. Amy Joyce, "Office Awareness Can Head Off Abuse at Home," *The Washington Post*, May 6, 2007.
74. Mind bridge, www.mindbridgebpo.com, accessed February 15, 2009.
75. U.S. Bureau of Labor Statistics, www.bls.gov, accessed February 17, 2009.

CHAPTER 13

1. John Q. Quelch and Katherine E. Jocz, "Marketing, Much Like Democracy, Is Good for You (Yes, Really)," *Advertising Age*, February 11, 2008; and The American Marketing Association's Marketing Power, www.marketingpower.com, accessed July 2010.
2. Michael S. Malone, "Taking On the World," *The Wall Street Journal*, April 5–6, 2008.
3. Frank T. Rothaermel, "Are You 'Pushing' in a 'Pull' World?" *Sloan Management Review*, Spring, 2010.
4. Michael Rubincam, "Marketing Matriculation," *The Washington Times*, May 1, 2008.
5. David Crokindale, "Mistakes Marketers Make," *The Wall Street Journal*, October 20, 2008.
6. Riva Richmond, "A Start-Ups Tale, Tweet by Tweet," *The Wall Street Journal*, September 28, 2009; and Emily Steel and Geoffrey A. Fowler, "Facebook Touts Selling Power of Friendship," www.wsj.com, accessed July 26, 2010.
7. Paul Sharma, "Advertising in the New Online World," *The Wall Street Journal*, July 14, 2010.
8. Ian Schafer, "We Better Start Monetizing Social Media Before It's Too Late," *Advertising Age*, May 5, 2008.
9. Dave Rich, "The New Normal: Your Customer Is in the Driver's Seat," www.forbes.com, accessed July 26, 2010.
10. Mark Johnson and Joe Sinfield, "Focusing on Consumer Needs Is Not Enough," *Advertising Age*, April 28, 2008.
11. Jerry Wind, "A Plan to Invent the Marketing We Need Today," *Sloan Management Review*, Summer 2008.
12. Mary E. Morrison, "Relationships Pay Dividends," *BtoB's Vertical Insight Guide*, 2008.
13. Eric Schneider, "Keep Customers by Maintaining Dialogue," *Advertising Age*, January 26, 2009.
14. Adrienne Graham, "Want to Succeed with Social Media? Get a Solid Strategy in Place First," www.forbes.com, accessed July 26, 2010.
15. Kate Maddox, "Marketers Look to Boost Customer Retention," *BtoB*, May 5, 2008.
16. Mikal E. Belicove, "A Community of One's Own," *Entrepreneur*, March 2010.
17. Steve Garmhausen, "Growing a Green Business," *Black Enterprise*, April 2008.
18. Jeffrey Smith, "Honda: Why We Chose Our New Home in Indiana," *The Wall Street Journal*, October 19, 2007.
19. Happycow.net, accessed June 2010.
20. Melanie Dabovich, "Farm Fertilizers Go Green," *The Washington Times*, June 20, 2008.
21. Ali McConnon, "No Bird in This Bucket," *BusinessWeek*, July 7, 2008.
22. Paola Singer, "'Vegetarians Have a Stake in Buenos Aires," *The Washington Post*, May 18, 2008.
23. Tom Marin, "Building a Better Brand: 5 Steps to Improve Identity of Goods, Services," *Orlando Business Journal*, December 11, 2009.
24. Doug Fuehne, "Using Pricing as a Competitive Advantage," *Industry Week*, May 1, 2010.
25. Geoff Colvin, "For Some Businesses, the Higher Price Is Right," *The Washington Post*, February 10, 2009.
26. Heather Clancy, "Web Sight Shipping 2.0," *Entrepreneur*, April 2008.
27. Mary E. Morrison, "Relationships Pay Dividends," *BtoB's Vertical Insight Guide*, 2008.
28. Maxine Clark, "Is the Customer Always Right?" *Inc.*, July 2008.
29. "Marketers Lag in Tracking Customers," *BtoB*, February 9, 2009.
30. Jack Neff, "Making Market Research Cool," *Advertising Age*, April 28, 2008.
31. Matthew Bandyk, "Now Even Small Firms Can Go Global," *U.S. News & World Report*, March 10, 2008.
32. Kelly Johnson, "Small Businesses Talk Social Media Strategy, Results," *Sacramento Business Journal*, May 7, 2010.
33. Matthew Creamer, "Consumers Curtail Consumption," *Advertising Age*, October 6, 2008.
34. Anita Elberse, "Should You Invest in the Long Tail?" *Harvard Business Review*, July–August 2008.
35. Erik K. Clemons, Paul F. Nunes, and Matt Reilly, "Six Strategies for Successful Niche Marketing," *The Wall Street Journal*, May 24, 2010.

CHAPTER 14

1. Alex Taylor III, "Hyundai Smokes the Competition," *Fortune*, January 18, 2010.
2. Emily Bryson York, "McD's Secret Sauce: It Embodies Value," *Advertising Age*, February 2, 2009.
3. Paul Ziobro, "Restaurants Push 'Value' Meals," *The Wall Street Journal*, October 1, 2008.
4. Patrick Barwise and Sean Meehan, "Is Your Company as Customer-Focused as You Think?" *MIT Sloan Management Review*, Spring 2010.
5. Rick Newman, "Road Testing Cars of the Future," *U.S. News & World Report*, April 2009.
6. James Skinner, "Hate the Food, Love the Stock?" *SmartMoney*, August 2008.
7. John Cloud and Oak Brook, "McDonald's Has a Chef?" *Time*, February 22, 2010.
8. Emily Bryson York, "Mc D's Secret Sauce."
9. Emily Bryson York, "Value Menus Cost Operators Dearly," *Advertising Age*, March 31, 2008.
10. Janet Adamy, "Wendy's Raises Its Coffee Profile," *The Wall Street Journal*, September 8, 2008.
11. Paul Ziobro and Janet Adamy, "Credit Crunch Squeezes Franchisees," *The Wall Street Journal*, September 29, 2008.
12. Emily Bryson York, "Starbucks' Surprise Success: Oatmeal," *Advertising Age*, October 13, 2008.
13. Janet Adamy, "Starbucks Plays Common Joe," *The Wall Street Journal*, February 2, 2009.
14. Janet Adamy, "Wendy's Comes Up with a New Strategic Recipe," *The Wall Street Journal*, September 30, 2008.
15. Emma Hall, "McD's Opened Dialogue to Turn Itself Around," *Advertising Age*, February 23, 2009.
16. Richard S. Tedlow, "Leaders in Denial," *Harvard Business Review*, July–August 2008.
17. Christopher Palmeri and Nanette Byrnes, "Code and Pepsi Try Reinventing Water," *BusinessWeek*, March 2, 2009.
18. Ari Levy and Joseph Galante, "Who Wants to Buy a Digital Elephant?" *Bloomberg BusinessWeek*, March 8, 2010.
19. Jessie Scanlon, "The Shape of a New Coke," *BusinessWeek*, September 8, 2008.
20. Amol Sharma, "AT&T, Verizon Make Different Calls," *The Wall Street Journal*, January 29, 2009.
21. Heather Clancy, "Web Sight Shipping 2.0," *Entrepreneur*, April 2008.
22. Jeremy Caplan, "Spice Girls," *Time*, July 14, 2008.
23. Erica Westley, "A Printed Silicon Chip," *Inc.*, February 2009.
24. Jane Stevenson, "Use Merchandising to Build Brand and Attract Consumers," *Advertising Age*, February 25, 2008.
25. Matthew Creamer, "Best Brand on Earth? Starts with a G . . . ," *Advertising Age*, April 21, 2008.
26. Jean Halliday, "Gas Buyers Pick Brand Over Price," *Advertising Age*, April 21, 2008.
27. Reena Jane, "Put a Patent on That Pleat," *BusinessWeek*, March 31, 2008.
28. Betsy D. Gelb and Partha Krishnamurthy, "Protect Your Product's Look and Feel from Imitators," *Harvard Business Review*, October 2008.
29. Keith Goldberg, "How You Can Stay in Control of Your Brand's Reputation," *Advertising Age*, February 9, 2009.
30. Samuel Fromartz, "5 Companies, 5 Strategies, 5 Transformations," *MIT Sloan Management Review*, Fall 2009.
31. Patrick Hanlon and Josh Hawkins, "Expand Your Brand Community Online," *Advertising Age*, January 7, 2008.
32. David Armano, "Brand Interactions Are the Future; Be Prepared with an Interaction Designer," *Advertising Age*, April 28, 2008.
33. Jennifer Hoyt, "99-Cent-Only Stores Find Wiggle Room on Pricing," *The Wall Street Journal*, September 10, 2008; and Jeoff Colvin, "Yes, You Can Raise Prices," *Fortune*, March 2, 2009.
34. Sandra Fleishman, "Maybe Not a 000-Sum Game," *The Washington Post*, February 16, 2008.
35. Jonathan Clements, "Price Fixing: In This Market, Selling a Home Requires Savvy," *The Wall Street Journal*, February 27, 2008.

CHAPTER 15

1. Carey Wilson, "Where Does It Go?" *Quality Digest*, March 2008.
2. "Bye Bye Bottled Water," *U.S. News & World Report*, January 7, 2008.
3. David M. Katz, "The Shortest Distance to Cash," *CFO*, March 2010.
4. Chris Burritt, Carol Wolf, and Matthew Boyle, "Why Wal-Mart Wants to Take the Driver's Seat," *Bloomberg BusinessWeek*, June 6, 2010.
5. Kate Betts, "Point-and-Shoot Shopping," *Time*, August 25, 2008.
6. Wendy Piersall, "What Is the Best Way to Start a Home Business Online?" Sparkplugging, www.sparkplugging.com, accessed April 2009.
7. Ken Favaro, Tim Romberger, and David Meer, "Five Rules for Retailing in a Recession," *Harvard Business Review*, April 2009.
8. Jen Haberkorn, "Web Sales May Hit $204 Billion," *The Washington Times*, April 8, 2008.
9. Marcia Layton Turner, "Get Sold on eBay," *Entrepreneur*, March 2008.
10. Ali McConnon, "Vending Machines Go Luxe," *BusinessWeek*, January 28, 2008.
11. Lawrence Delevingne, "Amway: Shining Up a Tarnished Name," *BusinessWeek*, August 11, 2008.
12. Emily Lambert and Klaus Kneale, "Climb to the Top," *Forbes*, August 11, 2008.
13. Tony Dokoupil, "A Drink's Purple Reign," *Newsweek*, August 11, 2008.
14. Russ Banham, "Managing the Strategic Supply Chain," *The Wall Street Journal*, April 27, 2010.
15. Charles H. Fine, "Collaborate or Race? How to Design the Value Chain You Need," *MIT Sloan Management Review*, Winter 2010.
16. Kent Garber, "Technology's Morning After," *U.S. News & World Report*, January 7, 2008.
17. Kia, www.kia.com/Sorento, accessed March 2009.
18. Matthew B. Myers and Mee-Shew Cheung, "Sharing Global Supply Chain Knowledge," *MIT Sloan Management Review*, Summer 2008.
19. Brian Slobodow, Omer Abdullah, and William C. Babuschak, "When Supplier Partnerships Aren't," *MIT Sloan Management Review*, Winter 2008.
20. Ben Worthen, "Weak Links in the Food (Supply) Chain," *The Wall Street Journal*, June 24, 2008.
21. David Simchi-Levi, "The 6 Forces Driving Supply Chain Design," *MIT Sloan Management Review*, Winter 2010.
22. Brian Hindo, "Cleaning Up with 'Reverse Logistics,'" *BusinessWeek*, August 4, 2008.
23. Manjeet Kripalani, "Weaving a New Kind of Company," *BusinessWeek*, March 23 and 30, 2009.
24. Jennifer Lawler, "The Logic of Thirds," *Entrepreneur*, March 2010.
25. Marc Gunther, "Union Pacific: 'Building America,'" *Fortune*, July 5, 2010.
26. Stephanie Chen, "Cargo Slump Bodes Ill for Supply Chain," *The Wall Street Journal*, March 20, 2008.

(36. Richard J. Harrington and Anthony K. Tjan, "Transforming Strategy One Customer at a Time," *Harvard Business Review*, March 2008.
37. Richard Karpinski, "Forrester Survey Finds Social Media Leading Way Toward CRM 2.0," *BtoB*, December 8, 2008.)

27. Moon Ihlwan, "What Makes Samsung Tops in TVs?" *BusinessWeek*, March 13, 2008.
28. Dan O'Shea, "A Scan-tastic App Goes Mainstream," *Entrepreneur*, May 2010.
29. Erica Westly, "A Printed Silicon Chip," *Inc.*, January–February 2009.

CHAPTER 16

1. Sarah E. Needleman, "Services Combine Social Media, Marketing," *The Wall Street Journal*, February 23, 2010.
2. Barbara Kiviat, "Starbucks Can Smell Growth," *Time*, February 1, 2010.
3. Jeffrey F. Rayport, "Where Is Advertising Going? Into 'Stitals,'" *Harvard Business Review*, May 2008.
4. Lena H. Sun, "Captivating an Audience," *The Washington Post*, April 6, 2008.
5. "Kraft Provides Recipe for Mobile-Marketing Success," *Advertising Age*, January 26, 2009.
6. Karen J. Bannan, "E-Mail Marketing Includes Placing Ads When Needed," *BtoB's E-Mail Marketer Insight Guide*, 2008.
7. Jeremy Mullman, "Yes, the Super Bowl Is Well Worth $3 Million a Spot," *Advertising Age*, January 26, 2009.
8. Emily Bryson York, "Denny's ROI on $5 Million: 2 Million Butts in Seats," *Advertising Age*, February 9, 2009.
9. Lisa de Moraes, "Super Bowl Yet a Bigger Winner," *The Washington Post*, February 4, 2009.
10. "What's New in Marketing? What's Not?" *Deliver*, March 2010.
11. Jack Neff, "Study Finds Mixed DVR Effects," *Advertising Age*, March 24, 2008.
12. Brian Steinberg, "What TV Metrics the Buyers Want," *Advertising Age*, May 12, 2008.
13. Brian Steinberg, "TV Clutter Dulls Product Placement," *Advertising Age*, April 7, 2008.
14. Amy Schatz and Suzanne Vranica, "Product Placements Get FCC Scrutiny," *The Wall Street Journal*, June 23, 2008.
15. John Gaudiosi, "I Want to Buy In-Game Ads. Why Are So Many Parties Involved?" *Advertising Age*, March 17, 2008.
16. Zorik Gordon, "The Future of Marketing," *Inc.*, April 2008.
17. Burt Helm, "Madison Avenue: At the Crossroads with the I-Way," *BusinessWeek*, March 17, 2008; Michael Learmonth, "Web Ad Growth Falls Off—and So Do the Salaries," *Advertising Age*, October 27, 2008; and Kate Maddox, "Outlook Bright for Online Advertising," *BtoB*, January 14, 2008.
18. Laredo, "How Older Pros Can Transition to Digital."
19. Ellis Booker, "Balancing Need to Send with Need to Suspend," *BtoB's E-Mail Marketer Insight Guide*, 2008.
20. Mark Frauenfelder and Seth Goldin, "Twitter: Thumbs Up or Thumbs Down?" *Entrepreneur*, June 2010.
21. Steve Sullivan, Bob Stohrer, Bob Liodice, and Jeff Bell, "TV Makes Strides While Marketers Experiment Widely," *Advertising Age*, March 24, 2008.
22. Phyllis Berman, "Food Fight," *Forbes*, October 13, 2008.
23. Abbey Klassen, "Forget Twitter: Your Best Marketing Tool Is the Humble Product Review," *Advertising Age*, June 29, 2009.
24. Marc De Swaan Arons, "What It Takes to Really Win Globally," *Advertising Age*, May 19, 2008.
25. Michael Port, "Know Who You Want to Know," *Entrepreneur*, April 2010.
26. "Two Ways to Find New Customers," *Inc.*, February 2009.
27. Russell Kern, "When It Comes to Lead Generation, Don't Fail. Mail," *BtoB*, 2008.
28. Karen J. Bannan, "Reaching the Right Prospects," *BtoB's Lead Generation Guide*, 2008.
29. Renee Oricchio, "Always Be Closing," *Inc.*, May 2010.
30. Ibid.
31. Jessi Hempel, "IBM's All-Star Salesman," *Fortune*, September 29, 2008.
32. Michael Bush, "PR Agencies Still Playing Catch-Up," *Advertising Age*, March 17, 2008.
33. April Joyner and J.J. McCorvey, "Spreading the News," *Inc.*, May 2010.
34. Sean Callahan, "Marketers Stay in the Conversation with PR," *BtoB*, February 9, 2009.
35. Paul Gillin, "New PR Reality: Link over Inc," *BtoB*, March 9, 2009.
36. John Jantsch, "Making Headlines," *Entrepreneur*, April 2008.
37. Andrew Park, "Jon Pritchett's Dream of Reviving Astro Turf Became a PR Nightmare," *Inc.*, September 2008.
38. Jason Del Rey, "The Groupon Avalanche," *Inc.*, April 2010.
39. Karen J. Bannan, "Objectworld Shifts from Trade Shows to Webinars," *BtoB*, October 13, 2008.
40. Heather Clancy, "Tell It to Me Straight," *Entrepreneurship*, June 2008.
41. Mikal E. Belicove, "The Best Blog Spot," *Entrepreneur*, July 2010.
42. Alice Z. Cuneo, "So Just What Is Mobile Marketing?" *Advertising Age*, March 17, 2008.
43. Gwen Moran, "My Smartphone Sent Me," *Entrepreneur*, March 2010.

CHAPTER 17

1. Norm Brodsky, "Our Irrational Fear of Numbers," *Inc.*, January–February 2009.
2. Roy Harris, "Not-for-Profit Accounting Goes to School," *CFO*, January 10, 2008; and Rebecca Tonn, "Colorado's Non-Profits Face Looming Deadline to File Financials," *Colorado Springs Business Journal*, May 8, 2010.
3. Clinton B. Douglas and Angella Sutthiwan, "The Conflicting Roles of Controllership and Compliance," *Strategic Finance*, July 1, 2008.
4. Kathy Williams, "New Guidance for Accountants in Business," *Strategic Finance*, July 1, 2008.
5. Institute of Management Accountants, www.imanet.org, accessed February 24, 2009.
6. American Institute of Certified Public Accountants, www.aicpa.org, accessed February 24, 2009; and John A. Kruglinski, "CPAs: Many Doors to Opportunity," *Pennsylvania CPA Journal*, January 1, 2009.
7. Mark Myring and Robert Bloom, "Charting the Future of the Accounting Profession," *CPA Journal*, June 1, 2008; and Maureen A. Renzi, "Beyond the Client: Looking to Consumers' Needs during Turbulent Times," *Pennsylvania CPA Journal*, January 1, 2009.
8. Financial Accounting Standards Board, www.fasb.org, accessed August 12, 2008; and Michael C. Toerner, "A Guide to Using the Accounting Standards Codification," *CPA Journal*, February 1, 2009.
9. Elizabeth MacDonald, "Figures Don't Lie, But Liars Figure," *Forbes*, March 14, 2007; "Accountant and S.E.C. Reach Deal in Enron Case," *Reuters*, January 29, 2008; and "New York's Closer Scrutiny of CPAs," *Practical Accountant*, February 1, 2009.
10. Larry O'Dell, "Virginia Whistleblower Loses Bid for Reinstatement," AP Online, August 5, 2008; and Brian Doherty, "Sarbanes-Oxley Revisited," *Reason*, January 1, 2009.
11. Helen M. Roybark, "PCAOB Inspection Report Card," *CPA Journal*, February 1, 2009.
12. Jane Bryant Quinn, "Lawsuit Threatens Sarbanes-Oxley Act," *The Washington Post*, July 20, 2008; and Jaclyn Jaeger, "High Court Weighs Fate of PCAOB, Future of SOX," *Compliance Week*, January 1, 2010.
13. "Want to Strengthen Your Business? Take the Time to Find a Certified Public Accountant," *Indiana Business Magazine*, March 1, 2008.
14. Alix Stewart, "Auditor Angst," *CFO Magazine*, May 1, 2008; and Dana R. Hermanson and Richard W. Houston, "Evidence from the PCAOB's Second Inspections of Small Firms," *CPA Journal*, February 1, 2009.

15. Ken Rankin, "Board Approves PCAOB Budget; Audit Overseer Seeks 9 Percent Raise," *Accounting Today*, January 5, 2009.
16. Martin Coe and John Delaney, "The Impact of Certification on Accounting Education," *Strategic Finance*, July 1, 2008.
17. "Qualities to Look For in a Tax Accountant," *Rocky Mountain News*, March 10, 2008.
18. Harvey M. Katz, "Who Will Pay the Cost of Government Employer Retiree Health Benefits?" *Labor Law Journal*, April 1, 2008; Jake W. Lorentz, "Report from GASB," *GAAFR Review*, January 1, 2009; and Gary Palmer, "Whistling Past the Fiscal Graveyard," *Birmingham Business Journal*, May 21, 2010.
19. William P. Barrett, "America's 200 Largest Charities," *Forbes*, November 21, 2007.
20. Matthew Goldstein, "Stanford: Where Was the SEC?" *BusinessWeek*, March 2, 2009; and Stewart Ain, "L.I. Nonprofits Try to Avoid Scams," *Long Island Business News*, June 23, 2010.
21. Isaac M. O'Bannion, "Remotely Speaking," *CPA Technology Advisor*, June 1, 2008; and Tim Mills-Groninger, "Accounting Alphabet Soup: Can Software Keep Up in Moving from FASB and GAAP to IASB and IFRS?" *Non-profit Times*, January 1, 2009.
22. Richard Moroshove, "The Right FIT," *CA Magazine*, March 1, 2008; and Karine Benzacar, "Accounting Made Easy," *CMA Management*, April 1, 2010.
23. Danielle Kost, "What's the Best Way to Prepare Returns: Accountant or Software?" *Boston Globe*, March 16, 2008; and Isaac M. O'Bannon, "Small Business Accounting Continues to Move Online," *The CPA Technology Advisor*, June 1, 2010.
24. Mona Amatie, James St. Clair, and Clifton A. Williams, "Adding Value to Annual Financial Statements," *Journal of Government Financial Management*, April 1, 2008.
25. Robert Frank, "Managing Intellectual Property," *Journal of Accountancy*, August 1, 2008; and Kurt Badenhausen, "The World's Most Valuable Brands," *Forbes*, www.forbes.com, accessed August 3, 2010.
26. Karen Kroll, "Numbers in the Sun," *Business Finance*, July 1, 2008.
27. Gene Marks, "What's Really Going On at Your Company?" Forbes.com, August 11, 2008; and Jim D'Addario, "Treasurers Can Protect Cash Flow during the Crisis," *Financial Executive*, January 1, 2009.
28. Enrique Brito, "To See Where Your Firm Is Headed, Follow Cash Flow," *Washington Business Journal*, April 25, 2008; and Chris James, "Controlling Your Business Cash," *Dallas Business Journal*, www.bizjournals.com, accessed July 28, 2010.
29. Shara Rutberg, "Lots of Money but Always Broke: The Importance of Creating and Understanding a Cash-Flow Statement," *Fortune Small Business*, April 21, 2008; and Gretchen Morgenson, "Cash Flow Is the True Reality Check," *International Herald Tribune*, January 11, 2010.
30. Alix Stuart, "A New Vision for Accounting," *CFO Magazine*, February 1, 2008.
31. Matt Hennis, "Cash Flow Often Ignored Lifeblood of Business," *Atlanta Business Chronicle*, May 2, 2008.
32. John C. Woosley, "Deductions Can Boost Small-Biz Cash Flow," *New Mexico Business Weekly*, June 27, 2008.
33. Gene Marks, "An Entrepreneur's Most Important Asset," Forbes.com, July 15, 2008.
34. "The Investor Professor," *American Association of Individual Investors Journal*, August 2007.
35. David C. Burns, Timothy J. Sale, and Jens A. Stephan, "A Better Way to Gauge Profitability; Systematic Ratio Analysis Using the Advanced DuPont Model," *Journal of Accountancy*, August 1, 2008.
36. Ellen Depasquale, "Managing Inventory for Profitability," Inc.com, January 22, 2008.

CHAPTER 18

1. Andre de Haan, "Time for CFOs to Lead," *CA Magazine*, August 1, 2008; and "Where Do You Look for a CFO and What Should You Know before Hiring One?" *Memphis Business Journal*, June 4, 2010.
2. Meta L. Levin, "Interim CFOs and Controllers Fill a Widening Gap," *The Wall Street Journal*, June 17, 2008.
3. Louise Mawhinney, "Working with Your CFO," *Research-Technology Management*, July 1, 2007.
4. Rick Newman, "How the Government Will Govern GM and Chrysler," *U.S. News & World Report*, December 19, 2008.
5. Kimberly Palmer, "Learning the Tricks of Managing Money," *U.S. News & World Report*, May 19, 2008.
6. Carol Tice, "It's Now or Never," *Entrepreneur*, August 2008; Jessica Marquez, "A Master Financial Plan; Special Report: Pension & Retirement Benefits," *Workforce Management*, January 19, 2009; and Dean Zerbe, "IRS Audits Small Biz More, Big Guys Less," *Forbes*, www.forbes.com, accessed July 30, 2010.
7. Sue Asci, "Taxes on the Mind," *Investment News*, August 25, 2008.
8. John Cummings, "10 Best Practices for Co-Sourcing Internal Audit," *Business Finance*, July 1, 2008.
9. Massimo Cecere, "Optimizing Internal Audit," *CA Magazine*, April 1, 2008.
10. Joyce M. Rosenberg, "January Gives Business Owners Time for Financial Planning," *Transport Topics*, January 7, 2008; and Marcia Banner, "Pre Budget Report and Financial Planning," *Money Management*, January 1, 2009.
11. Jason Balogh and Jason Logman, "7 Actions for Simplifying the Planning Cycle," *Financial Executive*, March 1, 2008.
12. Christina Le Beau, "The Quick and the Dead: Get Your Business in Order Before Things Turn Ugly," *Crain's Chicago Business*, April 14, 2008.
13. Joe McDonald, "Caterpillar Looks for Record Sales on China Demand," AP Worldstream, August 28, 2008; and Miguel Helft, "Intel Lowers Its Forecast for a Second Time," *New York Times*, January 8, 2009.
14. Kathy Williams, "What Are Your Budget Headaches?" *Strategic Finance*, January 1, 2008; "U.S. Bancorp Asks Managers to Trim Budgets," *Business First of Louisville*, February 9, 2009; and Steve Metzenthin, "Look at the Annual Budget from a Strategic Viewpoint," *Houston Business Journal*, July 30, 2010.
15. Ellen Simon, "Oil's Climb Forced Companies to Become Leaner," AP Online, September 4, 2008.
16. Tom Grandy, "The Law of Money: Grab That Cash with Both Hands and Make a Stash," *Reeves Journal*, April 1, 2008.
17. Monica Mehta, "Can They Pay?" *BusinessWeek SmallBiz*, January 2009.
18. Andrea Peiro, "Online Accounting," www.inc.com, accessed January 21, 2009.
19. "The Basics of Balance Sheets," www.inc.com, accessed January 21, 2009.
20. Nelson Wang, "Finance Keeps Cranking Away," *CFO*, February 2009.
21. National Federation of Independent Businesses, www.nfib.com, accessed February 24, 2009.
22. "CIT Group Provides Line of Credit to CHF Industries," Business Wire, May 7, 2008.
23. Eric Dash, "Big U.S. Finance Company Faces Credit Crisis and Shares Fall," *International Herald Tribune*, March 22, 2008; and "How to Improve Your Odds When Seeking a Commercial Loan," *Orlando Business Journal*, July 23, 2010.
24. General Electric, www.ge.com, accessed January 20, 2009.
25. Donald J. Korn, "Good to Get," Black Enterprise.com, accessed March 2009; and Katie Kuehner-Hebert, "Factoring: Portrait of an Industry," *The Secured Lender*, April 1, 2010.
26. C. J. Prince, "Currency New Money," *Entrepreneur*, March 2008; and Helen Coster and Maureen Farrell, "How to Raise Cash—Now!" *Forbes*, www.forbes.com, accessed August 1, 2010.
27. Aliza Earnshaw, "Businesses Turn to Factoring to Counter Cash Crunch," *Portland Business Journal*, June 27, 2008.
28. Kelly K. Spors and Simona Covel, "Slow Payments Squeeze Small-Business Owners," *The Wall Street Journal*, October 31, 2008.

29. Myra A. Thomas, "The Global Marketplace: A World of Opportunity and Challenge," *The Secured Lender*, July 1, 2008.
30. Chris Havens, "St. Paul Sues Merrill Lynch to Recover Investment Money," *Star Tribune (Minneapolis, MN)*, August 12, 2008; and "The Great Dilution; Corporate Finance," *The Economist*, January 17, 2009.
31. Dean Calbreath, "Credit Crunch Will Last into '09, Economists Say," *San Diego Union Tribune*, October 19, 2008.
32. "Credit Market and Entrepreneurship," Finance Wire, April 18, 2008; and Jeffrey Gangemi, "Changing Concerns for Entrepreneurs," *BusinessWeek*, April 24, 2007.
33. John Tozzi, "Credit Cards Replace Small Business Loans," *BusinessWeek*, August 20, 2008; and Nadia Oehlsen, "Risky Business: Issuers of Small-Business Cards Are Controlling Their Portfolios More Tightly Than Ever," *Cards & Payments*, February 1, 2009.
34. Pfizer, www.pfizer.com, accessed January 21, 2009.
35. Will Oremus, "Facebook to Move in Early 2009," *Oakland Tribune*, September 5, 2008; and Evan Hessel, "Venture's New Grail," *Forbes*, February 16, 2009.
36. Rebecca Buckman, "Venture to Nowhere," *Forbes*, January 12, 2009; and Bobbie Gossage, "An Insider's Guide to Venture Capital Financing," *Inc.*, www.inc.com, accessed August 1, 2010.
37. Aaron Luccretti and Robin Sidel, "Goldman, Morgan Now Stand Alone: Fight On or Fold?" *The Wall Street Journal*, September 16, 2008; and Andrew Beattie, "The Evolution Of Goldman Sachs" *Forbes*, www.forbes.com, accessed August 1, 2010.
38. "Seeking Balance Sheet Gold: Companies with Strong Dividend Potential Are Object of AFBA Fund," *Investment News*, September 1, 2008.

CHAPTER 19

1. Michael Liedtke, "Visa Stock Soars in Market Debut," AP Online, March 20, 2008; Robin Sidel, "Visa's $19 Billion IPO Swipe," *The Wall Street Journal*, February 26, 2008; and Tom Granahan, "It's Every IPO You Want It to Be; Groundbreaking Visa Offering Managed to Get Done as Wall Street's Dramatic Makeover Was Just Getting Started," *Investment Dealers' Digest*, January 19, 2009.
2. Bryant Ruiz Switzky, "Investment Banks Offer Multiple Options for Companies Seeking Funds," *Minneapolis/St. Paul Business Journal*, June 6, 2008.
3. Antony Curry and Una Galani, "Goldman Plays Job Cut Catch-Up," *The New York Times*, October 23, 2008.
4. Kent Hoover, "Institutional Investors Own 76% of Large Corporations," *Washington Business Journal*, September 15, 2008; and "Institutional Presence in U.S. Corporations at All-Time High," *Atlanta Business Chronicle*, September 2, 2008.
5. New York Stock Exchange, www.nyse.com, accessed March 4, 2009.
6. "NYSE Euronext Completes Acquisition of American Stock Exchange," Business Wire, October 1, 2008; and Nina Mehta, "New Lease on Life," *Traders*, January 1, 2009.
7. Sandra Ward, "Don't Bet against the House," *Barron's*, July 14, 2008; and NASDAQ, www.nasdaq.com, accessed March 3, 2009.
8. Frederick Balfour, "Nasdaq-NYSE Rivalry Comes to China," *Investing*, December 3, 2007; and "United States: Daimler to Delist from New York Stock Exchange," *TendersInfo*, May 15, 2010.
9. "Non-U.S. Company Delistings from NYSE Soared in 2007," U.S. Newswire, March 26, 2008; "Verso Receives Delisting Notice from NYSE," *U.S. Business Journal*, February 6, 2009; and David Cho, "Fannie, Freddie Ordered to Delist Shares from NYSE," *The Washington Post*, June 17, 2010.
10. Lynnley Browning, "Ex-UBS Counsel to Pay $6.5 Million to Settle Auction-Rate Trading Case," *The New York Times*, November 7, 2008; "Former UBS Exec Sentenced in NY," AP Online, November 3, 2008; and Liz Moyer, "Pequot's Samberg Charged with Insider Trading," *Forbes*, www.forbes.com, accessed August 1, 2010.
11. "Bondlike Stocks Offer Decent Yields," *Kiplinger's Retirement Report*, April 1, 2008.
12. Bennett Voyles, "Ask Not for Whom the Dow Tolls: How Will Advisors and Investors Behave after the Collapse of 2008," *On Wall Street*, November 1, 2008; and Patrice Hill, "U.S. Top Bond Rating Imperiled by Deficit; Moody's Sees Urgent Need to Narrow Gap," *The Washington Times* (Washington, DC), February 4, 2010.
13. Jane Sasseen, "Why Moody's and S&P Still Matter," *BusinessWeek*, July 21, 2008.
14. Daniel Lippincott, "Finding the Best Way to Invest in Municipal Bonds," *Daily Record (Rochester, NY)*, July 16, 2008.
15. Emily Lambert, "Busted but Good," *Forbes*, February 16, 2009.
16. Martin Skala, "Investors Seek Safer Ride with Convertible Funds," *Christian Science Monitor*, January 7, 2008.
17. Humberto Cruz, "Success in Investing Found in Sticking to Basic Principles," *Triangle Business Journal*, February 22, 2008; Clifford Alvares, "The Emotional Investor," *Business Today*, February 8, 2009; and Kelly Campbell, "Six Signs That You Should Fire Your Broker," *Forbes*, www.forbes.com, accessed August 1, 2010.
18. Jane Bryant Quinn, "Your New Rebalancing Act," *Newsweek*, February 18, 2008; and Frank Armstrong III, "How Much Diversification Is Enough?" *CPA Journal*, January 1, 2008.
19. Jane Bryant Quinn, "Planners Wanted ASAP," *Newsweek*, March 3, 2008.
20. Debra Silversmith and Don Silversmith, "We're Close to a Bear Market, but Hang On for Inevitable Fix," *Denver Business Journal*, March 31, 2008.
21. Kerry Hannon, "Plotting a Withdrawal Strategy: Tapping Retirement Funds Should Be Done with Great Care," *U.S. News & World Report*, November 3, 2008; and Dave Carpenter, "After End of Bear Market Looms Uncertainty," AP Worldstream, November 3, 2008.
22. Amy Feldman, "Financial Planning: What Higher Taxes Could Mean," *BusinessWeek*, October 16, 2008.
23. McDonald's, www.mcdonalds.com, accessed July 2, 2010.
24. Rachel L. Sheedy and Kathryn A. Watson, "How to Stay Afloat When Inflation Rises: Blue-Chip Stocks, Plus a Touch of Commodities and Real Estate, Help Keep a Portfolio above Water," *Kiplinger's Retirement Report*, July 1, 2008; Conrad De Aenlle, "Invest in Blue Chips and Cash at the Same Time," *The New York Times*, January 17, 2009; and Tom Demeropolis, "Investors Switching to Dividend Stocks," *Dayton Business Journal*, July 9, 2010.
25. Ben Silverman, "Dividends: The Sweet Spot," *BusinessWeek*, March 12, 2008.
26. David Phelps, "Stock Scam Illustrates Growing Problem: Penny-Stock Schemes, Like the One Allegedly Involving Berage Creations of Mendota Heights, Are on the Rise, the SEC Says," *Star Tribune (Minneapolis, MN)*, March 23, 2008.
27. "Stock Splits Help Keep Share Prices in Check," *Virginian Pilot*, May 4, 2008; and "T. Rowe to Split Stock," *Baltimore Business Journal*, June 8, 2006.
28. Josh Funk, "Berkshire Reports 77 Percent Drop in 3Q Earnings," AP Worldstream, November 8, 2008.
29. Tim Paradis, "Stocks Point Lower Open as Overseas Markets Slide," AP Online, October 27, 2008; and Renee Montagne, "Investors Fear Dreaded Margin Call," *NPR Morning Edition*, November 7, 2008.
30. Elizabeth Ody, "The Best Ways to Invest in Bonds," *Kiplinger's Personal Finance Magazine*, June 1, 2008.

31. E. S. Browning, "Corporate Bonds Become Fund Managers' Favorite," *The Wall Street Journal*, September 29, 2008; and Ben Levisohn, "A Bond Strategy for Volatile Times," *The Wall Street Journal*, www.wsj.com, accessed August 1, 2010.
32. Ilana Polyak, "Crazy for Junk: Julius Baer Global High Income Makes a Case for High-Yield Bonds—Even Now," *Financial Planning*, September 1, 2008.
33. Cynthia Koons, "Junk Bonds Encounter Short Supply of Buyers," *The Wall Street Journal*, October 3, 2008; David Hoffman, "Managers Tread Carefully in Making Picks: High-Grade Corporates, Munis Win Praise; Treasuries, Junk Offerings Get Thumbs-Down," *Investment News*, February 2, 2009; and Michael Aneiro, "Junk Bonds Caught in Downdraft," *The Wall Street Journal*, www.wsj.com, accessed August 1, 2010.
34. Katy Marquardt, "Why You Should Invest in ETFs: They're Cheap, Transparent, and Can Easily Plug Holes in Your Portfolio," *U.S. News & World Report*, July 31, 2008; and Michael Mazur, "Mutual Funds Continue to Be Popular," *Community Banker*, February 1, 2009.
35. "Two Simple Steps to Future Wealth," M2 Presswire, November 3, 2008; Katy Marquardt, "5 Smart Ways to Invest Your Extra Dough: Stash Your Cash in Index Funds, ETF, and Obama Stocks," *U.S. News & World Report*, January 2, 2009; and Richard A. Ferri, "Not Your Father's Index Fund," *Forbes*, www.forbes.com, accessed August 1, 2010.
36. Katy Marquardt, "Ten Things You Didn't Know about ETFs—But Should," *U.S. News & World Report*, May 15, 2008; and Jane Bryant Quinn, "Exchange-Traded Funds Beat Active Managers," *The Washington Post*, January 18, 2009.
37. Kathleen Gallagher, "Wholesale Panic Drives Dow Down 678 Points to 5-Year Low," *Milwaukee Journal Sentinel*, October 10, 2008.
38. Robert J. Samuelson, "Good Times Breed Bad Times," *Newsweek*, October 27, 2008.
39. Anthony Faiola, "Downturn Accelerates as It Circles the Globe," *The Washington Post*, January 24, 2009.

CHAPTER 20

1. Paul Vigna, "Tit for Tat on Inflation-Deflation Front," *The Wall Street Journal*, September 15, 2009.
2. Laura Cohn, "Battle Royal: Credit Vs. Debit," *Kiplinger's Personal Finance*, April 2010.
3. Currency.com, accessed July 2010.
4. Frank Ahrens and Howard Schneider, "Fears of New Recession Shake Markets Around the World," *The Washington Post*, June 30, 2010.
5. Sara Schaefer Munoz and Alistair MacDonald, "U.K. Takes Up 'Bad Bank' Concept," *The Wall Street Journal*, February 4, 2009.
6. Hans F. Sennholz, "The Origins of Money," *St. Croix Review*, April 2008.
7. Raymund Flandez, "Barter Fits the Bill for Strapped Firms," *The Wall Street Journal*, February 17, 2009.
8. Kevin Sullivan, "As Economy Plummets, Cashless Bartering Soars on the Internet," *The Washington Post*, March 14, 2009.
9. Michael Mandel and Peter Coy, "The Fed's Revolution," *BusinessWeek*, March 31, 2008.
10. Walter Williams, "Counterfeiting vs. Monetary Policy," *The Washington Times*, December 18, 2008.
11. Matt Woolsey, "Unscarcity Value," *Forbes*, February 16, 2009.
12. Robert J. Samuelson, "A New Specter: Deflation," *The Washington Post*, November 10, 2008.
13. Daniel Fisher, "Spend That Cash," *Forbes*, March 30, 2009.
14. Neil Irwin, "Fed Slashes Key Interest Rate, and Stocks Soar," *The Washington Post*, March 19, 2008.
15. "The Big Easy," *The Wall Street Journal*, May 1, 2008.
16. Karen Yourish and Tan Ly, "A Brief History of the Banking System," *The Washington Post*, April 1, 2008.
17. John Cassidy, "The Great Depression Debate," *Condé Nast Portfolio*, May 2008.
18. Neil Irwin, Brenda Maloney, and Todd Lindeman, "Recession 101," *The Washington Post*, October 31, 2008.
19. George Lesser, "Rebuild That Banking Wall," *The Washington Times*, May 8, 2008.
20. Binyamin Applebaum, "U.S. Aid Goes to Credit Unions," *The Washington Post*, January 29, 2009.
21. John J. McKechnie III, "A Credit Union May Be Better Than a Bank," *Bottom Line Personal*, March 1, 2008.
22. Michael Santoli, "Give Credit Where It's Due," *Barron's*, January 19, 2009.
23. "Buying Time," *The Washington Post*, November 26, 2008.
24. Russell Roberts, "How Government Stoked the Mania," *The Wall Street Journal*, October 3, 2008.
25. Kim Holmes, "Don't Count Out the Free Market," *The Washington Times*, October 23, 2008.
26. Tamara E. Holmes, "Did They Cause the Credit Crisis?" *Black Enterprise*, January 2009.
27. David Dreman, "Bailout Blues," *Forbes*, November 17, 2008.
28. Matthew Philips, "The Neighborhood That Wrecked the World," *Newsweek*, January 5, 2009.
29. Binyamin Applebaum, "Credit Unions to Get Federal Assistance," *The Washington Post*, December 2008.
30. Curtis Arnold, "Best Credit Cards for 2010," *Bottom Line Personal*, March 15, 2010.
31. Steve Hamm, "Will Go-Tags Make Your Wallet Obsolete?" *BusinessWeek*, September 8, 2008.
32. Christopher Palmeri, "Debit-Card Evolution," *BusinessWeek*, November 10, 2008.
33. Ben Levisohn, "Prepaid Cards: The Cleanup," *BusinessWeek*, March 13, 2008.
34. Justin Fox, "New World Order," *Time*, February 16, 2009; and International Monetary Fund, www.imf.org, accessed March 6, 2009.
35. "Back in Business," *The Washington Post*, October 30, 2008.
36. Howard Schneider, "IMF Considers a Restocked 'Tool Kit,'" *The Washington Post*, July 2, 2010.

APPENDIX

1. Rachelle Younglai, "Obama Budget Would Boost SEC, CFTC, FBI," *Daily News*, February 26, 2009; Michael W. Stocker, "SEC Measures to Prevent Flash Crashes Are Sensible, But Are They Enough?," *Forbes*, www.forbes.com, accessed July 30, 2010; and "Congressional Overhaul Maps the Future of Financial Regulation," *BusinessWeek*, www.businessweek.com, accessed August 3, 2010.
2. Justin Pope, "Law Schools Growing, Jobs Aren't," *Time*, June 17, 2008; and American Bankers Association www.aba.com, accessed March 2, 2009.
3. "Devices for Lawyers," *The Wall Street Journal*, August 13, 2008.
4. Alicia Mundy, "Plaintiffs' Lawyers Fight Restrictions on Product-Liability Suits," *The Wall Street Journal*, August 13, 2008.
5. Thomas C. Boehm and Jeffrey M. Ulmer, "Product Liability: Beyond Loss Control—an Argument for Quality Assurance," *Quality Management Journal*, April 1, 2008.
6. Kenneth Ross, "Know Your Liabilities: You Could Be Liable If You Sell a Defective Product," *Chiropractic Products*, January 1, 2008; and A. Mitchell Polinsky and Steven Shavell, "The Uneasy Case for Product Liability," *Harvard Law Review*, April 1, 2010.
7. Huhnsik Chung and Marc S. Voses, "Secondhand Asbestos," *Risk Management*, July 1, 2008; and Sally Roberts, "High Court Ruling in Asbestos Case a Big Win for Wisconsin Policyholders," *Business Insurance*, February 2, 2009.

8. "Rhode Island Supreme Court Overturns Lead Paint Verdict," *Paint & Coatings Industry Magazine*, September 1, 2008; and "Rhode Island Supreme Court Issues Landmark Lead Paint Ruling," *U.S. Federal News Service*, July 1, 2008.
9. Ben W. Heineman Jr., "Safety First Abroad," *Forbes*, June 29, 2008; and "State Settles with Mattel," *Mississippi Business Journal*, January 5, 2009.
10. Roseanne White Geisel, "Product Liability Rates Down for Smaller Pharmaceuticals," *Business Insurance*, July 28, 2008; and Joanne Wojcik, "Insurers to Get Portion of Vioxx Settlement," *Business Insurance*, January 26, 2009.
11. "Business Briefing," *The Washington Post*, October 18, 2008.
12. Sarah McBride, "Exiling the Happy Meal," *The Wall Street Journal*, July 22, 2008.
13. Sebastian Mallaby, "The Audacity of Growth," *The Washington Post*, June 2, 2008; and Janice Francis-Smith, "Tort Reform Takes Center Stage in Oklahoma Political Battle," *Oklahoma City Journal Record*, February 19, 2009.
14. Karen E. Klein, "The Flip Side of Unsolicited Ideas," *BusinessWeek*, July 30, 2008; and Alexander I. Poltorak, "Patent Reform Misses the Mark; Multi-tier System Is Needed for the 21st Century, *The Washington Times* (Washington, DC), May 25, 2010.
15. Lisa LaMotta, "Edison Would Be Happy," *Forbes*, November 1, 2007.
16. Maureen Farrell, "They Call This Intellectual Property?" *Forbes*, March 10, 2008.
17. Peter Benesh, "Attorney: High Court Finds Rules Patently Offensive," *Investors Business Daily*, January 28, 2008; and Peter Strozniak, "Unique by Design: A Recent Court Ruling Strengthens Design Patents for Inventors," *Inside Business*, January 1, 2009.
18. Kirk Teska, "DIY Patent: Want to Protect Your Idea with a Patent? You Can Draft It Yourself, but Be Aware of the Risks," *Mechanical Engineering-CIME*, May 1, 2008.
19. Stuart Weinberg, "What Business Owners Should Know about Patenting," *The Wall Street Journal*, August 11, 2008.
20. Howard Fine, "Billionaires—They Have to Work Hard with That Money," *Los Angeles Business Journal*, May 28, 2007; and David Whelan, "Animal Nut," *Forbes*, October 6, 2008.
21. George Pike, "The Fences of a Patent," *Information Today*, February 1, 2009.
22. Greg Griffin, "Trolling for Patents," *Denver Post*, March 16, 2006.
23. Scott Moritz, "Big Tech Gets Legal Aid in the Patent Wars," CNN Money.com, June 30, 2008; Allied Security Trust, www.alliedsecuritytrust.com, accessed March 3, 2009; and Sarah Tolkoff, "Patent Defender Acacia Embraces Industry Retort to Business Model," *Orange County Business Journal*, February 22, 2010.
24. S. Hemenway, "Patent Trolls Prey on Business Innovation," *Mondaq Business Briefing*, June 3, 2008.
25. Larry Neumeister, "Rowling Wins Lawsuit to Block Potter Encyclopedia," AP Online, September 8, 2008.
26. United States Patent and Trademark Office, www.uspto.gov, accessed March 1, 2009; and James Gallagher, "Colgate-Palmolive Sues Glaxosmithkline over Toothpaste Trademark," *Triangle Business Journal*, July 30, 2010.
27. "Company Name Not Same as Trademark," *SouthtownStar (Chicago, IL)*, January 25, 2008.
28. Michael Hooper, "Shoe Giant Takes a Hit," *Topeka-Capital Journal*, September 4, 2008; and Donna Goodison, "Sully's Sues Company over Green Monster Shirt," *Boston Herald*, January 3, 2009.
29. Nicholas C. Dranias, "Consideration as Contract: A Secular Natural Law of Contracts," *Texas Review of Law and Politics*, April 1, 2008.
30. "Justice Department Issues Report on Antitrust Monopoly Law," U.S. Newswire, September 8, 2008.
31. Todd Bishop, "Judge Extends Antitrust Scrutiny Microsoft 'On Notice' until November 2009," *Seattle Post-Intelligencer*, January 30, 2008; Peter Whoriskey, "Google Ad Deal Is under Scrutiny; Yahoo Agreement Subject of Antitrust Probe, Sources Say," *The Washington Post*, July 2, 2008; and Robert Wielaard, "Microsoft Loses E.U. Antitrust Case," *The Washington Post*, January 17, 2009.
32. Robert Weissman, "How Things Work: The FTC's Revolving Door," *Multinational Monitor*, July 1, 2008; and Susan Carey, "Snap, Crackle, Slap: FTC Objects to Kellogg's Rice Krispies Health Claim," *The Wall Street Journal*, www.wsj.com, accessed August 3, 2010.
33. "Drug Makers Sued," *MMR*, September 22, 2008.
34. Dan Browning, "Kia Dealer Sues Maker over Ad Aid to Rivals," *Star Tribune (Minneapolis, MN)*, March 26, 2008.
35. Peter Whoriskey, "Antitrust Inquiry Launched into Intel: FTC to Review Firm's Practices," *The Washington Post*, June 7, 2008.
36. Steve Lohr, "Google Tries to Allay Antitrust Concerns Deal with Yahoo Could Rouse Regulators," *International Herald Tribune*, May 23, 2008.
37. Dan Eggen, "Bush Defends Rescue Plan: Government Cash Infusion Was a Last Resort," *The Washington Post*, October 18, 2008; and "Growing Insecurities: The Securities and Exchange Commission," *The Economist*, January 17, 2009.
38. Peter J. Wallison and Edward Pinto, "Worse Than You Think: What Went Wrong at Fannie and Freddie—and What Still Might," *The National Review*, November 3, 2008; and Steve Forbes, "Bust Up These Beasts," *Forbes*, July 28, 2008.
39. Benjamin Stanley, "Main Street Bailout for the Common Taxpayer," U.S. Newswire, October 15, 2008.
40. Delen Goldberg, "Paying for Your Sins: Why Gov. Spitzer Wants to Raise Taxes—and Revenue—on New Yorkers' Guilty Pleasures," *Post Standard (Syracuse, NY)*, February 2, 2008; and Janet Novack, "Sin Taxes Are All the Rage," *Forbes*, May 10, 2010.
41. Valerie Bauman, "Amazon Sues NY over Internet Sales Tax Collection," AP Online, May 3, 2008; and Rachel Metz, "Buying on Web to Avoid Sales Taxes May End," *Deseret News (Salt Lake City)*, January 13, 2009.
42. Walt Williams, "States Look to Internet Retailers for Sales Taxes," *State Journal (Charleston, WV)*, May 30, 2008.
43. Thomas Evans and Paul B. Lewis, "An Empirical Economic Analysis of the 2005 Bankruptcy Reforms," *Emory Bankruptcy Developments Journal*, January 1, 2008.
44. Kristina Doss, "A Kinder Bankruptcy Law Is Sought as Filings Soar," *The Wall Street Journal*, January 21, 2009.
45. "Bankruptcy Reform: Dollar Costs Associated with the Bankruptcy Abuse Prevention and Consumer Protection Act of 2005," *General Accounting Office Reports & Testimony*, August 1, 2008.
46. Jenny Anderson, "Filings for Bankruptcy Up 18% in February," *The New York Times*, March 5, 2008; Jacqueline Palank, "U.S. Consumer Bankruptcies Expected to Exceed 1 Million in 2008," AP Worldstream, March 4, 2008; and Jeffrey Freedman, "Bankruptcy Becoming Common in the Middle Class," *Buffalo News*, January 21, 2010.
47. Brett Arends, "Some Bankruptcy Basics," *The Wall Street Journal*, October 23, 2008; and Richard Metcalf, "Bankruptcy: The Last Resort: New Mexico Saw Chapter 7 and Chapter 13 Filings Jump in 2008, Though Not as Much as the Rest of the Nation," *Albuquerque Journal*, February 1, 2009.
48. Bankruptcy Action, www.bankruptcyaction.com, accessed March 2, 2009.
49. "Airline Deregulation Deserves Another Look," *Honolulu Star-Bulletin*, April 14, 2008.

50. Bonnie Pfister, "3 Decades of Deregulated Flight Gets Mixed Reviews," *Pittsburg Tribune Review*, October 19, 2008; and Joan Lowy, "Congressmen Would Bring Back Airline Regulation," *Forbes*, www.forbes.com, accessed August 3, 2010.
51. Bruce M. Owen, "The Temptation of Media Regulation: Why Not Unbundle Episodes or Innings?" *Regulation*, March 22, 2008.
52. Robert J. Samuelson, "Good Times Breed Bad Times," *Newsweek*, October 27, 2008.
53. Michael Mandel, "Come On, Let's Regulate Again: Red Tape Is Back in Fashion in America," *The Independent*, September 21, 2008; and Katherine Mangu-Ward, "Is Deregulation to Blame? The New Washington Consensus Says 'Yes.' The Facts on the Ground Say Something Different," *Reason*, January 1, 2009.
54. "Repeal Utility Deregulation," *The Intelligencer*, August 14, 2008.

CHAPTER A (available online only)

1. Mary K. Pratt, "IT Careers: 5 Tips for Charting Your 100 Day Plan," *CIO*, October 2008.
2. Nick Wingfield and Don Clark, "Internet-Ready TVs Usher Web into Living Room," *The Wall Street Journal*, January 5, 2009.
3. Jon Fortt, "Netbooks Could Be the Next Hit Cell Phones," *Fortune*, January 28, 2009.
4. Richard Skrilet, "Business Intelligence Is More Than OLAP," BeyeNETWORK, www.b-eye-network.com, accessed February 11, 2009.
5. Michelle V. Rafter, "Document This: How to Organize Computer Data," www.technology.inc.com, accessed February 12, 2009; Christopher F. Chabris, "You Have Too Much Mail," *The Wall Street Journal*, December 14, 2008; and Elizabeth Wasserman, "TechTalk: E-mail Storage Sails for Boat Supplier," www.technology.inc.com, accessed February 12, 2009.
6. John P. Girard, "Diapers, Pop-Tarts, and Dog Food—The Case for Data Mining," *Prairie Business Magazine*, February 1, 2008.
7. Darren Dahl, "Trust Me: You're Gonna Love This," *Inc.*, November 2008.
8. Ben Worthen, "Mining for Gold," *The Wall Street Journal*, October 27, 2008.
9. Stephanie N. Mehta, "Tech Memo to Team Obama," *Fortune*, January 6, 2009.
10. Rochester Institute of Technology, "The Next Step in Health Care: Telemedicine Researchers Broadcast Live Surgery Using Internet2," *Ascribe Higher Education News Service*, November 12, 2008.
11. "Juniper Networks Powers U.S. Department of Energy's ESnet Network Supporting Global Research," *Business Wire*, February 11, 2009.
12. Brent Leary, "Social Media's Good, Bad, Ugly and Unexpected," *Inc.*, January 2009.
13. Unknown, "Social Networking: Brave New World or Revolution from Hell?" *ZDNet White Papers*, January 2008.
14. Salvatore Parise, Patricia J. Guinan, and Bruce D. Weinberg, "The Secrets of Marketing in a Web 2.0 World," *The Wall Street Journal*, January 1, 2009.
15. Jessi Hempel, "Web 2.0 Is So Over. Welcome to Web 3.0," *Fortune*, January 8, 2009.
16. Amol Sharma and Jessica E. Vascellaro, "Companies Eye Location-Services Market," *The Wall Street Journal*, November 28, 2009.
17. Charles J. Murray, "Faster Processors Pave Way for Vision, 3-D TV," *Design News*, January 5, 2009.
18. Jon Fortt, "Goodbye, PC (and Mac). Hello, Services," *Fortune*, February 4, 2009.
19. Mary O. Foley, "10 Hot Technologies for 2009," *Inc.*, December 2008.
20. Rachael King, "The Coming Desktop Revolution?" *BusinessWeek*, January 5, 2008.
21. Rob Preston, "Will Cloud Computing Rain on IT's Parade?" *InformationWeek*, February 18, 2008; and Jason Hiner, "Four Reasons Why 2009 Will Be a Watershed Year in Technology," *TechRepublic*, February 9, 2009.
22. Ryan Underwood, "Save the Planet—and Save the Company a Lot of Power and Paper," *Inc.*, June 2008.
23. Don Tapscott, "How to Teach and Manage 'Generation Net,'" *BusinessWeek*, November 30, 2008.
24. David Pauleen and Brian Harmer, "Away from the Desk . . . Always," *The Wall Street Journal*, December 15, 2008.
25. Michelle V. Rafter, "2009 Tech Security Forecast," www.technology.inc.com, accessed February 13, 2009.
26. Minda Zetlin, "Would Your Network Survive a Targeted Attack?" www.technology.inc.com, accessed February 9, 2009.
27. Ben Worthen, "New Data Privacy Laws Set for Firms," *The Wall Street Journal*, October 16, 2008.
28. Mary O. Foley, "Can Outsourcing Better Protect Customer Data?" www.technology.inc.com, accessed February 13, 2009; Bruce Schneier, "How to Prevent Digital Snooping," *The Wall Street Journal*, December 9, 2008; and Bruce Schneier, "Why Technology Won't Prevent Identity Theft," *The Wall Street Journal*, January 9, 2009.
29. Scott Austin, "Email with a Ribbon on It," *The Wall Street Journal*, December 7, 2008.
30. Julia Zappei, "Experts Warn of Cyberterrorism Threat," *Associated Press*, May 21, 2008.
31. "Prof. Howard A. Schmidt Appointed First President of the Information Security Forum," *M2 PressWire*, August 12, 2008.
32. Jia Lynn Yang, "Internet Search Engines Know a Lot about Their Users—Maybe Too Much," *Fortune*, January 6, 2009.

CHAPTER B (available online only)

1. Karl Lydersen, "Iowa Flooding Rivals 1993 Deluge," *The Washington Post*, June 14, 2008.
2. Liam Pleven, "State Farm Won't Cover Properties in Florida," *The Wall Street Journal*, January 28, 2009.
3. Kimberly Lankford, "Your ID-Theft Prevention Kit," *Kiplinger's Personal Finance*, April 2008.
4. Russ Banham, "ERM: Viewing Risk as Opportunity," *The Wall Street Journal*, April 21, 2009.
5. "Rising Trends in Risk Management," *The Wall Street Journal*, April 21, 2009.
6. Kevin Buehler, Andrew Freeman, and Ron Hulme, "The New Arsenal of Risk Management," *Harvard Business Review*, September 2008.
7. Eric Bellman, "Tata Protester Widens Her Focus," *The Wall Street Journal*, November 5, 2008.
8. Naazneen Karmali, "The Raja of Rooms," *Forbes*, January 12, 2009.
9. "15,000 Hens Killed in Bird-Flu Scare," *The Washington Times*, June 4, 2008.
10. Lyndsey Layton, "Suspect Peanuts Sent to Schools," *The Washington Post*, February 6, 2009.
11. Lauren Young, "Advocates Who Help You Negotiate Health Care," *BusinessWeek*, October 22, 2007.
12. "How to Choose a Health Care Provider for Your Company," *Inc. Guidebook* 1, no. 3 (2008).
13. Lauren Young, "Weaving That Safety Net," *BusinessWeek*, February 9, 2009.

14. Stacy Tillie, "What's Riding on Your Insurance Policy?" *AAA World*, January/February 2009.
15. Mya Frazier, "Who's in Charge of Green?" *Advertising Age*, June 9, 2008.

CHAPTER C (available online only)

1. David Bahnsen, "Preserve and Protect: Unnecessary Risk Leads to Failed Strategy," *World*, March 8/15, 2008.
2. Sara Wilson, "How to Make a Million," *Entrepreneur*, October 2008.
3. Claudia Buckl, "Teaching Financial Literacy," *The Washington Times*, May 5, 2008.
4. Jim McElhatton, "Community Colleges Seen as Essential," *The Washington Times*, April 14, 2008.
5. Glenn Ruffennach, "The Encore Quiz: How Much Do You Know?" *The Wall Street Journal*, May 3–4, 2008.
6. Claire Cain Miller, "Making a Mint," *Forbes*, May 5, 2008.
7. Nancy Trejos, "Majoring in Plastic," *The Washington Post*, April 13, 2008.
8. Mina Kimes, "Credit Cards Carte Blanche," *Fortune*, October 13, 2008.
9. Diane V. King, "Minding Their Money," *Black Enterprise*, April 2009.
10. James C. Cooper, "Hidden in the Bad News, Signs of Life," *BusinessWeek*, January 12, 2009.
11. Linda Stern, "To Your Credit," *Newsweek*, March 24, 2008.
12. Randy Myers, "A Guide to Annuities & Retirement Income," *The Wall Street Journal*, November 12, 2008.
13. "Choose a Health Care Plan for Your Company," *Inc. Guidebook* 1, no.3 (2008).
14. eHealthInsurance, www.ehealthinsurance.com, accessed March 19, 2009.
15. Peter Keating, "New Math for IRA Savings," *Smart Money*, April 2009.
16. Eric G. Meyers, "Slow and Steady Wins the Race," *Let's Talk Money*, March/April 2008.
17. Ashlea Ebeling, "7 Steps to Savings Sanity," *Forbes*, February 25, 2008.
18. Chris Taylor, "Master Your Money," *Black Enterprise*, April 2008.
19. Eric Schurenberg, "Why We Flunked 401(k)," *Money*, April 2008.
20. Mary Beth Franklin, "6 Simple Ways to Retire Rich," *Kiplinger's Personal Finance*, February 2008.
21. Amy Feldman, "Can This New 401(k) Save Retirement?" *BusinessWeek*, February 16, 2009.
22. Walecia Konrad, "Keep It in the Family," *Money*, January 2009.

glossary

401(k) plan (p. BC-14) A savings plan that allows you to deposit pretax dollars and whose earnings compound tax free until withdrawal, when the money is taxed at ordinary income tax rates.

absolute advantage (p. 62) The advantage that exists when a country has a monopoly on producing a specific product or is able to produce it more efficiently than all other countries.

accounting (p. 456) The recording, classifying, summarizing, and interpreting of financial events and transactions to provide management and other interested parties the information they need to make good decisions.

accounting cycle (p. 462) A six-step procedure that results in the preparation and analysis of the major financial statements.

accounts payable (p. 466) Current liabilities involving money owed to others for merchandise or services purchased on credit but not yet paid for.

acquisition (p. 129) One company's purchase of the property and obligations of another company.

administered distribution system (p. 416) A distribution system in which producers manage all of the marketing functions at the retail level.

administrative agencies (p. A-3) Federal or state institutions and other government organizations created by Congress or state legislatures with delegated power to pass rules and regulations within their mandated area of authority.

advertising (p. 431) Paid, nonpersonal communication through various media by organizations and individuals who are in some way identified in the advertising message.

affiliate marketing (p. 155) An Internet-based marketing strategy in which a business rewards individuals or other businesses (affiliates) for each visitor or customer the affiliate sends to its Web site.

affirmative action (p. 288) Employment activities designed to "right past wrongs" by increasing opportunities for minorities and women.

agency shop agreement (p. 324) Clause in a labor–management agreement that says employers may hire nonunion workers; employees are not required to join the union but must pay a union fee.

agents/brokers (p. 403) Marketing intermediaries who bring buyers and sellers together and assist in negotiating an exchange but don't take title to the goods.

American Federation of Labor (AFL) (p. 320) An organization of craft unions that championed fundamental labor issues; founded in 1886.

annual report (p. 458) A yearly statement of the financial condition, progress, and expectations of an organization.

annuity (p. BC-10) A contract to make regular payments to a person for life or for a fixed period.

apprentice programs (p. 298) Training programs involving a period during which a learner works alongside an experienced employee to master the skills and procedures of a craft.

arbitration (p. 327) The agreement to bring in an impartial third party (a single arbitrator or a panel of arbitrators) to render a binding decision in a labor dispute.

assembly process (p. 235) That part of the production process that puts together components.

assets (p. 466) Economic resources (things of value) owned by a firm.

auditing (p. 460) The job of reviewing and evaluating the records used to prepare a company's financial statements.

autocratic leadership (p. 191) Leadership style that involves making managerial decisions without consulting others.

balance of payments (p. 65) The difference between money coming into a country (from exports) and money leaving the country (for imports) plus money flows from other factors such

Note: Terms and definitions printed in italics are considered business slang, or jargon.

as tourism, foreign aid, military expenditures, and foreign investment.

balance of trade (p. 64) The total value of a nation's exports compared to its imports over a particular period.

balance sheet (p. 465) The financial statement that reports a firm's financial condition at a specific time.

ballyhooed Talked about in an exaggerated way.

banker's acceptance (p. 563) A promise that the bank will pay some specified amount at a particular time.

bankruptcy (p. A-14) The legal process by which a person, business, or government entity unable to meet financial obligations is relieved of those obligations by a court that divides any assets among creditors, allowing creditors to get at least part of their money and freeing the debtor to begin anew.

bargaining zone (p. 326) The range of options between the initial and final offer that each party will consider before negotiations dissolve or reach an impasse.

barter (p. 547) The direct trading of goods or services for other goods or services.

bear market Situation where the stock market is declining in value and investors feel it will continue to decline.

been there, done that Prior experience.

benchmarking (p. 218) Comparing an organization's practices, processes, and products against the world's best.

benefit segmentation (p. 362) Dividing the market by determining which benefits of the product to talk about.

blog (p. 445) An online diary (Web log) that looks like a Web page but is easier to create and update by posting text, photos, or links to other sites.

bond (p. 521) A corporate certificate indicating that a person has lent money to a firm.

bonds payable (p. 467) Long-term liabilities that represent money lent to the firm that must be paid back.

bookkeeping (p. 462) The recording of business transactions.

bottom line The last line in a profit and loss statement; it refers to net profit or loss.

brain drain (p. 41) The loss of the best and brightest people to other countries.

brainstorming (p. 186) Coming up with as many solutions to a problem as possible in a short period of time with no censoring of ideas.

brand (p. 382) A name, symbol, or design (or combination thereof) that identifies the goods or services of one seller or group of sellers and distinguishes them from the goods and services of competitors.

brand association (p. 385) The linking of a brand to other favorable images.

brand awareness (p. 384) How quickly or easily a given brand name comes to mind when a product category is mentioned.

brand equity (p. 384) The value of the brand name and associated symbols.

brand loyalty (p. 384) The degree to which customers are satisfied, like the brand, and are committed to further purchases.

brand manager (p. 385) A manager who has direct responsibility for one brand or one product line; called a product manager in some firms.

brand name (p. 353) A word, letter, or group of words or letters that differentiates one seller's goods and services from those of competitors.

breach of contract (p. A-10) When one party fails to follow the terms of a contract.

break-even analysis (p. 393) The process used to determine profitability at various levels of sales.

brightest days The best of times for a person or organization.

broadband technology (p. BA-10) Technology that offers users a continuous connection to the Internet and allows them to send and receive mammoth files that include voice, video, and data much faster than ever before.

budget (p. 490) A financial plan that sets forth management's expectations, and, on the basis of those expectations, allocates the use of specific resources throughout the firm.

bull market Situation where the stock market is increasing in value and investors feel it will continue to grow.

bundling (p. 382) Grouping two or more products together and pricing them as a unit.

bureaucracy (p. 207) An organization with many layers of managers who set rules and regulations and oversee all decisions.

business (p. 4) Any activity that seeks to provide goods and services to others while operating at a profit.

business cycles (p. 48) The periodic rises and falls that occur in economies over time.

business environment (p. 11) The surrounding factors that either help or hinder the development of businesses.

business intelligence (BI) (p. BA-3) Any of a variety of software applications that analyze an organization's raw data and take out useful insights from it.

business law (p. A-2) Rules, statutes, codes, and regulations that are established to provide a legal framework within which business may be conducted and that are enforceable by court action.

business plan (p. 162) A detailed written statement that describes the nature of the business, the target market, the advantages the business will have in relation to competition, and the resources and qualifications of the owner(s).

business-to-business (B2B) market (p. 359) All the individuals and organizations that want goods and services to use in producing other goods and services or to sell, rent, or supply goods to others.

buying stock on margin (p. 527) Purchasing stocks by borrowing some of the purchase cost from the brokerage firm.

cafeteria-style fringe benefits (p. 306) Fringe benefits plan that allows employees to choose the benefits they want up to a certain dollar amount.

cannibalize a business *One franchise pulls business away from another franchise, for example.*

capital budget (p. 490) A budget that highlights a firm's spending plans for major asset purchases that often require large sums of money.

capital expenditures (p. 495) Major investments in either tangible long-term assets such as land, buildings, and equipment or intangible assets such as patents, trademarks, and copyrights.

capital gains (p. 527) The positive difference between the purchase price of a stock and its sale price.

capitalism (p. 35) An economic system in which all or most of the factors of production and distribution are privately owned and operated for profit.

cash-and-carry wholesalers (p. 409) Wholesalers that serve mostly smaller retailers with a limited assortment of products.

cash budget (p. 490) A budget that estimates a firm's projected cash inflows and outflows that the firm can use to plan for any cash shortages or surpluses during a given period.

cash flow (p. 472) The difference between cash coming in and cash going out of a business.

cash flow forecast (p. 489) Forecast that predicts the cash inflows and outflows in future periods, usually months or quarters.

center stage *A very important position.*

centralized authority (p. 208) An organization structure in which decision-making authority is maintained at the top level of management at the company's headquarters.

certificate of deposit (CD) (p. 555) A time-deposit (savings) account that earns interest to be delivered at the end of the certificate's maturity date.

certification (p. 321) Formal process whereby a union is recognized by the National Labor Relations Board (NLRB) as the bargaining agent for a group of employees.

certified internal auditor (CIA) (p. 460) An accountant who has a bachelor's degree and two years of experience in internal auditing, and who has passed an exam administered by the Institute of Internal Auditors.

certified management accountant (CMA) (p. 458) A professional accountant who has met certain educational and experience requirements, passed a qualifying exam in the field, and been certified by the Institute of Certified Management Accountants.

certified public accountant (CPA) (p. 459) An accountant who passes a series of examinations established by the American Institute of Certified Public Accountants (AICPA).

chain of command (p. 207) The line of authority that moves from the top of a hierarchy to the lowest level.

channel of distribution (p. 402) A whole set of marketing intermediaries, such as agents, brokers, wholesalers, and retailers, that join together to transport and store goods in their path (or channel) from producers to consumers.

claim (p. BB-6) A statement of loss that the insured sends to the insurance company to request payment.

climate change (p. 19) The movement of the temperature of the planet up or down over time.

climbed the ladder Promoted to higher-level jobs.

closed shop agreement (p. 323) Clause in a labor–management agreement that specified workers had to be members of a union before being hired (was outlawed by the Taft-Hartley Act in 1947).

cloud computing (p. BA-13) A form of virtualization in which a company's data and applications are stored at offsite data centers that are accessed over the Internet (the cloud).

collective bargaining (p. 321) The process whereby union and management representatives form a labor–management agreement, or contract, for workers.

command economies (p. 42) Economic systems in which the government largely decides what goods and services will be produced, who will get them, and how the economy will grow.

commercial bank (p. 554) A profit-seeking organization that receives deposits from individuals and corporations in the form of checking and savings accounts and then uses some of these funds to make loans.

commercial finance companies (p. 499) Organizations that make short-term loans to borrowers who offer tangible assets as collateral.

commercialization (p. 387) Promoting a product to distributors and retailers to get wide distribution, and developing strong advertising and sales campaigns to generate and maintain interest in the product among distributors and consumers.

commercial paper (p. 500) Unsecured promissory notes of $100,000 and up that mature (come due) in 270 days or less.

common law (p. A-3) The body of law that comes from decisions handed down by judges; also referred to as unwritten law.

common market (p. 77) A regional group of countries that have a common external tariff, no internal tariffs, and a coordination of laws to facilitate exchange; also called a *trading bloc*. An example is the European Union.

common stock (p. 520) The most basic form of ownership in a firm; it confers voting rights and the right to share in the firm's profits through dividends, if offered by the firm's board of directors.

communism (p. 41) An economic and political system in which the government makes almost all economic decisions and owns almost all the major factors of production.

comparative advantage theory (p. 61) Theory that states that a country should sell to other countries those products that it produces most effectively and efficiently, and buy from other countries those products that it cannot produce as effectively or efficiently.

competition-based pricing (p. 392) A pricing strategy based on what all the other competitors are doing. The price can be set at, above, or below competitors' prices.

compliance-based ethics codes (p. 96) Ethical standards that emphasize preventing unlawful behavior by increasing control and by penalizing wrongdoers.

compressed workweek (p. 307) Work schedule that allows an employee to work a full number of hours per week but in fewer days.

computer-aided design (CAD) (p. 236) The use of computers in the design of products.

computer-aided manufacturing (CAM) (p. 236) The use of computers in the manufacturing of products.

computer-integrated manufacturing (CIM) (p. 236) The uniting of computer-aided design with computer-aided manufacturing.

concept testing (p. 387) Taking a product idea to consumers to test their reactions.

conceptual skills (p. 188) Skills that involve the ability to picture the organization as a whole and the relationship among its various parts.

conglomerate merger (p. 129) The joining of firms in completely unrelated industries.

Congress of Industrial Organizations (CIO) (p. 320) Union organization of unskilled workers; broke away from the American Federation of Labor (AFL) in 1935 and rejoined it in 1955.

consideration (p. A-9) Something of value; consideration is one of the requirements of a legal contract.

consumerism (p. A-12) A social movement that seeks to increase and strengthen the rights and powers of buyers in relation to sellers.

consumer market (p. 359) All the individuals or households that want goods and services for personal consumption or use.

consumer price index (CPI) (p. 47) Monthly statistics that measure the pace of inflation or deflation.

contingency planning (p. 185) The process of preparing alternative courses of action that may be used if the primary plans don't achieve the organization's objectives.

contingent workers (p. 296) Workers who do not have the expectation of regular, full-time employment.

continuous process (p. 235) A production process in which long production runs turn out finished goods over time.

contract (p. A-9) A legally enforceable agreement between two or more parties.

contract law (p. A-9) Set of laws that specify what constitutes a legally enforceable agreement.

contract manufacturing (p. 69) A foreign country's production of private-label goods to which a domestic company then attaches its brand name or trademark; part of the broad category of *outsourcing*.

contractual distribution system (p. 415) A distribution system in which members are bound to cooperate through contractual agreements.

contrarian approach (p. BC-8) Buying stock when everyone else is selling or vice versa.

controlling (p. 181) A management function that involves establishing clear standards to determine whether or not an organization is progressing toward its goals and objectives, rewarding people for doing a good job, and taking corrective action if they are not.

convenience goods and services (p. 378) Products that the consumer wants to purchase frequently and with a minimum of effort.

conventional (C) corporation (p. 121) A state-chartered legal entity with authority to act and have liability separate from its owners.

cookies (p. BA-18) Pieces of information, such as registration data or user preferences, sent by a Web site over the Internet to a Web browser that the browser software is expected to save and send back to the server whenever the user returns to that Web site.

cooking the books *Making accounting information look better than it actually is to outside observers and users of financial information of a company.*

cooling-off period (p. 328) When workers in a critical industry return to their jobs while the union and management continue negotiations.

cooperative (p. 137) A business owned and controlled by the people who use it—producers, consumers, or workers with similar needs who pool their resources for mutual gain.

copyright (p. A-7) A document that protects a creator's rights to materials such as books, articles, photos, and cartoons.

core competencies (p. 218) Those functions that the organization can do as well as or better than any other organization in the world.

core time (p. 306) In a flextime plan, the period when all employees are expected to be at their job stations.

corporate distribution system (p. 415) A distribution system in which all of the organizations in the channel of distribution are owned by one firm.

corporate philanthropy (p. 99) The dimension of social responsibility that includes charitable donations.

corporate policy (p. 100) The dimension of social responsibility that refers to the position a firm takes on social and political issues.

corporate responsibility (p. 100) The dimension of social responsibility that includes everything from hiring minority workers to making safe products.

corporate social initiatives (p. 99) Enhanced forms of corporate philanthropy directly related to the company's competencies.

corporate social responsibility (CSR) (p. 98) A business's concern for the welfare of society.

corporation (p. 115) A legal entity with authority to act and have liability separate from its owners.

cost of capital (p. 505) The rate of return a company must earn in order to meet the demands of its lenders and expectations of its equity holders.

cost of goods sold (or cost of goods manufactured) (p. 469) A measure of the cost of merchandise sold or cost of raw materials and supplies used for producing items for resale.

couch potatoes People who sit and watch TV for hours at a time.

countertrading (p. 74) A complex form of bartering in which several countries may be involved, each trading goods for goods or services for services.

counting on it Expecting it.

craft union (p. 319) An organization of skilled specialists in a particular craft or trade.

credit unions (p. 556) Nonprofit, member-owned financial cooperatives that offer the full variety of banking services to their members.

critical path (p. 247) In a PERT network, the sequence of tasks that takes the longest time to complete.

cross-functional self-managed teams (p. 216) Groups of employees from different departments who work together on a long-term basis.

current assets (p. 466) Items that can or will be converted into cash within one year.

customer relationship management (CRM) (p. 349) The process of learning as much as possible about customers and doing everything you can over time to satisfy them—or even exceed their expectations—with goods and services.

damages (p. A-10) The monetary settlement awarded to a person who is injured by a breach of contract.

database (p. 15) An electronic storage file for information.

data processing (DP) (p. BA-2) Name for business technology in the 1970s; included technology that supported an existing business and was primarily used to improve the flow of financial information.

dealer (private-label) brands (p. 383) Products that don't carry the manufacturer's name but carry a distributor or retailer's name instead.

debenture bonds (p. 523) Bonds that are unsecured (i.e., not backed by any collateral such as equipment).

debit card (p. 561) An electronic funds transfer tool that serves the same function as checks: it withdraws funds from a checking account.

debt financing (p. 495) Funds raised through various forms of borrowing that must be repaid.

decentralized authority (p. 208) An organization structure in which decision-making authority is delegated to lower-level managers more familiar with local conditions than headquarters management could be.

decertification (p. 321) The process by which workers take away a union's right to represent them.

decision making (p. 185) Choosing among two or more alternatives.

deflation (p. 47) A situation in which prices are declining.

demand (p. 37) The quantity of products that people are willing to buy at different prices at a specific time.

demand deposit (p. 555) The technical name for a checking account; the money in a demand deposit can be withdrawn anytime on demand from the depositor.

demographic segmentation (p. 362) Dividing the market by age, income, and education level.

demography (p. 17) The statistical study of the human population with regard to its size, density, and other characteristics such as age, race, gender, and income.

departmentalization (p. 210) The dividing of organizational functions into separate units.

depreciation (p. 469) The systematic write-off of the cost of a tangible asset over its estimated useful life.

depression (p. 49) A severe recession, usually accompanied by deflation.

deregulation (p. A-17) Government withdrawal of certain laws and regulations that seem to hinder competition.

devaluation (p. 74) Lowering the value of a nation's currency relative to other currencies.

digital natives (p. 219) Young people who have grown up using the Internet and social networking.

direct marketing (p. 414) Any activity that directly links manufacturers or intermediaries with the ultimate consumer.

direct selling (p. 414) Selling to consumers in their homes or where they work.

disability insurance (p. BC-11) Insurance that pays part of the cost of a long-term sickness or an accident.

discount rate (p. 551) The interest rate that the Fed charges for loans to member banks.

disinflation (p. 47) A situation in which price increases are slowing (the inflation rate is declining).

diversification (p. 525) Buying several different investment alternatives to spread the risk of investing.

dividends (p. 519) Part of a firm's profits that the firm may distribute to stockholders as either cash payments or additional shares of stock.

double-entry bookkeeping (p. 462) The concept of writing every business transaction in two places.

Dow Jones Industrial Average (the Dow) (p. 534) The average cost of 30 selected industrial stocks, used to give an indication of the direction (up or down) of the stock market over time.

drop shippers (p. 409) Wholesalers that solicit orders from retailers and other wholesalers and have the merchandise shipped directly from a producer to a buyer.

dumping (p. 65) Selling products in a foreign country at lower prices than those charged in the producing country.

e-commerce (p. 14) The buying and selling of goods over the Internet.

economic pie *The money available in the economy.*

economics (p. 30) The study of how society chooses to employ resources to produce goods and services and distribute them for consumption among various competing groups and individuals.

economies of scale (p. 205) The situation in which companies can reduce their production costs if they can purchase raw materials in bulk; the average cost of goods goes down as production levels increase.

electronic funds transfer (EFT) system (p. 561) A computerized system that electronically performs financial transactions such as making purchases, paying bills, and receiving paychecks.

electronic retailing (p. 412) Selling goods and services to ultimate customers (e.g., you and me) over the Internet.

e-mail snooped *When someone other than the addressee reads e-mail messages.*

embargo (p. 76) A complete ban on the import or export of a certain product, or the stopping of all trade with a particular country.

empowerment (p. 17) Giving frontline workers the responsibility, authority, freedom, training, and equipment they need to respond quickly to customer requests.

enabling (p. 192) Giving workers the education and tools they need to make decisions.

enterprise resource planning (ERP) (p. 242) A newer version of materials requirement planning (MRP) that combines the computerized functions of all the divisions and subsidiaries of the firm—such as finance, human resources, and order fulfillment—into a single integrated software program that uses a single database.

enterprise zones (p. 156) Specific geographic areas to which governments try to attract private business investment by offering lower taxes and other government support.

entrepreneur (p. 4) A person who risks time and money to start and manage a business.

entrepreneurial team (p. 150) A group of experienced people from different areas of business who join together to form a managerial team with the skills needed to develop, make, and market a new product.

entrepreneurship (p. 146) Accepting the risk of starting and running a business.

environmental scanning (p. 357) The process of identifying the factors that can affect marketing success.

equity financing (p. 495) Money raised from within the firm, or from operations through the sale of ownership in the firm (stock).

equity theory (p. 268) The idea that employees try to maintain equity between inputs and outputs compared to others in similar positions.

ethics (p. 92) Standards of moral behavior, that is, behavior accepted by society as right versus wrong.

everyday low pricing (EDLP) (p. 393) Setting prices lower than competitors and then not having any special sales.

exchange rate (p. 74) The value of one nation's currency relative to the currencies of other countries.

exchange-traded funds (ETFs) (p. 531) Collections of stocks that are traded on exchanges but are traded more like individual stocks than like mutual funds.

exclusive distribution (p. 412) Distribution that sends products to only one retail outlet in a given geographic area.

executor (p. BC-15) A person who assembles and values your estate, files income and other taxes, and distributes assets.

expectancy theory (p. 267) Victor Vroom's theory that the amount of effort employees exert on a specific task depends on their expectations of the outcome.

exporting (p. 61) Selling products to another country.

express warranties (p. A-8) Specific representations by the seller that buyers rely on regarding the goods they purchase.

external customers (p. 194) Dealers, who buy products to sell to others, and ultimate customers (or end users), who buy products for their own personal use.

extranet (p. BA-9) A semiprivate network that uses Internet technology and allows more than one company to access the same information or allows people on different servers to collaborate.

extrinsic reward (p. 257) Something given to you by someone else as recognition for good work; extrinsic rewards include pay increases, praise, and promotions.

facility layout (p. 241) The physical arrangement of resources (including people) in the production process.

facility location (p. 238) The process of selecting a geographic location for a company's operations.

factoring (p. 499) The process of selling accounts receivable for cash.

factors of production (p. 9) The resources used to create wealth: land, labor, capital, entrepreneurship, and knowledge.

Federal Deposit Insurance Corporation (FDIC) (p. 559) An independent agency of the U.S. government that insures bank deposits.

finance (p. 486) The function in a business that acquires funds for the firm and manages those funds within the firm.

financial accounting (p. 458) Accounting information and analyses prepared for people outside the organization.

financial control (p. 491) A process in which a firm periodically compares its actual revenues, costs, and expenses with its projected ones.

financial management (p. 486) The job of managing a firm's resources so it can meet its goals and objectives.

financial managers (p. 486) Managers who make recommendations to top executives regarding strategies for improving the financial strength of a firm.

financial statement (p. 463) A summary of all the transactions that have occurred over a particular period.

fiscal policy (p. 49) The federal government's efforts to keep the economy stable by increasing or decreasing taxes or government spending.

fixed assets (p. 466) Assets that are relatively permanent, such as land, buildings, and equipment.

flat organization structure (p. 209) An organization structure that has few layers of management and a broad span of control.

flexible manufacturing (p. 237) Designing machines to do multiple tasks so that they can produce a variety of products.

flextime plan (p. 306) Work schedule that gives employees some freedom to choose when to work, as long as they work the required number of hours.

focus group (p. 356) A small group of people who meet under the direction of a discussion leader to communicate their opinions about an organization, its products, or other given issues.

foreign direct investment (FDI) (p. 70) The buying of permanent property and businesses in foreign nations.

foreign subsidiary (p. 70) A company owned in a foreign country by another company, called the *parent company*.

formal organization (p. 221) The structure that details lines of responsibility, authority, and position; that is, the structure shown on organization charts.

form utility (p. 234) The value producers add to materials in the creation of finished goods and services.

franchise (p. 131) The right to use a specific business's name and sell its products or services in a given territory.

franchise agreement (p. 131) An arrangement whereby someone with a good idea for a business sells the rights to use the business name and sell a product or service to others in a given territory.

franchisee (p. 131) A person who buys a franchise.

franchisor (p. 131) A company that develops a product concept and sells others the rights to make and sell the products.

free-for-all atmosphere A situation where all order seems to be lost in conducting business.

free-market economies (p. 42) Economic systems in which the market largely determines what goods and services get produced, who gets them, and how the economy grows.

free-rein leadership (p. 192) Leadership style that involves managers setting objectives and employees being relatively free to do whatever it takes to accomplish those objectives.

free trade (p. 61) The movement of goods and services among nations without political or economic barriers.

freight forwarder (p. 419) An organization that puts many small shipments together to create a single large shipment that can be transported cost-effectively to the final destination.

fringe benefits (p. 305) Benefits such as sick-leave pay, vacation pay, pension plans, and health plans that represent additional compensation to employees beyond base wages.

from scratch From the beginning.

fundamental accounting equation (p. 464) Assets = Liabilities + Owners' equity; this is the basis for the balance sheet.

Gantt chart (p. 247) Bar graph showing production managers what projects are being worked on and what stage they are in at any given time.

General Agreement on Tariffs and Trade (GATT) (p. 77) A 1948 agreement that established an international forum for negotiating mutual reductions in trade restrictions.

general partner (p. 117) An owner (partner) who has unlimited liability and is active in managing the firm.

general partnership (p. 117) A partnership in which all owners share in operating the business and in assuming liability for the business's debts.

generic goods (p. 383) Nonbranded products that usually sell at a sizable discount compared to national or private-label brands.

geographic segmentation (p. 362) Dividing the market by cities, counties, states, or regions.

get in on the dough Take the opportunity to make some money.

givebacks (p. 329) Concessions made by union members to management; gains from labor negotiations are given back to management to help employers remain competitive and thereby save jobs.

go for the gold To work to be the very best (figuratively winning a gold medal).

go out with me Go with me to dinner or to a movie or some other entertainment.

goals (p. 181) The broad, long-term accomplishments an organization wishes to attain.

goal-setting theory (p. 267) The idea that setting ambitious but attainable goals can motivate workers and improve performance if the goals are accepted, accompanied by feedback, and facilitated by organizational conditions.

gone off the deep end Doing something risky, almost crazy—like jumping into the deep end of a swimming pool when you can't swim.

goods (p. 4) Tangible products such as computers, food, clothing, cars, and appliances.

goofing off Doing things at work not associated with the job, such as talking with others at the drinking fountain.

government and not-for-profit accounting (p. 461) Accounting system for organizations whose purpose is not generating a profit but serving ratepayers, taxpayers, and others according to a duly approved budget.

greening (p. 19) The trend toward saving energy and producing products that cause less harm to the environment.

grievance (p. 325) A charge by employees that management is not abiding by the terms of the negotiated labor–management agreement.

gross domestic product (GDP) (p. 47) The total value of final goods and services produced in a country in a given year.

gross profit (or gross margin) (p. 469) How much a firm earned by buying (or making) and selling merchandise.

hand over the keys Give access to others.

hard copy Copy printed on paper.

Hawthorne effect (p. 260) The tendency for people to behave differently when they know they are being studied.

health maintenance organizations (HMOs) (p. BB-7) Health care organizations that require members to choose from a restricted list of doctors.

health savings accounts (HSAs) (p. BB-9) Tax-deferred savings accounts linked to low-cost, high-deductible health insurance policies.

heart The most important part of something; the central force or idea.

hierarchy (p. 207) A system in which one person is at the top of the organization and there is a ranked or sequential ordering from the top down of managers who are responsible to that person.

high–low pricing strategy (p. 393) Setting prices that are higher than EDLP stores, but having many special sales where the prices are lower than competitors'.

horizontal merger (p. 129) The joining of two firms in the same industry.

hot second Immediately.

human relations skills (p. 188) Skills that involve communication and motivation; they enable managers to work through and with people.

human resource management (HRM) (p. 284) The process of determining human resource needs and then recruiting, selecting, developing, motivating, evaluating, compensating, and scheduling employees to achieve organizational goals.

hygiene factors (p. 262) In Herzberg's theory of motivating factors, job factors that can cause dissatisfaction if missing but that do not necessarily motivate employees if increased.

identity theft (p. 15) The obtaining of individuals' personal information, such as Social Security and credit card numbers, for illegal purposes.

If it isn't broken, don't fix it Don't risk making things worse by changing things that don't need to be changed.

implied warranties (p. A-8) Guarantees legally imposed on the seller.

importing (p. 60) Buying products from another country.

import quota (p. 76) A limit on the number of products in certain categories that a nation can import.

inbound logistics (p. 418) The area of logistics that involves bringing raw materials, packaging, other goods and services, and information from suppliers to producers.

income statement (p. 468) The financial statement that shows a firm's profit after costs, expenses, and taxes; it summarizes all of the resources that have come into the firm (revenue), all the resources that have left the firm, and the resulting net income.

incubators (p. 156) Centers that offer new businesses low-cost offices with basic business services.

indenture terms (p. 503) The terms of agreement in a bond issue.

independent audit (p. 460) An evaluation and unbiased opinion about the accuracy of a company's financial statements.

individual retirement account (IRA) (p. BC-12) A tax-deferred investment plan that enables you (and your spouse, if you are married) to save part of your income for retirement; a traditional IRA allows people who qualify to deduct from their reported income the money they put into an account.

industrial goods (p. 380) Products used in the production of other products. Sometimes called business goods or B2B goods.

industrial unions (p. 320) Labor organizations of unskilled and semiskilled workers in mass-production industries such as automobiles and mining.

inflation (p. 47) A general rise in the prices of goods and services over time.

infomercial (p. 435) A full-length TV program devoted exclusively to promoting goods or services.

informal organization (p. 221) The system that develops spontaneously as employees meet and form cliques, relationships, and lines of authority outside the formal organization; that is, the human side of the organization that does not appear on any organization chart.

information systems (IS) (p. BA-2) Technology that helps companies do business; includes such tools as automated teller machines (ATMs) and voice mail.

information technology (IT) (p. BA-2) Technology that helps companies change business by allowing them to use new methods.

information utility (p. 408) Adding value to products by opening two-way flows of information between marketing participants.

initial public offering (IPO) (p. 514) The first public offering of a corporation's stock.

injunction (p. 329) A court order directing someone to do something or to refrain from doing something.

insider trading (p. 101) An unethical activity in which insiders use private company information to further their own fortunes or those of their family and friends.

institutional investors (p. 515) Large organizations—such as pension funds, mutual funds, and insurance companies—that invest their own funds or the funds of others.

insurable interest (p. BB-5) The possibility of the policyholder to suffer a loss.

insurable risk (p. BB-5) A risk that the typical insurance company will cover.

insurance policy (p. BB-6) A written contract between the insured and an insurance company that promises to pay for all or part of a loss.

intangible assets (p. 466) Long-term assets (e.g., patents, trademarks, copyrights) that have no real physical form but do have value.

integrated marketing communication (IMC) (p. 430) A technique that combines all the promotional tools into one comprehensive and unified promotional strategy.

integrity-based ethics codes (p. 96) Ethical standards that define the organization's guiding values, create an environment that supports ethically sound behavior, and stress a shared accountability among employees.

intensive distribution (p. 412) Distribution that puts products into as many retail outlets as possible.

interactive promotion (p. 436) Promotion process that allows marketers to go beyond a monologue, where sellers try to persuade buyers to buy things, to a dialogue in which buyers and sellers work together to create mutually beneficial exchange relationships.

interest (p. 521) The payment the issuer of the bond makes to the bondholders for use of the borrowed money.

intermittent process (p. 235) A production process in which the production run is short and the machines are changed frequently to make different products.

intermodal shipping (p. 421) The use of multiple modes of transportation to complete a single long-distance movement of freight.

internal customers (p. 194) Individuals and units within the firm that receive services from other individuals or units.

International Monetary Fund (IMF) (p. 564) Organization that assists the smooth flow of money among nations.

Internet2 (p. BA-10) The private Internet system that links government supercomputer centers and a select group of universities; it runs more than 22,000 times faster than today's public infrastructure and supports heavy-duty applications.

intranet (p. BA-9) A companywide network, closed to public access, that uses Internet-type technology.

intrapreneurs (p. 155) Creative people who work as entrepreneurs within corporations.

intrinsic reward (p. 256) The personal satisfaction you feel when you perform well and complete goals.

inverted organization (p. 220) An organization that has contact people at the top and the chief executive officer at the bottom of the organization chart.

investment bankers (p. 515) Specialists who assist in the issue and sale of new securities.

invisible hand (p. 33) A phrase coined by Adam Smith to describe the process that turns self-directed gain into social and economic benefits for all.

involuntary bankruptcy (p. A-15) Bankruptcy procedures filed by a debtor's creditors.

IOUs *Debt; abbreviation for "I owe you."*

ISO 14000 (p. 246) A collection of the best practices for managing an organization's impact on the environment.

ISO 9000 (p. 246) The common name given to quality management and assurance standards.

job analysis (p. 290) A study of what is done by employees who hold various job titles.

job description (p. 291) A summary of the objectives of a job, the type of work to be done, the responsibilities and duties, the working conditions, and the relationship of the job to other functions.

job enlargement (p. 270) A job enrichment strategy that involves combining a series of tasks into one challenging and interesting assignment.

job enrichment (p. 270) A motivational strategy that emphasizes motivating the worker through the job itself.

job rotation (p. 270) A job enrichment strategy that involves moving employees from one job to another.

job sharing (p. 308) An arrangement whereby two part-time employees share one full-time job.

job simulation (p. 299) The use of equipment that duplicates job conditions and tasks so that trainees can learn skills before attempting them on the job.

job specifications (p. 291) A written summary of the minimum qualifications required of workers to do a particular job.

joint venture (p. 70) A partnership in which two or more companies (often from different countries) join to undertake a major project.

journal (p. 462) The record book or computer program where accounting data are first entered.

judiciary (p. A-2) The branch of government chosen to oversee the legal system through the court system.

jumped headfirst *Began quickly and eagerly without hesitation.*

junk bonds (p. 529) High-risk, high-interest bonds.

just-in-time (JIT) inventory control (p. 244) A production process in which a minimum of inventory is kept on the premises and parts, supplies, and other needs are delivered just in time to go on the assembly line.

Keynesian economic theory (p. 50) The theory that a government policy of increasing spending and cutting taxes could stimulate the economy in a recession.

key player *Important participant.*

kick back and relax *To take a rest.*

Knights of Labor (p. 320) The first national labor union; formed in 1869.

knockoff brands (p. 383) Illegal copies of national brand-name goods.

know-how *A level of specific expertise.*

knowledge management (p. 192) Finding the right information, keeping the information in a readily accessible place, and making the information known to everyone in the firm.

latchkey kids *School-age children who come home to empty houses since all of the adults are at work.*

law of large numbers (p. BB-6) Principle that if a large number of people are exposed to the same risk, a predictable number of losses will occur during a given period of time.

leading (p. 181) Creating a vision for the organization and guiding, training, coaching, and motivating others to work effectively to achieve the organization's goals and objectives.

lean manufacturing (p. 237) The production of goods using less of everything compared to mass production.

ledger (p. 462) A specialized accounting book or computer program in which information from accounting journals is accumulated into specific categories and posted so that managers can find all the information about one account in the same place.

letter of credit (p. 563) A promise by the bank to pay the seller a given amount if certain conditions are met.

level playing field *Treating everyone equally.*

leverage (p. 505) Raising needed funds through borrowing to increase a firm's rate of return.

leveraged buyout (LBO) (p. 130) An attempt by employees, management, or a group of investors to purchase an organization primarily through borrowing.

liabilities (p. 466) What the business owes to others (debts).

licensing (p. 66) A global strategy in which a firm (the licensor) allows a foreign company (the licensee) to produce its product in exchange for a fee (a royalty).

limited liability (p. 117) The responsibility of a business's owners for losses only up to the amount they invest; limited partners and shareholders have limited liability.

limited liability company (LLC) (p. 126) A company similar to an S corporation but without the special eligibility requirements.

limited liability partnership (LLP) (p. 118) A partnership that limits partners' risk of losing their personal assets to only their own acts and omissions and to the acts and omissions of people under their supervision.

limited partner (p. 117) An owner who invests money in the business but does not have any management responsibility or liability for losses beyond the investment.

limited partnership (p. 117) A partnership with one or more general partners and one or more limited partners.

line of credit (p. 498) A given amount of unsecured short-term funds a bank will lend to a business, provided the funds are readily available.

line organization (p. 213) An organization that has direct two-way lines of responsibility, authority, and communication running from the top to the bottom of the organization, with all people reporting to only one supervisor.

line personnel (p. 213) Employees who are part of the chain of command that is responsible for achieving organizational goals.

liquidity (p. 466) How fast an asset can be converted into cash.

lockout (p. 329) An attempt by management to put pressure on unions by temporarily closing the business.

logistics (p. 418) The marketing activity that involves planning, implementing, and controlling the physical flow of materials, final goods, and related information from points of origin to points of consumption to meet customer requirements at a profit.

long-term financing (p. 496) Funds needed for more than a year (usually 2 to 10 years).

long-term forecast (p. 490) Forecast that predicts revenues, costs, and expenses for a period longer than 1 year, and sometimes as far as 5 or 10 years into the future.

loss (p. 5) When a business's expenses are more than its revenues.

M-1 (p. 548) Money that can be accessed quickly and easily (coins and paper money, checks, traveler's checks, etc.).

M-2 (p. 548) Money included in M-1 plus money that may take a little more time to obtain (savings accounts, money market accounts, mutual funds, certificates of deposit, etc.).

M-3 (p. 548) M-2 plus big deposits like institutional money market funds.

Ma Bell *Telecommunication giant, AT&T.*

macroeconomics (p. 30) The part of economics study that looks at the operation of a nation's economy as a whole.

management (p. 179) The process used to accomplish organizational goals through planning, organizing, leading, and controlling people and other organizational resources.

management by objectives (MBO) (p. 267) Peter Drucker's system of goal setting and implementation; it involves a cycle of discussion, review, and evaluation of objectives among top and middle-level managers, supervisors, and employees.

management development (p. 300) The process of training and educating employees to become good managers and then monitoring the progress of their managerial skills over time.

managerial accounting (p. 457) Accounting used to provide information and analyses to managers within the organization to assist them in decision making.

manufacturers' brand names (p. 383) The brand names of manufacturers that distribute products nationally.

market (p. 166) People with unsatisfied wants and needs who have both the resources and the willingness to buy.

marketing (p. 346) The activity, set of institutions, and processes for creating, communicating, delivering, and exchanging offerings that have value for customers, clients, partners, and society at large.

marketing concept (p. 348) A three-part business philosophy: (1) a customer orientation, (2) a service orientation, and (3) a profit orientation.

marketing intermediaries (p. 402) Organizations that assist in moving goods and services from producers to businesses (B2B) and from businesses to consumers (B2C).

marketing mix (p. 350) The ingredients that go into a marketing program: product, price, place, and promotion.

marketing research (p. 354) The analysis of markets to determine opportunities and challenges, and to find the information needed to make good decisions.

market price (p. 39) The price determined by supply and demand.

market segmentation (p. 360) The process of dividing the total market into groups whose members have similar characteristics.

marriage of software, hardware, etc. Combination of various technologies.

Maslow's hierarchy of needs (p. 260) Theory of motivation based on unmet human needs from basic physiological needs to safety, social, and esteem needs to self-actualization needs.

mass customization (p. 237) Tailoring products to meet the needs of individual customers.

mass marketing (p. 362) Developing products and promotions to please large groups of people.

master limited partnership (MLP) (p. 117) A partnership that looks much like a corporation (in that it acts like a corporation and is traded on a stock exchange) but is taxed like a partnership and thus avoids the corporate income tax.

materials handling (p. 418) The movement of goods within a warehouse, from warehouses to the factory floor, and from the factory floor to various workstations.

materials requirement planning (MRP) (p. 242) A computer-based operations management system that uses sales forecasts to make sure that needed parts and materials are available at the right time and place.

matrix organization (p. 215) An organization in which specialists from different parts of the organization are brought together to work on specific projects but still remain part of a line-and-staff structure.

maturity date (p. 521) The exact date the issuer of a bond must pay the principal to the bondholder.

measuring stick Tool used to evaluate or compare something.

mediation (p. 326) The use of a third party, called a mediator, who encourages both sides in a dispute to continue negotiating and often makes suggestions for resolving the dispute.

mentor (p. 300) An experienced employee who supervises, coaches, and guides lower-level employees by introducing them to the right people and generally being their organizational sponsor.

merchant wholesalers (p. 409) Independently owned firms that take title to the goods they handle.

merger (p. 129) The result of two firms forming one company.

Mickey D's Nickname for McDonald's.

microeconomics (p. 30) The part of economics study that looks at the behavior of people and organizations in particular markets.

micropreneurs (p. 150) Entrepreneurs willing to accept the risk of starting and managing the type of business that remains small, lets them do the kind of work they want to do, and offers them a balanced lifestyle.

middle management (p. 187) The level of management that includes general managers, division managers, and branch and plant managers who are responsible for tactical planning and controlling.

mine the knowledge Make maximum use of the knowledge employees have.

mission statement (p. 181) An outline of the fundamental purposes of an organization.

mixed economies (p. 43) Economic systems in which some allocation of resources is made by the market and some by the government.

monetary policy (p. 51) The management of the money supply and interest rates by the Federal Reserve Bank.

money (p. 547) Anything that people generally accept as payment for goods and services.

money supply (p. 548) The amount of money the Federal Reserve Bank makes available for people to buy goods and services.

monopolistic competition (p. 39) The degree of competition in which a large number of sellers produce very similar products that buyers nevertheless perceive as different.

monopoly (p. 39) A degree of competition in which only one seller controls the total supply of a product or service, and sets the price.

more than meets the eye *More than one can see with his or her own eyes; much is happening that is not visible.*

motivators (p. 262) In Herzberg's theory of motivating factors, job factors that cause employees to be productive and that give them satisfaction.

mouse-click away *Ease of doing something by using the computer or Internet.*

muddy the water *Making things even more difficult than they currently are.*

multinational corporation (p. 71) An organization that manufactures and markets products in many different countries and has multinational stock ownership and multinational management.

mutual fund (p. 530) An organization that buys stocks and bonds and then sells shares in those securities to the public.

mutual insurance company (p. BB-7) A type of insurance company owned by its policyholders.

NASDAQ (p. 516) A nationwide electronic system that communicates over-the-counter trades to brokers.

national debt (p. 49) The sum of government deficits over time.

negligence (p. A-4) In tort law, behavior that causes unintentional harm or injury.

negotiable instruments (p. A-8) Forms of commercial paper (such as checks) that are transferable among businesses and individuals and represent a promise to pay a specified amount.

negotiated labor–management agreement (labor contract) (p. 323) Agreement that sets the tone and clarifies the terms under which management and labor agree to function over a period of time.

net income or net loss (p. 468) Revenue left over after all costs and expenses, including taxes, are paid.

network computing system (or client/server computing) (p. BA-12) Computer systems that allow personal computers (clients) to obtain needed information from huge databases in a central computer (the server).

networking (p. 300) The process of establishing and maintaining contacts with key managers in one's own organization and other organizations and using those contacts to weave strong relationships that serve as informal development systems.

niche marketing (p. 362) The process of finding small but profitable market segments and designing or finding products for them.

nonbanks (p. 557) Financial organizations that accept no deposits but offer many of the services provided by regular banks (pension funds, insurance companies, commercial finance companies, consumer finance companies, and brokerage houses).

nonprofit organization (p. 7) An organization whose goals do not include making a personal profit for its owners or organizers.

North American Free Trade Agreement (NAFTA) (p. 78) Agreement that created a free-trade area among the United States, Canada, and Mexico.

notes payable (p. 467) Short-term or long-term liabilities that a business promises to repay by a certain date.

objectives (p. 181) Specific, short-term statements detailing how to achieve the organization's goals.

off-the-job training (p. 299) Training that occurs away from the workplace and consists of internal or external programs to develop any of a variety of skills or to foster personal development.

oligopoly (p. 39) A degree of competition in which just a few sellers dominate the market.

one-to-one marketing (p. 362) Developing a unique mix of goods and services for each individual customer.

online training (p. 299) Training programs in which employees complete classes via the Internet.

on-the-job training (p. 298) Training at the workplace that lets the employee learn by doing or by watching others for a while and then imitating them.

open-market operations (p. 551) The buying and selling of U.S. government bonds by the Fed with the goal of regulating the money supply.

open shop agreement (p. 324) Agreement in right-to-work states that gives workers the option to join or not join a union, if one exists in their workplace.

operating (or master) budget (p. 490) The budget that ties together all of a firm's other budgets; it is the projection of dollar allocations to various costs and expenses needed to run or operate the business, given projected revenues.

operating expenses (p. 469) Costs involved in operating a business, such as rent, utilities, and salaries.

operational planning (p. 184) The process of setting work standards and schedules necessary to implement the company's tactical objectives.

operations management (p. 233) A specialized area in management that converts or transforms resources (including human resources) into goods and services.

organizational (or corporate) culture (p. 220) Widely shared values within an organization that provide unity and cooperation to achieve common goals.

organization chart (p. 187) A visual device that shows relationships among people and divides the organization's work; it shows who is accountable for the completion of specific work and who reports to whom.

organizing (p. 180) A management function that includes designing the structure of the organization and creating conditions and systems in which everyone and everything work together to achieve the organization's goals and objectives.

orientation (p. 298) The activity that introduces new employees to the organization; to fellow employees; to their immediate supervisors; and to the policies, practices, and objectives of the firm.

other side of the tracks *The area where people with less money live.*

out of the office loop *Out of the line of communication that occurs in the workplace.*

outbound logistics (p. 419) The area of logistics that involves managing the flow of finished products and information to business buyers and ultimate consumers (people like you and me).

outsourcing (p. 6) Contracting with other companies (often in other countries) to do some or all of the functions of a firm, like its production or accounting tasks.

over-the-counter (OTC) market (p. 515) Exchange that provides a means to trade stocks not listed on the national exchanges.

owners' equity (p. 467) The amount of the business that belongs to the owners minus any liabilities owed by the business.

participative (democratic) leadership (p. 191) Leadership style that consists of managers and employees working together to make decisions.

partnership (p. 114) A legal form of business with two or more owners.

patent (p. A-6) A document that gives inventors exclusive rights to their inventions for 20 years.

pave the way *Process of making a task easier.*

peanut butter and jelly *Popular combination for sandwich; the two are seen as perfect complementary products.*

penetration strategy (p. 393) Strategy in which a product is priced low to attract many customers and discourage competition.

pension funds (p. 558) Amounts of money put aside by corporations, nonprofit organizations, or unions to cover part of the financial needs of members when they retire.

perks *Short for* perquisites; *compensation in addition to salary, such as day care or a company car.*

perfect competition (p. 39) The degree of competition in which there are many sellers in a market and none is large enough to dictate the price of a product.

performance appraisal (p. 301) An evaluation that measures employee performance against established standards in order to make decisions about promotions, compensation, training, or termination.

personal selling (p. 437) The face-to-face presentation and promotion of goods and services.

pick economy (p. 447) Consumers who pick out their products from online outlets or who do online comparison shopping.

piece of the action A share in the opportunity.

pink slip A notice that you've lost your job.

pitch in To help as needed.

place utility (p. 407) Adding value to products by having them where people want them.

planning (p. 179) A management function that includes anticipating trends and determining the best strategies and tactics to achieve organizational goals and objectives.

PMI (p. 186) Listing all the pluses for a solution in one column, all the minuses in another, and the implications in a third column.

podcasting (p. 445) A means of distributing audio and video programs via the Internet that lets users subscribe to a number of files, also known as feeds, and then hear or view the material at the time they choose.

possession utility (p. 408) Doing whatever is necessary to transfer ownership from one party to another, including providing credit, delivery, installation, guarantees, and follow-up service.

poster child Best example.

precedent (p. A-3) Decisions judges have made in earlier cases that guide the handling of new cases.

preferred provider organizations (PPOs) (p. BB-9) Health care organizations similar to HMOs except that they allow members to choose their own physicians (for a fee).

preferred stock (p. 520) Stock that gives its owners preference in the payment of dividends and an earlier claim on assets than common stockholders if the company is forced out of business and its assets sold.

premium (p. BB-6) The fee charged by an insurance company for an insurance policy.

price leadership (p. 392) The strategy by which one or more dominant firms set the pricing practices that all competitors in an industry follow.

primary boycott (p. 328) When a union encourages both its members and the general public not to buy the products of a firm involved in a labor dispute.

primary data (p. 356) Data that you gather yourself (not from secondary sources such as books and magazines).

principle of motion economy (p. 257) Theory developed by Frank and Lillian Gilbreth that every job can be broken down into a series of elementary motions.

private accountant (p. 458) An accountant who works for a single firm, government agency, or nonprofit organization.

problem solving (p. 186) The process of solving the everyday problems that occur. Problem solving is less formal than decision making and usually calls for quicker action.

process manufacturing (p. 235) That part of the production process that physically or chemically changes materials.

producer price index (PPI) (p. 48) An index that measures prices at the wholesale level.

product (p. 352) Any physical good, service, or idea that satisfies a want or need plus anything that would enhance the product in the eyes of consumers, such as the brand name.

product analysis (p. 387) Making cost estimates and sales forecasts to get a feeling for profitability of new-product ideas.

product differentiation (p. 378) The creation of real or perceived product differences.

product liability (p. A-4) Part of tort law that holds businesses liable for harm that results from the production, design, sale, or use of products they market.

product life cycle (p. 388) A theoretical model of what happens to sales and profits for a product class over time; the four stages of the cycle are introduction, growth, maturity, and decline.

product line (p. 377) A group of products that are physically similar or are intended for a similar market.

product mix (p. 377) The combination of product lines offered by a manufacturer.

product placement (p. 434) Putting products into TV shows and movies where they will be seen.

product screening (p. 386) A process designed to reduce the number of new-product ideas being worked on at any one time.

production (p. 232) The creation of finished goods and services using the factors of production: land, labor, capital, entrepreneurship, and knowledge.

production management (p. 232) The term used to describe all the activities managers do to help their firms create goods.

productivity (p. 14) The amount of output you generate given the amount of input (e.g., hours worked).

profit (p. 5) The amount of money a business earns above and beyond what it spends for salaries and other expenses.

program evaluation and review technique (PERT) (p. 247) A method for analyzing the tasks involved in completing a given project, estimating the time needed to complete each task, and identifying the minimum time needed to complete the total project.

program trading (p. 535) Giving instructions to computers to automatically sell if the price of a stock dips to a certain point to avoid potential losses.

promissory note (p. 497) A written contract with a promise to pay a supplier a specific sum of money at a definite time.

promotion (p. 354) All the techniques sellers use to inform people about and motivate them to buy their products or services.

promotion mix (p. 430) The combination of promotional tools an organization uses.

pros and cons Arguments for and against something.

prospect (p. 438) A person with the means to buy a product, the authority to buy, and the willingness to listen to a sales message.

prospecting (p. 438) Researching potential buyers and choosing those most likely to buy.

prospectus (p. 517) A condensed version of economic and financial information that a company must file with the SEC before issuing stock; the prospectus must be sent to prospective investors.

psychographic segmentation (p. 362) Dividing the market using the group's values, attitudes, and interests.

psychological pricing (p. 394) Pricing goods and services at price points that make the product appear less expensive than it is.

public accountant (p. 459) An accountant who provides his or her accounting services to individuals or businesses on a fee basis.

public domain software (or freeware) (p. BA-14) Software that is free for the taking.

publicity (p. 441) Any information about an individual, product, or organization that's distributed to the public through the media and that's not paid for or controlled by the seller.

public relations (PR) (p. 441) The management function that evaluates public attitudes, changes policies and procedures in response to the public's requests, and executes a program of action and information to earn public understanding and acceptance.

pull strategy (p. 447) Promotional strategy in which heavy advertising and sales promotion efforts are directed toward consumers so that they'll request the products from retailers.

pump up the profits Making profits in a company appear larger than they actually are under recognized accounting rules.

purchasing (p. 244) The function in a firm that searches for quality material resources, finds the best suppliers, and negotiates the best price for goods and services.

pure risk (p. BB-3) The threat of loss with no chance for profit.

push strategy (p. 447) Promotional strategy in which the producer uses advertising, personal selling, sales promotion, and all other promotional tools to convince wholesalers and retailers to stock and sell merchandise.

qualifying (p. 438) In the selling process, making sure that people have a need for the product, the authority to buy, and the willingness to listen to a sales message.

quality (p. 244) Consistently producing what the customer wants while reducing errors before and after delivery to the customer.

quality of life (p. 6) The general well-being of a society in terms of its political freedom, natural environment, education, health care, safety, amount of leisure, and rewards that add to the satisfaction and joy that other goods and services provide.

quid pro quo Latin phrase meaning "something given in return for something else."

quite a stir Something that causes a feeling of concern.

rack jobbers (p. 409) Wholesalers that furnish racks or shelves full of merchandise to retailers, display products, and sell on consignment.

ratio analysis (p. 473) The assessment of a firm's financial condition and performance through calculations and interpretations of financial ratios developed from the firm's financial statements.

real time (p. 217) The present moment or the actual time in which something takes place.

recession (p. 48) Two or more consecutive quarters of decline in the GDP.

recruitment (p. 292) The set of activities used to obtain a sufficient number of the right people at the right time.

reinforcement theory (p. 268) Theory that positive and negative reinforcers motivate a person to behave in certain ways.

relationship marketing (p. 363) Marketing strategy with the goal of keeping individual customers over time by offering them products that exactly meet their requirements.

reserve requirement (p. 550) A percentage of commercial banks' checking and savings accounts that must be physically kept in the bank.

resource development (p. 31) The study of how to increase resources and to create the conditions that will make better use of those resources.

restructuring (p. 219) Redesigning an organization so that it can more effectively and efficiently serve its customers.

retailer (p. 403) An organization that sells to ultimate consumers.

retained earnings (p. 467) The accumulated earnings from a firm's profitable operations that were kept in the business and not paid out to stockholders in dividends.

revenue (p. 5) The value of what is received for goods sold, services rendered, and other financial sources.

reverse discrimination (p. 289) Discrimination against members of a dominant or majority group (e.g. white males) usually as a result of policies designed to correct discrimination against minority or disadvantaged groups.

reverse logistics (p. 419) The area of logistics that involves bringing goods back to the manufacturer because of defects or for recycling materials.

revolving credit agreement (p. 498) A line of credit that is guaranteed but usually comes with a fee.

right-to-work laws (p. 324) Legislation that gives workers the right, under an open shop, to join or not join a union if it is present.

risk (p. 5) The chance an entrepreneur takes of losing time and money on a business that may not prove profitable.

risk (p. BB-3) The chance of loss, the degree of probability of loss, and the amount of possible loss.

risk/return trade-off (p. 502) The principle that the greater the risk a lender takes in making a loan, the higher the interest rate required.

Roth IRA (p. BC-13) An IRA where you don't get upfront deductions on your taxes as you would with a traditional IRA, but the earnings grow tax-free and are also tax-free when they are withdrawn.

rule of indemnity (p. BB-6) Rule saying that an insured person or organization cannot collect more than the actual loss from an insurable risk.

rules-of-the-road orientation Introduction to the proper procedures within an organization.

sales promotion (p. 442) The promotional tool that stimulates consumer purchasing and dealer interest by means of short-term activities.

sampling (p. 444) A promotional tool in which a company lets consumers have a small sample of a product for no charge.

savings and loan association (S&L) (p. 556) A financial institution that accepts both savings and checking deposits and provides home mortgage loans.

Savings Association Insurance Fund (SAIF) (p. 560) The part of the FDIC that insures holders of accounts in savings and loan associations.

scientific management (p. 257) Studying workers to find the most efficient ways of doing things and then teaching people those techniques.

S corporation (p. 125) A unique government creation that looks like a corporation but is taxed like sole proprietorships and partnerships.

sea of information Lots of information, often too much to process.

secondary boycott (p. 329) An attempt by labor to convince others to stop doing business with a firm that is the subject of a primary boycott; prohibited by the Taft-Hartley Act.

secondary data (p. 355) Information that has already been compiled by others and published in journals and books or made available online.

secured bond (p. 503) A bond issued with some form of collateral.

secured loan (p. 498) A loan backed by something valuable, such as property.

Securities and Exchange Commission (SEC) (p. 516) Federal agency that has responsibility for regulating the various exchanges.

selection (p. 293) The process of gathering information and deciding who should be hired, under legal guidelines, for the best interests of the individual and the organization.

selective distribution (p. 412) Distribution that sends products to only a preferred group of retailers in an area.

self-insurance (p. BB-4) The practice of setting aside money to cover routine claims and buying only "catastrophe" policies to cover big losses.

Service Corps of Retired Executives (SCORE) (p. 168) An SBA office with volunteers from industry, trade associations, and education who counsel small businesses at no cost (except for expenses).

services (p. 4) Intangible products (i.e., products that can't be held in your hand) such as education, health care, insurance, recreation, and travel and tourism.

service utility (p. 408) Adding value by providing fast, friendly service during and after the sale and by teaching customers how to best use products over time.

sexual harassment (p. 335) Unwelcome sexual advances, requests for sexual favors, and other conduct (verbal or physical) of a sexual nature that creates a hostile work environment.

shaky ground Idea that possible problems lie ahead.

shareware (p. BA-14) Software that is copyrighted but distributed to potential customers free of charge.

Sherlock Holmes A famous fictional detective who was particularly adept at uncovering information to solve very difficult mysteries.

shoestring budget A budget that implies the company is short on funds and only includes a minimal amount of financial expenditures (i.e., it's as thin as a shoestring).

shopping goods and services (p. 378) Those products that the consumer buys only after comparing value, quality, price, and style from a variety of sellers.

shop stewards (p. 326) Union officials who work permanently in an organization and represent employee interests on a daily basis.

short-term financing (p. 496) Funds needed for a year or less.

short-term forecast (p. 489) Forecast that predicts revenues, costs, and expenses for a period of one year or less.

sift through mountains of information Sort through large volumes of information.

sin taxes Taxes used to discourage the use of goods like liquor or cigarettes.

sinking fund (p. 523) A reserve account in which the issuer of a bond periodically retires some part of the bond principal prior to maturity so that enough capital will be accumulated by the maturity date to pay off the bond.

Six Sigma quality (p. 244) A quality measure that allows only 3.4 defects per million opportunities.

skimming price strategy (p. 393) Strategy in which a new product is priced high to make optimum profit while there's little competition.

small business (p. 157) A business that is independently owned and operated, is not dominant in its field of operation, and meets certain standards of size (set by the Small Business Administration) in terms of employees or annual receipts.

Small Business Administration (SBA) (p. 165) A U.S. government agency that advises and assists small businesses by providing management training and financial advice and loans.

Small Business Investment Company (SBIC) Program (p. 165) A program through which private investment companies licensed by the Small Business Administration lend money to small businesses.

smart card (p. 562) An electronic funds transfer tool that is a combination credit card, debit card, phone card, driver's license card, and more.

smoking gun An issue or other disclosure that could prove a person or organization has done something wrong.

social audit (p. 104) A systematic evaluation of an organization's progress toward implementing socially responsible and responsive programs.

Social Security (p. BC-12) The term used to describe the Old-Age, Survivors, and Disability Insurance Program established by the Social Security Act of 1935.

socialism (p. 40) An economic system based on the premise that some, if not most, basic businesses should be owned by the government so that profits can be more evenly distributed among the people.

sole proprietorship (p. 114) A business that is owned, and usually managed, by one person.

sovereign wealth funds (SWFs) (p. 71) Investment funds controlled by governments holding large stakes in foreign companies.

span of control (p. 208) The optimum number of subordinates a manager supervises or should supervise.

specialty goods and services (p. 379) Consumer products with unique characteristics and brand identity. Because these products are perceived as having no reasonable substitute, the consumer puts forth a special effort to purchase them.

speculative risk (p. BB-3) A chance of either profit or loss.

squeezing franchisees' profits Tightening or reducing profits.

staffing (p. 189) A management function that includes hiring, motivating, and retaining the best people available to accomplish the company's objectives.

staff personnel (p. 213) Employees who advise and assist line personnel in meeting their goals.

stagflation (p. 47) A situation when the economy is slowing but prices are going up anyhow.

stakeholders (p. 6) All the people who stand to gain or lose by the policies and activities of a business and whose concerns the business needs to address.

standard of living (p. 6) The amount of goods and services people can buy with the money they have.

state-of-the-art The most modern type available.

statement of cash flows (p. 471) Financial statement that reports cash receipts and disbursements related to a firm's three major activities: operations, investments, and financing.

statistical process control (SPC) (p. 245) The process of taking statistical samples of product components at each stage of the production process and plotting those results on a graph. Any variances from quality standards are recognized and can be corrected if beyond the set standards.

statistical quality control (SQC) (p. 244) The process some managers use to continually monitor all phases of the production process to assure that quality is being built into the product from the beginning.

statutory law (p. A-3) State and federal constitutions, legislative enactments, treaties of the federal government, and ordinances—in short, written law.

staying afloat Staying in business during tough times.

stockbroker (p. 524) A registered representative who works as a market intermediary to buy and sell securities for clients.

stock certificate (p. 519) Evidence of stock ownership that specifies the name of the company, the number of shares it represents, and the type of stock being issued.

stock exchange (p. 515) An organization whose members can buy and sell (exchange) securities for companies and investors.

stock insurance company (p. BB-7) A type of insurance company owned by stockholders.

stocks (p. 519) Shares of ownership in a company.

stock splits (p. 527) An action by a company that gives stockholders two or more shares of stock for each one they own.

strategic alliance (p. 70) A long-term partnership between two or more companies established to help each company build competitive market advantages.

strategic planning (p. 183) The process of determining the major goals of the organization and the policies and strategies for obtaining and using resources to achieve those goals.

strict product liability (p. A-5) Legal responsibility for harm or injury caused by a product regardless of fault.

strike (p. 327) A union strategy in which workers refuse to go to work; the purpose is to further workers' objectives after an impasse in collective bargaining.

strikebreakers (p. 329) Workers hired to do the jobs of striking workers until the labor dispute is resolved.

supervisory management (p. 188) Managers who are directly responsible for supervising workers and evaluating their daily performance.

supply (p. 37) The quantity of products that manufacturers or owners are willing to sell at different prices at a specific time.

supply chain (or value chain) (p. 416) The sequence of linked activities that must be performed by various organizations to move goods from the sources of raw materials to ultimate consumers.

supply-chain management (p. 416) The process of managing the movement of raw materials, parts, work in progress, finished goods, and related information through all the organizations involved in the supply chain; managing the return of such goods, if necessary; and recycling materials when appropriate.

SWOT analysis (p. 182) A planning tool used to analyze an organization's strengths, weaknesses, opportunities, and threats.

tactical planning (p. 184) The process of developing detailed, short-term statements about what is to be done, who is to do it, and how it is to be done.

tall organization structure (p. 209) An organizational structure in which the pyramidal organization chart would be quite tall because of the various levels of management.

target costing (p. 391) Designing a product so that it satisfies customers and meets the profit margins desired by the firm.

target marketing (p. 361) Marketing directed toward those groups (market segments) an organization decides it can serve profitably.

tariff (p. 76) A tax imposed on imports.

tax accountant (p. 461) An accountant trained in tax law and responsible for preparing tax returns or developing tax strategies.

tax-deferred contributions (p. BC-12) Retirement account deposits for which you pay no current taxes, but the earnings gained are taxed as regular income when they are withdrawn at retirement.

taxes (p. A-13) How the government (federal, state, and local) raises money.

technical skills (p. 188) Skills that involve the ability to perform tasks in a specific discipline or department.

technology (p. 14) Everything from phones and copiers to computers, medical imaging devices, personal digital assistants, and the various software programs that make business processes more effective, efficient, and productive.

telecom Short for telecommunications.

telecommuting (p. 240) Working from home via computer and modem.

telemarketing (p. 413) The sale of goods and services by telephone.

telephone tag To leave a telephone message when you attempt to return a message left for you.

term insurance (p. BC-10) Pure insurance protection for a given number of years.

term-loan agreement (p. 502) A promissory note that requires the borrower to repay the loan in specified installments.

test marketing (p. 352) The process of testing products among potential users.

thorny issue An issue that can cause pain or difficulty (as a thorn on a rose bush may).

through the grapevine *Informal information communication; stories told by one person to the next.*

time deposit (p. 555) The technical name for a savings account; the bank can require prior notice before the owner withdraws money from a time deposit.

time in the trenches *Working with the other employees and experiencing what they contend with as opposed to managing from an office and relying solely on reports about what is happening in the workplace.*

time-motion studies (p. 257) Studies, begun by Frederick Taylor, of which tasks must be performed to complete a job and the time needed to do each task.

time utility (p. 407) Adding value to products by making them available when they're needed.

to take a break *To slow down and do something besides work.*

top management (p. 187) Highest level of management, consisting of the president and other key company executives who develop strategic plans.

tort (p. A-4) A wrongful act that causes injury to another person's body, property, or reputation.

total fixed costs (p. 393) All the expenses that remain the same no matter how many products are made or sold.

total product offer (p. 375) Everything that consumers evaluate when deciding whether to buy something; also called a *value package*.

trade credit (p. 496) The practice of buying goods and services now and paying for them later.

trade deficit (p. 64) An unfavorable balance of trade; occurs when the value of a country's imports exceeds that of its exports.

trademark (p. 382) A brand that has exclusive legal protection for both its brand name and its design.

trade protectionism (p. 76) The use of government regulations to limit the import of goods and services.

trade surplus (p. 64) A favorable balance of trade; occurs when the value of a country's exports exceeds that of its imports.

training and development (p. 297) All attempts to improve productivity by increasing an employee's ability to perform. Training focuses on short-term skills, whereas development focuses on long-term abilities.

transparency (p. 190) The presentation of a company's facts and figures in a way that is clear and apparent to all stakeholders.

trial balance (p. 462) A summary of all the data in the account ledgers to show whether the figures are correct and balanced.

trial close (p. 439) A step in the selling process that consists of a question or statement that moves the selling process toward the actual close.

trigger-happy *Term that refers to people reacting too fast to the circumstances facing them in a difficult situation.*

turn a blind eye *Ignore something of importance.*

turn the work off *Stop working.*

umbrella policy (p. BC-11) A broadly based insurance policy that saves you money because you buy all your insurance from one company.

unemployment rate (p. 46) The number of civilians at least 16 years old who are unemployed and tried to find a job within the prior four weeks.

Uniform Commercial Code (UCC) (p. A-8) A comprehensive commercial law, adopted by every state in the United States, that covers sales laws and other commercial laws.

uninsurable risk (p. BB-5) A risk that no insurance company will cover.

union (p. 318) An employee organization that has the main goal of representing members in employee–management bargaining over job-related issues.

union security clause (p. 323) Provision in a negotiated labor–management agreement that stipulates that employees who benefit from a union must either officially join or at least pay dues to the union.

union shop agreement (p. 324) Clause in a labor–management agreement that says workers do not have to be members of a union to be hired, but must agree to join the union within a prescribed period.

unlimited liability (p. 116) The responsibility of business owners for all of the debts of the business

unsecured bond (p. 503) A bond backed only by the reputation of the issuer; also called a debenture bond.

unsecured loan (p. 498) A loan that's not backed by any specific assets.

unsought goods and services (p. 379) Products that consumers are unaware of, haven't necessarily thought of buying, or find that they need to solve an unexpected problem.

utility (p. 407) In economics, the want-satisfying ability, or value, that organizations add to goods or services when the products are made more useful or accessible to consumers than they were before.

value (p. 374) Good quality at a fair price. When consumers calculate the value of a product, they look at the benefits and then subtract the cost to see if the benefits exceed the costs.

variable costs (p. 393) Costs that change according to the level of production.

variable life insurance (p. BC-10) Whole life insurance that invests the cash value of the policy in stocks or other high-yielding securities.

venture capital (p. 505) Money that is invested in new or emerging companies that are perceived as having great profit potential.

venture capitalists (p. 165) Individuals or companies that invest in new businesses in exchange for partial ownership of those businesses.

vertical merger (p. 129) The joining of two companies involved in different stages of related businesses.

vestibule training (p. 299) Training done in schools where employees are taught on equipment similar to that used on the job.

viral marketing (p. 445) The term now used to describe everything from paying customers to say positive things on the Internet to setting up multilevel selling schemes whereby consumers get commissions for directing friends to specific Web sites.

virtual corporation (p. 217) A temporary networked organization made up of replaceable firms that join and leave as needed.

virtualization (p. BA-13) A process that allows networked computers to run multiple operating systems and programs through one central computer at the same time.

virtual private network (VPN) (p. BA-9) A private data network that creates secure connections, or "tunnels," over regular Internet lines.

virus (p. BA-16) A piece of programming code inserted into other programming to cause some unexpected and, for the victim, usually undesirable event.

vision (p. 181) An encompassing explanation of why the organization exists and where it's trying to head.

volume (or usage) segmentation (p. 362) Dividing the market by usage (volume of use).

voluntary bankruptcy (p. A-15) Legal procedures initiated by a debtor.

walk out the door Leave the company; quit your job.

watching over your shoulder Looking at everything you do.

Web 2.0 (p. BA-11) The set of tools that allow people to build social and business connections, share information, and collaborate on projects online (including blogs, wikis, social networking sites and other online communities, and virtual worlds).

whistleblowers (p. 97) Insiders who report illegal or unethical behavior.

whole life insurance (p. BC-10) Life insurance that stays in effect until age 100.

wholesaler (p. 403) A marketing intermediary that sells to other organizations.

will (p. BC-15) A document that names the guardian for your children, states how you want your assets distributed, and names the executor for your estate.

word-of-mouth promotion (p. 444) A promotional tool that involves people telling other people about products they've purchased.

World Bank (p. 563) The bank primarily responsible for financing economic development; also known as the International Bank for Reconstruction and Development.

World Trade Organization (WTO) (p. 77) The international organization that replaced the General Agreement on Tariffs and Trade, and was assigned the duty to mediate trade disputes among nations.

yellow-dog contract (p. 320) A type of contract that required employees to agree as a condition of employment not to join a union; prohibited by the Norris-LaGuardia Act in 1932.

photo credits

CHAPTER 1

p.3: © John Cross/Mankato Free Press
p.5: © David W. Cerny/Reuters/Corbis
p.6: © Jack Hollingsworth/Getty Images
p.8: © Newscom Photos
p.10: Courtesy of Art For A Cause
p.11: © Jon Feingersh
p.13: © AP Photos
p.16: Courtesy of Cisco Systems, Inc.
p.18: Monkey Business Images Ltd/photolibrary
p.19: © Photoalto /photolibrary
p.21: Photo by Ward Perrin/Vancouver Sun

CHAPTER 2

p.29: © AP Photos
p.31 (left): © RF/Corbis
p.31 (right): © AP Photos
p.32: © Harris Barnes/AgStock Images/Corbis
p.33: © Frances Roberts/Alamy
p.35: © Ingram Publishing/Alamy
p.37: © AP Photos
p.41: © Francis Dean/The Image Works
p.42: © Alexander Demianchuk/Reuters/Landov
p.43: © AP Photos
p.45: © AP Photos
p.48: © Photodisc Collection/Getty Images
p.51: © Scott Olson/Getty Images

CHAPTER 3

p.59: © Jock Fistick/Bloomberg News/Getty Images
p.60: Photo by Bob Martin/Sports Illustrated/Getty Images
p.63: © AP Photos
p.65: © Scott Barbour/Getty Images
p.67: © AP Photos
p.68: © Alexander Nemenov/AFP/Getty Images
p.69: Courtesy of Domino's Pizza
p.70: © Gary Tramontina/The New York Times/Redux Pictures
p.74: © Timothy A. Clary/AFP/Getty Images
p.76: © AP Photos
p.77: © Prakash Singh/AFP/Getty Images
p.81: © Keren Su/Getty Images

CHAPTER 4

p.89: © AP Photos
p.90: © Doug Mills/The New York Times/Redux Pictures
p.92: © AP Photos
p.98: © AP Photos
p.99: © John Gillooly
p.101: © Rachel Epstein/PhotoEdit
p.102: Courtesy of Green Mountain Coffee Roasters
p.104: © Bill Hogan/MCT/Landov
p.105: © RF/Corbis
p.106: © AP Photos

CHAPTER 5

p.113: Brian Scudamore, Founder and CEO of 1-800-GOT-JUNK?
p.115: © James A. Parcell/TWP
p.116: GoGo Images/photolibrary

p.118: © Newscom Photos
p.121: © Newscom Photos
p.122: © Lucas Jackson/Reuters/Landov
p.126: Courtesy of Craftwood Inn
p.129: © Daniel Acker/Bloomberg News/Getty Images
p.131: © Jason Reed/Reuters/Landov
p.132: Door to Door Dry Cleaning Franchise Systems, LLC 2008
p.135: © Newscom Photos
p.136: © imagebroker.net/photolibrary

CHAPTER 6

p.145: © AP Photos
p.146: © 2005 Matthew Gilson/All rights reserved
p.148: © AP Photos
p.149: © PRNewsFoto/Stonyfield Farm/AP Photos
p.152: Courtesy Fonality
p.154: © Brian Smale Photography
p.155: © Paul Hardy/Corbis
p.156: Courtesy of the Business Development Center, Wausau, WI
p.158: © Steve Boyle/NewSport/Corbis
p.160: Courtesy Chef Lorena Garcia, Lorena Garcia Group
p.162: © AP Photos
p.164: Copyright 2005, USA TODAY. Reprinted with permission.
p.167: © Bloomberg News/Getty Images
p.168: Courtesy J&D's Bacon Salt

CHAPTER 7

p.177: © Jim Ruymen/UPI/Landov
p.178: © Digital Vision/Getty Images
p.180: © Creatas/photolibrary
p.184: Hiroko Masuike/The New York Times/Redux Pictures
p.185: © William Thomas Cain/Getty Images
p.189: Joanna M. Pineda, CEO/Chief Troublemaker, Matrix Group International, Inc.
p.191: © AP Photos
p.192: © Matthias Schrader/dpa/Landov
p.194: © Comstock Images/JupiterImages

CHAPTER 8

p.201: © 2006 Anne Ryan, zrIMAGES, Courtesy of Xerox
p.202: Photo by Getty Images for John Deere
p.205: Public Domain
p.206: © Interfoto/Alamy
p.210: © Sysoyev Grigory/ITAR-TASS/Landov
p.211: © Digital Vision
p.214: © Dave Carpenter, www.cartoonstock.com
p.216: © Photodisc Collection/Getty Images
p.219: Courtesy of Dell Inc.
p.221: Photo by Peter Macdiarmid/Getty Images
p.222 (top): © Brand X Pictures/PunchStock
p.222 (bottom): © AP Photos

CHAPTER 9

p.229: Paul Morse/Bloomberg News/Getty Images
p.232: Courtesy of Honda North America
p.233: © Michael Caronna/Reuters/Corbis
p.234: PRNewsFoto/The US Grant/AP Photos
p.235: Aly Song /Reuters/Landov
p.236: © Benoit Decout/REA/Redux Pictures

PC-1

p.237: Harrison McClary/Bloomberg News/Getty Images
p.239: © Lonnie Duka/age fotostock/photolibrary
p.241: Courtesy of Lockheed Martin
p.242: © Gary Reyes/San Jose Mercury News
p.245: Mercy Health Systems

CHAPTER 10

p.255: © AP Photos
p.256: © RF/Corbis
p.258: Copyright © 1994–2009 United Parcel Service of America, Inc. All rights reserved
p.259: Property of AT&T Archives. Reprinted with permission of AT&T
p.264: Courtesy of Ruckus Wireless
p.266: © AP Photos
p.270: © Robyn Beck/AFP/Getty Images
p.272: © Gabriel Bouys/AFP/Getty Images
p.273: Courtesy of Southwest Airlines
p.274: PRNewsFoto/Travelocity/AP Photos
p.276: © age fotostock/photolibrary

CHAPTER 11

p.283: Courtesy of CERTES FINANCIAL PROS (www.certespros.com)
p.286: © Michael Kappeler/AFP/Getty Images
p.289: © Keith Brofsky/Getty Images
p.292: © Paula Solloway/Alamy
p.295: © Juliana Sohn
p.298: © Joe Raedle/Getty Images
p.299: U.S. Air Force photo by Kristina Cilia
p.301: Erin Wigger for The New York Times/Redux Pictures
p.305: © Stan Honda/AFP/Getty Images
p.307: Courtesy of Caterpillar
p.308: © VEER/Mark Adams/Getty Images
p.310: © Steve Cole/Getty Images

CHAPTER 12

p.317: Sean Ryan/Maxppp/Landov
p.319: © Bettmann/Corbis
p.327: © AP Photos
p.328: © Justin Lane/epa/Corbis
p.330: © Edmonton Sun, Darryl Dyck, The Canadian Press Images
p.331: © AP Photos
p.332: © Newscom Photos
p.334: © Astrid Riecken/The Washington Times/Landov
p.335: © RF/Corbis
p.336: © AP Photos

CHAPTER 13

p.345: © Donna Alberico
p.349: © Bettmann/Corbis
p.350: Courtesy of National Highway Traffic Safety Administration and Ad Council
p.353 (top): © Jim Wilson/The New York Times/Redux Pictures
p.353 (bottom): © Burke Triolo/Brand X Pictures
p.354: © Janine Wiedel Photolibrary/Alamy
p.356: Courtesy RDA Group, Bloomfield Hills, Michigan
p.358: © iStockphotos.com/Mark Evans
p.360: Torsten Silz/AFP/Getty Images
p.363: Image provided by CafePress
p.365: Noel Hendrickson/Getty Images

CHAPTER 14

p.373: © AP Photos
p.375: Eduardo Penna
p.376: Courtesy of Apple
p.378: © Tim Boyle/Getty Images
p.379 (left): Jim Arbogast/Getty Images
p.379 (right): Comstock/PictureQuest

p.381: PRNewsFoto/Bumble Bee Tuna/AP Photos
p.382: Courtesy of C2 Group
p.383: © Tony Freeman/PhotoEdit
p.386: © Tony Kurdzuk/Star Ledger/Corbis
p.387: © AP Photos
p.391: © Newscom Photos
p.392: © RF/Corbis
p.394: © AP Photos

CHAPTER 15

p.401: Courtesy of Mark Stern
p.402: © AP Photos
p.407: © Zig Urbanski/Alamy
p.408: © Andy Kropa 2006/Redux Pictures
p.410: © Corbis/PunchStock
p.413 (left): The McGraw-Hill Companies, Inc./Andrew Resek, photographer
p.413 (right): Courtesy of Gamestop
p.414: © Newscom Photos
p.415: Courtesy Chocolate Chocolate Chocolate Company
p.417: Raul Vasquez/Bloomberg News/Getty Images
p.418: © RF/Corbis
p.420: © Steve Crise/Transtock/Transtock/Corbis
p.422: © AP Photos

CHAPTER 16

p.429: Courtesy Girl Scouts USA
p.434: Courtesy Kevin Zolkewicz
p.435: © Fox Broadcasting Co./Photofest
p.436: Brian Snyder/Reuters/Landov
p.437: Copyright © 2000–2009, bwgrewscale.com, All rights reserved.
p.438: © Blend Images/Getty Images
p.439: © age fotostock/photolibrary
p.442: © Maxine Hicks/The New York Times/Redux Pictures
p.443: International Manufacturing Technology Show
p.444: © Jeff Greenberg/PhotoEdit
p.446: © Laurence Mouton/age fotostock
p.448: Courtesy Mars Drinks UK

CHAPTER 17

p.455: Photo by David Plowden
p.458: © Michael Rosenfeld/Getty Images
p.460: © Stockbyte/Getty Images
p.461: © Jeff Henry/Corbis
p.464: © RF/Corbis
p.469: © Chip Litherland/The New York Times/Redux Pictures
p.470: ©The McGraw-Hill Companies, Inc., Andrew Resek, photographer
p.472: © AP Photos
p.475: © Matthew McDermott/Polaris Images
p.476: © age fotostock/SuperStock

CHAPTER 18

p.485: © Liz Hafalia/San Francisco Chronicle/Corbis
p.487: © AP Photos
p.488: © Image Source Black
p.494: © Piet Mall/Getty Images
p.495: © Adam Crowley/Getty Images
p.498: © Vic Bider/PhotoEdit
p.499: © SuperStock/photolibrary
p.503: © Peter Newcomb/Reuters/Corbis
p.504: © Steve Kagan/The New York Times/Redux Pictures

CHAPTER 19

p.513: © AP Photos
p.514: © Deborah Feingold/Corbis
p.516: Monika Graff/UPI/Landov
p.520: © Reuters/Landov

p.524: © Newscom Photos
p.526: © 2006 Charles Schwab & Co. All rights reserved
p.528: © Newscom Photos
p.531: © Paul Eekhoff/Getty Images

CHAPTER 20

p.545: © Matthew Cavanaugh/epa/Corbis
p.546: The U.S. Department of the Treasury Bureau of Engraving and Printing
p.547: © Wu Hong/epa/Corbis
p.551: © AP Photos
p.554: © Bettmann/Corbis
p.556: © Tannen Maury/Bloomberg News/Getty Images
p.559: Stan Honda/AFP/Getty Images
p.560: Viktoria Sinistra/AFP/Getty Images
p.561: © AP Photos
p.562: © AP Photos
p.564: © AP Photos

APPENDIX

p.A-1: © Reuters
p.A-3: Ron Chapple/Taxi/Getty Images
p.A-7: © Newscom Photos
p.A-8: Chris Rank/Bloomberg News/Getty Images
p.A-16: © AP Photos

BONUS CHAPTER A

p.BA-1: Courtesy of World Wide Technology, Inc.
p.BA-3: Courtesy of Apple
p.BA-6: Photo by Peter Macdiarmid/Getty Images
p.BA-8: © Jupiterimages/Imagesource
p.BA-10: Rune Hellestad/UPI/Landov
p.BA-11: Peter Cade/Getty Images
p.BA-12: Richard Perry/The New York Times/Redux Pictures
p.BA-13: © Newscom Photos
p.BA-15: BananaStock/Jupiterimages
p.BA-18: Douglas Healey/The New York Times/Redux Pictures

BONUS CHAPTER B

p.BB-1: © Bloomberg News/Getty Images
p.BB-3: © AP Photos
p.BB-5: © AP Photos
p.BB-6: © RF/Corbis
p.BB-7: Silvia Otte/Getty Images

BONUS CHAPTER C

p.BC-1: Don Farrall/Getty Images
p.BC-3: Purestock/Getty Images
p.BC-7: Phillip Spears/Getty Images
p.BC-9: © Keith Meyers/The New York Times/Redux Pictures
p.BC-12: © Brand X/JupiterImages/Getty Images
p.BC-13: © AP Photos
p.BC-15: © BananaStock/PunchStock

name index

A

Abdullah, Omer, N-12
Abelson, Alan, N-1, N-6
Adams, Steve, 134
Adams, Susan, N-7, N-8
Adams, William Lee, N-1
Adamy, Janet, N-12
Ahrens, Frank, N-6, N-16
Ain, Stewart, N-4, N-14
Albin, Tom, N-9
Aldrich, Mark E., N-10
Alexander, Bianca, 231
Alexander, Michael, 231
Alexander, White, 222
Allen, Paul, 484
Al-Qasimi, Sheikha Lubna, 58–59
Alvares, Clifford, N-15
Amadio, Jill, 351
Amatie, Mona, N-14
Anders, George, 384
Anderson, Chris, 362
Anderson, Jenny, N-17
Anderson, Joel E., N-8
Anderson, John, N-8
Anderson, Mark, N-8
Anderson, Tom, 147
Anderson, Troy, N-10
Aneiro, Michael, N-16
Angelini, Mary Pat, N-5
Ante, Spencer E., N-5
Antonucci, Tonya, 484–485
Applebaum, Binyamin, 557, N-16
Aratani, Lori, N-9
Archer, Leanna, 147
Arends, Brett, N-17
Ariall, Donald L., N-5
Aristotle, 92
Arlidge, John, 59
Armano, David, N-12
Armour, Stephanie, 287
Armstrong, Frank, III, N-15
Arnold, Curtis, N-16
Arons, Marc De Swaan, N-13
Arostegui, Martin, N-2
Asci, Sue, N-14
Atkins, Kimberly, N-10
Attoun, Marti, 3
Austin, Scott, N-18

B

Babuschak, William C., N-12
Bachman, Justin, N-2
Badenhausen, Kurt, N-10, N-14
Baghuvanshi, Gaurav, N-2
Bahnsen, David, N-19
Bajaj, Vikas, 536
Bajzek, Nick, N-11
Baker, Al, N-10
Baker, Stephen, N-5
Bakst, Dina, N-11
Bala, S., N-7
Balfour, Frederick, N-15
Balkin, David B., N-7
Balogh, Jason, N-14
Bandyk, Matthew, N-1, N-4, N-5, N-6, N-11
Banham, Russ, N-12, N-18
Bannan, Karen J., 434, N-13
Banner, Marcia, N-14
Barkley, Tom, N-1
Barnes, Brooks, N-3
Barney, Matt, N-6, N-7
Barrett, Amy, N-5
Barrett, William P., N-14
Barta, Patrick, N
Barwise, Patrick, N, N-12
Bashar, Tony, P-17
Baskin, Burton, 121
Batson, Andrew, N
Battersby, Mark E., N-4
Bauman, Valerie, N-17
Bawany, Sattar, N-1
Beach, William W., N
Beattie, Andrew, N-15
Beavers, Robyn, 254
Beck, Rachel, N-10
Becton, J. Bret, N-8
Behar, Jennifer, 469
Belicove, Mikal E., N-11, N-13
Bell, Jeff, N-13
Bellman, Eric, 373, N-2, N-18
Bendavid, Nafali, N-7
Benesh, Peter, N-17
Benzacar, Karine, N-14
Berggren, Kris, 149
Bergsten, C. Fred, 63
Berkley, Matt, N-5
Berman, Phyllis, N-13
Bernanke, Ben, 544–545, 546, 548
Bernard, Tara Siegel, N-10
Berners-Lee, Tim, BA-18
Berry, Bill, N-8
Bertani, Elizabeth, 487–488
Betrus, Michael, P-17
Bettencourt, Lance A., N-6
Betts, Kate, N-12
Bezos, Jeff, 146
Bidwell, Carol, N-5
Billups, Andrea, 104
Bird, Julie, N-9
Birk, Chris, N-5
Bishop, Todd, N-17
Bivins, Lawrence, N-4
Blake, Marilyn, N-11
Blakely, Stephanie, N-9
Blanchard, Dave, N-2
Blanchard, Kenneth, 94, N-3
Bloch, Nicolas, 180, 203, N-6
Bloom, Robert, N-13
Blow, Paul, N-6
Bo Ouyang, N-3
Boehm, Thomas C., N-16
Bogoslaw, David, 531
Boies, David, A–A-1
Bolles, Richard Nelson, P-17
Bonaminio, Jim, 146
Booker, Ellis, N-13
Botch, Matt, N-9
Boushey, Heather, 335
Bowie, David, 5
Boyar, Bill, N-9
Boyd, James, 494
Boyle, Matthew, 91, N-7, N-12
Brady, Diana, 201
Brant, Martha, 32
Breitfelder, Matthew D., N-8
Brewer, Miriam L., N-4
Breyfogle, Forrest W., III, N-7
Bridgeland, John M., N-3
Brimeyer, Rick, N-7
Brin, Sergey, 254–255
Brito, Enrique, N-14
Brodsky, Norm, 557, N-13
Brody, Mary Beth, N-4
Brohan, Mark, N-5
Brook, Oak, N-12
Brown, Roger, 337
Brown, Steven E. F., N-8
Brown, Warren, 32, 115
Browning, Dan, N-17
Browning, E. S., N-16
Browning, Lynnley, N-15
Brutto, Dan, N-1
Bucaro, Frank C., N-3
Buckl, Claudia, N-19
Buckley, Ronald M., 307
Buckman, Rebecca, N-15
Buehler, Kevin, N-18
Buffett, Warren, 512–513, 527, 533
Buhler, Patricia M., N-6
Bulik, Beth Snyder, N-6
Burke, Jacqueline A., N-2
Burn, Timothy, N-3
Burns, David C., N-14
Burr, Barry, N-10
Burritt, Chris, N-12
Burrows, Peter, N-2
Bush, George W., 50, 51, 58, 97, 100, 544, 559
Bush, Jason, N-2
Bush, Michael, N-13
Butrym, Daniel, 296–297
Butterfield, Stewart, 118
Byrnes, Nanette, N-12
Byron, Ellen, 429
Byus, Kent, N-3

C

Calbreath, Dean, N-15
Callahan, Sean, N-13

I

NAME INDEX

Calvey, Mark, N-5
Campbell, Kelly, N-15
Canli, Turhan, 295
Capell, Kerry, 384, 421, N-3
Caplan, Jeremy, N-12
Cardy, Robert L., N-7
Carey, Susan, N-17
Carlyle, Thomas, 31
Carpenter, Dave, N-15
Carraher, Charles E., 307
Carraher, Sarah C., 307
Carraher, Shawn M., 307
Carroll, Cynthia, 9
Caruso, Carmen, N-4
Carvin, Beth N., N-9
Cash, Martin, N-5
Cassano, Erik, N-7
Cassidy, John, N-10, N-16
Cassidy, Robert, N-5
Cater, John, N-6
Catlette, Bill, 102
Causey, Richard, 91
Cecere, Massimo, N-14
Celaschi, Robert, N-5
Cha, Ariana Eunjung, 560
Chabris, Christopher F., N-18
Chafkin, Max, 3, 127
Chandler, Matt, N-3
Chang, Ivy, N-4
Chansanchai, Athima, N-8
Chapnick, Nate, 351
Charan, Ram, N-6
Chemuturi, Vijay R., N-3
Chen, Gina, N-8
Chen, Jessica, BC-1
Chen, Shu-Ching Jean, N-2
Chen, Stephanie, N-12
Chen, Steve, 147
Cheung, Mee-Shew, N-12
Cho, David, 557, N-15
Choe Sang-Hun, N-2
Cholakis, Peter, N-11
Christmann, Samantha Maziarz, N-4
Chu, Jeff, 131
Chung, Huhnsik, N-16
Ciferri, Luca, N-2
Clancy, Heather, 358, 401, N-11, N-12, N-13
Clark, Andrew, 91
Clark, Charlie, 378
Clark, Don, N-18
Clark, Julie, 148
Clark, Maxine, N-11
Clegg, Roger, N-10
Clements, Jonathan, N-12
Clemons, Erik K., N-11
Clifford, Stephanie, 64
Clinton, Bill, 58
Cloud, John, N-12
Clough, Bethany, N-4, N-5
Coe, Martin, N-14
Cohen, Adrianne, 89
Cohen, Jessica, 222
Cohen, Robert J., 432
Cohn, Laura, N-16
Coleman, Nick, N-19
Collins, Chuck, N-10
Colvin, Geoff, 317, 333, 502, N-1, N-2, N-11

Colvin, Jeoff, N-12
Conant, Eve, N-12
Condon, Bernard, N
Confucius, 92
Conley, Chip, 261
Conlin, Michelle, 287, N-8
Connolly, Sean M., N-3
Conrad, Lee, N-4
Conroy, Erin, 153
Coody, Guerra DeBerry, N-11
Cooney, Elizabeth, N-4
Cooper, Andrea, 10, N
Cooper, James C., 545, N-1, N-7, N-19
Cooper, Matthew, N-10
Cooper, Robin, N-7
Coquillette, Carolyn, 353
Corkindale, Gill, N-3
Cose, Ellis, N-8
Costa, Hilary, N-5
Coster, Helen, N-14
Cotte, June, N-6
Covel, Simona, N-5, N-14
Cox, Trey, N-3
Coy, Peter, 545, N, N-1, N-2, N-16
Craft, Matthew, N-1
Cramer, Jim, P-5
Crawford, Cindy F., N-3
Creamer, Matthew, N-11, N-12
Creighton, Adam, N-4
Crokindale, David, N-11
Cross, Daniel, N-1
Croston, Glenn, 231
Crown, Judith, N-1
Crum, Rex, 229
Crutsinger, Martin, N-2
Cruz, Humberto, N-15
Cullen, Lisa Takeuchi, 43
Cummings, John, N-14
Cummins, Chip, 560
Cuneo, Alice Z., N-13
Cuneo, John, N
Curry, Antony, N-15
Curtsinger, Martin, N-1
Cutler, Thomas R., N-7
Czarnecki, John, 317

D

Dabovich, Melanie, N-11
D'Addario, Jim, N-14
Dahl, Darren, N-18
Dale, Arden, 20
Dame, Joey, 132
Dame, John, 132
Daniels, Mike, 229
Danielson, Ronald, N-6
Danko, William, BC, BC-2
Dash, Eric, A-1, N-14
Daskal, Melvin, N-4
Dauten, Dale, 150
David, Ruth, 36, N
Davis, Bob, 502
Davis, Gerald F., 107
Davis, Jerry, N-9
Dawson, Carol A., N-8
De Aenlle, Conrad, N-15
De Avila, Joseph, N-5

De Borchgrave, Arnaud, N-7
De Feo, Joseph A., N-6, N-7
De George, Richard T., 107
De Haan, Andre, N-14
De Moreas, Lisa, N-13
DeCarlo, Scott, N-10
Deepesh, Desai, N-9
Degenhardt-Burke, Carri, N-7
Deis, Donald, N-3
Del Rey, Jason, N-13
Delaney, John, N-14
Delevingne, Lawrence, N-12
DeLisi, Peter S., N-6
Dell, Michael, 147
Delune, Michael More, N-10
DeMasi, Michael, N-5
Demeropolis, Tom, N-15
Deming, W. Edwards, 245
Dentch, Courtney, N-4
Depasquale, Ellen, N-14
Depp, Johnny, 60, 332
DeWolfe, Chris, 147
Dikel, Margaret Riley, P-20
Dion, Celine, BB
Diskin, Colleen, N-9
Disney, Walt, 148
Dixon, Nancy M., N-6
Dizik, Alina, N, N-6
Doege, David, N-5
Doherty, Brian, N-13
Dokoupil, Tony, 421, N-12
Dorsey, Jack, 147
Doss, Kristina, N-17
Doty, David, 447
Dougherty, Conor, N-7
Douglas, Clinton B., N-13
Dow, Charles, 534
Dowling, Daisy Wademan, N-8
Dranias, Nicholas C., N-17
Dreman, David, N-16
Drucker, Peter, 9, 267, 333
Drueger, Brian D., P-17
Druxman, Lisa, N-5
Du Pont de Nemours, Éleuthère Irénée, 146
Duening, Thomas, N-4, N-5
Dvorak, Phred, N-10

E

Earnshaw, Aliza, N-14
Eastman, George, 146
Easton, Nina, N-1, N-9
Ebbers, Bernard, 91
Ebeling, Ashlea, N-19
Eckblad, Marshall, N-5
Edison, Thomas, 138
Eggen, Dan, N-17
Einhorn, Bruce, 82, N, N-2
Elberse, Anita, N-7, N-11
Elbow, Steve, N-9
Ellin, Abby, 147
Elliott, Kimberly, 325
Elliott, Michael, 43
Ellison, Larry, 332, 334
Ellos, William J., 107
Ells, Steve, 88–89
Endres, Grace M., N-7

Engardio, Pete, 79, 153, N-1, N-2, N-6, N-10
Epstein, Keith, N-1
Epstein, Richard, N-8
Erickson, Tamara J., N-6
Esch, Justin, 168
Evans, Kelly, N-1
Evans, Laura, 155
Evans, Thomas, N-17
Ewing, Jack, N-2

F

Faiola, Anthony, N-1, N-16
Fake, Caterina, 118
Falco, Randy, 447
Fallstrom, R. B., 485
Falvey, Ryan, 296
Fan, Maureen, 560
Farr, Michael, P-17
Farrell, Christopher, N-5
Farrell, Diana, N-2
Farrell, Maureen, N-14, N-17
Fattah, Hassan M., 59
Faulkner, Loren, N-11
Favaro, Ken, N-12
Fayol, Henri, 205–206, 223
Fedor, Liz, N-10
Feingold, Jerry, N-7
Feldman, Amy, N-15, N-19
Feldman, Henry, 136
Feldman, Paula, 136
Ferri, Richard A., N-16
Ferris, Gerald R., 307
Fey, Tina, 328
Fine, Charles H., N-12
Fine, Howard, N-17
Fineman, Josh, N-10
Fiorina, Carleton (Carly), 58
Fisher, Daniel, N, N-1, N-6, N-16
Fitzgerald, Beth, N-6
Flaherty, Michael, N-4
Flandez, Raymund, N-4, N-5, N-16
Fleishman, Sandra, N-12
Fletcher, Michael A., N-7
Flexman, Nancy, 148
Flinchbaugh, Jamie, N-7
Floyed, Tom, N-2
Foley, Mary O., N-18
Foley, Stephen, 93
Forbes, Malcolm, 138
Forbes, Steve, N, N-1, N-17
Ford, Henry, 138, 146
Forsee, Gary, 333
Fortt, Jon, N-18
Foudy, Julie, 484
Foust, Dean, 177, N-4
Fowler, Bree, N-2
Fowler, Geoffrey A., N-11
Fox, Adrienee, N-3
Fox, Jim, 304
Fox, Justin, N-16
Fraidin, Samuel N., N-2
Francis-Smith, Janice, N-17
Frank, Robert, N-14
Franklin, Mary Beth, BC-1, N-19
Frauenfelder, Mark, N-13
Frazier, Mya, 20, N-19
Free, Mitch, 64

Freedman, Jeffrey, N-17
Freeman, Andrew, N-18
Freeman, Sholnn, N-10
Frei, Frances X., N-7
Freifeld, Lorri, 222
Freston, Tom, 124
Fried, Lance, 348
Friedman, Caitlin, P-17
Friedman, Milton, 98
Frischmann, Don, N-3
Fromartz, Samuel, N-12
Fronstin, Paul, N-9
Froschheiser, Lee, N-8
Fry, Art, 155–156
Fuehne, Doug, N-11
Fuld, Richard, 333
Funk, Josh, N-15

G

Gadiesh, Orit, N-1
Galagan, Pat, N-3
Galani, Una, N-15
Galante, Joseph, N-12
Gallagher, James, N-17
Gallagher, Kathleen, N-16
Gamble, James, 146
Gangemi, Jeffrey, N-15
Gantt, Henry L., 247, 257, 277
Garber, Kent, N-12
Garcia, Lorena, 160
Gardner, David, 514
Gardner, Marilyn, N-9
Gardner, Tom, 514
Garmhausen, Steve, 231, N-11
Garvin, David A., N-6
Gates, Bill, 5, 40, 58, 138, 147, 148, 256, BA-5
Gates, Melinda, 40
Gaudiosi, John, N-13
Gavin, Brian, 358
Geisel, Roseanne White, N-17
Gelb, Betsy D., N-12
George, Bill, N, N-3
Gerard, Leo, 325
Ghemawat, Pankaj, N-6
Gilbreth, Frank, 257, 277
Gilbreth, Lillian, 257, 277
Gillers, Stephen, A-1
Gillette, Becky, N-8, N-9
Gillin, Paul, N-13
Girard, John P., N-18
Glater, Jonathan, A-1
Glenn, Don, 14
Goff, Delbert, N-3
Goff, Karen Goldberg, 153, N-5
Goldberg, Delen, N-17
Goldberg, Gabe, N-7
Goldberg, Keith, N-12
Goldern, K. C., P-17
Goldin, Seth, N-13
Goldman, Matt, 185
Goldsmith, Kelly, N
Goldsmith, Marshall, N, N-9
Goldstein, Matthew, N-14
Gomez-Mejia, Luis R., N-7
Gompers, Samuel, 320, 321
Gongloff, Mark, N, N-10
Goode, Robin White, N

Goodell, Charles E., 316
Goodell, Roger, 316–317
Goodison, Donna, N-17
Goodman, Peter S., N-4
Gordon, Zorik, N-13
Gore, Al, A
Gossage, Bobbie, N-15
Graham, Adrienne, N-11
Graham, Benjamin, 512
Graham, Nick, 2–3, 4, 5, 9
Granahan, Tom, N-15
Grandy, Tom, N-14
Graves, Alan B., N-3
Graves, Michael, 448
Gray, Farrah, N-5
Grayson, Katharine, N-10
Green, Heather, 384, 421, N-3
Greenberg, Duncan, 513, BC-1
Greenhouse, Steven, N-3, N-9, N-10
Greenspan, Alan, 544
Greenwald, Judy, N-8
Greenwell, Megan, 429
Griffin, Greg, N-17
Gross, Daniel, 392, 502
Grove, Andrew S., 235
Guinan, Patricia J., N-18
Gunn, Eileen, 273
Gunther, Marc, N-12
Gurchiek, Kathy, N-2
Guttentag, Michael D., N-2

H

Haberkorn, Jennifer, N-12
Hadden, Richard, 102
Haka, Sue, 477
Halkias, Maria, 345
Halko, John, 475
Hall, Emma, N-12
Halliday, Jean, N-12
Hals, Michael D., N-8
Hamel, Mary, N-6
Hamilton, Alexander, 553
Hamm, Steve, N, N-9, N-16
Hammersley, Jim, 162
Hammond, Dave, 169
Hancock, Dain, 241
Hanenel, Sam, N-10
Hanlon, Patrick, N-12
Hannagan, Charley, N-9
Hannon, Kerry, N-15
Harmer, Brian, N-18
Harper, Jennifer, N
Harrington, Richard J., N-12
Harris, Mike, 68
Harris, Roy, N-13
Harrison, Sheena, N-3
Hartley, Thomas, N-10
Harvey, Melissa, 148
Hastings, Rebecca R., N-8
Haven, Paul, N-2
Havens, Chris, N-15
Hawkins, Josh, N-12
Hay, Edward, 303
Healey, Douglas, BA-18
Heck, Josh, N-9
Heffes, Ellen M., N-7
Heineman, Ben W., Jr., N-17
Heintz, Nadine, N-6, N-11

Heisz, Deborah, N-4
Helft, Miguel, N-14
Helm, Burt, N-13
Hemenway, S., N-17
Hempel, Jessi, N-13, N-18
Hendrix, James P., P-17
Hennis, Matt, N-14
Hermanson, Dana R., N-13
Herzberg, Frederick, 261, 270, 277
Hessel, Evan, N-15
Heugens, A. R., N-2
Hickey, David T., N-3
Higgins, Michelle, N-2
Hill, Patrice, N-6, N-15
Hill, Patrick, 545
Hill, Terry, N-4
Hindo, Brian, N-12
Hiner, Jason, N-18
Hira, Nadira A., 258, N-7
Hirsh, Michael, 545
Hirshberg, Gary, 149
Hitt, Greg, N-7
Ho Ching, 9
Hoffa, James P., 320
Hoffman, David, N-16
Hofman, Mike, N-7
Hogan, Mike, 231
Holloway, Lindsay, BC-1
Holmes, Alexis, 147
Holmes, Kim, N-16
Holmes, Tamara, N-4
Holmes, Tamara E., N-5, N-16
Holtzman, Clay, N-3
Hooper, Michael, N-17
Hoover, Kent, N-15
Hopkins, Michael S., 351
Horn, Brian, N-7
Hosford, Christopher, N-6
Houlihan, Anne, N-8
Houston, Richard W., N-13
Hovanesian, Mara Der, 460
Hoyt, Jennifer, N-12
Hsieh, Tony, N-6
Huber, Tim, N-4
Hughes, Natalie, 165
Hulburt, Heather, N-3
Hulme, Ron, N-18
Hupp, Megan, N-5
Hurley, Chad, 147
Hurt, Christine, N-3
Hurtt, Rob, N-5
Huslin, Anita, 494, N-4
Huspeni, Dennis, N-3
Hyatt, Josh, N-7
Hymowitz, Carol, N-10

I

Ibarra, Herminia, N-6
Ihlwan, Moon, N-13
Ingrisano, John R., 273
Ip, Greg, N-1
Irvine, Diane, 154
Irwin, Nell, N, N-16
Isenberg, Daniel J., 43
Isenberg, Eugene, 333
Iwata, Edward, 477
Izzo, Phil, N-1

Jackson, Ira, N-7
Jackson, John, N-10
Jackson, Maggie, N-8
Jackson, Phil, 191
Jackson, Victoria, 166
Jaeger, Jaclyn, N-13
James, Andrea, N-3
James, Chris, N-14
Jane, Reena, N-12
Jantsch, John, N-13
Javitch, David, N-8
Jefferson, Thomas, 92
Jeter, Lynne, N-4
Jin, James, 64
Jobs, Steve, 124, 147, 150
Jocz, Katherine E., N-11
Johnson, Amy, N-3
Johnson, David R., 127
Johnson, Don, 392
Johnson, Kelly, N-11
Johnson, Mark, N-6, N-11
Johnson, Robert, 144
Johnson, Robert Wood, 97
Johnson, Sheila C., 144–145
Jones, Chris, 373
Jones, Pacman, 316
Joyce, Amy, N-11
Joyner, April, N-13
Judson, Whitcomb, 387
Jung, Andrea, 9

K

Kaganovich, Oleg, N-5
Kamdar, Mira, 373
Kanu, Kingsley, Jr., N-5
Kapadia, Reshma, N-1
Kapner, Suzanne, 358
Kapoor, Kunal, 519
Kaptein, Muel, N-2
Karabell, Zachary, 519
Karakowsky, Leonard, N-7
Karan, Donna, 9
Karatash, Abdullah, N-2
Karlgaard, Rich, N-1
Karmali, Naazneen, N-18
Karmin, Craig, N-10
Karpinski, Richard, N-11
Karsh, Brad, N-9
Kass, Danny, 158
Kass, Matt, 158
Katz, David, 477
Katz, David M., N-12
Katz, Harvey M., N-14
Kauffman, Cameron, N-7
Keasler, Terrill, N-3
Keating, Peter, N-19
Keating, Raymond J., 494
Keefe, Joe, 531
Keene, Tom, N-7
Kelly, Bretta, N-7
Kelly, Gary, 273
Kennedy, John F., 100
Kennedy, Simon, N-1
Kenshalo, Rachel, N-9
Kensicki, Peter R., N-3
Kern, Russell, N-13
Ketter, Paula, N-7
Key, Peter, N-2, N-4

Keynes, John Maynard, 50
Kibbe, Cindy, N-4
Kiley, David, 351
Killinger, Kerry, 333
Kimberly, James, N-8
Kimes, Mina, N-19
King, Diane V., N-19
King, Rachael, N-18
Kinglsey, Kanu, Jr., N-8
Kinnear, Thomas C., 410
Kiplinger, Knight, N-1, N-7
Kirby, Julia, N-6
Kirbyson, Geoff, N-3
Kirchhoff, Bruce, 158
Kirkland, Stephen D., N-9
Kiviat, Barbara, N-7, N-13
Kjetland, Ragnheld, BB-1
Klapper, Bradley S., N-2
Klassen, Abbey, N-13
Klein, Karen E., N-4, N-17
Klein, Sarah A., N-4
Kleinbaum, Adam M., 222
Klinger, Georgette, 150
Kneale, Klaus, N-12
Knowles, Francine, N-10
Konrad, Walecia, N-19
Koons, Cynthia, N-16
Kooser, Amanda C., BC-1
Korn, Donald J., N-14
Kost, Danielle, N-14
Kotter, John P., N-6
Kouzes, James M., N-6
Kozlowski, Dennis, 91
Kramer, Andrew, N-2
Krantz, Matt, N-1
Krasner, Jeffrey, N-10
Krell, Eric, N-3
Kreutzer, David, N
Kripalani, Manjeet, N-12
Krishnaiyer, Kartik, 485
Krishnamurthy, Partha, N-12
Krol, Carol, N
Kroll, Karen, 500, N-9, N-14
Kruglinski, John A., N-13
Kubica, Anthony J., N-9
Kuchment, Anna, 89
Kuehner-Hebert, Katie, N-14
Kugler, Logan, 358

L

Lafley, A. G., 202
Lahart, Justin, N
Lambert, Emily, N-12, N-15
LaMotta, Lisa, N-17
Lankford, Kimberly, N-18
Laredo, Leslie, N-6, N-13
Lawler, Edward, 268, N-7
Lawler, Jennifer, N-12
Lawrence, Joseph, N-10
Lay, Kenneth, 91
Layman, Tonya, N-6
Layton, Lyndsey, N-18
Le Beau, Christina, N-14
Learmonth, Michael, N-13
Leary, Brent, N-18
Lee, Cricket, 344–345, 348
Lee, Maria, 137
Lee, Min-Dong Paul, N-3

Lefkow, Dave, 168
Lehigh, Scot, N-2
Lemelson, Jerome, A-7
Lenet, Scott, N-5
Lesser, George, N-16
Leung, Sze, 408
Levering, Robert, 255
Levesque, Lynne C., N-6
Levin, Meta L., N-14
Levisohn, Ben, N-16
Levy, Ari, N-12
Lewis, Andy, N-10, N-11
Lewis, John L., 320
Lewis, Mark, N-10
Lewis, Paul B., N-17
Lewyt, Alex, BA-5
Liebman, Jessica, 373
Lied, Michael, 93
Liedtke, Michael, N-15
Lindblad, Cristina, 545
Lindborg, Hank, N-3
Lindeman, Todd, N-16
Lindsay, Greg, 82
Lindslay, Marsha, 201
Liodice, Bob, N-13
Lippincott, Daniel, N-15
Liptak, Adam, N-11
Llewellyn, Bronwyn, P-17
Lloyd, Edward, BB
Lloyd, Joan, N-8
Lo, Selina, 264
Lofton, Lynn, 460
Logman, Jason, N-14
Lohr, Steve, N-17
Lombardi, Vince, 149
Long, Teresa, N-11
Loomis, Carol J., N
Lorentz, Jake W., N-14
Low, Juliette Gordon, 428
Lowenstein, Roger, N-2
Lowy, Joan, N-18
Lublin, Joann S., N-10
Luccretti, Aaron, N-15
Luthar, Harsh K., N-11
Ly, Tan, N-16
Lydersen, Karl, N-18
Lykins, Gary, 266
Lyman, Chris, 152
Lynn, Jacquelyn, N-7
Lyons, Daniel, 147

M

MacDonald, Alistair, N-16
MacDonald, Elizabeth, N, N-13
MacGillis, Alec, N-9
Maddox, Kate, N-11, N-13
Madoff, Bernard, 461
Magaga, Pros, 36
Maidment, Godwin, N-1
Mailello, Michael, 333
Mainquist, Sally, 282–283
Mallaby, Sebastian, N-17
Mallory, Taylor, N-9
Malone, Michael S., N-11
Malone, Thomas W., N-7
Maloney, Brenda, N-16
Malthus, Thomas, 31–32, 33
Mandel, Michael, N-1, N-6, N-16, N-18

Mangelsdorf, Martha E., N-6
Mangu-Ward, Katherine, N-18
Mann, Sara L., N-7
Mannila, Chuck, N-11
Manzi, Jim, N
Marchetti, Mike, 294–295
Maremont, Mark, 333
Marin, Tom, N-11
Markkula, Mike, 150
Markowitz, Jack, N-10
Marks, Gene, N-14
Marquadt, Kay, 513
Marquardt, Katy, N-2, N-16
Marquez, Jessica, N-14
Marquez Estrada, Heron, N
Marr, Kendra, N-10
Marsden, Keith, N
Marshall, Samantha, N-3
Martin, Anya, N-11
Martin, Franny, 164
Martin, Roger L., N-6
Marx, Groucho, 256
Marx, Karl, 325
Masisak, Corey, N-10
Maskell, Brian, N-7
Maslia, Debrorah Held, N-5
Maslow, Abraham, 260, 270, 277
Mason, Laura, N-4
Mason, Linda, 337
Massey, Meg, N-10
Mast, Carlotta, N-4
Matsucia, Gaig, 446
Maurer, Harry, 545
Mawhinney, Louise, N-14
May, Sherri, N-8
Mayo, Elton, 259–260, 277
Maze, Jonathan, N-4
Mazur, Michael, N-16
McBride, Sarah, N-17
McCarthy, Michael, 317
McConnell, David, 146
McConnon, Ali, N-11, N-12
McCormick, Cyrus, 20
McCorvey, J. J., N-13
McDonald, Ian, BB-1
McDonald, Joe, N-2, N-14
McDonald, Leslie Rose, N-9
McDonnell, Sanford, 505
McElhatton, Jim, N, N-19
McFarland, Keith, N-4, N-6
McFeatters, Dale, N-1
McGregor, Douglas, 263, 277
McGregor, Jane, N-7
McGregor, Jena, 222, N, N-7
McIntyre, Douglas, N-10
McKechnie, John J., III, N-16
McKenzie, Meredyth, N-7
McKinnon, Gary, BB-3
Meany, George, 320
Meat Loaf, 93
Meece, Mickey, 494
Meehan, Sean, N, N-12
Meer, David, N-12
Mehta, Monica, N-14
Mehta, Nina, N-15
Mehta, Stephanie N., N-18
Metcalf, Richard, N-17
Metcalfe, Robert, BA-5
Mettler, Mike, 135

Metz, Rachel, N-17
Metzenthin, Steve, N-14
Meyer, Chris, N-6
Meyer, Harvey, N-9
Meyers, Eric G., N-19
Meyers, Jason, N
Meyerson, Harold, 325
Miards, Kelly, 434
Michelson, Gary, A-6
Mickey, John, 504
Middleton, Diana, N-9
Mihoubi, Bachir, N-4
Millard, Elizabeth, 283
Miller, Claire Cain, N-19
Miller, John W., N-1
Miller, Kerry, 455
Miller, Matthew, N, N-10
Miller, Rich, N-1
Mills, David, N-3
Mills, Heather, 501
Mills, James, 501
Mills-Groninger, Tim, N-14
Miner, Tim, N-6
Minow, Nell, 333
Missett, Judi Sheppard, 135
Moberg, Dennis, N-6
Modic, Stan, N-2
Moldroasser, Joan, 557
Molina, Joshua, N
Montagne, Renee, N-15
Montgomery, James, N-5
Moore, Gordon E., BA-11
Moore, Janet, N-2
Moorthy, R. S., 107
Moran, Gwen, N-13
Moresco, Justin, N-6
Morgenson, Gretchen, N-14
Moritz, Scott, N-17
Moroshove, Richard, N-14
Morris, Betsy, 177
Morrison, Mary E., N-11
Moskowitz, Milton, 255
Mount, Ian, N-4
Moyer, Liz, N-15
Mozilo, Angelo, 333
Mui, Ylan Q., N-7
Mujtaba, Bahaudin G., N-7
Mulcahey, Anne, 200–201
Mulcahey, Michael, 91
Muller, JoAnn, N-6
Mullman, Jeremy, N-13
Mundy, Alicia, N-16
Munk, Cheryl Winokur, N-3
Munoz, Sara Schaefer, N-16
Murdoch-Eaton, Deborah G., N-2
Murphy, Cait, N-6
Murray, Charles J., N-18
Myers, Matthew B., N-12
Myers, Randy, N-19
Myhrvold, Nathan, BA-5
Myring, Mark, N-13

N

Nadler, David, 268, N-7
Nakashima, Ryan, N-1
Nancherla, Aparna, N-9
Nardelli, Robert, 333
Neag, Mike, N-9

NAME INDEX

Needleman, Sarah E., N-9, N-13
Neering, Patricia, N-9
Neff, Jack, N-11, N-13
Nelson, Bob, N-8
Nelson, Todd, N-5
Neuman, Johanna, N-6
Neumeister, Larry, N-17
Neumesiter, Larry, 93
Newman, Richard, N-10
Newman, Rick, N-12, N-14
Newmark, Craig, 147
Nielsen, Tamera, N
Niemela, Jennifer, N-5
Niezen, Carlos, 417
Nooyi, Indra, 9, 176–177, 178
Norland, Rod, 392
Novack, Janet, N-17
Novelli, Bill, N
Nowicki, Michael, N-7
Nuernberg, Toni, N-3
Nunes, Paul F., N-11
Nyden, Paul J., N-1

O

Obama, Barack, 12, 14, 50, 51, 79, 156, 190, 230, 334, 559, 564, A-12, BA-10, BC-11
O'Bannion, Isaac M., N-14
Obodaru, Otila, N-6
O'Brien, Denis, 5
O'Brien, Elizabeth, 519
O'Brien, Jeffrey M., N-9
Ocker, Lisa, N-4
O'Dell, Larry, N-14
O'Driscoll, Gerald P., Jr., N-1
O'Driscoll, Tony, N-7
Ody, Elizabeth, N-15
Oehlsen, Nadia, N-15
Oelrich, Ludo, 99
Ogle, Maureen, N-4
O'Grady, Patrick, N-6
Ohtake, Miyoko, 32
Olsen, Ken, BA-5
O'Marah, Kevin, N-9, N-10
O'Neal, Stanley, 333
O'Neill, Danny, 394–395
Orda, Olga, 147
O'Reilly, Tim, BA-11
Oremus, Will, N-15
Orfalea, Paul, N-8
Oricchio, Renee, N-13
Ormiston, Charles, 180, N-6
O'Rourke, P. J., N
Orr, Kim, BC-1
Orrick, Dwayne, 294
O'Shea, Dan, N-13
O'Sullivan, Kate, 485
Otaka, Hideaki, 336
Otting, Laura Gassner, P-17
Ouchi, William, 265, 278
Ovens, David, N-6
Owen, Bruce M., N-18
Owens, Donna M., 145

P

Page, Larry, 254–255
Palank, Jacqueline, N-17
Palley, Thomas, N-1
Palmer, Gary, N-14
Palmer, Kimberly, N-14
Palmeri, Christopher, N-12, N-16
Palmisano, Sam, 228–229
Paradis, Tim, N-15
Parekh, Rupal, 429
Parise, Salvatore, N-18
Park, Andrew, N-13
Park, James, BC-1
Parker, Emily, 29
Pauleen, David, N-18
Paulson, Henry, 544
Payne, Stephen, N-3
Peale, Norman Vincent, 94, N-2
Pearce, Craig L., N-6
Pearlman, Russell, N-1
Pearlstein, Steve, N-10
Peiro, Andrea, N-14
Penney, J. C., 138
Penttila, Chris, 271
Perego, Martha, N-2
Perez, Angel, N-2
Perich, Sean, 454–455
Peters, Eric, 351
Peterson, William H., N
Pfister, Bonnie, N-18
Phalon, Joe, A-1
Phelps, David, N-15
Philips, Matthew, N-16
Phillips, Matthew, 131
Pierce, Sarah, N-4
Piersall, Wendy, N-12
Pike, George, N-17
Pineda, Joanna, 189
Pinto, Edward, N-17
Pisarenko, Natacha, N-2
Pleven, Liam, N-18
Polimeni, Ralph S., N-2
Polinsky, A. Mitchell, N-16
Pollock, Lauren, 203
Poltorak, Alexander I., N-17
Polyak, Ilana, N-16
Pope, Justin, N-16
Popeil, Ron, 435
Porath, Christine L., N-2
Port, Michael, N-13
Powell, Jennifer Heldt, N-5
Powell, Kurt A., N-3
Pozner, Barry Z., N-6
Prasso, Sheridan, 36
Pratt, Mary K., N-18
Presley, Elvis, 93
Preston, Rob, N-18
Prince, C. J., 557, N-14
Prince, Charles, 333
Prins, Nomi, 536
Procter, William, 146
Prodi, Romano, N
Pugh, Katrina, N-6
Puranam, Phanish, N
Pursey, P. M., N-3
Pyle, George, N-9

Q

Quelch, John Q., N-11
Quinet, Gregory R., N-5
Quinn, Jane Bryant, N-13, N-15, N-16
Quinn, Patricia, N-8
Quittner, Jeremy, N-4, N-5
Quittner, Josh, N-6

R

Rafter, Michelle V., N-18
Rahn, Richard, N
Ramberg, J. J., 10
Randall, David K., 333
Range, Jackie, 373
Rankin, Ken, N-14
Ranson, David, N-1
Rauber, Chris, N-10
Ray, Daryll E., N-2
Rayasam, Renuka, 325
Rayport, Jeffrey F., N-13
Reed, Lisa Knoppe, 10
Reed, Stanley, 502
Reed-Woodard, Marcia A., 447, N-8
Reese, Charley, N-10
Reeves, Amy, 447
Reeves, Byron, N-6
Reilly, Matt, N-11
Rein, Shaun, 513
Reinartz, Werner, N-7
Reingold, Jennifer, N-6
Reinhart, Carmen M., N-7
Rendon, Jim, N-8
Renzi, Maureen A., N-13
Resnik, Marc, 154–155
Reynolds, Dan, N-6
Ricardo, David, 61
Rice, Condoleezza, 58
Rich, Dave, N-11
Richie, Laurel, 428, 429
Richman, Mike, N-6
Richmond, Riva, N-11
Rigas, John, 91
Rigas, Michael, 91
Rigas, Timothy, 91
Riley, Anjanette, N-8
Robb, Greg, N-1
Robbins, Irvine, 121
Roberts, Julia, 60
Roberts, Russell, N-16
Roberts, Sally, N-16
Robinson, Tennile M., N-5
Robitaille, Suzanne, N-8
Rock, Brad, N-1
Rockefeller, John D., 442, 505
Rocks, David, N-1
Roddick, Anita, 150
Rodriquez, Julio, 417
Rodriquez, Robert, N-8
Roebuck, Alvah C., 138
Roehm, Frances E., P-20
Rogoff, Kenneth S., N-7
Romberger, Tim, N-12
Roos, Marty, N-4
Roosevelt, Franklin D., 35, 52, 554
Rosenberg, Arthur D., P-17
Rosenberg, Joyce, N-5
Rosenberg, Joyce M., N-14
Rosenberg, Larry, 408
Rosenwald, Michael S., N-7
Ross, Kenneth, N-16
Rotfeld, Herbert Jack, N-2
Rothermael, Frank T., N-11

Rovito, Rich, N-9
Rowling, J. K., 332, A-7
Roybark, Helen M., N-13
Rozelle, Pete, 316
Rubin, Courtney, N-1
Rubin, Harriett, N-10, N-11
Rubin, Neil, 531
Rubin, Paul H., 32
Rubinkam, Michael, N-7, N-11
Ruffennach, Glenn, N-19
Ruiz, Juanita, 407
Rutberg, Shara, N-14
Ryan, Beth Gorczyca, N-11
Ryan, Mari, N-11
Ryterband, Daniel J., N-10

S

Saad, Lydia, N-9
Sachs, Jeffrey D., N-1
Sale, Timothy J., N-14
Salkever, Alex, 392
Samuelson, Robert J., N, N-1, N-2, N-9, N-16, N-18
Sandella, Rick, N-4
Santoli, Michael, N-16
Sarowitz, Steve, 271
Sasseen, Jane, 79, N-2, N-10, N-15
Saxby, David, N-3
Scaggs, Ann, 444
Scaggs, James, 444
Scanlan, Thomas, 148
Scanlon, Jessie, N-12
Scarborough, Melanie, N-3, N-8
Schafer, Ian, N-11
Schaffer, Bryan, N-7
Schaffner, Dionn, 436
Schatz, Amy, N-13
Schaus, Robert, 180, N-6
Schenker, Jennifer L., 417
Scherber, Amy, 446
Schneider, Eric, N-11
Schneider, Howard, N-2, N-16
Schneier, Bruce, N-18
Schoenberger, Chana R., N
Schooley, Tim, N-4
Schraeder, Mike, N-8
Schreck, Adam, N-2
Schultz, Howard, 60, 63, 147, 177
Schumacher, Steve, N-7
Schuman, Nancy, P-17
Schumpeter, Joseph, 48
Schurenberg, Eric, N-19
Schuster, Jay, 304–305
Schwab, Andreas, N-6
Schwarz, Alan, N-10
Schweber, Howard, N-10
Scoble, Robert, 446
Scott, Mark, 560
Scudamore, Brian, 112–113, 114
Sears, Richard Warren, 138
Sellers, Patricia, N
Sennholz, Hans F., N-16
Serafin, Tatiana, 513, BC-1
Serwer, Andy, N-1
Shah, Rajiv, 417
Shankar, Satish, 180, 203, N-6
Shannon, Martin, N-11

Shapiro, Cynthia, P-17
Sharma, Amol, N-1, N-12, N-18
Sharma, Paul, N-11
Sharp, Sonja, 271
Shaus, Robert, 203
Shavell, Steven, N-16
Shaver, Tim, N-8
Shaw, Jennifer, N-11
Sheedy, Rachel L., N-15
Sheets, Mary Ellen, 114, 135
Shellenbarger, Sue, N-5
Sherwood, Pat, 487–488
Shin, Annys, N
Short, Jack, 147
Shugart, William, N-7
Shutts, Carole, 136
Sidel, Robin, N-15
Sidener, Jonathan, 348
Sidhu, Baijit, N-3
Silverman, Ben, N-15
Silversmith, Debra, N-15
Silversmith, Don, N-15
Simchi-Levi, David, N-12
Simmons, Russell, 149
Simms, Michelle, N-4
Simon, Ellen, N-14
Simon, Stephanie, 231
Simpson, Colin, N-8
Sinfield, Joe, N-6, N-11
Singer, Paola, N-11
Siwicki, Bill, N-5
Skala, Martin, N-15
Skilling, Jeffrey, 91
Skinner, James, N-12
Skinner, Launi, 112
Skrhak, K. Shelby, N-4
Skrilet, Richard, N-18
Slaughter, Matthew, N
Slavin, Nathan S., N-2
Slim, Carlos, 34
Sloan, Alan, 545, N-10
Slobodow, Brian, N-12
Small, Dan, N-2
Smigocki, Michael, N-3
Smith, Adam, 32, 33, 34, 99
Smith, Allen, N-8
Smith, Geri, 79, N-2, N-10
Smith, Jeffrey, N-11
Smith, Rebecca, 20
Smith, Steven Cole, N-8
Smith, Tom, N-3
Smith, Will, 60
Soder, Chuck, N-5
Solomon, Robert C., 107
Sorkin, Andrew Ross, N-4
Sowards, Dennis, N-7
Spector, Mike, N
Spiers, Elizabeth, 536, N-1
Spors, Kelly, N-8
Spors, Kelly K., N-14
Springen, Karen, N-8
Srikanth, Kannan, N
St. Anthony, Neal, N-5
St. Clair, James, N-14
St. John, Jeff, N-5
Stahl, Mila, 294, N-7
Stanley, Benjamin, N-17
Stanley, Thomas, BC, BC-2

Stanton, Phil, 185
Steel, Emily, N-11
Steinberg, Brian, N-13
Steinhoff, Jeffrey, 460
Steinke, H. Dean, 98
Stephan, Jens A., N-14
Stephens, Uriah Smith, 320
Stern, Andy, 325
Stern, Linda, N-19
Stern, Mark, 400
Stettner, Morey, 446, N-9
Stevenson, Jaclyn C., N-8
Stevenson, Jane, N-12
Steward, Michael, BA–BA-1
Stewart, Alix, N-13
Stewart, Martha, 101, 137, 144
Stier, Kenneth, 104
Stites, Eric, 113
Stocker, Michael W., N-16
Stohrer, Bob, N-13
Stolz, Richard F., N-2
Story, Louise, N-4
Strauss, Levi, 138
Stringer, David, 560
Stringer, Judy, N-9
Strohmeyer, Robert, BA-5
Strozniak, Peter, N-17
Stuart, Alix, 477, N-14
Stull, Elizabeth, N-8
Sugars, Brad, N-5
Sullivan, Bob, N-3
Sullivan, John, N-9
Sullivan, Kevin, N-16
Sullivan, Steve, N-13
Summers, Jim, N-7
Sun, Lena H., N-13
Superville, Darlene, 79
Sutthiwan, Angella, N-13
Sviokla, John, N-5
Swartz, John, N-10
Swartz, Mark, 91
Sweeney, John, 325
Swenson, Kyle, N-5
Swisher, Vicki, N-9
Switzky, Bryant Ruiz, N-15
Szakonyi, Mark, N-8
Szaky, Tom, 386

T

Tablac, Angela, N-5, N-9
Tagliabue, Paul, 316
Tait, Richard, 222
Talley, Ian, N-1
Tan, Maryann, N-8
Tapscott, Don, N-18
Tata, Ratan, 372–373, 374
Taylor, Alex, III, N-12
Taylor, Bill, N-8
Taylor, Chris, N-19
Taylor, Edward, 384
Taylor, Frederick, 257, 258, 259, 277
Tedlow, Richard S., N-12
Tennent, Devar, 407
Terlep, Sharon, N
Teska, Kirk, N-17
Thacker, Robert M., N-5
Thomas, Andrew, N-3

Thomas, Isiah, 335
Thomas, Ken, N-10
Thomas, Myra A., 500, N-15
Thompson, Chuck, N-8
Thornton, Emily, 502
Thurm, Scott, N-6
Tibken, Shara, N-5
Tice, Carol, N-14
Tillie, Stacy, N-19
Timmerman, Sandra, 337
Tjan, Anthony K., N-12
Tkaczyk, Christopher, 91, N-9
Toerner, Michael C., N-13
Tokarev, Alex, N
Tolkoff, Sarah, N-17
Tonn, Rebecca, N-13
Toral, Ruben, 82
Torres, Nichole L., BC-1
Tozzi, John, N-5, N-15
Tran, Tini, N-2
Trejos, Nancy, N-19
Triplett, William, N-2
Troianovski, Anton, N-8, N-9
Trudeau, Garry, 106
Trudel, Remi, N-6
Tsadik, Rebekah, 358
Tucker, Libby, N-3
Tully, Shawn, N-7
Tuna, Cari, N-7, N-9, N-10
Turner, Marcia Layton, N, N-12
Turner, Melanie, N-4
Tushman, Michael L., 222
Tyler, Kathryn, 283, N-8, N-9

U

Ulaga, Wolfgang, N-7
Ulman, Danielle, N-4
Ulmer, Jeffrey M., N-16
Ulwick, Anthony W., N-6
Underhill, William, N-6
Underwood, Anne, 20
Underwood, Ryan, N-18

V

Van Leeuwen, Brandi, N-4
Van Oosterhout, J. (Hans), N-2
Van Voorhis, Kenneth R., 152
Vanderbilt, Cornelius, 160
Vardi, Nathan, N-2
Vascellaro, Jessica E., N-18
Vella, Matt, N-6
Vembu, Venkatesan, N-4
Vernon, Lillian, 9
Vestring, Till, N-1
Viana, Liza Porteus, 485
Vick, Michael, 316
Vigna, Paul, N-16
Villhard, Cathy, 296
Vishwanath, Vijay, 180, 203, N-6
Vladen, Victor, 403

Vonasek, Wade, N-3
Voses, Marc S., N-16
Voyles, Bennett, N-15
Vranica, Suzanne, N-13
Vroom, Victor, 267, 278

W

Wachen, Mark, N
Walker, Scott, N-9
Wall, Emma, 82
Waller, Jeff, N-3
Wallison, Peter J., N-17
Walsh, Joe, N-3
Walsh, Kenneth T., 384
Walton, Sam, 4, 5
Wanetick, David, 258, N-7
Wang, Nelson, N-14
Ward, Richard, BB–BB-1, BB-2
Ward, Sandra, N-15
Warnholz, Jean-Louis, 417
Warnockm, Matt, N-3
Washington, Jerome, 408
Wasserman, Elizabeth, N-18
Watson, Kathryn A., N-15
Watson, Thomas, BA-5
Weber, Joseph, 392
Weber, Max, 206–207, 223
Weidenbaum, Murray, N-10
Weinberg, Bruce D., N-18
Weinberg, Neil, 333
Weinberg, Stuart, N-17
Weiner, Laura, N-9
Weingarten, Lucas, 149
Weisberg, Robert, N-3
Weiss, Tara, N-8
Weissman, Robert, N-17
Welch, Jack, 79, 180, N, N-2, N-6, N-8, N-10
Welch, Liz, 185
Welch, Suzy, 79, 180, N, N-2, N-6, N-8, N-10
West, John E., N-7
Westly, Erica, N-12, N-13
Wexler, Debra, 358
Whaley, Robert E., N-3
Whelan, David, N-17
White, Allen L., N-3
White, Erin, N-6, N-8
Whitman, Marina V., 107
Whitney, Eli, 20
Whitney, John, 303
Whittle, Sue R., N-2
Whoriskey, Peter, N-10, N-17
Wielaard, Robert, N-17
Wilburn, Nicola, 153
Wilburn, Randy, 153
Wildstrom, Stephen H., N-6
Will, George F., N, N-1
Williams, Armstrong, N-8
Williams, Clifton A., N-14
Williams, Erica, N-11

Williams, Kathy, N-13, N-14
Williams, Shirley, N-11
Williams, Walt, N-17
Williams, Walter, N-16
Willis, Richard H., N-3
Willmer, Dave, N-9
Willoughby, Martin, N-5
Wilson, Carey, 403, N-12
Wilson, Gary, N-6
Wilson, Sara, BC-1, N-19
Wilson, Sarah, BC-1
Wind, Jerry, N-11
Winfrey, Oprah, 9, 58, 113, 332
Wingfield, Brian, N-10
Wingfield, Nick, N-18
Winik, Lyric Wallwork, N-10
Wink, Chris, 185
Winograd, Morley, N-8
Wisman, Jonathan, N-7
Woetzel, Jonathan, N-2
Wojcik, Joanne, N-17
Wolf, Carol, N-12
Woods, Tiger, 332, 385
Woodyard, Chris, N-11
Woolsey, Matt, N-16
Woosley, John C., N-14
Worthen, Ben, N-12, N-18
Wozniack, Steve, 150
Wu, Nina, N-5

X

Xu Guiqi, N-1

Y

Yang, Jia Lynn, N-18
Yao Ming, 60
Yate, Martin, P-17
Yeaton, Kathryn, N-8
Yorio, Kimberly, P-17
York, Emily Bryson, N-12, N-13
Young, Lauren, N-18
Younglai, Rachelle, N-16
Yourish, Karen, N-16
Yunus, Muhammad, 7–8, 28–29, 36

Z

Zaid, Mayer N., 107
Zakaria, Fareed, N-2
Zanuck, Darryl, BA-5
Zappei, Julia, N-18
Zedillo, Ernesto, N-2
Zendrian, Alexandra, N-4
Zerbe, Dean, N-14
Zetlin, Minda, N-18
Zimmerman, Ann, 345
Ziobro, Paul, N-12
Zuckerberg, Mark, 147
Zumbrun, Joshua, N-8
ZZ Top, 93

organization index

A

A. H. Robins, A-5
A. M. Best, BC-11
AAA, 337
AAMCO, 415
AARP, 338
ABC, A-18
Abu Dhabi Investment Authority (ADIA), 502
Ace Hardware, 10, 138, 415
Adelphia Communications, 91
ADIA; see Abu Dhabi Investment Authority
Adidas, 237
Administaff, 306
Advertising Council, 350
AF Sachs AG, 416
Aflac, 298, A-7
AFL-CIO, 318, 320, 323, 331
AICPA; see American Institute of Certified Public Accountants
AIG; see American International Group
Albertson's, 411
Alcoa, 534
Allen-Bradley, 237
Alliance of Motion Picture and Television Producers, 328
Allied Pilot Association, 327
Allied Security Trust, A-7
Altria Group, 534
Amazon.com, 15, 146, 359, 445, BA-11, BA-14
American Airlines, 329
American Arbitration Association, 327
American Cotton Oil, 534
American Eagle, 21
American Express, 336, 428, 495, 534, 561, 563
American Institute of Certified Public Accountants (AICPA), 459
American International Group (AIG), 334, 487, 534, 536, A-18
American Marketing Association, 374
American Medical Association, 331
American Nurses Association, 331
American Solar Energy Society, 103
American Sugar Refining Co., 534
American Tobacco, 534, A-11
Ameritrade, 524, 525
Amtrak, 184
Amy's Bread, 446
Amy's Kitchen, 353
Anglo-American, 9
Anheuser-Busch, 130
Apex Fitness Group, 454
Apple Computer, 73, 124, 147, 150, 285, 376, 408, 436, 505, BA, BA-5, BA-13
Arby's, 375

Archipelago, 515
Arizona Beverage Company, 381
Arm & Hammer, 389
Armstrong, 445–446
Armstrong Foods, 2
Art for a Cause, 10
Arthur Andersen, 91, 459
Associated Grocers, 416
Associated Press, 138
Association of Certified Fraud Examiners, 102
AT&T, 191, 378, 534, A-11
Auntie Anne's Pretzels, 135, 137
Autobytel.com, 351
Autoliv Inc., 416
Autoweb.com, 351
Avon, 146
Avon Products, 9

B

Baby Einstein, 148
Bagel Works, 101
Bakery Barn, 454–455, 456
Bama Companies, 245
Bank of America, 148, 333, 334, 534, 536
Barnes & Noble, 359
Barney's New York, 502
Baskin-Robbins, 121, 132, 415
Bass Pro Shops, 411
Batter-Up Bakery, 296
Bayer, 383
Bear Stearns, 487, 536
Berkshire Hathaway, 512–513, 527
Bethlehem Steel, 534
Better Business Bureau, 168
Bill and Melinda Gates Foundation; see Gates Foundation
Black Entertainment Television (BET), 144
BLS; see Bureau of Labor Statistics
Blue Cross/Blue Shield, 82, BC-11
Blue Diamond, 138
Blue Man Group, 185
BlueNile.com, 154
Blurb, 273
Bob's Big Boy, 375
Body Shop, 150
Boeing, 62, 90, 178, 327, 505, 534
Boies, Schiller & Flexner, A-1
Boots, 384
Borden, 382
Borders Books, 359
BorgWarner, 416
Borsheims Fine Jewelry, 513
Boston Consulting Group, 176
BP, 80
Brandt's Cafe, 168
Brickwork India, 153

Bright Horizons Family Solutions, Inc., 337
Bristol-Myers Squibb, 336
British Airways, 19
Buffett Partnership Ltd, 512
Build-A-Bear Workshop Inc., 80
Bumble Bee, 381
Bumrungrand International Hospital, 82
Bureau of Alcohol, Tobacco, and Firearms, 418
Bureau of Labor Statistics (BLS), 296, 339
Burger King, 68, 88, 375

C

Cakelove, 115
California Nurses Association, 331
Calvin Klein, A
Campbell Soup Company, 70, 336, 360, 382, 428
Canadian Labour Congress, 330
Capital Protective Insurance (CPI), 238
Careerbuilder.com, 293, 294
Carl's Junior, 375
Caterpillar, 178, 328, 534
CBS, A, A-18
Celestial Seasonings, 101
Census Bureau, 92
Center for Women's Business Research, 134
Certes Financial Pros, 282–283, 296
Change to Win, 318, 320
Chevron, 70, 80, 534
Chicago Gas, 534
China Mobil, 71
Chipotle Mexican Grill, 88–89
Choco-Logo, 392
Chrysler, 72, 329, 487, 494
Ciba Specialty Chemicals, 103
CircleLending, 164
Circuit City, A-15, A-16
Cisco Systems, 191, 242, 305, 505, 516, A-7
CIT Group, 499
Citibank, BA-17
Citicorp, 544
Citigroup, 71, 333, 502, 534
City of Chesterfield Zoning Board, A-4
Clairol, 437
ClearCross, 418
Cleveland Indians, 131
CNOOC, 130
Coca-Cola, 13, 19, 67, 72–73, 176, 377, 383, 384, 417, 434, 466, 477, 513, 521, 527, 534
Coldwater Creek, 414
Colorado Rockies, 131
Companion Global Healthcare, 82

I-8

ORGANIZATION INDEX

Company Expert, 169
Conscious Planet Media, Inc., 231
Conseco, Inc., 308
Cook County Department of Revenue, 461
Cookies on Call, 164
Coors Brewing Company, 73, 437
Copart Inc., 403
Costco, 102, 409, 411
Council of Economic Advisers, 544
Council of Global Unions, 325
Country Garden, 520
Countrywide Financial, 333
Cox Enterprises, 287
CPI; see Capital Protective Insurance
Craftwood Inn, 126
Craigslist, 15
Cranium, 222
Crayola, 388
Critical Infrastructure Protection Board, BA-17–BA-18
Culpepper Compensation & Benefits Surveys, 306
Custom Foot, 237

D

Dairy Queen, 133, 513
Dangdang.com, 275
Dealtime.com, 394
Dean & DeLuca, 469
Decorating Den, 135
Def Jam Records, 149
Del Monte, 382
Dell Computer, 69, 73, 147, 200, 219, 237, 362, 383, 407, 516
Denny's, 433
Designed Dinners, 376
DHL, 358, 421
Digicel, 5
Digital Equipment Corporation, BA-5
Digitas, 447
Dip 'N' Strip, 137
Disney Company, 13, 67, 148, 274, 285, 521, 534, A-7
Distilling & Cattle Feeding Co., 534
Doggypads.com, 400
Domino's, 68, 69, 131, 135
Door-to-Door Dry Cleaning, 132
DOT; see U.S. Department of Transportation
Dow Chemical, 106, 109, 275, 287
Dow Jones & Company, 534
Dr Pepper, 447
Dream Dinners, 376
Drugstore.com, 448
Dubai Ports Authority, 58
Dun & Bradstreet, 158
Dunkin' Donuts, 68, 375
Dupont, 19, 146, 534, A-11
Dynamic Intranet, BA-22
Dyson, 448

E

E*Trade, 524, 525
E*Trade Bank, 562
Eastman Chemical Company, 305
Eastman Kodak, 146, 200, 383, 534

eBay, 15, 413, BA, BA-17
Economic Development Authority, 164
Economic Policy Institute, 335
Ecoprint, 294
Edgewater Technology, 339
Elance.com, 152, 153
Electrolux, 73
Elements Tierra, 160
Elite Foods, 70
EMC, 299
Emery, 421
Empress Mills, 372
Enron, 90, 91, 98, 456, 459, 460
Ernst & Young, 106, 148
e-Scrap Destruction, 442
ESPN, 484
Euronext, 515
Expedia, 349
Exxon Mobil, 71, 80, 122, 534

F

Fabindia, 419
Facebook, 14, 147, 168, 202, 219, 347, 406, 428, 435, 505, BA-10
Factory Green, 147
Famous Pies, 147
Fannie Mae; see Federal National Mortgage Association
Farmers Home Administration, 164
Federal Aviation Administration Academy, 299
Federal Home Loan Mortgage Corporation (Freddie Mac), 559, A-12, A-18
Federal National Mortgage Association (Fannie Mae), 536, 559, A-12, A-18
Fédération Internationale de Football Association, 484
FedEx, 191, 218, 258, 298, 358, 384, 404, 413, 419, 421, 422, 434, BA
FGX; see First Global Express
FINCA; see Foundation for International Community Assistance
Finish Line, 294–295
Firestone, BB-4
First Data, 561
First Global Express (FGX), 434
Fitlogic, 344–345, 346
Flextronics, 69, 240
Flickr, 118
Florida Power and Light, 39
Florida Public Service Commission, 39
FNMA; see Federal National Mortgage Association
Fonality, 152
Food and Drug Administration, 418
Football Association, 93
Ford Motor Company, 45, 62, 72, 74, 80–81, 146, 205, 219, 272, 373, 436–437, 494, A-5, BB-4
Forrester Research, 82
Foundation for International Community Assistance (FINCA), 36
Fox Lawson & Associates, 304
Freddie Mac; see Federal Home Loan Mortgage Corporation
Free Management Library, 233
Freestyle Audio, 348

Fresh Italy, 356
FridgeDoor.com, 362

G

Gap, 106
Garden.com, 436
Gates Foundation, 40, 99, 513
GE; see General Electric
GEICO, 512
General Electric Capital Corporation, 203, 499, 557
General Electric (GE), 19, 71, 121, 176, 180, 187, 203, 285, 300, 422, 534
General Motors (GM), 70, 72, 80, 122, 180, 205, 219, 329, 442, 494, 534, A-5
General Nutrition Center (GNC), 237
Gentle Giant Moving Company, 296
Girl Scouts, 428
Give More Media, 273–274
GlobeFunder, 164
Globoforce Ltd., 275
GM; see General Motors
GNC; see General Nutrition Center
Goldman Sachs, 506, 513, 530
Goodmail Systems, BA-17
Goodwill Industries, 487
Goodyear, 385, 534
Google, 15, 93, 189, 202, 239, 254–255, 285, 287, 305, 382, 384, 435, 505, 516, A-7, A-11, A-12, BA, BA-7, BA-11, BA-14, P-23
Grameen Bank, 7, 28–29, 36
Great Lakes Industry, 266
Green for All, 105
Green Marketing International Inc., BB-10
Green Mountain Coffee Roasters, 102
Greenpeace, 350
Grenade Gloves, 158
Guerra DeBerry Coody, 336–337
Guru.com, 153

H

H. B. Fuller Company, 74
HACE; see Hispanic Alliance for Career Enhancement
Hallmark, 10, 132
Harvard University, 259
Hasting.com, 152
HealthSouth, 90
Hershey Foods Corporation, 73, BA-19
Hewlett-Packard (HP), 58, 70, 222, 274, 534
Hispanic Alliance for Career Enhancement (HACE), 301
Hitachi, 70, 266
Holiday Inn, 68, 131, 136
Home Depot, 207, 208, 333, 393, 534
Home Instead Senior Care, 132
Honda, 7, 45, 70, 73, 232, 239
Honeywell, 534
Hoover's, P-23
Houston Rockets, 60
HP; see Hewlett-Packard
Hyundai, 7

ORGANIZATION INDEX

I

IASB; *see* International Accounting Standards Board
IBM, 15, 19, 62, 73, 100, 101, 121, 178, 191, 228–229, 232, 291–292, 336, 372, 534, A, BA-5, BA-13, BA-14
IGA, 415
Igus, 242
Ikea, 230
ImClone, 90
InBev, 130
Industrial and Commercial Bank of China, 71
Institute of Certified Management Accountants, 458
Institute of Internal Auditors, 460
Insurance Information Institute, BB-13
Intel, 73, 235, 385, 466, 492, 505, 516, 534, BA-11
InterActive Custom Clothes, 237–238
International Accounting Standards Board (IASB), 477
International Association of Machinists and Aerospace Workers, 327
International Franchise Association, 113, 134
International Franchise Association Education Foundation, 135
International Institute of St. Louis, 296
International Paper, 534
International Petroleum Exchange, BB
Intuit, 463, 494
Iowa State University, 421

J

J&D Bacon Salt, 168
Jack in the Box, A-5
Jazzercise, 133, 135
JCPenney, 208, 411
JetBlue Airways, 308, 387
Jiffy Lube, 131, 393
John Deere, 187
JohnsByrne, 236
Johnson & Johnson, 19, 96, 97, 98, 336, 492, 527, 534
Joie de Vivre, 261
Jones Apparel Group, 345
JPMorgan Chase, 105, 333, 336, 337, 487, 534, 536
Jungle Jim's International Market, 146

K

K2 Skis, 218
Kemper Auto and Home Group, 403
KFC, 43, 68, 69, 73, 131, 176, 375, 415
Kia, 416
Kinko's, 272–273
KLM Royal Dutch Airlines, 421
Kmart, 496
Kodak; *see* Eastman Kodak
KPMG, 273, 454
Kraft, 149, 416, 433, 448, 534
Krispy Kreme, 133, 375
Kroger, 411
K-Tec, 436

L

L. L. Bean, 414
Laclede Gas Light Co., 534
Land O Lakes, 138
Lands' End, 414
Leanna's, Inc., 147
LegalZoom, 127
Lehman Brothers, 333, 506, 536, A-15
Lemonade Inc., 155
Lending Club, 164
Lenovo Group Ltd., 19
Leo Burnett, 428, 447
Let's Dish, 376
Levi-Strauss, 82, 382
Lewyt Corporation, BA-5
LexisNexis, 295
Library of Congress, A-7
Likemind, 301
Lindley Group, 417
LinkedIn, BA-10
LivePerson.com, 358
Liz Claiborne, 411
Lloyd's, BB–BB-1, BB-2
Loanio, 557
Lockheed Martin Corporation, 156, 241
Los Angeles Lakers, 191
Lotus Development, 101
Lotus Public Relations, 274
Lowe's, 208
Lucas Group, 437
Luscious Garage, 353

M

Macy's, 208, 275, 345, 464, 499–500
Madison Square Garden, 335
Main Street Market, 2–3, 5
Major League Baseball (MLB), 60, 131, 503
Major League Soccer, 485
Maria's Bakery, 137
Maricopa County Planning Commission, A-4
Maritz, Inc., 274
Mars, 129
Mars Drinks North America, 434
Marvel Entertainment, 67
MasterCard, 495, 561, 563
Masterfoods USA, 437
Matrix Group, 189
Mattel, A-5
Maybelline, 437
McDonald's, 68, 72–73, 99, 106, 112, 131, 132, 133, 137, 208, 221, 233, 238, 257, 300, 374–375, 383, 415, 466, 527, 534, A-4, A-5–A-6, A-7
McDonnell Douglas, 505
MCI Inc., 91
Medtronic Inc., 82, A-6
Mercedes, 70, 239, 385
Merck, 98, 534, A-5
Mercy Health System, 245
Meridan Group, 63
Merrill Lynch, 222, 333, 536
Merry Maids, 137
MetLife Mature Market Institute, 337
MFG.com, 64
MHN PR & Internet Marketing, 501

Miami Dolphins, 60
Michelin, 416
Michelob, 382
Michigan State University School of Packaging, 381
Microsoft, 5, 40, 58, 71, 121, 147, 148, 189, 287, 506, 516, 528, 534, 548, A, A-11, A-12, BA-5
Mindbridge, 338–339
Minnesota Twins, 131
Minority Business Development Agency, 164
Missouri Department of Natural Resources, 461
Missouri Pacific Railroad, BA
Mistral, 144
Mitsubishi, 76, BA-5
Mitsui, 76
MLB; *see* Major League Baseball
MLP Sunoco Logistics (SXL), 117
Money Mailer, Inc., 136
Monster.com, 293, 294
Monte Jade, 301
Moody's Investor Services, 506, 522, 523, 529, BC-11, P-23
Morgan Stanley, 502
Morningstar Inc., 512
Motley Fool, 514
Motorola, 107, 176, 300
Mozy, BA-7
Mr. Rooter, 69
Mrs Fields Cookies, A-15
MTV, 124
Muhairy Group, 69
MySimon.com, 394
MySpace, 147, 155, 168, 347, 358, 428, 435, BA-10, BA-11

N

Nabors Industries, 333
Nakano Vinegar Company, 70
Napster, A
NASCAR, 384
Nathan's Famous, 137
National Basketball Association (NBA), 60, 191
National Bicycle Industrial Company, 237
National Business Incubator Association (NBIA), 156–157
National Cooperative Business Association, 137
National Education Association (NEA), 329
National Federation of Independent Business, 497
National Football League (NFL), 60, 316–317, 485
National Football League Players Association (NFLPA), 316, 317
National Hockey League (NHL), 328
National Institute of Health, 338
National Institute on Drug Abuse, 338
National Lead, 534
National Mediation Board, 326–327
National Park Service, 461
National Retail Federation, 154
National Small Business Association, 501

ORGANIZATION INDEX

National Venture Capital Association, 165
NBA; *see* National Basketball Association
NBC, A-18
NBC Universal, 203
NBIA; *see* National Business Incubator Association
NEA; *see* National Education Association
Nestlé, 19, 71, 477, 519
NetworkforGood.org, 100
New England Pottery Company, 80
New York Giants, 60
New York Knicks, 335
New York Mets, 131
New York Yankees, A
NewsCorp., BA-11
Nextel, 384
NFL; *see* National Football League
NHL; *see* National Hockey League
Nike, 69, 73, 82, 106, 219, 383, 411, A-7
Ning.com, BA-10
Nordstrom, 207, 411
Nordstrom Rack, 411
Nortel Networks, BA-13
North American Co., 534
Northwest Airlines, 130
Norton, BA-17
Nucor Steel, 305
NYSE Euronext, 515, 516

O

Oasis Center, 147
Occupational Safety and Health Administration (OSHA), 258, 338
Ocean Spray, 138
oDesk.com, 152
OECD; *see* Organization for Economic Cooperation and Development
Office Depot, 308, 411
Office of Federal Contract Compliance Programs, 289
Office of Personnel Management, 337
Ogilvy and Mather, 428
1-800-Got-Junk?, 112
Oracle Corporation, 332, 334
Organization for Economic Cooperation and Development (OECD), 75
Organization of American States, 108
Oriental Land Company, 67
Oscar Mayer, 428
OSHA; *see* Occupational Safety and Health Administration
Overnite Transit Company, 328

P

Packard Bell, BA-4
Palo Alto Software, 162
Parsley Patch, 487–488, 492
Partnership for a Drug-Free America, 428
Patagonia, 100, 106
Patek Philippe, 391
Patients Like Me, BA-10
Pax World, 531
Paylocity, 271

PayPal, 169, 548, BA-17
Peachtree, 493–494
Peanut Corporation of America, BB-4
PeopleSoft, 417
PepsiCo, 9, 70, 73, 103, 176–177, 178, 377, 384, 417, 444, 492, A-11
Perdue Chicken, 73
Peterson Institute for International Economics, 63, 325
Petro Canada, 330
Petrochina, 71
Pfizer, 501, 534, A-5
Phat Farm, 149
Phillips-Van Heusen, 106, 109
Physicians for Responsible Negotiations, 331
Pizza Hut, 43, 68, 69, 176
Playtex Company, A-5
Priceline.com, 349, 394
Procter & Gamble, 71, 80–81, 146, 202, 285, 305, 377, 527, 534
Prosper, 164, 557
Publicis Groupe, 447

Q

Quaker Oats, 176
Quanta Computer, 69
QVC, 345

R

Rainforest Action Network (RAN), 105
Randstad North America, 297
RCA, BA-4
Recording Industry Association of America (RIAA), A
Red Bull, 382
Red Cross, 234, 299, 350, 461
Resource Interactive, 155
RIAA; *see* Recording Industry Association of America
Riceland Foods, 138
Richardson Electronics, 417
Richland College, 245
Ritz-Carlton Hotel Company, 233
RJR Nabisco, 130
Rockwell Automation, 237
Rocky Mountain Chocolate Factory, 69, 136
Rollerblade, 383
Rowe Furniture, 209
Rubbish Boys, 112
Ruckus Wireless, 264
Rug Doctor Pro, 137
Rush Management, 149

S

S&P; *see* Standard & Poor's
Safeway, 411
Sage, 463
St. Louis Cardinals, 503
Saks Fifth Avenue, 366
Salamander Hospitality, 144–145
Salvation Army, 461
Sam's Club, 409, 411
Samsung, 70
Samuel Adams, 63

San Diego State University, 287
San Francisco Giants, 131
Sands Hotels, 506
Sanmina-SCI, 240
SAP, 417
Sara Lee Corporation, A-5
SBC Communications Inc., 534
Scott, 416
Scottrade, 525
Sears, Roebuck & Company, 106, 107, 109, 383, 411, 413, 414, 534
Seattle Mariners, 131
Second Bank of the United States, 553
Service Employees International Union (SEIU), 320, 325, 330, 331
7-Eleven, 131, 375, 378, 407, 411
Shakey's Pizza, 375
Shanghai Automotive Industrial Corporation, 70
Shanghai Electric, 19
Shell Oil, 19, 71, 519
Sherwin-Williams, 415
Shipwire Inc., 400–401
Siemens, 82, 519
Simply Cook It, 376
Six Flags, 184
Skyline Construction, 303
Skype, 219
Small Business and Entrepreneurship Council, 494
Small Business Exporters Association, 63
Sonoma Partners, 273
Sony, 189, 382, 383, 519
Southwest Airlines, 273
SpeeDee Oil Change & Tune-Up, 137
Sprint, 333
Sprout Group, 273
SRA International Inc., 132–133
Staffing Now, 282
Standard & Poor's, 506, 522, 523, 529, P-23
Standard Oil, 505, A-11
Staples, 167, 409
Starbucks, 63, 112, 147, 177, 181, 182, 353, 375, 383, 389, 407, 433, 466, 516, BA-11
StarKist, 103
Starwave, 484
State Farm, 403
State Farm Insurance, 338, BB-2
Stonyfield Farm, 149
Students for Responsible Business, 100
Substance Abuse & Mental Health Services Association, 338
Subway, 68, 133, 137
Sulekha, 301
Sun Microsystems, 307
Sunkist, 138
Sunny Fresh Foods, 245
Sunoco, Inc., 117
Superior Products, 74

T

T. Rowe Price, 532
Taco Bell, 43, 176, 184
Talon, Inc., 387
Target, 208, 218, 219, 366, 375, 378, 411, 422

Tata Group, 372–373
T.B.S. Inc., 134
TCBY, 133
Team, 414
Teamsters Union, 318, 328, 330
Tejari.com, 58
Temasek Holdings, 9
Tennessee Coal, Iron & Railroad Co., 534
TerraCycle, 386
Tesco, 384
Texaco, 534
Texas Instruments (TI), 419
3Com, BA-5
3M, 146, 155–156, 534
ThrowThings.com, 154–155
TIAA-CREF, 558
Timberland, 99, 384, 402
Time Warner, 222
TJ Maxx, 411
TNT, 99, 421
Toshiba, BA-14
Toyota Motor, 7, 32, 70, 72, 80–81, 267, 336, 351
Toys "R" Us, 130, 411
Transparency International, 75
Transportation Security Administration, 184
Transware Corporation, 63
Travelocity, 274, 349
Tripledge, 447
Tropical Blossom Honey Company, 63
Tropicana, 176
True Value Hardware, 138
Truman Development Corporation, 2
Trump Hotels and Casinos, 506
20th Century Fox, BA-5
Twitter, 147, 219, 445, BA-11
Two Men and a Truck, 135
Tyco International, 90, 91, 459
Tyson Foods, BB-4

U

Ugly Dolls, 63
Unilever, 519
Union Carbide, 534
United Airlines, 329
United American Nurses, 331
United Auto Workers, 328, 329
United Food and Commercial Workers Union, 325
United Healthcare, 82
United Parcel Service (UPS), 60, 187, 206, 218, 258–259, 295, 337, 358, 404, 413, 419, 421, 422, 434, 496
U.S. Air Force, 241
U.S. Department of Commerce, 62, 63, 67, 135, 169, 170
U.S. Department of Defense, 267

U.S. Department of Health and Human Services, 338
U.S. Department of Homeland Security, BA-17–BA-18
U.S. Department of Interior, 90
U.S. Department of Justice, 92, A, A-10–A-11, A-12
U.S. Department of Labor, 78, 102, 299, 338, P-17
U.S. Department of State, 422
U.S. Department of Transportation (DOT), 295
U.S. Department of Treasury, A-12, A-18
U.S. Government Printing Office, 63
U.S. Green Building Council, 131
U.S. Marines, 241
U.S. Navy, 241, 387
U.S. Patent and Trademark Office (USPTO), A-6, A-21
U.S. Postal Service, 339, 404, 419
U.S. Supreme Court, 91, 288, 289, 301, 329, 335, 459, A-3
United Steelworkers, 325
United Technologies, 534
Universal Studios, 67
University of California-Los Angeles, 265
University of Maryland, 168
University of Michigan, 335
University of Pittsburgh, 70
Unocal, 130
UPS; see United Parcel Service
UPS Store, 132
U.S. Leather, 534
U.S. Rubber Co., 534
U.S. Web Corporation, 136

V

Vehix, 346
VeriSign, BA-18
Verizon, 338, 534, A-7
Viacom, 93, 144, 147
Victoria Jackson Cosmetics Company, 166
Virgin Airlines, 382
Virgin Money, 164
Virginia Tech, 168
Visa, 495, 515, 561, 563, A-11
Vita-Mix, 436
Volkswagen, 70, 71, 239
VolunteerMatch.org, 100

W

Wachovia Bank, 544, A
Wagner Electric, BA
Wal-Mart, 4, 5, 19, 71, 73, 80, 102, 121, 146, 191, 218, 238, 382, 393, 411, 422, 534, BA-8

Walt Disney Company; see Disney Company
Warner Bros., 67
Washington Capitals, 144
Washington Mutual Bank, 333
Washington Mystics, 144
Washington Nationals, 131
Washington Opera Company, 394
Washington Wizards, 144
Watson Wyatt, 337
Wegman's Food Markets, 292
Weight Watchers, 131
Welch's, 138
Wells Fargo Bank, 100, 513, 544
Wendy's, 88, 233, 375
Western Australia Energy Research Alliance, 70
Western Electric, 259
Westinghouse, 534
Whiteflash.com, 358
Whole Foods Market, 180, 469
Will n' Roses LLC, 148
Wilson Sporting Goods, 230
Winn-Dixie, 294
Wipro Health Science, 82
Wizard Vending, 169
Women's Professional Soccer, 484–485
Women's United Soccer Association, 484–485
Woolworth, 534
Workforce Solutions, 306
Workz.com, 168
World Wide Technology (WWT), BA–BA-1
WorldCom, 90, 91, 101–102, 459, 460
Wrigley Company, 129
Wyeth, 218

X

Xerox Corporation, 100, 121, 200–201, 339, 383
Xporta, 418
XSAg.com, 14

Y

Yahoo, 118, 147, 391, 435, 484, 528, 530, 532, A-12, BA-8, P-23
YouTube, 93, 147, 219, 254, 428, 436, 445, A-7, BA-11
Yum! Brands, 43

Z

Zappos, 448
ZDNet.com, BA-21
Zopa, 164
Zuca Inc., 434

subject index

A

Absolute advantage, 62
ABSs; *see* Asset-backed securities
Accessory equipment, 380
Accountability, 190
Accountants
    certified management, 458
    certified public, 459, 460
    forensic, 460
    private, 458
    public, 459
Accounting
    areas
        auditing, 460, 488–489
        financial, 458–459
        forensic, 460
        government and not-for-profit, 461
        managerial, 457–458
        tax, 461
    defined, 456
    distinction from bookkeeping, 462
    ethical issues, 473
    fundamental equation, 464
    journals, 462
    ledgers, 462
    oversight of profession, 459, 460
    purposes, 456–457
    relationship to finance, 486
    reports, 457
    scandals, 459
    in small businesses, 167, 463
    technology used in, 463
    users of information, 456–457
Accounting cycle, 462–463
Accounting firms
    consulting work, 460
    scandals, 459
Accounting standards
    generally accepted principles, 459, 469–470, 477
    international, 477
Accounting system, 456, 457
Accounts payable, 466
Accounts receivable
    collecting, 494–495
    as current asset, 466
    factoring, 499–500
Acid-test (quick) ratio, 474
Acquisitions, 129; *see also* Mergers and acquisitions
Activity ratios, 475–476
ADA; *see* Americans with Disabilities Act
Administered distribution systems, 416
Administrative agencies, A-3, A-4
ADRs; *see* American depository receipts
Advantage
    absolute, 62
    comparative, 61–62
Advertising
    categories, 432
    celebrity endorsements, 385
    defined, 431
    direct mail; *see* Direct mail
    expenditures, 431, 432
    in foreign countries, 73
    global, 436–437
    greenwashing, 104
    infomercials, 435
    Internet, 432, 433, 435–436, 447
    magazine, 431–432, 433
    media, 431–433
    mobile, 433, 446
    newspaper, 431–432, 433
    outdoor, 433
    product placement, 434–435
    public benefits of, 432
    radio, 432–433
    television, 431, 432, 433–435
    testimonials, 445
    Yellow Pages, 432, 433
Advertising agencies, 447
Affiliate marketing, 155
Affirmative action, 288–289
Afghanistan, 19
AFL; *see* American Federation of Labor
AFL-CIO, 318, 320, 323, 331
African Americans; *see also* Minorities
    affirmative action, 288–289
    franchising opportunities, 135
    managers, 301
Age; *see* Aging of population; Demography
Age Discrimination in Employment Act of 1967, 288, 289–290
Agency shop agreements, 324
Agents/brokers, 403, 410–411
Aging of population
    baby boomers, 18
    of consumers, 17–18, 359
    discrimination issues, 289–290
    elder care, 337–338
    in United States, 17–18, 359
    of workforce, 289–290
Agriculture; *see also* Food industry
    biofuel production, 32
    cooperatives, 138
    history, 20–21
    number of farmers, 20–21
    technology used in, 14, 20
Air transportation, 421
Airlines
    costs of increased security, 19
    deregulation, A-17
Alcohol abuse, 338
Alcohol Labeling Legislation (1988), A-13
Alliances
    of Japanese firms, 76
    strategic, 70
Allocation model, 526
American depository receipts (ADRs), 519
American Federation of Labor (AFL), 320, 321
American Indians; *see* Minorities
American Inventor's Protection Act, A-6–A-7
American Stock Exchange (AMEX), 515
Americans with Disabilities Act (ADA) of 1990, 288, 289, 295, 310
Americans with Disabilities Amendments Act of 2008, 288, 289
AMEX; *see* American Stock Exchange
Andean Pact, 77
Angel investors, 164, 557
Annual reports, 458, 460, P-23
Annuities, BC-10
Antitrust laws, 39, A-10–A-12
Application forms, 294–295
Application service providers (ASPs), BA-12–BA-13
Application software; *see* Software
Apprentice programs, 298–299
Arbitration, 327
Argentina, Mercosur, 77
Articles of incorporation, 125
ASEAN Economic Community, 77
Asia; *see also individual countries*
    common markets, 77
    franchises, 136, 137
    manufacturing in, 19
    markets, 80, 81
    sweatshop labor, 106
Asian Americans; *see also* Minorities
    managers, 301
Asian tsunami, 99
ASPs; *see* Application service providers
Assembly line layouts, 241–242, 243
Assembly process, 235
Asset-backed securities (ABSs), 536
Assets
    accounts receivable, 498
    on balance sheet, 466
    capital expenditures, 495
    as collateral for loans, 498
    current, 466
    defined, 466
    depreciation, 469
    division of in bankruptcies, A-15–A-16
    fixed, 466
    goodwill, 466
    intangible, 466
    liquidity, 466
    personal, BC-3–BC-6
ATMs; *see* Automated teller machines
Auditing, 460, 488–489
Audits, social, 104–105
Authority
    centralized, 205–206, 208, 209
    decentralized, 208, 209
    line versus staff, 214
    managerial, 205
Autocratic leadership, 191
Automated teller machines (ATMs), 555, 563
Automation; *see* Technology

I-13

Automobile industry
  Chinese, 70, 80
  fuel-efficient cars, 32, 351
  hybrid cars, 32
  Indian, 372–373
  marketing, 351
  mass production, 205
  non-U.S. manufacturers, 7, 72, 232, 239
  recycling parts, 403
  supply chain management, 416
Automobile insurance, BC-11

B

B2B; *see* Business-to-business (B2B) market
B2C; *see* Business-to-consumer (B2C) transactions
Baby boomers
  aging of, 18
  births of, 348
  differences from Generation X members, 275, 276
Balance of payments, 64
Balance of trade, 64, 76
Balance sheets; *see also* Ratio analysis
  accounts, 477
  assets, 466
  defined, 464, 465
  liabilities and owners' equity, 466–467
  personal, 466, 467, BC-3
  sample, 465
Baldrige Awards, 245, 305
Bangladesh, Grameen Bank, 7, 28–29, 36
Banker's acceptances, 563
Bankruptcies; *see also* Business failures
  corporate, A-15–A-17
  defined, A-14
  division of assets, A-15–A-16
  in economic crisis of 2008–2009, 333, 506–507, 536, A-15
  involuntary, A-15
  laws, A-14–A-17
  number of, A-15
  procedures, A-15–A-17
  voluntary, A-15
Bankruptcy Abuse Prevention and Consumer Protection Act of 2005, A-15
Bankruptcy Amendments and Federal Judgeships Act of 1984, A-15
Bankruptcy Reform Act of 1994, A-15, A-16
Bankruptcy Reform Act of 2005, A-15
Banks; *see also* Central banks; Economic crisis of 2008–2009; Investment bankers
  automated teller machines (ATMs), 555, 563
  banker's acceptances, 563
  certificates of deposit (CDs), 555
  check-clearing, 551–552
  commercial, 554–556
  credit cards; *see* Credit cards
  debit cards, 561–562, BC-9
  demand deposits, 555
  deregulation, A-18
  failures, 553–554
  federal deposit insurance, 554, 557, 559–560
  fees, 561
  future of, 562
  history in United States, 553–554
  international, 563
  IRAs, BC-13
  letters of credit, 563
  loans; *see* Loans
  microcredit, 7, 28–29, 36
  online banking, 562
  relationships with, 472, 497–498
  reserve requirements, 550–551
  short-term financing, 497–498
  small businesses and, 162, 165, 168, 556
  technology used in, 561–562
  time deposits, 555
  trade financing, 563
  Troubled Assets Relief Program, 559
Bar codes, 381, 422
Bargaining zone, 326
Barriers to trade; *see* Trade barriers
Barron's, 533
Barter, 74, 547
Baseball
  major league, 60, 131, 503
  stadiums, 131, 503
Basic earnings per share, 475
"Basic Guide to Exporting," 63
Bears, 526
Benchmarking, 218
Benefit segmentation, 361, 362
Benefits; *see* Fringe benefits
BI; *see* Business intelligence
Bible, 92
Billboards, 433
Biofuels, 32
Biometric devices, BA-5
Black Enterprise magazine, 301, BA-1
Blogs, 445
Blue-chip stocks, 527
Boards of directors, 123, BB-4
Bolivia, 77
Bonds
  advantages and disadvantages, 522
  debenture, 523
  defined, 503, 521
  features
    call provisions, 523
    convertible, 524
    sinking funds, 523
  government, 522
  indenture terms, 503
  interest, 521–522, 529
  investing in, 529–530
  issuing, 503, 514–515
  junk, 529
  maturity dates, 521
  prices, 529
  quotations, 530
  ratings, 522, 523, 529
  secured, 503, 523
  unsecured, 503, 523
Bonds payable, 467
Bonus plans, 304
Bookkeeping, 462
Booms, 48
Borrowing; *see* Credit; Debt; Loans
Boycotts, 328
Brain drain, 41
Brainstorming, 186
Brand associations, 385
Brand awareness, 384
Brand equity, 384–385
Brand insistence, 385
Brand loyalty, 384
Brand managers, 385
Brand names, 353, 382, 466
Brand preferences, 385
Brands; *see also* Trademarks
  categories, 383
  defined, 382
  knockoff, 383
Brazil
  bribery, 105
  dumping disputes, 65
  Mercosur, 77
Breach of contract, A-10
Break-even analysis, 392–393
Breweries, 63
Bribery, 34, 75, 105, 106–107; *see also* Corruption
Britain, Defense Ministry, 241
Broadband technology, BA-10
Brokerage firms
  online, 524–525
  services, 558
  stockbrokers, 524
Brokers; *see* Agents/brokers; Stockbrokers
Brunei, 77
Budget deficits, 49–50
Budgets
  capital, 490
  cash, 490
  defined, 490
  developing, 490
  operating (master), 490
  personal, 492, BC-4–BC-5
Bulls, 526
Bundling, 382, 393
Bureaucracy, 204, 206, 207
Business
  benefits to community, 33–34
  defined, 4
  evolution in United States, 20–21
  future careers in, 21
Business cycle, 48–49
Business environment; *see also* Legal environment
  competitive, 16–17
  defined, 11
  ecological, 19
  economic and legal, 12–14, 73–75, 359
  elements of, 11, 12
  global, 18–19
  social, 17–18, 72–73, 359
  technological, 14–16
Business ethics; *see* Ethics
Business failures; *see also* Bankruptcies
  banks, 553–554
  causes, 158–159, 161–162, 487
  Internet companies, 155
  number of, 5, 158
  savings and loan associations, 556
  small businesses, 158–159, 161–162
Business information systems; *see* Information technology
Business intelligence (BI), BA-3–BA-4
Business law, A-2–A-3; *see also* Legal environment
Business leaders; *see also* Entrepreneurs
  successful, 138
Business ownership forms
  comparison, 128
  cooperatives, 137–138

corporations, 114–115; *see also* Corporations
franchises, 131–132; *see also* Franchises
numbers of and total receipts, 114, 115
partnerships, 114, 117–120
selecting, 138
sole proprietorships, 114, 115–116
Business Plan Pro, 162
Business plans, 162–164
Business process information, BA-5
Business Week, 531
Businesses, starting; *see also* Business ownership forms
business plans, 162–164
ethical issues, 161
number of new businesses, 114
organizing, 202–203
small businesses, 157
Web-based, 155
Business-to-business (B2B) companies, 14–15, 244; *see also* Marketing intermediaries
Business-to-business (B2B) market
channels of distribution, 404
comparison to consumer market, 365–366
defined, 359–360
industrial goods and services, 379–380, 404
personal selling, 362, 438–440
sales promotion techniques, 442
Business-to-business (B2B) transactions, 14–15
Business-to-consumer (B2C) transactions, 14–15, 440; *see also* Consumer market
Buying behavior; *see* Consumer behavior
Buying stock on margin, 527–528

C

C corporations, 121
CAD; *see* Computer-aided design
Cafeteria-style fringe benefits, 305–306
CAFTA; *see* Central American Free Trade Agreement
California
Silicon Valley, 239, 505, BA
utility deregulation, A-18
Callable bonds, 523
CAM; *see* Computer-aided manufacturing
Cambodia, 77
Canada; *see also* North American Free Trade Agreement
franchises, 136
Capital; *see also* Equity financing
cost of, 505–506
as factor of production, 9, 11
Capital budgets, 490
Capital expenditures, 495
Capital gains, 527
Capital items, 380
Capitalism; *see also* Markets
compared to other systems, 44
defined, 35, 42
foundations of, 35
rights in, 35
in United States, 34–35
wealth creation, 34–35, 40

Carbon footprints, 103, 384, 421
Card checks, 322
Careers
changing, P-26
in future, 21
in global business, 83, 180
information sources, P-16–P-17
in marketing, 366
in operations management, 248
self-assessments, P-4, P-14, P-15
in supply chain management, 423
working for large businesses, 8–9
Cars; *see* Automobile industry
Carts and kiosks, 413–414
Cash budgets, 490
Cash flow
defined, 472
personal, BC-3
problems with, 494
Cash flow analysis, 472
Cash flow forecasts, 489–490
Cash flow statement; *see* Statement of cash flows
Cash-and-carry wholesalers, 409
Catalog sales, 414–415
Category killer stores, 411
CDs; *see* Certificates of deposit
Celebrity endorsements, 385
Cell phones, 433, 446, 561, P-6–P-7
Cellular layouts; *see* Modular layouts
Central American Free Trade Agreement (CAFTA), 78–79, 323, 325
Central banks; *see also* Federal Reserve System
history, 553
influence on interest rates, 51, 551
Centralized authority, 205–206, 208, 209
CEOs (chief executive officers), 187; *see also* Managers
Certificates of deposit (CDs), 555
Certification, 321, 322
Certified financial planners (CFPs), 526, BC-15
Certified internal auditors (CIAs), 460
Certified management accountants (CMAs), 458
Certified public accountants (CPAs), 459, 460
CFOs; *see* Chief financial officers
CFPs; *see* Certified financial planners
Chain of command, 207
Change
adapting to, 202, 219–221
management of, 204
risk management and, BB-2–BB-3
Channels of distribution, 402–403, 404; *see also* Distribution; Supply chain management
Chapter 7 bankruptcies, A-15–A-16
Chapter 11 bankruptcies, A-15, A-16
Chapter 13 bankruptcies, A-15, A-16–A-17
Charitable giving; *see also* Nonprofit organizations
corporate philanthropy, 99
by entrepreneurs, 42
Check-clearing, 551–552
Chief executive officers (CEOs), 187, 332–334; *see also* Managers
Chief financial officers (CFOs), 187, 486
Chief information officers (CIOs), 187, BA-2–BA-3

Chief operating officers (COOs), 187
Child care benefits, 336–337
Child Protection Act (1966), A-13
Child Protection and Toy Safety Act (1969), A-13
Children
child care benefits, 336–337
guardians, BC-15
Children's Online Privacy Protection Act (2000), A-13
Chile, 77
China
automobile industry, 70, 80
bribery in, 105
business failures, 560
competition with United States, 19
economic reforms, 42
education, 82
exports, 60, 65, 80, 106
foreign investment, 43, 80
franchises in Hong Kong, 68, 69, 137
intellectual property issues, 80
Internet use, 15
joint ventures in, 70
manufacturing in, 19, 64, 80, 82
as market, 64
oil companies, 130
population, 80
prison labor, 106
sovereign wealth funds, 502
WTO membership, 80
CIAs; *see* Certified internal auditors
CIM; *see* Computer-integrated manufacturing
CIO; *see* Congress of Industrial Organizations
CIOs; *see* Chief information officers
Circuit breakers, 535
Citizens Corps, 100
Civil law, A-2
Civil Rights Act of 1964, 287, 288, 289
Civil Rights Act of 1991, 288, 289, 335
Class Action Fairness Act, A-6
Clayton Act of 1914, A-11
Client/server computing; *see* Network computing systems
Climate change, 19, 384
Closed shop agreements, 323–324
Closed-end mutual funds, 531
Clothing, T-shirt prices, 36
Cloud computing, BA-13–BA-14
CMAs; *see* Certified management accountants
Coattail effect, 133
Codes of ethics, 96, 97–98
Cognitive dissonance, 364
Collateral, 28–29
Collection procedures, 494–495
Collective bargaining, 321
Colleges and universities; *see also* Education; Students
Baldrige Award winners, 245
value of education, BC-2–BC-3, P-3
Colombia, 77
Command economies, 42; *see also* Communism; Socialism
Commercial banks, 554–556; *see also* Banks
Commercial finance companies, 499
Commercial law, A-8–A-9; *see also* Legal environment
Commercial paper, 500

Commercialization, 387
Commissions, 304
Common law, A-3
Common markets, 77; *see also* European Union
Common stock, 520; *see also* Stocks
Communication
  in large organizations, 222
  open, 270–272
Communications technology; *see* Cell phones; Internet; Networks; Technology
Communism, 41–42, 43, 44
Community service, 100
Comparable worth, 334–335
Comparative advantage theory, 61–62
Compensation; *see also* Fringe benefits
  comparable worth, 334–335
  employee retention and, 102
  executive, 332–334
  in foreign countries, 307
  as motivator, 260, 262
  objectives, 303
  pay equity, 334–335
  pay systems, 303–304
  of teams, 304–305
  wages, 304
Competition
  antitrust laws, 39, A-10–A-12
  effects on marketing, 359
  empowerment and, 16–17
  in free markets, 39
  global, 18–19
  monopolistic, 39
  nonprice, 394–395
  perfect, 39
Competition-based pricing, 392
Competitive environment, 16–17
Compliance-based ethics codes, 96, 97
Comprehensive Employment and Training Act of 1973, 288
Compressed workweek, 307–308
Comptrollers, 486
Computer chips, BA-11–BA-12
Computer viruses, BA-16–BA-17
Computer-aided design (CAD), 236
Computer-aided manufacturing (CAM), 236
Computer-integrated manufacturing (CIM), 236
Computers; *see* Information technology
Concept testing, 352–353, 387
Conceptual skills, 188
Conglomerate mergers, 129
Congress of Industrial Organizations (CIO), 320
Consideration, A-9
Constitution, U.S., A-15
Consultants, 460
Consumer behavior, 363–364
Consumer credit; *see* Credit cards; Personal financial planning
Consumer Credit Reporting Reform Act (1997), A-13
Consumer finance companies, 558
Consumer market; *see also* Green products; Retail industry
  brand preferences, 385
  channels of distribution, 404
  comparison to business-to-business market, 365–366
  defined, 359
  goods and services classification, 378–379, 380
  mass marketing, 363
  niche marketing, 362
  one-to-one marketing, 362
  relationship marketing, 363
  sales promotion techniques, 442–444
  segmentation, 360–362
Consumer price index (CPI), 47
Consumer Product Safety Act (1972), A-13
Consumer protection, A-12, A-13
Consumerism, A-12
Consumers; *see* Consumer market; Customers
Contingency planning, 184–185
Contingent workers, 296–297; *see also* Temporary employees
Continuous process, 235
Contract law, A-9–A-10
Contract manufacturing, 69–70
Contracts
  breach of, A-10
  conditions for legal enforcement, A-9
  defined, A-9
Contractual distribution systems, 415–416
Contrarian approach, BC-8
Control procedures
  Gantt charts, 247, 248
  PERT charts, 246–247
Controlling
  defined, 181
  performance standards, 193, 194
  steps, 193–194
Convenience goods and services, 378
Convenience stores, 411
Conventional (C) corporations, 121
Convertible bonds, 524
Convertible preferred stock, 521
Cookies, BA-18
Cooling-off periods, 328
Cooperatives
  agricultural, 138
  defined, 137
  food, 137, 416
  retail, 416
COOs; *see* Chief operating officers
Copyright Act of 1978, A-7
Copyrights, 93, A-7, BA-17; *see also* Intellectual property protection
Core competencies, 218–219
Core time, 306
Corporate and Criminal Fraud Accountability (Sarbanes-Oxley) Act, 97, 459, 460, A-12
Corporate bonds; *see* Bonds
Corporate distribution systems, 415
Corporate income taxes, 124, A-14
Corporate philanthropy, 99
Corporate policy, 100
Corporate responsibility, 100; *see also* Corporate social responsibility
Corporate scandals
  accounting-related, 91, 459
  executive compensation, 333
  motives for misconduct, 40
  recent, 90, 91, 101–102
Corporate social initiatives, 99
Corporate social responsibility (CSR)
  community service by employees, 100
  competitive benefits, 100
  debates on, 98–99
  defined, 98
  elements of, 99–100
  environmental issues, 103, 104, 105, 531
  international standards, 106, 108
  investors and, 104, 531
  reports, 105
  responsibilities to stakeholders
    customers, 100–101, 105
    employees, 102
    investors, 101–102
    society and environment, 102–103
  social audits, 104–105
  watchdogs, 104–105
Corporations
  advantages, 121–123
  articles of incorporation, 125
  boards of directors, 123, BB-4
  bylaws, 125
  conventional (C), 121
  defined, 115
  disadvantages, 123–124
  financing sources, 121
  incorporation process, 123–124, 125
  individuals as, 124
  limited liability companies, 126–127
  S, 125–126
  separation of ownership and management, 123
  sizes, 121, 122–123
  taking private, 129–130
  taxes, 124, A-14
  types, 122
  virtual, 127, 217–218
Corruption; *see also* Corporate scandals
  bribery, 34, 75, 105
  in business, 13, 34, 40
  in developing countries, 75
  in foreign countries, 105
  international agreements on, 108
  laws against, 13, 75, 108
  in U.S. government, 90
Cost accounting, 391
Cost of capital, 505–506
Cost of goods sold (or cost of goods manufactured), 469
Cost-based pricing, 391
Costs; *see also* Expenses
  cutting, 236
  forecasting, 489–490
  operating, 469–470
  total fixed, 393
  variable, 392, 393
Counterfeiting, 546
Countertrading, 74
Country of Origin Labeling Law (2009), A-13
Coupons, bond, 521–522
Court system, A-2; *see also* Legal environment
Cover letters, P-15, P-20–P-22
CPAs; *see* Certified public accountants
CPI; *see* Consumer price index
Craft unions, 319, 320
Credit; *see also* Debt; Loans; Short-term financing
  managing, BC-8–BC-9
  microlending firms, 28–29, 36
  peer-to-peer, 164
  for small businesses, 164–166, 494
  trade, 496–497

Credit cards
  accepting, 495
  financing small businesses, 501
  interest rates, BC-5, BC-9
  managing, BC-8–BC-9
  processing costs, 561
Credit lines, 498
Credit operations, 494–495
Credit unions, 556–557, 560–561, BC-13
Crime; *see also* Corruption
  cyber-, BA-17
  employee fraud, 102
  identity theft, 15–16, P-20
  insider trading, 101, 517–518
  intellectual property piracy, 80
Criminal law, A-2
Crisis planning, 184–185
Critical Infrastructure Information Act, BA-18
Critical path, 247
CRM; *see* Customer relationship management
Cross-functional teams; *see* Self-managed cross-functional teams
CSR; *see* Corporate social responsibility
Cuba
  economy, 42
  embargo on, 76
Cultural diversity; *see also* Diversity
  ethical issues, 107
  in global markets, 72–73
  motivational approaches, 274–275
  in United States, 17, 72, 359, 437
Culture; *see also* Organizational culture
  high- or low-context, 275
  influences on buying decisions, 364
  meaning, 72
Cumulative preferred stock, 521
Currencies
  convertible, 13
  devaluations, 74
  euro, 77, 549
  exchange rates, 73–74, 549
  exchanging, 563
  trading, 74, 546
  U.S. dollar, 73–74, 547, 549
Current assets, 466
Current liabilities, 466
Current ratio, 474
Customer databases, 15, 358
Customer group departmentalization, 211, 212
Customer relationship era, 349
Customer relationship management (CRM)
  activities, 354
  defined, 349
  software, 438
Customer service
  in corporate cultures, 221
  improving, 207
Customers
  aging of population, 17–18, 359
  buying decisions, 105, 363–364, BB-10
  complaints, 445
  consumer protection, A-12, A-13
  corporate responsibility to, 100–101, 105
  diverse population, 17, 359
  expectations, 16
  external, 194
  focus on, 221
  internal, 194
  involvement in product development, 216
  knowing, 166
  marketing to, 346–347
  online dialogues with, 436
  prospects, 438
  qualifying, 438
  responsiveness to, 15
  satisfaction, 194
  of small businesses, 166
Customization, 237–238
Cybercrime, BA-17
Cyberspace; *see* Internet
Cyberterrorism, BA-17
Cyclical unemployment, 46

D

Damages, A-10
Data
  managing, BA-7
  for marketing research, 355–356
  primary, 356
  secondary, 355–356
Data mining, BA-8
Data processing (DP), BA-2; *see also* Information technology
Data security, BA-9
Data warehouses, BA-8
Databases, 15; *see also* Customer databases
Day care; *see* Child care benefits
Dealer (private-label) brands, 383
Debenture bonds, 523
Debit cards, 561–562, BC-9
Debt; *see also* Bonds; Credit cards; Loans; Mortgages
  leverage ratios, 474–475, 505
  personal, BC-5
Debt financing
  balancing with equity, 506
  bonds, 503, 514–515
  compared to equity financing, 505–506
  defined, 495
  loans, 502–503
Debt to owners' equity ratio, 474–475
Decentralized authority, 208, 209
Decertification, 321, 322
Decision making
  centralized or decentralized, 205–206, 208, 209
  defined, 185
  empowering employees, 192, 207; *see also* Empowerment
  ethical, 93–94, 190
  rational model, 186
Defense industry, 19, 241
Deficits
  budget, 49–50
  trade, 64–65
Defined-contribution plans, BC-14
Deflation, 47
Demand, 37
Demand curve, 37–38
Demand deposits, 555
Demand-based pricing, 391–392
Deming cycle, 245
Democratic leadership, 191
Demographic segmentation, 361, 362
Demography; *see also* Aging of population; Diversity
  defined, 17
  population growth, 32
  single parents, 18
  world population by continent, 60, 61
Denmark, nontariff barriers, 76
Department of Motor Vehicles (DMV), 206
Department stores, 411
Departmentalization, 203, 210–212
Depreciation, 469
Depressions, 49; *see also* Great Depression
Deregulation, 39, A-17–A-18
Devaluations, 74
Developing countries
  corruption, 75
  countertrading, 74
  obstacles to trade with, 75
  population growth, 32
  poverty, 32
  products for markets in, 73
  promotion of entrepreneurship, 13
  retail distribution, 417
  standard of living, 73
  transportation and storage systems, 75
Digital Millennium Copyright Act (DMCA), 93
Digital natives, 219
Digital video recorders, 433–434
Diluted earnings per share, 475
Direct deposits, 562
Direct mail, 414
  advantages and disadvantages, 433
  expenditures, 431, 432
  franchises, 136
Direct marketing, 414–415
Direct payments, 562
Direct selling, 414
Directing, 192
Directors, corporate, 123, BB-4
Disability insurance, BB-9, BC-11
Disabled individuals; *see also* Diversity
  accommodations, 289
  laws protecting, 288, 289, 310
  telecommuting, BA-15
Disaster aid, 99
Discount rate, 551
Discount stores, 411
Discrimination
  age-related, 289–290
  in employment tests, 295
  gender-based, 334–335
  laws prohibiting, 287–288, 289–290, 310
  price, A-12
  reverse, 289
Disinflation, 47
Distance learning, 299
Distribution; *see also* Marketing intermediaries; Supply chain management
  administered systems, 416
  channels of, 402–403, 404
  contractual systems, 415–416
  cooperation in, 415–416
  corporate systems, 415
  in developing countries, 417
  for e-commerce transactions, 400–401, 413
  of new products, 353
  outsourcing, 419
  physical, 419–422
  retail strategies, 411–412

Distributor brands, 383
Distributors, 216–217; *see also* Marketing intermediaries
Diversification, 525–526
Diversity
   of customers, 17, 359
   in franchising, 134–135
     generational differences, 17–18, 275–276
     groups, 17
   in management development, 301
   of U.S. population, 17
   of workforce, 17
Dividends
     common stock, 519
     preferred stock, 520–521
Division of labor, 202–203, 205
DMCA; *see* Digital Millennium Copyright Act
DMV; *see* Department of Motor Vehicles
Doha Round, 77
Dollar, U.S., 73–74, 547, 549; *see also* Currencies
Dot-coms; *see* Internet companies
Double-entry bookkeeping, 462
Dow Jones Industrial Average, 534, 535
DP; *see* Data processing
Drop shippers, 409
Drug companies; *see* Pharmaceutical companies
Drug testing, 338
Dumping, 65
Durable power of attorney, BC-15

E

EACs; *see* Export Assistance Centers
Earnings; *see also* Compensation
   of college graduates, BC-2–BC-3, P-3
   gender differences, 334–335
   retained, 467, 504–505
Earnings per share (EPS)
     basic, 475
     diluted, 475
     price/earnings ratios, 528
Earnings statement; *see* Income statement
Ecological environment, 19; *see also* Environmental issues
E-commerce; *see also* Internet
     affiliate marketing, 155
     automobile shopping, 351
     combined with traditional retail stores (click-and-brick)
        competition from Internet-only retailers, 359
        competitiveness, 412–413
        distribution systems, 413
        Web kiosks in stores, 241
     customer relationships, 412, 436
     defined, 14
     distribution systems, 400–401, 413
     in franchising, 136
     global opportunities, 169
     growth, 14–15
     information captured, BA-6
     marketing, 358
     niche marketing, 362
     pick economy, 448
     price comparisons, 394
     risks, BB-3
     sales, 154
     setting up, 155
     social marketing, 358
     taxation of, A-14
Economic and legal environment, 12–14, 73–74, 359
Economic crisis of 2008–2009
     bankruptcies, 333, 506–507, 536, A-15
     causes, 13–14, 90, 536, 558–559
     credit crunch, 165, 491, 500, 557
     effects in retail, 208, 443
     effects on small businesses, 494, 557
     effects on workers, 178, 239
     federal bailout, 50, 334, 536, 559, A-18
     federal stimulus package, 50, 559, A-12
     fiscal policy responses, 50–51
     global effects, 536, 560, 564
     monetary policy, 544
     regulatory shortcomings, 559, A-12, A-18
     stock market decline, 525, 535
     subprime mortgages, 13, 165, 333, 535, 536
Economic systems; *see also* Capitalism; Markets
     command economies, 42
     communism, 41–42, 43, 44
     comparison, 44
     free-market, 42
     mixed economies, 43–45
     socialism, 40–41, 43
Economics
     allocation of resources, 31
     defined, 30
     as "dismal science," 31
     growth, 32
     macro-, 30–31
     micro-, 30
Economies of scale, 205
Ecuador, Andean Pact, 77
EDI; *see* Electronic data interchange
EDLP; *see* Everyday low pricing
Education; *see also* Students; Training and development
     economic development and, 32
     engineering, 82
     investing in, BC-2–BC-3
     tax incentives, BC-3
     value of, 82, BC-2–BC-3
EEOA; *see* Equal Employment Opportunity Act
EEOC; *see* Equal Employment Opportunity Commission
Efficiency, 15
EFT; *see* Electronic funds transfer (EFT) systems
Elder care, 337–338
Elderly; *see* Senior citizens
Electric utilities, 39; *see also* Utilities
Electronic cash, 548
Electronic data interchange (EDI), BA-9
Electronic funds transfer (EFT) systems, 561
Electronic retailing, 412–413; *see also* E-commerce
E-mail; *see also* Internet
     advertising, 433, 435
     managing, BA-7
     netiquette, P-6
     phishing scams, BA-17
     privacy issues, BA-18
     promotion via, 445–446
Embargoes, 76
Emerging markets; *see* Developing countries; Global markets
Employee benefits; *see* Fringe benefits
Employee Free Choice Act, 322
Employee Retirement Income Security Act (ERISA) of 1974, 288
Employee-management relations; *see also* Unions
     arbitration, 327
     bargaining zone, 326
     ethical values in, 94–96, 107, 204
     fairness in, 102
     future of, 329–332
     grievances, 325–326
     impact of technology, BA-16
     issues, 318–319
        child care, 336–337
        drug testing, 338
        elder care, 337–338
        e-mail privacy, BA-18
        executive compensation, 332–334
        pay equity, 334–335
        sexual harassment, 335–336
        violence in workplace, 338–339
     lockouts, 328
     mediation, 326–327
     resolving disagreements, 325–327
     in small businesses, 167
     tactics used in conflicts, 327–329
Employees; *see also* Compensation; Diversity; Empowerment; Human resource management; Labor; Recruitment; Staffing; Teams; Training and development
     aging of, 289–290
     community service, 100
     corporate responsibility to, 102
     e-mail use, BA-18
     enabling, 192
     engagement, 256
     fraud by, 102
     line personnel, 213–214
     losing, 311
     orientation, 298
     part-time, 296, 308
     performance appraisals, 301–302
     promotions, 309
     retention, 102, 311
     retirements, 290, 310–311
     safety issues, 204
     scheduling, 306–308
     staff personnel, 213–214
     terminating, 289, 310
     transfers, 309–310
Employment; *see* Careers; Jobs; Recruitment
Empowerment
     as competitive advantage, 16–17
     decision making, 192, 207
     defined, 17
     effects on managerial authority, 205
     increased span of control, 209
     knowledge needed for, 192
     as motivator, 264–265
     restructuring for, 219–220
     role of managers in, 180–181, 192
     of self-managed teams, 216
     Theory Y management and, 264–265
EMS; *see* Environmental management system
Enabling, 192
Endorsements, celebrity, 385

Energy use, BA-14; *see also* Greening
Engagement, employee, 256
England; *see* Britain
Enterprise portals, BA-9
Enterprise resource planning (ERP), 242
Enterprise risk management (ERM), BB-2
Enterprise zones, 156
Entertainment industry; *see* Movies; Television
Entrepreneur magazine, 135, 154
Entrepreneurial teams, 150
Entrepreneurs
 charitable giving, 40
 defined, 4
 innovation sources, 149–150
 micropreneurs, 150–153
 millionaires, BC
 minority group members, 9, 144–145
 opportunities for, 9
 personality traits, 148–149
 readiness questionnaire, 151–152
 retirement planning, BC-14
 social, 7–8
 successful, 4, 138, 146–147, 148–149
 wealth creation by, 9–11
 women, 9, 134–135
 young, 147
Entrepreneurship; *see also* Businesses, starting; Home-based businesses; Small businesses
 advantages, 9
 compared to working in large businesses, 8–9
 defined, 146
 as factor of production, 9, 10, 11
 within firms, 155–156
 government support of, 12–13, 156–157
 history, 146
 laws encouraging, 12–13, 156
 motivations, 147–148
 opportunities, 149–150
 socially responsible, 149
Environment; *see* Business environment
Environmental issues; *see also* Greening
 carbon cost of transportation, 420, 421
 climate change, 19, 384
 corporate responsibility and, 103, 104, 105, 531
 for individual companies, 204
 ISO 14000 standards, 246
 personal decisions, 20
 risks, BB-10
 tuna fishing, 103
Environmental management system (EMS), 246
Environmental scanning, 357
EPS; *see* Earnings per share
Equal Employment Opportunity Act (EEOA), 287, 288
Equal Employment Opportunity Commission (EEOC)
 affirmative action policies, 288–289
 age discrimination cases, 289
 influence on business, A-3
 powers, 287–288
 sexual harassment complaints to, 335–336

Equal Pay Act of 1963, 288, 334
Equilibrium prices, 37–39
Equipment, 380
Equity, owners'; *see* Owners' equity
Equity financing, 503–504; *see also* Stocks
 balancing with debt, 506
 compared to debt financing, 505–506
 defined, 495–496
 retained earnings, 504–505
 selling stock, 504, 514
 venture capital, 165, 505
Equity theory, 268–269
ERISA; *see* Employee Retirement Income Security Act
ERM; *see* Enterprise risk management
ERP; *see* Enterprise resource planning
Estate planning, BC-15
ETFs; *see* Exchange-traded funds
Ethics; *see also* Corporate scandals; Corporate social responsibility; Corruption
 in accounting, 473
 in banks, 555
 cheating by students, 92–93
 cultural differences and, 107
 defined, 92
 dilemmas, 93–94, 190
 enforcement, 98
 failures, 13–14
 in financial management, 493
 formal policies, 96
 in global markets, 75, 105–108
 improving, 96–98
 individual responsibility, 15, 92–93, P-7
 insider trading, 101, 517–518
 legality and, 90, 94
 in mortgage industry, 92
 organizational, 94–96, 190
 orientation questionnaire, 95
 outsourcing, 82, 240
 personal dilemmas, 15
 promoting, 190
 safety issues, 204
 standards, 92
 starting businesses, 161
 strikebreakers, 329
 values in organizational cultures, 204, 221
Ethics codes, 96, 97–98
Ethics offices, 97, 98
Ethnic groups, marketing to, 359; *see also* Cultural diversity; Minorities
Ethnocentricity, 72
Etiquette, P-5–P-7
Euro, 77, 549; *see also* Currencies
Europe; *see also individual countries*
 codetermination, 334
 executive compensation, 334
 financial institutions, 557
 unions, 325
European Economic Community, 77
European Union (EU); *see also* Euro
 history, 77
 Internet taxation, A-14
 members, 78
 quality standards, 246
Event marketing, 444
Everyday low pricing (EDLP), 393
Exchange rates, 73–74, 549
Exchanges; *see* Stock exchanges

Exchange-traded funds (ETFs), 531–532
Exclusive dealing, A-11
Exclusive distribution, 412
Executive compensation, 332–334
Executives; *see* Managers
Executors, BC-15
Exit interviews, 311
Expectancy theory, 267–268
Expenses; *see also* Costs
 forecasting, 489–490
 operating, 469–470
 personal, BC-3–BC-4, BC-6
Export Administration Act of 1979, 76
Export Assistance Centers (EACs), 67
Exporting; *see also* Global markets; Trade
 challenges, 169
 competition in, 61
 defined, 61
 export-trading companies, 67–68
 financing, 170, 500
 government assistance, 63, 67, 170
 information on, 63, 169
 jobs created by, 63
 letters of credit and, 563
 obstacles, 75
 opportunities, 63
 regulations, 76
 by small businesses, 67, 83, 169–170
Export-trading companies, 67–68
Express warranties, A-8
External customers, 194
Extranets, BA-9
Extrinsic rewards, 257

F

Facility layout, 241–242, 243
Facility location
 defined, 238
 factors, 239–240
 in foreign countries, 239
 in future, 240–241
 government incentives, 241
 for manufacturers, 239–240
 for service businesses, 238–239
Factoring, 499–500
Factors of production, 9–11, 35, 232
Failures; *see* Business failures
Fair Credit Reporting Act (1970), A-13
Fair Labor Standards Act of 1938, 288, 321
Fair Packaging and Labeling Act (1966), 382, A-13
Families; *see also* Children
 elder care, 337–338
 financing from, 497
 single parents, 18
Family and Medical Leave Act of 1993, 288
Family-friendly fringe benefits, 18
Farming; *see* Agriculture
FASB; *see* Financial Accounting Standards Board
FBI; *see* Federal Bureau of Investigation
FDA; *see* Food and Drug Administration
FDIC; *see* Federal Deposit Insurance Corporation
Federal budget deficit, 49–50
Federal Bureau of Investigation (FBI), 461

Federal Deposit Insurance Corporation (FDIC), 557, 559–560
Federal government; *see* U.S. government
Federal Housing Administration (FHA), BB-5
Federal Open Market Committee (FOMC), 549, 550
Federal Reserve Act of 1913, 553
Federal Reserve System
    banking crisis of 2008–2009 and, 558, 559, A-12, A-18
    banks, 549, 550
    Bernanke as chairman, 544–545, 548
    check-clearing role, 551–552
    control of money supply, 548–549, 550–551
    discount rate, 551
    financial crisis responses, 500
    formation, 553
    functions, 550, 553
    Greenspan as chairman, 544
    influence on business, A-3
    interest rates, 551, 558
    margin rates, 527
    monetary policy, 51, 550–551
    need for, 553
    open-market operations, 550, 551
    organization of, 549–550
    reserve requirements, 550–551
Federal Savings and Loan Insurance Corporation (FSLIC), 560
Federal Trade Commission Act of 1914, A-11–A-12
Federal Trade Commission (FTC), 15, 133, A-4, A-11–A-12, A-13
FHA; *see* Federal Housing Administration
FIFO (first in, first out), 470
Films; *see* Movies
Finance; *see also* Financial management
    defined, 486
    importance, 488–489
    relationship to accounting, 486
Financial accounting, 458–459; *see also* Accounting
Financial Accounting Standards Board (FASB), 459, 473, 475
Financial control, 491
Financial crises; *see* Economic crisis of 2008–2009
Financial institutions; *see* Banks; Credit unions; Nonbanks; Savings and loan associations
Financial leverage, 505
Financial management; *see also* Financial planning; Short-term financing
    debt financing, 495, 502–503
    defined, 486
    equity financing, 495–496, 503–505
    ethical issues, 493
    leverage, 505
    long-term financing, 496, 501–502
    operating funds, 492–494
    reasons for business failures, 487
    in recessions, 494, 506–507
    in small businesses, 164–166, 487, 494
    sources of funds, 495–496
    tax management, 488

Financial managers
    defined, 486
    tasks, 486–487, 488
    titles, 486
Financial markets; *see* Securities markets
Financial planning
    budgets, 490
    controls, 491
    forecasts, 489–490
    importance, 490
    personal; *see* Personal financial planning
    steps, 489
Financial ratios; *see* Ratio analysis
Financial services; *see* Banks
Financial statements
    annual reports, 458, 460, P-23
    auditing, 460
    balance sheet
        accounts, 477
        assets, 466
        defined, 464, 465
        liabilities and owners' equity, 466–467
        personal, 466, 467, BC-3
    defined, 463–464
    income statement, 477
        accounts, 477
        cost of goods sold, 469
        defined, 464, 468
        gross profit, 469
        net income, 468, 470
        operating expenses, 469–470
        personal, BC-3
        revenue, 469
    statement of cash flows, 464, 471–472
Firewalls, BA-9
Firing employees, 289, 310
Firms; *see* Corporations
First in, first out (FIFO), 470
First-line managers, 188, 190
Fiscal policy, 49–51
Fixed assets, 466
Fixed-position layouts, 242, 243
Flat organization structures, 209–210
Flexible manufacturing, 237
Flextime plans, 306–307
Floating exchange rates, 74
Focus groups, 356
FOMC; *see* Federal Open Market Committee
Food and Drug Administration (FDA), A-4, A-13
Food industry; *see also* Agriculture
    carbon cost, 421
    cooperatives, 137, 416
    environmental issues, 287
    healthy food, 287
    marketing intermediaries, 405–406
    meal preparation businesses, 376
    regulation of, A-13, A-17
    supermarkets, 292, 411, 444
    transportation, 421
Forecasts, 489–490
Foreign Corrupt Practices Act of 1978, 75, 108
Foreign currencies; *see* Currencies
Foreign direct investment
    advantages, 71
    defined, 70
    risks, 71
Foreign exchange; *see* Currencies

Foreign markets; *see* Global markets; Trade
Foreign stock exchanges, 518, 519
Foreign subsidiaries, 70–71
Forensic accountants, 460
Forfeiting, 500
Form utility, 234–235, 407
Formal organization, 221
Forms of business ownership; *see* Business ownership forms
Fortune, Best Companies to Work For, 255, 298, 305
Four Ps of marketing, 350–352
401(k) plans, BC-14
France, McDonald's stores, 375
Franchise agreements, 131
Franchise Business Review, 112
Franchisees, 131
Franchises
    advantages, 132–133
    defined, 131
    disadvantages, 133
    as distribution system, 415
    diversity in, 134–135
    e-commerce use, 136
    evaluation checklist, 134
    fast-growing, 132
    home-based, 135–136
    international, 68–69, 136–137
    scams, 133
    start-up costs, 132–133
    success rates, 133
    technology used in, 136
    Web sites, 136
Franchisors, 131
Fraud; *see also* Corporate scandals
    by franchisors, 133
    investigations, 460
    phishing scams, BA-17
Freakonomics, 445
Free markets; *see* Markets
Free trade; *see also* Trade
    defined, 61
    laws to ensure fairness, 65
    pros and cons, 62
Free trade agreements; *see* Central American Free Trade Agreement; Common markets; North American Free Trade Agreement
Freedom, 35
Freedom of Information Act, BA-18
Free-market economies, 42; *see also* Capitalism; Markets
Free-rein leadership, 191–192
Freight forwarders, 419–420
Frictional unemployment, 46
Fringe benefits
    cafeteria-style, 305–306
    child care, 336–337
    defined, 305
    employee retention and, 102
    family-friendly, 18
    in foreign countries, 307
    401(k) plans, BC-14
    health insurance, 305, BB-7–BB-9
    objectives, 303
    outsourcing, 294, 306
    pensions, 558
    vacation time, 305, 307
FSLIC; *see* Federal Savings and Loan Insurance Corporation
FTC; *see* Federal Trade Commission
Full-service wholesalers, 409, 410

Functional departmentalization, 211, 212
Fundamental accounting equation, 464
Funds; *see* Financial management; Mutual funds

G

GAAP; *see* Generally accepted accounting principles
Gain-sharing plans, 304, 305
Gantt charts, 247, 248
GASB; *see* Governmental Accounting Standards Board
GATT; *see* General Agreement on Tariffs and Trade
GDP (gross domestic product), 45–46
Gender discrimination, 334–335; *see also* Women
General Agreement on Tariffs and Trade (GATT), 76–77
General partners, 117
General partnerships, 117
Generally accepted accounting principles (GAAP), 459, 469–470, 477
Generation X, 275–276
Generation Y (Millennials), 275, 276, 362
Generational differences, 17–18, 275–276
Generic goods, 383
Generic names, 383
Geographic departmentalization, 211, 212
Geographical segmentation, 361–362
Germany
    automakers, 72
    codetermination, 334
    imported beer, 63
    standard of living, 6
Givebacks, 329
Global business; *see also* Multinational corporations
    accounting standards, 477
    careers in, 83, 180
    challenges, 180
    opportunities, 62–63
Global environment, 18–19
Global markets; *see also* Exporting; Importing; Trade
    adapting products for, 375
    adapting to other cultures, 68, 72–73, 436–437
    advertising, 436–437
    banking, 563
    business etiquette, P-7
    countertrading, 74
    currency markets, 73–74, 546
    developing countries, 73
    distribution, 417
    effects on marketing process, 358
    ethical concerns in, 75, 105–108
    forces affecting
        economic, 73–74
        legal and regulatory, 74–75
        physical and environmental, 75
        sociocultural, 72–73
    foreign direct investment, 70–71, 80–81
    large businesses, 62
    local contacts, 75
    logistics companies, 418–419
    marketing strategies, 73
    measuring, 64–65
    securities markets, 518, 519
    service sector, 43
    size of, 60
    small businesses, 62, 83, 169–170
    stock exchanges, 518, 519
    strategies for reaching, 66
        contract manufacturing, 69–70
        direct investment, 70–71
        franchises, 68–69
        joint ventures, 70
        licensing, 66–67
        strategic alliances, 70
Global warming, 19
Globalization, 18–19, 325
Goals, 181
Goal-setting theory, 267
Going public; *see* Initial public offerings; Stocks
Golden coffins, 333
Golden handshakes, 310, 333
Golden Rule, 92
Goods; *see also* Products
    defined, 4
    industrial, 379–380, 404
Goodwill, 466
Government and not-for-profit accounting, 461
Government bonds, 522
Governmental Accounting Standards Board (GASB), 461
Governments; *see also* Local governments; State governments; U.S. government
    accounting, 461
    bribery of officials, 75, 105
    competition to attract businesses, 241
    economic policies, 49–51
    entrepreneurship encouraged by, 12–13, 156–157
    fiscal policy, 49–51
    monetary policy, 51, 550–551
    regulations; *see* Regulations
    relations with businesses, 12–13
    sovereign wealth funds, 71, 502
    spending policies, 49–51
    taxes; *see* Taxes
Grapevine, 221
Great Britain; *see* Britain
Great Depression, 49, 553–554, 559
Green products
    business opportunities, 231
    business use of, 287
    carbon footprints, 103, 384, 421
    cars, 32, 351, 372
    consumer preferences, BB-10
    defining, 103
    promoting, 434
    purchasing, 20
Greening; *see also* Environmental issues
    business opportunities, 32, 231
    of company cafeterias, 287
    defined, 19
    employee involvement, 271
    energy efficiency, BA-14
    by entrepreneurs, 147, 149
    jobs created by, 103, 105
    LEED certification, 131
    personal decisions, 20
    promoting sustainability efforts, 434
    of sports stadiums, 131
    of technology, BA-14
Greenwashing, 104
Grievances, 325–326
Grocery stores; *see* Supermarkets
Gross domestic product (GDP), 45–46
Gross margin, 469
Gross profit, 469
Growth economics, 32
Growth stocks, 527

H

Hackers, BA-16, BA-17, BB-3
Haiti, 73
Hamburger University (McDonald's), 132, 300
Hardware, BA-11–BA-12
Hawthorne effect, 259–260
Hawthorne studies, 259–260
Health care; *see also* Pharmaceutical companies
    offshore outsourcing, 82
    unions, 331
Health insurance
    buying, BC-11
    for employees, 305, BB-7–BB-9
    types, BB-8
Health maintenance organizations (HMOs), BB-7–BB-9, BC-11
Health savings accounts (HSAs), BB-9, BC-11
Health threats, BB-2, BB-4
Herzberg's motivating factors, 261–263
Hierarchy, 187–188, 205, 207
Hierarchy of needs, 260–261, 263
High-context cultures, 275
Higher education; *see* Colleges and universities; Education
High-low pricing strategy, 393
High-tech companies; *see* Internet companies; Technology
Hiring; *see* Recruitment
Hispanic Americans, 9, 301, 437
HMOs; *see* Health maintenance organizations
Home countries, 70
Home-based businesses; *see also* Small businesses
    challenges, 152–153
    franchises, 135–136
    insurance coverage, BB-10
    number of, 152
    potential areas, 153
    reasons for growth of, 152
    scams, 154
    technology used in, 152
    types, 153
Home-based work; *see* Telecommuting
Homeowners insurance, BB-8, BB-10, BC-11
Homes, buying, BC-6–BC-8
Homosexuals; *see* Diversity
Hong Kong; *see also* China
Hong Kong, franchises, 68, 69, 137
Horizontal mergers, 129
Hotels, 233–234, 261
House brands, 383
Housing; *see* Mortgages; Real estate
HRM; *see* Human resource management
HSAs; *see* Health savings accounts
Human relations skills, 188

Human resource management; *see also* Recruitment; Training and development
  activities, 284, 285
  challenges, 286
  cultural differences, 73, 307
  defined, 284
  global workforce and, 307
  laws affecting, 287–290
  performance appraisals, 301–302
  planning, 290–292
  promotions and transfers, 309–310
  technology-related issues, BA-15–BA-16
  terminations, 289, 310
  trends, 284–285
Hurricane Katrina, 204
Hygiene factors, 262

I

Idea brokers, 222
Identity theft, 15–16, P-20
IFRS; *see* International Financial Reporting Standards
IMC; *see* Integrated marketing communication
IMF; *see* International Monetary Fund
Immigrants, 9, 156; *see also* Cultural diversity; Minorities
Immigration Act of 1990, 156
Immigration Reform and Control Act of 1986, 288
Implied warranties, A-8
Import quotas, 76
Importing; *see also* Global markets; Tariffs; Trade
  defined, 60–61
  letters of credit and, 563
  logistics companies and, 418
  opportunities, 63
Inbound logistics, 418
Income; *see also* Compensation; Earnings
  net, 468, 470
  retained earnings, 467, 504–505
Income statement
  accounts, 477
  cost of goods sold, 469
  defined, 464, 468
  gross profit, 469
  net income, 468, 470
  operating expenses, 469–470
  personal, BC-3
  revenue, 469
  sample, 468
Income stocks, 527
Income taxes; *see* Taxes
Incorporation; *see also* Corporations
  articles of, 125
  of individuals, 124
  process, 123–124, 125
Incubators, 156–157
Indenture terms, 503
Independent audits, 460
Index funds, 530–531
India
  automakers, 372–373
  competition with United States, 19
  education, 82
  incomes, 73
  as market, 80
  McDonald's franchises, 68

  outsourcing to, 82
  service industries, 82
Individual retirement accounts (IRAs)
  Roth, BC-13
  SEP plans, BC-14
  Simple, BC-14
  traditional, BC-12–BC-13
Indonesia
  ASEAN Economic Community, 77
  as market, 81
Industrial goods, 379–380, 404
Industrial Revolution, 319
Industrial unions, 320
Infant industries, 76
Inflation, 47–48, 548–549
Infomercials, 435
Informal organization, 221–222
Information
  distinction from knowledge, BA-3
  managing, BA-6–BA-8
  public, BA-6, BA-18
  storing and mining, BA-7–BA-8
  types, BA-5–BA-6
Information overload, BA-6
Information systems (IS), BA-2
Information technology (IT); *see also* Internet; Networks; Software; Technology
  computer-aided design and manufacturing, 236
  defined, BA-2
  effects on management, BA-15–BA-19
  for employee training and development, 299
  file management, BA-7
  green, BA-14
  hardware, BA-11–BA-12
  outsourcing, BA-12–BA-13
  privacy issues, BA-18–BA-19
  role in business, BA-2–BA-3, BA-4
  security issues, BA-9, BA-16–BA-18
  skills needed, BA-15, BA-19
  stability issues, BA-19
  training, 219, BA-15
  use in manufacturing, 236, 242
Information utility, 408
Initial public offerings (IPOs), 504, 514
Injunctions, 328–329
Innovation; *see also* Product development
  by entrepreneurs, 149–150
  in large organizations, 222
Insider trading, 101, 517–518
Insourcing, 7, 232
Installations, 380
Institutional investors, 515
Insurable interest, BB-5
Insurable risk, BB-5–BB-6
Insurance; *see also* Health insurance
  annuities, BC-10
  automobile, BC-11
  for boards of directors, BB-4
  business ownership policies, BB-5
  buying, BB-4–BB-6
  disability, BB-9, BC-11
  government programs, BB-5
  for home-based businesses, BB-10
  homeowners, BB-8, BB-10, BC-11
  liability, BB-8, BB-9–BB-10, BC-11
  life, BB-8, BB-10, BC-10
  premiums, BB-6
  property, BB-8

  renter's, BC-11
  rule of indemnity, BB-6
  self-, BB-4
  for small businesses, 168
  types, BB-8
  umbrella policies, BC-11
  uninsurable risks, BB-5
  workers' compensation, BB-9
Insurance companies
  IRAs with, BC-13
  life, 558
  mutual, BB-7
  ratings, BC-11
  stock, BB-7
Insurance policies, BB-6
Intangible assets, 466
Integrated marketing communication (IMC), 430–431
Integrity-based ethics codes, 96, 97
Intellectual property protection
  copyrights, 93, A-7, BA-17
  Internet issues, BA-17
  lack of in China, 80
  patents, A-6–A-7
  plagiarism from Internet, 92
  trademarks, 382, 383, A-7
Intensive distribution, 412
Interactive promotion, 436
Inter-American Convention Against Corruption, 108
Interest, on bonds, 521–522
Interest rates
  on bonds, 521–522, 529
  central bank influence on, 51, 551
  on credit cards, BC-5, BC-9
  discount rate, 551
Intermediaries; *see* Marketing intermediaries
Intermittent process, 235
Intermodal shipping, 421–422
Internal customers, 194
Internal Revenue Service (IRS), 126, 461, 469–470
International Bank for Reconstruction and Development; *see* World Bank
International banking, 563; *see also* Banks
International business; *see* Global business; Multinational corporations
International Financial Reporting Standards (IFRS), 477
International Manufacturing Trade Show, 443
International markets; *see* Global markets
International Monetary Fund (IMF), 560, 564
International Organization for Standardization (ISO), 108, 245–246
International trade; *see* Global markets; Trade
Internet; *see also* E-commerce
  advertising on, 432, 433, 435–436, 447
  agriculture-related Web sites, 14
  application service providers, BA-12–BA-13
  backup services, BA-7
  banking, 562
  blogs, 445
  business use, BA-8–BA-11
  connections to, BA-10
  consumer use for research, 346, 394, 448

cookies, BA-18
cybercrime, BA-17
dialogues with customers, 436
e-mail; *see* E-mail
employee familiarity with, 219
financial sites, 528
financing Web sites, 164, 557
future uses, BA-11
intellectual property violations, 93, BA-17
interactions among firms, 217, 240, 241
investment information, 528, 530, 532–533
job search resources, P-17
netiquette, P-6
online brokers, 524–525
operations management using, 240
phishing scams, BA-17
podcasting, 445
privacy issues, 15–16, BA-18–BA-19, P-20
recruiting employees, 293, 294
résumés posted on, P-18–P-20, P-21
security issues, BA-9, BA-16–BA-18
small business Web sites, 168, 169
social networking sites, 358, BA-10–BA-11
training programs, 299
viral marketing, 445
virtual trade shows, 443
viruses, BA-16–BA-17
Internet appliances, BA-12
Internet companies; *see also* E-commerce
  failures, 155
  setting up, 155
  successful, 154–155
  venture capital investments, 505
Internet2, BA-10
Interviews, 295, P-16, P-22–P-26
Intranets, BA-9
Intrapreneurs, 155–156
Intrinsic rewards, 256–257
Inventory
  acquiring, 495
  as collateral for loans, 498
  just-in-time, 244, 495
  valuation, 470
Inventory turnover ratio, 475–476
Inverted organizations, 220
Investing; *see also* Mutual funds; Securities markets
  in bonds, 529–530
  buying securities, 524
  capital gains, 527
  comparing investments, 533
  contrarian approach, BC-8
  diversification, 525–526
  401(k) plans, BC-14
  in global markets, 519
  information sources, 528–529, 530, 533
  IRAs, BC-12–BC-14
  in real estate, BC-6–BC-8
  risks, 525
  selling securities, 524
  in stocks, 526–529, BC-8
  strategies, 525
  in 21st century, 536–537
Investment
  foreign direct, 70–71, 80–81
  sovereign wealth funds, 71, 502

Investment bankers, 515
Investors; *see also* Owners' equity; Venture capitalists
  angels, 164, 557
  corporate responsibility to, 101–102
  institutional, 515
  socially conscious, 104, 531
Investor's Business Daily, 531, 533
Invisible hand, 33–34
Involuntary bankruptcy, A-15
IPOs; *see* Initial public offerings
Iraq war, 19
IRAs; *see* Individual retirement accounts
IRS; *see* Internal Revenue Service
IS; *see* Information systems
ISO 9000 standards, 245–246
ISO 14000 standards, 246
Israel, McDonald's franchises, 68
IT; *see* Information technology
Italy
  bribery in, 105
  joint ventures in, 70

J

Jamaica, 74
Japan
  automakers, 72
  bribery scandal, 105
  factors of production, 10
  joint ventures in, 70
  keiretsu (corporate alliances), 76
  management approach, 265
  mass customization, 237
  nontariff barriers, 76
  standard of living, 6
  Tokyo Disneyland, 67
  vending machines, 413
JIT; *see* Just-in-time inventory control
Job analysis, 290–291
Job descriptions, 291
Job enlargement, 270
Job enrichment, 270
Job interviews, 295
Job rotation, 270, 300
Job searches; *see also* Recruitment; Résumés
  Internet resources, P-17
  interviews, P-16, P-22–P-26
  self-assessments, P-4, P-14, P-15
  sources of jobs, P-16–P-17
  strategies, P-14–P-16
  traits sought by recruiters, P-24
Job simplification, 270
Job simulation, 299
Job specialization, 202–203
Job specifications, 291
Jobs; *see also* Careers; Outsourcing; Recruitment
  created by small businesses, 158
  displaced by technology, 21
  in green industries, 103, 105
  lost due to free-trade agreements, 78, 79
  in service industries, 21, 231
Job-sharing plans, 308
Joint Initiative on Corporate Accountability and Workers' Rights, 107
Joint ventures, international, 70
Journals, 462
Journeymen, 298

Judiciary, A-2; *see also* Legal environment
Junk bonds, 529
Just-in-time (JIT) inventory control, 244, 495

K

Keiretsu, 76
Keogh plans, BC-14–BC-15
Key economic indicators, 45–48
Keynesian economic theory, 50–51
Knights of Labor, 320
Knockoff brands, 383
Knowledge
  distinction from information, BA-3
  as factor of production, 9, 10, 11
  retention, P-5
Knowledge management, 192–193
Knowledge technology (KT), BA-3
Koran, 63, 73, 92
Korea; *see* North Korea; South Korea
KT; *see* Knowledge technology
Kuwait, 502

L

Labor; *see also* Employee-management relations; Employees; Unions
  as factor of production, 9, 10, 11
  international standards, 106
  legislation related to, 320–322, 328
  productivity, 14
  sweatshop conditions, 106, 319
Labor-Management Relations Act (Taft-Hartley Act), 320, 321, 324, 328
Labor-Management Reporting and Disclosure Act (Landrum-Griffin Act), 321
Land, as factor of production, 9, 10
Land banks, 553
Landrum-Griffin Act, 321
Lao People's Democratic Repubic, 77
Last in, first out (LIFO), 470
Latin America
  common markets, 77
  relations between managers and workers, 73, 107
Law of large numbers, BB-6
Laws; *see* Legal environment
Lawsuits
  product liability, A-4–A-5, BB-10
  threat of, BB-2, BB-4
  wrongful discharge, 310
Lawyers, 167–168, A-A-1
Layoffs; *see* Terminating employees
Layout, facility, 241–242, 243
LBOs; *see* Leveraged buyouts
Leadership
  autocratic, 191
  free-rein, 191–192
  need for, 189
  participative (democratic), 191
  styles, 190–192
Leading
  defined, 180–181
  empowering workers, 192
  knowledge management, 192–193
  need for, 189, 190
  roles, 189–190
  styles, 190–192
Lean manufacturing, 237
Ledgers, 462

Legal environment; *see also* Intellectual property protection; Lawsuits; Regulations; Taxes
  administrative agencies, A-3, A-4
  antitrust laws, 39, A-10–A-12
  bankruptcy laws, A-14–A-17
  business law, A-2–A-3
  consumer protection, A-12, A-13
  contract law, A-9–A-10
  cybercrime, BA-17
  deregulation, 39, A-17–A-18
  effects on global markets, 74–75
  ethical decisions, 90, 94
  human resource management, 287–290
  labor laws, 320–322, 328
  need for laws, A-2
  negotiable instruments, A-8–A-9
  partnership laws, 118, 120
  product liability, A-4–A-6
  punishment for corporate wrongdoing, 90, 91
  sales law, A-8–A-9
  tort law, A-4–A-6
  trade-related laws, 65
  types of laws, A-3
  warranties, A-8
Legislation; *see* Legal environment
Less-developed countries; *see* Developing countries
Letters of credit, 563
Leverage, 505
Leverage ratios, 474–475, 505
Leveraged buyouts (LBOs), 130
Liabilities; *see also* Debt
  current, 466
  defined, 466
  long-term, 466, 467
Liability
  limited, 117, 121
  unlimited, 116, 119
Liability insurance, BB-8, BB-9–BB-10, BC-11
Licensing, 66–67
Life cycle, product, 388–390
Life insurance, BB-8, BB-10, BC-10
Life insurance companies, 558
LIFO (last in, first out), 470
Limit orders, 527
Limited liability, 117, 121
Limited liability companies (LLCs), 126–127
Limited liability partnerships (LLPs), 118
Limited partners, 117
Limited partnerships, 117
Limited-function wholesalers, 409
Line organizations, 213
Line personnel, 213–214
Line-and-staff organizations, 213–214
Lines of credit, 498
Liquidity, 466
Liquidity ratios, 473–474
LLCs; *see* Limited liability companies
LLPs; *see* Limited liability partnerships
Loans; *see also* Credit; Debt; Mortgages
  bank, 556
  from commercial finance companies, 499
  long-term, 502–503
  microlending firms, 28–29, 36
  peer-to-peer, 557
  secured, 498
  short-term, 497–498
  unsecured, 498
Local governments
  administrative agencies, A-4
  municipal bonds, 522, 529
  taxes, A-14
Location, facility; *see* Facility location
Lockouts, 328, 329
Logistics
  defined, 418
  inbound, 418
  international, 418–419
  need for, 418
  outbound, 419
  reverse, 419
  storage, 422
  third-party, 419
Logistics companies, 419
Long-term financing
  balancing debt and equity, 506
  debt, 495, 502–503
  defined, 496
  equity, 495–496, 503–505
  objectives, 501
Long-term forecasts, 490
Long-term liabilities, 466, 467
Loss leaders, 391
Losses
  defined, 5
  net, 468, 470
Low-context cultures, 275

M

M-1, 548
M-2, 548
M-3, 548
M&A; *see* Mergers and acquisitions
Macroeconomics, 30–31
Magazine advertising, 431–432, 433
Magnuson-Moss Warranty-Federal Trade Commission Improvement Act (1975), A-13
Mail; *see* Direct mail; E-mail
Mail-order firms; *see* Catalog sales
Malaysia
  ASEAN Economic Community, 77
  as market, 81
Malcolm Baldrige National Quality Awards, 245, 305
Managed security services providers (MSSPs), BA-17
Management; *see also* Employee-management relations; Empowerment; Motivation; Small business management
  boards of directors, 123, BB-4
  challenges, 178, 180
  of change, 204
  contrast between American and Japanese styles, 265, 266
  controlling, 181, 193–194
  decision making, 185–186
  defined, 179
  directing, 192
  effects of information technology, BA-15–BA-19
  ethics in, 94–96, 190
  functions, 179–180
  leading
    defined, 180–181
    empowering workers, 192
    knowledge management, 192–193
  need for, 189
  styles, 190–192
  levels
    bureaucracies, 207
    middle, 187, 207
    number of, 209–210
    supervisory, 188, 190
    tasks and skills, 188
    top, 187
  organizing; *see* Organizing
  planning
    contingency, 184–185
    defined, 179
    forms, 183
    goals and objectives, 181–182
    importance, 181, 185
    mission statements, 181, 182
    operational, 184
    performance standards, 193, 194
    questions answered by, 182–183
    strategic, 183–184, 490
    SWOT analysis, 182–183
    tactical, 184
    vision creation, 181
  problem solving, 186
  separation from ownership, 123
  tactics used in conflicts with labor, 328–329
Management by objectives (MBO), 267
Management development, 300–301
Managerial accounting, 457–458
Managers
  authority, 205
  changing roles, 178–179
  compensation, 332–334
  differences from leaders, 189
  generational differences, 275–276
  in Latin America, 73
  mentors, 300
  progressive, 178, 192
  roles, 17
  span of control, 208–209, 211
  supervisory, 188, 190
Managing diversity; *see also* Diversity
Manpower Development and Training Act of 1962, 288
Manufacturer's agents, 410
Manufacturers' brand names, 383
Manufacturing; *see also* Automobile industry; Operations management
  competitiveness, 231–232
  contract, 69–70
  costs, 236
  facility layout, 241–242, 243
  facility location, 239–240
  foreign companies in United States, 232, 239
  jobs replaced by technology, 21
  mass production, 205
  operations management, 233
  output, 230
  outsourcing, 81–82
  production techniques
    computer-aided design and manufacturing, 236
    flexible manufacturing, 237
    improving, 236
    Internet purchasing, 244
    just-in-time inventory control, 244
    lean manufacturing, 237
    mass customization, 237–238
  productivity improvements, 20, 21, 48

technology used in, 21, 242
in United States, 230–231
Margin
    buying stock on, 527–528
    gross, 469
Market indices, 534
Market orders, 527
Market prices, 37–39, 394
Market segmentation, 360–361
Marketable securities; *see* Securities markets
Marketing; *see also* Personal selling; Promotion
    careers in, 366
    consultants, 168
    consumer decision-making process, 363–364
    defined, 346
    eras, 347–349
    evolution of, 347–349
    four Ps, 350–352
    greenwashing, 104
    helping buyers buy, 346–347
    on Internet, 358
    mass, 363
    by nonprofit organizations, 349–350
    one-to-one, 362
    by small businesses, 168
    test, 352–353
    value in, 374
Marketing concept, 348–349
Marketing concept era, 348–349
Marketing environment, 357–359
Marketing intermediaries; *see also* Business-to-business (B2B) companies; Retail industry; Wholesalers
    cooperation among, 415–416
    defined, 402
    exchange efficiency created by, 404–405
    in food industry, 405–406
    need for, 403–404, 406
    roles, 353
    sales promotion to, 443
    types, 403
    utilities created by, 407–408
    value versus cost of, 405–406
Marketing managers, 351
Marketing mix, 350–352, 389
Marketing research
    data analysis, 356
    data collection, 355–356
    data sources, 355
    defined, 354
    focus groups, 356
    process, 354–357
    by small businesses, 168
    strategy implementation, 356–357
    surveys, 356
Markets; *see also* Business-to-business (B2B) market; Consumer market; Global markets; Securities markets
    competition in, 39
    defined, 166
    demand, 37
    free, 39–40
    functioning of, 36–39
    inequality in, 40
    price determination, 36–38
    supply, 37
Maslow's hierarchy of needs, 260–261, 263
Mass customization, 237–238

Mass marketing, 363
Mass production, 205, 236
Master limited partnerships (MLPs), 117
Materials handling, 418
Materials requirement planning (MRP), 242
Matrix organizations, 214–216
Maturity dates, 521
MBO; *see* Management by objectives
Media, 441–442; *see also* Advertising; Television
Mediation, 326–327
Medical savings accounts (MSAs), BB-9
Medical tourism, 82
Medicine; *see* Health care
Mentors, 300
Mercantilism, 76
Merchant wholesalers, 409
Mercosur, 77
Mergers and acquisitions
    conglomerate mergers, 129
    defined, 129
    foreign companies involved in, 130
    horizontal mergers, 129
    in late 1990s, 129
    leveraged buyouts, 130
    types, 129, 130
    vertical mergers, 129
Mexico, 11, 43, 78; *see also* North American Free Trade Agreement
Microeconomics, 30; *see also* Prices
Microlending firms, 28–29, 36
Micropreneurs, 150–153
Middle management, 187, 207
Middlemen; *see* Marketing intermediaries
Millennial generation, 275, 276
Millionaires, BC–BC-1
MiniPlan, 162–164
Minorities; *see also* African Americans; Discrimination; Diversity
    entrepreneurs, 9, 144–145
    franchisees, 135
    Hispanic Americans, 9, 301
    managers, 301
Mission statements, 181, 182
Mississippi River, 420
Mixed economies, 43–45
MLM; *see* Multilevel marketing
MLPs; *see* Master limited partnerships
MNCs; *see* Multinational corporations
Mobile advertising, 433, 446
Model Business Corporation Act, 120
Modular layouts, 241–242, 243
Monetary policy, 51, 550–551
Money; *see also* Currencies
    coins, 547–548
    counterfeiting, 546
    defined, 547
    electronic cash, 548
    history, 547–548, 553
    importance, 546–547
    time value of, 493
Money magazine, 531
Money management; *see* Personal financial planning
Money supply, 51, 548–549, 550–551
Monopolies
    absolute advantage, 62
    antitrust laws, 39, A-10–A-12
    defined, 39
Monopolistic competition, 39

Moore's law, BA-11
Moral values, 92; *see also* Ethics
Morningstar Investor, 531
Mortgage bonds, 523
Mortgages
    FHA, BB-5
    fraud in industry, 92
    payments, BC-7
    securitization, 535, 536, 559
    subprime, 13–14, 333, 535, 536, 558
    tax deduction for interest payments, BC-8
Motion pictures; *see* Movies
Motivation
    cultural differences and, 274–275
    equity theory, 268–269
    ethical issues, 297
    expectancy theory, 267–268
    extrinsic rewards, 257
    generational differences, 275–276
    goal-setting theory, 267
    Herzberg's factors, 261–263
    importance, 256
    intrinsic rewards, 256–257
    job enrichment and, 270
    management by objectives, 267
    Maslow's hierarchy of needs, 260–261, 263
    by money, 260, 262
    personalizing, 274–276
    recognition, 272–274
    reinforcement theory, 268, 269
    in small businesses, 273
    of temporary employees, 297
    Theory X and Theory Y, 263–264, 266
    Theory Z, 265–266
Motivators, 262
Motor vehicles; *see* Automobile industry
Movies
    global market, 60
    product placement, 434
MRP; *see* Materials requirement planning
MSSPs; *see* Managed security services providers
Multicultural population, 359; *see also* Cultural diversity
Multilevel marketing (MLM), 414
Multinational corporations
    accounting standards, 477
    defined, 71
    ethical issues, 105–108
    foreign direct investment, 80–81
    foreign subsidiaries, 70–71
    largest, 71
Municipal bonds, 522, 529
Muslims, 63, 72–73
Mutual funds
    closed-end, 531
    defined, 530
    fees, 531
    index funds, 530–531
    international stocks, 519
    investing in, 530–532
    net asset values, 533
    no-load, 531
    objectives, 532
    quotations, 532–533
    socially responsible, 531
Mutual insurance companies, BB-7
Myanmar, 77

N

NAFTA; *see* North American Free Trade Agreement
Nanobots, BA-15–BA-16
NASDAQ
    defined, 516
    as electronic stock exchange, 516, BA-3
    stock quotations, 528
    stocks and bonds traded on, 516, 534
    Times Square price wall, 528
National Association of Securities Dealers Automated Quotations; *see* NASDAQ
National banks, 553
National Credit Union Administration (NCUA), 560–561
National debt, 49–50
National Flood Insurance Assocation, BB-5
National Labor Relations Act of 1935 (Wagner Act), 288, 320, 321, 323
National Labor Relations Board (NLRB), 321
Natural disasters, BB-2
NCUA; *see* National Credit Union Administration
Needs, hierarchy of, 260–261, 263
Negligence, A-4
Negotiable instruments, A-8–A-9
Negotiated labor-management agreements (labor contracts), 323–325
Neo-Malthusians, 32
Net; *see* Internet
Net income or net loss, 468, 470
Netiquette, P-6
Network computing systems (client/server computing), BA-12
Networking
    among firms, 216–217, 240
    in job searches, P-14–P-15
    by managers, 300
    online, BA-10
    social networking sites, BA-10–BA-11
    by students, P-5
Networks; *see also* Internet
    broadband, BA-10
    extranets, BA-9
    firewalls, BA-9
    intranets, BA-9
    portals, BA-9
    virtual private, BA-9
    virtualization, BA-13
    wireless, BA-12
New businesses; *see* Businesses, starting; Entrepreneurs
New product development; *see* Product development
New York Stock Exchange (NYSE)
    crashes, 534–535
    Dow Jones Industrial Average, 534, 535
    electronic trading, 516
    history, 515
    listing requirements, 516
    stock quotations, 528
New York Times, 294
News releases, 442
Newspapers
    advertising, 431–432, 433
    publicity in, 442, 446
    stock quotations, 528
Niche marketing, 362
NLRB; *see* National Labor Relations Board
No-load mutual funds, 531
Nonbanks, 499, 554, 557–558
Nonprice competition, 394–395
Nonprofit organizations; *see also* Charitable giving
    accounting, 461
    defined, 7
    marketing, 349–350
    objectives, 7
    using business principles in, 7–8
    volunteering for, 100
Nonstore retailing, 412–415
Nontariff barriers, 76
Norris-LaGuardia Act, 321
North American Free Trade Agreement (NAFTA), 78, 79, 323, 325
North Korea
    famine, 42
    incomes, 31
Notes payable, 467
Not-for-profit organizations; *see* Nonprofit organizations
Nurses, 331
Nutrition Labeling and Education Act (1990), A-13
NYSE; *see* New York Stock Exchange

O

Objectives, 181–182
Occupational Safety and Health Act of 1970, 288
Occupations; *see* Careers
Odd lots, 527
Off-the-job training, 299
Old-Age, Survivors, and Disability Insurance Program; *see* Social Security
Older customers, 17–18
Older employees, 289–290
Older Workers Benefit Protection Act, 288
Oligopolies, 39
One-to-one marketing, 362
Online banking, 562
Online brokers, 524–525
Online business; *see* E-commerce; Internet
Online training, 299
On-the-job training, 298
Open communication, 270–272
Open shop agreements, 324
Open-end mutual funds, 531
Open-market operations, 550, 551
Operating (master) budgets, 490
Operating expenses, 469–470
Operating funds
    for capital expenditures, 495
    credit operations, 494–495
    day-to-day needs, 493–494
    for inventory, 495
    need for, 492–493
    sources, 495–496
Operational planning, 184
Operations management
    careers in, 248
    control procedures, 246–247
    defined, 233
    in manufacturing, 233, 234–235
    in service industries, 233–234
    use of Internet, 240
Operations management planning
    facility layout, 241–242, 243
    facility location, 238–241
    materials requirement planning, 242
    quality control, 244
Opportunities; *see* SWOT analysis
Oprah Winfrey Show, 113, 115
Options, stock, 304, 332–333
Organization charts, 187, 203, 207
Organizational (or corporate) culture
    defined, 220
    informal organization, 221–222
    open communication in, 270–271
    values, 204
Organizational design; *see also* Teams
    bureaucracy, 204, 206, 207
    centralization, 205–206, 208, 209
    chain of command, 207
    decentralization, 208, 209
    departmentalization, 203, 210–212
    division of labor, 202–203, 205
    Fayol's principles, 205–206
    functional structures, 211
    hierarchy, 187–188, 205, 207
    historical development, 205–207
    hybrid forms, 211
    informal organization, 221–222
    inverted structures, 220
    line organizations, 213
    line-and-staff organizations, 213–214
    matrix organizations, 214–216
    principles, 202–203
    pyramid structures, 207, 209–210
    restructuring, 16–17, 203, 219–220
    span of control, 208–209, 211
    tall versus flat structures, 209–210
    traditional principles, 205–207
    Weber's principles, 206–207
Organized labor; *see* Unions
Organizing
    change in, 204, 219–221
    defined, 180
    interactions among firms, 217–218
    levels of management, 187–188, 207
    new businesses, 202–203
    stakeholder-oriented organizations, 194
Orientation, 298
OTC; *see* Over-the-counter (OTC) markets
Outbound logistics, 419
Outdoor advertising, 433
Outlet stores, 411
Outsourcing
    contract manufacturing, 69–70
    defined, 6–7, 218
    distribution, 419
    employee benefits, 294, 306
    ethical issues, 82, 240
    to home-based businesses, 152
    information technology services, BA-12–BA-13
    limits, 218–219
    logistics, 419
    offshore, 81–82
    problems with, 218
    production, 81–82, 239
    pros and cons, 81
    reversing decisions, 219

by small businesses, 153
supply chain management, 417
sweatshop labor issue, 106
training, BA-15
Web resources, 153
Over-the-counter (OTC) markets, 515–516
Owners' equity; *see also* Stocks
 defined, 467
 ratio of debt to, 474–475
 return on, 475
Ownership, separation from management, 123; *see also* Business ownership forms

P

Packaging, 381–382
Pakistan
 bribery in, 105
 foreign companies in, 73
 IMF loans, 560, 564
Par value, of stock, 519
Paraguay, 77
Parent companies, 70
Parents, single, 18; *see also* Children; Families
Participative (democratic) leadership, 191
Partnerships
 advantages, 118
 agreements, 119–120
 choosing partners, 119
 defined, 114
 disadvantages, 119
 general, 117
 limited, 117
 limited liability, 118
 master limited, 117
Part-time employees, 296, 308
Patents, A-6–A-7; *see also* Intellectual property protection
Pay equity, 334–335
Pay systems, 303–304; *see also* Compensation
Paycheck Fairness Act, 335
PCAOB; *see* Public Company Accounting Oversight Board
PDAs; *see* Personal digital assistants
P/E; *see* Price/earnings ratio
Penetration pricing strategy, 393
Penny stocks, 527
Pension Benefit Guaranty Corporation, BB-5
Pension funds, 558
Pentagon; *see* Defense Department, U.S.
People's Republic of China; *see* China
PEOs; *see* Professional employer organizations
Perfect competition, 39
Performance appraisals, 301–302
Performance ratios, 475
Performance standards, 193, 194
Personal digital assistants (PDAs), BA-11
Personal financial planning
 advisers, BC-15
 balance sheets, 466, 467, BC-3
 budgets, 492, BC-4–BC-5
 building financial base, BC-6–BC-7
 debts, BC-5
 estate planning, BC-15
 expenditures, BC-3–BC-4, BC-6

income statements, BC-3
insurance, BC-9–BC-11
investments; *see* Investing
need for, BC-2
real estate, BC-6–BC-8
retirement planning
 401(k) plans, BC-14
 IRAs, BC-12–BC-14
 Keogh plans, BC-14–BC-15
 Social Security, 18, BB-5, BC-12
savings, BC-5, BC-8
steps, BC-3–BC-6
Personal selling; *see also* Sales representatives
 benefits, 437–438
 in business-to-business market, 362, 438–440
 defined, 437
 relationships with customers, 439–440
 steps, 438–440
Personnel; *see* Human resource management
PERT (program evaluation and review technique) charts, 246–247
Peru
 Andean Pact, 77
 foreign companies in, 73
Pharmaceutical companies, A-5, A-12
Philanthropy; *see* Charitable giving
Philippines
 ASEAN Economic Community, 77
 franchises, 136
 as market, 81
Phishing, BA-17
Physical distribution; *see* Distribution
Physically challenged; *see* Disabled individuals
Pick economy, 448
Piecework pay systems, 304
Pipelines, 421
Place utility, 407
Planning; *see also* Financial planning; Operations management planning
 business plans, 162–164
 contingency, 184–185
 defined, 179
 forms, 183
 goals and objectives, 181–182
 human resources, 290–292
 importance, 181, 185
 mission statements, 181, 182
 operational, 184
 performance standards, 193, 194
 questions answered by, 182–183
 in small businesses, 162–164
 strategic, 183–184, 490
 SWOT analysis, 182–183
 tactical, 184
 vision creation, 181
Plastic money; *see* Credit cards
PMI (pluses, minuses, implications), 186
Podcasting, 445
Political economy, 76
Pollution; *see* Environmental issues
Population growth, 32; *see also* Demography
Portals, BA-9
Portfolio strategy, 526
Possession utility, 408
Post-it Notes, 155–156

Poverty
 in developing countries, 32
 relationship to population growth, 32
PPI; *see* Producer price index
PPOs; *see* Preferred provider organizations
PR; *see* Public relations
Precedents, A-3
Preferred provider organizations (PPOs), BB-9, BC-11
Preferred stock, 520–521
Premiums, BB-6
Press releases, 442
Price discrimination, A-12
Price indexes, 47–48
Price leadership, 392
Price/earnings ratio (P/E), 528
Prices
 comparing on Internet, 394
 determination of, 36–38
 equilibrium, 37–39
 inflation and deflation, 47
 market, 37–39, 394
 market forces and, 36–39, 394
 of new products, 353, 390–392
Pricing strategies
 break-even analysis, 392–393
 bundling, 382, 393
 competition-based pricing, 392
 cost-based pricing, 391
 demand-based pricing, 391–392
 everyday low pricing, 393
 high-low, 393
 objectives, 390–391
 penetration, 393
 psychological pricing, 394
 in retail, 393
 skimming, 393
Primary boycotts, 328
Primary data, 356
Principle of motion economy, 257
Privacy, on Internet, 15–16, BA-18–BA-19, P-20
Private accountants, 458
Private enterprise system; *see* Capitalism
Private property, 35
Private-label brands, 383
Problem solving, 186
Process departmentalization, 211, 212
Process layouts, 242, 243
Process manufacturing, 235
Processes, production, 234–235
Producer price index (PPI), 48
Product analysis, 387
Product departmentalization, 211, 212
Product development
 commercialization, 387
 concept testing, 352–353, 387
 design, 352–353
 for developing countries, 73
 process, 352–353, 385–386
 prototypes, 387
 test marketing, 352–353
 total product offer, 375–377
 value enhancers, 376, 377
Product differentiation, 39, 378
Product liability
 defined, A-4–A-5
 insurance, BB-10
 major awards, A-5
 strict, A-5
Product life cycle, 388–390

Product lines, 377–378
Product managers, 385
Product mix, 377–378
Product placement, 434–435
Product screening, 386–387
Production; see also Manufacturing; Quality
   computer-aided design and manufacturing, 236
   control procedures, 246–247
   costs, 391
   defined, 232
   factors of, 9–11, 35, 232
   flexible manufacturing, 237
   just-in-time inventory control, 244, 495
   lean manufacturing, 237
   mass, 205
   mass customization, 237–238
   outsourcing of, 81–82, 239
   processes, 234–235
Production era, 347–348
Production management, 232, 235
Productivity
   agricultural, 20
   benefits of flextime plans, 307
   defined, 14
   Hawthorne effect, 259–260
   impact of training, 297–298
   increases in
     in manufacturing, 20, 21, 48
     in United States, 48
     use of technology, 14, 48, 236
   labor, 14
   scientific management and, 257
   in service sector, 48, 232
   in United States, 48
Products
   adapting, 374–375
   brands, 382–385; see also Brand names
   complaints about, 445
   consumer goods and services, 378–379, 380
   customized, 237–238
   defined, 352
   development; see Product development
   distribution; see Distribution
   failures, 385–386
   generic goods, 383
   green
     business opportunities, 231
     business use of, 287
     carbon footprints, 103, 384, 421
     cars, 32, 351, 372
     consumer preferences, BB-10
     promoting, 434
   industrial goods and services, 379–380, 404
   packaging, 381–382
   pricing, 353
   tracking technology, 382, 422, BA-5
Professional behavior, P-5–P-7
Professional business strategies, P-5–P-6
Professional employer organizations (PEOs), 294, 306
Profit and loss statement; see Income statement
Profitability ratios, 475
Profits
   defined, 5

   gross, 469
   matching risk and, 5
   net, 470
Profit-sharing plans, 304
Program evaluation and review technique (PERT) charts, 246–247
Program trading, 535
Project management
   Gantt charts, 247, 248
   PERT charts, 246–247
Project managers, 215
Promissory notes, 497, 502
Promotion; see also Advertising; Personal selling
   campaign steps, 431
   defined, 354
   integrated marketing communication, 430–431
   interactive, 436
   on Internet, 435–436
   sales, 442–444
   strategies, 447–448
   of sustainability efforts, 434
   techniques, 354, 430
   word of mouth, 444–446
Promotion mix, 430, 446–447
Promotions, of employees, 309
Property, private ownership, 35
Property insurance, BB-8, BB-10, BC-11
Property taxes, A-14, BC-8
Prospecting, 438
Prospects, 438
Prospectuses, 517
Protectionism, 75–76
Protective tariffs, 76
Prototypes, 387
Psychographic segmentation, 361, 362
Psychological pricing, 394
Public, business responsibility to; see Corporate social responsibility
Public accountants, 459
Public Company Accounting Oversight Board (PCAOB), 459
Public domain software (freeware), BA-14
Public information, BA-6, BA-18
Public insurance, BB-5
Public relations (PR), 441
Public sector; see Governments
Public utilities; see Utilities
Publicity, 441–442, 446
Pull strategy, 447–448
Purchasing, 244; see also Suppliers; Supply chain management
Pure risk, BB-3
Push strategy, 447, 448

Q

Qualifying, 438
Quality
   Baldrige Awards, 245, 305
   as competitive advantage, 16
   defined, 244
   ISO 9000 standards, 245–246
   perceived, 384
   six sigma, 244
Quality control
   continuous improvement process, 244
   at end of production, 244
Quality Digest, BB-2

Quality of life, 6, 240
Quick ratio, 474

R

Race; see Diversity; Minorities
Rack jobbers, 409
Radio advertising, 432–433
Radio frequency identification (RFID), 382, 422, 562, BA-5
Railroads, 419–420
Ratio analysis
   activity ratios, 475–476
   defined, 473
   leverage ratios, 474–475, 505
   liquidity ratios
     acid-test (quick) ratio, 474
     current ratio, 474
     purpose, 473–474
   profitability ratios
     basic earnings per share, 475
     diluted earnings per share, 475
     return on equity, 475
     return on sales, 475
Real estate; see also Mortgages
   bubbles, 535–536, BC-7
   investing in, BC-6–BC-8
   property taxes, A-14, BC-8
Real time, 217
Realtors, 408
Recessions, 48–49, 230–231; see also Economic crisis of 2008–2009
Recognizing employees, 272–274
Recruitment, employee; see also Job searches
   affirmative action and, 288–289
   application forms, 294–295
   background investigations, 295
   challenges, 292–293
   of contingent workers, 296–297
   costs, 293
   defined, 292
   employment tests, 295
   interviews, P-16, P-22–P-26
   online services, 293, 294
   physical exams, 295
   selecting employees, 293–296
   by small businesses, 292–293, 294
   sources, 292, 293, 294
   traits sought, P-24
   trial periods, 296
Regulations; see also Legal environment
   consumer protection, A-12, A-13
   deregulation, 39, A-17–A-18
   effects on global markets, 74–75
   on hamburgers, A-17
   packaging, 382
   securities markets, 516–518
   support for, A-18
Reinforcement theory, 268, 269
Relationship marketing, 363
Religious differences, 72–73
Renter's insurance, BC-11
Research; see Marketing research; Product development
Reserve requirements, 550–551
Resignations, 311
Resource development, 31
Resource files, P-5
Resources; see Factors of production
Restrictions on trade; see Trade barriers

Restructuring
  competing with, 16–17
  for empowerment, 219–220
Résumés
  cover letters, P-15, P-20–P-22
  key words, P-18
  posting on Internet, P-18–P-20, P-21
  sample, P-19, P-21
  writing, P-15, P-17–P-18
Retail industry; *see also* E-commerce
  catalog companies, 414–415
  cooperatives, 416
  decentralized authority, 207
  in developing countries, 417
  distribution strategies, 411–412
  jobs in, 21
  nonstore retailing, 412–415
  number of stores in United States, 411
  pricing strategies, 393
  salespersons, 440
  supermarkets, 292, 411, 444
  types of stores, 411
Retailers, 403, 409
Retained earnings, 467, 504–505
Retirement planning
  defined-contribution plans, BC-14
  401(k) plans, BC-14
  IRAs, BC-12–BC-14
  Keogh plans, BC-14–BC-15
  Social Security, 18, BB-5, BC-12
Retirements, 290, 310–311
Return on equity (ROE), 475
Return on investment (ROI), 390
Return on sales, 475
Revenue tariffs, 76
Revenues
  defined, 5, 469
  forecasting, 489–490
Reverse discrimination, 289
Reverse logistics, 419
Revolving credit agreements, 498
RFID; *see* Radio frequency identification
Right-to-work laws, 324
Risk
  avoidance, BB-4
  defined, 5, BB-3
  insurable, BB-5–BB-6
  investment, 525
  matching profits and, 5
  pure, BB-3
  reduction, BB-3–BB-4
  return on equity, 475
  speculative, BB-3
  uninsurable, BB-5
Risk management; *see also* Insurance
  importance, BB-2
  options, BB-3–BB-5
  rapid change and, BB-2–BB-3
Risk/return trade-off, 502
Robinson-Patman Act of 1936, A-12
Rockefeller family, 505
ROE; *see* Return on equity
ROI; *see* Return on investment
Ronald McDonald Houses, 99
Roth IRAs, BC-13
Royalties, 66
Rule of indemnity, BB-6
Russia
  barter trade, 547
  dumping disputes, 65
  factors of production, 10
  income tax rates, 42
  as market, 80–81

S

S corporations, 125–126
S&Ls; *see* Savings and loan associations
Safety, 204, 258
SAIF; *see* Savings Association Insurance Fund
Salaries, 304; *see also* Compensation
Sales; *see also* Personal selling
  difference from revenues, 469
  gross, 469
  net, 469
  return on, 475
Sales agents, 410
Sales law, A-8–A-9
Sales promotion; *see also* Promotion
  defined, 442
  internal, 443
  to marketing intermediaries, 443
  sampling, 444
  techniques, 442–444
Sales representatives; *see also* Personal selling
  in retail stores, 440
  sales promotion to, 443
Sales taxes, 41, A-14
Sampling, 444
Sarbanes-Oxley Act, 97, 459, 460, A-12
Saudi Arabia
  franchises in, 72–73
  imports, 63
Savings; *see also* Retirement planning
  personal, BC-5, BC-8
  rates of return, BC-5
Savings accounts, 555
Savings and loan associations (S&Ls)
  defined, 556
  failures, 556
  federal deposit insurance, 560
  IRAs, BC-13
  as marketing intermediaries, 408
  services, 556
Savings Association Insurance Fund (SAIF), 560
SBA; *see* Small Business Administration
SBDCs; *see* Small Business Development Centers
SBIC; *see* Small Business Investment Company
Scandals; *see* Corporate scandals; Corruption
Scientific management
  Hawthorne studies, 259–260
  Taylor's work, 257
  at UPS, 258–259
SCM; *see* Supply chain management
SCORE; *see* Service Corps of Retired Executives
Seasonal unemployment, 46
Seasonal workers; *see* Temporary employees
SEC; *see* Securities and Exchange Commission
Secondary boycotts, 328, 329
Secondary data, 355–356
Secured bonds, 503, 523
Secured loans, 498
Securities; *see* Bonds; Securities markets; Stocks
Securities Act of 1933, 516

Securities and Exchange Act of 1934, 517
Securities and Exchange Commission (SEC)
  accounting investigations, 200
  accounting standards, 477
  Arthur Andersen investigation, 91
  banking crisis of 2008–2009 and, 559, A-12
  criticism of, A-12
  defined, 516
  establishment, 517
  fair disclosure regulation, 101
  influence on business, A-3
  insider trading regulations, 101, 517–518
  Public Company Accounting Oversight Board, 459
  regulation of markets, 516–518, 519
  regulation of stock and bond issuance, 504, 515, 517
Securities markets; *see also* Investing; Stock exchanges
  bubbles, 535
  functions, 514–515
  insider trading, 101, 517–518
  over-the-counter (OTC), 515–516
  primary, 514
  quotations, 528–529
  regulation of, 516–518
  secondary, 514
  volatility, 534–535
Security, information technology, BA-16–BA-18
Selection of employees, 293–296
Selective distribution, 412
Self-insurance, BB-4
Self-managed cross-functional teams, 216–217, 272
Selling; *see* Personal selling; Retail industry; Sales promotion
Selling era, 348
Senior citizens; *see also* Aging of population
  as consumers, 17–18, 359
  elder care, 337–338
  employees, 289–290
Service Corps of Retired Executives (SCORE), 168
Service industries
  competitiveness, 232
  facility layout, 241
  facility location, 238–239
  global markets, 43
  growth, 232–233
  home-based businesses, 152, 153
  inverted organizations, 220
  jobs in, 21, 231
  operations management, 233–234
  outsourcing jobs, 82
  packaging, 382
  product lines and product mixes, 378
  productivity, 48, 232
  types of organizations, 22
  in United States, 231, 232–233
Service utility, 408
Services, defined, 4
Sexual harassment, 335–336
Sexual orientation; *see* Diversity
Shadowing, 298
Shareholders; *see* Stockholders
Shareware, BA-14

Sherman Antitrust Act, A-11
Shipping; see Logistics; Transportation
Ships, 420–421
Shop stewards, 326
Shopping goods and services, 378–379
Short-term financing
   banks, 497–498
   commercial paper, 500
   defined, 496
   factoring, 499–500
   family and friends, 497
   lines of credit, 498
   loans, 497–498
   promissory notes, 497
   revolving credit agreements, 498
   for small businesses, 496–498
   trade credit, 496–497
Short-term forecasts, 489–490
Simple IRAs, BC-14
Sin taxes, A-13
Singapore
   ASEAN Economic Community, 77
   as market, 81
Single parents, 18
Sinking funds, 523
Site selection; see Facility location
Six sigma quality, 244
Skill-based pay, 305
Skills
   conceptual, 188
   human relations, 188
   management, 188
   technical, 188, BB-15, BA-19
Skimming price strategy, 393
Small Business Administration (SBA)
   business financing from, 164, 165–166, 557
   defined, 165
   definition of small business, 157
   export financing, 170
   information on exporting, 63, 169
   reasons for business failures, 161
   Service Corps of Retired Executives, 168
   Web site, 166, 168
Small Business Development Centers (SBDCs), 165
Small Business Investment Company (SBIC) Program, 165
Small business management
   accounting systems, 167, 463
   employee management, 167
   financial management, 164–166, 487
   financing
      bank loans, 165, 557
      credit cards, 501, 557
      retained earnings, 504–505
      short-term, 496–498
      sources, 164–166, 494, 557
      venture capital, 165, 505
   functions, 162
   importance, 161–162
   insurance, 168
   learning about, 160–161
   marketing, 166, 168
   MBA students as interns, 168
   planning, 162–164
   recruiting employees, 292–293, 294
   retirement plans, BC-14
   Web sites, 168

Small businesses; see also Businesses, starting; Entrepreneurship; Home-based businesses
   banks and, 162, 165, 168, 556, 557
   defined, 157
   exporting, 67, 83, 169–170
   failures, 158–159, 161–162
   family-run, 167
   global markets, 62, 83, 169–170
   importance, 157–158
   jobs created by, 158
   legal environment, 12–13
   legal help, 167–168
   markets, 166
   motivating employees, 273
   nonprice competition, 394–395
   number of, 157
   outsourcing by, 153
   product differentiation, 378
   promotion, 446
   success factors, 159
   taking over existing firms, 160–161
   Web sites, 168, 169
Smart cards, 562
Social audits, 104–105
Social entrepreneurs, 7–8
Social environment, 17–18, 72–73, 359
Social justice, 103
Social marketing, 358
Social networking, 222
Social networking sites, 358, BA-10–BA-11
Social responsibility, 34; see also Corporate social responsibility
Social Security, 18, BB-5, BC-12
Social Security Act of 1935, BC-12
Socialism
   benefits, 41
   command economies, 42
   compared to other systems, 44
   defined, 40–41
   government functions, 41, 43
   income redistribution, 41
   negative consequences, 41, 43
Socially responsible entrepreneurship, 149
Socially responsible investing (SRI), 104, 531
Society, responsibility to; see Corporate social responsibility
SOFFEX, BA-3
Soft benefits, 305
Software; see also Information technology
   accounting, 463
   antivirus, BA-16–BA-17
   business intelligence, BA-3–BA-4
   business plan, 162–164
   cookies, BA-18
   customer relationship management, 438
   employee application screening, 294–295
   functions, BA-14
   Microsoft's competitive practices, A, A-12
   public domain, BA-14
   shareware, BA-14
   supply chain management, 417
Sole proprietorships
   advantages, 115
   defined, 114
   disadvantages, 116–117
   owner's equity, 467

South Africa
   diamond production, 62
   franchises, 136
South Korea
   bribery in, 105
   incomes, 31
   as market, 81
   nontariff barriers, 76
Sovereign wealth funds (SWFs), 71, 502
Soviet Union (former); see Russia
Span of control, 208–209, 211
SPC; see Statistical process control
Specialty goods and services, 379
Specialty stores, 411
Speculative risk, BB-3
Spending; see Expenses
Spyware, BA-18
SQC; see Statistical quality control
SRI; see Socially responsible investing
Staff personnel, 213–214
Staffing; see also Employees; Recruitment
   defined, 189
   importance, 189
   retention, 102, 311
Stagflation, 47
Stakeholder-oriented organizations, 194
Stakeholders
   defined, 6
   relationships with, 441
   responding to, 6–7, 194
   responsibilities to, 100–103
Standard & Poor's 500, 534, BC-13
Standard of living
   contribution of business, 5–6
   defined, 6
   in developing countries, 73
   measuring, 6
Standards; see also Regulations
   accounting, 459, 469–470, 477
   ISO, 245–246
Start-up companies; see Businesses, starting
State governments
   administrative agencies, A-4
   competition to attract businesses, 241, 350
   right-to-work laws, 324
   support for entrepreneurs, 156
   taxes, A-14
Statement of cash flows, 464, 471–472
Statement of financial position; see Balance sheets
Statement of income and expenses; see Income statement
Statistical process control (SPC), 245
Statistical quality control (SQC), 244–245
Statutory law, A-3; see also Legal environment
Steel industry, 230
Stock certificates, 519
Stock exchanges; see also NASDAQ; New York Stock Exchange; Securities markets
   crash of 1929, 553
   defined, 515
   electronic, 516, BA-3
   global, 518, 519
   indicators, 533–534
   listing requirements, 516
   members, 515

program trading, 535
U.S., 515–516
volatility, 534–535
Stock insurance companies, BB-7
Stock options, 304, 332–333
Stock splits, 527
Stockbrokers, 524; *see also* Brokerage firms
Stockholders, 123, 467, 520; *see also* Owners' equity
Stocks
  advantages and disadvantages, 520
  American depository receipts, 519
  buying on margin, 527–528
  defined, 519
  dividends, 519
  in 401(k) plans, BC-14
  initial public offerings, 504, 514
  investing in, 526–529, BC-8
  issuing, 504, 514–515, 520–521
  preferred, 520–521
  price/earnings ratios, 528
  quotations, 528–529
Storage, 422
Stores; *see* Retail industry; Supermarkets
Strategic alliances, 70
Strategic planning, 183–184, 490
Strengths; *see* SWOT analysis
Strict product liability, A-5
Strikebreakers, 329
Strikes
  defined, 327
  laws prohibiting, 328
  use as tactic, 327–328
Structural unemployment, 46
Students
  cheating, 92–93
  employment, 296–297
  internships, 168
  knowledge retention, P-5
  professional behavior, P-5–P-7
  resource files, P-5
  study hints, P-7–P-9
  test-taking hints, P-9–P-10
  time management, P-10–P-11
Study hints, P-7–P-9
Subcontracting; *see* Outsourcing
Submarine patents, A-7
Subprime mortgage crisis, 13, 165, 333, 535, 536
Subsidiaries, foreign, 70–71
Substance abuse, 338
Supermarkets
  defined, 411
  employees, 292
  sampling, 444
Supervisory management, 188, 190
Suppliers
  financing from, 164
  including in cross-functional teams, 216–217
  just-in-time inventory control, 244
  locations, 239
  relationships with, 244
  sweatshop labor issue, 106
  use of Internet, 244
Supply, 37
Supply chain, 416; *see also* Marketing intermediaries
Supply chain management (SCM); *see also* Distribution
  careers in, 423
  defined, 416
  outsourcing, 417
  software, 417
Supply curve, 37–38
Surcharges; *see* Tariffs
Surface transportation, 419–420
Surveys, marketing research, 356
Sweatshop labor, 106, 319
SWFs; *see* Sovereign wealth funds
SWOT analysis, 182–183

T

Tactical planning, 184
Taft-Hartley Act; *see* Labor-Management Relations Act
Taiwan, computer manufacturing, 69
Tall organization structures, 209
Target costing, 391–392
Target marketing, 360–361
Tariffs
  in common markets, 77
  defined, 76
  lowered by international agreements, 77
  protective, 76
  revenue, 76
TARP; *see* Troubled Assets Relief Program
Tax accountants, 461
Tax credits, A-14
Tax-deferred contributions, BC-12
Taxes
  defined, A-13
  excise, A-14
  government policies, 49
  income
    corporate, 124, A-14
    deductions for homeowners, BC-8
    education incentives, BC-3
    federal, A-14
    personal, 40–41, A-14
    rates, 40–41
  on Internet transactions, A-14
  laws, A-13–A-14
  management of, 488
  property, A-14, BC-8
  sales, 41, A-14
  sin, A-13
  Social Security, BC-12
  types, A-13–A-14
  value-added, 41
Teams
  compensation, 304–305
  entrepreneurial, 150
  global, 216–217
  matrix organizations, 214–216
  open communication and, 272
  organizing, 203
  problem-solving, 186
  self-managed cross-functional, 216–217, 272
Technical skills, 188
Technological environment, impact on businesses, 14–16
Technology; *see also* Information technology; Internet; Networks; Telecommuting
  in banking, 561–562
  benefits, 14
  customer-responsiveness and, 15
  defined, 14
  digital video recorders, 433–434
  effects on marketing, 358
  jobs displaced by, 21
  in manufacturing, 21, 242
  predictions about, BA-5
  product tracking, 382, 422, BA-5
  productivity improvements, 14, 48, 236
  speed of evolution, BA-11–BA-12
Telecommunications Act of 1996, A-17
Telecommunications deregulation, A-17–A-18
Telecommuting
  benefits to employee, 308, 309, BA-15
  benefits to employer, 308, 309, BA-15
  challenges, 309, BA-15
  effects on facility location decisions, 240
  nanobots, BA-15–BA-16
Telemarketing, 413
Television
  advertising, 431, 432, 433–435
  digital video recorders, 433–434
  infomercials, 435
  online video sharing, 93
  Oprah Winfrey Show, 113, 115
  product placement, 434
Temporary employees
  agencies, 282–283
  hiring, 294, 296–297
  motivating, 297
  number of, 296
Ten Commandments, 92
Term insurance, BC-10
Terminating employees, 289, 310, 333
Term-loan agreements, 502
Terrorism
  companies linked to, 105
  costs of increased security, 19
  cyber-, BA-17
  threat of, 19, BB-2
Test marketing, 352–353
Testimonials, 445
Testing
  drug, 338
  of potential employees, 295
Test-taking hints, P-9–P-10
Text messaging, 433, 446
Thailand
  ASEAN Economic Community, 77
  as market, 81
  medical tourism, 82
Theory X management, 263–264, 266
Theory Y management, 264–265, 266
Theory Z management, 265–266
Therbligs, 257
Third-party logistics, 419
Threats; *see* SWOT analysis
360-degree reviews, 302
Thrift institutions; *see* Savings and loan associations
Time, A-1
Time deposits, 555
Time management, P-10–P-11
Time utility, 407
Time value of money, 493
Time-motion studies, 257
Title VII, Civil Rights Act of 1964, 287, 288, 289
Tobacco industry, A-4, A-5
Top management, 187
Tort law, A-4–A-6

Total fixed costs, 393
Total product offer, 375–377
Tourism, medical, 82; see also Travel industry
Trade; see also Exporting; Global markets; Importing
  balance of, 64
  common markets, 77
  comparative advantage theory, 61–62
  dumping disputes, 65
  financing, 563
  free, 61, 62
  future issues, 80–83
  growth, 18–19
  importance, 18–19, 60
  international agreements, 77–79
  largest trading countries, 65
  laws to ensure fairness, 65
  measuring, 64–65
  motives for, 61–62
  opportunities, 62–63
  organized labor and, 323, 325
  surpluses, 64, 76
Trade barriers; see also Tariffs
  embargoes, 76
  import quotas, 76
  nontariff, 76
Trade credit, 496–497
Trade deficits, 64–65
Trade protectionism, 75–76
Trade shows, 443
Trade unions; see Unions
Trademarks, 382, 383, A-7; see also Brand names; Intellectual property protection
Trading blocs, 77
Trading securities; see Brokerage firms; Securities markets
Training and development
  activities, 298
  apprentice programs, 298–299
  benefits, 297–298
  computer systems, 219, 299
  defined, 297
  by franchisors, 132
  job rotation and, 270
  job simulation, 299
  management development, 300–301
  mentoring, 300
  off-the-job, 299
  online programs, 299
  on-the-job, 298
  outsourcing, BA-15
  technical, BA-15
  vestibule training, 299
Transfers, employee, 309–310
Transparency, 190, 217
Transportation; see also Distribution; Logistics
  air, 421
  carbon cost, 420, 421
  intermodal, 421–422
  mode comparison, 419
  pipelines, 421
  railroads, 419–420
  surface, 419–420
  water, 420–421
Travel industry, 82
Treasurers, 486
Treasury bills, bonds, and notes, 522
Trial balances, 462–463
Trial close, 439, 440

Troubled Assets Relief Program (TARP), 536, 559
Trucking, 420
Truth-in-Lending Act (1968), A-13

U

UCC; see Uniform Commercial Code
Uganda, microlending in, 36
Umbrella policies, BC-11
Underemployed workers, 286
Unemployment, 46–47, 230
Unemployment compensation, BB-5
Unemployment rate, 46–47
Unethical behavior; see Ethics
Uniform Commercial Code (UCC), 13, A-8–A-9
Uniform Partnership Act (UPA), 118
Uninsurable risk, BB-5
Union security clause, 323
Union shop agreements, 324
Unions; see also Employee-management relations
  apprentice programs, 298
  boycotts, 328
  certification, 321, 322
  collective bargaining, 321
  contracts, 323–325
  corporate responsibility and, 105
  craft, 319, 320
  decertification, 321, 322
  decline of, 318, 329
  defined, 318
  in Europe, 325
  future of, 318, 324–325, 329–332
  givebacks, 329
  global links, 325
  history, 318, 319–320
  industrial, 320
  membership by state, 330
  objectives, 323–325
  organizing campaigns, 321, 322
  picketing, 327–328
  in professional sports, 316, 317
  protectionist views, 76
  resistance to management, 222
  shop stewards, 326
  strikes, 327–328
  tactics used in conflicts, 327–328
United Arab Emirates
  franchises, 69
  sovereign wealth fund, 502
  trade minister, 58–59
United Kingdom; see Britain
United Mine Workers, 320
United States
  comparative advantage, 61–62
  Constitution, A-15
  economic development, 20–21
  economic system
    business cycle, 48–49
    key economic indicators, 45–48
    mixed economy, 43–45
    productivity, 48
  exports, 61, 63, 64–65
  free trade agreements, 78–79
  imports, 61
  NAFTA and, 78, 79, 325
  standard of living, 6
  trade deficits, 64–65
  trade laws, 65
  trading partners, 65
  unemployment, 46–47

U.S. dollar, 73–74, 547, 549; see also Currencies
U.S. government
  administrative agencies, A-3, A-4
  assistance for exporters, 63, 67, 170
  budget deficits, 49–50
  corporate bailouts, 536, A-18
  corruption scandals, 90
  debt, 49–50
  employees, 43–45
  insurance programs, BB-5
  revenues and expenditures, 49–50
  role in economy, 43–45
U.S. government bonds, 522
United States v. American Tobacco, A-11
United States v. AT&T, A-11
United States v. E.I. du Pont de Nemours, A-11
United States v. Microsoft, A, A-11
United States v. Standard Oil, A-11
United Steelworkers Union, 76
Universal Product Codes (UPCs), 381, 422
Universities; see Colleges and universities
Unlimited liability, 116, 119
Unsecured bonds, 503, 523
Unsecured loans, 498
Unsought goods and services, 379
UPA; see Uniform Partnership Act
UPCs; see Universal Product Codes
Uruguay, Mercosur, 77
Uruguay Round, 77
USA Freedom Corps, 100
USA Today, 533
Usage segmentation, 362
Utilities
  cooperatives, 137
  deregulation of, 39, A-18
  electric, 39
  monopolies, 39
  regulators, A-4
Utility
  defined, 407
  form, 234–235, 407
  information, 408
  place, 407
  possession, 408
  service, 408
  time, 407

V

Value, 374
Value chain, 417; see also Supply chain
Value enhancers, 376, 377
Value package; see Total product offer
Value-added taxes, 41
Values, corporate, 189, 204, 221; see also Ethics
Variable costs, 392, 393
Variable life insurance, BC-10
Vending machines, 413
Vendors; see Suppliers
Venezuela, 77
Venture capital, 505
Venture capitalists, 165, 505
Vermont, virtual companies, 127
Vertical mergers, 129
Vestibule training, 299
Video games, 434–435
Video piracy, 93
Vietnam, 42, 77, 81

Violence in workplace, 338–339
Viral marketing, 445
Virtual corporations, 127, 217–218
Virtual private networks (VPNs), BA-9
Virtualization, BA-13
Viruses, BA-16–BA-17
Visions, 181, 189
Vocational Rehabilitation Act of 1973, 289
Volume, or usage, segmentation, 361, 362
Voluntary bankruptcy, A-15
Volunteerism; *see* Community service; Nonprofit organizations
VPNs; *see* Virtual private networks

W

Wages, 106, 304; *see also* Compensation
Wagner Act; *see* National Labor Relations Act of 1935
Wall Street Journal, 132, 347, 528, 531, 533
Warehouse clubs, 411
Warehouses, 422
Warranties, A-8
Wars, 19
Water transportation, 420–421
Weaknesses; *see* SWOT analysis

Wealth creation
  by entrepreneurs, 9–11
  millionaires, BC–BC-1
Web; *see* Internet
Web 2.0, BA-11
Web-based businesses; *see* E-commerce; Internet companies
Welfare Reform Act of 1996, 336
Western Europe; *see* Europe
Wheeler-Lea Amendment of 1938, A-12
Whistleblowers, 97
Whole life insurance, BC-10
Wholesale prices, 48
Wholesalers; *see also* Marketing intermediaries
  cash-and-carry, 409
  defined, 403
  difference from retailers, 409
  full-service, 409, 410
  limited-function, 409
  merchant, 409
  stores sponsored by, 415
Wi-Fi, BA-12
Wills, BC-15
Wireless technology, BA-12
Women
  business owners, 9, 134–135
  comparable worth, 334–335
  in labor force, 335–336

  managers, 301
  pay equity, 334–335
Word-of-mouth promotion, 444–446
Work teams; *see* Teams
Workers; *see* Employees; Labor
Workers' compensation insurance, BB-9
Workforce diversity; *see* Diversity
Working Mother magazine, 336
Workplace violence, 338–339
World Bank, 560, 563–564
World market; *see* Global markets
World trade; *see* Global markets; Trade
World Trade Organization (WTO), 76–77, 80
World Wide Web (WWW); *see* Internet
Wrongful discharge lawsuits, 310
WTO; *see* World Trade Organization
WWW (World Wide Web); *see* Internet

Y

Yankee bonds, 522
Yellow Pages, 432, 433
Yellow-dog contracts, 320, 321

Z

Zaire, bribery in, 105
Zippers, 387

Less managing. More teaching. Greater learning.

INSTRUCTORS...

Would you like your **students** to show up for class more **prepared**? *(Let's face it, class is much more fun if everyone is engaged and prepared...)*

Want ready-made application-level **interactive assignments,** student progress reporting, and auto-assignment grading? *(Less time grading means more time teaching...)*

Want an **instant view of student or class performance** relative to learning objectives? *(No more wondering if students understand...)*

Need to **collect data and generate reports** required for administration or accreditation? *(Say goodbye to manually tracking student learning outcomes...)*

Want to **record and post your lectures** for students to view online?

With **McGraw-Hill's *Connect* Plus Business,**

INSTRUCTORS GET:

- Interactive Applications – **book-specific interactive assignments** that require students to APPLY what they've learned.
- Simple **assignment management**, allowing you to spend more time teaching.
- **Auto-graded** assignments, quizzes, and tests.
- **Detailed Visual Reporting** where student and section results can be viewed and analyzed.
- Sophisticated **online testing** capability.
- A **filtering and reporting** function that allows you to easily assign and report on materials that are correlated to accreditation standards, learning outcomes, and Bloom's taxonomy.
- An easy-to-use **lecture capture** tool.

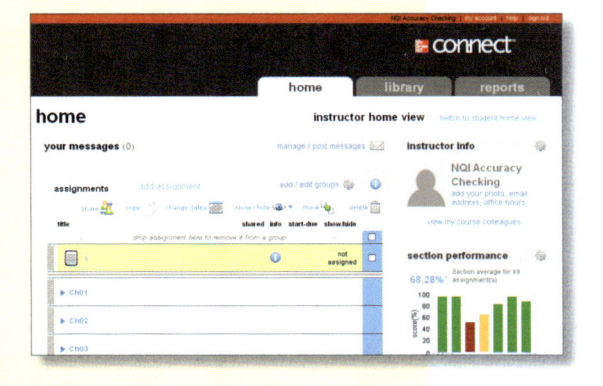

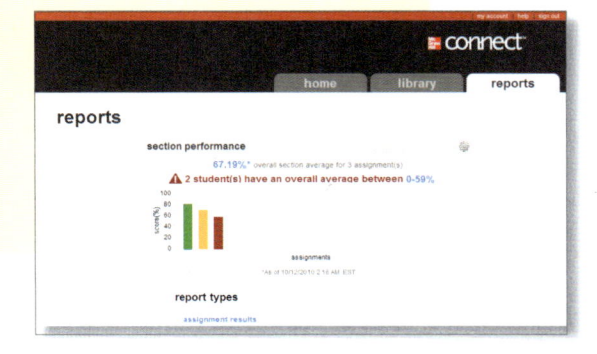

STUDENTS...

Want an online, **searchable version** of your textbook?

Wish your textbook could be **available online** while you're doing your assignments?

Connect™ Plus Business eBook

If you choose to use *Connect™ Plus Business*, you have an affordable and searchable online version of your book integrated with your other online tools.

Connect™ Plus Business eBook offers features like:

- Topic search
- Direct links from assignments
- Adjustable text size
- Jump to page number
- Print by section

STUDENTS...

Want to get more **value** from your textbook purchase?

Think learning about business should be a bit more **interesting**?

Check out the INTERACTIVE PRESENTATIONS found in *Connect*™.

Interactive Presentations are a great prep tool that teach each chapter's core learning objectives and concepts through a multimedia, professional presentation, which brings the text content to life. Come to class more prepared with knowledge of the chapter material, making you ready to participate in class.

Business

connecting principles to practice

William G. Nickels
University of Maryland

James M. McHugh
St. Louis Community College at Forest Park

Susan M. McHugh
Applied Learning Systems

McGraw-Hill Irwin

McGraw-Hill Irwin

BUSINESS: CONNECTING PRINCIPLES TO PRACTICE

Published by McGraw-Hill/Irwin, a business unit of The McGraw-Hill Companies, Inc., 1221 Avenue of the Americas, New York, NY, 10020. Copyright © 2012 by The McGraw-Hill Companies, Inc. All rights reserved. No part of this publication may be reproduced or distributed in any form or by any means, or stored in a database or retrieval system, without the prior written consent of The McGraw-Hill Companies, Inc., including, but not limited to, in any network or other electronic storage or transmission, or broadcast for distance learning.

Some ancillaries, including electronic and print components, may not be available to customers outside the United States.

This book is printed on acid-free paper.

1 2 3 4 5 6 7 8 9 0 QDB/QDB 1 0 9 8 7 6 5 4 3 2 1

ISBN 978-0-07-802312-5 (student edition)
MHID 0-07-802312-2 (student edition)

ISBN 978-0-07-748206-0 (annotated instructor edition)
MHID 0-07-748206-9 (annotated instructor edition)

Vice president and editor-in-chief: *Brent Gordon*
Editorial director: *Paul Ducham*
Executive director of development: *Ann Torbert*
Development editor II: *Kelly L. Delso*
Vice president and director of marketing: *Robin J. Zwettler*
Marketing director: *Amee Mosley*
Senior marketing manager: *Sarah Schuessler*
Vice president of editing, design, and production: *Sesha Bolisetty*
Senior project manager: *Bruce Gin*
Senior buyer: *Carol A. Bielski*
Lead designer: *Matthew Baldwin*
Senior photo research coordinator: *Jeremy Cheshareck*
Photo researcher: *Jennifer Blankenship*
Lead media project manager: *Brian Nacik*
Cover design: *Matthew Baldwin*
Interior design: *Kay Lieberherr*
Typeface: *10/12 New Aster*
Compositor: *Laserwords Private Limited*
Printer: *Quad/Graphics*

Library of Congress Cataloging-in-Publication Data

Nickels, William G.
   Business: connecting principles to practice / William G. Nickels, James M. McHugh, Susan M. McHugh.—1st ed.
     p.cm.
   Includes index.
   ISBN-13: 978-0-07-802312-5 (student ed. : alk. paper)
   ISBN-10: 0-07-802312-2 (student ed. : alk. paper)
   ISBN-13: 978-0-07-748206-0 (annotated instructor ed. : alk. paper)
   ISBN-10: 0-07-748206-9 (annotated instructor ed. : alk. paper)
   1. Industrial management. 2. Business. 1. McHugh, James M. II. McHugh, Susan M. III. Title.
HD31.N48952012
658—dc22

2010045064

www.mhhe.com